PENNSYLVANIA NEGLIGENCE

2015 Edition
Cases through 92 A.3d 833

Current edition by
JOHN M. POLENA, ESQ.
Member of the Allegheny County Bar

GEORGE T. BISEL COMPANY, INC.
710 S. WASHINGTON SQUARE

www.bisel.com

COPYRIGHT 2004, 2005, 2006, 2007, 2008, 2009, 2010, 2011, 2012, 2013, 2014, 2015

BY

GEORGE T. BISEL COMPANY, INC.

All Rights Reserved

The text of this publication, or any part thereof, may not be reproduced or transmitted in any form or by any means, electronic or mechanical, including photocopying, recording, storage in an information retrieval system, or otherwise, without the prior written permission of the publisher. The information contained herein is not intended to constitute legal advice generally or with respect to any particular set of facts or circumstances and should not be relied upon as such by the reader. Neither the authors nor the publisher assume responsibility for errors or omissions as may be contained herein, the use of the information contained herein, or any damages arising or resulting from the use of the information contained herein. Although the publisher intends to update this material from time to time, neither the authors nor the publisher assumes any obligation to do so and this material speaks only as of the date that research therefor was completed which necessarily preceded the publication date.

Printed in United States of America

Library of Congress Catalog Card Number: 00-135428
ISBN: 1-887024-82-4
ISSN: 1558-562X

HOW TO USE

First refer to main text, then check any supplement using the same reference numbers. Sections added subsequent to publication of the main text, if any, will be included in a supplemental table of contents in this pamphlet.

ALWAYS VERIFY CITATIONS BY CONSULTING THE OFFICIAL COURT DECISIONS, RULES, REGULATIONS AND STATUTES

If you have any questions, please call us at 800-247-3526. Contact the Bisel Editorial Department directly with your questions and suggestions at tonyd@bisel.com.

ACKNOWLEDGMENT

Thank you to my wife, Caroline, whose invaluable editing helped make this book possible. To my parents, John and Cory, thank you for all of your support in helping me get to where I am today. Finally, thank you to Tom Dempsey, Jr., for taking me under his wing and generously sharing all of his legal experience and knowledge with me.

John M. Polena, Editor

Breach of Duty

Recent or Seminal Cases for Elemental Analysis

Duty

Plaintiff bank sued defendant bank for failing to issue a suspicious activity report on an account that was later found to be involved in a check-kiting scheme, which caused plaintiff $900,000 in damages. The court held that as a general rule banks do not have a duty to inform each other of suspicions of illegal activity. The court also held that even if a duty were found, causation must be of a type a reasonable person would consider probable and fair. *Commerce Bank/Pennsylvania v. First Union National Bank*, 911 A.2d 133 (Pa. Super. 2006).

Parents, on behalf of their child, sued a fundraising company for failing to conform to the appropriate standard of care by not warning of the dangers inherent in fundraising activities, after their child was sexually assaulted while trying to solicit a subscription. The court reversed the dismissal of the complaint holding that the complaint on its face was sufficient to state a cause of action in negligence against the fund raising entity. *R.W. and C.W. v. Manzek*, 585 Pa. 335, 888 A.2d 740 (2005).

Contractor brought a negligent misrepresentation claim against an architect with whom he had no privity of contract, but upon whose plans he had reasonably relied in submitting a winning construction bid. The court held that businesses supplying information that will foreseeably be used and relied upon by third parties may be found to have a duty to the third parties that use that information to their detriment. *Bilt-Rite Contractors v. The Architectural Studio*, 581 Pa. 454, 866 A.2d 270 (2005).

Minor plaintiff and her parents sued psychiatrist for medical malpractice after the minor made allegations of parental sexual abuse in therapy that were found to be groundless. The court found that a psychiatrist owes no duty of care to a child's parents in a treatment setting where the child has allegedly been abused by those parents. *Althaus v. Cohen*, 562 Pa. 547, 756 A.2d 1166 (2000).

Breach of Duty

Plaintiff filed suit for injuries received while demolishing a bridge for the Port Authority of Allegheny County (PAT) in preparation for the construction of a busway. The court found that PAT was entitled to sovereign immunity and that the engineering firm under its contracts had no duty to the plaintiff and therefore no breach of duty had occurred. *Marshall v. Port Authority of Allegheny County*, 524 Pa. 1, 568 A.2d 931 (1990).

Underaged guest sued host for allegedly serving him alcohol after the minor was injured by a fall caused by his intoxication. The court held that the host had breached his duty of care by serving any amount of alcohol to a minor. *Orner v. Mallick*, 515 Pa. 132, 527 A.2d 521 (1987).

Causation

Causation

Plaintiff bank sued defendant bank for failing to issue a suspicious activity report on an account that was later found to be involved in a check-kiting scheme, which caused plaintiff $900,000 in damages. The court held that as a general rule banks do not have a duty to inform each other of suspicions of illegal activity. The court also held that even if a duty were found, causation must be of a type a reasonable person would consider probable and fair. ***Commerce Bank/Pennsylvania v. First Union National Bank*, 911 A.2d 133 (Pa. Super. 2006).**

Plaintiff's filed suit against the defendant after their child was injured by a train, when he climbed through fences owned by defendant onto a third party's land. The court held that defendant's improperly maintained fences had not caused the injury to plaintiff and therefore defendant was not the proximate cause of the plaintiff's injuries. ***Gardner v. Consolidated Rail Corporation SEPTA*, 524 Pa. 445, 573 A.2d 1016 (1990).**

Mother filed suit against the driver of an automobile that struck and killed her daughter for negligent infliction of emotional distress. The court held that the driver did not owe a duty of care to the mother and that the mother did not actually observe the accident, which was required to create an action for negligent infliction of emotional distress. ***Mazzagatti v. Everingham*, 512 Pa. 266, 516 A.2d 672 (1986).**

Plaintiffs filed suit against defendant for the breakdown of their marriage due to an erroneous diagnosis by defendant that their child had been born with syphilis. The court held that the misdiagnosis was not a substantial factor in the damages alleged by plaintiffs. ***Brown v. Philadelphia College of Osteopathic Medicine*, 760 A.2d 863 (Pa. Super. 2000).**

Damages

Administratrix for decedent filed suit after child used defendant's butane lighter, which lacked a child safety feature, to ignite linens in his home causing a fire that ultimately took his life. The court rejected plaintiff's breach of warranty claim and found that there was insufficient evidence to support a punitive damages award. ***Phillips v. Cricket Lighters*, 584 Pa. 179, 883 A.2d 439 (2005).**

Plaintiff rendered medical services to the decedent and then filed suit for compensation for services rendered. Decedent's estate sought to recover the amount paid on decedent's behalf by collateral sources and also the remaining unpaid amount as an expense. The court ruled that if the medical care provider charges less than the value of their services without intending a gift, the plaintiff's recovery is limited to the liability incurred. ***Moorhead v. Crozer Chester Medical Center*, 564 Pa. 156, 765 A.2d 786 (2001).**

A new trial was ordered after a jury award that "shocked the court's conscience" involving injuries received by a woman in a car accident. The court affirmed the grant of a new trial because there was no evidence to support the jury's decision not to award any pain and suffering damages to the injured woman in her negligence suit. ***Neison v. Hines,* 539 Pa. 516, 653 A.2d 634 (1994).**

General Analysis of Negligence

Plaintiff filed suit against defendant for negligently recording a urine sample, which led to him being denied employment. The court held that plaintiff had not contracted for defendant's services and therefore defendant owed no duty to the plaintiff. ***Ney v. Axelrod,* 723 A.2d 719 (Pa. Super. 1999).**

Plaintiff was injured while test driving a car being sold by the defendant. The court held that sufficient evidence of a breach of duty had not been produced to hold defendant liable on a theory of negligence. ***Ferry v. Fisher,* 709 A.2d 399 (Pa. Super. 1998).**

Plaintiff filed suit after a bone flap removed from his skull during surgery could not be reattached, due to contamination while being stored by defendant. The court held that the plaintiff had presented a prima facie case through expert testimony of negligence on some aspects of his case, but failed to present a prima facie case for his pain and fear. Additionally, the court held that the plaintiff's claim of battery due to lack of informed consent failed. ***Watkins v. Hospital of the University of Pennsylvania,* 737 A.2d 263 (Pa. Super. 1999).**

Absolute liability

—A—

Abandoned vehicle

Driver killed in collision with abandoned vehicle along turnpike. State Police immune in action for failure to remove vehicle. ***Bennett v. Pennsylvania Turnpike Commission*, 160 Pa. Cmwlth. 223, 634 A.2d 776.**

Minor plaintiff injured by bullets found in car in defendant's garage. Defendant towed and stored abandoned cars for City of Easton. Although owner knew that children played in his lot, had no knowledge of dangerous articles left in glove compartment. Nonsuit affirmed. ***Norton v. City of Easton*, 249 Pa. Super. 520, 378 A.2d 417.**

Abdominal aneurysm

Plaintiff's decedent died after his treating physician failed to diagnose a leaking abdominal aneurysm. An x-ray and radiologist's report clearly indicated the problem had not been forwarded to the treating physician by the hospital staff. There was uncontradicted evidence that, had the treating physician seen the x-ray and report, he would have treated the aneurysm and the patient would have survived. Held: summary judgment in favor of the hospital on the claim of corporate negligence was improper in light of the obvious failure of procedure to inform the treating physician. The verdict in favor of the treating physician was against the weight of the evidence where his negligence was admitted, but not found to be a cause of the injury. ***Cangemi v. Cone*, 774 A.2d 1262 (Pa. Super. 2001).**

Abduction from parking lot

Shopping center patron was abducted from parking lot and died from subsequent heart attack. Held: whether holder of easement was possessor with duty to protect invitee from criminal attack is question for the finder of fact. ***Leichter v. Eastern Realty Company*, 358 Pa. Super. 189, 516 A.2d 1247.**

Abortion

Pregnant woman injured in automobile accident brought wrongful death action after consenting to abortion. No liability. Non-viable fetus not person. ***Conelski v. Bubnis*, 535 Pa. 166, 634 A.2d 608.**

Absolute liability

Unexcused violation of dog law, allowing dog to run free, was negligence per se. Court did not impose absolute liability. Remanded for new trial. ***Miller v. Hurse*, 302 Pa. Super. 235, 448 A.2d 614.**

Azzarello case held to apply retroactively to cases pending at time of its filing, even as here where case was an appeal after trial. ***Leland v. Baker Chemical*, 282 Pa. Super. 573, 423 A.2d 393.**

§402A of Restatement (2d) Torts does not apply where employee of lessee injured on machine which was actually subject to a finance purchase agreement and

Absolute negligence

lessor not involved in installation or sale. Verdict against manufacturer upheld. ***Nath v. National Equipment*, 282 Pa. Super. 142, 422 A.2d 868.**

Industrial accident. Gloves caught in machine causing injury. Charge in error. Proper charge was that use of gloves must have been a "substantial factor" in bringing about the harm. New trial ordered. ***Takach v. Root Co.*, 279 Pa. Super. 167, 420 A.2d 1084.**

Employee of store loading a display on rack when it tipped over causing injury to plaintiff. Suit versus manufacturer based on defective design. Charge given on §402A of Restatement (2d) Torts. Verdict for defendant affirmed. ***Varner v. Pretty Products*, 270 Pa. Super. 86, 410 A.2d 1261.**

Plaintiff driving loaner car while his vehicle being serviced. Accident occurred allegedly due to defect in right rear axle shaft. Section 402A of Restatement (2d) Torts held to apply to supplier of chattel even if lease arrangement exists. ***Mandel v. Gulf Leasing*, 250 Pa. Super. 128, 378 A.2d 487.**

Defendant engaged in road building as an independent contractor—plaintiff's property allegedly damaged by blasting—recovery allowed—Supreme Court held that the fact that the matter was a public construction operation would not bring it into exception granted governmental bodies—doctrine of ultrahazardous occupations applied. ***Lobozzo v. Adam Eidemiller*, 437 Pa. 360, 263 A.2d 432.**

Absolute negligence

Verdict only against dog owner's boyfriend who did not have dog under control when it jumped on 67 year old pedestrian affirmed. Claims of absolute negligence by reason of mere ownership of dog and negligence per se denied. ***McCloud v. McLaughlin*, 837 A.2d 541 (Pa. Super. 2003).**

Accelerated speed

Plaintiff party to left—collision in intersection of two cars—plaintiff observing defendant's car approaching and slowing down—then suddenly accelerating and defendant's driver took hands off steering wheel and covered his face with hands—case for jury under facts of case. ***McCaffrey v. Philadelphia*, 421 Pa. 357, 219 A.2d 680.**

Accounting

Suit by clients against CPA firm claiming professional negligence in providing advice which resulted in federal criminal prosecution and guilty verdict for tax evasion and filing false returns. On determination that comparative negligence rule does not apply in cases involving loss of funds only and that contributory negligence rules apply, clients' guilty verdict establishes contributory negligence and precludes any recovery against CPA firm. ***Columbia Medical Group v. Herring & Roll, P.C.*, 829 A.2d 1184 (Pa. Super. 2003).**

Acidosis

Action to recover for death of child 11 months after birth where death caused by negligent failure to diagnose and act on dangerous condition in utero immediately before birth. Evidence to establish "corporate liability" of hospital under Thompson v. Nason Hospital, 527 Pa. 330, 591 A.2d 703 (1991) must be provided in the form of expert testimony where the negligence is not obvious but need not contain "magic words." The substance of all the expert testimony will be considered as a whole. The evidence must establish that the hospital, in its own duty to the patient, deviated from the accepted standard of care and that the deviation was a substantial factor in causing the harm to the plaintiff. ***Welsh v. Bulger*, 698 A.2d 581 (Pa. 1997).**

Actual loss

Case of first impression—An essential element of the cause of action for legal malpractice is proof of actual loss. Defendant attorney must be permitted to prove, by preponderance of evidence, that any potential claim for damages by the plaintiff was uncollectible. $2,300,000.00 verdict and judgment in favor of plaintiff reversed and remanded for hearing on collectibility of underlying judgment against tortfeasor in plaintiff's original claim. ***Kituskie v. Corbman*, 452 Pa. Super. 467, 682 A.2d 378 (1996).**

Adjacent property

Plaintiff's property damaged by reason of alleged defective condition of adjacent property of defendant—third party excavating in vicinity—cannot be said that act of third party was an intervening cause—nonsuit improperly entered. ***Bleman v. Gold*, 431 Pa. 348, 246 A.2d 376.**

Administrative remedy

Absent proof that an administrative remedy under the Workers' Compensation Act or Occupational Disease Act has been pursued or completed, a common law action by an employee against an employer will not be dismissed by entering judgment on the pleadings alone. Judgment on pleadings in favor of defendant reversed. ***Pollard v. Lord Corp.*, 445 Pa. Super. 109, 664 A.2d 1032 (1995).**

Adoption

Adoptive parents of son diagnosed with schizophrenia brought claims for negligent misrepresentation and negligent failure to disclose against their adoption agency for failing to disclose that their adoptive son's birth mother had a mental history of schizophrenia. At trial a jury found the agency negligent. The Superior Court reversed and remanded, holding that schizophrenia at the time of the adoption was not a known genetic disorder and therefore Plaintiffs could not prevail under a negligent misrepresentation theory. The Superior Court remanded on the negligent failure to disclose as the verdict sheet did not differentiate between the two theories of negligence. The Pennsylvania Supreme Court reversed the Superior Court and reinstated the verdict for the Plaintiffs, holding that where a general verdict is issued involving multiple issues the verdict may not be dismissed if at least one issue is supported by the verdict. ***Halper v. Jewish Family & Children's Service of Greater Philadelphia*, 963 A.2d 1282 (2009).**

Adoption of road

Reversal of order sustaining demurrer in favor of adoption agency to allow claims for negligent misrepresentation, intentional misrepresentation and negligent failure to disclose. Demurrer to claim of breach of duty to investigate sustained. ***Gibbs v. Ernst,* 538 Pa. 193, 647 A.2d 882 (1994).**

Parents who adopted child with severe psychological illness brought action against adoption agency and youth services agency. Held: demurrer to emotional distress but not negligent placement upheld. ***Gibbs v. Ernst,* 150 Pa. Cmwlth. 154, 615 A.2d 851.**

Adoption of road

In action against PennDOT and the city from which PennDOT had "adopted" a road for failure to install guard rails, summary judgment in favor of PennDOT was sustained. There was no proof by plaintiff of breach of a duty to plaintiff by PennDOT in the maintenance and care of the road surface between the curb lines—the only area for which PennDOT is statutorily responsible after "adoption" of the road from the city. ***Wallace v. Com., Dept. of Transp.,* 701 A.2d 307 (Pa. Cmwlth. 1997).**

Advertising

Plaintiff may proceed under theory of negligence against telephone company for placing old ad under expired contract in new yellow pages despite the existence of prior contractual relationship. ***McDole v. Bell Telephone of Pennsylvania,* 441 Pa. Super. 88, 656 A.2d 933 (1995).**

AED Good Samaritan Act

Elementary analysis of negligence claim by patron of tennis club who suffered brain damage due to stroke following heart attack. Plaintiffs allege that the club was negligent in not having an Automated External Defibrillator ("AED") on the premises and using the device to restart husband plaintiff's heart. Defendant club argued that the Emergency Medical Services Act precluded its untrained employees from using an AED even if it had one and the AED Good Samaritan Act had not yet been passed. Grant of summary judgment in favor of defendant club affirmed. ***Atcovitz v. Gulph Mills Tennis Club, Inc.,* 571 Pa. 580, 812 A.2d 1218 (Pa. 2002).**

Affirmative defense

Plaintiff filed legal malpractice action against attorney who missed statute of limitations date on the plaintiff's personal injury action. After the trial court determined that plaintiff's ability to collect damages from tortfeasor who had not been sued was not relevant to malpractice claim, jury returned verdict against defendant attorney in amount of $2,300,000. On appeal, Superior Court affirmed verdict and irrelevance of plaintiff's ability to collect damages; Supreme Court granted allocatur. In case of first impression in Pennsylvania, Supreme Court added fourth element to any legal malpractice case: (1) employment of attorney or another basis for duty: (2) failure of attorney to exercise reasonable skill and knowledge; (3) that such negligence was proximate cause of damage to plaintiff; and (4) affirmative defense of uncollectibility, i.e., that plaintiff in malpractice action would be unable to collect on claim which was "lost" by reason of legal malpractice. Burden of putting forward affirmative defense of uncollectibility is on attorney who asserts it. ***Kituskie v. Corbman*, 714 A.2d 1027 (Pa. 1998).**

Affirmative duty

Plaintiff, surviving husband, filed negligence action against credit union alleging that it breached an affirmative duty to inform him that only he would be provided credit life insurance on loan as first signatory rather than both husband and wife as co-obligors on loan. After verdict for plaintiffs in bench trial, Superior Court reversed holding that mere financial harm is not physical harm as required by §323 of Restatement (2d) Torts (negligent performance of undertaking to render services) nor was there proof of any fiduciary duty from the credit union to the husband nor is there any case law to define any affirmative duty to act in similar circumstances. ***Carlotti v. Employees of Credit Union*, 717 A.2d 564 (Pa. Super. 1998).**

Agency

Plaintiff alleged serious injury following in-office procedure performed by physician and nurse anesthetist who was an independent contractor assisting physician. At trial, judge granted non-suit in favor of physician on plaintiff's theory of the ostensible agency for liability of the nurse anesthetist. In issue of first impression, held that a patient who submits herself to the care of a doctor for the performance of an in-office medical procedure is be entitled to recover damages from the physician for the negligence of the doctor's independent contractors just as a patient who submits herself to the care of a hospital is entitled to recover damages from the hospital for the negligence of the independent contractors utilized by the hospital under the theory of ostensible agency. ***Parker v. Freilich*, 803 A.2d 738 (Pa. Super. 2002).**

Wife, who delivered brain-damaged child after Cesarean section with only local anesthetic, and husband, individually and as parents of child, sued anesthesiology group, obstetrician and hospital for malpractice. Nurses employed at hospital are not agents of the physicians when they act in the normal course of hospital services. Father's loss of consortium claim properly denied by trial court where his only testimony was that he had a subjective fear of engaging in sexual relations with his wife following her delivery of brain-damaged child, even though the damage may have been the result of medical malpractice. Father's claim for negligent infliction of emotional distress properly dismissed where he was not near the scene of the injuries to his wife and newborn child. Hearing his wife's cries of pain only, without any visual experience of her condition, was insufficient. ***Tiburzio-Kelly v. Montgomery*, 452 Pa. Super. 158, 681 A.2d 757 (1996).**

Passenger of intoxicated driver has no duty to third person killed by driver's negligence. Passenger's mere request that driver take her somewhere and driver's acquiescence does not establish driver as agent and passenger as principal so as to establish passenger's liability to third person killed by driver's negligence. Summary judgment affirmed. ***Clayton v. McCullough*, 448 Pa. Super. 126, 670 A.2d 710 (1996).**

Aggravating injury

Rear-end accident severely injuring passenger in front auto. Truck driver held to be agent of Department of Transportation and trucking business who leased driver and truck to PennDOT for liability purposes. ***Mineo v. Tancini,*** **349 Pa. Super. 115, 502 A.2d 1300.**

Plaintiff-decedent hanged himself with hospital robe ties while patient in psychiatric unit of defendant hospital, having been admitted after suicide attempt. Lower court erred in ruling as matter of law that treating physician was not agent of hospital. New trial as to doctor's agency and negligence only, and damages if appropriate. ***Simmons v. St. Clair Memorial Hospital,*** **332 Pa. Super. 444, 481 A.2d 870.**

Undisputed facts showed that injurious activity of individual defendant was outside the scope of employment. July 4th accident. Defendant, on errand for father, did not have permission to use vehicle. Summary judgment for employer affirmed. ***Johnson v. Glenn Sand & Gravel,*** **308 Pa. Super. 22, 453 A.2d 1048.**

Section 429 of Restatement (2d) Torts held applicable where patient enters hospital emergency room and is treated by a physician who is actually an independent contractor. Theory of ostensible or apparent agency. ***Capan v. Divine Providence Hospital,*** **287 Pa. Super. 364, 430 A.2d 647.**

Plaintiff injured by acts of an employee of defendant company—case tried not on theory of respondeat superior but on ground that defendant was negligent in employing its agent and failed to make proper investigation as to his character—held: under Section 317 of Restatement (2d) Torts, defendant was not negligent in employing its agent. ***Dempsy v. Walso Bureau, Inc.,*** **431 Pa. 562, 246 A.2d 418.**

Aggravating injury

Plaintiff employee accidentally injured in course of employment—alleged aggravation of injury by employer's medical department—held: remedy of employee against employer only under Act and not at common law. ***Vogel v. Jones & Laughlin Steel Co.,*** **221 Pa. Super. 157, 289 A.2d 158.**

Aiding injured person on highway

Co-defendant lost control of car and sideswiped other defendant's truck, severing its air line—co-defendant thrown to road surface—plaintiff and truck operator rushed to her assistance on foot—truck drifted back and injured plaintiff—jury found both defendants responsible—negligence of truck driver not a superseding cause—error to enter judgment n.o.v. for co-defendant—several sections of Restatement (2d) Torts cited by court. ***White v. Rosenberry,*** **441 Pa. 34, 271 A.2d 341.**

AIDS (HIV)

Plaintiff nursing care provider received a needle stick after giving an injection to a patient that she only later learned was afflicted with AIDs. In suit claiming negligent infliction of mental distress against organization that assigned her to provide care for patient without providing her with information on the patient's AIDs status or proper equipment, summary judgement in favor of defendant reversed. The court recognized that a cause of action for mental distress for fear of contracting AIDS will lie where there are circumstances that indicate the plaintiff was actually exposed to the AIDS virus. ***Shumosky v. Lutheran Welfare Services of Northeastern, PA., Inc.*, 784 A.2d 196 (Pa. Super. 2001).**

Plaintiff who was incorrectly informed that he had tested positive for HIV/AIDS sued community health agency, laboratory that performed tests, and others, claiming negligent infliction of emotional distress. Held: "fear of aids" which generated psychosomatic symptoms is not a cognizable injury in Pennsylvania. ***Doe v. Philadelphia Community Health Alternatives*, 745 A.2d 25 (Pa. Super. 2000).**

Trial court's discretion in matters of evidence and discovery is broad and will not be reversed absent clear abuse. Court's refusal to permit testimony regarding plaintiff's HIV status was reversible error where plaintiff opened the door to such evidence. Verdict affirmed as to liability; case remanded for new trial on damages. ***Aiello v. SEPTA*, ___ Pa. Cmwlth. ___, 687 A.2d 399 (1996).**

Plaintiff who contracted AIDS following transfusion of tainted blood filed suit against treating physicians and family physician for medical malpractice. Claim against one defendant dismissed for plaintiff's failure to establish through medical testimony that defendant's actions deviated from good and acceptable medical standards. Proof of compliance with medical standard of care need not be expressed in precisely the language used to annunciate the legal standard. Physician not required to obtain patient's informed consent before blood transfusion that was administered separately from a surgical procedure. ***Hoffman v. Brandywine Hospital*, 443 Pa. Super. 245, 661 A.2d 397 (1995).**

Patient received blood that tested positive for AIDS virus during in vitro fertilization procedure. Hospital and physician not liable for negligent infliction of emotional distress. ***Lubowitz v. Albert Einstein Medical Center*, 424 Pa. Super. 468, 623 A.2d 3.**

Patient notified he tested positive for AIDS as a result of erroneous blood test. Physician found not liable for lack of informed consent or intentional infliction of emotional distress. ***Doe v. Dyer-Goode*, 389 Pa. Super. 151, 566 A.2d 889.**

Airbags

Following in depth analysis of federal preemption law, Superior Court held that state common law causes of action are expressly not preempted by the National Traffic and Motor Vehicle Safety Act. Therefore, motorist may raise claim at trial that airbag that contributed to his injuries in head-on collision with another vehicle was defective, because Congress intended such issues to go to the jury. Order denying manufacturer's preliminary objections affirmed. ***Heiple v. C.R. Motors, Inc.*, 446 Pa. Super. 310, 666 A.2d 1066 (1995).**

Air conditioning unit

Plaintiff serviceman called to check air conditioning unit—general manager of defendant failed through lack of knowledge to operate proper thermostat—plaintiff injured when air conditioner started—improper to enter judgment on pleadings—plaintiff's pleading entitled him to a trial on the merits. ***Eckborg v. Hyde-Murphy Co.*, 442 Pa. 283, 276 A.2d 513.**

Aircraft accidents

Aircraft accidents

Plaintiff's decedent was killed when his helicopter crashed after receiving maintenance work by defendant corporation employee, assisted by corporation owner. Verdict in favor of plaintiff affirmed. Claim the corporate owner was individually liable on participation theory was not valid because the owner did not actively participate in the negligent action. Nonfeasance, rather than misfeasance, is not enough to allow individual liability of corporate officer. ***Shay v. Flight C Helicopter Services, Inc.*, 822 A.2d 1 (Pa. Super. 2003).**

Helicopter struck power line while conducting survey for electric company. Occupants brought action for failure to warn of dangerous condition. Electric company 64% negligent, pilot 35% negligent. ***Bailey v. Pennsylvania Electric Company*, 409 Pa. Super. 374, 598 A.2d 41.**

Pilot and wife injured when helicopter struck power line while spraying for department. ***Department immune. Dept. of Environmental Resources v. Meyers*, 135 Pa. Cmwlth. 526, 581 A.2d 696.**

During flight instruction, plane hit pole owned by PECO and crashed, killing instructor. Pilot survived. Estate of instructor settled, prior to trial with pilot. Error for Court to advise jury of settlement. Not reversible error since jury found that plaintiff, flight instructor, was the only negligent party, and therefore could not recover from remaining alleged tortfeasors. ***Weingrad v. Philadelphia Electric Co.*, 324 Pa. Super. 16, 471 A.2d 100.**

Airplane crash—fatal. Suit against estate of pilot. Lower court failed to charge on res ipsa loquitur—error. Under facts here, with no adequate explanation for crash other than pilot inexperience and negligence, charge should have been given. New trial ordered. ***Halsband v. Union National Bank*, 318 Pa. Super. 597, 465 A.2d 1014.**

Plaintiff killed when helicopter he was piloting crashed while in climbing flight. Seven foot section of one of the rotors separated. Defendant claimed failure due to fuel exhaustion and subsequent failure on plaintiff's part in not going into autorotation to effect a proper emergency landing. Seller under 402A includes suppliers and manufacturers. Entire 402A issue redefined by Court. Puffing advertisements in this instance dealing with ease of flying this product held not to be a misrepresentation under 402B. Defense verdict below. New trial ordered under redefined 402A. ***Berkebile v. Brantly Helicopter Corp.*, 462 Pa. 83, 337 A.2d 893.**

Airplane accident in airways over State of Georgia—plaintiff's decedent killed as result—suit against pilot—all parties residents of Pennsylvania and suit in that state—Pennsylvania law applicable under authority of Griffith v. United Airlines (416 Pa. 1). ***Kuchinic v. McCrory*, 422 Pa. 620, 222 A.2d 897.**

Airport tarmac

Airport tarmac is not a sidewalk under sidewalk exception to Political Subdivision Tort Claims Act. Plaintiff's allegation that airport authority's failure to design safety standards for tarmac is not sufficient allegation of defective design or construction of real estate so as to fall within real estate exception to Political Subdivision Tort Claims Act. Order granting summary judgment affirmed. ***Bullard v. Lehigh-Northampton Airport Authority***, ___ Pa. Cmwlth. ___, 668 A.2d 223 (1995).

Air quality testing

Plaintiffs were employees in office adjacent to school bus parking area and garage. Over a significant period of time, they all developed respiratory ailments that were eventually linked to exposure to fumes from diesel fuel and bus exhaust fumes. Plaintiffs filed suit against building architect, HVAC designer and installer and BMC, an environmental company that had been performing tests of building's air quality and certifying good air quality after plaintiffs' illness was established. The trial court granted BMC's motion for summary judgment because plaintiffs failed to institute suit within two years after plaintiffs discovered their illness. Held: discovery rule tolls statute of limitations in this case because defendant was not company that caused harm, but company hired to determine cause of plaintiffs' existing illnesses after they had complained to their supervisors. The two-year period ran from date BMC was negligent in performance of its tests, not date plaintiffs discovered their illness. The actual time that plaintiffs discovered that BMC was negligent in its testing is issue for jury and so prohibits summary judgment. ***Cappelli v. York Operating Co., Inc.***, 711 A.2d 481 (Pa. Super. 1998).

Air tank

Welder injured while repairing air tank which exploded when pressurized for testing. Nonsuit granted as to owner of tank. Section 388 of Restatement (2d) Torts applies. No reason to believe owner knew of dangerous condition or that experienced welder wouldn't himself realize the danger under facts here. Affirmed. ***Herleman v. Trumbauer Auto Sales***, 346 Pa. Super. 494, 499 A.2d 1109.

Alcoholism

Plaintiff called coroner to establish cause of death—court permitted counsel for defendant to develop connection of alcoholism in cause of death and refused plaintiff's attempt to attack this testimony—error and new trial awarded. ***Woodland v. Philadelphia T. Co.***, 428 Pa. 379, 238 A.2d 593.

Alighting from vehicle

Plaintiff injured when alighting from bus is not injured by reason of "operation of motor vehicle"; therefore suit against transit authority precluded. Order granting judgment notwithstanding the verdict affirmed. ***Rubenstein v. SEPTA***, ___ Pa. Cmwlth. ___, 668 A.2d 283 (1995).

Plaintiff alighting from bus is not engaged in operation of motor vehicle so claim for damages does not qualify under statutory exception to governmental immunity. Summary judgment affirmed. Legislative intent is to grant immunity; therefore interpretation of exceptions to governmental immunity should favor that outcome. ***Bazemore v. SEPTA***, ___ Pa. Cmwlth. ___, 657 A.2d 1323 (1995).

Recovery by bus passenger who fell from stationary bus steps is precluded by governmental immunity absent proof of movement of vehicle or any part of ve-

Allergic reaction

hicle. Summary judgment reversed on certified interlocutory appeal. *Simpkins v. SEPTA*, 167 Pa. Cmwlth. 451, 648 A.2d 591 (1994).

Passenger injured while alighting from bus. Vehicle exception to sovereign immunity not applicable. *Miller v. Erie Metropolitan Transit Authority*, 152 Pa. Cmwlth. 64, 618 A.2d 1095.

Passenger injured when bus door closed as she attempted to exit. Motor vehicle exception to government immunity applicable. *Sonnenberg v. Erie Metropolitan Transit Authority*, 137 Pa. Cmwlth. 533, 586 A.2d 1026.

Fatal injury to student struck by car after alighting from school bus. Held: school district immune from suit. *Aberant v. Wilkes-Barre Area School Dist.*, 89 Pa. Cmwlth. 516, 492 A.2d 1186.

Allergic reaction

Patient who suffered allergic reaction to medication brought action against hospital. Held: two-year statute of limitations and not six-year limitation under U.C.C. applied. *Stephenson v. Greenberg*, 421 Pa. Super. 1, 617 A.2d 364.

All-terrain vehicle (ATV)

Trial court granted defendant ATV manufacturer's and defendant premises owner's motions for summary judgment on basis of spoliation of evidence after theft of allegedly defectively designed ATV which was operated by minor plaintiff. Held: where neither plaintiff nor defendant was owner or in control of ATV after it had been recovered from accident scene and placed in storage at police facility, and because the allegation by plaintiff is defective design, there is inadequate proof of prejudice to defendant who could perform tests on another ATV of the same model. *Sebelin v. Yamaha Motor Corp*, U.S.A., 705 A.2d 904 (Pa. Super. 1998).

Alternate path

University owes no duty to students to control protestors. Student who sees open and obvious impediment to her path of travel should choose an alternate path, rather than attempting to jump from four-foot wall. Order granting summary judgment was affirmed. *Banks v. Trustees of University of Pennsylvania*, 446 Pa. Super. 99, 666 A.2d 329 (1995).

Ambiguous language

Plaintiff tripped and fell on a crack in sidewalk immediately adjacent to street level "head house" of subway entrance. Plaintiff sued SEPTA and City of Philadelphia, alleging that under lease between City and SEPTA, one or both of those entities was responsible for maintenance of sidewalk. Trial court determined that lease was ambiguous as to responsibility for area of sidewalk at issue and so allowed parol evidence. Jury found that SEPTA was responsible for maintenance. Jury verdict was entered against both City and SEPTA. Post trial motions by City and SEPTA were denied. On appeal, held: if SEPTA were found to be responsible, City should have been granted judgment n.o.v. Remand to enter judgment n.o.v. in favor of City of Philadelphia. *Smith v. SEPTA*, 707 A.2d 604 (Pa. Cmwlth. 1998).

Ambulance

Ambulance

Supreme court vacates Commonwealth Court decision that a volunteer ambulance service is not entitled to protection of Political Tort Claims Act and remands to trial court for evidence that ambulance service is local agency such as creation of the service by a political subdivision, municipal control of the service, benefits to the municipality, non-profit status and employee participation in municipal pension and benefit plans. ***Christy v. Cranberry Volunteer Ambulance Corps, Inc.*, 856 A.2d 43, 2004 WL 1822336 (Pa. 2004).**

Plaintiff's decedent died as a result of delay in arrival of EMS personnel who had been dispatched to the correct address with appropriate directions but went to another location. Held that failure to go to the correct address was not negligent operation of a motor vehicle under the motor vehicle exception to the Emergency Medical Services Act. EMS dispatching service operated by private hospital in the area is not afforded immunity under the act and there can be corporate liability. ***Regester v. County of Chester*, _____ Pa.____, 797 A.2d 898 (2002).**

A hospital is not within the definition of the Emergency Medical Services Act (35 P.S. § 6921) and so is not entitled to summary judgment in suit by plaintiff, alleging hospital's ambulance crew was negligent in failing to properly follow directions to plaintiff's decedent's house in response to 911 call about heart attack. ***Regester v. Longwood Ambulance*, 751 A.2d 694 (Pa. Super. 2000).**

General release of claims against emergency medical technician and ambulance service for overdose precluded claim of vicarious liability against hospital. Compulsory nonsuit in favor of hospital affirmed. ***Riffe v. Vereb Ambulance Service, Inc.*, 437 Pa. Super. 613, 650 A.2d 1076 (1994).**

Mental patient being transported to hospital escaped and died in fall from bridge. Held: evidence that ambulance crew left scene of accident admissible to show lack of training. ***Morrison v. Com., Dept. of Public Welfare*, 148 Pa. Cmwlth. 245, 610 A.2d 1082.**

Pedestrian struck by ambulance operated by volunteer ambulance service. Service liable. Not entitled to governmental immunity. ***Scrima v. Swissvale Area Emergency Service*, 143 Pa. Cmwlth. 500, 599 A.2d 301.**

Ambulance operated by contractor for municipality involved in accident in which two passengers were killed. Municipality not liable. ***Burnatoski v. Butler Ambulance Service*, 575 A.2d 1121.**

Paramedics, after transporting shooting victim to nearest hospital, refused (allegedly not told of emergency nature) to transfer to larger hospital due to company policy. Recommended private ambulance service. Plaintiff died at second hospital. Nonsuit affirmed based upon lack of evidence that paramedics were advised that inter-hospital transfer was an emergency. ***Morena v. South Hills Health System*, 501 Pa. 634, 462 A.2d 680.**

Ambulance had red light, but **h**ad siren and lights on. Fire company counterclaimed for property damage and won. Reversed. Error on counterclaim to charge

Amnesia

that fire company could recover even if negligent. True that plaintiff must show recklessness to recover, but reverse is not true for fire company as plaintiff. ***Junk v. East End Fire Dept.***, 262 Pa. Super. 473, 396 A.2d 1269.

Amnesia

Head-on collision. Verdict in favor of passenger against both drivers. Driver of car with passenger appealed. Other driver remembered nothing but that he was in proper lane shortly before accident. Appellant and passenger testified that they saw the other car in the wrong lane when fifty feet away. Photos by police confirmed this version. New trial granted only as to passenger's verdict against driver of his car as it was error to charge as to his contributory negligence without other evidence. ***Kulp v. Hess***, 227 Pa. Super. 603, 323 A.2d 217.

Evidence of plaintiff's lawyer's statement at pretrial conference to the effect that plaintiff had amnesia as to happening of accident not admissible after plaintiff remembers at trial. Psychiatrist had testified that this type of amnesia could disappear with time. ***Edgridge v. Melcher***, 226 Pa. Super. 381, 313 A.2d 750.

Plaintiff's vehicle struck by defendant's train at a grade crossing—plaintiff's testimony disclosed that plaintiff had a clear view from 1365 to 1849 feet before entering crossing—incontrovertible physical facts rule applied and action of court below entering nonsuit affirmed—the fact that plaintiff was suffering from traumatic amnesia not controlling. ***Reynolds v. Cen. R.R. of N.J. et al.***, 448 Pa. 415, 292 A.2d 924.

Minor plaintiff crossing rural highway when struck by defendant's car—minor had traversed within 2 inches of opposite side of highway—minor suffering from retrograde amnesia and unable to recall circumstances—defendant gave a questionable explanation why she did not see minor plaintiff—error to enter summary judgment—matter for jury on merits. ***Moore v. Zimmerman***, 221 Pa. Super. 359, 292 A.2d 458.

Amputation

Mother of child who received partial leg amputation at 8 days of age claimed damages for negligent infliction of emotional distress. Act that allegedly caused the distress was being informed by medical care providers that discoloration on child's lower leg believed to be bruising was actually evidence of blood clot. Held: being informed of likelihood of amputation if therapies were not successful was not the discrete and identifiable traumatic event contemporaneous to the injury to her child. ***Sonlin v. Abington Memorial Hospital***, 748 A.2d 213 (Pa. Super. 2000).

Anesthesia

Wife, who delivered brain-damaged child after Cesarean section with only local anesthetic, and husband, individually and as parents of child, sued anesthesiology group, obstetrician and hospital for malpractice. Nurses employed at hospital are not agents of the physicians when they act in the normal course of hospital services. Father's loss of consortium claim properly denied by trial court where his only testimony was that he had a subjective fear of engaging in sexual relations with his wife following her delivery of brain-damaged child, even though the damage may have been the result of medical malpractice. Father's claim for negligent infliction of emotional distress properly dismissed where he was not near the scene of the injuries to his wife and newborn child. Hearing his wife's cries of pain only, without any visual experience of her condition, was insufficient. ***Tiburzio-Kelly v. Montgomery*, 452 Pa. Super. 158, 681 A.2d 757 (1996).**

Patient brought action against surgeon for negligent administration of anesthetic. Summary judgment for surgeon inappropriate. ***Szabor v. Bryn Mawr Hospital*, 432 Pa. Super. 361, 638 A.2d 1004.**

Patient brought action against dentist for unanticipated result from injection of anesthetic based on negligence and lack of informed consent. Held: summary judgment on issue of negligence not appealable. Cause of action still remained. ***Garfolo v. Shah*, 400 Pa. Super. 456, 583 A.2d 1205.**

Angioplasty

Patient plaintiff sued physicians and hospital for injuries sustained after injection of Recombinant Tissue Plasminogen Activator (TPA) "clot buster" drugs into blood clots in his leg alleging lack of informed consent. Held that a claim that a health care provider failed to acquire informed consent is only available against the physician who performs a surgical procedure, not the health care facility. Court raises but does not answer the question of whether angioplasty is a "surgical" procedure which requires informed consent. Collateral issue of whether health care facility is liable for its own failure to acquire informed consent in trials of procedures which are under FDA supervision. ***Stalsitz v. Allentown Hospital*, 814 A.2d 766 (Pa. Super. 2002).**

Antenna

One man killed and another injured when antenna they were moving struck power line. Manufacturer not liable for failure to warn. Fact that regulation to provide warning was adopted later held irrelevant. ***Dunkle v. West Penn Power Company*, 400 Pa. Super. 334, 583 A.2d 814.**

Anticipating negligence

Individual contractor working on roof of smaller building within larger building, knocked off roof by crane. He knew of danger after years of working there. Held: crane operator not negligent, but employer-owner of crane/property owner (one entity) negligent for violation of §341A of Restatement (2d) Torts. Possessor should anticipate danger despite knowledge of danger to invitee. ***Skalos v. Higgins*, 303 Pa. Super. 107, 449 A.2d 601.**

Apartments

Apartment fire resulted in deaths of two tenants. Verdict for plaintiffs reversed. New trial ordered. Plaintiff's expert testified that a fire escape or other means of egress would have saved plaintiffs' lives. ***Mapp v. Dube*, 330 Pa. Super. 284, 479 A.2d 553.**

Apportionment of liability

Tenants brought action against apartment complex to recover for injuries resulting from criminal assault and kidnapping upon tenants. Act originated in apartment garage. Evidence of previous criminal activity and alleged inadequate security. Held: landlord does have to provide adequate security to protect tenants from foreseeable criminal activity of third persons. Landlord here held to have had sufficient notice. *Feld v. Merriam*, 314 Pa. Super. 414, 461 A.2d 225.

Apportionment of liability

Minor bicyclist injured when struck by car was granted new trial as to damages only after jury apportioned negligence 50/50 between driver and bicyclist and no negligence by parents but did not award damages. *Nykiel v. Heyl*, 838 A.2d 808 (Pa. Super. 2003).

In automobile accident, testimony by State Trooper with familiarity of truck inspection procedures properly disallowed as to standard of care required by truck driver. Comparative Negligence Act requires that jury apportion liability between plaintiff and all defendants against whom recovery is sought. Trial court's bifurcation to allow apportionment of liability between fewer than all defendants reversed. *Christiansen v. Silfies*, 446 Pa. Super. 464, 667 A.2d 396 (1995).

Plaintiff who fails to participate significantly in postoperative care risks loss of any claim for alleged negligence of physician in performing surgery. The Comparative Negligence Act is not applicable in such cases because of the inability to apportion liability between both parties. *Ferguson v. Panzarella*, 445 Pa. Super. 23, 664 A.2d 989 (1995).

Apportionment of liability for harm to plaintiff is question of law. Where tortious conduct of two or more persons causes a single harm that cannot be apportioned, the actors are joint tortfeasors even though they acted independently. Jury verdict in favor of driver injured as a result of two separate collisions affirmed. *Smith v. Pulcinella*, 440 Pa. Super. 525, 656 A.2d 494 (1995).

Standard of care for a child is the exercise of ordinary care appropriate for a child. Driver and Borough not liable where child who darts out into street found seventy percent negligent. *Smith v. Stribling*, 168 Pa. Cmwlth. 188, 649 A.2d 1003 (1994).

Arbitration

Administratrix of motorcyclist's estate brought a claim for negligence after the Pennsylvania motorcyclist was struck and killed by the New Jersey defendant in New Jersey. Defendant appealed the binding arbitration award based upon the lack of jurisdiction and a damage award against the defendant despite a finding that the decedent was 60% negligent. The Superior Court upheld the trial court's ruling that it had jurisdiction based upon the mutual agreement to arbitration in Pennsylvania. The Superior Court reversed and remanded with instructions to enter a judgment in favor of the Defendant on the basis of comparative negligence as a plaintiff cannot recover if they are found more than 50% negligent. *Rekun v. Pelaez*, 976 A.2d 578 (Pa. Super. 2009).

Architect

Plaintiff sued defendant architectural firm for negligence for a failure to use adequate fire resistant materials. The court held that claims sounding in professional liability require parties to submit a Certificate of Merit, even if the suit only states it is a claim for ordinary negligence. ***Varner v. Classic Communities Corp.*, 890 A.2d 1068 (Pa. Super. 2006).**

Architect has no duty to warn contractor employees of visible overhead power lines that came into contact with metal scaffolding killing or injuring workers. Summary judgment in favor of architect affirmed. ***Frampton v. Dauphin Distribution Services Co.*, 436 Pa. Super. 486, 648 A.2d 326 (1994).**

Arm

Verdict $25,000—reduced to $20,000 by remittitur below—arm extensively lacerated with fluid developing in elbow—two operations to remove glass—concussion—out-of-pocket expenses $2,929.43—not excessive. ***Herron v. Silbaugh*, 436 Pa. 339, 260 A.2d 755.**

Armed robbery

Delivery man injured in armed robbery on hospital property brought action for failure to provide adequate security. Hospital and security firms not liable. Plaintiff failed to establish notice of danger from criminal attacks. ***Kerns v. Methodist Hospital*, 393 Pa. Super. 533, 574 A.2d 1068.**

Arrest

Plaintiff awarded damages totalling $1,543.44 for injuries suffered during arrest. Verdict not inadequate nor inconsistent. ***Catalano v. Bujak*, 537 Pa. 155, 642 A.2d 448.**

Error to admit evidence of a police officer who arrived 20 minutes after accident and who testified that he took one of operators to office of a justice of the peace and arrested him for reckless driving—new trial granted. ***Eastern Express, Inc. v. Food Haulers, Inc. et al.*, 445 Pa. 432, 285 A.2d 152.**

Arthroscopic surgery

Patient suffered nerve damage after arthroscopic knee surgery. Held: doctrine of res ipsa loquitur applicable in medical malpractice cases. ***Leone v. Thomas*, 428 Pa. Super. 217, 630 A.2d 900.**

Asbestos

Employees brought claims against the Defendants for the contraction of mesothelioma due to their exposure of asbestos dust. The trial court denied Defendants' motions for summary judgment based upon the exclusivity of the Workers' Compensation Act. The Superior Court reversed. The Pennsylvania Supreme Court held that as the Workers' Compensation Act required an injury to manifest within 300 weeks, and all of the Defendant's manifestations occurred after that period, the

Assault and battery

Workers' Compensation Act exclusion did not apply to their injuries. ***Tooey v. AK Steel Corporation*, 81 A.3d 851 (Pa. Super. 2013)**.

Plaintiff brought lawsuit for negligence and strict liability against Defendant university for exposure to asbestos. The trial court granted summary judgment in favor of the Defendant on the basis that Plaintiff was a paid graduate student at the time of his exposure and immune based upon the Workers' Compensation Act. The Superior Court reversed holding that it was a question of fact for the jury as to what percentage of exposure occurred while Plaintiff was working in his capacity as an employee and when he was working in his capacity as a Ph.D. student. ***Sabol v. Allied Glove Corporation*, 37 A.3d 1198 (Pa. Super. 2011)**.

Assault and battery

Stock trader brought negligent supervision claim against a stock exchange after he was assaulted by another trader on the floor of the stock exchange. Pennsylvania Supreme Court reversed the Superior Court's grant of judgment as a matter of law holding that the Federal Securities Exchange Act did not preempt a state tort claim arising out of personal injuries suffered on a stock exchange floor by a securities industry employee. ***Dooner v. DiDonato*, 971 A.2d 1187 (Pa. 2009)**.

Administrator sued a night club for wrongful death when one of its bouncers smothered decedent. Defendant night club appealed the trial court's summary judgment ruling that the alleged conduct causing wrongful death was excluded under its insurance policy. Appellate court reversed holding that negligence leading to an intentional act may be held an accident. ***QBE Insurance Corp. v. M & S Landis Corp.*, 915 A.2d 1222 (Pa. Super. 2007)**.

Summary judgment entered against plaintiff who was shot by a robber while a passenger on defendant's stopped train. Plaintiff alleged that defendant's trainman's failure to open the door of the train to allow plaintiff to escape before he was shot was a concurrent cause of his injury and that failure to act involved the operation of the motor vehicle. The Commonwealth Court distinguishes concurrent negligent acts from a negligent act by defendant and a criminal assault by a third party and also holds by implication that the failure to open the door was not "operation" of the motor vehicle. ***Greenleaf v. SEPTA*, 698 A.2d 170 (Pa. Cmwlth. 1997)**.

Summary judgment in favor of defendant affirmed because plaintiff's allegations that she was injured by an unknown assailant on SEPTA platform do not constitute defect of the land itself so as to constitute waiver of sovereign immunity. ***Warnecki v. SEPTA*, 689 A.2d 1023 (Pa. Cmwlth. 1997)**.

Order granting summary judgment reversed on plaintiff's claims of battery, breach of contract, and lack of informed consent arising out of back surgery performed by or at the direction of physicians to whom plaintiff had never given consent. ***Grabowski v. Quigley*, 454 Pa. Super. 27, 684 A.2d 610 (1996)**.

Female plaintiff who "repressed" memory of assaults that occurred more than 21 years in the past was not entitled to tolling of two year statute of limitations under the discovery rule. Order sustaining preliminary objections affirmed. ***Pearce v. Salvation Army*, 449 Pa. Super. 654, 674 A.2d 1123 (1996)**.

Assault and battery

Oil company that supplied gasoline to independent contractor service station had no duty to service station attendant who was assaulted and raped during course of employment. Demurrer to complaint granted. *Smith v. Exxon Corporation*, **436 Pa. Super. 221, 647 A.2d 577 (1994).**

Resident brought action against housing authority for failure of security guards to come to his aid during assault. Authority not liable. *Battle v. Philadelphia Housing Authority*, **406 Pa. Super. 578, 594 A.2d 769.**

Delivery man injured in armed robbery on hospital property brought action for failure to provide adequate security. Hospital and security firms not liable. Plaintiff failed to establish notice of danger from criminal attacks. *Kerns v. Methodist Hospital*, **393 Pa. Super. 533, 574 A.2d 1068.**

Victim who was raped in building being renovated brought action against contractor. Contractor not liable. Duty to secure building was to owner and not plaintiff. *Glick v. Martin and Mohler, Inc.*, **369 Pa. Super. 428, 535 A.2d 626.**

Passenger assaulted in subway concourse. City not liable. Injury not the result of artificial condition or defect of the land. *Johnson v. SEPTA*, **516 Pa. 312, 532 A.2d 409.**

Suit against Schuylkill County and Boy Scouts for damages arising out of injuries sustained by retarded child on camping trip. County dismissed as defendant. Allegation of negligent supervision not within exception to Sovereign Immunity Act. *Silkowski v. Hacker*, **95 Pa. Cmwlth. 226, 504 A.2d 995.**

Plaintiff playing basketball in city-owned recreation center, injured when intruders entered building and assaulted him. Held: not within any exceptions to governmental immunity Act. *Johnson v. City of Philadelphia*, **93 Pa. Cmwlth. 87, 500 A.2d 520.**

Suit against SEPTA and city for injuries sustained by plaintiff in mugging which occurred in subway concourse. Held: complaint did state cause of action against city as possessor of land and within exception to Political Subdivision Tort Claims Act. *Johnson v. SEPTA*, **91 Pa. Cmwlth. 587, 498 A.2d 22.**

School district held not to be liable for injuries to person assaulted by unknown assailant on adjacent sidewalk, and subsequent assault on school grounds. Under circumstances here, criminal acts not foreseeable use of school property. *Joner v. Board of Education of Philadelphia*, **91 Pa. Cmwlth. 145, 496 A.2d 1288.**

Action against school district and hotel for drowning of student while on school trip in Virginia. Held: Pennsylvania law applied and school district immune from suit under facts here. *Davis v. School District of Philadelphia*, **91 Pa. Cmwlth. 27, 496 A.2d 903.**

Released mental patient assaulted plaintiff. Waiver of immunity as to physicians employed by Commonwealth allows suit by third parties against doctors for improper release of patient. *Allentown State Hospital v. Gill*, **88 Pa. Cmwlth. 331, 488 A.2d 1211.**

Assault and battery

Member of local union, on picket duty during labor dispute, injured in fight. Even assuming unions created atmosphere susceptible to violence, there is no duty to refrain from creating such an atmosphere. ***LaZar v. Rur Industries***, 337 Pa. Super. 445, 487 A.2d 29.

Tenants brought action against apartment complex to recover for injuries resulting from criminal assault upon and kidnapping of tenants. Act originated in apartment garage. Evidence of previous criminal activity and alleged inadequate security. Held: landlord does have duty to provide adequate security to protect tenants from foreseeable criminal activity. ***Feld v. Merriam***, 314 Pa. Super. 414, 461 A.2d 225.

Non-jury verdict of $150,000. Plaintiff told firemen responding to false alarm that the two boys apprehended were the wrong children. Fireman argued with plaintiff, struck him in knee with wrench, necessitating eventual surgical removal of kneecap. Specials quite low due to free medical care given. Verdict affirmed. ***Powell v. City of Philadelphia***, 311 Pa. Super. 526, 457 A.2d 1307.

Rape of wife plaintiff in Philadelphia's Suburban Station. Jury verdict $250,000 compensatory damages, $500,000 punitive damages. Husband awarded $25,000 compensatory damages. Delay damages award should be limited to compensatory damages only. ***Colodonato v. Conrail***, 307 Pa. Super. 478, 453 A.2d 987.

Defendants shot bullets into car with four plaintiffs. Tamar Dombach struck six times—pieces remain in buttocks. Verdict: $60 medical, $600 pain and suffering, $750 punitive damages. Sandra Helm suffered slight scratch on back. Verdict: $400 pain and suffering, $750 punitive damages. Car owner received $446.47 property damages. Both male passengers, uninjured, received $750 punitive damages. Affirmed. Charge on punitive damages affirmed. Permissible to award punitive damages without compensatory damages. ***Rhoads v. Heberling***, 306 Pa. Super. 35, 451 A.2d 1378.

Fight between two employees in parking lot of employer. Plaintiff may maintain action against co-employee. Action was intentional. ***Gillespie v. Vecenie***, 292 Pa. Super. 11, 436 A.2d 695.

Plaintiff assaulted on train platform in City. Demurrer of City granted. Duty to provide police protection is public and cannot be claimed by individual. ***Chapman v. City of Philadelphia***, 290 Pa. Super. 281, 434 A.2d 753.

Suit against bar owner for failure to protect patron from assault by patron known to be a trouble maker and frequent patron of bar. Bartender had custody of said patron's gun for a period of time. Somehow he got gun out during argument with plaintiff and shot him. Verdict for plaintiff affirmed. ***Prather v. H-K Corp.***, 282 Pa. Super. 556, 423 A.2d 385.

Customer of defendant raped by a former employee of defendant at plaintiff's home. Complaint dismissed, but reinstated on appeal. Although employee terminated, if employer negligently hired said person, he may owe duty to customers to whose homes employee had been previously sent, to warn of firing. ***Coath v. Jones***, 277 Pa. Super. 479, 419 A.2d 1249.

Assumption of the Risk Doctrine

Plaintiff stabbed in supermarket parking lot. Evidence of previous crimes within store and store policy to limit cash in registers. Verdict for plaintiff affirmed. ***Murphy v. Penn Fruit*, 274 Pa. Super. 427, 418 A.2d 480.**

Broken ankle sustained when insured knocked down by other driver's fists. Not entitled to coverage under uninsured motorist clause. ***Day v. State Farm*, 261 Pa. Super. 216, 396 A.2d 3.**

After making purchase at store, plaintiff detained by detective who thought plaintiff was a shoplifter. Later received an apology. Minor bruises, but emotional problems 6-1/2 years later at time of her death from unrelated causes. Out of pocket only $18.00. Verdict $35,000 affirmed. Husband's claim for loss of conjugal rights brought verdict of $25,000—remitted to $17,500—affirmed. ***Hannigan v. S. Klein Department Store*, 244 Pa. Super. 597, 371 A.2d 872.**

Suit against Commonwealth, various agencies, and individuals for assault and murder committed by individual allegedly improperly released by State Mental Hospital. Suit against Commonwealth barred. Suit against individuals permitted upon allegation of gross negligence. ***Freach v. Commonwealth*, 471 Pa. 558, 370 A.2d 1163.**

Karen Fishell, additional defendant, walked out of mental institution without being seen, went to her apartment, got gun, then went to boyfriend's apartment and shot and killed girl in apartment. Verdict against Karen Fishell only. Mental institution absolved. ***Evanuik v. U. of Pittsburgh Western Psychiatric Institute*, 234 Pa. Super. 287, 338 A.2d 636.**

Assumption of the Risk Doctrine

Bicyclist brought a claim against a tour organizer and PennDOT for injuries suffered during a bicycle tour, after his tire became caught in a groove in the road causing him to fall. The Commonwealth Court affirmed the trial court's grant of summary judgment on the basis that the bicyclist voluntarily assumed the risk inherent in the bicycle tour and that his injury was the same risk that he had appreciated and assumed. ***Vinikoor v. Pedal Pennsylvania, Inc.*, 974 A.2d 1233 (Pa. Cmwlth. 2009).**

Inmate brought claim for negligence against prison after he was injured in a fall from his bunk while trying to open a malfunctioning cell door. The trial court granted summary judgment in favor of the prison. The Commonwealth Court upheld the trial court's ruling holding that a prison only owed a duty to inmates for reasonably foreseeable harm and that it was not reasonably foreseeable that an inmate would try to open a cell door from the top bunk and also that the inmate assumed the risk of falling by attempting to open the cell door from the top bunk knowing of the danger that he could fall. ***Cochrane v. Kopko*, 975 A.2d 1203 (Pa. Cmwlth. 2009).**

A skier who was struck by an uphill skier while traversing the base of the hill towards a ski lift sued facility for injuries. Facility raised assumption of risk as an affirmative defense and also the Skier's Responsibility Act, 42 Pa.C.S. § 7102. Supreme Court analyzed sport of skiing under assumption of risk doctrine

Assured Clear Distance Rule

and legislation and held that participation in any aspect of sport of downhill skiing, even while not skiing "down" the hill, is covered by assumption of risk and statute. ***Hughes v. Seven Springs Farm, Inc.*, 762 A.2d 339 (Pa. 2000).**

Proof of assumption of the risk requires the following: the defendant establish that the plaintiff consciously appreciated the risk attendant to a certain endeavor; assumed the risk of injury by engaging in the endeavor despite the appreciation of the risk involved; and injury sustained was, in fact, the same risked injury that was appreciated and assumed. Case includes a thorough analysis of the doctrine and its history. The court addresses liability of an owner who alleges that he is "out of possession" of residence under construction when he actually has retained control of the project. ***Bullman v. Giuntoli*, 761 A.2d 566 (Pa. Super. 2000).**

The court ruled in verse, short but not terse, and addressed all the issues presented. Two dogs and their walker, came in for a shocker, when defendant's car made one dog dented. The vet's fee at issue, for damaged dog tissue, composed the poor plaintiff's pup's claim. Driver argued contrib, cut short for this squib, as the reason the poor dog was maimed. He loudly protested, the dog was molested, because it came into the road. Unfortunately, for the driver you see, the transcript defies that contention. Sudden emergency, last clear chance, both theories were raised and were argued. The superior court, to excuse the tort, found naught in the facts or the pleadings. Payment is due, from you know who, and the dogs and their owner keep strolling. Though written in verse, which some find perverse, this case is correct and controlling. ***Zangrando v. Sipula*, 756 A.2d 73 (Pa. Super. 2000).**

Employee was injured when he stepped backwards into a hole in a roof because he was compelled by job requirements to walk backwards and look forward. After thorough analysis of comparative negligence and assumption of risk theories, court determined that, in employment context—because reasonable minds could differ as to whether plaintiff/employee deliberately and with awareness of specific risks inherent in the activity nonetheless engaged in the activity that produced his injury—plaintiff's actions raise a fact question regarding comparative negligence, not a legal question regarding defendant's lack of duty to a person who assumes a risk. ***Staub v. Toy Factory, Inc.*, 749 A.2d 522 (Pa. Super. 2000).**

Assured Clear Distance Rule

Sudden Emergency Doctrine and Assured Clear Distance rule are mutually exclusive as the first relates to a moving instrumentality thrust into a driver's path of travel and the second relates to objects traveling in the same direction which are static in relation to each other. Driver's inability to see brake lights or turn signals in front of him is not a sudden emergency. ***Cunningham v. Byers*, 732 A.2d 655 (Pa. Super. 1999).**

In three-car accident, plaintiff was driver of car in front of which another car turned. Defendant driving behind plaintiff struck plaintiff's and other defendant's cars. Plaintiff was allowed by trial court to offer sudden emergency defense to turning defendant's claim of plaintiff's negligence but following defendant was not. Affirmed by Superior Court but reversed by Supreme Court in opinion which clearly explains difference and interrelationship between assured clear distance rule and

Assured Clear Distance Rule

sudden emergency doctrine. Both plaintiff and following driver are entitled to argue sudden emergency doctrine under facts of case. *Levey v. DeNardo*, **725 A.2d 733 (Pa. 1999).**

Plaintiff was rear-seat passenger in car driven by defendant which encountered fog bank, left road and struck tree, injuring plaintiff. Trial court charged on sudden emergency doctrine to which plaintiff objected. Plaintiff argued that defendant's summary citation for breaking statutory assured clear distance rule precluded her from claiming sudden emergency; a tree is not a sudden emergency and amount of time it took for defendant to react argues against any suddenness. Held: summary charges, particularly when defendant did not even attend hearing on charge, cannot be admitted in civil cases as a general rule. Tree was not sudden emergency, the fog was. There was adequate evidence that defendant acted quickly and thoroughly to minimize sudden appearance of fog. Plaintiff's second argument that jury's distaste with trial court's habit of chewing tobacco during trial and spitting into a cup as prejudicial to plaintiff is totally unfounded. *Dickens v. Barnhart*, **711 A.2d 513 (Pa. Super. 1998).**

Driver who collided with garbage truck situated diagonally on road was entitled to jury instruction on sudden emergency doctrine. Where evidence is such that reasonable minds could differ as to whether sudden emergency existed, both assured clear distance and sudden emergency instructions should be given. Assured clear distance charge to jury that failed to detail effect of presumption that rule applies where driver was proceeding in safe and prudent manner was legally insufficient. *Lockhart v. List*, **542 Pa. 141, 665 A.2d 1176 (1995).**

Real property exception to sovereign immunity does not apply in automobile accident involving motorcyclist and driver. PennDOT's design and construction of road, including length of passing lane and speed limits, were not defects that caused motorcyclist's injuries but merely facilitated occurrence of accident when combined with negligence of driver. Assured clear distance rule does not apply where instrumentality moves into driver's path within a distance short of the assured clear distance ahead. Driver does not need to anticipate negligence of another driver in calculating his assured clear distance. *Nestor v. Com., Dept. of Transp.*, **___ Pa. Cmwlth. ___, 658 A.2d 829 (1995).**

Automobile driver injured in collision with oncoming car alleged sufficient facts to preclude summary judgment under assured clear distance rule. *Anderson v. Moore*, **437 Pa. Super. 642, 650 A.2d 1090 (1994).**

Driver killed while attempting to avoid cars stopped in middle of road. Held: failure to comply with assured clear distance rule was negligence as matter of law. *Springer v. Luptowski*, **535 Pa. 332, 635 A.2d 134.**

Motorcyclist who lost control while rounding curve brought action against Commonwealth and township. Held: jury charge on assured clear distance rule not in error and testimony of expert concerning control of motorcycle admissable. *Wicks v. Com., Dept. of Transp.*, **139 Pa. Cmwlth. 336, 590 A.2d 832.**

Assured Clear Distance Rule

Rear-end accident severely injuring passenger in lead auto. Proper to charge on assured clear distance and refuse charge on sudden emergency where striking truck driver testified that he saw auto 100 feet away and that truck was capable of stopping within 50-60 feet. Plaintiff verdict affirmed. ***Mineo v. Tancini*, 349 Pa. Super. 115, 502 A.2d 1300.**

Head-on collision where each side claimed other came across center of highway first. Improper to charge on assured clear distance when cars are moving in opposite direction, as here. However, charge upheld since it was claimed that one vehicle hit a guard rail and then crossed over. ***Mickey v. Ayers*, 336 Pa. Super. 512, 485 A.2d 1199.**

Rear-end collision occurred, allegedly because borough stopped traffic on state highway for Memorial Day parade. Although error here to charge on sudden emergency (not a sudden confrontation of perilous situation), found to be harmless error. Sudden emergency doctrine and assured clear distance rule are mutually exclusive. Plaintiff's verdict affirmed. ***Elder v. Orluck*, 334 Pa. Super. 329, 483 A.2d 474.**

Defendant's auto struck plaintiff's garden tractor head-on, as he was plowing snow from driveway near berm of highway. Exact locations of vehicles at impact disputed. Held: assured clear distance rule does apply at night on snowy road. Driver must take attending circumstances into account, and must be able to stop automobile within range of his headlights. ***Fish v. Gosnell*, 316 Pa. Super. 565, 463 A.2d 1042.**

Rear-end collision. Plaintiff's vehicle in plain view for some period of time. No excuse given. Clear violation of assured clear distance. Defense verdict overturned and new trial ordered. ***Antolik v. Kerstetter*, 278 Pa. Super. 55, 419 A.2d 1353.**

Plaintiff came over crest of hill at night and struck defendant's vehicle backing out of driveway. Charge correct that if assured clear distance foreshortened by an act not under driver's control and not the result of his negligence, then rule does not apply. Both drivers found negligent. ***Johnson v. O'Leary*, 277 Pa. Super. 223, 419 A.2d 742.**

Clear evidence of violation of Section 1002 of the Vehicle Code as to operating within assured clear distance ahead—collision with an overturned rig in highway—nonsuit proper. ***Hollern v. Verhovsek*, 220 Pa. Super. 343, 387 A.2d 145.**

Plaintiff, passenger in defendant's car, injured when car went out of control on loose gravel. Error to charge on sudden emergency. Where gravel was stationary, proper charge should have been on assured clear distance doctrine. ***Brown v. Schriver*, 254 Pa. Super. 468, 386 A.2d 45.**

Assured clear distance doctrine does not apply when a sudden and clear emergency presents itself to driver. Where truck swerved into oncoming lane to avoid suddenly stopped vehicle, issue of whether sudden emergency applies for jury. ***Stacy v. Thrower Trucking*, 253 Pa. Super. 150, 384 A.2d 1274.**

Assured Clear Distance Rule

Grade crossing accident. Claim of strong glare for driver of auto. Error on these facts not to charge on assured clear distance and allow jury to determine whether or not plaintiff travelling too fast. ***Evans v. Reading Co.*, 242 Pa. Super. 209, 363 A.2d 1234.**

Apparent head-on collision. Error to charge on assured clear distance unless jury clearly instructed that doctrine does not apply to vehicles moving toward one another. ***Turner v. Smith*, 237 Pa. Super. 161, 346 A.2d 806.**

Collision of auto and motorcycle. Unclear whether cycle turned right to avoid collision or auto turned onto street and cycle was on wrong side of highway. In either event, erroneous to charge on assured clear distance where there is a sudden emergency, oncoming vehicles, or where vehicle moves into path of another vehicle short of the assured clear distance. ***Unangst v. Whitehouse*, 235 Pa. Super. 458, 344 A.2d 695.**

Plaintiff's car stopped in center of street, at night, and plaintiff talking to someone outside of car. Defendant came over top of hill, lights on high beam, with clear view for 300 to 400 feet. Struck side of plaintiff's car. Verdict for plaintiff affirmed for failure to stop within assured clear distance. ***Farbacher v. Frank*, 228 Pa. Super. 35, 323 A.2d 233.**

Plaintiff driving at approximately 50 miles per hour at night—colliding with an overturned rig in highway—testimony established that he saw a warning cloud of dust a sufficient distance away to have enabled him to stop—violation of section 1002 of the Vehicle Code as to operation of a vehicle within assured clear distance—nonsuit properly granted. ***Hollern v. Verhovsek*, 220 Pa. Super. 343, 287 A.2d 145.**

Defendant approaching the crest of a hill—view ahead partially obstructed—contacting a vehicle turning into a driveway and then the vehicle of plaintiffs—court did not err in instructing jury that assured clear distance rule applied—rule applies even though the vision of the operator is limited by the nature of the roadway. ***Bachman, et al. v. Bell, et al.*, 218 Pa. Super. 873, 279 A.2d 207.**

Plaintiff on a motorcycle was following a car ahead—that car suddenly swerved to avoid an excavation made by defendant and plaintiff unaware of excavation injured in jumping from his vehicle—court erred in instructing jury that existence of car ahead obstructing view would excuse plaintiff's otherwise violation of assured clear distance rule—new trial awarded. ***Koelle v. Philadelphia Electric Co.*, 443 Pa. 35, 277 A.2d 350.**

Operator of car in which passenger plaintiff situate contended that the reason that he did not observe tractor of defendant sooner was that it was so dirty as to be virtually camouflaged until he was within 20 feet of it—collision—verdict for passenger sustained but new trial granted as to suit by operator to determine whether contribution should be had. ***Stano v. Rearick*, 441 Pa. 72, 271 A.2d 251.**

Trial judge instructed jury that defendant was negligent as a matter of law in failing to maintain statutory assured clear distance ahead—error—oral testimony

Attorney - See Legal Malpractice

involved—court cannot so rule as a matter of law—matter for jury. *McElhinny v. Iliff*, 436 Pa. 506, 260 A.2d 739.

Plaintiff's decedents were passengers in car which passed tractor trailer unit of defendant on the Turnpike and while in passing lane lost control—skidded into path of tractor trailer which was still on berm lane—collision—assured clear distance rule not involved under facts—judgment n.o.v. for defendant on appeal. *Laborda v. Markel*, 434 Pa. 184, 252 A.2d 686.

Attorney - See Legal Malpractice
Attractive nuisances

Child injured at playground adjacent to underground cave. Owner immune under Recreation Act even though admission charged for entrance to cave but not playground. *Zackhery v. Crystal Cave Company, Inc.*, 391 Pa. Super. 471, 571 A.2d 464.

Minor plaintiff injured by bullets found in car in defendant's garage. Defendant towed and stored abandoned cars for City of Easton. Although owner knew that children played in his lot, had no knowledge of dangerous articles left in glove compartment. Nonsuit affirmed. *Norton v. City of Easton*, 249 Pa. Super. 520, 378 A.2d 417.

Child of 4 entered a partially constructed building being built by defendant contractor—fell to cellar while walking backward and was severely injured—no recovery—a house in course of construction is not an attractive nuisance. *Goll et al. v. Muscara*, 211 Pa. Super. 93, 235 A.2d 443.

Boy of 9-1/2 years fell from a concrete block wall of a building being constructed—Section 339 of Restatement (2d) Torts adopted by Supreme Court and action of the Superior Court in entering judgment n.o.v. affirmed—plaintiff did not bring case within the "utility" provision of Section 339. *Jesko v. Turk*, 421 Pa. 434, 219 A.2d 591.

Authority of client

Attorney settled case without authority of client; executed Order to Settle, Discontinue and End and took draft without giving money to client. Settlement properly overturned—burden on debtor who failed to ascertain whether attorney had authority. *Rothman v. Fillete*, 305 Pa. Super. 28, 451 A.2d 225.

Attorney apparently settled case without express client authority. Held: express authority required, therefore settlement not consummated. *Garnet v. D'Alonzo*, 55 Pa. Cmwlth. 263, 422 A.2d 1241.

Automated External Defibrillator

Elementary analysis of negligence claim by patron of tennis club who suffered brain damage due to stoke following heart attack. Plaintiffs allege that the club was negligent in not having an Automated External Defibrillator ("AED") on the premises and using the device to restart husband plaintiff's heart. Defendant club argued that the Emergency Medical Services Act precluded its untrained employees

Autopsy

from using an AED even if it had one and the AED Good Samaritan Act had not yet been passed. Grant of summary judgment in favor of defendant club affirmed. ***Atcovitz v. Gulph Mills Tennis Club*, Inc., 571 Pa. 580, 812 A.2d 1218 (Pa. 2002).**

Plaintiff patron alleged that the injuries he suffered from a heart attack were increased because defendant tennis club that did not have an automatic external defibrillator. Club pleaded that its employees were legally prohibited from using such a device under the Emergency Medical Services Act that relates to emergency medical service personnel. As there is no restriction on the use of such devices by lay persons, the elements of negligence were properly pleaded and the dismissal was reversed. ***Atcovitz v. Gulph Mills Tennis Club*, Inc., 766 A.2d 1280 (Pa. Super. 2001).**

Automatic door

Shopper injured when an automatic door closed on her while exiting a grocery store. In count against store for negligent treatment of a business invitee, plaintiff alleged that the automatic door posed an unreasonable risk of harm to some of its customers and that the store knew or should have known of the risk and failed to protect its customers. Opinion defines duty to business invitees and basic elements of negligence. ***Summers v. Giant Food Stores*, 743 A.2d 498 (Pa. Super. 1999).**

Patient injured when automatic door closed on leg. Held: compulsory nonsuit improper. Patient presented prima facia case. ***McDonald v. Aliquippa Hospital*, 414 Pa. Super. 317, 606 A.2d 1218.**

Plaintiff injured when struck in buttocks by automatic door at supermarket, as she bent over rail to reach for trading stamp book. Jury verdict for defendant affirmed. Held: not latent or unusual defect. ***Brancato v. Kroger Co., Inc.*, 312 Pa. Super. 448, 458 A.2d 1377.**

Automatic door locks

Car owner allowed to proceed to trial on theory that automatic door lock design was negligent in that it prevented her from being able to keep an attacker out of her car after the engine was turned off. ***Moroney v. General Motors Corporation*, 850 A.2d 629 (Pa. Super. 2004).**

Automobile dealer

Jury verdict as to liability only in favor of defendant used car dealership affirmed. Plaintiff injured by driver of stolen car failed to state a cause of action, where sole allegation of negligence was that dealership employees left keys in newly delivered vehicles in violation of unattended motor vehicle section of the Pennsylvania Vehicle Code. ***Santarlas v. Leaseway Motorcar Transport Company*, 456 Pa. Super. 34, 689 A.2d 311 (1997).**

Autopsy

Plaintiff's suit for negligence and negligent infliction of emotional distress against physician who performed autopsy on plaintiff's mother and same causes of action and respondeat superior against hospital. Autopsy report indicated that de-

Autopsy report changed

ceased mother's eyes had been "donated" despite insistence by plaintiff that eyes were not to be donated. Claims for emotional distress and respondeat superior dismissed on preliminary objections. Verdict in favor of plaintiff reversed on grounds that evidence was not adequate to prove that eyes had, in fact, been donated. The physician who had performed the autopsy amended report to indicate that he never looked to see if the eyes were in place. ***Van Zandt v. Holy Redeemer Hospital*, 806 A.2d 879 (Pa. Super. 2002).**

Autopsy report changed

Plaintiff's decedent had been in apparent health but became suddenly ill and condition diagnosed as gastroenteritis—discharged from hospital—died some 38 hours later—autopsy report changed to give cause of death as myocarditis—verdict for defendants—motions below properly dismissed—fair trial had been had. ***Brennan v. St. Luke's Hospital et al.*, 446 Pa. 339, 285 A.2d 471.**

B—

BB gun

Minor child who was in shared custody of separated parents negligently shot a friend with a BB gun. Suit brought against mother who had physical custody at the time of the shooting and father who did not have custody but who had purchased BB gun and was aware that the son had taken it to his mother's house. Held that father's status as a legal custodian is not, in and of itself, dispositive in establishing that he had the ability and opportunity to control his child's behavior at the time of the shooting. *K.H. and D.A.H. v. J.R. and N.R.*, 826 A.2d 863 (Pa. 2003).

Minor plaintiff injured when shot with a BB gun in possession of a friend, also a minor. In suit against non-custodial father and his son, the shooter, summary judgment was granted in favor of father on grounds that he was did not have custody or control of son. Reversed and remanded on grounds that lack of custody of minor is not a controlling issue where a jury may determine that father knew that son had the gun, (father had given it to him as a present), he knew the son had taken the gun to his mother's home without her knowledge and he knew that son might misuse the gun. *K.H. and D.A.H. v. J.R. and N.R.*, 778 A.2d 695 (Pa. Super. 2001).

Pedestrian injured by shot fired from BB gun by passenger in vehicle brought action against driver. Driver not liable. *Troutman v. Meschella*, 421 Pa. Super. 620, 618 A.2d 982.

Baby sitter

Baby sitter, while in employ of parents of small children, struck service station attendant while driving her own car. Action against parents of child disallowed. They neither expected nor gave permission for sitter to use car in scope of employment. *Ferrell v. Martin*, 276 Pa. Super. 175, 419 A.2d 152.

Backing

Decedent pedestrian struck at night by defendant's car backing into plaintiff's standing vehicle—verdict for defendant—new trial properly granted. *Dugan v. Niglo*, 436 Pa. 22, 258 A.2d 501.

Back injuries

Order granting summary judgment reversed on plaintiff's claims of battery, breach of contract, and lack of informed consent arising out of back surgery performed by or at the direction of physicians to whom plaintiff had never given consent. *Grabowski v. Quigley*, 454 Pa. Super. 27, 684 A.2d 610 (1996).

Back up warning

Products liability plaintiff whose foot was crushed by forklift that was not equipped with rear view mirrors or back-up warning device appealed verdict of $100,000.00 as inadequate in light of medical bills of more than $98,000, lost wages in excess of $145,000.00 and future lost wages in excess of $815,000.00. Plaintiff also argued that trial court should not have admitted evidence of plaintiff's alleged

Bailing wire

contributory negligence in strict product liability case and Superior Court agreed. ***Charlton v. Toyota Industrial Equipment*, 714 A.2d 1043 (Pa. Super. 1998).**

Bailing wire

Plaintiff injured by reason of a bailing wire striking him in the eye—only witness as to causation was an expert who would only say that occurrence "could have" or "probably" due to a defect claimed as cause—when further questioned he reiterated that "could" was the only term he could use—held: testimony inadmissible and judgment *n.o.v.* entered for defendant. ***Niggel v. Sears, Roebuck & Co.*, 219 Pa. Super. 353, 281 A.2d 718.**

Bailments

Welder injured while repairing air tank which exploded when pressurized for testing. Nonsuit granted as to owner of tank. Section 388 of Restatement (2d) Torts applies. No reason to believe owner knew of dangerous condition or that experienced welder wouldn't himself realize the danger under facts here. Affirmed. ***Herleman v. Trumbauer Auto Sales*, 346 Pa. Super. 494, 499 A.2d 1109.**

Plaintiff injured when wheel on machine he was using separated and struck him in head. §388 of Restatement (2d) Torts applies to defendant who contracted to repair. This was a bailment for repair. Duty on bailee to make reasonable inspections. Supplier then only liable for failure to warn of known dangers or dangers he had reason to know about. New trial granted due to improper charge. ***Lambert v. Pittsburgh Bridge and Iron Works*, 227 Pa. Super. 50, 323 A.2d 107.**

Plaintiff left car in defendant's parking lot—took claim check from machine and locked car—check was to be presented on removing car—car missing—not a bailment but error to enter summary judgment in favor of parking lot operator—plaintiff entitled to prove circumstances and whether attendant negligent in permitting car to be removed without presentation of claim check. ***Sparrow v. Airport Parking Co. of America*, 221 Pa. Super. 32, 289 A.2d 87.**

Bakery products

Defendant corporation supplied bakery articles to individual defendant for distribution—individual defendant owned and maintained vehicles—plaintiff injured by the vehicle operated by the individual defendant—individual defendant an independent contractor and corporate defendant not responsible. ***George v. Nemeth*, 426 Pa. 551, 233 A.2d 231.**

Bank

Bank employees, manager and assistant manager, held liable for undue influence in convincing depositor to name employees as sole beneficiaries of substantial accounts and bank held liable for negligent supervision of the employees. ***Owens v. Mazzei*, 847 A.2d 700 (Pa. Super. 2004).**

Negligence protections afforded to banks under the Uniform Fiduciaries Act are not available when the bank acts in bad faith. ***Melley v. Pioneer Bank, N.A.*, 834 A.2d 1191 (Pa. Super. 2003).**

Corporation brought action against bank for negligently permitting officer to withdraw funds and borrow money. Held: Corporation entitled to jury instruction on wanton misconduct. *Summit Fasteners, Inc. v. Harleysville National Bank*, 410 Pa. Super. 56, 599 A.2d 203.

Employee of bank allegedly injured when guard at bank, employed by detective agency, robbed bank and injured employee by tying her up and putting her in closet. State sued for not performing statutory duty to prevent known criminals from being employed by private detective agencies. Held: not an exception to Sovereign Immunity Act. Demurrer granted. *Nicholson v. M & S Detective Agency*, 94 Pa. Cmwlth. 521, 503 A.2d 1106.

Bankruptcy

Plaintiffs filed suit to recover for injuries suffered in a motor vehicle accident. The trial court granted summary judgment on the basis that Plaintiff's claim had been dismissed by a bankruptcy court order. The Superior Court affirmed holding that as Plaintiffs had failed to object to the bankruptcy court's notice of discharge of their claim against the Defendant they could not recover against the Defendant. *Gubbiotti v. Santey*, 2012 Pa. Super. 131 (Pa. Super. 2012).

Barricades

Child injured in street by car after being forced to leave sidewalk due to city-placed barricade. City not liable under exception to Political Subdivision Tort Claims Act because injuries not caused by care, custody, or control of real property or dangerous condition of sidewalk. *Kiley by Kiley v. City of Philadelphia*, 537 Pa. 502, 645 A.2d 184 (1994).

Barrier

Pedestrian who was injured by nylon rope strung between trees and signposts by police was entitled to bring action against city as the rope was a "traffic control device" under exceptions to governmental immunity. *Pettineio v. City of Philadelphia*, 721 A.2d 65 (Pa. Cmwlth. 1998).

Bathroom

In negligence action against corporate defendant and officers, officers are not liable for failing to maintain clean bathroom absent proof of their participation in creating or allowing continued existence of dangerous condition. Party's failure to answer request for admission that states a conclusion of law does not establish plaintiff's case. Judgment in favor of plaintiff vacated and remanded for consideration of scope of involvement and liability of owners. *Brindley v. Woodland Village Restaurant, Inc.*, 438 Pa. Super. 385, 652 A.2d 865 (1995).

Battery

Plaintiff injured when battery exploded while trying to jump-start vehicle. Trial court erred by instructing jury on malfunction doctrine and by not instructing on assumption of the risk. *Lonan v. Pep Boys, Manny, Moe, & Jack*, 371 Pa. Super. 291, 538 A.2d 22.

Bendectin

Bendectin

Plaintiffs parents and minor child received verdict against drug manufacturer on basis of allegations that mother's ingestion of Bendectin during pregnancy resulted in child being born with club feet. Denial of defendant's request for judgment not withstanding the verdict appealed and reversed by Superior Court with order to enter judgment *n.o.v.* Plaintiffs' expert's testimony did not meet standard of *Frye v. United States*, 293 F. 1013 (D.C Cir 1923) (scientific or medical testimony must draw its convincing force from some principle of science, mathematics and the like). **Blum v. Merrell Dow Pharmaceuticals, Inc., 705 A.2d 1314 (Pa. Super. 1997).**

Beryllium plant

Plaintiff allegedly injured by the emission of the fumes from a beryllium plant—court below granted judgment *n.o.v.*—Supreme Court reversed and held that the conduct of the defendant after 1950, the date when the Atomic Energy Commission prescribed unsafe toxicity levels, constituted actionable negligence. **Heck v. Beryllium Corp., 424 Pa. 140, 226 A.2d 87.**

Bicycles

Bicyclist brought a claim against a tour organizer and PennDOT for injuries suffered during a bicycle tour, after his tire became caught in a groove in the road causing him to fall. The Commonwealth Court affirmed the trial court's grant of summary judgment on the basis that the bicyclist voluntarily assumed the risk inherent in the bicycle tour and that his injury was the same risk that he had appreciated and assumed. **Vinikoor v. Pedal Pennsylvania, Inc., 974 A.2d 1233 (Pa. Cmwlth. 2009).**

Minor bicyclist injured when struck by car was granted new trial as to damages only after jury apportioned negligence 50/50 between driver and bicyclist and no negligence by parents but did not award damages. **Nykiel v. Heyl, 838 A.2d 808 (Pa. Super. 2003).**

Plaintiff was injured when struck by a bicycle being ridden by a police officer on patrol on the sidewalk. A municipal ordinance prohibited riding bicycles on sidewalks. Held, a bicycle is not a "motor vehicle" as defined in the motor vehicle exception to governmental immunity. All courts agree that this is a seemingly unjust result that must be remedied in the future by legislation. **Harding v. City of Philadelphia, 777 A.2d 1249 (Pa. Cmwlth. 2001)**.

Plaintiff bicyclist granted a new trial after review of trial record in which defendant automobile driver admitted striking plaintiff and causing injuries. Jury answered interrogatories that automobile driver was negligent but that negligence was not substantial factor in causing injury. In light of uncontradicted testimony by automobile driver that she had to back her car off the plaintiff's foot, the causal connection was clear. **Krucskowska v. Winter, 764 A.2d 627 (Pa. Super. 2000).**

Bicyclist alleged injuries as a result of being grabbed by police officer who was directing traffic on street where riding bicycles was expressly prohibited. Bi-

Bicycles

cyclist waived argument that governmental immunity defense did not exist under waiver provision of Philadelphia Code. Waiver provision of Philadelphia Code was invalidated as of the date of enactment of governmental immunity provisions of the Judicial Code. Police officer directing traffic is not a traffic control and therefore his acts do not fall within the traffic control exception to governmental immunity. Order granting summary judgment affirmed. ***Robinson v. City of Philadelphia,* ___ Pa. Cmwlth. ___, 666 A.2d 1141 (1995).**

Bicyclist brought action against motorist for injuries resulting from collision. Evidence of bicyclist's intoxication found not admissible. ***Locke v. Claypool,* 426 Pa. Super. 528, 627 A.2d 801.**

Bicycle rider injured when hay thrown from tractor pulled wagon caused him to collide with tree. Rider not entitled to uninsured motorist benefits. Injury did not arise out of ownership, maintenance or use of vehicle. ***Smith v. United Services Automobile Association,* 392 Pa. 248, 572 A.2d 785.**

Child injured when riding bicycle at city-owned tennis court. Genuine issues of material fact precluded dismissal of action. ***McNeill by McNeill v. City of Philadelphia,* 104 Pa. Cmwlth. 494, 522 A.2d 174.**

Bike accident occurred when dog chased and collided with bicycle. Reversed summary judgment for defendant. Material fact existed as to adequacy of restraint and due care taken by owners in restraining dog. ***Skowronski v. Bailey,* 330 Pa. Super. 83, 478 A.2d 1362.**

Plaintiff's fall on new bicycle caused by excessively wavy rear wheel, improperly assembled rear axle bearing and overly tightened rear brake. Verdict for plaintiff against manufacturer and retailer, although bicycle sent to retailer in partially unassembled condition; Strict liability. ***Ries v. MTD Products, Inc.,* 310 Pa. Super. 118, 456 A.2d 211.**

Auto-bicycle accident causing death to rider of bicycle. Defense verdict affirmed. Plaintiff found to be 79% at fault in somehow straying from berm onto highway. ***Yandrich v. Radic,* 291 Pa. Super. 75, 435 A.2d 226.**

Child killed by auto while riding her bicycle. Verdict for defendant affirmed. Defendant testified that he was going 20-25 m.p.h. when child appeared two to three feet away. Expert engineer computed auto's speed at time brakes locked of 11.3 m.p.h. Auto skid marks of 6 feet 9 inches. ***Haeberle v. Peterson,* 262 Pa. Super. 247, 396 A.2d 738.**

Wrongful death and survival action for death of 20 year old bicycle rider struck by auto. Error to exclude guilty plea on charge of driving under the influence. New trial ordered since verdict for plaintiff could have been compromise. ***Cromley v. Gardner,* 253 Pa. Super. 467, 385 A.2d 433.**

Verdict $8200 wrongful death and $35,000 survival action. Decedent 14 year old boy riding bicycle when struck and killed at intersection by auto. Plaintiff had stop sign. Reversed and new trial ordered. Evidentiary errors related to defendant's drinking. Error to allow counsel to mention insurance. Error to have stated that bi-

Bifurcation

cycle not subject to Vehicle Code, even though corrected later in charge. Required immediate correction. *Selby v. Brown,* **250 Pa. Super. 134, 378 A.2d 862.**

Auto-bicycle collision at night. New trial ordered. Bicycle not required to have headlight if on berm and not on highway. Failure to have light must be a proximate cause. General charge on lighting inadequate. *Adams v. Mackleer,* **239 Pa. Super. 244, 361 A.2d 439.**

Minor plaintiff on bicycle struck by defendant's truck—conflicting evidence—verdict for defendant—error to grant a new trial. *Burrell v. Phila. Electric Co.,* **438 Pa. 286, 265 A.2d 516.**

Minor plaintiff, aged 12, was operating his bicycle at night on berm of road—struck by car operated by defendant who had defective vision—case for jury. *Masters v. Alexander*, **424 Pa. 65, 225 A.2d 905.**

Bifurcation

In automobile accident, testimony by State Trooper with familiarity of truck inspection procedures properly disallowed as to standard of care required by truck driver. Comparative Negligence Act requires that jury apportion liability between plaintiff and all defendants against whom recovery is sought. Trial court's bifurcation to allow apportionment of liability between fewer than all defendants reversed. *Christiansen v. Silfies,* **446 Pa. Super. 464, 667 A.2d 396 (1995).**

Big Brother and Big Sister Organization

Local and national Big Brother/Big Sister organization does not owe minor who was sexually abused by organization member with prior history of abuse a duty to warn where minor does not have any ties to the organization. Summary judgment affirmed. *J.E.J. v. Tri-County Big Brothers/Big Sisters, Inc.,* ___ **Pa. Super.** ___, **692 A.2d 582 (1997).**

Bingo game

Plaintiff's decedent attended a club bingo game and on leaving allegedly fell on club's premises—plaintiff failed to establish defendant's negligence as the proximate cause of the fall—what caused fall only a guess or conjecture—nonsuit proper. *Watkins v. Sharon Aerie No. 327 F.O.E.,* **423 Pa. 396, 223 A.2d 742.**

Birth defect

Plaintiffs parents and minor child received verdict against drug manufacturer on basis of allegations that mother's ingestion of Bendectin during pregnancy resulted in child being born with club feet. Denial of defendant's request for judgment not withstanding the verdict appealed and reversed by Superior Court with order to enter judgment *n.o.v.* Plaintiffs' expert's testimony did not meet standard of *Frye v. United States*, 293 F. 1013 (D.C Cir 1923) (scientific or medical testimony must draw its convincing force from some principle of science, mathematics and the like). *Blum v. Merrell Dow Pharmaceuticals, Inc.*, **705 A.2d 1314 (Pa. Super. 1997).**

Parents of child who died from birth defects brought action against obstetricians. Held: since jury could not reach verdict, trial judge did not commit error by

Bleachers

failing to mold verdict in favor of defendants. ***Kreider v. Wellenbach*, 422 Pa. Super. 207, 619 A.2d 319.**

Damages for infant plaintiff, with birth defect not detected by early tests *in utero*, had no cause of action. Case dismissed. ***Ellis v. Sherman*, 330 Pa. Super. 42, 478 A.2d 1339.**

Child born with birth defect has no cause of action against lab or physician who allegedly failed to determine, prenatally, and in sufficient time to prevent birth, that child was afflicted with defect. ***Rubin v. Hamot Medical Center*, 329 Pa. Super. 439, 478 A.2d 869.**

Blast furnace

Two workers—one injured and one killed when jammed bricks in blast furnace on which they were working collapsed on them. Work not being done in usual course and posed unusual dangers. Verdict for plaintiffs reversed due to incomplete charge on Section 413 of Restatement (2d) Torts dealing with precautions necessary for work entrusted to contractors. ***Gonzalez v. U.S. Steel*, 248 Pa. Super. 95, 374 A.2d 1334.**

Blasting

Plaintiff injured by blasting operation in road construction—had an ulcer and contended occurrence aggravated condition—defendant urged other causes—court in error in charge—to escape liability defendant must show that contributing causes would have brought about injury without wrongful act—new trial granted. ***Boushell v. J.H. Beers, Inc.*, 215 Pa. Super. 439, 258 A.2d 682.**

Plaintiff owner of building damaged by fire—evidence from which jury could draw inference of negligent blasting causing an electrical fire—nonsuit improperly granted below—for jury. ***DeFrank v. Sullivan Trail Coal Co.*, 425 Pa. 512, 229 A.2d 899.**

Bleachers

Wooden bleachers from which plaintiff fell when they tipped over were not part of the real estate so as to allow suit to proceed against city under real estate exception to the Political Subdivision Tort Claims Act. ***Blocker v. City of Philadelphia*, 763 A.2d 373 (Pa. 2000).**

Plaintiff was injured when old bleachers on which she had been sitting collapsed. Summary judgment in favor of City granted based on determination by lower court that bleachers were personal property and not real estate and so did not fall under the real property exception to governmental immunity. Reversed on appeal because issue of whether bleachers were real or personal property was for jury. ***Blocker v. City of Philadelphia*, 729 A.2d 187 (Pa. Cmwlth. 1999).**

Because bleachers constituted a defective improvement to the land, Recreation Use of Land and Water Act did not bar spectator's claim against Township for injuries sustained in fall from bleachers at Township ball field. Order granting sum-

Blinded by lights

mary judgment reversed. ***Brown v. Tunkhannock Township,*** ___ **Pa. Cmwlth.** ___, **665 A.2d 1318 (1995).**

Blinded by lights

Pedestrian struck by car while he was walking in street. No sidewalks and steep embankments when prohibited walking off roadway. Driver claimed he was blinded by light of oncoming traffic. Verdict against driver affirmed. ***Drew v. Laber,*** **477 Pa. 297, 383 A.2d 941.**

Blindness

Legally blind patient fell on sidewalk outside of ophthalmologist's office. Patient found lying near hole in sidewalk. Held: summary judgment for defendants improper. ***Morlas v. Tasman,*** **527 Pa. 132, 589 A.2d 205.**

Blind solicitor of brooms falling into an areaway on defendant's property which was under construction and alteration—plaintiff a business invitee—case for jury. ***Argo v. Goodstein,*** **438 Pa. 468, 265 A.2d 783.**

Blood alcohol content

Driver of vehicle that collided with tree and utility pole brought action against Commonwealth and landowner. Driver found 70% negligent, Commonwealth 30% negligent. Evidence of driver's blood alcohol level properly admitted to show contributory negligence. ***Crosby v. Com., Dept. of Transp.,*** **378 Pa. Super. 72, 548 A.2d 281.**

Plaintiff a passenger in car that became disabled; struck while standing in center of road in front of car, attempting to wave on traffic. Plaintiff found 70% at fault. Proper to admit blood-alcohol of .185% taken two to three hours later at hospital, by the expert testimony given here. ***Emerick v. Carson,*** **325 Pa. Super. 308, 472 A.2d 1133.**

Defense verdict affirmed. Patron consumed three double shots of whiskey, plus beer; then had one-vehicle accident. Charge affirmed—no inference that plaintiff visibly intoxicated as a result of blood alcohol taken at hospital. Also proper to tell jury to disregard whether plaintiff was negligent in ordering or consuming the alcohol. Only issue was visible intoxication when served. ***Suskey v. Moose Lodge,*** **325 Pa. Super. 94, 472 A.2d 663.**

Court expressed skepticism in dictum of testimony which would interpolate back three hours the results of a blood alcohol test taken three hours post accident. ***Schwarzback v. Dunn,*** **252 Pa. Super. 454, 381 A.2d 1295.**

Offer of testimony of a physician that blood alcohol content of .14 would "affect" operator in his driving properly excluded—must establish a degree of intoxication which proves unfitness to drive. ***Billow v. Farmers Trust Co.,*** **438 Pa. 514, 266 A.2d 92.**

Boating accidents

Blood bank employee

Blood bank employee contracted AIDS after being splashed with HIV-infected blood. Blood not tested. Blood bank director negligent but not liable. ***James v. Nolan*, 418 Pa. Super. 425, 614 A.2d 709.**

Blood Shield Statute

In a case of first impression, plaintiff brought suit against supplier of platelets by which she was allegedly infected with hepatitis-B and hepatitis-C alleging strict liability, breach of warranty and negligence. Summary judgment granted on strict liability and breach of warranty claims based on Pennsylvania Blood Shield Statute 42 Pa.C.S. §8333. Negligence count dismissed for plaintiff's failure to provide expert report. Affirmed by Superior Court which held that manufacturer of blood products was included in defined class of "person" under the act. ***Weishorn v. Miles-Cutter*, 721 A.2d 811 (Pa. Super. 1998).**

Blood transfusion

Plaintiff who contracted AIDS following transfusion of tainted blood filed suit against treating physicians and family physician for medical malpractice. Claim against one defendant dismissed for plaintiff's failure to establish through medical testimony that defendant's actions deviated from good and acceptable medical standards. Proof of compliance with medical standard of care need not be expressed in precisely the language used to annunciate the legal standard. Physician not required to obtain patient's informed consent before blood transfusion which was administered separately from a surgical procedure. ***Hoffman v. Brandywine Hospital*, 443 Pa. Super. 245, 661 A.2d 397 (1995).**

Boating accidents

Plaintiff brought negligence action against owner of a public lake after plaintiff was injured when his boat was struck by another boat operator on the defendant's lake. The trial court entered summary judgment on behalf of the defendant. The Superior Court affirmed holding that a lake was "land" within the meaning of the Recreational Use of Land and Water Act and a landowner must have actual knowledge of a danger to be precluded from statutory immunity under the act. ***Ruspi v. Glatz*, 69 A.3d 680 (Pa. Super. 2013).**

Plaintiff's decedents were killed when their boat was trapped in the main channel of a dam on the Susquehanna River which created "Lake Frederick". Plaintiffs allege that the owner of the dam was negligent in failing to warn of the location of the dam. Defendants allege that they are immune from suit under the provisions of the Recreation Use of Land and Water Act (68 P.S. §477-1 *et seq.*). Trial court determined that the dam was a substantial improvement to the real property and therefore the immunity granted by the act was not available. Affirmed on basis that the act is designed to protect owners of large unimproved tracts of land that have not been altered. ***York Haven Power Co. v. Stone*, 715 A.2d 1164 (Pa. Super. 1998).**

Plaintiff fractured a lumbar vertebra in boating accident. Verdict of $500 awarded; nothing for loss of consortium claim of wife. Jury found 50% contributory

Body

negligence. Verdict held inadequate based upon loss of income, and pain and suffering evidence, which was uncontradicted. Failure to award loss of consortium also shocking. New trial on damages only. ***Deitrick v. Karnes,* 329 Pa. Super. 372, 478 A.2d 835.**

Compulsory nonsuit entered, reversed on appeal. Dredges had created sharp drop-off in Ohio River at boat launch area, where decedent had parked with girlfriend. Car rolled forward over drop-off. Presumption of due care precludes trial court from ruling decedent was contributorily negligent as a matter of law. ***Hawthorne v. Dravo Corp.,* 313 Pa. Super. 436, 460 A.2d 266.**

Case arose as the result of collision of two boats in water situated within Commonwealth—place and manner of collision highly disputed—verdict for defendant—new trial refused below—Supreme Court followed rule that such action will only be reversed where clear abuse of discretion exists or an error of law exists which is controlling. ***Chesko v. Steinbaugh,* 434 Pa. 82, 252 A.2d 644.**

Body

Defendants wantonly, intentionally and outrageously disposed of the body of the plaintiffs' son—held: a recovery could be had in tort for the emotional distress caused by such conduct. ***Papieves v. Kelly,* 437 Pa. 373, 263 A.2d 118.**

Boiler

In action arising from explosion of boiler caused by defective emergency shut off valve, manufacturer of valve held strictly liable for defective product. Manufacturer's liability for its defective product is outlined in Section 402A of Restatement (2nd) Torts, which provides that a plaintiff must prove that the product was sold in a defective condition dangerous to the user and that the defect was the proximate cause of the injury. An actor is relieved from liability owing to an intervening or superseding cause only if the intervening or superseding negligent acts were so extraordinary as not to have been reasonably foreseeable. Summary judgment affirmed in part and reversed in part. ***Dougherty v. Edward J. Meloney, Inc.,* 443 Pa. Super. 201, 661 A.2d 375 (1995).**

Plaintiff's decedent killed by reason of a boiler explosion—cause of explosion was due to a valve manufactured by added defendant—valve stuck and caused added pressure—suit was against owner of boiler who brought in value manufacturer—case falls within provisions of strict liability under Section 402A of Restatement (2d) Torts—verdict for plaintiff against boiler owner and over against added defendant on ground of indemnity. ***Burbage v. Boiler Eng. & Supp. Co. Inc. et al.,* 433 Pa. 319, 249 A.2d 563.**

Bone plate and screws

Plaintiff filed suit based on lack of informed consent where physicians implanted bone screws to aid in fixation of spinal column, a use of the bone screws that had not been specifically approved by the FDA in its review of bone screw technology. Plaintiff alleged that physician's failure to inform him of FDA status of bone screw use for spinal fixation prevented plaintiff from giving fully informed consent to implantation. Held that lack of FDA approval does not constitute a determination that an off-label use of a medical device is necessarily dangerous and that a patient must be informed of that use. ***Southard v. Temple University Hospital,* 566 Pa. 335, 781 A.2d 101 (2001)**.

State law claims for manufacture and sale of defective surgical repair screws and plates were not preempted by medical device amendments to federal food and drug act. Actions for failure to warn, strict liability, negligence, and implied warranty are preempted by medical device amendment to federal food and drug act. Summary judgment affirmed in part and reversed in part. ***Burgstahler v. Acromed Corporation,* 448 Pa. Super. 26, 670 A.2d 658 (1996)**.

Bone tumor

Accident victim brought malpractice action against hospital and physician for failure to diagnose bone tumor in skull. Hospital and physician not liable. Connection between negligence and injury not shown. ***Bowser v. Lee Hospital,* 399 Pa. Super. 332, 582 A.2d 369**.

Borrowed Servant Doctrine

Plaintiff, a trainee with a non-profit, brought negligence action against Defendant city after he slipped and fell while helping to clean up flood damage. The trial court granted summary judgment in favor of the city on the basis that the city had immunity under the Workers' Compensation Act. The Commonwealth Court affirmed holding that under the borrowed servant doctrine the city was the Plaintiff's employer, because the non-profit had loaned its workers to the city and the city had controlled the performance of the work and the Plaintiff's hours of work. ***Canot v. City of Easton,* 37 A.3d 53 (Pa. Cmwlth. Ct. 2012)**.

Bottles

Alleged drinking from soft drink bottle containing glass particles. Verdict for defendant. Without bottle and pieces of glass, plaintiff did not meet burden of proof. ***Williams v. Pepsi-Cola,* 240 Pa. Super. 578, 362 A.2d 314**.

Plaintiff, a retailer, was injured by explosion of a bottle of beer—defendant glass company manufactured bottle, defendant brewery company bottled the beer and defendant Kronzek was the distributor who sold the beer to the plaintiff—verdict for defendants—new trial granted—plaintiff's expert not entitled to give an opinion by the court below—held on appeal: he was entitled to give an opinion even though he had testified that he could not give an absolutely positive opinion. ***Bialek v. Pittsburgh Brewing Co. et al.,* 430 Pa. 176, 242 A.2d 231**.

Bowling

Plaintiff bowler slipped or failed to properly slide and was injured while using one of defendant's lanes—expert testimony was properly rejected and there being no other evidence of a defect, a nonsuit was properly entered. ***Houston v. Canon Bowl, Inc.,* 443 Pa. 383, 289 A.2d 908**.

Box-making machine

Box-making machine

Product liability plaintiff was cleaning a corrugated-box making machine when his gloved hand came in contact with moving parts and he lost two and one-half fingers. Prior to beginning cleaning process, plaintiff had "stopped" machine to best of his knowledge. On direct examination it was brought out that there was a label which warned of serious bodily injury if certain precautions were ignored and that those precautions were set forth in a manual. Despite court's refusal to admit manual, it was established on cross-examination that plaintiff had never read manual and that, although manual addressed potential for serious bodily injury, there was no warning about specific problem which injured plaintiff. Held: by eliciting testimony which suggested that reading manual would have prevented injuries, machine manufacturer opened door to evidence not otherwise admissible that manual would not have prevented the accident. Court also addressed appropriateness of subsequent repair rule in products liability cases despite its prohibition in negligence cases. ***Duchess v. Langston Corporation,*** **709 A.2d 410 (Pa. Super. 1999).**

Brain damage

Child suffered brain damage caused by use of forceps during birth. Physician not liable. Doctrine of informed consent not applicable. ***Sinclair by Sinclair v. Block,*** **534 Pa. Super. 563, 633 A.2d 1137.**

Brain surgery

Plaintiff who had a bone flap in skull replaced with titanium mesh sued to recover for pain, disfigurement and depression, alleging negligence by medical care providers in failing to preserve bone flap and battery for substituting titanium mesh for bone. Lower court's grant of summary judgment in favor of care providers reversed in part. Plaintiff's disfigurement was so obvious as to not require expert testimony and plaintiff's expert testified that psychological depression was caused by disfigurement resulting from surgery. Absent proof of causal relationship between pain and surgery, recovery for pain disallowed. ***Watkins v. Hospital of University of Pennsylvania,*** **737 A.2d 263 (Pa. Super. 1999).**

Husband suffering from seizures was treated by a partial lobectomy that resulted in more serious seizures and severe memory and speech problems. Informed consent to medical treatment requires that the patient have a "true understanding of the nature of the operation ... and the possible results." Judgment *n.o.v.* permitted only in "clear case." Judgment *n.o.v.* reversed and jury verdict reinstated. ***Rowinsky v. Sperling,*** **452 Pa. Super. 215, 681 A.2d 785 (1996).**

Brakes

Plaintiff and her decedents were passengers in a car driven by additional defendant who crossed over centerline of PennDOT road, crashed through guardrail and struck tree. Plaintiff alleged that brakes and engine had failed, that additional defendant driver was intoxicated and that PennDOT had failed to provide safe roadway because of inability of guardrail to prevent car from striking tree. Following grant of summary judgment in favor of PennDOT, plaintiff appealed. Held: PennDOT could not have adequate notice of combination of events leading to accident—loss of brakes and driver's intoxication—and therefore PennDOT had no duty to plaintiff and her decedents. *Baer v. Com., Dept. of Transp.*, 713 A.2d 189 (Pa. Cmwlth. 1998).

Sudden Emergency Doctrine and Assured Clear Distance Rule are mutually exclusive as the first relates to a moving instrumentality thrust into a driver's path of travel and the second relates to objects traveling in the same direction which are static in relation to each other. Driver's inability to see brake lights or turn signals in front of him is not a sudden emergency. *Cunningham v. Byers*, 732 A.2d 655 (Pa. Super. 1999).

Plaintiff was injured during operation of motorcycle and alleged in straight product liability case that defective brake caliper binder bolt was cause of accident. Defendant introduced evidence that plaintiff was intoxicated at the time of accident and that binder bolt broke as a result of the accident and argued that intoxication was the sole cause of the accident. Superior Court affirmed trial court's admission of evidence, holding that when defendant in product liability suit offers evidence to establish that injuries were caused solely by negligence of plaintiff without any involvement of defect alleged by plaintiff, such evidence is admissible. *Madonna v. Harley Davidson, Inc.*, 708 A.2d 507 (Pa. Super. 1998).

Summary judgment against plaintiff based on spoliation of evidence reversed where defendant, not plaintiff, was the owner of the missing brake master cylinder at issue and plaintiff never had control or possession of the part at any time. Wife passenger plaintiff who was struck by body of her husband at the time of impact which caused his death and her injury had standing under the impact and bystander governing wife plaintiff's claim for negligent infliction of emotional distress. *Long v. Yingling*, 700 A.2d 508 (Pa. Super. 1997).

Chain reaction collision caused by brake problems. Jury verdict for defendant. Held: error to charge on sudden emergency. Doctrine not to include sudden mechanical failures. New trial ordered. *Chiodo v. Gargloff & Downham Trucking*, 308 Pa. Super. 498, 454 A.2d 645.

Rear-end collision allegedly occurring when defendant's brakes failed. Expert testimony that ruptured brake hose could not have been determined in advance. No negligence. Verdict for defendant. *Floravit v. Kronenwetter*, 255 Pa. Super. 581, 389 A.2d 130.

Plaintiff killed when truck he was driving failed to negotiate curve and struck pole—photos of brake assembly admissible to show defect under §402A even though taken several months after accident. Verdict for plaintiff affirmed. *Woods v. Pleasant Hills Motor Co.*, 454 Pa. 224, 309 A.2d 698.

Plaintiff injured while using a car which left highway on application of brakes—brakes recently relined by defendant—testimony of plaintiff's expert refuted in part by plaintiff's exhibit of brake mechanism at trial—verdict for plaintiff—new trial granted on ground that credibility of witness was "devastated"—held: order properly entered—strong dissent. *Stover v. Fiveway S. Center*, 220 Pa. Super. 335, 286 A.2d 380.

Brawl

Truck purchased and used for 5 months before occurrence—brakes allegedly failing by reason of insufficient tightening of a nut on air supply line between reservoir and foot brake pedal—held: photographs of line taken much later and expert testimony inadmissible—new trial granted. ***Woods v. Pleasant Hills Motor Co., et al.*, 219 Pa. Super. 381, 281 A.2d 649.**

Rear-end collision—defendant operator explained that his brakes failed—verdict for defendant—new trial granted on ground "substantial justice warranted it"—abuse of discretion and grant reversed. ***Gilligan v. Shaw*, 441 Pa. 305, 272 A.2d 462.**

Defendant driver aware that brakes on his heavily loaded truck were defective and on application would not control speed of vehicle—continuing to operate truck with opportunity to have pulled to side of road—collision—new trial granted after verdict for defendant—not an abuse of discretion. ***Austin v. Ridge*, 435 Pa. 1, 255 A.2d 123.**

Auto agency sold car to one of defendants—within one-half hour after delivery of car, it collided with rear of another vehicle—evidence of defective brakes—lack of brake fluid—police officer permitted to testify as an expert—for jury as to both supplier and operator. ***Flavin v. Aldrich et al.*, 213 Pa. Super. 420, 250 A.2d 185.**

Police officer arrived on scene of accident some 10 to 15 minutes after occurrence—testifying as to brake failure of one of cars as a result of tests made after arrival—improperly admitted—such testimony hearsay—new trial properly granted. ***Andrews v. Jackson et al.*, 211 Pa. Super. 166, 235 A.2d 452.**

Brawl

Plaintiff a patron of defendant's club—slight barroom brawl with another patron—evidence did not apprise barkeeper of patron's intention to injure plaintiff—defendant not an insurer—judgment for defendant on record after a "hung" jury. ***Bahoric v. St. Lawrence Croatian No. 13*, 426 Pa. 90, 230 A.2d 725.**

Breach of guarantee

Six-year statute of limitations applies to claim for breach of guarantee by doctor that tubal ligation would prevent future pregnancies. Verdict for plaintiff affirmed. Economic losses were appropriate. Affirmed also non-economic award owing to failure to preserve issue properly on appeal. Verdict $21,000 for wife and $5,300 loss of consortium for husband. Subsequent pregnancy terminated by abortion followed by second tubal ligation. ***Murray v. University of Pennsylvania Hosp.*, 340 Pa. Super. 401, 490 A.2d 839.**

Breast cancer

Plaintiff's treating physician waited 15 months to order a biopsy of patient's breast after patient presented with substantial changes in breast condition after radiation therapy. Physician admitted at trial that he knew there was a 20% chance that the change in condition was caused by recurrence of cancer. Jury verdict in favor of doctor shocked the conscience of the court and new trial ordered. ***Vallone v. Creech*, 820 A.2d 760 (Pa. Super. 2003).**

Plaintiff's decedent wife was examined on numerous occasions by a physician's assistant who failed to diagnose properly or call in physician to examine a cancerous breast. Trial court entered a compulsory nonsuit after refusing to accept testimony of plaintiff's medical expert. Despite his twenty-five years of practice and experience as an oncologist familiar with the same condition that caused wife's death, expert could not provide a specific reference to his theory of liability in a medical text. Where plaintiff's expert expresses the opinion that defendants' actions increased the risk of harm to plaintiff, the question of causation must go to the jury. Superior Court also reversed procedural rulings by trial court that prevented plaintiff from providing relevant and material facts to the record despite a complete lack of prejudice to defendants. ***Smith v. Grab*, 705 A.2d 894 (Pa. Super. 1997).**

Physician's assistant's failure to refer patient complaining of breast pain to physician is not actionable without proof of causation in suit against medical practice group instituted after discovery of breast cancer. Board certified internist is qualified to render an opinion as to the duty of care of physician's assistant. Compulsory nonsuit affirmed. ***Montgomery v. So. Philadelphia Medical Group, Inc.*, 441 Pa. Super. 146, 656 A.2d 1385 (1995).**

Wrongful death and survival actions based on medical malpractice for failure to diagnose breast cancer are to be treated separately as to applicable statute of limitations. Failure to commence survival action within two years following death of decedent did not preclude wrongful death action filed within two years of death, as underlying cause of action for medical malpractice was not yet time barred as of decedent's death. ***Moyer v. Rubright*, 438 Pa. Super. 154, 651 A.2d 1139 (1994).**

Wrongful death and survival action brought against physician for failure to diagnose breast cancer. Summary judgment granted to physician. Held: order granting summary judgment appealable but action was time-barred. ***Holmes v. Lado*, 412 Pa. Super. 218, 602 A.2d 1389.**

Patient brought action against physician for failure to diagnose breast cancer. Physician not liable. Excluded evidence cumulative. Charge to jury not in error. ***Soda v. Baird*, 411 Pa. Super. 80, 600 A.2d 1274.**

Patient died after physician failed to order breast cancer screening. Physician not liable. Patient would have died anyway. ***Clayton v. Sabeh*, 406 Pa. Super. 335, 594 A.2d 365.**

Bridges

Child injured in fall from railroad bridge into creek on city-owned property. Railroad joined city. City immune. ***Consolidated Rail Corporation v. Shirk*, 143 Pa. Cmwlth. 422, 599 A.2d 262.**

Motorcyclist and minor pedestrian who fell from privately owned bridge brought action against owners and designer of bridge for failure to provide guard

Broken wrist

rails. Owners and designer not liable. No duty owed. Plaintiffs assumed risk. ***Himes v. New Enterprise Stone & Lime Company,* 399 Pa. Super. 301, 582 A.2d 353.**

Plaintiff decedent killed while riding on top of cab of work truck as truck passed under a bridge and his head struck bridge. Original clearance of 14 feet reduced by numerous road repairs. Railroad held negligent in not maintaining the required clearance. Contributory negligence for jury. Plaintiff's verdict affirmed. ***Marinelli v. Montour R.R. Co.,* 278 Pa. Super. 403, 420 A.2d 603.**

Plaintiff pedestrian fell while crossing a bridge maintained by Port Authority—notice that bridge was closed to pedestrians—notice frequently thrown down as bridge was notoriously used by pedestrians—verdict for plaintiff sustained—issue of contributory negligence was for the jury. ***Niemiec v. Allegheny County Port Authority et al.,* 223 Pa. Super. 435, 302 A.2d 439.**

Evidence that defendant negligently permitted a hole to exist in the planking of a bridge owned and maintained by it and that guard rails were decayed—plaintiff's truck going off bridge—case for jury—judgment for plaintiff affirmed. ***Cebulskie v. Lehigh Valley R.R. Co.,* 441 Pa. 230, 272 A.2d 171.**

Broken wrist

Medical malpractice claim for failure to diagnose fractured wrist. Liability admitted by radiologist. Jury improperly instructed on contributory negligence when insufficient facts plead or proven to support that instruction. Judgment in favor of radiologist reversed and new trial granted. ***Pascal v. Carter,* 436 Pa. Super. 40, 647 A.2d 231 (1994).**

Bucking traffic

Defendant pulled around standing cars to his left side and collided with car in which plaintiff riding—defendant "bucking traffic" at such time and held responsible for the injuries occasioned. ***Rogers v. Moody,* 430 Pa. 121, 242 A.2d 276.**

Building code

Plaintiff wife, school book salesperson, was injured when she attempted to gain entrance to school building which had been constructed in 1902. Plaintiff complained that entrance was not in compliance with current building codes and that noncompliance created an unsafe condition that caused her to fall and become injured. Trial court prohibited any testimony from plaintiff's building code compliance expert reasoning that school, because of its age, was not required to be in compliance with current building codes and to allow that issue to be raised to jury would confuse negligence issue. Additionally, photographs and plans of area in question were adequate to allow jury to make its own determination of whether landing and entrance were unsafe. Trial court's instructions as to defendant's duties to plaintiff were also adequate where they correctly described the plaintiff's status as business invitee and school's responsibilities to her as invitee. ***Kiehner v. School District of Philadelphia,* 712 A.2d 830 (Pa. Cmwlth. 1998).**

Burden of proof

Homeowner brought action against township for negligent inspection and failure to enforce building code. Government immunity statute held not retroactive. ***Saft v. Upper Dublin Township,* 161 Pa. Cmwlth. 158, 636 A.2d 284.**

Homeowner brought action against township for failure to enforce building code. Cause of action accrued before passage of Tort Claims Act. Act could not be applied retroactively. ***Garvey v. Rosanelli,* 144 Pa. Cmwlth. 588, 601 A.2d 1334.**

Worker fell through hole in floor at construction site. Employer immune from suit for intentional tort by Worker's Compensation Act. Municipality immune from suit for failure to enforce building code. ***Mentzer v. Ognibene,* 126 Pa. Cmwlth. 178, 559 A.2d 79.**

Burden of proof

Plaintiff was injured when car he was driving fell into 8"–12" ditch in road that resulted from settlement of fill deposited by local authority which had created hole. Plaintiff appeals from trial judge's decision to give instruction to jury which left question of whether local authority had actual or constructive notice of fill settling to jury. Plaintiff argued that because local authority created hole and installed fill that settled and caused dangerous condition, it had notice of condition as a matter of law. Instruction approved by Commonwealth Court which held that just because defendant created hole and installed fill that eventually resulted in dangerous condition does not mean that plaintiff is not required to show that defendant knew or should have known of the condition. ***Miller v. Lykens Borough Authority,* 712 A.2d 800 (Pa. Cmwlth. 1998).**

In medical malpractice action, the *Hamil/Mitzelfelt* two-pronged test "relaxing" a plaintiff's burden of proving causation should be applied to the entirety of plaintiff's expert's testimony regarding necessity of revised informed consent. Order removing compulsory nonsuit affirmed. ***Kratt v. Horrow,* 455 Pa. Super. 140, 687 A.2d 830 (1997).**

Plaintiff a passenger in auto involved in right angle collision. Verdict in favor of both drivers affirmed. Evidence conflicting and jury could have found that neither party at fault. Burden of proof on plaintiff to show negligence of one or both drivers. ***Platts v. Driscoll,* 245 Pa. Super. 235, 369 A.2d 381.**

Plaintiff allegedly drank bottle of soft drink containing glass particles. Without bottle and pieces of glass, plaintiff did not meet burden of proof. ***Williams v. Pepsi-Cola,* 240 Pa. Super. 578, 362 A.2d 314.**

Burden of proof on cause of alleged brain damage is on plaintiff, but medical testimony not necessary where injury was immediately and directly, or naturally and probably, the result of the accident. Here plaintiff hit on skull. Therefore, medical evidence by psychologist, although improper, not error. ***Simmons v. Mullen,* 231 Pa. Super. 199, 331 A.2d 892.**

Minor plaintiff lost sight of right eye during spitball battle on school bus. Verdict against school bus company sustained. Verdict in favor of minors who participated in fight reversed and new trial as to their culpability granted. Burden of

Burial

proof as to who threw the spitball was on these minor children once it was shown by plaintiff that one of them must have done it. Restatement (2d) Torts, §433B. *Sommers v. Hessler,* **227 Pa. Super. 41, 323 A.2d 17.**

Plaintiff—decedent a passenger in one of two cars, one of which crossed medial barrier. When a car crosses medial barrier, driver has burden to say why—in absence of exculpatory evidence, one of the drivers had to be negligent. Verdict for both defendant drivers reversed. *Fair v. Snowball Express,* **226 Pa. Super. 295, 310 A.2d 386.**

Burial

Wife of deceased brought action for intentional infliction of emotional distress against owner of mausoleum. Held: temporary burial of husbands remains against wife's wishes but in accordance with contract not extreme or outrageous conduct. *Baker v. Morjon, Inc.,* **393 Pa. Super. 409, 574 A.2d 676.**

Bus

Plaintiff brought negligence action against Defendant bus driver based upon a motor vehicle accident. The trial court entered judgment in favor of the Defendant following a jury verdict. The Superior Court affirmed holding in part that a negligence per se instruction due to violation of the Motor Vehicle Code was adequately covered by an assured clear distance instruction to the jury. *Phillips v. Lock,* **86 A.3d 906 (Pa. Super. 2014).**

Plaintiff brought negligence action against Defendant transportation authority after she tripped and fell while exiting a stopped bus. The trial court granted summary judgment for the Defendant. The Commonwealth Court affirmed holding that the vehicle liability exception to sovereign immunity did not apply as the bus was not in operation at the time of her fall. The Court also held that the bus did not fall under the personal property exception as it was not personal property. *Muldrow v. Southeastern Pennsylvania Transit Authority,* **88 A.3d 269 (Pa. Cmwlth 2014).**

Bus passenger brought negligence action against the Southeastern Pennsylvania Transportation Authority (SEPTA) for injuries suffered when the bus accelerated and stopped. The trial court granted summary judgment to the defendant based upon the "jerk and jolt" doctrine. The Commonwealth Court affirmed, holding that plaintiff had failed to produce evidence that the jerk or stop was so unusual and extraordinary as to exceed a passenger's reasonable anticipation. *Martin v. Southeastern Pennsylvania Transportation Authority,* **52 A.3d 385, No. 472 C.D. 2011 (Pa. Cmwlth. 2012).**

Bus passenger brought negligence action against Defendant Southeastern Pennsylvania Transportation Authority for injuries suffered when the bus accelerated and stopped. The trial court granted summary judgment to the Defendant based upon the "jerk and jolt" doctrine. The Commonwealth Court affirmed holding that Plaintiff had failed to produce evidence that the jerk or stop was so unusual and extraordinary as to exceed a passenger's reasonable anticipation. *Martin v. Southeastern Pennsylvania Transportation Authority,* **____ A.3d _____, No. 472 C.D. 2011 (Pa. Cmwlth. 2012).**

Bus

Plaintiff brought action against Defendant transportation authority for uninsured motorist benefits after he was injured when the bus he was riding in was struck from behind by an uninsured motorist while stopped. The trial court granted judgment in favor of the Defendant. The Commonwealth Court affirmed holding that the Defendant was immune from suit pursuant to sovereign immunity as the bus was not in operation at the time of the accident. ***Wright v. Denny,* 33 A.3d 687 (Pa. Cmwlth. 2011).**

Bus Passenger filed a negligence action against defendant port authority for injuries suffered as the result of the defendant's bus driver's slamming on the brakes. The trial court granted summary judgment to the defendant. The Commonwealth Court affirmed holding that pursuant to the "jerk or jolt" doctrine a bus passenger must establish an unusual or extraordinary movement beyond reasonable anticipation or evidence of an accident to recover for injuries. ***Jackson v. Port Authority of Allegheny County,* 17 A.3d 966 (Pa. Cmwlth. 2011).**

Passenger brought suit against defendant transportation authority after she fell while exiting a bus. Trial court granted summary judgment in favor of the defendant. The Commonwealth Court affirmed holding that the defendant was immune under the Sovereign Immunity Act, because the bus driver's failure to kneel a bus was not an act of actually operating the vehicle that would preclude immunity under the statute. ***Royal v. Southeastern Pennsylvania Transportation Authority,* 10 A.3d 927 (Pa. Cmwlth. 2010).**

Parent of deceased minor child brought suit against bus driver for negligence after the bus driver struck the minor child, while crossing the road. The jury rendered a verdict in favor of the Plaintiff. The Commonwealth Court on appeal reversed and remanded on the issue of damages, but held that the Defendants were not entitled to a directed verdict against the victim's uncle for his alleged contributory negligence as he was with the child and must have seen the bus. ***Cheng v. SEPTA,* 981 A.2d 371 (Pa. Cmwlth. 2009).**

Parents in their own right and on behalf of their minor son brought a negligence claim against a driver of a coach bus for injuries sustained in a collision. The appellate court upheld the jury verdict for the defendant bus driver holding that lay testimony from the bus passengers regarding the speed of the mother's oncoming car was properly admissible at trial. ***Fisher v. Central Cab Co.,* 945 A.2d 215 (Pa. Super. 2008).**

Plaintiff bus passenger suffered a broken femur when she fell on the floor of the bus as it began to move before she had been seated. Compulsory nonsuit for bus company affirmed based on lack of testimony that jerk or jolt of bus was so severe as to cause extraordinarily disturbing effect on other passengers. Plaintiff's medical expert's testimony that force of jerk or jolt of bus was severe because of nature of the injury is not sufficient. ***Asbury v. Port Authority Transit of Allegheny County,* 863 A.2d 84 (Pa. Cmwlth. 2004).**

Plaintiff who was struck by a car after alighting from a bus which had departed from its normal route was not permitted the advantage of the motor vehicle

Bus

exception to sovereign immunity. ***Mosley v. Southeastern Pennsylvania Transportation Authority*, 842 A.2d 473 (Pa. Cmwlth. 2004).**

Grant of new trial to plaintiff, bus passenger, reversed following trial judge's determination that he did not believe the testimony of the bus driver who alleged that sudden emergency necessitated sudden change of direction and contact of bus with Jersey barrier was incredible. Determination of credibility was for jury, regardless of the extraordinary difference in bus driver's story at time of trial as compared to reports immediately following accident. Analysis of sudden emergency doctrine. ***Divilly v. Port Authority of Allegheny County*, 810 A.2d 755 (Pa. Cmwlth. 2002).**

A plaintiff who was injured when she alighted from a bus was precluded from recovery because the bus was stopped and so not in "operation" as required to allow recovery based on an exception to sovereign immunity. ***Bottoms v. Southeastern Pennsylvania Transportation Authority*, 805 A.2d 47 (Pa. Cmwlth. 2002)**.

Plaintiff was injured when he fell on a bus that stopped suddenly. Trial court properly granted compulsory nonsuit when evidence of severity of stop failed to show that the stop had the "extraordinarily disturbing effect on other passengers" required to allow the case to go to the jury. ***Meussner v. Port Authority of Allegheny County*, 745 A.2d 719 (Pa. Cmwlth. 2000).**

Supreme Court affirms trial court grant of summary judgment in favor of SEPTA for actions of bus driver who discharged students into a busy street and not at a regular stop. Strong dissent by Justice Newman arguing that discharging passengers is part of operation of a transit bus. ***Warrick v. Pro Cor Ambulance, Inc.*, 739 A.2d 127 (Pa. 1999).**

Plaintiff appealed from jury award of $12,000.00 which she considered inadequate for injuries suffered when she inhaled smoke from Port Authority bus which caught fire in front of her car in tunnel. Plaintiff's expert testified to her affliction as Reactive Airways Dysfunction Syndrome ("RADS"). In hotly contested case relating to extent of her injury and when her condition improved to point of plaintiff being completely recovered, Held: there was adequate evidence for jury to accept Port Authority's version of facts rather than plaintiffs. Verdict was not so low as to shock the sense of justice. ***Labbett v. Port Authority of Allegheny County*, 714 A.2d 522 (Pa. Cmwlth. 1998).**

Plaintiff administratrix of deceased minor filed suit against SEPTA and ambulance company after child who had alighted from bus crossed in front of bus, with green light, and was struck by ambulance which was improperly passing bus on its left. After settling with ambulance service, SEPTA was granted summary judgment on basis of sovereign immunity as the act of stopping at an intersection, rather than at the appropriate bus stop in middle of block, then opening door to discharge child was not "operation" of motor vehicle under Sovereign Immunity Act. "...a temporary stop connected to the discharge of passengers is not part and parcel of the operation of a vehicle." Query, not even on a passenger transit bus? ***Warrick v. Pro Cor Ambulance, Inc.*, 709 A.2d 422 (Pa. Cmwlth. 1997).**

Bus

Plaintiff slipped, fell and sustained injury alighting from a bus. SEPTA bus driver's act of allowing bus to become "very crowded " was not an act which falls within the plain meaning of "operation" of a motor vehicle so as to survive nonsuit by Commonwealth agency defendant under sovereign immunity defense; act was merely ancillary to the actual operation of the vehicle. *Berman v. SEPTA*, **698 A.2d 1362 (Pa. Cmwlth. 1997).**

Order granting summary judgment in favor of Port Authority reversed where plaintiff's evidence, if credited, was sufficient to establish an unusual or extraordinary stopping of the bus. *Vuzzelli v. Port Authority of Allegheny County*, **___ Pa. Cmwlth. ___, 674 A.2d 1186 (1996).**

Plaintiff injured when alighting from bus is not injured by reason of "operation of motor vehicle"; therefore suit against transit authority precluded. Order granting judgment notwithstanding the verdict affirmed. *Rubenstein v. SEPTA*, **___ Pa. Cmwlth. ___, 668 A.2d 283 (1995).**

Plaintiff alighting from bus is not engaged in operation of motor vehicle so claim for damages does not qualify under statutory exception to governmental immunity. Summary judgment affirmed. Legislative intent is to grant immunity; therefore interpretation of exceptions to governmental immunity should favor that outcome. *Bazemore v. SEPTA*, **___ Pa. Cmwlth. ___, 657 A.2d 1323 (1995).**

Transportation authority not liable under operation of motor vehicle exception to governmental immunity where bus involved in accident with plaintiff was driven by unauthorized user and not employee of transportation authority. Summary judgment affirmed. *Pana v. SEPTA*, **___ Pa. Cmwlth. ___, 657 A.2d 1320 (1995).**

Recovery by bus passenger who fell from stationary bus steps is precluded by governmental immunity absent proof of movement of vehicle or any part of vehicle. Summary judgment reversed on certified interlocutory appeal. *Simpkins v. SEPTA*, **167 Pa. Cmwlth. 451, 648 A.2d 591 (1994).**

Passenger injured when tour bus started before she was seated. Held: release of principal acted as release of agent. *Pallante v. Harcourt Brace and Jovanovich, Inc.*, **427 Pa. Super. 371, 629 A.2d 146.**

Passenger injured while alighting from bus. Vehicle exception to sovereign immunity not applicable. *Miller v. Erie Metropolitan Transit Authority*, **152 Pa. Cmwlth. 64, 618 A.2d 1095.**

Pennsylvania residents injured in bus accident in New Jersey. Bus owned by New Jersey operator. Held: Venue in Pennsylvania improper. New Jersey Tort Claims Act controlling. *Flamer v. N.J. Transit*, **414 Pa. Super. 350, 607 A.2d 260.**

Passenger injured when bus door closed as she attempted to exit. Motor vehicle exception to government immunity applicable. *Sonnenberg v. Erie Metropolitan Transit Authority*, **137 Pa. Cmwlth. 533, 586 A.2d 1026.**

Passenger injured while entering bus. Trial court failed to instruct jury on duty of common carrier and on failure of driver to follow established procedure.

Bus

Vacated and remanded. ***Jones v. Port Authority of Allegheny County*, 136 Pa. Cmwlth. 445, 583 A.2d 512.**

Bus passenger and vehicle operator injured in separate accidents involving Port Authority busses. Port Authority entitled to damages-limiting provisions of Judiciary Act concerning pain and suffering. ***Rosenblum v. Port Authority of Allegheny County*, 127 Pa. Cmwlth. 38, 560 A.2d 912.**

Fatal injury to student struck by car after alighting from school bus. Held: school district immune from suit. Stopped school bus with flashing lights not a traffic control as defined by governmental immunity statute. ***Aberant v. Wilkes-Barre Area School Area School District*, 89 Pa. Cmwlth. 516, 492 A.2d 1186.**

Fourteen year old boy struck by auto passing bus allegedly after bus driver waved boy to cross in front of bus on snowy day. Sufficient evidence of driver's negligence to support verdict in favor of plaintiff. The issue as to relevance of Woods School's expenses, was one of conditional relevance, which under circumstances was for jury. New trial ordered on this issue, as to damages only, after determination of recusal issue. ***Reilly v. SEPTA*, 330 Pa. Super. 420, 479 A.2d 973.**

Elderly passenger boarded bus which then started forward allegedly before she was seated or supported. Issues of due care and duty owed for jury. Granting of defendant's motion for summary judgment reversed. ***LeGrand v. Lincoln Lines, Inc.*, 253 Pa. Super. 19, 384 A.2d 955.**

Minor plaintiffs passengers on bus. Bus had to travel through neighborhoods prone to violence. Injured when boys ran onto bus and randomly struck passengers. Common carrier has duty to repress disorder and to do whatever possible to restrain, and, if necessary, remove disorderly parties. Evidence that before boys boarded, they threw stones at bus. Negligent to open doors. Verdict for plaintiffs affirmed. ***Mangini v. SEPTA*, 235 Pa. Super. 478, 344 A.2d 621.**

Plaintiff a passenger in a bus—bus had been standing for red light—started up and stopped suddenly because car of other defendant had turned sharply in front—no contact—plaintiff thrown from seat—injury to neck—verdict against both defendants—motion of plaintiff based solely on inadequacy—motion dismissed—action affirmed on appeal. ***DiPietro v. Zeiders et al.*, 216 Pa. Super. 860, 266 A.2d 568.**

Plaintiff pedestrian allegedly struck by defendant's bus—evidence conflicting as to whether plaintiff was on sidewalk or in cartway when struck or whether she had been seized by an epileptic seizure and fell into side of bus—matter for jury to assess and reconcile opposing contentions. ***Auerbach v. Phila. Trans. Co.*, 421 Pa. 594, 221 A.2d 163.**

Plaintiff pedestrian traversing an alleyway without sidewalks and about 18 feet wide—defendant's bus turned into alleyway and allegedly caused plaintiff to escape contact to fall into a window well—for jury as to traction company but property owner not responsible. ***Murphy v. Pittsburgh Railways Co.*, 421 Pa. 252, 219 A.2d 303.**

Business invitee

Plaintiff was a passenger in defendant's bus which was very crowded—in endeavoring to alight plaintiff was thrown to pavement by a surging movement of passengers—defendant is responsible even though the acts of the passengers did not amount to a breach of the peace. ***Lasota v. Phila. Trans. Co.*, 421 Pa. 386, 219 A.2d 296.**

Plaintiff, a passenger in defendant's bus, was injured by its sudden stop—evidence that bus was traveling at an excessive speed in a congested area—sudden stop as the result of a truck cutting in front of bus—driver of bus did not testify—matter for jury. ***Connolly v. Phila. T. Co.*, 420 Pa. 280, 216 A.2d 60.**

Bus station

Police officer's failure to provide protection for specific individual shot on bus terminal platform is not a recognized exception to governmental immunity. Despite city ordinance purporting to waive governmental immunity for negligent acts of police officers, City cannot waive its immunity. Ordinance held retroactively invalid under *City of Philadelphia v. Gray*, 534 Pa. 467, 633 A.2d 1090 (1993). Summary judgment affirmed. ***Johnson v. City of Philadelphia*, ___ Pa. Cmwlth. ___, 657 A.2d 87 (1995).**

Business invitee

Delivery driver brought a claim for negligence against a University after he tripped and fell due to a raised bumper on the loading dock. On appeal the Superior Court affirmed the jury verdict in favor of the delivery driver on the basis that the University failed to warn its business invitee of a known unreasonably dangerous condition and failed to exercise reasonable care to protect the delivery driver as it had reason to expect that he might be distracted and fail to protect himself. ***Walker v. Drexel University*, 971 A.2d 521 (Pa. Super. 2009).**

Mall patron's suit for injuries sustained in fall caused by alleged "slippery substance" dismissed on summary judgment for lack of any proof that mall manager had constructive or actual notice of existence of any foreign matter on floors. ***Porro v. Century III Associates*, 846 A.2d 1282 (Pa. Super. 2004).**

Plaintiff's decedent, a bystander at an underage drinking party at a hotel on New Year's Eve, was shot by another visitor to hotel. In suit against hotel owners and security company, summary judgment in favor of defendants reversed on grounds that plaintiff's pleadings and deposition testimony established *prima facie* case of negligence, including, specifically, duty to protect decedent as business invitee from known dangerous conditions. Lethal actions of rowdy crowd of drunken underage party participants was foreseeable under the circumstances described. ***Rabutino v. Freedom State Realty Company, Inc.*, 809 A.2d 933 (Pa. Super. 2002).**

Shopper injured when an automatic door closed on her while exiting a grocery store. In count against store for negligent treatment of a business invitee, plaintiff alleged that the automatic door posed an unreasonable risk of harm to some of its customers and that the store knew or should have known of the risk and failed to protect its customers. Opinion defines duty to business invitees and basic elements of negligence. ***Summers v. Giant Food Stores*, 743 A.2d 498 (Pa. Super. 1999).**

Buyout agreement

79 year old plaintiff slipped and fell on "penny thin" black ice patch on parking lot of defendant's combination gasoline and convenience store while on the way back into the store to ask for a second time to use the private telephone in the store. After verdict for plaintiff, defendant appealed claiming that trial court's charge that plaintiff was a business invitee and court's refusal to charge on choice of ways doctrine were error. Held: by reason of defendant's directions to plaintiff to go outside onto its property to use the public phone and existence of a "welcome" sign on canopy established as a matter of law that plaintiff was a business invitee, not just a licensee. As to allegation of error in refusal to charge on choice of ways doctrine, the fact that the ice patch was very difficult to see, even for a much younger store employee who testified to that fact, precludes the charge on choice of ways if there was no way to discern the more dangerous of two paths. *Updyke v. BP Oil Co.*, 717 A.2d 546 (Pa. Super. 1998).

Buyout agreement

Law firm which represented shareholders with competing interests and drafted Buy Out Agreement more favorable to one shareholder than the other can be sued in action sounding in negligence or assumpsit. Date statute of limitations begins to run for negligence claim is date that actual loss is sustained. Compulsory nonsuit vacated and case remanded for new trial. *Fiorentino v. Rapoport*, ___ Pa. Super. ___, 693 A.2d 208 (1997).

Bystander

Defendant utility-pole inspection company did not have duty to protect bystander from injuries sustained when bystander came into contact with downed electrical wires while assisting victims of automobile accident which damaged utility pole. Defendant inspection company's alleged negligent inspection of pole was too remote to constitute proximate cause of bystander's injuries. Bystander was not third-party beneficiary of contract between inspection company and utility company, which required inspection company only to inspect and report condition of poles. Order sustaining preliminary objections of defendant inspection company affirmed. *Hicks v. Metropolitan Edison Company*, ___ Pa. Cmwlth. ___, 665 A.2d 529 (1995).

Driver may proceed with suit against Commonwealth for common law damages based on emotional and psychological distress following accident with PennDOT construction vehicle. *Tomikel v. Com., Dept. of Transp.*, ___ Pa. Cmwlth. ___, 658 A.2d 861 (1995).

Collision between automobile and a switch engine of defendant railroad—a police officer erroneously permitted to testify to what a bystander stated—held: it was not properly part of the *res gestae*. *Carney v. Penna. R.R. Co.*, 428 Pa. 489, 240 A.2d 71.

Bystander

Cadmium

—C—

Cadmium

The standards of proof established in asbestos actions apply to plaintiff's action for averred workplace cadmium exposure resulting in cancer. Plaintiff must establish that defendant's products were in use at work site to establish causal nexus element of action. Summary judgment affirmed. ***Jobe v. W.P. Metz Refining,*** **445 Pa. Super. 76, 664 A.2d 1015 (1995).**

Cannon

Student of military academy injured when toy cannon prematurely discharged did not assume the risk of injury where student had fired cannon more than 200 times without incident. Only necessary jury instruction was on comparative negligence. Judgment on jury verdict affirmed. ***Struble v. Valley Forge Military Academy,*** **445 Pa. Super. 224, 665 A.2d 4 (1995).**

Explosion of ceremonial cannon allegedly caused injuries. City of Pittsburgh and Commonwealth of Pennsylvania, joined. Commonwealth refused permission to amend Answer to include defense based upon Recreation Use of Land and Water Act. Affirmed denial. Commonwealth not meant to be included in definition of owner of land. ***Borgen v. Fort Pitt Museum,*** **83 Pa. Cmwlth. 207, 477 A.2d 36.**

Canon law

Parents of children expelled from Catholic grade school sued diocese, diocesan Board of Education and principal after diocese and bishop had confirmed expulsion following hearing before diocesan Board of Education. Trial court sustained preliminary objections of defendants on grounds that state court did not have jurisdiction to determine controversies under ecclesiastic rule, custom or law, as upheld and affirmed by bishop of Roman Catholic Church. Affirmed by Commonwealth Court pursuant to same reasoning as elucidated by Pennsylvania Supreme Court in *Presbytery of Beaver-Butler v. Middlesex Presbyterian Church*, 507 Pa. 255, 489 A.2d 1317, cert. denied, 474 U.S. 887, 106 S.Ct. 198, 88 L.Ed.2d 167. (1985). ***Gaston v. Diocese of Allentown,*** **712 A.2d 757 (Pa. Super. 1998).**

Captain of the Ship Doctrine

Plaintiff-decedent hanged himself with hospital robe ties while patient in psychiatric unit of defendant hospital, having been admitted after suicide attempt. Lower court erred in ruling as matter of law that treating physician was not agent of hospital. New trial as to doctor's agency and negligence only, and damages if appropriate. ***Simmons v. St. Clair Memorial Hospital,*** **332 Pa. Super. 444, 481 A.2d 870.**

Action by patient against surgeon and hospital for damages resulting from failure to remove hemostat. Verdict against doctor only. New trial ordered as to liability of hospital only since charge gave overly restrictive view of possible liability on part of hospital. Operating room personnel were hospital employees. ***Bilonoha v. Zubritzky,*** **233 Pa. Super. 136, 336 A.2d 351.**

Clamp left in abdomen during surgery. Binding instructions exonerating hospital held improper and new trial granted as to liability of hospital only. Jury could reasonably find that negligent party was at same time the servant of two masters. Verdict against operating doctor upheld. ***Jonsic v. Wagner,* 458 Pa. 246, 329 A.2d 497.**

Nurse is employee—agent of hospital and not doctor who ordered injection. Case tried against doctor only for injury resulting from injection. Nonsuit affirmed. ***Muller v. Likoff,* 225 Pa. Super. 111, 310 A.2d 303.**

Defendant's decedent the operating surgeon—left the closing of the surgical opening to orthopedic trainees—sponge left in wound—doctrine of captain of the ship did not require that the trial judge direct a verdict for the plaintiff—matter for jury—new trial awarded. ***Thomas v. Hutchinson,* 442 Pa. 118, 275 A.2d 23.**

Doctrine of "Captain of Ship" not applied to a physician who had no control or right to control those administering electric shock treatment. ***Collins v. Hand,* 431 Pa. 378, 246 A.2d 398.**

Car leaving highway

Truck purchased and used for 5 months before occurrence—brakes allegedly failing by reason of insufficient tightening of a nut on air supply line between reservoir and foot brake pedal—Held: photographs of line taken much later and expert testimony inadmissible—new trial granted. ***Woods v. Pleasant Hills Motor Co., et al.,* 219 Pa. Super. 381, 281 A.2d 649.**

Car wash

Plaintiff injured at car wash while vacuuming his car when struck by car exiting car wash. For jury whether owner satisfied duty of care in placement of vacuum by showing that 200,000 cars had used car wash without incident. ***Amabile v. Auto Kleen,* 249 Pa. Super. 240, 376 A.2d 247.**

Card game

Plaintiff, accompanying a club member to defendant's club, was severely injured as the result of an altercation arising from a disputed card game—Held: case for jury in suit against club, jury having exonerated the assailant. ***Doytek v. Bobtown R. & G. Club,* 216 Pa. Super. 368, 268 A.2d 149.**

Casino

Plaintiff brought negligence action against a casino after he tripped and fell over an electrical cord. The trial court transferred the case based upon preliminary objections to venue. The Superior Court affirmed holding that the operations of sister corporations could not be used to establish venue unless the Defendant itself actually conducted business in that venue as well. ***Wimble v. Parx Casino v. Greenwood Gaming & Entertainment, Inc.,* 40 A.3d 174 (Pa. Super. 2012).**

Cast

Cast

Patient with broken leg burned from quick-setting cast brought product liability and negligence action against manufacturer. Held: admission of report of prior occurrences not reversible error and award of delay damages for loss of consortium proper. ***Rogers v. Johnson & Johnson Products, Inc.,* 401 Pa. Super. 430, 585 A.2d 1004.**

Caterer

Plaintiffs injured while dancing allegedly as the result of asparagus on dance floor—caterer held responsible. ***Schwartz v. Warwick-Phila. Corp.,* 424 Pa. 185, 226 A.2d 484.**

Catheterization

Plaintiff alleged negligence on the part of the employees of defendant hospital in the insertion of a catheter. The court held that the complaint failed to allege that the hospital had any constructive or actual knowledge of the improper catheter insertion that created the plaintiff's injury. ***Kennedy v. Butler Memorial Hospital,* 901 A.2d 1042 (Pa. Super. 2006).**

Plaintiff's decedent died after a pediatrician performed a catheterization procedure when the patient's parents had given consent for the procedure to a cardiologist. The trial judge refused to charge on lack of informed consent on the basis that as long as consent to the procedure is adequate, the identity of the person who performs the procedure is irrelevant. Reversed and remanded for new trial to include liability and compensatory and punitive damages. ***Taylor v. Albert Einstein Medical Center,* 723 A.2d 1027 (Pa. Super. 1999).**

Failure to follow Department of Health standards which suggest 48 hour limit for catheterization is not negligence *per se*. Medical malpractice causation requires proof of increased risk of harm. Causation is question for trier of fact where artificial hip replacement patient developed staff infection from catheterization. ***Edwards v. Brandywine Hospital,* 438 Pa. Super. 673, 652 A.2d 1382 (1995).**

Patient brought malpractice action against hospital for negligent catheterization. Jury found hospital negligent but injuries not result of negligence and set damages at $50,000. New trial granted. ***Chiaverini v. Sewickley Valley Hospital,* 409 Pa. Super. 630, 598 A.2d 1021.**

Catholic grade school

Parents of student at Catholic grade school brought action for negligent infliction of emotional distress and defamation after their child was expelled for allegedly carrying a penknife to school. The trial court dismissed the complaint on preliminary objection. The Superior Court affirmed. The Pennsylvania Supreme Court reversed holding that the deference rule did not apply at the pleading stage as both the defamation and negligent infliction of emotional distress claims appeared to be able to be determined without requiring the court to decide ecclesiastical questions. ***Connor v. Archdiocese of Philadelphia*, 975 A.2d 1084 (Pa. 2009).**

Causation

Parents of children expelled from Catholic grade school sued diocese, diocesan Board of Education and principal after diocese and bishop had confirmed expulsion following hearing before diocesan Board of Education. Trial court sustained preliminary objections of defendants on grounds that state court did not have jurisdiction to determine controversies under ecclesiastic rule, custom or law, as upheld and affirmed by bishop of Roman Catholic Church. Affirmed by Commonwealth Court pursuant to same reasoning as elucidated by Pennsylvania Supreme Court in *Presbytery of Beaver-Butler v. Middlesex Presbyterian Church*, 507 Pa. 255, 489 A.2d 1317, cert. denied, 474 U.S. 887, 106 S.Ct. 198, 88 L.Ed.2d 167. (1985). ***Gaston v. Diocese of Allentown*, 712 A.2d 757 (Pa. Super. 1998).**

Catwalk

Employee of maintenance contractor injured when catwalk collapsed. Manufacturer not liable. Accident result of owner negligence. Owner not immune. Owner not statutory employer. ***Mathis v. United Engineers and Contractors, Inc.*, 381 Pa. Super. 467, 554 A.2d 96.**

Causation

Injured plaintiff/appellee entitled to new trial following jury instruction that failed to inform jury of ability to award damages if the defendant's negligent acts were a substantial factor in bringing about the harm to plaintiff. ***Mietelski v. Banks*, 854 A.2d 579 (Pa. Super. 2004).**

Where both parties' medical experts agree that some injury to plaintiff resulted from an accident and the jury finds that the defendant was negligent in his actions the jury cannot avoid a finding of substantial cause and deny damages. ***Kraner v. Kraner*, 841 A.2d 141 (Pa. Super. 2004).**

Elemental analysis of a negligence claim in a medical malpractice action for damages sustained in delivery of child. Superior Court further examines standards for proving causation of damages. ***Cruz v. Northeastern Hospital*, 801 A2d. 602 (Pa. Super. 2002).**

Plaintiff alleged injuries received in hospital from bed rail that repeatedly fell on her arm. Nonsuit granted and affirmed on grounds that plaintiff had failed to produce evidence in her case in chief to establish causation element of negligence claim. ***Kelly v. St. Mary Hospital*, 778 A.2d 1224 (Pa. Super. 2001).**

Expert testimony, expressed with reasonable medical certainty, that a physician's action increased the risk of harm creates an issue for the jury. Testimony need not be that physician's action "caused" the harm. ***Billman v. Saylor*, 761 A.2d 1208 (Pa. Super. 2000).**

Plaintiff bicyclist granted a new trial after review of trial record in which defendant automobile driver admitted striking plaintiff and causing injuries. Jury answered interrogatories that automobile driver was negligent but that negligence was not substantial factor in causing injury. In light of uncontradicted testimony by automobile driver that she had to back her car off the plaintiff's foot, the causal connection was clear. ***Krucskowska v. Winter*, 764 A.2d 627 (Pa. Super. 2000).**

Causation

Plaintiff was injured in an automobile accident for which defendant admitted negligence but disputed accident as cause of plaintiff's injuries. Jury returned verdict that there was no causal connection between accident and injuries despite testimony from medical experts for both parties that plaintiff's injuries were sustained in accident. Trial court granted plaintiff's motion for new trial on damages only as verdict was against weight of evidence. Superior Court affirmed new trial but remanded for new trial on both liability and damages. **Hixson v. Barlow, 723 A.2d 716 (Pa. Super. 1999).**

Plaintiff's decedent wife was examined on numerous occasions by a physician's assistant who failed to properly diagnose or call in physician to examine a cancerous breast. Trial court entered a compulsory nonsuit after refusing to accept testimony of plaintiff's medical expert. Despite his twenty-five years of practice and experience as an oncologist familiar with the same condition that caused wife's death, expert could not provide a specific reference to his theory of liability in a medical text. Where plaintiff's expert expresses the opinion that defendants' actions increased the risk of harm to plaintiff, the question of causation must go to the jury. Superior Court also reversed procedural rulings by trial court that prevented plaintiff from providing relevant and material facts to the record despite a complete lack of prejudice to defendants. **Smith v. Grab, 705 A.2d 894 (Pa. Super. 1997).**

Pennsylvania has not yet adopted the market share liability theory as an exception to the general rule of negligence law that a plaintiff must establish that a particular defendant proximately caused his or her injury. Summary judgment affirmed in favor of lead manufacturers and trade organization sued by minor injured by lead poisoning. **Skipworth v. Lead Industries Association, Inc., 547 Pa. 224, 690 A.2d 169 (1997).**

In medical malpractice action, the *Hamil/Mitzelfelt* two-pronged test "relaxing" a plaintiff's burden of proving causation should be applied to the entirety of plaintiff's expert's testimony regarding necessity of revised informed consent. Order removing compulsory nonsuit affirmed. **Kratt v. Horrow, 455 Pa. Super. 140, 687 A.2d 830 (1997).**

Not every wrong constitutes a legally cognizable cause of action. A physician who fails to remove sponges following an episiotomy resulting in no more than a foul odor is not subject to liability where no causal link between an act of negligence and legally cognizable injury is established. Order granting motion for nonsuit affirmed. **Gregorio v. Zeluck, 451 Pa. Super. 154, 678 A.2d 810 (1996).**

Order granting summary judgment in favor of school district affirmed where plaintiff who slipped on ice in school district parking lot failed to establish that injuries were caused by improper design, construction, deterioration, or inherent defect of real estate. Real property exception to Political Subdivision Tort Claims Act not applicable. **Metkus v. Pennsbury School District, ___ Pa. Cmwlth. ___, 674 A.2d 355 (1996).**

While PennDOT has a duty to make highways safe and possibly to install guard rails where necessary, in order to recover plaintiff must establish that lack of guardrail was cause of injuries rather than a contributing factor. Failure to allege

Causation

a defect "of" Commonwealth property precludes recovery under real property exception to sovereign immunity. Order granting partial summary judgment affirmed. ***Rothermel v. Com., Dept. of Transp.,* ___ Pa. Cmwlth. ___, 672 A.2d 837 (1996).**

Where recklessness or carelessness is at issue, proof of intoxication is relevant; however, evidence that plaintiff consumed alcohol is inadmissible unless it reasonably establishes intoxication. Order granting new trial inclusive of evidence of intoxication and denying judgment *n.o.v.* affirmed. ***Surowiec v. General Motors Corp.*, 448 Pa. Super. 510, 672 A.2d 333 (1996).**

In wrongful death and survival action by widow of motorist whose automobile crossed opposing lane and left highway, PennDOT entitled to jury charge on contributory negligence where no evidence presented regarding external cause of accident. Following plaintiff's inquiry into other causes of accident, State Trooper permitted to testify as to possibility of driver having fallen asleep. ***Burkholz v. Com., Dept. of Transp.,* ___ Pa. Cmwlth. ___, 667 A.2d 513 (1995).**

Nurse's opinion based on personal, unsupported medical diagnosis is inadequate expert testimony to establish prima facie evidence of causation in medical malpractice action. Order granting summary judgment affirmed. ***Flanagan v. Labe*, 446 Pa. Super. 107, 666 A.2d 333 (1995).**

Where patient who underwent perineal urethrotomy and cauterization, rather than planned transurethral prostatectomy, failed to establish a causal connection between resulting injuries and physician's conduct through expert testimony, compulsory nonsuit was proper. Patient should have been allowed to introduce evidence of alleged lack of consent to surgery that was admittedly not discussed by physician and patient prior to its performance. Order granting compulsory nonsuit on question of negligence affirmed. Case remanded on claim for lack of informed consent. ***Hoffman v. Mogil*, 445 Pa. Super. 252, 665 A.2d 478 (1995).**

Municipal defendants are neither afforded blanket immunity nor entitled to judgment as a matter of law in each and every tort claim where the victim's injuries were caused in part by the intervening criminal conduct of third parties or where the criminal acts of a third party merely form a link in the chain of causation. It is for the jury to determine whether municipal defendants' conduct was a substantial contributing factor in causing the victim's injuries and, if so, whether intervening criminal conduct of third parties was so extraordinary as not to be reasonably foreseeable by the municipal defendants. Summary judgment reversed. ***Jones v. Chieffo,* ___ Pa. Super. ___, 664 A.2d 1091 (1995).**

The standards of proof established in asbestos actions apply to plaintiff's action for averred workplace cadmium exposure resulting in cancer. Plaintiff must establish that defendant's products were in use at work site to establish causal nexus element of action. Summary judgment affirmed. ***Jobe v. W.P. Metz Refining*, 445 Pa. Super. 76, 664 A.2d 1015 (1995).**

Absent proof that patron was visibly intoxicated when served additional alcoholic beverages, no action for wrongful death or survival is established. Statutory violation of serving alcohol after hours does not establish liability for acts of third

Causation

parties absent proof that such service was proximate cause of the injury. *Hiles v. Brandywine Club,* **443 Pa. Super. 462, 662 A.2d 16 (1995).**

In action arising from explosion of boiler caused by defective emergency shut off valve, manufacturer of valve held strictly liable for defective product. Manufacturer's liability for its defective product is outlined in Section 402A of Restatement (2d) Torts, which provides that a plaintiff must prove that the product was sold in a defective condition dangerous to the user and that the defect was the proximate cause of the injury. An actor is relieved from liability owing to an intervening or superseding cause only if the intervening or superseding negligent acts were so extraordinary as not to have been reasonably foreseeable. Summary judgment affirmed in part and reversed in part. *Dougherty v. Edward J. Meloney, Inc.,* **443 Pa. Super. 201, 661 A.2d 375 (1995).**

Defendant injured when car struck dumpster he was rummaging through did not state cause of action against owners of property who lawfully placed dumpster in front of house and who had no awareness of plaintiff's presence. Plaintiff failed to show any proximate causation between owner's placement of dumpster and his injuries. Proximate causation exists where wrongful conduct is a substantial factor in bringing about the harm incurred. Order granting summary judgment affirmed. *Amarhanov v. Fassel,* **442 Pa. Super. 111, 658 A.2d 808 (1995).**

Physician's assistant's failure to refer patient complaining of breast pain to physician is not actionable without proof of causation in suit against medical practice group instituted after discovery of breast cancer. Board certified internist is qualified to render an opinion as to the duty of care of physician's assistant. Compulsory nonsuit affirmed. *Montgomery v. So. Philadelphia Medical Group, Inc.,* **441 Pa. Super. 146, 656 A.2d 1385 (1995).**

Apportionment of liability for harm to plaintiff is question of law. Where tortious conduct of two or more persons causes a single harm that cannot be apportioned, the actors are joint tortfeasors even though they acted independently. Jury verdict in favor of driver injured as a result of two separate collisions affirmed. *Smith v. Pulcinella,* **440 Pa. Super. 525, 656 A.2d 494 (1995).**

Police officer who enters upon another's land in his official capacity and in response to a call for assistance is a licensee. Landowner's duty is to inform licensee of dangerous, hidden conditions. Obviously rowdy crowd of patrons at social hall was not a dangerous, hidden condition. Although violation of Dram Shop Act is negligence *per se*, mere fact that patrons who assaulted police officer were intoxicated neither proves that they had been served when visibly intoxicated nor causation of officer's injuries. Summary judgment for defendant affirmed. *Holpp v. Fez, Inc.,* **440 Pa. Super. 512, 656 A.2d 147 (1995).**

In automobile accident case by decedent's administrator against intoxicated driver and PennDOT, whether PennDOT's alleged negligence for improper road design and maintenance was substantial factor in accident was question for jury. Existence of two tortfeasors does not automatically excuse one or the other from liability. Question of concurrent or joint causation and determination of whether an act is so extraordinary as to constitute a superseding cause are for the jury. Order

Causation

sustaining preliminary objections of PennDOT reversed. ***Powell v. Drumheller,* 539 Pa. 484, 653 A.2d 619 (1995).**

Failure to follow Department of Health standards that suggest 48 hour limit for catheterization is not negligence per se. Medical malpractice causation requires proof of increased risk of harm. Causation is question for trier of fact where artificial hip replacement patient developed staff infection from catheterization. ***Edwards v. Brandywine Hospital,* 438 Pa. Super. 673, 652 A.2d 1382 (1995).**

Action by passenger of stolen pizza delivery vehicle after vehicle crashed into pole dismissed against delivery driver and his employer for plaintiff's failure to establish causation. ***Matos v. Rivera,* 436 Pa. Super. 509, 648 A.2d 337 (1994).**

Plaintiff failed to prove that dangerous condition of a parking lot was causally related to injuries. Summary judgment in favor of volunteer fire department affirmed. ***West v. Kuneck,* 167 Pa. Cmwlth. 252, 647 A.2d 975 (1994).**

Summary judgment in favor of social host affirmed where no evidence that host had actual notice that minor's were consuming alcohol. Summary judgment in favor of telephone company affirmed because causal connection between location of pole and accident too remote in law to impose liability. ***Novak v. Kilby,* 167 Pa. Cmwlth. 217, 647 A.2d 687 (1994).**

Action of motorcyclist who crossed into oncoming lane while attempting to pass vehicle in his lane was sole cause of accident; order denying PennDOT's motion for post trial relief reversed. ***Glover v. Com., Dept. of Transp.,* 167 Pa. Cmwlth. 87, 647 A.2d 630 (1994).**

Motorcyclist failed to produce sufficient evidence in action against landowner, PennDOT and township to justify inference of negligence and causation owing to inability to identify reason his vehicle left roadway and struck fence post. Summary judgment affirmed. ***Saylor v. Green,* 165 Pa. Cmwlth. 249, 645 A.2d 318 (1994).**

Lengthy discussion of enterprise liability, civil conspiracy, and concert of action in D.E.S. case. Affirmed grant of summary judgment to numerous defendants of over 72 originally sued under one or more theories. ***Burnside v. Abbott Laboratories,* 351 Pa. Super. 264, 505 A.2d 973.**

Suit against employer of individual who allegedly caused auto accident while not on job. Alleged that employer failed to monitor employee's mental state and placed too much stress on employee, causing him to have emotional breakdown while driving. Demurrer sustained. ***Hill v. Acme,* 350 Pa. Super. 219, 504 A.2d 324.**

Alleged that excessively greasy doughnut caused severe gastritis and ulcer flare-up, leading to surgery. Defense verdict by jury affirmed. Court found that there was no evidence of causation, therefore all complaints of error were harmless. Expert opinion here did not have certainty required to allow jury to find causation. ***McCann v. Amy Joy Donut Shops,* 325 Pa. Super. 349, 472 A.2d 1149.**

Jury verdict $7,134—clear liability auto accident. Issue: whether plaintiff's alleged injuries in fact preexisted accident. Plaintiff alleged accident caused neurosis, leading to organic difficulties. Defendant contended preexisting condition's nat-

Causation

ural progression led to deterioration conditions—epileptic seizures and paralysis of one leg. New trial ordered due to inadequate charge on causation. ***Collins v. Cement Express, Inc.,* 301 Pa. Super. 139, 447 A.2d 987.**

Where plaintiff had a prescription refilled numerous times contrary to prescription and physician's instructions, sustaining loss of eyesight, proper for jury to exonerate physician as his actions not proximately related to damage. ***Malloy v. Shanahan,* 280 Pa. Super. 440, 421 A.2d 803.**

Workman injured in fall from temporary platform used for passage to house under construction. With no evidence as to cause of platform failure, jury verdict for plaintiff reversed. ***Szumsky v. Lohman Homes,* 267 Pa. Super. 478, 406 A.2d 1142.**

Plaintiff involved in one accident and pulled over to side of road. Standing between cars when another vehicle skidded into rear of stopped car pushing it into plaintiff. Antecedent negligence of plaintiff not a proximate cause of second accident. Error to charge on contributory negligence. ***Sullivan v. Wolson,* 262 Pa. Super. 397, 396 A.2d 1230.**

Liability admitted. Issue as to whether injury which manifested itself 2-1/2 months after accident must be proved by expert to have been connected to accident. Expert testimony required. New trial ordered on damages only. ***McArdle v. Panzels,* 262 Pa. Super. 88, 396 A.2d 658.**

Alleged failure to monitor vital signs of plaintiff after surgery. Temperature elevated to 105.2 degrees causing brain damage. Verdict against hospital only. Long discussion of causation in malpractice cases even though expert here testified with certainty as to causation here. Verdict affirmed. ***Robert v. Chodoff,* 259 Pa. Super. 332, 393 A.2d 853.**

In malpractice case, physician's testimony that earlier detection of cancer would have greatly decreased likelihood of amputation of arm that eventually occurred, not adequate to go to jury on causal connection between failure to diagnose and final result. ***Gradel v. Inouye,* 252 Pa. Super. 392, 381 A.2d 975.**

In malpractice case, trial judge correct in refusing suggested point for charge which in one sentence implied that plaintiff could recover by proving only negligence and increased risk of harm without adequately discussing causation in second sentence. ***Cohen v. Kalodner,* 236 Pa. Super. 124, 345 A.2d 235.**

F.E.L.A. case for back injuries sustained in two separate accidents. Previous chronic back problems of which defendant had no knowledge. Causation of back problems for jury. ***Ciarolla v. Union R.R.,* 235 Pa. Super. 137, 338 A.2d 669.**

Wife plaintiff injured in collision case—received extensive dental treatment—verdict $10,000 for wife plaintiff and $2,000 for husband—majority of court held evidence sufficient to establish causal connection. ***DiVirgiliis v. Gordon,* 212 Pa. Super. 548, 243 A.2d 459.**

Plaintiff was patient of defendant physician—had fracture of left femur—in hospital for 3 months—refractured leg while in bed—notified defendant who did not immediately respond—contended early discharge from hospital, failure to respond

Ceiling

to call and take x-rays as cause of reoccurrence—no expert testimony—causal connection not established. ***Dornon v. Johnson*, 421 Pa. 58, 218 A.2d 808.**

Cauterization

Where patient who underwent perineal urethrotomy and cauterization, rather than planned transurethral prostatectomy, failed to establish a causal connection between resulting injuries and physician's conduct through expert testimony, compulsory nonsuit was proper. Patient should have been allowed to introduce evidence of alleged lack of consent to surgery that was admittedly not discussed by physician and patient prior to its performance. Order granting compulsory nonsuit on question of negligence affirmed. Case remanded on claim for lack of informed consent. ***Hoffman v. Mogil*, 445 Pa. Super. 252, 665 A.2d 478 (1995).**

Cave in

In action by personal representative of plumbing contractor killed in cave-in at construction site, governmental immunity applies because plaintiff presented no proof that city exercised sufficient custody and control over site. Sanction order precluding city's filing of answer for failure to comply with discovery order does not compel waiver of real property exception to governmental immunity. Summary judgment in favor of city affirmed. ***Santori v. Snyder*, 165 Pa. Cmwlth. 505, 645 A.2d 443 (1994).**

Action brought against general contractor for death of plumbing contractor killed when walls of trench caved in. Held: Plumber did not assume risk by voluntarily working in dangerous trench. ***Handschuh v. Albert Development*, 393 Pa. Super. 444, 574 A.2d 693.**

Plaintiff, an employee of an independent contractor, injured by cave-in of a trench being dug for the laying of water pipe—plaintiff sued Authority defendant and several others—issue went off on the measure of control residing in Authority—court held such a matter of law as contract was clear and unambiguous—nonsuit entered—court below held employer a pure independent contractor and that Authority had no control over the manner in which contractor laid pipe—right of inspection not controlling—other defendants also held not responsible—action sustained on appeal. ***Giannetti v. Lower Bucks County Joint Municipal Authority et al.*, 439 Pa. 607, 266 A.2d 477.**

C.B. radio

Passenger injured when automobile struck by truck that went through red light. Truck driver liable. Evidence that truck driver relied on C.B. transmission as to status of traffic signal held admissible. ***Smith v. Brooks*, 394 Pa. Super. 327, 575 A.2d 926.**

Ceiling

Inmate who ran down hallway and jumped steps, hitting his head on ceiling, failed to establish that dangerous condition existed in ceiling above steps in hallway. Duty of care to inmate is that of owner to invitee. Compulsory nonsuit granted in

Cellar doors

favor of County affirmed. *Graf v. County of Northampton*, ___ Pa. Cmwlth. ___, 654 A.2d 131 (1995).

Cellar doors

Fall down steps in friend's home looking for restroom. Entered wrong door and fell as door opened onto cellar steps. Error to grant compulsory nonsuit. New trial ordered. *Fisher v. Findlay,* 319 Pa. Super. 214, 465 A.2d 1306.

Center of road

A three-vehicle accident. Clark vehicle fishtailed on ice, crossed the center of road, striking another vehicle, which was then rear-ended. Jury verdict only against crossing (Clark) vehicle. Passenger in the defendant's car was killed—(defendant's 14-year- old daughter). $30,000.00 was awarded to occupants of one car, but nothing to decedent's estate despite showing a high I.Q. and career plans to be a nurse. Net earning loss of $375,375 was proved. A new trial on damages only — verdict was inconsistent on damages. *McIntyre v. Clark,* 314 Pa. Super. 552, 461 A.2d 295.

Cervical sprain

Jury cannot disregard evidence of soft tissue damage, cervical sprain and herniated disk, which are injuries of the kind that normally cause pain and suffering for which plaintiff should be compensated. Order granting new trial on issue of damages reinstated. *Neison v. Hines,* 539 Pa. 516, 653 A.2d 634 (1995).

Cesarean section

Plaintiff's decedent died after a cesarean section where the evidence indicated pregnancy-induced hypertension, also known as preeclampsia. Corporate hospital negligence can take the form of a breach of any of four duties: to use reasonable care in the maintenance of safe and adequate facilities and equipment; to select and retain only competent physicians; to oversee all persons who practice medicine within its walls as to patient care; and to formulate, adopt and enforce adequate rules and policies to ensure quality care for the patients. A *prima facie* case of corporate negligence requires evidence that the hospital acted in deviation from the standard of care, had actual or constructive notice of the defects or procedures which created the harm and that the conduct was a substantial factor in bringing about the harm. *Whittington v. Episcopal Hospital*, 768 A.2d 1144, (Pa. Super. 2001).

Wife, who delivered a brain-damaged child after a Cesarean section with only local anesthetic, and husband, individually and as parents of the child, sued anesthesiology group, obstetrician and the hospital for malpractice. Nurses employed at the hospital are not agents of the physicians when they act in the normal course of hospital services. Father's loss of consortium claim was properly denied by the trial court where his only testimony was that he had a subjective fear of engaging in sexual relations with his wife following her delivery of the brain-damaged child, even though the damage may have been the result of medical malpractice. Father's claim for negligent infliction of emotional distress was properly dismissed where he was not near the scene of the injuries to his wife and newborn child. Hearing his wife's cries of pain only, without any visual experience of her condition, was insufficient. ***Tiburzio-Kelly v. Montgomery,* 452 Pa. Super. 158, 681 A.2d 757 (1996).**

In a medical malpractice action for failure to perform a Cesarean section in a timely manner, a registered nurse is a "medical witness" under Pa. Rule of Civil Procedure 4020(a)(5); therefore, her deposition testimony is admissible without her presence in court to contradict defendant doctor's testimony. Judgment reversed. ***Russell v. Albert Einstein Medical Center,* 543 Pa. 532, 673 A.2d 876 (1996).**

Infant injured at birth when physician attempted delivery with forceps before performing caesarean section. Physician not liable. Jury instruction on "two schools of thought" appropriate. Use of forceps did not require consent. ***Sinclair by Sinclair v. Block,* 406 Pa. Super. 540, 594 A.2d 750.**

Chain

In action where jury found plaintiff to be 30% negligent, one defendant to be 45% negligent and second defendant 25% negligent, plaintiff may still recover against defendant found to be less negligent than plaintiff because collectively defendants were more negligent than plaintiff. Where strictly liable defendant and negligent defendant acted as joint tortfeasors, contribution among them properly can be awarded. Judgment on molded jury verdict affirmed. ***Smith v. Weissenfels, Inc.,* 441 Pa. Super. 328, 657 A.2d 949 (1995).**

Chain collision

Action brought against vehicle drivers and state police arising out of chain reaction collision. Summary judgment based on intervening superseding cause precluded. ***Taylor v. Jackson,* 164 Pa. Cmwlth. 482, 643 A.2d 771.**

Chain reaction collision caused by brake problems. Jury verdict for defendant. Sudden emergency doctrine does not include sudden mechanical failures. Whether defects are attributable to negligence is determined by regular duty of care standards. New trial ordered. ***Chiodo v. Gargloff & Downham Trucking,* 308 Pa. Super. 498, 454 A.2d 645.**

Three car successive or chain collision—plaintiff's car in middle—car ahead stopped—plaintiff's car allegedly stopped suddenly—defendant's car, the third in line, collided with plaintiff's car—error for trial judge to remove question of plaintiff's possible contributory negligence from the jury—new trial granted. ***Toff v. Rohde,* 208 Pa. Super. 411, 222 A.2d 434.**

Chain sling

Plaintiff received permanent injury when metal tag on chain sling broke and struck his eye. Remaining parts of chain sling and metal tag were lost or misplaced. After filing suit against company which plaintiff alleged made sling, that company filed motion for summary judgment, alleging plaintiff could not prove whether that company or another manufactured the chain sling which actually caused his injury. Based on records of mine where plaintiff worked indicating that mine had purchased different chain slings from various companies over the years, trial court determined

Chair

there was no proof that chain sling at issue was supplied by defendant. Grant of summary judgment was affirmed on appeal. ***Payton v. Pennsylvania Sling Company*, 710 A.2d 1221 (Pa. Super. 1998).**

Chair

Verdict against injured plaintiff affirmed absent proof of unreasonably dangerous condition of chair. ***Steinhouse v. Herman Miller, Inc.*, 443 Pa. Super. 395, 661 A.2d 1379 (1995).**

Plaintiff injured when back of chair broke brought action against distributor. Verdict for distributor reversed. Court failed to instruct on malfunction theory. ***Brill v. Systems Resources, Inc.*, 405 Pa. Super. 603, 592 A.2d 1377.**

Where patient in hospital fell out of chair during a short absence by nurse, for jury as to whether, in view of plaintiff's condition, it was reasonable for nurse to leave even for short period of time. ***Hogan v. Bryn Mawr Hospital*, 250 Pa. Super. 109, 378 A.2d 477.**

Change of direction

Section 1012 of the Motor Vehicle Code requires signal 100 feet in advance of change of direction—Held: charge of court covering same adequate. ***Murphy v. Taylor*, 440 Pa. 186, 269 A.2d 486.**

Plaintiff instituted suit, inter alia, against Temple University—preliminary objections were sustained on ground of charitable immunity—petition to vacate judgment after change in applicable law—error to grant—a final judgment and appeal could have been taken from initial action. ***Love, Admr. v. Temple University*, 422 Pa. 30, 220 A.2d 838.**

Charities

Plaintiff fell on the sidewalk abutting defendant's church—Supreme Court extended the doctrine of *Flagiello v. Pennsylvania Hospital* (417 Pa. 486) to include church organizations and denied defendant synagogue a charitable immunity. ***Nolan v. Tifereth Israel Synagogue*, 425 Pa. 106, 227 A.2d 675.**

Plaintiff instituted suit, inter alia, against Temple University—preliminary objections were sustained on ground of charitable immunity—petition to vacate judgment after change in applicable law—error to grant—a final judgment and appeal could have been taken from initial action. ***Love, Admr. v. Temple University*, 422 Pa. 30, 220 A.2d 838.**

Charter school

Plaintiff was injured when struck by another student running through the hallway. The court affirmed that the charter school, which was established under the Charter School Law, was entitled to the same governmental immunity under the Political Subdivision Tort Claims Act as political subdivisions and local agencies. ***Warner v. Lawrence*, 900 A.2d 980 (Pa. Cmwlth. 2006).**

Children

Chase

Passenger in automobile injured in collision with vehicle being chased by another automobile. Held: sudden emergency rule not applicable where driver was being chased had other options available other than fleeing. *McKee by McKee v. Evans,* **380 Pa. Super. 120, 551 A.2d 260.**

Chemistry class - See Municipal liability: Schools and school districts

Chest tube

In medical malpractice case involving insertion of chest tube, nurse is not qualified to testify as an expert as to compliance with standards of medical care or to diagnose medical conditions. Summary judgment in favor of hospital affirmed. *Flanagan v. Labe,* **547 Pa. 254, 690 A.2d 183 (1997).**

Child abuse

Plaintiff, surrogate mother, sued infertility clinic under wrongful death and survival statutes, for negligent infliction of emotional distress, for fraud and for breach of fiduciary duty for the death of child murdered by sperm-donor father one month after the child's birth. After determining that clinic had waived any claim that mother lacked standing, Held: mother had stated cause of action under wrongful death and survival statutes but lacked sufficient factual basis for negligent infliction of emotional distress, fraud and breach of fiduciary duty. For-profit infertility clinic was in a "special relationship" with all parties to the transaction—surrogate mother, sperm-donor and resulting child—so as to create a duty imposed by law to effectively provide safeguards that might reasonably prevent foreseeable injuries to the parties, such as abuse of the child. *Huddleston v. Infertility Center of America,* **700 A.2d 453 (Pa. Super. 1997).**

Child Protective Services Act

Patient's unsubstantiated assertion of physical injury failed to establish negligent or intentional infliction of emotional distress. Doctor and medical center were immune from suit under Child Protective Services Law for disclosing plaintiff's admission that she had suffocated her child. Child Protective Services Law, which grants immunity for disclosures does not conflict with psychotherapist–patient privilege or the confidentiality provisions of the Mental Health Procedures Act. *Fewell v. Bresner,* **444 Pa. Super. 559, 664 A.2d 577 (1995).**

Children

Mother who filed suit for injuries to child born after failed abortion received permission from trial court to discontinue action without prejudice. On appeal, Superior Court reversed holding that delay during period of child's minority would unfairly prejudice defendants, particularly in light of the fact that plaintiff had already commenced the action. *Robinson v. Pennsylvania Hospital,* **737 A.2d 291 (Pa. Super. 1999).**

Children

Plaintiff minor was injured when his shoe was caught in escalator. Plaintiffs raised negligence and *res ipsa loquitur* claims in complaint (even though *res ipsa* is rule of evidence and not cause of action). Trial court refused to give *res ipsa* charge because plaintiffs had introduced evidence tending to show specific acts of negligence. Held: *res ipsa* charge is permissible as long as plaintiff has not presented evidence which tends to support a single cause of incident causing injury. When plaintiff presents as specific a case of negligence as possible, yet is unable to demonstrate exact cause of accident, plaintiff is entitled to *res ipsa loquitur* charge. **D'Arnenne v. Strawbridge & Clothier, 712 A.2d 318 (Pa. Super. 1998).**

Parents and child filed suit against psychiatrist who treated child and, after treatment, negligently embarked upon a course of action that directly affected both child and parents to their injury. Where psychiatrist goes well beyond treatment of minor (e.g., active participation in criminal proceedings directed against parents and maintaining silence when she knew patient was telling untruths and could not distinguish fact from fantasy), court will impose duty on psychiatrist to parents, breach of which may support determination of negligence. The lack of a psychiatrist–patient relationship with parents does not provide blanket immunity to psychiatrist. In instant case, it was also reasonably foreseeable to psychiatrist that her negligent actions would have harmful affect on patient's parents. **Althaus v. Cohen, 710 A.2d 1147 (Pa. Super. 1998).**

Parents of child injured in fall down stairs brought action against landlord. Held: summary judgment improper. Question of fact existed. **Kelly by Kelly v. Ickes, 427 Pa. Super. 542, 629 A.2d 1002.**

Child of tenant injured when companion closed fire door on hand. Plaintiff claimed door was faulty. Held: action of companion acted as superseding cause. **Bayard v. Philadelphia Housing Authority, 157 Pa. Cmwlth. 269, 629 A.2d 283.**

Child injured when struck by hand cart operated by city employee at recreation center. City not liable. **Benson v. City of Philadelphia, 146 Pa. Cmwlth. 388, 606 A.2d 550.**

Child injured in bicycle accident at playground owned by borough and school district. Both defendants jointly liable. **Dimino v. Borough of Pottstown, 142 Pa. Cmwlth. 683, 598 A.2d 357.**

Child had both legs amputated when run over by train. Child gained access to railroad tracks through hole in fence. Action brought against municipality for failure to maintain fence. Municipality not liable. Fence not on municipal property. **Scarborough v. Lewis, 523 Pa. 30, 565 A.2d 122.**

Child run over by train while lying on tracks. Permissive crossing theory held not applicable since child was lying on tracks and not crossing them. **Gaul v. Consolidated Rail Corp., 383 Pa. Super. 250, 556 A.2d 892.**

Child shot by playmate with unsecured police service revolver. Municipality not liable. Police officer-father not acting within scope of employment. **Natt v. Labor, 117 Pa. Cmwlth. 207, 543 A.2d 223.**

Child who exited city owned property through hole in fence was struck by train. City not liable for injuries that happened off city property or were inflicted by third parties. ***Lynch v. National Railroad Passenger Corporation,* 115 Pa. Cmwlth. 474, 540 A.2d 635.**

Child injured by other children at city-owned swimming pool. City not liable, injury did not arise out of custody or control of real property. ***Kasavage v. City of Philadelphia,* 105 Pa. Cmwlth. 554, 524 A.2d 1089.**

§328D of Restatement (2d) Torts accepted as law of Commonwealth. *Res ipsa loquitur* can be used under the terms and conditions set forth in Restatement. Exclusive control not required. Boy of four caught foot in escalator in store. Although Korvette's had day-to-day responsibility, Otis by contract assumed responsibility of regular maintenance, therefore proper to prove negligence circumstantially under §328D. Res ipsa doctrine is circumstantial evidence which creates a permissible inference of fault. Error to call it a rebuttable presumption. ***Gilbert v. Korvette's and Otis Elevator,* 457 Pa. 602, 327 A.2d 94.**

Minor plaintiff of 8 fell from the running board of a tractor and injured—trial court properly instructed jury that actual knowledge of presence of minor is not required to constitute wanton misconduct—charge as a whole correct and verdict for defendant upheld on appeal. ***Mount v. Bulifant,* 438 Pa. 265, 265 A.2d 627.**

Evidence disclosed that four persons were in front seat but one was a two year old child—court refused to charge that Section 1001 of Vehicle Code applied—error and new trial awarded. ***Atene v. Lawrence,* 428 Pa. 424, 239 A.2d 346.**

Child of 4 entered a partially constructed building being built by defendant contractor—fell to cellar while walking backward and was severely injured—no recovery—a house in course of construction is not an attractive nuisance. ***Goll et al. v. Muscara,* 211 Pa. Super. 93, 235 A.2d 443.**

Plaintiff struck and injured by an automobile driven by a 14 year old boy—car had been stolen from an airport limousine parking lot—majority of Superior Court felt that there existed no liability and that case was ruled by *Line v. Chestnut Motors, Inc.* (421 Pa. 26). ***Canavin v. Wilmington Trans. Co.,* 208 Pa. Super. 506, 223 A.2d 902.**

Children and alcohol

Summary judgment in favor of social host affirmed where no evidence that host had actual notice that minors were consuming alcohol. Summary judgment in favor of telephone company affirmed because causal connection between location of pole and accident too remote in law to impose liability. ***Novak v. Kilby,* 167 Pa. Cmwlth. 217, 647 A.2d 687 (1994).**

Minor injured after being served alcohol by another minor. Minor not liable as social host. ***Kapres v. Heller,* 536 Pa. 551, 640 A.2d 888.**

Teenager found liable for providing alcoholic beverages to other minor involved in automobile accident. ***Sperando v. Com., Dept. of Transp.,* 157 Pa. Cmwlth. 531, 630 A.2d 532.**

Children and Youth Services

Motorists injured in accident caused by intoxicated driver brought action against minors who served him alcohol. Minors liable. ***Muntz v. Com., Dept. of Transp.,*** **157 Pa. Cmwlth. 514, 630 A.2d 524.**

Minor plaintiff injured while intoxicated. Question of whether distributor was liable because he knew that beer was for consumption by minors was for jury to decide. ***Thomas v. Duquesne Light Company,*** **376 Pa. Super. 1, 545 A.2d 289.**

Passenger in vehicle driven by intoxicated minor killed in collision. Driver consumed alcohol purchased by other minor. Beer distributor who sold alcohol may be liable even though driver not purchaser. ***Matthews v. Konieczny,*** **515 Pa. 106, 527 A.2d 508.**

Landlord corporation not responsible for actions of licensee tenant in serving minors or visibly intoxicated persons who are later involved in accident. Corporate owner of real estate here granted nonsuit. ***McCrery v. Scioli,*** **336 Pa. Super. 455, 485 A.2d 1170.**

Summary judgment in favor of tavern owners in dram shop case, reversed. Affidavit of moving party that plaintiff was not visibly intoxicated when served alcoholic beverages, even if uncontradicted, will not support summary judgment. Credibility of testimony is still for jury. ***Peluso v. Walter,*** **334 Pa. Super. 609, 483 A.2d 905.**

Minor plaintiff injured while operating car—evidence that he had previously been served intoxicated liquor by defendants while visibly intoxicated—contrary to statute—case for jury—same case in 411 Pa. 142. ***Smith v. Evans,*** **421 Pa. 247, 219 A.2d 310.**

Children and Youth Services

Foster parents assigned by county Children and Youth Service agency were employees of agency and so entitled to immunity under Political Subdivision Tort Claims Act. ***Patterson v. Lycoming County,*** **815 A.2d 659 (Pa. Cmwlth. 2003).**

Doctrine of governmental immunity provides that liability may be imposed on a local agency only for negligent acts. Acts or conduct that constitute a crime, actual fraud, actual malice, or wilful misconduct do not subject a local agency to liability. Failure to disclose to adoptive parents information in CYS files that biological parents of adoptive child both suffered from mental illness, alcoholism, and drug abuse does not overcome governmental immunity of CYS. ***Zernhelt v. Lehigh County Office of CYS,*** **___ Pa. Cmwlth. ___, 659 A.2d 89 (1995).**

Children causing injury

Minor injured by a pellet fired from a gun held by another minor. In suit by parents of injured child and on his behalf against child who fired gun, trial court entered summary judgment on finding that the non-custodial mother of the child who fired the gun had no knowledge that the child had the gun in his possession while staying with his father. While the mere relation of parent and child imposes no duty upon the parent for the torts of the child, parents may be liable where negligence on the part of the parents makes an injury possible. If the injury ought to have been foreseen by the parents, their negligence is the proximate cause of the injury. *J.H. ex rel. Hoffman v. Pellak*, 764 A.2d 64 (Pa. Super. 2000).

A minor/owner who provides an air powered pellet gun to another minor may be liable to minor plaintiff injured by a pellet for providing the gun without instruction. The reasonably anticipated negligent firing of the pellet gun by other minor is not a superseding, intervening cause that insulates minor/owner from liability. Order sustaining preliminary objections reversed. *Frey v. Smith,* **454 Pa. Super. 242, 685 A.2d 169 (1996).**

Injuries resulting to child while playing with playmate on playground equipment will not be deemed to have been caused by negligence absent proof of playmate acting in an unreasonable or dangerous manner. *Schoymer v. Mexico Forge, Inc.,* **437 Pa. Super. 159, 649 A.2d 705 (1994).**

Fifth grade student struck in eye with pencil propelled by another student who tripped or fell. Teacher outside room, monitoring return of students. Non-jury verdict, $15,000, reversed. Momentary absence from room not negligent. Judgment reversed. *Simonetti v. School District of Philadelphia,* **308 Pa. Super. 555, 454 A.2d 1038.**

Six-year old injured by five-year old who swung a stick at him. Summary judgment for defendant affirmed. Conclusive presumption that five-year old incapable of negligence. *Dunn v. Teti,* **280 Pa. Super. 399, 421 A.2d 782.**

Spitball battle on school bus caused minor passenger to lose sight of one eye. Verdict in favor of minor participants reversed. Burden of proof on them to show which actually threw spitball once plaintiff showed it had to be one of them. Verdict against school bus company sustained. *Sommers v. Hessler,* **227 Pa. Super. 41, 323 A.2d 17.**

Plaintiff was a volunteer worker helping blacktop a parking lot—struck by tractor used to roll asphalt—defendant operator left tractor engine running—his 7 year old son started machine and plaintiff injured—owner of premises and operator of tractor properly held jointly responsible. *Glass v. Freeman,* **430 Pa. 21, 240 A.2d 825.**

Children contributorily negligence

An eleven year old boy was killed by passing automobile on narrow bridge. In suit against the driver who struck him and PennDOT for negligence in maintenance and operation of the bridge, trial court decisions to deny new trial as to driver affirmed and grant of new trial as to PennDOT reversed because determination of comparative negligence of minor child was within province of jury. *Stong v. PennDOT,* **817 A.2d 576 (Pa. Cmwlth. 2003).**

Plaintiff teenager brought suit against above ground pool owner for injuries suffered when she dove into four feet of water and suffered serious injuries to her neck. Order granting motion for compulsory nonsuit affirmed where evidence by plaintiff established that she was aware of danger of diving into shallow water; she was aware of depth of the water in the pool; and she proceeded to dive into the

Children in street

pool "on a dare". Plaintiff's status as licensee or trespasser not a factor in light of her knowledge of danger. Property owner's duty does not extend to those conditions the existence of which is obvious even to children, and the risk of which is fully realized by them, particularly when the child chooses to encounter the risk through recklessness or bravado. ***Long v. Manzo,* 452 Pa. Super. 451, 682 A.2d 370 (1996).**

Medical malpractice claim for failure to diagnose fractured wrist. Liability admitted by radiologist. Jury improperly instructed on contributory negligence when insufficient facts plead or proven to support that instruction. Judgment in favor of radiologist reversed and new trial granted. ***Pascal v. Carter,* 436 Pa. Super. 40, 647 A.2d 231 (1994).**

Issue of assumption of risk properly before jury where minor struck by stone thrown by playmate during horseplay. Defendant's verdict affirmed. ***McIntyre v. Cusick,* 247 Pa. Super. 354, 372 A.2d 864.**

A 7-1/2 year old pedestrian struck by auto while crossing street. Error to charge that if jury found that minor crossing against red light he was barred from recovering as a matter of law. ***Leopold v. Davies*, 246 Pa. Super. 176, 369 A.2d 868.**

Children in street

Plaintiff administratrix of deceased minor filed suit against SEPTA and ambulance company after child who had alighted from bus crossed in front of bus, with green light, and was struck by ambulance which was improperly passing bus on its left. After settling with ambulance service, SEPTA was granted summary judgment on basis of sovereign immunity as the act of stopping at an intersection, rather than at the appropriate bus stop in middle of block, then opening door to discharge child was not "operation" of motor vehicle under Sovereign Immunity Act. "...a temporary stop connected to the discharge of passengers is not part and parcel of the operation of a vehicle." Query, not even on a passenger transit bus? ***Warrick v. Pro Cor Ambulance, Inc.*, 709 A.2d 422 (Pa. Cmwlth. 1997).**

Parents of minor brought action against school district for injuries which resulted from minor being hit by school bus in authorized crossing zone. Failure to state common law or statutory cause of action against a political subdivision precludes recovery under the Political Subdivision Tort Claims Act. Order granting summary judgment affirmed. ***Dunaway v. South Eastern School District,* ___ Pa. Cmwlth. ___, 676 A.2d 1281 (1996).**

Standard of care for a child is the exercise of ordinary care appropriate for a child. Driver and Borough not liable where child who darts out into street found seventy percent negligent. ***Smith v. Stribling,* 168 Pa. Cmwlth. 188, 649 A.2d 1003 (1994).**

Child injured in street by car after being forced to leave sidewalk due to city-placed barricade. City not liable under exception to Political Subdivision Tort Claims Act because injuries not caused by care, custody, or control of real property or dangerous condition of sidewalk. ***Kiley by Kiley v. City of Philadelphia,* 537 Pa. 502, 645 A.2d 184 (1994).**

Children in street

Child struck by vehicle while crossing state highway after leaving city park. Held: city had no duty to regulate vehicular or pedestrian traffic. ***Hough v. Com., Dept. of Transp.,* 155 Pa. Cmwlth. 162, 624 A.2d 780.**

Mother brought action against driver who injured children in accident. Held: mother stated claim even though she did not witness accident or sustain physical injury. ***Krysmalski by Krysmalski v. Tarasovich,* 424 Pa. Super. 121, 622 A.2d 298.**

Six-year old crossing limited access highway, waited for traffic and crossed suddenly—struck by motorcycle driven by defendant. Verdict for plaintiff reversed, new trial ordered. Charge held misleading. Issue: Whether child was in place of danger for sufficient time or whether there was reasonable apprehension that child might run out. Duty of care required not adequately explained in charge. ***Fama v. Smith,* 303 Pa. Super. 413, 449 A.2d 755.**

Truck struck four-year old pedestrian visible 350 feet ahead of driver who thought child would continue across street. Child froze. Defense verdict overturned. ***Lamb v. Gibson,* 274 Pa. Super. 7, 417 A.2d 1224.**

Crossing guard leading children across street when defendant's car seen skidding towards them. Guard told children to go back to curb. Plaintiff ran wrong way and was struck. Verdict for plaintiff. Whether act of running was intervening cause and issue of overcoming presumption of no negligence of 11 year old were for jury. Affirmed. Verdict against driver, guard and city (employer). ***Ross v. Vereb,* 481 Pa. 446, 392 A.2d 1376.**

Minor plaintiff walking home from school. School zone—sidewalk being excavated. Crossed street to avoid excavation and she was struck within foot or two of opposite curb. Verdict for plaintiff sustained. ***Simmons v. Mullen,* 231 Pa. Super. 199, 331 A.2d 892.**

Four year old pedestrian struck by car. Testimony that boy asked for money to go to ice cream truck. Found in front of defendant's car, three feet from ice cream truck. From this it can be inferred that defendant was on wrong side of road. Enough to go to jury. Minor eleven years old at time of trial. Admission of his testimony within Court's discretion. ***Delio v. Hamilton,* 227 Pa. Super. 581, 308 A.2d 607.**

Minor plaintiff crossing rural highway when struck by defendant's car—minor had traversed within 2 inches of opposite side of highway—minor suffering from retrograde amnesia and unable to recall circumstances—defendant gave a questionable explanation why she did not see minor plaintiff—error to enter summary judgment—matter for jury on merits. ***Moore v. Zimmerman,* 221 Pa. Super. 359, 292 A.2d 458.**

Small boy struck and killed by defendant's car—only testimony that of defendant who stated that child came from in back of a car on her right side and immediately struck by front of car—not sufficient evidence of negligence to take case to jury—verdict for defendant upheld. ***Zechman v. Yerger,* 221 Pa. Super. 300, 292 A.2d 433.**

Children injured by conditions on property

Plaintiff's decedent, a boy of 6, broke from his father's hand and started across street—struck by defendant's truck in middle of street—jury could have found that defendant had a view of decedent, father and other brother for 200 feet and that defendant's version was not accurate—nonsuit improperly entered—case for jury. ***Cupelli v. Revtai*, 218 Pa. Super. 277, 275 A.2d 673.**

Minor child of additional defendant struck by defendant's car—defendant sought to join father as an additional defendant—preliminary objections sustained—father not negligent in permitting child of 9 to be on street. ***Reardon v. Wilbur*, 441 Pa. 551, 272 A.2d 888.**

Minor Plaintiff of 6 struck by defendant's truck—minor was either standing inside a parked vehicle or came from behind it—evidence from which a jury could have found that the minor ran into the side of defendant's passing truck—verdicts for defendant—motions denied by court below and action sustained on appeal. ***Caplan v. Option Supply Co.*, 438 Pa. 546, 264 A.2d 405.**

Minor aged 3 struck by truck owned by one defendant and operated by other—evidence that operator saw child in street about even with right front of truck—no evidence as to how long child was so located—error to enter nonsuit—for jury to pass on issue as to whether operator did or did not have reasonable opportunity to avoid accident. ***Jones et al. v. Spidle*, 213 Pa. Super. 81, 245 A.2d 677.**

Boy of 4 with young companion on sidewalk—cartway 34 feet wide—boy going into street to retrieve ball—child proceeded at least 17 feet in view of motorist—struck—facts sufficient to take case from purely darting out status—for jury. ***Schwegel v. Goldberg*, 209 Pa. Super. 280, 228 A.2d 405.**

Children injured by conditions on property

Plaintiff brought negligence suit on behalf of his daughter against Defendant property owner after she was injured when she fell into a decorative pond. Trial court granted summary judgment for the Defendant. The Superior Court affirmed holding that for a property owner to be liable for damages caused by an artificial condition on his property, as the result of a child trespassing, he must know or have reason to know that children were likely to trespass on their property. ***G.W.E. v. R.E.Z., Jr.*, 77 A.3d 43 (Pa. Super. 2013).**

Philadelphia Housing Authority found liable for injuries and damages suffered by minor child of tenant who suffered irreversible brain damage due to ingestion of lead based paint at public housing unit. ***Ford v. Philadelphia Housing Authority*, 848 A.2d 1038 (Pa. Cmwlth. 2004).**

Minor child injured by what may have been a part of a goal post lying "on" city-owned park property. Summary judgment in favor of city reversed because city may have been negligent in care, custody and control of real property for failure to remove the dangerous condition "on" the property. Local agency liability for negligent care, custody or control of real property does not require the instrumentality causing the harm to be "of" the real estate in the sense of being affixed to it. ***Martin v. City of Philadelphia*, 696 A.2d 909 (Pa. Cmwlth. 1997).**

Children injured by conditions on property

Minor student injured when a small knife blade in classroom carpet became imbedded in his knee. Summary judgment affirmed based on failure of circumstances to fall within real property exception to Political Subdivision Tort Claims Act. Liability may not be imposed upon a governmental entity for injuries caused by its negligent failure to remove foreign substances from its real estate. ***Wolfe v. Stroudsburg Area School District*, 688 A.2d 1245 (Pa. Cmwlth. 1997).**

Accumulation of water on school district property, which condition contributed to fall of high school student on crutches does not fall within real property exception to Political Subdivision Tort Claims Act. Order granting summary judgment for school district affirmed. ***Leonard v. Fox Chapel Area School District*, ___Pa. Cmwlth. ___, 674 A.2d 767 (1996).**

Administratrix of teenager who drowned in city-owned pond may not recover under Political Subdivision Tort Claims Act based on allegations of city's willful or malicious failure to warn of dangerous condition of pond. Recovery under Political Subdivision Tort Claims Acts is available only for acts of negligence. Public and private lands are covered by Recreation Use of Land and Water Act. Order refusing to grant judgment *n.o.v.* reversed. ***Lory v. City of Philadelphia*, 544 Pa. 38, 674 A.2d 673 (1996).**

Sidewalk exception to governmental immunity and real property exception to governmental immunity are to be read consistently. For real property exception to apply against school district, dangerous condition must be of or attached to the pavement or property and not on the subject pavement or property. Milk on sidewalk did not constitute dangerous condition of or attached to property. Jury verdict for defendant affirmed. ***DeLuca v. School District of Philadelphia*, ___ Pa. Cmwlth. ___, 654 A.2d 29 (1994).**

Willful or malicious failure to guard or warn exception to immunity under the Recreation Use of Land and Water Act applied to action by personal representative of minor's estate where minor drowned in natural pond located in city park. Evidence of prior unrelated swimming accidents inadmissable. Verdict for plaintiff reversed and remanded. ***Barr v. City and County of Philadelphia*, ___ Pa. Cmwlth. ___, 653 A.2d 1374 (1995).**

Five-year old playing on outside stairway fell through narrow opening in railing. Jury verdict for defendant. Charge of court approved stating that possessor of land not responsible for acts of bravado or immature recklessness, even in five-year old. Strong dissent. ***Slavish v. Ratajczak*, 277 Pa. Super. 272, 419 A.2d 767.**

Minor plaintiff injured by bullets found in car in defendant's garage. Defendant towed and stored abandoned cars for City of Easton. Although owner knew that children played in his lot, had no knowledge of dangerous articles left in glove compartments. Nonsuit affirmed. ***Norton v. City of Easton*, 249 Pa. Super. 520, 378 A.2d 417.**

Minor plaintiff trespassed on defendant's land at a point not used for play—injured by being impaled by a surveyor's stake—summary judgment prop-

Chiropractic

erly entered—Section 339 of Restatement (2d) Torts not complied with by plaintiff. ***Whigham v. Pyle*, 224 Pa. Super. 6, 302 A.2d 498.**

Minor plaintiff aged 13 climbed a pole of defendant electrical company carrying high voltage and was severely burned—pole located near a school ground—court below granted judgment *n.o.v.* for defendant on basis that the facts did not bring situation within Section 339 (e) of Restatement (2d) Torts—affirmed on appeal by an equally divided court. ***Felger v. Duquesne Light Co.*, 441 Pa. 421, 273 A.2d 738.**

Boy of 9-1/2 years fell from a concrete block wall of a building being constructed—children have knowledge of danger of falling—Supreme Court adopted Section 339 of Restatement (2d) Torts and denied recovery. ***Jesko v. Turk*, 421 Pa. 434, 219 A.2d 591.**

Chiropractic

A cause of action for failure to obtain informed consent has been steadfastly limited to "surgical or operative medical procedures." Lack of informed consent for a touching states cause of action for battery. Because chiropractors are statutorily proscribed from performing any surgical procedures, a cause of action against a chiropractor for failure to obtain informed consent before performing nonsurgical procedure will not lie as a matter of law. Order dismissing complaint affirmed. ***Matukonis v. Trainer*, 441 Pa. Super. 570, 657 A.2d 1314 (1995).**

Choice of Ways Doctrine

79 year old plaintiff slipped and fell on "penny thin" black ice patch on parking lot of defendant's combination gasoline and convenience store while on the way back into the store to ask for a second time to use the private telephone in the store. After verdict for plaintiff, defendant appealed claiming that trial court's charge that plaintiff was a business invitee and court's refusal to charge on choice of ways doctrine were error. Held: by reason of defendant's directions to plaintiff to go outside onto its property to use the public phone and existence of a "welcome" sign on canopy established as a matter of law that plaintiff was a business invitee, not just a licensee. As to allegation of error in refusal to charge on choice of ways doctrine, the fact that the ice patch was very difficult to see, even for a much younger store employee who testified to that fact, precludes the charge on choice of ways if there was no way to discern the more dangerous of two paths. ***Updyke v. BP Oil Co.*, 717 A.2d 546 (Pa. Super. 1998).**

University owes no duty to students to control protestors. Student who sees open and obvious impediment to her path of travel should choose an alternate path, rather than attempting to jump from four-foot wall. Order granting summary judgment affirmed. ***Banks v. Trustees of University of Pennsylvania*, 446 Pa. Super. 99, 666 A.2d 329 (1995).**

Plaintiff, real estate agent, fell through basement door. Error to charge on choice of ways since flush basement door was not obvious danger. Reason for choosing path over flush doorway was reasonable. Verdict for defendant reversed.

Church

New trial ordered. Charge held in error. ***Oswald v. Stewart*, 301 Pa. Super. 463, 448 A.2d 1.**

1972 accident. Pedestrian crossed street from behind illegally parked vehicle of city and struck by Booker vehicle. City vehicle partially on sidewalk. Plaintiff chose to walk in street. Held: contributorily negligent as matter of law. Plaintiff's verdict overturned. ***Stowe v. Booker and City of Philadelphia*, 284 Pa. Super. 53, 424 A.2d 1388.**

Plaintiff exiting from driveway—error to charge on choice of ways when turn in either direction provided a distinct hazard. New trial ordered. ***Downing v. Shaffer*, 246 Pa. Super. 512, 371 A.2d 953.**

Plaintiff pedestrian struck from rear while walking on roadway by car traveling in same direction—night—Held: error to charge that jury could conclude that if a safer street was available with sidewalks then plaintiff guilty of contributory negligence when no such evidence presented. Right of pedestrian on roadway equal to motor vehicles in absence of sidewalks. ***Eller v. Work*, 233 Pa. Super. 186, 336 A.2d 645.**

Plaintiff attempted to pass between the rear of his parked car and a car of the defendant parked to the rear of his car—testimony that defendant's driver had full view of plaintiff and knew that he intended to pass between cars—injured by forward movement of defendant's car—doctrine of choice of ways does not apply. ***Kinee v. Penn Radio Cab Co.*, 435 Pa. 387, 257 A.2d 554.**

Choking

Plaintiff sued a restaurant for failing to have choking treatment procedures in place after he choked on a piece of chicken in the restaurant. Court held that the defendant had satisfied its duty of care to plaintiff by summoning rescue personnel by calling 911. ***Campbell v. Eitak, Inc.*, 893 A.2d 749 (Pa. Super. 2006).**

In action by guardian of incapacitated, mental health patient for brain damages sustained as result of choking by restraining vest, immunity of physicians under Mental Health Procedures Act is not afforded to physician providing standard medical treatment at non-mental health facility. Judgment on jury verdict for defendant reversed and remanded. ***Allen v. Montgomery Hospital*, 447 Pa. Super. 158, 668 A.2d 565 (1995).**

Christmas party

Plaintiff's decedent was killed in automobile accident following employer-sponsored Christmas party. Where no factual determination as to whether injury was work-related, action against employer not barred by workers' compensation exclusivity provision. Order granting summary judgment in favor of employer reversed. ***Vetter v. Fun Footwear Co.*, 447 Pa. Super. 84, 668 A.2d 529 (1995).**

Church

Plaintiff fell on sidewalk abutting defendant's church—Supreme Court extended the doctrine of Flagiello v. Pennsylvania Hospital (417 Pa. 486) to include

Cigarette

church organizations and denied defendant synagogue a charitable immunity. *Nolan v. Tifereth Israel Synagogue,* **425 Pa. 106, 227 A.2d 675.**

Cigarette

Wrongful death action brought against cigarette manufacturer based on defective design and failure to warn. Held: 1) Federal Cigarette Labeling Act preempted state action for failure to warn; 2) while action for defective design not preempted, plaintiff failed to state cause of action. *Hite v. R. J. Reynolds Tobacco Company,* **396 Pa. Super. 82, 578 A.2d 417.**

Cigarette lighter

Lack of evidence to support a strict liability claim does not preclude a valid claim for negligent design of a lighter. *Phillips v. Cricket Lighters,* **841 A.2d 1000 (Pa. 2003).**

Clamp

Action by patient against surgeon and hospital for damages resulting from failure to remove hemostat from abdomen before concluding surgical procedure. Verdict against doctor only. Trial judge gave very restrictive view of hospital's possible liability. Charge precluded jury finding hospital negligent for not devising adequate rules and regulations. *Bilonoha v. Zubritzky,* **233 Pa. Super. 136, 336 A.2d 351.**

During surgery, clamp left in abdomen of plaintiff. Verdict against operating doctor. Binding instructions given exonerating hospital. Reversed, new trial as to liability of hospital only. Damages not to be tried over. *Tonsic v. Wagner,* **458 Pa. 246, 329 A.2d 497.**

Plaintiff patient required a second operation as the result of a clamp left in incision after initial operation—trial court charged jury that hospital's only negligence could be its failure to require an instrument count—verdict solely against operating surgeon—motion for a new trial as to hospital refused below and action affirmed on appeal—strong dissent. *Tonsic et vir v. Wagner,* **220 Pa. Super. 468, 288 A.2d 791.**

Class action

This is a class action suit for damages, including medical monitoring cost, by residents who lived within half a mile of lead processing plant against former and current owners of plant. Negligence per se requires that the law violated be designed to protect the interest of a group of individuals as opposed to the general public. Pennsylvania recognizes a cause of action for medical monitoring. Claims of negligence per se and for medical monitoring cannot be reached when the jury specifically finds no negligence on the part of the defendants. *Wagner v. Anzon, Inc.,* **453 Pa. Super. 619, 684 A.2d 570 (1996).**

Two-year statute of limitations for negligence action is tolled during period in which class certification is being determined, even if eventually denied. *Mu-*

nicipal Authority of Westmoreland County v. Moffat, **670 A.2d 747 (Pa. Cmwlth. 1996).**

Class action brought on behalf of estates of motorists killed in accidents in order to recover work-loss benefits. Held: action brought by estates represented by counsel time barred. Action by estate not represented not barred. ***Goll v. Insurance Company of North America,* 417 Pa. Super. 46, 611 A.2d 1255.**

Clear view

Plaintiff's vehicle struck by defendant's train at a grade crossing—plaintiff's testimony disclosed that plaintiff had a clear view from 1365 to 1849 feet before entering crossing—incontrovertible physical facts rule applied and action of court below entering nonsuit affirmed—the fact that plaintiff was suffering from traumatic amnesia not controlling. ***Reynolds v. Cen. R.R. of N.J. et al.,* 448 Pa. 415, 292 A.2d 924.**

Clearance

Railroad responsible for maintaining 14 foot clearance of bridge over roadway. Had been reduced to 10 feet 2 inches due to numerous road repairs. Plaintiff killed while riding on top of cab of truck which went under overpass. ***Marinelli v. Montour R.R. Co.,* 278 Pa. Super. 403, 420 A.2d 603.**

Clergy Sexual Abuse

Estate brought negligence action against Defendant after the decedent committed suicide when the Defendant stopped paying for the decedent's mental health treatment. The trial court dismissed the case. The Superior Court affirmed holding that that Plaintiff had failed to state a claim upon which relief can be granted as there was no allegation that the decedent was at a greater risk of harming himself due to the treatment provided by the Defendant. ***Unglo v. Zubik,* 29 A.3d 810 (Pa. Super. 2011).**

A minor who through his guardian brought suit against a priest for molestation and was awarded punitive damages appealed for post judgment interest on his punitive damages award. The appellate court held that the plaintiff was entitled to post-judgment interest on his punitive damages award from the date that the damages were awarded. ***Hutchison v. Luddy,* 946 A.2d 744 (Pa. Super. 2008).**

Plaintiff sued defendant archdiocese after a priest sexually abused him and the archdiocese never informed plaintiff's family of the priest's history of sexual abuse. The court held that to prove fraudulent concealment to toll the statute of limitations an affirmative act of concealment must occur that caused the plaintiff to not pursue a cause of action. ***Delaney v. Archdiocese of Philadelphia,* 924 A.2d 669 (Pa. Super. 2007).**

Plaintiff filed suit against archdiocese for negligent supervision after plaintiff was sexually abused by a priest of the archdiocese. Court held that in order for the two-year statute of limitations to be tolled in a personal injury action there must be fraud, deception, or concealment by the defendant that led to plaintiff's failure to file

Club

suit within the statutory period. *Lazarski v. Archdiocese of Philadelphia*, 926 A.2d 459 (Pa. Super. 2007).

The bishop and diocese demonstrated a pattern of ignoring complaints of molestation by priests and transferring priests to new parishes without warning of past molestations. The court held that the practices along with evidence that the bishop and diocese had reason to know of the high risk to children were sufficient to support a punitive damages award involving a negligent supervision claim in which a minor was molested by a priest. *Hutchinson v. Luddy,* 896 A.2d 1260 (Pa. Super. 2006).

Plaintiff filed a claim of sexual abuse by a priest that had occurred 20 years earlier. Plaintiff's argument to toll the statute of limitations due to repressed memories of the incident was denied. The court affirmed a default judgment against the priest for failure to respond. *Aquilino v. Philadelphia Catholic Archdiocese*, 884 A.2d 1269 (Pa. Super. 2005).

Twenty-six year old plaintiff brought suit against priest and church administration for injuries sustained as a result of alleged sexual abuse while plaintiff attended high school. Motions for judgment on the pleadings by all defendants sustained due to plaintiff's failure to timely file complaint following actual injury. *Baselice, III v. Franciscan Friars Assumption BVM Province, Inc.*, 879 A.2d 270 (Pa. Super. 2005).

Plaintiffs who did not file suit against clergy and church officials who participated in or covered up alleged clergy sexual abuse for at least twenty one years were barred by statute of limitations. *Meehan v. Archdiocese of Philadelphia*, 870 A.2d 912 (Pa. Super. 2005).

Club

Plaintiff a member of a club which served intoxicating liquors—no bartender—members mixed own drinks—plaintiff injured in a fight in club—nonsuit proper—no liability even if a business invitee—assumed risk. *Mike v. Lebanon Miridites League,* 421 Pa. 217, 218 A.2d 814.

Club foot

Plaintiffs parents and minor child received verdict against drug manufacturer on basis of allegations that mother's ingestion of Bendectin during pregnancy resulted in child being born with club feet. Denial of defendant's request for judgment not withstanding the verdict appealed and reversed by Superior Court with order to enter judgment *n.o.v.* Plaintiffs' expert's testimony did not meet standard of *Frye v. United States*, 293 F. 1013 (D.C Cir 1923) (scientific or medical testimony must draw its convincing force from some principle of science, mathematics and the like). *Blum v. Merrell Dow Pharmaceuticals, Inc.*, 705 A.2d 1314 (Pa. Super. 1997).

Coaching negligence

Plaintiff filed suit against softball pitching coach alleging negligence for teaching an illegal and dangerous pitching style. Summary judgment in favor of pitching coach reversed based on expert reports provided by plaintiff in support of her contentions of negligence. 42 Pa.C.S. § 8332.1 which establishes negligence standard for volunteer managers, coaches, umpires, referees or non-profit organizations only applies to volunteers, not paid personnel. ***Reeves v. Middletown Athletic Association*****, 866 A.2d 1115 (Pa. Super. 2005).**

Coin-operated machine

Plaintiffs were owners of a building—defendant installed and operated and serviced a coin operated vending machine in same—building destroyed by fire—plaintiff's experts postulated that same caused by defective maintenance of vending machine—Supreme Court found evidence sufficient to predicate liability. ***Marrazzo v. Scranton Nehi Bottling Co.*****, 422 Pa. 518, 223 A.2d 17.**

Coke oven

Immense coke oven door installed 35 years prior to accident which caused plaintiff's decedent's death and which is movable by means of wheels on tracks is still an "improvement" under statute of repose and so action by coke oven employee is extinguished. Trial court order denying motion for judgment *n.o.v.* reversed. ***Vargo v. Koppers Co., Inc.*****, 452 Pa. Super. 275, 681 A.2d 815 (1996).**

Collagen

A state claim that FDA requirements have not been met arising out of the use of a collagen implant is cognizable, despite preemption provisions of the medical device amendments to the Federal Food, Drug and Cosmetic Act. State negligence claims that mirror FDA standards for medical devices are not preempted. Order granting summary judgment reversed. ***Green v. Dolsky,*** **546 Pa. 400, 685 A.2d 110 (1996).**

Collapse

Plaintiff's decedent was killed in a trench collapse while a representative of the project design engineer was at the site. In affirming dismissal of the action against the engineer, the court held that a design professional does not have a duty to protect workers from hazards on a construction site unless there was an undertaking, either by contract or course of conduct, to supervise or control the construction and/or to maintain safe conditions at the site. ***Herczeg v. Hampton Township*****, 766 A.2d 866 (Pa. Super. 2001).**

Party wall of building under demolition collapsed, killing occupant of adjacent building. Jury verdict against contractor, landowner, and city. City hired alleged unapproved contractor and provided inadequate inspection for this emergency demolition. Under facts here, none of the concurrently negligent tortfeasors entitled to indemnity. ***Sirianni v. Nugent Brothers*****, 331 Pa. Super. 145, 480 A.2d 285.**

Plaintiff's verdict reduced by 40% for contributory negligence. Plaintiff was driving and attempted to avoid disabled truck. Drove onto berm which collapsed, causing car to tumble into ditch. Proper to submit issue of proper maintenance of guardrails and berm to jury. ***Merling v. Commonwealth,*** **79 Pa. Cmwlth. 121, 468 A.2d 894.**

Coma

Suit by brother against sister for injuries sustained in collapse of platform and steps outside door of sister's home. Verdict for sister upheld. No evidence of previous problems with steps. Brother a frequent visitor had in fact owned the house until four months prior to accident. ***Claycomb v. Claycomb*, 253 Pa. Super. 277, 397 A.2d 1207.**

Two workers—one injured and one killed when jammed bricks in blast furnace on which they were working collapsed on them. Work not being done in usual course and posed unusual dangers. Verdict for plaintiffs reversed due to incomplete charge on Section 413 of Restatement (2d) Torts dealing with precautions necessary for work entrusted to contractors. ***Gonzalez v. U.S. Steel*, 248 Pa. Super. 95, 374 A.2d 1334.**

Collapse of wall in a shopping center construction operation—workman injured—evidence that wall was weakened by cutting of a pipe chase—sufficient testimony to hold a piping contractor responsible. ***Abbott v. Steel City Piping Co.*, 437 Pa. 412, 263 A.2d 881.**

Coma

Coma patient suffered permanent flexion of elbows and hips. Held: judgment *n.o.v.* in favor of physician who failed to order drug therapy granted. New trial ordered for hospital and physician who directed physical therapy. ***Maurer v. Trustees of University of Pennsylvania*, 418 Pa. Super. 510, 614 A.2d 754.**

Combination of circumstances

Plaintiff and her decedents were passengers in a car driven by additional defendant who crossed over centerline of PennDOT road, crashed through guardrail and struck tree. Plaintiff alleged that brakes and engine had failed, that additional defendant driver was intoxicated and that PennDOT had failed to provide safe roadway because of inability of guardrail to prevent car from striking tree. Following grant of summary judgment in favor of PennDOT, plaintiff appealed. Held: PennDOT could not have adequate notice of combination of events leading to accident—loss of brakes and driver's intoxication—and therefore PennDOT had no duty to plaintiff and her decedents. ***Baer v. Com., Dept. of Transp.*, 713 A.2d 189 (Pa. Cmwlth. 1998).**

Combustible liquid

Plaintiff severely burned by flash fire caused when paint thinner used to clean paint from floor of volunteer fire department ignited was precluded from recovering for injuries because volunteer fire company entitled to governmental immunity. Real property exception to governmental immunity does not apply unless cause of action based on condition of real property or an actual defect of the property itself. Negligent mishandling of combustible liquids on property does not invoke real property exception. Denial of volunteer fire company's motion for summary judgment reversed and remanded. ***Grieff v. Reisinger*, ___ Pa. Cmwlth. ___, 654 A.2d 77 (1995).**

Commonwealth liability: Education

Common carrier

A common carrier has the highest duty of care to its passengers to carry them safely and enable them to alight safely at their intended destination. Bus company does not have a duty to intoxicated passengers who have disembarked from bus at their intended destination to insure that they travel safely after discharge. Trial court's refusal to grant summary judgment to bus company reversed and remanded. ***Knoud v. Galante*, 696 A.2d 854 (Pa.Super. 1997).**

Passenger injured while entering bus. Trial court failed to instruct jury on duty of common carrier and on failure of driver to follow established procedure. Vacated and remanded. ***Jones v. Port Authority of Allegheny County*, 136 Pa. Cmwlth. 445, 583 A.2d 512.**

Commonwealth liability: Care, custody and control of animals

Defendant appealed court ruling that it was not entitled to sovereign immunity and had negligently euthanized dogs owned by the plaintiff. The court held that in determining if an entity is a commonwealth entity deserving sovereign immunity the court must consider if the entity was created by the state to perform a state function. ***Snead v. Society for the Prevention of Cruelty to Animals of Pennsylvania*, 929 A.2d 1169 (Pa. Super. 2008).**

Philadelphia Housing Authority, a Commonwealth agency, did not have direct custody and control of tenant's dog which bit another tenant and so was shielded from liability by sovereign immunity. ***Govan v. Philadelphia Housing Authority*, 848 A.2d 193 (Pa. Cmwlth. 2004).**

Commonwealth liability: Education

Plaintiff professor brought defamation and various other tort claims against Defendant state university faculty members for their recommendations that he be denied a promotion. The trial court dismissed the complaint. The Commonwealth Court affirmed holding that the Defendants were entitled to sovereign immunity as they were acting within the course and scope of their employment in making their recommendations regarding the Plaintiff's promotion. ***Kull v. Guisse*, 81 A.3d 148 (Pa. Cmwlth 2013).**

Student sued school district when he was injured during gym class by a falling folding table improperly stored in the gym. The court ruled that the folding table was personalty and therefore the school district was immune under the Tort Claims Act. ***Repko v. Chichester School District*, 904 A.2d 1036 (Pa. Cmwlth. 2006).**

Student injured at school operated by Temple University. University not immune. Not Commonwealth agency. ***Doughty v. City of Philadelphia*, 141 Pa. Cmwlth. 659, 596 A.2d 1187.**

Handicapped swimmer drowned in university pool. University not liable. Failure to provide lifeguard did not fall into real property exception to sovereign immunity. ***Musheno v. Lock Haven University*, 132 Pa. Cmwlth. 643, 574 A.2d 129.**

Commonwealth liability: Emergency medical technicians

Suit against State College and professor for injuries sustained in lab explosion. Cause of action arose prior to passage of Sovereign Immunity Act, therefore error to dismiss complaint. ***Brungard v. Mansfield State*, 491 Pa. 114, 419 A.2d 1171.**

Suit against State College and professor for injuries suffered in explosion in chemistry lab. Suit permitted. ***Brungard v. Hartman*, 483 Pa. 200, 394 A.2d 1265.**

Suit against State College barred by doctrine of sovereign immunity. Complaint dismissed. ***Williams v. West Chester State*, 29 Pa. Cmwlth. 240, 370 A.2d 774.**

Commonwealth liability: Emergency medical technicians

Parents, individually and on behalf of their minor child, brought suit against emergency medical technicians of a volunteer fire company for birth defects suffered by the child during the emergency medical technicians' treatment of the child. The appellate court held that the volunteer fire company had sufficiently established that it was a local agency under the Political Subdivision Tort Claims Act. ***Flood v. Silfies*, 933 A.2d 1072 (Pa. Cmwlth. 2007).**

Commonwealth liability: Government function

Plaintiff state police officer brought negligence action against Defendant internal affairs investigator based upon an investigation performed by the Defendant that led to the Plaintiff being fired. The trial court denied Defendant's motion for summary judgment and they appealed. The Commonwealth Court reversed holding that the Defendant was entitled to sovereign immunity as the conduct forming the basis of the lawsuit occurred during the course and scope of his employment. ***Schell v. Guth*, 88 A.3d 1053 (Pa. Cmwlth. 2014).**

Plaintiff brought suit against engineer, code enforcement officers and township for tortious interference with contractual relations by refusing to inspect completed structures on lots in his subdivision. The code enforcement officer was a private business that had been contracted by the township to perform the township's code enforcement. The appellate court held that under the Political Subdivision Tort Claims Act an employee is required to be acting only on behalf of the governmental entity and therefore the code enforcement agent and engineer were entitled to immunity. ***Higby Development, LLC v. Sartor*, 954 A.2d 77 (Pa. Cmwlth. 2008).**

Plaintiff brought a claim of negligence along with several intentional tort claims against the county department of human services for notifying the police of her involuntary commitment denying her the right to bear arms. The appellate court upheld the trial court's ruling that the county department of human services was immune under the Political Subdivision Tort Claims Act to an action for that type of negligence alleged. ***R.H.S. v. Allegheny County Department of Human Services, Office of Mental Health*, 936 A.2d 1218 (Pa.Cmwlth. 2007).**

Minor died of drowning after drinking liquor bought by other minor. Held: 1) defense of contributory negligence permitted; 2) testimony that deceased consumed alcohol admissible; 3) testimony that purchaser appeared to be in mid-twen-

Commonwealth liability: Medical care

ties admissible. ***Barrie v. Pennsylvania Liquor Control Board*, 137 Pa. Cmwlth. 514, 586 A.2d 1017.**

Doctrine of sovereign immunity sustained as to Liquor Control Board sales of alcoholic beverages to a known alcoholic. Strong dissent, 403. ***McCoy v. Commonwealth*, 457 Pa. 513, 326 A.2d 396.**

Minor bought liquor from State Store—became drunk and fell eleven stories to his death—selling liquor a governmental, not proprietary function—suit barred by doctrine of sovereign immunity. ***Biello v. Pa. Liquor Control Board*, 454 Pa. 179, 301 A.2d 849.**

Plaintiff's decedent killed as a result of a collision of his vehicle and that of a vehicle of the Pennsylvania Turnpike Commission—preliminary objections in the nature of a demurrer sustained—Turnpike Commission engaged in a governmental function and immune to tort liability. ***Thomas v. Baird*, 433 Pa. 482, 252 A.2d 653.**

Commonwealth liability: Medical care

A residential care center operated by the Commonwealth's Department of Public Welfare is immune from suit alleging "institutional negligence" for failure to properly screen employee who sexually abused minor residents. Institutional negligence does not fall within the medical-professional liability exception to sovereign immunity. ***Dashner v. Hamburg Center of the Department of Public Welfare*, 845 A.2d 935 (Pa. Cmwlth. 2004).**

State prison inmate properly stated a cognizable cause of action for negligence against prison doctor and health system administrator under medical-professional exception to sovereign immunity. Inmate had been prescribed incorrect medication which resulted in low blood pressure and fall with injury to back and administrator transferred inmate to a facility that lacked capacity to care for inmate's resulting injuries. ***Williams v. Syed*, 782, 782 A.2d 1090 (Pa. Super. 2001).**

Sovereign immunity precludes a cause of action based on corporate liability against Commonwealth medical facilities. Suit against Commonwealth medical facility only, and not against medical care providers individually, is not included within the medical-professional liability exception to sovereign immunity. ***Moser v. Heistand*, 545 Pa. 554, 681 A.2d 1322 (1996).**

In action for alleged medical malpractice, plaintiff failed to state cause of action against state-employed physician, state hospital, and department of public welfare. Order sustaining preliminary objections affirmed because all defendants immune under sovereign immunity statute. ***Moser v. Heistand*, 168 Pa. Cmwlth. 109, 649 A.2d 177 (1994).**

Police officer shot by former mental patient brought action against state hospital and attending physician. Medical professional liability exclusion to sovereign immunity applicable. ***Sherk v. County of Dauphin*, 531 Pa. Super. 515, 614 A.2d 226.**

Commonwealth liability: Medical care

Patient at state hospital abducted and raped by unknown party. Commonwealth not liable. ***Alexander v. Com., Dept. of Public Welfare*, 137 Pa. Cmwlth. 342, 586 A.2d 475.**

Employee of state hospital raped by patient. Hospital not liable. Medical-professional exception to sovereign immunity did not apply. Workmen's Compensation only remedy. ***Holland v. Norristown State Hospital*, 136 Pa. Cmwlth. 655, 584 A.2d 1056.**

Police officer injured when attempting to arrest former state hospital patient. Hospital immune. Medical-professional exception to sovereign immunity applies only to patient injuries. ***Harrisburg State Hospital v. Sherk*, 128 Pa. Cmwlth. 150, 562 A.2d 1025.**

Negligent supervision of patient at state mental hospital, who was released and assaulted plaintiff. Held: within medical-professional liability exception to Sovereign Immunity Act. ***Yellen v. Philadelphia State Hospital*, 94 Pa. Cmwlth. 516, 503 A.2d 1108.**

Suit against county health facility dismissed. Facility immune pursuant to 42 Pa. C.S.A. §8541. Section upheld as being constitutional. ***Grill v. County of Southampton*, 88 Pa. Cmwlth. 327, 488 A.2d 1214.**

Waiver of immunity as applied to physicians employed by Commonwealth, allows suits by third parties against said physician for releasing mental patient improperly, which patient thereafter assaulted plaintiff. Denial of preliminary objections affirmed. ***Allentown State Hospital v. Gill*, 88 Pa. Cmwlth. 331, 488 A.2d 1211.**

Alleged malpractice case. Nurse employee of State Hospital dismissed as defendant. Since law has changed between ruling and appeal, case remanded for consideration under immunities act. ***Gregory v. Martyak*, 47 Pa. Cmwlth. 342, 408 A.2d 188.**

Wrongful death and survival action by estate of patient at mental hospital killed by another patient. Alleged failure to adequately supervise patient with known homicidal tendencies. Preliminary objections dismissed on allegation of gross negligence against officials and employees of state. ***Rhines v. Herzel*, 481 Pa. 165, 392 A.2d 298.**

Trespass action against State Hospital permitted. ***Poklemba v. Shamokin State Hospital*, 479 Pa. 414, 388 A.2d 722.**

Patient at State Hospital injured in fall from window. Suit v. Commonwealth dismissed. ***Wallace v. Commonwealth*, 32 Pa. Cmwlth. 615, 380 A.2d 930.**

Action brought against Commonwealth, Department of Public Welfare, and State Hospital for alleged improper treatment of plaintiff-decedent. Evenly divided court upheld finding of lower court that suit barred by doctrine of sovereign immunity. ***Tarantino v. Allentown State Hospital*, 465 Pa. 580, 351 A.2d 247.**

Commonwealth liability: Miscellaneous

Suit for personal injuries sustained by patient at state hospital who left grounds while unattended. Action based on gross negligence or incompetence under Mental Health Act not sufficient to take case out of doctrine of sovereign immunity. ***Coronia v. Greenfeder,* 30 Pa. Cmwlth. 337, 374 A.2d 741.**

Suit against Commonwealth and various agencies and individuals arising out of sexual assault and killing of two minors by individuals allegedly improperly released from State Mental Hospital. Held: suit versus Commonwealth barred. However, suit permitted against high public officials, doctors and parole officers upon allegation of gross negligence. ***Freach v. Commonwealth,* 471 Pa. 558, 370 A.2d 1163.**

Commonwealth liability: Miscellaneous

Plaintiff employees brought negligence lawsuits against the Southeastern Pennsylvania Transportation Authority (SEPTA) under the Federal Employees Liability Act. The trial court granted summary judgment for the defendant. The Commonwealth Court affirmed in part and reversed in part. The Pennsylvania Supreme Court held that SEPTA was not an arm of the government of the Commonwealth and thus not entitled to immunity from negligence suits under the *Federal Employees Liability Act.* ***Goldman v. Southeastern Pennsylvania Transportation Authority,* 57 A.3d 1154 (Pa. 2012).**

State police troopers owed no duty of care to motorist who fled during pursuit and was killed in collision with tree. Comparison of sovereign immunity act language with municipal immunity under Political Subdivision Tort Claim Act although the language is notably different in this particular type of case. ***Frazier v. Commonwealth of Pennsylvania*, 845 A.2d 253 (Pa. Cmwlth. 2004).**

Passenger injured by other passengers exiting train brought action for failure to control crowd. Authority found not liable for actions of third parties. ***SEPTA v. Hussey,* 138 Pa. Cmwlth. 436, 588 A.2d 110.**

Husband of deceased motorist brought wrongful death action against Department of Transportation. Held: damages recoverable against the Commonwealth are limited to those in a survival action and not a wrongful death action. ***Huda v. Kirk,* 536 A.2d 513.**

Plaintiff injured during National Guard training session while assembling machine gun. Summary judgment granted in favor of manufacturer based upon government contractor defense, affirmed. ***Mackey v. Maremont Corp.,* 350 Pa. Super. 415, 504 A.2d 908.**

Employee of bank allegedly injured when guard at bank, employed by detective agency, robbed bank and injured employee by tying her up and putting her in closet. State sued for not performing statutory duty to prevent known criminals from being employed by private detective agencies. Held: not an exception to Sovereign Immunity Act. Demurrer granted. ***Nicholson v. M & S Detective Agency,* 94 Pa. Cmwlth. 521, 503 A.2d 1106.**

Commonwealth liability: Motor vehicles

Sovereign Immunity Act, limiting awards against Commonwealth held prospective only to cause of action accruing after its effective date. Delay damages applicable to Commonwealth. ***Commonwealth v. Twenties,*** **76 Pa. Cmwlth. 537, 464 A.2d 642.**

Commonwealth liability: Motor vehicles

Plaintiff brought negligence suit against Defendant city after he was struck by a police cruiser stolen by an individual under arrest. The trail court granted dismissal. The Commonwealth Court affirmed holding that the motor vehicle exception to governmental immunity did not apply as the police officer was not operating the vehicle at the time of the accident. ***Gale v. City of Philadelphia,*** **86 A.3d 318 (Pa. Cmwlth. 2014).**

Plaintiffs filed suit to recover uninsured motorist benefits after being injured on a Port Authority bus, when it collided with an uninsured motorist. The court held that sovereign immunity did not bar a claim for uninsured motorist benefits against the Port Authority, where the Port Authority had not been found to be negligent. ***Lowery v. Port Authority of Allegheny County,*** **914 A.2d 953 (Pa. Cmwlth. 2006).**

Port Authority appealed a denial of a motion for post-trial relief awarding an injured passenger uninsured motorist benefits where the Port Authority's bus driver was found to be not negligent. The court held that the Port Authority's sovereign immunity did not protect it from paying uninsured motorist benefits when it was found not negligent. The court also held the statutory provision against stacking did not prevent a passenger from recovering underinsured motorist benefits from her automobile insurer. ***Paravati v. Port Authority of Allegheny County,*** **914 A.2d 946 (Pa. Cmwlth. 2006).**

Plaintiff who was struck by a car after alighting from a bus which had departed from its normal route was not permitted the advantage of the motor vehicle exception to sovereign immunity. ***Mosley v. Southeastern Pennsylvania Transportation Authority,*** **842 A.2d 473 (Pa. Cmwlth. 2004).**

Disabled plaintiff alleges he was injured when he lost control of the van he was driving because a company under contract with the Pennsylvania Department of Labor and Industry, Office of Vocational Rehabilitation was alleged to have negligently modified the van. In suit against the company that modified the van, the defendant pleaded immunity as a government contractor. Held: there is no government contractor immunity under Pennsylvania law. ***Connor v. Quality Coach, Inc.,*** **750 A.2d 823 (2000).**

Plaintiffs were injured when a grader's blade struck their car while plowing snow from the road during a state of emergency declared by the governor. Plaintiffs alleged negligence only, not willful misconduct. Under Section 7704(a) of the Pennsylvania Emergency Code, only willful misconduct is an exception to the general immunity afforded to Commonwealth employees. ***Zuppo v. Com., Dept. of Transp.,*** **739 A.2d 1148 (Pa. Cmwlth. 1999).**

Supreme Court affirms trial court grant of summary judgment in favor of SEPTA for actions of bus driver who discharged students into a busy street and not

Commonwealth liability: Motor vehicles

at a regular stop. Strong dissent by Justice Newman arguing that discharging passengers is part of operation of a transit bus. ***Warrick v. Pro Cor Ambulance, Inc.,* 739 A.2d 127 (Pa. 1999).**

Plaintiff was injured when she slipped and fell on floor of SEPTA train. Plaintiff argued that train was improperly cared for personal property of Commonwealth and so exempt from protection of Sovereign Immunity Act. Held: SEPTA train is vehicle for purposes of Sovereign Immunity Act and not personal property. Grant of compulsory nonsuit affirmed. ***Ross v. SEPTA,* 714 A.2d 1131 (Pa. Cmwlth. 1998).**

Plaintiff administratrix of deceased minor filed suit against SEPTA and ambulance company after child who had alighted from bus crossed in front of bus, with green light, and was struck by ambulance which was improperly passing bus on its left. After settling with ambulance service, SEPTA was granted summary judgment on basis of sovereign immunity as the act of stopping at an intersection, rather than at the appropriate bus stop in middle of block, then opening door to discharge child was not "operation" of motor vehicle under Sovereign Immunity Act. "...a temporary stop connected to the discharge of passengers is not part and parcel of the operation of a vehicle." Query, not even on a passenger transit bus? ***Warrick v. Pro Cor Ambulance, Inc.,* 709 A.2d 422 (Pa. Cmwlth. 1997).**

Plaintiff slipped, fell and sustained injury alighting from a bus. SEPTA bus driver's act of allowing bus to become "very crowded " was not an act which falls within the plain meaning of "operation" of a motor vehicle so as to survive nonsuit by Commonwealth agency defendant under sovereign immunity defense; act was merely ancillary to the actual operation of the vehicle. ***Berman v. SEPTA,* 698 A.2d 1362 (Pa. Cmwlth. 1997).**

Summary judgment entered against plaintiff who was shot by a robber while a passenger on defendant's stopped train. Plaintiff alleged that defendant's trainman's failure to open the door of the train to allow plaintiff to escape before he was shot was a concurrent cause of his injury and that failure to act involved the operation of the motor vehicle. The Commonwealth Court distinguishes concurrent negligent acts from a negligent act by defendant and a criminal assault by a third party and also holds by implication that the failure to open the door was not "operation" of the motor vehicle. ***Greenleaf v. SEPTA,* 698 A.2d 170 (Pa. Cmwlth. 1997).**

Plaintiff injured when alighting from bus is not injured by reason of "operation of motor vehicle"; therefore suit against transit authority precluded. Order granting judgment notwithstanding the verdict affirmed. ***Rubenstein v. SEPTA,* ___ Pa. Cmwlth. ___, 668 A.2d 283 (1995).**

Driver may proceed with suit against Commonwealth for common law damages based on emotional and psychological distress following accident with PennDOT construction vehicle. ***Tomikel v. Com., Dept. of Transp.,* ___ Pa. Cmwlth. ___, 658 A.2d 861 (1995).**

Plaintiff alighting from bus is not engaged in operation of motor vehicle so claim for damages does not qualify under statutory exception to governmental im-

Commonwealth liability: Personal property

munity. Summary judgment affirmed. Legislative intent is to grant immunity; therefore interpretation of exceptions to governmental immunity should favor that outcome. ***Bazemore v. SEPTA,*** **___ Pa. Cmwlth. ___, 657 A.2d 1323 (1995).**

Transportation authority not liable under operation of motor vehicle exception to governmental immunity where bus involved in accident with plaintiff was driven by unauthorized user and not employee of transportation authority. Summary judgment affirmed. ***Pana v. SEPTA,*** **___ Pa. Cmwlth. ___, 657 A.2d 1320 (1995).**

Passenger attacked on train. Vehicle liability exception to sovereign immunity not applicable. ***Evans v. SEPTA,*** **149 Pa. Cmwlth. 376, 613 A.2d 137.**

Pedestrian struck and killed by bus. Held: Since transportation authority could not waive immunity, limitation of damages provisions of Act 152 of 1978 applicable. Wrongful death and survival actions separate causes of action. ***Tulewicz v. SEPTA,*** **529 Pa. 588, 606 A.2d 427.**

Pedestrian hit by egg thrown from trolley brought action against transit authority. Authority held not liable. ***Hall v. SEPTA,*** **141 Pa. Cmwlth. 591, 596 A.2d 1153.**

Suit for injuries sustained in accident with State Police vehicle. Suit against employees remanded in light of *DuBree v. Commonwealth of Pa.,* 481 Pa. 540, 393 A.2d 293. ***Kenno v. Commonwealth,*** **481 Pa. 562, 393 A.2d 304.**

Injuries sustained in accident with State Police vehicle. Remanded for trial. ***Porr v. Pennsylvania State Police,*** **479 Pa. 419, 388 A.2d 725.**

Plaintiff sued Commonwealth and Turnpike Commission alleging injury arising out of collision caused entirely by negligence of Commission employee driving Commission owned vehicle. Court overruled previous decisions granting immunity to Turnpike Commission but upheld immunity of Commonwealth. ***Specter et ux v. Commonwealth,*** **462 Pa. 474, 341 A.2d 481.**

Plaintiff's decedent killed as a result of a collision of his vehicle and that of a vehicle of the Pennsylvania Turnpike Commission—preliminary objections in the nature of a demurrer sustained—Turnpike Commission engaged in a governmental function and immune to tort liability. ***Thomas v. Baird,*** **433 Pa. 482, 252 A.2d 653.**

Commonwealth liability: Personal property

Inmate in state police holding cell hanged himself with shoelaces that had not been removed far enough from his cell by state troopers. In survival action by parents against state police, held that shoelaces were not "personal property within the care, custody and control" of the commonwealth for personal property exception and holding cell that was not visible to troopers at all times so as to prevent suicide was not subject to real estate exception to sovereign immunity. Good dissent. ***Pennsylvania State Police v. Klimek,*** **839 A.2d 1173 (Pa. Cmwlth. 2003).**

Commonwealth liability: Police

Decedent-hunter's personal representative brought claim for negligent preservation of evidence against the State Police for failing to preserve evidence neces-

Commonwealth liability: Real estate

sary for products liability suit. The trial court granted summary judgment in favor of the Defendant. The Commonwealth Court affirmed holding that the personal property exception to sovereign immunity did not apply as the evidence caused the injury to the hunter and not the officer's mishandling of the evidence. *Pyeritz v. Commonwealth of Pennsylvania State Police Department*, **956 A.2d 1075 (Pa. Cmwlth. 2008).**

Administratrix filed suit against the state police for negligence in failing to wait for a PennDOT crew to correct a known icy road condition which contributed to plaintiff's decedent's death. The court held that the police only have a duty to an individual if they enter into a special relationship with that person. Troopers who had left the area of multiple accidents in the same section of road during the same night did not have an awareness of other motorists in the area sufficient to create a special relationship that could lead to liability. *Daubenspeck v. Commonwealth*, **894 A.2d 867 (Pa. Cmwlth. 2006).**

Sovereign immunity barred claim for intentional infliction of emotional distress in mother's case against state police for mishandling of daughter's remains. Pennsylvania law does not recognize an action for negligent mishandling of the dead. Mother's failure to allege that she witnessed any traumatic event involving her daughter's remains precluded claim for negligent infliction of emotional distress. Order sustaining defendants' preliminary objections affirmed. *Ray v. Pennsylvania State Police*, **___ Pa. Cmwlth. ___, 654 A.2d 140 (1995).**

State police failed to rescue passenger in vehicle carried away by flood waters. Police not liable. *Peak v. Petrovitch*, **161 Pa. Cmwlth. 261, 636 A.2d 1248.**

Driver killed in collision with abandoned vehicle along turnpike. State Police immune in action for failure to remove vehicle. *Bennett v. Pennsylvania Turnpike Commission*, **160 Pa. Cmwlth. 223, 634 A.2d 776.**

Commonwealth liability: Real estate

Plaintiff brought negligence action against PennDOT after he was injured in a crash due to ice that had accumulated on PennDOT's highway from a broken water pipe. The trial court granted summary judgment to PennDOT. The Commonwealth Court affirmed holding that the real estate exception to sovereign immunity did not apply as the formation of the ice on the road did not derive from the road itself. *Hall v. Southwestern Pennsylvania Water Authority*, **87 A.3d 998 (Pa. Cmwlth. 2014).**

Plaintiff brought negligence claim against Defendant transportation agency after she slipped on an icy wooden step on the train platform while attempting to board a train. The trial court entered summary judgment for the Defendant. The Commonwealth Court affirmed holding that allegations of improper maintenance resulting in ice were insufficient as the ice did not result from a defect in the real property itself. *Nardella v. Southeastern Pennsylvania Transportation Authority*, **34 A.3d 300 (Pa. Cmwlth. 2011).**

Decedent's estate brought negligence action against the defendant housing authority arising out of a fatal fall by the decedent for the housing authority's failure

Commonwealth liability: Real estate

to lock a door providing access to the roof of its building. The trial court entered summary judgment in favor of the defendant. The Commonwealth Court affirmed holding that even if the plaintiff had established a prima facie case of negligence, which it had not; the housing authority had not waived immunity under the real estate exception to the Sovereign Immunity Act as the decedent's physical injuries were not physically caused by the unlocked door. *Weckel v. Carbondale Housing Authority*, **20 A.3d 1245 (Pa. Cmwlth. 2011).**

Decedent's estate brought claim for negligence against defendant housing authority after the decedent died in an apartment fire allegedly due to the a disabled fire detection system and a lack of installed fire stops. The trial court denied Defendant's Motion for Summary Judgment. The Commonwealth Court affirmed holding that the allegations that the fire alarm system's malfunction and the lack of installed fire stops were sufficient to establish a dangerous condition of real estate that caused the decedent's death. ***Thornton v. Philadelphia Housing Authority*, 4 A.3d 1143 (Pa. Cmwlth. 2010.)**

Emergency Medical Technician sued the Luzerne County Housing Authority when, while responding to an emergency call, he was struck in the head by a metal bar that fell from a garage door at a housing authority property. The court held the plaintiff had failed to provide evidence that the commonwealth agency had actual or constructive notice of the dangerous condition or defect in the garage door necessary to sustain a negligence action. ***Gurnari v. Luzerne County Housing Authority*, 911 A.2d 236 (Pa. Cmwlth. 2006).**

City and housing authority both entitled to immunity under Political Subdivision Tort Claims Act and Sovereign Immunity Act. Plaintiff alleged that city's and housing authority's failure to maintain security systems on property constituted negligence related to the care, custody and control of the real estate. City and housing authority were not liable for failure to prevent criminal acts of third party who injured plaintiff. ***Williams v. Philadelphia Housing Authority*, 873 A.2d 81 (Pa. Cmwlth. 2005).**

Pennsylvania Turnpike Commission and contractors who adhered to Turnpike Commission standards in construction of 32" high median barriers are all entitled to sovereign immunity protection. ***Svege v. Interstate Safety Systems*, 862 A.2d 752 (Pa. Cmwlth. 2004).**

Inmate injured when he fell on wet, slippery waxed floor was not entitled to trial as the condition of floor was not "dangerous condition of real estate" under the real estate exception in the Sovereign Immunity Act. ***Raker v. Pa. Dept. of Corrections*, 844 A.2d 659 (Pa. Cmwlth. 2004).**

Inmate in state police holding cell hanged himself with shoelaces that had not been removed far enough from his cell by state troopers. In survival action by parents against state police, held that shoelaces were not "personal property within the care, custody and control" of the commonwealth for personal property exception and holding cell that was not visible to troopers at all times so as to prevent suicide was not subject to real estate exception to sovereign immunity. Good dissent. ***Pennsylvania State Police v. Klimek*, 839 A.2d 1173 (Pa. Cmwlth. 2003).**

Commonwealth liability: Real estate

Suit by car dealership for damages sustained when a creek overflowed its banks and damaged plaintiff's parking lot and inventory of new and used vehicles. Held that PennDOT's work in relocating road which abutted creek did not change the natural path of the watercourse and so was not a negligent act which might fit within an exception to sovereign immunity. ***Tom Clark Chevrolet, Inc. v. Pa. Dept. of Environmental Protection*, 816 A.2d 1246 (Pa. Cmwlth. 2003).**

Evaluation of the real estate exception to sovereign immunity statute and the historically applied "on/of" distinction. The proper method for determining whether the real estate exception to sovereign immunity applies is to focus on whether or not a dangerous condition created by rock salt on a train platform derived from, originated from, or had its source in the real estate itself and if not, the real estate exception did not apply. "On/of" analysis formally rejected. Important distinction between language of Sovereign Immunity Act and the Political Subdivision Tort Claims Act. ***Jones v. SEPTA*, 772 A.2d 435 (Pa. 2001).**

Absence of guardrail on Commonwealth highway adjacent to steep drop-off is not dangerous condition of Commonwealth realty and, therefore, not actionable under real estate exception to Sovereign Immunity. ***Dean v. PennDOT*, 751 A.2d 1130 (Pa. 2000).**

Plaintiff was injured when she slipped and fell on rock salt located *on* defendant's train platform. Held: "of / on" distinction continues to apply to cases where the real property exception to governmental immunity applies. ***Jones v. SEPTA*, 748 A.2d 1271 (Pa. Cmwlth. 2000).**

Plaintiff rendered quadriplegic after car in which she was a passenger fishtailed on snowy road and slid over embankment which did not have a guardrail. Plaintiff sued PennDOT for negligent failure to erect and maintain guardrail at curve. Lower court granted summary judgment to PennDOT based on *Rothermel v. Com.*, 531 Pa. 180, 672 A.2d 837 (Pa. Cmwlth, 1996) which held that a non-negligent circumstance which causes an accident precludes any recovery against sovereign even if negligent act of the sovereign which falls under real estate exception to sovereign immunity followed the cause and increased the damage. *Rothermel* overruled and judgment vacated with remand. ***Dean v. Com., Dept. of Transp.*, 718 A.2d 374 (Pa. Cmwlth. 1998).**

Plaintiff independent contractor, a sandblaster/painter, was injured when he fell from scaffolding below elevated rail tracks after the light on his sandblaster failed and he tripped on a hose he could not see. Plaintiff alleged that SEPTA was liable at common law for failure to provide a safe work area and that lack of lights on SEPTA property he was working on was a defect in SEPTA property. Held: there is no liability of an employer to an independent contractor absent special danger or peculiar risk conditions - working on a scaffold is neither - and that lack of lights on SEPTA is not a dangerous condition "of" the real estate. ***Donnelly v. SEPTA*, 708 A.2d 145 (Pa. Cmwlth. 1998).**

Summary judgment in favor of defendant affirmed because plaintiff's allegations that she was injured by an unknown assailant on SEPTA platform do not

Commonwealth liability: Real estate

constitute defect of the land itself so as to constitute waiver of sovereign immunity. ***Warnecki v. SEPTA*, 689 A.2d 1023 (Pa. Cmwlth. 1997).**

To recover against Commonwealth under real property exception to sovereign immunity, plaintiff, whose decedent was killed when tree limb on Commonwealth property fell on her car, must establish that PennDOT had actual or constructive notice of the dangerous condition. Trial court's refusal to charge on notice was reversible error. New trial granted. ***Com., Dept. of Transp., v. Patton*, 546 Pa. 561, 686 A.2d 1302 (1997).**

Failure of personal representative of decedent driver's estate to prove that tree which fell on decedent's car and killed her was located on Commonwealth property precluded recovery against Commonwealth under real property exception to sovereign immunity. Judgment reversed and judgment *n.o.v.* entered in favor of PennDOT. ***Marker v. Com., Dept. of Transp.*, 677 A.2d 345 (Pa. Cmwlth. 1996).**

While PennDOT has a duty to make highways safe and possibly to install guard rails where necessary, in order to recover plaintiff must establish that lack of guardrail was cause of injuries rather than a contributing factor. Failure to allege a defect "of" Commonwealth property precludes recovery under real property exception to sovereign immunity. Order granting partial summary judgment affirmed. ***Rothermel v. Com., Dept. of Transp.*, 672 A.2d 837 (Pa. Cmwlth. 1996).**

Plaintiff widower stated cause of action under real estate exception to sovereign immunity for death of motorist/wife caused by limb falling from tree that had been "topped" twenty years earlier and was growing above PennDOT's right of way at 45° angle. Judgment on verdict for plaintiff affirmed. ***Patton v. Com., Dept. of Transp.*, ___ Pa. Cmwlth. ___, 669 A.2d 1090 (1995).**

Plaintiff motorist whose automobile drifted into left lane and left the highway, traveling down an embankment and into a creek, failed to state a cause of action within real estate exception to sovereign immunity. PennDOT not required to erect guard rails along embankment where it could not foresee that motorist's vehicle would leave the highway. Order granting judgment on the pleadings affirmed. ***Felli v. Com., Dept. of Transp.*, ___ Pa. Cmwlth. ___, 666 A.2d 775 (1995).**

Plaintiff failed to allege PennDOT's constructive or actual notice of unsafe condition of excavation site. PennDOT protected by governmental immunity absent proof of its active fault. Motion to dismiss in favor of PennDOT affirmed. ***Miranda v. City of Philadelphia*, 166 Pa. Cmwlth. 181, 646 A.2d 71 (1994).**

Landslide from strip mine regulated by Department of Environmental Resources damaged railroad's right of way. Department immune. ***CSX Transportation Inc. v. Franty Construction*, 157 Pa. Cmwlth. 620, 630 A.2d 932.**

Passenger fell on slippery spot on subway platform. Held: whether dangerous condition was "on" or "off" platform was question of fact. ***Shubert v. SEPTA*, 155 Pa. Cmwlth. 129, 625 A.2d 102.**

Passenger injured in fall caused by debris left on stairway at subway station. Authority not liable. ***Hicks v. SEPTA*, 154 Pa. Cmwlth. 641, 624 A.2d 690.**

Commonwealth liability: Streets and highways

Passenger assaulted by third party while riding train. Transportation Authority not liable. ***Williamson v. SEPTA*, 154 Pa. Cmwlth. 448, 624 A.2d 218.**

Employee of subcontractor injured in fall from scaffold brought action against general contractor and Commonwealth. Held: Commonwealth immune, contractor may be liable and subcontractor not obligated to indemnify general contractor. ***Donaldson v. Com., Dept. of Transp.*, 141 Pa. Cmwlth. 474, 596 A.2d 269.**

Pilot and wife injured when helicopter struck power line while spraying for department. Department immune. ***Dept. of Environmental Resources v. Meyers*, 135 Pa. Cmwlth. 526, 581 A.2d 696.**

Tenant brought wrongful death action against housing authority for failure to inspect dwelling and discover condition that led to fatal fire. Housing authority Commonwealth agency and therefore immune. ***Crosby v. Kotch*, 135 Pa. Cmwlth. 470, 580 A.2d 1191.**

Plaintiffs injured when they fell into strip mine adjacent to state road brought action against Commonwealth. Commonwealth immune because injuries occurred on private property. ***Snyder v. Harmon*, 522 Pa. 424, 562 A.2d 307.**

Truck damaged in landslide on Commonwealth-owned property. Plaintiff established issues of material fact concerning negligent maintenance by Commonwealth. ***Trenco, Inc. v. Com., Dept. of Transp.*, 126 Pa. Cmwlth. 501, 560 A.2d 285.**

Commonwealth liability: Sidewalks

A state agency has no duty to remove or treat natural accumulations of ice and snow. A natural accumulation of ice, snow or frost on prison sidewalk is not a defect of property within the real property exception to governmental immunity; therefore, prisoner not entitled to recovery. Order granting summary judgment was affirmed. ***Hill v. Dragovich*, 679 A.2d 1382 (Pa. Cmwlth. 1996).**

Concert goer injured in fall caused by hole in sidewalk at recreation area. Owner of area not immune under Recreation Use of Land and Water Act. ***Mills v. Commonwealth*, 145 Pa. Cmwlth. 558, 604 A.2d 755.**

Fall on sidewalk in possession of state authority. Suit barred. ***King v. General State Authority*, 30 Pa. Cmwlth. 442, 373 A.2d 1185.**

Commonwealth liability: Streets and highways

Plaintiff brought negligence action against the Pennsylvania Department of Transportation for permitting water to accumulate on the highway causing him to crash. A jury found in favor of the defendant. The Commonwealth Court reversed and remanded. The Commonwealth Court held that a jury should not consider the plaintiff's contributory negligence in determining whether the Department of Transportation caused the plaintiff's accident. In addition, it found that the jury's finding that the defendant was not the cause of the plaintiff's accident was against the weight of the evidence as it was conceded at trial that the plaintiff lost control of his

Commonwealth liability: Streets and highways

vehicle due to water on the roadway. *Irey v. Commonwealth Department of Transportation,* **No. 2194 C.D. 2011 (Pa. Cmwlth. 2013).**

Plaintiff brought negligence action against the Pennsylvania Department of Transportation after she was injured when the driver of the vehicle she occupied swerved to avoid an animal in the road and was unable to regain control of her car due to a dropoff in the highway's shoulder. The trial court granted summary judgment. The Commonwealth Court affirmed, holding that the shoulder of the roadway was not intended for vehicular traffic and thus the defendant owed no duty to design, construct and maintain the shoulder drop off. ***Bubba v. Commonwealth of Pennsylvania Department of Transportation,* 61 A.3d 313 (Pa. Cmwlth. 2013).**

Decedent's estate brought negligence and wrongful death action against the Pennsylvania Department of Transportation for failing to install a median barrier on a highway after the decedent was struck by an oncoming vehicle that crossed a grassy median. The trial court granted summary judgment in favor of the defendant. The Commonwealth Court affirmed holding that the failure to install a guardrail or median did not create a dangerous condition to permit the real estate exception to sovereign immunity to apply. ***Rodriguez v. Commonwealth of Pennsylvania Department of Transportation,* 59 A.3d 45 (Pa. Cmwlth. 2013).**

Plaintiff brought negligence claims for defective design, construction and maintenance against Defendant Department of Transportation (DOT). Plaintiff was injured when another vehicle crossed the grass median of a divided highway and struck his vehicle. The trial court granted summary judgment in favor of the Defendant. The Commonwealth Court affirmed holding that (DOT) had no duty to erect median barriers. It also held that a median does not constitute a dangerous condition of Commonwealth real estate and that DOT had no duty to create a median that deterred crossovers. ***Quinones v. Commonwealth of Pennsylvania Department of Transportation,* 45 A.3d 467 (Pa. Cmwlth. 2012).**

Motorcyclist brought negligence claim against the Department of Transportation after he was injured when his motorcycle struck a pothole on the highway. The trial court granted summary judgment to the Defendant. The Commonwealth Court reversed holding that a letter from a state senator expressing concern over the condition of the roadway was sufficient to establish notice of a dangerous condition to preclude the defense of sovereign immunity. ***Walthour v. Commonwealth of Pennsylvania Department of Transportation,* 31 A.3d 762 (Pa. Cmwlth. 2011).**

Motorist brought lawsuit against the City of Philadelphia and Pennsylvania Department of Transportation after he lost control of his vehicle while driving on a city street due black ice caused by melt and refreeze from the highway. The trial court granted summary judgment in favor of both Defendants. The Commonwealth Court affirmed holding that the State Highway law did not impose a statutory duty on the Department of Transportation (DOT) to protect an individual from accumulations of snow and ice on the roads. In addition, the Court held that the natural formation of ice following DOT's treatment of the roadways with chemicals does not create an artificial condition waiving sovereign immunity. Finally, the Court held that the city was immune pursuant to the Political Subdivision Tort Claims Act as

Commonwealth liability: Streets and highways

the Plaintiff failed to establish the black ice was the result of improper construction, design, deterioration or inherent defect of the street itself. *Page v. City of Philadelphia*, 1542 C.D. 2010 (Pa. Cmwlth. 2011).

Plaintiffs brought negligence action against the Pennsylvania Department of Transportation for injuries suffered in a motor vehicle accident for the department's failure to install rumble strips on a road that ran along a steep embankment. The trial court entered summary judgment on behalf of the defendants. The Commonwealth Court affirmed holding that a failure to install rumble strips does not create a defect of the highway sufficient to waive immunity under the real estate exception to the defense of sovereign immunity. *Brown v. Commonwealth of Pennsylvania, Department of Transportation*, 11 A.3d 1054 (Pa. Cmwlth. 2011).

Decedents' estates brought negligence action against Defendant Department of Transportation for failing to maintain guardrails on the highway and for having a shoulder that was less than five feet wide. Trial Court granted summary judgment in favor of the defendant. The Commonwealth Court affirmed holding that where a local government installs a safety fixture it has no duty to provide it cannot be held liable for negligent installation of that fixture and a failure to provide a wider shoulder is not a dangerous condition of real estate. *Lambert v. Katz*, 8 A.3d 409 (Pa. Cmwlth. 2010).

Estate of driver killed when her vehicle left the road and struck a tree brought a claim for negligent failure to maintain against the Department of Transportation. The trial court dismissed the case on Defendant's Motion for Summary Judgment. The Commonwealth Court affirmed, holding that the Plaintiff's failure to allege that a dangerous condition of the highway caused the accident prevented the application of the real estate exception to sovereign immunity. *Pritts v. Commonwealth of Pennsylvania Department of Transportation*, 969 A.2d 1 (Pa. Cmwlth. 2009).

Driver brought a claim of negligence for injuries he suffered while driving on a state highway, after a decayed tree fell on his car. Trial Court granted a motion for nonsuit to Defendants based upon immunity. The Commonwealth Court affirmed, holding that PennDOT was entitled to sovereign immunity as the Plaintiff failed to establish that the decayed tree originated on Commonwealth property or that a part of the tree overhanging the highway constituted a dangerous condition that caused the accident. *Clark v. Pennsylvania Department of Transportation*, 962 A.2d 692 (Pa. Cmwlth. 2008).

Administrator brought suit on behalf of a deceased passenger against PennDOT for failing to use appropriate guardrails and failing to design appropriate roadway shoulders that resulted in the death of a passenger after the vehicle the deceased was traveling in went off the road. The appellate court upheld the trial court's ruling that failure to design and failure to maintain guardrails were not dangerous roadway conditions for which the Commonwealth has waived immunity. *Fagan v. Department of Transportation of the Commonwealth of Pennsylvania*, 946 A.2d 1123 (Pa. Cmwlth. 2008).

Commonwealth liability: Streets and highways

Plaintiff brought suit against the City of Philadelphia and the Pennsylvania Department of Transportation after she alleged she tripped and fell on an uneven portion of roadway. Plaintiff, in filing her suit, identified the Commonwealth of Pennsylvania as the Defendant, but in the body of her pleading named the Department of Transportation as a Defendant. The appellate court reversed a trial court ruling dismissing the complaint based upon sovereign immunity holding that the Plaintiff could correct the technical deficiency because the appropriate agency had actual notice of the suit. *Piehl v. City of Philadelphia*, 930 A.2d 607 (Pa. Commwlth. 2008).

Plaintiff crashed car through a highway guardrail and sued the Department of Transportation for failing to properly maintain the guardrail. The court upheld dismissal of plaintiff's claim for failing to establish causation because plaintiff could not establish how or why her car left the road. *Martinowski v. Commonwealth*, 916 A.2d 717 (Pa. Cmwlth 2006).

Plaintiff sued Pennsylvania Department of Transportation claiming that injuries he sustained due to his vehicle leaving the road were increased due to PennDOT's failure to provide a sufficient clear zone on the side of the road. The court granted summary judgment to PennDOT since the plaintiff had no evidence as to why his car left the road and could not therefore prove causation. *Fritz v. Glen Mills School*, 894 A.2d 172 (Pa. Cmwlth. 2006).

Plaintiff filed suit against the Pennsylvania Department of Transportation (PennDOT) for negligent infliction of emotional distress when his wife was killed by an object dropped from a highway overpass, which PennDOT knew had been the scene of several other similar incidents. The court affirmed judgment for PennDOT based upon the doctrine of sovereign immunity. The court found that to fall within the real property exception to sovereign immunity the defect in the real estate itself must cause the injury and not merely encourage or facilitate the act of another. *Cowell v. Commonwealth*, 883 A.2d 705 (Pa. Cmwlth. 2005).

Pennsylvania Turnpike Commission and contractors who adhered to Turnpike Commission standards in construction of 32" high median barriers are all entitled to sovereign immunity protection. *Svege v. Interstate Safety Systems*, 862 A.2d 752 (Pa. Cmwlth. 2004).

Verdict for estate of deceased driver affirmed against PennDOT upon proof that motor vehicle accident was caused by water sheeting across a PennDOT maintained road. *Vrabel v. Commonwealth Dept. of Transportation*, 844 A.2d 595 (Pa. Cmwlth. 2004).

Real estate exception to sovereign immunity held not to apply in suit against PennDOT for negligent design of road on which family was killed in "whiteout" snow conditions. *Kosmack v. Jones*, 807 A.2d 927 (Pa. Cmwlth. 2002).

Suit against PennDOT alleging negligence for failure to remove accumulations of ice and snow from state maintained road during declared Disaster Emergency in 1994. Summary judgment in favor of PennDOT affirmed on basis of sov-

Commonwealth liability: Streets and highways

ereign immunity and immunity under Pennsylvania's Emergency Management Services Code provisions. ***Kahres v. Henry,* 801 A.2d 650 (Pa. Super. 2002)**.

Reaffirmation of the position that the real estate exception to sovereign immunity does not require the Commonwealth to erect guard rails along embankments on state owned roads. ***Piazza v. Pennsylvania Department of Transportation,* 786 A.2d 328 (Pa. Cmwlth. 2001)**.

Plaintiff, individually and for deceased husband, filed suit against PennDOT and other defendants alleging that PennDOT's failure to remove snow and ice from roadway during proclaimed disaster emergency caused by excessive snowfall. Held, PennDOT had no duty to remove snow and ice from roads because that condition did not derive, originate or have as it's source the Commonwealth realty. While there is mention of the Disaster Emergency Act and it's limitations on liability, it was not part of the basis for the court's decision. ***Kahres v. Henry*, 801 A.2d 650 (Pa. Cmwlth. 2002)**.

Plaintiffs' decedent was killed when her vehicle was struck by a train at an un-gated, at-grade railroad crossing. In suit against borough where the crossing was located, PennDOT as owner of the crossing road and the railroad company, summary judgment motion by PennDOT was denied on the grounds that PennDOT had assumed liability for dangerous condition of the crossing when it entered into an agreement with the borough to seek upgrades to crossing from PA Public Utility Commission. Commonwealth Court reversed denial of summary judgment to PennDOT on grounds that the plaintiffs had not proved the applicability of the real estate exception to sovereign immunity as the crossing was not a dangerous condition of the highway under PennDOT's control. ***Sickles v. Consolidate Rail Corporation*, 777 A.2d 1240 (Pa. Cmwlth. 2001)**.

State highway law and the highway exceptions to sovereign immunity must be read in *pari materia*. Curb of a state highway that allegedly caused plaintiff's car to be catapulted into a stream bed, causing injuries, may be under control of PennDOT and so causation should go to jury. ***Shimko v. PennDOT*, 768 A.2d 413 (Pa. Cmwlth. 2001)**.

Plaintiff injured when a northbound truck struck her as she tried to cross two northbound lanes of traffic to head south. Plaintiff sued PennDOT, alleging the north-south roadway was negligently designed and maintained. PennDOT joined the municipality, alleging it was negligent for failing to install a traffic control device at the intersection. Appeal by municipality only after judgment against PennDOT and municipality. Held: because plaintiff did not provide sufficiently relevant and extensive expert testimony that signs or signals would have met the need of the intersection and the greater traffic needs, and there was no proof that the municipality could have, without PennDOT approval, erected signs restricting access to a state road, plaintiff could not prove negligence of municipality. ***Starr v. Veneziano*, 747 A.2d 867 (Pa. 2000)**.

Plaintiff's decedent killed when he struck stopped traffic on I-95 three miles in advance of a construction site. Plaintiff alleged that PennDOT was negligent in failing to place warning signs in advance of location where cars backed up and

Commonwealth liability: Streets and highways

stopped. Plaintiff also alleged PennDOT's failure to erect signs was negligence *per se*. Held: expert testimony as to need for advance signs three miles from construction site was required. PennDOT regulations that were silent on exact placement of warning signs could not be basis for claim of negligence *per se*, if PennDOT did not place the signs where plaintiff thought they should have been. ***Young v. PennDOT*, 744 A.2d 1276 (Pa. 2000).**

A muffler lying on a Commonwealth roadway is not a condition of or arising from Commonwealth real estate so as to allow plaintiff the benefit of the real property exception to sovereign immunity. ***Murphy v. Com., Dept. of Transp.*, 733 A.2d 688 (Pa. Cmwlth. 1999).**

Plaintiff and her decedents were passengers in a car driven by additional defendant who crossed over centerline of PennDOT road, crashed through guardrail and struck tree. Plaintiff alleged that brakes and engine had failed, that additional defendant driver was intoxicated and that PennDOT had failed to provide safe roadway because of inability of guardrail to prevent car from striking tree. Following grant of summary judgment in favor of PennDOT, plaintiff appealed. Held: PennDOT could not have adequate notice of combination of events leading to accident—loss of brakes and driver's intoxication—and therefore PennDOT had no duty to plaintiff and her decedents. ***Baer v. Com., Dept. of Transp.*, 713 A.2d 189 (Pa. Cmwlth. 1998).**

Plaintiff sued city for injuries sustained when she was caused to fall by defective condition of sidewalk that abutted state highway and city-owned property. Trial court granted city's summary judgment motion on grounds that city is immune from liability to suit for injuries sustained by plaintiff where defect is in sidewalk adjacent to state highway and not city street. Held: exception to governmental immunity for dangerous condition of sidewalk owned and maintained by city is unaffected by fact that sidewalk is adjacent to state highway and not city street. ***Wite v. City of Philadelphia*, 712 A.2d 345 (Pa. Cmwlth. 1998).**

Truck driver who drove onto very rough section of road in construction zone lost control of his vehicle and struck another truck that had jackknifed due to same conditions. First truck, in contravention of law, had not placed warning markers or flares 100 feet and 200 feet behind his vehicle to warn oncoming traffic of dangerous location of his truck immediately adjacent to the roadway. In consolidated suit by plaintiff and others against first truck driver, his trucking company and PennDOT, jury returned verdict in favor of plaintiff and against first driver's company only and allocated 41% liability to plaintiff. On appeal, Commonwealth Court held there was adequate evidence to support jury verdict in favor of plaintiff and against only one defendant. Affirmed with modification, allowing plaintiff's employer to file a subrogation according to Indiana law. ***Burlington Motor Carriers v. Com., Dept. of Transp.*, 710 A.2d 148 (Pa. Cmwlth. 1998).**

Plaintiff administratrix of deceased husband's estate filed suit against PennDOT and truck manufacturer, alleging negligence in condition of roadway/berm and design defect in truck which caught fire after roll-over accident. Summary judgment was granted in favor of PennDOT in negligence case and for manufacturer

Commonwealth liability: Streets and highways

in product liability case based on spoliation of evidence. Plaintiff transferred title to truck remains to scrap yard which parted out truck and then scrapped it before defendants had full opportunity to inspect so as to determine alternative theories of causation. Commonwealth Court affirmed. Supreme Court reversed on adopted reasoning of *Schmid v. Milwaukee Electric Tool Corp.* 13 F.3d 76 (3rd Cir. 1994) which established three-part test for spoliation cases: (1) the degree of fault of the party who altered or destroyed the evidence; (2) the degree of prejudice suffered by the opposing party, and (3) the availability of a lesser sanction that will protect the opposing party's rights and deter future similar conduct. **Schroeder v. Com., Dept. of Transp., 710 A.2d 23 (Pa. 1998).**

In action against PennDOT and the city from which PennDOT had "adopted" a road for failure to install guard rails, summary judgment in favor of PennDOT was sustained. There was no proof by plaintiff of breach of a duty to plaintiff by PennDOT in the maintenance and care of the road surface between the curb lines— the only area for which PennDOT is statutorily responsible after "adoption" of the road from the city. **Wallace v. Com., Dept. of Transp., 701 A.2d 307 (Pa. Cmwlth. 1997).**

Plaintiff's expert's report that state highway was defective in design, irrespective of plaintiff's claims of natural accumulations of ice and snow, creates factual question for jury relating to care and maintenance of DOT's real property and so precludes summary judgment in favor of DOT based on the Sovereign Immunity Act. **Smith v. Com., Dept. of Transp., 700 A.2d 587 (Pa. Cmwlth. 1997).**

A median on which alighting bus passenger tripped and sustained injuries is part of the highway and not a traffic control device; therefore, PennDOT, as owner of highway, may be subject to liability under exception to sovereign immunity. Verdict against City reversed; verdict against Commonwealth affirmed. **Slough v. Com., Dept. of Transp., 686 A.2d 62 (Pa. Cmwlth. 1996).**

While PennDOT has a duty to make highways safe and possibly to install guard rails where necessary, in order to recover plaintiff must establish that lack of guardrail was cause of injuries rather than a contributing factor. Failure to allege a defect "of" Commonwealth property precludes recovery under real property exception to sovereign immunity. Order granting partial summary judgment affirmed. **Rothermel v. Com., Dept. of Transp., 672 A.2d 837 (Pa. Cmwlth. 1996).**

In action by passenger against PennDOT for negligent design of road, judgment for PennDOT affirmed where plaintiff passenger determined to be negligent by exposing herself to an unreasonable risk in riding with a known intoxicated driver. Even minimal evidence of contributory negligence requires a charge on the issue. **Karchner v. Flaim, ___ Pa. Cmwlth. ___, 661 A.2d 928 (1995).**

Defect in a concrete median strip in the center of a PennDOT-maintained roadway constitutes a condition of the road allowing injured pedestrian's suit against PennDOT for defective maintenance of the median strip under real property exception to sovereign immunity. **Hubbard v. PennDOT, ___ Pa. Cmwlth. ___, 660 A.2d 201 (1995).**

Commonwealth liability: Streets and highways

Real property exception to sovereign immunity does not apply in automobile accident involving motorcyclist and driver. PennDOT's design and construction of road, including length of passing lane and speed limits, were not defects that caused motorcyclist's injuries but merely facilitated occurrence of accident when combined with negligence of driver. Assured clear distance rule does not apply where instrumentality moves into driver's path within a distance short of the assured clear distance ahead. Driver does not have to anticipate negligence of another driver in calculating his assured clear distance. ***Nestor v. Com., Dept. of Transp.,* ___ Pa. Cmwlth. ___, 658 A.2d 829 (1995).**

Summary judgment against plaintiffs who filed action against PennDOT for negligent design and maintenance of state highway reversed where amended complaint alleged facts sufficient to raise issue of whether government had maintained road in a condition safe for travel. ***Fidanza v. Com., Dept. of Transp.,* ___Pa. Cmwlth. ___, 655 A.2d 1076 (1995).**

In automobile accident case by decedent's administrator against intoxicated driver and PennDOT, whether PennDOT's alleged negligence for improper road design and maintenance was substantial factor in accident was question for jury. Existence of two tortfeasors does not automatically excuse one or the other from liability. Question of concurrent or joint causation and determination of whether an act is so extraordinary as to constitute a superseding cause are for the jury. Order sustaining preliminary objections of PennDOT reversed. ***Powell v. Drumheller,* 539 Pa. 484, 653 A.2d 619 (1995).**

In negligence action by truck driver for damages resulting from cow wandering onto roadway, turnpike commission had no duty of care, custody, or control of cow. Summary judgment affirmed. ***Mason & Dixon Lines, Inc. v. Mognet,* 166 Pa. Cmwlth. 1, 645 A.2d 1370 (1994).**

Accident victim brought action against township and Commonwealth for negligent maintenance, inspection, and design of roadway. Held: motion to amend caption to include PennDOT time barred. ***Gitto v. Plumstead Township,* 159 Pa. Cmwlth. 668, 634 A.2d 683.**

Parents of child struck and killed by automobile while riding bicycle brought action against Department of Transportation, municipality, and adjoining landowner. Defendants not liable. Failure to set speed limit below fifty-five and permitting vegetation to grow along highway not cause of accident. ***Salerno v. LaBarr,* 159 Pa. Cmwlth. 99, 632 A.2d 1002.**

Driver injured in intersection accident brought action against Commonwealth for failure to properly maintain and inspect intersection and for negligent design. Partial summary judgment granted for failure to maintain and inspect. Held: order not appealable. ***Stemper v. Com., Dept. of Transp.,* 159 Pa. Cmwlth. 31, 632 A.2d 971.**

Driver injured when vehicle struck log on embankment along highway. Department not liable. ***Babcock v. Com., Dept. of Transp.,* 156 Pa. Cmwlth. 69, 626 A.2d 672.**

Commonwealth liability: Streets and highways

Driver killed in collision with vehicle driven by intoxicated operator. Held: PennDOT not liable for negligent construction and maintenance of highway. ***Powell v. Drumheller,* 153 Pa. Cmwlth. 571, 621 A.2d 1197.**

Motorcyclist injured in collision at intersection brought action against county. County not liable. Roads designated state highways. ***Verna by Verna v. Commonwealth,* 149 Pa. Cmwlth. 449, 613 A.2d 174.**

Motorcycle operator injured in accident awarded delay damages in excess of $250,000. Held: statutory damage cap under Sovereign Immunity Act not applicable. ***Woods v. Com., Dept. of Transp.,* 531 Pa. 295, 612 A.2d 970.**

Truck driver injured in accident by tire left on turnpike after prior accident brought action against State Police and Turnpike Commission. Defendants immune. ***Nubert v. Pennsylvania State Police,* 148 Pa. Cmwlth. 505, 611 A.2d 1353.**

Passengers in vehicle driven by diabetic injured when driver lost consciousness. Held: Commonwealth and city not liable for failure to install warning and speed limit signs. Driver's loss of consciousness was superseding cause. ***Chacho v. Com., Dept. of Transp.,* 148 Pa. Cmwlth. 494, 611 A.2d 1346.**

Motorists injured in collision at intersection brought action against township and Commonwealth for failure to install traffic control device. Denial of defendants' motion for summary judgment upheld. ***Bendas v. Township of White Deer,* 531 Pa. 180, 611 A.2d 1184.**

Pedestrian killed while crossing highway between two townships. Action brought against both townships, Department of Transportation and driver. All government parties immune. ***Sloneker v. Martin,* 144 Pa. Cmwlth. 190, 604 A.2d 751.**

Insurance company sought contribution from Department of Transportation after settling accident alleging accident caused by dangerous condition of highway. Held: government unit may be jointly liable with other tortfeasor. ***Underwriters at Lloyds of London v. Com., Dept. of Transp.,* 145 Pa. Cmwlth. 268, 603 A.2d 241.**

Student struck by automobile while crossing state highway on way to school brought action against Commonwealth, school district and township for failure to provide crosswalks and traffic control devices. All defendants immune. ***Majestic v. Com., Dept. of Transp.,* 144 Pa. Cmwlth. 109, 601 A.2d 386.**

High school student struck by vehicle while crossing state highway brought action against school district, township, and Commonwealth. All defendants immune. ***Stein v. Com., Dept. of Transp.,* 144 Pa. Cmwlth. 105, 601 A.2d 384.**

Motorist injured in accident at intersection brought action against township and Department of Transportation for allowing a dangerous condition to exist. Township not liable. Motorist 51% negligent and Commonwealth 49% negligent. ***Wright v. Com., Dept. of Transp.,* 142 Pa. Cmwlth. 91, 596 A.2d 1241.**

Pedestrian struck by vehicle while crossing street. View of traffic was blocked by parked truck. Held: PennDOT and city not liable for negligent design

Commonwealth liability: Streets and highways

and maintenance of traffic signals. *Hillerman v. Com., Dept. of Transp.*, **141 Pa. Cmwlth. 14, 595 A.2d 204.**

Parents of child injured in automobile collision brought action against other driver and Department of Transportation. Both defendants not liable. Expert testimony required to show highway negligently designed. Testimony of other driver sufficient to show no negligence. *Tennis v. Fedorwicz,* **139 Pa. Cmwlth. 554, 592 A.2d 117.**

Motorists injured in collision brought action against each other and against Department of Transportation. Summary judgment in favor of department reversed. Governmental unit may be found jointly liable with non-governmental party. *Buschman v. Druch,* **139 Pa. Cmwlth. 182, 590 A.2d 53.**

Pedestrian injured in fall on roadbed of street railway located on state highway brought action against city, transportation authority and Department of Transportation Department. City found primarily liable, authority secondarily liable and department not liable. *Yackobovitz v. SEPTA,* **139 Pa. Cmwlth. 157, 590 A.2d 40.**

Motorcyclist injured in collision at intersection brought action against Commonwealth, township, and roadmaster for failure to replace stop sign and to remove vegetation from roadside. Summary judgment for defendants affirmed. *Bruce v. Com., Dept. of Transp.,* **138 Pa. Cmwlth. 187, 588 A.2d 974.**

Truck driver injured when vehicle skidded on ice and snow on highway. Department not liable for failure to clear ice and snow or for failure to warn. *Hunt v. Com., Dept. of Transp.,* **137 Pa. Cmwlth. 588, 587 A.2d 37.**

Child injured when struck by automobile brought action against Commonwealth alleging that highway was defective and dangerous owing to narrowing of curve and excessive drop off along berm. Real property exception to sovereign immunity applicable. Liability precluded on other grounds. *Bartell by Underhill v. Straub,* **134 Pa. Cmwlth. 43, 578 A.2d 72.**

Pedestrian who fell in pothole brought action against Commonwealth. Trial judge entered judgment *n.o.v.* in favor of Commonwealth. Commonwealth Court overturned judgment *n.o.v.* Jury had sufficient evidence to find Commonwealth had required notice of defect in highway. *Pallante v. City of Philadelphia,* **133 Pa. Cmwlth. 441, 575 A.2d 980.**

Police officer injured when motorcycle struck utility pole and brought action against electric company and Department of Transportation. Company and department not liable. Injuries would have occurred even if pole not present. Evidence of subsequent relocation of pole not admissible to show negligence. *Henry v. McCrudden,* **133 Pa. Cmwlth. 231, 575 A.2d 666.**

Passengers in automobile killed by drunken driver in collision at intersection. Action brought against Commonwealth for failure to install traffic signal. Commonwealth found negligent but not liable. Negligence not a substantial factor. *Roberts v. Dungan,* **133 Pa. Cmwlth. 98, 574 A.2d 1193.**

Commonwealth liability: Streets and highways

Motorcyclist injured in accident caused by potholes in highway. Commonwealth not liable. Statutory requirement that Department of Transportation be notified in writing of dangerous condition was held to be not unconstitutional. ***Ketterer v. Com., Dept. of Transp.,*** **133 Pa. Cmwlth. 92, 574 A.2d 735.**

Motorist killed when automobile went over guardrail owing to snow removed from highway left along berm. Commonwealth liable. Snow along berm was artificial condition caused by Department of Transportation. ***Com., Dept. of Transp. v. Weller,*** **133 Pa. Cmwlth. 18, 574 A.2d 728.**

Motorists injured or killed in accidents caused by ice and snow on highways. Commonwealth found not liable. Duty to remove ice and snow does not include duty to protect individuals from harm. ***Kilmer v. Com., Dept. of Transp.,*** **132 Pa. Cmwlth. 538, 573 A.2d 659.**

Motorist claimed that accident resulted from Department of Transportation's failure to install traffic signal at dangerous intersection. Held: Commonwealth may be liable under highway exception to sovereign immunity. ***Commonwealth v. Bendas,*** **131 Pa. Cmwlth. 488, 570 A.2d 1360.**

Plaintiffs injured when they fell into strip mine adjacent to state road brough action against Commonwealth. Commonwealth immune because injuries occurred on private property. ***Snyder v. Harmon,*** **522 Pa. 424, 562 A.2d 307.**

Jury verdict $750,000 against Commonwealth for quadriplegia suffered in auto accident allegedly caused by defective highway design. Verdict molded to $250,000 in accordance with section two of Sovereign Immunity Act. ***Lyles v. City of Philadelphia,*** **88 Pa. Cmwlth. 509, 490 A.2d 936.**

Multi-vehicle fatal accident at allegedly dangerous intersection on state highway. Trial judge directed verdict for PennDOT, reversed. Where a dangerous condition was developed and individuals are injured as a result, PennDOT cannot plead its discretion as absolute defense of liability. ***Wyke v. Ward,*** **81 Pa. Cmwlth. 392, 474 A.2d 375.**

Claim for damage and death against Commonwealth allegedly caused by deteriorated highway. Action barred by Act 152, since no evidence that Commonwealth had actual knowledge of dangerous condition. ***Lehnig v. Fleton,*** **278 Pa. Super. 12, 419 A.2d 1330.**

Plaintiffs injured by rocks thrown at their cars by unknown persons from bridge over state highway. History of similar incidents alleged. Held: as a matter of law to be a "condition" within the terms of 42 Pa. C.S.A. §5110(a)(4). ***Mistecka v. Commonwealth,*** **46 Pa. Cmwlth. 267, 408 A.2d 159.**

Motorist sued state for injuries received when large aluminum sign struck his car as he was driving along highway. Permissible cause of action under Act No. 152—1978. ***Lerner v. Com., Dept. of Transp.,*** **46 Pa. Cmwlth. 460, 406 A.2d 844.**

Suit against PennDOT now permitted. ***Reinerb v. Com., Dept. of Transp.,*** **482 Pa. 612, 394 A.2d 490.**

Commonwealth liability: Traffic control

Suit against employees of Department of Transportation for injuries allegedly as a result of deteriorated highway. Remanded for consideration in light of *DuBree*. **Lehnig v. Felton, 481 Pa. 559, 393 A.2d 303.**

Suit for death of driver of auto which plunged into excavation in public highway. Suit against Commonwealth permitted. Suit against officials of Department of Transportation remanded for further analysis. ***DuBree v. Commonwealth*, 481 Pa. 540, 393 A.2d 293.**

Appellant brought trespass action against appellee for damages incurred as a result of injuries allegedly caused by appellee's negligent maintenance of state highway. Supreme Court abolished the doctrine of sovereign immunity and overruled all inconsistent cases, stating, "Under the doctrine, plaintiff's opportunity depends, irrationally, not upon the nature of his injury or of the act which caused it, but upon the identity or status of the wrongdoer." ***Mayle v. Pennsylvania Dept. of Highways*, 479 Pa. 384, 388 A.2d 709 (1978).**

Injury during construction of bridge. Held: Port Authority can be sued—is not an "integral part of Commonwealth" as a public corporation and cannot claim immunity. ***Yancoskie v. Delaware River Port Authority*, 478 Pa. 396, 387 A.2d 41.**

Plaintiff injured while driving on allegedly defective state highway. Suit barred. ***Levine v. Commonwealth*, 34 Pa. Cmwlth. 385, 383 A.2d 1291.**

Suit against Department of Transportation and others to recover for alleged wrongful death of plaintiff's decedent because of allegedly negligence in the construction, maintenance and operation of highway. Suit barred by doctrine of sovereign immunity. ***Fischer v. Kassab*, 32 Pa. Cmwlth. 581, 380 A.2d 926.**

Accident allegedly caused by pot hole in state road. Suit barred. ***Greiser v. Commonwealth*, 30 Pa. Cmwlth. 436, 373 A.2d 1187.**

Suit v. Commonwealth and several state employees alleging negligent maintenance of highway as cause of fatal accident. Commonwealth dismissed. Remand or determination of case against individuals. ***Tokar v. Commonwealth*, 29 Pa. Cmwlth. 383, 371 A.2d 537.**

Injuries sustained in collision on turnpike allegedly caused by negligence of Pa. Turnpike Commission employee—action to recover against Commonwealth and Turnpike Commission—doctrine upheld as to Commonwealth, abolished as to Turnpike Commission, since "not a part of Commonwealth" as described in Constitution, Art. 1, §11—actions severable—action against Commission maintained. ***Specter et ux. v. Commonwealth and Turnpike Commission*, 462 Pa. 474, 341 A.2d 481.**

Plaintiff-decedent driving tractor-trailer which hit pot hole and went out of control. Suit against employees of Commonwealth. Summary judgment in favor of defendants affirmed. ***Lehnig v. Felton*, 235 Pa. Super. 100, 340 A.2d 564.**

Commonwealth liability: Traffic control

A median on which alighting bus passenger tripped and sustained injuries is part of the highway and not a traffic control device; therefore, PennDOT, as own-

Comparative negligence

er of highway, may be subject to liability under exception to sovereign immunity. Verdict against City reversed; verdict against Commonwealth affirmed. ***Slough v. Com., Dept. of Transp.,* 686 A.2d 62 (Pa. Cmwlth. 1996)**.

Pedestrian struck by vehicle while crossing street. View of traffic was blocked by parked truck. Held: Department of Transportation and city not liable for negligent design and maintenance of traffic signals. ***Hillerman v. Com., Dept. of Transp.,* 141 Pa. Cmwlth. 14, 595 A.2d 204.**

Passengers in automobile killed by drunken driver in collision at intersection. Action brought against Commonwealth for failure to install traffic signal. Commonwealth found negligent but not liable. Negligence not a substantial factor. ***Roberts v. Dungan,* 133 Pa. Cmwlth. 98, 574 A.2d 1193.**

Motorist claimed that accident resulted from Department of Transportation's failure to install traffic signal at dangerous intersection. Held: Commonwealth may be liable under highway exception to soverign immunity. ***Commonwealth v. Bendas,* 131 Pa. Cmwlth. 488, 570 A.2d 1360.**

Plaintiff injured alighting from trolley when struck by passing auto. Issue of City's duty to erect traffic island at dangerous trolley stops should be for jury. Nonsuit as to City reversed and new trial ordered on this issue only. ***Litwinko v. SEPTA,* 267 Pa. Super. 541, 407 A.2d 42.**

Suit v. Commonwealth for allegedly failing to place traffic signal at dangerous intersection—barred. ***McElwee v. Commonwealth,* 30 Pa. Cmwlth. 320, 373 A.2d 1163.**

Commonwealth liability: Utility service facilities

Directed verdict reversed and new trial granted to plaintiff injured when improperly backfilled water line trench settled, creating a three-foot wide, 18 inch deep ditch in PennDOT maintained road. Utility service facilities exception to sovereign immunity allows recovery because defect was a condition "of the facilities." ***Miller v. Com., Dept. of Transp.,* 690 A.2d 818 (Pa. Cmwlth. 1997).**

Company physician

Worker injured on job brought action against employer and company physician for failure to disclose previous injury. Employer immune. Physician not immune. ***Noyes v. Cooper,* 396 Pa. Super. 592, 579 A.2d 407.**

Comparative negligence

Plaintiff brought negligence claim against defendant forklift repair company after a backrest fell on his foot, while visiting the defendant's facility. A jury found in favor of the defendants. The Commonwealth Court reversed holding that plaintiff was entitled to a new trial, because the trial court included a question regarding plaintiff's own comparative negligence on the special verdict sheet without evidence of same. The Supreme Court overruled the Commonwealth Court holding that where a jury finds no negligence on the part of the defendant it is harmless error

Comparative negligence

to have a question of comparative negligence on a jury verdict slip. ***Boyle v. Independent Lift Truck, Inc.*, 6 A.3d 492 (Pa. 2010).**

Administratrix of motorcyclist's estate brought a claim for negligence after the Pennsylvania motorcyclist was struck and killed by the New Jersey defendant in New Jersey. Defendant appealed the binding arbitration award based upon the lack of jurisdiction and a damage award against the defendant despite a finding that the decedent was 60% negligent. The Superior Court upheld the trial court's ruling that it had jurisdiction based upon the mutual agreement to arbitration in Pennsylvania. The Superior Court reversed and remanded with instructions to enter a judgment in favor of the Defendant on the basis of comparative negligence as a plaintiff cannot recover if they are found more than 50% negligent. ***Rekun v. Pelaez*, 976 A.2d 578 (Pa. Super. 2009).**

Administrator appealed a trial court's molded verdict of zero dollars to the estate based upon health insurance benefits already received despite a jury verdict of fifty percent negligence on the part of both the plaintiff and defendants. The Pennsylvania Supreme Court held that the failure to present affirmative evidence does not make the other party's opinion evidence uncontroverted and the amount of damages is a question for the jury. ***Carroll v. Avallone*, 565 Pa. 676, 939 A.2d 872 (2007).**

Suit by clients against CPA firm claiming professional negligence in providing advice which resulted in federal criminal prosecution and guilty verdict for tax evasion and filing false returns. On determination that comparative negligence rule does not apply in cases involving loss of funds only and that contributory negligence rules apply, clients' guilty verdict establishes contributory negligence and precludes any recovery against CPA firm. ***Columbia Medical Group v. Herring & Roll, P.C.*, 829 A.2d 1184 (Pa. Super. 2003).**

An eleven year old boy was killed by passing automobile on narrow bridge. In suit against the driver who struck him and PennDOT for negligence in maintenance and operation of the bridge, trial court decisions to deny new trial as to driver affirmed and grant of new trial as to PennDOT reversed because determination of comparative negligence of minor child was within province of jury. ***Stong v. PennDOT*, 817 A.2d 576 (Pa. Cmwlth. 2003).**

In legal malpractice case, any contributory negligence of plaintiff client is a complete bar to recovery because the comparative negligence act only applies to cases involving death, injury or damage to tangible property. ***Gorski v. Smith*, 812 A.2d 683 (Pa. Super. 2003).**

Plaintiff driver was injured when his vehicle was broadsided by a police car responding to a call. Plaintiff claimed that defendant police officer was driving recklessly under the standards set by the emergency vehicle doctrine (75 Pa.C.S. § 3105). Defendant argued that plaintiff was contributorily negligent as he was driving under the influence of drugs. After verdict in favor of plaintiff, jury apportioned liability 55% to plaintiff and 45% to police officer. City and police officer presented motion to mold verdict to $0 under comparative negligence and court granted motion. New trial granted on appeal because the comparative negligence act cannot be

Comparative negligence

used to measure recklessness under emergency vehicle doctrine against plaintiff's negligence under the comparative negligence act. ***Johnson v. City of Philadelphia*, 808 A.2d 978 (Pa. Cmwlth Ct. 2002).**

Pedophilic sexual molestation is an intentional act and, as such, the doctrine of comparative negligence does not apply. Additionally, a victim of sexual abuse has no duty to avoid placing himself in the position to be harmed. ***Hutchinson ex rel. Hutchinson v. Luddy*, 763 A.2d 826 (Pa. Super. 2000).**

Employee was injured when he stepped backwards into a hole in a roof because he was compelled by job requirements to walk backwards and look forward. After thorough analysis of comparative negligence and assumption of risk theories, court determined that, in employment context—because reasonable minds could differ as to whether plaintiff/employee deliberately and with awareness of specific risks inherent in the activity nonetheless engaged in the activity that produced his injury—plaintiff's actions raise a fact question regarding comparative negligence, not a legal question regarding defendant's lack of duty to a person who assumes a risk. ***Staub v. Toy Factory, Inc.*, 749 A.2d 522 (Pa. Super. 2000).**

Plaintiff successfully sued physician for failure to diagnose. Doctor argued on appeal that trial court erred in failing to instruct jury on comparative negligence of plaintiff, when there was evidence that doctor had suggested a diagnostic test which plaintiff refused. Held: trial court must instruct the jury on comparative negligence where there is any evidence of comparative negligence on the part of the plaintiff. ***Zieber v. Bogert*, 747 A.2d 905 (Pa. Super. 2000).**

Plaintiff's decedent allegedly fell asleep at the wheel and his car, with his wife and family on board, crossed into opposing traffic, struck and slid along a guardrail and struck a bridge abutment causing his death. After verdict for plaintiff molded to reflect jury's finding of 40% comparative negligence of deceased driver, trial court granted new trial at request of PennDOT because it had failed to charge on superseding cause as PennDOT had requested. Commonwealth Court reversed trial court and Supreme Court held that superseding cause requires the act of a third party, not act of plaintiff or defendant. Acts of a plaintiff that contribute to the injury sustained are addressed by the law of comparative negligence, not superseding cause. ***Von Der Heide v. Com., Dept. of Transp.*, 718 A.2d 286 (Pa. 1998).**

Defense of decedent's contributory negligence is not eliminated from consideration merely because of negligence *per se* of tavern that served decedent while he was visibly intoxicated. Remand for new trial to determine plaintiffs' decedent's comparative negligence in driving while intoxicated after having been served while visibly intoxicated. Decedent could not have legally assumed risk of driving while intoxicated following determination of tavern's negligence in serving visibly intoxicated decedent. To pierce corporate veil, against which there is a strong legal presumption, plaintiff must prove undercapitalization, intermingling of individual and corporate affairs, failure to adhere to corporate formalities and use of the corporate form to perpetrate a fraud. ***Miller v. Brass Rail Tavern, Inc.*, 702 A.2d 1072 (Pa. Super. 1997).**

Comparative negligence

Patient treated by defendant orthopedic surgeon filed suit for negligently performed corrective surgery and continuing pain and suffering after the surgery. Verdict for plaintiff apportioning negligence 60/40 between defendant and plaintiff. New trial granted by trial court based on reasoning of *Gentile v. Devergilis*, 290 Pa. 50, 138 A. 540 in which it was held that where a patient refuses to follow directions for postoperative care, there can be no verdict against the treating physician who recommended the care for any negligent act because there can be no determination of which failure to treat- the original physician's or the patient's who refused to follow treatment directions - caused the harm. Superior Court affirmed and Supreme Court reversed stating that a patient's mere failure to attend postoperative appointments does not make it impossible as a matter of law for a jury to determine whether, and to what degree, the physician's negligence caused the injury. ***Ferguson v. Panzarella*, 700 A.2d 917 (Pa. 1997).**

In wrongful death and survival action by widow of motorist whose automobile crossed opposing lane and left highway, PennDOT entitled to jury charge on contributory negligence where no evidence presented regarding external cause of accident. Following plaintiff's inquiry into other causes of accident, State Trooper permitted to testify as to possibility of driver having fallen asleep. ***Burkholz v. Com., Dept. of Transp.*, ___ Pa. Cmwlth. ___, 667 A.2d 513 (1995).**

In automobile accident, testimony by State Trooper with familiarity of truck inspection procedures properly disallowed as to standard of care required by truck driver. Comparative Negligence Act requires that jury apportion liability between plaintiff and all defendants against whom recovery is sought. Trial court's bifurcation to allow apportionment of liability between fewer than all defendants reversed. ***Christiansen v. Silfies*, 446 Pa. Super. 464, 667 A.2d 396 (1995).**

In action by motorist for injuries sustained when she collided with side of a hopper car being pulled by defendant's train, railroad company whose train was actually on and moving over a crossing did not owe motorist a duty to warn of train's presence. Occupied crossing rule survived enactment of the Comparative Negligence Act. Order sustaining preliminary objections affirmed. ***Sprenkle v. Conrail*, 446 Pa. Super. 377, 666 A.2d 1099 (1995).**

Student of military academy injured when toy cannon prematurely discharged did not assume the risk of injury where student had fired cannon more than 200 times without incident. Only necessary jury instruction was on comparative negligence. Judgment on jury verdict affirmed. ***Struble v. Valley Forge Military Academy*, 445 Pa. Super. 224, 665 A.2d 4 (1995).**

Plaintiff who fails to participate significantly in postoperative care risks loss of any claim for alleged negligence of physician in performing surgery. The Comparative Negligence Act is not applicable in such cases because of the inability to apportion liability between both parties. ***Ferguson v. Panzarella*, 445 Pa. Super. 23, 664 A.2d 989 (1995).**

In action by passenger against PennDOT for negligent design of road, judgment for PennDOT affirmed where plaintiff passenger determined to be negligent by exposing herself to an unreasonable risk in riding with a known intoxicated driver.

Comparative negligence

Even minimal evidence of contributory negligence requires a charge on the issue. *Karchner v. Flaim*, ___ **Pa. Cmwlth.** ___, **661 A.2d 928 (1995).**

In an action where jury found plaintiff to be 30% negligent, one defendant to be 45% negligent and second defendant 25% negligent, plaintiff still may recover against defendant found to be less negligent than plaintiff because collectively defendants were more negligent than plaintiff. Where strictly liable defendant and negligent defendant acted as joint tortfeasors, contribution among them can be properly awarded. Judgment on molded jury verdict affirmed. ***Smith v. Weissenfels, Inc.*, 441 Pa. Super. 328, 657 A.2d 949 (1995).**

Truck driver who knew of propensity of radio to fall from overhead rack found to be seventy percent negligent for injuries sustained when radio fell from rack. Judgment for installer of radio affirmed. ***Dath v. Marano Truck Sales and Service, Inc.*, 437 Pa. Super. 571, 650 A.2d 901 (1994).**

Standard of care for a child is the exercise of ordinary care appropriate for a child. Driver and Borough not liable where child who darts out into street found seventy percent negligent. ***Smith v. Stribling*, 168 Pa. Cmwlth. 188, 649 A.2d 1003 (1994).**

Wife-plaintiff pedestrian struck by auto found 50% negligent. $5,000 award for wife-plaintiff adequate and $0 for husband-plaintiff supported by evidence. Order denying new trial affirmed. ***Nudelman v. Gilbride*, 436 Pa. Super. 44, 647 A.2d 233 (1994).**

Motorist injured in collision with portable generator. Damages reduced by 40% owing to plaintiff's negligence. Held: verdict sheet that allowed jury to list damages before deciding comparative negligence not reversible error. ***Floyd v. Philadelphia Electric Company*, 429 Pa. Super. 460, 632 A.2d 1314.**

Injured water skier brought action against operator of boat. Operator not liable. Doctrine of assumption of risk applicable in comparative negligence cases. ***Pagesh v. Ucman*, 403 Pa. Super. 549, 589 A.2d 747.**

Safety inspector injured in fall down elevator shaft. Held: fact that inspector proceeded to elevator through dark passageway did not raise his level of negligence to 51%. ***Ligon v. Middletown Area School District*, 136 Pa. Cmwlth. 566, 584 A.2d 376.**

Tenant injured in slip and fall on landlord's property. Tenant 58% negligent, landlord 42% negligent. Comparative negligence principles apply to implied warranty of habitability theory as well as negligence. ***Keck v. Doughman*, 392 Pa. Super. 127, 572 A.2d 724.**

Passenger injured when vehicle struck exit gate after hitting pothole on automobile dealer's lot. Dealer 60% negligent, driver 40% negligent. Remanded to determine delay damages. ***Kukowski v. Kukowski*, 358 Pa. Super. 172, 560 A.2d 222.**

Driver of vehicle that collided with tree and utility pole brought action against Commonwealth and landowner. Driver found 70% negligent, Commonwealth 30% negligent. Evidence of driver's blood alcohol level properly admitted to

Comparative negligence

show contributory negligence. ***Crosby v. Com., Dept. of Transp.,* 378 Pa. Super. 72, 548 A.2d 281.**

Patron injured while skating at roller skating rink. Defendant found 60% negligent, skater found 40% negligent. ***Berman v. Radnor Rolls, Inc.,* 374 Pa. Super. 118, 542 A.2d 525.**

Motorcycle driver injured in collision with automobile. Each party 50% negligent. Plaintiff entitled to collect 50% of his damages. ***Loper v. McGee,* 373 Pa. Super. 85, 540 A.2d 311.**

Motorcyclist struck by truck after crossing double yellow line in attempt to pass. Whether motorcycle rider was negligent was question for jury. Truck driver found 20% negligent, Motorcyclist found 80% negligent. ***Cervone v. Reading,* 371 Pa. Super. 279, 538 A.2d 16.**

Defendant unable to testify owing to injuries sustained in accident. Held: enactment of comparative negligence eliminated the presumption of due care arising in favor of a deceased or incapacitated defendant. ***Rice v. Shuman,* 513 Pa. 192, 519 A.2d 391.**

Under the Comparative Negligence Act, recovery by an injured plaintiff will be precluded only where plaintiff's negligence exceeds the combined negligence of all defendants. Each defendant is liable for his portion of negligence even if it is less than the negligence of plaintiff. ***Elder v. Orluck,* 511 Pa. 402, 515 A.2d 517.**

Rescuer injured during attempted rescue of driver of stopped automobile. Comparative Negligence Statute found to apply in cases involving rescue doctrine. Rescuer entitled to full recovery when rescue attempted in a reasonable manner. ***Pachesky v. Getz,* 353 Pa. Super. 505, 510 A.2d 776.**

Rear-end collision. Borough of Harrisville stopped traffic on state highway for Memorial Day parade. Alleged negligent traffic control (accident occurred before Tort Claims Act), negligence of striking vehicle, and negligence of plaintiff for defective tail lights. Jury found plaintiff 25% negligent, striking vehicle 60% negligent and Borough of Harrisville 15% negligent. Full analysis of Comparative Negligence Act as to issue of whether plaintiff found more negligent than a defendant can recover from that plaintiff. Held: yes, as long as plaintiff 50% or less at fault. ***Elder v. Orluck,* 334 Pa. Super. 329, 483 A.2d 474.**

In enacting the comparative negligence statute, the legislature did not intend to extend the application of the assumption of risk defense in cases that had been traditionally evaluated primarily according to contributory negligence principles. ***Fish v. Gosnell,* 316 Pa. Super. 565, 463 A.2d 1042 (1983).**

Handicapped plaintiff injured in her medical clinic parking lot. Fell on ice, fractured left hip. Charge on contributory negligence proper; charge on assumption or risk unnecessary and improper. Since fall on isolated ice patch between cars, proper *not* to charge on hills and ridges. Jury verdict $70,000—hip; $2,500—husband's loss of consortium. Reduced 35% for contributory negligence—$45,000 and $1,626. Affirmed. ***Carrender v. Fitterer,* 310 Pa. Super. 433, 456 A.2d 1013.**

Concurrent negligence

Fall down steps in darkened lavatory area of restaurant while searching for light switch, under facts here, does not constitute contributory negligence as a matter of law. Nonsuit removed. ***McNally v. Liebowitz,* 498 Pa. Super. 163, 445 A.2d 716.**

Where jury was confused as to how to present verdict in Jones Act case with setoff and comparative negligence, proper for judge to mold verdict. ***Richards v. Dravo Corp.,* 249 Pa. Super. 47, 375 A.2d 750.**

Comparative Negligence Act held to be applicable prospectively only—to be applied only to causes of actions arising on or after September 7, 1976. ***Costa v. Lair,* 241 Pa. Super. 517, 363 A.2d 1313.**

Concert patron

Concert goer injured in fall caused by hole in sidewalk at recreation area. Owner of area not immune under Recreation Use of Land and Water Act. ***Mills v. Commonwealth,* 145 Pa. Cmwlth. 558, 604 A.2d 755.**

Concurrent causation

Summary judgment reversed in case where plaintiff was injured by metal pole stump protruding from ground on housing authority property after she was pushed by a third party. Held: political subdivision can be liable despite the existence of a third party whose actions may constitute a concurrent cause of the injury. ***Wilson v. Philadelphia Housing Authority*, 735 A.2d 172 (Pa. Cmwlth. 1999).**

In automobile accident case by decedent's administrator against intoxicated driver and PennDOT, whether PennDOT's alleged negligence for improper road design and maintenance was substantial factor in accident was question for jury. Existence of two tortfeasors does not automatically excuse one or the other from liability. Question of concurrent or joint causation and determination of whether an act is so extraordinary as to constitute a superseding cause are for the jury. Order sustaining preliminary objections of PennDOT reversed. ***Powell v. Drumheller,* 539 Pa. 484, 653 A.2d 619 (1995).**

Concurrent negligence

Summary Judgment entered against plaintiff who was shot by a robber while a passenger on defendant's stopped train. Plaintiff alleged that defendant's trainman's failure to open the door of the train to allow plaintiff to escape before he was shot was a concurrent cause of his injury and that failure to act involved the operation of the motor vehicle. The Commonwealth Court distinguishes concurrent negligent acts from a negligent act by defendant and a criminal assault by a third party and also holds by implication that the failure to open the door was not "operation" of the motor vehicle. ***Greenleaf v. SEPTA,* 698 A.2d 170 (Pa. Cmwlth. 1997).**

Plaintiff was using a tire changing machine which exploded, causing tire and rim to strike him in the face. Verdict against Gulf Oil—owner of gas station, Duane Proctor—lessee of station, Seilon, Inc.—manufacturer of tire, and Calvin Hoffman—seller of tire. Verdict over in favor of Hoffman against Seilon. Verdict in favor of manufacturer of tire changing machine. Machine was old and worn, which

Condominium owner

was well-known to Gulf prior to its being given to Proctor. *Stewart v. Uniroyal,* **233 Pa. Super. 721, 339 A.2d 815.**

Condominium owner

Condominium association sued by owner who slipped and fell on accumulation of ice and snow between parked cars on the morning after the snow had fallen. After finding that the hills and ridges doctrine applied to the parties before it, the court determined that the condominium association's failure to remove the ice and snow from the parking lot before the cars had been moved the morning after a snow was nor unreasonable behavior. *Biernacki v. Presque Isle Condominiums Unit Owners Association,* **828 A.2d 1114 (Pa. Super. 2003).**

Condominium owner brought action against condominium association for damage caused by sewer backup. Compulsory nonsuit in favor of association upheld. *Smith v. King's Grant Condominium,* **418 Pa. Super. 260, 614 A.2d 261.**

Confidentiality

Patient, who signed an authorization to release her medical records for the calculation of medical expenses, brought claim for breach of confidentiality after medical practice disclosed her unrelated use of marijuana and unprescribed pain medication to her employer's workers' compensation carrier. At trial a jury awarded damages to the Plaintiff and the medical practice appealed on the basis that a breach of confidentiality was governed by a one-year statute of limitations. The Superior Court affirmed the trial court's holding denying the Defendant's motion for judgment not withstanding the verdict. The Pennsylvania Supreme Court affirmed, holding that a claim for breach of physician-patient confidentiality was governed by a two-year statute of limitations period. *Burger v. Blair Medical Associates, Inc.,* **964 A.2d 374 (2009).**

Consciously listening and observing

Minor plaintiff struck by defendant's train at a grade crossing—Supreme Court concluded that issues of visibility and warning were such as to make the matter one for the jury—jury could have found plaintiff consciously listening—evidence of lack of warning not negative and crossing one not affording a reasonable view—close case—strong dissent. *Fallon v. Penn Central Trans. Co.,* **444 Pa. 148, 279 A.2d 164.**

Consent

In a legal malpractice action based on negligence or contract, liability is not foreclosed by client's consent to settlement where agreement to settle was based on erroneous information from attorney. Superior Court's order reversing demurrer affirmed. *McMahon v. Shea,* **547 Pa. 124, 688 A.2d 1179 (1997).**

Plaintiff on entering hospital signed two consents for an operation—suit against operating doctor on an assault and battery claim and against hospital for negligence—nonsuits properly entered—consents sufficient on assault and battery charge and lack of expert testimony justified nonsuit in suit against hospital. *Chandler v. Cook,* **438 Pa. 447, 263 A.2d 794.**

Construction

Plaintiff had a serious back condition—he was advised that an exploratory operation was required—operation resulted in complete paralysis from the waist down—suit against neurosurgeon who operated on him—matter for jury as to whether consent given—verdict for plaintiff sustained on appeal. ***Gray v. Grunnagle***, **423 Pa. 144, 223 A.2d 663.**

Construction

Plaintiff, an employee of a subcontractor, brought a claim for negligence against the Defendant school district after he fell from a ladder when the decorative column he had leaned the ladder up against gave way. The trial court entered summary judgment for the defendant. The Commonwealth Court affirmed holding that a duty cannot be imposed upon a landowner if the defective condition was created by the work of the independent contractor. In addition, a landowner has no further liability where it turns work over to an independent contractor, who selects his own equipment and employees. ***Wombacher v. Greater Johnstown School District***, **20 A.3d 1240 (Pa. Cmwlth. 2011**).

Plaintiff filed negligence action against the defendant college, general contractor and subcontractor after he fell while climbing scaffolding erected by the subcontractor. A jury rendered a verdict against all three defendants. The Superior Court reversed and remanded for entry of judgment notwithstanding the verdict in favor of the college. On appeal the Superior Court affirmed its prior ruling holding that a property owner retaining a certain degree of authority over safety issues such as supervising and enforcing safety requirements or even imposing its own safety requirements does not constitute control sufficient to impose liability. In addition, regulating the use and access to a building is not sufficient to establish control regarding the manner or methods of the work being performed to impose liability. ***Beil v. Telesis Construction, Inc.***, **11 A.3d 456 (Pa. Super. 2011).**

Contractor brought suit against Defendant gas company for economic losses suffered when the company struck gas lines owned by the Defendant whose locations were improperly marked by an employee of the Defendant. The trial court dismissed the case based upon the economic loss doctrine on preliminary objections. The Superior Court affirmed. The Pennsylvania Supreme Court affirmed holding that the Defendant was not liable for economic losses under the Pennsylvania One Call Act as the Plaintiff had not suffered any personal injury or loss of property, but only economic damages. ***Excavation Technologies, Inc. v. Columbia Gas Company of Pennsylvania***, **985 A.2d 840 (Pa. 2009)**.

Administratrix sued Pennsylvania Turnpike Commission and Trumbull Corporation for failing to provide a safe work environment after her husband was killed while driving an unfamiliar truck type on the job site upon the order of his superiors. The court held; 1. That a possessor of land owes a duty of care to warn or correct dangers on his land unknown to a contractor or his employees; 2. Inspection of ongoing work at a construction site by a landowner is not evidence of control; 3. Driving a truck on a haul road is not a peculiar risk imparting liability onto a landowner. ***Farabaugh v. Pennsylvania Turnpike Commission***, **590 Pa. 46, 911 A.2d 1264 (2006).**

Construction

Bridge ironworker was injured when he fell from a construction site without a safety net or a connected safety line. In suit against the general contractor, summary judgment was entered because the contractors had no presence at the site and no contractual obligation to oversee safety standards and so no duty to plaintiff. Only subcontractor, plaintiff's employer, had a duty to insure his safety and in the event of a breach, workman's compensation provided recovery. ***Leonard v. Com., Dept. of Transp.*, 565 Pa. 101, 771 A.2d 1238 (Pa. 2001).**

Plaintiff injured when he fell from an I-beam at a PennDOT highway construction project. He alleged that general contractor and I-beam supplier were responsible to insure a safe workplace for him. Held: absent control over the workplace, general contractor and supplier have no duty to employees of other subcontractors. ***Leonard v. Com., Dept. of Transp.*, 723 A.2d 735 (Pa. Cmwlth. 1999).**

Plaintiffs appeal from grant of summary judgment to defendant PennDOT which was based on plaintiff's failure to procure expert report to support their claim that PennDOT was negligent in not placing warning signs in advance of construction zone. PennDOT argued successfully that it was immune from suit under Sovereign Immunity Act in that placement of warning signs was not necessary to insure safe condition of real estate for its intended use. Reversed by Commonwealth Court. Necessity of warning signs advising of stopped traffic on interstate highway in advance of traffic construction is within everyday knowledge of jury and so does not require expert testimony. Whether lack of warning signs, as described, constitutes dangerous condition of state maintained roadway for its intended purpose is proper question for jury. ***Young v. Com., Dept. of Transp.*, 714 A.2d 475 (Pa. Cmwlth. 1998).**

Summary judgment reversed where plaintiff insulation installer on stilts held not to have assumed the risk of slipping on construction debris left at job site by defendants. Assumption of risk should only preclude recovery where it is beyond question that the plaintiff voluntarily and knowingly proceeded in the face of an obvious and dangerous condition. ***Barrett v. Fredavid Builders, Inc.*, 454 Pa. Super. 162, 685 A.2d 129 (1996).**

Driver may proceed with suit against Commonwealth for common law damages based on emotional and psychological distress following accident with PennDOT construction vehicle. ***Tomikel v. Com., Dept. of Transp.*, ___ Pa. Cmwlth. ___, 658 A.2d 861 (1995).**

Six-year statute of limitations for latent defect in construction case runs from date injured party becomes aware, or by exercise of reasonable diligence should have become aware, of the defect. ***Romeo & Sons, Inc. v. P.C. Yezbak & Son, Inc.*, 539 Pa. 390, 652 A.2d 830 (1995).**

Architect has no duty to warn contractor employees of visible overhead power lines that came into contact with metal scaffolding killing or injuring workers. Summary judgment in favor of architect affirmed. ***Frampton v. Dauphin Distribution Services Co.*, 436 Pa. Super. 486, 648 A.2d 326 (1994).**

Continuing to operate truck

In action by personal representative of plumbing contractor killed in cave-in at construction site, governmental immunity applies because plaintiff presented no proof that city exercised sufficient custody and control over site. Sanction order precluding city's filing of answer for failure to comply with discovery order does not compel waiver of real property exception to governmental immunity. Summary judgment in favor of city affirmed. *Santori v. Snyder,* **165 Pa. Cmwlth. 505, 645 A.2d 443 (1994).**

Child injured in street by car after being forced to leave sidewalk due to city-placed barricade. City not liable under exception to Political Subdivision Tort Claims Act because injuries not caused by care, custody, or control of real property or dangerous condition of sidewalk. *Kiley by Kiley v. City of Philadelphia,* **537 Pa. 502, 645 A.2d 184 (1994).**

Purchaser of condominium brought action against builder for negligent construction. Builder not liable for negligence. Purely economic damages not recoverable. *Spivack v. Berks Ridge Corporation, Inc.,* **402 Pa. Super. 73, 586 A.2d 402.**

Contagious disease

Physician who treated woman with highly contagious, but common, viral infection has a duty to third persons to warn the patient about the risks associated with the disease, so patient may inform third persons who might come in contact with her about the risks. Order granting summary judgment in favor of defendants reversed and remanded to allow estate of minor who died as a result of coming into contact with contagious patient to proceed to trial. *Troxel v. A.I. DuPont Institute,* **450 Pa. Super. 71, 675 A.2d 314 (1996).**

Continuing negligence

Original medical malpractice case alleged treatment on one date only. At trial, before the evidence, attempted amendment to allege continuing treatment and malpractice. Permitted as extension of existing claim. *Laursen v. General Hospital of Monroe Co.,* **494 Pa. 238, 431 A.2d 237.**

Continuing to look

Operator observing approaching car but failing to continue to look during last 50 feet from intersection—making left turn—collision—no recovery—guilty of contributory negligence per se. *Leasure v. Heller,* **436 Pa. 108, 258 A.2d 855.**

Section 1014 (c) and 1016 (a) of the Motor Vehicle Code construed to require motorist on a stop street to yield right of way to vehicles on through highway—failing to look to observe approaching vehicles—guilty of contributory negligence as a matter of law. *Helfrich v. Brown,* **213 Pa. Super. 463, 249 A.2d 778.**

Continuing to operate truck

Defendant driver aware that brakes on his heavily loaded truck were defective and on application would not control speed of vehicle—continuing to operate truck with opportunity to have pulled to side of road—collision—new trial granted

Contract for specific result or cure

after verdict for defendant—not an abuse of discretion. *Austin v. Ridge*, 435 Pa. 1, 255 A.2d 123.

Contract for specific result or cure

Plaintiff who alleged that failed tubal ligation resulted in pregnancy was pursuing claim for breach of an express oral contract to provide a specific result—no future pregnancies. The Health Care Services Malpractice Act (40 P.S. §1301.606) requires that any contract for a specific cure or result must be in writing and because plaintiff's complaint alleged only breach of an oral contract, there can be no recovery. *Edwards v. Germantown Hospital*, 736 A.2d 612 (Pa. Super. 1999).

Contractors

Subcontractor brought negligence action against general contractor after falling 14 feet at a construction site. A jury found in favor of the subcontractor on the basis he was an independent contractor. The Superior Court affirmed. The Pennsylvania Supreme Court reversed holding that the statutory employer doctrine provided immunity for general contractors from suit by their subcontractors for injuries on the job based upon the Workers' Compensation Act. An independent contractor must contract with the owner of the property. *Patton v. Worthington Associates, Inc.*, 89 A.3d 643 (Pa. 2014).

Plaintiff subcontractor employee brought action against Defendant contractor after he was run over by a dump truck. Trial court granted summary judgment for the Defendant. The Superior Court reversed holding that there was a genuine issue of material fact as to whether the Defendant had a right to control the Plaintiff's work to preclude liability based upon the borrowed servant doctrine. *Shamis v. Moon*, 81 A.3d 962 (Pa. Super. 2013).

Plaintiff subcontractor brought negligence claim for injuries suffered in a fall against general contractor after he was injured when he drove a scissor lift into a hole in the floor at the construction site. A jury found in favor of the Plaintiff. The Superior Court affirmed holding that as the jury found, the Plaintiff was an independent contractor and the Defendant was not immune based upon the statutory employer defense. *Patton v. Worthington Associates, Inc.*, 43 A.3d 479 (Pa. Super. 2012).

In suit for injuries sustained by wife plaintiff against PennDOT and PennDOT contractor after settlement by PennDOT, held that contractor was not entitled to "government contractor defense" of governmental immunity when the work performed was not in accordance with government specifications. *Coolbaugh v. Com. of Pa., Dept. of Transportation*, 816 A.2 307 (Pa. Super. 2003).

Bridge ironworker was injured when he fell from a construction site without a safety net or a connected safety line. In suit against the general contractor, summary judgment was entered because the contractors had no presence at the site and no contractual obligation to oversee safety standards and so no duty to plaintiff. Only subcontractor, plaintiff's employer, had a duty to insure his safety and in the event of a breach, workman's compensation provided recovery. *Leonard v. Com., Dept. of Transp.*, 771 A.2d 1238 (Pa. 2001).

Contractors

Peculiar risk doctrine did not apply to make contractor liable for injuries sustained by subcontractor's employee who fell from roof of building on which he was working where both contractor and subcontractor were aware of dangerous condition of roof. ***Edwards v. Franklin and Marshall College*, 444 Pa. Super. 1, 663 A.2d 187 (1995).**

Pedestrian killed while crossing railroad tracks in non-designated area. Held: contractor out of possession may be liable for harm to third persons caused by defects in property. Whether deceased was more than 50% negligent was question for jury. ***Gilbert v. Consolidated Rail Corporation*, 154 Pa. Cmwlth. 249, 623 A.2d 873.**

Employee of contractor injured by crane operated by lessor-supplier of crane. Held: contractor not required to indemnify lessor. ***Bester v. Essex Crane Rental Corporation*, 422 Pa. Super. 178, 619 A.2d 304.**

Employee of contractor killed in elevator accident. Held: plant owner not entitled to indemnification from contractor. ***Hershey Foods Corporation v. General Electric Service Co.*, 422 Pa. Super. 143, 619 A.2d 285.**

Motorist injured when attempting to avoid automobile exiting from health care center. Center and architect and contractor who undertook renovations of center not liable. Elimination of second exit not cause of accident. ***Novack v. Jeannette District Memorial Hospital*, 410 Pa. Super. 603, 600 A.2d 616.**

Property owner brought action against township and firm contracted to act as sewage enforcement officer for negligently issuing permit. Township immune. Contractor not immune. ***Smith v. Porter Township*, 141 Pa. Cmwlth. 244, 595 A.2d 693.**

Commonwealth brought action against contractor and insurance company to defend and indemnify Transportation Department for accident that occurred on road where contractor made repairs. Defendants not liable. Department waived rights when it paid contractor in full. ***Com., Dept. of Transp. v. American States Insurance Company*, 138 Pa. Cmwlth. 11, 588 A.2d 1320.**

Truck driver injured when trailer struck bridge parapet in highway construction area. Held: contractor not liable. Government contractor defense applicable. ***DiBuono v. A. Barletta & Sons, Inc.*, 127 Pa. Cmwlth. 1, 560 A.2d 893.**

Contractor built a road in accordance with specifications with 6 inch drop-off to berm. Plaintiff was killed when car ran off road and he allegedly lost control due to drop-off. Summary judgment in favor of contractor reversed. Fact that contractor fulfilled contract does not relieve him of liability to third persons for creating a dangerous condition. ***St. Clair v. B & L Paving*, 270 Pa. Super. 277, 411 A.2d 525.**

Plaintiff fell while working at construction site—walking on wall which was incomplete and a portion gave way. Nonsuit affirmed by equally divided court. Plaintiff failed to show breach of industry standards, negligence in scheduling work or knowledge by defendants that he would be working on Saturday. Dissent felt con-

Contributory cause

tractor knew or should have known that wall was left in dangerous condition. ***McKenzie v. Cost Brothers*, 260 Pa. Super. 295, 394 A.2d 559.**

Plaintiff working remodeling building when ceiling installed 26 years earlier fell on him. Suit against company which designed and installed ceiling plus all owners from that time to time of injury. Motion for summary judgment by current owner under 12 P.S. §65.1 *et seq.,* which limits time for bringing suits to 12 years for injuries arising out of deficiencies in design, construction, etc., of improvements to real property against person performing construction or furnishing design. Owner, however, not protected by statute. Order granting motion reversed. ***Leach v. P.S.F.S.*, 234 Pa. Super. 486, 340 A.2d 491.**

Contractor doing work in fire house, removed brass pole from living quarters to ground floor and, then firemen covered hole with rug to keep dust down. Plaintiff, a fireman, was adjusting the rug and fell through hole. Verdict for plaintiff, affirmed. §343 of Restatement (2d) Torts—possessor liable where he should expect that invitees will fail to protect themselves against a danger. ***Bowman v. Fretts and Leeper Constr. Co.*, 227 Pa. Super. 347, 322 A.2d 719.**

An employee of a carpenter subcontractor injured by reason of improper shoring—general contractor had employed a subcontractor to do excavation work—this subcontractor employed a highlift truck and operator—Held: a verdict solely against excavating subcontractor proper as the operator was not a borrowed or loaned employee—whether general contractor was a statutory employer not passed upon appeal. ***Hamler v. Waldron et al.*, 445 Pa. 262, 284 A.2d 725.**

Contributory cause

Plaintiffs' decedent died as a result of injuries sustained in a motor vehicle accident when the driver, who was unlicensed and intoxicated, lost control of the vehicle. In suit against the bar, the driver and the owner of the car, held that owner was vicariously liable for negligence of driver even though owner's failure to insure that driver was licensed when there was reasonable cause to suspect lack of license was not a substantial factor in harm. Trial court also found driver liable and determined that plaintiffs' decedent was 20% negligent. Good discussion of vicarious liability as distinguished from contributory negligence. ***Terwilliger v. Kitchen*, 781 A.2d 1201 (Pa. Super. 2001)**.

Plaintiff allegedly struck on head by a stone from defendant's construction work—court below in error in charging that an ulcerous condition must have resulted without concurrence of a contributing cause—defendant only relieved if contributing cause would have produced the injury complained of independently of defendant's negligence. ***Boushell et ux. v. J. H. Beers, Inc.*, 215 Pa. Super. 439, 258 A.2d 682.**

Contributory negligence: Falling

Seaman brought action against employer for injuries suffered in fall down ladder. Held: contributory negligence need be only featherweight causative factor. ***Bunting v. Sun Company, Inc.*, 434 Pa. Super. 404, 643 A.2d 1085**.

Contributory negligence: Legal malpractice

Fall down steps in darkened lavatory area of restaurant while searching for light switch. Under facts here, no contributory negligence as a matter of law. Nonsuit removed. *McNally v. Liebowitz,* **498 Pa. 163, 445 A.2d 716.**

Plaintiff fell on deteriorated sidewalk. Had fallen in essentially the same spot 5 days earlier. Verdict for plaintiff reduced by 15% for comparative negligence. Charge proper that if plaintiff more than 50% negligent, she could not recover. Only in rare case should jury not consider apportionment of negligence. *Peair v. Home Assoc. of Enola,* **287 Pa. Super. 400, 430 A.2d 665.**

Compulsory nonsuit affirmed where patron at restaurant went to restroom area, entered unlit area and fell down steps. *McNally v. Liebowitz,* **274 Pa. Super. 386, 418 A.2d 460.**

Pedestrian-tenant fell on sidewalk defect which had been present for some time, although covered by leaves at time of accident. Compulsory nonsuit reversed. For jury whether plaintiff contributorily negligent. *Landy v. Romeo,* **274 Pa. Super. 75, 417 A.2d 1260.**

Fall due to water on restroom floor. Evidence that plaintiff had walked through the water upon entering restroom. Error not to charge on contributory negligence. *McCullough v. Monroeville Home Assoc.,* **270 Pa. Super. 428, 411 A.2d 794.**

Milk hauler slipped on manure on steps in milking pit of farm where he picked up milk. Hauler was a farmer familiar that manure was often in milking areas. Had descended steps a few minutes before accident but did not see the manure. Held: contributorily negligent as a matter of law. *Jewell v. Beckstine,* **255 Pa. Super. 238, 386 A.2d 597.**

Summary judgment granted and affirmed against woman who fell down dark stairs of hall during wedding reception. Contributorily negligent as a matter of law. *Just v. Sons of Italy Hall,* **240 Pa. Super. 416, 368 A.2d 308.**

Plaintiff fell while erecting a coal hopper. Contributory negligence of plaintiff in failing to use safety belt was for jury as there was testimony that it was not the custom to use one in job plaintiff was doing. Verdict for plaintiff on liability affirmed. *Lambert v. PBI Industries,* **244 Pa. Super. 118, 366 A.2d 944.**

Plaintiff pedestrian fell while crossing a bridge maintained by Port Authority—notice that bridge was closed to pedestrians—notice frequently thrown down and bridge was notoriously used by pedestrians—verdict for plaintiff sustained—issue of contributory negligence was for the jury. *Niemiec v. Allegheny County Port Authority et al.,* **223 Pa. Super. 435, 302 A.2d 439.**

Contributory negligence: Legal malpractice

In legal malpractice case, any contributory negligence of plaintiff client is a complete bar to recovery because the comparative negligence act only applies to cases involving death, injury or damage to tangible property. *Gorski v. Smith,* **812 A.2d 683 (Pa. Super. 2003).**

Contributory negligence: Medical malpractice

Contributory negligence: Medical malpractice

Plaintiff brought suit against his physician and hospital for delaying the diagnosis of his colon cancer. The appellate court affirmed the trial court's decision finding that there was no expert testimony that plaintiff's missing several appointments or failing to follow the doctor's prescribed colonoscopy plan contributed to the delay in his diagnosis. ***Rose v. Annabi*, 934 A.2d 743 (Pa. Super. 2007).**

Defendant physician who did not raise defense of plaintiffs' decedent's contributory negligence and record devoid of evidence of fact which might support contributory negligence prohibit charging jury with law on that defense. Decedent's failure to take actions recommended by physician were not substantial factors in causing his death. "It is not contributory negligence to fail to guard against the lack of ordinary care by another." ***Angelo v. Diamontoni*, 871 A.2d 1276 (Pa. Super. 2005).**

Contributory negligence: Miscellaneous

Contributory negligence of husband and wife physicians who sued their accountant for negligence in preparation of their corporate and personal tax returns precluded recovery, particularly in light of their criminal convictions for tax fraud. ***Columbia Medical Group v. Herring & Roll, P.C.*, 829 A.2d 1184 (Pa. Super. 2003).**

Savings and loan brought action against prothonotary and office of prothonotary for failure to index writ of revival of judgment. Prothonotary not personally liable for negligence of employees. Office of prothonotary not liable owing to plaintiff's contributory negligence. ***Commonwealth Federal Savings and Loan Association v. Pettit,* 137 Pa. Cmwlth. 523, 586 A.2d 1021.**

Minor died of drowning after drinking liquor bought by other minor. Held: 1) defense of contributory negligence permitted; 2) testimony that deceased consumed alcohol admissible; 3) testimony that purchaser appeared to be in mid-twenties admissible. ***Barrie v. Pennsylvania Liquor Control Board,* 137 Pa. Cmwlth. 514, 586 A.2d 1017.**

Plaintiff, then 16, injured during supervised summer football practice. No protective gear worn. Trial court held that plaintiff assumed risk as a matter of law. On appeal, assumption of risk doctrine abolished except where specifically preserved by statute. Issues should be limited to negligence and contributory negligence. ***Rutter v. Northeastern Beaver School,* 496 Pa. 590, 437 A.2d 1198.**

1972 accident. Pedestrian chose to cross street from behind an illegally parked city truck. Could have walked around truck on sidewalk. Struck in street by auto. Plaintiff held to be contributorily negligent as a matter of law. ***Stowe v. Booker & City of Philadelphia,* 284 Pa. Super. 53, 424 A.2d 1388.**

Plaintiff using tire changing machine which exploded causing tire and rim to strike him in face. Contributory negligence for jury even where machine in an obviously worn condition. §§388 and 392 of Restatement (2d) Torts applicable. ***Stewart v. Uniroyal, Inc.,* 233 Pa. Super. 721, 339 A.2d 815.**

Contributory negligence: Motor vehicles

The alleged contributory negligence of the plaintiff must be proximate to the occurrence—cases which have suggested a different rule repudiated and overruled. ***McCay v. Phila. Electric Co.*, 447 Pa. 490, 291 A.2d 759.**

Superior Court recognized change in the interpretation of contributory negligence—plaintiff's negligence to bar recovery must be a proximate cause. ***Harrison v. Nichols*, 219 Pa. Super. 428, 281 A.2d 696.**

Contributory negligence: Motor vehicles

Plaintiff who recovers 51% of verdict amount after jury determination that plaintiff was 49% negligent is entitled to delay damages calculated on molded verdict rather than full verdict. Jury verdict affirmed. ***Liberty v. Geneva College*, 456 Pa. Super. 544, 690 A.2d 1243 (1997).**

In wrongful death and survival action by widow of motorist whose automobile crossed opposing lane and left highway, PennDOT entitled to jury charge on contributory negligence where no evidence presented regarding external cause of accident. Following plaintiff's inquiry into other causes of accident, State Trooper permitted to testify as to possibility of driver having fallen asleep. ***Burkholz v. Com., Dept. of Transp.*, ___ Pa. Cmwlth. ___, 667 A.2d 513 (1995).**

In action by passenger against PennDOT for negligent design of road, judgment for PennDOT affirmed where plaintiff passenger determined to be negligent by exposing herself to an unreasonable risk in riding with a known intoxicated driver. Even minimal evidence of contributory negligence requires a charge on the issue. ***Karchner v. Flaim*, ___ Pa. Cmwlth. ___, 661 A.2d 928 (1995).**

Passenger who fell asleep was injured in automobile accident. The fact that passenger participated in all-night outing was admissible to show that she was contributorily negligent. ***Hill v. Reynolds*, 384 Pa. Super. 34, 557 A.2d 759.**

Seventeen-year old plaintiff riding on pickup truck running board—fell from truck. Cause of action prior to Comparative Negligence Act. Held: plaintiff contributorily negligent as matter of law. Proper holding, but new trial awarded. Jury to determine wanton and reckless conduct of plaintiff driver, or whether he had last clear chance to avoid injury. ***Hill v. Crawford*, 308 Pa. Super. 502, 454 A.2d 647.**

Pedestrian who testifies that he stepped off curb in middle of block after looking and seeing nothing, properly nonsuited. No evidence of negligence and clear contribution. ***Barney v. Foradas*, 305 Pa. Super. 404, 451 A.2d 710.**

Jury verdict $200,000. Crush injury—permanent disability to right heel of 53 year old. Male warehouse employee in dark parking lot, guiding tractor-trailer rigs in by voice. Had his hand on rig. Fell in parking lot hole. Issue of plaintiff's contributory negligence for jury. ***McDevitt v. Terminal Warehouse Co.*, 304 Pa. Super. 438, 450 A.2d 991.**

Bus driver waved plaintiff through intersection. Plaintiff had stopped for stop sign on cross street. Bus then moved prematurely and struck car. Plaintiff not

Contributory negligence: Motor vehicles

under duty to continue looking at bus once waved on. *Farley v. SEPTA,* **279 Pa. Super. 570, 421 A.2d 346.**

Plaintiff saw truck parked on private drive. Truck started moving and came into street causing collision. Plaintiff's contributory negligence for jury. *Fauzer v. Phila. Gas Works,* **279 Pa. Super. 310, 420 A.2d 1349.**

Failure of passenger in car to protest speed, standing alone, not evidence of contributory negligence. No evidence that he knew how fast vehicle was going, that he was a licensed driver, or knew how to operate car. *Palmer v. Brest,* **254 Pa. Super. 532, 386 A.2d 77.**

Where pedestrian crossed in middle of block in front of parked truck, which truck then started up striking pedestrian, contributory negligence for jury. Error to grant nonsuit on finding that pedestrian contributorily negligent as matter of law. *Lavely v. Wolota*, **253 Pa. Super. 196, 384 A.2d 1298.**

Plaintiff driving auto through intersection with green light. Construction barrier obstructed her view. Truck driven by defendant went through red light and struck plaintiff's car. Error for court below to hold plaintiff contributorily negligent. *Deer v. City of Pittsburgh,* **240 Pa. Super. 19, 367 A.2d 1119.**

Plaintiff standing on highway for about 10 minutes talking to driver of stopped auto when struck by truck. Night—plaintiff wearing dark clothes. Finding that plaintiff was contributorily negligent affirmed. *Trayer v. King,* **241 Pa. Super. 86, 359 A.2d 800.**

Defendant driving on turnpike when suddenly went into fog bank allegedly caused by cooling tower alongside road. Defendant jammed on brakes, skidded into opposite lanes and stopped at 90 degree angle to oncoming traffic when car stalled. Plaintiff encountered fog and slowed, but didn't see defendant's car until moment before impact. Contributory negligence for jury. Verdict for plaintiff sustained. *Westerman v. Stout, et al.,* **237 Pa. Super. 195, 335 A.2d 741.**

Plaintiff travelling on street which ends at "T" intersection. Defendant travelling on cross street. All three approaches have stop signs. Plaintiff stopped at stop sign with intention of turning left—looked both ways and, seeing nothing, proceeded. When turn almost completed, struck in rear by defendant who went through stop sign. Lower court entered compulsory nonsuit holding plaintiff contributorily negligent as a matter of law for failing to look again to his right before entering intersection. Reversed, new trial ordered. *Zumbo v. Ellis,* **232 Pa. Super. 566, 334 A.2d 770.**

Head on collision. One driver testified that he remembered nothing but being in proper lane shortly before accident. Other driver said he saw oncoming car in wrong lane fifty feet away and tried to swerve. Passenger in his car and police photos confirmed. Error to charge on contributory negligence of swerving driver. *Kulp v. Hess,* **227 Pa. Super. 603, 323 A.2d 217.**

Boy of 7 years and 3 months struck by car when allegedly he dashed into street to avoid a dog—verdict for defendant sustained on appeal by an equally divid-

Contributory negligence: Motor vehicles

ed court—dissenting opinion urged that charge should have covered sudden emergency and whether conduct of boy reasonable, citing Section 472 of Restatement (2d) Torts. ***Furby v. Novak*, 224 Pa. Super. 44, 302 A.2d 507.**

Minor plaintiff pedestrian standing on side of road where no sidewalk existed and was soliciting a ride—friendly vehicle stopped for him and while proceeding on right side of road to board same with back to defendant's vehicle was struck by same—Held: court below in error in granting nonsuit—minor plaintiff could not under the circumstances be held guilty of contributory negligence as a matter of law. ***South v. Gray*, 223 Pa. Super. 442, 302 A.2d 459.**

Continuing to operate a car at night after aware of a dust or cloud bank and colliding with an overturned rig in the highway is clear evidence of contributory negligence—nonsuit proper. ***Hollern v. Verhovsek*, 220 Pa. Super. 343, 287 A.2d 145.**

Plaintiff made a test of a snowmobile furnished by defendant—injured as a result of the condition of the track—court below treated plaintiff as testing a known danger and entered a nonsuit—case really involved an issue of contributory negligence and was for jury. ***Watson v. Zanotti Motor Co.*, 219 Pa. Super. 96, 280 A.2d 670.**

Plaintiff's truck went off a bridge owned and maintained allegedly defectively by defendant—court not in error in charging jury that any contributory negligence of plaintiff must be a proximate cause of the occurrence—doctrine of *Crane v. Neal* (389 Pa. 329) inferentially repudiated. ***Cebulskie v. Lehigh Valley R. R. Co.*, 441 Pa. 230, 272 A.2d 171.**

Plaintiff struck twice by two different cars—interval between first and second collision in dispute—for jury to determine whether sufficient time had elapsed to relieve plaintiff of contributory negligence as to claim against operator of second colliding car. ***Nebel v. Mauk*, 434 Pa. 315, 253 A.2d 249.**

Plaintiff testified in one instance that he did not look to his right until he was 2 or 3 feet over center of highway and in two other instances he testified that he looked as he reached the center of the highway—not confronted with the contradictions—entitled to go to the jury to reconcile—granting judgment *n.o.v.* in error. ***Gillingham v. Patz*, 429 Pa. 308, 239 A.2d 287.**

Three car chain collision—plaintiff's car in middle—car ahead stopped—plaintiff's car stopped allegedly very suddenly—defendant's car (the 3rd in line) collided with plaintiff's car—error for trial judge to remove question of plaintiff's possible contributory negligence from the jury—new trial granted. ***Toff v. Rohde*, 208 Pa. Super. 411, 222 A.2d 434.**

Plaintiff attempted to enter on street side of a car probably double parked in roadway—struck by defendant's car—proper to submit issue of contributory negligence to the jury—verdict for defendant—refusal of new trial motion proper. ***Prince v. McNeal*, 421 Pa. 126, 218 A.2d 775.**

Contributory negligence: Real estate

Contributory negligence: Real estate

Business invitee, a serviceman, not required to make an independent investigation to determine location of the thermostat controlling air conditioning—could rely on assumption defendant's general manager knew proper location of control—error to enter judgment on pleadings. *Eckborg v. Hyde-Murphy Co.,* **442 Pa. 283, 276 A.2d 513.**

Decedent assumed an awkward position in removing a spouting—contacting electrical line—evidence as to whether safer method and position should have been taken not sufficient evidence of contributory negligence to take the case from the jury. *Groh v. Phila. Electric Co.,* **441 Pa. 345, 271 A.2d 265.**

Control

Order granting summary judgment in favor of landowners and independent contractor-employer of injured trench digger affirmed. Injured employee may not recover against landowner when independent contractor has control of property on which trench was being dug and there was no "peculiar risk" to the trench digging operation of which the landowner had greater knowledge than the injured person. *Motter v. Meadows Limited Partnership,* **451 Pa. Super. 520, 680 A.2d 887 (1996).**

Plaintiffs pouring concrete in warehouse when recently constructed wall fell on them. Question of control as to owner. Whether he planned or designed wall in question and retained sufficient control over the project. Jury question. *Hargrove v. Frommeyer,* **229 Pa. Super. 298, 323 A.2d 300.**

Owner purchased building and hired contractors to renovate. His children seen playing on site and workmen complained to owner. Plaintiff injured when sixteen year old child of owner dropped staircase section on him. §414 of Restatement (2d) Torts—evidence that owner did exercise control over project. Verdict against owner. Granting of judgment *n.o.v.* as to owner reversed and verdict reinstated. Remanded for consideration of motion for new trial which had not been considered. *Byrd v. Merwin,* **456 Pa. 516, 317 A.2d 280.**

Control of vehicle

Cross over head-on accident. Verdict for defendant affirmed. Defendant testified that he pulled to berm to avoid accident in his lane, then tried to swerve around telephone pole when he lost control of his car, crossing four lanes of roadway and striking plaintiff. Although driver who crosses center line of highway is negligent *per se,* this can be rebutted by competent evidence that vehicle was there through no negligence on defendant's part. *Farelli v. Marko,* **349 Pa. Super. 102, 502 A.2d 1293.**

Plaintiff drove car over curb, across sidewalk, over six-inch retaining wall, through cyclone fence and into creek, in which he drowned. Held: City of Chester had no duty to maintain fence of such strength to withstand impact of car going in excess of 25 m.p.h. Events here so extraordinary as to be legally unforeseeable. *Merritt v. City of Chester,* **344 Pa. Super. 505, 496 A.2d 1220.**

Plaintiff-decedent in restaurant parking lot, at night went on wrong path with car, driving into canal, and drowned. Jury verdict $550,000 for wrongful death and $500,000 survival. ***Ehehalt v. Nyari O'Dette, Inc.,* 85 Pa. Cmwlth. 94, 481 A.2d 365.**

Plaintiff backed car into center of street on steep grade and stopped in center of street to talk. Defendant came over top of hill with clear view to plaintiff of 300 to 400 feet, yet struck plaintiff's car broadside. Night. Vehicle Code requires high beams to shine 350 feet. Defendant claimed lights on high beam. Verdict for plaintiff affirmed. ***Farbacher v. Frank,* 228 Pa. Super. 35, 323 A.2d 233.**

Driver veered slightly to right to allow car to pass in opposite direction at night and struck unlighted, unmarked utility pole. For jury as to negligence of driver and utility company. ***Scheel v. Tremblay and Phila. Electric Co.,* 226 Pa. Super. 45, 312 A.2d 45.**

Plaintiff driving at approximately 50 miles per hour at night—colliding with an overturned rig in highway—testimony established that he saw a warning cloud of dust a sufficient distance away to have enabled him to stop—violation of section 1002 of the Vehicle Code as to operation of a vehicle within assured clear distance—nonsuit properly granted. ***Hollern v. Verhovsek,* 220 Pa. Super. 343, 287 A.2d 145.**

Controlled Substance, Drug, Device, and Cosmetics Act

Hospital's duty to control access to drugs pursuant to the Controlled Substance, Drug, Device and Cosmetics Act, which classifies and controls access to drugs for protection of public at large, does not create duty to individual doctor employed by hospital who is, without knowledge of hospital, abusing drugs. ***Campo v. St. Luke's Hospital*, 755 A.2d 20 (Pa. Super. 2000).**

Convenience store

Patron did not assume risk of injury when she observed wet floor immediately before stepping on to it and falling. Nonsuit reversed. ***Hardy v. Southland Corporation,* 435 Pa. Super. 237, 645 A.2d 839 (1994).**

Conveyor belt

Workman injured when conveyor belt on which he was standing suddenly started, causing him to fall. Grant of motion for summary judgment in favor of contractor who installed electrical safety devices reversed. Held: material act issue as to emergency stop button and duty owed to third person other than parties to contract. ***Hess v. Fuellgraf Electric Co.,* 350 Pa. Super. 235, 504 A.2d 332.**

Coroner

A non-physician coroner properly qualified by experience is capable of testifying as to the time of death in an administrator's action against tavern for the death of patron. ***Miller v. Brass Rail Tavern, Inc.,* 541 Pa. 474, 664 A.2d 525 (1995).**

Corporate liability

Driver killed in one-car accident after being served alcohol. Held: non-physician coroner not competent to testify as to time of death. ***Miller v. Brass Rail Tavern, Inc.*, 434 Pa. Super. 383, 643 A.2d 694.**

Corporate liability

Estate of nursing home resident brought a wrongful death action against a nursing home for causing the death of a patient due to substandard care. A jury found against the nursing home on the basis of corporate and vicarious liability. The Superior Court upheld the trial court's decision holding that a nursing home was analogous to a hospital and it could be held liable under a theory of corporate negligence due to a failure to provide adequate staffing. ***Scampone v. Grane Healthcare Company*, 2010 Pa. Super. 124 (Pa. Super. 2010).**

Plaintiff appealed trial court's judgment of non pros for plaintiff's failure to file a certificate of merit in her action against defendant hospital for being sexually assaulted during her hospitalization. Appellate court reversed, holding that a certificate of merit is warranted only for claims raising questions involving medical judgment beyond the realm of common knowledge and experience. ***Smith v. Friends Hospital*, 928 A.2d 1072 (Pa. Super. 2007).**

Verdict in favor of plaintiff affirmed on appeal by physician who negligently applied splint to plaintiff's calf which caused burn or pressure sore which required plastic surgery to repair. Good analysis of elements of negligence and causation in medical malpractice case. "Corporate negligence" of hospital for physician's negligence not expanded to include corporate medical practice negligence for negligence of physician who was a member of the practice. ***Sutherland v. Monongahela Valley Hospital*, 856 A.2d 55 (Pa. Super. 2004).**

Action to recover for death of child 11 months after birth where death caused by negligent failure to diagnose and act on dangerous condition *in utero* immediately before birth. Evidence to establish "corporate liability" of hospital under *Thompson v. Nason Hospital* , 527 Pa. 330, 591 A.2d 703 (1991) must be provided in the form of expert testimony where the negligence is not obvious but need not contain "magic words." The substance of all the expert testimony will be considered as a whole. The evidence must establish that the hospital, in its own duty to the patient, deviated from the accepted standard of care and that that deviation was a substantial factor in causing the harm to the plaintiff. ***Welsh v. Bulger*, 698 A.2d 581 (Pa. 1997).**

Sovereign immunity precludes a cause of action based on corporate liability against Commonwealth medical facilities. Suit against Commonwealth medical facility only, and not against medical care providers individually, is not included within the medical-professional liability exception to sovereign immunity. ***Moser v. Heistand*, 545 Pa. 554, 681 A.2d 1322 (1996).**

In negligence action against corporate defendant and officers, officers are not liable for failing to maintain clean bathroom absent proof of their participation in creating or allowing continued existence of dangerous condition. Party's failure to answer request for admission that states a conclusion of law does not establish

Crane

plaintiff's case. Judgment in favor of plaintiff vacated and remanded for consideration of scope of involvement and liability of owners. ***Brindley v. Woodland Village Restaurant, Inc.*, 438 Pa. Super. 385, 652 A.2d 865 (1995).**

Corporate officer liability

Plaintiff brought action against managing shareholder for mismanaging their businesses and causing him to incur personal responsibility for the corporation's debts. The trial court dismissed the case on preliminary objections. The Superior Court held that the Plaintiff had no standing to sue a corporate officer for injuries unless the injuries were the result of a duty owed to the shareholder individually and not to the corporation as a whole. The Superior Court permitted Plaintiff an opportunity to amend his pleading. ***Hill v. Ofalt*, 85 A.3d 540 (Pa. Super. 2014).**

Plaintiff's decedent was killed when his helicopter crashed after receiving maintenance work by defendant corporation employee, assisted by corporation owner. Verdict in favor of plaintiff affirmed. Claim the corporate owner was individually liable on participation theory was not valid because the owner did not actively participate in the negligent action. Nonfeasance, rather than misfeasance, is not enough to allow individual liability of corporate officer. ***Shay v. Flight C Helicopter Services, Inc.*, 822 A.2d 1 (Pa. Super. 2003).**

County health facility

Suit against county health facility dismissed. Facility immune pursuant to 42 Pa. C.S.A. §8541. Section upheld as being constitutional. ***Gill v. County of Northampton*, 88 Pa. Cmwlth. 327, 488 A.2d 1214.**

Cousin

Plaintiff minor who witnessed his cousin's drowning is not sufficiently "closely related" under Pennsylvania law to allow standing for claim of negligent infliction of emotional distress. Order sustaining preliminary objections affirmed. ***Blanyar v. Pagnotti Enterprises, Inc.*, 451 Pa. Super 269, 679 A.2d 790 (1996).**

Cows

Milk production of farmer's cows declined because of stray electricity from power company's lines. Supplier of electricity owes highest duty of care in cases involving injury to property as well as injury to humans. ***Slater v. Pennsylvania Power Company*, 383 Pa. Super. 509, 557 A.2d 368.**

Crane

Where crane being operated by fellow employee, there can be no liability on leasing company unless accompanied by independent conduct on leasing company's part. Order dismissing complaint for indemnity here, affirmed under particular facts and pleadings. ***McKee v. McHugh Brothers*, 327 Pa. Super. 170, 475 A.2d 153.**

Jury verdict $490,000 to injured plaintiff and $47,000 to wife for loss of consortium. Plaintiff guiding rail for crane operator when crane hit high tension wires, causing severe electrical burns. Held: crane operator not coemployee of plaintiff under circumstances. Proper to submit negligence of operator to jury. Reversed 402A

Credit information provider

verdict as improperly submitted under facts here. Plaintiff's proof of negligence was a reasonable secondary cause. Negligence verdict affirmed. ***Thompson v. Anthony Crane Rental*, 325 Pa. Super. 386, 473 A.2d 120.**

Employee of crane company guiding load being moved by crane, injured when crane hit electric lines on property owner's land. Suit against property owner. Sufficient evidence of negligence of property owner in not properly warning crane operators that case should go to jury. Directed verdict overturned. New trial ordered. ***Beary v. Penna. Electric Co.*, 322 Pa. Super. 52, 469 A.2d 176.**

Individual contractor working on roof of smaller building within larger building, knocked off roof by crane. Knew of danger after years of working there. Held: crane operator not negligent, but employer-owner of crane/property owner (one entity) negligent for violation of §§341A and 343A of Restatement (2d) Torts. Possessor should anticipate danger despite knowledge of danger to invitee. ***Skalos v. Higgins*, 303 Pa. Super. 107, 449 A.2d 601.**

Plaintiff decedent electrocuted while in process of erecting steel beams when a crane operator brought crane too close to high voltage wires causing arc of electricity. Substantial verdict overturned due to apparent confusion of jury on issue of wrongful death and survival actions. ***Pniewski v. Kunda, et al.*, 237 Pa. Super. 438, 352 A.2d 462.**

Plaintiff injured when load of steel pipe fell from crane when its braking mechanism failed. Jury question, even after 20 years, as to whether defect attributable to manufacturer if plaintiff can show some evidence that it was present at time of delivery. New trial granted on other grounds after hung jury and defense judgment on record. ***Kuisis v. Baldwin-Lima-Hamilton*, 457 Pa. 321, 319 A.2d 914.**

Plaintiff, a laborer on a demolition project, injured by movement of a crane—verdict for plaintiff—new trial granted below—evidence sufficient to justify verdict—abuse of discretion—judgment ordered on verdict. ***Corbin v. M. Wilson & Son*, 421 Pa. 351, 219 A.2d 687.**

Credit information provider

Plaintiffs brought negligence and defamation action against Defendant after it made an inaccurate report on the Plaintiffs' mortgage payment history to a credit information provider. The trial court dismissed Plaintiffs' complaint. The Superior Court affirmed holding that negligence and defamation claims were preempted by the Fair Credit Reporting Act unless the information was furnished with malice or willful intent. ***Dietz v. Chase Home Finance, LLC*, 41 A.3d 882 (Pa. Super. 2012).**

Credit union

Plaintiff, surviving husband, filed negligence action against credit union alleging that it breached an affirmative duty to inform him that only he would be provided credit life insurance on loan as first signator rather than both husband and wife as co-obligors on loan. After verdict for plaintiffs in bench trial, Superior Court reversed holding that mere financial harm is not physical harm as required by §323 of Restatement (2d) Torts (negligent performance of undertaking to render services) nor was there proof of any fiduciary duty from the credit union to the husband nor is there any case law to define any affirmative duty to act in similar circumstances. *Carlotti v. Employees of Credit Union*, 717 A.2d 564 (Pa. Super. 1998).

Creeping disease

Creeping disease—inhalation of emissions causing cancer. Improper to grant summary judgment where genuine issue remains as to when administrator knew or should have known the cause of death. ***Anthony v. Koppers & Bethlehem Steel*, 284 Pa. Super. 81, 425 A.2d 428.**

Crest of hill

Defendant approaching the crest of a hill—view ahead partially obstructed—contacting a vehicle turning into a driveway and then the vehicle of plaintiffs—court did not err in instructing jury that assured clear distance rule applied—rule applies even though the vision of the operator is limited by the nature of the roadway. ***Bachman, et al. v. Bell, et al.*, 218 Pa. Super. 873, 279 A.2d 207.**

Criminal acts

Plaintiff, a psychiatric patient, brought suit against an ambulance service for negligently transporting him after he escaped from their care and later robbed a bank resulting in a criminal conviction. The appellate court reversed the trial court's ruling holding that under the no felony conviction recovery rule Plaintiff could not profit from his own criminal acts and also that his criminal acts were too remote to establish proximate causation. ***Holt v. Navarro*, 932 A.2d 915 (Pa. Super. 2007).**

City and housing authority both entitled to immunity under Political Subdivision Tort Claims Act and Sovereign Immunity Act. Plaintiff alleged that city's and housing authority's failure to maintain security systems on property constituted negligence related to the care, custody and control of the real estate. City and housing authority were not liable for failure to prevent criminal acts of third party who injured plaintiff. ***Williams v. Philadelphia Housing Authority*, 873 A.2d 81 (Pa. Cmwlth. 2005).**

Parents of deceased minor filed suit alleging negligence of babysitter in death based on conviction for first degree murder. Babysitter's homeowners insurance company, in declaratory judgment action, alleged that "intentional killing" element of criminal act eliminated its responsibility to defend or indemnify babysitter for negligence leading to death. Held that proper pleading of negligent acts before and after killing compelled insurer to provide defense, at least. ***Erie v. Muff*, 851 A.2d 919 (Pa. Super. 2004).**

Plaintiff was head of security at defendant hospital and was attacked by an employee who had been brought to supervisor's office for submission to urinalysis. Plaintiff alleged that tortfeasor was acting in his capacity as employee of the hospital and therefore hospital was liable under doctrine of *respondeat superior*. Defendant's motion for summary judgment sustained and affirmed on appeal. Tortfeasor's intentional act of injuring plaintiff was in no way related to his job description as laundry worker and there was no evidence from plaintiff of any expectation on the

Criminal assault

part of the defendant employer that the tortfeasor would act violently. *Costa v. Roxborough Memorial Hospital,* **708 A.2d 490 (Pa. Super. 1998).**

Plaintiff's decedent died after crashing into utility pole following high-speed chase. The decedent's criminal and negligent acts preclude imposition of liability on municipalities whose police officers were engaged in pursuit. Therefore, decedent's widow could not recover from municipalities under wrongful death theory because such action is derivative to any action the decedent may have had. Order granting summary judgment affirmed. *Tyree v. City of Pittsburgh,* **___ Pa. Cmwlth. ___, 669 A.2d 487 (1995).**

Co-owner of entireties property with actual knowledge of sexual abuse by other co-owner on their minor grandchildren within residence does not have duty to protect or warn grandchildren of grandfather's proclivities. Multimillion dollar compensatory and punitive damages award against grandmother reversed. While landowner may be liable for dangerous condition on the land, landowner is not liable for criminal or tortious acts of third parties. *T.A. v. Allen,* **447 Pa. Super. 302, 669 A.2d 360 (1995).**

Municipal defendants are neither afforded blanket immunity nor entitled to judgment as a matter of law in each and every tort claim where the victim's injuries were caused in part by the intervening criminal conduct of third parties or where the criminal acts of a third party merely form a link in the chain of causation. It is for the jury to determine whether municipal defendants' conduct was a substantial contributing factor in causing the victim's injuries and, if so, whether intervening criminal conduct of third parties was so extraordinary as not to be reasonably foreseeable by the municipal defendants. Summary judgment reversed. *Jones v. Chieffo,* **___ Pa. Super. ___, 664 A.2d 1091 (1995).**

A person is not liable for the criminal conduct of another in the absence of a special relationship imposing a preexisting duty. No special relationship exists between independent ice cream sales contractor and ice cream manufacturer that would impose duty on manufacturer to protect independent contractor from criminal acts of third person. Summary judgment affirmed. *Elbasher v. Simco Sales Service of Pennsylvania,* **441 Pa. Super. 397, 657 A.2d 983 (1995).**

Defendant's counsel attempting to establish that plaintiff under another name had a criminal record—within discretion of trial judge to refuse admission when identity not properly established. *Flowers v. Green,* **420 Pa. 481, 218 A.2d 219.**

Criminal assault

Summary judgment entered against plaintiff who was shot by a robber while a passenger on defendant's stopped train. Plaintiff alleged that defendant's trainman's failure to open the door of the train to allow plaintiff to escape before he was shot was a concurrent cause of his injury and that failure to act involved the operation of the motor vehicle. The Commonwealth Court distinguishes concurrent negligent acts from a negligent act by defendant and a criminal assault by a third party and also holds by implication that the failure to open the door was not "operation" of the motor vehicle. *Greenleaf v. SEPTA,* **698 A.2d 170 (Pa. Cmwlth. 1997).**

Criminal defense

In legal malpractice action by criminal defendant against his attorney, plaintiff's failure to allege facts in support of his claim that he was innocent of the criminal charges prohibits recovery. Plaintiff must demonstrate attorney's culpable negligent representation as the proximate cause of conviction. ***Slaughter v. Rushing*, 453 Pa. Super. 379, 683 A.2d 1234 (1996).**

Criminal suspect

Suspect who jumped out of window when police threatened to break down door brought action for negligence and intentional infliction of emotional distress. City not liable. Injuries not foreseeable and conduct not extreme or outrageous. ***Carson v. City of Philadelphia*, 133 Pa. Cmwlth. 74, 574 A.2d 1184.**

Crossing guard

Crossing guard leading children across street when defendant's car seen skidding towards them. Guard told children to go back to curb. Plaintiff ran wrong way and was struck. Verdict for plaintiff. Whether act of running was intervening cause and issue of overcoming presumption of no negligence of 11 year old were for jury. Affirmed. Verdict against driver, guard and city (employer). ***Ross v. Vereb*, 481 Pa. 446, 392 A.2d 1376.**

Crossing center line

Passing in a no-passing zone designated only by a double yellow line is negligence per se. ***Garcia v. Bang*, 375 Pa. Super. 356, 544 A.2d 509.**

Motorcyclist struck by truck after crossing double yellow line in attempt to pass. Whether motorcycle rider was negligent was question for jury. Truck driver found 20% negligent, Motorcyclist found 80% negligent. ***Cervone v. Reading*, 371 Pa. Super. 279, 538 A.2d 16.**

Cross over head-on accident. Verdict for defendant affirmed. Defendant testified that he pulled to berm to avoid accident in his lane, then tried to swerve around telephone pole when he lost control of his car, crossing four lanes of roadway and striking plaintiff. Although driver who crosses center line of highway is negligent *per se,* this can be rebutted by competent evidence that vehicle was there through no negligence on defendant's part. ***Farelli v. Marko*, 349 Pa. Super. 102, 502 A.2d 1293.**

Crossing zone

Parents of minor brought action against school district for injuries which resulted from minor being hit by school bus in authorized crossing zone. Failure to state common law or statutory cause of action against a political subdivision precludes recovery under the Political Subdivision Tort Claims Act. Order granting summary judgment affirmed. ***Dunaway v. South Eastern School District*, ___Pa. Cmwlth. ___, 676 A.2d 1281 (1996).**

Crosswalk

Crosswalk

Plaintiff was injured when a truck driven by the defendant struck her while she was crossing the street within a crosswalk. The appellate court held that it was error for the trial court not to include a jury instruction on negligence per se, since evidence had been presented that the plaintiff had been struck while in a crosswalk. ***Jenkins v. Wolf*, 911 A.2d 568 (Pa. Super. 2006).**

Suit by pedestrian against city and PennDOT for injuries sustained when she tripped on the raised "header" portion of a crosswalk on a city street that had been adopted by PennDOT as a state highway. Held that city-maintained crosswalk was a traffic control devise and so city was liable for negligent maintenance. ***Ryals v. City of Philadelphia*, 848 A.2d 1101 (Pa. Cmwlth. 2004).**

Plaintiff's decedent was killed when struck by an automobile while crossing a street at a crossing where the lines on the road delineating the cross-walk were faded and neither the bus stop to which he was walking nor the street was illuminated. Held: inadequate crossing area identification and lighting fell within the Trees, Traffic and Street Lighting exception to governmental immunity found at 42 Pa.C.S. § 8542(b)(4). ***Glenn v. Horan*, 765 A.2d 426 (Pa. Cmwlth. 2000).**

Crossing guard leading children across street. Observed skidding car and ordered children back to curb. 11 year old plaintiff ran wrong way. Verdict against driver, guard, and city (employer). ***Ross v. Vereb*, 481 Pa. 446, 392 A.2d 1376.**

Crowds

School held negligent in controlling crowd of parents who regularly came to pick up children at end of school. Plaintiff-parent jostled by workman in vestibule crowded with parents, causing her hand to be caught in door jamb. ***Swartley v. Tredyffrin Twp. School Dist.*, 287 Pa. Super. 499, 430 A.2d 1001.**

Curb

Plaintiff brought negligence action against the defendant landowners after she tripped and fell between two railroad ties the city had installed as curbing on a side street while trying to access the defendants' property for a yard sale. The trial court granted summary judgment in favor of the defendants. The Superior Court affirmed, holding that a gap between railroad ties did not constitute an unreasonably dangerous condition and there was no evidence the landowners knew the railroad ties were a danger to the plaintiff. ***Couto-Pressman v. Richards*, 63 A.3d 856 (Pa. Cmwlth. 2013).**

State highway law and the highway exceptions to sovereign immunity must be read in *pari materia*. Curb of a state highway that allegedly caused plaintiff's car to be catapulted into a stream bed, causing injuries, may be under control of PennDOT and so causation should go to jury. ***Shimko v. PennDOT*, 768 A.2d 413 (Pa. Cmwlth. 2001).**

Defect in a concrete median strip in the center of a PennDOT-maintained roadway constitutes a condition of the road allowing injured pedestrian's suit against PennDOT for defective maintenance of the median strip under real proper-

Custom and method

ty exception to sovereign immunity ***Hubbard v. Com., Dept. of Transp.,*** ___ **Pa. Cmwlth.** ___**, 660 A.2d 201 (1995).**

Plaintiffs injured when colliding with curbing which had been installed at an entrance previously used as an entrance to a shopping center—evidence of other occurrences improperly excluded—plaintiffs business invitees and evidence constituted some evidence of notice—nonsuit improperly entered. ***Colangelo v. Penn Hills Center, Inc.,* 221 Pa. Super. 381, 292 A.2d 490.**

Plaintiff pedestrian fell over a 1-3/8 inch protruding curb in city street—aware of defect before occurrence—allegedly distracted by sound of approaching traffic—insufficient excuse—guilty of contributory negligence as a matter of law. ***Knapp v. Bradford City,* 432 Pa. 172, 247 A.2d 575.**

Curve

Passenger warned driver of bad curve ahead. Accident a few second later when deer spotted and vehicle skidded on gravel. Error to charge on sudden emergency or contributory negligence of passenger. ***Hanlon v. Sorenson,* 289 Pa. Super. 268, 433 A.2d 60.**

Rounding curve and crossing center line striking plaintiff's vehicle. For jury. ***Edgridge v. Melcher,* 226 Pa. Super. 381, 313 A.2d 750.**

Plaintiffs passengers in a vehicle which veered right at dangerous curve to allow vehicle coming in opposite direction to pass. Struck utility pole. Pole unlit, no reflectors at night. Summary judgment against drivers and in favor of power company reversed. For jury. ***Scheel v. Tremblay and Phila. Electric Co.,* 226 Pa. Super. 45, 312 A.2d 45.**

When nature of highway does not call for a left turn to be made by motorist, it is error for trial judge to charge on the provisions of the Motor Vehicle Code as to left turns. ***Vescio v. Rubolino,* 433 Pa. 253, 249 A.2d 914.**

Custom and method

Police put out flares due to first accident. Second accident allegedly occurred due in part to the flares. Error to exclude testimony about custom and usage in placing and extinguishing flares. This is not expert testimony, but fact evidence. ***Kubit v. Russ,* 287 Pa. Super. 28, 429 A.2d 703.**

Plaintiff injured while defendant's employees were loading steel onto his truck. Verdict for defendant. Plaintiff's testimony on custom in industy properly excluded as he was unqualified only having been hauling steel 4 to 5 months. ***Pepin v. Bethlehem Steel,* 258 Pa. Super. 643, 390 A.2d 312.**

Dam

—D—

Dam

Downstream property owner sued reservoir and dam company for failure to contain water following heavy rains. The court confirmed that the owner of a reservoir is "required to exercise a degree of care commensurate with the risk of storing water in a reservoir and would be liable if its negligence made it possible for water to escape with resulting damage to property." Dam company's failure to comply with Dam Safety and Encroachments Act, 32 P.S. § 639.13 *et seq.* constituted negligence *per se*. ***Shamnoski v. PG Energy*, 765 A.2d 297 (Pa. Super. 2000).**

Municipal park which contains lake and low head dam are within purview of Recreation Use of Land and Water Act. Municipality given immunity for death and injury to two minors. Decided one month after *Stone v. York Haven Power Co.*, 749 A.2d 452 (Pa. 2000) but does not cite that decision. ***Pagnotti v. Lancaster Township*, 751 A.2d 1226 (Pa. Cmwlth. 2000).**

Recreation Use of Land and Water Act provides immunity to owner of man-made lake created when river is dammed to create a water supply for commercial venture, where lake is open to public free of charge. Dam that creates the lake is improvement to the real estate and so dam owner is not entitled to RULWA immunity afforded to lake owner. ***Stone v. York Haven Power Co.*, 749 A.2d 452 (Pa. 2000).**

Plaintiff's decedents were killed when their boat was trapped in the main channel of a dam on the Susquehanna River which created "Lake Frederick." Plaintiffs allege that the owner of the dam was negligent in failing to warn of the location of the dam. Defendants allege that they are immune from suit under the provisions of the Recreation Use of Land and Water Act (68 P.S. §477-1 *et seq.*) Trial court determined that the dam was a substantial improvement to the real property and therefore the immunity granted by the act was not available. Affirmed on basis that the act is designed to protect owners of large unimproved tracts of land that have not been altered. ***York Haven Power Co. v. Stone*, 715 A.2d 1164 (1998).**

Dance floor

In action by guest at wedding reception, testimony that there were two dangerous areas on portable dance floor is sufficient to preclude summary judgment where jury would not be required to speculate impermissibly as to cause of plaintiff's slip and fall on dance floor. Summary judgment reversed. ***First v. Zem Zem Temple*, 454 Pa. Super. 548, 686 A.2d 18 (1996).**

Plaintiffs injured while dancing allegedly as the result of asparagus on dance floor—caterer held responsible. ***Schwartz v. Warwick-Phila. Corp.*, 424 Pa. 185, 226 A.2d 484.**

Dangerous activity

Estate brought negligence claim against former owner of a steel plant on the basis that the former owner had failed to advise the new owner of a dangerous condition that later led to the death of a worker. The trial court dismissed the case on summary judgment. The Superior Court affirmed holding that the former owner had no reason to believe that the new owner would not become aware of the dangerous condition on the property as the entire workforce including management was retained after the sale of the plant. ***Gresik v. PA Partners, LP*, 989 A.2d 344 (Pa. Super. 2009).**

In buyers' action against seller of gasoline station equipment and property, action for strict liability based on leaking underground storage tanks will not lie. The operation of underground storage tanks at a gasoline station is not an abnormally dangerous activity. Order granting preliminary objection to strict liability claim affirmed. ***Smith v. Weaver*, ___ Pa. Super. ___, 665 A.2d 1215 (1995).**

Dangerous condition

Delivery driver brought a claim for negligence against a University after he tripped and fell due to a raised bumper on the loading dock. On appeal the Superior Court affirmed the jury verdict in favor of the delivery driver on the basis that the University failed to warn its business invitee of a known unreasonably dangerous condition and failed to exercise reasonable care to protect the delivery driver as it had reason to expect that he might be distracted and fail to protect himself. ***Walker v. Drexel University*, 971 A.2d 521 (Pa. Super. 2009).**

Building owner was liable to elevator mechanic who was injured when she fell from a ladder which was so close to the wall of an elevator shaft as to make it dangerous. Building owner was aware of danger by reason of prior complaints by other elevator mechanics but did not remedy problem. In granting new trial to defendant after verdict for plaintiff, trial court abused its discretion when it substituted its opinion of how the fall occurred for that of the jury. ***Mammoccio v. 1818 Market Partnership*, 734 A.2d 23 (Pa. Super. 1999).**

Decedent's failure to establish hospital's knowledge of water on floor in bathroom, which may represent a dangerous or defective condition of the property, prohibits recovery. A business invitee must prove either that the landowner created the harmful condition or had actual or constructive notice of the condition. Summary judgment affirmed. ***Swift v. Northeastern Hospital of Philadelphia*, 456 Pa. Super. 330, 690 A.2d 719 (1997).**

Plaintiff's decedent welder was killed when fumes inside gasoline tank truck in which he was working caught fire and exploded. Motion for compulsory nonsuit granted because plaintiff's decedent was fully aware of the risks attending the work he was performing. Recovery prohibited under Section 388 of Restatement (2d) Torts which imposes duty to warn owner of chattel who has reason to believe that those for whose use the chattel is supplied will not realize its dangerous condition. ***Erdos v. Bedford Valley Petroleum Co.*, 452 Pa. Super. 555, 682 A.2d 806 (1996).**

Peculiar risk doctrine did not apply to make contractor liable for injuries sustained by subcontractor's employee who fell from roof of building on which he was working where both contractor and subcontractor were aware of dangerous condition of roof. ***Edwards v. Franklin and Marshall College*, 444 Pa. Super. 1, 663 A.2d 187 (1995).**

Darkness

Verdict against injured plaintiff affirmed absent proof of unreasonably dangerous condition of chair. ***Steinhouse v. Herman Miller, Inc.,* 443 Pa. Super. 395, 661 A.2d 1379 (1995).**

Police officer who enters upon another's land in his official capacity and in response to a call for assistance is a licensee. Landowner's duty is to inform licensee of dangerous, hidden conditions. Obviously rowdy crowd of patrons at social hall was not a dangerous, hidden condition. Although violation of Dram Shop Act is negligence *per se*, mere fact that patrons who assaulted police officer were intoxicated neither proves that they had been served when visibly intoxicated nor causation of officer's injuries. Summary judgment for defendant affirmed. ***Holpp v. Fez, Inc.,* 440 Pa. Super. 512, 656 A.2d 147 (1995).**

In negligence action against corporate defendant and officers, officers are not liable for failing to maintain clean bathroom absent proof of their participation in creating or allowing continued existence of dangerous condition. Party's failure to answer request for admission that states a conclusion of law does not establish plaintiff's case. Judgment in favor of plaintiff vacated and remanded for consideration of scope of involvement and liability of owners. ***Brindley v. Woodland Village Restaurant, Inc.,* 438 Pa. Super. 385, 652 A.2d 865 (1995).**

Darkness

Safety inspector injured in fall down elevator shaft. Held: fact that inspector proceeded to elevator through dark passageway did not raise his level of negligence to 51%. ***Ligon v. Middletown Area School District,* 136 Pa. Cmwlth. 566, 584 A.2d 376.**

Fall down steps in friend's home, while looking for restroom. Entered wrong door; fell as door opened onto cellar steps. Error to grant compulsory nonsuit. New trial ordered. ***Fisher v. Findlay,* 319 Pa. Super. 214, 465 A.2d 1306.**

Jury verdict $200,000. Crush injury—permanent disability to right heel of 53-year old. Male warehouse employee in dark parking lot, guiding tractor-trailer rigs in by voice. Had his hand on rig. Fell in parking lot hole. Issue of plaintiff's contributory negligence for jury. ***McDevitt v. Terminal Warehouse Co.,* 304 Pa. Super. 438, 450 A.2d 991.**

Fall down steps in darkened lavatory area of restaurant while searching for light switch. Under facts here, no contributory negligence as a matter of law. Nonsuit removed. ***McNally v. Liebowitz,* 498 Pa. 163, 445 A.2d 716.**

Compulsory nonsuit entered where patron of restaurant went to restroom area, entered unlit area and fell down steps. Contributorily negligent as a matter of law. ***McNally v. Liebowitz,* 274 Pa. Super. 386, 418 A.2d 460.**

Summary judgment granted and affirmed against woman who fell down dark stairs of hall during wedding reception. Plaintiff relying on instructions given by niece. Contributorily negligent as a matter of law. ***Just v. Sons of Italy,* 240 Pa. Super. 416, 368 A.2d 308.**

Plaintiff killed while working at U.S. Steel. Employed by independent contractor, piling iron ore at night, atop huge piles, by truck. Only light that of headlights. Truck ran off edge and rolled over killing driver. Verdict for plaintiff affirmed. ***McDonough v. U.S. Steel Corp.,*** **228 Pa. Super. 268, 324 A.2d 542.**

Plaintiff employed by heating contractor. Injured when he stepped off roof in dark and fell to ground at night. Motion to remove nonsuit denied. Possessor of land only liable under §343 of Restatement (2d) Torts if dangerous condition is present involving unreasonable risk to invitees and he should expect invitee will fail to observe said condition. No emergency here requiring plaintiff to be on roof at night. No evidence of negligence on property owner. ***Kalin v. Delaware Valley Telephone Co.,*** **228 Pa. Super. 849, 316 A.2d 912.**

Plaintiff walking on well-defined but unimproved walkway adjacent to highway alongside defendant's plant. Came to bridge abutment and chose to walk to right rather than on highway and fell into stream. §342 of Restatement (2d) Torts. Failure to warn licensee of dangerous condition. Knowledge of condition proved by evidence of use by public over period of years. Inoperative light fixtures. Contributory negligence for jury. Only light was from across street. Verdict for plaintiff affirmed. ***Ciarimboli v. Walworth Co.,*** **228 Pa. Super. 766, 315 A.2d 292.**

Darting out

Standard of care for a child is the exercise of ordinary care appropriate for a child. Driver and Borough not liable where child who darts out into street found seventy percent negligent. ***Smith v. Stribling,*** **168 Pa. Cmwlth. 188, 649 A.2d 1003 (1994).**

Six and one-half year old boy struck by car in area where children were waiting for school bus as he "ran into street." Issue as to how quickly he entered street. Jury verdict in favor of motorist affirmed. ***Heffner v. Schad,*** **330 Pa. Super. 101, 478 A.2d 1372.**

Six-year old child was crossing limited access highway when struck by motorcycle. Girl had been standing, waiting for traffic, when she suddenly ran in front of defendant. Verdict for plaintiff reversed; new trial ordered. Issues of whether child was in place of danger for sufficient time, whether there was reasonable apprehension that child might run out, and the duty of care required, were not adequately explained by charge. ***Fama v. Smith,*** **303 Pa. Super. 414, 449 A.2d 755.**

11 year old boy crossing under supervision of crossing guard. Guard saw car skidding towards group of children and told them to return to curb. Plaintiff ran wrong way and was struck by car. For jury to determine whether plaintiff acted as reasonable 11 year old and whether presumption overcome. Verdict for plaintiff affirmed. ***Ross v. Vereb,*** **481 Pa. 446, 392 A.2d 1376.**

Unrefuted testimony of eyewitness showed three year old minor darted out from between parked cars into path of defendant's car which was travelling between 20 and 25 miles per hour. Child struck by left front of vehicle. Defendant testified that he did not see child until child suddenly came in front of his car. Nonsuit affirmed. ***Piccolo v. Weisenberger,*** **237 Pa. Super. 218, 352 A.2d 116.**

Daycare

Minor plaintiff walking home from school. School zone, Sidewalk being excavated so she crossed street to avoid the construction and was struck by defendant within foot or two of opposite curb. Verdict for plaintiff upheld. ***Simmons v. Mullen,*** **231 Pa. Super. 199, 331 A.2d 892.**

Small boy struck and killed by defendant's car—only testimony that of defendant who stated that child came from in back of a car on her right side and immediately struck by front of car—not sufficient evidence of negligence to take case to jury—verdict for defendant upheld. ***Zechman v. Yerger,*** **221 Pa. Super. 300, 292 A.2d 433.**

Hospital record of description of the accident disclosed minor plaintiff of three to be a darting out case—properly admitted under facts of the case—verdict for defendant upheld on appeal. ***Jones v. Spidle,*** **446 Pa. 103, 286 A.2d 366.**

Minor plaintiff aged 6 either came from inside a parked truck at intersection or came in front of it and ran into side of defendant's passing vehicle and sustained severe injuries—long trial—verdict for defendant—motion for new trial alleged inadequacy of charge and errors in transcript—court below refused motion and indicated that case would have justified a nonsuit—evidence apparently clear that minor ran into side of defendant's vehicle and was never in front of the same—action affirmed on appeal. ***Caplan v. Option Supply Co., et al.,*** **438 Pa. 546, 264 A.2d 405.**

Boy of 4 with young companions on sidewalk—cartway 34 feet wide—boy going into street to retrieve ball—child proceeded at least 17 feet in view of motorist—struck—facts sufficient to take case out of purely darting out status—for jury. ***Schwegel v. Goldberg,*** **209 Pa. Super. 280, 228 A.2d 405.**

Minor plaintiff was struck or ran into defendant's car—evidence that minor ran into street to retrieve a ball when defendant's car only 20 feet away—defendant swerved left to avoid minor but contact made—verdict for defendant—new trial refused—action proper. ***Wolf v. Needleman,*** **421 Pa. 113, 218 A.2d 321.**

Daycare

In action by parents against day care worker and center for molestation of child by worker, corporate entity not entitled to governmental immunity merely by reason of receipt of federal funds or designation by county as official community action program. Employer not vicariously liable for employee's outrageous conduct. Summary judgment reversed in part and affirmed in part. ***Sanchez by Rivera v. Montanez,*** **165 Pa. Cmwlth. 381, 645 A.2d 383 (1994).**

Dead body

Sovereign immunity barred claim for intentional infliction of emotional distress in mother's case against state police for mishandling of daughter's remains. Pennsylvania law does not recognize an action for negligent mishandling of the dead. Mother's failure to allege that she witnessed any traumatic event involving her daughter's remains precluded claim for negligent infliction of emotional distress. Order sustaining defendants' preliminary objections affirmed. ***Ray v. Pennsylvania State Police,*** **___ Pa. Cmwlth. ___, 654 A.2d 140 (1995).**

Relative of deceased brought action against city for failure to identify and release body. City immune. ***Kearney v. City of Philadelphia*, 150 Pa. Cmwlth. 517, 616 A.2d 72.**

Deck

Plaintiff's minor child was injured when he fell from a deck on a rented apartment. The deck was not designed or built in compliance with BOCA codes. On verdict for plaintiff defendant appeals alleging that exculpatory clause in lease releases landlord from liability. Held: exculpatory clause violates public policy as deck was built in violation of code and therefore void. ***Schultz v. DeVaux*, 715 A.2d 479 (1998).**

Deer

Passengers in automobile injured after driver attempted to avoid deer on highway brought action against Commonwealth. Questions of fact and law concerning Commonwealth's duty to maintain highway precluded judgment on the pleadings. ***Monzo v. Com., Dept. of Transp.*, 124 Pa. Cmwlth. 360, 556 A.2d 493.**

Plaintiff a passenger in auto involved in one vehicle accident. Skid on gravel. Error for judge to charge on contributory negligence of passenger who did warn driver of bad curve and accident occurred within a few seconds. Error also to charge on sudden emergency. Gravel was stationary and only subject to assured clear distance charge. Deer spotted 55 feet ahead, not an emergency. ***Hanlon v. Sorenson*, 289 Pa. Super. 268, 433 A.2d 60.**

Defamation

Plaintiff brought action against Defendant newspaper for defamation based upon newspaper's allegation his business was affiliated with organized crime. The trial court entered judgment in favor of the newspaper based upon a lack of proof of actual harm. The Superior Court, on appeal, reversed holding that the trial court failed to consider emotional distress, mental anguish, and personal humiliation as damages caused by the Defendant's publications and that the defamation merely needed to be a substantial cause of the Plaintiff's damages. ***Joseph v. Scranton Times, L.P.*, 89 A.3d 251 (Pa. Super. 2014).**

Plaintiff professor brought defamation and various other tort claims against Defendants state university faculty members for their recommendations that he be denied a promotion. The trial court dismissed the complaint. The Commonwealth Court affirmed holding that the Defendants were entitled to sovereign immunity as they were acting within the course and scope of their employment in making their recommendations regarding the Plaintiff's promotion. ***Kull v. Guisse*, 81 A.3d 148 (Pa. Cmwlth. 2013).**

Plaintiffs filed suit for defamation against multiple Defendants, including a deputy sheriff and assistant solicitor, for statements published in a newspaper speculating that the Plaintiffs might be anarchists or members of anti-government groups. The trial court dismissed Plaintiffs' complaint on preliminary objections. The Commonwealth Court affirmed holding that there was no cause of action for monetary

Defective assembly

damages for defamation based upon the Pennsylvania Constitution. It also held that calling a person a name that is descriptive of his political, economic or sociological philosophies does not give rise to a libel action. ***Balleta v. Spadoni*, 47 A.3d 183 (Pa. Cmwlth. 2012).**

Plaintiffs brought negligence and defamation action against Defendant after it made an inaccurate report on the Plaintiffs' mortgage payment history to a credit information provider. The trial court dismissed Plaintiffs' complaint. The Superior Court affirmed holding that negligence and defamation claims were preempted by the Fair Credit Reporting Act unless the information was furnished with malice or willful intent. ***Dietz v. Chase Home Finance, LLC*, 41 A.3d 882 (Pa. Super. 2012).**

Plaintiff a business newsletter publisher sued defendant Better Business Bureau over the issuance of a report on consumer complaints regarding the plaintiff. The court held that negligence may defeat a conditional privilege claim if the plaintiff is a private figure and the speech is not a matter of public concern. ***American Future Systems, Inc. v. Better Business Bureau of Eastern Pennsylvania*, 923 A.2d 389 (Pa. 2007).**

Plaintiff an assistant college basketball coach, sued a broadcaster and his network for defamation for reporting that plaintiff was involved in a theft at his place of employment. The court held failure to check sources, or negligence alone, was insufficient to show the actual malice necessary for a defamation claim involving a public figure. ***Blackwell v. Eskin*, 916 A.2d 1123 (Pa. Super. 2007)**.

Chiropractor brought action against newspaper that published defamatory letter. Held: newspaper had duty to ascertain truthfulness of statements contained in letter. ***Doughtery v. Boyertown Times*, 377 Pa. Super. 462, 547 A.2d 778.**

Defective assembly

One vehicle motorcycle accident. Jury verdict of $1,750,000. Driver of cycle suffered loss of most of right arm. Plaintiff alleged defective assembly of front-end assembly. New trial ordered on lower court error as to exclusion of evidence. ***Bascelli v. Randy, Inc.*, 339 Pa. Super. 254, 488 A.2d 1110.**

Defective condition

In action arising from explosion of boiler caused by defective emergency shut off valve, manufacturer of valve held strictly liable for defective product. An actor is relieved from liability owing to an intervening or superseding cause only if the intervening or superseding negligent acts were so extraordinary as not to have been reasonably foreseeable. Summary judgment affirmed in part and reversed in part. ***Dougherty v. Edward J. Meloney, Inc.*, 443 Pa. Super. 201, 661 A.2d 375 (1995).**

Where a pedestrian in broad daylight and with full knowledge of a defective pavement sidesteps to avoid another pedestrian and falls into a known defect which she observed, she will be held contributorily negligent as a matter of law. ***Kresovich v. Fitzsimmons*, 439 Pa. 10, 264 A.2d 585.**

Defective equipment

Plaintiff pedestrian aged 72 fell allegedly on a ridge of ice on pavement of individual defendants—daylight case—suit also against municipality—two theories of occurrence—one that pavement had been in a defective condition before occurrence and secondly that ice had formed in ridges from 1 to 2 inches in height—snowing at time—no evidence of constructive notice—nonsuit proper. *Silich v. Wissinger et al.,* **438 Pa. 548, 264 A.2d 169.**

Defective design

Plaintiff brought strict liability and negligence claims against defendant ATV manufacturer for injuries suffered when the rear fender of his ATV collapsed. The trial court granted summary judgment in favor of the defendant. The Superior Court reversed holding that there was a genuine issue of material fact regarding Plaintiff's negligence claims on the basis that Plaintiff's expert testified that there were other designs being used at the time of the accident that would have prevented the ATV's fender from collapsing. ***Smith v. Yamaha Motor Corp., U.S.A.,* 5 A.3d 314 (Pa.Super. 2010).**

Passenger injured in multi-vehicle collision alleged defect in design of auto caused more severe injury. Verdict against driver of striking car only. Held: films showing crash tests of another model of auto were properly admitted to demonstrate principles testified to be expert witness for auto manufacturer. Also proper to admit evidence of Federal Motor Vehicle standards, even though a products liability case. Compliance with standards were evidence for determination of whether or not there was defect. ***Jackson v. Spagnola,* 349 Pa. Super. 471, 503 A.2d 944.**

Plaintiff injured back while lifting 450 lb. barrel with drum truck made by defendant more than 20 years earlier. Claimed defective design put strain on user's back. Charge on "state of art" defense held in error. Reasonableness of what defendant should have known about the then "state of art" in the industry not the test. New trial ordered. ***Carrecter v. Colson Equipment Co.,* 346 Pa. Super. 95, 499 A.2d 326.**

Defective equipment

Car owner allowed to proceed to trial on theory that automatic door lock design was negligent in that it prevented her from being able to keep an attacker out of her car after the engine was turned off. ***Moroney v. General Motors Corporation,* 850 A.2d 629 (Pa. Super. 2004).**

Malpractice case allegedly due to defective drill used in neck surgery. Where joinder of manufacturer was first knowledge to plaintiff of defect, then statute of limitations did not begin to run until knowledge acquired. ***Grubb v. Einstein Medical Center,* 255 Pa. Super. 381, 387 A.2d 480.**

Plaintiff standing on clip which had been welded by defendant. Whether plaintiff's use of clip under the circumstances was foreseeable as a secondary use was for jury since primary use was to hold metal rods. Verdict for plaintiff affirmed. ***Lambert v. PBI Industries,* 244 Pa. Super. 118, 366 A.2d 944.**

Defective equipment

Plaintiff cut severely by power saw, when allegedly the telescoping guard jammed in the housing. Evidence sufficient to go to jury. Nonsuit removed. Saw was only a few months old. It is not necessary that defect manifest itself immediately upon purchase. *Agostino v. Rockwell Manufacturing Co.,* **236 Pa. Super. 434, 345 A.2d 735.**

Plaintiff using tire changing machine which exploded causing tire and rim to strike him in face. Machine was quite old and worn which was known to owner of gas station when it was put into service. Manufacturer exonerated. Owner, lessee and tire manufacturer found negligent. *Stewart v. Uniroyal,* **233 Pa. Super. 721, 339 A.2d 815.**

Helicopter crash—plaintiff pilot killed. Failure of seven foot section of one rotor. Entire 402 A doctrine clarified. Only two items of proof required: (1) product defective; and (2) defect was proximate cause of injuries. Plaintiff must also prove that defect existed when product left seller's hands. *Berkebile v. Brantly Helicopter Corp.,* **462 Pa. 83, 337 A.2d 893.**

Plaintiff operating forklift. Proceeding up a ramp to a truck, when truck rolled forward and forklift fell between truck and loading dock. Plaintiff proved that brakes and transmission defective. Defendant proved that truck was inspected one month earlier and brakes were 100%. Plaintiff rebuttal that inspection station had been decertified for having issued inspection certificates without performing inspections. Verdict of $225,000.00 affirmed. Strong dissent. *Tolentino v. Bailey,* **230 Pa. Super. 8, 326 A.2d 920.**

Exploding grinding wheel is such a malfunction as to be evidence of a defective condition sufficient to sustain recovery in absence of abnormal use. If machine altered, could manufacturer have reasonably foreseen such an alteration—here use of wheel of different manufacturer. For jury. *D'Antona v. Hampton Grinding Wheel Co.,* **225 Pa. Super. 120, 310 A.2d 307.**

Plaintiff killed when brakes failed and truck failed to negotiate curve—photos of brakes showed defect and were admissible upon expert's testimony that although taken months after accident they showed defect as it existed at time of crash. Verdict for plaintiff affirmed. *Woods v. Pleasant Hills Motor Co.,* **454 Pa. 224, 309 A.2d 698.**

Plaintiff injured while using a car which left highway on application of brakes—brakes recently relined by defendant—testimony of plaintiff's expert refuted in part by plaintiff's exhibit of brake mechanism at trial—verdict for plaintiff—new trial granted on ground that credibility of witness was "devastated"—Held: order properly entered—strong dissent. *Stover v. Five Way S. Center,* **220 Pa. Super. 335, 286 A.2d 380.**

Defendant owner of a dairy—plaintiff did odd jobs around same—engaged to unplug a clogged sewer—injured by defective equipment supplied by him—independent contractorship—defendant not responsible. *Funari v. Valentino,* **435 Pa. 363, 257 A.2d 259.**

Demolition

Delivery driver

A person is not liable for the criminal conduct of another in the absence of a special relationship imposing a preexisting duty. No special relationship exists between independent ice cream sales contractor and ice cream manufacturer that would impose duty on manufacturer to protect independent contractor from criminal acts of third person. Summary judgment affirmed. *Elbasher v. Simco Sales Service of Pennsylvania*, **441 Pa. Super. 397, 657 A.2d 983 (1995).**

Motorist injured in collision with vehicle delivering newspapers brought action against distributor. Distributor not liable. Delivery driver independent contractor. *Lutz v. Cybularz,* **414 Pa. Super. 579, 607 A.2d 1089.**

Delivery vehicle

Action by passenger of stolen pizza delivery vehicle after vehicle crashed into pole dismissed against delivery driver and his employer for plaintiff's failure to establish causation. *Matos v. Rivera,* **436 Pa. Super. 509, 648 A.2d 337 (1994).**

Demolition

Plaintiff brought claim for negligent demolition after the city tore down Plaintiff's home. A jury awarded the Plaintiff more than market value for the property. The Superior Court reversed, holding that the fundamental purpose of awarding damages for destruction of property by the tortious conduct of another is the actual loss suffered and therefore Plaintiff could only be awarded the actual market value of the property prior to demolition. *Oliver-Smith v. City of Philadelphia*, **962 A.2d 728 (Pa. Cmwlth. 2008).**

Plaintiffs whose building was partially damaged by fire in adjoining property and partially damaged by acts of demolition contractor hired by borough to tear down adjoining property filed suit against borough alleging negligent supervision and inspection of demolition contractor by borough. Held that negligent inspection or supervision is not an exception to municipal immunity act. *Moles v. Borough of Norristown,* **780 A.2d 787 (Pa. Cmwlth. 2001).**

Child injured in street by car after being forced to leave sidewalk due to city-placed barricade. City not liable under exception to Political Subdivision Tort Claims Act because injuries not caused by care, custody, or control of real property or dangerous condition of sidewalk. *Kiley by Kiley v. City of Philadelphia,* **537 Pa. 502, 645 A.2d 184 (1994).**

Fire-damaged elevator shaft collapsed during demolition and damaged adjoining property. Owner not liable. Causation to remote. *American Truck Leasing, Inc.,* **400 Pa. Super. 530, 583 A.2d 1242.**

Owner employed a competent demolition operator to dismantle a steel trestle—this operator employed a subcontractor to assist in dismantling trestle together with a crane and operator—plaintiff, an employee of dismantling contractor, injured by operator of crane—suit against owner steel company on ground that relationship was not an independent contractorship—nonsuit properly entered—no evidence of control by owner. *Brletich v. U.S. Steel Corp.,* **445 Pa. 525, 285 A.2d 133.**

D.E.S. case

Plaintiff, a laborer on a demolition project, injured by movement of a crane—verdict for the plaintiff—new trial granted below—evidence sufficient to justify verdict—abuse of discretion—judgment ordered entered on verdict. ***Corbin v. M. Wilson & Son,* 421 Pa. 351, 219 A.2d 687.**

D.E.S. case

Lengthy discussion of enterprise liability, civil conspiracy, and concert of action in D.E.S. case. Affirmed grant of summary judgment to numerous defendants of over 72 originally sued under one or more theories. ***Burnside v. Abbott Laboratories,* 351 Pa. Super. 264, 505 A.2d 973.**

Destruction of evidence

Employee, injured during the course of his employment, brought a claim for damages against his employer for negligently destroying parts of the truck that caused his injury, which the employee intended to use in a third party tort suit. The trial court dismissed the employee's claims on the basis that they were barred based on the Workers' Compensation Act. The Superior Court reversed, holding that the Workers' Compensation Act did not bar an employee's claim for negligent destruction of evidence against his employer as the injury did not arise during the course of the employee's employment. ***Minto v. J.B. Hunt Transportation Services, Inc.,* 971 A.2d 1280 (Pa. Super. 2009).**

Diabetes

Patient involved in automobile accident when returning from dental clinic brought action against dentist and hospital alleging negligent treatment of her diabetes. Patient failed to state cause of action. ***Waddell v. Bowers,* 415 Pa. Super. 469, 609 A.2d 847.**

Pedestrian injured when struck by vehicle driven by diabetic brought action against driver's physician for failure to properly diagnose and treat driver and for failure to notify Department of Transportation. Physician not liable. ***Crosby by Crosby v. Sultz,* 405 Pa. Super. 527, 592 A.2d 1337.**

Diesel fumes

Plaintiffs were employees in office adjacent to school bus parking area and garage. Over a significant period of time, they all developed respiratory ailments that were eventually linked to exposure to fumes from diesel fuel and bus exhaust fumes. Plaintiffs filed suit against building architect, HVAC designer and installer and BMC, an environmental company that had been performing tests of building's air quality and certifying good air quality after plaintiffs' illness was established. The trial court granted BMC's motion for summary judgment because plaintiffs failed to institute suit within two years after plaintiffs discovered their illness. Held: discovery rule tolls statute of limitations in this case because defendant was not company that caused harm, but company hired to determine cause of plaintiffs' existing illnesses after they had complained to their supervisors. The two-year period ran from date BMC was negligent in performance of its tests, not date plaintiffs discovered their illness. The actual time that plaintiffs discovered that BMC was negligent in its testing is issue for jury and so prohibits summary judgment. ***Cappelli v. York Operating Co., Inc.*, 711 A.2d 481 (Pa. Super. 1998).**

Dilapidated buildings

Inspection and demolition of dilapidated building is a governmental function—city immune from liability. ***Bleman v. Gold,* 431 Pa. 348, 246 A.2d 376.**

Director

Member of church board of directors injured in fall down church steps. Recovery denied. Negligence of church imputed to director. ***Zehner v. Wilkinson United Methodist Church,* 399 Pa. Super. 165, 581 A.2d 1388.**

Disability of party

Minor plaintiff injured—releases given—minor started suit some 6 years later and disaffirmed releases—statute of limitations applies and runs against one suffering a disability—verdict directed for defendant proper. ***Schmucker v. Naugle,* 426 Pa. 203, 231 A.2d 121.**

Disaster Emergency

Suit against PennDOT alleging negligence for failure to remove accumulations of ice and snow from state maintained road during declared Disaster Emergency in 1994. Summary judgment in favor of PennDOT affirmed on basis of sovereign immunity and immunity under Pennsylvania's Emergency Management Services Code provisions. ***Kahres v. Henry,* 801 A.2d 650 (Pa. Super. 2002).**

Discharge of passenger

Plaintiff administratrix of deceased minor filed suit against SEPTA and ambulance company after child who had alighted from bus crossed in front of bus, with green light, and was struck by ambulance which was improperly passing bus on its left. After settling with ambulance service, SEPTA was granted summary judgment on basis of sovereign immunity as the act of stopping at an intersection, rather than at the appropriate bus stop in middle of block, then opening door to discharge child was not "operation" of motor vehicle under Sovereign Immunity Act. "...a temporary stop connected to the discharge of passengers is not part and parcel of the operation of a vehicle." Query, not even on a passenger transit bus? ***Warrick v. Pro Cor Ambulance, Inc.*, 709 A.2d 422 (Pa. Cmwlth. 1997).**

Disclosure of statements

Patient's unsubstantiated assertion of physical injury failed to establish negligent or intentional infliction of emotional distress. Doctor and medical center were immune from suit under Child Protective Services Law for disclosing plaintiff's admission that she had suffocated her child. Child Protective Services Law, which grants immunity for disclosures does not conflict with psychotherapist–patient privilege or the confidentiality provisions of the Mental Health Procedures Act. ***Fewell v. Bresner,* 444 Pa. Super. 559, 664 A.2d 577 (1995).**

Discovered Peril Doctrine

Discovered Peril Doctrine

Plaintiff a passenger in car that became disabled at night in center of, and perpendicular to, road. Plaintiff struck while standing near center of road, at front of car, attempting to wave on traffic. Plaintiff found 70% at fault. Proper to refuse charge on "discovered peril" doctrine under facts here. No evidence that defendant knew or should have known of plaintiff's perilous position. Defense verdict affirmed. ***Emerick v. Carson*, 325 Pa. Super. 308, 472 A.2d 1133.**

Pedestrian stepped onto roadway allegedly in enough time to be avoided by defendant. Discovered peril doctrine charged. After several hours of deliberating, jury asked if both parties were negligent, must they find for defendant. Judge answered yes, which was error in view of previous charge, and it being last communication to jury. ***Smith v. Chardak*, 295 Pa. Super. 173, 435 A.2d 624.**

Discovery Rule

Plaintiffs filed suit on their own behalf and on behalf of decedent's estate for wrongful death due to prolonged exposure to sewage sludge. The court upheld dismissal on the basis that the Discovery Rule could not be applied to toll the statute of limitations in a wrongful death action. Death puts survivors on notice to determine the cause of death and any claims that might flow from it. ***Pennock v. Lenzi*, 882 A.2d 1057 (Pa. Cmwlth. 2005).**

Twenty-six year old plaintiff brought suit against priest and church administration for injuries sustained as a result of alleged sexual abuse while plaintiff attended high school. Motions for judgment on the pleadings by all defendants sustained due to plaintiff's failure to timely file complaint following actual injury. ***Baselice, III v. Franciscan Friars Assumption BVM Province, Inc.*, 879 A.2d 270 (Pa. Super. 2005)**.

Plaintiffs who did not file suit against clergy and church officials who participated in or covered up alleged clergy sexual abuse for at least twenty one years were barred by statute of limitations. ***Meehan v. Archdiocese of Philadelphia*, 870 A.2d 912 (Pa. Super. 2005).**

Discovery rule in medical malpractice cases is an exception to the limitations of action statutes which impose on plaintiffs a duty to bring suit within a set time after injury. If discovery of injury and cause is delayed despite the exercise of reasonable diligence, the limitation of action period is tolled. Because the determination of whether a party plaintiff is able, in the exercise of reasonable diligence, to know of his injury and its cause, it is for a jury to decide. It is not relevant to the application of the discovery rule whether or not the limitations period has expired. ***Fine v. Checcio*, 870 A.2d 850 (Pa. 2005)**.

Summary judgment against plaintiff whose medical malpractice case against surgeon who performed knee surgery reversed based on proof that plaintiff discovered injury and cause only after having seen third physician for another opinion on continued pain in knee. The fact that statute of limitations had not run from original surgery when plaintiff "lost confidence" in original physician is not relevant to toll statute of limitations. ***Caro v. Glah*, 867 A.2d 531 (Pa. Super. 2005).**

Discovery Rule

Dentist who continually gave assurances to Plaintiff that she would recover her sense of feeling of her tongue and lips "concealed" her true condition and so tolled the running of the statute of limitations. Only when plaintiff lost confidence in that doctor and sought another opinion did the statute of limitations begin to run again. ***Ward v. Rice*, 828 A.2d 1118 (Pa. Super. 2003).**

Plaintiffs were employees in office adjacent to school bus parking area and garage. Over a significant period of time, they all developed respiratory ailments that were eventually linked to exposure to fumes from diesel fuel and bus exhaust fumes. Plaintiffs filed suit against building architect, HVAC designer and installer and BMC, an environmental company that had been performing tests of building's air quality and certifying good air quality after plaintiffs' illness was established. The trial court granted BMC's motion for summary judgment because plaintiffs failed to institute suit within two years after plaintiffs discovered their illness. Held: Discovery Rule tolls statute of limitations in this case because defendant was not company that caused harm, but company hired to determine cause of plaintiffs' existing illnesses after they had complained to their supervisors. The two-year period ran from date BMC was negligent in performance of its tests, not date plaintiffs discovered their illness. The actual time that plaintiffs discovered that BMC was negligent in its testing is issue for jury and so prohibits summary judgment. ***Cappelli v. York Operating Co., Inc.*, 711 A.2d 481 (Pa. Super. 1998).**

Plaintiff, patient of psychiatrist, filed suit for damages resulting from psychiatrist's alleged sexual contact with patient. Motion for summary judgment granted, and affirmed by Superior Court, because plaintiff failed to file suit within two years of date when she could reasonably be expected to know of her injury with the exercise of reasonable diligence. Reasonable diligence is an objective and external standard that is the same for all persons. Plaintiff's allegation that she did not recognize inappropriateness of sexual contact by treating psychiatrist until informed by a later therapist is inadequate to toll statute of limitations. Discovery rule is not appropriate for plaintiff because she knew of existence of sexual contact at all times and a reasonable person would have recognized that such behavior was inappropriate. ***Haggart v. Cho*, 703 A.2d 522 (Pa. Super. 1997).**

Summary judgment for defendant reversed when limited tort plaintiff established that statute of limitations began not on date of accident but on date that she became aware or reasonably could have become aware that her injuries were "serious" under limited tort policy and so compensable under that statute. ***Walls v. Scheckler*, 700 A.2d 533 (Pa. Super. 1997).**

Female plaintiff who "repressed" memory of assaults that occurred more than 21 years in the past was not entitled to tolling of two year statute of limitations under the discovery rule. Order sustaining preliminary objections affirmed. ***Pearce v. Salvation Army,* 449 Pa. Super. 654, 674 A.2d 1123 (1996).**

Issue of plaintiff's discovery of asbestos-related injuries is one for jury. ***White v. Owens-Corning Fiberglass Corp.*, 447 Pa. Super. 5, 668 A.2d 136 (1995).**

Shipyard worker's failure to diligently ascertain cause of lung cancer prevents tolling of statute of limitations under discovery rule. Dissent opines that ma-

Disfigurement

jority opinion replaces "reasonably should have known" standard with "could have known" standard. Order granting summary judgment affirmed. ***Cochran v. GAF Corp.,* 542 Pa. 210, 666 A.2d 245 (1995).**

Plaintiff's decedent who was informed that mesothelioma was a rare asbestos-induced form of lung cancer is not entitled to benefit of discovery rule where products liability action commenced more than two years after diagnosis of lung cancer. ***Baumgart v. Keene Bldg. Products Corp.,* 542 Pa. 194, 666 A.2d 238 (1995).**

Where plaintiff knew before treating with dentist of periodontal disease, the "discovery rule" exception to the applicable statute of limitations is not available to plaintiff. ***Colanna v. Rice,* 445 Pa. Super. 1, 664 A.2d 979 (1995).**

The discovery rule tolls statute of limitations until date of discovery of negligent act. Where plaintiff was aware of injury to eye immediately upon occurrence but there was a delay in determining the extent of the injury, the discovery rule does not apply and statute runs from date of negligent act. Judgment entered on jury verdict reversed. ***Sterling v. St. Michael's School for Boys,* 442 Pa. Super. 437, 660 A.2d 64 (1995).**

Six-year statute of limitations for latent defect in construction case runs from date injured party becomes aware, or by exercise of reasonable diligence should have become aware, of the defect. ***Romeo & Sons, Inc. v. P.C. Yezbak & Son, Inc.,* 539 Pa. 390, 652 A.2d 830 (1995).**

"Discovery rule" applies to wrongful death and survival actions and therefore a determination must be made as to when personal representative knew or reasonably should have known cause of death. Remanded. ***Pastierik v. Duquesne Light Co.,* 341 Pa. Super. 329, 491 A.2d 841.**

Disfigurement

Plaintiff who had a bone flap in skull replaced with titanium mesh sued to recover for pain, disfigurement and depression, alleging negligence by medical care providers in failing to preserve bone flap and battery for substituting titanium mesh for bone. Lower court's grant of summary judgment in favor of care providers reversed in part. Plaintiff's disfigurement was so obvious as to not require expert testimony and plaintiff's expert testified that psychological depression was caused by disfigurement resulting from surgery. Absent proof of causal relationship between pain and surgery, recovery for pain disallowed. ***Watkins v. Hospital of University of Pennsylvania,* 737 A.2d 263 (Pa. Super. 1999).**

Display rack

Employee of store loading a display on rack when it tipped over causing injury to plaintiff. Suit versus manufacturer based on defective design. Charge given on §402A of Restatement (2d) Torts. Verdict for defendant affirmed. ***Varner v. Pretty Products,* 270 Pa. Super. 86, 410 A.2d 1261.**

Diving

Disregard of safety of others

Defendant police officer was pursuing a speed violator—proceeding at 80 miles per hour—applying brakes and jumping divider line—colliding with car of plaintiff's decedent—sufficient evidence for jury to find a "reckless disregard of the safety of others"—verdict for plaintiff sustained. ***Herron v. Silbaugh*, 436 Pa. 339, 260 A.2d 755.**

Dissolution of corporation

A dissolved corporation had agreed prior to dissolution to indemnify plaintiff, if plaintiff compelled to pay a verdict for personal injuries sustained in operation—not protected by Act of May 5, 1933 when suit brought within two years of dissolution. ***Westinghouse Elec. Co. v. Goodwin Corp.*, 432 Pa. 347, 247 A.2d 462.**

Ditch

Plaintiff was injured when car he was driving fell into 8"–12" ditch in road that resulted from settlement of fill deposited by local authority which had created hole. Plaintiff appeals from trial judge's decision to give instruction to jury which left question of whether local authority had actual or constructive notice of fill settling to jury. Plaintiff argued that because local authority created hole and installed fill that settled and caused dangerous condition, it had notice of condition as a matter of law. Instruction approved by Commonwealth Court which held that just because defendant created hole and installed fill that eventually resulted in dangerous condition does not mean that plaintiff is not required to show that defendant knew or should have known of the condition. ***Miller v. Lykens Borough Authority*, 712 A.2d 800 (Pa. Cmwlth. 1998).**

Directed verdict reversed and new trial granted to plaintiff injured when improperly backfilled water line trench settled, creating a three foot wide, 18 inch deep ditch in PennDOT maintained road. Utility service facilities exception to sovereign immunity allows recovery because defect was a condition "of the facilities." ***Miller v. Com., Dept. of Transp.*, 690 A.2d 818 (Pa. Cmwlth. 1997).**

Diversion of water

Land owner brought action against city for damage caused by backfilling and regrading adjacent parcel of land. City not liable under Storm Water Management Act. ***Bahor v. City of Pittsburgh*, 158 Pa. Cmwlth. 150, 631 A.2d 731.**

Diving

Swimmer injured while using diving board at county-owned pool. County not liable. ***County of Allegheny v. Fedunok*, 164 Pa. Cmwlth. 198, 642 A.2d 595.**

Plaintiff rendered quadriplegic as a result of dive off dock into a canal during private party. Error to instruct jury that plaintiff was an invitee. Should have been left to jury whether or not plaintiff was an invitee or licensee. Plaintiff was the husband of an invited guest. Verdict for plaintiff reversed and new trial ordered. ***Hager v. Etting*, 268 Pa. Super. 416, 408 A.2d 856.**

Divorce

Plaintiff injured when diving board located on platform of defendant's pool broke under his weight—pool operator and construction firm sued—plaintiff introduced expert testimony of faulty design—Held: pool operator had duty of doing more than visual inspection—nonsuit improperly entered—matter for jury. ***Starke v. Long,* 221 Pa. Super. 338, 292 A.2d 440.**

Defendant borough maintained a swimming pool—minor plaintiff dived from one meter board and struck bottom of pool and was seriously injured—evidence that depth of water at point was below standard of safe maintenance of a swimming pool—error for court below to enter judgment *n.o.v.* for defendant. ***Cummings v. Nazareth Borough,* 427 Pa. 14, 233 A.2d 874.**

Divorce

Attorney's failure to advise divorce client about well-established principles of law and the impact of a settlement agreement upon client's future obligations is sufficient ground for legal malpractice action. Mere existence of client's consent to settlement does not excuse malpractice. Miller v. Berschler, 423 Pa. Super. 405, 621 A.2d 595 (1993) expressly reversed. Summary judgment reversed. ***McMahon v. Shea,* 441 Pa. Super. 304, 657 A.2d 938 (1995).**

Dogs

Mother filed negligence lawsuit against a landlord after one of their tenant's dogs bit her child. The trial court entered summary judgment in favor of the Defendant. The Superior Court affirmed holding that a landlord that is out of possession cannot be liable for attacks by a tenant's animal without evidence that the landlord was aware the animal was dangerous.***Rosenberry v. Evans,* 48 A.3d 1255 (Pa. Super. 2012).**

Plaintiff brought action against the Society for the Prevention of Cruelty of Animals for illegally destroying her dogs. A jury found in favor of the Plaintiff and the Superior Court affirmed. The Pennsylvania Supreme Court affirmed holding that the SPCA did not have immunity under either the Sovereign Immunity Act or the Political Subdivision Tort Claims Act. ***Snead v. Society for the Prevention of Cruelty to Animals of Pennsylvania,* 985 A.2d 909 (Pa. 2009).**

Plaintiffs brought claims of negligence against dog owner and the landlord of the dog owner after a dog escaped from its owner's home and attacked the Plaintiffs. The trial court entered a monetary judgment for the Plaintiffs after a jury trial. The Superior Court held that a jury may consider the attack, which is the subject of the lawsuit, in determining whether a dog has dangerous propensities in determining whether a dog owner was negligent. However, the Superior Court reversed the trial court's holding against the landlord, holding that a landlord out of possession may be held liable for animals owned by a tenant only if the landlord has knowledge that the animal has dangerous propensities and the landlord has the right to remove the animal from the premises. ***Underwood v. Wind,* 954 A.2d 1199 (Pa. Super. 2008).**

Homeowner brought suit against his neighbors and his homeowner's association after his neighbor's unleashed dogs ran onto his property and attacked him. The appellate court upheld the trial court's grant of summary judgment for the homeowner's association, because it had not assumed a duty or have a duty to compel association members to confine their dogs. ***McMahon v. Pleasant Valley West Association*, 952 A.2d 731 (Pa. Cmwlth. 2008).**

Dog owner brought a negligence claim against the SPCA after it destroyed her dogs despite the fact that the dog fighting charges against the owner were dropped. The appellate court held that the SPCA had breached a duty to the dog owner to hold the animals until disposition of the dog fighting charges and that it had breached a duty to notify an owner that the dogs could be reclaimed if charges were dropped. ***Snead v. Society for Protection of Cruelty to Animals of Pennsylvania*, 929 A.2d 1169 (Pa. Super. 2008).**

Defendant private entity appealed court ruling that it was not entitled to sovereign immunity and had negligently euthanized dogs owned by the plaintiff. The court held that there was sufficient evidence of negligence on the part of the defendant in failing to notify the known owner of dogs being held by it as a result of criminal charges prior to the defendant's euthanization of the animals. ***Snead v. Society for the Prevention of Cruelty to Animals of Pennsylvania*, 929 A.2d 1169 (Pa. Super. 2007).**

Philadelphia Housing Authority, a Commonwealth agency, did not have direct custody and control of tenant's dog which bit another tenant and so was shielded from liability by sovereign immunity. ***Govan v. Philadelphia Housing Authority*, 848 A.2d 193 (Pa. Cmwlth. 2004).**

Verdict only against dog owner's boyfriend who did not have dog under control when it jumped on 67 year old pedestrian affirmed. Claims of absolute negligence by reason of mere ownership of dog and negligence *per se* denied. ***McCloud v. McLaughlin*, 837 A.2d 541 (Pa. Super. 2003).**

Plaintiffs were injured by a dog that had bitten people three or more times in the prior year. In suit against township and dog owner, township's motion for summary judgment was properly granted as there was no exception present to the governmental immunity afforded the township. Plaintiffs' arguments that government's breach of state Dog Law and Dog and Rabies Ordinance constituted violation of statutes which would give plaintiffs a right of recovery were incorrect as there is no private right of action under either act. Animal exception to governmental immunity does not apply because the township did not own the dog. ***Lerro v. Upper Darby Township*, 798 A.2d 871 (Pa. Cmwlth. 2002).**

The court ruled in verse, short but not terse, and addressed all the issues presented. Two dogs and their walker, came in for a shocker, when defendant's car made one dog dented. The vet's fee at issue, for damaged dog tissue, composed the poor plaintiff's pup's claim. Driver argued contrib, cut short for this squib, as the reason the poor dog was maimed. He loudly protested, the dog was molested, because it came into the road. Unfortunately, for the driver you see, the transcript defies that contention. Sudden emergency, last clear chance, both theories were raised and were argued. The superior court, to excuse the tort, found naught in the facts or the pleadings. Payment is due, from you know who, and the dogs and their owner

Dogs

keep strolling. Though written in verse, which some find perverse, this case is correct and controlling. ***Zangrando v. Sipula*, 756 A.2d 73 (Pa. Super. 2000).**

Owners of dog that was killed by veterinarian brought action for intentional infliction of emotional distress. Veterinarian not liable. ***Miller v. Peraino*, 426 Pa. Super. 189, 626 A.2d 637.**

Child bitten by neighbor's dog. Owner not liable. Absolute liability not applicable. ***Deardorff v. Burger*, 414 Pa. Super. 45, 606 A.2d 489.**

Moped rider injured by dog that was unrestrained. Held: evidence of violation of dog law can establish prima facie case of negligence. ***Liles v. Balmer*, 389 Pa. Super. 451, 567 A.2d 691.**

Mother of child attacked by dog brought action for negligent infliction of emotional distress. Held: dog owner not liable. Mother failed to show physical harm or injury resulting from distress. ***Wall v. Fisher*, 388 Pa. Super. 305, 565 A.2d 498.**

Plaintiff who was bitten by neighbor's dog received judgement only for cost of emergency treatment. Jury not compelled to believe that a dog bite or needle puncture causes compensable pain. ***Boggavarapu v. Ponsit*, 518 Pa. 162, 542 A.2d 516.**

Visitor to home bitten by dog owned by another visitor. Where young victim was warned only to be careful, *not* an assumption of risk to pet dog. Evidence of subsequent dog bites admitted only to show dangerous propensities. Verdict for plaintiff affirmed. ***Crance v. Sohanic*, 344 Pa. Super. 526, 496 A.2d 1230.**

Out-of-possession landlord held responsible for injuries to minor tenant inflicted by another tenant's dog. Dog owner was nephew of landlord and landlord knew of dog's dangerous propensities. ***Palerno v. Nails*, 334 Pa. Super. 544, 483 A.2d 871.**

Bike accident occurred when dog chased and collided with bicycle. Reversed summary judgment in favor of defendant. Material fact existed as to adequacy of restraint and due care taken by owners in restraining dog. ***Skowronski v. Bailey*, 330 Pa. Super. 83, 478 A.2d 1362.**

Unexcused violation of dog law, allowing dog to run free, was negligence per se. Court did not impose absolute liability. Remanded for new trial. ***Miller v. Hurst*, 302 Pa. Super. 235, 448 A.2d 614.**

Boy of nine attacked by guard dog. Evidence showed that dog was being restrained by a rope held by owner. Previous incident of dog having escaped and lunging at people. For jury. Nonsuit removed. ***Snyder v. Milton Auto Parts*, 285 Pa. Super. 559, 428 A.2d 186.**

Minor plaintiff bitten by dog. Only evidence showed that dog habitually chased cars and that on day of incident owner was watching the dog chase cars and was watching as biting occurred. No evidence of previous bite. Defendant testified that children threw stones at dog. Non-jury defendant's verdict affirmed. ***Freeman v. Terzya*, 229 Pa. Super. 254, 323 A.2d 186.**

Down's Syndrome

The owner of a dog with no known vicious propensities had dog secured by a chain attached to a dog collar—ring in collar broke and dog escaped and playfully jumped on plaintiff and injured her—no responsibility on dog owner as he had fully complied with the provisions of the Dog Law (3 P.S. 460-702)—retailer of dog collar also exonerated. **Oehler v. Davis, 223 Pa. Super. 333, 293 A.2d 895.**

Dolphin

Zoo volunteer whose fingertip was bitten off by Chuckles, a South American river dolphin, may not recover against City. City is immune from suit because care, custody, and control of animals exception to governmental immunity does not include wild animals. Order denying judgment *n.o.v.* reversed. **Sakach v. City of Pittsburgh, ___ Pa. Cmwlth. ___, 687 A.2d 34 (1996).**

Doors

Inmate brought claim for negligence against prison after he was injured in a fall from his bunk while trying to open a malfunctioning cell door. The trial court granted summary judgment in favor of the prison. The Commonwealth Court upheld the trial court's ruling holding that a prison only owed a duty to inmates for reasonably foreseeable harm and that it was not reasonably foreseeable that an inmate would try to open a cell door from the top bunk and also that the inmate assumed the risk of falling by attempting to open the cell door from the top bunk knowing of the danger that he could fall. **Cochrane v. Kopko, 975 A.2d 1203 (Pa. Cmwlth. 2009).**

Mother filed suit on behalf of her daughter against property owners after her daughter was injured when non-safety glass in the sliding door her daughter walked into shattered cutting her face. The appellate court vacated the trial court's judgment and remanded for rehearing based upon the exclusion of evidence of a prior incident involving a similar sliding door on the property. **Houdeshell v. Rice, 939 A.2d 981 (Pa. Super. 2007).**

Patient injured when automatic door closed on leg. Held: compulsory nonsuit improper. Patient presented prima facia case. **McDonald v. Aliquippa Hospital, 414 Pa. Super. 317, 606 A.2d 1218.**

Plaintiff injured when struck in buttocks by automatic door at supermarket, as she bent over rail to reach for trading stamp book. Jury verdict for defendant affirmed. Held: not to be latent or unusual defect. **Brancato v. Kroger Co., Inc., 312 Pa. Super. 448, 458 A.2d 1377.**

Down's Syndrome

Although entire complaint arising out of birth of Down's Syndrome child and sterilization was inartfully drafted, two distinct claims were asserted: one for wrongful birth and one for performance of sterilization procedure without informed consent. Plaintiff's proposed amendments to complaint did not create new cause of action but clarified and strengthened claim based on lack of informed consent and, therefore, should have been allowed. Order granting judgment on the pleadings and

Drag racing

denying leave to amend reversed. *Sejpal v. Corson, McKinley,* **445 Pa. Super. 427, 665 A.2d 1198 (1995).**

Drag racing

Driver of vehicle killed while drag racing. Held: the wanton nature of drag racing while intoxicated precludes recovery by one party from another. ***Lewis v. Miller,*** **374 Pa. Super. 515, 543 A.2d 590.**

Drain grate

Plaintiff who was injured when she tripped on a raised metal drain grate in a grocery store was not permitted by the trial court to raise the *res ipsa loquitur* defense in opposition to a motion for nonsuit. Following analysis of transitory defects versus a defect in the building itself, the court held that the existence of a defect that compromises the safety of the building itself permits the plaintiff, at the compulsory nonsuit stage, to raise *res ipsa loquitur* as a defense. ***Neve v. Insalaco's,*** **771 A.2d 786 (Pa. Super. 2001).**

Dram Shop Act

Plaintiff estate brought Dram Shop Act action against Defendant bar for injuries suffered by the decedent during a motor vehicle accident. A jury found in favor of the Plaintiff. On appeal, the Superior Court affirmed holding that it was admissible to introduce evidence of Liquor Code requirements, the legal blood alcohol content level to operate a vehicle, and that the owner had allowed underage patrons to enter its establishment. ***Schuenemann v. Dreemz, LLC,*** **34 A.3d 94 (Pa. Super. 2011).**

Plaintiffs' decedent died as a result of injuries sustained in a motor vehicle accident when the driver, who was unlicensed and intoxicated, lost control of the vehicle. In suit against the bar, the driver and the owner of the car, held that owner was vicariously liable for negligence of driver even though owner"s failure to insure that driver was licensed when there was reasonable cause to suspect lack of license was not a substantial factor in harm. Trial court also found driver liable and determined that plaintiffs" decedent was 20% negligent. Good discussion of vicarious liability as distinguished from contributory negligence. ***Terwilliger v. Kitchen,*** **781 A.2d 1201 (Pa. Super. 2001)**.

Plaintiffs who were personal representatives of decedent filed suit against bar for Dram Shop Act violations which led to the death of patron. Summary judgment granted to defendant due to lack of direct eyewitness evidence that decedent was served alcoholic beverages when visibly intoxicated. Held: circumstantial evidence indicating that decedent must have been visibly intoxicated when served is adequate to create question of fact for jury and so defeat summary judgment. In instant case, patrons testified decedent was visibly intoxicated when he left bar. Police testified plaintiff was still intoxicated at least 4 hours after he left bar. Medical evidence showed that decedent's blood alcohol content was twice legal limit at least 6 hours after he left bar. Scientific evidence showed that decedent must have consumed nearly fourteen twelve-ounce beers to achieve blood alcohol content he had. ***Fandozzi v. Kelly Hotel, Inc.,*** **711 A.2d 524 (Pa. Super. 1998).**

Dram Shop Act

Defense of decedent's contributory negligence is not eliminated from consideration merely because of negligence *per se* of tavern that served decedent while he was visibly intoxicated. Remand for new trial to determine plaintiffs' decedent's comparative negligence in driving while intoxicated after having been served while visibly intoxicated. Decedent could not have legally assumed risk of driving while intoxicated following determination of tavern's negligence in serving visibly intoxicated decedent. To pierce corporate veil, against which there is a strong legal presumption, plaintiff must prove undercapitalization, intermingling of individual and corporate affairs, failure to adhere to corporate formalities and use of the corporate form to perpetrate a fraud. ***Miller v. Brass Rail Tavern, Inc.*, 702 A.2d 1072 (Pa. Super. 1997).**

A non-physician coroner properly qualified by experience is capable of testifying as to time of death in administrator's action against tavern for death of patron. ***Miller v. Brass Rail Tavern, Inc.*, 541 Pa. 474, 664 A.2d 525 (1995).**

Absent proof that a patron was visibly intoxicated when served additional alcoholic beverages, no action for wrongful death or survival is established. Statutory violation of serving alcohol after hours does not establish liability for acts of third parties absent proof that such service was proximate cause of the injury. ***Hiles v. Brandywine Club*, 443 Pa. Super. 462, 662 A.2d 16 (1995).**

Pennsylvania Dram Shop Act does not insulate employees of licensee from liability for negligence in serving alcohol to visibly intoxicated patron. Order sustaining demurrer vacated. ***Detwiler v. Brumbaugh*, 441 Pa. Super. 110, 656 A.2d 944 (1995).**

Police officer who enters upon another's land in his official capacity and in response to a call for assistance is a licensee. Landowner's duty is to inform licensee of dangerous, hidden conditions. Obviously rowdy crowd of patrons at social hall was not a dangerous, hidden condition. Although violation of Dram Shop Act is negligence *per se*, mere fact that patrons who assaulted police officer were intoxicated neither proves that they had been served when visibly intoxicated nor causation of officer's injuries. Summary judgment for defendant affirmed. ***Holpp v. Fez, Inc.*, 440 Pa. Super. 512, 656 A.2d 147 (1995).**

Suit for violation of Dram Shop Act requires proof that person was visibly intoxicated when served additional alcoholic beverages. ***Conner v. Duffy*, 438 Pa. Super. 277, 652 A.2d 372 (1994).**

Summary judgment in favor of tavern owners in dram shop case, reversed. Affidavit of moving party that plaintiff was not visibly intoxicated when served alcoholic beverages, even if uncontradicted, will not support summary judgment. Credibility of testimony is still for jury. ***Peluso v. Walter*, 334 Pa. Super. 609, 483 A.2d 905.**

Dram shop-type complaint against private party dismissed as stating no cause of action. Pennsylvania does not recognize cause of action by persons injured by intoxicated driver against social host who had served intoxicants to driver. But

Drifting vehicle

see concurring opinion and footnotes on possibility of pure negligence action. *Klein v. Raysinger,* **298 Pa. Super. 246, 444 A.2d 753.**

Plaintiff a patron of defendant's club—slight barroom brawl with another patron—evidence did not apprise barkeeper of patron's intention to injure plaintiff—defendant not an insurer—judgment for defendant on record after a "hung" jury. *Bahoric v. St. Lawrence Croatian No. 13,* **426 Pa. 90, 230 A.2d 725.**

Drifting vehicle

Compulsory nonsuit entered, reversed on appeal. Dredger had created sharp drop-off in Ohio River at boat launch area. Decedent had parked there with girlfriend—car rolled forward over drop-off. Presumption of due care precludes trial court from ruling decedent was contributorily negligent as a matter of law. *Hawthorne v. Dravo Corp.,* **313 Pa. Super. 436, 460 A.2d 266.**

Defendant's operator left his rig in front of a restaurant with motor running—rig drifted into highway—decedent operating a tractor trailer unit with view of over 1000 feet collided with rig—verdict for defendant—new trial properly refused. *Hummel v. Womeldorf,* **426 Pa. 460, 233 A.2d 215.**

Drill

Plaintiff, an employee of the U.S. Steel Corporation, injured by an air drill—suit against alleged manufacturer—injury either caused by defective drill or because drill was unexpectedly started by a fellow employee—court instructed jury that only one of defendants could be held responsible under the circumstances of the case—verdict against employer only—judgment *n.o.v.* granted as to this defendant and refusal to grant a new trial as to manufacturer sustained on appeal. *Grasha v. Ingersoll-Rand Co.,* **439 Pa. 216, 266 A.2d 710.**

Drills and drilling

Plaintiff engaged in setting up equipment to drill a well—defendant's power lines overhead—plaintiff raised the mast to be used in drilling and contacted power line—injured as a result—nonsuit proper—no evidence of notice to defendant and plaintiff guilty of contributory negligence. *Kronk v. West Penn Power Co.,* **422 Pa. 458, 222 A.2d 720.**

Drive-in theater

Plaintiff was an invitee in a drive-in theater—while in rest room of theater his hearing was affected by explosion of a firecracker, the act of rowdy boys—theater held responsible under Section 344 of Restatement (2d) Torts. *Moran v. Valley F. Drive-In Theater, Inc.,* **431 Pa. 432, 246 A.2d 875.**

Driver

Dealer sold automobile to unlicensed and uninsured driver who was later involved in a collision. Held: other driver stated cause of action against dealer. *Pizzonia v. Colonial Motors, Inc.,* **433 Pa. Super. 9, 639 A.2d 1185.**

Driveway

Motorcyclist injured when struck by automobile making left turn at intersection. Automobile entered intersection after being signaled to proceed by driver of oncoming automobile. Whether driver who gave signal is negligent is question for trier of fact. Driver found not liable. ***Askew by Askew v. Zeller*, 361 Pa. Super. 34, 521 A.2d 459.**

Court below in error in admitting evidence that driver of one of vehicles involved was unlicensed in Pennsylvania—fact of license immaterial under facts—no allegation that driver was incompetent—new trial granted. ***Emanuel v. Ketner*, 440 Pa. 141, 269 A.2d 759.**

Driver's license

Physician was sued for a failure to follow his statutory duty to report a patient's lack of fitness to operate a motor vehicle to the Pennsylvania Department of Transportation. The court held that a physician's failure to comply with the Motor Vehicle Code's reporting requirements by not reporting seizures does not create a private cause of action against the physician for an accident caused by his patient. ***Hospodar v. Schick*, 885 A.2d 986 (Pa. Super. 2005).**

Ophthalmologist's failure to report patient's poor vision to PennDOT, despite statutory obligation to do so, does not give rise to a private cause of action to plaintiff's decedent, who was killed when struck by patient's car. ***Estate of Witthoeft v. Kiskaddon*, 733 A.2d 623 (Pa. 1999).**

Plaintiff's decedent was killed while driving intoxicated without a license in an uninspected, unregistered car at too high a rate of speed. He entered a highway ramp at twice the posted speed limit despite having been on the ramp on a daily basis. Jury returned verdict in the amount of $250,000.00 and apportioned liability to plaintiff and PennDOT at fifty percent each. Plaintiff appealed, alleging inadequacy of verdict. PennDOT appealed, alleging error by trial court in refusing to allow evidence of lack of license, registration, and inspection, error in refusing to find plaintiff's decedent to be a trespasser, and error in finding any duty on PennDOT because plaintiff's decedent was not a licensed driver. Affirmed on basis that verdict was a compromise by jury, PennDOT owes a duty to all persons operating vehicles on its roads regardless of the state of their license and lack of license, registration, and inspection were, while relevant, more prejudicial than probative. ***Quinn v. Com., Dept. of Transp.*, 719 A.2d 1105 (Pa. Cmwlth. 1998).**

Defendant rented a truck—lessee's passenger injured due to negligence of operator—lessee had a driver's license—sufficient evidence of his competency and experience to exculpate lessor from liability. ***Littles et al. v. Avis Rent-A-Car System*, 433 Pa. 72, 248 A.2d 837.**

Driveway

Motorist injured in collision with vehicle exiting driveway on commercial property. Property owner not liable for failure to warn of dangerous condition. ***Cruet v. Certain-Teed Corporation*, 432 Pa. Super. 554, 639 A.2d 478.**

Drowning

Passenger injured when vehicle collided with stone pillar at entrance to private driveway. Property owner not liable. ***Braxton v. Com., Dept. of Transp.*, 160 Pa. Cmwlth. 32, 634 A.2d 1150.**

Drowning

Municipal park which contains lake and low head dam are within purview of Recreation Use of Land and Water Act. Municipality given immunity for death and injury to two minors. Decided one month after *Stone v. York Haven Power Co.*, 749 A.2d 452 (Pa. 2000) but does not cite that decision. ***Pagnotti v. Lancaster Township*, 751 A.2d 1226 (Pa. Cmwlth. 2000).**

Plaintiff minor who witnessed his cousin's drowning is not sufficiently "closely related" under Pennsylvania law to allow standing for claim of negligent infliction of emotional distress. Order sustaining preliminary objections affirmed. ***Blanyar v. Pagnotti Enterprises, Inc.*, 451 Pa. Super 269, 679 A.2d 790 (1996).**

Administratrix of teenager who drowned in city-owned pond may not recover under Political Subdivision Tort Claims Act based on allegations of city's willful or malicious failure to warn of dangerous condition of pond. Recovery under Political Subdivision Tort Claims Acts is available only for acts of negligence. Public and private lands are covered by Recreation Use of Land and Water Act. Order refusing to grant judgment *n.o.v.* reversed. ***Lory v. City of Philadelphia*, 544 Pa. 38, 674 A.2d 673 (1996).**

Willful or malicious failure to guard or warn exception to immunity under the Recreation Use of Land and Water Act applied to action by personal representative of minor's estate where minor drowned in natural pond located in city park. Evidence of prior unrelated swimming accidents inadmissable. Verdict for plaintiff reversed and remanded. ***Barr v. City and County of Philadelphia*, ___ Pa. Cmwlth. ___, 653 A.2d 1374 (1995).**

Child drowned in swimming pool leased to township. Real estate exception to Tort Claims Act not applicable. ***Sims v. Silver Springs-Martin Luther School*, 155 Pa. Cmwlth. 619, 625 A.2d 1297.**

Altar boy drowned while swimming in seminary pool. Life guard not present. Seminary liable. Delay damages of 10% reduced to 6%. ***Rivera v. Philadelphia Theological Seminary*, 398 Pa. Super. 264, 580 A.2d 1342.**

Plaintiff assaulted in subway concourse. Held: real estate exception to the Tort Claims Act not applicable in cases of criminal assault by third party. ***Johnson v. SEPTA*, 516 Pa. 312, 532 A.2d 409.**

Altar boy drowned while attending swim party at seminary pool. Seminary not immune under Recreation Use of Land and Water Act. Failure to provide lifeguard violated standard of due care. ***Rivera v. Philadelphia Theological Seminary*, 510 Pa. 1, 507 A.2d 1.**

Stranded motorist drowned when swept into storm sewer. Settled before trial with adjacent landowner, township and PennDOT. Eventual jury verdict also included neighboring city from which it was proved that most of water came. Held: under

Drugs and drug companies

facts here City of Bethlehem not liable. Gradual orderly development resulting in incremental increase in rate of flow of surface waters through natural drainage swale does not give rise to liability. Other theories put forth by plaintiff not applicable under facts here. ***Laform v. Bethlehem Township,* 346 Pa. Super. 512, 499 A.2d 1373.**

Action against school district and hotel for drowning of student while on school trip to Virginia. Held: Pennsylvania law applied and school district immune from suit under facts here. ***Davis v. School District of Philadelphia,* 91 Pa. Cmwlth. 27, 496 A.2d 903.**

Plaintiff-decedent in restaurant parking lot, at night went on wrong path with car, driving into canal, and drowned. Jury verdict $550,000 for wrongful death and $500,000 survival. ***Ehehalt v. Nyari O'Dette, Inc.,* 85 Pa. Cmwlth. 94, 481 A.2d 365.**

Drug testing

Hospital which performed drug test resulting in allegedly false-positive result for Federal Express employee held to have a duty to employee, even absent privity of contract between hospital and employee, to exercise reasonable care in collection and handling of her urine sample for employment-related drug testing. ***Sharpe v. St. Luke's Hospital,* 821 A.2d 1215 (Pa. 2003).**

Drugs and drug companies

Class action lawsuit was brought against generic drug manufacturers in part for negligence after some consumers suffered permanent neurological disorders from taking the defendants' generic drug. The trial court overruled the defendants' preliminary objections that the plaintiffs' negligence claims were pre-empted by federal law. The Superior Court affirmed in part and reversed in part. The Superior Court held that the plaintiffs' state law negligence claim for misbranding arising prior to the Food and Drug Administration Amendments Act of 2007 were not pre-empted by federal law. ***In re: Reglan/Metoclopramide Litigation,* 2013 Pa. Super. 214 (Pa. Super. 2013).**

Plaintiff filed suit against a drug manufacturer for failing to warn drug users of cardiac problems regarding its diet drug therapy fen-phen. The court held that with prescription medications the duty to warn is to the prescribing doctor and not to the patient or public at large. To prove causation for a failure to warn regarding a prescription medication the plaintiff must show that the doctor would have altered his behavior and injury to the plaintiff would have been avoided. ***Lineberger v. Wyeth Corp.,* 894 A.2d 141 (Pa. Super. 2006).**

Hospital's duty to control access to drugs pursuant to the Controlled Substance, Drug, Device and Cosmetics Act, which classifies and controls access to drugs for protection of public at large, does not create duty to individual doctor employed by hospital who is, without knowledge of hospital, abusing drugs. ***Campo v. St. Luke's Hospital,* 755 A.2d 20 (Pa. Super. 2000).**

Plaintiff who was not hired because of positive drug test sued testing company alleging negligence in testing. Summary judgment in favor of testing company

Drugs and drug companies

affirmed due to lack of required therapeutic purpose for medical service provided by testing company and consequent lack of duty. *Ney v. Axelrod*, 723 A.2d 719 (Pa. Super. 1999).

Plaintiff pedestrian appeals verdict for defendant in negligence action where trial court admitted evidence of plaintiff's history of drug and alcohol abuse and his legal intoxication at time of accident which caused his injuries. Plaintiff argues that such evidence is prejudicial and irrelevant to his claim for damages and should have been excluded. Held: allowing plaintiff to pursue a claim for permanent injury, while simultaneously barring defendant from access to plaintiff's long history of drug and alcohol abuse, "would be manifestly unfair and grossly prejudicial." Further holding that evidence of plaintiff's intoxication "as a pedestrian" was relevant and admissible if evidence would prove unfitness to cross street. ***Kraus v. Taylor*, 710 A.2d 1142 (Pa. Super. 1998).**

In action against drug manufacturer where the only allegation of wrongdoing is failure to warn of dangers of prescription drug, proper cause of action is negligence, not product liability. Judgment for drug manufacturer affirmed. ***Hahn v. Richter*, 543 Pa. 558, 673 A.2d 888 (1996).**

Patient who developed aplastic anemia after treatment by drug Diamox brought malpractice action based on lack of informed consent. Held: issue of consent was not preserved on appeal. Judgment affirmed. ***Tarter v. Linn*, 396 Pa. Super. 155, 578 A.2d 453.**

Jury verdict $750,000 plus delay damage. Alleged improper prescribing of Butazolidin by defendant physician, without proper warnings and examinations, led to condition of aplastic anemia which required regular blood transfusions, shortened life expectancy and resulted in inability to bear children. Verdict against doctor only affirmed. Drug manufacturer's warnings held to be adequate. Reversed decision of Superior Court which had ordered new trial. ***Baldino v. Castagna*, 505 Pa. 239, 478 A.2d 807.**

Adverse reaction to drug. Verdict for drug company reversed as contrary to weight of evidence. Negligence alleged to be overpromotion of drug by detailmen, and the minimizing of side effects in drug's literature. New trial ordered. ***Baldino v. Castagna*, 308 Pa. Super. 506, 454 A.2d 1012.**

Error of court to refuse to allow plaintiff to put on rebuttal evidence where issue was proper administration of drug by treating physician. Grant of new trial affirmed. ***McNair v. Weikers*, 300 Pa. Super. 379, 446 A.2d 905.**

Suit originally by minor plaintiff (now deceased) against druggist who allegedly sold the drug "Chloromycetin" without a prescription—this defendant joined initial family doctor who prescribed the drug, a doctor who issued the prescription without seeing the minor plaintiff and the corporation compounding the drug—minor died of aplastic anemia—verdict against additional defendants only—long opinion as to the defenses and liability of the additional defendants—Held: matter for the jury—verdict for the plaintiffs upheld on appeal. ***Incollingo v. Ewing*, 444 Pa. 263, 282 A.2d 206.**

Drunk driver

Pedestrian plaintiff injured by drunken driver sued passengers who may have been aware of driver's intoxication. Summary judgment in favor of defendants affirmed because a passenger does not owe a duty to a third person where driver of vehicle is intoxicated, absent a special relationship, joint enterprise, joint venture or a right to control the vehicle. ***Brandjord v. Hopper,*** **455 Pa. Super. 426, 688 A.2d 721 (1997).**

In suit by decedent's estate against minor passenger in other vehicle, an individual who is simply a passenger in a vehicle operated by an intoxicated driver may not be held responsible for the driver's negligence. Rather, liability may only be imposed where sufficient facts indicate that the passenger substantially assisted or encouraged the driver's negligent conduct. Order granting summary judgment in favor of minor passenger affirmed. ***Welc v. Porter,*** **450 Pa. Super. 112, 675 A.2d 334 (1996).**

Passenger of intoxicated driver has no duty to third person killed by driver's negligence. Passenger's mere request that driver take her somewhere and driver's acquiescence does not establish driver as agent and passenger as principal so as to establish passenger's liability to third person killed by driver's negligence. Summary judgment affirmed. ***Clayton v. McCullough,*** **448 Pa. Super. 126, 670 A.2d 710 (1996).**

In action by passenger against PennDOT for negligent design of road, judgment for PennDOT affirmed where plaintiff passenger determined to be negligent by exposing herself to an unreasonable risk in riding with a known intoxicated driver. Even minimal evidence of contributory negligence requires a charge on the issue. ***Karchner v. Flaim,*** **___ Pa. Cmwlth. ___, 661 A.2d 928 (1995).**

In automobile accident involving drunk driver who struck a stone-wall culvert that did not bear reflectors, issue of dangerous nature of stone wall precludes summary judgment in favor of PennDOT. ***Com., Dept. of Transp. v. Koons,*** **___ Pa. Cmwlth. ___, 661 A.2d 490 (1995).**

Pennsylvania Dram Shop Act does not insulate employees of licensee from liability for negligence in serving alcohol to visibly intoxicated patron. Order sustaining demurrer vacated. ***Detwiler v. Brumbaugh,*** **441 Pa. Super. 110, 656 A.2d 944 (1995).**

New trial granted on issue of damages only following grossly inadequate award of $25,000.00 for death of 18 year old passenger in car driven by drunk driver. ***Kiser v. Schulte,*** **538 Pa. 219, 648 A.2d 1 (1994).**

Plaintiff sued Commonwealth and Turnpike Commission alleging injury arising out of collision caused entirely by negligence of Commission employee driving Commission owned vehicle. Court overruled previous decisions granting immunity to Turnpike Commission but upheld immunity of Commonwealth. ***Specter v. Commonwealth,*** **462 Pa. 474, 341 A.2d 481.**

# Dumpster

Dumpster

Plaintiff filed negligence action against the food service company that operated the plant's cafeteria after he slipped and fell on cooking oil that had leaked from a dumpster. The trial court entered summary judgment for the Defendant. The Superior Court held that as the Defendant had undertaken a duty to dispose of cooking oil in sealed containers and since cooking oil had been found in the dumpster not in a sealed container it was a question of fact for the jury to determine if the Defendant was negligent. *Casselbury v. American Food Service*, 30 A.3d 510 (Pa. Super. 2011).

Defendant injured when car struck dumpster he was rummaging through did not state cause of action against owners of property who lawfully placed dumpster in front of house and who had no awareness of plaintiff's presence. Plaintiff failed to show any proximate causation between owner's placement of dumpster and his injuries. Proximate causation exists where wrongful conduct is a substantial factor in bringing about the harm incurred. Order granting summary judgment affirmed. *Amarhanov v. Fassel*, 442 Pa. Super. 111, 658 A.2d 808 (1995).

Dursban

Husband and wife sued pest-control company and Dow chemical company for injuries suffered by husband and wife as a result of husband's exposure to Dursban 2E pesticide. Only causes of action specifically or by necessary implication preempted by federal legislation are unavailable to a state court plaintiff. If plaintiff can establish a violation of Federal Insecticide, Fungicide and Rodenticide Act not predicated on failure to warn or inadequate labeling (e.g., gross negligence in reporting to EPA or negligence in testing regimen), that claim is actionable in state court. Plaintiffs' failure to cite additional newly-discovered facts in support of a new cause of action or lack of proof that additional facts were unavailable to plaintiff until disclosed by defendant precludes amendment of complaint after statute of limitations had passed. If plaintiff could establish that defendant prevented plaintiff from acquiring knowledge that would support new cause of action, and there was no other reasonable source for such information, statute of limitation would be tolled. *Romah v. Hygienic Sanitation, Inc.*, 705 A.2d 841 (Pa. Super. 1997).

Duty of care: Drug testing

Hospital which performed drug test resulting in allegedly false-positive result for Federal Express employee held to have a duty to employee, even absent privity of contract between hospital and employee, to exercise reasonable care in collection and handling of her urine sample for employment-related drug testing. *Sharpe v. St. Luke's Hospital*, 821 A.2d 1215 (Pa. 2003).

Duty of care: Miscellaneous

Co-executors sued medical center for negligence after the decedent died from a methadone overdose cause by methadone stolen from the medical center's patient. The court held that a federal statute registering and regulating medical centers distributing methadone did not create a duty of care to the public. *McCandless v. Edwards*, 908 A.2d 900 (Pa. Super. 2006).

Duty of care: Miscellaneous

Defendant insurance company had acquired title to a previously stolen vehicle which it had insured. After sale of the recovered car to an auction house, plaintiff, who purchased the car from a subsequent dealer, was arrested for driving a stolen vehicle because "stolen" status of title had not be revoked by police department. In suit by plaintiff against insurance company: held, no duty of insurance company to plaintiff to clear title to vehicle. *Salvatore v. State Farm Mutual Automobile Insurance Company*, 869 A.2d 511 (Pa. Super. 2005).

Plaintiff's decedent was killed in an automobile accident while joyriding with a 15 year old unlicenced driver who had taken his mother's car after failing to attend a court-mandated weekend residential treatment program. Summary judgment motion by the residential treatment program organization was granted on the grounds that it had no duty to the plaintiff as the delinquent driver was not under the care, custody or control of the program and the accident was not foreseeable. *Brisbane v. Outside In School of Experiential Education, Inc.*, 799 A.2d 89 (Pa. Super. 2002).

Bridge ironworker was injured when he fell from a construction site without a safety net or a connected safety line. In suit against the general contractor, summary judgment was entered because the contractors had no presence at the site and no contractual obligation to oversee safety standards and so no duty to plaintiff. Only subcontractor, plaintiff's employer, had a duty to insure his safety and in the event of a breach, workman's compensation provided recovery. *Leonard v. Com., Dept. of Transp.*, 771 A.2d 1238 (Pa. 2001).

Painting contractor sued by property owner in contract and negligence for failure to abate lead paint during job. Dismissal of contract claim affirmed. Dismissal of negligence claim reversed on grounds that a party to a contract has two duties: a contractual duty and a legal duty to act without negligence towards both the other party to the contract and third parties. One who creates a condition on behalf of a possessor of land has the same liability as the possessor of the land for physical harm to others caused by the dangerous condition. *Reformed Church v. Hooven*, 764 A.2d 1106 (Pa. Super. 2000).

Plaintiffs/home sellers and third party to transaction sued buyers' title/closing company and mortgagee bank for negligence, conversion, and intentional/negligent infliction of emotional distress. Title/closing company, after undertaking to clear title by payoff of secured and unsecured loan, only paid off unsecured loan and then mortgagee bank attached funds held by third party to real estate transaction to satisfy remaining secured loan. Court determined that plaintiffs had standing to bring negligence action against title/closing company which had undertaken duty to clear title and all outstanding loans prior to sale. *McKeeman v. Corestates Bank, N.A.*, 751 A.2d 655 (Pa. Super. 2000).

Plaintiff injured when he fell from an I-beam at a PennDOT highway construction project. He alleged that general contractor and I-beam supplier were responsible to insure a safe workplace for him. Held: absent control over the workplace, general contractor and supplier have no duty to employees of other subcontractors. *Leonard v. Com., Dept. of Transp.*, 723 A.2d 735 (Pa. Cmwlth. 1999).

Duty of care: Miscellaneous

Plaintiff who was not hired because of positive drug test sued testing company alleging negligence in testing. Summary judgment in favor of testing company affirmed due to lack of required therapeutic purpose for medical service provided by testing company and consequent lack of duty. *Ney v. Axelrod*, 723 A.2d 719 (Pa. Super. 1999).

Plaintiff was a professional football game spectator who was tackled and trampled after he caught a football that had cleared the goal posts after a field goal. Summary judgment in favor of security company responsible for fan control and stadium authority reversed on basis that no-duty rule relied on by trial court only applies to hazardous circumstances that are common, frequent and expected. Disorderly fans of which stadium authority and security company were previously aware are not a regular part of a football game. *Telega v. Security Bureau, Inc.*, 719 A.2d 372 (Pa. Super. 1998).

Pedestrian plaintiff injured by drunken driver sued passengers who may have been aware of driver's intoxication. Summary judgment in favor of defendants affirmed because a passenger does not owe a duty to a third person where driver of vehicle is intoxicated, absent a special relationship, joint enterprise, joint venture or a right to control the vehicle. *Brandjord v. Hopper,* 455 Pa. Super. 426, 688 A.2d 721 (1997).

Passenger of intoxicated driver has no duty to third person killed by driver's negligence. Passenger's mere request that driver take her somewhere and driver's acquiescence does not establish driver as agent and passenger as principal so as to establish passenger's liability to third person killed by driver's negligence. Summary judgment affirmed. *Clayton v. McCullough,* 448 Pa. Super. 126, 670 A.2d 710 (1996).

Defendant utility pole inspection company did not have duty to protect bystander from injuries sustained when bystander came into contact with downed electrical wires while assisting victims of automobile accident that damaged utility pole. Defendant inspection company's alleged negligent inspection of pole was too remote to constitute proximate cause of bystander's injuries. Bystander was not third-party beneficiary of contract between inspection company and utility company, which required inspection company only to inspect and report condition of poles. Order sustaining preliminary objections of defendant inspection company affirmed. *Hicks v. Metropolitan Edison Company,* ___ Pa. Cmwlth. ___, 665 A.2d 529 (1995).

Hospital has no duty independent of physicians to establish practice and procedure for obtaining informed consent from patients. Doctrine of informed consent applied only to physicians and surgeons who perform operations. Hospitals owe four specifically enumerated duties to all patients. Preliminary objections sustained. *Kelly v. Methodist Hospital,* 444 Pa. Super. 427, 664 A.2d 148 (1995).

In action against Recorder of Deeds by title insurance company, Recorder of Deeds has no duty to index mortgage by location. Summary judgment affirmed. *Penn Title Ins. Co. v. Deshler,* ___ Pa. Cmwlth. ___, 661 A.2d 481 (1995).

Duty of care: Miscellaneous

A person is not liable for the criminal conduct of another in the absence of a special relationship imposing a preexisting duty. No special relationship exists between independent ice cream sales contractor and ice cream manufacturer that would impose duty on manufacturer to protect independent contractor from criminal acts of third person. Summary judgment affirmed. *Elbasher v. Simco Sales Service of Pennsylvania,* **441 Pa. Super. 397, 657 A.2d 983 (1995).**

Tenant broke ankle when board broke on front porch used in common by all tenants in building. Although charge of court in error as to duty of landlord where independent contractor hired to make repairs, here verdict showed independent negligence on part of landlord, therefore error harmless. *Speer v. Barry,* **349 Pa. Super. 365, 503 A.2d 409.**

Plaintiff drove car over curb, across sidewalk, over six-inch retaining wall, through cyclone fence and into creek, in which he drowned. Held: City of Chester had no duty to maintain fence of such strength to withstand impact of car going in excess of 25 m.p.h. Events here so extraordinary as to be legally unforeseeable. *Merritt v. City of Chester,* **344 Pa. Super. 505, 496 A.2d 1220.**

During labor dispute, picketing member of local union injured in fight. Sued defendant for failing to control employees or have adequate security. Defendant joined unions. Sustained of demurrer filed by unions affirmed. Even assuming unions created atmosphere where there was susceptibility to violence, there is no duty to refrain from creating such atmosphere. *Lazar v. Rur Industries,* **337 Pa. Super. 445, 487 A.2d 29.**

Six-year old crossing limited access highway, waited for traffic and crossed suddenly—struck by motorcycle driven by defendant. Verdict for plaintiff reversed, new trial ordered. Charge held misleading. Issue: Whether child was in place of danger for sufficient time or whether there was reasonable apprehension that child might run out. Duty of care required not adequately explained in charge. *Fama v. Smith,* **303 Pa. Super. 414, 449 A.2d 755.**

Jury verdict $95,000. 1970 accident—plaintiff an 11th grade student, cut hand on circular saw, amputating one finger, severely injuring another. Guard on saw had been removed by shop instructor. Verdict against principal and school district. Guard had been off for several months. Verdict affirmed. *McKnight v. City of Philadelphia,* **299 Pa. Super. 327, 445 A.2d 778.**

Inadequate supply of gas to plaintiff's house caused pilot on heater to go out while plaintiff away causing water pipes to freeze and burst. Could be inferred that gas company had statutory duty to supply gas. Jury question. Directed verdict by court below reversed. *Cox v. Equitable Gas Co.,* **227 Pa. Super. 153, 324 A.2d 516.**

No negligence claim can be passed upon a state of facts on which the law does not impose a duty upon the defendant in favor of the plaintiff. Section 323 of Restatement (2d) Torts cannot be invoked to provide a duty or undertaking which does not exist. *Boyce v. U.S. Steel Corp.,* **446 Pa. 226, 285 A.2d 459.**

Duty of care: Of business proprietor

Duty of care: Of business proprietor

Police officer severely injured by delinquent minor driving stolen car filed suit against auto dealer/owner who had left locked car on auto auction lot. Summary judgment in favor of auto dealer and auto auction affirmed based on lack of duty to police officer. ***Roche v. Ugly Duckling Car Sales, Inc.,* 879 A.2d 785 (Pa. Super. 2005).**

Plaintiff's decedent, a bystander at an underage drinking party at a hotel on New Year's Eve, was shot by another visitor to hotel. In suit against hotel owners and security company, summary judgment in favor of defendants reversed on grounds that plaintiff's pleadings and deposition testimony established *prima facie* case of negligence, including, specifically, duty to protect decedent as business invitee from known dangerous conditions. Lethal actions of rowdy crowd of drunken underage party participants was foreseeable under the circumstances described. ***Rabutino v. Freedom State Realty Company, Inc.,* 809 A.2d 933 (Pa. Super. 2002).**

While in hospital, psychiatric patient started fire killing another patient. Granting of hospital's demurrer by lower court reversed. Issues of hospital's negligence and superseding cause for jury. ***Vattimo v. Lower Bucks Hosp.,* 59 Pa. Cmwlth. 1, 428 A.2d 765.**

Plaintiff injured at car wash while vacuuming his car when struck by car exiting car wash. For jury whether owner satisfied duty of care in placement of vacuum by showing that 200,000 cars had used car wash without incident. ***Amabile v. Auto Kleen,* 249 Pa. Super. 240, 376 A.2d 247.**

Plaintiff employed by an independent contractor to haul slag from defendant's mill—arm caught in dump truck device and situation not discovered for some 8 hours—defendant steel company held not responsible as no duty on it to see to plaintiff's safety—that duty by contract was imposed on his employer—summary judgment properly entered for defendant. ***Boyce v. U.S. Steel Corp.,* 446 Pa. 226, 285 A.2d 459.**

Duty of care: Of carrier

A common carrier has the highest duty of care to its passengers to carry them safely and enable them to alight safely at their intended destination. Bus company does not have a duty to intoxicated passengers who have disembarked from bus at their intended destination to insure that they travel safely after discharge. Trial court's refusal to grant summary judgment to bus company reversed and remanded. ***Knoud v. Galante,* ___ Pa. Super. ___, 696 A.2d 854 (1997).**

69 year old woman injured while entering terminal of defendant when door was let go by another patron. Issue of whether plaintiff was a passenger or licensee for jury. Error to charge that plaintiff was a passenger. ***Kiely v. SEPTA,* 485 Pa. Super. 205, 401 A.2d 366.**

Trackless trolley struck open door of parked vehicle while turning. Point of contact with rear of trolley. Operator must be aware that rear of vehicle can be dan-

Duty of care: Of professional

gerous while making turn. §290 of Restatement (2d) Torts. *Lebesco v. SEPTA,* **251 Pa. Super. 415, 380 A.2d 848.**

Passengers on bus injured when boys entered bus and randomly struck passengers. Common carrier has duty to repress disorder and to do whatever possible to restrain and, if necessary, remove disorderly parties. Negligent to open doors when same boys had earlier thrown stones at bus. Evidence that driver did nothing to quell disturbance. Plaintiff verdict sustained. *Mangini v. SEPTA,* **235 Pa. Super. 478, 344 A.2d 621.**

Duty of care: Of professional

Plaintiff's decedent was killed in a trench collapse while a representative of the project design engineer was at the site. In affirming dismissal of the action against the engineer, the court held that a design professional does not have a duty to protect workers from hazards on a construction site unless there was an undertaking, either by contract or course of conduct, to supervise or control the construction and/or to maintain safe conditions at the site. *Herczeg v. Hampton Township*, **766 A.2d 866 (Pa. Super. 2001).**

Hospital's duty to control access to drugs pursuant to the Controlled Substance, Drug, Device and Cosmetics Act, which classifies and controls access to drugs for protection of public at large, does not create duty to individual doctor employed by hospital who is, without knowledge of hospital, abusing drugs. *Campo v. St. Luke's Hospital*, **755 A.2d 20 (Pa. Super. 2000).**

Plaintiff's pacemaker wires were broken as a result of a fall. After going to the hospital, broken wires were removed and new ones installed. Plaintiff did not ask for old wires until almost two years later and before he had filed suit against the pacemaker manufacturer, alleging a defective product. Plaintiff never sued the pacemaker manufacturer, but did sue the hospital, alleging negligent spoliation of evidence he would have required to prosecute his case against the pacemaker manufacturer. Hospital's preliminary objections for failure to state a cause of action were sustained and affirmed on appeal. Absent some special relationship such as agreement, contract, statute or other special circumstances where one voluntarily assumes a duty by affirmative conduct, the law will not recognize a duty in a third party to preserve evidence. *Elias v. Lancaster General Hospital*, **710 A.2d 65 (Pa. Super. 1998).**

In action by estate of decedent hit by automobile while bicycling, ophthalmologist has no duty to patient to inform PennDOT of patient's poor vision. Order sustaining preliminary objections affirmed. *Estate of Witthoeft v. Kiskaddon,* **450 Pa. Super. 364, 676 A.2d 1223 (1996).**

Physician who treated woman with highly contagious, but common, viral infection has a duty to third persons to warn the patient about the risks associated with the disease, so patient may inform third persons who might come in contact with her about the risks. Order granting summary judgment in favor of defendants reversed and remanded to allow estate of minor who died as a result of coming into contact

Duty of care: Of property owner

with contagious patient to proceed to trial. ***Troxel v. A.I. DuPont Institute,* 450 Pa. Super. 71, 675 A.2d 314 (1996).**

Hospital does not have duty to ensure that its staff maintains professional liability insurance coverage. Order granting summary judgment affirmed. ***Domineck v. Mercy Hospital,* 449 Pa. Super. 313, 673 A.2d 959 (1996).**

Mental health care providers had no duty to police officer for injuries caused by patient who, one day after visiting health care facility in agitated state, drove his car into police van while experiencing a psychotic episode, injuring officer. Summary judgment affirmed. ***Heil v. Brown,* 443 Pa. Super. 502, 662 A.2d 669 (1995).**

Physician's assistant's failure to refer patient complaining of breast pain to physician is not actionable without proof of causation in suit against medical practice group instituted after discovery of breast cancer. Board certified internist is qualified to render an opinion as to the duty of care of physician's assistant. Compulsory nonsuit affirmed. ***Montgomery v. So. Philadelphia Medical Group, Inc.,* 441 Pa. Super. 146, 656 A.2d 1385 (1995).**

Duty of care: Of property owner

Plaintiff, an employee of a subcontractor, brought a claim for negligence against the Defendant school district after he fell from a ladder when the decorative column he had leaned the ladder up against gave way. The trial court entered summary judgment for the defendant. The Commonwealth Court affirmed holding that a duty cannot be imposed upon a landowner if the defective condition was created by the work of the independent contractor. In addition, a landowner has no further liability where it turns work over to an independent contractor, who selects his own equipment and employees. ***Wombacher v. Greater Johnstown School District,* 20 A.3d 1240 (Pa. Cmwlth. 2011).**

Plaintiff filed negligence action against the defendant college, general contractor and subcontractor after he fell while climbing scaffolding erected by the subcontractor. A jury rendered a verdict against all three defendants. The Superior Court reversed and remanded for entry of judgment notwithstanding the verdict in favor of the college. On appeal the Superior Court affirmed its prior ruling holding that a property owner retaining a certain degree of authority over safety issues such as supervising and enforcing safety requirements or even imposing its own safety requirements does not constitute control sufficient to impose liability. In addition, regulating the use and access to a building is not sufficient to establish control regarding the manner or methods of the work being performed to impose liability. ***Beil v. Telesis Construction, Inc.*, 11 A.3d 456 (Pa. Super. 2011).**

Administratrix sued Pennsylvania Turnpike Commission and Trumbull Corporation for failing to provide a safe work environment after her husband was killed while driving an unfamiliar truck type on the job site upon the order of his superiors. The court held; 1. That a possessor of land owes a duty of care to warn or correct dangers on his land unknown to a contractor or his employees; 2. Inspection of ongoing work at a construction site by a landowner is not evidence of control; 3. Driv-

Duty of care: Of property owner

ing a truck on a haul road is not a peculiar risk imparting liability onto a landowner. *Farabaugh v. Pennsylvania Turnpike Commission*, 590 Pa. 46 (2006).

Inherent danger of attending a baseball game is that you may be hit by a foul ball and injured as happened to plaintiff. Sports team had no duty to protect plaintiff from inherent danger of foul ball. *Pakett v. The Phillies, L.P.*, 871 A.2d 304 (Pa. Cmwlth. 2005).

Plaintiff and her decedents were passengers in a car driven by additional defendant who crossed over centerline of PennDOT road, crashed through guardrail and struck tree. Plaintiff alleged that brakes and engine had failed, that additional defendant driver was intoxicated and that PennDOT had failed to provide safe roadway because of inability of guardrail to prevent car from striking tree. Following grant of summary judgment in favor of PennDOT, plaintiff appealed. Held: PennDOT could not have adequate notice of combination of events leading to accident—loss of brakes and driver's intoxication—and therefore PennDOT had no duty to plaintiff and her decedents. *Baer v. Com., Dept. of Transp.*, 713 A.2d 189 (Pa. Cmwlth. 1998).

Co-owner of entireties property with actual knowledge of sexual abuse by other co-owner on their minor grandchildren within residence does not have duty to protect or warn grandchildren of grandfather's proclivities. Multimillion dollar compensatory and punitive damages award against grandmother reversed. While landowner may be liable for dangerous condition on the land, landowner is not liable for criminal or tortious acts of third parties. *T.A. v. Allen*, 447 Pa. Super. 302, 669 A.2d 360 (1995).

University owes no duty to students to control protestors. Student who sees open and obvious impediment to her path of travel should choose an alternate path, rather than attempting to jump from four foot wall. Order granting summary judgment affirmed. *Banks v. Trustees of University of Pennsylvania*, 446 Pa. Super. 99, 666 A.2d 329 (1995).

The determination of whether an individual is a trespasser, licensee, or invitee is for the jury. A licensee may become an invitee, thereby increasing duty of care owed by landowner. Plaintiff may recover damages where two or more substantial causes combine to cause an injury, even if no one cause standing alone would have brought about the injury. Although action of third party in pushing plaintiff off a guide wall was an intervening cause, its occurrence was not so extraordinary or unforeseeable as to make it a superseding cause which would excuse property owner for negligent maintenance of wall, which condition substantially contributed to plaintiff's injuries. *Trude v. Martin*, 442 Pa. Super. 614, 660 A.2d 626 (1995).

Inmate who ran down hallway and jumped steps, hitting his head on ceiling, failed to establish that dangerous condition existed in ceiling above steps in hallway. Duty of care to inmate is that of owner to invitee. Compulsory nonsuit granted in favor of County affirmed. *Graf v. County of Northampton*, ___ Pa. Cmwlth. ___, 654 A.2d 131 (1995).

Duty of care: To children

Plaintiff injured when vehicle in which he was a passenger skidded on icy overpass. Commonwealth has exclusive jurisdiction over control and maintenance of state highways. Township through which highway passes has no duty, even to warn of known dangers. Dismissal of Newtown Township affirmed. *Haas v. Comm. of Pa.,* **84 Pa. Cmwlth. 522, 479 A.2d 100.**

Independent contractor working on roof of smaller building within larger building. Knocked off roof by crane. He knew of danger after years of working there. Held: crane operator not negligent, but employer-owner of crane/property owner (one entity) negligent for violation of §341A of Restatement (2d) Torts. Possessor should anticipate danger despite knowledge of danger to invitee. *Skalos v. Higgins,* **303 Pa. Super. 107, 449 A.2d 601.**

Railroad responsible for maintaining 14 foot clearance of bridge over roadway. Had been reduced to 10 feet 2 inches due to numerous road repairs. Plaintiff killed while riding on top of cab of truck which went under overpass. *Marinelli v. Montour R.R. Co.,* **278 Pa. Super. 403, 420 A.2d 603.**

Employee of independent contractor injured when employee of plant owner started a machine which plaintiff was adjusting. Court below refused to charge on duty owed by possessor of land to business visitor. Error on these facts—new trial ordered. Landowner's duty toward a business visitor is the highest duty owed to any entrant upon the land. *Crotty v. Reading Industries,* **237 Pa. Super. 1, 345 A.2d 259.**

Fog emanating from cooling tower caused auto accident on turnpike. Tower originally constructed for use during spring and summer only but was being used all year long. Property owners owed duty to those using abutting highway and plaintiff's verdict affirmed. *Westerman v. Stout,* **237 Pa. Super. 195, 335 A.2d 741.**

Limb of tree fell on plaintiff's car travelling on highway killing plaintiff. Suit against owner of property and against Electric Company which performed inspections and maintenance on trees near power lines. Verdict against both defendants. Appeal only by electric company. Evidence showed that they had inspected trees along highway for 24 years and had removed limbs and branches. Tree in question has been decaying for four years. §324A(c) of Restatement (2d) Torts—gratuitously or for consideration taking over or rendering services to another and then failing to exercise reasonable care. Verdict affirmed. *Beury v. Hicks,* **227 Pa. Super. 476, 323 A.2d 788.**

Duty of care: To children

Co-owner of entireties property with actual knowledge of sexual abuse by other co-owner on their minor grandchildren within residence does not have duty to protect or warn grandchildren of grandfather's proclivities. Multimillion dollar compensatory and punitive damages award against grandmother reversed. While landowner may be liable for dangerous condition on the land, landowner is not liable for criminal or tortious acts of third parties. *T.A. v. Allen,* **447 Pa. Super. 302, 669 A.2d 360 (1995).**

Duty of care: To licensee

Injuries resulting to child while playing with playmate on playground equipment will not be deemed to have been caused by negligence absent proof of playmate acting in an unreasonable or dangerous manner. ***Schoymer v. Mexico Forge, Inc.,* 437 Pa. Super. 159, 649 A.2d 705 (1994).**

Service of any amount of alcohol in contravention of crimes code by adult host to minor is a breach of duty to care. ***Orner v. Mallick,* 515 Pa. 132, 527 A.2d 521.**

Jury verdict $95,000. 1970 accident—plaintiff an 11th grade student, cut hand on circular saw, amputating one finger, severely injuring another. Guard on saw had been removed by shop instructor. Verdict against principal and school district. Guard had been off for several months. Verdict affirmed. ***McKnight v. City of Philadelphia,* 299 Pa. Super. 327, 445 A.2d 778.**

Duty of care: To fraternity initiate

Elemental analysis of negligence and factors establishing duty between parties. Fraternity initiate sued national fraternity and local fraternity members seeking compensation for injuries sustained in hazing activities (paddling) which resulted in renal failure, hospitalization and kidney dialysis. Summary judgment in favor of all defendants reversed as to local chapter advisor who failed to properly oversee and monitor the membership process. ***Kenner v. Kappa Alpha Psi Fraternity, Inc.,* 808 A.2d 178 (Pa. Super. 2002).**

Duty of care: To invitee

Plaintiff sued a restaurant for failing to have choking treatment procedures in place after he choked on a piece of chicken in the restaurant. Court held that the defendant had satisfied its duty of care to plaintiff by summoning rescue personnel by calling 911. ***Campbell v. Eitak, Inc.,* 893 A.2d 749 (Pa. Super. 2006).**

Duty of care: To licensee

The determination of whether an individual is a trespasser, licensee or invitee is for the jury. A licensee may become an invitee, thereby increasing duty of care owed by landowner. Plaintiff may recover damages where two or more substantial causes combine to cause an injury, even if no one cause standing alone would have brought about the injury. Although action of third party in pushing plaintiff off a guide wall was an intervening cause, its occurrence was not so extraordinary or unforeseeable as to make it a superseding cause that would excuse property owner for negligent maintenance of wall, which condition substantially contributed to plaintiff's injuries. ***Trude v. Martin,* 442 Pa. Super. 614, 660 A.2d 626 (1995).**

Police officer who enters upon another's land in his official capacity and in response to a call for assistance is a licensee. Landowner's duty is to inform licensee of dangerous, hidden conditions. Obviously rowdy crowd of patrons at social hall was not a dangerous, hidden condition. Although violation of Dram Shop Act is negligence *per se,* mere fact that patrons who assaulted police officer were intoxicated neither proves that they had been served when visibly intoxicated nor causa-

Duty of care: To motor vehicle operator

tion of officer's injuries. Summary judgment for defendant affirmed. *Holpp v. Fez, Inc.,* **440 Pa. Super. 512, 656 A.2d 147 (1995).**

Duty of care: To motor vehicle operator

No duty of care by police to driver fleeing police. Utility company not liable for placement of utility pole struck by fleeing driver. *Beck v. Zabrowski,* **168 Pa. Cmwlth. 385, 650 A.2d 1152 (1994).**

County has duty to make highway reasonably safe for its intended purpose. In case for injuries arising out of automobile accident, question as to whether dangerous condition existed on highway is for jury. *McCalla v. Mura,* **538 Pa. 527, 649 A.2d 646 (1994).**

Defendant repaved highway pursuant to contract with State, causing a six inch drop-off at berm. No contract violation. Plaintiff driving on highway, lost control of vehicle and was killed allegedly due to drop-off. Fact that contractor fulfilled contract properly did not relieve him of liability to third persons if he created dangerous condition. For jury. *St. Clair v. B & L Paving,* **270 Pa. Super. 277, 411 A.2d 525.**

Duty of care: To trespasser

The determination of whether an individual is a trespasser, licensee, or invitee is for the jury. A licensee may become an invitee, thereby increasing duty of care owed by landowner. Plaintiff may recover damages where two or more substantial causes combine to cause an injury, even if no one cause standing alone would have brought about the injury. Although action of third party in pushing plaintiff off a guide wall was an intervening cause, its occurrence was not so extraordinary or unforeseeable as to make it a superseding cause which would excuse property owner for negligent maintenance of wall, which condition substantially contributed to plaintiff's injuries. *Trude v. Martin,* **442 Pa. Super. 614, 660 A.2d 626 (1995).**

Political Subdivision Tort Claims Act exception for dangerous condition of property does not extend to plaintiff who became trespasser when he climbed to roof of school building to retrieve tennis ball. School district took sufficient steps to prevent entry onto roof. Summary judgment in favor of school district affirmed. *Longbottom v. Sim-Kar Lighting Fixture Co.,* **___ Pa. Cmwlth. ___, 651 A.2d 621 (1994).**

Duty of care: To worker

Oil company who supplied gasoline to independent contractor service station had no duty to service station attendant who was assaulted and raped during course of employment. Demurrer to complaint granted. *Smith v. Exxon Corporation,* **436 Pa. Super. 221, 647 A.2d 577 (1994).**

Examining physician for worker's compensation carrier owes no duty to injured worker other than to perform examination with professional skill and to issue a report to party engaging him. *Craddock v. Gross,* **350 Pa. Super. 575, 504 A.2d 1300.**

Duty to warn

Workman injured when conveyor belt on which he was standing suddenly started, causing him to fall. Grant of motion for summary judgment in favor of contractor who installed electrical safety devices reversed. Held: material act issue as to emergency stop button and duty owed to third person other than parties to contract. ***Hess v. Fuellgraf Electric Co.,*** **350 Pa. Super. 235, 504 A.2d 332.**

Dairy farm employee who slipped and fell outside milk house sued Milk Co-operative which allegedly had duty to inspect. Held: duty to inspect went to protection of public with regard to sanitation of milk products. Summary judgment in favor of defendants affirmed. ***Johnson v. Baker,*** **346 Pa. Super. 183, 499 A.2d 372.**

During labor dispute, picketing member of local union injured in fight. Sued defendant for failing to control employees or have adequate security. Defendant joined unions. Sustained of demurrer filed by unions affirmed. Even assuming unions created atmosphere where there was susceptibility to violence, there is no duty to refrain from creating such atmosphere. ***Lazar v. Rur Industries,*** **337 Pa. Super. 445, 487 A.2d 29.**

Jury verdict $200,000. Crush injury—permanent disability to right heel of 53-year old, male warehouse employee. Dark parking lot. Employee guiding tractor-trailer rigs by voice. Had hand on rig. Fell in hole in parking lot. Issue of contributory negligence for jury. With lease silent, lessor has, over years, undertaken to keep parking area in repair. Held: a continuing duty to keep area reasonably safe for tenant's use. ***McDevitt v. Terminal Warehouse Company,*** **304 Pa. Super. 438, 450 A.2d 991.**

Jury verdict $151,000. Truck driver, rented with truck, to steel company. Driver injured while helping load truck, although not a required duty. Held: contractor engaged in independent business—not statutory employee. Held: casual employee, not subject to compensation, but causing employer to be open to liability under traditional tort principles. Held: negligent to request overweight, untrained man to do job he was physically ill-equipped to perform. ***Ashman v. Sharon Steel Corporation,*** **302 Pa. Super. 305, 448 A.2d 1054 (1982).**

Plaintiff killed when trench in which he was working collapsed. Defendant by contract required to supervise and inspect. §324(a) of Restatement (2d) Torts applicable. Plaintiff's verdict affirmed. ***Heath v. Huth Engineers,*** **279 Pa. Super. 90, 420 A.2d 758 (1980).**

Housing Authority inspector injured in fall on premises he was inspecting for safety defects. Judgment *n.o.v.* after plaintiff's verdict affirmed. Cannot hold property owner responsible for defect plaintiff was supposed to discover. ***Atkins v. Urban Redevelopment Authority,*** **489 Pa. 344, 414 A.2d 100 (1980).**

Duty to warn

A corrections officer brought a negligence action against a physician for failing to warn her that an inmate had a communicable disease. The trial court dismissed the complaint on preliminary objections. The Superior Court vacated the trial's court decision and remanded. The Pennsylvania Supreme Court on a matter of first impression held that a physician had no duty to warn a corrections officer that

Duty to warn

an inmate had a communicable disease. ***Seebold v. Prison Health Services, Inc.*, 57 A.3d 1232 (Pa. 2012).**

Plaintiff sued grocery store for negligence when plaintiff tripped over the store's blind employee's cane and was injured. The court held that obstacles are a known or obvious danger when exiting an aisle in a grocery store. A grocery store has no duty to warn of risks arising from entering or exiting its aisles. ***Campisi v. Acme Markets, Inc.*, 915 A.2d 117 (Pa. Super. 2006).**

Parents of minor child sued a fund raising company for failing to conform to the appropriate standard of care by not warning of the dangers inherent in fund raising activities, after their child was sexually assaulted while trying to solicit a subscription. The court reversed the dismissal of the complaint holding that the complaint on its face was sufficient to state a cause of action in negligence against the fund raising entity. ***R.W. and C.W. v. Manzek*, 585 Pa. 335, 888 A.2d 740 (2005).**

Plaintiff filed suit against a drug manufacturer for failing to warn drug users of cardiac problems regarding its diet drug therapy fen-phen. The court held that with prescription medications the duty to warn is to the prescribing doctor and not to the patient or public at large. To prove causation for a failure to warn regarding a prescription medication the plaintiff must show that the doctor would have altered his behavior and injury to the plaintiff would have been avoided. ***Lineberger v. Wyeth Corp.*, 894 A.2d 141 (Pa. Super. 2006).**

Plaintiff's decedent killed by her mentally ill husband after the husband informed his therapist that he was going to kill his wife. Suit commenced alleging professional negligence by therapist in failing to warn wife or inform police. After judgment on pleadings in favor of defendants, Superior Court affirmed, as did Supreme Court. Supreme Court formally adopts duty to warn doctrine in Pennsylvania if there is a specific and immediate threat of serious bodily injury to a specifically identified victim that has been communicated to the professional. While the Supreme Court found that both criteria to establish a duty to warn were met, it also determined that the telephonic warning that had been given by the therapist to the wife-victim was adequate. Two dissents suggest adequacy of warning should have gone to jury and legal standard for adequacy of warning was too broad and too ineffective. ***Emerich v. Philadelphia Center for Human Development*, 720 A.2d 1032 (Pa. 1999).**

Truck driver who drove onto very rough section of road in construction zone lost control of his vehicle and struck another truck that had jackknifed due to same conditions. First truck, in contravention of law, had not placed warning markers or flares 100 feet and 200 feet behind his vehicle to warn oncoming traffic of dangerous location of his truck immediately adjacent to the roadway. In consolidated suit by plaintiff and others against first truck driver, his trucking company and PennDOT, jury returned verdict in favor of plaintiff and against first driver's company only and allocated 41% liability to plaintiff. On appeal, Commonwealth Court held there was adequate evidence to support jury verdict in favor of plaintiff and against only one defendant. Affirmed with modification, allowing plaintiff's em-

Duty to warn

ployer to file a subrogation according to Indiana law. ***Burlington Motor Carriers v. Com., Dept. of Transp.*, 710 A.2d 148 (Pa. Cmwlth. 1998).**

Local and national Big Brother/Big Sister organization does not owe minor who was sexually abused by organization member with prior history of abuse a duty to warn where minor does not have any ties to the organization. Summary judgment affirmed. ***J.E.J. v. Tri-County Big Brothers/Big Sisters, Inc.*, ___ Pa. Super. ___, 692 A.2d 582 (1997).**

State law claims for manufacture and sale of defective surgical repair screws and plates were not preempted by medical device amendments to federal food and drug act. Actions for failure to warn, strict liability, negligence, and implied warranty are preempted by medical device amendment to federal food and drug act. Summary judgment affirmed in part and reversed in part. ***Burgstahler v. Acromed Corporation*, 448 Pa. Super. 26, 670 A.2d 658 (1996).**

Co-owner of entireties property with actual knowledge of sexual abuse by other co-owner on their minor grandchildren within residence does not have duty to protect or warn grandchildren of grandfather's proclivities. Multimillion dollar compensatory and punitive damages award against grandmother reversed. While landowner may be liable for dangerous condition on the land, landowner is not liable for criminal or tortious acts of third parties. ***T.A. v. Allen*, 447 Pa. Super. 302, 669 A.2d 360 (1995).**

In action by motorist for injuries sustained when she collided with side of a hopper car being pulled by defendant's train, railroad company whose train was actually on and moving over a crossing did not owe motorist a duty to warn of train's presence. Occupied crossing rule survived enactment of the Comparative Negligence Act. Order sustaining preliminary objections affirmed. ***Sprenkle v. Conrail*, 446 Pa. Super. 377, 666 A.2d 1099 (1995).**

Where evidence indicates that foundry worker knew that silicosis was a risk associated with being exposed to silica sand and voluntary exposed himself to the risk, employer could not be held strictly liable for failure to warn of dangers associated with silica sand as a matter of law. Order entering judgment notwithstanding the verdict in favor of employer affirmed. ***Phillips v. A-Best Products Company*, 542 Pa. 124, 665 A.2d 1167 (1995).**

Architect has no duty to warn contractor employees of visible overhead power lines that came into contact with metal scaffolding killing or injuring workers. Summary judgment in favor of architect affirmed. ***Frampton v. Dauphin Distribution Services Co.*, 436 Pa. Super. 486, 648 A.2d 326 (1994).**

Longshoreman crushed to death while attempting to load irregularly-shaped iron plates. Held: danger was obvious. No duty to warn. ***Ellis v. Chicago Bridge and Iron Company*, 376 Pa. Super. 220, 545 A.2d 906 (1988).**

Error to dismiss plaintiff's claim based upon inadequate warnings by manufacturer as to the lack of visibility of cycle to other vehicles on road without giving leave to amend or present evidence on inadequacy of warnings. Dismissal of neg-

Duty to warn

ligence claim on inadequate warnings or safety devices also held premature under circumstances. *Fravel v. Suzuki Motor Co., Ltd.,* **337 Pa. Super. 97, 486 A.2d 498.**

Plaintiff injured when vehicle in which he was a passenger skidded on icy overpass. Commonwealth has exclusive jurisdiction over control and maintenance of state highways. Township through which highway passes has no duty even to warn of known dangers. Dismissal of Newtown Twp. affirmed. *Haas v. Commonwealth,* **84 Pa. Cmwlth. 522, 479 A.2d 100.**

Jury verdict $750,000 plus delay damage. Alleged improper prescribing of Butazolidin by defendant physician, without proper warnings and examinations lead to condition of aplastic anemia which required regular blood transfusions, shortened life expectancy, and resulted in inability to bear children. Verdict against doctor only affirmed. Drug manufacturer's warnings held to be adequate. Reversed decision to Superior Court which had ordered new trial. *Baldino v. Castagna,* **505 Pa. 239, 478 A.2d 807.**

Jury verdict $220,000 plus delay damages. Plaintiff, inmate at House of Corrections, assigned to garbage detail. All toes of left foot traumatically amputated by compactor blade. Warning buzzer not working. Further issue of negligent structural modification of rear step. *Mattox v. City of Philadelphia,* **308 Pa. Super. 111, 454 A.2d 46.**

Fourteen-year old boys playing with BB gun. One killed in horseplay. Boy who shot gun testified that he knew of gun's lethal propensity. Liability therefore cannot be imposed upon manufacturer for failure to warn of propensity. *Sherk v. Daisy-Heddon,* **498 Pa. 594, 450 A.2d 615.**

Pedestrian struck by auto. Error to refuse charge that if driver saw pedestrian standing ahead, and perceived possibility that pedestrian might cross in front of auto, there was a duty to sound horn in warning. *Morris v. Moss,* **290 Pa. Super. 587, 435 A.2d 184.**

Defendant vehicle collided with embankment in construction area then struck plaintiff's car. Construction company held liable for not placing warning Plaintiff walking on well-defined but unimproved walkway adjacent to defendant's plant and the public highway. Dark—plaintiff took wrong way around bridge abutment and fell into stream. §342 of Restatement (2d) Torts—failure to warn licensee of dangerous condition. Knowledge shown by evidence of use by public for years. *Ciarimboli v. Walworth Co.,* **228 Pa. Super. 766, 315 A.2d 292.**

Proper to allow highway engineer to testify on necessity of putting warnings signs on roadway to warn of pedestrians walking in roadway. *Drew v. Labor,* **277 Pa. Super. 419, 419 A.2d 1216.**

Plaintiff's verdict in case where plaintiff robbed at train station, clothes thrown on top of train and plaintiff injured climbing on top of car to get clothes and coming in contact with electric wires. Error not to charge the duty to warn licensee extends only to that which property owner may reasonably anticipate. *Carpenter v. Penn Central,* **269 Pa. Super. 9, 409 A.2d 37.**

Duty to warn

Duty of passenger to warn driver of impending danger does not arise when it is clear that driver was fully cognizant of impending danger. ***Yannuzzi v. Mitchell,* 260 Pa. Super. 47, 393 A.2d 1005.**

Rear-end collision with parked dump truck which was parked on highway to protect workers. Driver in stopped truck and driver of auto sued contractor for failure to properly post warnings. New trial ordered due to confusing charge. ***Osterritter v. Holl,* 259 Pa. Super. 112, 393 A.2d 742.**

City employee stole quantity of swimming pool sanitizer and gave it to another employee in brown bag. While in car, plaintiff, a passenger, was severely burned when chemical spontaneously ignited. Improper to direct verdict against manufacturer. Theft irrelevant. Adequacy of warnings still at issue. ***Pegg v. General Motors,* 258 Pa. Super. 59, 391 A.2d 1074.**

Plaintiff employed by heating contractor injured when he stepped off roof of customer in dark and fell to ground. §343 of Restatement (2d) Torts—possessor of land only liable if there is a dangerous condition involving unreasonable risk to invitees and if he should expect that invitee will fail to observe condition. Motion to remove nonsuit denied. ***Kalin v. Delaware Valley Telephone Co.,* 228 Pa. Super. 849, 316 A.2d 912.**

E. coli bacteria

—E—

E. coli bacteria

Plaintiff's children were made ill by exposure to E. coli bacteria on farm during a tour. Defendant farm sought to join county Health Department as defendant alleging that the department was liable under one of two exceptions to governmental immunity – care, custody and control or real estate and care, custody and control of animals – on grounds that the department made regular inspections of the property and the animals. Held that such inspections are insufficient to constitute ownership or control of the real estate or animals and so no exception applies to allow recovery against department. *Sweeney v. Merrymead Farm, Inc.*, **799 A.2d 972 (Pa. Cmwlth. 2002)**.

Easement

Plaintiff minor's guardians filed suit against easement holder for negligence, after the minor plaintiff was injured while riding a motorbike on defendant electric utility's easement. The court held that under the Recreational Use of Land and Water Act (RULWA) private owners of undeveloped land that open it up to recreational public use free of charge are entitled to immunity. The court found that easement holders that exercised control over the easement were for statutory purposes within the definition of owners used by the statute and entitled to immunity under RULWA. ***Stanton v. Lackawanna Energy, LTD.*, 585 Pa. 550 (2005)**.

Minor injured when his motorcycle struck a fence while riding on 123 acres of vacant land. Electric power utility which had 70' easement over the area for transmission line purposes held to be an "owner or possessor" under the Recreation Use of Land and Water Act and so immune from suit on basis of compliance with other terms of the act. Allegation of mere negligence rather than willful or malicious conduct, preclude relief from bar of RULWA. ***Stanton v. Lackawanna Energy, Ltd.*, 820 A.2d 1256 (Pa. Super. 2003)**.

Summary judgment reversed where owners of property adjoining parking lot on which plaintiff slipped and fell had easement across parking lot and, therefore, question existed as to whether property owners were liable as possessor of parking lot. ***Blackman v. Federal Realty Inv. Trust*, 444 Pa. Super. 411, 664 A.2d 139 (1995)**.

Economic Loss Doctrine

Contractor brought suit against Defendant gas company for economic losses suffered when the company struck gas lines owned by the Defendant whose locations were improperly marked by an employee of the Defendant. The trial court dismissed the case based upon the economic loss doctrine on preliminary objections. The Superior Court affirmed. The Pennsylvania Supreme Court affirmed holding that the Defendant was not liable for economic losses under the Pennsylvania One Call Act as the Plaintiff had not suffered any personal injury or loss of property, but only economic damages. ***Excavation Technologies, Inc. v. Columbia Gas Company of Pennsylvania*, 985 A.2d 840 (Pa. 2009)**.

Electricity

Suit by electric company for purely economic losses suffered when water company negligently released chlorine gas into the atmosphere requiring evacuation and shut-down of electric generating plant. Summary judgment for water company affirmed on basis that there is no recovery for purely economic loss resulting from negligent acts. Additionally, Pennsylvania does not recognize private right of action for public nuisance. ***Duquesne Light Company v. Pennsylvania American Water Company*, 850 A.2d 701 (Pa. Super. 2004).**

Excavation subcontractor who had improperly relied on incorrect drawings sued companies that performed subsurface testing for the township which was building a new library. Complaint alleged purely economic damages in negligent misrepresentation claim. No cause of action exists in negligence to recover purely economic damages. ***David Pflumm Paving and Excavating, Inc. v. Foundation Services Company, F.T.*, 816 A.2d 1164 (Pa. Super. 2003).**

250 employees of a tire manufacturing plant sued landowners whose property abutted the plant property for loss of wages and benefits during repair and reconstruction of the plant necessitated by storm water runoff redirected by construction performed by one or more of the adjoining landowners. Held that the Economic Loss Doctrine provides that no cause of action exists in negligence absent physical injury or property damage. Purely economic losses alleged by plaintiffs are not recoverable. ***Adams v. Copper Beach Townhome Communities, L.P.*, 816 A.2d 301 (Pa. Super. 2003).**

Electric Utility

Electrician filed a claim for gross negligence against Defendant regional transmission organization for failing to de-energize a nearby transmission line that caused the line the electrician was working on to become energized and electrocute him. Trial court denied the Defendant's motion for summary judgment. The Superior Court on appeal held that the Federal Energy Regulatory Commission granted immunity to a regional transmission organization for liability except in cases of gross negligence or willful misconduct. ***Yorty v. PJM Interconnection, L.L.C.*, 79 A.3d 655 (Pa. Super. 2013).**

Plaintiff utility customers brought claims for negligence, strict liability, breach of contract and breach of warranty against defendant electric utility to recover damages caused from a power surge. The trial court entered summary judgment in favor of the defendant. The Superior Court affirmed in part and reversed in part. The Superior Court held that the exculpatory clause in the public utility's tariff did limit its maximum damages for a negligence action, but did not entirely preclude a claim for that cause of action. ***State Farm Fire & Casualty Co. v. PECO*, 54 A.3d 921 (Pa. Super. 2012).**

Electricity

Plaintiffs' estates filed a negligence action against Defendant power company for causing the deaths of the decedents on the basis that the power company disconnected the electricity to its customer's home. Plaintiffs claimed that the de-

Electricity

fendant caused the deaths of the decedent, because the fire was caused by a candle being used by one of the plaintiff's due to the lack of electricity. The trial court granted summary judgment in favor of the defendant. The Superior Court affirmed holding that the disconnecting of electricity was not the proximate cause of plaintiffs' deaths. ***Eckroth v. Pennsylvania Electric, Inc.*, 12 A.3d 422 (Pa. Super. 2010).**

Painting contractor and spouse filed suit against electric utility for injuries sustained as a result of electric shock and fall. Utility company's failure to object to inclusion of negligence language in jury charge on punitive damages precludes appellate review of alleged error. Superior Court affirmance of trial court's finding that defendant timely objected to flawed punitive damages charge reversed. ***Takes v. Metropolitan Edison Company*, ___Pa. ___, 695 A.2d 397 (1997).**

Plaintiff's decedent electrocuted while applying stucco to building in proximity to uninsulated electrical wires. Political Subdivision Tort Claims Act precludes imposition of liability upon governmental unit based on a theory of vicarious liability for work performed by contractor. Order granting summary judgment affirmed. ***Thomas v. City of Philadelphia*, ___ Pa. Cmwlth. ___, 668 A.2d 292 (1995).**

Barn owners' suit against electric utility for oversupply of electricity that allegedly caused fire properly initiated in Common Pleas Court. Court of Common Pleas has original jurisdiction to entertain a suit for damages against a public utility, based on its asserted failure to provide adequate services, even though subject matter of complaint against public utility is encompassed by the public utility code. P.U.C. order dismissing complaint vacated and remanded. ***Poorbaugh v. Pennsylvania P.U.C.*, ___ Pa. Cmwlth. ___, 666 A.2d 744 (1995).**

Defendant utility pole inspection company did not have duty to protect bystander from injuries sustained when bystander came into contact with downed electrical wires while assisting victims of automobile accident that damaged utility pole. Defendant inspection company's alleged negligent inspection of pole was too remote to constitute proximate cause of bystander's injuries. Bystander was not third-party beneficiary of contract between inspection company and utility company, which required inspection company only to inspect and report condition of poles. Order sustaining preliminary objections of defendant inspection company affirmed. ***Hicks v. Metropolitan Edison Company*, ___ Pa. Cmwlth. ___, 665 A.2d 529 (1995).**

Political Subdivision Tort Claims Act exception for dangerous condition of property does not extend to plaintiff who became trespasser when he climbed to roof of school building to retrieve tennis ball. School district took sufficient steps to prevent entry onto roof. Summary judgment in favor of school district affirmed. ***Longbottom v. Sim-Kar Lighting Fixture Co.*, ___ Pa. Cmwlth. ___, 651 A.2d 621 (1994).**

Where plaintiff sustained injuries after striking utility pole, utility company liable for improper placement of electric pole in highway right-of-way. Compulsory nonsuit reversed. ***Talarico v. Bonham*, 168 Pa. Cmwlth. 467, 650 A.2d 1192 (1994).**

Electricity

Architect has no duty to warn contractor employees of visible overhead power lines that came into contact with metal scaffolding killing or injuring workers. Summary judgment in favor of architect affirmed. ***Frampton v. Dauphin Distribution Services Co.,* 436 Pa. Super. 486, 648 A.2d 326 (1994).**

Trespasser electrocuted while attempting to steal copper cable. Property owner not liable. ***Dudley v. USX Corporation,* 414 Pa. Super. 160, 606 A.2d 916.**

Film processing company brought action against power company for supplying defective electrical power. Held: trial court's transfer of action to Public Utility Commission proper. ***Optimum Image, Inc. v. Philadelphia Electric Company,* 410 Pa. Super. 475, 600 A.2d 553.**

Milk production of farmer's cows declined because of stray electricity from power company's lines. Supplier of electricity owes highest duty of care in cases involving injury to property as well as injury to humans. ***Slater v. Pennsylvania Power Company,* 383 Pa. Super. 509, 557 A.2d 368.**

Employee of independent contractor was injured when he came in contact with uninsulated high voltage lines. Owner found liable even if danger was obvious. ***Beary v. Container General Corporation,* 368 Pa. Super. 61, 533 A.2d 716.**

Jury verdict $490,000 to injured plaintiff; $47,000 to wife for loss of consortium. Plaintiff guiding rail for crane operator when crane hit high tension wires causing severe electrical burns. Held: crane operator not co-employee of plaintiff under circumstances. ***Thompson v. Anthony Crane Rental,* 325 Pa. Super. 386, 473 A.2d 120.**

Employee of crane company guiding load being moved by crane, injured when crane hit electric lines on property owner's land. Suit against property owner. Sufficient evidence of negligence of property owner in not properly warning crane operators. For jury. Directed verdict overturned. New trial ordered. ***Beary v. Pennsylvania Electric Co.,* 322 Pa. Super. 52, 469 A.2d 176.**

Plaintiff decedent electrocuted while in process of erecting steel beams. Crane operator brought crane too close to high voltage wires causing arc of electricity to ground. Plaintiff's verdict reversed due to confusion evident in jury's verdict. ***Pniewski v. Kunda et al.,* 237 Pa. Super. 438, 352 A.2d 462.**

Nonsuit reversed. Plaintiff on electric pole working on cable TV cable which was on pole by virtue of license agreement. TV cable came in contact with high voltage wire and plaintiff badly burned. Lower court too narrowly restricted testimony of plaintiff's expert and should have allowed into evidence the defendant's safety manual. ***Densler v. Metropolitan Edison,* 235 Pa. Super. 585, 345 A.2d 758.**

Violation of National Electrical Code by utility company requiring 2400 volt line to be at least 8 feet from the peak or crest of a roof. Issue as to whether new owners had sufficient time to know of danger properly submitted to jury. Plaintiff's verdict affirmed. ***Yocum v. Honold,* 234 Pa. Super. 766, 345 A.2d 741.**

Verdict of $900,000.00 affirmed. Plaintiff painting electrical towers of defendant. Told by his employer that power was off. Received severe burns over 35 per

Electricity

cent of body resulting in extensive injuries. *Piso v. Weirton Steel Co., et al.*, **235 Pa. Super. 517, 345 A.2d 728.**

Plaintiff injured when aluminum siding he was installing came into contact with uninsulated electric wire of defendant. Fell off scaffold. Plaintiff's employer (additional defendant) had not provided scaffold with railing. Plaintiff's expert testified that although wires conformed to Codes, they did not constitute good engineering practice. Jury had Code before them. For jury. Plaintiff's verdict reversed on other grounds. *Burke v. Duquesne Light Co.*, **231 Pa. Super. 412, 332 A.2d 544.**

Door of elevator came in contact with plaintiff and gave him a shock—accident of nature as to not ordinarily happen in absence of negligence on part of company in charge of maintenance—$4,000.00 verdict sustained. Exclusive control applied. *Johnson v. Otis Elevator*, **225 Pa. Super. 500, 311 A.2d 656.**

Minor plaintiff aged 13 climbed a pole of defendant electrical company carrying high voltage and was severely burned—pole located near a school ground—court below granted judgment *n.o.v.* for defendant on basis that the facts did not bring situation within Section 339 (e) of Restatement (2d) Torts—affirmed on appeal by an equally divided court. *Felger v. Duquesne Light Co.*, **441 Pa. 421, 273 A.2d 738.**

Decedent, a workman, was removing a piece of spouting and contacted defendant's 13.2 KV transmission line—sustaining injuries which resulted in his death—line 6 feet, 3 inches from side of building and not 8 feet—conflicting expert testimony—held: case for jury as to death action only. *Groh v. Phila. Electric Co.*, **441 Pa. 345, 271 A.2d 265.**

Plaintiff was connected with an electrical contractor firm—injured while working in defendant's establishment—wiring antiquated and defective to plaintiff's knowledge—his work was to correct same—defendant as the possessor of land was under no duty to protect plaintiff under the circumstances—judgment *n.o.v.* for defendant properly entered. *Palenscar v. Michael J. Bobb, Inc.*, **439 Pa. 101, 266 A.2d 478.**

Plaintiff was an employee of an independent contractor on defendant's premises and engaged as a painter on a scaffold—an electric wire owned and placed by defendant arced and severed cable supporting scaffold and plaintiff injured in fall—case for jury—verdict for plaintiff upheld—maintenance of wire contrary to provisions of National Electrical Code. *Janowicz v. Crucible Steel Co. of America*, **433 Pa. 304, 249 A.2d 773.**

Hypothetical question must be based on matters which appear of record and on facts warranted by evidence—electrical fire—expert testimony by hypothetical question to connect it with blasting operation of defendant admissible. *DeFrank v. Sullivan Trail Coal Co.*, **425 Pa. 512, 229 A.2d 899.**

Plaintiff, an electrician while at work, came in contact with defendant's service wiring which was allegedly defectively insulated—plaintiff received a shock and was thrown off ladder—court below in error in directing a verdict for the defendant—matter for jury. *Meehan v. Phila. Electric Co.*, **424 Pa. 51, 225 A.2d 900.**

Elevators

Plaintiffs were owners of a building—defendant installed and operated and serviced a coin operated vending machine in same—building destroyed by fire—plaintiff's experts postulated that same caused by defective maintenance of vending machine—Supreme Court found evidence sufficient to predicate liability. ***Marrazzo v. Scranton Nehi Bottling Co.*, 422 Pa. 518, 223 A.2d 17.**

Plaintiff engaged in setting up equipment to drill a well—defendant's power lines overhead—plaintiff raised the mast to be used in drilling and contacted power line—injured as a result—nonsuit proper—no evidence of notice to defendant and plaintiff guilty of contributory negligence. ***Kronk v. West Penn Power Co.*, 422 Pa. 458, 222 A.2d 720.**

Elements of negligence

Police officer severely injured by delinquent minor driving stolen car filed suit against auto dealer/owner who had left locked car on auto auction lot. Summary judgment in favor of auto dealer and auto auction affirmed based on lack of duty to police officer. ***Roche v. Ugly Duckling Car Sales, Inc.*, 879 A.2d 785 (Pa. Super. 2005).**

Plaintiff filed suit against softball pitching coach alleging negligence for teaching an illegal and dangerous pitching style. Summary judgment in favor of pitching coach reversed based on expert reports provided by plaintiff in support of her contentions of negligence. 42 Pa.C.S. § 8332.1 which establishes negligence standard for volunteer managers, coaches, umpires, referees or non-profit organizations only applies to volunteers, not paid personnel. ***Reeves v. Middletown Athletic Association*, 866 A.2d 1115 (Pa. Super. 2005).**

Verdict in favor of plaintiff affirmed on appeal by physician who negligently applied splint to plaintiff's calf which caused burn or pressure sore which required plastic surgery to repair. Good analysis of elements of negligence and causation in medical malpractice case. "Corporate negligence" of hospital for physician's negligence not expanded to include corporate medical practice negligence for negligence of physician who was a member of the practice. ***Sutherland v. Monongahela Valley Hospital*, 856 A.2d 55 (Pa. Super. 2004).**

Injured plaintiff/appellee entitled to new trial following jury instruction that failed to inform jury of ability to award damages if the defendant's negligent acts were a substantial factor in bringing about the harm to plaintiff. ***Mietelski v. Banks*, 854 A.2d 579 (Pa. Super. 2004).**

Elemental analysis of a negligence claim in a medical malpractice action for damages sustained in delivery of child. Superior Court further examines standards for proving causation of damages. ***Cruz v. Northeastern Hospital*, 801 A.2d 602 (Pa. Super. 2002).**

Elevators

Building owner was liable to elevator mechanic who was injured when she fell from a ladder which was so close to the wall of an elevator shaft as to make it dangerous. Building owner was aware of danger by reason of prior complaints by

Elevators

other elevator mechanics but did not remedy problem. In granting new trial to defendant after verdict for plaintiff, trial court abused its discretion when it substituted its opinion of how the fall occurred for that of the jury. ***Mammoccio v. 1818 Market Partnership,* 734 A.2d 23 (Pa. Super. 1999).**

Plaintiff elevator inspector who tripped on misaligned elevator floor failed to produce evidence that product was defective and that defendant was seller. Products liability claim dismissed and verdict for defendant affirmed. ***Micciche v. Eastern Elevator Co.,* 435 Pa. Super. 219, 645 A.2d 278 (1994).**

Passenger injured when elevator lurched as she was exiting. Company that maintained elevator found negligent. ***Williams v. Otis Elevator Company,* 409 Pa. Super. 486, 598 A.2d 302.**

Jury was presented with sufficient evidence from which to infer that defendants were negligent in failing to include photoelectric cell in elevator door. ***Dallas v. F. M. Oxford, Inc.,* 381 Pa. Super. 89, 552 A.2d 1109.**

Employee who was struck in head by elevator assumed the risk when he placed his head in the elevator shaft thereby relieving employer's insurer of duty to warn. ***Malinder v. Jenkins Elevator & Machine Company,* 371 Pa. Super. 509, 538 A.2d 414.**

Passenger was crushed when elevator door suddenly closed. Held: doctrine of *res ipsa loquitor* applicable in this case. ***Carney v. Otis Elevator Company,* 370 Pa. Super. 394, 536 A.2d 804.**

Employee of subcontractor who was injured in fall down uncovered elevator shaft brought action against other subcontractor. Defendant had no duty of care and therefore was not liable. ***Weiser v. Bethlehem Steel Corporation,* 353 Pa. Super. 10, 508 A.2d 1241.**

Plaintiff, 93 years old with failing vision, fell stepping onto elevator which stopped 10-12 inches below level. Verdict affirmed against defendant responsible for maintenance (obtained by default). Nonsuit granted as to building owner. Verdict against elevator designer and installer reversed as elevator was installed 24 years earlier and hence barred by 12 year statute of limitations for improvements to real estate. ***Mitchell v. United Elevator,* 290 Pa. Super. 476, 434 A.2d 1243.**

Tenant in apartment injured when self-service elevator bucked as she was stepping off with doors opened. Duty of owner similar to common carrier. Verdict against owner only. Inspecting company exonerated as they had duty only to inspect, not make routine repairs. ***McGowan v. Devonshire Hall Apt.,* 278 Pa. Super. 229, 420 A.2d 514.**

10 year old boy fell to his death down elevator shaft in project. Doors had operated improperly for years. Other evidence of negligence and knowledge of condition and children playing with elevators. Verdict for plaintiff affirmed. ***Bethay v. Phila. Housing Authority,* 271 Pa. Super. 366, 413 A.2d 710.**

Plaintiff, passenger on freight elevator allegedly injured in fall when elevator started shaking causing his body to be compressed between elevator and wall. El-

Emergency Management Service Code

evator had no front gate. Absence of gate enough to raise issue of negligence. Nonsuit removed. For jury. ***Williams v. Eastern Elevator,* 254 Pa. Super. 393, 386 A.2d 7.**

Door of elevator came in contact with plaintiff and gave him a shock—accident of nature as to not ordinarily happen in absence of negligence on part of company in charge of maintenance—$4,000.00 verdict sustained. Exclusive control applied. ***Johnson v. Otis Elevator,* 225 Pa. Super. 500, 311 A.2d 656.**

Wife plaintiff was a practical nurse in attendance on a patient in defendant's medical center—allegedly struck by door of an elevator which could be automatically or manually operated—one Morgan was a volunteer worker and was in elevator at time of occurrence—his agency denied—verdict for plaintiff—judgment *n.o.v.* for defendant on ground that no negligence shown—solely an injury sustained in an automatic elevator without evidence of any negligent operation—affirmed on appeal. ***Linaberry v. Muhlenberg Medical Center,* 216 Pa. Super. 861, 266 A.2d 508.**

Plaintiff's decedent was an elevator operator in defendant's business property—a tenant moved elevator to 4th floor—decedent attempted to enter elevator at lobby level and fell some 15 to 18 feet into shaft—clearly guilty of contributory negligence as a matter of law—no recovery. ***Allison v. Snelling & Snelling, Inc.,* 425 Pa. 519, 229 A.2d 861.**

Embankment

Park visitor who slipped on embankment between picnic pavilion and parking lot in County park was precluded from any recovery for injuries sustained against the County under Recreation Use of Land and Water Act. Land was unimproved and no fee was charged to plaintiff for use of the park. Order denying summary judgment reversed and complaint dismissed. ***Brezinski v. County of Allegheny,* 694 A.2d 388 (Pa. Cmwlth. 1997).**

Plaintiff motorist whose automobile drifted into left lane and left the highway, traveling down an embankment and into a creek, failed to state a cause of action within real estate exception to sovereign immunity. PennDOT not required to erect guardrails along embankment where it could not foresee that motorist's vehicle would leave the highway. Order granting judgment on the pleadings affirmed. ***Felli v. Com., Dept. of Transp.,* ___ Pa. Cmwlth. ___, 666 A.2d 775 (1995).**

Embolism

Alleged failure to diagnose pulmonary embolism allegedly causing plaintiff's death. Defense verdict affirmed. Proper to cross-examine plaintiff's expert on facts tending to refute inferences or deductions, even if beyond direct, by using information in hospital record not relied upon by expert. ***Kemp v. Qualls,* 326 Pa. Super. 1369, 473 A.2d 1369.**

Emergency Management Service Code

Suit against PennDOT alleging negligence for failure to remove accumulations of ice and snow from state maintained road during declared Disaster Emergency in 1994. Summary judgment in favor of PennDOT affirmed on basis of sov-

Emergency medical care

ereign immunity and immunity under Pennsylvania's Emergency Management Services Code provisions. ***Kahres v. Henry,* 801 A.2d 650 (Pa. Super. 2002).**

Plaintiffs were injured when a grader's blade struck their car while plowing snow from the road during a state of emergency declared by the governor. Plaintiff's alleged negligence only, not willful misconduct. Under Section 7704(a) of the Pennsylvania Emergency Code, only willful misconduct is an exception to the general immunity afforded to Commonwealth employees. ***Zuppo v. Com., Dept. of Transp.*, 739 A.2d 1148 (Pa. Cmwlth. 1999).**

Emergency medical care

Assault and fight in bar led to death of plaintiff. City a defendant for failure of police to provide needed medical care. Evidence of blood alcohol, visible intoxication, bleeding from nose and mouth sufficient to go to jury. ***Furman v. Frankie,* 268 Pa. Super. 305, 408 A.2d 478.**

Emergency Medical Services Act

Elementary analysis of negligence claim by patron of tennis club who suffered brain damage due to stroke following heart attack. Plaintiffs allege that the club was negligent in not having an Automated External Defibrillator ("AED") on the premises and using the device to restart husband plaintiff's heart. Defendant club argued that the Emergency Medical Services Act precluded its untrained employees from using an AED even if it had one and the AED Good Samaritan Act had not yet been passed. Grant of summary judgment in favor of defendant club affirmed. ***Atcovitz v. Gulph Mills Tennis Club, Inc.*, 571 Pa. 580, 812 A.2d 1218 (Pa. 2002).**

Plaintiff's decedent died as a result of delay in arrival of EMS personnel who had been dispatched to the correct address with appropriate directions but went to another location. Held that failure to go to the correct address was not negligent operation of a motor vehicle under the motor vehicle exception to the Emergency Medical Services Act. EMS dispatching service operated by private hospital in the area is not afforded immunity under the act and there can be corporate liability. ***Regester v. County of Chester*, 568 Pa.410, 797 A.2d 898 (2002).**

Plaintiff patron alleged that the injuries he suffered from a heart attack were increased because defendant tennis club that did not have an automatic external defibrillator. Club pleaded that its employees were legally prohibited from using such a device under the Emergency Medical Services Act that relates to emergency medical service personnel. As there is no restriction on the use of such devices by lay persons, the elements of negligence were properly pleaded and the dismissal was reversed. ***Atcovitz v. Gulph Mills Tennis Club*, 766 A.2d 1280 (Pa. Super. 2001).**

A hospital is not within the definition of the Emergency Medical Services Act (35 P.S. § 6921) and so is not entitled to summary judgment in suit by plaintiff, alleging hospital's ambulance crew was negligent in failing to properly follow directions to plaintiff's decedent's house in response to 911 call about heart attack. ***Regester v. Longwood Ambulance*, 751 A.2d 694 (Pa. Super. 2000).**

Emergency room

Emergency medical technician

Parents, individually and on behalf of their minor child, brought suit against emergency medical technicians of a volunteer fire company for birth defects suffered by the child during the emergency medical technicians' treatment of the child. The appellate court held that the volunteer fire company had sufficiently established that it was a local agency under the Political Subdivision Tort Claims Act. *Flood v. Silfies*, **933 A.2d 1072 (Pa. Cmwlth. 2007).**

Emergency Medical Technician sued the Luzerne County Housing Authority when, while responding to an emergency call, he was struck in the head by a metal bar that fell from a garage door at a housing authority property. The court held the plaintiff had failed to provide evidence that the commonwealth agency had actual or constructive notice of the dangerous condition or defect in the garage door necessary to sustain a negligence action. *Gurnari v. Luzerne County Housing Authority*, **911 A.2d 236 (Pa. Cmwth. 2006).**

Supreme court vacates Commonwealth Court decision that a volunteer ambulance service is not entitled to protection of Political Tort Claims act and remands to trial court for evidence that ambulance service is local agency such as creation of the service by a political subdivision, municipal control of the service, benefits to the municipality, non-profit status and employee participation in municipal pension and benefit plans. *Christy v. Cranberry Volunteer Ambulance Corps,Inc.* **856 A.2d 43, 2004 WL 1822336 (Pa. 2004).**

General release of claims against emergency medical technician and ambulance service for overdose precluded claim of vicarious liability against hospital. Compulsory nonsuit in favor of hospital affirmed. *Riffe v. Vereb Ambulance Service, Inc.,* **437 Pa. Super. 613, 650 A.2d 1076 (1994).**

Emergency medical technician injured by automobile accident victim while providing treatment. Held: neither pedestrian victim nor driver tortfeasor liable due to lack of proximate cause. *Bell v. Irace,* **422 Pa. Super. 298, 619 A.2d 365.**

Emergency responder

Plaintiff firefighter brought a claim against his insurer for underinsured motorist benefits after he was injured traveling to the scene of an accident when a bridge on his own property collapsed. The trial court affirmed an arbitration panel denial of benefits on the basis that the bridge collapse was a supervening cause extinguishing liability on behalf of the driver that caused the accident to which the plaintiff was responding. The Pennsylvania Supreme Court affirmed, holding that an original tortfeasor could not be held liable for injuries attributable to a superseding cause. *Bole v. Erie Ins. Exchange*, **50 A.3d 1256 (Pa. 2012).**

Emergency room

Charge of court, on issue of hospital's responsibility to patient suffering heart attack in emergency room, held to be inadequate. Patient under care of non-staff physician who allegedly due to misinformation caused patient to be transported

Emergency Vehicle Doctrine

to another hospital. Plaintiff died en route. New trial ordered. ***Dohan v. Stahlnecker*, 313 Pa. Super. 279, 459 A.2d 1228.**

Section 429 of Restatement (2d) Torts held applicable where patient enters hospital emergency room and is treated by a physician who is actually an independent contractor. Theory of ostensible or apparent agency. ***Capan v. Divine Providence Hospital*, 287 Pa. Super. 364, 430 A.2d 647.**

Emergency Vehicle Doctrine

Plaintiff driver was injured when his vehicle was broadsided by a police car responding to a call. Plaintiff claimed that defendant police officer was driving recklessly under the standards set by the emergency vehicle doctrine (75 Pa.C.S. § 3105). Defendant argued that plaintiff was contributorily negligent as he was driving under the influence of drugs. After verdict in favor of plaintiff, jury apportioned liability 55% to plaintiff and 45% to police officer. City and police officer presented motion to mold verdict to $0 under comparative negligence and court granted motion. New trial granted on appeal because the comparative negligence act cannot be used to measure recklessness under emergency vehicle doctrine against plaintiff's negligence under the comparative negligence act. ***Johnson v. City of Philadelphia*, 808 A.2d 978 (Pa. Cmwlth. 2002).**

Emergency vehicles

Driver who was injured while fleeing police brought a negligence action against a police officer that collided with his ATV while attempting to apprehend him for traffic violations. The trial court granted summary judgment in favor of the Defendant. The Commonwealth Court affirmed holding that there was no statutory duty owed to a fleeing motorist by an officer. ***Kuniskas v. Commonwealth of Pennsylvania*, 977 A.2d 602 (Pa. Cmwlth. 2009).**

Paramedics, after transporting shooting victim to nearest hospital, refused (allegedly not told of emergency nature) to transfer to larger hospital due to company policy. Recommended private ambulance service. Plaintiff died at second hospital. Nonsuit affirmed based upon lack of evidence that paramedics were advised that inter-hospital transfer was an emergency. ***Morena v. South Hills Health System*, 501 Pa. 634, 462 A.2d 680.**

Intersection accident—auto and ambulance. Ambulance had red light, but had siren and lights on. Fire company counterclaimed for property damage and won. Reversed. Error on counterclaim to charge that fire company could recover even if negligent. True that plaintiff must show recklessness to recover, but reverse is not true for fire company as plaintiff. ***Junk v. East End Fire Department*, 262 Pa. Super. 473, 396 A.2d 1269.**

Emotional distress

Plaintiff nursing care provider received a needle stick after giving an injection to a patient that she only later learned was afflicted with AIDS. In suit claiming negligent infliction of mental distress against organization that assigned her to provide care for patient without providing her with information on the patient's AIDS

Emotional distress

status or proper equipment, summary judgement in favor of defendant reversed. The court recognized that a cause of action for mental distress for fear of contracting AIDS will lie where there are circumstances that indicate the plaintiff was actually exposed to the AIDS virus. ***Shumosky v. Lutheran Welfare Services of Northeastern, PA., Inc.* 784 A.2d 196 (Pa. Super. 2001)**.

Summary judgment against plaintiff based on spoliation of evidence reversed where defendant, not plaintiff, was the owner of the missing brake master cylinder at issue and plaintiff never had control or possession of the part at any time. Wife passenger plaintiff who was struck by body of her husband at the time of impact which caused his death and her injury had standing under the impact and bystander governing wife plaintiff's claim for negligent infliction of emotional distress. ***Long v. Yingling,* 700 A.2d 508 (Pa. Super. 1997)**.

Plaintiff, surrogate mother, sued infertility clinic under wrongful death and survival statutes, for negligent infliction of emotional distress, for fraud and for breach of fiduciary duty for the death of child murdered by sperm-donor father one month after the child's birth. After determining that clinic had waived any claim that mother lacked standing, Held: mother had stated cause of action under wrongful death and survival statutes but lacked sufficient factual basis for negligent infliction of emotional distress, fraud and breach of fiduciary duty. For-profit infertility clinic was in a "special relationship" with all parties to the transaction—surrogate mother, sperm-donor and resulting child—so as to create a duty imposed by law to effectively provide safeguards that might reasonably prevent foreseeable injuries to the parties, such as abuse of the child. ***Huddleston v. Infertility Center of America,* 700 A.2d 453 (Pa. Super. 1997)**.

Wife plaintiff who was left unattended in emergency room during miscarriage and then handed corpse of miscarried fetus while nurse took pictures established sufficient evidence of physical impact to allow recovery for negligent infliction of emotional distress. Case remanded for new trial on damages. ***Brown v. Philadelphia College of Osteopathic Medicine,* 449 Pa. Super. 667, 674 A.2d 1130 (1996)**.

Negligent infliction of emotional distress requires proof of physical contact or contemporaneous sensory observance of family member being physically injured. Employee discharged by employer has no cause of action of negligent infliction of emotional distress absent any possibility of physical impact. Summary judgment affirmed. ***Hunger v. Grand Central Sanitation,* 447 Pa. Super. 575, 670 A.2d 173 (1996)**.

Damages for future harm, embarrassment, and humiliation are appropriate in asbestos products liability case. Jury verdicts within range of $150,000.00 to $275,000.00 are not excessive for asbestosis cases. ***Giordano v. A.C.&S. Inc.,* 446 Pa. Super. 232, 666 A.2d 710 (1995)**.

Patient's unsubstantiated assertion of physical injury failed to establish negligent or intentional infliction of emotional distress. Doctor and medical center were immune from suit under Child Protective Services Law for disclosing plaintiff's admission that she had suffocated her child. Child Protective Services Law, which

Emotional distress

grants immunity for disclosures does not conflict with psychotherapist–patient privilege or the confidentiality provisions of the Mental Health Procedures Act. ***Fewell v. Bresner,* 444 Pa. Super. 559, 664 A.2d 577 (1995).**

Driver may proceed with suit against Commonwealth for common law damages based on emotional and psychological distress following accident with PennDOT construction vehicle. ***Tomikel v. Com., Dept. of Transp.,*** ___ **Pa. Cmwlth.** ___**, 658 A.2d 861 (1995).**

Sovereign immunity barred claim for intentional infliction of emotional distress in mother's case against state police for mishandling of daughter's remains. Pennsylvania law does not recognize an action for negligent mishandling of the dead. Mother's failure to allege that she witnessed any traumatic event involving her daughter's remains precluded claim for negligent infliction of emotional distress. Order sustaining defendants' preliminary objections affirmed. ***Ray v. Pennsylvania State Police,*** ___ **Pa. Cmwlth.** ___**, 654 A.2d 140 (1995).**

Physician discharged from employment brought action for intentional infliction of emotional distress. Employer not liable. ***Zikria v. Association of Thoracic and Cardiovascular Surgeons, P.C.,* 432 Pa. Super. 248, 637 A.2d 1367.**

Wife brought action for negligent infliction of emotional distress after being erroneously informed that husband was injured. Hospital not liable. ***Armstrong v. Paoli Memorial Hospital,* 430 Pa. Super. 36, 633 A.2d 605.**

Student brought action for intentional infliction of emotional distress. College not liable. Student did not seek medical treatment. ***Britt v. Chestnut College,* 429 Pa. Super. 263, 632 A.2d 557.**

Owners of dog that was killed by veterinarian brought action for intentional infliction of emotional distress. Veterinarian not liable. ***Miller v. Peraino,* 426 Pa. Super. 189, 626 A.2d 637.**

Victim of sexual harassment brought action against employer claiming attack by third party and intentional infliction of emotional distress. Employer not liable. ***Kryeski v. Schott Glass Technologies, Inc.,* 426 Pa. Super. 105, 626 A.2d 595.**

Parents of altar boy sexually assaulted by priest brought action against diocese, parish, and priest for intentional infliction of emotional distress. Defendants not liable. ***Johnson v. Caparelli,* 425 Pa. Super. 404, 625 A.2d 668.**

Patient received blood that tested positive for AIDS virus during in vitro fertilization procedure. Hospital and physician not liable for negligent infliction of emotional distress. ***Lubowitz v. Albert Einstein Medical Center,* 424 Pa. Super. 468, 623 A.2d 3.**

Mother brought action against driver who injured children in accident. Held: mother stated claim even though she did not witness accident or sustain physical injury. ***Krysmalski by Krysmalski v. Tarasovich,* 424 Pa. Super. 121, 622 A.2d 298.**

Emotional distress

Employee brought action for intentional infliction of emotional distress. Employer granted judgment *n.o.v.* Reversed. Expert testimony as to damages not required under facts of case. **Hackney v. Woodring, 424 Pa. Super. 96, 622 A.2d 286.**

Dismissed employee brought action for intentional infliction of emotional distress. Employer not liable. Conduct not outrageous. **Jacques v. Akzo International Salt, Inc., 422 Pa. Super. 419, 619 A.2d 748.**

Parents who adopted child with severe psychological illness brought action against adoption agency and youth services agency. Held: demurrer to emotional distress but not negligent placement upheld. **Gibbs v. Ernst, 150 Pa. Cmwlth. 154, 615 A.2d 851.**

Daughter witnessed negligent medical treatment of mother. Held: no recovery against nursing home and physician for infliction of emotional distress. **Kelly v. Resource Housing of America, 419 Pa. Super. 393, 615 A.2d 423.**

Worker attempted suicide after negotiations on his workman's compensation claim collapsed. Insurance carrier not liable for negligent and intentional infliction of emotional distress. **Santiago v. Pennsylvania National Mutual Casualty Insurance Company, 418 Pa. Super. 178, 613 A.2d 1235.**

Police officer who witnessed man being crushed to death in trash compactor brought action for negligent infliction of emotional distress. Owner of compactor not liable. **Covello v. Weis Markets, Inc., 415 Pa. Super. 610, 610 A.2d 50.**

Daughter of deceased brought action against physician for negligent infliction of emotional distress after witnessing mother's death. Held: cause of action stated. Dismissal inappropriate. **Love v. Cramer, 414 Pa. Super. 231, 606 A.2d 1175.**

Worker brought action against employer for intentional infliction of emotional distress claiming harassment after on-job injury. Employer not liable. **Shaffer v. Procter & Gamble, 412 Pa. Super. 630, 604 A.2d 289.**

City employee who was harassed by coworkers brought action against supervisor for intentional infliction of emotional distress and against city for negligent supervision. Neither defendant liable. **McNeal v. City of Easton, 143 Pa. Cmwlth. 151, 598 A.2d 638.**

Hospital patient who attempted suicide was found by husband. Hospital not immune under Mental Health Procedures Act and not liable for negligent infliction of emotional distress. **Bloom v. Dubois Regional Medical Center, 409 Pa. Super. 83, 597 A.2d 671.**

Patient who suffered miscarriage brought actions for malpractice and for intentional and negligent infliction of emotional distress against obstetrician and physician who covered when he was unavailable. Neither physician liable. **Strain v. Ferroni, 405 Pa. Super. 349, 592 A.2d 698.**

Captain of barge brought action against employer for emotional injury caused by hiring of unstable seaman. Employer not liable. **Klineburger v. Maritrans, 404 Pa. Super. 490, 591 A.2d 314.**

Emotional distress

Patient brought action against hospital for negligent and intentional infliction of emotional distress caused by noise from employee's birthday party. Hospital not liable. ***Abadie v. Riddle Memorial Hospital*, 404 Pa. Super. 8, 589 A.2d 1143.**

Employee brought action for intentional infliction of emotional distress against employer. Action barred by Workmen's Compensation Act. ***Papa v. Franklin Mint Corporation*, 400 Pa. Super. 358, 583 A.2d 826.**

Suspect who jumped out of window when police threatened to break down door brought action for negligence and intentional infliction of emotional distress. City not liable. Injuries not foreseeable and conduct not extreme or outrageous. ***Carson v. City of Philadelphia*, 133 Pa. Cmwlth. 74, 574 A.2d 1184.**

Wife of deceased brought action for intentional infliction of emotional distress against owner of mausoleum. Held: temporary burial of husbands remains against wife's wishes but in accordance with contract not extreme or outrageous conduct. ***Baker v. Morjon, Inc.*, 393 Pa. Super. 409, 574 A.2d 676.**

Patient notified he tested positive for AIDS as a result of erroneous blood test. Physician found not liable for lack of informed consent or intentional infliction of emotional distress. ***Doe v. Dyer-Goode*, 389 Pa. Super. 151, 566 A.2d 889.**

Mother of child attacked by dog brought action for negligent infliction of emotional distress. Held: dog owner not liable. Mother failed to show physical harm or injury resulting from distress. ***Wall v. Fisher*, 388 Pa. Super. 305, 565 A.2d 498.**

Wife saw husband's vehicle being followed by speeding vehicle and heard, but did not see, the following collision. Held: plaintiff stated a cause of action for negligent infliction of emotional distress. ***Neff v. Lasso*, 382 Pa. Super. 487, 555 A.2d 1304.**

Petroleum products from service station contaminated neighbors' wells. Neighbors brought action for negligent infliction of emotional distress. Held: there can be no recovery in the absence of attendant physical injury. ***Houston v. Texaco, Inc.*, 371 Pa. Super. 399, 538 A.2d 502.**

Employee who was wrongfully reassigned for allegedly making suggestive remarks to a customer brought action for intentional infliction of emotional distress against employer. Held: there is no liability for the mere negligent infliction of emotional distress. ***Jackson v. Sun Oil Company*, 361 Pa. Super. 54, 521 A.2d 469.**

Mother who was informed of daughter's involvement in automobile accident by telephone and who later arrived at the scene could not recover for negligent infliction of emotional distress. ***Mazzagotti v. Everingham*, 512 Pa. 266, 516 A.2d 672.**

Patient died of complications following elective surgery. Husband and daughter asserted claims for negligent infliction of emotional distress. Held: action will not lie unless the bystander personally observes an identifiable traumatic event. ***Halliday v. Beltz*, 356 Pa. Super. 375, 514 A.2d 906.**

Employee

Estate of stillborn child has no action for damages which allegedly occurred owing to negligent prenatal care. Parents have no cause of action for emotional stress without showing of physical injury. *Justice v. Booth Maternity Center,* **345 Pa. Super. 529, 498 A.2d 950.**

Emphysema

Plaintiff suffered from emphysema caused by cigarette smoking and from asbestosis. Experts testified that determination of relative contributions of asbestos exposure and cigarette smoking to disability not possible. Held: jury not capable of apportioning damages in this case. *Martin v. Owens-Corning Fiberglas,* **515 Pa. 377, 528 A.2d 947.**

Employee

An employee injured in an automobile accident driven by a co-employee who had consumed alcoholic beverages brought suit against the co-employee driver. Trial court held that the injured employee's third party tort claim against the co-employee driver was barred by the Workers' Compensation Act. Superior Court affirmed in part and reversed in part, holding that consumption of alcoholic beverages does not per se take an employee's actions outside the scope of employment for purposes of the exclusivity of the Workers' Compensation Act. *Employers Mutual Casualty Co. v. Boiler Erection and Repair Co.,* **964 A.2d 381 (Pa. Super. 2008).**

Foster parents assigned by county Children and Youth Service agency were employees of agency and so entitled to immunity under Political Subdivision Tort Claims Act. *Patterson v. Lycoming County,* **815 A.2d 659 (Pa. Cmwlth. 2003).**

Employee injured in fall down steps brought action against building owners. Owners officers in corporation employing plaintiff. Held: issues of material fact existed that precluded summary judgment. *Fern v. Usser,* **428 Pa. Super. 210, 630 A.2d 896.**

Employee of independent contractor injured in fall from ladder. Telephone company not liable. Peculiar Risk Doctrine not applicable. *Steiner v. Bell of Pennsylvania,* **426 Pa. Super. 84, 626 A.2d 584.**

Employee of independent contractor injured in fall from ladder. Owner of land not liable. Peculiar Risk Doctrine not applicable. *Lorah v. Luppold Roofing Company, Inc.,* **424 Pa. Super. 439, 622 A.2d 1383.**

Employee injured on job brought action against employer's landlord. Employer did not obtain workman's compensation insurance. Landlord not liable. *Deeter v. Dull Corporation, Inc.,* **420 Pa. Super. 576, 617 A.2d 336.**

Employee who fell down stairs leading to employer's office brought action against owner and builder of office building. Defendants not liable. *Dilauro v. One Bala Avenue Associates,* **419 Pa. Super. 191, 615 A.2d 90.**

Suit against employer of individual who allegedly caused auto accident while not on job. Alleged that employer failed to monitor employee's mental state

Employee of contractor or subcontractor

and placed too much stress on employee, causing him to have emotional breakdown while driving. Demurrer sustained. ***Hill v. Acme,* 350 Pa. Super. 219, 504 A.2d 324.**

Dairy farm employee who slipped and fell outside milk house sued Milk Co-operative which allegedly had duty to inspect. Held: duty to inspect went to protection of public with regard to sanitation of milk products. Summary judgment in favor of defendants affirmed. ***Johnson v. Baker,* 346 Pa. Super. 183, 499 A.2d 372.**

Employee of contractor or subcontractor

Plaintiff subcontractor's employee brought negligence action against general contractor for injuries suffered in a fall at the work site. Trial court entered judgment on the verdict in favor of the Plaintiff. The Superior Court, on appeal, held that the general contractor was entitled to statutory immunity under the Workers' Compensation Act based upon the statutory employer doctrine. ***Sheard v. J.J. De-Luca Co., Inc.*, 92 A.3d 68 (Pa. Super. 2014).**

Reversal of trial court decision to sustain school district's preliminary objections where pleadings indicated that plaintiff field service engineer was not in any better position than school district to see whether elevated catwalk was safe to walk on. ***Beaver v. Coatesville Area School District*, 845 A.2d 955 (Pa. Cmwlth. 2004).**

Employee of contractor injured in fall at work site owned by city. City not liable. ***Canizares v. City of Philadelphia,* 162 Pa. Cmwlth. 444, 639 A.2d 882.**

Employee of contractor injured in fall brought action against owner of construction site based on §§411, 416, and 427 of Restatement (2d) Torts. Owner not liable. ***Mentzer v. Ognibene,* 408 Pa. Super. 578, 597 A.2d 604.**

Employee of subcontractor injured in fall from ladder brought action against owner of construction site. Owner not liable. ***Peffer v. Penn 21 Associates,* 406 Pa. Super. 460, 594 A.2d 711.**

Employee of subcontractor brought negligence action against general contractor for on job injury. General contractor was statutory employer and therefore not liable. Contract language to the contrary not controlling. ***Pastore v. Anjo Construction Company,* 396 Pa. Super. 58, 578 A.2d 21.**

Employee of subcontractor injured on job brought action against engineering firm that signed contract on behalf of power company. Engineering firm not immune. Was not party to contract and not statutory employer. ***Travaglia v. C. H. Schwertner & Son, Inc.,* 391 Pa. Super. 61, 570 A.2d 513.**

Employee of subcontractor injured while riding in hoist brought action against general contractor. Judgment for plaintiff. Hoist operated contrary to safety regulations. General contractor not statutory employer. ***Cox v. Turner Construction Company,* 373 Pa. Super. 214, 540 A.2d 944.**

Worker's Compensation Act does not bar wrongful death action in case where employee of subcontractor is killed as a result of negligence of different subcontractor. ***Grant v. Riverside Corp.,* 364 Pa. Super. 593, 528 A.2d 962.**

Employer's liability

An employee of a carpenter subcontractor injured by reason of improper shoring—general contractor had employed a subcontractor to do excavation work—this subcontractor employed a highlift truck and operator—Held: a verdict solely against excavating subcontractor proper as the operator was not a borrowed or loaned employee—whether general contractor was a statutory employer not passed upon on appeal. ***Hamler v. Waldron et al.,*** **445 Pa. 262, 284 A.2d 725.**

Employee pension plan

Medical corporation filed legal malpractice action against law firm for inadequate preparation and filing of corporation's employee pension plan. Order granting summary judgment for defendant firm affirmed on grounds that statute of limitations had expired. Statute began to run on date that pension plan was denied by Internal Revenue Service. Subsequent administrative appeal to IRS did not toll statute. ***Robbins & Seventko Orthopedic Surgeons, Inc. v. Geisenberger,*** **449 Pa. Super. 367, 674 A.2d 244 (1996).**

Employer's duty

Trial court properly granted summary judgment in favor of employer of schizophrenic truck driver who shot and killed one man and wounded another after driving employer's truck into front yard of first victim. Driver's criminal activity was wholly outside scope of his employment. Employer's failure to investigate driver's past criminal behavior, other than his driving record, was permitted. Employer's duty is simply to hire competent drivers. Employer is not required to insure safety of those who come into contact with employee by reason other than his employment. ***Brezenski v. World Truck Transfer, Inc.,*** **755 A.2d 36 (Pa. Super. 2000).**

Member of local union, on picket duty during labor dispute, injured in fight. Even assuming unions created atmosphere susceptible to violence, there is no duty to refrain from creating such an atmosphere. ***LaZar v. Rur Industries,*** **337 Pa. Super. 445, 487 A.2d 29.**

Employer's liability

Plaintiff brought negligence action against out of state employer after its employee stuck Plaintiff's vehicle. The trial court dismissed the case based upon a lack of personal jurisdiction. The Superior Court reversed holding that as the employee was acting within the scope of his employment the court had jurisdiction over the out-of-state employer under Pennsylvania's Long-Arm Statute. ***Sciavone v. Aveta,*** **41 A.3d 861 (Pa. Super. 2012).**

Plaintiff brought lawsuit against Defendant employer after he was injured operating a machine manufactured by the successor in interest to his employer. The trial court dismissed Plaintiff's complaint. The Superior Court affirmed holding that the Pennsylvania Supreme Court has not accepted the Dual Persona Doctrine exception to the exclusivity of the Workers' Compensation Act. ***Soto v. Nabisco, Inc.,*** **32 A.3d 787 (Pa. Super. 2011).**

Employer's liability

Plaintiff brought lawsuit for negligence and strict liability against Defendant university for exposure to asbestos. The trial court granted summary judgment in favor of the Defendant on the basis that Plaintiff was a paid graduate student at the time of his exposure and immune based upon the Workers' Compensation Act. The Superior Court reversed holding that it was a question of fact for the jury as to what percentage of exposure occurred while Plaintiff was working in his capacity as an employee and when he was working in his capacity as a Ph.D. student. *Sabol v. Allied Glove Corporation,* **37 A.3d 1198 (Pa. Super. 2011).**

Employee, injured during the course of his employment, brought a claim for damages against his employer for negligently destroying parts of the truck that caused his injury, which the employee intended to use in a third party tort suit. The trial court dismissed the employee's claims on the basis that they were barred based on the Workers' Compensation Act. The Superior Court reversed, holding that the Workers' Compensation Act did not bar an employee's claim for negligent destruction of evidence against his employer as the injury did not arise during the course of the employee's employment. *Minto v. J.B. Hunt Transportation Services, Inc.,* **971 A.2d 1280 (Pa. Super. 2009).**

An employee who is sexually assaulted and raped by a co-employee may still pursue a negligence claim against the employer under the "personal animus" or "third party attack" exception to the exclusivity provisions of the workers compensation act. Because the attack in the instant case was based on purely personal motives, unrelated to the employment, plaintiff was entitled to proceed with her common law action. *Krasevic v. Goodwill Industries, Inc.,* **764 A.2d 561 (Pa. Super. 2000).**

Plaintiff was head of security at defendant hospital and was attacked by an employee who had been brought to supervisor's office for submission to urinalysis. Plaintiff alleged that tortfeasor was acting in his capacity as employee of the hospital and therefore hospital was liable under doctrine of *respondeat superior*. Defendant's motion for summary judgment sustained and affirmed on appeal. Tortfeasor's intentional act of injuring plaintiff was in no way related to his job description as laundry worker and there was no evidence from plaintiff of any expectation on the part of the defendant employer that the tortfeasor would act violently. *Costa v. Roxborough Memorial Hospital,* **708 A.2d 490 (Pa. Super. 1998).**

Action by passenger of stolen pizza delivery vehicle after vehicle crashed into pole dismissed against delivery driver and his employer for plaintiff's failure to establish causation. *Matos v. Rivera,* **436 Pa. Super. 509, 648 A.2d 337 (1994).**

Employee brought action against employer for wrongfully identifying her as thief. Employer not liable. *Jaindl v. Mohr,* **432 Pa. Super. 220, 637 A.2d 1353.**

Tenant in apartment complex murdered by maintenance worker. Held: management company that originally hired worker not liable for wrongful death. *Pittsburgh National Bank v. Perr,* **431 Pa. Super. 580, 637 A.2d 334.**

Fight between two employees in parking lot of employer. Employer held in suit between employees as it was a jury question as to employer's independent negligence in this personal matter. ***Gillespie v. Vecenie***, **292 Pa. Super. 11, 436 A.2d 695.**

Customer of defendant raped in her home by former employee. Demurrer sustained by lower court—reversed. Even though employer-employee relationship terminated, if employer had negligently hired said person, he may owe duty to customers to whose homes employee had been sent while employed, to warn of firing and circumstances. ***Coath v. Jones,*** **277 Pa. Super. 479, 419 A.2d 1249.**

Baby sitter, while in employ of parents of small children, struck service station attendant while driving her own car. Action against parents of child disallowed. They neither expected nor gave permission for sitter to use car in scope of employment. ***Ferrell v. Martin,*** **276 Pa. Super. 175, 419 A.2d 152.**

Duty of employer to instruct an inexperienced driver how to operate a tractor on a freshly graded road—failure to do evidence of negligence. ***Michaels v. Tubbs,*** **221 Pa. Super. 255, 289 A.2d 738.**

Plaintiff injured by acts of an employee of defendant company—case tried not on theory of *respondeat superior* but on ground that defendant was negligent in employing its agent and failed to make proper investigation as to his character—held: under Section 317 of Restatement (2d) Torts defendant was not negligent in employing its agent. ***Dempsy v. Walso Bureau, Inc.,*** **431 Pa. 562, 246 A.2d 418.**

Encephalitis

Plaintiffs are parents of a son who developed mental and physical limitations as a result of encephalitis following administration of a measles, mumps and rubella vaccination. Suit against hospital and physician who administered vaccination. After suit first brought, plaintiffs accepted judgment under federal National Vaccine Injury Compensation Program and then recommenced suit in state court. Held: acceptance of judgment in federal program bars recovery in state action absent some claim that an action other than administration or effect of vaccination was cause of injury. ***Harman v. Borah***, **720 A.2d 1058 (Pa. Super. 1998).**

Engine running

Plaintiff was a volunteer worker helping blacktop a parking lot—struck by tractor used to roll asphalt—defendant operator left tractor engine running—his 7 year old son started machine and plaintiff injured—owner of premises and operator of tractor properly held jointly responsible. ***Glass v. Freeman,*** **430 Pa. 21, 240 A.2d 825.**

Entering highway

Operator of a car entering main highway from a side driveway must continue to look as he enters highway—failure to do constitutes evidence of negligence—collision with car on main highway—nonsuit proper. ***Billow v. Farmers Trust Co.,*** **438 Pa. 514, 266 A.2d 92.**

En ventre sa mere

En ventre sa mere

Injuries received by child while *en ventre sa mere* formerly could form basis for survival or wrongful death actions as maintained only on behalf of child born alive. Live birth now held no longer to be a limiting prerequisite to maintenance of such action. Case remanded for further proceedings. ***Amadio v. Levin,* 509 Pa. 199, 501 A.2d 1085.**

Epilepsy

Verdict $22,000—collision case—plaintiff alleged that traumatic epilepsy resulted from the trauma of the accident—out-of-pocket expenses and loss of wages disputed—motion of plaintiff on ground of inadequacy refused. ***Wilson v. Nelson,* 437 Pa. 254, 258 A.2d 657.**

Proper to permit physician to testify from statistical knowledge the probability of a child with a skull fracture and brain damage having epileptic seizures in the future. ***Schwegel v. Goldberg,* 209 Pa. Super. 280, 228 A.2d 405.**

Episiotomy

Not every wrong constitutes a legally cognizable cause of action. A physician who fails to remove sponges following an episiotomy resulting in no more than a foul odor is not subject to liability where no causal link between an act of negligence and legally cognizable injury is established. Order granting motion for nonsuit affirmed. ***Gregorio v. Zeluck,* 451 Pa. Super. 154, 678 A.2d 810 (1996).**

ERISA

When a Health Maintenance Organization makes a treatment decision that affects the type of care or the time in which a patient receives care, the HMO may be liable for negligence under state law for injuries sustained as a result of that decision. Federal preemption under the Employee Retirement Income Security Act of 1974 relates to eligibility determinations only. ***Pappas v. Asbel,* 768 A.2d 1089 (Pa. 2001).**

Federal Employee Retirement Income Security Act provisions regarding federal preemption of state laws which "relate to" ERISA benefits and plans do not preempt negligence claims against HMO for failure to timely approve emergency treatment to patient-plaintiff who suffered permanent injury by reason of delay. ***Pappas v. Asbel,* 724 A.2d 889 (Pa. 1998).**

Errand

Undisputed facts showed injurious activity of individual defendant to be outside scope of employment. Accident on July 4th; defendant did not have permission to use vehicle; was on errand for father. Summary judgment for employer affirmed. ***Johnson v. Glenn Sand and Gravel,* 308 Pa. Super. 22, 453 A.2d 1048.**

Escalators

Plaintiff minor was injured when his shoe was caught in escalator. Plaintiffs raised negligence and *res ipsa loquitur* claims in complaint (even though *res ipsa* is rule of evidence and not cause of action). Trial court refused to give *res ipsa* charge because plaintiffs had introduced evidence tending to show specific acts of negligence. Held: *res ipsa* charge is permissible as long as plaintiff has not presented evidence which tends to support a single cause of incident causing injury. When plaintiff presents as specific a case of negligence as possible, yet is unable to demonstrate exact cause of accident, plaintiff is entitled to *res ipsa loquitur* charge. **D'Arnenne v. Strawbridge & Clothier, 712 A.2d 318 (Pa. Super. 1998).**

Escalator maintenance company appealed verdict because jury's answers to interrogatories inconsistent. Company's failure to object at time of verdict constituted waiver. **Curran v. Greate Bay Hotel and Casino, 434 Pa. Super. 368, 643 A.2d 687.**

Boy of four had foot caught in escalator in defendant's store. §328D of Restatement (2d) Torts accepted a law of Commonwealth. *Res ipsa loquitur* can be used under terms and conditions set forth in Restatement. Exclusive control not required. Although Korvette's had day-to-day responsibility for safe function of escalator, Otis by contract assumed responsibility of regular maintenance. New trial as to Otis ordered due to error in charge. **Gilbert v. Korvette's and Otis Elevator, 457 Pa. 602, 327 A.2d 94.**

Escaped patient

Additional defendant walked out of defendant institution without being seen, went to her apartment and got a gun, then went to her boyfriend's apartment and shot and killed a girl in that apartment. Verdict against additional defendant only, affirmed. **Evanuik v. University of Pittsburgh Western Psychiatric Institute, 234 Pa. Super. 287, 338 A.2d 636.**

Escaped prisoner

Local government not liable for injury caused by escaped criminal. Real Estate exception to Tort Claims Act not applicable. **Mascoro v. Youth Study Center, 514 Pa. 351, 523 A.2d 1118.**

Estate planning

Administratrix brought lawsuit against County Register of Wills for issuing a grant of letters of administration without securing a bond resulting in the estate losing funds. The trial court granted summary judgment on the basis that the register was immune under the Political Subdivision Tort Claims Act. The Commonwealth Court reversed and remanded. The Pennsylvania Supreme Court affirmed the Commonwealth Court holding that the Political Subdivision Tort Claims Act does not immunize Registers for violations of the Probate Estates and Fiduciary Code §3712. **Dorsey v. Redman, 96 A.3d 332 (Pa. 2014).**

Executors sought witness fees, costs, and attorney's fees after the trial court denied a petition to have them removed as executors. The trial court dismissed the motion for fees on the basis that the motion was not filed within 20 days of its final order. The Superior Court, on appeal, held that the Orphans' Court retained jurisdic-

Excavation

tion for 30 days after the entry of a final order on a petition for removal of an executor. *In re: Estate of Mary L. Bechtel*, **92 A.3d 833 (Pa. Super. 2014)**.

Suit by deceased's husband who was executor and legatee of decedent's estate against attorney who drafted will was dismissed on summary judgment because there was no evidence by plaintiff that effect of will was inconsistent with testatrix's wishes. *Jones v. Wilt*, **871 A.2d 210 (Pa. Super. 2005)**.

Excavation

Excavator brought a claim against a gas utility company for negligent misrepresentation for purely economic damages associated with the gas utility company's improper marking of gas lines under the Pennsylvania One Call Act. The appellate court sustained the trial court's decision holding that under the economic loss rule some physical harm must occur to the Plaintiff's property or person to recover in a negligence action. *Excavation Technologies, Inc. v. Columbia Gas Co.*, **936 A.2d 111 (Pa. Super. 2007)**.

Excavation subcontractor who had improperly relied on incorrect drawings sued companies that performed subsurface testing for the township which was building a new library. Complaint alleged purely economic damages in negligent misrepresentation claim. No cause of action exists in negligence to recover purely economic damages. *David Pflumm Paving and Excavating, Inc. v. Foundation Services Company, F.T.*, **816 A.2d 1164 (Pa. Super. 2003)**.

Plaintiff failed to allege PennDOT's constructive or actual notice of unsafe condition of excavation site. PennDOT protected by governmental immunity absent proof of its active fault. Motion to dismiss in favor of PennDOT affirmed. *Miranda v. City of Philadelphia*, **166 Pa. Cmwlth. 181, 646 A.2d 71 (1994)**.

In action by personal representative of plumbing contractor killed in cave-in at construction site, governmental immunity applies as plaintiff presented no proof that city exercised sufficient custody and control over site. Sanction order precluding city's filing of answer for failure to comply with discovery order does not compel waiver of real property exception to governmental immunity. Summary judgment in favor of city affirmed. *Santori v. Snyder*, **165 Pa. Cmwlth. 505, 645 A.2d 443 (1994)**.

Plaintiff motorcyclist injured by reason of an unlighted excavation created by defendant in highway—case for jury but error in charge that existence of car ahead obscuring view could excuse plaintiff from otherwise complying with assured clear distance rule. *Koelle v. Phila. Electric Co.*, **443 Pa. 35, 277 A.2d 350**.

Exclusive Control Doctrine

Broken water main—damage to nearby property—verdict for defendant upheld by evenly divided court—failure to charge on exclusive control affirmed. *Banet v. City of Philadelphia*, **226 Pa. Super. 452, 313 A.2d 253**.

Door of elevator came in contact with plaintiff and gave him a shock—accident of nature as to not ordinarily happen in absence of negligence on part of com-

Expert testimony required or allowed

pany in charge of maintenance—$4,000.00 verdict sustained. Exclusive control applied. ***Johnson v. Otis Elevator*, 225 Pa. Super. 500, 311 A.2d 656.**

Boy of 3 in a class for child care and development suffered an eye injury while apparently at play—suit against teacher and school principal—held: doctrine of exclusive control will not apply—situation did not meet requirements to invoke the doctrine—verdict for defendants upheld. ***Greathouse v. Horowitz*, 439 Pa. 62, 264 A.2d 665.**

Plaintiff, a patient in defendant's hospital, allegedly fell out of bed and was injured—verdict for defendant—doctrine does not apply. ***Miller v. Delaware County Mem. Hospital*, 428 Pa. 504, 239 A.2d 340.**

Fire originating in defendants' premises—plaintiff's property damaged—opportunity to inspect—doctrine of exclusive control not applicable. ***Githens Rexsamer & Co. Inc., v. Wildstein*, 428 Pa. 201, 236 A.2d 792.**

Expansion joint

Plaintiff automobile operator sued PennDOT for damages sustained when his car struck a metal expansion joint that had risen approximately two feet above the roadway. On res ipsa loquitur claim, held that plaintiff did not prove the elements set forth in Restatement (Second) of Torts, § 328(d) (1965). ***Biddle v. PennDOT*, 817 A.2d 1213 (Pa. Cmwlth. 2003).**

Expectation of violence

Plaintiff was head of security at defendant hospital and was attacked by an employee who had been brought to supervisor's office for submission to urinalysis. Plaintiff alleged that tortfeasor was acting in his capacity as employee of the hospital and therefore hospital was liable under doctrine of *respondeat superior*. Defendant's motion for summary judgment sustained and affirmed on appeal. Tortfeasor's intentional act of injuring plaintiff was in no way related to his job description as laundry worker and there was no evidence from plaintiff of any expectation on the part of the defendant employer that the tortfeasor would act violently. ***Costa v. Roxborough Memorial Hospital*, 708 A.2d 490 (Pa. Super. 1998).**

Experimental procedure

Patient who suffered complications from implantation of experimental lens in eye brought action against hospital based on lack of informed consent. Held: judgment *n.o.v.* in favor of hospital in error. ***Friter v. Iolab Corporation*, 414 Pa. Super. 622, 607 A.2d 1111.**

Expert testimony required or allowed

Plaintiff brought negligence action against Defendant after the front wheel of the vehicle it leased to Plaintiff's employer fell off while Plaintiff was driving it. The trial court entered summary judgment in favor of the Defendant. The Superior Court affirmed holding that Plaintiff had to provide expert testimony to prove the existence of a mechanical defect in the vehicle that caused the front wheel to fall off. ***Brandon v. Ryder Truck Rental, Inc.*, 34 A.3d 104 (Pa. Super. 2011).**

Expert testimony required or allowed

Patient brought a medical malpractice suit against her orthopedic surgeon over injuries sustained in surgery to remove a bunion. The court ruled that the Medical Care Availability and Reduction Error Act ("MCARE Act") governing expert qualifications applied in medical malpractice trials and that under the MCARE Act a podiatrist was not a qualified expert. ***Wexler v. Hecht*, 928 A.2d 973 (Pa. 2007).**

Plaintiff filed suit after defendant doctor removed an abnormal portion of her small bowel during a diagnostic laparoscopy. The court found dismissal of a directed verdict was appropriate since it could not be found as a matter of law that defendant had exceeded the scope of plaintiff's signed consent statement. The court also held that expert testimony was necessary to determine if there was a duty to consult during a surgical procedure. ***McSorley v. Deger*, 905 A.2d 524 (Pa. Super. 2006).**

Plaintiff filed a negligence suit based upon a doctor's failure to follow up with the plaintiff after learning the result of an abnormal CT scan. The court held that the plaintiff was required to present an expert report on the standard of care to be used and to show that the standard was breached proximately causing the injury to plaintiff. The standard of care of a family practitioner verbally advised of an abnormal CT scan was not within the comprehension or experience of ordinary persons. ***Papach v. Mercy Suburban Hospital*, 887 A.2d 233 (Pa. Super. 2005).**

Hotel guest permitted to go to jury on question of negligent security measures at hotel without an expert witness. ***Ovitsky v. Captial City Economic Development Corporation*, 846 A.2d 124 (Pa. Super. 2004).**

Plaintiff's decedent killed when he struck stopped traffic on I-95 three miles in advance of a construction site. Plaintiff alleged that PennDOT was negligent in failing to place warning signs in advance of location where cars backed up and stopped. Plaintiff also alleged PennDOT's failure to erect signs was negligence *per se*. Held: expert testimony as to need for advance signs three miles from construction site was required. PennDOT regulations that were silent on exact placement of warning signs could not be basis for claim of negligence *per se*, if PennDOT did not place the signs where plaintiff thought they should have been. ***Young v. PennDOT*, 744 A.2d 1276 (Pa. 2000).**

Plaintiff who had a bone flap in skull replaced with titanium mesh sued to recover for pain, disfigurement and depression, alleging negligence by medical care providers in failing to preserve bone flap and battery for substituting titanium mesh for bone. Lower court's grant of summary judgment in favor of care providers reversed in part. Plaintiff's disfigurement was so obvious as to not require expert testimony and plaintiff's expert testified that psychological depression was caused by disfigurement resulting from surgery. Absent proof of causal relationship between pain and surgery, recovery for pain disallowed. ***Watkins v. Hospital of University of Pennsylvania*, 737 A.2d 263 (Pa. Super. 1999).**

Parents of child born with hyaline membrane disease, a condition relating to immaturity of the lung tissue, filed suit against hospital and physicians alleging that lack of immediate steps to insure adequate oxygenation resulted in child's autism, mental retardation and other neurological dysfunction. Summary judgment granted to defendants on basis that plaintiffs' experts' testimony was, by reason of its lack of foundation in established medical literature and acceptance in the field, intrinsically unreliable and so inadmissable. ***Checchio v. Frankford Hospital*, 717 A.2d 1058 (Pa. Super. 1998).**

Plaintiffs appeal from grant of summary judgment to defendant PennDOT which was based on plaintiff's failure to procure expert report to support their claim that PennDOT was negligent in not placing warning signs in advance of construction zone. PennDOT argued successfully that it was immune from suit under Sovereign Immunity Act in that placement of warning signs was not necessary to insure safe condition of real estate for its intended use. Reversed by Commonwealth Court. Necessity of warning signs advising of stopped traffic on interstate highway in advance of traffic construction is within everyday knowledge of jury and so does not require expert testimony. Whether lack of warning signs, as described, constitutes dangerous condition of state maintained roadway for its intended purpose is proper question for jury. ***Young v. Com., Dept. of Transp.*, 714 A.2d 475 (Pa. Cmwlth. 1998).**

Police officer who did not see accident in question would not be qualified by experience or training as expert unless foundation were laid for that qualification. Even if officer was qualified as expert, his deposition testimony based on post-accident interviews with parties to accident is inadmissible without his own independent knowledge of actual circumstances of accident. ***Bennett v. Graham*, 714 A.2d 393 (Pa. 1998).**

Summary judgment affirmed against plaintiff which flagrantly ignored order of trial court to hire experts and file reports within sixty days or be precluded from introducing expert testimony in support of claims that defendant's furnace was defective, when even fourteen months after reports were available, they still had not been presented to defendant. ***Croydon Plastics v. Lower Bucks Cooling & Heating*, 698 A.2d 625 (Pa. Super. 1997).**

In medical malpractice case involving insertion of chest tube, nurse is not qualified to testify as an expert as to compliance with standards of medical care or to diagnose medical conditions. Summary judgment in favor of hospital affirmed. ***Flanagan v. Labe*, 547 Pa. 254, 690 A.2d 183 (1997).**

Nurse's opinion based on personal, unsupported medical diagnosis is inadequate expert testimony to establish prima facie evidence of causation in medical malpractice action. Order granting summary judgment affirmed. ***Flanagan v. Labe*, 446 Pa. Super. 107, 666 A.2d 333 (1995).**

Where patient who underwent perineal urethrotomy and cauterization, rather than planned transurethral prostatectomy, failed to establish a causal connection between resulting injuries and physician's conduct through expert testimony, compulsory nonsuit was proper. Patient should have been allowed to introduce evidence of alleged lack of consent to surgery that was admittedly not discussed by physician and patient prior to its performance. Order granting compulsory nonsuit on question of negligence affirmed. Case remanded on claim for lack of informed consent. ***Hoffman v. Mogil*, 445 Pa. Super. 252, 665 A.2d 478 (1995).**

Expert testimony required or allowed

A non-physician coroner properly qualified by experience is capable of testifying as to time of death in administrator's action against tavern for death of patron. ***Miller v. Brass Rail Tavern, Inc.,* 541 Pa. 474, 664 A.2d 525 (1995).**

In action against orthopedic surgeon for injury resulting from improperly performed back surgery, defendant physician's expert's report failed to address necessity of surgery and therefore expert was precluded from testifying on that issue. Judgment for plaintiff affirmed. ***Walsh v. Kubiak,* 443 Pa. Super. 284, 661 A.2d 416 (1995).**

Plaintiff who contracted AIDS following transfusion of tainted blood filed suit against treating physicians and family physician for medical malpractice. Claim against one defendant dismissed for plaintiff's failure to establish through medical testimony that defendant's actions deviated from good and acceptable medical standards. Proof of compliance with medical standard of care need not be expressed in precisely the language used to annunciate the legal standard. Physician not required to obtain patient's informed consent before blood transfusion that was administered separately from a surgical procedure. ***Hoffman v. Brandywine Hospital,* 443 Pa. Super. 245, 661 A.2d 397 (1995).**

Shipyard worker brought action against manufacturer of products containing encapsulated asbestos. Trial court granted summary judgment based on failure of plaintiff to offer testimony by industrial hygienist. Reversed. ***Junge v. Garlock, Inc.,* 427 Pa. Super. 592, 629 A.2d 1027.**

Patient suffered facial paralysis after undergoing microvascular decompression surgery. Nonsuit found improper. Expert medical testimony essential. ***Levy v. Jannetta,* 423 Pa. Super. 384, 621 A.2d 585.**

Patient who had nerve severed during surgery brought action based on lack of informed consent and *res ipsa loquitur*. Summary judgment based on patients intention not to call expert witnesses upheld. ***Bearfield v. Hauch,* 407 Pa. Super. 624, 595 A.2d 1320.**

Parents of child injured in automobile collision brought action against other driver and Department of Transportation. Both defendants not liable. Expert testimony required to show highway negligently designed. Testimony of other driver sufficient to show no negligence. ***Tennis v. Fedorwicz,* 139 Pa. Cmwlth. 554, 592 A.2d 117.**

Motorcyclist who lost control while rounding curve brought action against Commonwealth and township. Held: jury charge on assured clear distance rule not in error and testimony of expert concerning control of motorcycle admissible. ***Wicks v. Com., Dept. of Transp.,* 139 Pa. Cmwlth. 336, 590 A.2d 832.**

Pedestrian fell into tree well on sidewalk outside stadium. Dark and raining. Non-jury verdict in favor of plaintiff with one-third comparative negligence. Held: plaintiff needed no expert as to proper design of tree well on sidewalk. ***Barns v. City of Philadelphia,* 350 Pa. Super. 615, 504 A.2d 1321.**

Expert testimony required or allowed

Passenger injured in multi-vehicle collision. Alleged defect in design of auto caused more severe injury. Verdict against driver of striking car only. Held: films showing crash tests of another model auto were properly admitted to demonstrate principles testified to by expert witness for auto manufacturer. *Jackson v. Spagnola*, **349 Pa. Super. 471, 503 A.2d 944.**

Jury verdict $203,000 to wife and $105,000 to husband for loss of consortium. Reversed owing to erroneous charge on damages. Alleged negligent suturing of ureter during hysterectomy caused subsequent loss of kidney. Proper to allow urologist, under facts here, to testify as to malpractice even though defendant was a gynecologist. ***Kearns v. Clark,* 343 Pa. Super. 30, 493 A.2d 1358.**

Jury verdict $800,000 for 16 year old female passenger in car involved in accident and rendered quadriplegic due to fracture dislocation of cervical spine. Alleged cause of accident was combining radial and non-radial tire on front axle. New trial ordered. Held: plaintiff's expert witnesses not properly qualified to testify under facts here. In products liability case, it is for court to rule as matter of social policy whether product is one on which strict liability may be imposed. Tests outlined in opinion. ***Dambacher v. Mallis,* 336 Pa. Super. 22, 485 A.2d 408.**

Auto accident. Issue of whether vehicle negligently hit guardrail and thereafter front wheel came off car, or whether wheel came off car, causing it to go out of control. Defense verdict after officer was qualified as expert and opined that wheel came off first. Error to qualify police officer as expert under these circumstances. New trial ordered. ***Reed v. Hutchinson,* 331 Pa. Super. 404, 480 A.2d 1096.**

Apartment fire resulted in deaths of two tenants. Verdict for plaintiff reversed. New trial ordered. Plaintiff's expert testified that fire escape or other means of egress would have saved plaintiffs' lives. Error not to let defense expert testify to contrary. Pretrial summary of defense did cover this area broadly. ***Mapp v. Dube,* 330 Pa. Super. 284, 479 A.2d 553.**

Malpractice case—alleged negligence in damaging facial nerve during ear operation. Nonsuit entered. Expert witness deposition excluded due to failure to comply with pretrial order. *Res ipsa loquitur* theory rejected due to lack of evidence and finding of no common fund of knowledge from which jury could reach conclusion of negligence. Nonsuit affirmed. ***Gallegor v. Felder,* 329 Pa. Super. 204, 478 A.2d 34.**

Jury verdict $1,500,000—$837,000 (wrongful death); $663,000 (survival). 31 year old married male injured in auto accident with survivable chest injuries, died in hospital due to failure to diagnose pneumothorax. Nonsuit as to one of the physicians properly granted where plaintiff offered no evidence and defendant had no previous expert report placing any liability on that physician. Inference from failure to call expert witness improperly charged, since no showing that he was unavailable or uncooperative to plaintiff. ***Richardson v. LaBuz,* 81 Pa. Cmwlth. 436, 474 A.2d 1181.**

Expert testimony required or allowed

Injury to worker on rear step of trash truck. Proper to allow plaintiff's expert to testify about proper engineering of step. Field was beyond common knowledge of jury. **Mattox v. City of Philadelphia, 308 Pa. Super. 111, 454 A.2d 46.**

Expert required on issue of whether injured person was conscious upon admission to hospital. Error to allow chart entry into evidence alone on that issue. **Morris v. Moss, 290 Pa. Super. 587, 435 A.2d 184.**

Evidence of custom and usage is not expert opinion requiring expert testimony. **Kubit v. Russ, 287 Pa. Super. 28, 429 A.2d 703.**

High school football player injured in touch football game. Within discretion of trial court to exclude expert witness of plaintiff who was to testify on football safety equipment. Within common knowledge of jury to understand common game of touch football. **Rutter v. Northeastern Beaver County School, 283 Pa. Super. 155, 423 A.2d 1035.**

Proper to admit evidence of expert highway engineer on necessity of putting signs on road warning of pedestrians walking on roadway due to construction. **Drew v. Laber, 277 Pa. Super. 419, 419 A.2d 1216.**

Malpractice case against hospital. Failure of hospital personnel to advise promptly of changes in vital signs needs no expert testimony to prove negligence. **Brannan v. Lankenau Hospital, 490 Pa. 588, 417 A.2d 196.**

Assault and fight in bar led to death of plaintiff. Expert testimony not required where injury and death followed immediately and directly. **Furman v. Frankie, 268 Pa. Super. 305, 408 A.2d 478.**

Plaintiff on electric pole working on cable TV cable. Badly shocked. Lower court held to have too narrowly restricted plaintiff's expert's testimony as to whether the 7.43 foot distance between TV cable and electric wire was adequate despite various codes. Further he should have been permitted to testify as to whether plaintiff was qualified under the National Electric Safety Code or whether he was considered general public. **Densler v. Metropolitan Edison, 235 Pa. Super. 585, 345 A.2d 758.**

Suit against car dealer for selling allegedly defective car to plaintiff. Sole issue on appeal was exclusion of testimony of plaintiff's expert who was to testify as to defect. Evidence excluded by trial court since there was no evidence as to how vehicle was towed from scene or how vehicle was stored for the three weeks before expert saw car. Expert said at side bar that tampering or damage was unlikely due to grease buildup in area of alleged defect. Reversed. New trial ordered. Expert permitted to testify. **Ritson v. Don Allen Chevrolet, 233 Pa. Super. 112, 336 A.2d 359.**

Plaintiff injured when he struck portion of defendant's pool when diving. Expert in water safety and pool design not permitted to testify since the descriptions of the pool, water content and design from the lay witnesses were such that it was possible for jury to apply their own experience and not be swayed by conclusion of expert. Defense verdict affirmed. **Maholland v. Bird, 230 Pa. Super. 431, 326 A.2d 528.**

Explosions

Police officer expert testified as to who was driving from after-accident photographs. Judge should have permitted other side to produce expert to say that photographs were inconclusive even though general rule is that expert should not be permitted to state inference or judgment as to ultimate facts for jury determination. ***Ryan v. Furey,* 225 Pa. Super. 294, 303 A.2d 221.**

Failure to call doctor-expert—even though testimony probably cumulative, requires charge that there is an inference that evidence would be unfavorable, but tempered with charge that other side had subpoena power. ***Downey v. Weston,* 451 Pa. 259, 301 A.2d 635.**

Plaintiff received as one of her injuries a splitting of the retina—causal connection with trauma of occurrence established—error to refuse to permit expert to express an opinion as to the possible effect of such an injury on a future operation or the removal of a cataract—also error to refuse to permit expert to express an opinion to the possibility of effect on the good eye—new trial granted. ***Walsh v. Brody,* 220 Pa. Super. 293, 286 A.2d 666.**

Expert testimony of a witness with 25 years experience with fiber rugs permitted where testimony established a curled condition of rug on floor of defendant's premises—not a matter capable of valuation by a jury alone. ***Reardon v. Meehan,* 424 Pa. 460, 227 A.2d 667.**

Trial judge permitted testimony of an engineer as to the rate of speed and distance traversed by a pedestrian crossing a roadway 18 feet in width—error—matter for jury to pass on—verdict for defendant—new trial granted. ***Collins v. Zediker,* 421 Pa. 52, 218 A.2d 776.**

Explosions

Plaintiff brought negligence action against former steel mill owner for injuries suffered in an explosion even though the steel mill was no longer owned by the Defendant at the time of the accident. Plaintiff claimed the removal of an emergency drawbridge by the Defendant led to his injuries while he was employed by current mill owner. The trial court entered summary judgment for the Defendant. The Superior Court affirmed. The Pennsylvania Supreme Court affirmed holding that a former property owner could not be liable for negligent construction based upon alterations it made to property it no longer owned. ***Gresik v. PA Partners, LP,* 33 A.3d 594 (Pa. 2011).**

Plaintiff's decedent welder was killed when fumes inside gasoline tank truck in which he was working caught fire and exploded. Motion for compulsory nonsuit granted because plaintiff's decedent was fully aware of the risks attending the work he was performing. Recovery prohibited under Section 388 of Restatement (2d) Torts which imposes duty to warn owner of chattel who has reason to believe that those for whose use the chattel is supplied will not realize its dangerous condition. ***Erdos v. Bedford Valley Petroleum Co.,* 452 Pa. Super. 555, 682 A.2d 806 (1996).**

In homeowner's action against gas utility for damages to home following gas explosion, gas utility's effort to join as additional defendant original contractor who performed allegedly negligent work was time-barred. Twelve-year statute of repose

Explosions

is not unconstitutional. Order granting judgment on pleadings in favor of additional defendants affirmed. ***Columbia Gas of PA, Inc. v. Carl E. Baker, Inc.*, 446 Pa. Super. 481, 667 A.2d 404 (1995).**

Referee's determination in Workers' Compensation case that plaintiff's injury was not caused by exploding lighter and was not work related collaterally estops plaintiff from seeking recovery for same injuries in products liability action against lighter manufacturer. Order granting summary judgment affirmed. ***Capobianchi v. Bic Corp.*, 446 Pa. Super. 130, 666 A.2d 344 (1995).**

Contributory negligence does not preclude recovery in a products liability case. In action arising out of tire explosion that injured garage mechanic, defendant failed to prove that plaintiff assumed the specific risk attendant to the procedure of changing a tire. Voluntary assumption of a risk is a defense in a products liability case and requires proof that the plaintiff fully understands the specific risk and yet chooses voluntarily to encounter the risk. ***Robinson v. B.F. Goodrich Tire Company*, 444 Pa. Super. 640, 664 A.2d 616 (1995).**

In action arising out of explosion of boiler caused by defective emergency shut-off valve, manufacturer of valve held strictly liable for defective product. Manufacturer's liability for its defective product is outlined in Section 402A of Restatement (2d) Torts, which provides that a plaintiff must prove that the product was sold in a defective condition dangerous to the user and that the defect was the proximate cause of the injury. An actor is relieved from liability due to an intervening or superseding cause only if the intervening or superseding negligent acts were so extraordinary as not to have been reasonably foreseeable. Summary judgment affirmed in part and reversed in part. ***Dougherty v. Edward J. Meloney, Inc.*, 443 Pa. Super. 201, 661 A.2d 375 (1995).**

There is but one standard of care in a negligence action, which is reasonable care. Reasonable care will vary based on the circumstances and instrumentalities in each situation. Action by customer against garage and mechanic for injuries sustained when gasoline exploded after being poured into carburetor did not warrant a jury instruction on a standard of care higher than reasonable care. Judgment for defendants affirmed. ***Stewart v. Motts*, 539 Pa. 596, 654 A.2d 535 (1995).**

Welder injured when air tank he was repairing exploded when pressurized for testing. Nonsuit granted as to owner of tank. Section 388 of Restatement (2d) Torts applies. No reason to believe that either owner knew of dangerous condition or that experienced welder wouldn't himself realize danger under facts here. Affirmed. ***Herleman v. Trumbauer Auto Sales*, 346 Pa. Super. 494, 499 A.2d 1109.**

Explosion of ceremonial cannon allegedly caused injuries. City of Pittsburgh and Commonwealth of Pennsylvania, joined. Commonwealth refused permission to amend Answer to include defense based upon Recreation Use of Land and Water Act. Affirmed denial. Commonwealth not meant to be included in definition of owner of land. ***Borgen v. Fort Pitt Museum*, 83 Pa. Cmwlth. 207, 477 A.2d 36.**

Explosion from propane heater while lighting pilot. Gas allegedly not odorized. §402A claim. Verdict for defendant affirmed. Issue of odor and defect alleged for not odorizing. Properly before jury. *Evans v. Thomas,* **304 Pa. Super. 338, 450 A.2d 710.**

Gas range sold and installed by gas company exploded, injuring plaintiff and causing property damage. Verdict for plaintiff on breach of implied warranty of merchantability—not negligence or product liability. Verdict not inconsistent. Jury could have found insufficient proof of negligence and no defect, but still breach of warranty. *Walsh v. Pa. Gas and Water,* **303 Pa. Super. 52, 449 A.2d 573.**

Plaintiff connecting sewer line when there was an explosion of gasoline fumes which had collected in trench. Evidence of leak in tanks of nearby gasoline station. Also evidence of inadequate repairs and complaints to sewer authority of fumes. Verdict for plaintiff. *O'Malley v. Peerless Petroleum,* **283 Pa. Super. 272, 423 A.2d 1251.**

Explosion of underground tanks at gas station. Personal injuries to wife of owner. Grant of summary judgment in favor of former owner, reversed. Issue of his knowledge of defect at time of sale was for jury. *Bonneau v. Ralph Martin Oil,* **259 Pa. Super. 428, 393 A.2d 901.**

Plaintiff injured by explosion of propane gas upon entering defendant's slaughter house—no concrete evidence of actual cause of explosion and any breach of defendant's duty to plaintiff as a business invitee—mere happening of an accident—nonsuit affirmed. *Shirley v. Clark,* **441 Pa. 508, 271 A.2d 868.**

Plaintiffs' property damaged by gas explosion—employee of gas company had inspected property two days before explosion and neglected to warn plaintiffs of certain gas leaks and shut off gas at meter and not at curb—gas company held responsible. *Fore v. United Nat. Gas Co.,* **436 Pa. 499, 261 A.2d 316.**

Plaintiff, a retailer, was injured by explosion of a bottle of beer—defendant glass company manufactured bottle, defendant brewery company bottled the beer and defendant Kronzek was the distributor who sold the beer to the plaintiff—verdict for defendants—new trial granted—plaintiff's expert not entitled to give an opinion by the court below—held on appeal: he was entitled to give an opinion even though he had testified that he could not give an absolutely positive opinion. *Bialek v. Pittsburgh Brewing Co. et al.,* **430 Pa. 176, 242 A.2d 231.**

Extramarital affair

Motion to dismiss sustained against Plaintiff husband who sued family physician in negligence for physician's adulterous affair with plaintiff's wife. Held, that Pennsylvania does not recognize a claim of negligence against a physician under these facts because the physician does not owe a duty of care to the husband to avoid the relationship with husband's wife. *Long v. Ostroff,* **854 A.2d 524 (Pa. Super. 2004)**.

Eye injuries

Fifth grade student struck in eye with pencil propelled by another student, who tripped or fell. Teacher outside room monitoring return of students. Non-jury verdict of $15,000 reversed. Momentary absence from room not negligent. Judg-

Eyewitness

ment reversed. *Simonetti v. School District of Philadelphia,* 308 Pa. Super. 555, 454 A.2d 1038.

Jury verdict $37,000. Loss of eye struck by object ejected from lawn mower. Plaintiff a passerby. *Lavin v. Mylecraine,* 307 Pa. Super. 564, 453 A.2d 1031.

Eyewitness

Plaintiffs who were personal representatives of decedent filed suit against bar for Dram Shop Act violations which led to the death of patron. Summary judgment granted to defendant due to lack of direct eyewitness evidence that decedent was served alcoholic beverages when visibly intoxicated. Held: circumstantial evidence indicating that decedent must have been visibly intoxicated when served is adequate to create question of fact for jury and so defeat summary judgment. In instant case, patrons testified decedent was visibly intoxicated when he left bar. Police testified plaintiff was still intoxicated at least 4 hours after he left bar. Medical evidence showed that decedent's blood alcohol content was twice legal limit at least 6 hours after he left bar. Scientific evidence showed that decedent must have consumed nearly fourteen twelve-ounce beers to achieve blood alcohol content he had. *Fandozzi v. Kelly Hotel, Inc.,* 711 A.2d 524 (Pa. Super. 1998).

Plaintiff's decedent died as the result of an automobile collision—no eye witnesses—each car found on proper side of road but facing in opposite directions after occurrence from that originally proceeding—cars originally going in opposite directions—nonsuit proper—mere happening of an accident. *Laubach v. Haigh,* 433 Pa. 487, 252 A.2d 682 (1969).

—F—

Failing to observe

Defendant on through highway and plaintiff on stop street—plaintiff testified that he came to a stop about 8 to 10 feet from sign situated some 30 feet from intersecting highway—made observation to his left and observed no approaching vehicles—proceeding and struck by defendant's car approaching on through highway—view of plaintiff partly obstructed by fog and buildings—did not stop again before entering highway—did not observe defendant's car until almost point of contact—verdict for defendant—motions dismissed—affirmed on appeal. *Martin v. Mihalko*, **439 Pa. 612, 266 A.2d 269.**

Failing to stop

Plaintiff's tractor-trailer collided with defendant's train at a grade crossing—foggy weather—plaintiff did not stop—various highway signs advised of the crossing—familiar with crossing—judgment on pleadings and depositions for defendant. *Scott v. Reading Co.*, **432 Pa. 240, 248 A.2d 43.**

Failure to discover defect

The defense of contributory negligence which consists merely in failure to discover defect cannot be asserted in an action under Section 402A of Restatement (2d) Torts. *Burbage v. Boiler Eng. & Sup. Co., Inc. et al.*, **433 Pa. 319, 249 A.2d 563.**

Failure to inspect

Plaintiffs brought negligence action against Defendant after they were injured in a fall when an exterior stairway gave out at the Defendant's facility due to rusted bolts. A jury found in favor of the Plaintiffs. On appeal the Superior Court affirmed holding that the Defendant owed a duty to the Plaintiffs to inspect its exterior stairway for signs of failure. *Gillingham v. Consol Energy, Inc.*, **2012 Pa. Super. 133 (Pa. Super. 2012).**

Corrosion of large underground oil tank causing seepage to adjacent properties and stream—public nuisance—negligent failure to inspect and maintain. *Lerro v. Thomas Wynne, Inc.*, **451 Pa. 37, 301 A.2d 705.**

Failure to supervise

Plaintiffs were potential buyers of one of defendant's custom homes who were "fleeced" by defendant's agent in scam he ran without defendant's knowledge. Evidence established that defendant's agent had enticed plaintiffs to invest nearly $49,000 of their money with agent in "get rich quick" scheme designed to allow plaintiffs to upgrade home they were going to pay defendant to build. Trial court found that evidence also established defendant completely failed to supervise their agent when there was substantial evidence that agent was fleecing many clients. Superior Court affirmed on basis of defendant's failure to supervise agent. *Heller v. Patwil Homes, Inc.*, **713 A.2d 105 (Pa. Super. 1998).**

Failure to warn

Failure to warn

Plaintiff filed suit against a part supplier after he was injured when a graphitizer exploded. The court affirmed the dismissal of plaintiff's suit for failure to warn, because it found that employees were well aware of the dangers of the product and injury was due to inadequate training. Summary judgment for defendant uniform supplier for negligence was also affirmed for a lack of evidence that the uniform company had assumed any responsibility in choosing the uniform to be purchased. ***Stephens v. Paris Cleaners, Inc.*, 885 A.2d 59 (Pa. Super. 2005)**

Summary judgment for defendant truck driver affirmed where there was no evidence that he knew that driving on an under-inflated tire would create or increase the risk of injury to a mechanic who was severely injured while reinflating the tire during the repair process. Without more, driver's knowledge that he drove on tire that was low or "super low" is inadequate to establish negligence. §388 of Restatement (2d) Torts requires both knowledge of dangerous condition and failure to inform the person to whom control of the chattel in the dangerous condition is transferred. ***Overbeck v. Cates*, 700 A.2d 970 (Pa. Super. 1997).**

Administratrix of teenager who drowned in city-owned pond may not recover under Political Subdivision Tort Claims Act based on allegations of city's willful or malicious failure to warn of dangerous condition of pond. Recovery under Political Subdivision Tort Claims Acts is available only for acts of negligence. Public and private lands are covered by Recreation Use of Land and Water Act. Order refusing to grant judgment *n.o.v.* reversed. ***Lory v. City of Philadelphia*, 544 Pa. 38, 674 A.2d 673 (1996).**

State law claims for manufacture and sale of defective surgical repair screws and plates were not preempted by medical device amendments to Federal Food and Drug Act. Actions for failure to warn, strict liability, negligence, and implied warranty are preempted by medical device amendment to federal food and drug act. Summary judgment affirmed in part and reversed in part. ***Burgstahler v. Acromed Corporation*, 448 Pa. Super. 26, 670 A.2d 658 (1996).**

Willful or malicious failure to guard or warn exception to immunity under the Recreation Use of Land and Water Act applied to action by personal representative of minor's estate where minor drowned in natural pond located in city park. Evidence of prior unrelated swimming accidents inadmissable. Verdict for plaintiff reversed and remanded. ***Barr v. City and County of Philadelphia*, ___ Pa. Cmwlth. ___, 653 A.2d 1374 (1995).**

Motorist injured in collision with vehicle exiting driveway on commercial property. Property owner not liable for failure to warn of dangerous condition. ***Cruet v. Certain-Teed Corporation*, 432 Pa. Super. 554, 639 A.2d 478.**

Passenger injured in head-on collision. Passenger not negligent for failure to warn driver of danger from oncoming vehicle. ***Phillips v. Schoenberger*, 369 Pa. Super. 52, 534 A.2d 1075.**

Fall: By business invitee

Road narrowed due to snow on berm. Two vehicles hit left front to left front. Charge on contributory negligence of passenger inadequate. Duty does not arise where driver fully cognizant of impending danger. Failure to warn, further, not an assumption of risk and charge on that was error. Charge on contributory negligence error also since it said that if contributory negligence, however slight, contributed to the accident, plaintiff cannot recover. Causality for contributory negligence and negligence the same. ***Yannuzzi v. Mitchell,*** **260 Pa. Super. 47, 393 A.2d 1005.**

Plaintiff injured while operating punch press machine—defendant a supplier—not a 402A case. Section 388 of Restatement (2d) Torts applies—one who supplies chattel must take reasonable steps to warn of known or reasonably known danger—for jury. ***McKenna v. Art Pearl Works,*** **225 Pa. Super. 362, 310 A.2d 677.**

Fall: By business invitee

Recovery by bus passenger who fell from stationary bus steps is precluded by governmental immunity absent proof of movement of vehicle or any part of vehicle. Summary judgment reversed on certified interlocutory appeal. ***Simpkins v. SEPTA,*** **167 Pa. Cmwlth. 451, 648 A.2d 591 (1994).**

Plaintiff elevator inspector who tripped on misaligned elevator floor failed to produce evidence that product was defective and that defendant was seller. Products liability claim dismissed and verdict for defendant affirmed. ***Micciche v. Eastern Elevator Co.,*** **435 Pa. Super. 219, 645 A.2d 278 (1994).**

Plaintiff tripped and fell while attempting to enter bank. No defect in steps other than uneven heights. Some evidence that a pillar blocked view of steps as plaintiff approached. Plaintiff held contributorily negligent as a matter of law. ***Villano v. Security Savings Assoc.,*** **268 Pa. Super. 67, 407 A.2d 440.**

Plaintiff fell in defendant's parking lot. Daylight. Tripped over exposed wires which may or may not have been in shadow. Judgment on the record, after hung jury, reversed. Retrial ordered. ***Gregoris v. Stockwell Rubber,*** **235 Pa. Super. 71, 340 A.2d 570.**

Plaintiff a fireman. Contractor renovating fire house removed pole from living quarters to ground floor. Plaintiff knew of hole and was straightening rug covering hole to keep dust down and fell through hole. §343 of Restatement (2d) Torts. Possessor liable where he should expect that invitees will fail to protect themselves against danger. Plaintiff verdict affirmed. ***Bowman v. Fretts and Leeper Constr. Co.,*** **227 Pa. Super. 347, 322 A.2d 719.**

Plaintiff while waiting for his gas tank to be filled and following directions to a rest room, fell into an open repair pit in service station—alleged that poor lighting and shadow obscured opening—nonsuit improper—matter for the jury. ***Latch v. Reburn,*** **220 Pa. Super. 396, 281 A.2d 673.**

Plaintiff, a business invitee in defendant's garage and service station, falling down a flight of steps into basement when he entered an unlocked door—testifying on deposition that he did not even look where he was going and walked into space—summary judgment granted for defendant on pleadings, depositions and

Fall: Caused by objects or foreign matter

photographs—action affirmed on appeal. ***Simmons v. Doll's Garage, Inc.,* 440 Pa. 635, 269 A.2d 509.**

Plaintiff entered defendant's store to purchase meat and on leaving fell on steps—evidence that sawdust, wood chips and fine gravel were on steps—no handrail—jury disagreed—judgment entered on whole record—reversed on appeal—matter for jury. ***Kuminkoski v. Daum,* 429 Pa. 494, 240 A.2d 524.**

Wife plaintiff fell while leaving defendant club—she alleged that mat slipped and moved when tread upon and that ice was under surface of mat—evidence strongly disputed—verdict for defendant—refusal of new trial proper. ***Maher v. College Club of Pittsburgh,* 427 Pa. 621, 235 A.2d 134.**

Plaintiff's decedent attended a club bingo game and on leaving allegedly fell on club's premises—plaintiff failed to establish defendant's negligence as the proximate cause of the fall—what caused fall only a guess or conjecture—nonsuit proper. ***Watkins v. Sharon Aerie No. 327 F.O.E.,* 423 Pa. 396, 223 A.2d 742.**

Wife plaintiff was a business invitee in defendant's funeral parlor—on leaving she allegedly, as result of deceptive lighting and slight drop in level of porch from main parlor, fell on porch—judgment *n.o.v.* properly entered below and affirmed on appeal. ***O'Neill v. Batchelor Bros. Inc. Funeral Homes,* 421 Pa. 413, 219 A.2d 682.**

Plaintiff, a business invitee in defendant's office building, fell on water in hallway—result of snow brought in by others or from snow blown in through an opened window—condition existing for at least 3-1/2 hours—recovery allowed. ***Papa v. Pittsburgh Penn-Center Corp.,* 421 Pa. 228, 218 A.2d 783.**

Fall: Caused by objects or foreign matter

Build-up of grease and oil on city-owned sidewalk is not a dangerous condition "of" the sidewalk; therefore, city is immune from liability under the Political Subdivision Tort Claims Act for injuries sustained by pedestrian who slipped and fell on sidewalk. ***Finn v. City of Philadelphia,* 541 Pa. 596, 664 A.2d 1342 (1995).**

Hills and ridges of ice on school district property are not dangerous condition of the property itself and, therefore, do not fall within real property exception to Political Subdivision Tort Claims Act. Order granting judgment on pleadings affirmed. ***McRae for School District of Philadelphia,* ___ Pa. Cmwlth. ___, 660 A.2d 209 (1995).**

For real property exception to apply against school district, dangerous condition must be of or attached to the pavement or property and not on the subject pavement or property. Rainwater on floor of school building did not constitute dangerous condition of or attached to property. Directed verdict for defendant affirmed. Dissent would apply exception based on school district's use of terrazzo floor tile which school district knew became dangerously slippery when wet. ***Shedrick v. William Penn School District,* ___ Pa. Cmwlth. ___, 654 A.2d 163 (1995).**

Sidewalk exception to governmental immunity and real property exception to governmental immunity are to be read consistently. For real property exception

Fall: In industrial setting

to apply against school district, dangerous condition must be of or attached to the pavement or property and not on the subject pavement or property. Milk on sidewalk did not constitute dangerous condition of or attached to property. Jury verdict for defendant affirmed. ***DeLuca v. School District of Philadelphia*, ___ Pa. Cmwlth. ___, 654 A.2d 29 (1994).**

In negligence action against corporate defendant and officers, officers are not liable for failing to maintain clean bathroom absent proof of their participation in creating or allowing continued existence of dangerous condition. Party's failure to answer request for admission that states a conclusion of law does not establish plaintiff's case. Judgment in favor of plaintiff vacated and remanded for consideration of scope of involvement and liability of owners. ***Brindley v. Woodland Village Restaurant, Inc.*, 438 Pa. Super. 385, 652 A.2d 865 (1995).**

Municipality immune from liability to plaintiff who slipped and fell on grease on sidewalk. Verdict in favor of plaintiff reversed. ***Finn v. City of Philadelphia*, 165 Pa. Cmwlth. 255, 645 A.2d 320 (1994).**

Plaintiff allegedly fell on accumulation of petroleum products on sidewalk of Exxon station. Summary judgment in favor of Exxon reversed. Liability of Exxon as owner out of possession for jury. Suit to proceed against lessee operator and Exxon. ***Juarbe v. City of Philadelphia*, 288 Pa. Super. 330, 431 A.2d 1073.**

Plaintiff slipped and fell on cherry on floor of supermarket. Nonsuit affirmed. No evidence of notice or negligence of defendant's employees. ***Moultry v. A&P*, 281 Pa. Super. 525, 422 A.2d 593.**

Fall due to water on restroom floor. Fell on way out. Plaintiff had seen water on way in. Error not to charge on contributory negligence. ***McCullough v. Monroeville Home Assoc.*, 270 Pa. Super. 428, 411 A.2d 794.**

Slip and fall at race track. Floor of betting room became increasingly littered as evening progressed. Plaintiff did not identify exactly what she slipped on but her trousers were wet after fall. For jury. ***McMillan v. Mountain Laurel Racing*, 240 Pa. Super. 248, 367 A.2d 1106.**

Plaintiff on alighting from a car allegedly slipped on defendant's pavement during a snow storm—alleged existence of an isolated patch of ice as cause of fall not established—nonsuit proper. ***Tolbert v. Gillette*, 438 Pa. 63, 260 A.2d 463.**

Fall: In industrial setting

Subcontractor brought negligence action against general contractor after falling 14 feet at a construction site. A jury found in favor of the subcontractor on the basis he was an independent contractor. The Superior Court affirmed. The Pennsylvania Supreme Court reversed holding that the statutory employer doctrine provided immunity for general contractors from suit by their subcontractors for injuries on the job based upon the Workers' Compensation Act. An independent contractor must contract with the owner of the property. ***Patton v. Worthington Associates, Inc.*, 89 A.3d 643 (Pa. 2014).**

Fall: On personal property

Workman injured in fall from temporary platform used for passage to house under construction. With no evidence as to cause of platform failure, jury verdict for plaintiff reversed. ***Szumsky v. Lohman Homes,*** **267 Pa. Super. 478, 406 A.2d 1142.**

Plaintiff injured when steel plate running from loading platform to compactor gave way. Suit against installer who joined employer and trash hauler. Verdict against installer and employee only. ***Hinton v. Waste Techniques,*** **243 Pa. Super. 189, 364 A.2d 724.**

Plaintiff workman employed by general contractor—injured by the fall of a wall—evidence that cutting a pipe chase in wall so weakened it as to cause collapse—sufficient evidence in record for jury to find that defendant Steel City cut the chase—verdict for plaintiff sustained. ***Abbott v. Steel City Piping Co.,*** **437 Pa. 412, 263 A.2d 881.**

Plaintiff fell from scaffold because a brace slipped suddenly—plaintiff fell into a hole 16 feet deep which defendant had dug and failed to cover—existence of hole not the proximate cause—preliminary objections properly sustained. ***Barber v. Kohler Co.,*** **428 Pa. 219, 237 A.2d 224.**

Plaintiff, a stevedore, fell in defendant's warehouse—claim of defective lighting and lack of toe boards—failure to establish breach of General Safety Act of 1937—verdict for defendant—refusal of a new trial proper—no abuse of discretion. ***Matulonis v. Reading Railroad Co.,*** **421 Pa. 230, 219 A.2d 301.**

Fall: On personal property

Summary judgment reversed where owners of property adjoining parking lot on which plaintiff slipped and fell had easement across parking lot and, therefore, question existed as to whether property owners were liable as possessor of parking lot. ***Blackman v. Federal Realty Inv. Trust,*** **444 Pa. Super. 411, 664 A.2d 139 (1995).**

Bar patron injured in fall down defective staircase. Seller of property retained title until all payments made. Seller not liable. ***Welz v. Wong,*** **413 Pa. Super. 299, 605 A.2d 368.**

Employee of tenant brought action against landlord for injuries resulting from fall on stairs caused by rainwater tracked in by people using stairway. Landlord not liable. No hidden defect. ***Dorsey v. Continental Associates,*** **404 Pa. Super. 525, 591 A.2d 716.**

Tenant injured in slip and fall on landlord's property. Tenant 58% negligent, landlord 42% negligent. Comparative negligence principles apply to implied warranty of habitability theory as well as negligence. ***Keck v. Doughman,*** **392 Pa. Super. 127, 572 A.2d 724.**

Volunteer fireman injured when he fell into window well. Held: fireman's rule not adopted in Pennsylvania. Firemen do not assume the risk of on-duty injuries. ***Mull v. Kerstetter,*** **373 Pa. Super. 228, 540 A.2d 951.**

Fall: On public property

Tenant broke ankle when board broke on front porch used in common by all tenants in building. Jury verdict $38,695. Although charge of court error as to duty of landlord where independent contractor hired to make repairs, here verdict showed independent negligence of landlord. Therefore, error harmless. ***Speer v. Barry,*** **349 Pa. Super. 365, 503 A.2d 409.**

Plaintiff allegedly fell on accumulation of petroleum products on sidewalk of Exxon station. Summary judgment in favor of Exxon reversed. Liability of Exxon as owner out of possession for jury. Suit to proceed against lessee operator and Exxon. ***Juarbe v. City of Philadelphia,*** **288 Pa. Super. 330, 431 A.2d 1073.**

Plaintiff fell on deteriorated sidewalk and was injured. Had fallen in essentially the same place 5 days earlier. Plaintiff held 15% at fault. Condition had existed for years. Proper for jury to apportion responsibility. ***Peair v. Home Assoc. of Enola,*** **287 Pa. Super. 400, 430 A.2d 665.**

Wife plaintiff fell on an outside flight of steps while descending same—evidence of defective condition of steps—only means of access to place of employment—verdict for plaintiff sustained—motion for new trial and judgment *n.o.v.* refused. ***Naponic v. Carlton Motel, Inc.,*** **221 Pa. Super. 287, 289 A.2d 473.**

Plaintiff lodged car in defendant's automobile sales and service station building—walking to rear of building to pick up car and entered an unlocked door and fell down a flight of steps to basement with severe injuries—plaintiff testified on deposition that he had not "even looked" where he was going—motion for summary judgment on pleadings, deposition and photographs—motion granted below and sustained on appeal. ***Simmons v. Doll's Garage, Inc.,*** **440 Pa. 635, 269 A.2d 509.**

Plaintiff, a patient in defendant's hospital, allegedly fell out of bed and was injured—verdict for defendant—doctrine does not apply. ***Miller v. Delaware County Mem. Hospital,*** **428 Pa. 504, 239 A.2d 340.**

Plaintiff while making a delivery allegedly tripped and fell over a rug on floor of defendant's premises and was seriously injured—recovery allowed—court found actionable negligence. ***Reardon v. Meehan,*** **424 Pa. 460, 227 A.2d 667.**

Plaintiff, a nurse, entered a private hospital and fell at emergency entrance—evidence that water had entered entrance and attendant had removed mat to mop up—case for jury. ***Kerwood v. Rolling Hill Corp.,*** **424 Pa. 59, 225 A.2d 918.**

Fall: On public property

Wife plaintiff filed suit against school district alleging that water left from "damp mopping" of school hallway caused her to slip and fall and suffer injuries. After grant of motion for summary judgment by defendant based on plaintiffs' failure to prove facts which would take case under real estate exception to governmental immunity, Commonwealth Court affirmed. On appeal, Supreme Court reversed and remanded to Commonwealth Court which reversed and remanded its prior affirmance of trial court grant of summary judgment. Held: "...for government immunity purposes, it is no longer of any consequence that the injury does not result from a defect in, or condition of, the real property itself, and that the real property

Fall: On public property

exception should no longer be considered *in pari materia* with the sidewalk exception to governmental immunity or the real estate exception to sovereign immunity". ***Hanna v. West Shore School District*, 717 A.2d 626 (Pa. Cmwlth. 1998).**

"Dangerous condition of real estate" exception to governmental immunity was fact question for jury. Summary judgment in favor of defendant reversed. ***Berhane v. SEPTA*, 166 Pa. Cmwlth. 196, 646 A.2d 1268 (1994).**

Plaintiff elevator inspector who tripped on misaligned elevator floor failed to produce evidence that product was defective and that defendant was seller. Products liability claim dismissed and verdict for defendant affirmed. ***Micciche v. Eastern Elevator Co.*, 435 Pa. Super. 219, 645 A.2d 278 (1994).**

Passenger fell on slippery spot on subway platform. Held: whether dangerous condition was "on" or "off" platform was question of fact. ***Shubert v. SEPTA*, 155 Pa. Cmwlth. 129, 625 A.2d 102.**

Pedestrian injured in fall on roadbed of street railway located on state highway brought action against city, transportation authority, and Department of Transportation. City found primarily liable, authority secondarily liable, and department not liable. ***Yackobovitz v. SEPTA*, 139 Pa. Cmwlth. 157, 590 A.2d 40.**

Plaintiff injured when she fell from temporary stage. Defendant's negligence not substantial factor in injury. Order for new trial reversed and jury verdict reinstated. ***Arcidiacono v. Timeless Towns of America, Inc.*, 363 Pa. Super. 521, 526 A.2d 804.**

Pedestrian tripped over sidewalk that was raised because of roots from tree planted by city. Property owner and not city held primarily liable. ***Pischos v. Sauvion*, 103 Pa. Cmwlth. 517, 520 A.2d 945.**

Pedestrian fell into tree well on sidewalk outside stadium. Dark and rainy. Non-jury verdict for plaintiff with one-third comparative negligence. Held: plaintiff needed no expert as to proper design of tree well or sidewalk. Affirmed. ***Burns v. City of Philadelphia*, 350 Pa. Super. 615, 504 A.2d 1321.**

Summary judgment for city affirmed. Minor fell from billboard on land owned by SEPTA adjacent to city playground. Held: city under no obligation to erect fence to prevent minors from entering SEPTA's land on which billboard located. ***Kearns v. Rollins Outdoor Advertising*, 89 Pa. Cmwlth. 596, 492 A.2d 1204.**

Fall down steps in darkened lavatory area of restaurant while searching for light switch. Under facts here, does not constitute contributory negligence as a matter of law. Nonsuit removed. ***McNally v. Liebowitz*, 498 Pa. 163, 445 A.2d 716.**

Plaintiff fell on deteriorated sidewalk and was injured. Had fallen in essentially the same place 5 days earlier. Plaintiff held 15% at fault. Condition had existed for years. Proper for jury to apportion responsibility. ***Peair v. Home Assoc. of Enola*, 287 Pa. Super. 400, 430 A.2d 665.**

Fall: On public property

Pedestrian who falls on a cartway and proves nothing else cannot recover. ***Bullick v. City of Scranton*, 224 Pa. Super. 173, 302 A.2d 849.**

Pedestrian falling allegedly due to drop in level of sidewalk—four inch overhang of building held sufficient excuse for not seeing drop—verdict for plaintiff sustained. ***Kobi v. Bau*, 218 Pa. Super. 139, 279 A.2d 297.**

Plaintiff pedestrian fell on pavement abutting defendant's garage premises—evidence that cause of fall was a patch of ice in a crack in pavement—not required to establish "hills or ridges" under facts of case—matter for jury—plaintiff not guilty of contributory negligence in choice of way. ***Tonik v. Apex Garages, Inc.*, 442 Pa. 373, 275 A.2d 296.**

Wife plaintiff pedestrian fell on a bright sunny day, allegedly as the result of a crack in the blacktop one inch wide, one inch deep and six or seven inches long—no explanation for not seeing defect—evidence produced in depositions—judgment on pleadings for defendant affirmed on appeal. ***Lang v. Butler*, 441 Pa. 331, 271 A.2d 338.**

Female pedestrian walking an accustomed route in broad daylight with knowledge that defendant's pavement was partly defective—alleging presence of another pedestrian obscured view—sidestepping and falling—judgment *n.o.v.*—plaintiff had already observed defective condition—distraction not an excuse. ***Kresovich v. Fitzsimmons*, 439 Pa. 10, 264 A.2d 585.**

Plaintiff pedestrian aged 72 fell allegedly on a ridge of ice on pavement of individual defendants—daylight case—suit also against municipality—two theories of occurrence—one that pavement had been in a defective condition before occurrence and secondly that ice had formed in ridges from 1 to 2 inches in height—snowing at time—no evidence of constructive notice—nonsuit proper. ***Silich v. Wissinger et al.*, 438 Pa. 548, 264 A.2d 169.**

Plaintiff attempted to prove case by using certain paragraphs of an answer admitting ownership of alleged property in front of which plaintiff allegedly fell—refusal of admission proper—plaintiff must establish negligence by affirmative proof. ***Rosenson v. Lyle*, 436 Pa. 354, 261 A.2d 79.**

Plaintiff's decedent was a pedestrian on a city street—bright day—stepping down from curb into an excavation 6 feet long, 4 feet wide and 3 inches deep and within such area a manhole cover—decedent guilty of contributory negligence—should have seen excavation—judgment *n.o.v.* properly entered in suit against municipality. ***Cerino v. Philadelphia*, 435 Pa. 355, 257 A.2d 571.**

Plaintiff fell while on pavement by reason allegedly of a raised concrete sewer cover—in broad daylight—no excuse for not seeing condition—guilty of contributory negligence—nonsuit proper. ***Beil v. Allentown*, 434 Pa. 10, 252 A.2d 692.**

Plaintiff pedestrian fell over a 1-3/8 inch protruding curb in city street—aware of defect before occurrence—allegedly distracted by sound of approaching traffic—insufficient excuse—guilty of contributory negligence as a matter of law. ***Knapp v. Bradford City*, 432 Pa. 172, 247 A.2d 575.**

Falling asleep

Pedestrian allegedly fell as the result of the existence of hole in cartway 36 inches long, 24 inches wide and from 4 to 5 inches deep—at night—photograph of hole disclosed a ruler inserted showing only 1½ inches in depth—case still for the jury. ***Teagle v. Philadelphia*, 430 Pa. 395, 243 A.2d 342.**

Plaintiffs injured while dancing allegedly as the result of asparagus on dance floor—caterer held responsible. ***Schwartz v. Warwick-Phila. Corp.*, 424 Pa. 185, 226 A.2d 484.**

Falling asleep

In wrongful death and survival action by widow of motorist whose automobile crossed opposing lane and left highway, PennDOT entitled to jury charge on contributory negligence where no evidence presented regarding external cause of accident. Following plaintiff's inquiry into other causes of accident, State Trooper permitted to testify as to possibility of driver having fallen asleep. ***Burkholz v. Com., Dept. of Transp.*, ___ Pa. Cmwlth. ___, 667 A.2d 513 (1995).**

Falling objects

Where no evidence that trunk was too large or unwieldy to be placed in overhead rack of railroad car, employee could not maintain action for negligence of employer in providing safe place to work when trunk fell on employee's foot causing injury. Summary judgment affirmed. ***Lehman v. National R.R. Passenger Corp.*, 443 Pa. Super. 185, 661 A.2d 17 (1995).**

Longshoreman crushed to death while attempting to load irregularly-shaped iron plates. Held: danger was obvious. No duty to warn. ***Ellis v. Chicago Bridge and Iron Company*, 376 Pa. Super. 220, 545 A.2d 906.**

Plaintiff died in hospital after being injured by roll of fencing that fell from a vehicle. After settlement with individual who secured fencing, court ordered dismissal of settled defendants from case, they not being joint tortfeasors under the circumstances. ***Harka v. Nabati*, 337 Pa. Super. 617, 487 A.2d 432.**

Plaintiff a patron in self-service toy store when struck by box falling from shelf. Error to charge on contributory negligence where there was no testimony that plaintiff had done anything to cause box to fall. New trial ordered. ***Davis v. Liberto*, 240 Pa. Super. 132, 368 A.2d 332.**

Limb of tree fell onto plaintiff's car while travelling on highway. Suit versus owner of property and Phila. Electric Co. Verdict against both affirmed. Electric company responsible since they had, for 24 years, inspected trees along highway and removed limbs and branches. Further there was evidence that tree in question had been decaying for four years. ***Beury v. Hicks*, 227 Pa. Super. 476, 323 A.2d 788.**

Mannequin fell on plaintiff while shopping in defendant's store. No evidence as to how and why it fell. Nonsuit reversed. Jury could reasonably infer that store was negligent in allowing mannequin to be in such a position and improperly secured. Proof need be slight. ***Paul v. Hess Bros., Inc.*, 226 Pa. Super. 92, 312 A.2d 65.**

Faulty construction or condition

False representations

Plaintiff injured in a cab accident—on next day after occurrence an adjuster obtained a release from plaintiff on payment of $20—release allegedly obtained by false representations—plaintiff in serious pain at time of execution—jury's verdict finding release invalid upheld by a divided court. ***Jenkins v. Peoples Cab Co. et al.,*** **208 Pa. Super. 131, 220 A.2d 669.**

Family Use Doctrine

Pedestrian struck by wife defendant driving auto. No family use doctrine in Pennsylvania. Mere fact of spousal relationship insufficient to impose liability upon husband owner of auto. In non-commercial use of vehicle, vicarious liability imposed only where master had right to control servant's acts. Summary judgment for absent husband owner of auto affirmed. ***Breslin v. Ridarelli,*** **308 Pa. Super. 179, 454 A.2d 80.**

Farm

Plaintiffs brought nuisance, negligence, and trespass action against Defendant farmer based upon his use of sewage sludge on his fields causing foul odors and harmful effects on their properties. The trial court granted summary judgment for the Defendant. The Superior Court reversed and remanded holding that a farmer had no duty to use his property to protect neighbors from offensive odors emanating from his property, but the facts could constitute a nuisance claim. ***Gilbert v. Synagro Central, LLC.,*** **90 A.3d 37 (Pa. Super. 2014).**

Farm tractor

Boy injured on farm tractor. Suit versus tractor owner and manufacturer. Nonsuit granted as to manufacturer. Jury verdict for owner. Reversed Superior Court's grant of new trial on all issues. Plaintiff's cause of action against owner not affected by joinder of manufacturer or subsequent removal. ***Meyer v. Heilman,*** **503 Pa. 472, 469 A.2d 1037.**

Plaintiff's decedent, a minor of 16 years of age, killed as result of operation of a tractor and cutter by husband defendant—shield covering connecting shaft propelled through air and striking decedent—verdict for defendant—new trial properly granted below—verdict against weight of evidence—explanation of defendant husband contrary to physical facts—doctrine of exclusive control does not apply. ***Getz v. Balliet,*** **431 Pa. 441, 246 A.2d 108.**

Faulty construction or condition

In action against PennDOT and the city from which PennDOT had "adopted" a road for failure to install guard rails, summary judgment in favor of PennDOT was sustained. There was no proof by plaintiff of breach of a duty to plaintiff by PennDOT in the maintenance and care of the road surface between the curb lines—the only area for which PennDOT is statutorily responsible after "adoption" of the road from the city. ***Wallace v. Com., Dept. of Transp.,*** **701 A.2d 307 (Pa. Cmwlth. 1997).**

Fear or fright

Plaintiff's expert's report that state highway was defective in design, irrespective of plaintiff's claims of natural accumulations of ice and snow, creates factual question for jury relating to care and maintenance of DOT's real property and so precludes summary judgment in favor of DOT based on Sovereign Immunity Act. ***Smith v. Com., Dept. of Transp.*, 700 A.2d 587 (Pa. Cmwlth. 1997).**

Plaintiff was injured in an automobile accident allegedly caused by defective road design and condition. On the day of trial, the trial court granted PennDOT's motion for nonsuit based on plaintiff's failure to notify PennDOT of action within six months of accident under 42 Pa. C.S. §5522(a)(1) based on presumption of prejudice and hardship for failure to notify PennDOT. Held: presentation of motion on day of trial was untimely given substantial amount of time during which PennDOT could earlier have made the same motion, there is no presumption of prejudice or hardship attendant to lack of required notice. Negligence of plaintiff's counsel in providing notice coupled with lack of undue hardship to Commonwealth constituted adequate reason for delay in providing notice. Remanded to trial court for hearing on actual prejudice on PennDOT with burden of proof on PennDOT. ***Leedom v. Com., Dept. of Transp.*, 699 A.2d 815 (Pa. Cmwlth. 1997).**

Pedestrian fell into tree well on sidewalk outside stadium. Dark and rainy. Non-jury verdict for plaintiff with one-third comparative negligence. Held: plaintiff needed no expert as to proper design of tree well or sidewalk. Affirmed. ***Burns v. City of Philadelphia*, 350 Pa. Super. 615, 504 A.2d 1321.**

Accident allegedly occurred owing to pothole in state highway. Evidence of repair five days after accident and that pothole was located 1-1/2 miles from Department's local maintenance shed, insufficient to charge department with actual notice as required by statute. Nonsuit as to Commonwealth affirmed. ***Stevens v. Commonwealth*, 89 Pa. Cmwlth. 309, 492 A.2d 490.**

Jury verdict $750,000 against Commonwealth in favor of plaintiff rendered quadriplegic in auto accident allegedly caused by defective highway design. Previous settlement with City for $500,000. No negligence found against City and driver of vehicle in which she was a passenger. Verdict only against Commonwealth. Verdict however molded to $250,000 in accordance with Section 2 of the Sovereign Immunity Act. ***Lyles v. City of Philadelphia*, 88 Pa. Cmwlth. 509, 490 A.2d 936.**

Fear or fright

Auto accident caused death of driver and passenger. Sideswipe forced car onto guardrail and thereafter into head-on collision. Evidence of instantaneous death. Verdict exceeded proven money damages, therefore new trial on damages only ordered. ***Nye v. Com., Dept. of Transp.*, 331 Pa. Super. 209, 480 A.2d 318.**

Plaintiff saw her child eating from loaf of bread from which she had previously eaten. Saw string and "brown stuff"—emotional reaction—gastritis. Verdict for plaintiff affirmed. ***Wisniewski v. Great A & P Tea Co.*, 226 Pa. Super. 574, 323 A.2d 744.**

Uncontrolled car skidded onto sidewalk, struck plaintiff's son and inflicted other damage in plaintiff's presence—no impact with plaintiff—plaintiff developed

Federal statutes

an acute heart condition variously diagnosed by evidence of causal relationship with occurrence—previous no impact rule abolished—case for jury. ***Niederman v. Brodsky,* 436 Pa. 401, 261 A.2d 84.**

Plaintiff in reasonable well-grounded fear of his position in a steam room of defendant premises, injured hand in an attempt to attract attention—case still for the jury as to operator of steam room. ***Stebner v. Young Men's Christian Assn.*, 428 Pa. 370, 238 A.2d 19.**

Federal agency

In action by parents against day care worker and center for molestation of child by worker, corporate entity not entitled to governmental immunity merely by reason of receipt of federal funds or designation by county as official community action program. Employer not vicariously liable for employee's outrageous conduct. Summary judgment reversed in part and affirmed in part. ***Sanchez by Rivera v. Montanez,* 165 Pa. Cmwlth. 381, 645 A.2d 383 (1994).**

Federal Employee's Health Benefits Act

Federal employee brought negligence and malpractice action against health maintenance organization. State tort claim preempted by Federal Employee's Health Benefits Act. ***Fink v. Delaware Valley HMO.* 417 Pa. Super. 287, 612 A.2d 485.**

Federal Insecticide, Fungicide and Rodenticide Act (FIFRA)

Husband and wife sued pest-control company and Dow chemical company for injuries suffered by husband and wife as a result of husband's exposure to Dursban 2E pesticide. Only causes of action specifically or by necessary implication preempted by federal legislation are unavailable to a state court plaintiff. If plaintiff can establish a violation of Federal Insecticide, Fungicide and Rodenticide Act not predicated on failure to warn or inadequate labeling (*e.g.*, gross negligence in reporting to EPA or negligence in testing regimen), that claim is actionable in state court. Plaintiffs' failure to cite additional newly-discovered facts in support of a new cause of action or lack of proof that additional facts were unavailable to plaintiff until disclosed by defendant precludes amendment of complaint after statute of limitations had passed. If plaintiff could establish that defendant prevented plaintiff from acquiring knowledge that would support new cause of action, and there was no other reasonable source for such information, statute of limitation would be tolled. ***Romah v. Hygienic Sanitation, Inc.*, 705 A.2d 841 (Pa. Super. 1997).**

Federal statutes

Co-executors sued medical center for negligence after the decedent died from a methadone overdose cause by methadone stolen from the medical center's patient. The court held that a federal statute registering and regulating medical centers distributing methadone did not create a duty of care to the public. ***McCandless v. Edwards*, 908 A.2d 900 (Pa. Super. 2006).**

Negligence claim by plaintiff who drove his vehicle under a train stopped at a crossing and was injured when the train moved and dragged his vehicle barred by Occupied Crossing Rule which provides that the existence of a train in a cross-

Federal statutes

ing is warning enough of its presence. Negligence *per se* claim of plaintiff was also barred by federal preemption of Federal Rail Safety Act, 49 U.S.C. § 20101, *et seq.* ***Krentz v. Consolidated Rail Corporation*, 865 A.2d 889 (Pa. Super. 2005)**.

Husband and wife sued pest-control company and Dow chemical company for injuries suffered by husband and wife as a result of husband's exposure to Dursban 2E pesticide. Only causes of action specifically or by necessary implication preempted by federal legislation are unavailable to a state court plaintiff. If plaintiff can establish a violation of Federal Insecticide, Fungicide and Rodenticide Act not predicated on failure to warn or inadequate labeling (e.g., gross negligence in reporting to EPA or negligence in testing regimen), that claim is actionable in state court. Plaintiffs' failure to cite additional newly-discovered facts in support of a new cause of action or lack of proof that additional facts were unavailable to plaintiff until disclosed by defendant precludes amendment of complaint after statute of limitations had passed. If plaintiff could establish that defendant prevented plaintiff from acquiring knowledge that would support new cause of action, and there was no other reasonable source for such information, statute of limitation would be tolled. ***Romah v. Hygienic Sanitation, Inc.*, 705 A.2d 841 (Pa. Super. 1997)**.

A state claim that FDA requirements have not been met arising out of the use of a collagen implant is cognizable, despite preemption provisions of the medical device amendments to the Federal Food, Drug and Cosmetic Act. State negligence claims that mirror FDA standards for medical devices are not preempted. Order granting summary judgment reversed. ***Green v. Dolsky,* 546 Pa. 400, 685 A.2d 110 (1996)**.

In an action by passenger against PennDOT and vehicle manufacturer, compliance with federal motor vehicle safety standards and regulations does not preclude state cause of action sounding in negligence for failure to incorporate additional safety features. Order granting summary judgment against manufacturer reversed. ***Muntz v. Com., Dept. of Transp.,* ___ Pa. Cmwlth. ___, 674 A.2d 328 (1996)**.

State law claims for manufacture and sale of defective surgical repair screws and plates were not preempted by medical device amendments to Federal Food and Drug Act. Actions for failure to warn, strict liability, negligence, and implied warranty are preempted by medical device amendment to federal food and drug act. Summary judgment affirmed in part and reversed in part. ***Burgstahler v. Acromed Corporation,* 448 Pa. Super. 26, 670 A.2d 658 (1996)**.

Medical device amendments to the Federal Food, Drug and Cosmetic Act of 1938 preempt state court action for breach of implied warranties of merchantability and fitness for a particular purpose regarding surgical bone plates and screws. Express warranties as to condition or properties of bone plates and screws are not preempted by the amendments. Learned intermediary doctrine does not preclude patient's suit against manufacturer on an express warranty made in connection with the sale of a prescription device. Order granting summary judgment affirmed in part and reversed in part. ***Rosci v. Acromed, Inc.,* ___ Pa. Super. ___, 669 A.2d 959 (1995)**.

Fellow Servant Rule

Following in depth analysis of federal preemption law, Superior Court held that state common law causes of action are expressly not preempted by the National Traffic and Motor Vehicle Safety Act. Therefore, motorist may raise claim at trial that airbag that contributed to his injuries in head-on collision with another vehicle was defective, because Congress intended such issues to go to the jury. Order denying manufacturer's preliminary objections affirmed. **Heiple v. C.R. Motors, Inc., 446 Pa. Super. 310, 666 A.2d 1066 (1995).**

Where no evidence that trunk was too large or unwieldy to be placed in overhead rack of railroad car, employee could not maintain action for negligence of employer in providing safe place to work when trunk fell on employee's foot, causing injury. Summary judgment affirmed. **Lehman v. National R.R. Passenger Corp., 443 Pa. Super. 185, 661 A.2d 17 (1995).**

In action by parents against day care worker and center for molestation of child by worker, corporate entity not entitled to governmental immunity merely by reason of receipt of federal funds or designation by county as official community action program. Employer not vicariously liable for employee's outrageous conduct. Summary judgment reversed in part and affirmed in part. **Sanchez by Rivera v. Montanez, 165 Pa. Cmwlth. 381, 645 A.2d 383 (1994).**

Federal Tort Claims Act

In action by parents against day care worker and center for molestation of child by worker, corporate entity not entitled to governmental immunity merely by reason of receipt of federal funds or designation by county as official community action program. Employer not vicariously liable for employee's outrageous conduct. Summary judgment reversed in part and affirmed in part. **Sanchez by Rivera v. Montanez, 165 Pa. Cmwlth. 381, 645 A.2d 383 (1994).**

Fellow Servant Rule

Pennsylvania National Guardsmen granted state compensation when injured during active service. Amount of compensation determined by Pennsylvania Workmen's Compensation Law. Therefore, suit against fellow guardsmen, in tort, is barred. See Pennsylvania Military Code, 51 Pa. C.S.A. §3501 as exclusive remedy. **Knauer v. Salter, 313 Pa. Super. 289, 459 A.2d 1233.**

Employer provided transportation to and from work in company vehicle. Workmen's Compensation held to be exclusive remedy especially where transportation was a negotiated benefit. Strong dissent. **Sylvester v. Peruso, 286 Pa. Super. 225, 428 A.2d 653.**

Fellow volunteer fireman struck plaintiff who was directing traffic as defendant was responding to alarm. Held: both in course of employment. Workmen's Compensation exclusive remedy. **DeLong v. Miller, 285 Pa. Super. 120, 426 A.2d 1171.**

Fence

Fence

In negligence action by truck driver for damages resulting from cow wandering onto roadway, turnpike commission had no duty of care, custody, or control of cow. Summary judgment affirmed. ***Mason & Dixon Lines, Inc. v. Mognet,* 166 Pa. Cmwlth. 1, 645 A.2d 1370 (1994).**

Motorcyclist failed to produce sufficient evidence in action against landowner, PennDOT, and township to justify inference of negligence and causation owing to inability to identify reason his vehicle left roadway and struck fence post. Summary judgment affirmed. ***Saylor v. Green,* 165 Pa. Cmwlth. 249, 645 A.2d 318 (1994).**

Child injured by train after crawling through hole in city-owned fence. City not liable. Owed no duty to child. ***Gardner v. Consolidated Rail Corporation,* 524 Pa. 445, 573 A.2d 1016.**

Fetus

Wife plaintiff who was left unattended in emergency room during miscarriage and then handed corpse of miscarried fetus while nurse took pictures established sufficient evidence of physical impact to allow recovery for negligent infliction of emotional distress. Case remanded for new trial on damages. ***Brown v. Philadelphia College of Osteopathic Medicine,* 449 Pa. Super. 667, 674 A.2d 1130 (1996).**

Accident involving school bus resulted in death of ten-week-old fetus. Death of non-viable fetus not applicable. ***Askew v. Cruciani,* 149 Pa. Cmwlth. 397, 613 A.2d 147.**

Pregnant woman injured in automobile accident brought action to recover for injuries to herself and to fetus. Fetus was aborted to avoid risk of damage. Held: wrongful death and survival action may not be brought on behalf of non-viable fetus. ***Coveleski v. Bubnis,* 391 Pa. Super. 409, 571 A.2d 433.**

Fiduciary negligence

Plaintiff trustee brought breach of fiduciary duty action against investment advisor for mishandling auction rate securities entrusted to him. After a bench trial the trial court found in favor of the plaintiff on the breach of fiduciary duty claim. The Superior Court affirmed, holding that the investment advisor's breach of fiduciary duty occurred when he decided not to inform the trustee that it did not have auction rights to securities that had been purchased for the trust. ***In re: Jerome Markowitz Trust,* 2013 Pa. Super. 128 (Pa. Super. 2013).**

Limited partners brought suit against a general partner for breach of fiduciary duty for excluding them from their proper share of benefits from the partnership. The trial court granted judgment in favor of the defendant. The Superior Court affirmed, holding that a limited partner has no standing to bring claims in his individual capacity against a limited partnership's general partner as the harms alleged were suffered to the limited partnership entity itself and not the limited partner individually. ***Weston v. Northhampton Personal Care, Inc.,* 62 A.3d 947 (Pa. 2013).**

Fire

Plaintiff, a former CEO, brought a breach of fiduciary duty lawsuit against defendant corporate directors for preventing the board of directors from functioning independently and for engaging the company in a self-dealing transaction. The trial court granted summary judgment in favor of the defendants. The Superior Court affirmed, holding that the plaintiff had failed to produce evidence that the defendants had actual control of the corporation's conduct to establish a breach of fiduciary duty. ***Rock v. Rangos*, 61 A.3d 239 (Pa. Super. 2013).**

Executor of estate failed to properly maintain real estate of decedent—left property be vandalized and failed to rent same—held: such circumstances constituted fiduciary negligence and subjected fiduciary to a surcharge—case remanded to determine amount of surcharge. ***Denlinger Estate*, 449 Pa. 393, 297 A.2d 478.**

Fighting

Broken ankle sustained when insured knocked down by other driver's fists. Not entitled to coverage under uninsured motorist clause. ***Day v. State Farm*, 261 Pa. Super. 216, 396 A.2d 3**.

Decedent became drunk and got involved in fight and was killed. Suit against hotel which served him last two drinks. Verdict for defendant in survival action and $1,995.00 in wrongful death. Decedent 21 years old earning $3.25 per hour. Spent $55.00 per week for food, lodging and entertainment. Separated from wife and giving her no support. No evidence of savings. No tax records or payroll stubs produced. No evidence of pain and suffering. Verdict sustained as compromise. ***Gallagher v. Four Winds Motor-Hotel*, 233 Pa. Super. 1, 335 A.2d 394.**

Fill

Plaintiff was injured when car he was driving fell into 8"–12" ditch in road that resulted from settlement of fill deposited by local authority which had created hole. Plaintiff appeals from trial judge's decision to give instruction to jury which left question of whether local authority had actual or constructive notice of fill settling to jury. Plaintiff argued that because local authority created hole and installed fill that settled and caused dangerous condition, it had notice of condition as a matter of law. Instruction approved by Commonwealth Court which held that just because defendant created hole and installed fill that eventually resulted in dangerous condition does not mean that plaintiff is not required to show that defendant knew or should have known of the condition. ***Miller v. Lykens Borough Authority*, 712 A.2d 800 (Pa. Cmwlth. 1998).**

Fire

Plaintiff brought a negligence action against Defendant electric utility after Defendant repaired a utility pole damaged in an accident and a fire broke out in the Plaintiff's basement electrical panel after the Defendant restored power to the Plaintiff's building. The trial court entered summary judgment in favor of the electric utility. The Superior Court reversed holding that there was a genuine issue of material fact as to whether an electric utility owes a duty to warn its customers that it would be reconnecting electrical lines to its property or owes a duty to inspect its

Fire

customers electrical system prior to restoring power. *Alderwoods, Inc. v. Duquesne Light Co.,* **2012 Pa. Super. 153 (Pa Super. 2012).**

Plaintiffs' estates filed a negligence action against Defendant power company for causing the deaths of the decedents on the basis that the power company disconnected the electricity to its customer's home. Plaintiffs claimed that the defendant caused the deaths of the decedent, because the fire was caused by a candle being used by one of the plaintiff's due to the lack of electricity. The trial court granted summary judgment in favor of the defendant. The Superior Court affirmed holding that the disconnecting of electricity was not the proximate cause of plaintiffs' deaths. *Eckroth v. Pennsylvania Electric, Inc.,* **12 A.3d 422 (Pa. Super. 2010).**

Decedent's estate brought claim for negligence against defendant housing authority after the decedent died in an apartment fire allegedly due to the a disabled fire detection system and a lack of installed fire stops. The trial court denied Defendant's Motion for Summary Judgment. The Commonwealth Court affirmed holding that the allegations that the fire alarm system's malfunction and the lack of installed fire stops were sufficient to establish a dangerous condition of real estate that caused the decedent's death. *Thornton v. Philadelphia Housing Authority,* **4 A.3d 1143 (Pa. Cmwlth. 2010).**

Plaintiff produce warehouse owner appealed jury verdict in favor of defendant electrical contractors who had allegedly improperly installed connections inside a metering box. Superior Court affirmed trial court's spoliation charge to jury in light of plaintiff's failure to preserve all electrical equipment that could have been investigated and found to be an alternative cause of the fire. Such a charge was less restrictive than a grant of summary judgment and therefore appropriate after application of three pronged test set forth in prior cases. *Pia v. Perrotti,* **718 A.2d 321 (Pa. Super. 1998).**

Summary judgment in favor of volunteer fire department based on Political Subdivision Tort Claims Act reversed, where fire department chief's act of spreading paint thinner on the floor at fire department, which caught fire and injured visitor/plaintiff, constituted "care, custody or control of real property" and so provided an exception to immunity. Reversing Commonwealth Court. *Grieff v. Reisinger,* **___ Pa. ___, 693 A.2d 195 (1997).**

Barn owners' suit against electric utility for oversupply of electricity that allegedly caused fire properly initiated in Common Pleas Court. Court of Common Pleas has original jurisdiction to entertain a suit for damages against a public utility, based on its asserted failure to provide adequate services, even though subject matter of complaint against public utility is encompassed by the public utility code. P.U.C. order dismissing complaint vacated and remanded. *Poorbaugh v. Pennsylvania P.U.C.,* **___ Pa. Cmwlth. ___, 666 A.2d 744 (1995).**

Plaintiff severely burned by flash fire caused when paint thinner used to clean paint from floor of volunteer fire department ignited was precluded from recovering for injuries because volunteer fire company entitled to governmental immunity. Real property exception to governmental immunity does not apply unless

Fire

cause of action based on condition of real property or an actual defect of the property itself. Negligent mishandling of combustible liquids on property does not invoke real property exception. Denial of volunteer fire company's motion for summary judgment reversed and remanded. ***Grieff v. Reisinger,*** ___ **Pa. Cmwlth.** ___, **654 A.2d 77 (1995).**

Tenant brought wrongful death action against housing authority for failure to inspect dwelling and discover condition that led to fatal fire. Housing authority Commonwealth agency and therefore immune. ***Crosby v. Kotch,*** **135 Pa. Cmwlth. 470, 580 A.2d 1191.**

Shopping-center owner and tenants brought action against carpet store and foam manufacturer for damage resulting from fire caused by improper storage of foam padding. Store found 80% negligent. Manufacturer 20% negligent for failure to warn. ***Remy v. Michael D's Carpet Outlets,*** **391 Pa. Super. 476, 571 A.2d 466.**

Apartment fire resulted in deaths of two tenants. Verdict for plaintiffs reversed. New trial ordered. Plaintiff's expert testified that a fire escape or other means of egress would have saved plaintiffs' lives. ***Mapp v. Dube,*** **330 Pa. Super. 284, 479 A.2d 553.**

Death in fire at leased premises. Under circumstances, Fire and Panic Act, 35 P.S. §1222 does not apply. Complaint, however, does state cause of action in negligence—§17.6 of Restatement (2d) Property. Case remanded for new trial. ***Asper v. Haffley,*** **312 Pa. Super. 424, 458 A.2d 1364.**

City employee stole quantity of swimming pool sanitizer and gave it to another employee in brown paper bag. While in car, plaintiff, a passenger was burned when chemical spontaneously ignited. Improper to direct verdict against manufacturer. Theft irrelevant since adequacy of warnings still at issue as was defect in design which allowed flash fires. ***Pegg v. General Motors,*** **258 Pa. Super. 59, 391 A.2d 1074.**

Plaintiff employed defendant janitorial company to police his building—evidence that employee of company put ashes from incinerator into a cardboard box—fire ensued—evidence that employee had stirred ashes with his bare fingers to determine whether hot—sufficient evidence to take case to jury for fire loss. ***Duffy v. Nat. Janitorial Services, Inc.,*** **429 Pa. 334, 340 A.2d 527.**

Sufficient evidence from which jury could infer that a fire destroying plaintiff's plant originated from the negligent repair of a box car loaded with cornstarch—matter for the jury. ***Connelly Containers, Inc. v. Penna. R.R. Co.,*** **222 Pa. Super. 7, 292 A.2d 528.**

Fire department tore holes in plaintiff's roof to prevent fire on adjoining property from spreading—nonsuit in case against adjoining property owner affirmed—mere violation of Fire Code not negligence *per se* without showing that there is a connection between the spread or cause of the fire and the violation. ***Githens R.&Co. v. Wilstein,*** **43 Pa. 480, 277 A.2d 157.**

Fire and Panic Act

A number of firemen killed or injured in a service station gasoline explosion—held: under facts supplier of gasoline and repair company responsible—*per curiam* opinion—several concurring opinions—procedure issues also involved. **Walsh et al. v. Sun Oil Co., 437 Pa. 80, 262 A.2d 128.**

Plaintiff's premises damaged by fire originating in defendant's warehouse—evidence that electrical equipment was defective—trial court admitted certain evidence prepared by a city employee not required by his duties to make such a report and who was deceased at time of trial—also trial court ruled matter as one of exclusive control—error and new trial properly granted. **Githens, Rexsamer & Co. Inc. v. Wildstein, 428 Pa. 201, 236 A.2d 792.**

Plaintiff owner of building damaged by fire—evidence from which jury could draw inference of negligent blasting causing an electrical fire—nonsuit improperly granted below—for jury. **DeFrank v. Sullivan Trail Coal Co., 425 Pa. 512, 229 A.2d 899.**

Fire and Panic Act

Death in fire at leased premises. Under circumstances, Fire and Panic Act, 35 P.S. §1222 does not apply. Complaint, however, does state cause of action in negligence—§17.6 of Restatement (2d) Property. Case remanded for new trial. *Asper v. Haffley,* **312 Pa. Super. 424, 458 A.2d 1364.**

Fire department

Plaintiff firefighter brought a claim against his insurer for underinsured motorist benefits after he was injured traveling to the scene of an accident when a bridge on his own property collapsed. The trial court affirmed an arbitration panel denial of benefits on the basis that the bridge collapse was a supervening cause extinguishing liability on behalf of the driver that caused the accident to which the Plaintiff was responding. The Pennsylvania Supreme Court affirmed holding that an original tortfeasor could not be held liable for injuries attributable to a superseding cause. **Bole v. Erie Ins. Exchange, _____ A.3d _____, No. 24 WAP 2011 (Pa. 2012).**

Plaintiff was injured when she tripped on a box under a table located in a blocked-off street during a fire department street fair. Grant of summary judgment in favor of fire department due to lack of exception to governmental immunity under Political Subdivision Tort Claims Act affirmed. Care, custody and control of real estate exception to governmental immunity does not apply to streets. **Granchi v. Borough of North Braddock, 810 A.2d 747 (Pa. Cmwlth. 2002).**

Vehicle exception to governmental immunity does not apply when alleged cause of accident in which plaintiff was injured was valve that fell from back of fire truck en route to station. **Swartz v. Hilltown Township V.F.D., 721 A.2d 819 (Pa. Cmwlth. 1998).**

Plaintiff filed suit against multiple defendants, including volunteer fire company for injuries sustained after sale of alcohol to defendant. After review of legal and factual basis of fire company's status as local agency entitled to protection of

Fire department

Political Subdivision Tort Claims Act, court determined that illegal sale of alcohol on fire company property does not constitute "care, custody or control" standard related in *Grieff v. Reisinger*, 548 Pa. 13, 693 A.2d 195 (1997) and so immunity available and grant of summary judgment in favor of volunteer fire company affirmed. **Eger v. Lynch, 714 A.2d 1149 (Pa. Cmwlth. 1998).**

Plaintiff sued city for injuries sustained while being driven to hospital by fire fighter in fire rescue van. During trip to hospital, left rear tandem wheels feel off van, causing an accident and plaintiff's injuries. Parties stipulated that firefighter was not driving negligently and that repair and maintenance of vehicle by city was negligent. Plaintiff's motion for summary judgment granted and affirmed by Commonwealth Court. Supreme Court held that maintenance and repair of van is included in exception to Political Subdivision Tort Claims act relating to injuries caused by negligent acts of local agency or its employees with respect to the operation of a motor vehicle. Negligence related to the operation of a vehicle encompasses not only how a person drives, but also whether he should be driving a particular vehicle in the first place. ***Mickle v. City of Philadelphia*, 707 A.2d 1124 (Pa. 1998).**

Summary judgment in favor of volunteer fire department based on Political Subdivision Tort Claims Act reversed, where fire department chief's act of spreading paint thinner on the floor at fire department, which caught fire and injured visitor/plaintiff, constituted "care, custody or control of real property" and so provided an exception to immunity. Reversing Commonwealth Court. ***Grieff v. Reisinger*, ___ Pa. ___, 693 A.2d 195 (1997).**

Plaintiff severely burned by flash fire caused when paint thinner used to clean paint from floor of volunteer fire department ignited was precluded from recovering for injuries because volunteer fire company entitled to governmental immunity. Real property exception to governmental immunity does not apply unless cause of action based on condition of real property or an actual defect of the property itself. Negligent mishandling of combustible liquids on property does not invoke real property exception. Denial of volunteer fire company's motion for summary judgment reversed and remanded. ***Grieff v. Reisinger*, ___ Pa. Cmwlth. ___, 654 A.2d 77 (1995).**

Plaintiff failed to prove that dangerous condition of a parking lot was causally related to injuries. Summary judgment in favor of volunteer fire department affirmed. ***West v. Kuneck*, 167 Pa. Cmwlth. 252, 647 A.2d 975 (1994).**

Amount of damage recoverable from fire department limited by local agency status. Purchase of liability insurance in excess of statutory limit is not a waiver. ***Dunaj v. Selective Insurance Co. of America*, 167 Pa. Cmwlth. 93, 647 A.2d 633 (1994).**

Wedding guest injured at reception held in fire hall. Held: volunteer fire department not political subdivision within meaning of venue statute. ***Estate of Harkins v. Romito Caterers, Inc.*, 152 Pa. Cmwlth. 600, 620 A.2d 570.**

Fire fighter - See Fire department

Spectator at fire department carnival assaulted by employee of amusement operator. Matter remanded in order to establish official status of fire department. ***Miller by Miller,* 152 Pa. Cmwlth. 159, 618 A.2d 1143.**

City resident treated by fire department unit brought action against city and department for improper care. Defendants immune. Judgment on pleadings should have been granted. ***City of Philadelphia v. Glim,* 149 Pa. Cmwlth. 491, 613 A.2d 613.**

Spectator at fire injured when hose burst. Borough not liable. ***Speece v. Borough of North Braddock,* 145 Pa. Cmwlth. 568, 604 A.2d 760.**

Volunteer fireman injured when he fell into window well. Held: fireman's rule not adopted in Pennsylvania. Firemen do not assume the risk of on-duty injuries. ***Mull v. Kerstetter,* 373 Pa. Super. 228, 540 A.2d 951.**

Intersection collision with off-duty fire truck. Plaintiff looked only once for traffic and then did not continue to look. Nonsuit reversed and new trial granted. No duty to continue looking under the circumstances. ***Imes v. Empire Hook and Ladder,* 247 Pa. Super. 470, 372 A.2d 922.**

Contractor doing work in fire house, removed brass pole from living quarters to ground floor and, then firemen covered hole with rug to keep dust down. Plaintiff, a fireman, was adjusting the rug and fell through hole. Verdict for plaintiff, affirmed. §343 of Restatement (2d) Torts—possessor liable where he should expect that invitees will fail to protect themselves against a danger. ***Bowman v. Fretts and Leeper Constr. Co.,* 227 Pa. Super. 347, 322 A.2d 719.**

A number of firemen killed or injured in a service station gasoline explosion—held: under facts supplier of gasoline and repair company responsible—*per curiam* opinion—several concurring opinions—procedure issues also involved. ***Walsh et al. v. Sun Oil Co.,* 437 Pa. 80, 262 A.2d 128.**

Fire fighter - See Fire department

Firearms

Pistol accidentally discharged injuring owner. Evidence of similar occurrences with other models held admissible. ***DiFrancesco v. Excam, Inc.,* 434 Pa. Super. 173, 642 A.2d 529.**

Member of hunting club killed by other member during hunt. Held: club members not liable for actions of individual who fired fatal shot. ***Johnson v. Johnson,* 410 Pa. Super. 631, 600 A.2d 965.**

Defendant shot eight bullets into car with four plaintiffs. Tamar Dombach struck six times in buttocks—pieces of metal remain in body. Verdict: $60 medical, $600 pain and suffering, $750 punitive damages. Sandra Helm suffered slight scratch on back—verdict: $400 pain and suffering, $750 punitive damages. Owner of car received $446.47 property damages. Both male passengers, uninjured, each received $750 punitive damages. ***Rhoads v. Heberling,* 306 Pa. Super. 35, 451 A.2d 1378.**

Fourteen-year old boys playing with BB gun. One killed in horseplay. Boy who shot gun testified that he knew of gun's lethal propensity. Liability therefore cannot be imposed upon manufacturer for failure to warn of that propensity. ***Sherk v. Daisy-Heddon*, 498 Pa. 594, 450 A.2d 615.**

Wrongful death and survival action instituted against employer of decedent who killed himself with loaded gun which employer kept in unlocked locker. Nonsuit affirmed. ***Malloy v. Girard Bank*, 292 Pa. Super. 34, 436 A.2d 991.**

14 year old boy killed by BB gun accidentally shot at him by friend. Suit against manufacturer allowed under strict liability theory and negligence. Theory was that gun was of a higher power than public expected. ***Sherk v. Daisy-Heddon*, 285 Pa. Super. 320, 427 A.2d 657.**

Suit against bar owner for failure to protect patron from assault and battery and gunshot by another person. Bartender had custody of gun for a short while, but somehow in fracas it ended up in assailant's hands. Verdict for plaintiff. ***Prather v. H-K Corp.*, 282 Pa. Super. 556, 423 A.2d 385.**

Death action. Verdict for plaintiff sustained by equally divided court. Plaintiff shot by police officer while lying face down and spread eagle. Officer's cocked gun discharged. Reasonable care here held to be extraordinary car when dealing with loaded firearm. ***Everett v. City of New Kensington*, 262 Pa. Super. 28, 396 A.2d 467.**

Minor plaintiff injured by bullets found in car in defendant's garage. Defendant towed abandoned cars for City of Easton. Nonsuit affirmed. Although owner knew children played in lot, no knowledge of dangerous articles left in glove compartments. Only liable to trespassers for known dangers or those of which he should have known. ***Norton v. City of Easton*, 249 Pa. Super. 520, 378 A.2d 417.**

Complete loss of sight in right eye due to gunshot wound. Night manager in motel attempted to protect himself with mace pen which failed to stop intruder as advertised. Action of criminal intruder not a superseding cause. Verdict for plaintiff against mace pen manufacturer ***Klages v. General Ordnance Equipment Corp.*, 240 Pa. Super. 356, 367 A.2d 304.**

Additional defendant walked out of defendant institution without being seen, went to her apartment and got a gun, then went to her boyfriend's apartment and shot and killed a girl in that apartment. Verdict against additional defendant only, affirmed. ***Evanuik v. University of Pittsburgh Western Psychiatric Institute*, 234 Pa. Super. 287, 338 A.2d 636.**

Fireworks

Plaintiff assistant firework technician brought suit against Defendant lead firework technician after he was injured while setting off a fireworks display. The trial court entered summary judgment in favor of the Defendant. The Superior Court reversed and remanded on the basis that there was a genuine issue of material fact as to whether the lead technician had negligently used an oversized tube causing the Plaintiff's injury. The Superior Court also held that the doctrine of as-

Fixture

sumption of the risk was a determination for a jury unless the evidence was clear. ***Thompson v. Ginkel*, 2014 Pa. Super. 125 (Pa. Super. 2014).**

Guest at party injured when fireworks cannon exploded. Host not liable. Guest assumed risk. ***Howell v. Clyde*, 533 Pa. 151, 620 A.2d 1107.**

Minor plaintiff injured by explosion of an aerial bomb fireworks—occurrence took place in a public park after a fireworks display—court below properly held township immune from liability—strong dissent. ***Flisek et al. v. Star Fireworks, Inc. et al.*, 220 Pa. Super. 350, 286 A.2d 673.**

Children of plaintiff found an unexploded aerial bomb—plaintiff to determine whether safe poured out part of contents which would not ignite but remainder in bomb suddenly exploded, injuring plaintiff—judgment on pleadings reversed—matter for jury—not testing a known danger. ***Karns v. T. Vitale Fireworks Corp.*, 436 Pa. 181, 259 A.2d 687.**

Fixture

Plaintiff's decedent was killed when he was struck by the door to a coke oven battery. Issue before the court was whether the door, which was of massive size and rolled on wheels, was a fixture and therefore subject to the 12 year statute of repose or personalty subject to suit for defective design or construction. Held: door was not a fixture and 12 year statute of repose did not apply. **Vargo v. Koppers, 715 A.2d 423 (1998).**

Immense coke oven door installed 35 years prior to accident which caused plaintiff's decedent's death and which is movable by means of wheels on tracks is still an "improvement" under statute of repose and so action by coke oven employee is extinguished. Trial court order denying motion for judgment *n.o.v.* reversed. ***Vargo v. Koppers Co., Inc.*, 452 Pa. Super. 275, 681 A.2d 815 (1996).**

Flares

Truck driver who drove onto very rough section of road in construction zone lost control of his vehicle and struck another truck that had jack-knifed due to same conditions. First truck, in contravention of law, had not placed warning markers or flares 100 feet and 200 feet behind his vehicle to warn oncoming traffic of dangerous location of his truck immediately adjacent to the roadway. In consolidated suit by plaintiff and others against first truck driver, his trucking company and PennDOT, jury returned verdict in favor of plaintiff and against first driver's company only and allocated 41% liability to plaintiff. On appeal, Commonwealth Court held there was adequate evidence to support jury verdict in favor of plaintiff and against only one defendant. Affirmed with modification, allowing plaintiff's employer to file a subrogation according to Indiana law. ***Burlington Motor Carriers v. Com., Dept. of Transp.*, 710 A.2d 148 (Pa. Cmwlth. 1998).**

Police put out flares due to first accident. Second accident allegedly occurred due in part to the flares. Error to exclude testimony about custom and usage in placing and extinguishing flares. This is not expert testimony, but fact evidence. ***Kubit v. Russ*, 287 Pa. Super. 28, 429 A.2d 703.**

Floors

Flooding

Suit by car dealership for damages sustained when a creek overflowed its banks and damaged plaintiff's parking lot and inventory of new and used vehicles. Held that PennDOT's work in relocating road which abutted creek did not change the natural path of the watercourse and so was not a negligent act which might fit within an exception to sovereign immunity. ***Tom Clark Chevrolet, Inc. v. Pa. Dept. of Environmental Protection*, 816 A.2d 1246 (Pa. Cmwlth. 2003).**

250 employees of a tire manufacturing plant sued landowners whose property abutted the plant property for loss of wages and benefits during repair and reconstruction of the plant necessitated by storm water runoff redirected by construction performed by one or more of the adjoining landowners. Held that the Economic Loss Doctrine provides that no cause of action exists in negligence absent physical injury or property damage. Recovery of purely economic losses alleged by plaintiffs are not recoverable. ***Adams v. Copper Beach Townhome Communities, L.P.*, 816 A.2d 301 (Pa. Super. 2003).**

Downstream property owner sued reservoir and dam company for failure to contain water following heavy rains. The court confirmed that the owner of a reservoir is "required to exercise a degree of care commensurate with the risk of storing water in a reservoir and would be liable if its negligence made it possible for water to escape with resulting damage to property." Dam company's failure to comply with Dam Safety and Encroachments Act, 32 P.S. § 639.13 *et seq.* constituted negligence *per se*. ***Shamnoski v. PG Energy*, 765 A.2d 297 (Pa. Super. 2000).**

Class action suit brought against power company for damage caused by flood waters released from company's dam. Company not liable. Evidence of property damage upstream of dam properly admitted. ***Engle v. West Penn Power Company*, 409 Pa. Super. 486, 598 A.2d 291.**

Stranded motorist drowned when swept into storm sewer. Settled before trial with adjacent landowner, township and PennDOT. Eventual jury verdict also included neighboring city from which it was proved that most of water came. Held: under facts City of Bethlehem not liable. Gradual orderly development resulting in incremental increase in rate of flow of surface waters through natural drainage swale does not give rise to liability. Other theories put forth by plaintiff not applicable under facts here. ***Laform v. Bethlehem Township*, 346 Pa. Super. 512, 499 A.2d 1373.**

Head-on collision with multiple deaths allegedly due to flooded road. Evidence of state widening road without doing anything to control already existing problem with runoff. Subsequent negligence not a superseding cause insulating township from liability if original negligence was a contributing factor. ***Piekarski v. Club Overlook*, 281 Pa. Super. 162, 421 A.2d 1198.**

Floors

Inmate injured when he fell on wet, slippery waxed floor was not entitled to trial as condition of floor was not "dangerous condition of real estate" under the real estate exception in the Sovereign Immunity Act. ***Raker v. Pa. Dept. of Corrections*, 844 A.2d 659 (Pa. Cmwlth. 2004).**

Floors

Wife plaintiff filed suit against school district alleging that water left from "damp mopping" of school hallway caused her to slip and fall and suffer injuries. After grant of motion for summary judgment by defendant based on plaintiffs' failure to prove facts which would take case under real estate exception to governmental immunity, Commonwealth Court affirmed. On appeal, Supreme Court reversed and remanded to Commonwealth Court which reversed and remanded its prior affirmance of trial court grant of summary judgment. Held: "...for government immunity purposes, it is no longer of any consequence that the injury does not result from a defect in, or condition of, the real property itself, and that the real property exception should no longer be considered *in pari materia* with the sidewalk exception to governmental immunity or the real estate exception to sovereign immunity". ***Hanna v. West Shore School District*, 717 A.2d 626 (Pa. Cmwlth. 1998).**

Plaintiff was injured when she slipped and fell on floor of SEPTA train. Plaintiff argued that train was improperly cared for personal property of Commonwealth and so exempt from protection of Sovereign Immunity Act. Held: SEPTA train is vehicle for purposes of Sovereign Immunity Act and not personal property. Grant of compulsory nonsuit affirmed. ***Ross v. SEPTA*, 714 A.2d 1131 (Pa. Cmwlth. 1998).**

For real property exception to apply against school district, dangerous condition must be of or attached to the pavement or property and not on the subject pavement or property. Rainwater on floor of school building did not constitute dangerous condition of or attached to property. Directed verdict for defendant affirmed. Dissent would apply exception based on school district's use of terrazzo floor tile which school district knew became dangerously slippery when wet. ***Shedrick v. William Penn School District*, ___ Pa. Cmwlth. ___, 654 A.2d 163 (1995).**

Plaintiff severely burned by flash fire caused when paint thinner used to clean paint from floor of volunteer fire department ignited was precluded from recovering for injuries because volunteer fire company entitled to governmental immunity. Real property exception to governmental immunity does not apply unless cause of action based on condition of real property or an actual defect of the property itself. Negligent mishandling of combustible liquids on property does not invoke real property exception. Denial of volunteer fire company's motion for summary judgment reversed and remanded. ***Grieff v. Reisinger*, ___ Pa. Cmwlth. ___, 654 A.2d 77 (1995).**

Patron did not assume risk of injury when she observed wet floor immediately before stepping on to it and falling. Nonsuit reversed. ***Hardy v. Southland Corporation*, 435 Pa. Super. 237, 645 A.2d 839 (1994).**

Plaintiff, a relative of defendants, fell on a heavily waxed floor—rug skidded when stepped on—sufficient evidence of notice and unusual application of wax—case for jury—verdict for plaintiff upheld. ***Farrell v. Bonner*, 424 Pa. 301, 227 A.2d 683.**

Flow of traffic

Plaintiff motorist injured in collision with township garbage truck entitled to new trial after trial court incorrectly instructed jury that garbage truck driver was entitled to drive against traffic flow in the same manner as Motor Vehicle Code defined Type I and Type II vehicles such as emergency vehicles. New trial granted. ***Sawchzuk-Serge v. Township of Cheltenham,*** ___ **Pa. Super.** ___, **670 A.2d 210 (1996).**

Foam padding

Shopping-center owner and tenants brought action against carpet store and foam manufacturer for damage resulting from fire caused by improper storage of foam padding. Store found 80% negligent. Manufacturer 20% negligent for failure to warn. ***Remy v. Michael D's Carpet Outlets,* 391 Pa. Super. 476, 571 A.2d 466.**

Fog

Plaintiff was rear seat passenger in car driven by defendant which encountered fog bank, left road and struck tree, injuring plaintiff. Trial court charged on sudden emergency doctrine to which plaintiff objected. Plaintiff argued that defendant's summary citation for breaking statutory assured clear distance rule precluded her from claiming sudden emergency; a tree is not a sudden emergency and amount of time it took for defendant to react argues against any suddenness. Held: summary charges, particularly when defendant did not even attend hearing on charge, cannot be admitted in civil cases as a general rule. Tree was not sudden emergency, the fog was. There was adequate evidence that defendant acted quickly and thoroughly to minimize sudden appearance of fog. Plaintiff's second argument that jury's distaste with trial court's habit of chewing tobacco during trial and spitting into a cup as prejudicial to plaintiff is totally unfounded. ***Dickens v. Barnhart,* 711 A.2d 513 (Pa. Super. 1998).**

Mrs. Stout, with husband as passenger, driving on turnpike. Road free of fog when suddenly car entered dense fog—night. Mrs. Stout jammed on brakes, skidded into opposite lanes and stopped at 90 degree angle to oncoming traffic. Plaintiff encountered fog and slowed but still didn't see Stout car until too late to avoid impact. Fog emanating from cooling tower owned by defendant United Aircraft. Plaintiff verdict against both defendants. ***Westerman v. Stout, et al.,* 237 Pa. Super. 195, 335 A.2d 741.**

Food

In negligence and products liability case against foreign defendant, general jurisdiction requires sufficient contacts with forum relating to activities alleged to be negligent or products alleged to be dangerous. ***McCall v. Formu-3 Intern'l, Inc.,* 437 Pa. Super. 575, 650 A.2d 903 (1994).**

Food and Drug Administration

A physician may be required to include in his description of an operative procedure the use of Food and Drug Administration classification of a device intended to be used in the procedure. A hospital has no duty to a patient under Pennsylvania's informed consent doctrine; that duty is on the physician who is to perform

Food, Drug and Cosmetic Act of 1938

the procedure. ***Southard v. Temple University Hospital*, 731 A.2d 603 (Pa. Super. 1999).**

Food, Drug and Cosmetic Act of 1938

Plaintiff who was disfigured by injections of silicone sued doctor who had violated FDA prohibition against using silicone for such a purpose. Trial court granted a new trial on plaintiff's motion after a verdict in favor of the physician. Breach of FDA prohibition is negligence *per se* and FDA is not prohibited from regulating medical treatment. ***Cabiroy v. Scipione*, 767 A.2d 1078 (Pa. Super. 2001).**

A state claim that FDA requirements have not been met arising out of the use of a collagen implant is cognizable, despite preemption provisions of the medical device amendments to the Federal Food, Drug and Cosmetic Act. State negligence claims that mirror FDA standards for medical devices are not preempted. Order granting summary judgment reversed. ***Green v. Dolsky*, 546 Pa. 400, 685 A.2d 110 (1996).**

State law claims for manufacture and sale of defective surgical repair screws and plates were not preempted by medical device amendments to Federal Food and Drug Act. Actions for failure to warn, strict liability, negligence, and implied warranty are preempted by medical device amendment to federal food and drug act. Summary judgment affirmed in part and reversed in part. ***Burgstahler v. Acromed Corporation*, 448 Pa. Super. 26, 670 A.2d 658 (1996).**

Medical device amendments to the Federal Food, Drug and Cosmetic Act of 1938 preempt state court action for breach of implied warranties of merchantability and fitness for a particular purpose regarding surgical bone plates and screws. Express warranties as to condition or properties of bone plates and screws are not preempted by the amendments. Learned intermediary doctrine does not preclude patient's suit against manufacturer on an express warranty made in connection with the sale of a prescription device. Order granting summary judgment affirmed in part and reversed in part. ***Rosci v. Acromed, Inc.*, ___ Pa. Super. ___, 669 A.2d 959 (1995).**

Food poisoning

Plaintiff sued sausage packer, restaurant supplier and restaurant for injuries from eating allegedly tainted pork. Granting of demurrer reversed. Cause of action stated on allegation of negligence for failure to inspect and breach of implied warranty. ***Clouser v. Shamokin Packing*, 240 Pa. Super. 268, 361 A.2d 836.**

Foot

Railroad worker had foot amputated by railroad car. Employer liable under Federal Employer's Liability Act. ***Harding v. Consolidated Rail Corporation*, 423 Pa. Super. 208, 620 A.2d 1185.**

Boy of four had foot caught in escalator in defendant's store. §328D of Restatement (2d) Torts accepted a law of Commonwealth. *Res ipsa loquitur* can be used under terms and conditions set forth in the Restatement. Exclusive control not required. Although Korvette's had day-to-day responsibility for safe function of escalator, Otis by contract assumed responsibility of regular maintenance. New trial as to Otis ordered due to error in charge. *Gilbert v. Korvette's and Otis Elevator*, **457 Pa. 602, 327 A.2d 94.**

Foreclosure

Plaintiffs brought tort action against real estate agency, lender and personal property removal service for removing their personal property and locking them out of a home after a foreclosure. The trial court granted the defendants' motion to dismiss. The Superior Court affirmed, holding that tort claims related to the removal of personal property and trespass had been resolved in the prior foreclosure action requiring dismissal of any civil actions related to the process of removal of property from a foreclosed home. *Gray v. Buonopane*, **53 A.3d 829 (Pa. Super. 2012).**

Foreign defendant

In negligence and products liability case against foreign defendant, general jurisdiction requires sufficient contacts with forum relating to activities alleged to be negligent or products alleged to be dangerous. *McCall v. Formu-3 Intern'l, Inc.*, **437 Pa. Super. 575, 650 A.2d 903 (1994).**

Plaintiff injured in forklift accident brought action against manufacturer, a Japanese corporation. Held: court did not have personal jurisdiction over manufacturer. *Graham v. Machinery Distribution, Inc.*, **410 Pa. Super. 267, 599 A.2d 984.**

Plaintiff injured in auto accident while in Subaru. Subaru manufacturer held to be subject to *in personam* jurisdiction in Pennsylvania even though a Japanese corporation selling cars through U.S. corporation. *Hewitt v. Eicheliman's Subaru*, **341 Pa. Super. 589, 492 A.2d 23.**

Indiana insurance carrier not subject to *in personam* jurisdiction in declaratory judgment action to determine No-Fault benefits responsibility. Company not licensed in Pennsylvania. Merely has clause providing it to indemnify insureds in accordance with financial responsibility laws of any state in which accident may occur. *United Farm Bureau Mutual v. U.S.F. & G.*, **501 Pa. 646, 462 A.2d 1300.**

Foreign Sovereign Immunities Act

Hotel in Bahamas established and owned by foreign country with coverage under Foreign Sovereign Immunities Act is therefore immune from jurisdiction. *Tucker v. Whitaker Travel, Ltd.*, **348 Pa. Super. 55, 501 A.2d 643.**

Foreign substance

Alleged that excessively greasy doughnut caused severe gastritis and ulcer flare-up, leading to surgery. Defense verdict by jury, affirmed. Court found no evidence of causation, therefore all complaints of error were harmless. *McCann v. Amy Joy Donut Shops*, **325 Pa. Super. 340, 472 A.2d 1149.**

Plaintiff allegedly drank bottle of soft drink containing glass particles. Without bottle and particles, court found that plaintiff did not meet burden of proof. Defense verdict entered by court. *Williams v. Pepsi-Cola*, **240 Pa. Super. 578, 362 A.2d 314.**

Foreseeability

Plaintiff sued sausage packer, restaurant supplier and restaurant for injuries from eating allegedly tainted pork. Granting of demurrer reversed. Cause of action stated on allegation of negligence for failure to inspect and breach of implied warranty. ***Clouser v. Shamokin Packing*, 240 Pa. Super. 268, 361 A.2d 836.**

Plaintiff saw her child eating from loaf of bread from which she had previously eaten. Saw string and "brown stuff"—emotional reaction—gastritis. Verdict for plaintiff affirmed. ***Wisniewski v. Great A & P Tea Co.*, 226 Pa. Super. 574, 323 A.2d 744.**

Foreseeability

Parents and child filed suit against psychiatrist who treated child and, after treatment, negligently embarked upon a course of action that directly affected both child and parents to their injury. Where psychiatrist goes well beyond treatment of minor (*e.g.*, active participation in criminal proceedings directed against parents and maintaining silence when she knew patient was telling untruths and could not distinguish fact from fantasy), court will impose duty on psychiatrist to parents, breach of which may support determination of negligence. The lack of a psychiatrist–patient relationship with parents does not provide blanket immunity to psychiatrist. In instant case, it was also reasonably foreseeable to psychiatrist that her negligent actions would have harmful affect on patient's parents. ***Althaus v. Cohen*, 710 A.2d 1147 (Pa. Super. 1998).**

Plaintiff motorist whose automobile drifted into left lane and left the highway, traveling down an embankment and into a creek, failed to state a cause of action within real estate exception to sovereign immunity. PennDOT not required to erect guardrails along embankment where it could not foresee that motorist's vehicle would leave the highway. Order granting judgment on the pleadings affirmed. ***Felli v. Com., Dept. of Transp.*, ___ Pa. Cmwlth. ___, 666 A.2d 775 (1995).**

Municipal defendants are neither afforded blanket immunity nor entitled to judgment as a matter of law in each and every tort claim where the victim's injuries were caused in part by the intervening criminal conduct of third parties or where the criminal acts of a third party merely form a link in the chain of causation. It is for the jury to determine whether municipal defendants' conduct was a substantial contributing factor in causing the victim's injuries and, if so, whether intervening criminal conduct of third parties was so extraordinary as not to be reasonably foreseeable by the municipal defendants. Summary judgment reversed. ***Jones v. Chieffo*, ___ Pa. Super. ___, 664 A.2d 1091 (1995).**

Mental health care providers had no duty to police officer for injuries caused by patient who, one day after visiting health care facility in agitated state, drove his car into police van while experiencing a psychotic episode, injuring officer. Summary judgment affirmed. ***Heil v. Brown*, 443 Pa. Super. 502, 662 A.2d 669 (1995).**

In action arising out of explosion of boiler caused by defective emergency shut-off valve, manufacturer of valve held strictly liable for defective product. Manufacturer's liability for its defective product is outlined in Section 402A of Restatement (2d) Torts, which provides that a plaintiff must prove that the product was sold

Foreseeability

in a defective condition dangerous to the user and that the defect was the proximate cause of the injury. An actor is relieved from liability owing to an intervening or superseding cause only if the intervening or superseding negligent acts were so extraordinary as not to have been reasonably foreseeable. Summary judgment affirmed in part and reversed in part. ***Dougherty v. Edward J. Meloney, Inc.,* 443 Pa. Super. 201, 661 A.2d 375 (1995).**

School district held not liable for injuries to person assaulted by unknown assailant on adjacent sidewalk or for subsequent assault on school grounds. Under circumstances here, criminal acts not foreseeable. Criminal acts not a foreseeable use of school property. ***Joner v. Board of Education,* 91 Pa. Cmwlth. 145, 496 A.2d 1288.**

Plaintiff drove car over curb, across sidewalk, over six-inch retaining wall, through cyclone fence and into creek, in which he drowned. Held: City of Chester had no duty to maintain fence of such strength to withstand impact of car going in excess of 25 m.p.h. Events here so extraordinary as to be legally unforeseeable. ***Merritt v. City of Chester,* 344 Pa. Super. 505, 496 A.2d 1220.**

Action against school district and hotel for drowning of student while on school trip in Virginia. Held: Pennsylvania law applied and school district immune from suit under facts here. ***Davis v. School District of Philadelphia,* 91 Pa. Cmwlth. 27, 496 A.2d 903.**

Jury verdict—$500,000 ($400,000 survival; $100,000 wrongful death). Death of middle-aged male. Truck crashed through guardrail and fell on top of plaintiff's vehicle. Evidence indicated city was aware of need for stronger guardrail—reasonable foreseeability for jury. Lower Court molded verdict to apportion negligence. City and Commonwealth held negligent for confusing signs on expressway and exit. ***Thompson v. City of Philadelphia,* 502 Pa. 473, 466 A.2d 1349.**

Plaintiff-decedent driving auto which was rear-ended. Gas tank exploded. Chrysler exonerated by jury. Reversed. Charge on strict liability in error since it injected foreseeability and reasonableness. ***Smialeli v. Chrysler,* 290 Pa. Super. 496, 434 A.2d 1253.**

Vial of nitric acid taken from school lab, burned plaintiff when later found by two boys engaged in horseplay. Foreseeability of this occurrence relevant only to jury's determination of negligence. It was not highly extraordinary that acid would burn plaintiff—charge on §435(2) of Restatement (2d) Torts in error. ***Brown v. Tinneny,* 280 Pa. Super. 512, 421 A.2d 839.**

Plaintiff suffered heart attack several months after injury in auto accident. Judge charged that foreseeability of injuries a test for determining proximate cause. Since jury never instructed on causation, charge on foreseeability reversible error. ***McCloy v. Penn Fruit,* 245 Pa. Super. 251, 369 A.2d 389.**

Plaintiff fell while erecting coal hopper suffering serious injuries. Standing on a clip which had been designed to hold metal rods—clip gave way. For jury as to whether standing on clip was a secondary use foreseeable to manufacturer. ***Lambert v. PBI Industries,* 244 Pa. Super. 118, 366 A.2d 944.**

Foul ball

Plaintiff on electric pole working on cable TV cable. Severely shocked as he threw cable. Defendant's safety manual should have been admitted for purpose of showing foreseeability of this action since manual prohibited it on the part of its employees. Nonsuit reversed. ***Densler v. Metropolitan Edison,* 235 Pa. Super. 585, 345 A.2d 758.**

Failure of rotor of helicopter. Pilot killed. 402A clarified. Foreseeability of seller held to be irrelevant in strict liability case. ***Berkebile v. Brantly Helicopter Corp.,* 462 Pa. 83, 337 A.2d 893.**

Foul ball

Plaintiff was injured when struck in the face by a foul ball at a baseball game. The Superior Court affirmed the trial court's decision to sustain the defendant's preliminary objections for failure to state a cause of action under the "no-duty" theory applied to baseball and other sports venues where a patron is injured in circumstances commonly understood to entail some risk of harm. ***Romeo v. The Pittsburgh Associates,* 787 A.2d 1027 (Pa. Super. 2001).**

Four in front seat

Evidence that a child, being the fourth occupant of the front seat, detracted the attention of the operator and that her milk bottle interfered with the brakes of the car—violation of Section 1001 of the Vehicle Code and established the negligence of the operator per se—nonsuit as to him proper. ***Little v. Jarvis,* 219 Pa. Super. 158, 280 A.2d 617.**

Evidence disclosed that four persons were in front seat but one was a two year old child—court refused to charge that Section 1001 of Vehicle Code applied—error and new trial awarded. ***Atene v. Lawrence,* 428 Pa. 424, 239 A.2d 346.**

Fraternity

Elemental analysis of negligence and factors establishing duty between parties. Fraternity initiate sued national fraternity and local fraternity members seeking compensation for injuries sustained in hazing activities (paddling) which resulted in renal failure, hospitalization and kidney dialysis. Summary judgment in favor of all defendants reversed as to local chapter advisor who failed to properly oversee and monitor the membership process. ***Kenner v. Kappa Alpha Psi Fraternity, Inc.,* 808 A.2d 178 (Pa. Super. 2002).**

Minor injured after being served liquor at fraternity party. Held: national fraternity may be found civilly liable as social host. ***Jefferies v. Commonwealth,* 371 Pa. Super. 12, 537 A.2d 355.**

Fraudulent Concealment

Five patients' estates brought claims for wrongful death against a hospital after one of its nurses confessed to killing the patients. The trial court denied the hospital's motion for summary judgment. The Superior Court upheld the trial court's ruling holding that the hospital had an affirmative duty to inform a patient or their next of kin when it knows or should have known that one of its employees either killed or attempted to kill a patient. *Krapf v. St. Luke's Hospital*, _____ A.2d _____, 2010 WL 2902744 (Pa. Super. 2010).

Fraudulent Misrepresentation

Plaintiffs filed suit against Plaintiff-husband's employer for fraudulent misrepresentation resulting in the aggravation of his chronic beryllium disease. Plaintiffs maintained that the Defendant knew of the dangers associated with beryllium-based products and failed to introduce a testing program for chronic beryllium disease allowing Plaintiff-husband's pre-existing condition to be aggravated. The trial court granted summary judgment on the basis that Plaintiffs had failed to establish that the Defendant knew Plaintiff had chronic beryllium disease. The Superior Court affirmed holding that Plaintiffs had failed to establish a prima facie case for fraudulent misrepresentation, which was necessary to avoid the exclusivity of the Workers' Compensation Act. *Kostryckyj v. Pentron Laboratory Technologies, LLC*, 2012 Pa. Super. 152 (Pa. Super. 2012).

Freezing

Inadequate supply of gas to plaintiff's house caused pilot on heater to go out while plaintiff away causing water pipes to freeze and burst. Could be inferred that gas company had statutory duty to supply gas. Jury question. Directed verdict by court below reversed. *Cox v. Equitable Gas Co.*, 227 Pa. Super. 153, 324 A.2d 516.

Fumes

Plaintiff's decedent welder was killed when fumes inside gasoline tank truck in which he was working caught fire and exploded. Motion for compulsory nonsuit granted because plaintiff's decedent was fully aware of the risks attending the work he was performing. Recovery prohibited under section 388 of Restatement (2d) Torts which imposes duty to warn owner of chattel who has reason to believe that those for whose use the chattel is supplied will not realize its dangerous condition. *Erdos v. Bedford Valley Petroleum Co.*, 452 Pa. Super. 555, 682 A.2d 806 (1996).

In homeowner's action against gas utility for damages to home following gas explosion, gas utility's effort to join as additional defendant original contractor who performed allegedly negligent work was time-barred. Twelve-year statute of repose is not unconstitutional. Order granting judgment on pleadings in favor of additional defendants affirmed. *Columbia Gas of PA, Inc. v. Carl E. Baker, Inc.*, 446 Pa. Super. 481, 667 A.2d 404 (1995).

In action arising out of explosion of boiler caused by defective emergency shut-off valve, manufacturer of valve held strictly liable for defective product. Manufacturer's liability for its defective product is outlined in Section 402A of Restatement (2d) Torts, which provides that a plaintiff must prove that the product was sold in a defective condition dangerous to the user and that the defect was the proximate cause of the injury. An actor is relieved from liability owing to an intervening or superseding cause only if the intervening or superseding negligent acts were so extraordinary as not to have been reasonably foreseeable. Summary judgment affirmed in part and reversed in part. *Dougherty v. Edward J. Meloney, Inc.*, 443 Pa. Super. 201, 661 A.2d 375 (1995).

Fundraising

Defendant gas company had converted a gas range in plaintiff's residence—minor daughter of 12 allegedly burned when a flare-up occurred and flames shot out 2 feet from burner—case for fact finders—judgment *n.o.v.* improperly entered below—judgment directed on verdict. ***Handfinger v. Phila. Gas Works Co.*, 439 Pa. 130, 266 A.2d 769.**

Plaintiffs' property damaged by gas explosion—employee of gas company had inspected property two days before explosion and neglected to warn plaintiffs of certain gas leaks and shut off gas at meter and not at curb—gas company held responsible. ***Fore v. United Nat. Gas Co.*, 436 Pa. 499, 261 A.2d 316.**

Plaintiff maintained a high pressure underground gas main along highway—road contractor sublet part of work—subcontractor damaged gas main—contractor knew of existence of main and failed to warn subcontractor—contractor held responsible under Sections 416 and 427 of Restatement (2d) Torts. ***Phila. Electric Co. v. Julian*, 425 Pa. 217, 228 A.2d 669.**

Plaintiff allegedly injured by the emission of the fumes from a beryllium plant—court below granted judgment *n.o.v.*—Supreme Court reversed and held that the conduct of the defendant after 1950, the date when the Atomic Energy Commission prescribed unsafe toxicity levels, constituted actionable negligence. ***Heck v. Beryllium Corp.*, 424 Pa. 140, 226 A.2d 87.**

Plaintiff householders were injured by the explosion of gas in their home—evidence that a coupling was seriously corroded—coupling located one foot from foundation of dwelling and was laid about 18 inches above a water pipe in detritus soil—pipe sagged causing break—for jury in suit against gas company—sufficient evidence of negligence. ***Hemrock v. Peoples Nat. Gas Co.*, 423 Pa. 259, 223 A.2d 687.**

Fundraising

Parents, on behalf of their child, sued a fundraising company for failing to conform to the appropriate standard of care by not warning of the dangers inherent in fundraising activities, after their child was sexually assaulted while trying to solicit a subscription. The court reversed the dismissal of the complaint, holding that the complaint on its face was sufficient to state a cause of action in negligence against the fund raising entity. ***R.W. and C.W. v. Manzek*, 585 Pa. 335 (2005).**

Funeral parlor

Wife plaintiff was a business invitee in defendant's funeral parlor—on leaving she allegedly, as result of deceptive lighting and slight drop in level of porch from main parlor, fell on porch—judgment *n.o.v.* properly entered below and affirmed on appeal. ***O'Neill v. Batchelor Bros. Inc. Funeral Homes*, 421 Pa. 413, 219 A.2d 682 (1966).**

—G—

Garbage truck

Plaintiff motorist injured in collision with township garbage truck entitled to new trial after trial court incorrectly instructed jury that garbage truck driver was entitled to drive against traffic flow in same manner as Motor Vehicle Code defined Type I and Type II vehicles such as emergency vehicles. New trial granted. ***Sawchzuk-Serge v. Township of Cheltenham,*** ___ **Pa. Super.** ___, **670 A.2d 210 (1996).**

Driver who collided with garbage truck situated diagonally on road was entitled to jury instruction on sudden emergency doctrine. Where evidence is such that reasonable minds could differ as to whether sudden emergency existed, both assured clear distance and sudden emergency instructions should be given. Assured clear distance charge to jury that failed to detail effect of presumption that rule applies where driver was proceeding in safe and prudent manner was legally insufficient. ***Lockhart v. List,* 542 Pa. 141, 665 A.2d 1176 (1995).**

Gas main

Plaintiff maintained a high pressure underground gas main along highway—road contractor sublet part of work—subcontractor damaged gas main—contractor knew of existence of main and failed to warn subcontractor—contractor held responsible under Sections 416 and 427 of Restatement (2d) Torts. ***Phila. Electric Co. v. Julian,* 425 Pa. 217, 228 A.2d 669.**

Gas range

Gas range sold and installed by gas company exploded, injuring plaintiff and causing property damage. Verdict for plaintiff on breach of implied warranty of merchantability—not negligence or product liability. Verdict not inconsistent. Jury could have found insufficient proof of negligence and no defect, but still breach of warranty. ***Walsh v. Pa. Gas and Water,* 303 Pa. Super. 52, 449 A.2d 573.**

Defendant gas company had converted a gas range in plaintiff's residence—minor daughter of 12 allegedly burned when a flare-up occurred and flames shot out 2 feet from burner—case for fact finders—judgment *n.o.v.* improperly entered below—judgment directed on verdict. ***Handfinger v. Phila. Gas Works Co.,* 439 Pa. 130, 266 A.2d 769.**

Gas station

In buyers' action against seller of gasoline station equipment and property, action for strict liability based on leaking underground storage tanks will not lie. The operation of underground storage tanks at a gasoline station is not an abnormally dangerous activity. Order granting preliminary objection to strict liability claim affirmed. ***Smith v. Weaver,*** ___ **Pa. Super.** ___, **665 A.2d 1215 (1995).**

Plaintiff allegedly fell on accumulation of petroleum products on sidewalk of Exxon station. Summary judgment in favor of Exxon reversed. Liability of Exxon as owner out of possession for jury. Suit to proceed against lessee operator and Exxon. ***Juarbe v. City of Philadelphia,* 288 Pa. Super. 330, 431 A.2d 1073.**

Gas tank

Plaintiff struck and killed by auto while he was standing at gas pump located adjacent to highway. Theory of plaintiff that pumps were negligently located for jury. Summary judgment in favor of service station reversed. ***Migyanko v. Thistlethwaite,* 275 Pa. Super. 500, 419 A.2d 12.**

Explosion of underground tanks at gas station. Personal injuries to wife of owner. Grant of summary judgment in favor of former owner, reversed. Issue of his knowledge of defect at time of sale was for jury. ***Bonneau v. Ralph Martin Oil,* 259 Pa. Super. 428, 393 A.2d 901.**

Gas tank

Plaintiff's decedent welder was killed when fumes inside gasoline tank truck in which he was working caught fire and exploded. Motion for compulsory nonsuit granted because plaintiff's decedent was fully aware of the risks attending the work he was performing. Recovery prohibited under Section 388 of Restatement (2d) Torts which imposes duty to warn owner of chattel who has reason to believe that those for whose use the chattel is supplied will not realize its dangerous condition. ***Erdos v. Bedford Valley Petroleum Co.,* 452 Pa. Super. 555, 682 A.2d 806 (1996).**

Rear-end collision—gas tank exploded. Charge of court on strict liability in error since it injected foreseeability and reasonableness into design defect theory. Verdict in favor of Chrysler reversed. ***Smialek v. Chrysler Motors,* 290 Pa. Super. 496, 434 A.2d 1253.**

In homeowner's action against gas utility for damages to home following gas explosion, gas utility's effort to join as additional defendant original contractor who performed allegedly negligent work was time-barred. Twelve-year statute of repose is not unconstitutional. Order granting judgment on pleadings in favor of additional defendants affirmed. ***Columbia Gas of PA, Inc. v. Carl E. Baker, Inc.,* 446 Pa. Super. 481, 667 A.2d 404 (1995).**

Gas utility

Excavator brought a claim against a gas utility company for negligent misrepresentation for purely economic damages associated with the gas utility company's improper marking of gas lines under the Pennsylvania One Call Act. The appellate court sustained the trial court's decision holding that under the economic loss rule some physical harm must occur to the Plaintiff's property or person to recover in a negligence action. ***Excavation Technologies, Inc. v. Columbia Gas Co.,* 936 A.2d 111 (Pa. Super. 2007).**

Gas valve

In action arising out of explosion of boiler caused by defective emergency shut-off valve, manufacturer of valve held strictly liable for defective product. Manufacturer's liability for its defective product is outlined in Section 402A of Restatement (2d) Torts, which provides that a plaintiff must prove that the product was sold in a defective condition dangerous to the user and that the defect was the proximate cause of the injury. An actor is relieved from liability due to an intervening or superseding cause only if the intervening or superseding negligent acts were so extraordinary as not to have been reasonably foreseeable. Summary judgment affirmed in part and reversed in part. ***Dougherty v. Edward J. Meloney, Inc.,* 443 Pa. Super. 201, 661. A.2d 375 (1995).**

There is but one standard of care in a negligence action, which is reasonable care. Reasonable care will vary based on the circumstances and instrumentalities in each situation. Action by customer against garage and mechanic for injuries sustained when gasoline exploded after being poured into carburetor did not warrant a jury instruction on a standard of care higher than reasonable care. Judgment for defendants affirmed. ***Stewart v. Motts,* 539 Pa. 596, 654 A.2d 535 (1995).**

Gastric-bypass surgery

Plaintiff filed suit against physician who had performed gastric-bypass surgery alleging that she had not received adequate information on which to base an informed consent. Held: question of adequacy of information is for jury to decide. The nature of the information provided, not the identity or position of the person who provides it, nurse rather than physician, is important. ***Foflygen v. Allegheny General Hospital,* 723 A.2d 705 (Pa. Super. 1999).**

Gastroscopic examination

Plaintiff patient injured as the result of a gastroscopic examination—court below held to be in error in submitting to jury the standard of information to be given to patient in order for patient to give an informed consent—basis is not accepted medical practice—matter is contractual and fiduciary in character and issue is whether patient gave an effective informed consent. ***Cooper v. Roberts,* 220 Pa. Super. 260, 286 A.2d 647.**

General contractor

Summary judgment against employee of subcontractor sustained after he filed negligence action against property owner and general contractor who was afforded immunity as statutory employer. ***Emery v. Leavesly McCollum,* 725 A.2d 807 (Pa. Super. 1999).**

General contractor is "statutory employer" of employee of subcontractor and so is immune from suit for negligence under Workers' Compensation Act. ***McCarthy v. Lepore,* 724 A.2d 938 (Pa. Super. 1998).**

Summary judgment in favor of general contractor who was sued for negligence by worker injured on job site was affirmed by Superior and Supreme courts on basis that general contractor was a statutory employer under Workers' Compensation Act even though the subcontractor who hired worker carried his workers' compensation insurance. ***Fonner v. Shandon, Inc.,* 724 A.2d 903 (Pa. 1999).**

Defendant purchased building. Hired general and electrical contractors to renovate. Defendant owner's children played on site and plaintiff, workman complained. Plaintiff injured when 16 year old dropped staircase section on leg. Verdict by jury in favor of plaintiff against owner and general contractor. Motion for judgment *n.o.v.* by contractor denied and this was affirmed by Supreme Court. Motion

Gist of the Action Doctrine

for judgment *n.o.v.* as to owner granted, but this reversed by Supreme Court and jury award reinstated. ***Byrd v. Merwin*, 456 Pa. 516, 317 A.2d 280.**

Gist of the Action Doctrine

General contractor brought breach of contract action against a developer. The developer brought a counterclaim for fraud against the plaintiff. The trial court entered a judgment in favor of the defendant. The Superior Court on appeal held that the gist of the action doctrine did not preclude the developer's fraud claim as it arose from the plaintiff's submission of fraudulent invoices as opposed to duties imposed by the contract itself. ***J.J. Deluca Co., Inc. v. Toll Naval Associates*, 56 A.3d 402 (Pa. Super. 2012).**

Mortgagor brought suit against mortgagee for breach of contract, negligence, and fraud and misrepresentation alleging that the mortgagee was negligent in supervising its employees, who engaged in fraud. The court dismissed the negligence claim under the gist of the action doctrine, because the claim was rooted in the fraud and misrepresentation claim. ***Strausser v. Pramco, III & Manufacturers and Traders Trust Co.*, 944 A.2d 761 (Pa. Super. 2008).**

"Gist of the Action Doctrine" provides that a contract claim cannot be couched in terms of a negligence action. In suit for damages resulting from breach of contract to provide a suitable log home kit, allegations that bad advice on repairs constituted negligence is actually a part of a contract claim, not negligence. ***Freestone v. New England Log Homes, Inc.*, 819 A.2d 550 (Pa. Super 2003).**

Glass

Plaintiff allegedly drank bottle of soft drink containing glass particles. Without bottle and particles, court found that plaintiff did not meet burden of proof. Defense verdict entered by court. ***Williams v. Pepsi-Cola*, 240 Pa. Super. 578, 362 A.2d 314.**

Gloves

Industrial accident. Gloves caught in machine causing injury. Charge in error. Proper charge was that use of gloves must have been a "substantial factor" in bringing about the harm. New trial ordered. ***Takach v. Root Co.*, 279 Pa. Super. 167, 420 A.2d 1084.**

Good Samaritan Rule

Elementary analysis of negligence claim by patron of tennis club who suffered brain damage due to stroke following heart attack. Plaintiffs allege that the club was negligent in not having an Automated External Defibrillator ("AED") on the premises and using the device to restart husband plaintiff's heart. Defendant club argued that the Emergency Medical Services Act precluded its untrained employees from using an AED even if it had one and the AED Good Samaritan Act had not yet been passed. Grant of summary judgment in favor of defendant club affirmed. ***Atcovitz v. Gulph Mills Tennis Club, Inc.*, 571 Pa. 580, 812 A.2d 1218 (Pa. 2002).**

Good Samaritan rule applied to homeowner who failed to take reasonable steps to care for party guest who was knocked unconscious after falling and striking head on concrete floor. Placing guest on couch while still unconscious and going to bed was inadequate care. ***Filter v. McCabe*, 733 A.2d 1274 (Pa. Super. 1999).**

Government contractor defense

Pennsylvania Turnpike Commission and contractors who adhered to Turnpike Commission standards in construction of 32" high median barriers are all entitled to sovereign immunity protection. ***Svege v. Interstate Safety Systems*, 862 A.2d 752 (Pa. Cmwlth. 2004).**

In suit for injuries sustained by wife plaintiff against PennDOT and PennDOT contractor after settlement by PennDOT, held that contractor was not entitled to "government contractor defense" of governmental immunity when the work performed was not in accordance with government specifications. ***Coolbaugh v. Com. of Pa., Dept. of Transportation*, 816 A.2 307 (Pa. Super. 2003).**

Disabled plaintiff alleges he was injured when he lost control of the van he was driving because a company under contract with the Pennsylvania Department of Labor and Industry, Office of Vocational Rehabilitation was alleged to have negligently modified the van. In suit against the company that modified the van, the defendant pleaded immunity as a government contractor. Held: there is no government contractor immunity under Pennsylvania law. ***Connor v. Quality Coach, Inc.*, 750 A.2d 823 (2000).**

Truck driver injured when trailer struck bridge parapet in highway construction area. Held: contractor not liable. Government contractor defense applicable. ***DiBuono v. A. Barletta & Sons, Inc.*, 127 Pa. Cmwlth. 1, 560 A.2d 893.**

Plaintiff injured during National Guard training session while assembling machine gun. Summary judgment granted in favor of manufacturer based upon government contractor defense, affirmed. ***Mackey v. Maremont Corp.*, 350 Pa. Super. 415, 504 A.2d 908.**

Grab bar

Inmate filed suit against county correctional facility for injury to his head received when the "grab bar" in the prison shower broke free causing him to fall. Despite county's argument that the shower stall was only personal property, lack of evidence by county that shower stall was not a fixture and resulting presumption that it was in the nature of real property maintained by the county, precludes summary judgment under Political Subdivision Tort Claims Act. ***Davis v. Brennan*, 698 A.2d 1382 (Pa. Cmwlth. 1997).**

Grade crossings

Grade crossing on limited access 4 lane highway. Posted speed limit 60 M.P.H. Issue of whether flashing lights were working. Drivers unable to see down trucks approaching crossing. 20 M.P.H. speed limit at grade crossing abrogated by posted 60 M.P.H. limit. Issue whether crossing inherently dangerous. Substantial

Grade crossings

plaintiff's verdict affirmed. ***Burhecker v. Reading Co.*, 271 Pa. Super. 35, 412 A.2d 147.**

Tractor-trailer driven by plaintiff struck by train at crossing—plaintiff killed. Neither plaintiff nor train operator attempted to stop before impact. Evidence of strong glare for plaintiff, high foliage at crossing and inoperative flashing lights. Contradicted by witnesses for defendant that flashers working and blowing of whistle by train. For jury. Verdict for plaintiff. ***Evans v. Reading Co.*, 242 Pa. Super. 209, 363 A.2d 1234.**

Plaintiff's vehicle struck by defendant's train at a grade crossing—plaintiff's testimony disclosed that plaintiff had a clear view from 1365 to 1849 feet before entering crossing—incontrovertible physical facts rule applied and action of court below entering nonsuit affirmed—the fact that plaintiff was suffering from traumatic amnesia not controlling. ***Reynolds v. Cen. R.R. of N.J. et al.*, 448 Pa. 415, 292 A.2d 924.**

Plaintiff, an occupant of a truck, was injured as a result of defendant's locomotive colliding with truck at a grade crossing in City of Philadelphia—evidence that visibility was poor and lack of warning, although same denied—case for jury—trial errors assigned held not sufficient to call for a new trial. ***Dollison v. B. & O. R.R. Co.*, 446 Pa. 96, 284 A.2d 704.**

Plaintiff's railroad train struck a tractor-trailer stalled on a grade crossing—rig remained on tracks some 15 or 20 minutes—operator failing to set out flares or otherwise warn train crew—damage to leading diesel engine—some evidence of defects in crossing—verdict for plaintiff sustained on appeal. ***Baltimore & Ohio R.R. Co. v. Campbell and Taylor Lumber Co.*, 218 Pa. Super. 904, 279 A.2d 215.**

Minor plaintiff struck by defendant's train at a grade crossing—Supreme Court concluded that issues of visibility and warning were such as to make the matter one for the jury—jury could have found plaintiff consciously listening—evidence of lack of warning not negative and crossing one not affording a reasonable view—close case—strong dissent. ***Fallon v. Penn Central Trans. Co.*, 444 Pa. 148, 279 A.2d 164.**

Plaintiff's tractor-trailer collided with defendant's train at a grade crossing—foggy weather—plaintiff did not stop—various highway signs advised of the crossing—familiar with crossing—judgment on pleadings and depositions for defendant. ***Scott v. Reading Co.*, 432 Pa. 240, 248 A.2d 43.**

Decedent operator with two passengers approached a grade crossing and collided with a locomotive on crossing—clear evidence of failure to stop, look and listen—guests familiar with crossing—verdict for defendant railroad and estate of operator proper—error to grant a new trial as to estate of operator. ***Tomasek v. Monongahela Rwy. Co.*, 427 Pa. 371, 235 A.2d 359.**

Plaintiff's decedent killed at a grade crossing—verdict for defendant railroad—motion for new trial refused—action sustained on appeal—charge of court as a whole proper—failure of plaintiff's counsel to object as to certain unfavorable actions of trial court will not permit raising same on appeal. *Wilson v. Penna. R.R. Co.*, **421 Pa. 419, 219 A.2d 666.**

Grading of property

Township sued in negligence for poor grading and construction on plaintiffs' property. Trial court's determination that landowner/plaintiff's proper relief was under Eminent Domain Code reversed. ***Poole v. Township of District*, 843 A.2d 422 (Pa. Cmwlth. 2004).**

Grease

Buildup of grease and oil on city-owned sidewalk is not a dangerous condition "of" the sidewalk; therefore, city is immune from liability under the Political Subdivision Tort Claims Act for injuries sustained by pedestrian who slipped and fell on sidewalk. ***Finn v. City of Philadelphia*, 541 Pa. 596, 664 A.2d 1342 (1995).**

Municipality immune from liability to plaintiff who slipped and fell on grease on sidewalk. Verdict in favor of plaintiff reversed. ***Finn v. City of Philadelphia*, 165 Pa. Cmwlth. 255, 645 A.2d 320 (1994).**

Gross negligence

Summary judgment against plaintiff psychiatric patient affirmed based on lack of proof that physician's actions amounted to gross negligence rather than simple negligence. Discussion of applicability of immunity under Mental Health Procedures Act to voluntary admissions. ***Walsh v. Borczon*, 881 A.2d 1 (Pa. Super. 2005).**

Under the Mental Health Procedures Act, a physician may only be liable for injury to a patient when gross negligence occurs. A physician's failure to speak to a non-minor patient's mother about the likely effect of alcohol consumption when combined psychiatric medications does not rise to the level of gross negligence. ***Alphonsi v. Huntington Hospital, Inc.*, 798 A.2d 216 (Pa. Super. 2002).**

Immunity granted to those who provide examination or treatment of a person under the Mental Health Procedures Act extends to physical health medical care providers and hospital referred to treat patient's medical condition, as well as those treating for mental illnesses, absent willful misconduct or gross negligence. ***Allen v. Montgomery Hospital*, ___ Pa. ___, 696 A.2d 1175 (1997).**

Hospital's immunity from suit under Mental Health Procedures Act may be decided on summary judgment. Hospital's actions after plaintiff's decedent failed to attend an outpatient appointment did not rise to level of gross negligence. ***Albright v. Abington Memorial Hospital*, ___ Pa. ___, 696 A.2d 1159 (1997).**

Group home

Estate brought action against facility providing care for her mentally retarded daughter after daughter died while in the facility's care. The trial court dismissed Plaintiff's case and the Superior Court reversed and remanded. The Superior Court held that Plaintiff had alleged actions sufficient to establish gross negligence and

Guard rails

incompetence where the complaint alleged that, despite express instructions to do so, employees failed to contact a nurse after the decedent vomited. ***Potts v. Step by Step, Inc.,* 26 A.3d 1115 (Pa. Super. 2011).**

Guard rails

Motorist's estate brought a claim for negligent design against Pennsylvania Turnpike Commission after the decedent's vehicle hydroplaned on the roadway and crashed. The trial court granted summary judgment in favor of the Defendant. The Commonwealth Court affirmed holding that the Commonwealth was immune from suit where the guardrail folds back and impales a vehicle based upon the Sovereign Immunity Act. ***Stein v. Pennsylvania Turnpike Commission,* 989 A.2d 80 (Pa. Cmwlth. 2010).**

Reaffirmation of the position that the real estate exception to sovereign immunity does not require the Commonwealth to erect guard rails along embankments on state owned roads. ***Piazza v. Pennsylvania Department of Transportation,* 786 A.2d 328 (Pa. Cmwlth. 2001).**

City's failure to install guard rail along curved section of street with drop-off is not dangerous condition of municipal street and, therefore, not actionable under streets exception to Political Subdivision Tort Claims Act. ***Lockwood v. City of Pittsburgh,* 751 A.2d 1136 (Pa. 2000).**

Absence of guard rail on Commonwealth highway adjacent to steep drop-off is not dangerous condition of Commonwealth realty and, therefore, not actionable under real estate exception to Sovereign Immunity. ***Dean v. PennDOT,* 751 A.2d 1130 (Pa. 2000).**

Plaintiff rendered quadriplegic after car in which she was a passenger fishtailed on snowy road and slid over embankment which did not have a guard rail. Plaintiff sued PennDOT for negligent failure to erect and maintain guard rail at curve. Lower court granted summary judgment to PennDOT based on *Rothermel v. Com.*, 531 Pa. 180, 672 A.2d 837 (Pa. Cmwlth, 1996) which held that a non-negligent circumstance which causes an accident precludes any recovery against sovereign even if negligent act of the sovereign which falls under real estate exception to sovereign immunity followed the cause and increased the damage. *Rothermel* overruled and judgment vacated with remand. ***Dean v. Com., Dept. of Transp.,* 718 A.2d 374 (Pa. Cmwlth. 1998).**

Plaintiff and her decedents were passengers in car driven by additional defendant who crossed over center line of PennDOT road, crashed through guard rail and struck tree. Plaintiff alleged that brakes and engine had failed, that additional defendant driver was intoxicated and that PennDOT had failed to provide safe roadway because of inability of guard rail to prevent car from striking tree. Following grant of summary judgment in favor of PennDOT, plaintiff appealed. Held: PennDOT could not have adequate notice of combination of events leading to accident—loss of brakes and driver's intoxication—and therefore PennDOT had no duty to plaintiff and her decedents. ***Baer v. Com., Dept. of Transp.,* 713 A.2d 189 (Pa. Cmwlth. 1998).**

Guests

In action against PennDOT and the city from which PennDOT had "adopted" a road for failure to install guard rails, summary judgment in favor of PennDOT was sustained. There was no proof by plaintiff of breach of a duty to plaintiff by PennDOT in the maintenance and care of the road surface between the curb lines - the only area for which PennDOT is statutorily responsible after "adoption" of the road from the city. ***Wallace v. Com., Dept. of Transp.*, 701 A.2d 307 (Pa. Cmwlth. 1997).**

While PennDOT has a duty to make highways safe and possibly to install guard rails where necessary, in order to recover plaintiff must establish that lack of guard rail was cause of injuries rather than a contributing factor. Failure to allege a defect "of" Commonwealth property precludes recovery under real property exception to sovereign immunity. Order granting partial summary judgment affirmed. ***Rothermel v. Com., Dept. of Transp.*, ___ Pa. Cmwlth. ___, 672 A.2d 837 (1996).**

Plaintiff motorist whose automobile drifted into left lane and left the highway, traveling down an embankment and into a creek, failed to state a cause of action within real estate exception to sovereign immunity. PennDOT not required to erect guard rails along embankment where it could not foresee that motorist's vehicle would leave the highway. Order granting judgment on the pleadings affirmed. ***Felli v. Com., Dept. of Transp.*, ___ Pa. Cmwlth. ___, 666 A.2d 775 (1995).**

Suit against Commonwealth and certain officials. Vehicle went through missing portion of guard rail striking plaintiff's taxi head-on—killing plaintiff. Jury verdict $17,354 (survival); $625,021 (wrongful death). Married male—earning loss approximately $16,000/year. Guard rail missing for extended period of time. ***Pine v. Synkonis,* 79 Pa. Cmwlth. 479, 470 A.2d 1074.**

Jury verdict $111,205.14 including delay damage. Actual verdict $150,000 (40% contributory negligence). Plaintiff driving and in attempting to avoid disabled truck, drove onto berm which collapsed causing car to tumble into ditch. Proper to submit maintenance of guard rails and berm to jury, for determination of whether it was reasonable. ***Merling v. Commonwealth,* 79 Pa. Cmwlth. 121, 468 A.2d 894.**

Jury verdict, $500,000 ($400,000 survival and $100,000 wrongful death). Death of middle-aged male killed when truck crashed through guard rail on top of his vehicle. Evidence indicated city aware of need for stronger guard rail—reasonable foreseeability for jury. Lower Court molded verdict to apportion negligence. City and Commonwealth held negligent for confusing signs on expressway and exit. ***Thompson v. City of Philadelphia,* 320 Pa. Super. 124, 466 A.2d 1349.**

Guests

Good Samaritan rule applied to homeowner who failed to take reasonable steps to care for a party guest who was knocked unconscious after falling and striking head on concrete floor. Placing guest on couch while still unconscious and going to bed was inadequate care. ***Filter v. McCabe,* 733 A.2d 1274 (Pa. Super. 1999).**

Guest at party injured when fireworks cannon exploded. Host not liable. Guest assumed risk. ***Howell v. Clyde,* 533 Pa. 151, 620 A.2d 1107.**

Guilty plea

Accident in Delaware which has guest statute. Defendant a Pennsylvania resident; plaintiff a Delaware resident. Held: Delaware's guest statute applies, thereby barring action. Lower court's reason for dismissing action based upon *forum non conveniens*, in error under circumstances, but result proper. **Miller v. Gay, 323 Pa. Super. 466, 470 A.2d 1353.**

Two car collision—passenger in one vehicle killed—each driver claimed other crossed center line—defense verdict reversed—new trial ordered—one of the drivers must have been negligent and with evidence that each crossed center line, each had burden to show freedom from negligence. **Fair v. Snowball Express, 226 Pa. Super. 295, 310 A.2d 386.**

Guest requested operator to turn on courtesy light so that she might look for house key—accident allegedly resulting from detraction of operator's attention—verdict for defendant—upheld by an equally divided court with dissenting opinion finding such conduct not evidence of contributory negligence. **Reagan v. Love, 219 Pa. Super. 432, 281 A.2d 761.**

Plaintiff, a resident of Pennsylvania, was injured in Delaware while riding as guest in car operated by defendant, a Delaware resident—car owned by defendant's father, also a Delaware resident and car registered in that state—Delaware has a guest statute and Pennsylvania does not—Held: Delaware law applies as that state has the greater interests and contacts. **Cipolla v. Shaposka, 439 Pa. 563, 267 A.2d 854.**

Female plaintiff aged 25 was guest in the car of the defendant Stawski—occurrence took place on a rainy and foggy night—the Stawski car collided with the stopped automobile of the additional defendant—this car stopped on fast lane as the result of a blown-off hood—verdict solely against Stawski—motions denied—action affirmed on appeal. **Arras v. Stawski et al., 439 Pa. 611, 266 A.2d 268.**

Plaintiff's decedent killed in an automobile accident with his wife operating car—bad weather—windshield wiper defective—driving into guard rail—suit against wife—verdict for defendant—refusal to grant a new trial affirmed on appeal. **Campana v. Bower, 424 Pa. 383, 227 A.2d 887.**

Guilty plea

Wrongful death and survival action for death of 20 year old bicycle rider struck by auto. Error to exclude guilty plea on charge of driving under the influence. New trial ordered since verdict for plaintiff could have been compromise. **Cromley v. Gardner, 253 Pa. Super. 467, 385 A.2d 433.**

Gum disease

Where plaintiff knew before treating with dentist of periodontal disease, the "Discovery Rule" exception to the applicable statute of limitations is not available to plaintiff. **Colanna v. Rice, 445 Pa. Super. 1, 664 A.2d 979 (1995).**

Gunshot

Plaintiff injured in a shooting brought a negligence action against the parents of the adult man who shot him on the basis that he resided with the parents and that the parents had confiscated their son's gun and returned it to him. The trial court granted Defendant's motion for summary judgment. The Superior Court affirmed, holding that temporary confiscation of their son's gun did not render the parents liable as the parents had no right to control the gun owned by their son and their confiscation did not support Plaintiff's theory that the son could only use the gun with his parent's consent. *Wittrien v. Burkholder,* **965 A.2d 1229 (2009).**

Child died of wounds from shot fired from crowd that police failed to disperse. City not liable. *Yates v. City of Philadelphia,* **134 Pa. Cmwlth. 282, 578 A.2d 609.**

Habitability

—H—

Habitability

Tenant injured in slip and fall on landlord's property. Tenant 58% negligent, landlord 42% negligent. Comparative negligence principles apply to implied warranty of habitability theory as well as negligence. **Keck v. Doughman,** 392 Pa. Super. 127, 572 A.2d 724.

Hallway

Inmate who ran down hallway and jumped steps, hitting head on ceiling, failed to establish that dangerous condition existed in ceiling above hallway steps. Duty of care to inmate is of owner to invitee. Compulsory nonsuit granted in favor of County affirmed. **Graf v. County of Northampton,** 654 A.2d 131 (Pa. Cmwlth. 1995).

Hamil/Mitzelfelt Test

In medical malpractice action, the *Hamil/Mitzelfelt* two-pronged test "relaxing" a plaintiff's burden of proving causation should be applied to the entirety of plaintiff's expert's testimony regarding necessity of revised informed consent. Order removing compulsory nonsuit affirmed. **Kratt v. Horrow,** 455 Pa. Super. 140, 687 A.2d 830 (1997).

Handicapped child

Handicapped child paralyzed after falling on school sidewalk. Held: school authority immune. Action was based on negligent supervision and not defect in real property. **Houston v. Central Bucks School Authority,** 119 Pa. Cmwlth. 48, 546 A.2d 1286.

Handicapped curb cuts

Failure of school district to install handicapped curb cuts may constitute a dangerous condition of sidewalks so as to fall within exceptions to governmental immunity. **Gilson v. Doe,** 143 Pa. Cmwlth. 591, 600 A.2d 267.

Handrails

Steps leading from store has no handrails—foreign matter on steps—plaintiff invitee falling—failure to provide handrails some evidence of negligence. **Kuminkoski v. Daum,** 429 Pa. 494, 240 A.2d 524.

Hands off steering wheel

Plaintiff party to left—collision in intersection of two cars—plaintiff observing defendant's car approaching and slowing down—then suddenly accelerating and defendant's driver took hands off steering wheel and covered his face with hands—case for jury under facts of case. **McCaffrey v. Philadelphia,** 421 Pa. 357, 219 A.2d 680.

Harrassment

Worker brought action against employer for intentional infliction of emotional distress claiming harassment after on-job injury. Employer not liable. ***Shaffer v. Procter & Gamble,* 412 Pa. Super. 630, 604 A.2d 289.**

Hazards created by contractor

Employees of a contractor of a sewerage disposal plant injured by reason of the presence allegedly of explosive gas in vault—Sewer Authority not responsible—it could not be held responsible to protect employees of an independent contractor from hazards created by contractor—nonsuit proper. ***Celender et al. v. Allegheny County Sanitary Authority,* 208 Pa. Super. 390, 222 A.2d 461.**

Headlights

Plaintiff motorcyclist injured when he struck car that pulled out in front of him. Driver of car alleged he did not see motorcycle because its headlight was not operating. Plaintiff admitted that he frequently drove without operating headlight. Judgment in favor of plaintiff against motorcycle re-seller and car driver vacated on basis that plaintiff assumed the risks that attend riding a motorcycle without a functioning headlight. ***Frey v. Harley Davidson,* 734 A.2d 1 (Pa. Super. 1999).**

Under the assured clear distance ahead doctrine, the driver of an automobile at night must be able to stop within the range of his headlights. ***Fish v. Gosnell,* 316 Pa. Super. 565, 463 A.2d 1042.**

Vehicle Code requires high beam to shine 350 feet ahead. Where defendant had clear view of 300 to 400 feet and claimed he had lights on high beam, it was for jury to determine negligence for striking side of plaintiff's car stopped in highway. Verdict for plaintiff affirmed. ***Farbacher v. Frank,* 228 Pa. Super. 35, 323 A.2d 233.**

Head-on collision

Following in-depth analysis of federal preemption law, Superior Court held state common law causes of action expressly not preempted by the National Traffic and Motor Vehicle Safety Act. So, motorist may raise claim at trial that airbag that contributed to his injuries in head-on collision with another vehicle was defective because Congress intended such issues to go to jury. Order denying manufacturer's preliminary objections affirmed. ***Heiple v. C.R. Motors, Inc.,* 446 Pa. Super. 310, 666 A.2d 1066 (1995).**

Automobile driver injured in collision with oncoming car alleged sufficient facts to preclude summary judgment under assured clear distance rule. ***Anderson v. Moore,* 437 Pa. Super. 642, 650 A.2d 1090 (1994).**

Passenger injured in head-on collision. Passenger not negligent for failure to warn driver of danger from oncoming vehicle. ***Phillips v. Schoenberger,* 369 Pa. Super. 52, 534 A.2d 1075.**

Cross over head-on accident. Verdict for defendant affirmed. Defendant testified he pulled to berm to avoid accident in his lane, then tried to swerve around tele-

Head-on collision

phone pole when he lost control of his car, crossing four lanes of roadway and striking plaintiff. Although driver who crosses center line of highway is negligent *per se,* this can be rebutted by competent evidence that vehicle was there through no negligence on defendant's part. **Farelli v. Marko, 349 Pa. Super. 102, 502 A.2d 1293.**

Head-on collision where each side claimed other came across center of highway first. For jury to determine which version of facts they believed. **Mickey v. Ayers, 336 Pa. Super. 512, 485 A.2d 1199.**

Fatal accident to operator of motorcycle in collision with truck. Alleged defect in street caused cycle to lose control after collision with truck. Verdict against plaintiff. New trial as to truck driver only, affirmed. Evidence of post-accident repairs to defect properly excluded under facts here. None of the alleged trial errors goes to negligence of the City. **Robinson v. City of Philadelphia, 329 Pa. Super. 139, 478 A.2d 1.**

Jury verdict $80,000—reduced to $64,000 due to finding of 20% contributory negligence. Defendant's auto struck plaintiff's garden tractor head-on, as he was plowing snow from driveway near berm. Exact locations of vehicles at impact disputed. Held: assured clear distance rule does apply at night on snowy road. Driver must take attending circumstances into account. **Fish v. Gosnell, 316 Pa. Super. 565, 463 A.2d 1042.**

Head-on collision. Both drivers and passenger killed. Passenger's estate sued. Driver of passenger's car intoxicated as both driver and passenger had spent afternoon drinking. Verdict for defendant on basis that plaintiff had assumed risk. **Weaver v. Clabaugh, 255 Pa. Super. 532, 388 A.2d 1094.**

Defendant's truck swerved into oncoming traffic to avoid suddenly stopped vehicle. Verdict for defendant truck driver affirmed. For jury as to whether clear emergency existed, thereby superseding assured clear distance doctrine. **Stacy v. Thrower Trucking, 253 Pa. Super. 150, 384 A.2d 1274.**

Head-on collision. Truck driver claimed auto swerved into his lane. Auto driver claims truck swerved into her lane so that she swerved left, then truck turned back into his lane where impact occurred. Verdict against truck driver. **Lininger v. Kromer, 238 Pa. Super. 259, 358 A.2d 89.**

Head-on collision. Error to charge on assured clear distance ahead unless jury also instructed that doctrine does not apply to vehicles moving toward one another. Defendant in wrong lane approaching blind intersection, without due regard for the situation is sufficient evidence to submit issue of reckless conduct to jury. New trial ordered. **Turner v. Smith, 237 Pa. Super. 161, 346 A.2d 806.**

Head-on collision. Verdict in favor of passenger against both drivers. Driver of car with passenger appealed. Other driver remembered nothing but that he was in proper lane shortly before accident. Appellant and passenger testified they saw other car in wrong lane when fifty feet away. Photos by police confirmed this version. New trial granted only as to passenger's verdict against driver of his car as it was error to charge as to his contributory negligence without other evidence. **Kulp v. Hess, 227 Pa. Super. 603, 323 A.2d 217.**

Head-on collision at curve—evidence that defendant crossed center line—for jury. ***Edgridge v. Melcher,*** **226 Pa. Super. 381, 313 A.2d 750.**

Head-on collision—each driver claimed other crossed center line—for jury. As against passenger, jury must find that at least one defendant was negligent. ***Fair v. Snowball Express,*** **226 Pa. Super. 295, 310 A.2d 386.**

Cars going in opposite directions—head-on collision—each driver contended that other car was on wrong side of road—trial court in error in not charging on the doctrine of contributory negligence. ***Walker v. Martin,*** **214 Pa. Super. 287, 257 A.2d 619.**

Plaintiff occupant of one of colliding cars—rainy day—defendant testified that his car had skidded but was stopped at time of occurrence with machine one to one and a half feet over center line—driver of other car allegedly came over brow of hill and collided with him—version of other operator was that car was on her side of road and moving at time of collision—verdict for defendant—new trial properly refused. ***Cwiakala v. Paal,*** **427 Pa. 322, 235 A.2d 145.**

Health care centers

Preliminary objections filed almost two years after original complaint filed still timely, timeliness being a determination within discretion of court, where there was intervening removal to federal court, subsequent remand to state court and confusion among all parties as to ongoing status of amended complaint. Hospital corporation that operates health care centers in numerous counties, including that in which plaintiff filed medical malpractice action, subject to venue of plaintiff's choosing so long as one of its health care centers meets the standard criteria for allowing venue in county where plaintiff brings suit, even if hospital named in the complaint, where the alleged negligence occurred, not located in the county where venue is sought. ***Gale v. Mercy Catholic Medical Center***, **698 A.2d 647 (Pa. Super. 1997).**

Health Care Services Malpractice Act

Plaintiff who alleged that failed tubal ligation resulted in pregnancy was pursuing claim for breach of an express oral contract to provide a specific result—no future pregnancies. The Health Care Services Malpractice Act (40 P.S. §1301.606) requires that any contract for a specific cure or result must be in writing and because plaintiff's complaint alleged only breach of an oral contract, there can be no recovery. ***Edwards v. Germantown Hospital***, **736 A.2d 612 (Pa. Super. 1999).**

Health regulations

City's duty to inspect privately-owned property to insure compliance with health and safety regulations does not constitute "care, custody and control" or "possession" of real property so as to except City from immunity provided by Political Subdivision Tort Claims Act. Order sustaining preliminary objections reversed. ***City of Pittsburgh v. Stahlman,*** **___ Pa. Cmwlth. ___, 677 A.2d 384 (1996).**

Health spas

Health spas

Suit for personal injury allegedly caused by spa employee during therapy following back surgery. Contract with spa had exculpatory clause. Error to grant summary judgment where plaintiff claims clause violative of public policy. ***Leidy v. Deseret Enterprises*, 252 Pa. Super. 162, 381 A.2d 164.**

Heart attack

Police officer suffered heart attack shortly after arriving at police station with fleeing driver defendant. Defense verdict affirmed. Held: risk that officer would have heart attack could not reasonably be foreseen. Driver owed officer no duty of care for purposes of negligence action. ***Zanine v. Gallegher*, 345 Pa. Super. 119, 497 A.2d 1332.**

Defense verdict. Alleged improper treatment and advice to heart patient who returned to work as cement truck driver, and suffered heart attack. Died three years later (after suit started) of second heart attack. Verdict affirmed. Proper for trial judge in certain instances to charge on questions of law not requested by either party. Proper here, where patient was heavy smoker and very overweight, to charge on contributory negligence. ***Berry v. Friday*, 324 Pa. Super. 499, 472 A.2d 191.**

Heart valve

Heart valve replacement patient brought action against surgeons for lack of informed consent. Surgeons liable. ***Stover v. Association of Thoracic and Cardiovascular Surgeons*, 431 Pa. Super. 11, 635 A.2d 1047.**

Heparin lock

Failure to follow Department of Health standards that suggest 48 hour limit for catheterization is not negligence *per se*. Medical malpractice causation requires proof of increased risk of harm. Causation is question for trier of fact where artificial hip replacement patient developed staff infection from catheterization. ***Edwards v. Brandywine Hospital*, 438 Pa. Super. 673, 652 A.2d 1382 (1995).**

Hepatitis

Husband who contracted hepatitis from wife brought malpractice action against wife's physician. Held: physician had duty to advise wife of her ability to transmit disease to others. ***DiMarco v. Lynch-Homes—Chester County*, 384 Pa. Super. 463, 559 A.2d 530.**

Herniated disk

Jury cannot disregard evidence of soft-tissue damage, cervical sprain, and herniated disk, which are injuries of the kind that normally cause pain and suffering for which plaintiff should be compensated. Order granting new trial on issue of damages reinstated. ***Neison v. Hines*, 539 Pa. 516, 653 A.2d 634 (1995).**

Hidden approach

Plaintiff on through highway—embankment prevented a view of vehicles on stop street—observant—first observing defendant in middle of intersection when plaintiff 10 to 15 feet from intersection—collision—matter still for the jury. ***Rhode v. Kearney,*** **208 Pa. Super. 8, 220 A.2d 378.**

High beams

Defendant came over crest of hill at night with high beams on. Had clear view of 300 to 400 feet. Plaintiff stopped car in street to talk. Vehicle Code requires 350 feet visibility on high beams. Verdict for plaintiff affirmed. ***Farbacher v. Frank,*** **228 Pa. Super. 35, 323 A.2d 233.**

Highway construction

Plaintiff brought negligence action against PennDOT after he was injured in a crash due to ice that had accumulated on PennDOT's highway from a broken water pipe. The trial court granted summary judgment to PennDOT. The Commonwealth Court affirmed holding that the real estate exception to sovereign immunity did not apply as the formation of the ice on the road did not derive from the road itself. ***Hall v. Southwestern Pennsylvania Water Authority,*** **87 A.3d 998 (Pa. Cmwlth. 2014).**

Plaintiffs brought negligence suit against PennDOT for failing to install a traffic signal at an intersection. Jury found PennDOT partially negligent. The Commonwealth Court held that PennDOT's regulation placing financial responsibility on local municipalities to install traffic signals did not relieve it of its duty to drivers for dangerous conditions existing on its roadways. ***Tate v. Commonwealth of Pennsylvania Department of Transportation,*** **84 A.3d 762 (Pa. Cmwlth. 2014).**

Plaintiff brought negligence claims for defective design, construction and maintenance against Defendant Department of Transportation (DOT). Plaintiff was injured when another vehicle crossed the grass median of a divided highway and struck his vehicle. The trial court granted summary judgment in favor of the Defendant. The Commonwealth Court affirmed holding that DOT had no duty to erect median barriers. It also held that a median does not constitute a dangerous condition of Commonwealth real estate and that DOT had no duty to create a median that deterred crossovers. ***Quinones v. Commonwealth of Pennsylvania Department of Transportation,*** **45 A.3d 467 (Pa. Cmwlth. 2012).**

Administrator brought suit on behalf of a deceased passenger against the Pennsylvania Department of Transportation (PennDotOT) for failing to use appropriate guardrails and failing to design appropriate roadway shoulders that resulted in the death of a passenger after the vehicle the deceased was traveling in went off the road. The appellate court upheld the trial court's ruling that failure to design and failure to maintain guardrails were not dangerous roadway conditions for which the Commonwealth has waived immunity. ***Fagan v. Department of Transportation of the Commonwealth of Pennsylvania,*** **946 A.2d 1123 (Pa. Cmwlth. 2008).**

Driver was sued for negligence after he struck a flag person working a paving project. The court held that, given the facts of the case, jury instructions did not require an instruction on the duty of care required of an ordinary person outside a work zone. ***McManamon v. Washko,*** **906 A.2d 1259 (Pa. Super. 2006).**

Hitchhiker

Contractor built road in accordance with specifications with 6 inch drop-off to berm. Plaintiff killed when car ran off road and he allegedly lost control due to drop-off. Summary judgment in favor of contractor reversed. Fact that contractor fulfilled contract does not relieve him of liability to third persons for creating a dangerous condition. ***St. Clair v. B & L Paving,* 270 Pa. Super. 277, 411 A.2d 525.**

Hitchhiker

Plaintiff, a hitchhiker, riding on a tractor trailer unit—injured in an apparent collision—evidence not clear whether operator of car in which riding had permission or authority to permit plaintiff to ride in car—failure to file answer to pleading not conclusive—new trial granted. ***Noel v. Puckett,* 427 Pa. 328, 235 A.2d 380.**

HMO liability

Federal Employee Retirement Income Security Act provisions regarding federal preemption of state laws which "relate to" ERISA benefits and plans do not preempt negligence claims against HMO for failure to timely approve emergency treatment to patient-plaintiff who suffered permanent injury by reason of delay. ***Pappas v. Asbel,* 724 A.2d 889 (Pa. 1998).**

Plaintiff parents of minor son who died following premature delivery sued obstetrician and HMO alleging medical negligence by obstetrician in failing to diagnose pre-term labor and vicarious liability of HMO for negligence of nursing staff and corporate liability for failure to properly supervise obstetrician and maintain adequate procedures and protocols. After plaintiff had closed and defendant had presented two of its witnesses, the trial court, *sua sponte,* granted defendants' motion for nonsuit. Superior court reversed on grounds that nonsuit was improper after defendant had presented witnesses and plaintiffs had made out a *prima facie* case of negligence against HMO for vicarious and direct corporate liability. ***Shannon v. McNulty,* 718 A.2d 828 (Pa. Super. 1998).**

Hoarseness

Expert medical testimony in a medical malpractice case involving damage to a laryngeal nerve and resulting hoarseness which establishes (1) that the type of injury complained of does not usually occur without negligence, (2) that other responsible causes, including the conduct of plaintiff or other persons are sufficiently eliminated by evidence, and (3) that the indicated negligent act was performed within the scope of the defendant's duty to the plaintiff, prohibits a compulsory nonsuit and calls for an instruction on *res ipsa loquitur. **Hightower-Warren v. Silk,* 698 A.2d 52 (Pa. 1997).**

Hockey puck - See Sports injuries

Holes and depressions

Uncovered drainage hole located within public right of way but outside paved street is not part of highway for purposes of highway exception to governmental immunity provision of Political Subdivision Tort Claims Act. Fact that drainage hole was located in public right of way that was in possession of abutting landowner means that municipality did not have possession and so real estate exception is not applicable to provide injured plaintiff with relief. *Gramlich v. Lower Southampton Township*, 838 A.2d 843 (Pa. Cmwlth. 2003).

Pedestrian injured after stepping into hole created where tree trunk removed from township-owned park grounds may not recover against township which has immunity under both Political Subdivision Tort Claims Act and Recreation Use of Land and Water Act. Summary judgment for township affirmed. *Wilkinson v. Conoy Township*, 677 A.2d 876 (Pa. Cmwlth. 1996).

Pedestrian fell into tree well on sidewalk outside stadium. Dark and rainy. Non-jury verdict for plaintiff with one-third comparative negligence. Held: plaintiff needed no expert as to proper design of tree well or sidewalk. Affirmed. *Barnes v. City of Philadelphia*, 350 Pa. Super. 615, 504 A.2d 1321.

Worker fell in three foot hole in floor of her office near desk. Had previously complained. Was distracted at time of fall by movement of desk chairs toward her. Compulsory nonsuit in error. For jury. *Weitz v. Baurkot*, 267 Pa. Super. 471, 406 A.2d 1138.

Plaintiff fell from scaffold because a brace slipped suddenly—plaintiff fell into a hole 16 feet deep which defendant had dug and failed to cover—existence of hole not the proximate cause—preliminary objections properly sustained. *Barber v. Kohler Co.*, 428 Pa. 219, 237 A.2d 224.

Homeowner's association

Homeowner brought suit against his neighbors and his homeowner's association after his neighbor's unleashed dogs ran onto his property and attacked him. The appellate court upheld the trial court's grant of summary judgment for the homeowner's association, because the association had not assumed a duty or have a duty to compel association members to confine their dogs. *McMahon v. Pleasant Valley West Association*, 952 A.2d 731 (Pa. Cmwlth. 2008).

Horseplay

School student prank—one of group dared other to knock trash can off balcony railing. Was tapped inadvertently during horseplay, falling on plaintiff below. Nonsuit affirmed. Settled before trial with two obvious participants. Suit tried against others present who allegedly encouraged and dared actors. Held: evidence did not present fault of individuals or group as a whole. *Kline v. Ball*, 306 Pa. Super. 284, 452 A.2d 727.

Horses

Summary judgment properly granted against plaintiff when she presented no evidence that stallion which bit her had shown any prior propensity for viciousness which would have put stallion's owner on notice and created liability for harm. *Kinley v. Bierly*, 876 A.2d 419 (Pa. Super. 2005).

Host liability

Social hosts can be held liable to minors injured as a result of being served alcoholic beverages, and to third parties injured by the action of the intoxicated

Hotel

minor. Liability, cannot, however, be based upon negligent entrustment of a non-owned auto or on duty as a landowner. ***Congini v. Portersville Valve Co.*, 504 Pa. 157, 470 A.2d 515.**

Hotel

Hotel guest permitted to go to jury on question of negligent security measures at hotel without an expert witness. ***Ovitsky v. Captial City Economic Development Corporation*, 846 A.2d 124 (Pa. Super. 2004).**

Plaintiff's decedent, a bystander at an underage drinking party at a hotel on New Year's Eve, was shot by another visitor to hotel. In suit against hotel owners and security company, summary judgment in favor of defendants reversed on grounds that plaintiff's pleadings and deposition testimony established *prima facie* case of negligence, including, specifically, duty to protect decedent as business invitee from known dangerous conditions. Lethal actions of rowdy crowd of drunken underage party participants was foreseeable under the circumstances described. ***Rabutino v. Freedom State Realty Company, Inc.*, 809 A.2d 933 (Pa. Super. 2002).**

Release entered into with hotel defendant for injuries sustained in federal slip and fall case did not release defendants in subsequent state court action for medical malpractice in surgery to repair wrist injured during slip and fall at hotel, where release specifically designated federal court action and caption as subject of release. Summary judgment for physicians and surgeons reversed. ***Harrity v. Medical College of Pennsylvania Hospital*, 439 Pa. Super. 10, 653 A.2d 5 (1995).**

Hunter

Member of hunting club killed by other member during hunt. Held: club members not liable for actions of individual who fired fatal shot. ***Johnson v. Johnson*, 410 Pa. Super. 631, 600 A.2d 965.**

Husband and wife

Shipyard worker died from lung cancer caused by exposure to asbestos. Widow not entitled to damages for loss of consortium for period after husband's death. Award of delay damages for consortium claim proper. ***Novelli v. Johns-Manville Corporation*, 395 Pa. Super. 144, 576 A.2d 1085.**

Pedestrian struck by wife defendant driving auto. Family use doctrine not part of Pennsylvania law. Mere fact of spousal relationship insufficient to impose liability upon husband, owner of auto. Affirmed summary judgment for absent husband/owner of auto. ***Breslin v. Ridarelli*, 308 Pa. Super. 179, 454 A.2d 80.**

Auto accident. Dismissal of suit by wife passenger against husband, overturned. ***Miller v. Miller*, 495 Pa. 611, 435 A.2d 173.**

Wife brought action in trespass to recover against husband and others for personal injuries in auto accident in which wife a passenger in car driven by husband—trial court granted husband motion for summary judgment—Superior Court affirmed—Supreme Court held defense of interspousal immunity abolished—reversed Superior Court; remanded to trial court. ***Hack v. Hack,* 495 Pa. 300, 433 A.2d 859.**

Passenger in auto driven by husband which collided with another auto brought suit and husband joined. Verdict against husband only. Judgment entered and no appeal filed. Motion to Strike Judgment granted. Reversed. Interspousal immunity waived as not timely filed. ***Policino v. Ehrlich,* 478 Pa. 5, 385 A.2d 968.**

Wife injured in auto accident prior to marriage, brought suit against her husband after marriage. Dismissal affirmed. ***Smith v. Smith,* 240 Pa. Super. 97, 361 A.2d 756.**

Plaintiff, passenger in auto operated by fiance. Involved in accident. Trial occurred after their marriage. Verdict against husband—additional defendant—only. Stricken as violative of statute on interspousal immunity. ***Policino v. Ehrlich,* 236 Pa. Super. 19, 345 A.2d 224.**

Wife is entitled to compensation for loss of her husband's consortium—New position required by Article I, Section 27 of the Pennsylvania Constitution guaranteeing equal rights. The rights of both spouses must be redressed in one action hereafter. ***Hopkins v. Blanco,* 457 Pa. 90, 320 A.2d 139.**

Interspousal immunity—premarital tort—subsequent marriage—suit barred. ***Kelso v. Mielcarek,* 226 Pa. Super. 476, 313 A.2d 324.**

Failure of one spouse to join in the other spouse's personal injury action will bar any claim of the non-joining spouse for loss of consortium. ***Hopkins v. Blanco,* 224 Pa. Super. 116, 302 A.2d 855.**

The interspousal immunity for personal injuries applies to a premarital tort—strong dissent. ***DiGirolamo, et ux. v. Apanavage,* 222 Pa. Super. 74, 293 A.2d 96.**

Court below in error in charging in a suit for injuries to a minor child that the contributory negligence of the wife plaintiff would bar recovery by husband for expenses sustained by him for his daughter's injuries—case reversed by court on appeal—husband not vicariously liable for negligence of his wife—new trial awarded as to damages only. ***Idzojtic v. Catalucci,* 222 Pa. Super. 47, 292 A.2d 464.**

Verdict for plaintiff husband included $3,000 for loss of wife's consortium—by equally divided Supreme Court judgment for amount affirmed. ***Brown v. Phila. T. Co.,* 437 Pa. 348, 263 A.2d 423.**

Hydraulic lift

Plaintiff injured after he slipped while dodging lowering hydraulic lift that he knew lowered sporadically was entitled to jury determination on question of assumption of the risk. Order granting summary judgment reversed. ***Long v. Norriton Hydraulics, Inc.,* 443 Pa. Super. 532, 662 A.2d 1089 (1995).**

Hydroplaning

Motorist injured when vehicle hydroplaned on highway leading to bridge owned by commission. Commission incorporated in New Jersey. Commission liable

Hypoxia

since it voluntarily attempted to correct dangerous condition of highway. ***Laconis v. Burlington County Bridge Commission,* 400 Pa. Super. 483, 583 A.2d 1218.**

Hypoxia

Action to recover for death of child 11 months after birth where death caused by negligent failure to diagnose and act on dangerous condition *in utero* immediately before birth. Evidence to establish "corporate liability" of hospital under *Thompson v. Nason Hospital*, 527 Pa. 330, 591 A.2d 703 (1991) must be provided in the form of expert testimony where the negligence is not obvious but need not contain "magic words." The substance of all the expert testimony will be considered as a whole. The evidence must establish that the hospital, in its own duty to the patient, deviated from the accepted standard of care and that that deviation was a substantial factor in causing the harm to the plaintiff. ***Welsh v. Bulger,* 698 A.2d 581 (Pa. 1997).**

Ice and snow

—I—

Ice and snow

Plaintiff sued defendant business owner and city after he slipped and fell on freshly fallen snow on a public sidewalk ramp adjoining the business owner's property. The trial court granted summary judgment. The Superior Court affirmed, holding that based upon the hills and ridges doctrine the plaintiff could not recover as the ice he slipped on was smooth and had not accumulated in hills and ridges. In addition, there was no evidence that the business owner had actual or constructive notice of the ramp's condition and it owed no duty as the time to clear the sidewalk had not expired under the city's ordinance. ***Alexander v. City of Meadville*, 61 A.3d 218 (Pa. Super. 2012).**

Plaintiff brought negligence claim against Defendant transportation agency after she slipped on an icy wooden step on the train platform, while attempting to board a train. The trial court entered summary judgment for the Defendant. The Commonwealth Court affirmed holding that allegations of improper maintenance resulting in ice were insufficient as the ice did not result from a defect in the real property itself. ***Nardella v. Southeastern Pennsylvania Transportation Authority*, 34 A.3d 300 (Pa. Cmwlth. 2011).**

Motorist brought lawsuit against the City of Philadelphia and Pennsylvania Department of Transportation after he lost control of his vehicle while driving on a city street due to black ice caused by melt and refreeze from the highway. The trial court granted summary judgment in favor of both Defendants. The Commonwealth Court affirmed holding that the State Highway law did not impose a statutory duty on the Department of Transportation (DOT) to protect an individual from accumulations of snow and ice on the roads. In addition, the Court held that the natural formation of ice following DOT's treatment of the roadways with chemicals does not create an artificial condition waiving sovereign immunity. Finally, the Court held that the city was immune pursuant to the Political Subdivision Tort Claims Act as the Plaintiff failed to establish the black ice was the result of improper construction, design, deterioration or inherent defect of the street itself. ***Page v. City of Philadelphia*, 1542 C.D. 2010 (Pa. Cmwlth. 2011).**

Plaintiff brought suit against school district after she slipped and fell on snow and ice in their parking lot. A jury found in favor of the Defendant. The Commonwealth Court affirmed holding that the law does not require a property owner to keep their parking lot free and clear of ice at all times and the evidence presented was sufficient to find that the slippery surface was the result of a generally icy condition. ***Tucker v. Bensalem Township School District*, 987 A.2d 198 (Pa. Cmwlth. 2009).**

Plaintiffs injured in a slip and fall crossing a sidewalk brought a negligence claim against the city for failing to remove snow and ice from the sidewalk abutting the city's police station. The trial court found in favor of the Plaintiffs and the Commonwealth Court affirmed. The Supreme Court reversed, holding that the real property exception to governmental immunity does not apply to injuries arising

Ice and snow

from sidewalks even if the sidewalk abuts local agency property. ***Reid v. City of Philadelphia*, 598 Pa. 389, 957 A.2d 232 (2008).**

Plaintiff brought a claim against a property owner after he slipped and fell on ice in their parking lot. The appellate court reversed the trial court's grant of summary judgment holding that when a property owner retains control of a part of the leased premises he is liable for physical harm caused by dangerous conditions that exist on that part of the property over whichthat he retained control. ***Jones v. Levin*, 940 A.2d 451 (Pa. Super. 2007).**

Plaintiff slipped and fell on black ice, while walking on a recently plowed road owned by a subdivision developer. The court held that based upon the "hills and ridges" doctrine the developer was protected from liability, since the developer had not permitted the ice to unreasonably accumulate to create the dangerous condition. ***Harvey v. Rouse Chamberlain, LTD.*, 901 A.2d 523 (Pa. Super. 2006).**

Summary judgment affirmed against pedestrian whose complaint failed to allege that slip and fall on ice and snow on sidewalk "resulted from a condition of the sidewalk or derived from, originated from or had as its source, the sidewalk. Mere allegations of dangerous condition, causation, and damage are inadequate. ***Cohen v. City of Philadelphia*, 847 A.2d 778 (Pa. Cmwlth. 2004).**

Hills and ridges doctrine is not applicable when the dangerous condition of the walking surface is inside a structure. ***Heasley v. Carter Lumber*, 843 A.2d 1274 (Pa. Super. 2004).**

Hills and ridges doctrine regarding ice and snow accumulations applies to landlord and tenant relationships. ***Biernacki v. Presque Isle Condominiums Unit Owners Association, Inc.*, 828 A.2d 1114 (Pa. Super. 2003).**

Real estate exception to sovereign immunity held not to apply in suit against PennDOT for negligent design of road on which family was killed in "whiteout" snow conditions. ***Kosmack v. Jones*, 807 A.2d 927 (Pa. Cmwlth. 2002).**

Suit against PennDOT alleging negligence for failure to remove accumulations of ice and snow from state maintained road during declared Disaster Emergency in 1994. Summary judgment in favor of PennDOT affirmed on basis of sovereign immunity and immunity under Pennsylvania's Emergency Management Services Code provisions. ***Kahres v. Henry*, 801 A.2d 650 (Pa. Super. 2002).**

Tenant of county housing authority who was injured when she slipped and fell on snow and ice-covered parking area could not recover against local agency, because snow and ice were condition *on* the real estate, not condition *of* the real estate. Supreme Court's seemingly different determination on similar facts under the Sovereign Immunity Act does not control under different language of the Political Subdivision Tort Claims Act. ***Irish v. Lehigh County Housing Authority*, 751 A.2d 1201 (Pa. Cmwlth. 2000).**

Plaintiff was injured when she slipped on ice on public street and fell while going towards church. Summary judgment for church granted and affirmed on appeal because church was not "possessor" of street on which plaintiff fell. Summa-

Ice and snow

ry judgment for municipality affirmed on basis that snow and ice on street was not a condition "of" the street and therefore action fell outside of streets exception to governmental immunity. ***Walinsky v. St. Nicholas Ukranian Catholic Church*, 740 A.2d 318 (Pa. Cmwlth. 1999).**

Plaintiff injured when she fell on ice and snow-covered school district concrete landing received jury verdict. School District appealed claiming that place of fall was a sidewalk and so the "on or of" test applies. Commonwealth Court affirmed based on school district's failure to exercise proper care and control of real property. ***Snyder v. North Allegheny School District*, 722 A.2d 239 (Pa. Cmwlth. 1998).**

79 year old plaintiff slipped and fell on "penny thin" black ice patch on parking lot of defendant's combination gasoline and convenience store while on the way back into the store to ask for a second time to use the private telephone in the store. After verdict for plaintiff, defendant appealed claiming that trial court's charge that plaintiff was a business invitee and court's refusal to charge on choice of ways doctrine were error. Held: by reason of defendant's directions to plaintiff to go outside onto its property to use the public phone and existence of a "welcome" sign on canopy established as a matter of law that plaintiff was a business invitee, not just a licensee. As to allegation of error in refusal to charge on choice of ways doctrine, the fact that the ice patch was very difficult to see, even for a much younger store employee who testified to that fact, precludes the charge on choice of ways if there was no way to discern the more dangerous of two paths. ***Updyke v. BP Oil Co.*, 717 A.2d 546 (Pa. Super. 1998).**

After slip and fall on accumulated ice and snow at airport, plaintiff sued City of Philadelphia which had control of area where accident occurred. Trial court granted summary judgment in favor of city on basis of lack of evidence to support claim under real property exception to Political Subdivision Tort Claims Act. Commonwealth Court affirmed in an unpublished decision and Supreme Court reversed, holding that summary judgment was improper where there exists a genuine issue of material fact as to whether the city was negligent under the real property exception for a dangerous condition *on* the property. This case, as pointed out by Justice Castille and Chief Justice Flaherty in the dissent, arguably overrules Finn v. City of Philadelphia, 541 Pa. 596, 664 A.2d 1342 (1995) which required a showing of a dangerous condition *of* the real property. ***Kilgore v. City of Philadelphia*, 717 A.2d 514 (Pa. 1998).**

Plaintiff appeals from grant of summary judgment to defendants based on common-enemy doctrine relating to natural surface water runoff in urban area. Plaintiff was injured when she slipped and fell on ice that had accumulated in alley next to defendant's business location. Held: so long as defendant had not artificially changed natural course of water or substantially changed quality or quantity of surface water, no injury will fall to lower landowner or to another. The record is devoid of evidence that defendants modified natural course of water in any way. ***Fazio v. Fegley Oil Co, Inc.*, 714 A.2d 510 (Pa. Cmwlth. 1998).**

Ice and snow

Plaintiff who fell on thin layer of "black ice" in motel parking lot suffered injuries and sued motel owner. Plaintiff argued that "hills and ridges" doctrine, which requires showing of accumulation of ice and snow, should not apply to business premises; they are not so burdened by substantial size of area to be cleared of ice and snow as are municipalities and local agencies, which organizations the doctrine is designed to protect. Plaintiff also argued that custodian who had placed salt and sand on portions of premises was negligent for not salting and sanding entire parking lot. Held: "hills and ridges" applies to business invitees and local agencies equally and because plaintiff could not show accumulation had been allowed to form without any effort to cure problem, summary judgment was proper. *Morin v. Travelers Rest Motel, Inc.*, **704 A.2d 1085 (Pa. Super. 1997).**

Accumulation of ice and snow into ridges and hills on which plaintiff slipped, fell and was injured is not a dangerous condition *of* the sidewalk under sovereign immunity act and summary judgment in favor of Commonwealth sustained. The Court closely reviewed *Grieff v. Reisinger*, 548 Pa. 13, 693 A.2d 195 (1997) but remains bound by facts of this case and those in *Finn v. Philadelphia,* 541 Pa. 596, 664 A.2d 1342 (1995) as distinguished from those in *Grieff, supra*. *Abella v. City of Philadelphia*, **703 A.2d 547 (Pa. Cmwlth. 1997).**

Plaintiff's expert's report that state highway was defective in design, irrespective of plaintiff's claims of natural accumulations of ice and snow, creates factual question for jury relating to care and maintenance of PennDOT's real property and so precludes summary judgment in favor of PennDOT based on Sovereign Immunity Act. *Smith v. Com., Dept. of Transp.*, **700 A.2d 587 (Pa. Cmwlth. 1997).**

A state agency has no duty to remove or treat natural accumulations of ice and snow. A natural accumulation of ice, snow or frost on prison sidewalk is not a defect of property within the real property exception to governmental immunity; therefore, prisoner not entitled to recovery. Order granting summary judgment affirmed. *Hill v. Dragovich*, **___Pa. Cmwlth. ___, 679 A.2d 1382 (1996).**

Order granting summary judgment in favor of school district affirmed where plaintiff who slipped on ice in school district parking lot failed to establish that injuries were caused by improper design, construction, deterioration, or inherent defect of real estate. Real property exception to Political Subdivision Tort Claims Act not applicable. *Metkus v. Pennsbury School District*, **___ Pa. Cmwlth. ___, 674 A.2d 355 (1996).**

Hills and ridges of ice on school district property are not dangerous condition of the property itself and, therefore, do not fall within real property exception to Political Subdivision Tort Claims Act. Order granting judgment on pleadings affirmed. *McRae for School District of Philadelphia*, **___ Pa. Cmwlth. ___, 660 A.2d 209 (1995).**

Striking worker injured when he fell on snow-covered sidewalk while pickting. School district liable. *Giosa v. School District of Philadelphia,* **157 Pa. Cmwlth. 489, 630 A.2d 511.**

Ice and snow

Truck driver injured when vehicle skidded on ice and snow on highway. Department not liable for failure to clear ice and snow or for failure to warn. ***Hunt v. Com., Dept. of Transp.*, 137 Pa. Cmwlth. 588, 587 A.2d 37.**

Student injured in fall on snow-covered lawn while walking to gymnasium. University not liable. Doctrine of hills and ridges not applicable. ***Gilligan v. Villanova University*, 401 Pa. Super. 113, 584 A.2d 1005.**

Landowner sued by pedestrian who fell on ice on sidewalk filed third-party complaint against PennDOT, alleging negligence in snow removal. Department not liable. ***Miller v. Kistler*, 135 Pa. Cmwlth. 647, 582 A.2d 416.**

Trolley passenger slipped and fell on ice or frost present on platform. Authority not liable. ***Bowles v. SEPTA*, 135 Pa. Cmwlth. 534, 581 A.2d 700.**

Pedestrian who slipped and fell on ice and snow while taking short cut through parking lot brought action against tenant freight company and landlord. Neither landlord nor tenant liable. No duty owed. Pedestrian assumed risk. ***Ott v. Unclaimed Freight Company*, 395 Pa. Super. 483, 577 A.2d 894.**

Motorist killed when automobile went over guardrail owing to snow removed from highway left along berm. Commonwealth liable. Snow along berm was artificial condition caused by PennDOT. ***Com., Dept. of Transp. v. Weller*, 133 Pa. Cmwlth. 18, 574 A.2d 728.**

Motorists injured or killed in accidents caused by ice and snow on highways. Commonwealth found not liable. Duty to remove ice and snow does not include duty to protect individuals from harm. ***Kilmer v. Com., Dept. of Transp.*, 132 Pa. Cmwlth. 538, 573 A.2d 659.**

Pedestrian tripped and fell on ice and snow on city street. City not liable. Ice and snow are natural conditions even if shoveled onto street. ***Vitelli v. City of Chester*, 119 Pa. Cmwlth. 58, 545 A.2d 1011.**

Delivery man slipped and fell on snow-covered private walkway. Held: doctrine of hills and ridges applies to private, as well as public, walks. ***Wentz v. Pennwood Apartments*, 359 Pa. Super. 1, 518 A.2d 314.**

Customer slipped and fell in shopping center parking lot. Property owner not liable owing to absence of ridges and elevations in ice covering lot. ***Roland v. Kravco, Inc.*, 355 Pa. Super. 493, 513 A.2d 1029.**

Owner of land definition in Recreation Use of Land and Water Act does not apply to Commonwealth. Therefore, plaintiff injured on snowmobile when he struck concealed tree stump can maintain action against Commonwealth. Grant of Commonwealth's preliminary objections reversed. ***Auresto v. Commonwealth*, 88 Pa. Cmwlth. 476, 490 A.2d 492.**

Non-jury verdict of $319,419.92 against PennDOT and $39,927.49 each against Logan Fire Co. and PennDOT assistant county superintendent. Decedent, husband and father of four minor children, in accident on ice patch, causing his vehicle to spin out of control. Ice patch created by fire company pumping out flooded

Ice and snow

basement of adjacent landowner. Twenty-seven hours before this accident, another accident occurred at same location. PennDOT was notified and sent employee who put up trestle with light (which did not work) and left scene. PennDOT assistant county superintendent on routine patrol, failed to correct condition adequately. PennDOT found 80% liable and other two defendants each found 10% liable. ***Commonwealth v. Phillips,* 87 Pa. Cmwlth. 504, 488 A.2d 77.**

Plaintiff injured when vehicle in which he was a passenger skidded on icy overpass. Commonwealth has exclusive jurisdiction over control and maintenance of state highways. Township through which highway passes has no duty, even to warn of known dangers. Dismissal of Newtown Township affirmed. ***Haas v. Comm. of Pa.,* 84 Pa. Cmwlth. 522, 479 A.2d 100.**

Auto accident allegedly caused by ice on state highway—a recurring problem caused by runoff from abutting private property. Passenger in car injured. Summary judgment as to borough affirmed. Borough not secondarily liable for repairs to state highway. Duty to warn, not raised below—cannot be considered on appeal. Affirmed. ***Janosko v. Pittsburgh National Corp.,* 83 Pa. Cmwlth. 636, 478 A.2d 160.**

Fall on ice patch in parking lot of chiropractic clinic. Jury verdict $70,000, reflecting 35% for comparative negligence. Ice was next to car although rest of lot was clear. Plaintiff became aware of ice while still seated in car. Wore prosthesis at time—fractured left hip. Verdict reversed. Where plaintiff sees risk, possessor of land relieved of responsibility and duty of care to invitee who, under circumstances here, was held to have assumed risk as matter of law. Comparative negligence statute not applicable. ***Carrender v. Fitterer,* 503 Pa. 178, 469 A.2d 120.**

Truck coming down steep hill unable to stop at stop sign—skidded on ice through intersection causing accident. Jury verdict for defendant. Held: unavoidable accident. Negligence *per se*—going through sign not same as strict liability. Error to grant new trial. Verdict reinstated. ***Bumbarger v. Kaminsky,* 311 Pa. Super. 177, 457 A.2d 552.**

Handicapped plaintiff injured in parking lot of medical clinic. Had artificial lower leg, fell on ice and fractured hip. Charge on comparative negligence proper. Charge on assumption of risk would have been unnecessary and improper. Because fall was on isolated patch of ice between cars, proper *not* to charge on hills and ridges. Jury verdict, $70,000 hip, $2,500 for husband's loss of consortium. Reduced 35% for contribution, $45,000 and $1,626. Affirmed. ***Carrender v. Fitterer,* 310 Pa. Super. 433, 456 A.2d 1013.**

Business visitor slipped and fell on snow-covered metal plate in front of entrance. Metal plate not visible due to snow. Error to grant nonsuit. For jury as to whether metal plate, combined with wet snow, was a dangerous condition requiring warning. ***Treadway v. Ebert Motor Co.,* 292 Pa. Super. 41, 436 A.2d 994.**

Plaintiff fell on snow covered ice on sidewalk. 8 years earlier City had approved repair to sidewalk caused by tree root. Repair inadequate. Depression remained or returned. Property owner held primarily liable and City secondarily liable on jury verdict. ***Clayton v. Durham,* 273 Pa. Super. 571, 417 A.2d 1196.**

Ice and snow

Minor child injured by snowball. Verdict in favor of parents for reimbursement of expenses but against minor found contributorily negligent. Held: not inconsistent. **Gould v. Nickel, 268 Pa. Super. 183, 407 A.2d 891.**

Testimony as to slip on ice sufficient as to causation and relationship to ridges of ice to go to jury. Nonsuit reversed. **Izzo v. Meyer, 259 Pa. Super. 95, 393 A.2d 733.**

Slip and fall on ice. Nonsuit entered by lower court. Reversed. Plaintiff testified that he got out of car, that entire sidewalk was icy, that it had not snowed for two days, that there had been freezing and thawing and that he felt a 3 to 4 inch ridge of ice as he fell. Not contributorily negligent as a matter of law. **Strother v. Binkele, 256 Pa. Super. 404, 389 A.2d 1186.**

Plaintiff—a crossing guard—allegedly struck on sidewalk when defendant's car skidded on ice. Defense was that car stopped at curb and did not strike plaintiff. Charge on unavoidable accident proper under the circumstances. **Kenworthy v. Burghart, 241 Pa. Super. 267, 361 A.2d 335.**

Plaintiff forced to walk in street due to failure of property owner to clear sidewalk and further required to walk out in roadway due to three foot high bank of snow caused by city plows. While walking in street possibly struck by auto driven by Barnes. Verdict against city and property owner only. Conflict in testimony as to whether plaintiff slipped or was struck by car. **Bacsick v. Barnes, et al., 234 Pa. Super. 616, 341 A.2d 157.**

A 65 year old pedestrian fell at night on pieces of ice on a roadway which did not have sidewalks—street light not working—not sufficient evidence of negligence—nonsuit sustained—dissenting opinion. **Familiari v. Lancaster City, 442 Pa. 535, 277 A.2d 763.**

Plaintiff pedestrian fell on pavement abutting defendant's garage premises—evidence that cause of fall was a patch of ice in a crack in pavement—not required to establish "hills or ridges" under facts of case—matter for jury—plaintiff not guilty of contributory negligence in choice of way. **Tonik v. Apex Garages, Inc., 442 Pa. 373, 275 A.2d 296.**

Plaintiff on alighting from a car allegedly slipped on defendant's pavement during a snow storm—alleged existence of an isolated patch of ice as cause of fall not established—nonsuit proper. **Tolbert v. Gillette, 438 Pa. 63, 260 A.2d 463.**

Car passed by a bus which threw up a snow swirl—driver of passed car continued on and collided with rear of another car, injuring plaintiff, a passenger therein—jury held both operator of car colliding and bus company responsible—judgment *n.o.v.* properly entered for bus company as its bus was some 1500 to 2000 feet ahead when collision took place. **Metts v. Griglak, 438 Pa. 392, 264 A.2d 684.**

Plaintiff was 72 years of age and a retired miner—fell on defendant's abutting sidewalk—evidence that it was snowing at time or shortly before—plaintiff attempted to prove notice by offering two photographs taken some 6 months later—photographs disclosed unevenness of pavement and were rejected—action proper—

Ice skating

mere unevenness not sufficient to take case to the jury—nonsuit entered—motions dismissed and action affirmed on appeal. ***Silich v. Wissinger,* 438 Pa. 548, 264 A.2d 169.**

Suit against property owner for injuries resulting from fall, allegedly as result of an accumulation of ice and snow on abutting pavement—no proof of hills and ridges—nonsuit improperly entered below—rule that there must be proof of hills and ridges only applicable when general slippery conditions prevail by reason of recent precipitation. ***Williams v. Shultz,* 429 Pa. 429, 240 A.2d 812.**

Plaintiff truck driver maintained that he fell and was injured as the result of "wet slippery ice"—no "ridges or grooves"—business invitee—nonsuit proper—no evidence of notice or how long condition existed. ***Wilson v. Howard Johnson Restaurant,* 421 Pa. 455, 219 A.2d 676.**

Ice skating

Minor injured while ice skating on public lake in borough. Held: borough's alleged failure to supervise was alleged cause of injury and therefore not within exception to Political Subdivision Tort Claims Act. ***Fizzano v. Ridley Park,* 94 Pa. Cmwlth. 179, 503 A.2d 57.**

Plaintiff, a business invitee in a skating rink owned and operated by defendant, fell allegedly as the result of a "soft spot" in ice—evidence that ice manufacturing machine was defective—operator held responsible. ***Dean v. Allegheny County,* 209 Pa. Super. 310, 228 A.2d 40.**

Identity

There is no legally cognizable cause of action in Pennsylvania for negligent identification of a criminal defendant. Summary judgment affirmed. ***Jaindl v. Mohr,* 541 Pa. 163, 661 A.2d 1362 (1995).**

Imputed negligence

Pedestrian injured by shot fired from BB gun by passenger in vehicle brought action against driver. Driver not liable. ***Troutman v. Meschella,* 421 Pa. Super. 620, 618 A.2d 982.**

Member of church board of directors injured in fall down church steps. Recovery denied. Negligence of church imputed to director. ***Zehner v. Wilkinson United Methodist Church,* 399 Pa. Super. 165, 581 A.2d 1388.**

Passengers in automobile injured in collision at intersection. Held: trial court erred in refusing to instruct jury that negligence of driver may not be imputed against passenger-guest. ***Ellis v. Graves,* 385 Pa. Super. 168, 560 A.2d 220.**

Plaintiffs—children were passengers in their mother's car which collided with defendant's car. Mother and other driver negligent. Mother's negligence cannot be imputed to children. Verdict denying them a recovery against the weight of the evidence. ***Lind v. Thomas,* 265 Pa. Super. 121, 401 A.2d 830.**

Independent contractor

The doctrine of imputing the negligence of the operator of the vehicle to the owner present in the car modified to apply only where the relationship is that of master and servant or where a joint enterprise exists—for jury to determine under proper instruction—judgment *n.o.v.* improperly entered under facts of case. ***Smalich v. Westfall,*** **440 Pa. 409, 269 A.2d 476.**

Incontrovertible Physical Facts Rule

Plaintiff walked between parked truck and his car, intending to enter car through left door. Truck turned to left, allegedly causing plaintiff to be struck by right rear. Argument that accident could not have happened as described was rejected with no supporting evidence. ***Siravo v. AAA Trucking,*** **306 Pa. Super. 217, 452 A.2d 521.**

Plaintiff's vehicle struck by defendant's train at a grade crossing—plaintiff's testimony disclosed that plaintiff had a clear view from 1365 to 1849 feet before entering crossing—incontrovertible physical facts rule applied and action of court below entering nonsuit affirmed—the fact that plaintiff was suffering from traumatic amnesia not controlling. ***Reynolds v. Cen. R.R. of N.J. et al.,*** **448 Pa. 415, 292 A.2d 924.**

Independent contractor

Subcontractor brought negligence action against general contractor after falling 14 feet at a construction site. A jury found in favor of the subcontractor on the basis he was an independent contractor. The Superior Court affirmed. The Pennsylvania Supreme Court reversed holding that the statutory employer doctrine provided immunity for general contractors from suit by their subcontractors for injuries on the job based upon the Workers' Compensation Act. An independent contractor must contract with the owner of the property. ***Patton v. Worthington Associates, Inc.***, **89 A.3d 643 (Pa. 2014).**

Absent proof that a particular trenching effort presented a peculiar risk or danger, an employer, in this case a municipal sewer authority, will not beheld vicariously liable for the negligent conduct of its contractors. ***Dunkle v. Middleburg Municipal Authority*, 842 A.2d 477 (Pa. Cmwlth. 2004).**

Plaintiff independent contractor, a sandblaster/painter, was injured when he fell from scaffolding below elevated rail tracks after the light on his sandblaster failed and he tripped on a hose he could not see. Plaintiff alleged that SEPTA was liable at common law for failure to provide a safe work area and that lack of lights on SEPTA property he was working on was a defect in SEPTA property. Held: there is no liability of an employer to an independent contractor absent special danger or peculiar risk conditions - working on a scaffold is neither - and that lack of lights on SEPTA is not a dangerous condition "of" the real estate. ***Donnelly v. SEPTA*, 708 A.2d 145 (Pa. Cmwlth. 1998).**

Order granting summary judgment in favor of landowners and independent contractor-employer of injured trench digger affirmed. Injured employee may not recover against landowner when independent contractor has control of property on which trench was being dug and there was no "peculiar risk" to the trench-digging

Independent contractor

operation of which the landowner had greater knowledge than did the injured person. ***Motter v. Meadows Limited Partnership,* 451 Pa. Super. 520, 680 A.2d 887 (1996).**

A person is not liable for the criminal conduct of another in the absence of a special relationship imposing a pre-existing duty. No special relationship exists between independent ice cream sales contractor and ice cream manufacturer that would impose duty on manufacturer to protect independent contractor from criminal acts of third person. Summary judgment affirmed. ***Elbasher v. Simco Sales Service of Pennsylvania,* 441 Pa. Super. 397, 657 A.2d 983 (1995).**

Oil company who supplied gasoline to independent contractor service station had no duty to service station attendant who was assaulted and raped during course of employment. Demurrer to complaint granted. ***Smith v. Exxon Corporation,* 436 Pa. Super. 221, 647 A.2d 577 (1994).**

Tenant broke ankle when board broke on the front porch used in common by all tenants in building. Jury verdict $38,695. Although charge of court in error as to duty of landlord where independent contractor hired to make repairs, here verdict showed independent negligence on part of landlord. Therefore, error harmless. ***Speer v. Barry,* 349 Pa. Super. 365, 503 A.2d 409.**

Jury verdict $151,000. Truck driver, rented with truck, to steel company. Driver injured while helping load truck, although not one of his required duties. Held: to be contractor engaged in independent business—not statutory employee; not subject to compensation, but causing employer to be open to liability under traditional tort principles. ***Ashman v. Sharon Steel Corporation,* 302 Pa. Super. 305, 448 A.2d 1054.**

Private duty nurse joined by hospital as independent contractor in negligence case where plaintiff fell out of bed. For jury as to whether nurse justified in leaving room. ***Hogan v. Bryn Mawr Hospital,* 250 Pa. Super. 109, 378 A.2d 477.**

Two workers, one injured and one killed when jammed bricks in blast furnace collapsed. Unusual dangers on job. Verdict for plaintiffs reversed on basis of Section 413 of Restatement (2d) Torts—relating to duty to provide for taking precautions against dangers involved in work entrusted to contractors. Charge inadequate. ***Gonzalez v. U.S. Steel,* 248 Pa. Super. 95, 374 A.2d 1334.**

Owner employed a competent demolition operator to dismantle a steel trestle—this operator employed a subcontractor to assist in dismantling trestle together with a crane and operator—plaintiff, an employee of dismantling contractor, injured by operator of crane—suit against owner steel company on ground that relationship was not an independent contractorship—nonsuit properly entered—no evidence of control by owner. ***Brletich v. U.S. Steel Corp.,* 445 Pa. 525, 285 A.2d 133.**

General contractor defendant engaged other defendant to do certain specialized stone work in a home improvement operation—subcontractor specialized in this type of work, was paid a lump sum, furnished his own tools and equipment and own employees—general contractor interested only in result—Held: relationship was that of independent contractorship and general contractor not responsible for operation of a car by subcontractor—Superior Court reversed. *Cox v. Caeti*, **444 Pa. 143, 279 A.2d 756.**

Plaintiff serviceman called to check air conditioning unit—general manager of defendant failed through lack of knowledge to operate proper thermostat—plaintiff injured when air conditioner started—improper to enter judgment on pleadings—plaintiff's pleading entitled him to a trial on the merits. *Eckborg v. Hyde-Murphy Co.,* **442 Pa. 283, 276 A.2d 513.**

Plaintiff, an employee of a contractor, injured by cave-in of a trench being dug for the laying of water pipe—plaintiff sued Authority defendant and several others—issue as to the measure of control residing in Authority—court held such a matter of law as contract was clear and unambiguous—nonsuit entered—court below held employer a pure contractor (independent) and that Authority had no control over the manner in which contractor laid pipe—right of inspection not controlling. *Giannetti v. Lower Bucks Joint Municipal Authority, et al.,* **439 Pa. 607, 266 A.2d 447.**

One defendant engaged in remodeling a home—engaged other defendant to do some stone work of a special character—latter defendant had an automobile accident—jury's verdict held both defendants responsible—upheld by a divided court on appeal—strong dissent—criteria for determining relationship set forth at large in dissenting opinion. *Cox v. Caeti,* **216 Pa. Super. 214, 263 A.2d 765.** *Reversed by Supreme Court.*

Driver of truck owned same—had own P.U.C. permit and paid for oil and gas—compensated on mileage basis—no evidence of control—consistent with independent contractorship. *Dugan v. Niglio,* **436 Pa. 22, 258 A.2d 501.**

Defendant owner of a dairy—plaintiff did odd jobs around same—engaged to unplug a clogged sewer—injured by defective equipment supplied by him—independent contractorship—defendant not responsible. *Funari v. Valentino,* **435 Pa. 363, 257 A.2d 259.**

Defendant corporation supplied bakery articles to individual defendant for distribution—individual defendant owned and maintained vehicles—plaintiff injured by the vehicle operated by the individual defendant—individual defendant an independent contractor and corporate defendant not responsible. *George v. Nemeth,* **426 Pa. 551, 233 A.2d 231.**

Industrial accidents

Plaintiff injured when industrial split-wheel separated and struck him in head. Plaintiff worked for a company which replaced tires on forklift trucks with this split-wheel. Wheel separated violently while new tire being inflated. New trial ordered to improper charge. §388 of Restatement (2d) Torts should have been applied dealing with duty of bailee. *Lambert v. Pittsburgh Bridge and Iron Works,* **227 Pa. Super. 50, 323 A.2d 107.**

Plaintiff, an employee of the U.S. Steel Corporation, injured by an air drill—suit against alleged manufacturer—injury either caused by defective drill or because

Industrial accidents

drill was unexpectedly started by a fellow employee—court instructed jury that only one of defendants could be held responsible under the circumstances of the case—verdict against employer only—judgment *n.o.v.* granted as to this defendant and refusal to grant a new trial as to manufacturer sustained on appeal. ***Grasha v. Ingersoll-Rand Co.*, 439 Pa. 216, 266 A.2d 710.**

Plaintiff workman employed by general contractor—injured by the fall of a wall—evidence that cutting a pipe chase in wall so weakened it as to cause collapse—sufficient evidence in record for jury to find that defendant Steel City cut the chase—verdict for plaintiff sustained. ***Abbott v. Steel City Piping Co.*, 437 Pa. 412, 263 A.2d 881.**

Plaintiff, a structural steel worker at a shopping center erection operation, was injured by the collapse of "bar joists"—the defendant, a subcontractor, held responsible by the jury, had placed bundles of steel decking on joists at a point too far removed from supporting beams—case for jury and defendant's motion properly refused. ***Quinn v. Kumar*, 437 Pa. 268, 263 A.2d 458.**

Plaintiff was an employee of an independent contractor on defendant's premises and engaged as a painter on a scaffold—an electric wire owned and placed by defendant arced and severed cable supporting scaffold and plaintiff injured in fall—case for jury—verdict for plaintiff upheld—maintenance of wire contrary to provisions of National Electrical Code. ***Janowicz v. Crucible Steel Co. of America*, 433 Pa. 304, 249 A.2d 773.**

Plaintiff's decedent killed by reason of a boiler explosion—cause of explosion was due to a valve manufactured by added defendant—valve stuck and caused added pressure—suit was against owner of boiler who brought in value manufacturer—case falls within provisions of strict liability under Section 402A of Restatement (2d) Torts—verdict for plaintiff against boiler owner and over against added defendant on ground of indemnity. ***Burbage v. Boiler Eng. & Supp. Co. Inc. et al.*, 433 Pa. 319, 249 A.2d 563.**

Plaintiff's decedent, a minor of 16 years of age, killed as result of operation of a tractor and cutter by husband defendant—shield covering connecting shaft propelled through air and struck decedent—verdict for defendant—new trial properly granted below—verdict against weight of evidence—explanation of defendant husband contrary to physical facts—doctrine of exclusive control does not apply. ***Getz v. Balliet*, 431 Pa. 441, 246 A.2d 108.**

Plaintiff, a laborer on a demolition project, injured by movement of a crane—verdict for the plaintiff—new trial granted below—evidence sufficient to justify verdict—abuse of discretion—judgment ordered entered on verdict. ***Corbin v. M. Wilson & Son*, 421 Pa. 351, 219 A.2d 687.**

Plaintiff electrician injured by fall from ladder—suit against property owner and contractor—contention that locking device defective—a ladder photographed 52 days after occurrence but not shown to be ladder involved—plaintiff did not see locking device—nonsuit proper. ***Semet v. Andorra Nurseries, Inc.*, 421 Pa. 484, 219 A.2d 357.**

Injury without damage

Industrial development corporation

Westmoreland County Industrial Development Corporation which is alleged to have acted negligently in the sale of real estate is a "local agency" and therefore entitled to immunity under the Political Subdivision Tort Claims act. ***Green Valley Dry Cleaners, Inc. v. Westmoreland County Industrial Development Corporation*, 832 A.2d 1143 (Pa. Cmwlth. 2003).**

Industrial standards

Worker injured in fall from crane brought products liability and negligence action against manufacturer and seller. Held: trial court did not commit error by admitting evidence of industry standards. Evidence of subsequent repair by employer was properly excluded. ***Leaphart v. Whiting Corporation*, 387 Pa. Super. 253, 564 A.2d 165.**

Minor plaintiff injured alighting from trampoline in neighbor's backyard. Defense verdict reversed. Held: error to exclude evidence of industry standard on safe use of both recreational and instructional trampolines. New trial ordered. ***Walheim v. Kirkpatrick*, 305 Pa. Super. 590, 451 A.2d 1033.**

Inherent risks

Amateur softball player brought suit against an amateur softball association for breach of duty for failing to recommend that a helmet be worn during games. The appellate court affirmed the trial court's ruling that under the no duty rule the softball association had no duty to warn of a risk inherent in softball. ***Craig v. Amateur Softball Association of America*, 951 A.2d 372 (Pa. Super. 2008).**

Inherent danger of attending a baseball game is that you may be hit by a foul ball and injured as happened to plaintiff. Sports team had no duty to protect plaintiff from inherent danger of foul ball. ***Pakett v. The Phillies, L.P.*, 871 A.2d 304 (Pa. Cmwlth. 2005).**

Injection

Plaintiff who was disfigured by injections of silicone sued doctor who had violated FDA prohibition against using silicone for such a purpose. Trial court granted a new trial on plaintiff's motion after a verdict in favor of the physician. Breach of FDA prohibition is negligence *per se* and FDA is not prohibited from regulating medical treatment. ***Cabiroy v. Scipione*, 767 A.2d 1078 (Pa. Super. 2001).**

While informed consent is required from a patient in any surgical or operative procedure, it is not required when only nonsurgical procedures are performed. Administration of anesthetics, steroids or other medications by injection does not require informed consent. ***Morgan v. MacPhail*, 704 A.2d 617 (Pa. 1997).**

Injury without damage

Where both plaintiff's and defendant's medical expert opine that the plaintiff suffered some physical injury as a result of an automobile accident, and the jury determines that the defendant's negligence caused the accident, a defense verdict based on the jury's belief that the accident was not a substantial factor in causing

Innkeeper

the injuries is against the weight of the evidence and must be vacated. *Campagna v. Rogan*, 829 A.2d 322 (Pa. Super. 2003).

Where all medical experts testify that the plaintiff passenger suffered injury in an automobile accident caused by defendant, a jury's determination that the defendant's negligence was not a substantial factor in causing plaintiff's injuries is against the weight of the evidence. *Lemmon v. Ernst*, 822 A.2d 768 (Pa. Super. 2003).

Reversal of j.n.o.v. in favor of plaintiff following verdict for defendant where plaintiff alleged injury resulting from automobile accident. Following testimony of plaintiff's expert and no expert testimony from defendant, the trial court held that defense verdict in face of plaintiff's claim of injury was against the weight of the evidence. Held that where plaintiff's and defendant's experts agree that injury followed accident, failure to award damages is not permitted, but where there is no agreement between competing experts as to existence of injury caused by accident, defense verdict may stand, even in the face of injury. *Peterson v. Shreiner*, 822 A.2d 833 (Pa. Super. 2003).

Where medical experts retained by both parties testify that plaintiff was injured in a motor vehicle accident, the jury must find that the plaintiff was injured. Jury may still find that injury was not so severe as to warrant compensation. *Andrews v. Jackson*, 800 A.2d 959 (Pa. Super. 2002).

Innkeeper

Guest, who was sexually assaulted at a fraternity party at a motel, filed suit against the motel, fraternity and attacker. The appellate court held that the motel breached its duty of care, because it knew that a fraternity party was going to be held at its establishment, which could include underage drinking, and did not provide personnel to monitor the premises. *Paliometros v. Loyola*, 923 A.2d 128 (Pa. Super. 2007).

An innkeeper's liability at common law for the safety of the goods of his guests is absolute—negligence need not be established—failure of the innkeeper to comply with the provisions of the Act of June 12, 1913, P.L. 481, as to location of a safe place to deposit possessions—summary judgment entered for plaintiff as to liability but innkeeper entitled to jury trial as to extent of damages. *Buck v. Hankin*, 217 Pa. Super. 262, 269 A.2d 344.

Plaintiff a patron of defendant's club—slight barroom brawl with another patron—evidence did not apprise barkeeper of patron's intention to injure plaintiff—defendant not an insurer—judgment for defendant on record after a "hung" jury. *Bahoric v. St. Lawrence Croatian No. 13*, 426 Pa. 90, 230 A.2d 725.

Inspection

City's duty to inspect privately-owned property to insure compliance with health and safety regulations does not constitute "care, custody and control" or "possession" of real property so as to except City from immunity provided by Political Subdivision Tort Claims Act. Order sustaining preliminary objections reversed. *City of Pittsburgh v. Stahlman,* ___ Pa. Cmwlth. ___, 677 A.2d 384 (1996).

Defendant utility-pole inspection company did not have duty to protect bystander from injuries sustained when bystander came into contact with downed electrical wires while assisting victims of automobile accident which damaged utility pole. Defendant inspection company's alleged negligent inspection of pole was too remote to constitute proximate cause of bystander's injuries. Bystander was not third-party beneficiary of contract between inspection company and utility company, which required inspection company only to inspect and report condition of poles. Order sustaining preliminary objections of defendant inspection company affirmed. *Hicks v. Metropolitan Edison Company,* ___ Pa. Cmwlth. ___, 665 A.2d 529 (1995).

Dairy farm employee who slipped and fell outside milk house sued Milk Cooperative which allegedly had duty to inspect. Held: duty to inspect went only to protection of public with regard to sanitation of milk products. Summary judgment in favor of defendants affirmed. *Johnson v. Baker,* 346 Pa. Super. 183, 499 A.2d 372.

Fire originating in defendants' premises—plaintiff's property damaged—opportunity to inspect—doctrine of exclusive control not applicable. *Githens Rexsamer & Co. Inc., v. Wildstein,* 428 Pa. 201, 236 A.2d 792.

Institutional negligence

A residential care center operated by the Commonwealth's Department of Public Welfare is immune from suit alleging "institutional negligence" for failure to properly screen employee who sexually abused minor residents. Institutional negligence does not fall within the medical-professional liability exception to sovereign immunity. *Dashner v. Hamburg Center of the Department of Public Welfare*, 845 A.2d 935 (Pa. Cmwlth. 2004).

Insurance

Plaintiff brought claim for personal injuries as a result of a rear end collision by the Defendant. Defendant appealed the trial court's ruling that she was collaterally estopped at trial from disputing the amount of damages suffered by the Plaintiff based upon a prior UIM arbitration proceeding as both the Plaintiff and Defendant had the same insurance carrier. The Superior Court reversed the trial court's decision holding that there was no privity at the UIM arbitration proceeding between the Defendant and her insurance carrier as she did not participate in the proceeding. *Catroppa v. Carlton,* 998 A.2d 643 (Pa. Super. 2010).

Administrator sued a night club for wrongful death when one of its bouncers smothered decedent. Defendant night club appealed the trial court's summary judgment ruling that the alleged conduct causing wrongful death was excluded under its insurance policy. The appellate court reversed holding that negligence leading to an intentional act may be held an accident. *QBE Insurance Corp. v. M & S Landis Corp.*, 915 A.2d 1222 (Pa. Super. 2007).

Insurance agent/Broker malpractice

Plaintiffs filed suit to recover uninsured motorist benefits after being injured on a Port Authority bus when it collided with an uninsured motorist. The court held that sovereign immunity did not bar a claim for uninsured motorist benefits against the Port Authority, where the Port Authority had not been found to be negligent. *Lowery v. Port Authority of Allegheny County*, 914 A.2d 953 (Pa. Cmwlth. 2006).

Port Authority appealed a denial of a motion for post-trial relief awarding an injured passenger uninsured motorist benefits where the Port Authority's bus driver was found to be not negligent. The court held that the Port Authority's sovereign immunity did not protect it from paying uninsured motorist benefits when it was found not negligent. The court also held the statutory provision against stacking did not prevent a passenger from recovering underinsured motorist benefits from her automobile insurer. *Paravati v. Port Authority of Allegheny County*, 914 A.2d 946 (Pa. Cmwlth. 2006).

Parents of deceased minor filed suit alleging negligence of babysitter in death based on conviction for first degree murder. Babysitter's homeowners insurance company, in declaratory judgment action, alleged that "intentional killing" element of criminal act eliminated its responsibility to defend of indemnify babysitter for negligence leading to death. Held that proper pleading of negligent acts before and after killing compelled insurer to provide defense, at least. *Erie v. Muff*, 851 A.2d 919 (Pa. Super. 2004).

Home owner brought action against mortgagee for failure to obtain disability insurance. Home owner disabled in accident. Held: contributory negligence of plaintiff bars recovery. Comparative Negligence Act did not apply. *Wescoat v. Northwest Savings Association*, 378 Pa. Super. 295, 548 A.2d 619.

Defendant in personal injury action can join his insurance agent as additional defendant when agent fails to obtain or renew liability coverage and defendant can join insurer as additional defendant when insurer allegedly breaches his own contract. *Stokes v. Loyal Order of Moose Lodge*, 302 Pa. Super. 256, 488 A.2d 624.

Insurance agent/Broker malpractice

An insurance agent or broker has a duty not to misrepresent the coverage procured. Failure to properly provide appropriate insurance may amount to negligent misrepresentation. The failure to comply with applicable statutes and regulations governing the selling of insurance may provide a basis for a finding of negligence *per se*. An insurance broker has an obligation to investigate the financial soundness of an insurance carrier and to refrain from placing insurance with a carrier that the agent/broker knows or should know to be financially unsound. *Al's Café v. Sanders Insurance Agency*, 820 A.2d 745 (Pa. Super. 2003).

Intentional acts

Plaintiff was head of security at defendant hospital and was attacked by an employee who had been brought to supervisor's office for submission to urinalysis. Plaintiff alleged that tortfeasor was acting in his capacity as employee of the hospital and therefore hospital was liable under doctrine of *respondeat superior*. Defendant's motion for summary judgment sustained and affirmed on appeal. Tortfeasor's

Intentional infliction of emotional distress

intentional act of injuring plaintiff was in no way related to his job description as laundry worker and there was no evidence from plaintiff of any expectation on the part of the defendant employer that the tortfeasor would act violently. **Costa v. Roxborough Memorial Hospital, 708 A.2d 490 (Pa. Super. 1998).**

Doctrine of governmental immunity provides that liability may be imposed on a local agency only for negligent acts. Acts or conduct that constitute a crime, actual fraud, actual malice, or wilful misconduct do not subject a local agency to liability. Failure to disclose to adoptive parents information in CYS files that biological parents of adoptive child both suffered from mental illness, alcoholism, and drug abuse does not overcome governmental immunity of CYS. **Zernhelt v. Lehigh County Office of CYS, ___ Pa. Cmwlth. ___, 659 A.2d 89 (1995).**

Intentional infliction of emotional distress

Plaintiff brought a claim of intentional infliction of emotional distress against Defendant hospital after it transferred his deceased father's body to the co-Defendant medical school where post-mortem operations were performed on the body without his consent. The trial court dismissed the case based upon preliminary objections. The Superior Court affirmed the dismissal of the intentional infliction of emotional distress claim on the basis that the Plaintiff was not present at the time the post-mortem operations that caused him distress occurred. **Weiley v. Albert Einstein Medical Center, 2012 Pa. Super. 106 (Pa. Super. 2012).**

Mother, who gave birth to a son with physical deformities, brought claims of negligent infliction of emotional distress and intentional infliction of emotional distress against a radiologist who reported that the results of her ultrasound were normal and revealed no fetal abnormalities. The trial court dismissed all the Defendants on preliminary objections. The Superior Court affirmed in part and reversed in part holding that the Plaintiff had sufficiently pled a prima facie case for negligent infliction of emotional distress, but she had failed to set forth outrageous conduct sufficient for a claim for intentional infliction of emotional distress. Toney v. Chester County Hospital, 961 A.2d 192 (Pa. Super. 2008). Because mother of minor who died during surgical procedure performed by doctor to whom she had not given informed consent was not present at time of procedure, she could not recover for intentional infliction of emotional distress. §46 of Restatement (2d) Torts requires that person who is claiming emotional distress plead presence at time of incident causing distress. **Taylor v. Albert Einstein Medical Center, 754 A.2d 650 (Pa. 2000).**

Patient's unsubstantiated assertion of physical injury failed to establish negligent or intentional infliction of emotional distress. Doctor and medical center were immune from suit under Child Protective Services Law for disclosing plaintiff's admission that she had suffocated her child. Child Protective Services Law, which grants immunity for disclosures does not conflict with psychotherapist–patient privilege or the confidentiality provisions of the Mental Health Procedures Act. **Fewell v. Bresner, 444 Pa. Super. 559, 664 A.2d 577 (1995).**

Sovereign immunity barred claim for intentional infliction of emotional distress in mother's case against state police for mishandling of daughter's remains. Pennsylvania law does not recognize an action for negligent mishandling of the

Intersection accidents: Between intersections

dead. Mother's failure to allege that she witnessed any traumatic event involving her daughter's remains precluded claim for negligent infliction of emotional distress. Order sustaining defendants' preliminary objections affirmed. ***Ray v. Pennsylvania State Police,* ___ Pa. Cmwlth. ___, 654 A.2d 140 (1995).**

Plaintiff taken to hospital with inability to walk. Emergency physician found nothing and left him on floor for one and one-half to two hours. Verdict $14,000 compensatory for intentional infliction of emotional distress. Held: charge on "intentional" as defined in §46 of Restatement (2d) Torts held inadequate; failure to charge on punitive damages, under facts here, improper. ***Hoffman v. Memorial Osteopathic Hospital,* 342 Pa. Super. 375, 492 A.2d 1382.**

Intersection accidents: Between intersections

Plaintiff brought a claim against defendant after the defendant inched forward into the intersection to see around illegally parked cars and was subsequently struck by the plaintiff, who had the right of way. The appellate court remanded the case back to the trial court after the jury found the defendant driver negligent, but then also found that the defendant driver was not a factual cause in bringing about the plaintiff driver's injuries. The court held that the jury's verdict was against the weight of the evidence. ***Bostanic v. Barker-Barto*, 936 A.2d 1084 (Pa. Super. 2007).**

Plaintiff—pedestrian crossing in middle of street. Defendant testified that plaintiff ran across street. Jury found both parties negligent. Plaintiff testified that she was hurrying, but not running. Verdict for defendant affirmed. ***Rosato v. Nationwide*, 263 Pa. Super. 340, 397 A.2d 1238.**

Plaintiff crossed street in downtown Pittsburgh, mid-day, in front of stopped truck, in middle of block immediately after another pedestrian crossed in same path. Defendant truck started forward and struck plaintiff. Plaintiff not contributorily negligent as matter of law. For jury as to whether driver maintained proper vigilance. Granting of nonsuit reversed. New trial ordered. ***Lavely v. Wolota*, 253 Pa. Super. 196, 384 A.2d 1298.**

Pedestrian struck at night by defendant's vehicle—plaintiff carrying flashlight and had crossed part of 48 foot wide highway—for jury if plaintiff on highway long enough so that defendant as careful driver should have seen him and avoided impact. ***Berry v. Lintner*, 226 Pa. Super. 562, 323 A.2d 253.**

Plaintiff and his deceased wife obviously walking across street between intersections—struck by defendant's car—error for trial court to refuse a point based on section 101 and section 1013(c) of Vehicle Code as to rights of vehicles and pedestrians between intersections—new trial granted. ***Gaev et al., v. Mandell*, 219 Pa. Super. 397, 281 A.2d 699.**

Defendant attempted to turn truck in highway with view blocked—evidence that decedent was thrown 63 feet through the air—jury could infer excessive speed from such testimony—nonsuit improperly entered—case for jury. ***McNett v. Briggs*, 217 Pa. Super. 322, 272 A.2d 202.**

Intersection accidents: Location of parties

Intersection accidents: Location of parties

Motorcycle and auto intersection accident. Auto making left turn. Passenger testified that she said at scene that accident was the fault of driver of motorcycle. Had there been objection, might not have been admissible. Verdict against driver of motorcycle only. Evidence of high speed and no headlights at night. ***Carl v. Kurtz,* 255 Pa. Super. 198, 386 A.2d 577.**

Collision of auto and motorcycle. Unclear whether cycle turned right to avoid collision or auto turned onto street and cycle was on wrong side of highway. In either event, erroneous to charge on doctrine of assured clear distance. New trial ordered. ***Unangst v. Whitehouse,* 235 Pa. Super. 458, 344 A.2d 695.**

Plaintiff stopped at intersection. View blocked by parked truck of defendant Johanna Farms. Edged out and saw defendant Cohen 150-175 feet away travelling at 40 m.p.h. Plaintiff stopped but Cohen continued and struck plaintiff's car on right side three seconds later. Verdict against both defendants affirmed. ***Bell v. Cohen,* 228 Pa. Super. 872, 322 A.2d 704.**

Defendant entering a through highway from a private road—colliding with plaintiff's car, allegedly being driven on main highway without lights at night—trial court on facts properly submitted plaintiff's possible contributory negligence to jury—verdict for defendant sustained. ***Kern v. Arnold,* 218 Pa. Super. 143, 279 A.2d 229.**

Defendant on through highway and plaintiff on stop street—plaintiff testified that he came to a stop about 8 to 10 feet from sign situated some 30 feet from intersecting highway—made observation to his left and observed no approaching vehicles—proceeding and struck by defendant's car approaching on through highway—view of plaintiff partly obstructed by fog and buildings—did not stop again before entering highway—did not observe defendant's car until almost point of contact—verdict for defendant—motions dismissed—affirmed on appeal. ***Martin v. Mihalko,* 439 Pa. 612, 266 A.2d 269.**

Plaintiff on stop street—starting across a four lane through highway with his vision obscured by approaching cars—failing to continue to look—struck by defendant's car which passed observed vehicles—guilty of contributory negligence—judgment *n.o.v.* on appeal. ***Helfrich v. Brown,* 213 Pa. Super. 463, 249 A.2d 778.**

Plaintiff on stop street—stopping at curb and observing no vehicles in intersecting street—while in center saw defendant's car 200 feet distant—struck when rear of car within 5 feet of opposite curb line—for jury—plaintiff not guilty of contributory negligence as a matter of law in proceeding. ***Wynkoop v. McLendon,* 208 Pa. Super. 81, 220 A.2d 904.**

Plaintiff on through highway—embankment prevented a view of vehicles on stop street—observant—first observing defendant in middle of intersection when plaintiff 10 to 15 feet from intersection—collision—matter still for the jury. ***Rhode v. Kearney,* 208 Pa. Super. 8, 220 A.2d 378.**

Intersection accidents: Miscellaneous

Plaintiff party to left—collision in intersection of two cars—plaintiff observing defendant's car approaching and slowing down—then suddenly accelerating and defendant's driver took hands off steering wheel and covered his face with hands—case for jury under facts of case. ***McCaffrey v. Philadelphia,* 421 Pa. 357, 219 A.2d 680.**

Intersection accidents: Miscellaneous

Plaintiffs injured in motor vehicle accident at dangerous intersection filed suit against municipality which had responsibility for entire intersection. Plaintiffs' expert testimony about condition of intersection, appropriate remedy for dangerous condition and ability to erect control devices was adequate to preclude summary judgment for municipality. ***Wenger v. West Pennsboro Township*, 868 A.2d 638 (Pa. Cmwlth. 2005).**

Plaintiff was injured in a motor vehicle accident at a notoriously dangerous "five points" intersection. Plaintiff was traveling from a state highway across another state highway towards, but not yet on, a township road when he was hit. Held that the fact that a township road is part of the intersection in which a party injured as a result of an automobile accident does not require that the township be held in the case. Township properly dismissed from suit. ***Griffith v. Snader*, 795 A.2d 502 (Pa. Cmwlth. 2002).**

PennDOT had never been requested to approve a sign by township despite repeated township inquiries concerning available ways to make the intersection safer. Commonwealth Court affirmed denial of township's post trial motion on basis of township's affirmative duty to make its roads safe for intended users pursuant to *McCalla v. Mura*, 538 Pa. 527, 649 A.2d 646 (1994) and *Bendas v. Township of White Deer*, 531 Pa. 180, 611 A.2d 1184 (1992). Trial court order denying plaintiff's post trial motion to allow increase in delay damages affirmed when plaintiff's consent to stay of delay damage period, and plaintiff's own delay, were factors which increased delay. ***Starr v. Veneziano*, 705 A.2d 950 (Pa. Cmwlth. 1998).**

Driver injured in intersection accident brought action against Commonwealth for failure to properly maintain and inspect intersection and for negligent design. Partial summary judgment granted for failure to maintain and inspect. Held: order not appealable. ***Stemper v. Com., Dept. of Transp.*, 159 Pa. Cmwlth. 31, 632 A.2d 971.**

Driver injured in collision at intersection brought action against township for failure to remove obstructions from private property. Township not liable. ***Voren v. Bell Telephone Company of Pennsylvania*, 150 Pa. Cmwlth. 507, 616 A.2d 66.**

Motorist injured in accident at intersection brought action against township and PennDOT for allowing a dangerous condition to exist. Township not liable. Motorist 51% negligent and Commonwealth 49% negligent. ***Wright v. Com., Dept. of Transp.*, 142 Pa. Cmwlth. 91, 596 A.2d 1241.**

Motorist injured in collision at intersection of public and private roadways brought action against owner of private road for failure to clear foliage on adjacent

Intersection accidents: Traffic control device present

property. Owner not liable. No duty to clear foliage on property owned by another. ***Okkerse v. Howe,* 405 Pa. Super. 608, 593 A.2d 431.**

Motorcyclist injured in collision at intersection brought action against Commonwealth, township, and road master for failure to replace stop sign and to remove vegetation from roadside. Summary judgment for defendants affirmed. ***Bruce v. Com., Dept. of Transp.,* 138 Pa. Cmwlth. 352, 588 A.2d 974.**

Motorcyclist injured when struck by automobile making left turn at intersection. Automobile entered intersection after being signaled to proceed by driver of oncoming automobile. Whether driver who gave signal is negligent is question for trier of fact. Driver found not liable. ***Askew by Askew v. Zeller,* 361 Pa. Super. 34, 521 A.2d 459.**

Multi-vehicle fatal accident at allegedly dangerous intersection on state highway. At trial, evidence of dangerous condition was excluded in nature of letters of complaint, evidence of previous accidents, surveys and the like. Trial judge directed verdict for PennDOT, reversed. Where dangerous condition has developed and individuals injured as a result, PennDOT cannot plead its discretion as absolute defense against liability. ***Wyke v. Ward,* 81 Pa. Cmwlth. 392, 474 A.2d 375.**

Two vehicles collided at intersection. Plaintiff sued abutting property owner among others for maintaining shrub and trees which obstructed view. Lower court granted summary judgment in favor of property owner. Reversed. Issues of superceding cause, comparative negligence and violations of statutes, for jury. ***Harvey v. Hansen,* 299 Pa. Super. 474, 445 A.2d 1228.**

Section 1014 (c) and 1016 (a) of the Motor Vehicle Code construed to require motorist on a stop street to yield right of way to vehicles on through highway—failing to look to observe approaching vehicles—guilty of contributory negligence as a matter of law. ***Helfrich v. Brown,* 213 Pa. Super. 463, 249 A.2d 778.**

Intersection accidents: Traffic control device present

Drivers injured in intersection accident each claimed they had green light. Held: jury instruction on assured clear distance rule in error. ***Cannon v. Tabor,* 434 Pa. Super. 232, 642 A.2d 1108.**

Motorist injured in collision at intersection. Defendant went through red light at high rate of speed. Plaintiff did not look to left. Defendant found 75% negligent, plaintiff 25% negligent. ***Cooper v. Burns,* 376 Pa. Super. 276, 545 A.2d 935.**

Intersection collision. Question of who had green light. Jury found defendant's negligence not to be substantial factor in bringing about plaintiff's injuries, but found him to be 10% at fault. Proper to mold defense verdict. Award of new trial by lower court reversed. Intent of jury clear. ***Goertel v. Muth,* 331 Pa. Super. 179, 480 A.2d 303.**

Accident at intersection where admittedly, overhead traffic signal turned green in two directions at once. Correspondence between City of Scranton and

Intersection accidents: Traffic control device present

PennDOT was admissible concerning maintenance of signals at this intersection. ***Whitman v. Riddell*, 324 Pa. Super. 177, 471 A.2d 521.**

Jury verdict against driver with red light in favor of passengers. Right angle collision. Jury found car with green light not negligent, even though driver did not look for traffic just before entering intersection. Affirmed. ***Spraggins v. Shields*, 310 Pa. Super. 408, 456 A.2d 1000.**

Plaintiff going through blinking yellow when defendant came from left, through stop sign and blinking red, striking rear of plaintiff's vehicle. Plaintiff's verdict affirmed. Judge charged *sua sponte* on wanton and reckless misconduct. ***Perigo v. Deegan*, 288 Pa. Super. 93, 431 A.2d 303.**

Intersection accident—auto and ambulance. Ambulance had red light, but had siren and lights on. Fire company counterclaimed for property damage and won. Reversed. True that plaintiff must prove recklessness to recover but reverse is not true. Negligence under the circumstances the test on counterclaim. ***Junk v. East End Fire Department*, 262 Pa. Super. 473, 396 A.2d 1269.**

Intersection collision with off-duty fire truck. Plaintiff had green light. Plaintiff admitted that after looking for traffic once, he never looked again. Nonsuit reversed. For jury whether plaintiff should have looked again under the circumstances. ***Imes v. Empire Hook & Ladder*, 247 Pa. Super. 470, 372 A.2d 922.**

Plaintiff decedent passenger in vehicle which had blinking red and truck which struck auto had blinking yellow. Whether actions of truck driver were negligent in how and when he looked for traffic was for jury. Verdict only against driver of auto affirmed. ***Bascelli v. Bucci*, 244 Pa. Super. 355, 368 A.2d 754.**

Stop sign for defendant. Conflict as to which vehicle was the striking vehicle. Plaintiff testified that he looked before entering intersection and saw defendant, but did not look again. For jury. ***Jurich v. United Parcel*, 239 Pa. Super. 306, 361 A.2d 650.**

Plaintiff passenger in defendant's car involved in accident with second car whose driver was not a party. Defendant had flashing yellow light. Other car went through flashing red light. Sole issue was negligence of defendant who testified that he did not see other car until it was 15 feet from him. Trial judge charged that defendant did not exercise proper care in proceeding on yellow flasher. Grant of new trial after defense verdict affirmed. ***Hayter v. Sileo*, 230 Pa. Super. 329, 326 A.2d 462.**

Minor plaintiff, passenger in car driven by Mrs. Troup who was killed in collision with defendant's truck. Car had stop sign and truck on through street. Minor testified that Mrs. Troup stopped; that minor plaintiff looked to left and saw defendant's truck 40-50 feet away as Mrs. Troup entered intersection and that a few seconds later there was impact. Wheels of truck went over top of car. On this testimony there was evidence of negligence on part of truck driver, especially with evidence of severity of impact. Nonsuit removed. New trial ordered. ***Kauffman v. Carlisle Cement Products Co., Inc.*, 227 Pa. Super. 320, 323 A.2d 754.**

Intervening negligence or cause

Plaintiff on road making a "T" intersection with another highway—proceeding with green light to make a right turn—struck by defendant proceeding on highway to which plaintiff was entering—court below in error in entering judgment *n.o.v.* for defendant—plaintiff did make an observation and could rely on light, although not blindly. ***Fowler v. Smith,* 217 Pa. Super. 244, 269 A.2d 340.**

Plaintiff to right had his view blocked by a truck turning right—had green light in his favor—struck by car from left when he had traversed more than half of the intersection—evidence such that it could not be ruled as a matter of law that he did not look and relied solely on the light—nonsuit improperly granted—case for jury. ***Robinson v. Raab,* 216 Pa. Super. 397, 268 A.2d 225.**

Wife plaintiff stopped for red light near intersection and when light changed made an observation at a point where a view could be had—observing defendant's car to left at 2 feet from intersection—applied brakes and struck when about 2 feet in intersection—court below properly held that her possible contributory negligence was for jury—court below held case properly distinguished from *Smith v. United News Co.*, 413 Pa. 243, where operator made no observation. ***DeBellis v. Malley,* 218 Pa. Super. 720, 266 A.2d 548.**

Plaintiff to right stopped for red light at intersection—when light changed looked in both directions and saw nothing approaching—then proceeded and did not see defendant's car until about point of contact—defendant's car proceeding against a red light—Held: plaintiff was entering an unoccupied intersection and was not apprised that defendant would disregard light—verdict for plaintiff—motions refused below and action affirmed on appeal. ***Fouser v. Cantola,* 438 Pa. 549, 264 A.2d 169.**

Collision in intersection between tractor trailer and a sedan automobile—operator of sedan automobile maintained that he had a green light and made proper observation before entering intersection—operator probably did not make any further observation—case still for jury—drivers at controlled intersections not held to as high degree of care as where intersection is not controlled. ***Ridley v. Boyer et al.,* 426 Pa. 28, 231 A.2d 307.**

Plaintiff proceeding at an intersection with traffic light in his favor—defendant's truck 80 feet to his left when plaintiff 15 feet from intersection—proceeding—collision—plaintiff's possible contributory negligence was for the jury. ***Andrews v. Long,* 425 Pa. 152, 228 A.2d 760.**

Plaintiffs were proceeding on a through highway—plaintiffs' evidence that defendant disregarded a stop sign and collided with their car in intersection—defendant's version substantially different—verdict for defendants—new trial granted below in the interests of justice—action affirmed on appeal. ***Wylie v. Powaski,* 422 Pa. 285, 220 A.2d 842.**

Intervening negligence or cause

Plaintiff was injured and his wife was killed when their car was struck by a vehicle fleeing a police vehicle that was operating its emergency lights but no siren.

Intervening negligence or cause

The trial court granted summary judgment to the pursuing officer, his superiors and city under the Political Subdivision Tort Claims Act pursuant to *Dickens v. Horner,* 531 Pa. 127, 611 A.2d 693 (1992). Supreme Court affirmed Commonwealth Court reversal of trial court and overruling of *Dickens, supra,* holding that it is a question for the jury to decide whether the police officer/supervisors/city's negligence was a substantial factor causing plaintiffs' harm and whether the fleeing driver's actions were a superseding cause precluding governmental liability. ***Jones v. Chieffo,* 700 A.2d 417 (Pa. 1997).**

A minor/owner who provides an air powered pellet gun to another minor may be liable to minor plaintiff injured by a pellet for providing the gun without instruction. The reasonably anticipated negligent firing of the pellet gun by other minor is not a superseding, intervening cause that insulates minor/owner from liability. Order sustaining preliminary objections reversed. ***Frey v. Smith,* 454 Pa. Super. 242, 685 A.2d 169 (1996).**

Municipal defendants are neither afforded blanket immunity nor entitled to judgment as a matter of law in each and every tort claim where the victim's injuries were caused in part by the intervening criminal conduct of third parties or where the criminal acts of a third party merely form a link in the chain of causation. It is for the jury to determine whether municipal defendants' conduct was a substantial contributing factor in causing the victim's injuries and, if so, whether intervening criminal conduct of third parties was so extraordinary as not to be reasonably foreseeable by the municipal defendants. Summary judgment reversed. ***Jones v. Chieffo,* ___ Pa. Super. ___, 664 A.2d 1091 (1995).**

In action arising out of explosion of boiler caused by defective emergency shut-off valve, manufacturer of valve held strictly liable for defective product. Manufacturer's liability for its defective product is outlined in Section 402A of Restatement (2d) Torts, which provides that a plaintiff must prove that the product was sold in a defective condition dangerous to the user and that the defect was the proximate cause of the injury. An actor is relieved from liability due to an intervening or superseding cause only if the intervening or superseding negligent acts were so extraordinary as not to have been reasonably foreseeable. Summary judgment affirmed in part and reversed in part. ***Dougherty v. Edward J. Meloney, Inc.,* 443 Pa. Super. 201, 661 A.2d 375 (1995).**

The determination of whether an individual is a trespasser, licensee or invitee is for the jury. A licensee may become an invitee, thereby increasing duty of care owed by landowner. Plaintiff may recover damages where two or more substantial causes combine to cause an injury, even if no one cause standing alone would have brought about the injury. Although action of third party in pushing plaintiff off a guide wall was an intervening cause, its occurrence was not so extraordinary or unforeseeable as to make it a superseding cause, which would excuse property owner for negligent maintenance of wall, which condition substantially contributed to plaintiff's injuries. ***Trude v. Martin,* 442 Pa. Super. 614, 660 A.2d 626 (1995).**

Intoxication

Action brought against vehicle drivers and state police arising out of chain reaction collision. Summary judgment based on intervening superseding cause precluded. ***Taylor v. Jackson,*** **164 Pa. Cmwlth. 482, 643 A.2d 771.**

Crossing guard leading children across street. Saw car skidding on ice and ordered children back to curb. Plaintiff, 11 year old boy, ran wrong way. Whether plaintiff's intervening act of running was a superseding cause was for jury. Verdict against driver, guard, and city (employer) affirmed. ***Ross v. Vereb,*** **481 Pa. 446, 392 A.2d 1376.**

Suit versus owner of tavern where decedent had been drinking. Later in evening at friend's home, decedent fell down steps, hit head and died. For jury despite defense of intervening cause. $60,000 verdict affirmed. ***Connelly v. Ziegler,*** **251 Pa. Super. 521, 380 A.2d 902.**

Plaintiff-patron at car wash injured in vacuum area when struck by car exiting from wash area. For jury on intervening cause—failure of auto's brakes vis-a-vis location of vacuum area and lengthy period of no accidents prior to this incident. ***Amabile v. Auto Kleen,*** **249 Pa. Super. 240, 376 A.2d 247.**

Wire of telephone company pulled down by passing truck and blocked street. Plaintiff was attempting to clear wire from street. Defendant taxi, although asked to stop by plaintiff, did not stop and caught wire which then tangled in plaintiff's feet causing him to fall and be injured. Negligence of telephone company based on previous occasion of trucks hitting wire. Superior Court affirmed judgment *n.o.v.* in favor of phone company. Supreme Court reversed and reinstated verdict against all defendants. Properly submitted to jury. ***Miller v. Checker Yellow Cab, et al.,*** **465 Pa. 82, 348 A.2d 128.**

Plaintiff veered to right to allow vehicle passing in opposite direction on curve to clear. Struck unmarked, unlit utility pole. Night. Intervening act—for jury as to liability of utility company. ***Scheel v.Tremblay and Phila. Elec. Co.,*** **226 Pa. Super. 45, 312 A.2d 45.**

Plaintiff's property damaged by reason of alleged defective condition of adjacent property of defendant—third party excavating in vicinity—cannot be said that act of third party was an intervening cause—nonsuit improperly entered. ***Bleman v. Gold,*** **431 Pa. 348, 246 A.2d 376.**

Intoxication

Plaintiff's estate brought lawsuit against the Defendant casino after casino's valet failed to prevent the intoxicated decedent from driving and he was later killed in a car accident. The trial court granted summary judgment to the casino. The Superior Court affirmed holding that a casino valet has no affirmative duty to refuse to return car keys to a drunk driver. ***Moranko v. Downs Racing L.P.,*** **2014 Pa. Super. 128 (Pa. Super. 2014).**

Plaintiffs filed negligence lawsuit against Decedent's estate for injuries suffered in a head on collision where the decedent crossed over into oncoming traffic. The jury found in favor of plaintiffs after a trial on damages only. The Superior

Intoxication

Court affirmed holding that it was harmless error to permit the introduction of evidence of the decedent's intoxication of cocaine and alcohol prior to the accident despite the fact that the decedent had conceded liability. ***Knowles v. Levan*, 15 A.3d 504 (Pa. Super. 2011).**

Guardian of ironworker injured on a construction project filed negligence claim after falling from a beam. The trial court entered judgment in favor of the building owner. The Superior Court affirmed holding that evidence of the Plaintiff's intoxication was relevant in a suit for negligence. ***Braun v. Target Corporation*, 983 A.2d 752 (Pa. Super. 2009).**

Plaintiff appealed a ruling allowing the introduction of evidence of his alcohol consumption and blood alcohol content in a case involving a contributory negligence defense by the City. An admission by the plaintiff of consumption of alcohol, testimony by an officer that plaintiff's breath smelled of alcohol, and testimony plaintiff's speech was impaired were sufficient independent evidence at trial of intoxication to admit plaintiff's blood alcohol content and alcohol consumption. ***Lock v. City of Philadelphia*, 895 A.2d 660 (Pa. Cmwlth. 2006).**

Plaintiff's acceptance of the inherent risks of skiing does not include acceptance of the risk that he would be hit from behind by a fellow sportsman using the resort's facilities while under the influence of alcohol. ***Crews v. Seven Springs Mountain Resort*, 874 A.2d 100 (Pa. Super. 2005).**

Verdict entered against plaintiff injured when struck by train while walking on tracks affirmed despite plaintiff's appeal that trial court should not have allowed into evidence any testimony about "suspected" cocaine use without a medical determination of intoxication. Held: while mere evidence of use of a controlled substance is inadmissible to prove recklessness or carelessness, intoxication and physical impairment may be established by circumstantial evidence. ***Chicchi v. SEPTA*, 727 A.2d 604 (Pa. Cmwlth. 1999).**

Plaintiff and her decedents were passengers in a car driven by additional defendant who crossed over center line of PennDOT road, crashed through guardrail and struck tree. Plaintiff alleged that brakes and engine had failed, that additional defendant driver was intoxicated and that PennDOT had failed to provide safe roadway because of inability of guardrail to prevent car from striking tree. Following grant of summary judgment in favor of PennDOT, plaintiff appealed. Held: PennDOT could not have adequate notice of combination of events leading to accident—loss of brakes and driver's intoxication—and therefore PennDOT had no duty to plaintiff and her decedents. ***Baer v. Com., Dept. of Transp.*, 713 A.2d 189 (Pa. Cmwlth. 1998).**

Plaintiff filed suit against multiple defendants, including volunteer fire company for injuries sustained after sale of alcohol to defendant. After review of legal and factual basis of fire company's status as local agency entitled to protection of Political Subdivision Tort Claims Act, court determined that illegal sale of alcohol on fire company property does not constitute "care, custody or control" standard related in *Grieff v. Reisinger*, 548 Pa. 13, 693 A.2d 195 (1997) and so immunity available and grant of summary judgment in favor of volunteer fire company affirmed. ***Eger v. Lynch,*** **714 A.2d 1149 (Pa. Cmwlth. 1998).**

Plaintiffs who were personal representatives of decedent filed suit against bar for Dram Shop Act violations which led to the death of patron. Summary judgment granted to defendant due to lack of direct eyewitness evidence that decedent was served alcoholic beverages when visibly intoxicated. Held: circumstantial evidence indicating that decedent must have been visibly intoxicated when served is adequate to create question of fact for jury and so defeat summary judgment. In instant case, patrons testified decedent was visibly intoxicated when he left bar. Police testified plaintiff was still intoxicated at least 4 hours after he left bar. Medical evidence showed that decedent's blood alcohol content was twice legal limit at least 6 hours after he left bar. Scientific evidence showed that decedent must have consumed nearly fourteen twelve ounce beers to achieve blood alcohol content he had. ***Fandozzi v. Kelly Hotel, Inc.*,** **711 A.2d 524 (Pa. Super. 1998)**

Plaintiff pedestrian appeals verdict for defendant in negligence action where trial court admitted evidence of plaintiff's history of drug and alcohol abuse and his legal intoxication at time of accident which caused his injuries. Plaintiff argues that such evidence is prejudicial and irrelevant to his claim for damages and should have been excluded. Held: allowing plaintiff to pursue a claim for permanent injury, while simultaneously barring defendant from access to plaintiff's long history of drug and alcohol abuse, "would be manifestly unfair and grossly prejudicial." Further holding that evidence of plaintiff's intoxication "as a pedestrian" was relevant and admissible if evidence would prove unfitness to cross street. ***Kraus v. Taylor,*** **710 A.2d 1142 (Pa. Super. 1998).**

Plaintiff was injured during operation of motorcycle and alleged in straight product liability case that defective brake caliper binder bolt was cause of accident. Defendant introduced evidence that plaintiff was intoxicated at the time of accident and that binder bolt broke as a result of the accident and argued that that intoxication was the sole cause of the accident. Superior Court affirmed trial court's admission of evidence, holding that when defendant in product liability suit offers evidence to establish that injuries were caused solely by negligence of plaintiff without any involvement of defect alleged by plaintiff, such evidence is admissible. ***Madonna v. Harley Davidson, Inc.*, 708 A.2d 507 (Pa. Super. 1998).**

Defense of decedent's contributory negligence is not eliminated from consideration merely because of negligence *per se* of tavern that served decedent while he was visibly intoxicated. Remand for new trial to determine plaintiffs' decedent's comparative negligence in driving while intoxicated after having been served while visibly intoxicated. Decedent could not have legally assumed risk of driving while intoxicated following determination of tavern's negligence in serving visibly intoxicated decedent. ***Miller v. Brass Rail Tavern, Inc.*, 702 A.2d 1072 (Pa. Super. 1997).**

A common carrier has the highest duty of care to its passengers to carry them safely and enable them to alight safely at their intended destination. Bus company does not have a duty to intoxicated passengers who have disembarked from bus at their intended destination to insure that they travel safely after discharge. Trial

Intoxication

court's refusal to grant summary judgment to bus company reversed and remanded. ***Knoud v. Galante*, 696 A.2d 854 (Pa. Super. 1997).**

Pedestrian plaintiff injured by drunken driver sued passengers who may have been aware of driver's intoxication. Summary judgment in favor of defendants affirmed because a passenger does not owe a duty to a third person where driver of vehicle is intoxicated, absent a special relationship, joint enterprise, joint venture or a right to control the vehicle. ***Brandjord v. Hopper*, 455 Pa. Super. 426, 688 A.2d 721 (1997).**

In suit by decedent's estate against minor passenger in other vehicle, an individual who is simply a passenger in a vehicle operated by an intoxicated driver may not be held responsible for the driver's negligence. Rather, liability may only be imposed where sufficient facts indicate that the passenger substantially assisted or encouraged the driver's negligent conduct. Order granting summary judgment in favor of minor passenger affirmed. ***Welc v. Porter*, 450 Pa. Super. 112, 675 A.2d 334 (1996).**

Where recklessness or carelessness is at issue, proof of intoxication is relevant; however, evidence that plaintiff consumed alcohol is inadmissible unless it reasonably establishes intoxication. Order granting new trial inclusive of evidence of intoxication and denying judgment *n.o.v.* affirmed. ***Surowiec v. General Motors Corp.*, 448 Pa. Super. 510, 672 A.2d 333 (1996).**

Plaintiff's decedent was killed in automobile accident following employer-sponsored Christmas party. Where no factual determination as to whether injury was work-related, action against employer not barred by workers' compensation exclusivity provision. Order granting summary judgment in favor of employer reversed. ***Vetter v. Fun Footwear Co.*, 447 Pa. Super. 84, 668 A.2d 529 (1995).**

Absent proof that a patron was visibly intoxicated when served additional alcoholic beverages, no action for wrongful death or survival is established. Statutory violation of serving alcohol after hours does not establish liability for acts of third parties absent proof that such service was proximate cause of the injury. ***Hiles v. Brandywine Club*, 443 Pa. Super. 462, 662 A.2d 16 (1995).**

In action by passenger against PennDOT for negligent design of road, judgment for PennDOT affirmed where plaintiff passenger determined to be negligent by exposing herself to an unreasonable risk in riding with a known intoxicated driver. Even minimal evidence of contributory negligence requires a charge on the issue. ***Karchner v. Flaim*, 661 A.2d 928 (Pa. Cmwlth. 1995).**

Pennsylvania Dram Shop Act does not insulate employees of licensee from liability for negligence in serving alcohol to visibly intoxicated patron. Order sustaining demurrer vacated. ***Detwiler v. Brumbaugh*, 441 Pa. Super. 110, 656 A.2d 944 (1995).**

Police officer who enters upon another's land in his official capacity and in response to a call for assistance is a licensee. Landowner's duty is to inform licensee of dangerous, hidden conditions. Obviously rowdy crowd of patrons at social hall was not a dangerous, hidden condition. Although violation of Dram Shop Act is

Intoxication

negligence *per se*, mere fact that patrons who assaulted police officer were intoxicated neither proves that they had been served when visibly intoxicated nor causation of officer's injuries. Summary judgment for defendant affirmed. ***Holpp v. Fez, Inc.*, 440 Pa. Super. 512, 656 A.2d 147 (1995).**

In automobile accident case by decedent's administrator against intoxicated driver and PennDOT, whether PennDOT's alleged negligence for improper road design and maintenance was substantial factor in accident was question for jury. Existence of two tortfeasors does not automatically excuse one or the other from liability. Question of concurrent or joint causation and determination of whether an act is so extraordinary as to constitute a superseding cause are for the jury. Order sustaining preliminary objections of PennDOT reversed. ***Powell v. Drumheller,* 539 Pa. 484, 653 A.2d 619 (1995).**

Suit for violation of Dram Shop Act requires proof that person was visibly intoxicated when served additional alcoholic beverages. ***Conner v. Duffy,* 438 Pa. Super. 277, 652 A.2d 372 (1994).**

New trial granted on issue of damages only following grossly inadequate award of $25,000.00 for death of 18 year old passenger in car driven by drunk driver. ***Kiser v. Schulte,* 538 Pa. 219, 648 A.2d 1 (1994).**

Summary judgment in favor of social host affirmed where no evidence that host had actual notice that minor's were consuming alcohol. Summary judgment in favor of telephone company affirmed because causal connection between location of pole and accident too remote in law to impose liability. ***Novak v. Kilby,* 167 Pa. Cmwlth. 217, 647 A.2d 687 (1994).**

Minor injured after being served alcohol by other minor. Minor not liable as social host. ***Kapres v. Heller,* 536 Pa. 551, 640 A.2d 888 (1994).**

Guest murdered by intoxicated minor while parents away. Parents not liable. ***Maxwell v. Keas,* 433 Pa. Super. 70, 639 A.2d 1215 (1994).**

Minor served alcohol at graduation parties injured in fall. Host not liable. ***Orner v. Mallick,* 432 Pa. Super. 580, 639 A.2d 491 (1994).**

Intoxicated minor shot by police after threatening parents brought action against sellers of alcoholic beverages. Sellers not liable. ***Reilly v. Tiergarten, Inc.,* 430 Pa. Super. 10, 633 A.2d 208 (1993).**

Teenager found liable for providing alcoholic beverages to other minor involved in automobile accident. ***Sperando v. Com., Dept. of Transp.,* 157 Pa. Cmwlth. 531, 630 A.2d 532.**

Motorists injured in accident caused by intoxicated driver brought action against minors who served him alcohol. Minors liable. ***Muntz v. Com., Dept. of Transp.,* 157 Pa. Cmwlth. 514, 630 A.2d 524.**

Bicyclist brought action against motorist for injuries resulting from collision. Evidence of bicyclist's intoxication found not admissible. ***Locke v. Claypool,* 426 Pa. Super. 528, 627 A.2d 801.**

Intoxication

Driver killed in collision with vehicle driven by intoxicated operator. Held: PennDOT not liable for negligent construction and maintenance of highway. ***Powell v. Drumheller,* 153 Pa. Cmwlth. 571, 621 A.2d 1197.**

Pedestrian struck by vehicle awarded damages for lost wages but not pain and suffering. Held: evidence of pedestrian's intoxication incompetent and insufficient. Reversed and remanded. ***Whyte v. Robinson,* 421 Pa. Super. 33, 617 A.2d 380.**

Passenger in vehicle involved in one-car accident brought action based on Dram Shop Act. Tavern owner not liable. Driver not visibly intoxicated. ***Johnson v. Harris,* 419 Pa. Super. 541, 615 A.2d 771.**

Pedestrian struck by automobile after being served alcohol at volunteer fire department function. Department held immune. ***Guinn v. Albertis Fire Company,* 531 Pa. 500, 614 A.2d 218.**

Estate of murdered college student brought action against other student who served the alcohol. Defendant not liable. Minor not liable as social host. ***Goldberg v. Delta Tau Delta,* 418 Pa. Super. 207, 613 A.2d 1250.**

Minor injured after consuming alcohol provided by other minor. Social host liability did not extend to minor who served alcohol. ***Kapres v. Heller,* 417 Pa. Super. 371, 612 A.2d 987.**

Minor killed in motorcycle accident after drinking alcohol at fraternity party. Summary judgment granted to college and fraternity upheld. ***Millard v. Osborne and Lambda Chi Alpha,* 416 Pa. Super. 475, 611 A.2d 715.**

Intoxicated driver injured in accident brought action against volunteer fire department for serving him alcohol. Department not entitled to immunity. ***Buchanan v. Littlehales,* 146 Pa. Cmwlth. 423, 606 A.2d 567.**

Child injured in accident caused by intoxicated driver. Manufacturer of alcoholic beverages found not liable. ***Dauphin Deposit Bank and Trust Company v. Toyota,* 408 Pa. Super. 256, 596 A.2d 845.**

Passenger in vehicle operated by intoxicated driver brought action against driver and city for injuries caused by vehicle striking headwall along highway. City not liable. Driver 75% liable, passenger 25% liable. ***Hannon v. City of Philadelphia,* 138 Pa. Cmwlth. 166, 587 A.2d 845.**

Minor died of drowning after drinking liquor bought by other minor. Held: 1) defense of contributory negligence permitted; 2) testimony that deceased consumed alcohol admissible; 3) testimony that purchaser appeared to be in mid-twenties admissible. ***Barrie v. Pennsylvania Liquor Control Board,* 137 Pa. Cmwlth. 514, 586 A.2d 1017.**

Motorist killed in accident after being served alcohol at volunteer fire department function. Fire department not immune. Not in performance of fire fighting duties. ***Salazar v. Tayler's Dining Room, Inc.,* 136 Pa. Cmwlth. 527, 583 A.2d 1264.**

Intoxication

Owner loaned automobile to unlicensed driver who was killed in accident while intoxicated. Department brought wrongful death action on behalf of driver's child. Owner not liable. Only causal negligence that of driver. ***Com., Dept. of Public Welfare v. Hickey,* 136 Pa. Cmwlth. 223, 582 A.2d 734.**

College student died of alcohol poisoning as a result of being served alcohol by friends on day before 21st birthday. Held: serving alcohol on day before 21st birthday negligence *per se*. ***Herr v. Booten,* 398 Pa. Super. 166, 580 A.2d 1115.**

Pedestrian struck by automobile while walking home from fire department where he was served alcohol. Held: actions of department may have been outside scope of its duties and therefore immunity would not attach. ***Guinn v. Albertis Fire Company,* 134 Pa. Cmwlth. 270, 577 A.2d 971.**

College student convicted of murder brought action against estate of victim and against fraternity for negligently enticing him to party and for serving him drugs and alcohol. Dismissal of complaint upheld. ***Van Mastright v. Delta Tau Delta,* 393 Pa. Super. 142, 573 A.2d 1128.**

Minor student who was served alcohol in university dormitory and at fraternity house started fire that destroyed building. University and fraternity not liable to owner of building. Did not furnish alcohol. ***Alumni Association v. Sullivan,* 524 Pa. 356, 572 A.2d 1209.**

Testimony concerning driver's fatigue and intoxication provided circumstantial evidence of his negligence; sufficient to preclude a nonsuit. ***Harvilla v. Delcamp,* 521 Pa. 21, 555 A.2d 763.**

Minor plaintiff injured while intoxicated. Question of whether distributor was liable because he knew that beer was for consumption by minors was for jury to decide. ***Thomas v. Duquesne Light Company,* 376 Pa. Super. 1, 545 A.2d 289.**

Occupants of vehicle involved in accident brought negligent entrustment action against owner of other automobile. Held: evidence of driver's intoxication at the time he borrowed automobile was admissible to show negligent entrustment. ***Wertz v. Kephart,* 374 Pa. Super. 274, 542 A.2d 1019.**

Minor injured after being served liquor at fraternity party. Held: national fraternity may be found civilly liable as social host. ***Jefferies v. Commonwealth,* 371 Pa. Super. 12, 537 A.2d 355.**

Social host who serves alcohol to minor may be found liable for damages caused by fire started by intoxicated minor. ***Alumni Association v. Sullivan,* 369 Pa. Super. 585, 535 A.2d 1095.**

Service of any amount of alcohol in contravention of crimes code by adult host to minor is a breach of duty to care. ***Orner v. Mallick,* 515 Pa. 132, 527 A.2d 521.**

Passenger in vehicle driven by intoxicated minor killed in collision. Driver consumed alcohol purchased by other minor. Beer distributor who sold alcohol may

Intoxication

be liable even though driver not purchaser. ***Matthews v. Konieczny,*** **515 Pa. 106, 527 A.2d 508.**

Employee killed in automobile accident after being served alcohol by employer at business meeting. Held: a social host is not liable for serving alcoholic beverages to an adult guest. ***Burkhart v. Brockway Glass Company,*** **352 Pa. Super. 204, 507 A.2d 844.**

Minor purchased case of beer from distributor. Three minors then consumed some of the beer and one, who was driving, had accident in which one of the other two was killed. Driver not purchaser of beer. Purchaser not visibly intoxicated when purchase made. Summary judgment in favor of defendant affirmed. ***Mathews v. Konieczny,*** **338 Pa. Super. 504, 488 A.2d 5.**

Minor bought beer from distributor and gave it to another minor who then got drunk and had auto accident. Distributor held not liable to third party plaintiff owing to language of 47 P.S. §4-497. ***Mancuso v. Bradshaw,*** **338 Pa. Super. 328, 487 A.2d 990.**

Pedestrian struck by auto. Evidence admitted at trial that pedestrian was intoxicated. Charge given based upon presumption of intoxication contained in Vehicle Code. Held: error to charge on presumption of intoxication. Verdict for defendant reversed. Under facts, however, evidence of blood alcohol and other evidence of intoxication is relevant. ***Ackerman v. Delcomico,*** **336 Pa. Super. 569, 486 A.2d 410.**

Landlord corporation not responsible for actions of licensee tenant in serving minors or visibly intoxicated persons who are later involved in accident. Corporate owner of real estate here granted nonsuit. ***McCrery v. Scioli,*** **336 Pa. Super. 455, 485 A.2d 1170.**

Summary judgment in favor of tavern owners in dram shop case, reversed. Affidavit of moving party that plaintiff was not visibly intoxicated when served alcoholic beverages, even if uncontradicted, will not support summary judgment. Credibility of testimony is still for jury. ***Peluso v. Walter,*** **334 Pa. Super. 609, 483 A.2d 905.**

Minor passenger in auto killed in accident. Driver intoxicated—also a minor. Joinder of individuals who, in addition to licensee, served alcoholic beverages to driver. Serving minors held to be actionable. ***Douglas v. Schwenk,*** **330 Pa. Super. 392, 479 A.2d 608.**

Noncommercial organization which sponsored private social gathering and which acted strictly as social host supplying liquor, with no sales and no license under liquor code involved, could not be held liable to third party injured by intoxicated guest. ***Sites v. Cloonan,*** **328 Pa. Super. 481, 477 A.2d 547.**

Plaintiff a passenger in car that became disabled; struck while standing in center of road in front of car, attempting to wave on traffic. Plaintiff found 70% at fault. Proper to admit blood-alcohol of .185% taken two to three hours later at hos-

Intoxication

pital, by the expert testimony given here. ***Emerick v. Carson*, 325 Pa. Super. 308, 472 A.2d 1133.**

Defense verdict affirmed. Patron consumed three double shots of whiskey, plus beer; then, had one-vehicle accident. Charge affirmed—no inference that plaintiff visibly intoxicated as a result of blood alcohol taken at hospital. Also proper to tell jury to disregard whether plaintiff was negligent in ordering or consuming the alcohol. Only issue was visible intoxication when served. ***Suskey v. Moose Lodge*, 325 Pa. Super. 94, 472 A.2d 663.**

Defendants are negligent per se in serving alcohol to the point of intoxication to a person less than 21 years of age, and they can be held liable for injuries proximately resulting from the minor's intoxication. ***Congini v. Portersville Value Co.*, 504 Pa. 157, 470 A.2d 515.** (Distinguished from *Klein v. Raysinger,* holding no liability of social host as to *adult* guests).

Social hosts who serve alcoholic beverages held not responsible in third-party actions by later-injured plaintiffs. ***Klein v. Raysinger*, 504 Pa. 141, 470 A.2d 507.**

Dram shop-type complaint against private party dismissed as stating no cause of action. Pennsylvania does not recognize cause of action by persons injured by intoxicated driver against social host who had served intoxicants to driver. But see concurring opinion and footnotes on possibility of pure negligence action. ***Klein v. Raysinger*, 298 Pa. Super. 246, 444 A.2d 753; and 302 Pa. Super. 248, 448 A.2d 620.**

Driver left defendant tavern, and within 10 minutes involved in motor vehicle accident. Police and independent witnesses describe clearly visible intoxication. Enough to go to jury. Error to grant nonsuit exonerating taproom. ***Speicher v. Reda*, 290 Pa. Super. 168, 434 A.2d 183.**

Auto accident killed plaintiff. Defendant driver was intoxicated. Lower court granted nonsuit against server of alcoholic beverages. Although no evidence of visible intoxication at time of last drink, clear evidence of intoxication at scene of accident. Blood alcohol taken shortly thereafter at .12. All relevant as circumstantial evidence of visible intoxication at time of last drink. ***Couts v. Ghion*, 281 Pa. Super. 135, 421 A.2d 1184.**

Decedent killed in auto accident by intoxicated minor. Suit against taproom, among others. Mere fact that a minor was served, in violation of law is not evidence of negligence under 47 P.S. §4-497. ***Simon v. Shirely*, 269 Pa. Super. 364, 409 A.2d 1365.**

Intersection accident. Error to exclude evidence of intoxication where breathalyzer one hour after accident was .14, where police smelled alcohol on breath at scene, where defendant's gait was impaired at scene and where defendant admitted consuming wine earlier in evening. ***Custatis v. Reichert*, 267 Pa. Super. 247, 406 A.2d 787.**

Head-on collision. Both drivers and passenger killed. Passenger sued. Driver of passenger's car intoxicated as he and passenger had spent afternoon drinking.

Intra-family immunity

Verdict for defendant on basis of assumption of risk. Although charge in error, it was stated as submitted by plaintiff. Affirmed. ***Weaver v. Clabaugh,* 255 Pa. 532, 388 A.2d 1094.**

Error in civil personal injury case to exclude guilty plea on charge of driving under the influence. ***Cronley v. Gardner,* 253 Pa. 467, 385 A.2d 433.**

Court in dictum expressed skepticism of testimony which would interpolate back three hours the results of blood alcohol test taken three hours post accident. ***Schwarzbach v. Dunn,* 252 Pa. Super. 454, 381 A.2d 1295.**

Suit versus owner of tavern where decedent had been drinking all afternoon and evening. Later, at friend's home decedent fell down steps, hit head and died. Verdict against tavern owner of $60,000 affirmed. ***Connelly v. Ziegler,* 251 Pa. Super. 521, 380 A.2d 902.**

Error to have police testify that defendant driver had been drinking without evidence that he was unfit to drive. ***Selby v. Brown,* 250 Pa. Super. 134, 378 A.2d 862.**

Plaintiff lying prone in roadway after spending day in several bars. Struck by two cars within minutes of one another. No proof as to how decedent got into roadway, therefore evidence of drinking properly excluded. ***Lehman v. McCleary,* 229 Pa. Super. 508, 329 A.2d 862.**

Plaintiff injured when auto crashed in which he was passenger. Driver drunk. Both had come from party at employer. Law only imposes liability on licensee of state when serving visibly intoxicated person. Complaint against employer dismissed. ***Manning v. Andy,* 454 Pa. 237, 310 A.2d 75.**

Defendant admittedly negligent—offer of proof to establish intoxication of operator to entitle plaintiff to punitive damages—offer rejected below in error—new trial awarded—driving while intoxicated may entitle injured party to punitive damages. ***Focht v. Rabada,* 217 Pa. Super. 35, 268 A.2d 157.**

Offer of testimony of a physician that blood alcohol content of .14 would "affect" operator in his driving properly excluded—must establish a degree of intoxication which proves unfitness to drive. ***Billow v. Farmers Trust Co.,* 438 Pa. 514, 266 A.2d 92.**

Court below erred in permitting evidence that defendant had been in a bar prior to occurrence—prejudicial as creating inference that defendant was intoxicated. ***Morreale v. Prince,* 436 Pa. 51, 258 A.2d 508.**

Minor plaintiff injured while operating car—evidence that he had previously been served intoxicated liquor by defendants while visibly intoxicated—contrary to statute—case for jury. ***Smith v. Evans,* 421 Pa. 247, 219 A.2d 310.**

Intra-family immunity

Wife filed action in trespass against husband as result of auto accident in which wife's personal injuries charged caused by husband's negligence as driver. Supreme Court concluded tortfeasor's immunity from liability due to marital relationship with injured party not sustainable on basis of law, logic or public policy—therefore, abolished defense of interspousal immunity. ***Hack v. Hack,*** **495 Pa. 300, 433 A.2d 859.**

Husband and wife in accident. Husband joined as additional defendant. Verdict against husband only. No request for charge on interspousal immunity. Defense waived. ***Ciarrocca v. Campbell,*** **282 Pa. Super. 60, 422 A.2d 675.**

Doctrine of interspousal immunity waived as not timely filed. ***Policino v. Ehrlich,*** **478 Pa. 5, 385 A.2d 968.**

Wife injured in auto accident prior to marriage. Suit barred by subsequent marriage to defendant. ***Smith v. Smith,*** **240 Pa. Super. 97, 361 A.2d 756.**

Interspousal immunity—premarital tort—subsequent marriage—suit barred. ***Kelso v. Mielcarek,*** **226 Pa. Super. 476, 313 A.2d 324.**

The doctrine of intra-family immunity is abolished in Pennsylvania at least insofar as it would bar a recovery where a child is injured allegedly as the result of her mother's tortious acts—all previous decisions overruled. ***Falco v. Pados,*** **444 Pa. 372, 282 A.2d 351.**

Intubation

Verdict in favor of woman whose voice was irreparably damaged following intubation procedure vacated, and judgment entered for appellant hospital where plaintiff's complaint stated cause of action in negligence against hospital, but proof at trial focused only on family physician's negligence in follow-up care of plaintiff; no amendment to plaintiff's original complaint was filed. ***Reynolds v. Thomas Jefferson University Hospital,*** **450 Pa. Super. 327, 676 A.2d 1205 (1996).**

Invitees

Plaintiffs brought negligence action against Defendant after they were injured in a fall when an exterior stairway gave out at the Defendant's facility due to rusted bolts. A jury found in favor of the Plaintiffs. On appeal the Superior Court affirmed holding that the Defendant owed a duty to the Plaintiffs to inspect its exterior stairway for signs of failure. The Superior Court also held that the Plaintiffs were invitees as they were on the Defendant's property to perform services for the Defendant. ***Gillingham v. Consol Energy, Inc.,*** **2012 Pa. Super. 133 (Pa. Super. 2012).**

Meter reader who fell into a window well and was injured was a licensee on property, not an invitee. The standard of care due by homeowners required that they exercise reasonable care to make unreasonably dangerous conditions safe and to warn licensees of the conditions. Existence of window well was known to reader and was not an unreasonably dangerous condition. ***Cresswell v. End,*** **931 A.2d 673 (Pa. Super. 2003).**

Plaintiff wife, school book salesperson, was injured when she attempted to gain entrance to school building which had been constructed in 1902. Plaintiff complained that entrance was not in compliance with current building codes and that

Invitees

noncompliance created an unsafe condition that caused her to fall and become injured. Trial court prohibited any testimony from plaintiff's building code compliance expert reasoning that school, because of its age, was not required to be in compliance with current building codes and to allow that issue to be raised to jury would confuse negligence issue. Additionally, photographs and plans of area in question were adequate to allow jury to make its own determination of whether landing and entrance were unsafe. Trial court's instructions as to defendant's duties to plaintiff were also adequate where they correctly described the plaintiff's status as business invitee and the school's responsibilities to her as invitee. ***Kiehner v. School District of Philadelphia*, 712 A.2d 830 (Pa. Cmwlth. 1998).**

Plaintiff roofing supply salesman was injured when he stepped into unguarded hole in floor of defendant's house that was under construction. At conclusion of plaintiff's case against homeowner, trial court granted compulsory nonsuit on grounds that plaintiff had not presented adequate evidence to establish he was entitled to status greater than trespasser. Record contained references to defendant homeowner's approval of plaintiff's offer to deliver roof vents to plaintiff's house and to implication from workmen at house that plaintiff was permitted to enter house to leave roof vents inside, safe from theft and exposure. Reversal of nonsuit because there were adequate facts to take issue of plaintiff's status as business invitee to jury. ***Emge v. Hagosky*, 712 A.2d 315 (Pa. Super. 1998).**

Plaintiff who fell on thin layer of "black ice" in motel parking lot suffered injuries and sued motel owner. Plaintiff argued that "hills and ridges" doctrine, which requires showing of accumulation of ice and snow, should not apply to business premises; they are not so burdened by substantial size of area to be cleared of ice and snow as are municipalities and local agencies, which organizations the doctrine is designed to protect. Plaintiff also argued that custodian who had placed salt and sand on portions of premises was negligent for not salting and sanding entire parking lot. Held: "hills and ridges" applies to business invitees and local agencies equally and because plaintiff could not show accumulation had been allowed to form without any effort to cure problem, summary judgment was proper. ***Morin v. Travelers Rest Motel, Inc.*, 704 A.2d 1085 (Pa. Super. 1997).**

Decedent's failure to establish hospital's knowledge of water on floor in bathroom, which may represent a dangerous or defective condition of the property, prohibits recovery. A business invitee must prove either that the landowner created the harmful condition or had actual or constructive notice of the condition. Summary judgment affirmed. ***Swift v. Northeastern Hospital of Philadelphia*, 456 Pa. Super. 330, 690 A.2d 719 (1997).**

The determination of whether an individual is a trespasser, licensee or invitee is for the jury. A licensee may become an invitee, thereby increasing duty of care owed by landowner. Plaintiff may recover damages where two or more substantial causes combine to cause an injury, even if no one cause standing alone would have brought about the injury. Although action of third party in pushing plaintiff off a guide wall was an intervening cause, its occurrence was not so extraordinary or unforeseeable as to make it a superseding cause which would excuse property owner for negligent maintenance of wall, which condition substantially contributed to plaintiff's injuries. ***Trude v. Martin,* 442 Pa. Super. 614, 660 A.2d 626 (1995).**

Inmate who ran down hallway and jumped steps, hitting his head on ceiling, failed to establish that dangerous condition existed in ceiling above steps in hallway. Duty of care to inmate is that of owner to invitee. Compulsory nonsuit granted in favor of County affirmed. ***Graf v. County of Northampton,* ___ Pa. Cmwlth. ___, 654 A.2d 131 (1995).**

Customer who fell in supermarket brought action claiming injuries caused by excess wax or presence of grapes on floor. Market not liable. ***Myers v. Penn Traffic Company,* 414 Pa. Super. 181, 606 A.2d 926.**

Customer who slipped on water in front of ice machine brought action against store owner and contractor who stocked machine. New trial ordered. Evidence of post-accident remedial measures improperly admitted. ***Miller v. Peter J. Schmitt & Company, Inc.,* 405 Pa. Super. 502, 592 A.2d 1324.**

Customer slipped and fell in supermarket. Supermarket not liable. Failure of trial court to grant judgment *n.o.v.* and new trial not error. ***Goldman v. Acme Markets, Inc.,* 393 Pa. Super. 245, 574 A.2d 100.**

Fall on ice patch of chiropractic clinic parking lot. Jury verdict $70,000, reflecting 35% comparative negligence. Ice was next to car although rest of lot was clear. Plaintiff became aware of ice while still seated in car. Wore prosthesis at time—fractured left hip. Verdict reversed. Where plaintiff sees risk, possessor of land relieved of responsibility and duty of care to invitee who, under circumstances here held to have assumed risk as matter of law. Comparative negligence statute not applicable. ***Carrender v. Fitterer,* 503 Pa. 178, 469 A.2d 120.**

Nine-year old struck in head with bat while playing softball in school yard. Not organized school activity. Alleged improperly painted markings on ground required catcher to be too close to plate. Plaintiff held to be public invitee. School district said painting done for ball game with no bat. Granting summary judgment in favor of school district, reversed. Jury issue. ***Bersani v. School District of Philadelphia,* 310 Pa. Super. 1, 456 A.2d 151.**

Plaintiff rendered quadriplegic as a result of dive off dock into a canal during private party. Error to instruct jury that plaintiff was an invitee. Should have been left to jury whether or not plaintiff was an invitee or licensee. Plaintiff was the husband of an invited guest. Verdict for plaintiff reversed and new trial ordered. ***Hager v. Etting,* 268 Pa. Super. 416, 408 A.2d 856.**

Injuries sustained by spectator when struck by foul ball. Absent showing that defendant deviated from customary practice, defendants not negligent. ***Jones v. Three Rivers Management Corp.,* 251 Pa. Super. 82, 380 A.2d 387.**

Slip and fall on freshly mopped hospital floor. Plaintiff had observed floor being mopped upon entering hospital. Verdict for plaintiff affirmed. ***Calhoun v. Jersey Shore Hospital,* 250 Pa. Super. 567, 378 A.2d 1294.**

Invitees

Plaintiff mistaken for shoplifter by store employee. Later received apology. Bruises to arm, recurrence of arthritis and ulcer flare-up. Physically recovered within five months but never recovered emotionally until time of her death 6-1/2 years later of unrelated causes. Substantial verdict including punitive damages. **Hannigan v. S. Klein Department Stores, 244 Pa. Super. 597, 371 A.2d 872.**

Mannequin fell on plaintiff while shopping—jury could reasonably infer that store negligent in allowing such an object to be in such a position improperly secured—proof need be slight—defendant's verdict reversed. **Paul v. Hess Bros. Inc., 226 Pa. Super. 92, 312 A.2d 65.**

Proprietor of a shopping center must exercise reasonable care—previous entrance to center blocked off by high curbing—plaintiffs injured—previous occurrences—case for jury. **Colangelo v. Penn Hills Center, Inc., 221 Pa. Super. 381, 292 A.2d 490.**

Plaintiff bowler slipped or failed to properly slide and was injured while using one of defendant's lanes—expert testimony was properly rejected and there being no other evidence of a defect, a nonsuit was properly entered. **Houston v. Canon Bowl, Inc., 443 Pa. 383, 289 A.2d 908.**

Jar of olives fell from a high shelf above the ordinary reach of a customer and struck plaintiff—Held: the stocking of merchandise in such a manner may subject customers to unwarranted risk and entry of nonsuit below as in error—matter for jury. **Dougherty v. Great A. & P. Tea Co., 221 Pa. Super. 221, 289 A.2d 747.**

Plaintiff while waiting for his gas tank to be filled and while following directions to a rest room, fell into an open repair pit in service station—alleged that poor lighting and shadow obscured opening—nonsuit improper—matter for jury. **Latch v. Reburn, 220 Pa. Super. 396, 281 A.2d 673.**

Plaintiff on premises to inspect plywood—falling into open trapdoor and injured—case for jury against parties in control of building—error to direct verdict for defendant. **Pastuszek v. Murphy Plywood Corp. et al., 219 Pa. Super. 59, 280 A.2d 644.**

Plaintiff, a member of an expert independent contractor rigging operator, injured allegedly as the result of the presence of a rack in moving area—owner possessor held not responsible—no duty on owner to warn or remove rack—plaintiff an expert rigger, condition evident and injury resulted from an act of a fellow employee. **Crane v. I.T.E. Circuit Breaker Co., 443 Pa. 442, 278 A.2d 362.**

Customer fell down a step in store as the result of a shifting shopping cart—fractured hip—Held: cross-examination concerning a prior accident not error—verdict of $2,500.00 with expenses of $2,013.49 not inadequate—new trial refused plaintiff—strong dissent. **Levant v. L. Wasserman, Inc., 218 Pa. Super. 116, 275 A.2d 678.**

Plaintiff customer in a shopping center—fell on a discarded hot dog in a common aisle—lease provided landlord would police aisles—proprietor of a grocery store, a tenant, held not responsible—operator of shopping center, the lessor, had settled his liability—ordinary rules of landlord and tenant applied in situations of multiple leasing *Leary v. Lawrence Sales Corp.* **442 Pa. 389, 275 A.2d 32.**

Plaintiff lodged car in defendant's automobile sales and service station building—walking to rear of building to pick up car and entered an unlocked door and fell down a flight of steps to basement with severe injuries—plaintiff testified on deposition that he had not "even looked" where he was going—motion for summary judgment on pleadings, deposition and photographs—motion granted below and action sustained on appeal. *Simmons v. Doll's Garage, Inc.,* **440 Pa. 635, 269 A.2d 509.**

Plaintiff, accompanying a club member to defendant's club, was severely injured as the result of an altercation arising from a disputed card game—Held: case for jury in suit against club, jury having exonerated the assailant. *Doytek v. Bobtown R. & G. Club,* **216 Pa. Super. 368, 268 A.2d 149.**

Blind solicitor of brooms falling into an areaway on defendant's property which was under construction and alteration—plaintiff a business invitee—case for jury. *Argo v. Goodstein,* **438 Pa. 468, 265 A.2d 783.**

Plaintiff entered defendant's store to purchase meat and on leaving fell on steps—evidence that sawdust, wood chips and fine gravel were on steps—jury disagreed—also evidence of no handrail—judgment entered on whole record—reversed on appeal—matter for the jury. *Kuminkoski v. Daum,* **429 Pa. 494, 240 A.2d 524.**

Plaintiffs injured while dancing allegedly as the result of asparagus on dance floor—caterer held responsible. *Schwartz v. Warwick-Phila. Corp.,* **424 Pa. 185, 226 A.2d 484.**

Plaintiff injured while entering store of defendant by reason of acts of children shoving and pushing a swinging door—preliminary objections improperly sustained—matter for jury. *Regelski v. F. W. Woolworth Co.,* **423 Pa. 524, 225 A.2d 561.**

Plaintiff a member of club which served intoxicating liquors—no bartender—members mixed own drinks—plaintiff injured in fight in club—nonsuit proper—no liability even if business invitee—assumed risk. *Mike v. Lebanon Miridites League,* **421 Pa. 217, 218 A.2d 814.**

Ischemia

Action to recover for death of child 11 months after birth where death caused by negligent failure to diagnose and act on dangerous condition *in utero* immediately before birth. Evidence to establish "corporate liability" of hospital under *Thompson v. Nason Hospital*, 527 Pa. 330, 591 A.2d 703 (1991) must be provided in the form of expert testimony where the negligence is not obvious but need not contain "magic words." The substance of all the expert testimony will be considered as a whole. The evidence must establish that the hospital, in its own duty to the patient, deviated from the accepted standard of care and that that deviation was a

Ischemia

substantial factor in causing the harm to the plaintiff. ***Welsh v. Bulger,* 698 A.2d 581 (Pa. 1997).**

—J—

Janitor

Plaintiff employed defendant janitorial company to police his building—evidence that employee of company put ashes from incinerator into a cardboard box—fire ensued—evidence that employee had stirred ashes with his bare fingers to determine whether hot—sufficient evidence to take case to jury for fire loss. ***Duffy v. Nat. Janitorial Services, Inc.*, 429 Pa. 334, 340 A.2d 527.**

Jar

Jar of olives fell from a high shelf above the ordinary reach of a customer and struck plaintiff—held the stocking of merchandise in such a manner may subject customers to unwarranted risk and entry of nonsuit below as in error—matter for jury. ***Dougherty v. Great A. & P. Tea Co.*, 221 Pa. Super. 221, 289 A.2d 747.**

Jerk or Jolt Doctrine

Plaintiff bus passenger suffered a broken femur when she fell on the floor of the bus as it began to move before she had been seated. Compulsory nonsuit for bus company affirmed based on lack of testimony that jerk or jolt of bus was so severe as to cause extraordinarily disturbing effect on other passengers. Plaintiff's medical expert's testimony that force of jerk or jolt of bus was severe because of nature of the injury is not sufficient. ***Asbury v. Port Authority Transit of Allegheny County*, 863 A.2d 84 (Pa. Cmwlth. 2004).**

Joint enterprise

Pedestrian plaintiff injured by drunken driver sued passengers who may have been aware of driver's intoxication. Summary judgment in favor of defendants affirmed because a passenger does not owe a duty to a third person where driver of vehicle is intoxicated, absent a special relationship, joint enterprise, joint venture or a right to control the vehicle. ***Brandjord v. Hopper*, 455 Pa. Super. 426, 688 A.2d 721 (1997).**

Joint tortfeasors

Defendant appealed an order of joint and several damages, where the claims against defendants were based upon distinct theories of negligence and crashworthiness involving a car accident. The court found that damages could be apportioned jointly and severally since the jury determined that the actions of both defendants had been substantial factors in causing the deaths to the plaintiffs' family. ***Harsh v. Petroll*, 584 Pa. 606 (2005).**

Plaintiff sued driver of car that veered into her lane and hit her car, used car salesman who had authorized defendant driver to test drive the car, and dealership for which used car salesman worked. Jury returned verdict against all three parties and apportioned liability among them, which was molded to joint and several liability by trial court. On appeal, Superior Court reversed denial of post trial motions of salesman and dealership who argued that they had no knowledge that defendant driver was other than a licensed driver (which he was) and so no duty to plaintiff

Joint tortfeasors

which would support a claim of negligent entrustment by plaintiff. *Ferry v. Fisher*, **709 A.2d 399 (Pa. Super. 1998).**

Where vehicle owner knows or should know that its employee driver has had his operator's license suspended, owner is, by statute, jointly and severally liable with the driver for the driver's negligence. Summary judgment in favor of owner reversed. *Shomo v. Scribe*, **546 Pa. 542, 686 A.2d 1292 (1996).**

The determination of whether an individual is a trespasser, licensee or invitee is for the jury. A licensee may become an invitee, thereby increasing duty of care owed by landowner. Plaintiff may recover damages where two or more substantial causes combine to cause an injury, even if no one cause standing alone would have brought about the injury. Although action of third party in pushing plaintiff off a guide wall was an intervening cause, its occurrence was not so extraordinary or unforeseeable as to make it a superseding cause which would excuse property owner for negligent maintenance of wall, which condition substantially contributed to plaintiff's injuries. *Trude v. Martin*, **442 Pa. Super. 614, 660 A.2d 626 (1995).**

In action where jury found plaintiff to be 30% negligent, one defendant to be 45% negligent, and second defendant 25% negligent, plaintiff still may recover against defendant found to be less negligent than plaintiff because collectively defendants were more negligent than plaintiff. Where strictly liable defendant and negligent defendant acted as joint tortfeasors, contribution among them can be properly awarded. Judgment on molded jury verdict affirmed. *Smith v. Weissenfels, Inc.*, **441 Pa. Super. 328, 657 A.2d 949 (1995).**

Apportionment of liability for harm to plaintiff is question of law. Where tortious conduct of two or more persons causes a single harm that cannot be apportioned, the actors are joint tortfeasors even though they acted independently. Jury verdict in favor of driver injured as a result of two separate collisions affirmed. *Smith v. Pulcinella*, **440 Pa. Super. 525, 656 A.2d 494 (1995).**

In automobile accident case by decedent's administrator against intoxicated driver and PennDOT, whether PennDOT's alleged negligence for improper road design and maintenance was substantial factor in accident was question for jury. Existence of two tortfeasors does not automatically excuse one or the other from liability. Question of concurrent or joint causation and determination of whether an act is so extraordinary as to constitute a superseding cause are for the jury. Order sustaining preliminary objections of PennDOT reversed. *Powell v. Drumheller*, **539 Pa. 484, 653 A.2d 619 (1995).**

Motorists injured in collision brought action against each other and against PennDOT. Summary judgment in favor of department reversed. Governmental unit may be found jointly liable with non-governmental party. *Buschman v. Druch*, **139 Pa. Cmwlth. 182, 590 A.2d 53.**

Wrongful death and survival actions brought against manufacturers and distributors of asbestos products. Manufacturers settled for amount greater than pro-rata share. Non-settling defendants liable for full amount of their pro-rata shares of

Joint tortfeasors

damages. Punitive damages inappropriate. ***Moran v. G. & W.H. Corson, Inc.***, **402 Pa. Super. 101, 586 A.2d 416.**

Driver injured in multi-vehicle accident settled with one joint tortfeasor. Other joint tortfeasors held liable for full amount of damages minus amount of settlement and for full amount of delayed damages. ***Wirth v. Miller***, **398 Pa. Super. 244, 580 A.2d 1154.**

A joint tortfeasor who satisfies more than his equitable share of the joint liability may recover the excess from his fellow joint tortfeasor. ***Ariondo v. Munsey***, **112 Pa. Cmwlth. 475, 553 A.2d 94**

Under the Comparative Negligence Act recovery by an injured plaintiff will be precluded only where plaintiff's negligence exceeds the combined negligence of all defendants. Each defendant is liable for his portion of negligence even if it is less than the negligence of plaintiff. ***Elder v. Orluck***, **511 Pa. 402, 515 A.2d 517**

A joint tortfeasor who satisfies more than his equitable share of the joint liability may recover the excess from his fellow joint tortfeasor. ***Ariondo v. Munsey***, **112 Pa. Cmwlth. 475, 553 A.2d 94.**

Plaintiff injured in garage when employee was assembling multi-piece truck rim which blew apart. Rim eventually mounted on truck without its manufacturer being known. Suit against all manufacturers of multi-piece rims must fail owing to lack of common design. Dismissal of certain defendants affirmed. ***Cummins v. Firestone***, **344 Pa. Super. 9, 495 A.2d 963.**

Where three physicians misdiagnosed fracture, release of one does not release other tortfeasors whose joint negligence, even though independent, is not able to be apportioned. Verdict may have to be reduced by amount of settlement however. See 42 Pa. C.S.A. §8326. ***Capone v. Donovan,*** **332 Pa. Super. 185, 480 A.2d 1249.**

Reversed Superior Court's allowance of joinder of insurance company and agent on basis of wrongful denial of claim. Claims do not arise out of same transaction as underlying tort for damages due to slip and fall of guest. ***Stokes v. Loyal Order of Moose***, **502 Pa. 460, 466 A.2d 1341.**

Jury verdict $37,000. Loss of eye—struck by object ejected from lawn mower. Plaintiff, a passerby. For purposes of delay damages rule, joint tortfeasor may not take advantage of separate offer made by other defendant. True, even where other tortfeasor settled, with joint-tortfeasor release, and verdict is within 125% of that settlement, but against non-settling defendant. ***Lavin v. Mylecraine***, **307 Pa. Super. 564, 453 A.2d 1031.**

School student prank—one of group dared other to knock trash can off balcony railing. Was tapped inadvertently during horseplay, falling on plaintiff below. Nonsuit affirmed. Settled before trial with two obvious participants. Suit tried against others present who allegedly encouraged and dared actors. Held: evidence did not present fault of individuals or group as a whole. ***Kline v. Ball***, **306 Pa. Super. 284, 452 A.2d 727.**

Joint tortfeasors

Jury verdict $500,000; $50,000 to husband for loss of consortium. Complications from hysterectomy led to loss of one kidney and ureter damage. Alleged postoperative negligence led to amputation of right leg. Two doctors, both involved in patient care, correctly held to be jointly and severally liable—not case of primary or secondary liability. Charge on causation based upon Hamil v. Bashline, III, affirmed. ***Hoeke v. Mercy Hospital of Pittsburgh*, 299 Pa. Super. 47, 445 A.2d 140.**

Injured plaintiff released operator of motor vehicle. Thereafter sued doctors for malpractice in treating injury. Not a joint tort. Improper to join released driver. Doctors liable only for those injuries attributable to their negligence. ***Voyles v. Corwin, et al.*, 295 Pa. Super. 126, 441 A.2d 381.**

Pedestrian struck and killed by one or more autos as he stepped off medial strip at night. Settled with first striking vehicle. Nonsuit as to all others. Evidence insufficient as to whether others actually struck plaintiff, or whether he died from first impact. ***Pio v. Letarec*, 294 Pa. Super. 196, 439 A.2d 818.**

Malpractice action. Where joint tortfeasor release signed before trial as to hospital and its employee, they are considered one entity for determination of pro-rata contribution. ***Jones v. Harrisburg Polyclinic*, 496 Pa. 465, 437 A.2d 1134.**

Spitball battle on school bus. Minor passenger lost sight of right eye. Verdict against bus company and driver. Other students not held in by jury. Reversed as to other minors only and new trial granted. Burden of proof as to who threw spitball was on the minor children, once it was shown that one of them must have done it, to show the innocence of each one. §433B of Restatement (2d) Torts. ***Sommers v. Hessler*, 227 Pa. Super. 41, 323 A.2d 17.**

Injury to passenger occupant as the result of a collision of vehicles of original and added defendants—court in error in refusing point which called for a finding against one or both defendants—verdict for defendants—no evidence of contributory negligence or evidence that would exonerate both defendants—new trial granted. ***Weinstein v. Phila. Trans. Co.*, 222 Pa. Super. 448, 295 A.2d 111.**

Minor plaintiff injured by a stone probably thrown by one of additional defendants—contractor and land owner sued—defendants brought in 12 boys who were throwing stones—court below in error in sustaining preliminary objections on ground that it was not averred which boy threw the stone—matter controlled by Section 433 B (3) of Restatement (2d) Torts involving two or more actors—all additional defendants could be sued—leave to amend should have been given. ***Snoparsky v. Baer*, 439 Pa. 140, 266 A.2d 707.**

One defendant engaged in remodeling a home—engaged other defendant to do some stone work of a special character—latter defendant had an automobile accident—jury's verdict held both defendants responsible—upheld by a divided court on appeal—strong dissent—criteria for determining relationship set forth at large in dissenting opinion. ***Cox v. Caeti*, 216 Pa. Super. 214, 263 A.2d 765.**

Judicial Immunity

Joists

Plaintiff, a structural steel worker at a shopping center erection operation, was injured by the collapse of "bar joists"—the defendant, a subcontractor, held responsible by the jury, had placed bundles of steel decking on joists at a point too far removed from supporting beams—case for jury and defendant's motion properly refused. ***Quinn v. Kumar*, 437 Pa. 268, 263 A.2d 458.**

Jones Act

Seaman brought action against employer for injuries suffered in fall down ladder. Held: contributory negligence need be only featherweight causative factor. ***Bunting v. Sun Company, Inc.*, 434 Pa. Super. 404, 643 A.2d 1085.**

Captain of barge brought action against employer for emotional injury caused by hiring of unstable seaman. Employer not liable. ***Klineburger v. Maritrans*, 404 Pa. Super. 490, 591 A.2d 314.**

Judicial Immunity

Plaintiff sued an investigative consultant for the Bureau of Program Integrity for negligently conducting his investigation into the Plaintiff's dental practice on behalf of the Department of Public Welfare. The trial court denied the investigator's preliminary objections asserting judicial immunity. The Superior Court affirmed holding that investigation for the Bureau of Program Integrity did not involve impending or pending judicial acts permitting judicial immunity. ***Pollina v. Dishong*, 2014 Pa. Super. 153 (2014).**

Knee

—K—

Knee

Plaintiff brought negligence action against marketing firm and knee replacement manufacturer for injuries she suffered while riding an exercise bike in a promotional video. A jury found in favor of the Plaintiff. The Superior Court reversed on appeal holding that a treating physician's opinions on causation could not be shielded from the required expert disclosure in a pre-trial statement. It also held that as a matter of impression a physician could be cross-examined based upon an agreement signed with the Plaintiff to toll the statute of limitations for lawsuits to be filed against him by the Plaintiff. ***Polett v. Public Communications, Inc.*, 83 A.3d 205 (Pa. Super. 2013).**

Plaintiff who fails to participate significantly in postoperative care of knee risks loss of any claim for alleged negligence of physician in performing surgery. The Comparative Negligence Act is not applicable in such cases because of the inability to apportion liability between both parties. ***Ferguson v. Panzarella*, 445 Pa. Super. 23, 664 A.2d 989 (1995).**

Knee immobilizer

In medical malpractice action for failure of physician to inform physical therapy provider not to remove a knee immobilizer from patient's knee, order granting motion for nonsuit reversed where defendant offered self-serving testimony and exhibits during plaintiffs' case in chief. Plaintiffs' expert's testimony offered in first person form is sufficient to establish deviation from standard of care and so precludes entry of nonsuit. ***Joyce v. Boulevard Physical Therapy*, ___ Pa. Super. ___, 694 A.2d 648 (1997).**

Knife

Minor student injured when a small knife blade in classroom carpet became imbedded in his knee. Summary judgment affirmed based on failure of circumstances to fall within real property exception to Political Subdivision Tort Claims Act. Liability may not be imposed upon a governmental entity for injuries caused by its negligent failure to remove foreign substances from its real estate. ***Wolfe v. Stroudsburg Area School District*, 688 A.2d 1245 (Pa. Cmwlth. 1997).**

Knockdown at crosswalk

Crossing guard leading children across street. Observed skidding car and ordered children back to curb. 11 year old plaintiff ran wrong way. Verdict against driver, guard, and city (employer). ***Ross v. Vereb*, 481 Pa. 446, 392 A.2d 1376.**

Knowledge of danger

Plaintiff sued grocery store for negligence when plaintiff tripped over the store's blind employee's cane and was injured. The court held that obstacles are a known or obvious danger when exiting an aisle in a grocery store. A grocery store has no duty to warn of risks arising from entering or exiting its aisles. ***Campisi v. Acme Markets, Inc.*, 915 A.2d 117 (Pa. Super. 2006).**

Knowledge of danger

Plaintiff teenager brought suit against above ground pool owner for injuries suffered when she dove into four feet of water and suffered serious injuries to her neck. Order granting motion for compulsory nonsuit affirmed where evidence by plaintiff established that she was aware of danger of diving into shallow water; she was aware of depth of the water in the pool; and she proceeded to dive into the pool "on a dare". Plaintiff's status as licensee or trespasser not a factor in light of her knowledge of danger. Property owner's duty does not extend to those conditions the existence of which is obvious even to children, and the risk of which is fully realized by them, particularly when the child chooses to encounter the risk through recklessness or bravado. ***Long v. Manzo*, 452 Pa. Super. 451, 682 A.2d 370 (1996).**

Order granting summary judgment in favor of landowners and independent contractor-employer of injured trench digger affirmed. Injured employee may not recover against landowner when independent contractor has control of property on which trench was being dug and there was no "peculiar risk" to the trench digging operation of which the landowner had greater knowledge than the injured person. ***Motter v. Meadows Limited Partnership*, 451 Pa. Super. 520, 680 A.2d 887 (1996).**

In action by bus passenger who stepped off of bus and onto broken storm sewer, possessor of land may be liable for physical harm to a licensee caused by conditions on land of which possessor has actual or constructive knowledge. Order granting motion for nonsuit affirmed. ***Colston v. SEPTA*, ___ Pa. Cmwlth. ___, 679 A.2d 299 (1996).**

Jury verdict for plaintiff reduced 20% for contributory negligence. Defendant's auto struck plaintiff's garden tractor head-on as he was plowing snow from his driveway near berm of highway. Exact locations of vehicles at impact disputed. Essence of assumption of risk defense is not fault, but a knowledgeable change of position by plaintiff by acquiescing in a known danger. Exposing one's self to traffic is not a consent to drivers, that they abandon their duty of care. The exposure is a factor only in the negligence analysis. ***Fish v. Gosnell*, 316 Pa. Super. 565, 463 A.2d 1042.**

Pedestrian-tenant fell on defect in sidewalk which had been present for some time. Covered by leaves at time of injury. Compulsory nonsuit reversed. ***Landy v. Romeo*, 274 Pa. Super. 75, 417 A.2d 1260.**

Suit by brother against sister for injuries sustained in collapse of platform and steps outside door of sister's home. Verdict for defendant. Brother a frequent visitor and had owned house until four months before accident. No evidence of previous problems. ***Claycomb v. Claycomb*, 263 Pa. Super. 277, 397 A.2d 1207.**

Explosion at gas station injured wife of owner. Summary judgment in favor of former owner reversed. For jury as to who may have had knowledge of defect at time of sale. ***Bonneau v. Ralph and Martin Oil*, 259 Pa. Super. 428, 393 A.2d 901.**

Female pedestrian walking an accustomed route in broad daylight with knowledge that defendant's pavement was partly defective—alleging presence of another pedestrian obscured view—sidestepping and falling—judgment n.o.v.—

Knowledge of danger

plaintiff had already observed defective condition—distraction not an excuse. *Kresovich v. Fitzsimmons*, **439 Pa. 10, 264 A.2d 585.**

Landlord and tenant

—L—

Labor dispute

Member of local union, on picket duty during labor dispute, injured in fight. Even assuming unions created atmosphere susceptible to violence, there is no duty to refrain from creating such an atmosphere. ***LaZar v. Rur Industries*, 337 Pa. Super. 445, 487 A.2d 29.**

Laches

Court below granted a nonsuit as to one defendant—post trial motions filed but not ordered down for argument for seven years—court below within its discretion in dismissing motion on ground, inter alia, of laches. ***Shrum v. Penns. Elec. Co.*, 440 Pa. 383, 269 A.2d 502.**

Ladder

Falling from ladder—sidewalk cement giving way—improper filling by water department authority—authority held responsible but new trial as to landlord who was out of possession. ***Dinio v. Goshorn*, 437 Pa. 224, 270 A.2d 203.**

Plaintiff given privilege by defendant to store certain property in a hay loft—no charge for same—ladder to loft provided access—ladder slipped and plaintiff injured—no evidence of a latent defect—nonsuit proper—plaintiff but a gratuitous licensee. ***Sharp v. Luksa*, 440 Pa. 125, 269 A.2d 658.**

Plaintiff electrician injured by fall from ladder—suit against property owner and contractor—contention that locking device defective—a ladder photographed 52 days after occurrence but not shown to be ladder involved—plaintiff did not see locking device—nonsuit proper. ***Semet v. Andorra Nurseries, Inc.*, 421 Pa. 484, 219 A.2d 357.**

Landlord and tenant

Mother filed negligence lawsuit against a landlord after one of their tenant's dogs bit her child. The trial court entered summary judgment in favor of the Defendant. The Superior Court affirmed holding that a landlord that is out of possession cannot be liable for attacks by tenant's animal without evidence that the landlord was aware the animal was dangerous. ***Rosenberry v. Evans*, 48 A.3d 1255 (Pa. Super. 2012).**

Tenant sued landlord for breach of duty for failing to repair a leaking basement on the leased premise after promising to repair it. Trial court dismissed plaintiff's negligence claim because it reasoned the liability arose out of the signed lease and was a contract claim, not a negligence claim. The Superior Court reversed holding that the negligence claim arose from the landlord having a legal duty to exercise reasonable care when repairing a known dangerous condition on a leased premises, which arose from her promise to repair. ***Reed v. Dupuis*, 920 A.2d 861 (Pa. Super. 2007).**

Landlord and tenant

Hills and ridges doctrine regarding ice and snow accumulations applies to landlord and tenant relationships. ***Biernacki v. Presque Isle Condominiums Unit Owners Association, Inc.*, 828 A.2d 1114 (Pa. Super. 2003).**

In action on behalf of minor for injuries sustained by exposure to lead-based paint in Philadelphia Housing Authority property, distinction drawn between contract claim of breach of the implied warranty of habitability and negligence claims against landlord for care and condition of property. Delay damages awarded on basis of negligence claim under breach of implied warranty of habitability reversed as unavailable in contract action. ***McIntyre v. Philadelphia Housing Authority*, 816 A.2d 1204 (Pa. Cmwlth. 2003).**

Plaintiff's minor child was injured when he fell from a deck on a rented apartment. The deck was not designed or built in compliance with BOCA codes. On verdict for plaintiff, defendant appeals alleging that exculpatory clause in lease releases landlord from liability. Held: exculpatory clause violates public policy as deck was built in violation of code. ***Schultz v. DeVaux*, 715 A.2d 479 (1998).**

City's failure to supervise and control criminal detainee who left work release facility and murdered plaintiffs' decedent is not a recognized exception to governmental immunity. City's indemnification of lessor of work release facility was not a waiver of governmental immunity in favor of plaintiffs. Summary judgment affirmed. ***Rodriguez v. City of Philadelphia, Dept. of Human Services*, ___ Pa. Cmwlth. ___, 657 A.2d 105 (1995).**

Tenant's grandchild injured after eating lead-based paint chips. Landlord not liable. ***Felton by Felton v. Spratley*, 433 Pa. Super. 474, 640 A.2d 1358.**

Employee of tenant brought action against landlord for injuries sustained in fall. Held: 2 year statute of limitations applied. ***Ritchy v. Pratt*, 431 Pa. Super. 219, 636 A.2d 208.**

Tenant slipped and fell in parking lot. Summary judgment for landlord reversed. ***Bleam v. Gateway Professional Center Associates*, 431 Pa. Super. 145, 636 A.2d 172.**

Tenant slipped on bag covering greasy substance on stairway. Housing authority not liable. ***Walker v. Philadelphia Housing Authority*, 158 Pa. Cmwlth. 497, 631 A.2d 1117.**

Parents of child injured in fall down stairs brought action against landlord. Held: summary judgment improper. Question of fact existed. ***Kelly by Kelly v. Ickes*, 427 Pa. Super. 542, 629 A.2d 1002.**

Tenant brought action against landlord for damage caused by water leak. Exculpatory clause in lease enforceable. ***Topp Copy Products, Inc. v. Singletary*, 533 Pa. 468, 626 A.2d 98.**

Guest at party brought action against owner of party site. Owner leased premises to fraternity. Question of whether owner was landlord out of possession was disputed issue. ***Forgang v. Universal Gym Company*, 423 Pa. Super. 416, 621 A.2d 601.**

Landlord and tenant

Tenant suffered spontaneous abortion of seventeen-week fetus due to collapse of apartment. Actions for wrongful death, survivorship, and loss of consortium not maintainable. ***McCaskill v. Philadelphia Housing Authority*, 419 Pa. Super. 313, 615 A.2d 382.**

Employee of tenant brought action against landlord for injuries resulting from fall on stairs caused by rainwater tracked in by people using stairway. Landlord not liable. No hidden defect. ***Dorsey v. Continental Associates*, 404 Pa. Super. 525, 591 A.2d 716.**

Commercial tenant brought negligence action against landlord for damage caused by leaking water in apartment above. Landlord liable. Exculpatory clause in lease not enforceable. ***Topp Copy Products, Inc. v. Singletory*, 404 Pa. Super. 459, 591 A.2d 298.**

Tenant was victim of criminal attack on stairway outside her apartment. Question of whether landlord was negligent for failing to repair lock on front door after promising to do so was for jury to decide. ***Reider v. Martin*, 359 Pa. Super. 586, 519 A.2d 507.**

Social guest of tenant injured in fall in stairwell. Held: landlord out of possession not liable for injuries to third party. ***Kobylinski v. Hipps*, 359 Pa. Super. 549, 519 A.2d 488.**

Service-station customer slipped and fell in doorway. Held: landlord out of possession is not liable for conditions that are not apparent during inspection. ***Henze v. Texaco, Inc.*, 352 Pa. Super. 538, 508 A.2d 1200.**

Philadelphia Housing Authority was both a lessor and lessee of complex on which repairman fell while going to repair a tenant's appliance. Under facts, improper to direct verdict for P.H.A. ***Pierce v. Philadelphia Housing Authority*, 519 Pa. Super. 491, 486 A.2d 1004.**

Landlord corporation not responsible for actions of licensee tenant in serving minors and visibly intoxicated persons who are later involved in accident. Corporate owner of real estate here granted nonsuit. ***McCreny v. Scioli*, 336 Pa. Super. 455, 485 A.2d 1170.**

Reverses Superior Court decision and vacates verdict. Landlord's duty to protect tenants from criminal acts of third persons held to be very limited. Tenants may rely only on protection offered within the reasonable expectations of the program. A tenant may not expect more than is offered. Under facts, error to submit punitive damages to jury as to landlord. No evidence of evil motive or reckless indifference to safety of tenants. ***Feld v. Merriam*, 506 Pa. 383, 485 A.2d 742.**

Out-of-possession landlord held responsible for injuries to minor tenant inflicted by another tenant's dog. Dog owner was nephew of landlord and landlord knew of dog's dangerous propensities. ***Palerno v. Nails*, 334 Pa. Super. 544, 483 A.2d 871.**

Tenants brought action against apartment complex to recover for injuries resulting from criminal assault and kidnapping of tenants. Act originated in apart-

Landlord and tenant

ment garage. Evidence of previous criminal activity and alleged inadequate security. Held: landlord does have duty to provide adequate security to protect tenants from foreseeable criminal activity of third persons. Landlord here held to have had sufficient notice. **Feld v. Merriam, 314 Pa. Super. 414, 461 A.2d 225.**

Death in fire at leased premises. Under circumstances, Fire and Panic Act, 35 P.S. §1222, does not apply. Complaint, however, does state cause of action in negligence—§17.6 of Restatement (2d) Property. Case remanded for trial. **Asper v. Haffley, 312 Pa. Super. 424, 458 A.2d 1364.**

Jury verdict $200,000 for crush injury with permanent disability—male warehouse employee, in dark parking lot. Employee guiding tractor-trailer rigs, by voice, with hand on rig. Fell in parking lot hole. Issue of plaintiff's circumstances with lease silent. Lessor has, over years, undertaken to keep parking area in repair. Held: therefore, a continuing duty to keep it reasonably safe for tenants use. **McDevitt v. Terminal Warehouse Co., 304 Pa. Super. 438, 450 A.2d 991.**

Plaintiff insurance carrier covered its assured for damages by water—claim paid and company subrogated—damage resulted from defects in sprinkler system which allegedly existed prior to the date of leasing—exculpatory clause in lease held not to necessarily relieve landlord from responsibility—nonsuit improper. **Employers L.A.C. Ltd. v. Greenville Business Mens Association, 423 Pa. 288, 423 A.2d 620.**

Plaintiff tenant fell as the result of a breaking off of a small piece of concrete at the entrance of his rented property—nonsuit improperly entered—case falls within Section 357 of Restatement (2d) Torts when landlord agrees to make repairs. **Walters v. Char-Mar, Inc., 220 Pa. Super. 79, 284 A.2d 139.**

An employee of a tenant fell from a ladder placed on sidewalk abutting premises owned by one of defendants—such defendant out of possession and held not legally responsible by Supreme Court but only new trial granted as the defendant had filed no motion n.o.v. **Dinio v. Goshorn, 437 Pa. 224, 270 A.2d 203.**

Plaintiffs were tenants of first four floors of building owned by one of defendants—rental agents also defendants—a sprinkler pipe broke as a result of freezing on fifth floor and damaged plaintiff's property—exculpatory clause in lease agreements held not to exculpate agents as release clause did not expressly include negligence prior to leasing. **Kotwasinski et al. v. Rasner et al., 436 Pa. 32, 258 A.2d 865.**

Exculpatory clause in lease agreement—plaintiff's land damaged by fumes and smoke—land covered by lease agreement not included in damage clause—error for court to sustain preliminary objections to the pleadings—matter for the jury. **King v. U. S. Steel Corporation, 432 Pa. 140, 247 A.2d 563.**

Plaintiff fell in driveway in front of a market operated by defendant but owned by added defendant—added defendant as owner only responsible if there existed a failure to inspect or a failure to repair after knowledge of defect—neither condition averred in complaint to add additional defendant—complaint as stated did not state a cause of action against added defendant. **Presley v. Acme Markets, Inc., 213 Pa. Super. 265, 247 A.2d 478.**

Laryngeal nerve

Landlord leased premises in an admittedly defective condition—orally promising to repair—wife plaintiff fell as result of defective condition—Supreme Court reversed Harris v. Lewistown Trust Co. (326 Pa. 145) and held that a recovery may be had. ***Reitmeyer v. Sprecher*, 431 Pa. 284, 243 A.2d 395.**

Property leased to parents of deceased minor—child ate paint which had peeled from living room woodwork and child died as the result of lead poisoning—preliminary objections in the nature of a demurrer sustained—no liability on either landlord or rental agent—use of lead paint not basis for an action—no covenant to repair and no warrant that premises were habitable. ***Kolojeski v. John Deisher, Inc.*, 429 Pa. 191, 239 A.2d 329.**

Plaintiff, a tenant of defendant's multiple leased premises, injured while attempting to adjust a heating vent—no notice of defective condition given to landlord—perhaps also guilty of contributory negligence—nonsuit proper. ***Smith v. M.P.W. Realty Company, Inc.*, 423 Pa. 536, 225 A.2d 227.**

Tenant fell on lawn abutting defendant's apartment house—exculpatory clause in lease agreement did not specifically mention lawn—Supreme Court by divided court held clause insufficient to support judgment on pleadings for the defendant. ***Galligan v. Arovitch*, 421 Pa. 301, 219 A.2d 463.**

Defendant landlord leased part of an industrial building and retained part for its own use—plaintiff injured by cave-in of part of first floor—landlord held responsible—evidence of notice of defective condition. ***Pratt v. Scott Enterprises, Inc.*, 421 Pa. 46, 218 A.2d 795.**

Landslide

Landslide from strip mine regulated by Department of Environmental Resources damaged railroad's right of way. Department immune. ***CSX Transportation Inc. v. Franty Construction*, 157 Pa. Cmwlth. 620, 630 A.2d 932.**

Truck damaged in landslide on Commonwealth-owned property. Plaintiff established issues of material fact concerning negligent maintenance by Commonwealth. ***Trenco, Inc. v. Com., Dept. of Transp.*, 126 Pa. Cmwlth. 501, 560 A.2d 285.**

Lanes of travel

Entry of nonsuit reversed. Three lane highway. Plaintiff went into middle lane to make left turn. Defendant cut ahead without signal. Plaintiff swerved, lost control, collided with parked van and was killed. For jury. ***Herman v. Horst*, 255 Pa. Super. 232, 386 A.2d 594.**

Laryngeal nerve

Expert medical testimony in a medical malpractice case involving damage to a laryngeal nerve and resulting hoarseness which establishes (1) that the type of injury complained of does not usually occur without negligence, (2) that other responsible causes, including the conduct of plaintiff or other persons are sufficiently eliminated by evidence and (3) that the indicated negligent act was performed with-

Last Clear Chance Doctrine

in the scope of the defendant's duty to the plaintiff prohibits a compulsory nonsuit and calls for an instruction on res ipsa loquitur. ***Hightower-Warren v. Silk*, 698 A.2d 52 (Pa. 1997).**

Last Clear Chance Doctrine

The court ruled in verse, short but not terse, and addressed all the issues presented. Two dogs and their walker, came in for a shocker, when defendant's car made one dog dented. The vet's fee at issue, for damaged dog tissue, composed the poor plaintiff's pup's claim. Driver argued contrib, cut short for this squib, as the reason the poor dog was maimed. He loudly protested, the dog was molested, because it came into the road. Unfortunately, for the driver you see, the transcript defies that contention. Sudden emergency, last clear chance, both theories were raised and were argued. The superior court, to excuse the tort, found naught in the facts or the pleadings. Payment is due, from you know who, and the dogs and their owner keep strolling. Though written in verse, which some find perverse, this case is correct and controlling. ***Zangrando v. Sipula*, 756 A.2d 73 (Pa. Super. 2000).**

Seventeen-year old plaintiff riding on running board of pickup truck—fell from truck. Cause of action prior to Comparative Negligence Act. Plaintiff held contributorily negligent as matter of law. Proper holding but new trial awarded. Jury to determine wanton, reckless conduct of defendant/driver or whether he had last clear chance to avoid injury. ***Hill v. Crawford*, 308 Pa. Super. 502, 454 A.2d 647.**

Where pedestrian stepped onto roadway in front of car, for jury to determine if driver had enough time to avoid accident. ***Smith v. Chardale*, 295 Pa. Super. 173, 435 A.2d 624.**

Latent defects

Six-year statute of limitations for latent defect in construction case runs from date injured party becomes aware, or by exercise of reasonable diligence should have become aware, of the defect. ***Romeo & Sons, Inc. v. P.C. Yezbak & Son, Inc.*, 539 Pa. 390, 652 A.2d 830 (1995).**

Tenant broke ankle when board broke on front porch used in common by all tenants in building. Jury verdict $38,695. Although charge of court in error as to duty of landlord where independent contractor hired to make repairs, here verdict showed independent negligence on part of landlord, therefore error harmless. ***Speer v. Barry*, 349 Pa. Super. 365, 503 A.2d 409.**

Lawn

Tenant fell on lawn abutting defendant's apartment house—exculpatory clause in lease agreement did not specifically mention lawn—Supreme Court by divided court held clause insufficient to support judgment on pleadings for the defendant. ***Galligan v. Arovitch*, 421 Pa. 301, 219 A.2d 463.**

Lawn mower

Trial court's grant of new trial reversed where testimony offered by rebuttal witness was proper evidence of facts different from those on which defendant's experts relied in forming their opinions of how accident involving lawn mover occurred. Jury confusion as to procedure for allocating damages between multiple defendants involved in multiple theories of liability is insignificant when jury clearly establishes in polling that the verdict, as deciphered by trial judge in presence of all counsel, is the verdict upon which they agreed. ***Mitchell v. Gravely International, Inc.*, 698 A.2d 618 (Pa. Super. 1997).**

Jury verdict $37,000. Loss of eye struck by object ejected from lawn mower. Plaintiff a passerby. ***Lavin v. Mylecraine*, 307 Pa. Super. 564, 453 A.2d 1031.**

Lead poisoning

Philadelphia Housing Authority found liable for injuries and damages suffered by minor child of tenant who suffered irreversible brain damage due to ingestion of lead-based paint at public housing unit. ***Ford v. Philadelphia Housing Authority*, 848 A.2d 1038 (Pa. Cmwlth. 2004).**

In action on behalf of minor for injuries sustained by exposure to lead-based paint in Philadelphia Housing Authority property, distinction drawn between contract claim of breach of the implied warranty of habitability and negligence claims against landlord for care and condition of property. Delay damages awarded on basis of negligence claim under breach of implied warranty of habitability reversed as unavailable in contract action. ***McIntyre v. Philadelphia Housing Authority*, 816 A.2d 1204 (Pa. Cmwlth. 2003).**

Painting contractor sued by property owner in contract and negligence for failure to abate lead paint during job. Dismissal of contract claim affirmed. Dismissal of negligence claim reversed on grounds that a party to a contract has two duties: a contractual duty and a legal duty to act without negligence towards both the other party to the contract and third parties. One who creates a condition on behalf of a possessor of land has the same liability as the possessor of the land for physical harm to others caused by the dangerous condition. ***Reformed Church v. Hooven*, 764 A.2d 1106 (Pa. Super. 2000).**

Pennsylvania has not yet adopted the market share liability theory as an exception to the general rule of negligence law that a plaintiff must establish that a particular defendant proximately caused his or her injury. Summary judgment affirmed in favor of lead manufacturers and trade organization sued by minor injured by lead poisoning. ***Skipworth v. Lead Industries Association, Inc.*, 547 Pa. 224, 690 A.2d 169 (1997).**

Pennsylvania has not adopted the use of market share liability as a theory of recovery. Action for injuries suffered by minor child as a result of lead poisoning dismissed because of plaintiff's failure to allege identity of suppliers of lead-based paint and lack of causal connection. Summary judgment affirmed. ***Skipworth v. Lead Industries Association, Inc.*, 445 Pa. Super. 610, 665 A.2d 1288 (1995).**

Property leased to parents of deceased minor—child ate paint which had peeled from living room woodwork and child died as the result of lead poisoning—preliminary objections in the nature of a demurrer sustained—no liability on either landlord or rental agent—use of lead paint not basis for an action—no covenant to

Learned Intermediary Doctrine

repair and no warrant that premises were habitable. ***Kolojeski v. John Deisher, Inc.*, 429 Pa. 191, 239 A.2d 329.**

Learned Intermediary Doctrine

Medical device amendments to the Federal Food, Drug and Cosmetic Act of 1938 preempt state court action for breach of implied warranties of merchantability and fitness for a particular purpose regarding surgical bone plates and screws. Express warranties as to condition or properties of bone plates and screws are not preempted by the amendments. Learned intermediary doctrine does not preclude patient's suit against manufacturer on an express warranty made in connection with the sale of a prescription device. Order granting summary judgment affirmed in part and reversed in part. ***Rosci v. Acromed, Inc.*, ___ Pa. Super. ___, 669 A.2d 959 (1995).**

Leased equipment or vehicle

Plaintiff brought negligence action against Defendant after the front wheel of the vehicle it leased to Plaintiff's employer fell off while Plaintiff was driving it. The trial court entered summary judgment in favor of the Defendant. The Superior Court affirmed holding that Plaintiff had to provide expert testimony to prove the existence of a mechanical defect in the vehicle that caused the front wheel to fall off. ***Brandon v. Ryder Truck Rental, Inc.*, 34 A.3d 104 (Pa. Super. 2011).**

Plaintiff driving loaner car while his vehicle being serviced. Accident occurred allegedly due to defect in right rear axle shaft. Section 402A of Restatement (2d) Torts held to apply to supplier of chattel even if lease arrangement exists. ***Mandel v. Gulf Leasing*, 250 Pa. Super. 128, 378 A.2d 487.**

Leases

Plaintiff tripped and fell on a crack in sidewalk immediately adjacent to street level "head house" of subway entrance. Plaintiff sued SEPTA and City of Philadelphia, alleging that under lease between City and SEPTA, one or both of those entities was responsible for maintenance of sidewalk. Trial court determined that lease was ambiguous as to responsibility for area of sidewalk at issue and so allowed parol evidence. Jury found that SEPTA was responsible for maintenance. Jury verdict was entered against both City and SEPTA. Post trial motions by City and SEPTA were denied. Held on appeal: if SEPTA were found to be responsible, City should have been granted judgment n.o.v. Remand to enter judgment n.o.v. in favor of City of Philadelphia. ***Smith v. SEPTA*, 707 A.2d 604 (Pa. Cmwlth. 1998).**

No-Fault Act does not impose liability upon lessor of automobile caused by lessee's negligence. ***Jahn v. O'Neill et al.*, 327 Pa. Super. 357, 475 A.2d 837.**

Where crane was being operated by fellow employee, there can be no liability on leasing company unless accompanied by independent conduct on leasing company's part. Order dismissing complaint for indemnity here affirmed under particular facts and pleadings. ***McKee v. McHugh Brothers*, 327 Pa. Super. 170, 475 A.2d 153.**

Plaintiff insurance carrier covered its assured for damages by water—claim paid and company subrogated—damage resulted from defects in sprinkler system which allegedly existed prior to the date of leasing—exculpatory clause in lease held not to necessarily relieve landlord from responsibility—nonsuit improper. ***Employers L.A.C. Ltd. v. Greenville Business Mens Association*, 423 Pa. 288, 423 A.2d 620.**

Plaintiff rented ski equipment and later fell. Bindings did not release. Signed lease had exculpatory clause. Summary judgment as to count under lease in favor of defendant affirmed. ***Zimmer v. Mitchell and Ness*, 253 Pa. Super. 474, 385 A.2d 437.**

Court reaffirmed applicability of §402A of Restatement (2d) Torts to supplier of defective chattel even though chattel was leased. ***Nath v. National Equipment*, 473 Pa. 178, 373 A.2d 1105.**

Defendant made a lease to rent an 8 ton truck to one K. K struck an overhead railroad bridge with top of truck—plaintiff passenger injured—no recovery from defendant lessor. ***Littles et al. v. Avis Rent-A-Car System*, 433 Pa. 72, 248 A.2d 837.**

Leaves

Pedestrian-tenant fell on defect in sidewalk which had been present for some time although covered by leaves at time of injury. Held: issue of contributory negligence for jury. Entry of compulsory nonsuit reversed. ***Landy v. Romeo*, 274 Pa. Super. 75, 417 A.2d 1260.**

Left turn

PennDOT had never been requested to approve such a sign by township despite repeated township inquiries concerning available ways to make the intersection safer. Commonwealth Court affirmed denial of township's post trial motion on basis of township's affirmative duty to make its roads safe for intended users pursuant to McCalla v. Mura, 538 Pa. 527, 649 A.2d 646 (1994) and Bendas v. Township of White Deer, 531 Pa. 180, 611 A.2d 1184 (1992). ***Starr v. Veneziano*, 705 A.2d 950 (Pa. Cmwlth. 1998).**

Driver of automobile injured in collision with truck while making left turn into store parking lot. Owner of store not liable. Highway under control of PennDOT. ***Allen v. Mellinger*, 156 Pa. Cmwlth. 113, 625 A.2d 1326.**

Motorcycle passenger sued driver of auto making left turn into path of motorcycle. Judge at trial entered nonsuit in favor of motorcycle driver who was joined as additional defendant. Jury verdict then in favor of original defendant. Trial judge granted new trial on damages only, since jury was prejudiced against motorcycles. Superior Court reversed nonsuit in favor of additional defendant and ordered new trial on all issues as to defendant. Affirmed finding that verdict was the result of biased jury. ***Eagleson v. Malone*, 319 Pa. Super. 163, 465 A.2d 1280.**

Collision between auto and bicycle. Improper for court not to charge on duty of auto making left turn where there was a dispute as to whether accident occurred during or after left turn completed. ***Adams v. Mackleer*, 239 Pa. Super. 244, 361 A.2d 439.**

Legal malpractice

Compulsory nonsuit of lower court reversed. Plaintiff remembered nothing after entering intersection with green light. Police testified point of impact in plaintiff's lane and concluded that defendant attempting left turn. For jury. *Zevas v. Poniktera*, 238 Pa. Super. 375, 357 A.2d 654.

Plaintiff stopped car preparatory to making a left turn into supermarket—defendant's car colliding with plaintiff's stopped vehicle—court must charge on duty of driver making left turn—Section 1012, as amended, of Vehicle Code applies—new trial granted. *McMahon v. Young*, 442 Pa. 484, 276 A.2d 534.

Operator continued to observe car approaching from opposite direction until 50 feet from intersection—then making no further observation and started left turn at intersection—collision—violating Section 1012 of Vehicle Code—guilty of contributory negligence as a matter of law. *Leasure v. Heller*, 436 Pa. 108, 258 A.2d 855.

When nature of highway does not call for a left turn to be made by motorist, it is error for trial judge to charge on the provisions of the Motor Vehicle Code as to left turns. *Vescio v. Rubolino*, 433 Pa. 253, 249 A.2d 914.

Plaintiff traveling south and defendant north on same street—plaintiff started left turn when defendant about 100 to 150 feet away—plaintiff's car struck on right rear fender—case for fact finders—verdict for plaintiff affirmed. *Pascucci v. Derenick*, 213 Pa. Super. 49, 245 A.2d 474.

Legal malpractice

Plaintiff brought legal malpractice claim against her attorneys after they failed to file her medical malpractice claim within the statute of limitations. The trial court granted summary judgment for the Defendants. The Superior Court reversed and remanded holding that the Plaintiff had shown sufficient evidence to maintain medical malpractice claims against both her hospital and nursing home. *Sokolsky v. Eidelman*, 93 A.3d 858 (Pa. Super. 2014).

Plaintiff brought a legal malpractice action against an attorney for failing to finalize the plaintiff's alimony agreement. A jury found in favor of the plaintiff. The Superior Court affirmed, holding that an attorney's failure to finalize a tentative alimony agreement after the essential terms of the agreement had been agreed upon was sufficient to establish legal malpractice. *O'Kelly v. Dawson*, 62 A.3d 414 (Pa. Super. 2013).

Plaintiffs brought legal malpractice claim against a law firm and attorney for mishandling the sale of the plaintiffs' company leaving them personally liable for unpaid corporate taxes. The trial court granted judgment on the pleadings for the defendant. The Superior Court reversed, holding that in a legal malpractice claim based upon breach of an attorney-client agreement a continued tax liability could constitute an actual loss to establish legal malpractice and damages were not limited only to attorneys' fees paid. *Coleman v. Duane Morris, LLP.*, 58 A.3d 833 (Pa. Super. 2012).

Legal malpractice

Plaintiff-mother and Plaintiff-son brought professional negligence action against their former attorney for simultaneously representing both of them when they had adverse interests in the estate of Plaintiff-mother's husband. A jury found in favor of the Defendants. The Superior Court on appeal upheld the trial court's ruling holding that the Rules of Professional Conduct could not be used as jury instructions. ***Smith v. Morrison*, 47 A.3d 131 (Pa. Super. 2012).**

Plaintiff bankruptcy trustee brought professional negligence action against Defendant law firm alleging that it had negligently conducted its investigation into allegations of fraud at the bankrupt corporation. The trial court dismissed the case on preliminary objections. The Superior Court reversed holding that allegations the Defendant law firm had negligently conducted its investigation into the looting of the firm leading to ongoing looting of the company were sufficient to establish a prima facie case of professional negligence. ***Kirschner v. K & L Gates LLP*, 46 A.3d 737 (Pa. Super. 2012).**

Plaintiff brought a claim for legal malpractice against Defendant attorney, which was dismissed by the trial court as the statute of limitations had passed. The Superior Court sua sponte held that the Plaintiff's Complaint set forth a claim for breach of contract despite the fact that only legal malpractice had been raised in the pleadings. Pennsylvania Supreme Court reversed the Superior Court, holding that an appellate court could not raise an issue on appeal that had not been argued and preserved by the parties. ***Steiner v. Markel*, 968 A.2d 1253 (Pa. 2009).**

Bank brought claim against attorney for legal malpractice for failing to mark a judgment satisfied, which resulted in a judgment against the bank when it was sued for that failure. The appellate court held that the malpractice claim accrued at the time the bank could have reasonably been aware of the breach and not when judgment was entered against the bank and therefore the statute of limitations prevented judgment against the attorney. ***Wachovia Bank, N.A. v. Ferretti*, 935 A.2d 565 (Pa. Super. 2007).**

Plaintiffs sued defendant attorney for legal malpractice for negligently drafting their mother's will leading to their diminished inheritance. Court held that an attorney-client relationship must be shown between plaintiff and defendant to maintain a legal malpractice action. ***Hess v. Fox Rothschild, L.L.P.*, 925 A.2d 798 (Pa. Super. 2007).**

Suit by deceased's husband who was executor and legatee of decedent's estate against attorney who drafted will was dismissed on summary judgment because there was no evidence by plaintiff that effect of will was inconsistent with testatrix's wishes. ***Jones v. Wilt*, 871 A.2d 210 (Pa. Super. 2005).**

Elemental analysis of legal malpractice and nature of attorney-client relationship. ***Capital Care Corporation v. Hunt*, 847 A.2d 75 (Pa. Super. 2004).**

Failure of recorder of deed's docketing clerk to correctly index a mortgage led to financial damages to plaintiff. In granting j.n.o.v. to recorder as defedant, held that Political Subdivision Tort Claims Act applies to actions of recorder of deeds alleged to be negligent and alleged negligence was not within exceptions to

Legal malpractice

immunity conferred by act. Affirmed holding that mortgagee's attorney's failure to check that mortgage was properly recorded was negligent. ***Antonis v. Liberati*, 821 A.2d 666 (Pa. Cmwlth. 2003).**

Son of deceased mother filed suit alleging legal malpractice against attorney for his father because attorney did not immediately probate mother's will which established substantial trust for son. Son alleged two theories: He was third party beneficiary of contract between father and attorney and incurred damages in being required to force probate of mother's will and attorney was negligent per se because he had, prior to son's forcing of probate of will, concealed the existence of mother's will. Held that criminal statute imposing criminal penalty for concealment of a will is designed to protect society at large, not beneficiaries and so there can be no negligence per se for violation; and son was not owed any duty by attorney, despite his beneficiary status, as father's interests in managing his deceased wife's estate was primarily obligation of attorney's representation. ***Minnich v. Yost*, 817 A.2d 538 (Pa. Super. 2003).**

In legal malpractice case, any contributory negligence of plaintiff client is a complete bar to recovery because the comparative negligence act only applies to cases involving death, injury or damage to tangible property. ***Gorski v. Smith*, 812 A.2d 683 (Pa. Super. 2003).**

Elemental analysis of legal malpractice claim in suit by client against attorney who failed to timely file suit against third party tortfeasor in worker's compensation claim. On issue of whether decision against plaintiff in worker's compensation claim collaterally estopped suit against attorney for failure to file the third party claim, held that the decision of the worker's compensation judge that plaintiff was not disabled was not a determination that he was not injured and so action against third party tortfeasor would have been able to proceed. ***Nelson v. Neslin*, 806 A.2d 873 (Pa. Super. 2002).**

In legal malpractice case, plaintiff must establish employment of attorney or another basis for duty, failure of attorney to exercise ordinary skill and knowledge, and that such negligence was proximate cause of damages to plaintiff. Plaintiff must also establish that she would have recovered in underlying action. Failure to plead or prove any element precludes claim of legal malpractice. The increased risk of harm standard for determining negligence does not apply in legal malpractice case. ***Myers v. Robert Lewis Seigle, P.C.*, 751 A.2d 1182 (Pa. Super. 2000).**

Suit by plaintiff against bar association lawyer referral service for negligent referral to an attorney who failed to file plaintiff's suit within statute of limitations period. Pennsylvania law does not recognize a claim for "negligent referral." ***Bourke v. Kazaras*, 746 A.2d 642 (Pa. Super. 2000).**

Plaintiff filed legal malpractice action against attorney who missed statute of limitations date on plaintiff's personal injury action. After the trial court determined that plaintiff's ability to collect damages from tortfeasor who had not been sued was not relevant to malpractice claim, jury returned verdict against defendant attorney in amount of $2,300,00. On appeal, Superior Court affirmed verdict and irrelevance

Legal malpractice

of plaintiff's ability to collect damages; Supreme Court granted allocatur. In case of first impression in Pennsylvania, Supreme Court added fourth element to any legal malpractice case: (1) employment of attorney or another basis for duty: (2) failure of attorney to exercise reasonable skill and knowledge; (3) that such negligence was proximate cause of damage to plaintiff; and (4) affirmative defense of non-collectibility, i.e., that plaintiff in malpractice action would be unable to collect on claim which was "lost" by reason of legal malpractice. Burden of putting forward affirmative defense of non-collectibility is on attorney who asserts it. ***Kituskie v. Corbman*, 714 A.2d 1027 (Pa. 1998).**

Plaintiff in legal malpractice action failed to establish he had suffered any discernible injury or damage. Fact that plaintiff lost security interest in property as junior lienholder does not establish that he was unable to enforce his security purely by reason of attorney's failure to provide him with notice of sheriff's sale by senior lienholder. ***Boyer v. Walker*, 714 A.2d 458 (Pa. Super. 1998).**

In legal malpractice action following an approved settlement where plaintiff is unsatisfied with amount of the settlement, plaintiff must establish that attorney induced client to settle by fraud or made some negligent representation, unfounded in law, to induce client to settle. Explaining Muhammad v. Strassburger, et al., 526 Pa.. 541, 587 A.2d 1346. ***Banks v. Jerome Taylor & Associates*, 700 A.2d 1329 (Pa. Super. 1997).**

Law firm which represented shareholders with competing interests and drafted Buy Out Agreement more favorable to one shareholder than the other can be sued in action sounding in negligence or assumpsit. Date statute of limitations begins to run for negligence claim is date that actual loss is sustained. Compulsory nonsuit vacated and case remanded for new trial. ***Fiorentino v. Rapoport*, ___ Pa. Super. ___, 693 A.2d 208 (1997).**

In a legal malpractice action based on negligence or contract, liability is not foreclosed by client's consent to settlement where agreement to settle was based on erroneous information from attorney. Superior Court's order reversing demurrer affirmed. ***McMahon v. Shea*, 547 Pa. 124, 688 A.2d 1179 (1997).**

In legal malpractice action by criminal defendant against his attorney, plaintiff's failure to allege facts in support of his claim that he was innocent of the criminal charges prohibits recovery. Plaintiff must demonstrate attorney's culpable negligent representation as the proximate cause of conviction. ***Slaughter v. Rushing*, 453 Pa. Super. 379, 683 A.2d 1234 (1996).**

A party's subjective belief that they are represented by an attorney and their failure to plead the basic elements of negligence preclude recovery against the attorney. Order sustaining preliminary objections affirmed. ***Cost v. Cost*, 450 Pa. Super. 685, 677 A.2d 1250 (1996).**

Case of first impression - An essential element of the cause of action for legal malpractice is proof of actual loss. Defendant attorney must be permitted to prove, by preponderance of evidence, that any potential claim for damages by the plaintiff was uncollectible. $2,300,000.00 verdict and judgment in favor of plaintiff

Legal malpractice

reversed and remanded for hearing on collectibility of underlying judgment against tortfeasor in plaintiff's original claim. ***Kituskie v. Corbman*, 452 Pa. Super. 467, 682 A.2d 378 (1996).**

Medical corporation filed legal malpractice action against law firm for inadequate preparation and filing of corporation's employee pension plan. Order granting summary judgment for defendant firm affirmed on grounds that statute of limitations had expired. Statute began to run on date that pension plan was denied by Internal Revenue Service. Subsequent administrative appeal to IRS did not toll statute. ***Robbins & Seventko Orthopedic Surgeons, Inc. v. Geisenberger*, 449 Pa. Super. 367, 674 A.2d 244 (1996).**

Attorney who agrees to "prepare and prosecute [an] appeal" is required to inform clients of result of appeal. Order sustaining preliminary objections reversed and remanded in part. ***Perkovic v. Barrett*, 448 Pa. Super. 356, 671 A.2d 740 (1996).**

Attorney's failure to advise divorce client about well-established principles of law and the impact of a settlement agreement upon client's future obligations is sufficient ground for legal malpractice action. Mere existence of client's consent to settlement does not excuse malpractice. Miller v. Berschler, 423 Pa. Super. 405, 621 A.2d 595 (1993) expressly reversed. Summary judgment reversed. ***McMahon v. Shea*, 441 Pa. Super. 304, 657 A.2d 938 (1995).**

To establish negligence for legal malpractice, plaintiff must show employment of lawyer, failure of lawyer to exercise ordinary skill and knowledge, and proximate causation between such failure and damage to plaintiff. Plaintiff-assignee of defendant-assignor's malpractice claim against defendant's counsel will not lie where plaintiff waived right to enforce judgment against defendant in exchange for assignment of right to sue defendant's counsel. Upon forgiveness of judgment by plaintiff in exchange for right to sue, defendant and therefore plaintiff-assignee lost damages element of legal malpractice claim. ***Ammon v. McCloskey*, 440 Pa. Super. 251, 655 A.2d 549 (1995).**

Policy that prevents recovery by disgruntled client against attorney after settlement approved by client extends to derivative claims by third parties against attorney or attempt to join attorney as additional defendant. ***Goodman v. Kotzen*, 436 Pa. Super. 71, 647 A.2d 247 (1994).**

Client dissatisfied with settlement brought malpractice action against attorney. Attorney not liable. ***Spirer v. Freeland & Kronz*, 434 Pa. Super. 341, 643 A.2d 673**

Client who brought malpractice action against attorney for allowing statute of limitation to expire sought delay damages. Recovery denied. ***Wagner v. Orie and Zivic*, 431 Pa. Super. 337, 636 A.2d 679.**

Client dissatisfied with marital settlement agreement brought malpractice action against attorney. Attorney not liable. ***Martos v. Concilio*, 427 Pa. Super. 612, 629 A.2d 1037.**

Legal malpractice

Client brought malpractice action against attorney for negligent advice regarding the effect of a release. Lawyer not immune even though release part of prior separate action. ***Collas v. Garnick*, 425 Pa. Super. 8, 624 A.2d 117.**

Investor brought malpractice action against partner, an attorney, after investment failed. Attorney not liable. No attorney-client relationship. ***Atherson v. Haug*, 424 Pa. Super. 406, 622 A.2d 983.**

Prisoner brought malpractice action against public defender for failure to file petition for allowance of appeal. Defendant not liable even though not immune. ***Veneri v. Pappano*, 424 Pa. Super. 394, 622 A.2d 977.**

Husband involved in alimony settlement brought action against attorney for failure to explain consequences of settlement. Attorney not liable. ***Miller v. Berschler*, 423 Pa. Super. 405, 621 A.2d 595.**

Criminal defendants brought malpractice actions against attorneys. Action time barred. Supreme Court delineated elements for such actions. ***Baily v. Tucker*, 533 Pa. 237, 621 A.2d 108.**

Attorney failed to advise client that deportation could result from guilty plea. Attorney not liable. ***Rogers v. Williams*, 420 Pa. Super. 396, 616 A.2d 1031.**

Clients brought malpractice action against attorneys because of dissatisfaction with settlement in medical malpractice case. Attorneys not liable. Plaintiffs failed to state cause of action. Did not plead fraud in the inducement. ***Muhammed v. Strassburger et al.*, 526 Pa. Super. 541, 587 A.2d 1346.**

Bank brought malpractice action against attorney whose advice led to loan of $1,000,000 to debtor who became insolvent. Held: bank stated cause of action even though remedies against debtor had not been exhausted. ***Liberty Bank v. Ruder*, 402 Pa. Super. 561, 587 A.2d 761.**

Prisoner brought negligent representation action against public defender who represented him. Public defender not immune. ***Williams v. Office of the Public Defender of the County of Lehigh*, 402 Pa. Super. 188, 586 A.2d 924.**

Union brought malpractice action against attorney who erroneously advised that payment of criminal defense fees for union officials was proper. Attorney not liable. ***Composition Roofers Local 30/30B v. Katz*, 398 Pa. Super. 564, 581 A.2d 607.**

Children of testator brought malpractice action against attorneys who drafted parent's will. Attorneys not liable. No attorney–client relationship with children. ***Hatbob v. Brown*, 394 Pa. Super. 234, 575 A.2d 607.**

Husband and wife brought malpractice action against attorney for failure to properly serve complaint in wife's consortium action. Attorney liable. Consortium actions by wife mandated by Pennsylvania Equal Rights Amendment even though amendment took effect while action was pending. ***McHugh v. Litvin, Blumberg, Matusow & Young*, 525 Pa. 1, 574 A.2d 1040.**

Legal malpractice

Client's suicide was not a reasonably foreseeable consequence of attorney's alleged negligent representation. *McPeake v. Cannon, Esquire P.C.*, 381 Pa. Super. 227, 553 A.2d 439

Allegation that during divorce settlement, claimant's lawyer (defendant here) gave woman incorrect valuation of husband's stock, thereby reducing her ultimate settlement. Summary judgment granted for defendant affirmed. Effect of information on ability to obtain better settlement too speculative to allow recovery for attorney's alleged malpractice. *Marisotti v. Tinari*, 335 Pa. Super. 595, 485 A.2d 54.

Alleged failure of attorney for purchaser of land to secure the expected 45 acres, but 33 acres instead. Non-jury verdict in favor of defendant, affirmed. *Hoyer v. Frazee*, 323 Pa. Super. 421, 470 A.2d 990.

Attorney settled without client's permission, absconded with funds and discontinued action. Attempt, five years later to overturn order to discontinue. Petition to strike order dismissed. Plaintiff left only with claim against now-disbarred attorney. *Rothman v. Fillette*, 503 Pa. 259, 469 A.2d 543.

Where lawyers, allegedly in conspiracy with clients, offered bribe to witness to ignore subpoena in labor proceeding, client has cause of action against attorney if attorney has, by immoral or illegal conduct, violated his professional obligations to client. Claim is for legal fees paid to client. Clients may not maintain claim for other damages since they too were involved in the immoral and illegal act. *Feld and Sons v. Pechner, Dorfman, et al.*, 312 Pa. Super. 125, 458 A.2d 545.

Failure to advise clients that activities may or would violate Pennsylvania Securities Act is cause of action which can be brought against attorney. Action should be decided on basis of common law negligence theories. *Brennan v. Reed, Smith, Shaw & McClay*, 304 Pa. Super. 398, 450 A.2d 740.

After settlement of longshoreman injury case and contrary to attorney's advice, statutory benefits apparently terminated. Held: damages or loss too conjectural to sustain cause of action. *Pashak v. Barish*, 303 Pa. Super. 559, 450 A.2d 67.

Where attorney missed statute of limitations and, thereafter, without telling client, secured $9,000 from his own malpractice carrier, then told his client recovery was from auto case and deducted 40% contingent fee—this was for jury. *O'Callaghan v. Weitzman*, 291 Pa. Super. 471, 436 A.2d 212.

Suit against lawyer by residuary legatee and devisee under will prepared by defendant—plaintiff also attesting witness barring her from taking under will. Plaintiff alleged had lost devise to which entitled by reason of legal malpractice of defendant. Defendant filed preliminary objections alleging lack of privity. Superior Court held privity not essential element of assumpsit action based on third-party beneficiary theory, stating an attorney may be liable for damage caused by his negligence to person intended to be benefitted by his performance, irrespective of any lack of privity. *Guy v. Liederbach*, 279 Pa. Super. 543, 421 A.2d 333.

Underlying case was auto accident. Alleged malpractice in failing to sue defendant's corporate employer. Jury verdict $9500. Insurance coverage $10,000.

Licensee

During negotiations, a judge had estimated value of $75,000 if there were coverage and a defense lawyer placed value of $25,000. Alleged failure to have corporate defendant reduced verdict. Summary judgment for defendant affirmed. Presence or absence of other defendants should not have affected the verdict. ***Schenkel v. Monheit*, 266 Pa. Super. 396, 405 A.2d 493.**

Lawyer appointed to represent indigent defendant in federal criminal case under Federal Criminal Justice Act, immune from tort liability based upon alleged failure to raise statute of limitations. ***Ferri v. Ackerman*, 483 Pa. 90, 394 A.2d 553.**

Suit against attorney for letting statue of limitations lapse. Defendant's attorney filed answer raising defenses that: (1) Dead Man's rule precluded plaintiff from prevailing in original case; (2) no attorney-client relationship existed; and (3) plaintiff failed to state cause of action. These were legal conclusions. Judgment on pleadings granted by court below reversed and case remanded for further proceedings. ***Watson v. Green*, 231 Pa. Super. 115, 331 A.2d 790.**

Default judgment entered for failure to file an appearance—petition to open granted—evidence of neglect of attorney—not an abuse of discretion—order affirmed. ***Stephens v. Bartholomew*, 422 Pa. 311, 220 A.2d 617.**

Lessor of vehicle

Unlicensed driver of leased vehicle involved in accident. Lessor not liable. ***Burkholder v. Genway Corporation*, 432 Pa. Super. 36, 637 A.2d 650.**

Defendant rented a truck—lessee's passenger injured due to negligence of operator—lessee had a driver's license—sufficient evidence of his competency and experience to exculpate lessor from liability. ***Littles et al. v. Avis Rent-A-Car System*, 433 Pa. 72, 248 A.2d 837.**

Plaintiff operating a leased truck which was not equipped with flares, flashers and flags—truck stalled—plaintiff directing traffic—struck by car of one of defendants who saw disabled truck 100 yards away—lessor defendant not legally responsible as its negligence was not proximate cause. ***Klena v. Rutkowski*, 432 Pa. 509, 248 A.2d 9.**

Licensee

Meter reader who fell into a window well and was injured was a licensee on property, not an invitee. The standard of care due by homeowners required that they exercise reasonable care to make unreasonably dangerous conditions safe and to warn licensees of the conditions. Existence of window well was known to reader and was not an unreasonably dangerous condition. ***Cresswell v. End*, 931 A.2d 673 (Pa. Super. 2003).**

Plaintiff teenager brought suit against above ground pool owner for injuries suffered when she dove into four feet of water and suffered serious injuries to her neck. Order granting motion for compulsory nonsuit affirmed where evidence by plaintiff established that she was aware of danger of diving into shallow water; she was aware of depth of the water in the pool; and she proceeded to dive into the pool "on a dare". Plaintiff's status as licensee or trespasser not a factor in light of

Licensee

her knowledge of danger. Property owner's duty does not extend to those conditions the existence of which is obvious even to children, and the risk of which is fully realized by them, particularly when the child chooses to encounter the risk through recklessness or bravado. **Long v. Manzo, 452 Pa. Super. 451, 682 A.2d 370 (1996).**

In action by bus passenger who stepped off of bus and onto broken storm sewer, possessor of land may be liable for physical harm to a licensee caused by conditions on land of which possessor has actual or constructive knowledge. Order granting motion for nonsuit affirmed. **Colston v. SEPTA, 679 A.2d 299 (Pa. Cmwlth. 1996).**

Political Subdivision Tort Claims Act exception for dangerous condition of property does not extend to plaintiff who became trespasser when he climbed to roof of school building to retrieve tennis ball. School district took sufficient steps to prevent entry onto roof. Summary judgment in favor of school district affirmed. **Longbottom v. Sim-Kar Lighting Fixture Co., ___ Pa. Cmwlth. ___, 651 A.2d 621 (1994).**

Pennsylvania Dram Shop Act does not insulate employees of licensee from liability for negligence in serving alcohol to visibly intoxicated patron. Order sustaining demurrer vacated. **Detwiler v. Brumbaugh, 441 Pa. Super. 110, 656 A.2d 944 (1995).**

Police officer who enters upon another's land in his official capacity and in response to a call for assistance is a licensee. Landowner's duty is to inform licensee of dangerous, hidden conditions. Obviously rowdy crowd of patrons at social hall was not a dangerous, hidden condition. Although violation of Dram Shop Act is negligence per se, mere fact that patrons who assaulted police officer were intoxicated neither proves that they had been served when visibly intoxicated nor causation of officer's injuries. Summary judgment for defendant affirmed. **Holpp v. Fez, Inc., 440 Pa. Super. 512, 656 A.2d 147 (1995).**

The determination of whether an individual is a trespasser, licensee or invitee is for the jury. A licensee may become an invitee, thereby increasing duty of care owed by landowner. Plaintiff may recover damages where two or more substantial causes combine to cause an injury, even if no one cause standing alone would have brought about the injury. Although action of third party in pushing plaintiff off a guide wall was an intervening cause, its occurrence was not so extraordinary or unforeseeable as to make it a superseding cause which would excuse property owner for negligent maintenance of wall, which condition substantially contributed to plaintiff's injuries. **Trude v. Martin, 442 Pa. Super. 614, 660 A.2d 626 (1995).**

Co-owner of entireties property with actual knowledge of sexual abuse by other co-owner on their minor grandchildren within residence does not have duty to protect or warn grandchildren of grandfather's proclivities. Multimillion dollar compensatory and punitive damages award against grandmother reversed. While landowner may be liable for dangerous condition on the land, landowner is not liable for criminal or tortious acts of third parties. **T.A. v. Allen, 447 Pa. Super. 302, 669 A.2d 360 (1995).**

Limited tort option

Empty lot across street from, and owned, by bank used by teenagers to play football. Boy tripped over stake in ground, injured. Nonsuit affirmed. Held: plaintiff a licensee and defendant held reasonably unaware of condition, under circumstances. ***Wiegand v. Mars National Bank*, 308 Pa. Super. 218, 454 A.2d 99.**

Plaintiff's decedent robbed in train station and clothing thrown on top of commuter car. Electrocuted trying to retrieve clothing. Verdict for plaintiff reversed. Duty to warn licensee extends only to what property owner may reasonably anticipate. ***Carpenter v. Penn Central*, 269 Pa. Super. 9, 409 A.2d 37.**

Plaintiff rendered quadriplegic as a result of dive off dock into a canal during private party. Error to instruct jury that plaintiff was an invitee. Should have been left to jury whether or not plaintiff was an invitee or licensee. Plaintiff was the husband of an invited guest. Verdict for plaintiff reversed and new trial ordered. ***Hager v. Etting*, 268 Pa. Super. 416, 408 A.2d 856.**

Plaintiff given privilege by defendant to store certain property in a hay loft—no charge for same—ladder to loft provided access—ladder slipped and plaintiff injured—no evidence of a latent defect—nonsuit proper—plaintiff but a gratuitous licensee. ***Sharp v. Luks*a, 440 Pa. 125, 269 A.2d 659.**

Lights and lighting

Student injured by baseball hit by coach at high speed in poorly lit gymnasium was not barred by political subdivision immunity, if inadequate lighting—a condition of the gymnasium—was under the care, custody and control of the school district and the school district could have been held jointly liable. ***Kevan v. Manesiotis*, 728 A.2d 1006 (Pa. Cmwlth. 1999).**

Jury verdict $200,000 for crush injury with permanent disability—male warehouse employee, in dark parking lot. Employee guiding tractor-trailer rigs, by voice, with hand on rig. Fell in parking lot hole. Issue of plaintiff's circumstances with lease silent. Lessor has, over years, undertaken to keep parking area in repair. Held: therefore, a continuing duty to keep it reasonably safe for tenants use. ***McDevitt v. Terminal Warehouse Co.*, 304 Pa. Super. 438, 450 A.2d 991.**

Fall down steps in darkened lavatory area of restaurant while searching for light switch, under facts here, does not constitute contributory negligence as a matter of law. Nonsuit removed. ***McNally v. Liebowitz*, 498 Pa. Super. 163, 445 A.2d 716.**

Limited tort option

Plaintiff brought negligence action against Defendant after he was rear-ended. The trial court entered judgment in favor of the Defendant. The Superior Court reversed holding that a serious injury need not be permanent to meet the exception for recovery of non-economic damages based upon a limited tort selection. The Superior Court noted that: 1) the extent of impairment; 2) length of time the impairment lasted; 3) the treatment required to correct the impairment; and, 4) other relevant factors should be considered in determining if an injury was "serious." ***Cadena v. Latch*, 78 A.3d 636 (Pa. Super. 2013).**

Liver disease

Summary judgment for defendant reversed when limited tort plaintiff established that statute of limitations began not on date of accident but on date that she became aware or reasonably could have become aware that her injuries were "serious" under limited tort policy and so compensable under that statute. ***Walls v. Scheckler*, 700 A.2d 533 (Pa. Super. 1997).**

Plaintiff injured in motor vehicle accident offered four medical reports that showed that she had suffered serious soft tissue injury in the accident. Trial court granted defendant's motion for summary judgment based on findings in law that plaintiffs injuries were not compensable under the statutorily imposed limited tort restrictions. Superior Court reversed on its own review of reports by physicians and testimony adduced in summary judgment proceeding. ***Leonelli v. McMullen*, 700 A.2d 525 (Pa. Super. 1997).**

Summary judgment reversed where trial court failed to consider medical evidence of psychic injuries that may have qualified as serious impairment of a bodily function under limited tort coverage provided for in Motor Vehicle Financial Responsibility Law before granting summary judgment. Minor children injured in accident while riding in their mother's uninsured vehicle are held to have the same deemed limited tort coverage as their uninsured mother. ***Hames v. Philadelphia Housing Authority*, 696 A.2d 880 (Pa. Cmwlth. 1997).**

Pedestrian struck by automobile failed to establish serious injury or serious impairment of bodily function. Factors to be considered in determining severity of bodily impairment for purposes of recovery under limited tort option include extent of the impairment, particular body function impaired, duration of the impairment, treatment required to correct the impairment and any other relevant factors. Judgment in favor of plaintiff for only out-of-pocket medical expenses affirmed. ***Murray v. McCann*, 442 Pa. Super. 30, 658 A.2d 404 (1995).**

Liver disease

In medical malpractice action for delayed diagnosis of liver disease, the "two disease rule" from asbestos-related cases will be applied to preclude plaintiff's claim for increased risk and fear of liver cancer until such disease actually occurs. Second judge's grant of summary judgment on plaintiff's claim for increased risk of harm after first judge denied summary judgment on the same issue is reversible error. Order granting summary judgment as to increased risk of harm reversed. ***Klein v. Weisberg*, ___ Pa. Super. ___, 694 A.2d 644 (1997).**

Livestock

In negligence action by truck driver for damages resulting from cow wandering onto roadway, turnpike commission had no duty of care, custody, or control of cow. Summary judgment affirmed. ***Mason & Dixon Lines, Inc. v. Mognet*, 166 Pa. Cmwlth. 1, 645 A.2d 1370 (1994).**

Loading and unloading

Plaintiff injured while defendant's employees were loading steel on his truck. Defendant claimed employees following plaintiff's instructions. Evidence on

Looking—Observation

custom excluded as plaintiff not qualified as expert. Verdict for defendant. ***Pepin v. Bethlehem Steel*, 257 Pa. Super. 643, 390 A.2d 312.**

Plaintiff injured while unloading a truck—no evidence of how accident happened—contended improper loading but expert testimony insufficient to establish causal relationship—judgment n.o.v. entered on appeal. ***Warden v. Lyons Trans. Lines, Inc. et al.*, 432 Pa. 495, 248 A.2d 313.**

Plaintiff unloading box car on defendant's siding—some of contents fell on him—evidence insufficient to establish that defendant's crew pushed another car into standing box car—court below properly granted judgment n.o.v. for defendant. ***Flaherty v. Penna. R.R. Co.*, 426 Pa. 83, 231 A.2d 179.**

Lobectomy

Husband suffering from seizures was treated by a partial lobectomy that resulted in more serious seizures and severe memory and speech problems. Informed consent to medical treatment requires that the patient have a "true understanding of the nature of the operation ... and the possible results." Judgment n.o.v. permitted only in "clear case." Judgment n.o.v. reversed and jury verdict reinstated. ***Rowinsky v. Sperling*, 452 Pa. Super. 215, 681 A.2d 785 (1996).**

Lock

Defendant Y.M.C.A. conducted a steam room on its premises—plaintiff a patron—lock of room defective and known to defendant Y.M.C.A.—plaintiff injured in an effort to attract attention—court in error in granting a nonsuit as to Y.M.C.A. but proper as to defendant company which constructed steam room. ***Stebner v. Young Men's Christian Assn.*, 428 Pa. 370, 238 A.2d 19.**

Log

Driver injured when vehicle struck log on embankment along highway. PennDOT not liable. ***Babcock v. Com., Dept. of Transp.*, 156 Pa. Cmwlth. 69, 626 A.2d 672.**

Log homes

"Gist of the Action Doctrine" provides that a contract claim cannot be couched in terms of a negligence action. In suit for damages resulting from breach of contract to provide a suitable log home kit, allegations that bad advice on repairs constituted negligence is actually a part of a contract claim, not negligence. ***Freestone v. New England Log Homes, Inc.*, 819 A.2d 550 (Pa. Super. 2003).**

Looking—Observation

Intersection collision. Plaintiff admitted that after looking for traffic once, he never looked again. Plaintiff had green light. For jury whether plaintiff should have continued looking under the circumstances. Nonsuit reversed. ***Imes v. Empire Hook and Ladder*, 247 Pa. Super. 470, 372 A.2d 922.**

Operator of a car entering main highway from a side driveway must continue to look as he enters highway—failure to do constitutes evidence of negligence—col-

Loss of consortium

lision with car on main highway—nonsuit proper. ***Billow v. Farmers Trust Co.*, 438 Pa. 514, 266 A.2d 92.**

Operator observing approaching car but failing to continue to look during last 50 feet from intersection—making left turn—collision—no recovery—guilty of contributory negligence per se. ***Leasure v. Heller*, 436 Pa. 108, 258 A.2d 855.**

Plaintiff testified in one instance that he did not look until he was 2 or 3 feet over center of highway and in two other instances he testified that he looked as he reached the center of the highway—not confronted with contradiction—entitled to go to the jury to reconcile—granting of judgment n.o.v. in error. ***Gillingham v. Patz*, 429 Pa. 308, 239 A.2d 287.**

A pedestrian crossing a street need not be so observant as to substantially look in both directions simultaneously, like the Janus of mythology—case for jury under facts of case. ***Flowers v. Green*, 20 Pa. 481, 218 A.2d 219.**

Loss of consortium

Wife, who delivered brain-damaged child after Cesarean section with only local anesthetic, and husband, individually and as parents of child, sued anesthesiology group, obstetrician and hospital for malpractice. Nurses employed at hospital are not agents of the physicians when they act in the normal course of hospital services. Father's loss of consortium claim properly denied by trial court where his only testimony was that he had a subjective fear of engaging in sexual relations with his wife following her delivery of brain-damaged child, even though the damage may have been the result of medical malpractice. Father's claim for negligent infliction of emotional distress properly dismissed where he was not near the scene of the injuries to his wife and newborn child. Hearing his wife's cries of pain only, without any visual experience of her condition, was insufficient. ***Tiburzio-Kelly v. Montgomery*, 452 Pa. Super. 158, 681 A.2d 757 (1996).**

Wife brought loss of consortium claim against physician who treated husband before marriage. Held: physician may be liable. Claim did not ripen until after marriage. ***Vazquez v. Friedberg*, 431 Pa. Super. 523, 637 A.2d 300.**

Wife brought action for loss of consortium. Defendant attempted to join husband who was contributorily negligent. Held: joinder of husband not permissible. ***Barchfeld v. Nunly by Nunly*, 395 Pa. Super. 517, 577 A.2d 910.**

Shipyard worker died from lung cancer caused by exposure to asbestos. Widow not entitled to damages for loss of consortium for period after husband's death. Award of delay damages for consortium claim proper. ***Novelli v. Johns-Manville Corporation*, 395 Pa. Super. 144, 576 A.2d 1085.**

Husband and wife brought a malpractice action against attorney for failure to properly serve complaint in wife's consortium action. Attorney liable. Consortium actions by wife mandated by Pennsylvania Equal Rights Amendment even though amendment took effect while action was pending. ***McHugh v. Litvin, Blumberg, Matusow & Young*, 525 Pa. 1, 574 A.2d 1040.**

Plaintiff fractured a lumbar vertebra in boating accident. Verdict of $500 awarded; nothing for loss of consortium claim of wife. Jury found 50% contributory negligence. Verdict held inadequate based upon loss of income, and pain and suffering evidence, which was uncontradicted. Failure to award loss of consortium also shocking. New trial on damages only. **Deitrick v. Karnes**, 329 Pa. Super. 372, 478 A.2d 835.

Premarital tort—subsequent marriage—suit barred. **Keso v. Mielcarek**, 226 Pa. Super. 476, 313 A.2d 324.

Failure of one spouse to join in the other spouse's personal injury action will bar any claim of the non-joining spouse for loss of consortium. **Hopkins v. Blanco**, 224 Pa. Super. 116, 302 A.2d 855.

Verdict for plaintiff husband included $3,000 for loss of wife's consortium—by equally divided Supreme Court judgment for amount affirmed. **Brown v. Phila. T. Co.**, 437 Pa. 348, 263 A.2d 423.

Wife filed claim for loss of consortium—court below sustained preliminary objections thereto—such an appealable order but under facts solely within the jurisdiction of the Superior Court—matter remanded. **DeAngeli v. Fitzgerald**, 433 Pa. 529, 252 A.2d 706.

Loss of control

Plaintiff's decedents were passengers in car which passed tractor trailer unit of defendant on the Turnpike and while in passing lane lost control—skidded into path of tractor trailer which was still on berm lane—collision—assured clear distance rule not involved under facts—judgment n.o.v. for defendant on appeal. **Laborda v. Markel**, 434 Pa. 184, 252 A.2d 686.

Plaintiff, driver of an automobile, allegedly lost control of car by reason of a hole in cartway the size of a manhole and 4 inches deep—filled with water—case for jury—not necessary that every fact points unerringly to liability. **Fringer v. West York Borough**, 421 Pa. 579, 220 A.2d 849.

Lung disease

Wife plaintiff diagnosed with lung cancer filed suit against radiology association and radiologist who had taken and interpreted chest x-ray at request of insurance company for failure to diagnose cancerous tumor. No physician-patient relationship is created where a physician examines a patient at the request of an insurance company. Summary judgment affirmed. **Promubol v. Hackett**, 454 Pa. Super. 622, 686 A.2d 417 (1996).

Shipyard worker's failure to diligently ascertain cause of lung cancer prevents tolling of statute of limitations under discovery rule. Dissent opines that majority opinion replaces "reasonably should have known" standard with "could have known" standard. Order granting summary judgment affirmed. **Cochran v. GAF Corp.**, 542 Pa. 210, 666 A.2d 245 (1995).

Lying in roadway

Wrongful death and survival actions allegedly due to lung disease from working at coke ovens. Requirement of wrongful death statute that action be brought within two years of death leaves no room for construction. Similar ruling as to survival action. Suits brought more than two years after death are barred. ***Anthony v. Koppers Co., Inc.*, 496 Pa. 119, 436 A.2d 181.**

Lying in roadway

McCleary struck plaintiff's body with his car. Plaintiff lying prone in roadway after spending the day in several bars. A few minutes later second defendant Senft struck the prone body. No evidence to conclude that one defendant did more damage than the other. Verdict properly molded to be shared equally by both defendants. ***Lehman v. McCleary*, 229 Pa. Super. 508, 329 A.2d 862.**

Plaintiff decedent left party and a few minutes later defendant left. Plaintiff walking home. Defendant driving. Dark night. As defendant pulled from curb he felt drag under wheels. Thinking he ran over trash bag, he backed up. Drag still present so he got out and discovered plaintiff's body. No evidence of how plaintiff got under wheels. Defendant's verdict affirmed. ***Rost v. Wickenheiser*, 229 Pa. Super. 84, 323 A.2d 154.**

—M—

Machinery

Plaintiff brought lawsuit against Defendant employer after he was injured operating a machine manufactured by the successor in interest to his employer. The trial court dismissed Plaintiff's complaint. The Superior Court affirmed holding that the Pennsylvania Supreme Court has not accepted the Dual Persona Doctrine exception to the exclusivity of the Workers' Compensation Act. ***Soto v. Nabisco, Inc.,* 32 A.3d 787 (Pa. Super. 2011).**

Immense coke oven door installed 35 years prior to accident which caused plaintiff's decedent's death and which is movable by means of wheels on tracks is still an "improvement" under statute of repose and so action by coke oven employee is extinguished. Trial court order denying motion for judgment *n.o.v.* reversed. ***Vargo v. Koppers Co., Inc.,* 452 Pa. Super. 275, 681 A.2d 815 (1996).**

Maintenance of vehicle

Plaintiff sued city for injuries sustained while being driven to hospital by fire fighter in fire rescue van. During trip to hospital, left rear tandem wheels feel off van, causing an accident and plaintiff's injuries. Parties stipulated that fire fighter was not driving negligently and that repair and maintenance of vehicle by city was negligent. Plaintiff's motion for summary judgment granted and affirmed by Commonwealth Court. Supreme Court held that maintenance and repair of van is included in exception to Political Subdivision Tort Claims act relating to injuries caused by negligent acts of local agency or its employees with respect to the operation of a motor vehicle. Negligence related to the operation of a vehicle encompasses not only how a person drives, but also whether he should be driving a particular vehicle in the first place. ***Mickle v. City of Philadelphia,* 707 A.2d 1124 (Pa. 1998).**

Empty lot across street from and owned by bank used by teenagers to play football. Boy tripped over stake in ground, injured. Nonsuit affirmed. Plaintiff held to be licensee. Defendant held reasonably to be unaware of condition under circumstances. ***Wiegand v. Mars National Bank,* 308 Pa. Super. 218, 454 A.2d 99.**

Two vehicles collided at intersection. Plaintiff sued, among others, abutting property owner for maintenance of shrubs and trees which obstructed view. Lower court granted summary judgment in favor of property owner. Reversed. Issues of superceding cause, comparative negligence and violations of statutes, for jury. ***Harvey v. Hansen,* 299 Pa. Super. 474, 445 A.2d 1228.**

Malfunction theory

Cross-claim plaintiff who built hog barn with roof trusses designed and manufactured by two additional defendants sued designer and manufacturer after trusses collapsed causing damages to plaintiff's barn and personalty. Trial court granted additional defendants' motion for summary judgment on basis of spoliation of evidence after cross-claim plaintiff failed to preserve allegedly defective trusses for both additional defendants' inspection. Held that because cross-claim plaintiff was proceeding under design defect or malfunction theories, lack of actual trusses was

Malingering

not so prejudicial as to warrant dismissal of claim. A court deciding spoliation issues must consider (1) the degree of fault of the offending party, (2) prejudice to the opposing party, and (3) the appropriateness of sanctions in light of those circumstances. ***Troup v. Tri-county Confinement Systems*, 708 A.2d 825 (Pa. Super. 1998).**

Malingering

Rear-end collision. No treatment for two weeks then admission to Harrisburg Hospital—diagnosis: psychoneurotic conversion reaction. Defense expert said plaintiff a malingerer. Verdict of $2,145.00 affirmed. Alleged specials $2,400.00. ***Rose v. Hoover*, 231 Pa. Super. 251, 331 A.2d 878.**

Mammogram

Patient brought action against physician for failure to diagnose breast cancer. Held: "two schools of thought" applicable to failure to order yearly mammogram but not failure to diagnose from symptoms. ***Levine v. Rosen*, 532 Pa. 512, 616 A.2d 623.**

Man-made lake

Recreation Use of Land and Water Act provides immunity to owner of man-made lake created when river is dammed to create a water supply for commercial venture, where lake is open to public free of charge. Dam that creates the lake is improvement to the real estate and so dam owner is not entitled to RULWA immunity afforded to lake owner. ***Stone v. York Haven Power Co.*, 749 A.2d 452 (Pa. 2000).**

Manhole cover

Plaintiff sued contractor who allegedly replaced manhole cover incorrectly, which placement caused plaintiff to lose control of his vehicle and crash, sustaining injuries. Defendant contractor filed cross-claim against city for which it was performing work and city moved to transfer venue to county where it was located from original situs of action, the county where the contractor had its place of business. Held: any local agency must be sued in the county in which it is located, whether local agency is an original or additional defendant. ***Smith v. Agentis*, 704 A.2d 737 (Pa. Cmwlth. 1998).**

Manure

Milk hauler slipped on manure on steps in milking pit of farm where he picked up milk. Hauler was a farmer familiar that manure was often in milking areas. Had descended steps a few minutes before accident but did not see the manure. Held contributorily negligent as a matter of law. ***Jewell v. Beckstine*, 255 Pa. Super. 238, 386 A.2d 597.**

Market share liability

Pennsylvania has not yet adopted the market share liability theory as an exception to the general rule of negligence law that a plaintiff must establish that a particular defendant proximately caused his or her injury. Summary judgment affirmed in favor of lead manufacturers and trade organization sued by minor injured

Master and servant

by lead poisoning. ***Skipworth v. Lead Industries Association, Inc.,*** **547 Pa. 224, 690 A.2d 169 (1997).**

Pennsylvania has not adopted the use of market share liability as a theory of recovery. Action for injuries suffered by minor child as a result of lead poisoning dismissed because of plaintiff's failure to allege identity of suppliers of lead-based paint and lack of causal connection. Summary judgment affirmed. ***Skipworth v. Lead Industries Association, Inc.,*** **445 Pa. Super. 610, 665 A.2d 1288 (1995).**

Mastectomy

Plaintiff filed suit against plastic surgeon for surgery without providing informed consent. Following verdict for plaintiff, defendants appeal arguing that trial court had erred in refusing to grant judgment *n.o.v.* for plaintiff's failure to present expert evidence as to the probability of the risks involved, that the risks actually occurred and that her injuries were caused by the surgery. Superior Court affirmed holding that, recovery on theory of informed consent is permitted regardless of causation because it is the conduct of the unauthorized procedure that constitutes the tort. ***Boute v. Seitchik,*** **719 A.2d 320 (Pa. Super. 1998).**

Master and servant

Where vehicle owner knows or should know that its employee driver has had his operator's license suspended, owner is, by statute, jointly and severally liable with the driver for the driver's negligence. Summary judgment in favor of owner reversed. ***Shomo v. Scribe,*** **546 Pa. 542, 686 A.2d 1292 (1996).**

While Section 317 of Restatement (2d) Torts imposes liability upon a master for acts of a servant committed outside the scope of the servant's employment, liability will not lie unless the acts are performed by the servant "upon the premises in possession of the master." Church and religious officials not liable for conduct of priest who molested minor on non-diocesan property. Judgment against Church, bishop and diocese vacated. ***Hutchison v. Luddy,*** **453 Pa. Super. 420, 683 A.2d 1254 (1996).**

Peculiar risk doctrine did not apply to make contractor liable for injuries sustained by subcontractor's employee who fell from roof of building on which he was working where both contractor and subcontractor were aware of dangerous condition of roof. ***Edwards v. Franklin and Marshall College,*** **444 Pa. Super. 1, 663 A.2d 187 (1995).**

Pennsylvania Dram Shop Act does not insulate employees of licensee from liability for negligence in serving alcohol to visibly intoxicated patron. Order sustaining demurrer vacated. ***Detwiler v. Brumbaugh,*** **441 Pa. Super. 110, 656 A.2d 944 (1995).**

Respiratory therapist who contracted tuberculosis from exposure to patient brought negligence action against employer hospital for failure to diagnosis and treat her condition promptly and not to obtain remedy for contracting disease. Jury verdict for plaintiff reversed on grounds that her sole remedy was workers' com-

Master and servant

pensation. ***Snyder v. Pocono Medical Center,*** **440 Pa. Super. 606, 656 A.2d 534 (1995).**

Motor Vehicle Financial Responsibility Law precludes employee injured during the scope of his employment as a result of automobile accident in which co-employee was driving from recovering common law damages against coemployee in addition to workers' compensation benefits. ***Ducjai v. Dennis,*** **540 Pa. 103, 656 A.2d 102 (1995).**

Action by passenger of stolen pizza-delivery vehicle after vehicle crashed into pole by thief dismissed against delivery driver and his employer for plaintiff's failure to establish causation. ***Matos v. Rivera,*** **436 Pa. Super. 509, 648 A.2d 337 (1994).**

Suit against employer of individual who allegedly caused auto accident while not on job. Alleged that employer failed to monitor employee's mental state and placed too much stress on employee, causing him to have emotional breakdown while driving. Demurrer sustained. ***Hill v. Acme,*** **350 Pa. Super. 219, 504 A.2d 324.**

Undisputed facts showed that injurious activity of individual defendant was outside the scope of employment. July 4th accident. Defendant, on errand for father, did not have permission to use vehicle. Summary judgment for employer affirmed. ***Johnson v. Glenn Sand & Gravel,*** **308 Pa. Super. 22, 453 A.2d 1048.**

Minor plaintiff worked for defendant two to three times per week—trash hauling business. Plaintiff stood on running board of truck and helped line it up with containers. Injured when pulled under truck's wheels. No express contract of employment, no fixed salary—sometimes no salary at all. Granting of defendant's motion for summary judgment, alleging defense of workmen's compensation, reversed and case remanded for trial. ***Stewart v. Uryc,*** **237 Pa. Super. 258, 352 A.2d 465.**

Duty of employer to instruct an inexperienced driver how to operate a tractor on a freshly graded road—failure to do evidence of negligence. ***Michaels v. Tubbs,*** **221 Pa. Super. 255, 289 A.2d 738.**

Minor plaintiff of 14 was a "candy-striper" in defendant's hospital—injured while at work—held that she was not an employee under Workmen's Compensation Act but that hospital owed a duty to her as a general master and servant relationship and matter for jury—equally divided court. ***Marcus v. Frankford Hospital,*** **445 Pa. 206, 283 A.2d 69.**

Plaintiff's decedent, a minor, killed by being struck by shield of a tractor and cutter—farm laborer—verdict for defendant—new trial ordered—explanation of defendant operator contrary to physical facts—doctrine of exclusive control does not apply. ***Getz v. Balliet,*** **431 Pa. 441, 246 A.2d 108.**

Plaintiff, a hitchhiker, riding on a tractor trailer unit—injured in an apparent collision—evidence not clear whether operator of car in which riding had permission or authority to permit plaintiff to ride in car—failure to file answer to pleading not conclusive—new trial granted. ***Noel v. Puckett,*** **427 Pa. 328, 235 A.2d 380.**

Mat

A high school cheerleader was injured when she fell to the hardwood gymnasium floor during rehearsal and struck her face and jaw. Suit was brought alleging that failure to have mats in place during the practice constituted a defective condition of the real estate and therefore an exception to governmental immunity. Held: failure to place mats which are personal property, does not fall within the real estate exception to governmental immunity following *Blocker v. City of Philadelphia,* 563 Pa. 559, 763 A.2d 373 (2000). ***Rieger v. Altoona Area School District*, 768 A.2d 912 (Pa. Cmwlth. 2001).**

Wife plaintiff fell while leaving defendant club—she alleged that mat slipped and moved when tread upon and that ice was under surface of mat—evidence strongly disputed—verdict for defendant—refusal of new trial proper. ***Maher v. College Club of Pittsburgh*, 427 Pa. 621, 235 A.2d 134.**

Mechanic

Contributory negligence does not preclude recovery in a products liability case. In action arising out of tire explosion that injured garage mechanic, defendant failed to prove that plaintiff assumed the specific risk attendant to the procedure of changing a tire. Voluntary assumption of a risk is a defense in a products liability case and requires proof that the plaintiff fully understands the specific risk and yet chooses voluntarily to encounter the risk. ***Robinson v. B.F. Goodrich Tire Company*, 444 Pa. Super. 640, 664 A.2d 616 (1995).**

Mechanical failure

Chain reaction collision caused by brake problems. Jury verdict for defendant. Held: error to charge on sudden emergency. Doctrine not to include sudden mechanical failures. New trial ordered. ***Chiodo v. Gargloff & Downham Trucking*, 308 Pa. Super. 498, 454 A.2d 645.**

Mechanical signal

Rear-end collision—plaintiff in forward car injured—error for trial judge to charge that plaintiff might be found guilty of contributory negligence if she did not give a hand signal of intention to stop—Code also provides for mechanical signals. ***Buckalew v. DeAngelis*, 424 Pa. 292, 227 A.2d 672.**

Medial barrier

Pennsylvania Turnpike Commission and contractors who adhered to Turnpike Commission standards in construction of 32" high median barriers are all entitled to sovereign immunity protection. ***Svege v. Interstate Safety Systems*, 862 A.2d 752 (Pa. Cmwlth. 2004).**

Plaintiff/decedent a passenger in one of two cars, one of which crossed medial barrier. When a car crosses medial barrier, driver has burden to say why—in absence of exculpatory evidence, one of the drivers had to be negligent. Verdict for

Median strip

both defendant drivers reversed. *Fair v. Snowball Express,* **226 Pa. Super. 295, 310 A.2d 386.**

Median strip

A median on which alighting bus passenger tripped and sustained injuries is part of the highway and not a traffic control device; therefore, PennDOT, as owner of highway, may be subject to liability under exception to sovereign immunity. Verdict against City reversed; verdict against Commonwealth affirmed. ***Slough v. Com., Dept. of Transp.,* 686 A.2d 62 (Pa. Cmwlth. 1996).**

Defect in a concrete median strip in the center of a PennDOT-maintained roadway constitutes a condition of the road allowing injured pedestrian's suit against PennDOT for defective maintenance of the median strip under real property exception to sovereign immunity ***Hubbard v. Com., Dept. of Transp.,* ___ Pa. Cmwlth. ___, 660 A.2d 201 (1995).**

Medical Device Amendments of 1976

A physician may be required to include in his description of an operative procedure the use of Food and Drug Administration classification of a device intended to be used in the procedure. A hospital has no duty to a patient under Pennsylvania's informed consent doctrine; that duty is on the physician who is to perform the procedure. ***Southard v. Temple University Hospital,* 731 A.2d 603 (Pa. Super. 1999).**

A state claim that FDA requirements have not been met arising out of the use of a collagen implant is cognizable, despite preemption provisions of the medical device amendments to the Federal Food, Drug and Cosmetic Act. State negligence claims that mirror FDA standards for medical devices are not preempted. Order granting summary judgment reversed. ***Green v. Dolsky,* 546 Pa. 400, 685 A.2d 110 (1996).**

State law claims for manufacture and sale of defective surgical repair screws and plates were not preempted by medical device amendments to Federal Food, Drug and Cosmetic Act. Actions for failure to warn, strict liability, negligence, and implied warranty are preempted by medical device amendment to federal food and drug act. Summary judgment affirmed in part and reversed in part. ***Burgstahler v. Acromed Corporation,* 448 Pa. Super. 26, 670 A.2d 658 (1996).**

Medical device amendments to the Federal Food, Drug and Cosmetic Act of 1938 preempt state court action for breach of implied warranties of merchantability and fitness for a particular purpose regarding surgical bone plates and screws. Express warranties as to condition or properties of bone plates and screws are not preempted by the amendments. Learned intermediary doctrine does not preclude patient's suit against manufacturer on an express warranty made in connection with the sale of a prescription device. Order granting summary judgment affirmed in part and reversed in part. ***Rosci v. Acromed, Inc.,* ___ Pa. Super. ___, 669 A.2d 959 (1995).**

Medical malpractice: Dental

Medical malpractice: Abatement of action

Defendant filed for an abatement of medical malpractice action after the minor plaintiff died and plaintiff's parents failed to substitute a personal representative within one year of the plaintiff's death. The court held that a defendant may petition for an abatement of action if a personal representative is not appointed within one year of the filing of a suggestion of death and that the abatement shall be granted unless plaintiff presents a reasonable explanation for the delay in appointing a personal representative. *Salvidia v. Ashbrook*, 923 A.2d 436 (Pa. Super. 2007).

Medical malpractice: Anesthesia

Administrator of decedent's estate filed suit against decedent's physician for negligence for failing to diagnose an obstruction in decedent's coronary artery leading to decedent's death. The court held that medical malpractice is a form of negligence requiring that; 1) the physician owed a duty to the patient; 2) the physician breached the duty; 3) the breach was the proximate cause of the harm to the patient; 4) damages suffered by the patient due to the harm. *Winschel v. Jain*, 925 A.2d 782 (Pa. Super. 2007).

Plaintiff alleged serious injury following in-office procedure performed by physician and nurse anesthetist who was an independent contractor assisting physician. At trial, judge granted non-suit in favor of physician on plaintiff's theory of the ostensible agency for liability of the nurse anesthetist. In issue of first impression, held that a patient who submits herself to the care of a doctor for the performance of an in-office medical procedure is be entitled to recover damages from the physician for the negligence of the doctor's independent contractors just as a patient who submits herself to the care of a hospital is entitled to recover damages from the hospital for the negligence of the independent contractors utilized by the hospital under the theory of ostensible agency. *Parker v. Freilich*, 803 A.2d 738 (Pa. Super. 2002).

Medical malpractice: Dental

Discovery rule in medical malpractice cases is an exception to the limitations of action statutes which impose on plaintiffs a duty to bring suit within a set time after injury. If discovery of injury and cause is delayed despite the exercise of reasonable diligence, the limitation of action period is tolled. Because the determination of whether a party plaintiff is able, in the exercise of reasonable diligence, to know of his injury and its cause, it is for a jury to decide. It is not relevant to the application of the discovery rule whether or not the limitations period has expired. *Fine v. Checcio*, 870 A.2d 850 (Pa. 2005).

Dentist who continually gave assurances to Plaintiff that she would recover her sense of feeling of her tongue and lips "concealed" her true condition and so tolled the running of the statute of limitations. Only when plaintiff lost confidence in that doctor and sought another opinion did the statute of limitations begin to run again. *Ward v. Rice*, 828 A.2d 1118 (Pa. Super. 2003).

In case of dental malpractice, including issue of first impression in the Commonwealth, held that a root canal is a "surgical" or "operative procedure" and there-

Medical malpractice: Dental

for a trigger for requirement of patient's informed consent. ***Perkins v. Disipio*, 736 A.2d 6098 (Pa. Super. 1999).**

Where plaintiff knew before treating with dentist of periodontal disease, the "discovery rule" exception to the applicable statute of limitations is not available to plaintiff. ***Colanna v. Rice*, 445 Pa. Super. 1, 664 A.2d 979 (1995).**

Plaintiff failed to properly prosecute dental malpractice action where service was not effected until two years after original filing of writ of summons and fours years after surgery for proplast implant. A dentist may not be held strictly liable for alleged defects in dental implants. Manufacturer and not physician should be pursued for products liability claim. Order granting summary judgment affirmed. ***Bigansky v. Thomas Jefferson University Hospital*, 442 Pa. Super. 69, 658 A.2d 423 (1995).**

$2.7 million verdict for patient of oral surgeon who was negligent in administering an injection that damaged patient's trigeminal nerve not subject to remittitur. No new trial granted. ***Tesauro v. Perrige*, 437 Pa. Super. 620, 650 A.2d 1079 (1994).**

Patient brought malpractice action against dentist for failure to diagnose periodontal disease. Held: patient had sufficient knowledge to bring suit within statute of limitations. ***Brooks v. Sagovia*, 431 Pa. Super. 508, 636 A.2d 1201.**

Patient with heart disease died from infection after dentist failed to prescribe penicillin before dental procedure. Dentist liable. ***Bonavitacola v. Chiver*, 422 Pa. Super. 556, 619 A.2d 1363.**

Patient involved in automobile accident when returning from dental clinic brought action against dentist and hospital alleging negligent treatment of her diabetes. Patient failed to state cause of action. ***Waddell v. Bowers*, 415 Pa. Super. 469, 609 A.2d 847.**

Patient brought action against dentist for unanticipated result from injection of anesthetic based on negligence and lack of informed consent. Held: summary judgment on issue of negligence not appealable. Cause of action still remained. ***Garfolo v. Shah*, 400 Pa. Super. 456, 583 A.2d 1205.**

Surgery for removal of impacted wisdom teeth. Left with loss of sensation in tongue. No assertion of negligent performance ever alleged. Verdict for defendant affirmed. Informed consent can be given even though information on risks is communicated by assistant or nurse. Failure of defendant to testify does not entitle plaintiff to negative inference charge—defendant being subject to subpoena and further present in courtroom during trial. ***Bulman v. Myers*, 321 Pa. Super. 261, 467 A.2d 1353.**

23 year old woman had many teeth extracted under general anesthesia and died during recovery. Procedure performed in office and anesthesia administered by surgeon. Error not to charge on lack of informed consent even though consent form signed. ***Sauro v. Shea*, 257 Pa. Super. 87, 390 A.2d 259.**

Medical malpractice: Failure to diagnose

Wife plaintiff injured in collision case—received extensive dental treatment—verdict $10,000 for wife plaintiff and $2,000 for husband—majority of court held evidence sufficient to establish causal connection. ***DiVirgiliis v. Gordon,*** **212 Pa. Super. 548, 243 A.2d 459.**

Plaintiff consulted defendant dentist as to condition of certain of her teeth—contention of plaintiff that in the treatment of her teeth, the needle was injected too far and that defendant failed to x-ray her teeth—as result plaintiff claimed that she lost all of her teeth—no expert testimony—nonsuit proper. ***Lambert v. Soltis,*** **422 Pa. 304, 221 A.2d 173.**

Medical malpractice: Failure to diagnose

Plaintiff brought medical malpractice action against physician for failing to diagnose her breast cancer due to the physician's choice to use a fine needle aspiration biopsy. A jury found in favor of the plaintiff. The Superior Court affirmed, holding that a pathologist and oncologist were qualified to testify under the Medical Availability and Reduction of Error Act regarding the standard of care for a surgeon in choosing a biopsy method despite neither practicing as surgeons. ***Renna v. Schadt,* 64 A.3d 658 (Pa. Super. 2013).**

Plaintiff filed a medical malpractice action against Defendants New Jersey hospital and physician for failing to treat an epidural abscess, which was later discovered in Pennsylvania and resulted in paralysis. The Superior Court held that it had no specific jurisdiction over the New Jersey Defendants because the harm for failing to treat or diagnose arose in New Jersey. The Court held that the discovery of the harm in Pennsylvania did not alter the fact that it originated in New Jersey. The Court also held that there were no facts suggesting that the Defendants had any contact with Pennsylvania regarding Plaintiff's treatment. ***Mendel v. Williams,* 2012 Pa. Super. 171 (Pa. Super. 2012).**

Estate brought medical malpractice claim against Defendant physician for failure to diagnose decedent's acute viral myocarditis. A jury found in favor of Defendant. The Superior Court reversed holding that the trial court erred in providing a jury instruction to weigh the subjective state of mind of the physician when treating the decedent. ***Passarello v. Grumbine,* 29 A.3d 1158 (Pa. Super. 2011).**

Patient who suffered a stroke brought suit against radiology group after the radiologists failed to detect a carotid artery blockage based upon an MRI. A jury found in favor of the Plaintiff. The Superior Court held that it was a question of fact for the jury as to whether the Plaintiff was discharged by the hospital based upon the Defendant's MRI interpretation. ***Whitaker v. Frankford Hospital of the City of Philadelphia*, 984 A.2d 512 (Pa. Super. 2009).**

Plaintiff brought medical malpractice claim against physician for failing to diagnosis his knee cancer until a year after it had first been suggested in a radiology report. The jury found for the Plaintiffs and the trial court denied the physician's motion for judgment not withstanding the verdict. The Superior Court affirmed, holding that the radiologist report indicated the possibility that the abnormality was benign, but the Defendant physician failed to eliminate the possibility that it was

Medical malpractice: Failure to diagnose

malignant and therefore the physician was not entitled to judgment as a matter of law. ***Tindall v. Friedman*, 970 A.2d 1159 (Pa. Super. 2009).**

Plaintiff filed suit against hospital for failing to consult a neurologist, delaying her diagnosis, and delaying treatment, which could have prevented her stroke. The court reversed the lower court's dismissal of plaintiff's corporate negligence theory holding that the plaintiff had established the elements for a prima facie case through expert testimony and additional evidence. ***Brodowski v. Ryave*, 885 A.2d 1045 (Pa. Super. 2005).**

Defendant physician who did not raise defense of plaintiffs' decedent's contributory negligence and record devoid of evidence of fact which might support contributory negligence prohibit charging jury with law on that defense. Decedent's failure to take actions recommended by physician were not substantial factors in causing his death. "It is not contributory negligence to fail to guard against the lack of ordinary care by another." ***Angelo v. Diamontoni*, 871 A.2d 1276 (Pa. Super. 2005).**

Summary judgment against plaintiff whose medical malpractice case against surgeon who performed knee surgery reversed based on proof that plaintiff discovered injury and cause only after having seen third physician for another opinion on continued pain in knee. The fact that statute of limitations had not run from original surgery when plaintiff "lost confidence" in original physician is not relevant to toll statute of limitations. ***Caro v. Glah*, 867 A.2d 531 (Pa. Super. 2005).**

Plaintiff's decedent died after his treating physician failed to diagnose a leaking abdominal aneurysm. An x-ray and radiologist's report clearly indicated the problem had not been forwarded to the treating physician by the hospital staff. There was uncontradicted evidence that, had the treating physician seen the x-ray and report, he would have treated the aneurysm and the patient would have survived. Held: summary judgment in favor of the hospital on the claim of corporate negligence was improper in light of the obvious failure of procedure to inform the treating physician. The verdict in favor of the treating physician was against the weight of the evidence where his negligence was admitted, but not found to be a cause of the injury. ***Cangemi v. Cone*, 774 A.2d 1262 (Pa. Super. 2001).**

Plaintiff successfully sued physician for failure to diagnose. Doctor argued on appeal that trial court erred in failing to instruct jury on comparative negligence of plaintiff, when there was evidence that doctor had suggested a diagnostic test which plaintiff refused. Held: trial court must instruct the jury on comparative negligence where there is any evidence of comparative negligence on the part of the plaintiff. ***Zieber v. Bogert*, 747 A.2d 905 (Pa. Super. 2000).**

Plaintiff's decedent wife was examined on numerous occasions by a physician's assistant who failed to properly diagnose or call in physician to examine a cancerous breast. Trial court entered a compulsory nonsuit after refusing to accept testimony of plaintiff's medical expert. Despite his twenty-five years of practice and experience as an oncologist familiar with the same condition that caused wife's death, expert could not provide a specific reference to his theory of liability in a medical text. Where plaintiff's expert expresses the opinion that defendants' actions

Medical malpractice: Failure to diagnose

increased the risk of harm to plaintiff, the question of causation must go to the jury. Superior Court also reversed procedural rulings by trial court that prevented plaintiff from providing relevant and material facts to the record despite a complete lack of prejudice to defendants. ***Smith v. Grab,*** **705 A.2d 894 (Pa. Super. 1997).**

Action to recover for death of child 11 months after birth where death caused by negligent failure to diagnose and act on dangerous condition *in utero* immediately before birth. Evidence to establish "corporate liability" of hospital under *Thompson v. Nason Hospital*, 527 Pa. 330, 591 A.2d 703 (1991) must be provided in the form of expert testimony where the negligence is not obvious but need not contain "magic words." The substance of all the expert testimony will be considered as a whole. The evidence must establish that the hospital, in its own duty to the patient, deviated from the accepted standard of care and that that deviation was a substantial factor in causing the harm to the plaintiff. ***Welsh v. Bulger,*** **698 A.2d 581 (Pa. 1997).**

In medical malpractice action for delayed diagnosis of liver disease, the "two disease rule" from asbestos-related cases will be applied to preclude plaintiff's claim for increased risk and fear of liver cancer until such disease actually occurs. Second judge's grant of summary judgment on plaintiff's claim for increased risk of harm after first judge denied summary judgment on the same issue is reversible error. Order granting summary judgment as to increased risk of harm reversed. ***Klein v. Weisberg,*** ___ **Pa. Super.** ___**, 694 A.2d 644 (1997).**

Nurse who sought treatment at employer/hospital for tuberculosis contracted at hospital must seek recovery for injuries sustained as a result of misdiagnosis and mistreatment through workers compensation proceedings. Superior Court order reversing verdict for plaintiff affirmed by equally divided court. ***Snyder v. Pocono Medical Center,*** **547 Pa. 415, 690 A.2d 1152 (1997).**

Wife plaintiff diagnosed with lung cancer filed suit against radiology association and radiologist who had taken and interpreted chest x-ray at request of insurance company for failure to diagnose cancerous tumor. No physician-patient relationship is created where a physician examines a patient at the request of an insurance company. Summary judgment affirmed. ***Promubol v. Hackett,*** **454 Pa. Super. 622, 686 A.2d 417 (1996).**

Physician's assistant's failure to refer patient complaining of breast pain to physician is not actionable without proof of causation in suit against medical practice group instituted after discovery of breast cancer. Board-certified internist is qualified to render an opinion as to the duty of care of physician's assistant. Compulsory nonsuit affirmed. ***Montgomery v. So. Philadelphia Medical Group, Inc.,*** **441 Pa. Super. 146, 656 A.2d 1385 (1995).**

Respiratory therapist who contracted tuberculosis from exposure to patient brought negligence action against employer hospital for failure to diagnosis and treat her condition promptly and not to obtain remedy for contracting disease. Jury verdict for plaintiff reversed on grounds that her sole remedy was workers' compensation. ***Snyder v. Pocono Medical Center,*** **440 Pa. Super. 606, 656 A.2d 534 (1995).**

Medical malpractice: Failure to diagnose

Wrongful death and survival actions based on medical malpractice for failure to diagnose breast cancer are to be treated separately as to applicable statute of limitations. Failure to commence survival action within two years following death of decedent did not preclude wrongful death action filed within two years of death, because underlying cause of action for medical malpractice was not yet time-barred as of decedent's death. ***Moyer v. Rubright,* 438 Pa. Super. 154, 651 A.2d 1139 (1994).**

Medical malpractice claim for failure to diagnose fractured wrist. Liability admitted by radiologist. Jury improperly instructed on contributory negligence when insufficient facts pled or proven to support that instruction. Judgment in favor of radiologist reversed and new trial granted. ***Pascal v. Carter,* 436 Pa. Super. 40, 647 A.2d 231 (1994).**

Patient sought damages based on cost of treatment resulting from failure to diagnose acute appendicitis. Held: defendant not entitled to reduction in damages based on free care provided by affiliated medical center. ***Kashner v. Geisinger Clinic,* ____ Pa. Super. ____, 638 A.2d 980.**

Patient brought malpractice action for failure to diagnose breast cancer. Action barred by statute of limitations. Statute began to run when she was informed that tumor was cancerous. ***Bradley v. Ragheb,* 429 Pa. Super. 616, 633 A.2d 192.**

Action brought against physician for failure to diagnose colon cancer. Physician not liable. Jury instruction on failure to administer blood test not error. ***Sacks v. Mambu,* 429 Pa. Super. 498, 632 A.2d 1333.**

Physician found negligent in failing to diagnose rectal cancer but no damages awarded. Conflicting testimony supported verdict. ***Gallagher v. Marguglio,* 429 Pa. Super. 451, 632 A.2d 1309.**

Parents of child born with severe diabetes brought action for failure to perform ultrasound test. Physicians not liable. ***Bianchini v. N.K.D.S. Associates LTD.,* 420 Pa. Super. 294, 616 A.2d 700.**

Patient brought action against physician for failure to diagnose breast cancer. Held: "two schools of thought" applicable to failure to order yearly mammogram but not failure to diagnose from symptoms. ***Levine v. Rosen,* 532 Pa. 512, 616 A.2d 623.**

Wrongful death and survival action brought against physician for failure to diagnose breast cancer. Summary judgment granted to physician. Held: order granting summary judgment appealable but action was time-barred. ***Holmes v. Lado,* 412 Pa. Super. 218, 602 A.2d 1389.**

Physician failed to diagnose patient's cancer after reading x-ray taken during pre-employment physical. Physician not liable. ***Tomko v. Marks,* 412 Pa. Super. 54, 602 A.2d 890.**

Patient brought action against physician for failure to diagnose breast cancer. Physician not liable. Excluded evidence cumulative. Charge to jury not in error. ***Soda v. Baird,* 411 Pa. Super. 80, 600 A.2d 1274.**

Medical malpractice: Failure to diagnose

Malpractice action brought against city and health department for improperly diagnosing child's illness. Defendants not liable. Tort Claims Act does not deny equal protection. ***Gallagher v. City of Philadelphia,* 142 Pa. Cmwlth. 487, 597 A.2d 747.**

Survival action filed against physician for failure to diagnose and treat breast cancer. Held: survival action not barred by action filed during decedent's lifetime. ***Walker v. Roney,* 407 Pa. Super. 620, 595 A.2d 1318.**

Patient died after physician failed to order breast cancer screening. Physician not liable. Patient would have died anyway. ***Clayton v. Sabeh,* 406 Pa. Super. 335, 594 A.2d 365.**

Accident victim brought malpractice action against hospital and physician for failure to diagnose bone tumor in skull. Hospital and physician not liable. Connection between negligence and injury not shown. ***Bowser v. Lee Hospital,* 399 Pa. Super. 332, 582 A.2d 369.**

Worker injured on job brought action against employer and company physician for failure to disclose previous injury. Employer immune. Physician not immune. ***Noyes v. Cooper,* 396 Pa. Super. 592, 579 A.2d 407.**

Patient brought malpractice action against physician for failure to diagnose breast cancer. Trial court's instruction on contributory negligence not in error. Instructions on irrelevant considerations and "two schools of thought" constituted reversible error. ***Levine v. Rosen,* 394 Pa. Super. 178, 575 A.2d 579.**

Mother brought action for negligent infliction of emotional distress based on physician's failure to diagnose and treat son's illness. Judgement for defendant. Mother did not witness traumatic event. ***Tackett v. Enke,* 353 Pa. Super. 349, 509 A.2d 1310.**

Jury verdict $1,500,000—$837,000 (wrongful death); $663,000 (survival). Thirty-one year old married male injured in auto accident with survivable chest injuries died in hospital due to failure to diagnose pneumothorax. ***Richardson v. LaBuz,* 81 Pa. Cmwlth. 436, 474 A.2d 1181.**

Alleged failure to diagnose pulmonary embolism allegedly causing plaintiff's death. Defense verdict, affirmed. Diagnosis in subsequent hospital record properly admitted to show difficulty in making proper diagnosis. Not introduced for purpose of inherent veracity. Subsequent hospital also failed to promptly make proper diagnosis. ***Kemp v. Qualls,* 326 Pa. Super. 319, 473 A.2d 1369.**

Non-jury verdict $7,500. Alleged, failure to diagnose promptly regional ileitis. Increase in medical expenses in excess of $10,000 plus lost wages of $1,700. Evidence that defendant should have conducted certain tests supports verdict. Such failure increased risk of harm to plaintiff. ***Denardo v. Carneval,* 297 Pa. Super. 484, 444 A.2d 135.**

Malpractice case involving failure to diagnose cancer. Proper for jury to consider risk of metastasis even though eight years elapsed. There was expert testimony that metastasis still a possibility. ***Gradel v. Inouye,* 491 Pa. 534, 421 A.2d 674.**

Medical malpractice: HMO

Defense verdict in malpractice case. Although plaintiff's expert testified that defendant negligently failed to make a proper diagnosis of a fracture with subsequent permanent sequelae, jury believed otherwise. Affirmed. ***Quinlan v. Brown*, 277 Pa. Super. 525, 419 A.2d 1274.**

Alleged failure to detect mass in breast. Case not tried on theory of *Hamil v. Bashline*. Theory of case was that negligence caused cancer to develop. Defense verdict. Affirmed. ***Jones v. Montefiore Hosp.*, 275 Pa. Super. 422, 418 A.2d 1361.**

Verdict $1,500,000 for malpractice allegedly occurring from preoperative administration of anesthesia causing severe brain damage. Four attempts made to place endotracheal tube in trachea. 10 minutes after 4th attempt, plaintiff suffered cardiac arrest. Expert testified that tube was negligently placed and that physicians failed to diagnose mechanical blockage. Surgeon held in as "captain of ship." ***Schneider v. Einstein Medical Center*, 257 Pa. Super. 348, 390 A.2d 1271.**

Plaintiff fractured arm and thereafter developed cancer at fracture site which physician allegedly failed to diagnose. Thereafter arm had to be amputated. Expert testified that earlier detection would have greatly decreased likelihood of amputation—Held: not adequate to go to jury. Where evidence was that metastasis highly unlikely, should not have been submitted to jury. ***Gradel v. Inouye*, 252 Pa. Super. 392, 381 A.2d 975.**

Suit for damages for injuries sustained by minor during birth alleging late diagnosis of breech and further improper delivery techniques. Defense expert testified care was of high quality. Verdict for defendant. ***Freed v. Priore*, 247 Pa. Super. 418, 372 A.2d 895.**

Plaintiff's decedent had been in apparent health but became suddenly ill and condition diagnosed as gastroenteritis—discharged from hospital—died some 38 hours later—autopsy report changed to give cause of death as myocarditis—verdict for defendants—motions below properly dismissed—fair trial had been had. ***Brennan v. St. Luke's Hospital et al.*, 446 Pa. 339, 285 A.2d 471.**

Minor plaintiff strained himself while lifting—first doctor diagnosed case under several possibilities—second doctor saw minor only once—condition became worse and surgery required to remove a testicle—no expert testimony to develop that doctors should have diagnosed condition as a torsion and have taken surgical measures of relief—judgment *n.o.v.* properly entered as to both defendants. ***Carl v. Matzko*, 213 Pa. Super. 446, 249 A.2d 808.**

Plaintiffs, executrices, brought suit for the death of their decedent allegedly due to failure of defendant physician to properly diagnose and treat decedent—court charged that there existed a presumption against negligence of treating doctor—error—verdict for defendant—new trial ordered by Supreme Court. ***Richmond v. A.F. of L. Medical Service Plan of Philadelphia et al.*, 421 Pa. 269, 218 A.2d 303.**

Medical malpractice: HMO

Executrix brought wrongful death action against medical care provider after the decedent died of gastrointestinal bleeding as a result of a failure by the Defen-

Medical malpractice: Hospital

dant professional corporation to assign a physician to care for the decedent on the hospital's floor that it was supervising. A jury found in favor of the Plaintiff. The Superior Court affirmed holding that a professional corporation responsible for arranging and coordinating patient care in a unit of a hospital could be found negligent for failing to deliver the comprehensive care it was contractually obligated to provide. *Hyrcza v. West Penn Allegheny Health System*, **978 A.2d 961 (Pa. Super. 2009).**

    A hospital may not be held vicariously liable for the negligence of its agents and employees if they have been previously been absolved of liability in a prior proceeding. *Bordlemay v. Keystone Health Plans, Inc.*, **789 A.2d 748 (Pa. Super. 2001).**

    When a Health Maintenance Organization makes a treatment decision that affects the type of care or the time in which a patient receives care, the HMO may be liable for negligence under state law for injuries sustained as a result of that decision. Federal preemption under the Employee Retirement Income Security Act of 1974 relates to eligibility determinations only. *Pappas v. Asbel*, **768 A.2d 1089 (Pa. 2001).**

    Federal employee brought negligence and malpractice action against health maintenance organization. State tort claim preempted by Federal Employee's Health Benefits Act. *Fink v. Delaware Valley HMO.* **417 Pa. Super. 287, 612 A.2d 485.**

Medical malpractice: Hospital

    Plaintiff brought medical malpractice lawsuit against the Defendant hospital alleging a surgical sponge was left inside him after surgery. The trial court dismissed on the basis that no expert testimony was produced by the Plaintiff. The Superior Court reversed holding that the doctrine of res ipsa loquitur could be applied in medical malpractice cases of obvious negligence. *Fessenden v. Robert Packer Hospital*, **2014 Pa. Super. 154 (2014).**

    Plaintiff parents and estate administrators filed a medical malpractice wrongful death action against defendant hospital for injuries suffered by the minor decedent during a Caesarean section. A jury found in favor of the plaintiffs. The Superior Court affirmed holding that a jury could award damages under the Wrongful Death Act for plaintiff parents' loss of society and companionship of their child. The Superior Court also reiterated that in a professional negligence action against a hospital or physician the plaintiff was only required to produce evidence that the defendant's conduct increased the risk of harm to the plaintiff. *Hatwood v. Hospital of the University of Pennsylvania*, **55 A.3d 1229 (Pa. Super. 2012).**

    Plaintiff filed a medical malpractice action against Defendant New Jersey hospital for failing to treat an epidural abscess, which was later discovered in Pennsylvania and resulted in paralysis. The Superior Court held that it had no specific jurisdiction over the New Jersey hospital because the harm for failing to treat or diagnose arose in New Jersey. The Court held that the discovery of the harm in Pennsylvania did not alter the fact that it originated in New Jersey. The Court also held that there were no facts suggesting that the hospital had any contact with Penn-

Medical malpractice: Hospital

sylvania regarding Plaintiff's treatment. *Mendel v. Williams*, 2012 Pa. Super. 171 (Pa. Super. 2012).

Plaintiff brought a claim for negligence against the defendant hospital for injuries suffered by the decedent when he fell from a hospital bed due to not being restrained. Plaintiff's Complaint was dismissed for a failure to file a certificate of merit. The Superior Court affirmed holding that Plaintiff's Complaint alleged failures to train staff assisting in the care of patients, which was an allegation of professional liability requiring a certificate of merit. The Pennsylvania Supreme Court affirmed the Superior Court's ruling without opinion. *Ditch v. Waynesboro Hospital*, 17 A.3d 310 (Pa. 2011).

Five patients' estates brought claims for wrongful death against a hospital after one of its nurses confessed to killing the patients. The trial court denied the hospital's motion for summary judgment. The Superior Court upheld the trial court's ruling holding that the hospital had an affirmative duty to inform a patient or their next of kin when it knows or should have known that one of its employees either killed or attempted to kill a patient. *Krapf v. St. Luke's Hospital*, _____ A.2d _____, 2010 WL 2902744 (Pa. Super 2010).

Plaintiff injured due to a wrist surgery brought medical malpractice claim against medical providers. Trial court granted summary judgment on the basis that the Plaintiff failed to file her complaint within the two years she should have reasonably discovered or actually discovered the cause of her injury. The Superior Court affirmed. The Pennsylvania Supreme Court reversed, holding that summary judgment was improperly granted as there was a question of fact as to whether or not the Plaintiff should have discovered the cause of her injury to commence the running of the statute of limitations. *Wilson v. El-Daief*, 964 A.2d 354 (Pa. 2009).

Plaintiff brought suit under a res ipsa loquitor theory against a hospital after she was admitted for a complaint related to Crohn's disease, and later while in the hospital developed a shoulder injury requiring surgery. The appellate court reversed the trial court's judgment on the basis that Plaintiff could not proceed on a res ipsa loquitor theory, because she had failed to rule out other responsible causes for her shoulder injury including herself. *Griffin v. University of Pittsburgh Medical Center-Braddock Hospital*, 950 A.2d 996 (Pa. Super. 2008).

Hospital filed suit for indemnification against defendant physicians after a judgment was entered against the hospital in a medical malpractice case and defendant physicians were never joined. The appellate court held that in order to succeed on an indemnity claim against the unjoined physicians, expert reports were required to establish the negligence of the unjoined physicians. *MIIX Insurance Co. v. Epstein*, 937 A.2d 469 (Pa. Super. 2007).

Plaintiff brought suit against a physician and hospital after he suffered a chemical burn to his shoulder while he was unconscious during surgery. The appellate court held that the doctrine of res ipsa loquitor could not be used by the Plaintiff to create an inference of negligence, because the defense expert testified that the injury was an outbreak of shingles and therefore could have occurred without neg-

Medical malpractice: Hospital

ligence. *MacNutt v. Temple University Hospital, Inc.*, 932 A.2d 980 (Pa. Super. 2008).

Co-executors brought a suit for medical malpractice against the hospital for failure to transmit x-rays showing a possible cancerous mass and failure to investigate against the treating physician. The court held that the substance of the complaint controls whether a claim a claim is for ordinary negligence or professional malpractice. ***Rostock v. Anzalone*, 904 A.2d 943 (Pa. Super. 2006).**

Patient filed suit against defendant hospital for medical malpractice after she went into respiratory arrest due to a reaction from a combination of morphine and anti-nausea medication. The court held that in establishing a prima facie case the plaintiff had introduced sufficient evidence of a failure to monitor her respiratory rate to show that the defendant's acts had increased the risk of harm to her. ***Vogelsberger v. Magee-Womens Hospital of UPMC Health System*, 903 A.2d 540 (Pa. Super. 2006).**

Plaintiff alleged negligence on the part of the employees of defendant hospital in the insertion of a catheter. The court held that the complaint failed to allege that the hospital had any constructive or actual knowledge of the improper catheter insertion that created the plaintiff's injury. ***Kennedy v. Butler Memorial Hospital*, 901 A.2d 1042 (Pa. Super. 2006).**

Plaintiff filed suit against hospital for failing to consult a neurologist, delaying her diagnosis, and delaying treatment, which could have prevented her stroke. The court reversed the lower court's dismissal of plaintiff's corporate negligence theory holding that the plaintiff had established the elements for a prima facie case through expert testimony and additional evidence. ***Brodowski v. Ryave*, 885 A.2d 1045 (Pa. Super. 2005).**

Patient committed to hospital under Mental Health Procedures Act died by drowning while taking an unsupervised bath. Despite clear medical testimony by affidavit that the staff of the hospital breached their duty of care to the patient, it was held that mere negligence was not established to be the "gross negligence" required to be proved to avoid the immunity set forth in the Mental Health Procedures Act. ***Downey v. Crozer-Chester Medical Center*, 817 A.2d 517 (Pa. Super. 2003).**

Plaintiff's suit for negligence and negligent infliction of emotional distress against physician who performed autopsy on plaintiff's mother and same causes of action and respondeat superior against hospital. Autopsy report indicated that deceased mother's eyes had been "donated" despite insistence by plaintiff that eyes were not to be donated. Claims for emotional distress and respondeat superior dismissed on preliminary objections. Verdict in favor of plaintiff reversed on grounds that evidence was not adequate to prove that eyes had, in fact, been donated. The physician who had performed the autopsy amended report to indicate that he never looked to see if the eyes were in place. ***Van Zandt v. Holy Redeemer Hospital*, 806 A.2d 879 (Pa. Super. 2002).**

Suit by personal representative against medical facility and physician on behalf of decedent who died after allegedly negligent surgical placement of a catheter

Medical malpractice: Hospital

and alleged battery due to lack of informed consent by decedent for earlier treatment. Held that a medical facility cannot be held vicariously liable for a physician's failure to obtain informed consent. It is the individual physician's responsibility, in his or her special relationship with the patient, to obtain the consent. ***Valles v. Albert Einstein Medical Center*, 805 A.2d 1232 (Pa. 2002).**

Plaintiff's decedent died after general anesthesia and surgery to repair injured elbow. Physician's had determined prior to surgery that patient was suffering from various serious ailments that compromised her ability to survive general anesthesia and surgery. Summary judgement in favor of all individual and corporate defendants reversed on determination that testimony of plaintiff's medical witnesses was adequate to state a *prima facie* case of medical and corporate malpractice despite the absence of "magic words". ***Rauch v. Mike-Mayer*, 783 A.2d 815 (Pa. Super. 2001).**

Decedent died as a result of a burst abdominal aortic aneurysm that had not been properly diagnosed well before it burst. Suit was against hospital that took x-ray that clearly showed aneurysm and physician that did not review the x-ray. Summary judgment in favor of hospital and verdict in favor of physician were reversed on determination that question of whether hospital properly notified physician of results of x-ray was for jury and jury's finding that doctor was negligent but that negligence was not a substantial factor was obvious error. ***Cangemi v. Cone*, 774 A.2d 1262 (Pa. Super. 2001).**

Plaintiff's decedent died after his treating physician failed to diagnose a leaking abdominal aneurysm. An x-ray and radiologist's report clearly indicated the problem had not been forwarded to the treating physician by the hospital staff. There was uncontradicted evidence that, had the treating physician seen the x-ray and report, he would have treated the aneurysm and the patient would have survived. Held: summary judgment in favor of the hospital on the claim of corporate negligence was improper in light of the obvious failure of procedure to inform the treating physician. The verdict in favor of the treating physician was against the weight of the evidence where his negligence was admitted, but not found to be a cause of the injury. ***Cangemi v. Cone*, 774 A.2d 1262 (Pa. Super. 2001).**

Plaintiff's decedent died after caesarian section where evidence indicated pregnancy-induced hypertension, also known as preeclampsia. Corporate hospital negligence can take the form of a breach of any of four duties: to use reasonable care in the maintenance of safe and adequate facilities and equipment; to select and retain only competent physicians; to oversee all persons who practice medicine within its walls as to patient care; and to formulate, adopt and enforce adequate rules and policies to ensure quality care for the patients. A *prima facie* case of corporate negligence requires evidence that the hospital acted in deviation from the standard of care, had actual or constructive notice of the defects or procedures which created the harm and that the conduct was a substantial factor in bringing about the harm. ***Whittington v. Episcopal Hospital*, 768 A.2d 1144, (Pa. Super. 2001).**

Medical malpractice: Hospital

Wife, who delivered brain-damaged child after Cesarean section with only local anesthetic, and husband, individually and as parents of child, sued anesthesiology group, obstetrician and hospital for malpractice. Nurses employed at hospital are not agents of the physicians when they act in the normal course of hospital services. Father's loss of consortium claim properly denied by trial court where his only testimony was that he had a subjective fear of engaging in sexual relations with his wife following her delivery of brain-damaged child, even though the damage may have been the result of medical malpractice. Father's claim for negligent infliction of emotional distress properly dismissed where he was not near the scene of the injuries to his wife and newborn child. Hearing his wife's cries of pain only, without any visual experience of her condition, was insufficient. *Tiburzio-Kelly v. Montgomery,* **452 Pa. Super. 158, 681 A.2d 757 (1996).**

Verdict in favor of woman whose voice was irreparably damaged following intubation procedure vacated, and judgment entered for appellant hospital where plaintiff's complaint stated cause of action in negligence against hospital, but proof at trial focused only on family physician's negligence in follow-up care of plaintiff; no amendment to plaintiff's original complaint was filed. *Reynolds v. Thomas Jefferson University Hospital,* **450 Pa. Super. 327, 676 A.2d 1205 (1996).**

Wife plaintiff who was left unattended in emergency room during miscarriage and then handed corpse of miscarried fetus while nurse took pictures established sufficient evidence of physical impact to allow recovery for negligent infliction of emotional distress. Case remanded for new trial on damages. *Brown v. Philadelphia College of Osteopathic Medicine,* **449 Pa. Super. 667, 674 A.2d 1130 (1996).**

Hospital does not have duty to ensure that its staff maintains professional liability insurance coverage. Order granting summary judgment affirmed. *Domineck v. Mercy Hospital,* **449 Pa. Super. 313, 673 A.2d 959 (1996).**

Hospital has no duty independent of physicians to establish practice and procedure for obtaining informed consent from patients. Doctrine of informed consent applied only to physicians and surgeons who perform operations. Hospitals owe four specifically enumerated duties to all patients. Preliminary objections sustained. *Kelly v. Methodist Hospital,* **444 Pa. Super. 427, 664 A.2d 148 (1995).**

In action for alleged medical malpractice, plaintiff failed to state cause of action against state-employed physician, state hospital, and department of public welfare. Order sustaining preliminary objections affirmed because all defendants immune under sovereign immunity statute. *Moser v. Heistand,* **168 Pa. Cmwlth. 109, 649 A.2d 177 (1994).**

Patient injured in fall while walking to bathroom after administration of preoperative injections. Hospital negligent but not liable. *Atkins v. Pottstown Medical Center,* **430 Pa. Super. 279, 634 A.2d 258.**

Patient brought action against orthopedic surgeon and hospital. Claim against surgeon discontinued by plaintiff. Hospital not liable. *Walls v. Hazleton State General Hospital,* **157 Pa. Cmwlth. 170, 629 A.2d 232.**

Medical malpractice: Hospital

Children of mother killed by former mental patient brought action against hospital and psychiatrist for failure to warn of patient's violent tendencies. Defendants not liable. ***Leonard v. Latrobe Hospital,* 425 Pa. Super. 540, 625 A.2d 1228.**

Mother of infant who died shortly after birth brought action against hospital. Held: jury could reasonably infer that hospital staff did not inform physician that fetus was in distress. Productivity factor of 1.1 applied to child's potential earning capacity. ***Greer v. Bryant,* 423 Pa. Super. 608, 621 A.2d 999.**

Patient who suffered allergic reaction to medication brought action against hospital. Held: two-year statute of limitation and not six-year limitation under U.C.C. applied. ***Stephenson v. Greenberg,* 421 Pa. Super. 1, 617 A.2d 364.**

Patient who suffered complications from implantation of experimental lens in eye brought action against hospital based on lack of informed consent. Held: judgment *n.o.v.* in favor of hospital in error. ***Friter v. Iolab Corporation,* 414 Pa. Super. 622, 607 A.2d 1111.**

Patient brought malpractice action against hospital for negligent catheterization. Jury found hospital negligent but injuries not result of negligence and set damages at $50,000. New trial granted. ***Chiaverini v. Sewickley Valley Hospital,* 409 Pa. Super. 630, 598 A.2d 1021.**

Hospital patient who attempted suicide was found by husband. Hospital not immune under Mental Health Procedures Act and not liable for negligent infliction of emotional distress. ***Bloom v. Dubois Regional Medical Center,* 409 Pa. Super. 83, 597 A.2d 671.**

Patient brought malpractice action against hospital for negligently supervising care. Theory of corporate liability as it relates to hospitals adopted. ***Thompson v. Nason Hospital,* 527 Pa. 330, 591 A.2d 703.**

Patient who suffered paralysis after neurosurgery brought malpractice action against surgeon and hospital. Surgeon settled before trial. Held: hospital may be found liable if risk of injury was increased because of its negligence. ***Mitzelfelt v. Kamin,* 526 Pa. 54, 584 A.2d 888.**

Patient suffered injuries as the result of negligence of staff physician. Held: hospital may be held liable even though physician not employee. ***Thompson v. Nason Hospital,* 370 Pa. Super. 115, 535 A.2d 1177.**

Alleged negligent supervision of patient at state mental hospital who was released and then assaulted plaintiff. Held: within medical professional liability exception to Sovereign Immunity Act. Preliminary objections denied. ***Yellen v. Philadelphia State Hospital,* 94 Pa. Cmwlth. 576, 503 A.2d 1108.**

Negligent infliction of emotional distress and malpractice adequately pleaded here against psychiatric hospital allegedly treating plaintiff's drug dependency condition. ***Crivellaro v. Pennsylvania Power and Light,* 341 Pa. Super. 173, 491 A.2d 207.**

Medical malpractice: Hospital

Plaintiff's decedent brought to emergency room, with heart attack. Family doctor had him transferred to Lankenau—doctor had no privileges at Riddle. Transfer allegedly occurred in view of Riddle personnel, and without proper written release forms signed. Plaintiff died en route. Verdict for hospital affirmed. **Riddle Memorial Hospital v. Dohan, 504 Pa. 571, 475 A.2d 1314.**

Charge of court held to be inadequate on issue of hospital's responsibility to patient suffering heart attack in emergency room. Patient was under care of non-staff physician who, allegedly due to misinformation, caused patient to be transported to another hospital. Plaintiff died en route. New trial ordered. **Dohan v. Stahlnecker, 313 Pa. Super. 279, 459 A.2d 1228.**

Jury verdict $1,000,000—malpractice action; $10,000—auto negligence action. Rear end collision—injuries to neck and back. Low back surgery. Infection followed—neomycin antibiotic allegedly caused kidney failure, partial paralysis of lower limbs and total hearing loss. Plaintiff could walk on crutches at time of trial. Verdict affirmed. Plaintiff, truck driver, earned $3.00/hr. at time of accident. Special damages $294,000. Hospital held in case because hospital resident-employee actively participated in neomycin therapy and made some dosage decisions. Residents held to standard of specialist, not general practitioner. **Pratt v. Stein, 298 Pa. Super. 92, 444 A.2d 674.**

Hospital physician treated victim of altercation. Patient died. Records allegedly falsified to lay blame upon other actor in fight rather than on the malpractice of the physicians. Actor-plaintiff charged with a homicide. Charges if proven are actionable against hospital—§46 of Restatement (2d) Torts. **Banyas v. Lower Bucks Hospital, 293 Pa. Super. 122, 437 A.2d 1236.**

Original complaint alleged only date of his hospital admission. Error not to allow amendment at trial so that proof could go to continuing negligence, even though statute had run. **Laursen v. General Hospital of Monroe Co., 494 Pa. 238, 431 A.2d 237.**

Section 429 of Restatement (2d) Torts held applicable where patient enters hospital and is treated by staff physician who is actually independent contractor. Hospital responsible under theory of ostensible agency. **Capan v. Divine Providence Hospital, 287 Pa. Super. 364, 430 A.2d 647.**

Fourteen-year old boy in hospital due to exhibition of bizarre behavior. While in hospital he set a fire killing roommate. Found not guilty by reason of insanity. Issue of negligence of hospital and superseding cause for jury. **Vattimo v. Lower Bucks Hosp., 59 Pa. Cmwlth. 1, 428 A.2d 765.**

Chronic alcoholic presented himself at hospital with nose bleed. Developed delirium tremors due to lack of alcohol and died 6 days later due to heart failure. No evidence of negligence. Verdicts for defendants affirmed. **Capan v. Divine Providence Hospital, 270 Pa. Super. 127, 410 A.2d 1282.**

Husband-decedent died at office of private physician after defendant hospital allegedly was negligent in treating apparent heart attack. Sufficient to go to jury if expert believes that negligent action or inaction of defendant was a "substantial fac-

Medical malpractice: Hospital

tor" in bringing about harm or demise of plaintiff. ***Hamil v. Bashline*, 481 Pa. 256, 392 A.2d 1280.**

Verdict $450,000 for 50 year old woman rendered quadriplegic during neck surgery. Drill went too far damaging spinal cord—alleged defect in drill, alleged lack of informed consent. Verdict against resident and surgeon, hospital, and drill manufacturer. New drill—not tested prior to operation. Affirmed. ***Grubb v. Eistein Medical Center*, 255 Pa. Super. 381, 381 A.2d 480.**

Plaintiff-decedent taken to defendant hospital complaining of severe chest pains. Doctor ordered EKG—machine malfunctioned and doctor ordered use of second machine which was never found. Plaintiff died on way to private physician for EKG. Expert opinion that conduct of defendant may have caused the harm insufficient since it would require jury to speculate. Evidence of increased risk not adequate. ***Hamil v. Bashline Hospital*, 243 Pa. Super. 227, 364 A.2d 1366.**

Plaintiff-decedent admitted for surgery on internal male sex organs. Surgery not completed upon discovery of terminal cancer. Numerous x-rays taken during remaining 11 months of plaintiff's life showed two hemostats left inside. None of the three defendants nor the doctors who cared for plaintiff until his death advised him of their presence. An x-ray technician told him only 10 weeks before his death, but by then his condition precluded surgery for removal. Defense was that hemostats caused no discomfort nor hastened death. Verdict $49,000.00, compensatory damages. ***Easter v. Hancock*, 237 Pa. Super. 31, 346 A.2d 323.**

Plaintiff's husband called private hospital and asked that his wife be admitted. Hospital refused unless ordered by a physician on staff. Three days later wife sustained cerebral hemorrhage with permanent damage. Summary judgment in favor of hospital granted. Private hospital under no duty to accept non-emergency case. ***Fabian v. Matzko*, 236 Pa. Super. 267, 344 A.2d 569.**

Action by patient against surgeon and hospital for damages resulting from failure to remove hemostat from abdomen before concluding surgical procedure. Verdict against doctor only. Trial judge gave very restrictive view of hospital's possible liability. Charge precluded jury finding hospital negligent for not devising adequate rules and regulations. ***Bilonoha v. Zubritzky*, 233 Pa. Super. 136, 336 A.2d 351.**

During surgery, clamp left in abdomen of plaintiff. Verdict against operating doctor. Binding instructions given exonerating hospital. Reversed, new trial as to liability of hospital only. Damages not to be tried over. ***Tonsic v. Wagner*, 458 Pa. 246, 329 A.2d 497.**

Nurse giving injection pursuant to physician's instructions is employee of hospital—nonsuit in suit versus doctor sustained. ***Muller v. Likoff*, 225 Pa. Super. 111, 310 A.2d 303.**

Plaintiff patient required a second operation as the result of a clamp left in incision after initial operation—trial court charged jury that hospital's only negligence could be its failure to require an instrument count—verdict solely against operating surgeon—motion for a new trial as to hospital refused below and action af-

Medical malpractice: Informed Consent Doctrine

firmed on appeal—strong dissent. *Tonsic et vir v. Wagner,* **220 Pa. Super. 468, 288 A.2d 791.**

Plaintiff on entering hospital signed two consents for an operation—suit against operating doctor on an assault and battery claim and against hospital for negligence—nonsuits properly entered—consents sufficient on assault and battery charge and lack of expert testimony justified nonsuit in suit against hospital. *Chandler v. Cook,* **438 Pa. 447, 263 A.2d 794.**

Plaintiff, a nurse, entered a private hospital and fell at emergency entrance—evidence that water had entered entrance and attendant had removed mat to mop up—case for jury. *Kerwood v. Rolling Hill Corp.,* **424 Pa. 59, 225 A.2d 918.**

Medical malpractice: Informed Consent Doctrine

Patient brought medical malpractice action against medical providers for lack of informed consent after a drug pump used to treat her multiple sclerosis left her paraplegic. Trial court granted judgment for the medical providers despite a jury verdict in the Plaintiff's favor and the Superior Court affirmed. The Pennsylvania Supreme Court reversed, holding that circumstantial evidence is sufficient to prove elements of a medical malpractice action, but expert testimony is required to establish that a reasonable physician would have informed a patient of the likely risk prior to surgery. *Fitzpatrick v. Natter,* **599 Pa. 465, 961 A.2d 1229 (2008).**

Plaintiff brought suit against physician and hospital for lack of informed consent after the physician performed a tubal ligation procedure on her and her other physician failed to inform the surgeon that she no longer consented to have a tubal ligation performed. *Isaac v. Jameson Memorial Hospital,* **932 A.2d 924 (Pa. Super. 2007).**

Plaintiff filed suit after defendant doctor removed an abnormal portion of her small bowel during a diagnostic laparoscopy. The court found dismissal of a directed verdict was appropriate since it could not be found as a matter of law that defendant had exceeded the scope of plaintiff's signed consent statement. The court also held that expert testimony was necessary to determine if there was a duty to consult during a surgical procedure. *McSorley v. Deger,* **905 A.2d 524 (Pa. Super. 2006).**

Patient plaintiff sued physicians and hospital for injuries sustained after injection of Recombinant Tissue Plasminogen Activator (TPA) "clot buster" drugs into blood clots in his leg alleging lack of informed consent. Held that a claim that a health care provider failed to acquire informed consent is only available against the physician who performs a surgical procedure, not the health care facility. Court raises but does not answer the question of whether angioplasty is a "surgical" procedure which requires informed consent. Collateral issue of whether health care facility is liable for its own failure to acquire informed consent in trials of procedures which are under FDA supervision. *Stalsitz v. Allentown Hospital,* **814 A.2d 766 (Pa. Super. 2002).**

Elemental analysis of informed consent doctrine in case of a woman who sued her cancer surgeon for failure to give adequate information to support an informed consent on whether to proceed with second excisional biopsy to remove a

Medical malpractice: Informed Consent Doctrine

mass from plaintiff's breast following earlier discovery of cancerous tissue in same breast. Jury determined that physician had failed to obtain an informed consent but that failure was not a substantial factor in plaintiff's decision to undergo the biopsy. ***Hohns v. Gain*, 806 A.2d 16 (Pa. Super. 2002).**

Suit by personal representative against medical facility and physician on behalf of decedent who died after allegedly negligent surgical placement of a catheter and alleged battery due to lack of informed consent by decedent for earlier treatment. Held that a medical facility cannot be held vicariously liable for a physician's failure to obtain informed consent. It is the individual physician's responsibility, in his or her special relationship with the patient, to obtain the consent. ***Valles v. Albert Einstein Medical Center*, 805 A.2d 1232 (Pa. 2002).**

Plaintiff patient who awoke from anesthesia following surgery for revascularization of his penis to increase blood flow was presented with a warranty card for the penile implant and pump which had been placed without his consent. In suit for damages based on lack of informed consent, trial court granted motion for directed verdict on grounds that plaintiff did not present expert testimony that his injuries were the causally connected to the implant. On appeal from reversal by Superior Court, the Supreme Court thoroughly analyzed the doctrine of informed consent as a battery theory rather than a negligence and affirmed Superior Court decision vacating the directed verdict. ***Montgomery v. Bazaz-Sehgal*, _____ Pa. _____, 798 A.2d 742 (2002).**

Pennsylvania courts continue to rely on the battery standard for informed consent cases. ***Bey v. Sacks*, 789 A.2d 232 (Pa. Super 2001).**

Plaintiff filed suit based on lack of informed consent where physicians implanted bone screws to aid in fixation of spinal column, a use of the bone screws that had not been specifically approved by the FDA in its review of bone screw technology. Plaintiff alleged that physician's failure to inform him of FDA status of bone screw use for spinal fixation prevented plaintiff from giving fully informed consent to implantation. Held that lack of FDA approval does not constitute a determination that an off-label use of a medical device is necessarily dangerous and that a patient must be informed of that use. ***Southard v. Temple University Hospital*, 566 Pa. 335, 781 A.2d 101 (2001).**

Following injuries resulting from a leaking suture, plaintiff sued surgeon, alleging that his misrepresentation about how many times he had performed the surgery vitiated her informed consent when he had in fact only performed the surgery a limited number of times. Held: surgeon's experience was not a factor in determining whether informed consent was properly given. The only relevant issue is whether a full explanation of the risks was conveyed by the surgeon to the patient. ***Duttry v. Patterson*, 771 A.2d 1255 (Pa. 2001).**

In action by plaintiff who was injured following spinal fusion surgery, the court held that Pennsylvania has adopted the prudent patient standard for informed consent cases. A physician must inform a patient of the "material facts, risks, complications and alternatives to surgery, which a reasonable person in the patient's po-

Medical malpractice: Informed Consent Doctrine

sition would have considered significant in deciding whether to have the operation." *Cosmo v. Marcotte,* **760 A.2d 886 (Pa. Super. 2000).**

Because mother of minor who died during surgical procedure performed by doctor to whom she had not given informed consent was not present at time of procedure, she could not recover for intentional infliction of emotional distress. §46 of Restatement (2d) Torts requires that person who is claiming emotional distress plead presence at time of incident causing distress. *Taylor v. Albert Einstein Medical Center,* **754 A.2d 650 (Pa. 2000).**

In case of dental malpractice, including issue of first impression in the Commonwealth, held that a root canal is a "surgical" or "operative procedure" and therefor a trigger for requirement of patient's informed consent. *Perkins v. Disipio,* **736 A.2d 6098 (Pa. Super. 1999).**

A physician may be required to include in his description of an operative procedure the use of Food and Drug Administration classification of a device intended to be used in the procedure. A hospital has no duty to a patient under Pennsylvania's informed consent doctrine; that duty is on the physician who is to perform the procedure. *Southard v. Temple University Hospital,* **731 A.2d 603 (Pa. Super. 1999).**

Plaintiff's decedent died after a pediatrician performed a catheterization procedure when the patient's parents had given consent for the procedure to a cardiologist. The trial judge refused to charge on lack of informed consent on the basis that as long as consent to the procedure is adequate, the identity of the person who performs the procedure is irrelevant. Reversed and remanded for new trial to include liability and compensatory and punitive damages. *Taylor v. Albert Einstein Medical Center,* **723 A.2d 1027 (Pa. Super. 1999).**

Plaintiff filed suit against physician who had performed gastric-bypass surgery alleging that she had not received adequate information on which to base an informed consent. Held: question of adequacy of information is for jury to decide. The nature of the information provided, not the identity or position of the person who provides it, nurse rather than physician, is important. *Foflygen v. Allegheny General Hospital,* **723 A.2d 705 (Pa. Super. 1999).**

Plaintiff filed suit against plastic surgeon for surgery without providing informed consent. Following verdict for plaintiff, defendants appeal arguing that trial court had erred in refusing to grant judgment *n.o.v.* for plaintiff's failure to present expert evidence as to the probability of the risks involved, that the risks actually occurred and that her injuries were caused by the surgery. Superior Court affirmed holding that, recovery on theory of informed consent is permitted regardless of causation because it is the conduct of the unauthorized procedure that constitutes the tort. *Boute v. Seitchik,* **719 A.2d 320 (Pa. Super. 1998).**

While informed consent is required from a patient in any surgical or operative procedure, it is not required when only nonsurgical procedures are performed. Administration of anesthetics, steroids or other medications by injection does not require informed consent. *Morgan v. MacPhail,* **704 A.2d 617 (Pa. 1997).**

Medical malpractice: Informed Consent Doctrine

In medical malpractice action, jury verdict slip poorly drafted by counsel for defendant and plaintiff resulted in inconsistent verdict. Plaintiff was required to provide medical testimony of informed consent and evidence was for jury on whether physician was negligent. Order granting new trial on liability only reversed; entire case remanded for new trial. ***Nogowski v. Alemo-Hammad,* 456 Pa. Super. 750, 691 A.2d 950 (1997).**

In medical malpractice action, the *Hamil/Mitzelfelt* two-pronged test "relaxing" a plaintiff's burden of proving causation should be applied to the entirety of plaintiff's expert's testimony regarding necessity of revised informed consent. Order removing compulsory nonsuit affirmed. ***Kratt v. Horrow,* 455 Pa. Super. 140, 687 A.2d 830 (1997).**

Order granting summary judgment reversed on plaintiff's claims of battery, breach of contract, and lack of informed consent arising out of back surgery performed by or at the direction of physicians to whom plaintiff had never given consent. ***Grabowski v. Quigley,* 454 Pa. Super. 27, 684 A.2d 610 (1996).**

Husband suffering from seizures was treated by a partial lobectomy that resulted in more serious seizures and severe memory and speech problems. Informed consent to medical treatment requires that the patient have a "true understanding of the nature of the operation ... and the possible results." Judgment *n.o.v.* permitted only in "clear case." Judgment *n.o.v.* reversed and jury verdict reinstated. ***Rowinsky v. Sperling,* 452 Pa. Super. 215, 681 A.2d 785 (1996).**

Although entire complaint arising out of birth of Down's Syndrome child and sterilization was inartfully drafted, two distinct claims were asserted: one for wrongful birth and one for performance of sterilization procedure without informed consent. Plaintiff's proposed amendments to complaint did not create new cause of action but clarified and strengthened claim based on lack of informed consent and, therefore, should have been allowed. Order granting judgment on the pleadings and denying leave to amend reversed. ***Sejpal v. Corson, McKinley,* 445 Pa. Super. 427, 665 A.2d 1198 (1995).**

Where patient who underwent perineal urethrotomy and cauterization, rather than planned transurethral prostatectomy, failed to establish a causal connection between resulting injuries and physician's conduct through expert testimony, compulsory nonsuit was proper. Patient should have been allowed to introduce evidence of alleged lack of consent to surgery that was admittedly not discussed by physician and patient prior to its performance. Order granting compulsory nonsuit on question of negligence affirmed. Case remanded on claim for lack of informed consent. ***Hoffman v. Mogil,* 445 Pa. Super. 252, 665 A.2d 478 (1995).**

Hospital has no duty independent of physicians to establish practice and procedure for obtaining informed consent from patients. Doctrine of informed consent applied only to physicians and surgeons who perform operations. Hospitals owe four specifically enumerated duties to all patients. Preliminary objections sustained. ***Kelly v. Methodist Hospital,* 444 Pa. Super. 427, 664 A.2d 148 (1995).**

Medical malpractice: Informed Consent Doctrine

In action against orthopedic surgeon for injury resulting from improperly performed back surgery, defendant physician's expert's report failed to address necessity of surgery and therefore expert was precluded from testifying on that issue. Judgment for plaintiff affirmed. *Walsh v. Kubiak,* **443 Pa. Super. 284, 661 A.2d 416 (1995).**

Plaintiff who contracted AIDS following transfusion of tainted blood filed suit against treating physicians and family physician for medical malpractice. Claim against one defendant dismissed for plaintiff's failure to establish through medical testimony that defendant's actions deviated from good and acceptable medical standards. Proof of compliance with medical standard of care need not be expressed in precisely the language used to annunciate the legal standard. Physician not required to obtain patient's informed consent before blood transfusion that was administered separately from a surgical procedure. *Hoffman v. Brandywine Hospital,* **443 Pa. Super. 245, 661 A.2d 397 (1995).**

A cause of action for failure to obtain informed consent has been steadfastly limited to "surgical or operative medical procedures." Lack of informed consent for a touching states cause of action for battery. Because chiropractors are statutorily proscribed from performing any surgical procedures, a cause of action against a chiropractor for failure to obtain informed consent before performing nonsurgical procedure will not lie as a matter of law. Order dismissing complaint affirmed. *Matukonis v. Trainer,* **441 Pa. Super. 570, 657 A.2d 1314 (1995).**

A referring physician cannot be held liable under theory of failure to obtain informed consent where he had no physical contact with plaintiff who suffered injury as a result of recommended surgery. Suit for failure to obtain informed consent grounded in battery, not negligence. Verdict for plaintiff vacated and remanded. *Shaw v. Kirschbaum,* **439 Pa. Super. 24, 653 A.2d 12 (1994).**

Patient who suffered complications after stomach stapling surgery brought action against physician and nurse based on lack of informed consent. Nurse not liable. Negligence theory of informed consent not recognized. *Foflygen v. R. Zemel, M.D. (PC),* **420 Pa. Super. 18, 615 A.2d 1345.**

Patient who suffered complications after surgery brought action based on lack of informed consent. Held: physician must disclose factors that a reasonable man would consider significant. *Gouse v. Cassell,* **532 Pa. 197, 615 A.2d 331.**

Patient brought malpractice action against surgeon and radiologist for treatment of cancer. Informed consent doctrine found not applicable to radiation treatment. *Dible v. Vagley,* **417 Pa. Super. 302, 612 A.2d 493.**

Patient suffered adverse reaction to intravenous drug administration. Held: doctrine of informed consent not applicable in drug cases. *Wu v. Spence,* **413 Pa. Super. 352, 605 A.2d 395.**

During course of laparoscopy and tubal potency test surgeon performed procedure to open and drain fallopian tubes. Action based on lack of informed consent. Surgeon not liable. *Moure v. Raeuchle,* **529 Pa. 394, 604 A.2d 1003.**

Medical malpractice: Informed Consent Doctrine

Patient who had nerve severed during surgery brought action based on lack of informed consent and *res ipsa loquitur*. Summary judgment based on patient's intention not to call expert witnesses upheld. **Bearfield v. Hauch, 407 Pa. Super. 624, 595 A.2d 1320.**

Physician performed additional procedures during back surgery. Patient brought action based on lack of consent. Physician not liable. **Sanderson v. Frank S. Bryan, M.D. LTD., 406 Pa. Super. 310, 594 A.2d 353.**

Patient who had sciatic nerve severed during surgery brought action against surgeon based on lack of informed consent and *res ipsa loquitur*. Held: standard of care for informed consent is that of reasonable man and *res ipsa loquitur* is applicable in medical malpractice cases. **Clemons v. Tranovich, 403 Pa. Super. 427, 589 A.2d 260.**

Patient who had enlarged ovary removed during operation to repair bladder brought action for lack of consent. Instruction to jury on implied consent based on reasonable man standard held in error. **Millard v. Nagle, 402 Pa. Super. 376, 587 A.2d 10.**

Patient who developed aplastic anemia after treatment by drug Diamox brought malpractice action based on lack of informed consent. Held: issue of consent was not preserved on appeal. Judgment affirmed. **Tarter v. Linn, 396 Pa. Super. 155, 578 A.2d 453.**

Patient was notified he tested positive for AIDS as a result of erroneous blood test. Physician found not liable for lack of informed consent or intentional infliction of emotional distress. **Doe v. Dyer-Goode, 389 Pa. Super. 151, 566 A.2d 889.**

Doctrine of informed consent does not apply to cases solely involving administrator of therapeutic drugs. Limited only to surgical and operative medical procedures. Cause of action for negligence only still available. Defense verdict here where plaintiff had adverse reaction to butazolidin, but no adequate proof of negligent administration of drug by physician. **Boyer v. Smith, 345 Pa. Super. 66, 497 A.2d 646.**

Elective surgery to correct bend in little finger failed, necessitating eventual amputation of finger. Question of informed consent. Verdict for physician reversed. New trial ordered. **Rogers v. Lu, 335 Pa. Super. 595, 485 A.2d 54.**

Surgery for removal of impacted wisdom teeth. Left with loss of sensation in tongue. No assertion of negligent performance ever alleged. Verdict for defendant affirmed. Informed consent can be given even though information on risks is communicated by assistant or nurse. Failure of defendant to testify does not entitle plaintiff to negative inference charge—defendant being subject to subpoena and further present in courtroom during trial. **Bulman v. Myers, 321 Pa. Super. 261, 467 A.2d 1353.**

Medical malpractice: Miscellaneous

Patient admitted for biopsy of parotid gland. Told of one-inch incision. Defendant removed gland due to small growth leaving depression in neck and six-inch scar. Verdict $50,000. ***DeFulvio v. Host*, 272 Pa. Super. 221, 414 A.2d 1087.**

Tooth extraction in office. Plaintiff died under anesthesia. Patient allegedly not advised of risks. Error to fail to charge on lack of informed consent even though consent form signed. ***Sauro v. Shea*, 257 Pa. Super. 87, 390 A.2d 259.**

Alleged failure to obtain patient's informed consent before performing prostatectomy. For jury to determine whether defendant's conversation with plaintiff was adequate for a "reasonable man" to make his consent valid. ***Jeffies v. McCague*, 242 Pa. Super. 76, 363 A.2d 1167.**

Plaintiff patient injured as the result of a gastroscopic examination—court below held to be in error in submitting to jury the standard of information to be given to patient in order for patient to give an informed consent—basis is not accepted medical practice—matter is contractual and fiduciary in character and issue is whether patient gave an effective informed consent. ***Cooper v. Roberts*, 220 Pa. Super. 260, 286 A.2d 647.**

Plaintiff had a serious back condition—he was advised that an exploratory operation was required—operation resulted in complete paralysis from the waist down—suit against neurosurgeon who operated on him—matter for jury as to whether consent given—verdict for plaintiff sustained on appeal. ***Gray v. Grunnagle*, 423 Pa. 144, 223 A.2d 663.**

Medical malpractice: Miscellaneous

Patient, who signed an authorization to release her medical records for the calculation of medical expenses, brought claim for breach of confidentiality after medical practice disclosed her unrelated use of marijuana and unprescribed pain medication to her employer's workers' compensation carrier. At trial a jury awarded damages to the Plaintiff and the medical practice appealed on the basis that a breach of confidentiality was governed by a one-year statute of limitations. The Superior Court affirmed the trial court's holding denying the Defendant's motion for judgment not withstanding the verdict. The Pennsylvania Supreme Court affirmed, holding that a claim for breach of physician-patient confidentiality was governed by a two-year statute of limitations period. ***Burger v. Blair Medical Associates, Inc.*, 964 A.2d 374 (2009).**

Decedent's personal representative brought medical malpractice claim against physicians and hospital. Claim was dismissed after plaintiff's counsel failed to file a certificate of merit within the appropriate statutory period. The trial court entered judgment of non pros and denied a petition to open the judgment. The Superior Court reversed and remanded, holding that counsel's mistake in believing his paralegal had filed the certificates of merit, which were completed prior to the statutory deadline, was due to reasonable inadvertence warranting the opening of the judgment of non pros. ***Sabo v. Worrall, III*, 959 A.2d 347 (Pa. Super. 2008).**

Plaintiff sued defendant psychiatrist for disclosing confidential information received during treatment to another patient. The court held that to establish a prima

Medical malpractice: Nurse

facie medical malpractice case the plaintiff must prove; 1. The physician owed a duty to the patient; 2. The physician breached that duty; 3. The breach of duty was a proximate cause in harming the patient; 4. The patient's damages were a result of that harm. Expert testimony in a medical malpractice action is generally required unless the matter is obviously within the comprehension of a lay person. ***Rohrer v. Pope*, 918 A.2d 122 (Pa. Super. 2007).**

Administratrix of deceased patient brought a claim for medical malpractice against physician for negligent treatment of decedent's condition. The court held that plaintiff could amend the complaint, after the statute of limitations had run, but the underlying averments or theories within the complaint could not be changed. ***Chaney v. Meadville Medical Center*, 912 A.2d 300 (Pa. Super. 2006).**

Plaintiff sued for lack of informed consent and negligence after suffering permanent vision loss as a result of corrective surgery performed by defendant ophthalmologist. The Pennsylvania Supreme Court held that trial courts have latitude to overlook procedural defects that do not prejudice other parties, but not to a party that entirely disregards a rule. ***Womer v. Hilliker*, 589 Pa. 256, 908 A.2d 269 (2006).**

Physician was sued for a failure to follow his statutory duty to report a patient's lack of fitness to operate a motor vehicle to the Pennsylvania Department of Transportation. The court held that a physician's failure to comply with the Motor Vehicle Code's reporting requirements by not reporting seizures does not create a private cause of action against the physician for an accident caused by his patient. ***Hospodar v. Schick*, 885 A.2d 986 (Pa. Super. 2005).**

Motion to dismiss sustained against Plaintiff husband who sued family physician in negligence for physician's adulterous affair with plaintiff's wife. Held, that Pennsylvania does not recognize a claim of negligence against a physician under these facts because the physician does not owe a duty of care to the husband to avoid the relationship with husband's wife. ***Long v. Ostroff*, 854 A.2d 524 (Pa. Super. 2004).**

Plaintiff's deceased quadriplegic husband suffered head injuries when he fell from an exam table after he was left alone in his doctor's examination room. Where evidence was presented that he could not move independently and he fell from the table, trial court's failure to charge on res ipsa loquitur was reversible. ***Quinby v. Burmeister*, 850 A.2d 667 (Pa. Super. 2004).**

Medical malpractice: Nurse

Executors of decedent's estate sued hospital for wrongful death and professional negligence after the decedent died in the hospital as a result of a brain herniation that was not appropriately treated due to a failure by the nurse to relay the appropriate information to the decedent's surgeon. A jury rendered a verdict in favor of the decedent. The Superior Court affirmed on appeal holding that a hospital could be held liable failure to comply with standard medical practice where a nurse fails to report changes in a patient's condition or fails to question a doctor's order

Medical malpractice: Nurse

and a patient is injured. *Rettiger v. UPMC Shadyside*, 991 A.2d 915 (Pa. Super. 2010).

Paraplegic sued medical center for pressure wounds incurred during his rehabilitation stay allegedly caused by substandard nursing care. Trial court granted compulsory nonsuit against Plaintiff due to lack of causation after the Plaintiff presented a registered nurse to testify regarding the relevant standard of care without presenting a doctor. The Superior Court reversed. The Pennsylvania Supreme Court affirmed the Superior Court holding that a properly qualified nurse could testify as to medical causation under the Professional Nursing Law. The proper test for a nurse to testify regarding causation and the relevant nursing standard of care was whether the witness had specialized knowledge on the subject of testimony set forth in *Miller v. Brass Rail Tavern, Inc.*, 541 Pa. 474, 480, 664 A.2d 525, 528 (1995). *Freed v. Geisinger Medical Center*, 971 A.2d 1202 (Pa. 2009).

Paraplegic sued medical center for pressure wounds incurred during his rehabilitation stay by allegedly substandard nursing care. The court reversed the trial court's decision to bar a nurse from testifying as an expert witness as to a breach of standard of care in treating the plaintiff. The court held that a qualified non-medical expert could give a medical opinion as long as the witness had sufficient specialized knowledge to aid the jury in determining the facts of the case. *Freed v. Geisinger Medical Center*, 910 A.2d 68 (Pa. Super. 2006).

Elemental analysis of a negligence claim in a medical malpractice action for damages sustained in delivery of child. Superior Court further examines standards for proving causation of damages. *Cruz v. Northeastern Hospital*, 801 A2d. 602 (Pa. Super. 2002).

Medical malpractice action by parents for injuries suffered by newborn before delivery resulting from nurses failure to monitor and recognize signs of fetal distress. Very clear elemental analysis of negligence law. *Cruz v. Northeastern Hospital*, 801 A.2d 602 (Pa. Super. 2002).

Wife, who delivered brain-damaged child after Cesarean section with only local anesthetic, and husband, individually and as parents of child, sued anesthesiology group, obstetrician and hospital for malpractice. Nurses employed at hospital are not agents of the physicians when they act in the normal course of hospital services. *Tiburzio-Kelly v. Montgomery,* 452 Pa. Super. 158, 681 A.2d 757 (1996).

Patient who suffered complications after stomach stapling surgery brought action against physician and nurse based on lack of informed consent. Nurse not liable. Negligence theory of informed consent not recognized. *Foflygen v. R. Zemel, M.D. (PC),* 420 Pa. Super. 18, 615 A.2d 1345.

Inmate brought action against prison nurse for dispensing improper medication. Nurse not liable. *Navarro v. George,* 150 Pa. Cmwlth. 229, 615 A.2d 890.

Patient suffered nerve damage to arm after injection given by nurse. Trial court refused to admit evidence of plaintiff's mental illness (Munchausen Syndrome). Reversed. Evidence of mental illness admissable. *Cohen v. Albert Einstein Medical Center,* 405 Pa. Super. 392, 592 A.2d 720.

Medical malpractice: Nursing home

Following surgery, vital signs allegedly not monitored in accordance with physician's instructions and temperature went up to 105.2 degrees before action was taken. Alleged brain damage. Nurse allegedly put Kleenex in seeping operative wound. Verdict against hospital only affirmed. ***Robert v. Chodoff,* 259 Pa. Super. 332, 393 A.2d 853.**

Death of plaintiff following auto accident owing to malpractice and not auto accident. Physicians and nurses failed to diagnose injury properly and failed to place plaintiff on ventilator. Died 5 days later in extreme pain. Expert characterized malpractice as gross. Verdict for plaintiff. ***Embrey v. Borough of West Mifflin,* 257 Pa. Super. 168, 390 A.2d 765.**

Where patient in hospital fell out of chair during a short absence by nurse, for jury as to whether, in view of plaintiff's condition, it was reasonable for nurse to leave even for short period of time. ***Hogan v. Bryn Mawr Hospital,* 250 Pa. Super. 109, 378 A.2d 477.**

Five year old boy entered hospital for tonsillectomy in otherwise excellent health. Anesthesiologist left operating room during surgery and nurse negligently monitored administration of anesthesia causing death six weeks later. Verdict against hospital. Reversed as to damages only. ***Willinger v. Mercy Catholic Medical Center,* 241 Pa. Super. 456, 362 A.2d 280.**

Nurse giving injection pursuant to physician's instructions is employee of hospital—nonsuit in suit versus doctor sustained. ***Muller v. Likoff,* 225 Pa. Super. 111, 310 A.2d 303.**

Medical malpractice: Nursing home

A private, independent contractor organization that managed and set administrative and medical policy and procedure for a county-owned nursing home was not clothed with the governmental immunity afforded by the Political Subdivision Tort Claims Act. ***Helsel v. Complete Care Services, L.P.,* 797 A.2d 1051 (Pa. Cmwlth. 2002).**

Medical malpractice: Physician

Plaintiff brought medical malpractice lawsuit against the Defendant physician alleging a surgical sponge was left inside him after surgery. The trial court dismissed on the basis that no expert testimony was produced by the Plaintiff. The Superior Court reversed holding that the doctrine of res ipsa loquitur could be applied in medical malpractice cases of obvious negligence. ***Fessenden v. Robert Packer Hospital*, 2014 Pa. Super. 154 (2014).**

Plaintiffs brought medical malpractice action against their child's treating physician for failing to diagnose their child with acute viral myocarditis. A jury found in favor of the Defendant. The Superior Court reversed and remanded based upon the trial court's decision to give an "error in judgment" charge. The Supreme Court held that an "error in judgment" instruction should not be given in medical malpractice cases and that the holding should be applied retroactively. ***Passarello v. Grumbine*, 87 A.3d 285 (Pa. 2014).**

Medical malpractice: Physician

Plaintiffs brought wrongful death and survival action against Defendant physician after their child died due to the physician's failure to administer a RhoGAM injection 9 years prior and despite the Defendant no longer being her physician. The trial court granted partial summary judgment in favor of the Defendant and the Superior Court affirmed. The Pennsylvania Supreme Court held that the 7-year statute of repose in the MCARE Act does not apply to a wrongful death and survival action. It also held that a third party could bring a cause of action for the negligent performance of a service where the doctor should recognize that the service provided to the patient is needed for their protection. *Matharu v. Muir*, 86 A.3d 250 (Pa. Super. 2014).

Patient brought medical malpractice action against her physician for causing her kidney failure due to long-term ingestion of a prescription drug. The trial court entered judgment in the physician's favor. The Superior Court reversed holding that a Plaintiff may pursue both a direct cause and increased risk theories in the same medical malpractice action and receive jury instructions on both theories. *Klein v. Aronchick*, 85 A.3d 487 (Pa. Super. 2014).

Plaintiff brought medical malpractice action against her podiatrist after the surgery he performed on her did not resolve her complaints. A jury found in favor of the podiatrist. The Superior Court reversed holding that evidence of the Plaintiff's informed consent to the surgeries and signed acknowledgement of the potential risks was irrelevant and reversible error. *Brady v. Urbas*, 80 A.3d 480 (Pa. Super. 2014).

Plaintiff's estate brought medical malpractice action against Defendants chiropractors after the Decedent suffered a vertebral artery dissection and stroke the morning after her chiropractor visit. The trial court entered judgment in favor of the Defendants following a jury trial. The Superior Court affirmed holding that the 2-year statute of limitations for a survival action begins to run at latest upon the death of the decedent and as the estate sought to amend after 2 years the survival action must be dismissed. *Bell v. Willis*, 80 A.3d 476 (Pa. Super. 2013).

Patient filed a medical malpractice case against her physician for lack of informed consent due to surgeries performed on her in 1985 and 1989. The trial court denied the Defendant physician's motion for summary judgment based upon the statute of repose set forth in the Medical Care Availability and Reduction of Error (MCARE) Act. The Superior Court affirmed holding that the MCARE Act's statute of repose does not apply to causes of action where the negligent act and date of discovery of injury were prior to the effective date of the MCARE Act statute. *Bulebosh v. Flannery*, 91 A.3d 1241 (Pa. Super. 2014).

Plaintiff brought medical malpractice action against physician for failing to diagnose her breast cancer due to the physician's choice to use a fine needle aspiration biopsy. A jury found in favor of the plaintiff. The Superior Court affirmed, holding that a pathologist and oncologist were qualified to testify under the Medical Availability and Reduction of Error Act regarding the standard of care for a sur-

Medical malpractice: Physician

geon in choosing a biopsy method despite neither practicing as surgeons. *Renna v. Schadt*, 64 A.3d 658 (Pa. Super. 2013).

Plaintiff brought medical malpractice action against physician for an injury suffered during laser eye surgery. The trial court denied the defendant's motion for summary judgment based upon the statute of repose. The Superior Court held the denial of summary judgment was immediately appealable and that the seven-year statute of repose in the Medical Care Availability and Reduction of Error Act applied to an injury that manifested itself after the adoption of the MCARE Act even though the surgery was performed prior to the act's adoption. *Osborne v. Lewis*, 59 A.3d 1109 (Pa. Super. 2012).

A corrections officer brought a negligence action against a physician for failing to warn her that an inmate had a communicable disease. The trial court dismissed the complaint on preliminary objections. The Superior Court vacated the trial's court decision and remanded. The Pennsylvania Supreme Court on a matter of first impression held that a physician had no duty to warn a corrections officer that an inmate had a communicable disease. *Seebold v. Prison Health Services, Inc.*, 57 A.3d 1232 (Pa. 2012).

Plaintiff brought a medical malpractice action against a physician for negligently performing a sterilization procedure claiming damages related to her choosing to undergo an abortion because the fetus was determined to have congenital defects. The trial court entered summary judgment in favor of the defendant as the plaintiff's expert failed to cite medical literature in his expert opinion. The Superior Court reversed holding that plaintiff's expert's experience in the relevant field of medicine was sufficient to support his opinions. The Superior Court also held that where an unwanted pregnancy is not carried to term there was no limitation on the damages recoverable after the termination of the pregnancy. *Catlin v. Hamburg*, 56 A.3d 914 (Pa. Super. 2012).

Plaintiff parents and estate administrators filed a medical malpractice wrongful death action against defendant hospital for injuries suffered by the minor decedent during a Caesarean section. A jury found in favor of the plaintiffs. The Superior Court affirmed holding that a jury could award damages under the Wrongful Death Act for plaintiff parents' loss of society and companionship of their child. The Superior Court also reiterated that in a professional negligence action against a hospital or physician the plaintiff was only required to produce evidence that the defendant's conduct increased the risk of harm to the plaintiff. *Hatwood v. Hospital of the University of Pennsylvania*, 55 A.3d 1229 (Pa. Super. 2012).

Plaintiff brought tort action against physician for medical malpractice after the physician had a consensual sexual relationship with the plaintiff, while treating her as a general practitioner for anxiety and depression. The trial court granted dismissal of the action on preliminary objections. The Superior Court affirmed. The Pennsylvania Supreme Court in a matter of first impression held that a general practitioner providing incidental mental health treatment was under no heightened duty to refrain from having consensual sexual relations with a patient. *Thierfelder v. Wolfert*, 52 A.3d 1251 (Pa. 2012).

Medical malpractice: Physician

Plaintiff filed a medical malpractice action against Defendant New Jersey hospital for failing to treat an epidural abscess, which was later discovered in Pennsylvania and resulted in paralysis. The Superior Court held that it had no specific jurisdiction over the New Jersey hospital because the harm for failing to treat or diagnose arose in New Jersey. The Court held that the discovery of the harm in Pennsylvania did not alter the fact that it originated in New Jersey. The Court also held that there were no facts suggesting that the hospital had any contact with Pennsylvania regarding Plaintiff's treatment. ***Mendel v. Williams*, 2012 Pa. Super. 171 (Pa. Super. 2012).**

Estate brought medical malpractice claim against Defendant physician for failure to diagnose decedent's acute viral myocarditis. A jury found in favor of Defendant. The Superior Court reversed holding that the trial court erred in providing a jury instruction to weigh the subjective state of mind of the physician when treating the decedent. ***Passarello v. Grumbine*, 29 A.3d 1158 (Pa. Super. 2011).**

Patient brought medical malpractice and intentional infliction of emotional distress claims against general practitioner treating her for anxiety and depression after he had consensual sex with her, while treating her. The trial court dismissed Plaintiff's complaint on preliminary objections. Superior Court reversed holding that there is a potential cause of action where a patient being treated for emotional symptoms experiences a worsening of their symptoms due to a sexual relationship with a physician providing treatment for those specific emotional symptoms. ***Thierfelder v. Wolfert*, 978 A.2d 361 (Pa. Super. 2009).**

Plaintiff brought medical malpractice claim against physician for failing to diagnosis his knee cancer until a year after it had first been suggested in a radiology report. The jury found for the Plaintiffs and the trial court denied the physician's motion for judgment not withstanding the verdict. The Superior Court affirmed, holding that the radiologist report indicated the possibility that the abnormality was benign, but the Defendant physician failed to eliminate the possibility that it was malignant and therefore the physician was not entitled to judgment as a matter of law. ***Tindall v. Friedman*, 970 A.2d 1159 (Pa. Super. 2009).**

Plaintiff injured due to a wrist surgery brought medical malpractice claim against medical providers. The trial court granted summary judgment on the basis that the Plaintiff failed to file her complaint within the two years she should have reasonably discovered or actually discovered the cause of her injury. The Superior Court affirmed. The Pennsylvania Supreme Court reversed, holding that summary judgment was improperly granted as there was a question of fact as to whether or not the Plaintiff should have discovered the cause of her injury for the statute of limitations to begin to commence. ***Wilson v. El-Daief*, 964 A.2d 354 (2009).**

Patient brought a medical malpractice claim against physician for failing to diagnose her with breast cancer in a timely manner. A jury found in favor of the defendant. The Superior Court affirmed, holding that the record was sufficient to find that the Defendant had not breached the standard of care as there was disagreement among the six experts as to whether there was an abnormality prior to the physician's ultimate diagnosis. ***Wytiaz v. Deitrick*, 954 A.2d 643 (Pa. Super. 2008).**

Medical malpractice: Physician

Hospital filed suit for indemnification against defendant physicians after a judgment was entered against the hospital in a medical malpractice case and defendant physicians were never joined. The appellate court held that in order to succeed on an indemnity claim against the unjoined physicians, expert reports were required to establish the negligence of the unjoined physicians. *MIIX Insurance Co. v. Epstein*, **937 A.2d 469 (Pa. Super. 2007).**

Plaintiff sued her surgeon for problems alleged to be the result of the removal of an abnormal section of her small intestines discovered by the surgeon during an unrelated surgery. The court held that an expert witness was required to determine if the physician deviated from the standard of care in performing the bowel resection surgery and in whether the procedure had exceeded the scope of the patient's informed consent. *McSorley v. Deger*, **905 A.2d 524 (Pa. Super. 2006).**

Co-executors brought a suit for medical malpractice against the hospital for failure to transmit x-rays showing a possible cancerous mass and failure to investigate against the treating physician. The court held that the substance of the complaint controls whether a claim a claim is for ordinary negligence or professional malpractice. *Rostock v. Anzalone*, **904 A.2d 943 (Pa. Super. 2006).**

Verdict in favor of plaintiff affirmed on appeal by physician who negligently applied splint to plaintiff's calf which caused burn or pressure sore which required plastic surgery to repair. Good analysis of elements of negligence and causation in medical malpractice case. "Corporate negligence" of hospital for physician's negligence not expanded to include corporate medical practice negligence for negligence of physician who was a member of the practice. *Sutherland v. Monongahela Valley Hospital*, **856 A.2d 55 (Pa. Super. 2004).**

Plaintiff who suffered pneumothorax resulting in a collapsed lung sued physician who administered injection that allegedly caused the problem. Due to plaintiff's failure to produce expert medical testimony as to standard of care in the procedure, plaintiff went to trial on theory of *res ipsa loquitur*. After verdict in favor of plaintiff was affirmed by Superior Court, Supreme Court reversed on grounds that failure to provide expert medical testimony on standard of care precludes *res ipsa loquitur* case based purely on jury's lay knowledge or expectations. *Toogood v. Rogal*, **824 A.2d 1140 (Pa. 2003).**

Plaintiff's treating physician waited 15 months to order a biopsy of patient's breast after patient presented with substantial changes in breast condition after radiation therapy. Physician admitted at trial that he knew there was a 20% chance that the change in condition was caused by recurrence of cancer. Jury verdict in favor of doctor shocked the conscience of the court and new trial ordered. *Vallone v. Creech*, **820 A.2d 760 (Pa. Super. 2003).**

Plaintiff's suit for negligence and negligent infliction of emotional distress against physician who performed autopsy on plaintiff's mother and same causes of action and respondeat superior against hospital. Autopsy report indicated that deceased mother's eyes had been "donated" despite insistence by plaintiff that eyes were not to be donated. Claims for emotional distress and respondeat superior dismissed on preliminary objections. Verdict in favor of plaintiff reversed on grounds

Medical malpractice: Physician

that evidence was not adequate to prove that eyes had, in fact, been donated. The physician who had performed the autopsy amended report to indicate that he never looked to see if the eyes were in place. *Van Zandt v. Holy Redeemer Hospital*, 806 A.2d 879 (Pa. Super. 2002).

Suit by personal representative against medical facility and physician on behalf of decedent who died after allegedly negligent surgical placement of a catheter and alleged battery due to lack of informed consent by decedent for earlier treatment. Held that a medical facility cannot be held vicariously liable for a physician's failure to obtain informed consent. It is the individual physician's responsibility, in his or her special relationship with the patient, to obtain the consent. *Valles v. Albert Einstein Medical Center*, 805 A.2d 1232 (Pa. 2002).

Under the Mental Health Procedures Act, a physician may only be liable for injury to a patient when gross negligence occurs. A physician's failure to speak to a non-minor patient's mother about the likely effect of alcohol consumption when combined psychiatric medications does not rise to the level of gross negligence. *Alphonsi v. Huntington Hospital, Inc.*, 798 A.2d 216 (Pa. Super. 2002).

Plaintiff's decedent died after general anesthesia and surgery to repair injured elbow. Physician's had determined prior to surgery that patient was suffering from various serious ailments that compromised her ability to survive general anesthesia and surgery. Summary judgement in favor of all individual and corporate defendants reversed on determination that testimony of plaintiff's medical witnesses was adequate to state a *prima facie* case of medical and corporate malpractice despite the absence of "magic words". *Rauch v. Mike-Mayer*, 783 A.2d 815 (Pa. Super. 2001).

Decedent died as a result of a burst abdominal aortic aneurysm that had not been properly diagnosed well before it burst. Suit was against hospital that took x-ray that clearly showed aneurysm and physician that did not review the x-ray. Summary judgment in favor of hospital and verdict in favor of physician were reversed on determination that question of whether hospital properly notified physician of results of x-ray was for jury and jury's finding that doctor was negligent but that negligence was not a substantial factor was obvious error. *Cangemi v. Cone*, 774 A.2d 1262 (Pa. Super. 2001).

Expert testimony, expressed with reasonable medical certainty, that a physician's action increased the risk of harm creates an issue for the jury. Testimony need not be that physician's action "caused" the harm. *Billman v. Saylor*, 761 A.2d 1208 (Pa. Super. 2000).

Therapeutic psychiatrist treating child who claimed to have been sexually abused by her parents owes no duty to non-patient parents of child for misdiagnosis of alleged sexual abuse. *Althaus, ex rel. Althaus v. Cohen*, 756 A.2d 1166 (Pa. 2000).

Plaintiff who alleged that failed tubal ligation resulted in pregnancy was pursuing claim for breach of an express oral contract to provide a specific result—no future pregnancies. The Health Care Services Malpractice Act (40 P.S. §1301.606)

Medical malpractice: Physician

requires that any contract for a specific cure or result must be in writing and because plaintiff's complaint alleged only breach of an oral contract, there can be no recovery. *Edwards v. Germantown Hospital*, **736 A.2d 612 (Pa. Super. 1999).**

Parents and child filed suit against psychiatrist who treated child and, after treatment, negligently embarked upon a course of action that directly affected both child and parents to their injury. Where psychiatrist goes well beyond treatment of minor (*e.g.*, active participation in criminal proceedings directed against parents and maintaining silence when she knew patient was telling untruths and could not distinguish fact from fantasy), court will impose duty on psychiatrist to parents, breach of which may support determination of negligence. The lack of a psychiatrist–patient relationship with parents does not provide blanket immunity to psychiatrist. In instant case, it was also reasonably foreseeable to psychiatrist that her negligent actions would have harmful affect on patient's parents. ***Althaus v. Cohen*, 710 A.2d 1147 (Pa. Super. 1998).**

Patient treated by defendant orthopedic surgeon filed suit for negligently performed corrective surgery and continuing pain and suffering after the surgery. Verdict for plaintiff apportioning negligence 60/40 between defendant and plaintiff. New trial granted by trial court based on reasoning of *Gentile v. Devergilis*, 290 Pa. 50, 138 A. 540 in which it was held that where a patient refuses to follow directions for postoperative care, there can be no verdict against the treating physician who recommended the care for any negligent act because there can be no determination of which failure to treat- the original physician's or the patient's who refused to follow treatment directions - caused the harm. Superior Court affirmed and Supreme Court reversed stating that a patient's mere failure to attend postoperative appointments does not make it impossible as a matter of law for a jury to determine whether, and to what degree, the physician's negligence caused the injury. ***Ferguson v. Panzarella*, 700 A.2d 917 (Pa. 1997).**

Order granting summary judgment reversed on plaintiff's claims of battery, breach of contract, and lack of informed consent arising out of back surgery performed by or at the direction of physicians to whom plaintiff had never given consent. ***Grabowski v. Quigley,* 454 Pa. Super. 27, 684 A.2d 610 (1996).**

Husband suffering from seizures was treated by a partial lobectomy that resulted in more serious seizures and severe memory and speech problems. Informed consent to medical treatment requires that the patient have a "true understanding of the nature of the operation ... and the possible results." Judgment *n.o.v.* permitted only in "clear case." Judgment *n.o.v.* reversed and jury verdict reinstated. ***Rowinsky v. Sperling,* 452 Pa. Super. 215, 681 A.2d 785 (1996).**

Wife, who delivered brain-damaged child after Cesarean section with only local anesthetic, and husband, individually and as parents of child, sued anesthesiology group, obstetrician and hospital for malpractice. Nurses employed at hospital are not agents of the physicians when they act in the normal course of hospital services. Father's loss of consortium claim properly denied by trial court where his only testimony was that he had a subjective fear of engaging in sexual relations with his wife following her delivery of brain-damaged child, even though the dam-

Medical malpractice: Physician

age may have been the result of medical malpractice. Father's claim for negligent infliction of emotional distress properly dismissed where he was not near the scene of the injuries to his wife and newborn child. Hearing his wife's cries of pain only, without any visual experience of her condition, was insufficient. ***Tiburzio-Kelly v. Montgomery,* 452 Pa. Super. 158, 681 A.2d 757 (1996).**

Not every wrong constitutes a legally cognizable cause of action. A physician who fails to remove sponges following an episiotomy resulting in no more than a foul odor is not subject to liability where no causal link between an act of negligence and legally cognizable injury is established. Order granting motion for nonsuit affirmed. ***Gregorio v. Zeluck,* 451 Pa. Super. 154, 678 A.2d 810 (1996).**

Verdict in favor of woman whose voice was irreparably damaged following intubation procedure vacated, and judgment entered for appellant hospital where plaintiff's complaint stated cause of action in negligence against hospital, but proof at trial focused only on family physician's negligence in follow-up care of plaintiff; no amendment to plaintiff's original complaint was filed. ***Reynolds v. Thomas Jefferson University Hospital,* 450 Pa. Super. 327, 676 A.2d 1205 (1996).**

Physician who treated woman with highly contagious, but common, viral infection has a duty to third persons to warn the patient about the risks associated with the disease, so patient may inform third persons who might come in contact with her about the risks. Order granting summary judgment in favor of defendants reversed and remanded to allow estate of minor who died as a result of coming into contact with contagious patient to proceed to trial. ***Troxel v. A.I. DuPont Institute,* 450 Pa. Super. 71, 675 A.2d 314 (1996).**

In action by guardian of incapacitated, mental health patient for brain damages sustained as result of choking by restraining vest, immunity of physicians under Mental Health Procedures Act is not afforded to physician providing standard medical treatment at non-mental health facility. Judgment on jury verdict for defendant reversed and remanded. ***Allen v. Montgomery Hospital,* 447 Pa. Super. 158, 668 A.2d 565 (1995).**

Where patient who underwent perineal urethrotomy and cauterization, rather than planned transurethral prostatectomy, failed to establish a causal connection between resulting injuries and physician's conduct through expert testimony, compulsory nonsuit was proper. Patient should have been allowed to introduce evidence of alleged lack of consent to surgery that was admittedly not discussed by physician and patient prior to its performance. Order granting compulsory nonsuit on question of negligence affirmed. Case remanded on claim for lack of informed consent. ***Hoffman v. Mogil,* 445 Pa. Super. 252, 665 A.2d 478 (1995).**

Plaintiff who fails to participate significantly in postoperative care risks loss of any claim for alleged negligence of physician in performing surgery. The Comparative Negligence Act is not applicable in such cases because of the inability to apportion liability between both parties. ***Ferguson v. Panzarella,* 445 Pa. Super. 23, 664 A.2d 989 (1995).**

Medical malpractice: Physician

In action against orthopedic surgeon for injury resulting from improperly performed back surgery, defendant physician's expert's report failed to address necessity of surgery and therefore expert was precluded from testifying on that issue. Judgment for plaintiff affirmed. ***Walsh v. Kubiak,*** **443 Pa. Super. 284, 661 A.2d 416 (1995).**

Plaintiff who contracted AIDS following transfusion of tainted blood filed suit against treating physicians and family physician for medical malpractice. Claim against one defendant dismissed for plaintiff's failure to establish through medical testimony that defendant's actions deviated from good and acceptable medical standards. Proof of compliance with medical standard of care need not be expressed in precisely the language used to annunciate the legal standard. Physician not required to obtain patient's informed consent before blood transfusion that was administered separately from a surgical procedure. ***Hoffman v. Brandywine Hospital,*** **443 Pa. Super. 245, 661 A.2d 397 (1995).**

A referring physician cannot be held liable under theory of failure to obtain informed consent where he had no physical contact with plaintiff who suffered injury as a result of recommended surgery. Suit for failure to obtain informed consent grounded in battery, not negligence. Verdict for plaintiff vacated and remanded. ***Shaw v. Kirschbaum,*** **439 Pa. Super. 24, 653 A.2d 12 (1994).**

Release entered into with hotel defendant for injuries sustained in federal slip and fall case did not release defendants in subsequent state court action for medical practice in surgery to repair wrist injured during slip-and-fall at hotel, where release specifically designated federal court action and caption as subject of release. Summary judgment for physicians and surgeons reversed. ***Harrity v. Medical College of Pennsylvania Hospital,*** **439 Pa. Super. 10, 653 A.2d 5 (1995).**

Failure to follow Department of Health standards that suggest 48-hour limit for catheterization is not negligence *per se*. Medical malpractice causation requires proof of increased risk of harm. Causation is question for trier of fact where artificial hip replacement patient developed staff infection from catheterization. ***Edwards v. Brandywine Hospital,*** **438 Pa. Super. 673, 652 A.2d 1382 (1995).**

In action for alleged medical malpractice, plaintiff failed to state cause of action against state-employed physician, state hospital, and department of public welfare. Order sustaining preliminary objections affirmed because all defendants immune under sovereign immunity statute. ***Moser v. Heistand,*** **168 Pa. Cmwlth. 109, 649 A.2d 177 (1994).**

New trial granted in medical malpractice case for failure to perform timely caesarean section. Deposition testimony of witness not shown to be unavailable admitted. ***Russel v. Albert Einstein Medical Center,*** **434 Pa. Super. 295, 643 A.2d 102.**

Patient brought action against surgeon for negligent administration of anesthetic. Summary judgment for surgeon inappropriate. ***Szabor v. Bryn Mawr Hospital,*** **432 Pa. Super. 361, 638 A.2d 1004.**

Medical malpractice: Physician

Wife brought loss of consortium claim against physician who treated husband before marriage. Held: physician may be liable. Claim did not ripen until after marriage. ***Vazquez v. Friedberg,*** **431 Pa. Super. 523, 637 A.2d 300.**

Heart valve replacement patient brought action against surgeons for lack of informed consent. Surgeons liable. ***Stover v. Association of Thoracic and Cardiovascular Surgeons,*** **431 Pa. Super. 11, 635 A.2d 1047.**

Child suffered brain damage caused by use of forceps during birth. Physician not liable. Doctrine of informed consent not applicable. ***Sinclair by Sinclair v. Block,*** **534 Pa. Super. 563, 633 A.2d 1137.**

Patient suffered nerve damage after arthroscopic knee surgery. Held: doctrine of *res ipsa loquitur* applicable in medical malpractice cases. ***Leone v. Thomas,*** **428 Pa. Super. 217, 630 A.2d 900.**

Patient brought action against orthopedic surgeon and hospital. Claim against surgeon discontinued by plaintiff. Hospital not liable. ***Walls v. Hazleton State General Hospital,*** **157 Pa. Cmwlth. 170, 629 A.2d 232.**

Action brought against physician who treated guest who died of injuries in fall down stairs. Held: release of host released physician. ***Holmes v. Lankenau Hospital,*** **426 Pa. Super. 452, 627 A.2d 763.**

Children of mother killed by former mental patient brought action against hospital and psychiatrist for failure to warn of patient's violent tendencies. Defendants not liable. ***Leonard v. Latrobe Hospital,*** **425 Pa. Super. 540, 625 A.2d 1228.**

Patient suffered facial paralysis after undergoing microvascular decompression surgery. Nonsuit found improper. Expert medical testimony essential. ***Levy v. Jannetta,*** **423 Pa. Super. 384, 621 A.2d 585.**

Patient who suffered complications after stomach stapling surgery brought action against physician and nurse based on lack of informed consent. Nurse not liable. Negligence theory of informed consent not recognized. ***Foflygen v. R. Zemel, M.D. (PC),*** **420 Pa. Super. 18, 615 A.2d 1345.**

Patient who suffered complications after surgery brought action based on lack of informed consent. Held: physician must disclose factors that a reasonable man would consider significant. ***Gouse v. Cassell,*** **532 Pa. 197, 615 A.2d 331.**

Coma patient suffered permanent flexion of elbows and hips. Held: judgment *n.o.v.* in favor of physician who failed to order drug therapy granted. New trial ordered for hospital and physician who directed physical therapy. ***Maurer v. Trustees of University of Pennsylvania,*** **418 Pa. Super. 510, 614 A.2d 754.**

Patient brought malpractice action against surgeon and radiologist for treatment of cancer. Informed consent doctrine found not applicable to radiation treatment. ***Dible v. Vagley,*** **417 Pa. Super. 302, 612 A.2d 493.**

Patient injured by use of tourniquet during surgery. Held: two-schools doctrine requires advocacy by considerable number of recognized and respected professionals. ***Jones v. Chidester,*** **531 Pa. 31, 610 A.2d 964.**

Medical malpractice: Physician

During course of laparoscopy and tubal potency test surgeon performed procedure to open and drain fallopian tubes. Action based on lack of informed consent. Surgeon not liable. *Moure v. Raeuchle,* **529 Pa. 394, 604 A.2d 1003.**

Patient suffered stroke following surgery. Physician found negligent but not liable. Failure to instruct jury on missing witness rule not in error. *O'Rourke on Behalf of O'Rourke v. Rao,* **411 Pa. Super. 609, 602 A.2d 362.**

Infant injured at birth when physician attempted delivery with forceps before performing caesarean section. Physician not liable. Jury instruction on "two schools of thought" appropriate. Use of forceps did not require consent. *Sinclair by Sinclair v. Block,* **406 Pa. Super. 540, 594 A.2d 750.**

Physician performed additional procedures during back surgery. Patient brought action based on lack of consent. Physician not liable. *Sanderson v. Frank S. Bryan, M.D. LTD.,* **406 Pa. Super. 310, 594 A.2d 353.**

Pedestrian injured when struck by vehicle driven by diabetic brought action against driver's physician for failure to properly diagnose and treat driver and for failure to notify Department of Transportation. Physician not liable. *Crosby by Crosby v. Sultz,* **405 Pa. Super. 527, 592 A.2d 1337.**

Patient who suffered miscarriage brought actions for malpractice and for intentional and negligent infliction of emotional distress against obstetrician and physician who covered when he was unavailable. Neither physician liable. *Strain v. Ferroni,* **405 Pa. Super. 349, 592 A.2d 698.**

Patient brought malpractice action against surgeon for damage to vocal cords. Trial court refused to give instruction on *res ipsa loquitur*. Reversed and remanded. *Sedlitsky v. Pareso,* **400 Pa. Super. 1, 582 A.2d 1314.**

Parents of child injured by prescription drug brought malpractice action against partner of prescribing physician. Held: partner not individually liable. *Keech v. Mead Johnson and Company,* **398 Pa. Super. 329, 580 A.2d 1374.**

Husband who contracted hepatitis from wife brought malpractice action against wife's physician. Held: physician had duty to advise wife of her ability to transmit disease to others. *DiMarco v. Lynch-Homes—Chester County,* **384 Pa. Super. 463, 559 A.2d 530.**

Injuries received by child while *en ventre sa mere* formerly could form basis for survival or wrongful death actions as maintained only on behalf of child born alive. Live birth now held no longer to be a limiting prerequisite to maintenance of such action. Case remanded for further proceedings. *Amadio v. Levin,* **509 Pa. 199, 501 A.2d 1085.**

Estate of stillborn child has no action for damages which allegedly occurred owing to negligent prenatal care. Parents have no cause of action for emotional distress without showing of physical injury. *Justice v. Booth Maternity Center,* **345 Pa. Super. 529, 498 A.2d 950.**

Medical malpractice: Physician

Jury verdict $203,000 for wife, $105,000 for husband for loss of consortium. Reversed due to erroneous charge on damages. New trial on damages only. Alleged negligent suturing of ureter during hysterectomy caused subsequent loss of one kidney. Proper to allow urologist, under facts here, to testify as to malpractice. ***Kearns v. Clark,* 343 Pa. Super. 30, 493 A.2d 1358.**

Verdict $14,000 compensatory damages for tort of intentional infliction of emotional distress. Plaintiff taken to hospital with inability to walk. Emergency physician found nothing and left patient on floor for 1-1/2 to 2-1/2 hours. Stipulated that delay in diagnosing actual condition had no effect on medical condition. ***Hoffman v. Memorial Osteopathic Hospital,* 342 Pa. Super. 375, 492 A.2d 1382.**

Jury verdict $750,000 plus delay damage. Alleged improper prescribing of Butazolidin by defendant physician, without proper warnings and examinations. Led to condition of aplastic anemia which required regular blood transfusions, shortened life expectancy and resulted in inability to bear children. Verdict against doctor only, affirmed. Drug manufacturer's warnings held to be adequate. Reversed decision of Superior Court which had ordered new trial. ***Baldino v. Castagna,* 505 Pa. 239, 478 A.2d 807.**

Alleged negligence in damaging facial nerve during ear operation. Nonsuit entered. Affirmed. Expert witness deposition excluded due to failure to comply with pretrial order. ***Gallegor v. Felder,* 329 Pa. Super. 204, 478 A.2d 34.**

Plaintiff's decedent brought to emergency room, with heart attack. Family doctor had him transferred to Lankenau—doctor had no privileges at Riddle. Transfer allegedly occurred in view of Riddle personnel, and without proper written release forms signed. Plaintiff died en route. Verdict for hospital affirmed. ***Riddle Memorial Hospital v. Dohan,* 504 Pa. 571, 475 A.2d 1314.**

Jury verdict of $75,000 for allegedly performing unnecessary abdominal surgery. Reversed. The improper admission of opinion of expert, not qualified on specific issue (which opinion goes to heart of case), cannot be cured by corrective charge. ***Furey v. Jefferson Hospital,* 325 Pa. Super. 212, 472 A.2d 1083.**

Defense verdict. Alleged improper treatment and advice to heart patient who returned to work as cement truck driver, and suffered heart attack. Died three years later (after suit started) of second heart attack. Verdict affirmed. Proper here, where patient was heavy smoker and very overweight, to charge on contributory negligence. ***Berry v. Friday,* 324 Pa. Super. 499, 472 A.2d 191.**

Suit alleging damage due to negligent supervision of psychiatric patient, who needed additional care following fatal fire which he set, sufficiently sets forth cause of action. Demurrer denied. ***Vattimo v. Lower Bucks Hospital,* 502 Pa. 240, 465 A.2d 1231.**

Alleged mistreatment of accidental gunshot wound which caused loss of leg. Defense verdict affirmed. Jury found treatment negligent, but not substantial factor in loss of leg. Affirmed lower court's rulings on expert testimony, cross examination. Approved lower court's charge taken as a whole on causation. ***Brozana v. Flanigan,* 309 Pa. Super. 145, 454 A.2d 1125.**

Medical malpractice: Physician

Jury verdict $429,960 reversed on evidentiary grounds. Alleged malpractice; failure to correct promptly internal bleeding and negligence during surgery causing bleeding which lead to ulcerative colitis and neurosis. Plaintiff testified that in recovery room she heard nonparty physician shout into phone that she was critical and that defendant physician was unable to be reached. This was hearsay—prejudicial and reversible error to admit. Proper to grant judgment *n.o.v.* as to verdict of hospital negligence. **Reichman v. Wallach, 306 Pa. Super. 177, 452 A.2d 501.**

Jury verdict $500,000; $50,000 to husband for loss of consortium. Complications from hysterectomy led to loss of one kidney and ureter damage. Alleged postoperative negligence led to amputation of right leg. Two doctors, both involved in patient care, correctly held jointly and severally liable. Not a case of primary or secondary liability. Charge on causation based upon *Hamil v. Bashline, III*, affirmed. **Hoeke v. Mercy Hospital of Pittsburgh, 299 Pa. Super. 47, 445 A.2d 140.**

Jury verdict $1,000,000—malpractice action; $10,000—auto negligence action. Rear end collision—injuries to neck and back. Low back surgery. Infection followed—neomycin antibiotic allegedly caused kidney failure, partial paralysis of lower limbs and total hearing loss. Plaintiff could walk on crutches at time of trial. Verdict affirmed. Plaintiff, truck driver, earned $3.00/hr. at time of accident. Special damages $294,000. Hospital held in case because hospital resident-employee actively participated in neomycin therapy and made some dosage decisions. Residents held to standard of specialist, not general practitioner. **Pratt v. Stein, 298 Pa. Super. 92, 444 A.2d 674.**

Res ipsa loquitur may be applied to medical malpractice cases. **Jones v. Harrisburg Polyclinic, 496 Pa. 465, 437 A.2d 1134.**

Patient refilled prescription numerous times contrary to law and physician's instructions and the prescription. Loss of eyesight. Refills without knowledge of physician. Defense verdict affirmed. **Malloy v. Shanahan, 280 Pa. Super. 440, 421 A.2d 803.**

Plant physician sued for malpractice for allegedly mistreating work-related injury. Suit barred where physician is on salary and therefore fellow employee of plaintiff. **Babich v. Pavich, 270 Pa. Super. 140, 411 A.2d 218.**

During surgery, plaintiff allegedly mispositioned causing severe neck pain, and pain in left shoulder and arm due to nerve palsy. Verdict $56,000.00 reversed. *Res ipsa loquitur* applied to malpractice case but reversed due to failure of plaintiff to eliminate other responsible causes or actions of third persons. **Jones v. Harrisburg Polyclinic, 269 Pa. Super. 373, 410 A.2d 303.**

Plaintiff sustained collapsed lung allegedly due to negligent injection of cortisone into back of shoulder. Needle allegedly pierced pleural cavity. Although defendant testified that needle was too small to pierce cavity, plaintiff's expert testified to the contrary. Defendant had no record of needle size. Verdict for plaintiff. **Earlin v. Cravetz, 264 Pa. Super. 294, 399 A.2d 783.**

Verdict $1,500,000 for malpractice allegedly occurring from preoperative administration of anesthesia causing severe brain damage. Four attempts made to

Medical malpractice: Physician

place endotracheal tube in trachea. 10 minutes after 4th attempt, plaintiff suffered cardiac arrest. Expert testified that tube was negligently placed and that physicians failed to diagnose mechanical blockage. Surgeon held in as "captain of ship." ***Schneider v. Einstein Medical Center,*** **257 Pa. Super. 348, 390 A.2d 1271.**

Death of plaintiff following auto accident owing to malpractice and not auto accident. Physicians and nurses failed to diagnose injury properly and failed to place plaintiff on ventilator. Died 5 days later in extreme pain. Expert characterized malpractice as gross. Verdict for plaintiff. ***Embrey v. Borough of West Mifflin,*** **257 Pa. Super. 168, 390 A.2d 765.**

Plaintiff treated for removal of growth on neck. Shortly after surgery experienced pain in area and some loss of function in left arm. Another doctor diagnosed severed nerve. Defendant denied that he severed nerve. Verdict for defendant. Where testimony in conflict, for jury. ***Sindler v. Goldman,*** **256 Pa. Super. 417, 389 A.2d 1192.**

Where doctor left orders to be notified of any change in vital signs, a 0.2 raise in body temperature is not so alarming as to indicate call should have been made without expert testimony so indicating. ***Brannan v. Lankenau Hospital,*** **254 Pa. Super. 352, 385 A.2d 1376.**

Physician's attempt to join non-health care provider as additional defendant improper under Malpractice Arbitration Act. ***Gillette v. Redinger,*** **34 Pa. Cmwlth. 469, 383 A.2d 1295.**

Elderly plaintiff receiving physical therapy following hip surgery and fell fracturing left leg and arm. Surgeon testified injury was a stress fracture. Therapist several feet from plaintiff when incident occurred. Verdict for defendant. ***McAvenue v. Bryn Mawr Hospital,*** **245 Pa. Super. 507, 369 A.2d 743.**

Wife-plaintiff in hospital for delivery of fourth child. Labor inducing drug given. Admitting physician allegedly not present and further improper monitoring by staff alleged. Tear of uterus required hysterectomy and infectious hepatitis. Verdict for plaintiff. ***Stack v. Wapner,*** **244 Pa. Super. 286, 368 A.2d 292.**

Radiology treatments given for colony of plantar warts. Blister developed and healed. Two years and two months later skin decomposed at site of treatment requiring surgery and leaving permanent disability. Expert testified that result could only have come from overdose of radiation. Verdict for plaintiff against doctor and hospital. ***Ragan v. Steen,*** **229 Pa. Super. 515, 331 A.2d 724.**

Surgery on middle ear—immediate pain and rawness of tongue—continued treatment and assurance by doctor that condition temporary. Surgery 4/25/61. Last treatment March 1963. Suit 2/9/65. Compulsory nonsuit affirmed by evenly divided court. ***Barshay v. Schlosser,*** **226 Pa. Super. 260, 313 A.2d 296.**

Plaintiff patient required a second operation as the result of a clamp left in incision after initial operation—trial court charged jury that hospital's only negligence could be its failure to require an instrument count—verdict solely against operating surgeon—motion for a new trial as to hospital refused below and action af-

Medical malpractice: Physician's assistant

firmed on appeal—strong dissent. ***Tonsic et vir v. Wagner*, 220 Pa. Super. 468, 288 A.2d 791.**

Suit originally by minor plaintiff (now deceased) against druggist who allegedly sold the drug "Chloromycetin" without a prescription—this defendant joined initial family doctor who prescribed the drug, a doctor who issued the prescription without seeing the minor plaintiff and the corporation compounding the drug—minor died of aplastic anemia—verdict against additional defendants only—long opinion as to the defenses and liability of the additional defendants—Held: matter for the jury—verdict for the plaintiffs upheld on appeal. ***Incollingo v. Ewing*, 444 Pa. 263, 282 A.2d 206.**

Plaintiff operated on for a disc removal—defendant's decedent, the operating surgeon, left the closing of the surgical opening to resident trainees—sponge left in plaintiff's body—new operation required—court below in error in directing verdict for plaintiff—matter for jury under the facts—new trial awarded. ***Thomas v. Hutchinson*, 442 Pa. 118, 275 A.2d 23.**

Plaintiff on entering hospital signed two consents for an operation—suit against operating doctor on an assault and battery claim and against hospital for negligence—nonsuits properly entered—consents sufficient on assault and battery charge and lack of expert testimony justified nonsuit in suit against hospital. ***Chandler v. Cook*, 438 Pa. 447, 263 A.2d 794.**

Plaintiff, an aged woman, was suffering from a mental condition known as agitated depression—the defendant, her physician, recommended shock treatment and referred her to a hospital equipped to give such treatment—while receiving treatment plaintiff sustained bilateral fractures of the acetabulae—Held on appeal: defendant was not personally negligent and not responsible under doctrine of *respondeat superior* as not having control of those administering treatment. ***Collins v. Hand*, 431 Pa. 378, 246 A.2d 398.**

Plaintiff had an attack of nose bleeding of pronounced proportions—defendant performed an emergency operation and a partial paralysis developed—verdict for defendant—new trial properly refused—conflicting medical testimony for the jury. ***Horst v. Shearburn*, 426 Pa. 439, 233 A.2d 236.**

Medical malpractice: Physician's assistant

Plaintiff brought medical malpractice action based upon a physician's assistant leaving a catheter fragment in her left shoulder. The trial court granted summary judgment based upon Plaintiff's failure to provide expert medical testimony. The Superior Court affirmed holding that Plaintiff could not rely on the doctrine of res ipsa loquitur as the standard of care to remove a catheter was beyond the knowledge of a jury and thus required expert testimony. ***Vazquez v. CHS Professional Practice, P.C.*, 39 A.3d 395 (Pa. Super. 2012).**

Plaintiff's decedent wife was examined on numerous occasions by a physician's assistant who failed to properly diagnose or call in physician to examine a cancerous breast. Trial court entered a compulsory nonsuit after refusing to accept testimony of plaintiff's medical expert. Despite his twenty-five years of practice

Medical reports

and experience as an oncologist familiar with the same condition that caused wife's death, expert could not provide a specific reference to his theory of liability in a medical text. Where plaintiff's expert expresses the opinion that defendants' actions increased the risk of harm to plaintiff, the question of causation must go to the jury. Superior Court also reversed procedural rulings by trial court that prevented plaintiff from providing relevant and material facts to the record despite a complete lack of prejudice to defendants. ***Smith v. Grab*, 705 A.2d 894 (Pa. Super. 1997).**

Physician's assistant's failure to refer patient complaining of breast pain to physician is not actionable without proof of causation in suit against medical practice group instituted after discovery of breast cancer. Board certified internist is qualified to render an opinion as to the duty of care of physician's assistant. Compulsory nonsuit affirmed. ***Montgomery v. So. Philadelphia Medical Group, Inc.*, 441 Pa. Super. 146, 656 A.2d 1385 (1995).**

Medical monitoring

This is a class action suit for damages, including medical monitoring cost, by residents who lived within half a mile of lead processing plant against former and current owners of plant. Negligence *per se* requires that the law violated be designed to protect the interest of a group of individuals as opposed to the general public. Pennsylvania recognizes a cause of action for medical monitoring. Claims of negligence *per se* and for medical monitoring cannot be reached when the jury specifically finds no negligence on the part of the defendants. ***Wagner v. Anzon, Inc.*, 453 Pa. Super. 619, 684 A.2d 570 (1996).**

Medical records

Patient, who signed an authorization to release her medical records for the calculation of medical expenses, brought claim for breach of confidentiality after medical practice disclosed her unrelated use of marijuana and unprescribed pain medication to her employer's workers' compensation carrier. At trial a jury awarded damages to the Plaintiff and the medical practice appealed on the basis that a breach of confidentiality was governed by a one-year statute of limitations. The Superior Court affirmed the trial court's holding denying the Defendant's motion for judgment not withstanding the verdict. The Pennsylvania Supreme Court affirmed, holding that a claim for breach of physician-patient confidentiality was governed by a two-year statute of limitations period. ***Burger v. Blair Medical Associates, Inc.*, 964 A.2d 374 (2009).**

Medical reports

Plaintiff injured in motor vehicle accident offered four medical reports that showed that she had suffered serious soft tissue injury in the accident. Trial court granted defendant's motion for summary judgment based on findings in law that plaintiff's injuries were not compensable under the statutorily imposed limited tort restrictions. Superior Court reversed on its own review of reports by physicians and testimony adduced in summary judgment proceeding. ***Leonelli v. McMullen*, 700 A.2d 525 (Pa. Super. 1997).**

Memory

Plaintiff in a malpractice case did not furnish defendant with a copy of a medical report of a physician who did not treat, examine or had been consulted relative to plaintiff's injuries—doctor only to give opinion evidence as to negligence of defendant—did not fall within rule of court requiring exchange of medical reports—compulsory nonsuit improperly entered. ***Coffey v. Faix,* 426 Pa. 421, 233 A.2d 229.**

Memory

Female plaintiff who "repressed" memory of assaults that occurred more than 21 years in the past was not entitled to tolling of two year statute of limitations under the discovery rule. Order sustaining preliminary objections affirmed. ***Pearce v. Salvation Army,* 449 Pa. Super. 654, 674 A.2d 1123 (1996).**

Mental distress damages

Nineteen-year old son of plaintiff killed by auto. Father did not witness accident. Father committed suicide three months later. Suit by father's estate against driver of auto dismissed. ***Yandrich v. Radic,* 495 Pa. 243, 433 A.2d 459.**

Mental Health and Mental Retardation Act

Estate brought action against facility providing care for her mentally retarded daughter after daughter died while in the facility's care. The trial court dismissed Plaintiff's case and the Superior Court reversed and remanded. The Superior Court held that Plaintiff had alleged actions sufficient to establish gross negligence and incompetence where the complaint alleged that, despite express instructions to do so, employees failed to contact a nurse after the decedent vomited. ***Potts v. Step by Step, Inc.,* 26 A.3d 1115 (Pa. Super. 2011).**

Mental Health Procedures Act

Summary judgment against plaintiff psychiatric patient affirmed based on lack of proof that physician's actions amounted to gross negligence rather than simple negligence. Discussion of applicability of immunity under Mental Health Procedures Act to voluntary admissions. ***Walsh v. Borczon*, 881 A.2d 1 (Pa. Super. 2005).**

Patient committed to hospital under Mental Health Procedures Act died by drowning while taking an unsupervised bath. Despite clear medical testimony by affidavit that the staff of the hospital breached their duty of care to the patient, it was held that such negligence was not established to be the "gross negligence" required to be proved to avoid the immunity set forth in the Mental Health Procedures Act. ***Downey v. Crozer-Chester Medical Center*, 817 A.2d 517 (Pa. Super. 2003).**

Suit by parents of minor child who was raped by a mental health patient who had been released from a residential treatment facility to the community without adequate supervision. Plaintiffs claimed that base service unit and residential treatment facility were negligent in allow individual defendant into community without adequate supervision and with knowledge of his propensity to deviant sexual behavior. Held that mental health facilities and staff have no duty to unknown and unforeseen victims absent some special relationship. Held further that only a showing of

Mental illness

gross negligence will allow recovery from mental health professionals. *F.D.P. and J.A.P. v. Ferrara*, **804 A.2d 1221 (Pa. Super. 2002)**.

Under the Mental Health Procedures Act, a physician may only be liable for injury to a patient when gross negligence occurs. A physician's failure to speak to a non-minor patient's mother about the likely effect of alcohol consumption when combined psychiatric medications does not rise to the level of gross negligence. *Alphonsi v. Huntington Hospital, Inc.*, **798 A.2d 216 (Pa. Super. 2002)**.

Immunity granted to those who provide examination or treatment of a person under the Mental Health Procedures Act extends to physical health medical care providers and hospital referred to treat patient's medical condition, as well as those treating for mental illnesses, absent willful misconduct or gross negligence. *Allen v. Montgomery Hospital*, ___ **Pa.** ___, **696 A.2d 1175 (1997)**.

Hospital's immunity from suit under Mental Health Procedures Act may be decided on summary judgment. Hospital's actions after plaintiff's decedent failed to attend an outpatient appointment did not rise to level of gross negligence. *Albright v. Abington Memorial Hospital*, **548 Pa. 268, 696 A.2d 1159 (1997)**.

Psychiatric patient who died from injuries suffered as a result of crashing through second floor window of hospital and falling two stories was not being treated by hospital so as to clothe hospital with immunity under Mental Health Procedures Act. Judgment affirmed. *Fogg v. Paoli Memorial Hospital*, **455 Pa. Super. 81, 686 A.2d 1355 (1996)**.

In action by guardian of incapacitated, mental health patient for brain damages sustained as result of choking by restraining vest, immunity of physicians under Mental Health Procedures Act is not afforded to physician providing standard medical treatment at non-mental health facility. Judgment on jury verdict for defendant reversed and remanded. *Allen v. Montgomery Hospital*, **447 Pa. Super. 158, 668 A.2d 565 (1995)**.

Patient's unsubstantiated assertion of physical injury failed to establish negligent or intentional infliction of emotional distress. Doctor and medical center were immune from suit under Child Protective Services Law for disclosing plaintiff's admission that she had suffocated her child. Child Protective Services Law, which grants immunity for disclosures does not conflict with psychotherapist–patient privilege or the confidentiality provisions of the Mental Health Procedures Act. *Fewell v. Bresner*, **444 Pa. Super. 559, 664 A.2d 577 (1995)**.

Mental illness

Plaintiffs filed a negligence action against Defendant motorist after Plaintiff-husband was struck by Defendant's vehicle. Defendants sought mental health records of Plaintiff-husband based upon an allegation in the police report that he had attempted suicide but Plaintiffs refused to release his records. The trial court refused to grant an order releasing the mental health records based upon the confidentiality provisions of the Mental Health Procedures Act. The Commonwealth Court reversed holding that by filing the lawsuit Plaintiff had directly placed his past mental health history at issue waiving the confidentiality provisions of the Mental Health

Mental shock and anguish

Procedures Act. *Octave ex. rel. Octave v. Walker*, **37 A.3d 604 (Pa. Cmwlth. 2011).**

In action by guardian of incapacitated, mental health patient for brain damages sustained as result of choking by restraining vest, immunity of physicians under Mental Health Procedures Act is not afforded to physician providing standard medical treatment at non-mental health facility. Judgment on jury verdict for defendant reversed and remanded. ***Allen v. Montgomery Hospital*, 447 Pa. Super. 158, 668 A.2d 565 (1995).**

Mental health care providers had no duty to police officer for injuries caused by patient who, one day after visiting health care facility in agitated state, drove his car into a police van while experiencing a psychotic episode, injuring officer. Summary judgment affirmed. ***Heil v. Brown*, 443 Pa. Super. 502, 662 A.2d 669 (1995).**

Police officer shot by former mental patient brought action against state hospital and attending physician. Medical professional liability exclusion to sovereign applicable. ***Sherk v. County of Dauphin*, 531 Pa. Super. 515, 614 A.2d 226.**

Patient suffered nerve damage to arm after injection given by nurse. Trial court refused to admit evidence of plaintiff's mental illness (Munchausen Syndrome). Reversed. Evidence of mental illness admissable. ***Cohen v. Albert Einstein Medical Center*, 405 Pa. Super. 392, 592 A.2d 720.**

Mental shock and anguish

Plaintiffs father, mother and sister of deceased boy, witnessed his sudden death by being struck by defendant's car—no physical impact as to plaintiffs—claim solely for mental shock and anguish—preliminary objections properly sustained—no recovery for such loss in Pennsylvania. ***Knaub v. Gotwalt*, 422 Pa. 267, 220 A.2d 646.**

Mere happening of accident

Plaintiff property owner employed defendant to install gas heat in place of oil heat—tank disconnected—supplier of oil notified to make no further deliveries of oil—oil delivered by unknown party and plaintiff's cellar flooded—defendant repairman not responsible—mere happening of an accident. ***Raibley v. Marvin E. Kanze, Inc.*, 221 Pa. Super. 234, 289 A.2d 161.**

Plaintiff injured by explosion of propane gas upon entering defendant's slaughter house—no concrete evidence of actual cause of explosion and any breach of defendant's duty to plaintiff as a business invitee—mere happening of an accident—nonsuit affirmed. ***Shirley v. Clark*, 441 Pa. 508, 271 A.2d 868.**

Collision between truck of plaintiff's decedent and bus—no eye witnesses—testimony only of nature of the highway, collision, final resting place of vehicles and skid marks on highway—nonsuit proper. ***Kester v. Rutt*, 439 Pa. 546, 266 A.2d 713.**

Plaintiff's decedent jumped to her death from roof of defendant's high rise apartment—complaint averred a failure to restrict access to roof as ground for negligence—preliminary objections in the nature of a demurrer properly sustained—defendant apartment house operator had breached no duty owed to decedent. *Engel v. Parkway Co.*, **439 Pa. 559, 266 A.2d 685.**

Plaintiff's decedent died as the result of an automobile collision—no eye witnesses—each car found on proper side of road but facing in opposite directions after occurrence from that originally proceeding—cars originally going in opposite directions—nonsuit proper—mere happening of an accident. *Laubach v. Haigh*, **433 Pa. 487, 252 A.2d 682.**

Defendant's agent operating a tractor trailer unit across an intersection at a reasonable speed—feeling a contact the operator stopped and then found body of plaintiff's decedent partly under trailer—mere happening of an accident—nonsuit proper. *Hardy v. Clover Leaf Mills*, **426 Pa. 206, 232 A.2d 755.**

Wife plaintiff's and defendant's machines collided in intersection—wife had no knowledge of how accident happened and defendant did not testify—nonsuit proper—mere happening of an accident. *Engle v. Spino*, **425 Pa. 254, 228 A.2d 745.**

Decedent pedestrian crossing street near intersection—defendant's cab made a left turn and contacted decedent—no evidence of speed, awareness of decedent's presence or proof of inattentiveness—nonsuit proper—mere happening of an accident. *Antonson v. Johnson*, **420 Pa. 558, 218 A.2d 123.**

Mesothelioma

Plaintiff's decedent who was informed that mesothelioma was a rare, asbestos-induced form of lung cancer is not entitled to benefit of discovery rule where products liability action commenced more than two years after diagnosis of lung cancer. *Baumgart v. Keene Bldg. Products Corp.*, **542 Pa. 194, 666 A.2d 238 (1995).**

Metastasis

Reverses Superior Court ruling. Proper for jury to consider risk of metastasis even though 8 years had elapsed since failure to diagnose cancer without evidence of metastasis. Expert testimony that it was still a possibility. Verdict in excess of $700,000 reinstated. *Gradel v. Inouye*, **491 Pa. 534, 421 A.2d 674.**

Meter reader

Meter reader who fell into a window well and was injured was a licensee on property, not an invitee. The standard of care due by homeowners required that they exercise reasonable care to make unreasonably dangerous conditions safe and to warn licensees of the conditions. Existence of window well was known to reader and was not an unreasonably dangerous condition. *Cresswell v. End*, **931 A.2d 673 (Pa. Super. 2003).**

Microvascular decompression surgery

Microvascular decompression surgery

Patient suffered facial paralysis after undergoing microvascular decompression surgery. Nonsuit found improper. Expert medical testimony essential. ***Levy v. Jannetta,*** **423 Pa. Super. 384, 621 A.2d 585.**

Minority Tolling Statute

Plaintiff parents of minor who acquired streptococcus infection soon after birth commenced action against medical care providers and hospitals by praecipe for writ of summons and began discovery. After 16 months of discovery and motions, and before a complaint had been filed, parents requested permission to discontinue action without prejudice so they could have time to engage in additional discovery, have their experts review the additional information, and acquire funds on their own for that purpose or engage counsel who would advance the discovery costs. Court granted an additional four months to engage in discovery and file a complaint, which plaintiffs were unable to do; common pleas court entered *non pros*. The Superior Court held that lower court's decision to discontinue without prejudice a case that was 16 months old did not outweigh the burden already imposed on defendants and the additional burden of the potentially long wait for plaintiffs to recommence suit. The Minority Tolling Statute does not preclude compelling a case to proceed rather than allowing a reversion to the protection of tolled status, once a case filed on behalf of a minor has been commenced. ***Fancsali v. University Health Center of Pittsburgh*, 700 A.2d 962 (Pa. Super. 1997).**

Mirror of car

Pedestrian while standing on sidewalk allegedly struck by protruding mirror of defendant's truck—trial court in error in excluding from jury's consideration the fact that mirror may have extended over sidewalk even though the truck was still on the travelled portion of the cartway—new trial awarded to plaintiff. ***Russell v. Helm's Express, Inc.,*** **221 Pa. Super. 292, 293 A.2d 78.**

Miscarriage

Wife plaintiff who was left unattended in emergency room during miscarriage and then handed corpse of miscarried fetus while nurse took pictures established sufficient evidence of physical impact to allow recovery for negligent infliction of emotional distress. Case remanded for new trial on damages. ***Brown v. Philadelphia College of Osteopathic Medicine,*** **449 Pa. Super. 667, 674 A.2d 1130 (1996).**

Patient who suffered miscarriage brought actions for malpractice and for intentional and negligent infliction of emotional distress against obstetrician and physician who covered when he was unavailable. Neither physician liable. ***Strain v. Ferroni,*** **405 Pa. Super. 349, 592 A.2d 698.**

Missing plank

Plaintiff, while using a railroad bridge, fell through same as the result of a missing plank—railroad company held responsible and Pennsylvania rule as to not having permissive rights to use right of way longitudinally seriously questioned or abrogated. ***Franc v. Penna. R.R. Co.*, 424 Pa. 99, 225 A.2d 528.**

Mistaken identity

Plaintiff mistaken for shoplifter by store employee. Later received apology. Bruises to arm, recurrence of arthritis and ulcer flare-up. Physically recovered within five months but never recovered emotionally until time of her death 6-1/2 years later of unrelated causes. Substantial verdict including punitive damages. ***Hannigan v. S. Klein Department Stores*, 244 Pa. Super. 597, 371 A.2d 872.**

Molestation

While Section 317 of Restatement (2d) Torts imposes liability upon a master for acts of a servant committed outside the scope of the servant's employment, liability will not lie unless the acts are performed by the servant "upon the premises in possession of the master." Church and religious officials not liable for conduct of priest who molested minor on non-diocesan property. Judgment against Church, bishop and diocese vacated. ***Hutchison v. Luddy*, 453 Pa. Super. 420, 683 A.2d 1254 (1996).**

In action by parents against day care worker and center for molestation of child by worker, corporate entity not entitled to governmental immunity merely by reason of receipt of federal funds or designation by county as official community action program. Employer not vicariously liable for employee's outrageous conduct. Summary judgment reversed in part and affirmed in part. ***Sanchez by Rivera v. Montanez*, 165 Pa. Cmwlth. 381, 645 A.2d 383 (1994).**

Moral duty

Plaintiff a passenger in defendant's cab injured by action of unknown third party—failure of defendant's driver to secure name of operator of offending car did not create a right of action against cab company—only a moral duty involved—right of action has never been extended to a situation where only financial well being involved. ***Stupka v. Peoples Cab Co.*, 437 Pa. 509, 260 A.2d 759.**

Mortality tables

Patron of race track injured when bench collapsed. Mortality tables held admissible to determine future damages. ***Helm v. Eagle Downs-Keystone Racetrack*, 385 Pa. Super. 550, 561 A.2d 812.**

Mortgages and mortgagees

Plaintiffs brought negligence and defamation action against Defendant after it made an inaccurate report on the Plaintiffs' mortgage payment history to a credit information provider. The trial court dismissed Plaintiffs' complaint. The Superior Court affirmed holding that negligence and defamation claims were preempted by the Fair Credit Reporting Act unless the information was furnished with malice or willful intent. ***Dietz v. Chase Home Finance, LLC*, 41 A.3d 882 (Pa. Super. 2012).**

Mortgagor brought suit against mortgagee for breach of contract, negligence, and fraud and misrepresentation alleging that the mortgagee was negligent in su-

Motor Vehicle Financial Responsibility Act

pervising its employees, who engaged in fraud. The court dismissed the negligence claim under the gist of the action doctrine, because the negligence claim was rooted entirely in the fraud and misrepresentation claim. *Strausser v. Pramco, III & Manufacturers and Traders Trust Co.*, 944 A.2d 761 (Pa. Super. 2008).

Mere negligence is all that is required to assign liability for mortgagee's failure to satisfy paid off mortgage within 45 day time limit imposed by 21 P.S. §§ 681,682. *Kornfeld v. Atlantic Financial Federal*, 856 A.2d 170 (Pa. Super. 2004).

Failure of recorder of deed's docketing clerk to correctly index a mortgage led to financial damages to plaintiff. In granting j.n.o.v. to recorder as defedant, held that Political Subdivision Tort Claims Act applies to actions of recorder of deeds alleged to be negligent and alleged negligence was not within exceptions to immunity conferred by act. Affirmed holding that mortgagee's attorney's failure to check that mortgage was properly recorded was negligent. *Antonis v. Liberati*, 821 A.2d 666 (Pa. Cmwlth. 2003).

In action against Recorder of Deeds by title insurance company, Recorder of Deeds has no duty to index mortgage by location. Summary judgment affirmed. *Penn Title Ins. Co. v. Deshler*, ___ Pa. Cmwlth. ___, 661 A.2d 481 (1995).

Motor Vehicle Financial Responsibility Act

Police officer brought a declaratory action seeking a ruling that the city could not seek reimbursement under the Motor Vehicle Financial Responsibility Act for benefits it paid under the Heart and Lung Act for a third party recovery obtained by the officer. The trial court granted summary judgment for the Plaintiff. The Commonwealth Court reversed holding that the city could assert a subrogation lien for benefits it paid under the Heart and Lung Act against a settlement obtained by an officer from a third party tortfeasor as the Heart and Lung Act was similar to a payment of workers' compensation benefits. *Oliver v. City of Pittsburgh*, 977 A.2d 1232 (Pa. Cmwlth. 2009).

Pedestrian injured by automobile is not precluded from recovery of less than "serious bodily injury" damages because of her mother's limited tort coverage selection on mother's automobile. *L.S., a minor v. Eschbach*, 874 A.2d 1150 (Pa. 2005).

Summary judgment reversed where trial court failed to consider medical evidence of psychic injuries that may have qualified as serious impairment of a body function under limited tort coverage provided for in Motor Vehicle Financial Responsibility Law before granting summary judgment. Minor children injured in accident while riding in their mother's uninsured vehicle are held to have the same deemed limited tort coverage as their uninsured mother. *Hames v. Philadelphia Housing Authority*, 696 A.2d 880 (Pa. Cmwlth. 1997).

Motor Vehicle Financial Responsibility Law precludes employee injured during the scope of his employment as a result of automobile accident in which co-employee was driving from recovering common law damages against co-employee in addition to workers' compensation benefits. *Ducjai v. Dennis*, 540 Pa. 103, 656 A.2d 102 (1995).

Motorcycles and motorscooters

Motorcycles and motorscooters

Motorcyclists brought negligence claim against the Department of Transportation after he was injured when his motorcycle struck a pothole on the highway. The trial court granted summary judgment to the Defendant. The Commonwealth Court reversed holding that a letter from a state senator expressing concern over the condition of the roadway was sufficient to establish notice of a dangerous condition to preclude the defense of sovereign immunity. ***Walthour v. Commonwealth of Pennsylvania Department of Transportation*, 31 A.3d 762 (Pa. Cmwlth. 2011)**.

Administratrix of motorcyclist's estate brought a claim for negligence after the Pennsylvania motorcyclist was struck and killed by the New Jersey defendant in New Jersey. Defendant appealed the binding arbitration award based upon the lack of jurisdiction and a damage award against the defendant despite a finding that the decedent was 60% negligent. The Superior Court upheld the trial court's ruling that it had jurisdiction based upon the mutual agreement to arbitration in Pennsylvania. The Superior Court reversed and remanded with instructions to enter a judgment in favor of the Defendant on the basis of comparative negligence as a plaintiff cannot recover if they are found more than 50% negligent. ***Rekun v. Pelaez*, 976 A.2d 578 (Pa. Super. 2009).**

Parents brought suit on behalf of their minor child against a power company whose easement their child injured himself on while riding a motor bike when he struck a gate the power company had erected on the easement. The appellate court upheld the trial court's decision that a gate on an easement was insufficient to remove the immunity provided by the Recreational Use of Land and Water Act, because the land remained in a vastly unaltered original state. ***Stanton v. Lackawanna Energy, Ltd.*, 951A.2d 1181 (Pa. Super. 2008).**

Member of motorcycle club sued his motorcycle club for negligence after he crashed into a tractor that was on the club's racetrack. The court held that the indemnification clause signed by the club member explicitly gave up all right to sue for damages incurred from an injury sustained on the club's track. ***Nissley v. Candytown Motorcycle Club, Inc.*, 913 A.2d 887 (Pa. Super. 2006).**

Plaintiff minor's guardians filed suit against easement holder for negligence, after the minor plaintiff was injured while riding a motorbike on defendant electric utility's easement. The court held that under the Recreation Use of Land and Water Act (RULWA) private owners of undeveloped land that open it up to recreational public use free of charge are entitled to immunity. The court found that easement holders that exercised control over the easement were for statutory purposes within the definition of owners used by the statute and entitled to immunity under RULWA. ***Stanton v. Lackawanna Energy, LTD.*, 584 Pa. 550, 886 A.2d 667 (2005).**

Minor injured when his motorcycle struck a fence while riding on 123 acres of vacant land. Electric power utility which had 70' easement over the area for transmission line purposes held to be an "owner or possessor" under the Recreation Use of Land and Water Act and so immune from suit on basis of compliance with other terms of the act. Allegation of mere negligence rather than willful or malicious

Motorcycles and motorscooters

conduct, precludes relief from bar of RULWA. *Stanton v. Lackawanna Energy, Ltd.*, **820 A.2d 1256 (Pa. Super. 2003).**

Plaintiff motorcyclist was injured when he struck a car that pulled out in front of him. Driver of car alleged that he did not see motorcycle because its headlight was not operating. Plaintiff admitted that he frequently drove without operating headlight. Judgment in favor of plaintiff against motorcycle reseller and car driver vacated on basis that plaintiff assumed the risks that attend riding a motorcycle without a functioning headlight. ***Frey v. Harley Davidson*, 734 A.2d 1 (Pa. Super. 1999).**

Plaintiff was injured during operation of motorcycle and alleged in straight product liability case that defective brake caliper binder bolt was cause of accident. Defendant introduced evidence that plaintiff was intoxicated at the time of accident and that binder bolt broke as a result of the accident and argued that that intoxication was the sole cause of the accident. Superior Court affirmed trial court's admission of evidence, holding that when defendant in product liability suit offers evidence to establish that injuries were caused solely by negligence of plaintiff without any involvement of defect alleged by plaintiff, such evidence is admissible. ***Madonna v. Harley Davidson, Inc.*, 708 A.2d 507 (Pa. Super. 1998).**

Real property exception to sovereign immunity does not apply in automobile accident involving motorcyclist and driver. PennDOT's design and construction of road, including length of passing lane and speed limits, were not defects that caused motorcyclist's injuries but merely facilitated occurrence of accident when combined with negligence of driver. Assured clear distance rule does not apply where instrumentality moves into driver's path within a distance short of the assured clear distance ahead. Driver does not have to anticipate negligence of another driver in calculating assured clear distance. ***Nestor v. Com., Dept. of Transp.*, ___ Pa. Cmwlth. ___, 658 A.2d 829 (1995).**

Action of motorcyclist who crossed into oncoming lane while attempting to pass vehicle in his lane was sole cause of accident; order denying PennDOT's motion for post-trial relief reversed. ***Glover v. Com., Dept. of Transp.*, 167 Pa. Cmwlth. 87, 647 A.2d 630 (1994).**

Motorcyclist failed to produce sufficient evidence in action against landowner, PennDOT and township to justify inference of negligence and causation due to inability to identify reason his vehicle left roadway and struck fence post. Summary judgment affirmed. ***Saylor v. Green*, 165 Pa. Cmwlth. 249, 645 A.2d 318 (1994).**

Dirt bike rider injured when bike fell into rut. Land owner immune under Recreation Use of Land and Water Act. ***Zlakowski v. Com., Dept. of Transp.*, 154 Pa. Cmwlth. 528, 624 A.2d 259.**

Motorcyclist and passenger injured in accident caused by fluids left on highway from previous accident. Driver of automobile involved in previous accident and State Police not liable. No duty to plaintiffs. ***Susko v. Pennsylvania State Police*, 132 Pa. Cmwlth. 263, 572 A.2d 831.**

Motorcycles and motorscooters

One vehicle motorcycle accident. Jury verdict of $1,750,000. Driver of cycle suffered loss of most of right arm. Plaintiff alleged defective assembly of front-end assembly. New trial ordered on lower court error as to exclusion of evidence. *Bascelli v. Randy, Inc.,* **339 Pa. Super. 254, 488 A.2d 1110.**

Error to dismiss plaintiff's claim based upon inadequate warnings by manufacturer as to lack of visibility of cycle to other vehicle on road without giving leave to amend or present evidence on inadequacy of warnings. Dismissal of negligence claim on inadequate warning or safety devices also held premature under circumstances. *Frauel v. Suzuki Motor Co., Ltd.,* **337 Pa. Super. 97, 486 A.2d 498.**

Fatal accident to operator of motorcycle in collision with truck. Alleged defect in street caused cycle to lose control after collision with truck. Verdict against plaintiff. New trial as to truck driver only, affirmed. Evidence of post-accident repairs to defect properly excluded under facts here. None of the alleged trial errors goes to negligence of the City. *Robinson v. City of Philadelphia.,* **329 Pa. Super. 139, 478 A.2d 1.**

Jury verdict with 50% contributory negligence. Verdict $89,000 reduced by half. Plaintiff rendered paraplegic at age 21, when his motorcycle collided with another vehicle at T-intersection. Stop sign missing for plaintiff's direction of travel. Speed limit 25 mph. Plaintiff's own expert and other witnesses put plaintiff at higher rate of speed. Grant of unrestricted new trial, affirmed. Within proper discretion of lower court, under facts here, to hold verdict contrary to weight of evidence. Speed of motorcycle estimated at 50-60 mph. *Buck v. Scott Twp.,* **325 Pa. Super. 148, 472 A.2d 691.**

Motorcyclist riding on private property ran into a 1-1/2 inch steel cable strung across roadway to deter trespassers. Admitted, plaintiff was trespasser. Duty to trespasser is not to act in reckless disregard for safety. Landowner knew dirt bikes traversed property. New trial ordered. Submission of case to jury on negligence theory—misleading. Court questions viability of doctrine of landowner immunity. *Antonace v. Ferri Contracting Co.,* **320 Pa. Super. 519, 467 A.2d 833.**

Motorcycle passenger sued driver of auto making left turn into path of motorcycle. Trial judge entered nonsuit in favor of motorcycle driver who was joined as additional defendant. Jury verdict then in favor of original defendant. Trial judge granted new trial on damages only, feeling jury was prejudiced against motorcycles. Superior Court reversed nonsuit in favor of additional defendant and ordered new trial on all issues as to defendant. Affirmed finding that verdict was the result of biased jury. *Eagleson v. Malone,* **319 Pa. Super. 163, 465 A.2d 1280.**

Motorcycle and auto intersection collision. Auto making left turn. Passenger on motorcycle said at scene it was fault of motorcycle—going fast, at night, without lights. Verdict against motorcycle driver only. *Carl v. Kurtz,* **255 Pa. Super. 198, 386 A.2d 577.**

Large pile of dirt alongside parking lot. Driver of vehicle pulled out striking plaintiff going by on motorcycle and killing him. Verdict against defendant who piled dirt affirmed. Piling dirt alongside parking lot is negligent and driver's coming

Moving machinery

out behind it does not as a matter of law relieve defendant of negligence—not as a matter of law a superseding cause. ***Flickinger Estate v. Ritsky,* 452 Pa. 69, 305 A.2d 40.**

Plaintiff motorcyclist injured by reason of an unlighted excavation created by defendant in highway—case for jury but error in charge that existence of car ahead obscuring view could excuse plaintiff from otherwise complying with assured clear distance rule. ***Koelle v. Phila. Electric Co.,* 443 Pa. 35, 277 A.2d 350.**

Moving machinery

Plaintiff injured while unclogging electric lawn mower—started spontaneously. Design defect claimed for lack of "deadman's switch." Amputation of index and middle fingers; ring finger immobilized. Thumb and little finger shortened. Lower court entered order requiring General Electric to wholly indemnify Sears. Held: jury to determine whether plaintiff, by inserting hand into stalled mower, had assumed risk of injury. Court affirmed verdict and holding, requiring complete indemnification. ***Burch v. Sears, Roebuck & Co.,* 320 Pa. Super. 444, 467 A.2d 615.**

Muffler

A muffler lying on a Commonwealth roadway is not a condition of or arising from Commonwealth real estate so as to allow plaintiff the benefit of the real estate exception to sovereign immunity. ***Murphy v. Com., Dept. of Transp.,* 733 A.2d 688 (Pa. Cmwlth. 1999).**

Multiple impacts

Apportionment of liability for harm to plaintiff is question of law. Where tortious conduct of two or more persons causes a single harm that cannot be apportioned, the actors are joint tortfeasors even though they acted independently. Jury verdict in favor of driver injured as a result of two separate collisions affirmed. ***Smith v. Pulcinella,* 440 Pa. Super. 525, 656 A.2d 494 (1995).**

Multi-vehicle accident

Plaintiff's discontinuance of her action against all defendants in a multi-vehicle accident case does not affect the right of a defendant to continue to prosecute a claim against another defendant on a cross-claim. After settlement by plaintiff, case was discontinued as to all claims and removed from trial list. Order vacated and remanded for trial on cross-claims separate from plaintiff's settled claims. ***Ross v. Tomlin,* ___ Pa. Super. ___, 696 A.2d 230 (1997).**

Municipal liability: Care, custody, and control of animals

Plaintiff brought action against the Society for the Prevention of Cruelty of Animals for illegally destroying her dogs. A jury found in favor of the Plaintiff and the Superior Court affirmed. The Pennsylvania Supreme Court affirmed holding that the SPCA did not have immunity under either Sovereign Immunity Act or the Political Subdivision Tort Claims Act. ***Snead v. Society for the Prevention of Cruelty to Animals of Pennsylvania,* 985 A.2d 909 (Pa. 2009).**

Municipal liability: Fire departments and fire fighters

Plaintiff's children were made ill by exposure to E-coli bacteria on farm during a tour. Defendant farm sought to join county Health Department as defendant alleging that the department was liable under one of two exceptions to governmental immunity – care, custody and control or real estate and care, custody and control of animals – on grounds that the department made regular inspections of the property and the animals. Held that such inspections are insufficient to constitute ownership or control of the real estate or animals and so no exception applies to allow recovery against department. *Sweeney v. Merrymead Farm, Inc.*, **799 A.2d 972 (Pa. Cmwlth. 2002)**.

Plaintiffs were injured by a dog that had bitten people three or more times in the prior year. In suit against township and dog owner, township's motion for summary judgment was properly granted as there was no exception present to the governmental immunity afforded the township. Plaintiffs' arguments that government's breach of state Dog Law and Dog and Rabies Ordinance constituted violation of statutes which would give plaintiffs a right of recovery were incorrect as there is no private right of action under either act. Animal exception to governmental immunity does not apply because the township did not own the dog. *Lerro v. Upper Darby Township*, **798 A.2d 871 (Pa. Cmwlth. 2002)**.

Zoo volunteer whose fingertip was bitten off by Chuckles, a South American river dolphin, may not recover against City. City is immune from suit because care, custody, and control of animals exception to governmental immunity does not include wild animals. Order denying judgment *n.o.v.* reversed. *Sakach v. City of Pittsburgh*, ___ Pa. Cmwlth. ___, **687 A.2d 34 (1996)**.

Municipal liability: Fire departments and fire fighters

Plaintiff filed suit against multiple defendants, including volunteer fire company for injuries sustained after sale of alcohol to defendant. After review of legal and factual basis of fire company's status as local agency entitled to protection of Political Subdivision Tort Claims Act, court determined that illegal sale of alcohol on fire company property does not constitute "care, custody or control" standard related in *Grieff v. Reisinger*, 548 Pa. 13, 693 A.2d 195 (1997) and so immunity available and grant of summary judgment in favor of volunteer fire company affirmed. *Eger v. Lynch*, **714 A.2d 1149 (Pa. Cmwlth. 1998)**.

Summary judgment in favor of volunteer fire department denied based on Political Subdivision Tort Claims Act, where fire department chief's act of spreading paint thinner on the floor at fire department, which caught fire and injured visitor/plaintiff, constituted "care, custody or control of real property" and so provided an exception to immunity. *Grieff v. Reisinger*, ___ Pa. ___, **693 A.2d 195 (1997)**.

Plaintiff severely burned by flash fire caused when paint thinner used to clean paint from floor of volunteer fire department ignited was precluded from recovering for injuries because volunteer fire company entitled to governmental immunity. Real property exception to governmental immunity does not apply unless cause of action based on condition of real property or an actual defect of the property itself. Negligent mishandling of combustible liquids on property does not invoke real property exception. Denial of volunteer fire company's motion for sum-

Municipal liability: Government function

mary judgment reversed and remanded. *Grieff v. Reisinger*, ___ Pa. Cmwlth. ___, 654 A.2d 77 (1995).

Plaintiff failed to prove that dangerous condition of a parking lot was causally related to injuries. Summary judgment in favor of volunteer fire department affirmed. *West v. Kuneck*, **167 Pa. Cmwlth. 252, 647 A.2d 975 (1994).**

Amount of damage recoverable from fire department limited by local agency status. Purchase of liability insurance in excess of statutory limit is not a waiver. *Dunaj v. Selective Insurance Co. of America*, **167 Pa. Cmwlth. 93, 647 A.2d 633 (1994).**

Police and fire personnel took no action to resuscitate subway passenger who died of heart attack. City not liable. *Welsh v. City of Philadelphia*, **156 Pa. Cmwlth. 299, 627 A.2d 248.**

Spectator at fire department carnival assaulted by employee of amusement operator. Matter remanded in order to establish official status of fire department. *Miller by Miller*, **152 Pa. Cmwlth. 159, 618 A.2d 1143.**

City resident treated by fire department unit brought action against city and department for improper care. Defendants immune. Judgment on pleadings should have been granted. *City of Philadelphia v. Glim*, **149 Pa. Cmwlth. 491, 613 A.2d 613.**

Spectator at fire injured when hose burst. Borough not liable. *Speece v. Borough of North Braddock*, **145 Pa. Cmwlth. 568, 604 A.2d 760.**

Driver of automobile injured in collision with fire truck. Plaintiff settled with truck driver and fire department. Fire Dispatcher immune. *Keesey v. Longwood Volunteer Fire Company, Inc.*, **144 Pa. Cmwlth. 466, 601 A.2d 921.**

Non-jury verdict, $150,000. Firemen responding to false alarm were told by plaintiff that they had apprehended wrong children. Fireman argued with plaintiff, and struck him in knee with wrench, causing eventual surgical removal of kneecap. Verdict affirmed. *Powell v. City of Philadelphia*, **311 Pa. Super. 526, 457 A.2d 1307.**

Municipal liability: Government function

Inmate filed a claim of negligence against Franklin County for failing to transmit records and docket pleadings. The court held the alleged actions of defendant did not fall into any of the enumerated exceptions to governmental immunity under 42 Pa.C.S. § 8541 and dismissed the negligence claim. *Weaver v. Franklin County*, **918 A.2d 194 (Pa. Cmwlth. 2007).**

Prisoner filed claim in negligence against correction officers for the destruction of his television, which was broken while being held in their custody. The trial court dismissed the claim on governmental immunity grounds, but was reversed. The appellate court held that personal property damaged while in possession of a Commonwealth party is an enumerated exception to sovereign immunity in Pennsylvania. *Williams v. Stickman*, **917 A.2d 915 (Pa. Cmwlth. 2007).**

Municipal liability: Government function

Westmoreland County Industrial Development Corporation which is alleged to have acted negligently in the sale of real estate is a "local agency" and therefore entitled to immunity under the Political Subdivision Tort Claims act. ***Green Valley Dry Cleaners, Inc. v. Westmoreland County Industrial Development Corporation,* 832 A.2d 1143 (Pa. Cmwlth. 2003).**

Plaintiffs sued local sewage enforcement officer for negligent performance of his duty. Individual and borough defendants' motion for judgment on the pleadings granted because of governmental immunity. Trial court's denial of plaintiff's motion to amend complaint to allege intentional acts by sewage enforcement officer also affirmed because six month statute of limitation had expired before amendment. ***Stoppie v. Johns,* 720 A.2d 808 (Pa. Cmwlth. 1998).**

Plaintiff's decedent electrocuted while applying stucco to building in proximity to uninsulated electrical wires. Political Subdivision Tort Claims Act precludes imposition of liability upon governmental unit based on a theory of vicarious liability for work performed by contractor. Order granting summary judgment affirmed. ***Thomas v. City of Philadelphia,* ___ Pa. Cmwlth. ___, 668 A.2d 292 (1995).**

Passage of Political Subdivision Tort Claims Act precludes any governmental waiver of immunity. ***Davis v. City of Philadelphia,* 168 Pa. Cmwlth. 334, 650 A.2d 1127 (1994).**

Homeowner brought action against township for negligent inspection and failure to enforce building code. Government immunity statute held not retroactive. ***Saft v. Upper Dublin Township,* 161 Pa. Cmwlth. 158, 636 A.2d 284.**

Homeowner brought action against township for failure to enforce building code. Cause of action accrued before passage of Tort Claims Act. Act could not be applied retroactively. ***Garvey v. Rosanelli,* 144 Pa. Cmwlth. 588, 601 A.2d 1334.**

Property owner brought action against township and firm contracted to act as sewage enforcement officer for negligently issuing permit. Township immune. Contractor not immune. ***Smith v. Porter Township,* 141 Pa. Cmwlth. 244, 595 A.2d 693.**

Resident brought action against housing authority for failure of security guards to come to his aid during assault. Authority not liable. ***Battle v. Philadelphia Housing Authority,* 406 Pa. Super. 578, 594 A.2d 769.**

Savings and Loan brought action against prothonotary and office of prothonotary for failure to index writ of revival of judgment. Prothonotary not personally liable for negligence of employees. Office of prothonotary not liable owing to plaintiff's contributory negligence. ***Commonwealth Federal Savings and Loan Association v. Pettit,* 137 Pa. Cmwlth. 523, 586 A.2d 1021.**

Spectator brought action against city for injuries resulting from fall from temporary bleachers. City immune. Alleged negligence of police improperly pleaded. ***DeRitis v. City of Philadelphia,* 136 Pa. Cmwlth. 244, 582 A.2d 738.**

Minor injured while ice skating on public lake in Borough. Held: Borough's alleged failure to supervise was alleged cause of injury and therefore not within ex-

Municipal liability: Miscellaneous

ception to Political Subdivision Tort Claims Act. *Fizzano v. Ridley Park*, **94 Pa. Cmwlth. 179, 503 A.2d 57.**

Jury verdict $220,000 plus delay damage against City of Philadelphia. Plaintiff, inmate at House of Correction, had all toes of left foot traumatically amputated while on garbage detail. Warning buzzer not working; issue of negligent structural modification of rear step. Verdict affirmed. *Mattox v. City of Philadelphia*, **308 Pa. Super. 111, 454 A.2d 46.**

Political Subdivision Tort Claims Act held to be valid exercise of legislative authority. Suit against county for failure to place decedent in properly supervised area of Detention Center not covered by Act. *Carroll v. County of York*, **496 Pa. 363, 437 A.2d 394.**

Plaintiff assaulted on train platform in city. Demurrer of city sustained. Duty of city to provide police protection is a public one and may not be claimed by an individual unless special relationship exists. Does not exist because plaintiff is in high crime area. *Chapman v. City of Philadelphia*, **290 Pa. Super. 281, 434 A.2d 753.**

Inspection and demolition of dilapidated building is a governmental function—city immune from liability. *Bleman v. Gold*, **431 Pa. 348, 246 A.2d 376.**

Municipal liability: Miscellaneous

Plaintiff rehabilitation facility brought wrongful use of civil proceedings, abuse of process and intentional interference with a contract claims against city and its solicitor. The trial court dismissed the case on preliminary objections. The Commonwealth Court affirmed holding that the Political Subdivision Tort Claims Act provides immunity to local agencies for all claims except for 8 enumerated exceptions sounding in negligence. *Orange Stones Co. v. City of Reading*, **87 A.3d 1014 (Pa. Cmwlth 2014).**

Plaintiff brought negligence action against defendant borough after she fell over a picnic table in a public park. The trial court granted summary judgment for the defendant. The Commonwealth Court affirmed, holding the real property exception to governmental immunity did not apply to personalty that was not affixed to the property. *Mandakis v. Borough of Matamoras*, **1914 C.D. 2012 (Pa. Cmwlth. 2013).**

Plaintiff, a trainee with a non-profit, brought negligence action against Defendant city after he slipped and fell while helping to clean up flood damage. The trial court granted summary judgment in favor of the city on the basis that the city had immunity under the Workers' Compensation Act. The Commonwealth Court affirmed holding that under the Borrowed Servant Doctrine the city was the Plaintiff's employer because the non-profit had loaned its workers to the city and the city had controlled the performance of the work and the Plaintiff's hours of work. *Canot v. City of Easton*, **37 A.3d 53 (Pa. Cmwlth. 2012).**

City of Philadelphia employees brought a class action suit claiming breach of fiduciary duty when a series of actions by the city led to a decrease in the Deferred Compensation Plan of the employees. The trial court dismissed two counts

Municipal liability: Miscellaneous

of negligence, but permitted a third count of breach of contract to proceed. The Commonwealth Court affirmed the trial court's dismissal of the negligence claims, but reversed dismissing the breach of contract claim on the basis of the gist of the action doctrine. The Pennsylvania Supreme Court held that the breach of contract claim was appropriately dismissed and that the personal property exception to the Tort Claims Act did not apply to deferred compensation funds it held as it had legal and equitable ownership over the fund itself. *McShea v. City of Philadelphia*, 995 A.2d 334 (Pa. 2010).

Political Subdivision Tort Claims Act bars suit for medical negligence against a county owned and operated nursing home. The exception for medical or professional negligence found in the Sovereign Immunity Act is not in the Political Subdivision Tort Claims Act. *Davis v. County of Westmoreland*, 844 A.2d 54 (Pa. Cmwlth. 2004).

Township sued in negligence for poor grading and construction on plaintiffs' property. Trial court's determination that landowner/plaintiff's proper relief was under Eminent Domain Code reversed. *Poole v. Township of District*, 843 A.2d 422 (Pa. Cmwlth. 2004).

Foster parents assigned by county Children and Youth Service agency were employees of agency and so entitled to immunity under Political Subdivision Tort Claims Act. *Patterson v. Lycoming County*, 815 A.2d 659 (Pa. Cmwlth. 2003).

Plaintiffs whose building was partially damaged by fire in adjoining property and partially damaged by acts of demolition contractor hired by borough to tear down adjoining property filed suit against borough alleging negligent supervision and inspection of demolition contractor by borough. Held that negligent inspection or supervision is not an exception to municipal immunity act. *Moles v. Borough of Norristown*, 780 A.2d 787 (Pa. Cmwlth. 2001).

The question of whether a plaintiff has sustained a permanent loss of a bodily function as required by section 8553 of the Judicial Code, 42 Pa.C.S. §8553, in a claim against a local agency under the Political Subdivision Tort Claims Act is a question for the jury. *Laich v. Bracey*, 776 A.2d 1022 (Pa. Cmwlth. 2001).

Doctrine of governmental immunity provides that liability may be imposed on a local agency only for negligent acts. Acts or conduct that constitute a crime, actual fraud, actual malice, or wilful misconduct do not subject a local agency to liability. Failure to disclose to adoptive parents information in CYS files that biological parents of adoptive child both suffered from mental illness, alcoholism, and drug abuse does not overcome governmental immunity of CYS. *Zernhelt v. Lehigh County Office of CYS*, ___ Pa. Cmwlth. ___, 659 A.2d 89 (1995).

City's failure to supervise and control criminal detainee in work-release facility who left facility and murdered plaintiffs' decedent is not a recognized exception to governmental immunity. City's indemnification of lessor of work release facility was not a waiver of governmental immunity in favor of plaintiffs. Summary judgment affirmed. *Rodriguez v. City of Philadelphia, Dept. of Human Services*, ___ Pa. Cmwlth. ___, 657 A.2d 105 (1995).

Municipal liability: Motor vehicles

Prisoner committed suicide shortly after being counseled by parole officer. City and officer not liable. Parole officers not health care personnel under exceptions to government immunity. ***Freedman v. City of Allentown*, 128 Pa. Cmwlth. 126, 562 A.2d 1012.**

Suit against Schuylkill County and Boy Scouts for damages arising out of injuries sustained by retarded child on camping trip. County dismissed as defendant. Allegation of negligent supervision not within exception to Sovereign Immunity Act. ***Silkowski v. Hacker*, 95 Pa. Cmwlth. 226, 504 A.2d 995.**

Minor plaintiff injured as the result of the explosion of an aerial bomb fire cracker—occurrence took place in a public park after a fireworks display—court below held township immune to liability—affirmed on appeal with a strong dissent. ***Flisek et al. v. Star Fireworks, Inc. et al.*, 220 Pa. Super. 350, 286 A.2d 673.**

Suit instituted against Allegheny County by mother of a deceased child—action based on alleged lack of proper care of child, an emotionally disturbed individual—preliminary objections properly sustained on ground of governmental immunity—strong dissents. ***Laughner v. Allegheny County*, 436 Pa. 572, 261 A.2d 607.**

Municipal liability: Motor vehicles

Plaintiff brought a claim for negligence against transportation agency and its driver after he was struck by a car while crossing the road, because the van driver let him out on the opposite side of the road from his house. The trial court granted summary judgment in favor of the Defendants. The Commonwealth Court affirmed holding that in order to fall within the motor vehicle exception to the Political Subdivision Tort Claims Act the injuries must be caused by a moving vehicle or a moving part of a vehicle. ***Phillips v. Washington County Transportation Authority*, 986 A.2d 925 (Pa. Cmwlth. 2009).**

Plaintiff bus passenger brought a claim for negligence against the Defendant Port Authority for injuries suffered when the Plaintiff fell out of his wheelchair due to the driver deploying the wheelchair ramp uneven with the ground. The trial court denied Defendant's motion for summary judgment. The Commonwealth Court reversed the trial court's decision holding that as the bus ramp was not moving when the passenger fell the vehicle exception to liability did not apply. ***Mannella v. Port Authority of Allegheny County*, 982 A.2d 130 (Pa. Cmwlth. 2009).**

Plaintiff injured when she fell over in her wheel chair while being transported in a local transportation agency van. Summary judgment in favor of local agency by reason of governmental immunity defense sustained because plaintiff did not provide proof of permanent loss of a bodily function. ***Smith v. Endless Mountain Transportation Authority*, 878 A.2d 177 (Pa. Cmwlth. 2005).**

Minor injured when struck by a school bus sustained a permanent 4 millimeter scar on his right wrist. In suit against school bus owned and operated by school district, jury's determination that the scar, although permanent, was not disfiguring was proper and so kept case out of governmental immunity exception for injuries

Municipal liability: Motor vehicles

which cause permanent loss of a bodily function or permanent disfigurement. *Alexander v. Benson*, 812 A.2d 785 (Pa. Cmwlth. 2002).

A plaintiff who was injured when she alighted from a bus was precluded from recovery because the bus was stopped and so not in "operation" as required to allow recovery based on an exception to sovereign immunity. *Bottoms v. Southeastern Pennsylvania Transportation Authority*, 805 A.2d 47 (Pa. Cmwlth. 2002).

Supreme Court affirms trial court grant of summary judgment in favor of SEPTA for actions of bus driver who discharged students into a busy street and not at a regular stop. Strong dissent by Justice Newman arguing that discharging passengers is part of operation of a transit bus. *Warrick v. Pro Cor Ambulance, Inc.*, 739 A.2d 127 (Pa. 1999).

Plaintiff was injured when she struck a vacant police car with its engine running and warning lights operating which was parked in the left lane of a multi-lane road. In suit against city, summary judgment in favor of city affirmed on grounds that officer who had left car to attend to a motorist on traffic lanes traveling in opposite direction was not operating vehicle under motor vehicle exception to governmental immunity. Commonwealth Court also affirmed trial court's order sustaining preliminary objections in favor of driver on other side of the road that officer was attending because his actions were to remote in law to be cause of plaintiff's injuries. *Beiter v. City of Philadelphia*, 738 A.2d 37 (Pa. Cmwlth. 1999).

In suit by plaintiff injured when struck by a police car that had been pursuing him, motion for summary judgment for municipality affirmed. Motor vehicle exception to governmental immunity under the Political Subdivision Tort Claims Act is not applicable to a person who was fleeing a police officer or in flight from apprehension. *Forgione v. Heck*, 736 A.2d 759 (Pa. Cmwlth. 1999).

Vehicle exception to governmental immunity does not apply when alleged cause of accident in which plaintiff was injured was valve that fell from back of fire truck en route to station. *Swartz v. Hilltown Township V.F.D.*, 721 A.2d 819 (Pa. Cmwlth. 1998).

Plaintiff injured when he collided with a stopped and abandoned city-owned truck could not recover because the truck's position and abandoned status removed it from the "operation of a motor vehicle" exception to political subdivision tort claims act immunity. *Merz v. City of Philadelphia*, 719 A.2d 1131 (Pa. Cmwlth. 1998).

Plaintiff's minor son was injured when crossing the street in front of a school bus from which he had just disembarked after having been "waved across" by the bus driver. Lower court granted summary judgment to school district of Philadelphia on basis that bus driver waving to student was not "operation" of the motor vehicle and so not an exception to governmental immunity. Commonwealth Court reversed and Supreme Court reversed Commonwealth Court holding that the driver's wave was not part of the "operation" of the motor vehicle. *White v. School District of Philadelphia*, 718 A.2d 778 (Pa. 1998).

Municipal liability: Motor vehicles

Plaintiff sued city for injuries sustained while being driven to hospital by fire fighter in fire rescue van. During trip to hospital, left rear tandem wheels feel off van, causing an accident and plaintiff's injuries. Parties stipulated that fire fighter was not driving negligently and that repair and maintenance of vehicle by city was negligent. Plaintiff's motion for summary judgment granted and affirmed by Commonwealth Court. Supreme Court held that maintenance and repair of van is included in exception to Political Subdivision Tort Claims act relating to injuries caused by negligent acts of local agency or its employees with respect to the operation of a motor vehicle. Negligence related to the operation of a vehicle encompasses not only how a person drives, but also whether he should be driving a particular vehicle in the first place. *Mickle v. City of Philadelphia*, **707 A.2d 1124 (Pa. 1998).**

Homeowners may recover for damage to property caused by city-owned truck that rolled backward into plaintiffs' home. Truck was improperly parked and left unattended with engine running and therefore was in "operation" under motor vehicle exception to Political Subdivision Tort Claims Act. Judgment on the pleadings against City affirmed and remanded for trial. *Cacchione v. Wieczorek*, **___ Pa. Cmwlth. ___, 674 A.2d 773 (1996).**

Plaintiff motorist injured in collision with township garbage truck entitled to new trial after trial court incorrectly instructed jury that garbage truck driver was entitled to drive against traffic flow in the same manner as Motor Vehicle Code defined Type I and Type II vehicles such as emergency vehicles. New trial granted. *Sawchzuk-Serge v. Township of Cheltenham*, **___ Pa. Super. ___, 670 A.2d 210 (1996).**

Negligent maintenance of city's fire department rescue van falls within operation of motor vehicle exception to governmental immunity. "Operation" requires only that the vehicle be in motion. Order granting summary judgment in favor of plaintiff affirmed. *Mickle v. City of Philadelphia*, **___ Pa. Cmwlth. ___, 669 A.2d 520 (1995).**

Plaintiff's decedent died after crashing into utility pole following high speed chase. The decedent's criminal and negligent acts preclude imposition of liability on municipalities whose police officers were engaged in pursuit. Therefore, decedent's widow could not recover from municipalities under wrongful death theory as such action is derivative to any action the decedent may have had. Order granting summary judgment affirmed. *Tyree v. City of Pittsburgh*, **___ Pa. Cmwlth. ___, 669 A.2d 487 (1995).**

Passenger injured while exiting bus. Held: vehicle exception to sovereign immunity not applicable. Authority not liable for first party benefits under Financial Responsibility Law. *Gielarowski v. Port Authority of Allegheny County,* **159 Pa. Cmwlth. 214, 632 A.2d 1054.**

Motorist entering street from driveway involved in collision caused by unlawfully parked city vehicle. City not liable. *City of Philadelphia v. Melendez,* **156 Pa. Cmwlth. 271, 627 A.2d 234.**

Motorist injured back when automobile struck from behind by vehicle driven by city employee. Held: medical testimony sufficient to find permanent injury and

Municipal liability: Police

delay damages in excess of statutory maximum recoverable against municipality. ***Robinson v. Jackson,*** **145 Pa. Cmwlth. 211, 602 A.2d 917.**

Motorist injured when vehicle struck from behind by trash truck. City found negligent but not liable. ***Kaufman v. City of Philadelphia,*** **144 Pa. Cmwlth. 444, 601 A.2d 910.**

Student injured when struck by automobile while crossing street after alighting from Transportation Authority bus. Authority immune. ***Lehman v. County of Lebanon Transportation Authority,*** **143 Pa. Cmwlth. 416, 599 A.2d 259.**

Passenger injured when bus door closed as she attempted to exit. Motor vehicle exception to government immunity applicable. ***Sonnenberg v. Erie Metropolitan Transit Authority,*** **137 Pa. Cmwlth. 533, 586 A.2d 1026.**

Motorist injured in collision with police car. City liable. City waived immunity when it enacted Chapter 21–700 of the Philadelphia Code. ***City of Philadelphia v. Gray,*** **133 Pa. Cmwlth. 396, 576 A.2d 411.**

Ambulance operated by contractor for municipality involved in accident in which two passengers were killed. Municipality not liable. ***Burnatoski v. Butler Ambulance Service,*** **575 A.2d 1121.**

Municipal liability: Nursing home

A private, independent contractor organization that managed and set administrative and medical policy and procedure for a county-owned nursing home was not clothed with the governmental immunity afforded by the Political Subdivision Tort Claims Act. ***Helsel v. Complete Care Services, L.P.,*** **797 A.2d 1051 (Pa. Cmwlth. 2002).**

Municipal liability: Police

Decedent's estate brought action against municipality after the decedent was killed in a collision with a police officer involved in a high speed chase of another motorist. The trial court dismissed the preliminary objections to dismiss the action. The Commonwealth Court affirmed. The Commonwealth Court held that under the Political Subdivision Tort Claims Act a municipality was immune only if the action of the officer in operating his vehicle in pursuit of the fleeing suspect was not a substantial factor in causing the injured individual's injuries. ***Cornelius v. Roberts,*** **71 A.3d 345 (Pa. Cmwlth. 2013).**

Plaintiff alleged police failed to adequately investigate a robbery and attempted shooting committed against the plaintiff. A private party cannot recover in a personal injury suit for monetary damages based upon a police officer's failure to prevent or vigorously investigate a crime, since there is no general duty of care on the part of the government to protect private citizens from the criminal acts of third parties. ***Murphy v. City of Duquesne,*** **898 A.2d 676 (Pa. Cmwth. 2006).**

The Commonwealth Court determined that a police officer's car, stopped on the road facing against traffic at night, with its lights pointing at oncoming traffic, was not "operating" under motor vehicle exception to governmental immunity and

Municipal liability: Police

so suit by motorcycle operator for injuries sustained when rider struck police car should have been dismissed. ***North Sewickley Township v. LaValle*, 786 A.2d 325 (Pa. Cmwlth. 2001)**.

Plaintiff was injured when struck by a bicycle being ridden by a police officer on patrol on the sidewalk. A municipal ordinance prohibited riding bicycles on sidewalks. Held, a bicycle is not a "motor vehicle" as defined in the motor vehicle exception to governmental immunity. All courts agree that this is a seemingly unjust result that must be remedied in the future by legislation. ***Harding v. City of Philadelphia*, 777 A.2d 1249 (Pa. Cmwlth. 2001)**.

Police owe no duty of care to a fleeing driver. ***Lindstrom v. City of Corry*, 763 A.2d 394 (Pa. 2000)**.

Plaintiff police officer was injured when he tripped on old fencing on lot adjacent to house at which a search warrant was being served. Lower court granted summary judgment to defendant property owners holding that police officer was a trespasser and so defendants had a duty only to avoid wanton or willful negligence or misconduct. Superior Court affirmed and Supreme Court granted allocatur and also affirmed holding that Section 345 of Restatement (2d) Torts relating to duty to trespassers entering pursuant to a privilege is not adopted in Pennsylvania and police and fire fighters are to be accorded trespasser status. ***Rossino v. Kovacs*, 718 A.2d 755 (Pa. 1998)**.

Police officer who did not see accident in question would not be qualified by experience or training as expert unless foundation were laid for that qualification. Even if officer was qualified as expert, his deposition testimony based on post-accident interviews with parties to accident is inadmissible without his own independent knowledge of actual circumstances of accident. ***Bennett v. Graham*, 714 A.2d 393 (Pa. 1998)**.

Plaintiff pedestrian injured by impact of police car is entitled to reversal of nonsuit where evidence indicates that all elements of negligence claim were established at trial. Trial court's determination that plaintiff failed to prove that his injury was permanent or of a serious nature so as to impair a bodily function is reversible abuse of discretion. Nonsuit removed; remanded for new trial. ***Boyer v. City of Philadelphia*, 692 A.2d 259 (Pa. Cmwlth. 1997)**.

Police officer's failure to provide protection for specific individual shot on bus terminal platform is not a recognized exception to governmental immunity. Despite city ordinance purporting to waive governmental immunity for negligent acts of police officers, City cannot waive its immunity. Ordinance held retroactively invalid under *City of Philadelphia v. Gray*, 534 Pa. 467, 633 A.2d 1090 (1993). Summary judgment affirmed. ***Johnson v. City of Philadelphia*, ___ Pa. Cmwlth. ___, 657 A.2d 87 (1995)**.

Police officer who enters upon another's land in his official capacity and in response to a call for assistance is a licensee. Landowner's duty is to inform licensee of dangerous, hidden conditions. Obviously rowdy crowd of patrons at social hall was not a dangerous, hidden condition. Although violation of Dram Shop Act is

Municipal liability: Police

negligence *per se*, mere fact that patrons who assaulted police officer were intoxicated neither proves that they had been served when visibly intoxicated nor causation of officer's injuries. Summary judgment for defendant affirmed. ***Holpp v. Fez, Inc.,* 440 Pa. Super. 512, 656 A.2d 147 (1995).**

State police failed to rescue passenger in vehicle carried away by flood waters. Police not liable. ***Peak v. Petrovitch,* 161 Pa. Cmwlth. 261, 636 A.2d 1248.**

Woman died of hypothermia after being left outside by police. Police not liable. ***Philadelphia v. Estate of Dennis,* 161 Pa. Cmwlth. 69, 636 A.2d 240.**

Plaintiffs injured in collision with police vehicles brought actions based on city code section waiving immunity. Code section invalid. ***City of Philadelphia Police Department v. Williams,* 534 Pa. 467, 633 A.2d 1090.**

Detainee brought action against police for injuries suffered while unconscious. Held: presence of blood in cell would not support inference of negligence. Real property exception to governmental immunity not applicable. ***Diaz v. Houck,* 159 Pa. Cmwlth. 274, 632 A.2d 1081.**

Police and fire personnel took no action to resuscitate subway passenger who died of heart attack. City not liable. ***Welsh v. City of Philadelphia,* 156 Pa. Cmwlth. 299, 627 A.2d 248.**

Police officer not liable for injuries to third parties involved in collision with fleeing vehicle. ***White v. Mayo Laverda (S.R.L.),* 152 Pa. Cmwlth. 488, 620 A.2d 52.**

Pedestrian injured in hit-and-run accident. Held: inability of plaintiff to produce police report did not preclude recovery. ***Hatcher v. Travelers Insurance Company,* 421 Pa. Super. 225, 617 A.2d 808.**

Shooting victim killed by spouse of police officer with officer's revolver. Summary judgment in favor of city and officer vacated. ***Nelson v. City of Philadelphia,* 149 Pa. Cmwlth. 611, 613 A.2d 674.**

Police officer who witnessed man being crushed to death in trash compactor brought action for negligent infliction of emotional distress. Owner of compactor not liable. ***Covello v. Weis Markets, Inc.,* 415 Pa. Super. 610, 610 A.2d 50.**

Motorist brought action against police for failure to adequately warn of icy highway and vehicles blocking highway. Police not liable. ***Miseo v. Ross Township Police Department,* 147 Pa. Cmwlth. 263, 607 A.2d 806.**

Subway passenger stabbed by other passenger. Police officer helped victim from train then ceased assistance. Held: summary judgment for city inappropriate. Officer owed duty to victim. ***Rankin v. SEPTA,* 146 Pa. Cmwlth. 429, 606 A.2d 536.**

Bystander shot and killed by police officer during arrest. Administratrix brought actions for wrongful death, survival and loss of consortium. Separate recovery for loss of consortium denied. ***Mease v. Commonwealth,* 145 Pa. Cmwlth. 407, 603 A.2d 679.**

Municipal liability: Police

Suspect committed suicide with police officer's firearm while being detained by township and county police. Officers and departments immune. ***Simmons v. Township of Moon,* 144 Pa. Cmwlth. 198, 601 A.2d 425.**

Passenger killed when automobile struck tree that had fallen across state road. Township police placed flares and cones around tree. Township immune. ***Mylett v. Adamsky,* 139 Pa. Cmwlth. 637, 591 A.2d 341.**

Police officer injured in fall while chasing trespasser. Landowner not liable. No duty to erect fence to protect from hazards on adjacent land. ***Hauch v. Samuel Geltman & Company,* 400 Pa. Super. 534, 583 A.2d 1244.**

Inmate being held for intoxication hanged herself in police cell. City not liable. Chapter 21–701 of City Code not applicable. ***City of Philadelphia v. Kluska,* 134 Pa. Cmwlth. 511, 579 A.2d 1006.**

Child died of wounds from shot fired from crowd that police failed to disperse. City not liable. ***Yates v. City of Philadelphia,* 134 Pa. Cmwlth. 282, 578 A.2d 609.**

Motorist injured in collision with police car. City liable. City waived immunity when it enacted Chapter 21–700 of the Philadelphia Code. ***City of Philadelphia v. Gray,* 133 Pa. Cmwlth. 396, 576 A.2d 411.**

Police officer injured when attempting to arrest former state hospital patient. Hospital immune. Medical-professional exception to sovereign immunity applies only to patient injuries. ***Harrisburg State Hospital v. Sherk,* 128 Pa. Cmwlth. 150, 562 A.2d 1025.**

City police officers, allegedly responding to call to pick up "hospital case," instead took decedent to jail where he died three hours later. Held: city *not* immune from suit for alleged negligence of policy which causes injury. Grant of city's preliminary objections reversed. ***Capanna v. City of Philadelphia,* 89 Pa. Cmwlth. 349, 492 A.2d 761.**

Auto accident. Issue of whether vehicle negligently hit guardrail and thereafter front wheel came off car, or whether wheel came off car, causing it to go out of control. Defense verdict after officer was qualified as expert and opined that wheel came off first. Error to qualify police officer as expert under these circumstances. New trial ordered. ***Reed v. Hutchinson,* 331 Pa. Super. 404, 480 A.2d 1096.**

Child shot in eye by neighbor. Racial tension in neighborhood. Suit against city for nonfeasance of police and Human Relations Commission. Plaintiff unable to establish that special relationship existed between individual and city. No such relationship shown. ***Melendez v. City of Philadelphia,* 320 Pa. Super. 59, 466 A.2d 1060.**

Plaintiff assaulted on train platform in city. Demurrer of city sustained. Duty of city to provide police protection is a public one and may not be claimed by an individual unless special relationship exists. Does not exist because plaintiff is in high crime area. ***Chapman v. City of Philadelphia,* 290 Pa. Super. 281, 434 A.2d 753.**

Municipal liability: Police

Off-duty police officer shot neighbor during argument with gun that was not issued by police department. Verdict against individual and City employer. Denial of judgment *n.o.v.* as to City reversed for lack of evidence of connection between tortious act and employer. ***Fitzgerald v. McCutcheon,*** **270 Pa. Super. 102, 410 A.2d 1270.**

Assault and fight in bar led to death of plaintiff. City a defendant for failure of police to provide needed medical care. Evidence of blood alcohol, visible intoxication, bleeding from nose and mouth sufficient to go to jury. ***Furman v. Frankie,*** **268 Pa. Super. 305, 408 A.2d 478.**

Death action. Verdict for plaintiff sustained by equally divided court. Plaintiff shot by police officer while lying face down and spread eagle. Cocked gun discharged. Extraordinary care required when dealing with loaded firearm. ***Everette v. City of New Kensington,*** **262 Pa. Super. 28, 396 A.2d 467.**

Police officer expert testified as to who was driving from after-accident photographs. Judge should have permitted other side to produce expert to say that photographs were inconclusive even though general rule is that expert should not be permitted to state inference or judgment as to ultimate facts for jury determination. ***Ryan v. Furey,*** **225 Pa. Super. 294, 303 A.2d 221.**

Plaintiff's decedent, a boy of 18, found wandering semiconscious in cold weather and taken into police custody—boy given no attention and died next day—amended complaint held on appeal to state a cause of action against police officers—good discussion of liability of public officers. ***Ammlung v. Platt,*** **224 Pa. Super. 47, 302 A.2d 491.**

Plaintiff operating a police vehicle going to a fire—collision in intersection with vehicle of defendant—cross suits by defendant and borough for property damage—jury denied claims of all contending parties—error assigned was failure to charge that police officer would only be responsible if operating car in a reckless manner—verdicts sustained below on ground that trial judge had properly charged as to the operation of the police car—action sustained on appeal. ***Fullen v. Boory,*** **440 Pa. 644, 270 A.2d 624.**

Police officer of City of Harrisburg shot and killed plaintiff's decedent—City sued—preliminary objections properly sustained—City not responsible as matter involved a governmental function. ***Smeltz v. Harrisburg,*** **440 Pa. 224, 269 A.2d 466.**

Police officer had automobile mechanical experience prior to entering police service—he tested brakes of car involved in occurrence and found them defective—within discretion of trial court to permit him to testify as an expert. ***Flavin v. Aldrich et al.,*** **213 Pa. Super. 420, 250 A.2d 185.**

Police officer arrived on scene of accident some 10 to 15 minutes after occurrence—testifying as to brake failure of one of cars as a result of tests made after arrival—improperly admitted—such testimony hearsay—new trial properly granted. ***Andrews v. Jackson et al.,*** **211 Pa. Super. 166, 235 A.2d 452.**

Municipal liability: Police pursuit

Plaintiff's decedent killed by a policeman who was attempting to restore order—Supreme Court refused to overrule the cases establishing governmental immunity to municipalities. ***Graysneck v. Heard*, 422 Pa. 111, 220 A.2d 893.**

Municipal liability: Police pursuit

Driver who was injured while fleeing police brought a negligence action against a police officer who collided with his ATV while attempting to apprehend him for traffic violations. The trial court granted summary judgment in favor of the Defendant. The Commonwealth Court affirmed holding that there was no statutory duty owed to a fleeing motorist by an officer. ***Kuniskas v. Commonwealth of Pennsylvania*, 977 A.2d 602 (Pa. Cmwlth. 2009).**

Plaintiff driver was injured when his vehicle was broadsided by a police car responding to a call. Plaintiff claimed that defendant police officer was driving recklessly under the standards set by the emergency vehicle doctrine (75 Pa.C.S. § 3105). Defendant argued that plaintiff was contributorily negligent as he was driving under the influence of drugs. After verdict in favor of plaintiff, jury apportioned liability 55% to plaintiff and 45% to police officer. City and police officer presented motion to mold verdict to $0 under comparative negligence and court granted motion. New trial granted on appeal because the comparative negligence act cannot be used to measure recklessness under emergency vehicle doctrine against plaintiff's negligence under the comparative negligence act. ***Johnson v. City of Philadelphia*, 808 A.2d 978 (Pa. Cmwlth. 2002).**

Police owe no duty of care to a fleeing driver. ***Lindstrom v. City of Corry*, 763 A.2d 394 (Pa. 2000).**

Plaintiff injured when a car driven by a criminal suspect fleeing police officers struck his car. Plaintiff filed suit against municipalities whose police were involved in chase. Held: motor vehicle exception to Political Subdivision Tort Claims Act applies to high-speed police pursuit in residential neighborhoods and commercial districts. Question of appropriateness of chase is for jury. ***Aiken v. Borough of Blawnox*, 747 A.2d 1282 (Pa. Cmwlth. 2000).**

In suit by plaintiff injured when struck by a police car that had been pursuing him, motion for summary judgment for municipality affirmed. Motor vehicle exception to governmental immunity under the Political Subdivision Tort Claims Act is not applicable to a person who was fleeing a police officer or in flight from apprehension. ***Forgione v. Heck*, 736 A.2d 759 (Pa. Cmwlth. 1999).**

Plaintiff was injured and his wife was killed when their car was struck by a vehicle fleeing a police vehicle that was operating its emergency lights but no siren. The trial court granted summary judgment to the pursuing officer, his superiors and city under the Political Subdivision Tort Claims Act pursuant to *Dickens v. Horner,* 531 Pa. 127, 611 A.2d 693 (1992). Supreme Court affirmed Commonwealth Court reversal of trial court and overruling of *Dickens, supra,* holding that it is a question for the jury to decide whether the police officer/supervisors/city's negligence was a substantial factor causing plaintiffs' harm and whether the fleeing driver's actions

Municipal liability: Police pursuit

were a superseding cause precluding governmental liability. ***Jones v. Chieffo,*** **700 A.2d 417 (Pa. 1997).**

In negligence action against City for injuries sustained by plaintiffs as a result of high speed chase by unmarked City police car without lights or siren, discovery judge's entry of judgment against City on issue of liability was not an inappropriate sanction. Although City properly raised governmental immunity defense, its repeated failure to comply with discovery requests and defiance of court orders warranted entry of judgment. Mere fact that procedural discovery sanction touches on City's substantive right to immunity defense does not constitute a waiver of the defense. Whether a case proceeds as a "case stated" or as a "trial without a jury upon stipulated facts" dramatically affects the rights of the parties to appeal. ***Taylor v. City of Philadelphia,*** **692 A.2d 308 (Pa. Cmwlth. 1997).**

In action by injured passenger and estate of deceased passenger against police officers and municipalities for injuries and death resulting from high speed chase, the criminal act of flight alone does not constitute a superseding cause as a matter of law, so as to preclude recovery under motor vehicle exception to Political Subdivision Tort Claims Act. Order sustaining preliminary objections reversed. ***Black v. Shrewsbury Borough,*** **675 A.2d 381 (Pa. Cmwlth. 1996).**

Plaintiff's decedent died after crashing into utility pole following high-speed chase. The decedent's criminal and negligent acts preclude imposition of liability on municipalities whose police officers were engaged in pursuit. Therefore, decedent's widow could not recover from municipalities under wrongful death theory because such action is derivative to any action the decedent may have had. Order granting summary judgment affirmed. ***Tyree v. City of Pittsburgh,*** ___ **Pa. Cmwlth.** ___**, 669 A.2d 487 (1995).**

No duty of care by police to driver fleeing police. Utility company not liable for placement of utility pole struck by fleeing driver. ***Beck v. Zabrowski,*** **168 Pa. Cmwlth. 385, 650 A.2d 1152 (1994).**

Motorist injured in collision with vehicle involved in high speed police chase. City not liable even though police may have violated vehicle code. ***Foster v. City of Pittsburgh,*** **162 Pa. Cmwlth. 553, 639 A.2d 929.**

Plaintiffs injured in collision with police vehicles brought actions based on city code section waiving immunity. Code section invalid. ***City of Philadelphia Police Department v. Williams,*** **534 Pa. 467, 633 A.2d 1090.**

Suspect killed during police chase following unsuccessful arrest. City liable. Police did not follow proper procedures. ***Agresta v. Gillespie,*** **158 Pa. Cmwlth. 230, 631 A.2d 772.**

Unlicensed driver injured in collision during police chase. Municipality and police officer not liable. ***Hawks by Hawks v. Livermore,*** **157 Pa. Cmwlth. 243, 629 A.2d 270.**

Municipal liability: Police pursuit

Driver killed and passenger injured when struck by vehicle involved in police chase. Officer, department and municipality not liable. ***Angle v. Miller,*** **157 Pa. Cmwlth. 181, 629 A.2d 238.**

Driver and passenger injured in collision with vehicle involved in high speed police chase. Police officers and department not liable. ***Tobay v. Crossland,*** **153 Pa. Cmwlth. 103, 620 A.2d 636.**

City not liable for injuries to third party resulting from collision with vehicle involved in high speed police chase. ***Dennis v. City of Philadelphia,*** **153 Pa. Cmwlth. 81, 620 A.2d 625.**

Motorist injured when struck by vehicle involved in police chase. City not liable. ***Conroy v. City of Philadelphia,*** **152 Pa. Cmwlth. 486, 620 A.2d 51.**

Driver and passenger injured when struck by vehicle that ran red light during police chase. City not liable. ***Burnett v. City of Philadelphia,*** **152 Pa. Cmwlth. 483, 620 A.2d 50.**

Motorist injured when struck by vehicle involved in police chase. Police officer and township immune. ***Dickens v. Horner,*** **531 Pa. 127, 611 A.2d 693.**

Motorcyclist pursued by police injured while attempting to avoid roadblock. Judgment against city reversed. City may have been immune. ***City of Pittsburgh v. Judges,*** **147 Pa. Cmwlth. 234, 607 A.2d 339.**

Passenger in vehicle injured during high speed police chase. Held: passenger stated cause of action against police officer and department. Judgment on the pleadings not appropriate. ***Baker v. Hawks,*** **127 Pa. Cmwlth. 92, 560 A.2d 939.**

Police officer suffered heart attack shortly after arriving at police station with fleeing driver defendant. Defense verdict affirmed. Held: risk that officer would have heart attack could not reasonably be foreseen. Driver owed officer no duty of care for purposes of negligence action. ***Zanine v. Gallegher,*** **345 Pa. Super. 119, 497 A.2d 1332.**

During high speed police chase, pursued vehicle ran red light and struck car in which plaintiff was a passenger. Error to enter compulsory nonsuit in favor of city. Merely because it was the pursued vehicle in the accident, still a jury question, especially where summary offense is involved. ***Kuzmics v. Santiago,*** **256 Pa. Super. 35, 389 A.2d 587.**

High-speed police chase caused death of innocent bystander. Fugitive had eluded police earlier in high speed chase. No precautions taken in second chase. For jury. Verdict for plaintiff affirmed. ***Emery v. Borough of Lewistown,*** **247 Pa. Super. 623, 373 A.2d 1145.**

Plaintiff painting a building—City policeman chasing suspect and shot plaintiff. Sovereign immunity abolished—preliminary objections overruled. ***Laughlin v. Pittsburgh,*** **226 Pa. Super. 431, 310 A.2d 289.**

Defendant police officer was pursuing a speed violator—proceeding at 80 miles per hour—applying brakes and jumping divider line—colliding with car of

Municipal liability: Real estate

plaintiff's decedent—sufficient evidence for jury to find a "reckless disregard of the safety of others"—verdict for plaintiff sustained. ***Herron v. Silbaugh*, 436 Pa. 339, 260 A.2d 755.**

Plaintiff's decedent was a guest passenger in defendant's car—car went out of control on curve and left highway—verdict for defendant—new trial properly granted—car being pursued by police and going 90 miles per hour just before occurrence—jury should have been instructed as to wanton misconduct. ***Fugagli v. Camasi*, 426 Pa. 1, 229 A.2d 735.**

Municipal liability: Prisons

Prisoner brought negligence action against county prison after he was injured when another prisoner backed into him with a tractor while mowing the lawn. Trial court dismissed the complaint. The Commonwealth Court reversed holding that a prisoner operating a tractor was a county employee that permitted an exception to governmental immunity. The Court also held that the county's failure to maintain the back-up warning signal could constitute an exception to governmental immunity. ***Allen v. County of Wayne*, 88 A.3d 1035 (Pa. Cmwlth. 2013).**

Municipal liability: Real estate

Plaintiff brought negligence action against Defendant airport after she tripped and fell on a stage in the airport. The trial court granted summary judgment to the Defendant. The Commonwealth Court affirmed holding that for the real property exception to immunity to apply the dangerous condition must be attached to the floor. ***Sanchez-Guardiola v. City of Philadelphia*, 87 A.3d 934 (Pa. Cmwlth 2014).**

Plaintiff brought a negligence action against the Defendant parking authority for fractures to her foot suffered while exiting a parking shuttle on a ramp in the parking lot. The trial court found in favor of the Plaintiff. The Commonwealth Court reversed holding that the parking authority was immune as the claim did not fall under the real property exception to governmental immunity as the Plaintiff's injury did not result from the parking authority's property. The injury was the result of the shuttle bus driver letting her exit on a ramp. ***Oliver v. Tropiano Transportation, Inc.*, 79 A.3d 1233 (Pa. Cmwlth 2013).**

Plaintiff brought negligence action against the defendant city after she tripped and fell between two railroad ties the city had installed as curbing on a side street. The trial court granted summary judgment in favor of the defendant city. The Commonwealth Court affirmed, holding that under the Political Subdivision Tort Claims Act the plaintiff was required to establish that a dangerous condition existed and the political subdivision was on notice of the issue. The Superior Court held that a gap between railroad ties did not present a dangerous condition. ***Couto-Pressman v. Richards*, 63 A.3d 856 (Pa. Cmwlth. 2013).**

Condo Association brought claim of negligence against county port authority resulting from a landslide on a hillside it owned. A jury found in favor of the Defendant. The Commonwealth Court affirmed holding that, while earth movement was

Municipal liability: Real estate

a dangerous condition that satisfied the Sovereign Immunity Act's real estate exception, there is no liability for failing to provide lateral support to a neighbor where the neighbor has done nothing to change the contour of their property. ***Morewood Point Community Association v. Port Authority of Allegheny County*, 993 A.2d 323 (Pa. Cmwlth. 2010).**

     Management company employee sued the city after he was injured at a city-owned golf course in the course of his employment maintaining the course in a garden built by an independent contractor. A jury found in favor of the city. The Commonwealth Court affirmed finding that under the Political Subdivision Tort Claims Act the city could not be held liable for the acts of a person who is not an employee of the city, such as an independent contractor. ***Nardo v. City of Philadelphia*, 988 A.2d 740 (Pa. Cmwlth. 2010).**

     Plaintiff brought suit against the city and sports club after he broke his leg in a flag football league game when he tripped and fell in a depression on a field owned by the City of Philadelphia. The trial court entered summary judgment in favor of the Defendants. The Commonwealth Court affirmed because the mere fact that the field was regularly mowed did not remove the field from exemption of liability for the city under the Recreational Use of Land and Water Act. ***Davis v. City of Philadelphia*, 987 A.2d 1274 (Pa. Cmwlth. 2010).**

     Employee of subcontractor brought suit against the borough, fire company, contractor, and inspection company after he was injured in a fall from scaffolding while building the borough's firehouse. The trial court granted summary judgment in favor of the Defendants. The Commonwealth Court held that the real property exception to government immunity applied as scaffolding was not real property. ***Hain v. Borough of West Reading*, 986 A.2d 961 (Pa. Cmwlth. 2009).**

     Plaintiff brought suit against a municipality after the swing set she was using broke causing her to suffer brain damage. The appellate court affirmed the trial court's decision that brain damage was a loss of bodily function and therefore Plaintiff could prevail on her claim, because her injury was an enumerated exception to immunity under the Political Subdivision Tort Claims Act. ***Sider v. Borough of Waynesboro*, 933 A.2d 681 (Pa. Cmwlth. 2007).**

     City and housing authority both entitled to immunity under Political Subdivision Tort Claims Act and Sovereign Immunity Act. Plaintiff alleged that city's and housing authority's failure to maintain security systems on property constituted negligence related to the care, custody and control of the real estate. City and housing authority were not liable for failure to prevent criminal acts of third party who injured plaintiff. ***Williams v. Philadelphia Housing Authority*, 873 A.2d 81 (Pa. Cmwlth. 2005).**

     County was shielded by governmental immunity under Political Subdivision Tort Claims Act in suit by pedestrians struck by runaway vehicle on walking path adjacent to road where there was no intervening guard rail. ***Simko v. County of Allegheny*, 869 A.2d 571 (Pa. Cmwlth. 2005).**

Municipal liability: Real estate

Summary judgment in favor of volunteer fire department affirmed against child who was injured by a softball hit beyond the boundaries of a softball into a display area near the field. The condition of the fire department's real estate was not itself the cause of the injury, it merely facilitated the injury by a third party. *Gaylord v. Morris Township Fire Department*, 853 A.2d 1112 (Pa. Cmwlth. 2004).

Uncovered drainage hole located within public right of way but outside paved street is not part of highway for purposes of highway exception to governmental immunity provision of Political Subdivision Tort Claims Act. Fact that drainage hole was located in public right of way that was in possession of abutting landowner means that municipality did not have possession and so real estate exception is not applicable to provide injured plaintiff with relief. *Gramlich v. Lower Southampton Township*, 838 A.2d 843 (Pa. Cmwlth. 2003).

Debris and dead cat which had accumulated on steps leading into basement of building owned by Philadelphia Housing Authority were not conditions that "derived, originated or had as their source" the municipal realty itself so as to fall within the real estate exception to governmental immunity. *Lingo v. Philadelphia Housing Authority*, 820 A.2d 859 (Pa. Cmwlth. 2003).

Plaintiff was injured when she tripped on a box under a table located in a blocked-off street during a fire department street fair. Grant of summary judgment in favor of fire department due to lack of exception to governmental immunity under Political Subdivision Tort Claims Act affirmed. Care, custody and control of real estate exception to governmental immunity does not apply to streets. *Granchi v. Borough of North Braddock*, 810 A.2d 747 (Pa. Cmwlth. 2002).

Plaintiff's children were made ill by exposure to E-coli bacteria on farm during a tour. Defendant farm sought to join county Health Department as defendant alleging that the department was liable under one of two exceptions to governmental immunity – care, custody and control or real estate and care, custody and control of animals – on grounds that the department made regular inspections of the property and the animals. Held that such inspections are insufficient to constitute ownership or control of the real estate or animals and so no exception applies to allow recovery against department. *Sweeney v. Merrymead Farm, Inc.*, 799 A.2d 972 (Pa. Cmwlth. 2002).

Wooden bleachers from which plaintiff fell when they tipped over were not part of the real estate so as to allow suit to proceed against city under real estate exception to Political Subdivision Tort Claims Act. *Blocker v. City of Philadelphia*, 763 A.2d 373 Pa. 2000).

Tenant of county housing authority who was injured when she slipped and fell on snow and ice-covered parking area could not recover against local agency, because snow and ice were condition *on* the real estate, not condition *of* the real estate. Supreme Court's seemingly different determination on similar facts under the Sovereign Immunity Act does not control under different language of the Political Subdivision Tort Claims Act. *Irish v. Lehigh County Housing Authority*, 751 A.2d 1201 (Pa. Cmwlth. 2000).

Municipal liability: Real estate

Plaintiff slipped and fell on sidewalk in front of city building that fronted on Commonwealth highway. City argued it was immune from liability under the sidewalk exception to the governmental immunity statute because the sidewalk did not abut a city-owned street. After a very thorough review of the history of the sovereign and governmental immunity acts and cases, the court held that the city could be liable under the real estate exception to governmental immunity. ***Sherman v. City of Philadelphia***, **745 A.2d 95 (Pa. Cmwlth. 2000).**

Summary judgment reversed in case where plaintiff was injured by metal pole stump protruding from ground on housing authority property after she was pushed by a third party. Held: political subdivision can be liable despite the existence of a third party whose actions may constitute a concurrent cause of the injury. ***Wilson v. Philadelphia Housing Authority*, 735 A.2d 172 (Pa. Cmwlth. 1999).**

Plaintiff was accosted and injured by a city employee while working on city property. After suit by plaintiff against city, alleging that city was negligent in allowing a dangerous condition on its property—the city employee—summary judgment was granted in favor of city. Affirmed on the basis that a human employee is not a condition arising from the city's real property itself or from the care, custody or control of it. ***Tiedeman v. City of Philadelphia*, 732 A.2d 696 (Pa. Cmwlth. 1999).**

Plaintiff was injured when old bleachers on which she had been sitting collapsed. Summary judgment in favor of City granted based on determination by lower court that bleachers were personal property and not real estate and so did not fall under the real property exception to governmental immunity. Reversed on appeal because issue of whether bleachers were real or personal property was for jury. ***Blocker v. City of Philadelphia*, 729 A.2d 187 (Pa. Cmwlth. 1999).**

After slip and fall on accumulated ice and snow at airport, plaintiff sued City of Philadelphia which had control of area where accident occurred. Trial court granted summary judgment in favor of city on basis of lack of evidence to support claim under real property exception to Political Subdivision Tort Claims Act. Commonwealth Court affirmed in an unpublished decision and Supreme Court reversed holding that summary judgment was improper where there exists a genuine issue of material fact as to whether the city was negligent under the real property exception for a dangerous condition *on* the property. This case, as pointed out by Justice Castille and Chief Justice Flaherty in the dissent, arguably overrules *Finn v. City of Philadelphia*, 541 Pa. 596, 664 A.2d 1342 (1995) which required a showing of a dangerous condition *of* the real property. ***Kilgore v. City of Philadelphia*, 717 A.2d 514 (Pa. 1998).**

Plaintiff filed suit against multiple defendants, including volunteer fire company for injuries sustained after sale of alcohol to defendant. After review of legal and factual basis of fire company's status as local agency entitled to protection of Political Subdivision Tort Claims Act, court determined that illegal sale of alcohol on fire company property does not constitute "care, custody or control" standard related in *Grieff v. Reisinger*, 548 Pa. 13, 693 A.2d 195 (1997) and so immunity avail-

Municipal liability: Real estate

able and grant of summary judgment in favor of volunteer fire company affirmed. ***Eger v. Lynch,* 714 A.2d 1149 (Pa. Cmwlth. 1998).**

Plaintiff who was injured when he fell on defective or missing city-owned and maintained steps presented proof that city employees cleaned or shoveled damaged steps four or five times per year and that those employees were obligated to report defects or problems with steps. Plaintiff also offered credible evidence that there was a continuous deterioration of the steps from the date of the last repair more than one and one-half years before plaintiff's injury; therefore, city had actual or constructive notice of defective condition. City's defense of Political Subdivision Tort Claims Act was inadequate in light of plaintiff's evidence of defective condition of steps and notice to city. ***Ellis v. City of Pittsburgh,* 703 A.2d 593, (Pa. Cmwlth. 1997).**

Inmate filed suit against county correctional facility for injury to his head received when the "grab bar" in the prison shower broke free causing him to fall. Despite county's argument that the shower stall was only personal property, lack of evidence by county that shower stall was not a fixture and resulting presumption that it was in the nature of real property maintained by the county, precludes summary judgment under Political Subdivision Tort Claims Act. ***Davis v. Brennan,* 698 A.2d 1382 (Pa. Cmwlth. 1997).**

Summary judgment in favor of volunteer fire department denied based on Political Subdivision Tort Claims Act, where fire department chief's act of spreading paint thinner on the floor at fire department, which caught fire and injured visitor/plaintiff, constituted "care, custody or control of real property" and so provided an exception to immunity. ***Grieff v. Reisinger,* ___ Pa. ___, 693 A.2d 195 (1997).**

City's duty to inspect privately-owned property to insure compliance with health and safety regulations does not constitute "care, custody and control" or "possession" of real property so as to except City from immunity provided by Political Subdivision Tort Claims Act. Order sustaining preliminary objections reversed. ***City of Pittsburgh v. Stahlman,* ___ Pa. Cmwlth. ___, 677 A.2d 384 (1996).**

Minor child injured by what may have been a part of a goal post lying "on" city-owned park property. Summary judgment in favor of city reversed because city may have been negligent in care, custody and control of real property for failure to remove the dangerous condition "on" the property. Local agency liability for negligent care, custody or control of real property does not require the instrumentality causing the harm to be "of" the real estate in the sense of being affixed to it. ***Martin v. City of Philadelphia,* 696 A.2d 909 (Pa. Cmwlth. 1997).**

Pedestrian injured after stepping into hole created where tree trunk removed from township-owned park grounds may not recover against township which has immunity under both Political Subdivision Tort Claims Act and Recreation Use of Land and Water Act. Summary judgment for township affirmed. ***Wilkinson v. Conoy Township,* 677 A.2d 876 (Pa. Cmwlth. 1996).**

Municipal liability: Real estate

Administratrix of teenager who drowned in city-owned pond may not recover under Political Subdivision Tort Claims Act based on allegations of city's willful or malicious failure to warn of dangerous condition of pond. Recovery under Political Subdivision Tort Claims Acts is available only for acts of negligence. Public and private lands are covered by Recreation Use of Land and Water Act. Order refusing to grant judgment *n.o.v.* reversed. ***Lory v. City of Philadelphia*, 544 Pa. 38, 674 A.2d 673 (1996).**

County's failure to install nonslip tile in drying off area of county prison shower constituted improper design or inherent defect of the governmental real estate. Therefore, inmate may recover under real property exception to Political Subdivision Tort Claims Act for injuries sustained in fall. Order granting summary judgment in favor of defendant reversed. ***Bradley v. Franklin County Prison*, ___ Pa. Cmwlth. ___, 674 A.2d 363 (1996).**

Plaintiff severely burned by flash fire caused when paint thinner used to clean paint from floor of volunteer fire department ignited was precluded from recovering for injuries because volunteer fire company entitled to governmental immunity. Real property exception to governmental immunity does not apply unless cause of action based on condition of real property or an actual defect of the property itself. Negligent mishandling of combustible liquids on property does not invoke real property exception. Denial of volunteer fire company's motion for summary judgment reversed and remanded. ***Grieff v. Reisinger*, ___ Pa. Cmwlth. ___, 654 A.2d 77 (1995).**

In action by personal representative of plumbing contractor killed in cave-in at construction site, governmental immunity applies as plaintiff presented no proof that city exercised sufficient custody and control over site. Sanction order precluding city's filing of answer for failure to comply with discovery order does not compel waiver of real property exception to governmental immunity. Summary judgment in favor of city affirmed. ***Santori v. Snyder*, 165 Pa. Cmwlth. 505, 645 A.2d 443 (1994).**

Tenant slipped on bag covering greasy substance on stairway. Housing authority not liable. ***Walker v. Philadelphia Housing Authority*, 158 Pa. Cmwlth. 497, 631 A.2d 1117.**

Patron assaulted in parking lot operated by city. Held: Political Subdivision Tort Claims Act precludes liability of city for acts of third parties. ***Chevalier v. City of Philadelphia*, 516 Pa. 316, 532 A.2d 411.**

Patron assaulted in garage owned by parking authority. Held: parking authority as government agency immune from suit. ***Rhoads v. Lancaster Parking Authority*, 103 Pa. Cmwlth. 278, 520 A.2d 122.**

Plaintiff playing basketball in city-owned recreation center was injured when intruders entered building and assaulted him. Held: not within any exceptions to governmental immunity act (Political Subdivision Tort Claims Act). ***Johnson v. City of Philadelphia*, 93 Pa. Cmwlth. 87, 500 A.2d 520.**

Municipal liability: Schools and school districts

Stranded motorist drowned when swept into storm sewer. Settled before trial with adjacent landowner, township and PennDOT. Eventual jury verdict also included neighboring city from which it was proved that most of the water came. Held: under facts here City of Bethlehem not liable. Gradual orderly development resulting in incremental increase in rate of flow of surface waters through normal drainage swale does not give rise to liability. ***Laform v. Bethlehem Township,* 346 Pa. Super. 512, 499 A.2d 1373.**

Suit against SEPTA and City for injuries sustained by plaintiff in mugging which occurred in subway concourse. Held: complaint did state a cause of action against City as possessor of land and within exception to Political Subdivision Tort Claims Act. ***Johnson v. SEPTA,* 91 Pa. Cmwlth. 587, 498 A.2d 22.**

Broken water main—plaintiff must prove specific negligence—exclusive control not applicable—defendant's verdict affirmed by evenly divided court. ***Banet v. City of Philadelphia,* 226 Pa. Super. 452, 313 A.2d 253.**

Plaintiff, an employee of an independent contractor, injured by cave-in of a trench being dug for the laying of water pipe—plaintiff sued Authority defendant and several others—issue went off on the measure of control residing in Authority—court held such a matter of law as contract was clear and unambiguous—nonsuit entered—court below held employer a pure independent contractor and that Authority had no control over the manner in which contractor laid pipe—right of inspection not controlling—other defendants also held not responsible—action sustained on appeal. ***Giannetti v. Lower Bucks County Joint Municipal Authority et al.,* 439 Pa. 607, 266 A.2d 477.**

Municipal liability: Schools and school districts

Plaintiff filed suit against the school district after she was injured by a table in the school gymnasium. The court held that under the Tort Claims Act the school district was immune from liability. A free standing table was an item of personalty and therefore did not fall under the real property exception of the Tort Claims Act. ***Repko v. Chichester School District,* 904 A.2d 1036 (Pa. Cmwlth. 2006).**

Plaintiff was injured when struck by another student running through the hallway. The court affirmed that the charter school, which was established under the Charter School Law, was entitled to the same governmental immunity under the Political Subdivision Tort Claims Act as political subdivisions and local agencies. ***Warner v. Lawrence,* 900 A.2d 980 (Pa. Cmwlth. 2006).**

Plaintiff's hand was severely injured while attempting a "groove cut" in woodshop class on a table saw. The court affirmed judgment for the plaintiff under the real property exception to immunity under the Political Subdivision Tort Claims Act because the saw was real property under the definition used within the act. ***Wells v. Harrisburg Area School District,* 884 A.2d 946 (Pa. Cmwlth. 2005).**

Reversal of trial court decision to sustain school district's preliminary objections where pleadings indicated that plaintiff field service engineer was not in any

Municipal liability: Schools and school districts

better position than school district to see whether elevated catwalk was safe to walk on. ***Beaver v. Coatesville Area School District*, 845 A.2d 955 (Pa. Cmwlth. 2004).**

Minor injured when struck by a school bus sustained a permanent 4 millimeter scar on his right wrist. In suit against school bus owned and operated by school district, jury's determination that the scar, although permanent, was not disfiguring was proper and so kept case out of governmental immunity exception for injuries which cause permanent loss of a bodily function or permanent disfigurement. ***Alexander v. Benson*, 812 A.2d 785 (Pa. Cmwlth. 2002).**

Plaintiff student was injured when the pulleys on a scroll saw he had just cleaned in shop class caught and amputated a finger. The power to the saw had not been disconnected during the cleaning process. Because the saw was hardwired to the electrical system, bolted to the floor, it had not been moved since its installation in 1987 and there was no intent to remove it from the shop class it was part of the real estate of the school. Following evolving governmental immunity law, the real estate exception to immunity was properly applied. ***Cureton v. Philadelphia School District*, 798 A.2d 279 (Pa. Cmwlth. 2002).**

Plaintiff was severely burned when fellow students in advanced chemistry lab ignited ethyl alcohol. Plaintiff claimed the laboratory lacked adequate safety systems to prevent burns and that deficiency constituted a dangerous condition of the school district real estate, an exception to municipal immunity. Held that summary judgment entered in favor of school district and teacher was appropriate. Any negligence would have been in lack of supervision, not a dangerous condition of the real estate or a condition arising from the care, custody or control of the real estate itself. ***Tackett v. Pine Richland School District*, 793 A.2d 1022 (Pa. Cmwlth. 2002).**

Plaintiff was injured when she fell on interior school steps while participating in a relay race in hallways and stairwells at the direction of the field hockey coach. Grant of compulsory nonsuit affirmed on basis that coach's directions that children race in halls and on stairs was not evidence of actionable conduct under the real estate exception to governmental immunity. ***Wilson v. Norristown Area School District*, 783 S.2d 871 (Pa. Cmwlth. 2001).**

Plaintiff injured when the school bus she was alighting from as its operator was struck from behind by a minivan owned and operated by a school district. In suit against the minivan driver and the district, summary judgment was entered in favor of both defendants on the grounds that the plaintiff had failed to establish permanent loss of a bodily function as required by 42 Pa.C.S. § 8542(b)(1). Reversed on the determination that the question of permanent loss of bodily function is for the jury and therefore not grounds for summary judgment. ***Laich v. Bracey*, 776 A.2d 1022 (Pa. Cmwlth. 2001).**

A high school cheerleader was injured when she fell to the hardwood gymnasium floor during rehearsal and struck her face and jaw. Suit was brought, alleging that failure to have mats in place during the practice constituted a defective condition of the real estate and therefore an exception to governmental immunity. Held: failure to place mats which are personal property, does not fall within the real estate

Municipal liability: Schools and school districts

exception to governmental immunity following *Blocker v. City of Philadelphia,* 563 Pa. 559, 763 A.2d 373 (2000). **Rieger v. Altoona Area School District, 768 A.2d 912 (Pa. Cmwlth. 2001).**

Student injured by baseball hit by coach at high speed in poorly lit gymnasium was not barred by political subdivision immunity, if inadequate lighting—a condition of the gymnasium—was under the care, custody and control of the school district and the school district could have been held jointly liable. **Kevan v. Manesiotis, 728 A.2d 1006 (Pa. Cmwlth. 1999).**

Minor student injured when a small knife blade in classroom carpet became imbedded in his knee. Summary judgment affirmed based on failure of circumstances to fall within real property exception to Political Subdivision Tort Claims Act. Liability may not be imposed upon a governmental entity for injuries caused by its negligent failure to remove foreign substances from its real estate. **Wolfe v. Stroudsburg Area School District, 688 A.2d 1245 (Pa. Cmwlth. 1997).**

Parents of minor brought action against school district for injuries which resulted from minor being hit by school bus in authorized crossing zone. Failure to state common law or statutory cause of action against a political subdivision precludes recovery under the Political Subdivision Tort Claims Act. Order granting summary judgment affirmed. **Dunaway v. South Eastern School District, 676 A.2d 1281 (Pa. Cmwlth. 1996).**

Accumulation of water on school district property, which condition contributed to fall of high school student on crutches does not fall within real property exception to Political Subdivision Tort Claims Act. Order granting summary judgment for school district affirmed. **Leonard v. Fox Chapel Area School District, 674 A.2d 767 (Pa. Cmwlth. 1996).**

Order granting summary judgment in favor of school district affirmed where plaintiff who slipped on ice in school district parking lot failed to establish that injuries were caused by improper design, construction, deterioration, or inherent defect of real estate. Real property exception to Political Subdivision Tort Claims Act not applicable. **Metkus v. Pennsbury School District, 674 A.2d 355 (Pa. Cmwlth. 1996).**

Hills and ridges of ice on school district property are not dangerous condition of the property itself and, therefore, do not fall within real property exception to Political Subdivision Tort Claims Act. Order granting judgment on pleadings affirmed. **McRae for School District of Philadelphia, ___ Pa. Cmwlth. ___, 660 A.2d 209 (1995).**

For real property exception to apply against school district, dangerous condition must be of or attached to the pavement or property and not on the subject pavement or property. Rainwater on floor of school building did not constitute dangerous condition of or attached to property. Directed verdict for defendant affirmed. Dissent would apply exception based on school district's use of terrazzo floor tile that school district knew became dangerously slippery when wet. **Shedrick v. William Penn School District, ___ Pa. Cmwlth. ___, 654 A.2d 163 (1995).**

Municipal liability: Schools and school districts

Political Subdivision Tort Claims Act exception for dangerous condition of property does not extend to plaintiff who became trespasser when he climbed to roof of school building to retrieve tennis ball. School district took sufficient steps to prevent entry onto roof. Summary judgment in favor of school district affirmed. **Longbottom v. Sim-Kar Lighting Fixture Co.,** ___ **Pa. Cmwlth.** ___, **651 A.2d 621 (1994).**

Striking worker injured when he fell on snow-covered sidewalk while picketing. School district liable. **Giosa v. School District of Philadelphia, 157 Pa. Cmwlth. 489, 630 A.2d 511.**

Student injured on merry-go-round in school playground. District not immune. Question of permanent disfigurement for jury. **Norwin School District v. Cortazzo, 155 Pa. Cmwlth. 432, 625 A.2d 183.**

Child injured crossing highway at school bus stop. School district not liable for selecting stop location. **Combs v. Borough of Ellsworth, 151 Pa. Cmwlth. 21, 615 A.2d 462.**

Student injured while crossing street on way to school bus stop. School district not liable for negligently selecting location of bus stop. **Brelish v. Clarks Green Borough, 146 Pa. Cmwlth. 232, 604 A.2d 1235.**

Spectator at high school sporting event injured in fall on ice. Summary judgment for school district not appropriate. Doctrine of hills and ridges probably not applicable. **Mahoney Area School District v. Budwash, 146 Pa. Cmwlth. 72, 604 A.2d 1156.**

Student injured when he stepped into hole in field during lacrosse practice. Held: school district not immune under Recreation Use of Land and Water Act. **Seifirth v. Downingtown Area School District, 145 Pa. Cmwlth. 562, 604 A.2d 757.**

Patient injured by student nurse brought action against community college. College immune. **Community College of Allegheny County v. Seibert, 144 Pa. Cmwlth. 616, 601 A.2d 1348.**

High School student struck by vehicle while crossing state highway brought action against school district, township and Commonwealth. All defendants immune. **Stein v. Com., Dept. of Transp., 144 Pa. Cmwlth. 105, 601 A.2d 384.**

Failure of school district to install handicapped curb cuts may constitute a dangerous condition of sidewalks so as to fall within exceptions to governmental immunity. **Gilson v. Doe, 143 Pa. Cmwlth. 591, 600 A.2d 267.**

Child injured in bicycle accident at playground owned by borough and school district. Both defendants jointly liable. **Dimino v. Borough of Pottstown, 142 Pa. Cmwlth. 683, 598 A.2d 357.**

Spectator injured when struck by football during pregame activities. School district immune. **Johnson v. Woodland Hills School District, 135 Pa. Cmwlth. 43, 582 A.2d 395.**

Municipal liability: Schools and school districts

Student injured in fall during school-sponsored race. Held: real property exception to governmental immunity did not apply. Injury not caused by artificial condition or defect in land. *Faber v. Pennsbury School District,* **131 Pa. Cmwlth. 642, 571 A.2d 546.**

Student sexually assaulted by another student. School district immune from suit for actions of third party and for negligent supervision. *Cotter v. School District of Philadelphia,* **125 Pa. Cmwlth. 596, 562 A.2d 1029.**

Motorist killed in accident involving students driving between schools. School district not liable. Vehicle exception to governmental immunity did not apply. *Capuzzi v. Heller,* **125 Pa. Cmwlth. 678, 558 A.2d 596.**

Highschool wrestler was injured by door during running drill inside school. Held: plaintiff brought claim that fell within the real property exception to the Political Subdivision Tort Claims Act. *Gump v. Chartiers-Houston School District,* **125 Pa. Cmwlth. 596, 558 A.2d 589.**

Handicapped child paralyzed after falling on school sidewalk. Held: school authority immune. Action was based on negligent supervision and not defect in real property. *Houston v. Central Bucks School Authority,* **119 Pa. Cmwlth. 48, 546 A.2d 1286.**

Student injured while performing stunt in school gymnasium. Held: since complaint alleged negligence concerning care, custody and control of landing surface around vaulting horse, the real property exception to governmental immunity applies. *Singer v. School District of Philadelphia,* **99 Pa. Cmwlth. 553, 513 A.2d 1108.**

Child struck by baseball at high school baseball game. Owner of land immune under Recreation Use Act. School District may be liable under real property exception to the Tort Claims Act. *Lowman v. Indiana School District,* **96 Pa. Cmwlth. 389, 507 A.2d 1270.**

Plaintiff injured during cheerleading practice at school. Suit against school district dismissed by granting of order of summary judgment. School district immune where allegation was lack of supervision. *Messina v. Blairsville-Saltsburg School District,* **94 Pa. Cmwlth. 100, 503 A.2d 89.**

Student suffered injury sliding into second base during high school baseball game. Judgment on pleadings in favor of school district reversed. Issue remanded as to whether base was realty or personalty. *Beardell v. Western Wayne School District,* **91 Pa. Cmwlth. 348, 496 A.2d 1373.**

School district held not liable for injuries to person assaulted by unknown assailant on adjacent sidewalk and subsequent assault on school grounds. Under circumstances here, criminal acts not a foreseeable use of school property. *Joner v. Board of Education of Philadelphia,* **91 Pa. Cmwlth. 145, 496 A.2d 1288.**

Action against school district and hotel for drowning of student while on school trip in Virginia. Held: Pennsylvania law applied and school district im-

Municipal liability: Schools and school districts

mune from suit under facts here. ***Davis v. School District of Philadelphia*, 91 Pa. Cmwlth. 27, 496 A.2d 903.**

School simulating hostage crisis with blindfolded students. One student injured in fall. Held: suit barred by Political Subdivision Immunity Act. Not within one of its exceptions. ***Mooney v. North Penn School District*, 90 Pa. Cmwlth. 27, 493 A.2d 795.**

Injury to student in gym class while doing vault from springboard over vaulting horse. Suit against teacher and school district. Complaint dismissed. Teacher entitled to immunity and injury did not come within exception to immunity of local agencies. ***Brown v. Quaker Valley School*, 86 Pa. Super. 496, 486 A.2d 526.**

In action of trespass against school district for injury sustained by student at the hands of a fellow student, held that the provisions of Political Subdivision Tort Claims Act (42 Pa. C.S.A. §8541) operated to immunize school district from claims of an alleged failure on the part of the district to take adequate measures to protect the student's safety or to supervise the fellow students. ***Auerbach v. Council Rock School District*, 74 Pa. Cmwlth. 507, 459 A.2d 1376 (1983).**

Non-jury verdict of $83,190.00 to minor; $1,810 to parents. Minor plaintiff, 5th grade, 11 year old student, injured in school floor hockey game (organized extracurricular activity). Struck in mouth by hockey stick, severing five teeth. Held: negligent not to supply mouth guards. Requests were made, but denied by school board. Minor plaintiff unaware of any injuries in previous games. Held: presumption that he was incapable of contributory negligence not rebutted. ***Berman v. Philadelphia Board of Education*, 310 Pa. Super. 153, 456 A.2d 545.**

Nine-year old struck in head with bat while playing softball in school-yard. Not organized school activity. Alleged that improperly painted markings on ground required catcher to be too close to plate. School district said painting was for another game with no bat. Reversed, granting summary judgment in favor of school district. Jury issue. ***Bersani v. School District of Philadelphia*, 310 Pa. Super. 1, 456 A.2d 151.**

Fifth grade student struck in eye with pencil propelled by another student, who tripped or fell. Teacher outside room monitoring return of students. Non-jury verdict of $15,000 reversed. Momentary absence from room not negligent. Judgment reversed. ***Simonetti v. School District of Philadelphia*, 308 Pa. Super. 555, 454 A.2d 1038.**

Student stabbed to death by fellow student. Demurrer sustained—complaint dismissed. Activities constituting alleged negligence not a cause of action under Political Subdivision Tort Claims Act, and complaint failed to state cause of action under statute for deprivation of constitutional rights. ***Close v. Voorhees*, 67 Pa. Cmwlth. 205, 446 A.2d 728.**

Jury verdict, $95,000. 1970 accident—plaintiff, 11th grade high school student, cut hand on circular saw, amputating one finger and severely injuring another. Guard on saw had been removed by shop instructor. Verdict against principal and

Municipal liability: Schools and school districts

school district. Guard had been off for several months. Verdict affirmed. ***McKnight v. City of Philadelphia,* 299 Pa. Super. 327, 445 A.2d 778.**

Student struck in eye by pencil thrown by classmate—parents sued school district—statute allows recovery from political subdivisions only if death, permanent disfigurement or loss occurs, or medical expenses over $1500 are incurred. Parents contended statute did not give equal protection—allowing some to recover and others not—court held legislative classification was reasonable—no recovery. ***Robson v. Penn Hills School District,* 63 Pa. Cmwlth. 250, 437 A.2d 1273.**

Plaintiff injured in summer football practice. Trial court held that plaintiff assumed risk of injury. Reversed. Assumption of risk abolished except where specifically preserved by statute. ***Rutter v. Northeastern Beaver School District,* 496 Pa. 590, 437 A.2d 1198.**

Parent broke finger in door jamb while exiting with crowd of parents who normally came to pick up children. Jostled by workman in vestibule. School held negligent in controlling crowd. ***Swartley v. Tredyffrin Twp. School Dist.,* 287 Pa. Super. 499, 430 A.2d 1001.**

Minor plaintiff injured in art class when candle mold fell over spilling hot wax on his back. Jury verdict for defendants, school district and teacher. Lower court's grant of plaintiff's motion for judgment *n.o.v.* reversed but remanded for consideration of motion for new trial. ***Bottorf v. Waltz,* 245 Pa. Super. 139, 369 A.2d 332.**

Failure to properly supervise students on school grounds—preliminary objections overruled. ***Cromley v. Loyalsock Twp. School District,* 226 Pa. Super. 433, 310 A.2d 330.**

Minor plaintiff injured at school—arm caught in shredding machine at shop—sovereign immunity abolished as to local government units, municipal corporations and quasi-corporations—order sustaining preliminary objections reversed. ***Ayala v. Phila. Board of Education,* 453 Pa. 584, 305 A.2d 877.**

Minor plaintiff injured in physical education class—preliminary objections sustained in suit against school district—doctrine of sovereign immunity reaffirmed—strong dissenting opinion. ***Hill v. North Hills S.D.,* 223 Pa. Super. 254, 299 A.2d 350.**

Minor plaintiff injured while operating a machine in a vocational school—suit against school district—preliminary objections properly sustained—sovereign immunity—for Supreme Court or Legislature to change. ***Ayala v. Phila. Board of Education,* 223 Pa. Super. 171, 297 A.2d 495.**

School district provided premises for summer recreation program—made no charge—minor plaintiffs injured on premises—preliminary objections sustained—Held: governmental function—affirmed on appeal with strong dissent. ***Kitchen v. Wilkinsburg School District,* 222 Pa. Super. 479, 293 A.2d 84.**

Minor plaintiff injured in school gymnasium when another pupil tripped her and she fell into a rack of gymnasium equipment—plaintiff contended that school

Municipal liability: Sidewalks

was maintaining a nuisance as gymnasium was being repaired and that "pieces of wood," "nails" and other debris on floor—preliminary objections properly sustained—case not within "nuisance exception." ***Young v. Philadelphia School District,* 442 Pa. 638, 276 A.2d 301.**

School district and school authority invited public to view improvements of school property—falling accident on grounds of school—demurrer properly sustained in suit against both defendants as one involving a governmental function. ***Flinchbaugh v. Cornwall-Lebanon Suburban Joint School Authority,* 438 Pa. 407, 264 A.2d 708.**

Minor plaintiff attended school in defendant school district—set upon by a group of rowdy youths and severely injured—no recovery from school district—situation not a nuisance. ***Husser v. Pittsburgh School Dist.,* 425 Pa. 249, 228 A.2d 910.**

Suit against school district—court below sustained preliminary objections—action affirmed on appeal—up to Legislature to change rule of municipal immunity from tort liability if public policy demands it. ***Dillon v. York City S.D.,* 422 Pa. 103, 220 A.2d 896.**

Municipal liability: Sidewalks

Plaintiff sued defendant business owner and city after he slipped and fell on freshly fallen snow on a public sidewalk ramp adjoining the business owner's property. The trial court granted summary judgment. The Superior Court affirmed, holding that based upon the hills and ridges doctrine the plaintiff could not recover as the ice he slipped on was smooth and had not accumulated in hills and ridges. In addition, there was no evidence that the city had actual or constructive notice of the ramp's condition. ***Alexander v. City of Meadville,* 61 A.3d 218 (Pa. Super. 2012).**

Plaintiff brought a negligence claim against defendant city after suffering an injury on the sidewalk portion of a bridge. The trial court denied defendant's motion for summary judgment. The Commonwealth Court affirmed holding that ownership remains with a municipality where a designated roadway is located, because the legislature has not indicated any intent for the state to acquire an ownership interest in a roadway that is designated a state highway. ***Burke v. City of Bethlehem,* 10 A.3d 377 (Pa. Cmwlth. 2010).**

Plaintiff slipped and fell on the sidewalk outside of the defendant's police station. The court held that the city could be held liabile, because it had violated its own snow removal ordinance and had notice of the condition through the city custodian's testimony of his awareness of the snow accumulation. ***Reid v. City of Philadelphi*a, 904 A.2d 54 (Pa. Cmwlth. 2006).**

County was shielded by governmental immunity under Political Subdivision Tort Claims Act in suit by pedestrians struck by runaway vehicle on walking path adjacent to road where there was no intervening guard rail. ***Simko v. County of Allegheny,* 869 A.2d 571 (Pa. Cmwlth. 2005).**

Municipal liability: Sidewalks

City which owns sidewalk abutted by private owner and Commonwealth highway is liable for maintenance of sidewalk, regardless of dedication of the highway. Under the Political Subdivision Tort Claims Act, it is control of the sidewalk, not ownership that determines liability for maintenance and injuries. This case abrogates a substantial number of prior cases. ***Walker v. Eleby*, 842 A.2d 389 (Pa. 2004).**

Summary judgment affirmed against pedestrian whose complaint failed to allege that slip and fall on ice and snow on sidewalk "resulted from a condition of the sidewalk or derived from, originated from or had as its source, the sidewalk. Mere allegations of dangerous condition, causation, and damage are inadequate. ***Cohen v. City of Philadelphia*, 847 A.2d 778 (Pa. Cmwlth. 2004).**

Plaintiff filed suit against city alleging that injuries she sustained when she tripped on a curb-stop box located in the sidewalk located between a state highway and a privately-owned residence were caused by the city"s failure to maintain the curb-stop box. Summary judgment entered in favor of city because the offending box was not owned by the city as required under the utility service facilities exception to governmental immunity. The city did not own the sidewalk either and so the sidewalk exception to governmental immunity does not apply. ***Jackson v. City of Philadelphia*, 782 A.2d 1115 (Pa. Cmwlth. 2001).**

Plaintiff slipped and fell on sidewalk in front of city building that fronted on Commonwealth highway. City argued it was immune from liability under the sidewalk exception to the governmental immunity statute, because the sidewalk did not abut a city-owned street. After a very thorough review of the history of the sovereign and governmental immunity acts and cases, the court held that the city could be liable under the real estate exception to governmental immunity. ***Sherman v. City of Philadelphia*, 745 A.2d 95 (Pa. Cmwlth. 2000).**

Plaintiff who was injured after tripping and falling on sidewalk sued property owner and city. On proof of release to property owner who was primarily liable for care and maintenance of sidewalk, summary judgment for city granted under Political Subdivision Tort Claims Act which extinguishes liability of city on release of primarily liable landowner. ***Burns v. Crossman*, 740 A.2d 773 (Pa. Cmwlth. 1999).**

Plaintiff injured when she fell on ice and snow covered school district concrete landing received jury verdict. School district appealed claiming that place of fall was a sidewalk and so the "on or of" test applies. Commonwealth Court affirmed based on school district's failure to exercise proper care and control of real property. ***Snyder v. North Allegheny School District*, 722 A.2d 239 (Pa. Cmwlth. 1998).**

Plaintiff sued city for injuries sustained when she was caused to fall by defective condition of sidewalk that abutted state highway and city-owned property. Trial court granted city's summary judgment motion on grounds that city is immune from liability to suit for injuries sustained by plaintiff where defect is in sidewalk adjacent to state highway and not city street. Held: exception to governmental immunity for dangerous condition of sidewalk owned and maintained by city is unaffected by fact that sidewalk is adjacent to state highway and not city street. ***White v. City of Philadelphia*, 712 A.2d 345 (Pa. Cmwlth. 1998).**

Municipal liability: Sidewalks

Accumulation of ice and snow into ridges and hills on which plaintiff slipped, fell and was injured is not a dangerous condition of the sidewalk under sovereign immunity act and summary judgment in favor of Commonwealth sustained. The Court closely reviewed *Grieff v. Reisinger*, 548 Pa. 13, 693 A.2d 195 (1997) but remains bound by facts of this case and those in *Finn v. Philadelphia,* 541 Pa. 596, 664 A.2d 1342 (1995) as distinguished from those in *Grieff.* ***Abella v. City of Philadelphia,* 703 A.2d 547 (Pa. Cmwlth. 1997).**

Airport tarmac is not a sidewalk under sidewalk exception to Political Subdivision Tort Claims Act. Plaintiff's allegation that airport authority's failure to design safety standards for tarmac is not sufficient allegation of defective design or construction of real estate so as to fall within real estate exception to Political Subdivision Tort Claims Act. Order granting summary judgment affirmed. ***Bullard v. Lehigh-Northampton Airport Authority,* ___ Pa. Cmwlth. ___, 668 A.2d 223 (1995).**

Buildup of grease and oil on city-owned sidewalk is not a dangerous condition "of" the sidewalk; therefore, city is immune from liability under the Political Subdivision Tort Claims Act for injuries sustained by pedestrian who slipped and fell on sidewalk. ***Finn v. City of Philadelphia,* 541 Pa. 596, 664 A.2d 1342 (1995).**

For real property exception to governmental immunity to apply to municipality, sidewalk must be within right of way of a street owned by the municipality. Pedestrian who tripped on pipe projecting from sidewalk that was owned by municipality could not recover from municipality because underlying street right of way was owned by PennDOT. Because sidewalk was not realty for purposes of exception, pipe was not realty by reason of its connection to sidewalk. Summary judgment in favor of borough affirmed. ***Gray v. Logue,* ___ Pa. Cmwlth. ___, 654 A.2d 109 (1995).**

Sidewalk exception and real property exception to governmental immunity are to be read consistently. For real property exception to apply against school district, dangerous condition must be of or attached to the pavement or property and not on the subject pavement or property. Milk on sidewalk did not constitute dangerous condition of or attached to property. Jury verdict for defendant affirmed. ***DeLuca v. School District of Philadelphia,* ___ Pa. Cmwlth. ___, 654 A.2d 29 (1994).**

Municipality immune from liability to plaintiff who slipped and fell on grease on sidewalk. Verdict in favor of plaintiff reversed. ***Finn v. City of Philadelphia,* 165 Pa. Cmwlth. 255, 645 A.2d 320 (1994).**

Child injured in street by car after being forced to leave sidewalk due to city-placed barricade. City not liable under exception to Political Subdivision Tort Claims Act because injuries not caused by care, custody, or control of real property or dangerous condition of sidewalk. ***Kiley by Kiley v. City of Philadelphia,* 537 Pa. 502, 645 A.2d 184 (1994).**

Pedestrian injured after stepping in hole in sidewalk brought action against city. City neither primarily nor secondarily liable. ***Lyons v. City of Philadelphia,* ___ Pa. Cmwlth. ___, 632 A.2d 1006.**

Municipal liability: Streets and highways

Pedestrian who fell on sidewalk brought action against city for failure to maintain and repair. City subject to suit even though secondarily liable. ***Restifo v. City of Philadelphia,*** **151 Pa. Cmwlth. 27, 617 A.2d 818.**

Pedestrian injured from slip and fall on sidewalk. City immune. Sidewalk not within right-of-way of city owned street. ***Bruce v. Gadson,*** **127 Pa. Cmwlth. 162, 561 A.2d 75.**

Pedestrian fell into tree well on sidewalk outside stadium. Dark and raining. Non-jury verdict in favor of plaintiff with one-third comparative negligence. Held: plaintiff needed no expert as to proper design of tree well or sidewalk. ***Burns v. City of Philadelphia,*** **350 Pa. Super. 615, 504 A.2d 1321.**

Fall on sidewalk. Suit against property owners. Property owners sought to join city. Joinder disallowed as liability of city only secondary to property owners abutting public sidewalk. ***Graham v. Roberts,*** **254 Pa. Super. 589, 386 A.2d 610.**

Pedestrian struck by car while walking in street with no sidewalks. Embankment prohibited walking off roadway. Theory against township was design defect especially in light of increased usage since construction. Verdict against driver. ***Drew v. Laber,*** **477 Pa. 297, 383 A.2d 941.**

Municipal liability: Streets and highways

Motorist brought lawsuit against the City of Philadelphia and Pennsylvania Department of Transportation after he lost control of his vehicle while driving on a city street due to black ice caused by melt and refreeze from the highway. The trial court granted summary judgment in favor of both Defendants. The Commonwealth Court affirmed holding that the State Highway law did not impose a statutory duty on the Department of Transportation (DOT) to protect an individual from accumulations of snow and ice on the roads. In addition, the Court held that the natural formation of ice following DOT's treatment of the roadways with chemicals does not create an artificial condition waiving sovereign immunity. Finally, the Court held that the city was immune pursuant to the Political Subdivision Tort Claims Act as the Plaintiff failed to establish the black ice was the result of improper construction, design, deterioration or inherent defect of the street itself. ***Page v. City of Philadelphia,*** **1542 C.D. 2010 (Pa. Cmwlth. 2011).**

Motorist's estate brought a claim for negligent design against Pennsylvania Turnpike Commission after the decedent's vehicle hydroplaned on the roadway and crashed. The trial court granted summary judgment in favor of the Defendant. The Commonwealth Court affirmed holding that the Commonwealth was immune from suit where the guardrail folds back and impales a vehicle based upon the Sovereign Immunity Act. ***Stein v. Pennsylvania Turnpike Commission,*** **989 A.2d 80 (Pa. Cmwlth. 2010).**

Pedestrian brought suit against the city and Commonwealth after tripping on an uneven portion of road. Trial Court dismissed the Complaint on the basis of the sovereign immunity act. The Commonwealth Court reversed. The Pennsylvania Supreme Court on a matter of first impression held that a Complaint naming the Commonwealth as a Defendant in the case caption, but identifying a Common-

Municipal liability: Streets and highways

wealth agency as a party throughout could be amended by the Plaintiff despite the statute of limitation having run. ***Piehl v. City of Philadelphia*, 987 A.2d 146 (Pa. 2009).**

Pedestrian injured in a trip and fall due to street resurfacing brought negligence action against the city. The trial court found for the Plaintiff. The Superior Court reversed, holding that the city was not the owner of the street as it was designated a state highway and also that the Plaintiff had failed to prove a contractual relationship between the city and Commonwealth to maintain the road, which was required for the street exception to the Political Subdivision Tort Claims Act to be applied to the city. ***Leiphart v. City of Philadelphia*, 972 A.2d 1239 (Pa. Cmwlth. 2009).**

Plaintiffs injured in motor vehicle accident at dangerous intersection filed suit against municipality which had responsibility for entire intersection. Plaintiffs' expert testimony about condition of intersection, appropriate remedy for dangerous condition and ability to erect control devices was adequate to preclude summary judgment for municipality. ***Wenger v. West Pennsboro Township*, 868 A.2d 638 (Pa. Cmwlth. 2005).**

Uncovered drainage hole located within public right of way but outside paved street is not part of highway for purposes of highway exception to governmental immunity provision of Political Subdivision Tort Claims Act. Fact that drainage hole was located in public right of way that was in possession of abutting landowner means that municipality did not have possession and so real estate exception is not applicable to provide injured plaintiff with relief. ***Gramlich v. Lower Southampton Township*, 838 A.2d 843 (Pa. Cmwlth. 2003).**

Plaintiff was injured when she tripped on a box under a table located in a blocked-off street during a fire department street fair. Grant of summary judgment in favor of fire department due to lack of exception to governmental immunity under Political Subdivision Tort Claims Act affirmed. Care, custody and control of real estate exception to governmental immunity does not apply to streets. ***Granchi v. Borough of North Braddock*, 810 A.2d 747 (Pa. Cmwlth. 2002).**

Directed verdict against automobile passenger who sued City of Pittsburgh affirmed on basis of municipal immunity from suit under Political Subdivision Tort Claims Act. Trial court determination that "wedge curb" next to street, which was not a part of the traveled portion of the city street, was not a portion of the street included in the streets exception to the act. ***Smith v. Manson*, 806 A.2d 518 (Pa. Cmwlth. 2002).**

Plaintiff's decedent was killed when struck by an automobile while crossing a street at a crossing where the lines on the road delineating the cross-walk were faded and neither the bus stop to which he was walking nor the street was illuminated. Held: inadequate crossing area identification and lighting fell within the Trees, Traffic and Street Lighting exception to governmental immunity found at 42 Pa.C.S. § 8542(b)(4). ***Glenn v. Horan*, 765 A.2d 426 (Pa. Cmwlth. 2000).**

Municipal liability: Streets and highways

City's failure to install guard rail along curved section of street with drop-off is not dangerous condition of municipal street and, therefore, not actionable under streets exception to Political Subdivision Tort Claims Act. ***Lockwood v. City of Pittsburgh***, 751 A.2d 1136 (Pa. 2000).

Plaintiff was injured when she slipped on ice on public street and fell while going towards church. Summary judgment for church granted and affirmed on appeal because church was not "possessor" of street on which plaintiff fell. Summary judgment for municipality affirmed on basis that snow and ice on street was not a condition "of" the street and therefore action fell outside of streets exception to governmental immunity. ***Walinsky v. St. Nicholas Ukranian Catholic Church***, 740 A.2d 318 (Pa. Cmwlth. 1999).

Plaintiff's decedent was killed when his truck struck a tree that had fallen across the road. After verdict for plaintiff, municipality appealed claiming that it was entitled to governmental immunity because the tree "on" the road was not a condition "of" the road. Commonwealth Court reversed on that basis following *Finn v. City of Philadelphia*, 541 Pa. 596, 664 A.2d 1342 (1995). ***Osborne v. Cambridge Township***, 736 A.2d 715 (Pa. Cmwlth. 1999).

Plaintiff was injured when car he was driving fell into 8"–12" ditch in road that resulted from settlement of fill deposited by local authority which had created hole. Plaintiff appeals from trial judge's decision to give instruction to jury which left question of whether local authority had actual or constructive notice of fill settling to jury. Plaintiff argued that because local authority created hole and installed fill that settled and caused dangerous condition, it had notice of condition as a matter of law. Instruction approved by Commonwealth Court which held that just because defendant created hole and installed fill that eventually resulted in dangerous condition does not mean that plaintiff is not required to show that defendant knew or should have known of the condition. ***Miller v. Lykens Borough Authority***, 712 A.2d 800 (Pa. Cmwlth. 1998).

PennDOT had never been requested to approve such a sign by township despite repeated township inquiries concerning available ways to make the intersection safer. Commonwealth Court affirmed denial of township's post trial motion on basis of township's affirmative duty to make its roads safe for intended users pursuant to *McCalla v. Mura*, 538 Pa. 527, 649 A.2d 646 (1994) and *Bendas v. Township of White Deer*, 531 Pa. 180, 611 A.2d 1184 (1992). Trial court order denying plaintiff's post trial motion to allow increase in delay damages affirmed when plaintiff's consent to stay of delay damage period, and plaintiff's own delay, were factors which increased delay. ***Starr v. Veneziano***, 705 A.2d 950 (Pa. Cmwlth. 1998).

Plaintiff's expert's report that state highway was defective in design, irrespective of plaintiff's claims of natural accumulations of ice and snow, creates factual question for jury relating to care and maintenance of PennDOT's real property and so precludes summary judgment in favor of PennDOT based on Sovereign Immunity Act. ***Smith v. Com., Dept. of Transp.***, 700 A.2d 587 (Pa. Cmwlth. 1997).

County has duty to make highway reasonably safe for its intended purpose. In case for injuries arising out of automobile accident, question as to whether dan-

Municipal liability: Streets and highways

gerous condition existed on highway is for jury. ***McCalla v. Mura*, 538 Pa. 527, 649 A.2d 646 (1994).**

Driver and passenger injured in accident caused by streetcar tracks. City liable. Evidence of prior accident and subsequent repairs admissible. ***Fernandez v. City of Pittsburgh*, 164 Pa. Cmwlth. 622, 643 A.2d 1176.**

Operator injured when trolly derailed brought action against city for negligent maintenance of road bed. City not liable. ***Smick v. City of Philadelphia*, 161 Pa. Cmwlth. 622, 638 A.2d 287.**

Pedestrian struck by vehicle along state road. Action brought against city for installing inadequate and misleading traffic control markings. City immune. ***Kennedy v. City of Philadelphia*, 160 Pa. Cmwlth. 558, 635 A.2d 1105.**

Child struck by vehicle while crossing state highway after leaving city park. Held: city had no duty to regulate vehicular or pedestrian traffic. ***Hough v. Com., Dept. of Transp.*, 155 Pa. Cmwlth. 162, 624 A.2d 780.**

Motorcyclist injured in collision at intersection brought action against county. County not liable. Roads designated state highways. ***Verna by Verna v. Commonwealth*, 149 Pa. Cmwlth. 449, 613 A.2d 174.**

Pedestrian tripped over pothole in state road brought action against city based on home rule charter. City not liable. ***Phillips v. City of Philadelphia*, 148 Pa. Cmwlth. 175, 610 A.2d 509.**

Pedestrian killed while crossing highway between two townships. Action brought against both townships, PennDOT, and driver. All government parties immune. ***Sloneker v. Martin*, 144 Pa. Cmwlth. 190, 604 A.2d 751.**

High School student struck by vehicle while crossing state highway brought action against school district, township, and Commonwealth. All defendants immune. ***Stein v. Com., Dept. of Transp.*, 144 Pa. Cmwlth. 105, 601 A.2d 384.**

Motorist injured in accident at intersection brought action against township and PennDOT for allowing a dangerous condition to exist. Township not liable. Motorist 51% negligent and Commonwealth 49% negligent. ***Wright v. Com., Dept. of Transp.*, 142 Pa. Cmwlth. 91, 596 A.2d 1241.**

Motorist injured when struck by vehicle traveling wrong direction on one way street brought action against city for negligent design of intersection. City not liable. Accident caused by other driver. ***Burton v. Terry*, 140 Pa. Cmwlth. 336, 592 A.2d 1380.**

Pedestrian injured in fall on roadbed of street railway located on state highway brought action against city, transportation authority, and PennDOT. City found primarily liable, authority secondarily liable, and department not liable. ***Yackobovitz v. SEPTA*, 139 Pa. Cmwlth. 157, 590 A.2d 40.**

Passenger in vehicle operated by intoxicated driver brought action against driver and city for injuries caused by vehicle striking head wall along highway. City

Municipal liability: Streets and highways

not liable. Driver 75% liable, passenger 25% liable. ***Hannon v. City of Philadelphia,* 138 Pa. Cmwlth. 166, 587 A.2d 845.**

City immune from suit for failure to correct dangerous condition of highway since actual or constructive notice of condition not shown. ***Fenton v. City of Philadelphia,* 127 Pa. Cmwlth. 466, 561 A.2d 1334.**

Pedestrian tripped and fell on ice and snow on city street. City not liable. Ice and snow are natural conditions even if shoveled onto street. ***Vitelli v. City of Chester,* 119 Pa. Cmwlth. 58, 545 A.2d 1011.**

Plaintiff drove car over curb, across sidewalk, over six-inch retaining wall, through cyclone fence and into creek in which he drowned. Held: City of Chester had no duty to maintain a fence of such strength to withstand impact of car going in excess of 25 m.p.h. Events here so extraordinary as to be legally unforeseeable. City obligated to maintain streets to be reasonably safe for normal use. ***Merritt v. City of Chester,* 344 Pa. Super. 505, 496 A.2d 1220.**

Plaintiff injured when vehicle in which he was a passenger skidded on icy overpass. Commonwealth has exclusive jurisdiction over control and maintenance of state highways. Township through which highway passes has not duty even to warn of known dangers. Dismissal of Newtown Twp. affirmed. ***Haas v. Commonwealth,* 84 Pa. Cmwlth. 522, 479 A.2d 100.**

Auto accident allegedly caused by ice on state highway—was a recurring problem caused by runoff from abutting private property. Passenger in car injured. Summary judgment as to borough affirmed. Borough not secondarily liable for repairs. Duty to warn not raised below, therefore, cannot be considered on appeal. Affirmed. ***Janosko v. Pittsburgh Nat'l Corp.,* 83 Pa. 636, 478 A.2d 160.**

Multi-vehicle fatal accident at allegedly dangerous intersection on state highway. Trial judge directed verdict for PennDOT, reversed. Where a dangerous condition was developed and individuals are injured as a result, PennDOT cannot plead its discretion as absolute defense of liability. ***Wyke v. Ward,* 81 Pa. Cmwlth. 392, 474 A.2d 375.**

Single vehicle accident. Alleged negligent design of highway. Held: township cannot be held liable for negligent design or construction of a highway which has been adopted as a state highway. ***Swank v. Bensalem Twp.,* 504 Pa. 291, 472 A.2d 1065.**

Suit against Commonwealth and certain officials. Vehicle went through missing portion of guardrail, striking plaintiff's taxi head-on, killing plaintiff. Jury verdict $17,354 (survival); $625,021 (wrongful death). Guardrail missing for extended period of time. Qualified immunity given to certain state officials. Department supervisor for Philadelphia County and his assistant held accountable. ***Pine v. Synkonis,* 79 Pa. Cmwlth. 479, 470 A.2d 1074.**

Pedestrian struck by car while walking in street with no sidewalks. Embankment prohibited walking off roadway. Theory against township was design defect

Municipal liability: Structures

especially in light of increased usage since construction. Verdict against driver. *Drew v. Laber,* **477 Pa. 297, 383 A.2d 941.**

Branch of tree extended into cartway and injured an occupant of a passing van—suit against municipality and property owners—verdict against both sustained on appeal—property owner not primarily responsible—joint obligation of both defendants. *Green v. Freeport Borough,* **218 Pa. Super. 334, 280 A.2d 412.**

Pedestrian fell allegedly as the result of the existence of a hole in cartway 36 inches long, 2 feet wide and 4 or 5 inches in depth—at night—photograph of hole disclosed a ruler inserted showing only 1-1/2 inches in depth—case still for jury. *Teagle v. Philadelphia,* **430 Pa. 395, 243 A.2d 342.**

Plaintiff, driver of an automobile, allegedly lost control of car by reason of a hole in cartway the size of a manhole and 4 inches deep—filled with water—case for jury—not necessary that every fact points unerringly to liability. *Fringer v. West York Borough,* **421 Pa. 579, 220 A.2d 849.**

Municipal liability: Structures

Immense coke oven door installed 35 years prior to accident which caused plaintiff's decedent's death and which is movable by means of wheels on tracks is still an "improvement" under statute of repose and so action by coke oven employee is extinguished. Trial court order denying motion for judgment *n.o.v.* reversed. *Vargo v. Koppers Co., Inc.,* **452 Pa. Super. 275, 681 A.2d 815 (1996).**

Because bleachers constituted a defective improvement to the land, Recreation Use of Land and Water Act did not bar spectator's claim against Township for injuries sustained in fall from bleachers at Township ball field. Order granting summary judgment reversed. *Brown v. Tunkhannock Township,* **___ Pa. Cmwlth. ___, 665 A.2d 1318 (1995).**

Inmate who ran down hallway and jumped steps, hitting his head on ceiling, failed to establish that dangerous condition existed in ceiling above steps in hallway. Duty of care to inmate is that of owner to invitee. Compulsory nonsuit granted in favor of County affirmed. *Graf v. County of Northampton,* **___ Pa. Cmwlth. ___, 654 A.2d 131 (1995).**

Child of tenant injured when companion closed fire door on hand. Plaintiff claimed door was faulty. Held: action of companion acted as superseding cause. *Bayard v. Philadelphia Housing Authority,* **157 Pa. Cmwlth. 269, 629 A.2d 283.**

Municipal liability: Traffic control

Suit by pedestrian against city and PennDOT for injuries sustained when she tripped on the raised "header" portion of a crosswalk on a city street that had been adopted by PennDOT as a state highway. Held that city-maintained crosswalk was a traffic-control device and so city was liable for negligent maintenance. *Ryals v. City of Philadelphia,* **848 A.2d 1101 (Pa. Cmwlth. 2004).**

Plaintiff injured when a northbound truck struck her as she tried to cross two northbound lanes of traffic to head south. Plaintiff sued PennDOT, alleg-

Municipal liability: Traffic control

ing the north-south roadway was negligently designed and maintained. PennDOT joined the municipality, alleging it was negligent for failing to install a traffic control device at the intersection. Appeal by municipality only after judgment against PennDOT and municipality. Held: because plaintiff did not provide sufficiently relevant and extensive expert testimony that signs or signals would have met the needs of the intersection and the greater traffic needs, and there was no proof that the municipality could have, without PennDOT approval, erected signs restricting access to a state road, plaintiff could not prove negligence of municipality. *Starr v. Veneziano*, 747 A.2d 867 (Pa. 2000).

Pedestrian who was injured by nylon rope strung between trees and signposts by police was entitled to bring action against city as the rope was a "traffic control device" under exceptions to governmental immunity. *Pettineio v. City of Philadelphia*, 721 A.2d 65 (Pa. Cmwlth. 1998).

Bicyclist alleged injuries as a result of being grabbed by police officer who was directing traffic on street where riding bicycles was expressly prohibited. Bicyclist waived argument that governmental immunity defense did not exist under waiver provision of Philadelphia Code. Waiver provision of Philadelphia Code was invalidated as of the date of enactment of governmental immunity provisions of the Judicial Code. Police officer directing traffic is not a traffic control and therefore his acts do not fall within the traffic control exception to governmental immunity. Order granting summary judgment affirmed. *Robinson v. City of Philadelphia*, ___ Pa. Cmwlth. ___, 666 A.2d 1141 (1995).

County has duty to make highway reasonably safe for its intended purpose. In case of injuries arising out of automobile accident, question as to whether dangerous condition existed on highway is for jury. *McCalla v. Mura*, 538 Pa. 527, 649 A.2d 646 (1994).

Pedestrian struck by vehicle along state road. Action brought against city for installing inadequate and misleading traffic control markings. City immune. *Kennedy v. City of Philadelphia*, 160 Pa. Cmwlth. 558, 635 A.2d 1105.

Motorist injured in accident caused by malfunctioning traffic signal received jury award in excess of statutory maximum. Held: township did not waive cap by purchasing liability insurance. *Spisak v. Downey*, 152 Pa. Cmwlth. 220, 618 A.2d 1174.

Minor passenger killed in automobile accident caused by drunk driver. Improperly placed traffic sign contributed to accident. City jointly liable because of negligently placed sign. *Crowell v. City of Philadelphia*, 531 Pa. 400, 613 A.2d 1178.

Passengers in vehicle driven by diabetic injured when driver lost consciousness. Held: Commonwealth and city not liable for failure to install warning and speed limit signs. Driver's loss of consciousness superseding cause. *Chacho v. Com., Dept. of Transp.*, 148 Pa. Cmwlth. 494, 611 A.2d 1346.

Motorists injured in collision at intersection brought action against township and Commonwealth for failure to install traffic control device. Denial of defendants'

Municipal liability: Traffic control

motion for summary judgment upheld. ***Bendas v. Township of White Deer*, 531 Pa. 180, 611 A.2d 1184.**

Student struck by automobile while crossing state highway on way to school brought action against Commonwealth, school district and township for failure to provide crosswalks and traffic control devices. All defendants immune. ***Majestic v. Com., Dept. of Transp.*, 144 Pa. Cmwlth. 109, 601 A.2d 386.**

Motorist injured in collision at intersection caused by faulty traffic signal. Township and company that maintained signal liable. ***United States Fidelity & Guaranty Company v. Royer*, 143 Pa. Cmwlth. 31, 598 A.2d 583.**

Pedestrian struck by vehicle while crossing street. View of traffic was blocked by parked truck. Held: PennDOT and city not liable for negligent design and maintenance of traffic signals. ***Hillerman v. Com., Dept. of Transp.*, 141 Pa. Cmwlth. 14, 595 A.2d 204.**

Motorcyclist injured in collision at intersection brought action against Commonwealth, township, and roadmaster for failure to replace stop sign and to remove vegetation from roadside. Summary judgment for defendants affirmed. ***Bruce v. Com., Dept. of Transp.*, 138 Pa. Cmwlth. 352, 588 A.2d 974.**

Motorist injured in accident on state highway brought action against city and PennDOT for failure to erect sign warning of curve. City immune. No duty to erect sign even though highway within city limits. ***Carter v. City of Philadelphia*, 137 Pa. Cmwlth. 152, 585 A.2d 578.**

Driver and passenger injured in collision with other vehicle brought action against city for installation of incorrect traffic sign. City not liable. Other driver direct cause of injuries. ***Crowell v. City of Philadelphia*, 131 Pa. Cmwlth. 418, 570 A.2d 626.**

Pedestrian killed by trolley while crossing State highway. City found not liable for failure to provide safety or traffic control devices. ***Jackson v. SEPTA*, 129 Pa. Cmwlth. 596, 566 A.2d 638.**

Fatal injury to student struck by car after alighting from school bus. Held: school district immune from suit. Stopped school bus with flashing lights not a traffic control as defined by governmental immunity statute. ***Aberant v. Wilkes-Barre Area School Area School District*, 89 Pa. Cmwlth. 516, 492 A.2d 1186.**

Jury verdict with 50% contributory negligence. Verdict $89,000 reduced by half. Plaintiff rendered paraplegic at age 21 when his motorcycle collided with another vehicle at T-intersection. Stop sign missing for plaintiff's direction of travel. Speed limit 25 mph. Plaintiff's own expert and other witnesses put plaintiff at higher rate of speed. Grant of unrestricted new trial affirmed. Within proper discretion of lower under facts here to hold verdict contrary to weight of evidence. Speed of motorcycle estimated to be 50–60 mph. ***Buck v. Scott Twp.*, 325 Pa. Super. 148, 472 A.2d 691.**

Jury verdict $500,000 ($400,000 survival; $100,000 wrongful death). Death of middle-aged male killed when truck crashed through guard rail on top of his ve-

Municipal liability: Utility service facilities

hicle. City and Commonwealth held negligent for confusing signs on expressway and exit. ***Thompson v. City of Philadelphia,* 320 Pa. Super. 124, 466 A.2d 1349.**

Traffic signal malfunction caused light to be green for both streets at intersection. Jury found improper maintenance. Verdict against Borough and Traffic Control. ***Embrey v. Borough of West Mifflin,* 257 Pa. Super. 168, 390 A.2d 765.**

Municipal liability: Utility service facilities

Plaintiff filed a contract action against the municipal water authority for failing to shut off water to their property resulting in damages to the property after the pipes froze and burst. The court held that plaintiff's claim sounded in tort and that a municipal water authority had immunity under the Pennsylvania's Tort Claims Act. ***Matarazzo v. Millers Mutual Group, Inc.*, 927 A.2d 689 (Pa. Cmwlth. 2007).**

Department of Transportation sued the Borough of West View for damages caused to a state highway by the Borough's water main breaking. The court held that the Tort Claims Act did not provide a defense to liability for the Borough, since it was contractually obligated to repair the damages to the highway as a condition of its occupancy of the right-of-way. ***Commonwealth v. Municipal Authority of the Borough of West View*, 919 A.2d 343 (Pa. Cmwlth. 2007).**

Plaintiff filed suit against Latrobe Municipal Authority for breach of a statutory duty when plaintiff struck and damaged an underground sewer, which Latrobe failed to notify it about. The court upheld dismissal of the case because the plaintiff failed to allege a dangerous condition of the utility system required under the Political Subdivision Tort Claims Act to allow municipal liability. ***Le Nature's, Inc. v. Latrobe Municipal Authority*, 913 A.2d 988 (Pa. Cmwlth. 2006).**

Absent proof that a particular trenching effort presented a peculiar risk or danger, an employer, in this case a municipal sewer authority, will not be held vicariously liable for the negligent conduct of its contractors. ***Dunkle v. Middleburg Municipal Authority*, 842 A.2d 477 (Pa. Cmwlth. 2004).**

Plaintiff filed suit against city alleging that injuries she sustained when she tripped on a curb-stop box located in the sidewalk located between a state highway and a privately-owned residence were caused by the city"s failure to maintain the curb-stop box. Summary judgment entered in favor of city because the offending box was not owned by the city as required under the utility service facilities exception to governmental immunity. The city did not own the sidewalk either and so the sidewalk exception to governmental immunity does not apply. ***Jackson v. City of Philadelphia*, 782 A.2d 1115 (Pa. Cmwlth. 2001).**

Plaintiff was injured when he tripped on a pile of dirt left on Commonwealth owned street by a water line repair contractor. In suit against city and others, court held that nonsuit in favor of city was proper. Plaintiff failed to prove that utility exception to municipal immunity was applicable as water line break was on private property, not city property, and real estate exception to immunity did not apply as plaintiff failed to prove that city had contractual obligation to Commonwealth to maintain Commonwealth owned street. ***Leone v. Commonwealth Department of Transportaion*, 780 A.2d 754 (Pa. Cmwlth. 2001).**

Municipal liability: Volunteer ambulance company

Plaintiff recovered from city water authority after establishing that city's water meter located in plaintiff's residence was defective when it broke and flooded plaintiff's basement. Held: broken water meter was a dangerous condition of a utility service facility under the Political Subdivision Tort Claims Act and that it was located on a "right of way" owned by the city, even though it was in plaintiff's residence. *Primiano v. City of Philadelphia*, **739 A.2d 1172 (Pa. Cmwlth. 1999).**

Municipal liability: Volunteer ambulance company

Supreme court vacates Commonwealth Court decision that a volunteer ambulance service is not entitled to protection of Political Tort Claims Act and remands to trial court for evidence that ambulance service is local agency such as creation of the service by a political subdivision, municipal control of the service, benefits to the municipality, non-profit status and employee participation in municipal pension and benefit plans. ***Christy v. Cranberry Volunteer Ambulance Corps, Inc.* 856 A.2d 43, 2004 WL 1822336 (Pa. 2004).**

Murder

Tenant in apartment complex murdered by maintenance worker. Held: management company that originally hired worker not liable for wrongful death. ***Pittsburgh National Bank v. Perr*, 431 Pa. Super. 580, 637 A.2d 334.**

---N---

Nail

Evidence that plaintiff workman was injured by slipping on nail or screw in floor of a moving van owned by defendant—finding for defendant by court sitting without jury—affirmed on appeal. ***Schofield v. Crossman*, 420 Pa. 196, 216 A.2d 455.**

National Traffic and Motor Vehicle Safety Act

Following in-depth analysis of federal preemption law, Superior Court held that state common law causes of action are expressly not preempted by the National Traffic and Motor Vehicle Safety Act. Therefore, motorist may raise claim at trial that airbag that contributed to his injuries in head-on collision with another vehicle was defective, because Congress intended such issues to go to the jury. Order denying manufacturer's preliminary objections affirmed. ***Heiple v. C.R. Motors, Inc.*, 446 Pa. Super. 310, 666 A.2d 1066 (1995).**

Neck surgery

Plaintiff claimed medical negligence resulting in injury from selection of local rather than general anesthesia in an operation to remove a schwannoma growth around one of the nerves in his neck. After instruction by trial court that a physician may follow either of two recognized schools of thought, the jury returned a verdict for the defendant. Affirmed by Superior Court. Supreme Court granted allocatur and held that evidence of two schools of thought may be adduced by oral testimony alone and that documentary evidence of existence of second school of thought is not necessary. ***Gala v. Hamilton*, 715 A.2d 1108 (1998).**

Negligence *per se*

Plaintiff driver filed suit after the Defendant driver swerved into the Plaintiff's lane as the Plaintiff was passing the Defendant on the left. The trial court denied instructions on the sudden emergency doctrine and negligence per se. The Superior Court, on appeal, held that evidence that the Motor Vehicle Code was violated supported a negligence per se jury instruction at trial. ***Drew v. Work*, 2014 Pa. Super. 137 (Pa. Super. 2014).**

Plaintiff brought suit against Defendant police officer after he was struck making a left turn at an intersection by the Defendant. The officer was responding to a disturbance call and exceeding the speed limit but was not using his lights or siren. The jury found in favor of the Defendant. The Commonwealth Court reversed holding that the trial court had erred in failing to provide a negligence per se instruction as the officer was responding to a non-emergency call and had been exceeding the posted speed limit without emergency lights or a siren. ***Sodders v. Fry*, 32 A.3d 882 (Pa. Cmwlth. 2011).**

Driver brought personal injury action for a motor vehicle accident against the Defendant driver after the Defendant's vehicle crossed the center line. A jury found in favor of the Plaintiff. The Commonwealth Court held that the fact that there was evidence that the Defendant lost control as a result of ice on the road

Negligence per se

prevented the Plaintiff from establishing that the Defendant was negligent per se. ***Behney v. Bolich*, 986 A.2d 944 (Pa. Cmwlth. 2009)**.

Driver struck and injured by a police officer driving the wrong way down a one-way road while in pursuit of a suspect brought a claim of negligence against the officer. The trial court entered a directed verdict in favor of the Plaintiff, granting a new trial on the issue of contributory negligence. The Superior Court affirmed, holding that the Defendant had failed to meet its burden at trial that it qualified for special privileges to disregard the speed and directional mandates of the vehicle code and therefore the Defendant was negligent per se for violating these statutes. ***Lahr v. City of York*, 972 A.2d 41 (Pa. Super. 2009)**.

Plaintiff was injured when a truck driven by the defendant struck her while she was crossing the street within a crosswalk. The appellate court held that it was error for the trial court not to include a jury instruction on negligence per se, since evidence had been presented that the plaintiff had been struck while in a crosswalk. ***Jenkins v. Wolf*, 911 A.2d 568 (Pa. Super. 2006)**.

Plaintiff rescue worker was struck and injured by a second driver who fell asleep at the wheel and struck plaintiff as he attended to an earlier hit and run accident. Plaintiff filed suit against the hit and run driver claiming his actions were the proximate cause of plaintiff's injuries, because his flight forced the only officer securing the accident scene to leave, increasing the danger to plaintiff. The court held that the hit and run driver's flight was too remote to have brought about plaintiff's injury, since the actual cause was the second motorist falling asleep at the wheel. Additionally, the court found that plaintiff's claim of negligence per se based upon the defendant's violation of a hit and run statute still required proximate causation and ultimately failed as well. ***Lux v. Gerald Ort Trucking, Inc.*, 887 A.2d 1281 (Pa. Super. 2005)**.

Verdict only against dog owner's boyfriend who did not have dog under control when it jumped on 67 year old pedestrian affirmed. Claims of absolute negligence by reason of mere ownership of dog and negligence *per se* denied. ***McCloud v. McLaughlin*, 837 A.2d 541 (Pa. Super. 2003)**.

Son of deceased mother filed suit alleging legal malpractice against attorney for his father because attorney did not immediately probate mother's will which established substantial trust for son. Son alleged two theories: He was third party beneficiary of contract between father and attorney and incurred damages in being required to force probate of mother's will and attorney was negligent *per se* because he had, prior to son's forcing of probate of will, concealed the existence of mother's will. Held that criminal statute imposing criminal penalty for concealment of a will is designed to protect society at large, not beneficiaries and so there can be no negligence *per se* for violation; and son was not owed any duty by attorney, despite his beneficiary status, as father's interests in managing his deceased wife's estate was primarily obligation of attorney's representation. ***Minnich v. Yost*, 817 A.2d 538 (Pa. Super. 2003)**.

Plaintiff who was disfigured by injections of silicone sued doctor who had violated FDA prohibition against using silicone for such a purpose. Trial court

Negligence per se

granted a new trial on plaintiff's motion after a verdict in favor of the physician. Breach of FDA prohibition is negligence *per se* and FDA is not prohibited from regulating medical treatment. ***Cabiroy v. Scipione*, 767 A.2d 1078 (Pa. Super. 2001).**

Downstream property owner sued reservoir and dam company for failure to contain water following heavy rains. The court confirmed that the owner of a reservoir is "required to exercise a degree of care commensurate with the risk of storing water in a reservoir and would be liable if its negligence made it possible for water to escape with resulting damage to property." Dam company's failure to comply with Dam Safety and Encroachments Act, 32 P.S. § 639.13 *et seq.* constituted negligence *per se*. ***Shamnoski v PG Energy*, 765 A.2d 297 (Pa. Super. 2000).**

Plaintiff's decedent killed when he struck stopped traffic on I-95 three miles in advance of a construction site. Plaintiff alleged that PennDOT was negligent in failing to place warning signs in advance of location where cars backed up and stopped. Plaintiff also alleged PennDOT's failure to erect signs was negligence *per se*. Held: expert testimony as to need for advance signs three miles from construction site was required. PennDOT regulations that were silent on exact placement of warning signs could not be basis for claim of negligence *per se*, if PennDOT did not place the signs where plaintiff thought they should have been. ***Young v. PennDOT*, 744 A.2d 1276 (Pa. 2000).**

This is a class action suit for damages, including medical monitoring cost, by residents who lived within half a mile of lead processing plant against former and current owners of plant. Negligence *per se* requires that the law violated be designed to protect the interest of a group of individuals as opposed to the general public. Pennsylvania recognizes a cause of action for medical monitoring. Claims of negligence per se and for medical monitoring cannot be reached when the jury specifically finds no negligence on the part of the defendants. ***Wagner v. Anzon, Inc.*, 453 Pa. Super. 619, 684 A.2d 570 (1996).**

Violation of a statute, although negligence *per se*, does not constitute a ground for imposing liability unless it can be shown to be a substantial factor in causing plaintiff's injuries which resulted from a trip and fall. Failure to produce evidence of separate and distinct damages attributable to a scar precludes a specific jury instruction regarding the scar. Judgment affirmed. ***Gravlin v. Fredavid Builders and Developers*, 450 Pa. Super. 655, 677 A.2d 1235 (1996).**

Absent proof that a patron was visibly intoxicated when served additional alcoholic beverages, no action for wrongful death or survival is established. Statutory violation of serving alcohol after hours does not establish liability for acts of third parties absent proof that such service was proximate cause of the injury. ***Hiles v. Brandywine Club*, 443 Pa. Super. 462, 662 A.2d 16 (1995).**

Failure to follow Department of Health standards that suggest 48-hour limit for catheterization is not negligence *per se*. Medical malpractice causation requires proof of increased risk of harm. Causation is question for trier of fact where artificial hip replacement patient developed staff infection from catheterization. ***Edwards v. Brandywine Hospital*, 438 Pa. Super. 673, 652 A.2d 1382 (1995).**

Negligent design

Driving at unsafe speed in violation of statute constituted negligence *per se* in personal injury action brought by occupants of vehicle with which defendant collided. **Folino v. Young, 368 Pa. Super. 220, 553 A.2d 1034.**

Truck coming down steep hill unable to stop at stop sign; skidded on ice through intersection, causing accident. Jury verdict for defendant. Held: unavoidable accident. Negligence *per se* (going through sign) is not same as strict liability. Jury could find valid excuse, despite due care, for going past sign. Error for judge to grant new trial. Verdict reinstated. **Bumbarger v. Kaminsky, 311 Pa. Super. 177, 457 A.2d 552.**

Mere fact that taproom served minor in violation of law is not evidence of negligence as to third party claim of estate of motorist killed by minor in auto accident. **Simon v. Shirely, 269 Pa. Super. 364, 409 A.2d 1365.**

Violation of Section 1001 of the Vehicle Code as to four in the front seat constitutes negligence *per se* where such violation established a causal connection with the occurrence. **Little v. Jarvis, 219 Pa. Super. 156, 280 A.2d 617.**

Negligent design

Lack of evidence to support a strict liability claim does not preclude a valid claim for negligent design of a lighter. **Phillips v. Cricket Lighters, 841 A.2d 1000 (Pa. 2003).**

Negligent destruction of evidence

Employee, injured during the course of his employment, brought a claim for damages against his employer for negligently destroying parts of the truck that caused his injury, which the employee intended to use in a third party tort suit. The trial court dismissed the employee's claims on the basis that they were barred based on the Workers' Compensation Act. The Superior Court reversed, holding that the Workers' Compensation Act did not bar an employee's claim for negligent destruction of evidence against his employer as the injury did not arise during the course of the employee's employment. **Minto v. J.B. Hunt Transportation Services, Inc., 971 A.2d 1280 (Pa. Super. 2009).**

Negligent entrustment

Driver brought personal injury action against owner of a vehicle involved in a hit and run accident driven by an unlicensed driver. The trial court entered judgment in favor of the Plaintiff. The Superior Court affirmed the trial court's holding that the trial court's finding that a claim for negligent entrustment could be encompassed by the general language of the original complaint that the Defendant had violated various statutes pertaining to the operation of a motor vehicle. **Graham v. Campo, 990 A.2d 9 (Pa. Super. 2010).**

Plaintiff injured in a shooting brought a negligence action against the parents of the adult man who shot him on the basis that he resided with the parents and that the parents had confiscated their son's gun and returned it to him. The trial court granted Defendant's motion for summary judgment. The Superior Court affirmed, holding that temporary confiscation of their son's gun did not render the parents li-

Negligent hiring or supervision

able as the parents had no right to control the gun owned by their son and their confiscation did not support Plaintiff's theory that the son could only use the gun with his parent's consent. *Wittrien v. Burkholder*, **965 A.2d 1229 (2009).**

Decedent-hunter's personal representative brought claim for negligent preservation of evidence against the State Police for failing to preserve evidence necessary for products liability suit. The trial court granted summary judgment in favor of the Defendant. The Commonwealth Court affirmed holding that the personal property exception to sovereign immunity did not apply as the evidence caused the injury to the hunter and not the officer's mishandling of the evidence. *Pyeritz v. Commonwealth of Pennsylvania State Police Department*, **956 A.2d 1075 (Pa. Cmwlth. 2008).**

Plaintiff sued driver of car that veered into her lane and hit her car, used car salesman who had authorized defendant driver to test drive the car, and dealership for which used car salesman worked. Jury returned verdict against all three parties and apportioned liability among them, which was molded to joint and several liability by trial court. On appeal, Superior Court reversed denial of post trial motions of salesman and dealership who argued that they had no knowledge that defendant driver was other than a licensed driver (which he was) and so no duty to plaintiff which would support a claim of negligent entrustment by plaintiff. *Ferry v. Fisher*, **709 A.2d 399 (Pa. Super. 1998).**

Occupants of vehicle involved in accident brought negligent entrustment action against owner of other automobile. Held: evidence of driver's intoxication at the time he borrowed automobile was admissible to show negligent entrustment. *Wertz v. Kephart*, **374 Pa. Super. 274, 542 A.2d 1019.**

Negligent hiring or supervision

Plaintiff appealed trial court's judgment of non pros for plaintiff's failure to file a certificate of merit in her action against defendant hospital for being sexually assaulted during her hospitalization. Appellate court reversed, holding that a certificate of merit is warranted only for claims raising questions involving medical judgment beyond the realm of common knowledge and experience. *Smith v. Friends Hospital*, **928 A.2d 1072 (Pa. Super. 2007).**

Twenty-six year old plaintiff brought suit against priest and church administration for injuries sustained as a result of alleged sexual abuse while plaintiff attended high school. Motions for judgment on the pleadings by all defendants sustained due to plaintiff's failure to timely file complaint following actual injury. *Baselice, III v. Franciscan Friars Assumption BVM Province, Inc.*, **879 A.2d 270 (Pa. Super. 2005).**

Plaintiffs who did not file suit against clergy and church officials who participated in or covered up alleged clergy sexual abuse for at least twenty one years were barred by statute of limitations. *Meehan v. Archdiocese of Philadelphia*, **870 A.2d 912 (Pa. Super. 2005).**

Bank employees, manager and assistant manager held liable for undue influence in convincing depositor to name employees as sole beneficiaries of substantial

Negligent identification

accounts and bank held liable for negligent supervision of the employees. ***Owens v. Mazzei*, 847 A.2d 700 (Pa. Super. 2004).**

Verdict for bank teller plaintiff in suit against security company for negligent and negligent *per se* hiring of security guard who robbed bank during off-duty hours reversed because bank robber's unforeseeable violent criminal act was a superseding cause of the harm. ***Maban v. Am-Guard, Inc.*, 841 A.2d 1052 (Pa. Super. 2004).**

Plaintiff nursing care provider received a needle stick after giving an injection to a patient that she only later learned was afflicted with AIDs. In suit claiming negligent infliction of mental distress against organization that assigned her to provide care for patient without providing her with information on the patient's AIDs status or proper equipment, summary judgement in favor of defendant reversed. The court recognized that a cause of action for mental distress for fear of contracting AIDS will lie where there are circumstances that indicate the plaintiff was actually exposed to the AIDS virus. ***Shumosky v. Lutheran Welfare Services of Northeastern, PA., Inc.* 784 A.2d 196 (Pa. Super. 2001).**

Plaintiffs sued minister and church alleging minister had sexually molested their daughter, and church had been negligent in investigation prior to hiring minister and in monitoring his behavior after his employment. On appeal from grant of summary judgment in favor of church, the court held that evidence presented by plaintiffs was insufficient to present a question of fact for the jury to decide as to either negligent hiring or supervision. ***R.A. v. First Church of Christ*, 748 A.2d 692 (Pa. Super. 2000).**

Negligent identification

There is no legally cognizable cause of action in Pennsylvania for negligent identification of a criminal defendant. Summary judgment affirmed. ***Jaindl v. Mohr*, 541 Pa. 163, 661 A.2d 1362 (1995).**

Negligent infliction of emotional distress

Plaintiff brought a claim of intentional infliction of emotional distress against Defendant hospital after it transferred his deceased father's body to the co-Defendant medical school where post-mortem operations were performed on the body without his consent. The trial court dismissed the case based upon preliminary objections. The Superior Court affirmed the dismissal of the negligent infliction of emotional distress claim on the basis that the Plaintiff had failed to sufficiently plead facts sufficient to support that the hospital owed him a fiduciary duty. ***Weiley v. Albert Einstein Medical Center*, 2012 Pa. Super. 106 (Pa. Super. 2012).**

Parents of a minor child brought a claim of negligent infliction of emotional distress and defamation among other claims for a parochial school's expulsion of their child for bringing a weapon to school and the school's communication of the child's expulsion to the community. The trial court dismissed all claims after preliminary objections, raising lack of jurisdiction based upon the deference rule and the Superior Court affirmed the trial court's dismissal. The Pennsylvania Supreme Court reversed and remanded holding that the deference rule did not apply at the

Negligent infliction of emotional distress

pleading stage to the negligent infliction of emotional distress claim or the defamation claims as the pleadings did not allege facts that would require the court to decide an ecclesiastical question. ***Connor v. Archdiocese of Philadelphia*, 975 A.2d 1084 (Pa. 2009).**

Mother, who gave birth to a son with physical deformities, brought claims of negligent infliction of emotional distress and intentional infliction of emotional distress against a radiologist who reported that the results of her ultrasound were normal and revealed no fetal abnormalities. The trial court dismissed all the Defendants on preliminary objections. The Superior Court affirmed in part and reversed in part holding that the Plaintiff had sufficiently pled a prima facie case for negligent infliction of emotional distress, but she had failed to set forth outrageous conduct sufficient for a claim for intentional infliction of emotional distress. ***Toney v. Chester County Hospital*, 961 A.2d 192 (Pa. Super. 2008).**

Parents of minor student brought a claim of negligent infliction of emotional distress and defamation against parochial elementary school for expulsion of their son for carrying a penknife to school. The appellate court held that the decision to expel the student was a disciplinary matter involving ecclesiastical matters that under the "deference rule" was prohibited from judicial review. ***Connor v. Archdiocese of Philadelphia*, 933 A.2d 92 (Pa. Super. 2007).**

Plaintiff filed suit against the Pennsylvania Department of Transportation (PennDOT) for negligent infliction of emotional distress when his wife was killed by an object dropped from a highway overpass, which PennDOT knew had been the scene of several other similar incidents. The court affirmed judgment for PennDOT based upon the doctrine of sovereign immunity. The court found that to fall within the real property exception to sovereign immunity the defect in the real estate itself must cause the injury and not merely encourage or facilitate the act of another. ***Cowell v. Commonwealth*, 883 A.2d 705 (Pa. Cmwlth. 2005).**

Defendant doctor who prescribed medications and ordered another physician to perform a gynecological examination of his mother, where no negligence alleged, cannot be liable for negligent infliction of emotional distress. In order to prove negligent infliction of emotional distress, the plaintiff must first show that some act of negligence took place in proximity to or resulted in some physical impact on the plaintiff's body. Absent such an act, no cause of action can be maintained. ***Paves v. Corson*, 765 A.2d 1128 (Pa. Super. 2000).**

Mother of child who received partial leg amputation at 8 days of age claimed damages for negligent infliction of emotional distress. Act that allegedly caused the distress was being informed by medical care providers that discoloration on child's lower leg believed to be bruising was actually evidence of blood clot. Held: being informed of likelihood of amputation if therapies were not successful was not the discrete and identifiable traumatic event contemporaneous to the injury to her child. ***Sonlin v. Abington Memorial Hospital*, 748 A.2d 213 (Pa. Super. 2000).**

Plaintiff who was incorrectly informed that he had tested positive for HIV/AIDS sued community health agency, laboratory that performed tests, and others, claiming negligent infliction of emotional distress. Held: "fear of aids" which gen-

Negligent infliction of emotional distress

erated psychosomatic symptoms is not a cognizable injury in Pennsylvania. *Doe v. Philadelphia Community Health Alternatives*, 745 A.2d 25 (Pa. Super. 2000).

Wife plaintiff diagnosed with lung cancer filed suit against radiology association and radiologist who had taken and interpreted chest x-ray at request of insurance company for failure to diagnose cancerous tumor. No physician-patient relationship is created where a physician examines a patient at the request of an insurance company. Summary judgment affirmed. *Promubol v. Hackett,* **454 Pa. Super. 622, 686 A.2d 417 (1996).**

Wife, who delivered brain-damaged child after Cesarean section with only local anesthetic, and husband, individually and as parents of child, sued anesthesiology group, obstetrician and hospital for malpractice. Nurses employed at hospital are not agents of the physicians when they act in the normal course of hospital services. Father's loss of consortium claim properly denied by trial court where his only testimony was that he had a subjective fear of engaging in sexual relations with his wife following her delivery of brain-damaged child, even though the damage may have been the result of medical malpractice. Father's claim for negligent infliction of emotional distress properly dismissed where he was not near the scene of the injuries to his wife and newborn child. Hearing his wife's cries of pain only, without any visual experience of her condition, was insufficient. *Tiburzio-Kelly v. Montgomery,* **452 Pa. Super. 158, 681 A.2d 757 (1996).**

Plaintiff minor who witnessed his cousin's drowning is not sufficiently "closely related" under Pennsylvania law to allow standing for claim of negligent infliction of emotional distress. Order sustaining preliminary objections affirmed. *Blanyar v. Pagnotti Enterprises, Inc.,* **451 Pa. Super 269, 679 A.2d 790 (1996).**

Wife plaintiff who was left unattended in emergency room during miscarriage and then handed corpse of miscarried fetus while nurse took pictures established sufficient evidence of physical impact to allow recovery for negligent infliction of emotional distress. Case remanded for new trial on damages. *Brown v. Philadelphia College of Osteopathic Medicine,* **449 Pa. Super. 667, 674 A.2d 1130 (1996).**

Negligent infliction of emotional distress requires proof of physical contact or contemporaneous sensory observance of family member being physically injured. Employee discharged by employer has no cause of action of negligent infliction of emotional distress absent any possibility of physical impact. Summary judgment affirmed. *Hunger v. Grand Central Sanitation,* **447 Pa. Super. 575, 670 A.2d 173 (1996).**

Patient's unsubstantiated assertion of physical injury failed to establish negligent or intentional infliction of emotional distress. Doctor and medical center were immune from suit under Child Protective Services Law for disclosing plaintiff's admission that she had suffocated her child. Child Protective Services Law, which grants immunity for disclosures does not conflict with psychotherapist–patient privilege or the confidentiality provisions of the Mental Health Procedures Act. *Fewell v. Bresner,* **444 Pa. Super. 559, 664 A.2d 577 (1995).**

Negligent infliction of emotional distress

Sovereign immunity barred claim for intentional infliction of emotional distress in mother's case against state police for mishandling of daughter's remains. Pennsylvania law does not recognize an action for negligent mishandling of the dead. Mother's failure to allege that she witnessed any traumatic event involving her daughter's remains precluded claim for negligent infliction of emotional distress. Order sustaining defendants' preliminary objections affirmed. *Ray v. Pennsylvania State Police,* ___ Pa. Cmwlth. ___, 654 A.2d 140 (1995).

Nineteen-year old son of plaintiff killed by auto. Father did not witness accident. Father committed suicide three months later. Suit by father's estate against driver of auto dismissed. *Yandrich v. Radic,* 495 Pa. 243, 433 A.2d 459.

Claim by identical twin and mother for their own emotional distress resulting from the injuries sustained by their sister/daughter dismissed. Neither near scene of accident. *Hoffner v. Hodge,* 47 Pa. Cmwlth. 277, 407 A.2d 940.

Mother seeking damages for her own emotional distress from driver of car which killed her child. She observed accident. Zone of danger no longer the exclusive test. Damage must be foreseeable. Where mother sees child being killed, as a matter of law, emotional distress is foreseeable. *Sinn v. Burd,* 486 Pa. 146, 404 A.2d 672.

Where plaintiff's theory was that he was struck by defendant's vehicle and defense was that plaintiff was never struck, error for court to charge that there did not have to be a touching for plaintiff to recover. New trial ordered. *Hrivnak v. Perrone,* 472 Pa. 348, 372 A.2d 730.

Mother watched store employees accost her two daughters and remove them from shopping area. Mother alleges she became fearful for her own safety and of physical impact and suffered heart attack shortly after daughters released one-half hour later. For jury. Summary judgment for defendant reversed. *Bowman v. Sears,* 245 Pa. Super. 530, 369 A.2d 754.

Wife witnessed husband being struck by car and suffered heart attack from which she died. No recovery on behalf of wife where she was not herself in danger of physical impact or harm or in fear of such impact. *Scarf v. Koltoff,* 242 Pa. Super. 294, 363 A.2d 1276.

A wife and mother who allegedly suffered a nervous breakdown when informed of accident involving her husband and three children, in which accident she was not involved nor present, is not entitled to damages. Preliminary objections sustained. *Beck v. Brennan,* 228 Pa. Super. 804, 316 A.2d 906.

Uncontrolled car skidded onto pavement, struck plaintiff's son and inflicted other damage in plaintiff's presence—no impact with plaintiff—plaintiff developed an acute heart condition variously diagnosed but evidence of causal relationship with occurrence—previous impact rule abolished—case for jury. *Niederman v. Brodsky,* 436 Pa. 401, 261 A.2d 84.

Negligent misrepresentation

Negligent misrepresentation

Adoptive parents of son diagnosed with schizophrenia brought claims for negligent misrepresentation and negligent failure to disclose against their adoption agency for failing to disclose that their adoptive son's birth mother had a mental history of schizophrenia. At trial a jury found the agency negligent. The Superior Court reversed and remanded, holding that schizophrenia at the time of the adoption was not a known genetic disorder and therefore Plaintiff's could not prevail under a negligent misrepresentation theory. The Superior Court remanded on the negligent failure to disclose as the verdict sheet did not differentiate between the two theories of negligence. The Pennsylvania Supreme Court reversed the Superior Court and reinstated the verdict for the Plaintiffs, holding that where a general verdict is issued involving multiple issues the verdict may not be dismissed if at least one issue is supported by the verdict. *Halper v. Jewish Family & Children's Service of Greater Philadelphia*, **963 A.2d 1282 (2009).**

Excavator brought a claim against a gas utility company for negligent misrepresentation for purely economic damages associated with the gas utility company's improper marking of gas lines under the Pennsylvania One Call Act. The appellate court sustained the trial court's decision holding that under the economic loss rule some physical harm must occur to the Plaintiff's property or person to recover in a negligence action. ***Excavation Technologies, Inc. v. Columbia Gas Co.*, 936 A.2d 111 (Pa. Super. 2007).**

Excavation subcontractor who had improperly relied on incorrect drawings sued companies that performed subsurface testing for the township which was building a new library. Complaint alleged purely economic damages in negligent misrepresentation claim. No cause of action exists in negligence to recover purely economic damages. ***David Pflumm Paving and Excavating, Inc. v. Foundation Services Company, F.T.*, 816 A.2d 1164 (Pa. Super. 2003).**

In legal malpractice action following an approved settlement where plaintiff is unsatisfied with amount of the settlement, plaintiff must establish that attorney induced client to settle by fraud or made some negligent representation, unfounded in law, to induce client to settle. Explaining *Muhammad v. Strassburger, et al.*, 526 Pa.. 541, 587 A.2d 1346. ***Banks v. Jerome Taylor & Associates*, 700 A.2d 1329 (Pa. Super. 1997).**

Reversal of order sustaining demurrer in favor of adoption agency to allow claims for negligent misrepresentation, intentional misrepresentation and negligent failure to disclose. Demurrer to claim of breach of duty to investigate sustained. ***Gibbs v. Ernst*, 538 Pa. 193, 647 A.2d 882 (1994).**

Negligent referral

Suit by plaintiff against bar association lawyer referral service for negligent referral to an attorney who failed to file plaintiff's suit within statute of limitations period. Pennsylvania law does not recognize a claim for "negligent referral." *Bourke v. Kazaras*, 746 A.2d 642 (Pa. Super. 2000).

Negligent supervision

Stock trader brought negligent supervision claim against a stock exchange after he was assaulted by another trader on the floor of the stock exchange. Pennsylvania Supreme Court reversed the Superior Court's grant of judgment as a matter of law holding that the Federal Securities Exchange Act did not preempt a state tort claim arising out of personal injuries suffered on a stock exchange floor by a securities industry employee. ***Dooner v. DiDonato*, 971 A.2d 1187 (PA 2009).**

Neither driver negligent

Left turn accident. Jury found neither driver negligent. Lower court refused to grant new trial. This held proper as to drivers, but not as to the one passenger. Evidence of negligence of both drivers. ***Myers v. Gold*, 77 Pa. Super. 66, 419 A.2d 663.**

Neomycin

Jury verdict $1,000,000—malpractice action; $10,000—auto negligence action. Rear end collision—injuries to neck and back. Low back surgery. Infection followed—neomycin antibiotic used allegedly caused kidney failure, partial paralysis of lower limbs and total hearing loss. Could walk on crutches at time of trial. Verdict affirmed. Hospital held in case because hospital resident-employee actively participated in neomycin therapy, and made some dosage decisions. Charge on agency of residents upheld. Charge on damages affirmed, discussing as independent items of damages—loss of life's pleasures, inconvenience and embarrassment. ***Pratt v. Stein*, 298 Pa. Super. 92, 444 A.2d 674.**

New injuries

Plaintiffs, husband and wife, executed a release which covered property damage of husband's car but by its terms covered unknown personal injuries—wife plaintiff later developed disc trouble—proper to submit issue to jury—release held not conclusive. ***Cady v. Mitchell*, 208 Pa. Super. 16, 220 A.2d 373.**

Newspaper delivery driver

Motorist injured in collision with vehicle delivering newspapers brought action against distributor. Distributor not liable. Delivery driver independent contractor. ***Lutz v. Cybularz*, 414 Pa. Super. 579, 607 A.2d 1089.**

Not looking

Plaintiff, a business invitee in defendant's garage and service station, falling down a flight of steps into basement when he entered an unlocked door—testifying on deposition that he did not even look where he was going and walked into space—summary judgment granted for defendant on pleadings, depositions and photographs—action affirmed on appeal. ***Simmons v. Doll's Garage, Inc.*, 440 Pa. 635, 269 A.2d 509.**

Notice of condition

Notice of condition

Emergency Medical Technician sued the Luzerne County Housing Authority when, while responding to an emergency call, he was struck in the head by a metal bar that fell from a garage door at a housing authority property. The court held the plaintiff had failed to provide evidence that the commonwealth agency had actual or constructive notice of the dangerous condition or defect in the garage door necessary to sustain a negligence action. ***Gurnari v. Luzerne County Housing Authority*, 911 A.2d 236 (Pa. Cmwlth. 2006).**

Mall patron's suit for injuries sustained in fall caused by alleged "slippery substance" dismissed on summary judgment for lack of any proof that mall manager had constructive or actual notice of existence of any foreign matter on floors. ***Porro v. Century III Associates*, 846 A.2d 1282 (Pa. Super. 2004).**

Plaintiff in legal malpractice action failed to establish he had suffered any discernible injury or damage. Fact that plaintiff lost security interest in property as junior lienholder does not establish that he was unable to enforce his security purely by reason of attorney's failure to provide him with notice of sheriff's sale by senior lienholder. ***Boyer v. Walker*, 714 A.2d 458 (Pa. Super. 1998).**

Plaintiff was injured when car he was driving fell into 8"-12" ditch in road that resulted from settlement of fill deposited by local authority which had created hole. Plaintiff appeals from trial judge's decision to give instruction to jury which left question of whether local authority had actual or constructive notice of fill settling to jury. Plaintiff argued that because local authority created hole and installed fill that settled and caused dangerous condition, it had notice of condition as a matter of law. Instruction approved by Commonwealth Court which held that just because defendant created hole and installed fill that eventually resulted in dangerous condition does not mean that plaintiff is not required to show that defendant knew or should have known of the condition. ***Miller v. Lykens Borough Authority*, 712 A.2d 800 (Pa. Cmwlth. 1998).**

Plaintiff who was injured when he fell on defective or missing city-owned and maintained steps presented proof that city employees cleaned or shoveled damaged steps four or five times per year and that those employees were obligated to report defects or problems with steps. Plaintiff also offered credible evidence that there was a continuous deterioration of the steps from the date of the last repair more than one and one-half years before plaintiff's injury; therefore, city had actual or constructive notice of defective condition. City's defense of Political Subdivision Tort Claims Act was inadequate in light of plaintiff's evidence of defective condition of steps and notice to city. ***Ellis v. City of Pittsburgh*, 703 A.2d 593, (Pa. Cmwlth. 1997).**

Plaintiff was injured in an automobile accident allegedly caused by defective road design and condition. On the day of trial, the trial court granted PennDOT's motion for nonsuit based on plaintiff's failure to notify PennDOT of action within six months of accident under 42 Pa.C.S. §5522(a)(1) based on presumption of prejudice and hardship for failure to notify PennDOT. Held: presentation of motion on day of trial was untimely given substantial amount of time during which PennDOT

Notice of condition

could earlier have made the same motion, there is no presumption of prejudice or hardship attendant to lack of required notice. Negligence of plaintiff's counsel in providing notice coupled with lack of undue hardship to Commonwealth constituted adequate reason for delay in providing notice. Remanded to trial court for hearing on actual prejudice on PennDOT with burden of proof on PennDOT. ***Leedom v. Com., Dept. of Transp.*****, 699 A.2d 815 (Pa. Cmwlth. 1997).**

Decedent's failure to establish hospital's knowledge of water on floor in bathroom, which may represent a dangerous or defective condition of the property, prohibits recovery. A business invitee must prove either that the landowner created the harmful condition or had actual or constructive notice of the condition. Summary judgment affirmed. ***Swift v. Northeastern Hospital of Philadelphia*****, 456 Pa. Super. 330, 690 A.2d 719 (1997).**

To recover against Commonwealth under real property exception to sovereign immunity, plaintiff, whose decedent was killed when tree limb on Commonwealth property fell on her car, must establish that PennDOT had actual or constructive notice of the dangerous condition. Trial court's refusal to charge on notice was reversible error. New trial granted. ***Com., Dept. of Transp. v. Patton*****, 546 Pa. 561, 686 A.2d 1302 (1997).**

Truck driver who knew of propensity of radio to fall from overhead rack found to be seventy percent negligent for injuries sustained when radio fell from rack. Judgment for installer of radio affirmed. ***Dath v. Marano Truck Sales and Service, Inc.*****, 437 Pa. Super. 571, 650 A.2d 901 (1994).**

Summary judgment in favor of social host affirmed where no evidence that host had actual notice that minors were consuming alcohol. Summary judgment in favor of telephone company affirmed because causal connection between location of pole and accident too remote in law to impose liability. ***Novak v. Kilby*****, 167 Pa. Cmwlth. 217, 647 A.2d 687 (1994).**

Plaintiff failed to allege PennDOT's constructive or actual notice of unsafe condition of excavation site. PennDOT protected by governmental immunity absent proof of its active fault. Motion to dismiss in favor of PennDOT affirmed. ***Miranda v. City of Philadelphia*****, 166 Pa. Cmwlth. 181, 646 A.2d 71 (1994).**

Plaintiff slipped and fell on cherry on floor of supermarket. Absent proof of actual or constructive notice or negligence, plaintiff cannot recover. ***Moultrey v. A&P*****, 281 Pa. Super. 525, 422 A.2d 593.**

Suit against SEPTA and City of Philadelphia. Proper notice given to city but none to SEPTA. SEPTA did not have actual notice of dangerous condition in area where plaintiff fell. Suit not filed until 10 days before expiration of statute of limitations. Summary judgment in favor of SEPTA upheld under §36 of Metropolitan Transportation Authorities Act. ***Irrera v. SEPTA*****, 231 Pa. Super. 508, 331 A.2d 705.**

Nullum tempus

Nullum tempus

School district brought action for cost of removing asbestos against installing contractor. Trial court granted new trial to district. Held: doctrine of *nullum tempus* applicable. ***Mt. Lebanon School District v. W. R. Grace and Company*, 414 Pa. Super. 455, 607 A.2d 756.**

Numerous accidents

Evidence that numerous accidents had occurred as result of erection of a high curbing at a previous entrance to a shopping center improperly rejected—admissible to establish notice and knowledge of a dangerous condition. ***Colangelo v. Penn Hills Center, Inc.*, 221 Pa. Super. 381, 292 A.2d 490.**

Nursing home

Decedent's estate brought a negligence and wrongful death action against a nursing home and its management company on the basis that dehydration and malnutrition caused the decedent's heart attack. A jury found the nursing home both corporately and vicariously liable for the decedent's death. The Superior Court affirmed, holding that the management company and nursing home owners could be held liable for corporate negligence. The Pennsylvania Supreme Court affirmed, holding that a skilled nursing facility and a management company could be held directly liable for corporate negligence in the death of a resident and were not immune from suit. ***Scampone v. Highland Park Care Center*, 57 A.3d 582 (Pa. 2012).**

Estate of decedent brought negligence action against a nursing home for the death of the decedent. A jury found in favor of the plaintiff and awarded punitive damages. The Superior Court affirmed, holding that a nursing home could be held directly liable for corporate negligence for understaffing resulting in the decedent's death and also for the actions of its employees. The Superior Court also held that punitive damages could be awarded against a company operating a nursing home on the basis of its understaffing. ***Hall v. Episcopal Long Term Care*, 54 A.3d 381 (Pa. Super. 2012).**

Estate of nursing home resident brought a wrongful death action against a nursing home for causing the death of resident due to substandard care. A jury found against the nursing home on the basis of corporate and vicarious liability. The Superior Court upheld the trial court's decision holding that a nursing home was analogous to a hospital and it could be held liable under a theory of corporate negligence due to a failure to provide adequate staffing. ***Scampone v. Grane Healthcare Company*, 2010 Pa. Super. 124 (Pa. Super. 2010).**

Political Subdivision Tort Claims act bars suit for medical negligence against a county owned and operated nursing home. The exception for medical or professional negligence found in the Sovereign Immunity Act is not in the Political Subdivision Tort Claims Act. ***Davis v. County of Westmoreland*, 844 A.2d 54 (Pa. Cmwlth. 2004).**

A private, independent contractor organization that managed and set administrative and medical policy and procedure for a county-owned nursing home was not clothed with the governmental immunity afforded by the Political Subdivision Tort Claims Act. ***Helsel v. Complete Care Services, L.P.*, 797 A.2d 1051 (Pa. Cmwlth. 2002)**.

Obstructed view

—O—

Obstructed view

Two vehicles collided at intersection. Plaintiff sued abutting property owner among others for maintaining shrub and trees which obstructed view. Lower court granted summary judgment in favor of property owner. Reversed. Issues of superceding cause, comparative negligence and violations of statutes, for jury. ***Harvey v. Hansen,* 299 Pa. Super. 474, 445 A.2d 1228.**

Plaintiff driving auto through intersection with green light. Construction barrier obstructed view. Truck ran red light. Error for court to charge that plaintiff was contributorily negligent as a matter of law since she explained reason for failing to see defendant. For jury. ***Deer v. City of Pittsburgh,* 240 Pa. Super. 19, 367 A.2d 1119.**

Nonsuit overturned. New trial ordered. Plaintiff's decedent struck by defendant's driver and killed. Evidence that a wall obstructed driver's view in direction of decedent's approach to scene. Police found scratches on bumper. Witness heard a crash, looked up and saw plaintiff in street and defendant's truck stopped. *Res gestae* statement of driver: "I did see him, but when I saw him it was too late." For jury. ***Esposito v. Dairyman's League Cooperative,* 236 Pa. Super. 401, 344 A.2d 505.**

Plaintiff stopped car at intersection. View blocked by truck of defendant Johanna Farms parked at corner. Plaintiff edged out and stopped then struck by car driven by defendant Cohen. Verdict for plaintiff against both defendants. ***Bell v. Cohen, et al.,* 228 Pa. Super. 872, 322 A.2d 704.**

Additional defendant brought in on ground of illegal parking alleged to be the cause of the collision—possible negligence of defendant construed not to be a superceding cause as a matter of law—case for fact finders. ***Clevenstein v. Rizzuto,* 439 Pa. 397, 266 A.2d 623.**

Obstruction

Group of boy scouts walking on highway. Excavation on berm forced boys on highway. Truck pulled around boys but pulled back too soon striking plaintiff. Driver and construction company held responsible. ***Grainy v. Campbell,* 493 Pa. 88, 425 A.2d 379.**

Defendant's auto struck embankment in construction area of state highway and then struck plaintiff's car at night. Held: construction company liable for not placing warning signs on highway. ***Dietterle v. Harding,* 279 Pa. Super. 530, 421 A.2d 326.**

Large pile of dirt alongside parking lot. Driver of vehicle pulled out striking plaintiff going by on motorcycle and killing him. Verdict against defendant who piled dirt affirmed. Piling dirt alongside parking lot is negligent and driver's coming out behind it does not as a matter of law relieve defendant of negligence—not as a matter of law a superseding cause. ***Flickinger Estate v. Ritsky,* 452 Pa. 69, 305 A.2d 40.**

Only Reasonable Inference Rule

Occupied Crossing Rule

Plaintiff sued railroad after he drove into a stationary freight train and then was dragged several feet when the train began moving again. The court held that the adoption of comparative negligence by the Pennsylvania General Assembly did not negate the continued viability of the occupied crossing rule, which ordinarily absolves a railroad of its duty to warn of its train obstructing a highway. The court also held that the Federal Railroad Safety Act preempted Pennsylvania's blocked-crossing statute. **Krentz v. Consolidated Rail Corporation, 589 Pa. 576, 910 A.2d 20 (2006).**

Negligence claim by plaintiff who drove his vehicle under a train stopped at a crossing and was injured when the train moved and dragged his vehicle barred by Occupied Crossing Rule which provides that the existence of a train in a crossing is warning enough of its presence. Negligence *per se* claim of plaintiff was also barred by federal preemption of Federal Rail Safety Act, 49 U.S.C. § 20101, *et seq.* **Krentz v. Consolidated Rail Corporation, 865 A.2d 889 (Pa. Super. 2005).**

In action by motorist for injuries sustained when she collided with side of a hopper car being pulled by defendant's train, railroad company whose train was actually on and moving over a crossing did not owe motorist a duty to warn of train's presence. Occupied crossing rule survived enactment of the Comparative Negligence Act. Order sustaining preliminary objections affirmed. **Sprenkle v. Conrail, 446 Pa. Super. 377, 666 A.2d 1099 (1995).**

Odor

Not every wrong constitutes a legally cognizable cause of action. A physician who fails to remove sponges following an episiotomy resulting in no more than a foul odor is not subject to liability where no causal link between an act of negligence and legally cognizable injury is established. Order granting motion for nonsuit affirmed. **Gregorio v. Zeluck, 451 Pa. Super. 154, 678 A.2d 810 (1996).**

Odorizing gas

Explosion from propane heater while lighting pilot. Gas allegedly not odorized. §402A of Restatement (2d) Torts claim. Verdict for defendant affirmed. Issue of odor and defect alleged for not odorizing. Properly before jury. **Evans v. Thomas, 304 Pa. Super. 338, 450 A.2d 710.**

Only Reasonable Inference Rule

Jury could have inferred from the evidence that negligently repaired box car originated the fire which destroyed plaintiff's plant, even though other causes could have caused same—present rule of *Smith v. Bell Telephone Co.*, 397 Pa. 134 reaffirmed. **Connelly Containers, Inc. v. Penna. R.R. Co., 222 Pa. Super. 7, 292 A.2d 528.**

The Pennsylvania modification of the rule invoked where a pedestrian injured by glass falling from a plate glass window as the result of a wind storm—plaintiff's expert testified that the defective construction of the building was the

Open and obvious danger

proximate cause of the window blowing out—Superior Court reversed. *Jones v. Treegobb,* **433 Pa. 225, 249 A.2d 352.**

Rule applied where plaintiff was struck by a ball while standing near a concession where balls were thrown at a fair—evidence that management permitted boys to throw back balls and plaintiff was standing near to the area where such balls were thrown—nonsuit improper. *Devenney v. North Franklin Twp. V.F. Dept.,* **209 Pa. Super. 378, 228 A.2d 61.**

Open and obvious danger

Plaintiff subcontractor brought negligence claim for injuries suffered in a fall against general contractor after he was injured when he drove a scissor lift into a hole in the floor at the construction site. A jury found in favor of the Plaintiff. The Superior Court affirmed holding that it was a question of fact for the jury as to whether Plaintiff being distracted was sufficient to establish he was not aware of the holes in the floor to make them an open and obvious danger. *Patton v. Worthington Associates, Inc.,* **43 A.3d 479 (Pa. Super. 2012).**

University owes no duty to students to control protestors. Student who sees open and obvious impediment to her path of travel should choose an alternate path, rather than attempting to jump from four-foot wall. Order granting summary judgment affirmed. *Banks v. Trustees of University of Pennsylvania,* **446 Pa. Super. 99, 666 A.2d 329 (1995).**

Opportunity and occasion

Testimony that warning at a grade crossing was not heard is positive and not negative when sufficient opportunity and occasion for hearing and where jury could have found witness consciously listening. *Fallon v. Penn Central Trans. Co.,* **444 Pa. 148, 279 A.2d 164.**

Opposite lane

Action of motorcyclist who crossed into oncoming lane while attempting to pass vehicle in his lane was sole cause of accident; order denying PennDOT's motion for post trial relief reversed. *Glover v. Com., Dept. of Transp.,* **167 Pa. Cmwlth. 87, 647 A.2d 630 (1994).**

Ophthalmologist

Ophthalmologist's failure to report patient's poor vision to PennDOT, despite statutory obligation to do so, does not give rise to a private cause of action to plaintiff's decedent, who was killed when struck by patient's car. *Estate of Witthoeft v. Kiskaddon,* **733 A.2d 623 (Pa. 1999).**

In action by estate of decedent hit by automobile while bicycling, ophthalmologist has no duty to patient to inform PennDOT of patient's poor vision. Order sustaining preliminary objections affirmed. *Estate of Witthoeft v. Kiskaddon,* **450 Pa. Super. 364, 676 A.2d 1223 (1996).**

Overhanging limb

Other accidents or occurrences

Evidence that numerous accidents had occurred as result of erection of a high curbing at a previous entrance to a shopping center improperly rejected—admissible to establish notice and knowledge of a dangerous condition. ***Colangelo v. Penn Hills Center, Inc.*, 221 Pa. Super. 381, 292 A.2d 490.**

Evidence admissible to establish that plaintiff had a prior rear-end automobile accident involving injury to her back—claiming in instant case similar injuries—cross-examination involving same permitted. ***McCay v. Phila. Electric Co.*, 447 Pa. 490, 291 A.2d 759.**

Plaintiff further injured by a fall down steps some three months after occurrence—expert testimony that fall resulted from injuries sustained in occurrence sued on—matter properly left to jury. ***Kinee v. Penn Radio Cab Co.*, 435 Pa. 387, 257 A.2d 554.**

Other causes

Jury could have inferred from the evidence that negligently repaired box car originated the fire which destroyed plaintiff's plant, even though other causes could have caused same—present rule of *Smith v. Bell Telephone Co.*, 397 Pa. 134 reaffirmed. ***Connelly Containers, Inc. v. Penna. R.R. Co.*, 222 Pa. Super. 7, 292 A.2d 528.**

Out of possession

Falling from ladder—sidewalk cement giving way—improper filling by water department authority—authority held responsible but new trial as to landlord who was out of possession. ***Dinio v. Goshorn*, 437 Pa. 224, 270 A.2d 203.**

Oven door

Plaintiff's decedent was killed when he was struck by the door to a coke oven battery. Issue before the court was whether the door, which was of massive size and rolled on wheels, was a fixture and therefore subject to the 12 year statute of repose or personalty subject to suit for defective design or construction. Held: door was not a fixture and 12 year statute of repose did not apply. ***Vargo v. Koppers*, 715 A.2d 423 (1998).**

Overdose

General release of claims against emergency medical technician and ambulance service for overdose precluded claim of vicarious liability against hospital. Compulsory nonsuit in favor of hospital affirmed. ***Riffe v. Vereb Ambulance Service, Inc.*, 437 Pa. Super. 613, 650 A.2d 1076 (1994).**

Overhanging limb

Plaintiff widower stated cause of action under real estate exception to sovereign immunity for death of motorist/wife caused by limb falling from tree that had been "topped" twenty years earlier and was growing above PennDOT's right of way

Overpass

at 45° angle. Judgment on verdict for plaintiff affirmed. ***Patton v. Com., Dept. of Transp.,*** **___ Pa. Cmwlth. ___, 669 A.2d 1090 (1995).**

Overpass

Plaintiff filed suit against the Pennsylvania Department of Transportation (PennDOT) for negligent infliction of emotional distress when his wife was killed by an object dropped from a highway overpass, which PennDOT knew had been the scene of several other similar incidents. The court affirmed judgment for PennDOT based upon the doctrine of sovereign immunity. The court found that to fall within the real property exception to sovereign immunity the defect in the real estate itself must cause the injury and not merely encourage or facilitate the act of another. ***Cowell v. Commonwealth,*** **883 A.2d 705 (Pa. Cmwlth. 2005).**

Overturned rig on highway

Plaintiff driving at approximately 50 miles per hour at night—colliding with an overturned rig in highway—testimony established that he saw a warning cloud of dust a sufficient distance away to have enabled him to stop—violation of section 1002 of the Vehicle Code as to operation of a vehicle within assured clear distance—nonsuit properly granted. ***Hollern v. Verhovsek,*** **220 Pa. Super. 343, 287 A.2d 145.**

Painter

—P—

Paint

Plaintiff injured after slip and fall on wet porch sued homeowner and paint company. Inconsistencies between two releases executed by plaintiff on the same day, one of which released paint company and "all others who may be liable," preserved genuine issue of material fact as to which of the two releases took precedence. Summary judgment reversed. ***Mackay v. Sauerland,*** **454 Pa. Super. 666, 686 A.2d 840 (1996).**

Tenant's grandchild injured after eating lead-based paint chips. Landlord not liable. ***Felton by Felton v. Spratley,*** **433 Pa. Super. 474, 640 A.2d 1358.**

Property leased to parents of deceased minor—child ate paint which had peeled from living room woodwork and child died as the result of lead poisoning—preliminary objections in the nature of a demurrer sustained—no liability on either landlord or rental agent—use of lead paint not basis for an action—no covenant to repair and no warrant that premises were habitable. ***Kolojeski v. John Deisher, Inc.,*** **429 Pa. 191, 239 A.2d 329.**

Defendant supplied a paint product to plaintiff's employer—plaintiff allegedly sustained serious injury to his eyes in using product—ample warning given plaintiff's employer—suit against supplier and manufacturer and employer joined—verdict against employer only—affirmed on appeal. ***Thomas v. Arvon Products Co.,*** **424 Pa. 365, 227 A.2d 897.**

Paint thinner

Summary judgment in favor of volunteer fire department denied based on Political Subdivision Tort Claims Act, where fire department chief's act of spreading paint thinner on the floor at fire department, which caught fire and injured visitor/plaintiff, constituted "care, custody or control of real property" and so provided an exception to immunity. ***Grieff v. Reisinger,*** **___ Pa. ___, 693 A.2d 195 (1997).**

Plaintiff severely burned by flash fire caused when paint thinner used to clean paint from floor of volunteer fire department ignited was precluded from recovering for injuries because volunteer fire company entitled to governmental immunity. Real property exception to governmental immunity does not apply unless cause of action based on condition of real property or an actual defect of the property itself. Negligent mishandling of combustible liquids on property does not invoke real property exception. Denial of volunteer fire company's motion for summary judgment reversed and remanded. ***Grieff v. Reisinger,*** **___ Pa. Cmwlth. ___, 654 A.2d 77 (1995).**

Painter

Painting contractor and spouse filed suit against electric utility for injuries sustained as a result of electric shock and fall. Utility company's failure to object to inclusion of negligence language in jury charge on punitive damages precludes appellate review of alleged error. Superior Court affirmance of trial court's finding

Panicked driver

that defendant timely objected to flawed punitive damages charge reversed. *Takes v. Metropolitan Edison Company*, ___ Pa. ___, 695 A.2d 397 (1997).

Plaintiff was an employee of an independent contractor on defendant's premises and engaged as a painter on a scaffold—an electric wire owned and placed by defendant arced and severed cable supporting scaffold and plaintiff injured in fall—case for jury—verdict for plaintiff upheld—maintenance of wire contrary to provisions of National Electrical Code. ***Janowicz v. Crucible Steel Co. of America*, 433 Pa. 304, 249 A.2d 773.**

Panicked driver

Plaintiff's and defendant's cars going in opposite directions—cars rounding a curve—defendant testified that he panicked, slammed on the brakes and skidded into plaintiff's car on plaintiff's side of the road—verdict for defendant—new trial awarded on appeal—court below abused its discretion in not granting same. ***Anzelone v. Jesperson*, 436 Pa. 28, 258 A.2d 510.**

Paralysis

Patient who suffered paralysis after neurosurgery brought malpractice action against surgeon and hospital. Surgeon settled before trial. Held: hospital may be found liable if risk of injury was increased because of its negligence. ***Mitzelfelt v. Kamin*, 526 Pa. 54, 584 A.2d 888.**

Paramedics

Paramedics, after transporting shooting victim to nearest hospital, refused (allegedly not told of emergency nature) to transfer to larger hospital due to company policy. Recommended private ambulance service. Plaintiff died at second hospital. Nonsuit affirmed based upon lack of evidence that paramedics were advised that inter-hospital transfer was an emergency. ***Morena v. South Hills Health System*, 501 Pa. 634, 462 A.2d 680.**

Paranoid psychosis

Verdict $130,000.00—grade crossing case—plaintiff an occupant of a truck—diagnosis of paranoid psychosis—disputed medical testimony—special damages $43,385—future medical expense estimated at $4,000—future wage loss based on work life expectancy reduced to present worth totalled $65,889—Held: not excessive. ***Dollison v. B. & O. R.R. Co.*, 447 Pa. 96, 284 A.2d 704.**

Parents

Minor child who was in shared custody of separated parents negligently shot a friend with a BB gun. Suit brought against mother who had physical custody at the time of the shooting and father who did not have custody but who had purchased BB gun and was aware that the son had taken it to his mother's house. Held that father's status as a legal custodian is not, in and of itself, dispositive in establishing that he had the ability and opportunity to control his child's behavior at the time of the shooting. ***K.H. and D.A.H. v. J.R. and N.R.*, 826 A.2d 863 (Pa. 2003).**

Parked cars

Minor injured by a pellet fired from a gun held by another minor. In suit by parents of injured child and on his behalf against child who fired gun, trial court entered summary judgment on finding that the non-custodial mother of the child who fired the gun had no knowledge that the child had the gun in his possession while staying with his father. While the mere relation of parent and child imposes no duty upon the parent for the torts of the child, parents may be liable where negligence on the part of the parents makes an injury possible. If the injury ought to have been foreseen by the parents, their negligence is the proximate cause of the injury. ***J.H. ex rel. Hoffman v. Pellak*, 764 A.2d 64 (Pa. Super. 2000).**

Plaintiffs—children in their mother's car which was involved in accident. Mother's negligence could not be imputed to children. Clear that children could not be guilty of contributory negligence. ***Lind v. Thomas*, 265 Pa. Super. 121, 401 A.2d 830.**

The doctrine of intra-family immunity is overruled at least insofar as barring a recovery where a child is injured, allegedly as the result of the tortious conduct of her mother—all previous decisions to the contrary overruled. ***Falco v. Pados*, 444 Pa. 372, 282 A.2d 351.**

Minor child of additional defendant struck by defendant's car—defendant sought to join father as an additional defendant—preliminary objections sustained—father not negligent in permitting child of 9 to be on street. ***Reardon v. Wilbur*, 441 Pa. 551, 272 A.2d 888.**

Parked cars

Jury verdict as to liability only in favor of defendant used car dealership affirmed. Plaintiff injured by driver of stolen car failed to state a cause of action, where sole allegation of negligence was that dealership employees left keys in newly delivered vehicles in violation of unattended motor vehicle section of the Pennsylvania Vehicle Code. ***Santarlas v. Leaseway Motorcar Transport Company*, 456 Pa. Super. 34, 689 A.2d 311 (1997).**

Plaintiff seated in parked auto with door open when struck by trackless trolley which turned. Contact at rear of vehicle. Verdict for plaintiff affirmed. Operator of vehicle must be aware that rear can be dangerous while turning. ***Lebesco v. SEPTA*, 251 Pa. Super. 415, 380 A.2d 848.**

Plaintiff stopped car at intersection. View blocked by truck of defendant Johanna Farms parked at corner. Plaintiff edged out and stopped then struck by car driven by defendant Cohen. Verdict for plaintiff against both defendants. ***Bell v. Cohen, et al.*, 228 Pa. Super. 872, 322 A.2d 704.**

Plaintiff injured by collision with defendant's car at an intersection—defendant joined one Williams on ground that his car was illegally parked and obstructed defendant's view—court below in error in sustaining additional defendant's demurrer—matter for jury. ***Clevenstein v. Rizzuto*, 439 Pa. 397, 266 A.2d 623.**

Parking garage or lot

Charge as a whole did not instruct jury that burden of proving contributory negligence was on defendant—jury from charge could infer the contrary—error—new trial awarded. ***Franchetti v. Johnson,* 215 Pa. Super. 14, 257 A.2d 261.**

Defendant's operator left his rig in front of a restaurant with motor running—rig drifted into highway—decedent operating a tractor trailer unit with view of over 1000 feet collided with rig—verdict for defendant—new trial properly refused. ***Hummel v. Womeldorf,* 426 Pa. 460, 233 A.2d 215.**

Plaintiff while properly operating his car forced to swerve by the action of an unknown car and to collide with an unlighted trailer illegally parked—Supreme Court by a divided court held that the illegally parking of unlighted trailer the proximate cause. ***Slawson v. C.A.B.Y. Trans.,* 425 Pa. 489, 229 A.2d 888.**

Defendant proceeding southward and was passing a double parked car—pulling into northbound lane and injured plaintiff alighting from his car—case for jury—new trial properly granted where jury found for defendant. ***Green v. Johnson,* 424 Pa. 296, 227 A.2d 644.**

Parking garage or lot

Plaintiff and her daughter were injured when the vehicle in which they were traveling in a mall parking lot was struck from the side by another vehicle in the same lot. There was no traffic control device at the intersection of the trafficways on which they were each traveling. In remanding for a new trial, the court stated that a non-public parking area is not a highway for purposes of determining right of way under Pennsylvania traffic law. ***Marsico v. Dibileo,* 796 A.2d 997 (Pa. Super. 2002)**.

Plaintiff who fell on thin layer of "black ice" in motel parking lot suffered injuries and sued motel owner. Plaintiff argued that "hills and ridges" doctrine, which requires showing of accumulation of ice and snow, should not apply to business premises; they are not so burdened by substantial size of area to be cleared of ice and snow as municipalities and local agencies, which organizations the doctrine is designed to protect. Plaintiff also argued that custodian who had placed salt and sand on portions of premises was negligent for not salting and sanding entire parking lot. Held: "hills and ridges" applies to business invitees and local agencies equally and because plaintiff could not show accumulation had been allowed to form without any effort to cure problem, summary judgment was proper. ***Morin v. Travelers Rest Motel, Inc.,* 704 A.2d 1085 (Pa. Super. 1997).**

Park visitor who slipped on embankment between picnic pavilion and parking lot in County park was precluded from any recovery for injuries sustained against the County under Recreation Use of Land and Water Act. Land was unimproved and no fee was charged to plaintiff for use of the park. Order denying summary judgment reversed and complaint dismissed. ***Brezinski v. County of Allegheny,* 694 A.2d 388 (Pa. Cmwlth. 1997).**

Order granting summary judgment in favor of school district affirmed where plaintiff who slipped on ice in school district parking lot failed to establish that injuries were caused by improper design, construction, deterioration, or inherent de-

Parking garage or lot

fect of real estate. Real property exception to Political Subdivision Tort Claims Act not applicable. *Metkus v. Pennsbury School District,* **674 A.2d 355 (Pa. Cmwlth. 1996).**

Pedestrian employee in company parking lot struck by coemployee vehicle may not recover in tort action against coemployee driver. Workers' compensation is exclusive remedy. Order granting summary judgment affirmed. *Albright v. Fagan,* **448 Pa. Super. 395, 671 A.2d 760 (1996).**

Summary judgment reversed where owners of property adjoining parking lot on which plaintiff slipped and fell had easement across parking lot and, therefore, question existed as to whether property owners were liable as possessor of parking lot. *Blackman v. Federal Realty Inv. Trust,* **444 Pa. Super. 411, 664 A.2d 139 (1995).**

Plaintiff failed to prove that dangerous condition of a parking lot was causally related to injuries. Summary judgment in favor of volunteer fire department affirmed. *West v. Kuneck,* **167 Pa. Cmwlth. 252, 647 A.2d 975 (1994).**

Driver of automobile injured in collision with truck while making left turn into store parking lot. Owner of store not liable. Highway under control of PennDOT. *Allen v. Mellinger,* **156 Pa. Cmwlth. 113, 625 A.2d 1326.**

Motorist injured when attempting to avoid automobile exiting from health care center. Center and architect and contractor who undertook renovations of center not liable. Elimination of second exit not cause of accident. *Novack v. Jeannette District Memorial Hospital,* **410 Pa. Super. 603, 600 A.2d 616.**

Pedestrian who slipped and fell on ice and snow while taking short cut through parking lot brought action against tenant freight company and landlord. Neither landlord nor tenant liable. No duty owed. Pedestrian assumed risk. *Ott v. Unclaimed Freight Company,* **395 Pa. Super. 483, 577 A.2d 894.**

Plaintiff mugged in city-operated parking lot that was inadequately lighted. Under Tort Claims Act city not liable for actions of third parties. *Chevalier v. City of Philadelphia,* **516 Pa. 316, 532 A.2d 411.**

Patron assaulted in garage owned by parking authority. Held: parking authority as government agency immune from suit. *Rhoads v. Lancaster Parking Authority,* **103 Pa. Cmwlth. 278, 520 A.2d 122.**

Shopping Center patron was abducted from parking lot and died from subsequent heart attack. Held: whether holder of easement was possessor with duty to protect invitee from criminal attack is question for the finder of fact. *Leichter v. Eastern Realty Company,* **358 Pa. Super. 189, 516 A.2d 1247.**

Customer slipped and fell in shopping center parking lot. Property owner not liable owing to absence of ridges and elevations in ice covering lot. *Roland v. Kravco, Inc.,* **355 Pa. Super. 493, 513 A.2d 1029.**

Passenger in automobile was injured in collision with vehicle stolen from parking lot. Owner of lot not liable because injury was not foreseeable. Local or-

Parking garage or lot

dinance concerning negligence of parking lot operators did not alter foreseeability requirement. *Jamison v. City of Philadelphia,* **355 Pa. Super. 376, 513 A.2d 479.**

Plaintiff-decedent in restaurant parking lot at night went on wrong path with car, drove into canal and drowned. Verdict by jury of $550,000 wrongful death, $500,000 survival. *Ehehalt v. Nyari O'Dette, Inc.,* **85 Pa. Cmwlth. 94, 481 A.2d 365.**

Plaintiff fell on patch of ice in parking lot of chiropractic clinic. Jury verdict $70,000 reflecting 35% comparative negligence. Ice was next to car, although rest of lot was clear. Plaintiff became aware of ice while still seated in car. Wore prosthesis at time—fractured left hip. Verdict reversed. Where plaintiff sees risk, possessor of land relieved of responsibility and duty of care to invitee who, under circumstances here was held to have assumed risk as matter of law. Comparative negligence statute not applicable. *Carrender v. Fitterer,* **503 Pa. 178, 469 A.2d 120.**

Handicapped plaintiff injured in parking lot of clinic where she went for medical care. Plaintiff had artificial lower leg and fell on ice. Fall was on isolated patch of ice between cars. Jury verdict $70,000 for hip, $2,500 for husband's loss of consortium. Reduced 35% for contribution. Affirmed. *Carrender v. Fitterer,* **310 Pa. Super. 433, 456 A.2d 1013.**

Jury verdict $200,000, crush injury with permanent disability. Male warehouse employee in dark parking lot guiding tractor-trailer rigs by voice, with hand on rig. Fell in parking lot hole. Issue of plaintiff's contributory negligence for jury under circumstances. With lease silent, lessor has over years undertaken to keep parking area in repair. Held: a continuing duty to keep area reasonably safe for tenant's use. *McDevitt v. Terminal Warehouse Co.,* **304 Pa. Super. 438, 450 A.2d 991.**

Plaintiff stabbed in parking lot of supermarket. Evidence of previous crimes within store and limitation of amount of cash permitted in cash registers. Substantial verdict for plaintiff affirmed. *Murphy v. Penn Fruit,* **274 Pa. Super. 427, 418 A.2d 480.**

Pile of dirt left near highway by contractor which allegedly obstructed view of driver leaving parking lot—operator struck motorcyclist on highway—judgment *n.o.v.* reversed and verdict against contractor reinstated. *Flickinger, et al. v. Ritsky and Marona Construction Co.,* **452 Pa. 69, 305 A.2d 40.**

Plaintiff left car in defendant's parking lot—took claim check from machine and locked car—check was to be presented on removing car—car missing—not a bailment but error to enter summary judgment in favor of parking lot operator—plaintiff entitled to prove circumstances and whether attendant negligent in permitting car to be removed without presentation of claim check. *Sparrow v. Airport Parking Co. of America,* **221 Pa. Super. 32, 289 A.2d 87.**

Plaintiff's car collided with defendant's car in a parking lot of a shopping center—court below granted judgment *n.o.v.*—in error—facts of case not so clear as to justify such disposition—facts of case could explain why plaintiff did not see defendant's car until too late to avoid a collision. *Gerisch v. McElhone,* **209 Pa. Super. 79, 223 A.2d 923.**

Passengers

Partially constructed building

Child of 4 entered a partially constructed building being built by defendant contractor—fell to cellar while walking backward and was severely injured—no recovery—a house in course of construction is not an attractive nuisance. ***Goll et al. v. Muscara*, 211 Pa. Super. 93, 235 A.2d 443.**

Participation theory

In negligence action against corporate defendant and officers, officers are not liable for failing to maintain clean bathroom absent proof of their participation in creating or allowing continued existence of dangerous condition. Party's failure to answer request for admission that states a conclusion of law does not establish plaintiff's case. Judgment in favor of plaintiff vacated and remanded for consideration of scope of involvement and liability of owners. ***Brindley v. Woodland Village Restaurant, Inc.*, 438 Pa. Super. 385, 652 A.2d 865 (1995).**

Partners

Parents of child injured by prescription drug brought malpractice action against partner of prescribing physician. Held: partner not individually liable. ***Keech v. Mead Johnson and Company*, 398 Pa. Super. 329, 580 A.2d 1374.**

Partnership brought personal injury action against physician who treated one of the partners. Held: Partnership may not recover economic damages against third-party tortfeasor. ***Margolis v. Jackson*, 375 Pa. Super. 182, 543 A.2d 1238.**

Passengers

Plaintiff passenger brought negligence action against the unlicensed intoxicated driver of the vehicle she was in and a dram shop action against the bar where they had been drinking. The trial court granted summary judgment on behalf of the Defendant. The Superior Court affirmed holding that the Plaintiff passenger was vicariously liable for the intoxicated driver's actions as she permitted him to drive her vehicle knowing he did not have a license. ***Price v. Leibfried*, 34 A.3d 1279 (Pa. Super. 2011).**

Plaintiff bus passenger suffered a broken femur when she fell on the floor of the bus as it began to move before she had been seated. Compulsory nonsuit for bus company affirmed based on lack of testimony that jerk or jolt of bus was so severe as to cause extraordinarily disturbing effect on other passengers. Plaintiff's medical expert's testimony that force of jerk or jolt of bus was severe because of nature of the injury is not sufficient. ***Asbury v. Port Authority Transit of Allegheny County*, 863 A.2d 84 (Pa. Cmwlth. 2004).**

Summary judgment entered against plaintiff who was shot by a robber while a passenger on defendant's stopped train. Plaintiff alleged that defendant's trainman's failure to open the door of the train to allow plaintiff to escape before he was shot was a concurrent cause of his injury and that failure to act involved the operation of the motor vehicle. The Commonwealth Court distinguishes concurrent negligent acts from a negligent act by defendant and a criminal assault by a third party

Passengers

and also holds by implication that the failure to open the door was not "operation" of the motor vehicle. ***Greenleaf v. SEPTA*, 698 A.2d 170 (Pa. Cmwlth. 1997).**

Summary judgment reversed where trial court failed to consider medical evidence of psychic injuries that may have qualified as serious impairment of a body function under limited tort coverage provided for in Motor Vehicle Financial Responsibility Law before granting summary judgment. Minor children injured in accident while riding in their mother's uninsured vehicle are held to have the same deemed limited tort coverage as their uninsured mother. ***Hames v. Philadelphia Housing Authority*, 696 A.2d 880 (Pa. Cmwlth. 1997).**

A common carrier has the highest duty of care to its passengers to carry them safely and enable them to alight safely at their intended destination. Bus company does not have a duty to intoxicated passengers who have disembarked from bus at their intended destination to insure that they travel safely after discharge. Trial court's refusal to grant summary judgment to bus company reversed and remanded. ***Knoud v. Galante*, ___ Pa. Super. ___, 696 A.2d 854 (1997).**

Pedestrian plaintiff injured by drunken driver sued passengers who may have been aware of driver's intoxication. Summary judgment in favor of defendants affirmed because a passenger does not owe a duty to a third person where driver of vehicle is intoxicated, absent a special relationship, joint enterprise, joint venture or a right to control the vehicle. ***Brandjord v. Hopper*, 455 Pa. Super. 426, 688 A.2d 721 (1997).**

In suit by decedent's estate against minor passenger in other vehicle, an individual who is simply a passenger in a vehicle operated by an intoxicated driver may not be held responsible for the driver's negligence. Rather, liability may only be imposed where sufficient facts indicate that the passenger substantially assisted or encouraged the driver's negligent conduct. Order granting summary judgment in favor of minor passenger affirmed. ***Welc v. Porter*, 450 Pa. Super. 112, 675 A.2d 334 (1996).**

Passenger of intoxicated driver has no duty to third person killed by driver's negligence. Passenger's mere request that driver take her somewhere and driver's acquiescence does not establish driver as agent and passenger as principal so as to establish passenger's liability to third person killed by driver's negligence. Summary judgment affirmed. ***Clayton v. McCullough*, 448 Pa. Super. 126, 670 A.2d 710 (1996).**

Plaintiff injured when alighting from bus is not injured by reason of "operation of motor vehicle"; therefore suit against transit authority precluded. Order granting judgment notwithstanding the verdict affirmed. ***Rubenstein v. SEPTA*, ___ Pa. Cmwlth. ___, 668 A.2d 283 (1995).**

In action by passenger against PennDOT for negligent design of road, judgment for PennDOT affirmed where plaintiff passenger determined to be negligent by exposing herself to an unreasonable risk in riding with a known intoxicated driver.

Passengers

Even minimal evidence of contributory negligence requires a charge on the issue. ***Karchner v. Flaim,*** **___ Pa. Cmwlth. ___, 661 A.2d 928 (1995).**

Plaintiff alighting from bus is not engaged in operation of motor vehicle so claim for damages does not qualify under statutory exception to governmental immunity. Summary judgment affirmed. Legislative intent is to grant immunity; therefore interpretation of exceptions to governmental immunity should favor that outcome. ***Bazemore v. SEPTA,*** **___ Pa. Cmwlth. ___, 657 A.2d 1323 (1995).**

Passenger injured while exiting bus. Held: vehicle exception to sovereign immunity not applicable. Authority not liable for first party benefits under Financial Responsibility Law. ***Gielarowski v. Port Authority of Allegheny County,* 159 Pa. Cmwlth. 214, 632 A.2d 1054.**

Passenger assaulted by third party while riding train. Transportation Authority not liable. ***Williamson v. SEPTA,* 154 Pa. Cmwlth. 448, 624 A.2d 218.**

Passenger attacked on train. Vehicle liability exception to sovereign immunity not applicable. ***Evans v. SEPTA,* 149 Pa. Cmwlth. 376, 613 A.2d 137.**

Passenger injured by other passengers exiting train brought action for failure to control crowd. Authority found not liable for actions of third parties. ***SEPTA v. Hussey,* 138 Pa. Cmwlth. 436, 588 A.2d 110.**

Passenger in vehicle operated by intoxicated driver brought action against driver and city for injuries caused by vehicle striking headwall along highway. City not liable. Driver 75% liable, passenger 25% liable. ***Hannon v. City of Philadelphia,* 138 Pa. Cmwlth. 166, 587 A.2d 845.**

Passenger on trolley injured in collision with automobiles brought action against insurance company under Financial Responsibility Law. Insurance company found not liable. Trolley on tracks not motor vehicle within statute. ***Ellis v. SEPTA,* 524 Pa. 398, 573 A.2d 216.**

Passengers in automobile injured in collision at intersection. Held: trial court erred in refusing to instruct jury that negligence of driver may not be imputed against passenger-guest. ***Ellis v. Graves,* 385 Pa. Super. 168, 560 A.2d 220.**

Passenger who fell asleep was injured in automobile accident. The fact that passenger participated in all-night outing was admissible to show that she was contributorily negligent. ***Hill v. Reynolds,* 384 Pa. Super. 34, 557 A.2d 759.**

Passenger in truck leased to carrier was injured when brakes failed. Lessee held vicariously liable under Interstate Common Carrier Act for injury to member of the traveling public. ***Wilkerson v. Allied Van Lines,* 360 Pa. Super. 523, 521 A.2d 25.**

Plaintiff passenger on bus travelling through construction zone when bump threw plaintiff violently up and down. SEPTA joined City but lower court entered directed verdict at close of evidence in favor of City. Verdict in favor of plaintiff against SEPTA affirmed. ***Farness v. SEPTA,* 338 Pa. Super. 130, 487 A.2d 887.**

Passing

Jury verdict $800,000 for 16 year old female passenger in car involved in accident, rendered quadriplegic due to fracture-dislocation of cervical spine. New trial ordered. Held: plaintiff's expert witnesses not properly qualified to testify under facts here. ***Dambaher v. Mallis,* 336 Pa. Super. 22, 485 A.2d 408.**

Plaintiff was a passenger in defendant's bus which was very crowded—in endeavoring to alight plaintiff was thrown to pavement by a surging movement of passengers—defendant is responsible even though the acts of the passengers did not amount to a breach of the peace. ***Lasota v. Phila. Trans. Co.,* 421 Pa. 386, 219 A.2d 296.**

Passing

Plaintiff driver filed suit after the Defendant driver swerved into the Plaintiff's lane as the Plaintiff was passing the Defendant on the left. The trial court denied instructions on the sudden emergency doctrine and negligence per se. The Superior Court, on appeal, held that evidence that the Motor Vehicle Code was violated supported a negligence per se jury instruction at trial. ***Drew v. Work*, 2014 Pa. Super. 137 (Pa. Super. 2014).**

Real property exception to sovereign immunity does not apply in automobile accident involving motorcyclist and driver. PennDOT's design and construction of road, including length of passing lane and speed limits, were not defects that caused motorcyclist's injuries but merely facilitated occurrence of accident when combined with negligence of driver. Assured clear distance rule does not apply where instrumentality moves into driver's path within a distance short of the assured clear distance ahead. Driver does not have to anticipate negligence of another driver in calculating his assured clear distance. ***Nestor v. Com., Dept. of Transp.,* ___ Pa. Cmwlth. ___, 658 A.2d 829 (1995).**

Action of motorcyclist who crossed into oncoming lane while attempting to pass vehicle in his lane was sole cause of accident; order denying PennDOT's motion for post trial relief reversed. ***Glover v. Com., Dept. of Transp.,* 167 Pa. Cmwlth. 87, 647 A.2d 630 (1994).**

Passing in a no-passing zone designated only by a double yellow line is negligence *per se*. ***Garcia v. Bang,* 375 Pa. Super. 356, 544 A.2d 509.**

Motorcyclist struck by truck after crossing double yellow line in attempt to pass. Whether motorcycle rider was negligent was question for jury. Truck driver found 20% negligent, Motorcyclist found 80% negligent. ***Cervone v. Reading,* 371 Pa. Super. 279, 538 A.2d 16.**

Auto in passing lane. Bus in right lane passed on right and then veered into left lane striking auto. No evidence of negligence on auto driver. Error to charge on contributory negligence. ***Smith v. Port Authority Transit,* 257 Pa. Super. 66, 390 A.2d 249.**

Passengers on bus injured when boys entered bus and randomly struck passengers. Common carrier has duty to repress disorder and to do whatever possible to restrain and, if necessary, remove disorderly parties. Negligent to open doors when same boys had earlier thrown stones at bus. Evidence that driver did nothing to quell disturbance. Plaintiff verdict sustained. ***Mangini v. SEPTA*****, 235 Pa. Super. 478, 344 A.2d 621.**

Eakin driving north on highway. Passed on right by Polimeni which struck Eakin vehicle and then crossed highway and struck Caldwell vehicle. Three suits and cross-claims. After all tried, only Polimeni found negligent. Verdict sustained. ***Churchill v. Eakin, et al.*****, 233 Pa. Super. 466, 335 A.2d 378.**

Plaintiff struck by truck going between two stopped buses. Truck partially on wrong side of road. Plaintiff had no recollection of accident. For jury. ***Gregorich v. Pepsi-Cola*****, 230 Pa. Super. 144, 327 A.2d 171.**

Plaintiff injured by reason of contact with a tractor-trailer—one of named defendants skidded into opposite lane and stopped—tractor-trailer endeavored to pass stalled vehicle and caused contact with plaintiff's car—jury exonerated defendant who had skidded and held owner of tractor-trailer and its operator responsible—such finding upheld on appeal. ***Boyd v. Hertz Corp. et al.*****, 219 Pa. Super. 488, 281 A.2d 679.**

Plaintiff in car to rear of a dump truck proceeding in same direction—plaintiff operator pulled out to pass when defendant dump truck operator pulled out to pass a car ahead and collided with plaintiff's passing car—verdict against plaintiff operator and inadequate verdicts for passengers—court below granted a new trial without an opinion—affirmed on appeal. ***Eagleson v. Hoffman*****, 217 Pa. Super. 721, 266 A.2d 549.**

A bus passed a car on a snowy roadway and had proceeded some 1500 to 2000 feet before car to rear ran into a snow bank and become uncontrollable, resulting in a rear-end collision with another car—that operator held negligent but judgment *n.o.v.* entered as to bus company. ***Metts v. Griglak*****, 438 Pa. 392, 264 A.2d 684.**

Plaintiff attempted to pass between the rear of his parked car and a car of the defendant parked to the rear of his car—testimony that defendant's driver had full view of plaintiff and knew that he intended to pass between cars—injured by forward movement of defendant's car—doctrine of choice of ways does not apply. ***Kinee v. Penn Radio Cab Co.*****, 435 Pa. 387, 257 A.2d 554.**

Defendant proceeding southward and was passing a double parked car—pulling into northbound lane and injured plaintiff alighting from his car—case for jury—new trial properly granted where jury found for defendant. ***Green v. Johnson*****, 424 Pa. 296, 227 A.2d 644.**

Passing lane

Real property exception to sovereign immunity does not apply in automobile accident involving motorcyclist and driver. PennDOT's design and construction of road, including length of passing lane and speed limits, were not defects that caused motorcyclist's injuries but merely facilitated occurrence of accident when combined with negligence of driver. Assured clear distance rule does not apply where instrumentality moves into driver's path within a distance short of the assured clear

Patella

distance ahead. Driver does not have to anticipate negligence of another driver in calculating his assured clear distance. ***Nestor v. Com., Dept. of Transp.,* ___ Pa. Cmwlth. ___, 658 A.2d 829 (1995).**

Patella

Plaintiff who fails to participate significantly in postoperative care risks loss of any claim for alleged negligence of physician in performing surgery. The Comparative Negligence Act is not applicable in such cases because of the inability to apportion liability between both parties. ***Ferguson v. Panzarella,* 445 Pa. Super. 23, 664 A.2d 989 (1995).**

Peculiar Risk Doctrine

Administratrix sued Pennsylvania Turnpike Commission and Trumbull Corporation for failing to provide a safe work environment after her husband was killed while driving an unfamiliar truck type on the job site upon the order of his superiors. The court held; 1. That a possessor of land owes a duty of care to warn or correct dangers on his land unknown to a contractor or his employees; 2. Inspection of ongoing work at a construction site by a landowner is not evidence of control; 3. Driving a truck on a haul road is not a peculiar risk imparting liability onto a landowner. ***Farabaugh v. Pennsylvania Turnpike Commission,* 590 Pa. 46, 911 A.2d 1264 (2006).**

Peculiar risk doctrine did not apply to make contractor liable for injuries sustained by subcontractor's employee who fell from roof of building on which he was working where both contractor and subcontractor were aware of dangerous condition of roof. ***Edwards v. Franklin and Marshall College,* 444 Pa. Super. 1, 663 A.2d 187 (1995).**

Pedestrian

Decedent's estate brought negligence action against a motorist after the decedent was struck and killed by the defendant. The trial court granted summary judgment in favor of the defendant. The Superior Court reversed, holding that plaintiff's expert report, which opined that the defendant should have observed the plaintiff in sufficient time to stop his vehicle, was enough to preclude summary judgment in favor of the defendant. ***Wright v. Eastman,* 63 A.3d 281 (Pa. Super. 2013).**

Parent of deceased minor child brought suit against bus driver for negligence after the bus driver struck the minor child, while crossing the road. The jury rendered a verdict in favor of the Plaintiff. The Commonwealth Court on appeal reversed and remanded on the issue of damages, but held that the Defendants were not entitled to a directed verdict against the victim's uncle who was allegedly contributorily negligent as he was with the child and must have seen the bus. ***Cheng v. SEPTA,* 981 A.2d 371 (Pa. Cmwlth. 2009).**

Plaintiff brought a claim against a property owner after he tripped and fell on sidewalk outside of the property owner's home. The appellate court reversed the trial court's denial for a new trial solely on damages, because the jury's award of zero dollars to the plaintiff, despite a holding of 50% negligence on the part of both parties, was against the weight of the evidence. *Casselli v. Powlen*, **937 A.2d 1137 (Pa. Super. 2007).**

Pedestrian injured by automobile is not precluded from recovery of less than "serious bodily injury" damages because of her mother's limited tort coverage selection on mother's automobile. *L.S., a minor v. Eschbach*, **874 A.2d 1150 (Pa. 2005)**.

County was shielded by governmental immunity under Political Subdivision Tort Claims Act in suit by pedestrians struck by runaway vehicle on walking path adjacent to road where there was no intervening guard rail. *Simko v. County of Allegheny*, **869 A.2d 571 (Pa. Cmwlth. 2005)**.

Pedestrian plaintiff injured by drunken driver sued passengers who may have been aware of driver's intoxication. Summary judgment in favor of defendants affirmed because a passenger does not owe a duty to a third person where driver of vehicle is intoxicated, absent a special relationship, joint enterprise, joint venture or a right to control the vehicle. *Brandjord v. Hopper*, **455 Pa. Super. 426, 688 A.2d 721 (1997).**

Pedestrian employee in company parking lot struck by coemployee vehicle may not recover in tort action against coemployee driver. Workers' compensation is exclusive remedy. Order granting summary judgment affirmed. *Albright v. Fagan*, **448 Pa. Super. 395, 671 A.2d 760 (1996).**

Pedestrian struck by automobile failed to establish serious injury or serious impairment of bodily function. Factors to be considered in determining severity of bodily impairment for purposes of recovery under limited tort option include extent of the impairment, particular body function impaired, duration of the impairment, treatment required to correct the impairment, and any other relevant factors. Judgment in favor of plaintiff for only out-of-pocket medical expenses affirmed. *Murray v. McCann*, **442 Pa. Super. 30, 658 A.2d 404 (1995).**

Wife-plaintiff pedestrian struck by auto found 50% negligent. A $5,000 award for wife-plaintiff adequate and $0 for husband-plaintiff supported by evidence. Order denying new trial affirmed. *Nudelman v. Gilbride*, **436 Pa. Super. 44, 647 A.2d 233 (1994).**

Pedestrian tripped over raised grate in sidewalk in front of restaurant. Pedestrian licensee and not invitee. *Palange v. City of Philadelphia Law Department*, **433 Pa. Super. 373, 640 A.2d 1305.**

Pedestrian injured after stepping in hole in sidewalk brought action against city. City neither primarily nor secondarily liable. *Lyons v. City of Philadelphia*, **___ Pa. Cmwlth. ___, 632 A.2d 1006.**

Pedestrian killed while crossing highway between two townships. Action brought against both townships, PennDOT, and driver. All government parties immune. *Sloneker v. Martin*, **144 Pa. Cmwlth. 190, 604 A.2d 751.**

Pedestrian who fell on sidewalk adjacent to property owned by school district appealed decision that district was immune to Superior Court. Appeal trans-

Pedestrian

ferred to Commonwealth Court. *Wilson v. School District of Philadelphia,* **410 Pa. Super. 416, 600 A.2d 210.**

Pedestrian hit by egg thrown from trolley brought action against transit authority. Authority held not liable. *Hall v. SEPTA,* **141 Pa. Cmwlth. 591, 596 A.2d 1153.**

Pedestrian hit on head by ham bone while on premises owned by authority. Authority not liable. Real estate exception to government immunity did not apply. *Douglas v. Philadelphia Housing Authority,* **134 Pa. Cmwlth. 441, 578 A.2d 1011.**

Pedestrian crossing street in middle of block struck by delivery truck backing into parking space. Held: fact that pedestrian crossed between intersection insufficient to establish negligence. *Bressler v. Dannon Yogurt,* **392 Pa. Super. 475, 573 A.2d 562.**

Uninsured pedestrian injured when struck by stolen automobile. Held: insurer of owner of stolen automobile liable for uninsured motorist benefits. *Ector v. Motorist Insurance Companies,* **391 Pa. Super. 458, 571 A.2d 457.**

Pedestrian killed by trolley while crossing State highway. City found not liable for failure to provide safety or traffic control devices. *Jackson v. SEPTA,* **129 Pa. Cmwlth. 596, 566 A.2d 638.**

Pedestrian fell into tree well on sidewalk outside stadium. Dark and rainy. Non-jury verdict for plaintiff with one-third comparative negligence. Held: plaintiff needed no expert as to proper design of tree well or sidewalk. Affirmed. *Burns v. City of Philadelphia,* **350 Pa. Super. 615, 504 A.2d 1321.**

Fatal injury to student struck by car after alighting from school bus. Held: school district immune from suit. Stopped school bus with flashing lights is not a traffic control as defined by governmental immunity statute. *Aberant v. Wilkes-Barre Area School Dist.,* **89 Pa. Cmwlth. 516, 492 A.2d 1186.**

Pedestrian struck by auto. Evidence admitted at trial that pedestrian was intoxicated. Verdict for defendant reversed. Charge given using presumption of intoxication from Vehicle Code. This was error. Under facts here however, evidence of blood alcohol and other evidence of intoxication was relevant. *Ackerman v. Delcomico,* **336 Pa. Super. 569, 486 A.2d 410.**

Pedestrian-bus accident. Verdict for defense. New trial denied. All witnesses agreed that pedestrian struck bus between front and rear passenger door while crossing street on red light. *Klyman v. SEPTA,* **331 Pa. Super. 172, 480 A.2d 299.**

Fourteen-year old boy struck by auto passing bus, allegedly after bus driver waved boy to cross in front of bus on snowy day. Sufficient evidence of driver's negligence to support verdict in favor of plaintiff. Held: driver of auto 65% negligent; SEPTA 30%; plaintiff 5%. Verdict $7,875,000. New trial ordered on issue of school's expenses being conditionally relevant (as to damages only) after determination of recusal issue. *Reilly v. SEPTA,* **330 Pa. Super. 420, 479 A.2d 973.**

Pedestrian

Six and one-half year old boy struck by car in area where children were waiting for school bus. Child "ran into street." Issue as to how quickly child entered street. Jury verdict for motorist, affirmed. **Heffner v. Schad, 330 Pa. Super. 101, 478 A.2d 1372.**

Trial judge granted new trial based on inadequate instruction. Plaintiff standing on berm when struck by overhanging mirror on defendant's truck. Charge did not clearly state that plaintiff could recover even though defendant did not leave highway. New trial ordered. **Saylor v. Rose, 319 Pa. Super. 560, 466 A.2d 686.**

Jury verdict $45,000 wrongful death, $250,000 survival. Decedent standing on sidewalk was run over by defendant who had consumed significant amount of alcohol. Decedent a 31 year old male, married with two children. Compensatory damage award affirmed. **Harvey v. Hassinger, 315 Pa. Super. 97, 461 A.2d 814.**

Pedestrian struck by wife defendant driving auto. Family use doctrine not part of Pennsylvania law. Mere fact of spousal relationship insufficient to impose liability on husband owner of auto. Affirmed summary judgment in favor of absent husband owner of auto. **Breslin v. Ridarelli, 308 Pa. Super. 179, 454 A.2d 80.**

Plaintiff walking between parked truck and his car, intended to enter his car through left door, struck by truck which moved as he was about to enter his car. Plaintiff's verdict affirmed. Defense argument that accident could not happen as described was rejected, with no supporting evidence. Court says *res ipsa* may apply to case—dissent on this issue. **Siravo v. AAA Trucking, 306 Pa. Super. 217, 452 A.2d 521.**

Pedestrian who testifies that he stepped off curb in middle of block after looking and seeing nothing, properly nonsuited. No evidence of negligence and clear contribution. **Barney v. Foradas, 305 Pa. Super. 404, 451 A.2d 710.**

Pedestrian struck and killed by one or more vehicles as he stepped off medial strip of four-lane highway at night. Settled with first striking vehicle. Nonsuit entered as to all others. Evidence insufficient as to whether any other vehicles struck plaintiff. **Pio v. Letaavec, 294 Pa. Super. 196, 439 A.2d 818.**

Pedestrian struck by auto. Defense verdict overturned. Where plaintiff stepped into roadway in enough time for defendant to avoid accident, jury to consider if defendant could have avoided the accident. **Smith v. Chardak, 295 Pa. Super. 173, 435 A.2d 624.**

Pedestrian struck by auto. Defense verdict reversed. Proper, within discretion of trial judge, to allow police officer to estimate speed from skid marks. Error to refuse charge that if driver saw pedestrian standing ahead, and perceived possibility of crossing, there was a duty to sound horn. **Morris v. Moss, 290 Pa. Super. 587, 435 A.2d 184.**

Group of boy scouts walking on highway due to construction on berm. Truck moved to left to avoid them but moved back too soon and struck plaintiff. Verdict against driver and construction company. Contractor should have recognized potential for this type of occurrence. **Grainy v. Campbell, 493 Pa. 88, 425 A.2d 379.**

Pedestrian

Pedestrian struck twice by two successive vehicles at night on Interstate Highway. Verdict against second driver only. New trial order on charge of court relating to sudden emergency. ***Potenburg v. Varner and Petka*, 284 Pa. Super. 19, 424 A.2d 1370.**

Truck struck 4 year old pedestrian who froze on highway 350 feet ahead of driver. Defense verdict overturned by court *en banc*. Affirmed. ***Lamb v. Gibson*, 274 Pa. Super. 7, 417 A.2d 1224.**

Plaintiff and five Boy Scouts hiking along two lane road. Came to open ditch in berm and walked on roadway. Defendant saw ditch and plaintiff and moved into left lane, but cut back to right lane too soon striking plaintiff. Driver's actions were a superseding cause to any negligence. ***Grainy v. Campbell*, 269 Pa. Super. 225, 409 A.2d 860.**

Pedestrian crossing in middle of block struck by auto in middle of street; some evidence of running. Jury found both plaintiff and defendant negligent. ***Rosato v. Nationwide*, 263 Pa. Super. 340, 397 A.2d 1238.**

Plaintiff on shoulder of road after accident exchanging information. Another car then skidded into his parked car which struck him. Antecedent negligence of plaintiff not a proximate cause of injuries or second accident. Error to charge on contributory negligence or sudden emergency. New trial ordered. ***Sullivan v. Wolson*, 262 Pa. Super. 397, 396 A.2d 1230.**

Plaintiff crossed street in downtown Pittsburgh, mid-day, in front of stopped truck, in middle of block. Granting of nonsuit reversed. Not contributorily negligent as matter of law. For jury. ***Lavely v. Wolota*, 253 Pa. Super. 196, 384 A.2d 1298.**

Pedestrian struck by car while walking in street which had no sidewalks. Embankments prohibited walking off roadway. Driver blinded by oncoming lights. Theory against township was design defect in roadway in light of increased usage. Verdict against driver and township. ***Drew v. Laber*, 477 Pa. 297, 383 A.2d 941.**

Plaintiff, a crossing guard, allegedly struck by auto which skidded on ice. Defense was that auto stopped at curb and did not strike plaintiff. Charge on unavoidable accident proper. Verdict for defendant. ***Kenworthy v. Burghart*, 241 Pa. Super. 267, 361 A.2d 335.**

Plaintiff standing on highway for about 10 minutes talking to driver of stopped auto when struck by oncoming truck. Night—plaintiff wearing dark clothes. Jury found defendant negligent and plaintiff guilty of contributory negligence. ***Trayer v. King*, 241 Pa. Super. 86, 359 A.2d 800.**

Plaintiff's decedent struck by defendant's driver and killed. Evidence that wall obstructed driver's view in direction of decedent's approach to scene. Police found scratches on bumper. Witness heard crash, looked up and saw plaintiff in street and defendant's truck stopped. *Res gestae* statement of driver:: "I did see him, but when I saw him, it was too late." For jury. ***Exposito v. Dairyman's League Cooperative*, 236 Pa. Super. 401, 344 A.2d 505.**

Pedestrian

Thirteen-year old plaintiff walking in street—no sidewalks—night. Defendant driving in same direction and struck him from behind. For jury. Right of pedestrian in street equal to that of motor vehicles in absence of sidewalks. ***Eller v. Work*, 233 Pa. Super. 186, 336 A.2d 645.**

Minor plaintiff walking home from school. Sidewalk being excavated. School zone. Minor plaintiff crossed street to avoid excavation when struck by defendant's auto when within foot or two of opposite curb. Verdict for plaintiff sustained. ***Simmons v. Mullen*, 231 Pa. Super. 199, 331 A.2d 892.**

Plaintiff struck by defendant's truck which was pulling between buses stopped on opposite sides of street discharging passengers. Evidence that truck partially on wrong side of street. Plaintiff had no recollection of accident. For jury. ***Gregorich v. Pepsi-Cola*, 230 Pa. 144, 327 A.2d 171.**

Pedestrian struck at night by defendant's vehicle—plaintiff carrying flashlight and had crossed part of 48 foot wide highway—for jury if plaintiff on highway long enough so that defendant as careful driver should have seen him and avoided impact. ***Berry v. Lintner*, 226 Pa. Super. 562, 323 A.2d 253.**

Minor crossing street from east to west. Defendant driving south. No parked cars. Plaintiff struck by right front bumper. Body picked up one foot from west berm. No other traffic. For jury. ***McAuliffe v. Constantine*, 228 Pa. Super. 52, 323 A.2d 158.**

Plaintiff decedent left party and a few minutes later defendant left. Plaintiff walking home. Defendant driving. Dark night. As defendant pulled from curb he felt drag under wheels. Thinking he ran over trash bag, he backed up. Drag still present so he got out and discovered plaintiff's body. No evidence of how plaintiff got under wheels. Defendant's verdict affirmed. ***Rost v. Wickenheiser*, 229 Pa. Super. 84, 323 A.2d 154.**

Minor asked for ice cream money. Picked up in front of defendant's car, three feet from ice cream truck. From this it could be inferred that defendant was on wrong side of road. For jury. ***DeLio v. Hamilton*, 227 Pa. Super. 581, 308 A.2d 607.**

A pedestrian is not contributorily negligent as a matter of law in walking longitudinally on an icy highway on the right hand side with back to approaching traffic where no sidewalk exists. ***South v. Gray*, 223 Pa. Super. 442, 302 A.2d 459.**

Plaintiff pedestrian fell while crossing a bridge maintained by Port Authority—notice that bridge was closed to pedestrians—notice frequently thrown down as bridge was notoriously used by pedestrians—verdict for plaintiff sustained—issue of contributory negligence was for the jury. ***Niemiec v. Allegheny County Port Authority et al.*, 223 Pa. Super. 435, 302 A.2d 439.**

Pedestrian while standing on sidewalk allegedly struck by protruding mirror of defendant's truck—trial court in error in excluding from jury's consideration the fact that mirror may have extended over sidewalk even though the truck was still on the travelled portion of the cartway—new trial awarded to plaintiff. ***Russell v. Helm's Express, Inc.*, 221 Pa. Super. 292, 293 A.2d 78.**

Pellet gun

Plaintiff's decedent had been a passenger in a car which stalled in highway—decedent got out to help push car to a nearby gas station—at night—decedent struck by defendant's car coming from rear while he was pushing car—for jury—decedent could not be said to be contributorily negligent as a matter of law. *Schofield v. Scott,* **442 Pa. 642, 277 A.2d 143.**

Decedent pedestrian struck at night by defendant's car between intersections—evident that decedent was thrown 63 feet through the air—jury could infer excessive speed from such testimony—nonsuit improperly entered—case for jury. *McNett v. Briggs,* **217 Pa. Super. 322, 272 A.2d 202.**

Pedestrian crossing four lane main highway (two lanes each way)—stopping in medial strip and then running across two remaining lanes without looking—struck—guilty of contributory negligence—jury found for defendant—error to grant a new trial. *Parker v. Jones,* **423 Pa. 15, 223 A.2d 229.**

Plaintiff's pedestrian crossing street—apparently not at a crosswalk—struck by defendant's car when having traversed eight-ninths of distance between curbs—defendant's explanation that he did not see plaintiff—at night but street well lighted—case for jury. *Kmetz v. Lochiatto,* **421 Pa. 363, 219 A.2d 588.**

Decedent pedestrian crossing street near intersection—defendant's car made a left turn and contacted decedent—no evidence of speed, awareness of decedent's presence or proof of inattentiveness—nonsuit proper—mere happening of an accident. *Antonson v. Johnson,* **420 Pa. 558, 218 A.2d 123.**

Pellet gun

Minor injured by a pellet fired from a gun held by another minor. In suit by parents of injured child and on his behalf against child who fired gun, trial court entered summary judgment on finding that the non-custodial mother of the child who fired the gun had no knowledge that the child had the gun in his possession while staying with his father. While the mere relation of parent and child imposes no duty upon the parent for the torts of the child, parents may be liable where negligence on the part of the parents makes an injury possible. If the injury ought to have been foreseen by the parents, their negligence is the proximate cause of the injury. *J.H. ex rel. Hoffman v. Pellak,* **764 A.2d 64 (Pa. Super. 2000).**

A minor/owner who provides an air powered pellet gun to another minor may be liable to minor plaintiff injured by a pellet for providing the gun without instruction. The reasonably anticipated negligent firing of the pellet gun by other minor is not a superseding, intervening cause that insulates minor/owner from liability. Order sustaining preliminary objections reversed. *Frey v. Smith,* **454 Pa. Super. 242, 685 A.2d 169 (1996).**

Pennsylvania National Guardsmen

Pennsylvania National Guardsmen granted state compensation when injured during active service. Amount of compensation determined by Pennsylvania Workmen's Compensation Law. Therefore, suit against fellow guardsmen, in tort, is barred. See Pennsylvania Military Code, 51 Pa. C.S.A. §3501 as exclusive remedy. *Knauer v. Salter,* **313 Pa. Super. 289, 459 A.2d 1233.**

Perineal urethrotomy

Where patient who underwent perineal urethrotomy and cauterization, rather than planned transurethral prostatectomy, failed to establish a causal connection between resulting injuries and physician's conduct through expert testimony, compulsory nonsuit was proper. Patient should have been allowed to introduce evidence of alleged lack of consent to surgery that was admittedly not discussed by physician and patient prior to its performance. Order granting compulsory nonsuit on question of negligence affirmed. Case remanded on claim for lack of informed consent. *Hoffman v. Mogil,* **445 Pa. Super. 252, 665 A.2d 478 (1995).**

Permanent disfigurement

Minor injured when struck by a school bus sustained a permanent 4 millimeter scar on his right wrist. In suit against school bus owned and operated by school district, jury's determination that the scar, although permanent, was not disfiguring was proper and so kept case out of governmental immunity exception for injuries which cause permanent loss of a bodily function or permanent disfigurement. *Alexander v. Benson,* **812 A.2d 785 (Pa. Cmwlth. 2002).**

Permissive path and ways

Plaintiff, while using a railroad bridge, fell through same as the result of a missing plank—railroad company held responsible and Pennsylvania rule as to not having permissive rights to use right of way longitudinally seriously questioned or abrogated. *Franc v. Penna. R.R. Co.,* **424 Pa. 99, 225 A.2d 528.**

Summary judgment reversed where owners of property adjoining parking lot on which plaintiff slipped and fell had easement across parking lot and, therefore, question existed as to whether property owners were liable as possessor of parking lot. *Blackman v. Federal Realty Inv. Trust,* **444 Pa. Super. 411, 664 A.2d 139 (1995).**

Personal care home

Personal representative of estate of deceased personal care home resident brought suit alleging negligence of PCH, staff and administration under § 323 of Restatement 2nd Torts, negligent performance of an undertaking to render services, after the resident was not prevented from leaving the PCH without medications, becoming lost and drowning in a local river. Summary judgment in favor of PCH reversed. *Feeney v. Disston Manor Personal Care Home,* **849 A.2d 590 (Pa. Super. 2004).**

Patient at personal care home injured when he wandered away. Home not liable. *Mohler v. Jeke,* **407 Pa. Super. 478, 595 A.2d 1247.**

Personal property

Personal property

Plaintiff was injured when she slipped and fell on floor of SEPTA train. Plaintiff argued that train was improperly cared for personal property of Commonwealth and so exempt from protection of Sovereign Immunity Act. Held: SEPTA train is vehicle for purposes of Sovereign Immunity Act and not personal property. Grant of compulsory nonsuit affirmed. ***Ross v. SEPTA*, 714 A.2d 1131 (Pa. Cmwlth. 1998).**

Inmate filed suit against county correctional facility for injury to his head received when the "grab bar" in the prison shower broke free causing him to fall. Despite county's argument that the shower stall was only personal property, lack of evidence by county that shower stall was not a fixture and resulting presumption that it was in the nature of real property maintained by the county, precludes summary judgment under Political Subdivision Tort Claims Act. ***Davis v. Brennan*, 698 A.2d 1382 (Pa. Cmwlth. 1997).**

Personality change

Cross suits filed—plaintiff in one of suits had been severely injured and admittedly had a personality change—court below erred in admitting testimony from a divorce hearing to establish another reason for personality change without competent medical testimony to connect it up with condition. ***Smith v. German*, 434 Pa. 47, 253 A.2d 107.**

Physical education class

Minor plaintiff injured in physical education class—preliminary objections sustained in suit against school district—doctrine of sovereign immunity reaffirmed—strong dissenting opinion. ***Hill v. North Hills S.D.*, 223 Pa. Super. 254, 299 A.2d 350.**

Physical therapy

In medical malpractice action for failure of physician to inform physical therapy provider not to remove a knee immobilizer from patient's knee, order granting motion for nonsuit reversed where defendant offered self-serving testimony and exhibits during plaintiffs' case in chief. Plaintiffs' expert's testimony offered in first person form is sufficient to establish deviation from standard of care and so precludes entry of nonsuit. ***Joyce v. Boulevard Physical Therapy*, ___ Pa. Super. ___, 694 A.2d 648 (1997).**

Physician-patient confidentiality

Medical Group was sued by its patient for breach of physician-patient confidentiality after medical records were released to the patient's employer that resulted in the patient being terminated by their employer. The court held that a two-year statute of limitation applied to breach of physician-patient confidentiality. ***Burger v. Blair Medical Associates, Inc.*, 928 A.2d 246 (Pa. Super. 2007).**

Plaintiff wife sued doctor who had disclosed to wife's husband that test results were consistent with sexually transmitted disease. Plaintiff's claim that physician breached physician-patient relationship was recognized as valid but its dismissal was affirmed on grounds that wife had impliedly consented to disclosure of medical information to husband. Doctrine of tortious interference with the marital relationship abolished. ***Haddad v. Gopal*, 787 A.2d 975 (Pa. Super. 2002)**.

A physician who has participated in the care of a patient may not be contacted by a defendant in a case brought by the patient by other means than formal discovery. This protects patient-physician confidentiality and supports rules prohibiting *ex parte* communications with physicians who have treated a plaintiff patient. ***Marek v. Ketyer*, 733 A.2d 1268 (Pa. Super. 1999)**.

Physician's assistant

Plaintiff brought medical malpractice action based upon a physician's assistant leaving a catheter fragment in her left shoulder. The trial court granted summary judgment based upon Plaintiff's failure to provide expert medical testimony. The Superior Court affirmed holding that Plaintiff could not rely on the doctrine of res ipsa loquitur as the standard of care to remove a catheter was beyond the knowledge of a jury and thus required expert testimony. ***Vazquez v. CHS Professional Practice, P.C.*, 39 A.3d 395 (Pa. Super. 2012)**.

Piercing corporate veil

Defense of decedent's contributory negligence is not eliminated from consideration merely because of negligence *per se* of tavern that served decedent while he was visibly intoxicated. Remand for new trial to determine plaintiffs' decedent's comparative negligence in driving while intoxicated after having been served while visibly intoxicated. Decedent could not have legally assumed risk of driving while intoxicated following determination of tavern's negligence in serving visibly intoxicated decedent. To pierce corporate veil, against which there is a strong legal presumption, plaintiff must prove undercapitalization, intermingling of individual and corporate affairs, failure to adhere to corporate formalities and use of the corporate form to perpetrate a fraud. ***Miller v. Brass Rail Tavern, Inc.*, 702 A.2d 1072 (Pa. Super. 1997)**.

Pile of dirt

Large pile of dirt alongside parking lot. Driver of vehicle pulled out striking plaintiff going by on motorcycle and killing him. Verdict against defendant who piled dirt affirmed. Piling dirt alongside parking lot is negligent and driver's coming out behind it does not as a matter of law relieve defendant of negligence—not as a matter of law a superseding cause. ***Flickinger Estate v. Ritsky*, 452 Pa. 69, 305 A.2d 40**.

Pipe and pipeline

Building owner sued Defendant contractor based upon a violation of the Storage Tank and Spill Prevention Act for failing to repair his underground fuel oil product lines correctly. The trial court granted summary judgment to the contractor. The Superior Court reversed in part and affirmed in part holding that under the Storage Tank and Spill Prevention Act the claim had been filed timely as it was filed be-

Plain view

fore the 6- or 20-year statute of limitations period. *Morgan v. Petroleum Products Equipment Co.*, 92 A.3d 823 (Pa. Super. 2014).

For real property exception to governmental immunity to apply to municipality, sidewalk must be within right of way of a street owned by the municipality. Pedestrian who tripped on pipe projecting from sidewalk that was owned by municipality could not recover from municipality because underlying street right of way was owned by PennDOT. Because sidewalk was not realty for purposes of exception, pipe was not realty by reason of its connection to sidewalk. Summary judgment in favor of borough affirmed. *Gray v. Logue*, ___ Pa. Cmwlth. ___, 654 A.2d 109 (1995).

Pipeline carrying gasoline under housing development ruptured by workman laying television cable. Pipeline company not liable. Pipeline not abnormally dangerous. Injury caused by action of others. *Melso v. Sun Pipe Line Company*, 394 Pa. Super. 578, 576 A.2d 999.

Cable television company ruptured pipeline while laying cable. Pipeline company negligent for failure to mark and supervise pipeline. Township engineer liable for failure to advise cable company of presence of pipeline. *Cipriani v. Sup Pipe Line Co.*, 393 Pa. Super. 471, 574 A.2d 706.

Plain view

Rear-end collision. Plaintiff in plain view for some period. No excuse given by defendant. No evidence of contributory negligence. Defense verdict overturned and new trial ordered. *Antolik v. Kerstetter*, 278 Pa. Super. 55, 419 A.2d 1353.

Plaintiff's own testimony

Court in charge failed to inform jury, as requested, that jury could find against plaintiff, if by plaintiff's own testimony he revealed factors which would convict him of contributory negligence. *Matteo v. Sharon Hill Lanes, Inc.*, 216 Pa. Super. 188, 263 A.2d 910.

Plate glass window

Plaintiff, a pedestrian, injured by a large glass window of defendant's building falling on him—wind of high velocity with gusts 45 to 46 miles per hour—Held: no liability—defendant not negligent in construction of building nor as occupiers in failing to protect windows. *Jones v. Treegoob*, 212 Pa. Super. 482, 243 A.2d 161. Reversed: 433 Pa. 225.

Platelets

In a case of first impression, plaintiff brought suit against supplier of platelets by which she was allegedly infected with hepatitis-B and hepatitis-C alleging strict liability, breach of warranty and negligence. Summary judgment granted on strict liability and breach of warranty claims based on Pennsylvania Blood Shield Statute 42 Pa.C.S. §8333. Negligence count dismissed for plaintiff's failure to provide expert report. Affirmed by Superior Court which held that manufacturer of

Playgrounds, parks, and recreation areas

blood products was included in defined class of "person" under the act. *Weishorn v. Miles-Cutter*, 721 A.2d 811 (Pa. Super. 1998).

Playgrounds, parks, and recreation areas

Plaintiff injured when she stopped suddenly and was thrown forward at the bottom of a "Giant Slide" located on county-owned property. County claimed immunity under Recreation Use of Land and Water Act. Held: giant slide was improvement to real estate outside RULWA immunity in that county recognized its obligation to perform daily maintenance on the slide to insure safety of visitors. **Bashioum v. County of Westmoreland**, 747 A.2d 441 (Pa. Cmwlth. 2000).

Minor child injured by what may have been a part of a goal post lying "on" city-owned park property. Summary judgment in favor of city reversed because city may have been negligent in care, custody and control of real property for failure to remove the dangerous condition "on" the property. Local agency liability for negligent care, custody or control of real property does not require the instrumentality causing the harm to be "of" the real estate in the sense of being affixed to it. **Martin v. City of Philadelphia**, 696 A.2d 909 (Pa. Cmwlth. 1997).

Park visitor who slipped on embankment between picnic pavilion and parking lot in County park was precluded from any recovery for injuries sustained against the County under Recreation Use of Land and Water Act. Land was unimproved and no fee was charged to plaintiff for use of the park. Order denying summary judgment reversed and complaint dismissed. **Brezinski v. County of Allegheny**, 694 A.2d 388 (Pa. Cmwlth. 1997).

Pedestrian injured after stepping into hole created where tree trunk removed from township-owned park grounds may not recover against township which has immunity under both Political Subdivision Tort Claims Act and Recreation Use of Land and Water Act. Summary judgment for township affirmed. **Wilkinson v. Conoy Township**, 677 A.2d 876 (Pa. Cmwlth. 1996).

Because bleachers constituted a defective improvement to the land, Recreation Use of Land and Water Act did not bar spectator's claim against Township for injuries sustained in fall from bleachers at Township ball field. Order granting summary judgment reversed. **Brown v. Tunkhannock Township**, ___ Pa. Cmwlth. ___, 665 A.2d 1318 (1995).

Injuries resulting to child while playing with playmate on playground equipment will not be deemed to have been caused by negligence absent proof of playmate acting in an unreasonable or dangerous manner. **Schoymer v. Mexico Forge, Inc.**, 437 Pa. Super. 159, 649 A.2d 705 (1994).

Swimmer injured while using diving board at county-owned pool. County not liable. **County of Allegheny v. Fedunok**, 164 Pa. Cmwlth. 198, 642 A.2d 595.

Guest injured when table collapsed at volunteer fire department picnic. Park owned by borough. Fire department and borough immune. **Kniaz v. Benton Borough**, 164 Pa. Cmwlth. 109, 642 A.2d 551.

Playgrounds, parks, and recreation areas

Pedestrians injured in falls at Penn's Landing Recreation Area. No immunity under Recreation Use of Land and Water Act because land was improved. ***Mills v. Commonwealth*, 534 Pa. 519, 633 A.2d 1115.**

Fan assaulted at football game in view of security guard. City not liable. ***Poulos v. City of Philadelphia*, 156 Pa. Cmwlth. 648, 628 A.2d 1198.**

Child drowned in swimming pool leased to township. Real estate exception to Tort Claims Act not applicable. ***Sims v. Silver Springs-Martin Luther School*, 155 Pa. Cmwlth. 619, 625 A.2d 1297.**

Child injured while playing on spin-around at swim club. Spin-around was improvement to real estate under statute of repose. ***Schmoyer v. Mexico Forge, Inc.*, 423 Pa. Super. 593, 621 A.2d 692.**

Softball player injured on field owned by borough. Held: facts insufficient to determine whether Recreation Use of Land and Water Act applied. ***Thomas v. Borough of Blossburg*, 146 Pa. Super. 220, 604 A.2d 1230.**

Child injured in bicycle accident at playground owned by borough and school district. Both defendants jointly liable. ***Dimino v. Borough of Pottstown*, 142 Pa. Cmwlth. 683, 598 A.2d 357.**

Trespasser at city-owned swimming pool died as a result of injuries. City not immune under Recreation Use of Land and Water Act but is immune under Tort Claims Act. ***Mitchell v. City of Philadelphia*, 141 Pa. Cmwlth. 695, 596 A.2d 1205.**

Child injured when she dived into swimming pool owned by city. City not immune under Recreation Use of Land and Water Act. Real estate exception to government immunity applicable. ***City of Philadelphia v. Duda*, 141 Pa. Cmwlth. 88, 595 A.2d 206.**

Spectator at roller hockey game played in city-owned facility injured while attempting to break up fight. City not liable. ***City of Philadelphia v. Buck*, 138 Pa. Cmwlth. 250, 587 A.2d 875.**

Basketball player injured at city-owned playground. City not immune. Recreation Use of Land and Water Act not applicable. Real property exception to governmental immunity applied. ***Walsh v. City of Philadelphia*, 526 Pa. 226, 585 A.2d 445.**

Child injured at city-owned playground. City not immune under Recreation Use of Land and Water Act. Real property exception to governmental immunity may also apply. ***Wurth by Wurth v. City of Philadelphia*, 136 Pa. Cmwlth. 629, 584 A.2d 403.**

Child injured in fall from exercise bars at city-owned playground. City found not liable. Recreation Use of Land and Water Act applies to small inner-city playgrounds. City also immune if injury resulted from willful or malicious conduct of employee. ***Marko v. City of Philadelphia*, 133 Pa. Cmwlth. 574, 576 A.2d 1193.**

Playgrounds, parks, and recreation areas

Child injured by train after crawling through hole in city-owned fence. City not liable. Owed no duty to child. **Gardner v. Consolidated Rail Corporation, 524 Pa. 445, 573 A.2d 1016.**

Child injured in playground operated by borough and school district. Held: defendants immune under the Recreation Use of Land and Water Act. **DiMino v. Borough of Pottstown, 129 Pa. Cmwlth. 154, 564 A.2d 1329.**

Basketball player injured when he stepped into hole at city-owned recreation center. City immune under Recreation Use of Land and Water Act. **Walsh v. City of Philadelphia, 126 Pa. Cmwlth. 27, 558 A.2d 192.**

Child drowned while swimming in creek at township-owned park. Township immune from suit under Recreation Use of Land and Water Act. **Jones v. Cheltenham Township, 117 Pa. Cmwlth. 440, 543 A.2d 1258.**

Plaintiff injured while attending volunteer fire department picnic in borough-owned park. Held: borough immune under the Recreation Use of Land and Water Act even though fee charged for bingo game. **Kniaz v. Benton Borough, 112 Pa. Cmwlth. 416, 535 A.2d 308.**

Child injured by other children at city-owned swimming pool. City not liable. Injury did not arise out of custody or control of real property. **Kasavage v. City of Philadelphia, 105 Pa. Cmwlth. 554, 524 A.2d 1089.**

Child injured when riding bicycle at city-owned tennis court. Genuine issues of material fact precluded dismissal of action. **McNeill by McNeill v. City of Philadelphia, 104 Pa. Cmwlth. 494, 522 A.2d 174.**

Minor injured while ice skating on public lake in borough. Held: borough's alleged failure to supervise was alleged cause of injury and therefore not within exception to Political Subdivision Tort Claims Act. **Fizzano v. Ridley Park, 94 Pa. Cmwlth. 179, 503 A.2d 57.**

Plaintiff playing basketball in city-owned recreation center injured when intruders entered building and assaulted him. Held: not within any exceptions to governmental immunity act (Political Subdivision Tort Claims Act). **Johnston v. City of Philadelphia, 93 Pa. Cmwlth. 87, 500 A.2d 520.**

Summary judgment for city affirmed. Minor fell from billboard on land owned by SEPTA adjacent to city playground. Held: city under no obligation to erect fence to prevent minors from entering SEPTA's land on which billboard located. **Kearns v. Rollins Outdoor Advertising, 89 Pa. Cmwlth. 596, 492 A.2d 1204.**

Plaintiff injured when diving board located on platform of defendant's pool broke under his weight—pool operator and construction firm sued—plaintiff introduced expert testimony of faulty design—Held: pool operator had duty of doing more than visual inspection—nonsuit improperly entered—matter for jury. **Starke v. Long, 221 Pa. Super. 338, 292 A.2d 440.**

Minor plaintiff of two years attended a picnic with parents—apparently struck in eye by a piece of glass and lost sight of eye—some evidence of rowdyism

Plumber

in park—operator of park held responsible—strong dissent. ***Barakos v. Kollas,*** **433 Pa. 258, 249 A.2d 568.**

Plaintiff was an invitee in a drive-in theater—while in rest room of theater his hearing was affected by explosion of a firecracker, the act of rowdy boys—theater held responsible under Section 344 of Restatement (2d) Torts. ***Moran v. Valley F. Drive-In Theater, Inc.,*** **431 Pa. 432, 246 A.2d 875.**

Plaintiff injured in diving into a swimming pool allegedly because water was not of sufficient depth—Supreme Court had previously passed on matter and had refused judgment *n.o.v.*, reversing court below but remanding case for court to pass on motion for a new trial—new trial refused with trial judge dissenting—Supreme Court affirmed action—the issue cannot be litigated again. ***Cummings v. Nazareth Borough,*** **430 Pa. 255, 242 A.2d 460.**

Defendant borough maintained a swimming pool—minor plaintiff dived from one meter board and struck bottom of pool and was seriously injured—evidence that depth of water at point was below standard of safe maintenance of a swimming pool—error for court below to enter judgment *n.o.v.* for defendant. ***Cummings v. Nazareth Borough,*** **427 Pa. 14, 233 A.2d 874.**

Municipality maintained a public swimming pool—minor plaintiff pushed into pool allegedly as result of rowdyism of other boys—minor seriously injured—verdict for defendant—case properly submitted to the jury—refusal of new trial not error. ***Zeman v. Canonsburg Borough,*** **423 Pa. 450, 223 A.2d 728.**

Plumber

In action by personal representative of plumbing contractor killed in cave-in at construction site, governmental immunity applies because plaintiff presented no proof that city exercised sufficient custody and control over site. Sanction order precluding city's filing of answer for failure to comply with discovery order does not compel waiver of real property exception to governmental immunity. Summary judgment in favor of city affirmed. ***Santori v. Snyder,*** **165 Pa. Cmwlth. 505, 645 A.2d 443 (1994).**

Poles

Plaintiff's decedent died after crashing into utility pole following high-speed chase. The decedent's criminal and negligent acts preclude imposition of liability on municipalities whose police officers were engaged in pursuit. Therefore, decedent's widow could not recover from municipalities under wrongful death theory as such action is derivative to any action the decedent may have had. Order granting summary judgment affirmed. ***Tyree v. City of Pittsburgh,*** ___ **Pa. Cmwlth.** ___**, 669 A.2d 487 (1995).**

Defendant utility pole inspection company did not have duty to protect bystander from injuries sustained when bystander came into contact with downed electrical wires while assisting victims of automobile accident which damaged utility pole. Defendant inspection company's alleged negligent inspection of pole was too remote to constitute proximate cause of bystander's injuries. Bystander was not third-party beneficiary of contract between inspection company and utility company that required inspection company only to inspect and report condition of poles. Order sustaining preliminary objections of defendant inspection company affirmed. *Hicks v. Metropolitan Edison Company,* ___ Pa. Cmwlth. ___, 665 A.2d 529 (1995).

Where plaintiff sustained injuries after striking utility pole, utility company liable for improper placement of electric pole in highway right-of-way. Compulsory nonsuit reversed. *Talarico v. Bonham,* 168 Pa. Cmwlth. 467, 650 A.2d 1192 (1994).

No duty of care by police to driver fleeing police. Utility company not liable for placement of utility pole struck by fleeing driver. *Beck v. Zabrowski,* 168 Pa. Cmwlth. 385, 650 A.2d 1152 (1994).

Summary judgment in favor of social host affirmed where no evidence that host had actual notice that minors were consuming alcohol. Summary judgment in favor of telephone company affirmed because causal connection between location of pole and accident too remote in law to impose liability. *Novak v. Kilby,* 167 Pa. Cmwlth. 217, 647 A.2d 687 (1994).

Plaintiff—driver struck unmarked, unlit pole at night at dangerous curve—pole 10 inches from paved road—for jury as to negligence of utility company and/or driver as to passenger. *Scheel v. Tremblay and Phila. Elec. Co.,* 226 Pa. Super. 45, 312 A.2d 45.

Police

Plaintiff state police officer brought negligence action against Defendant internal affairs investigator based upon an investigation performed by the Defendant that led to the Plaintiff being fired. The trial court denied Defendant's motion for summary judgment and they appealed. The Commonwealth Court reversed holding that the Defendant was entitled to sovereign immunity as the conduct forming the basis of the lawsuit occurred during the course and scope of his employment. *Schell v. Guth,* 88 A.3d 1053 (Pa. Cmwlth. 2014).

Plaintiff brought negligence suit against Defendant city after he was struck by a police cruiser stolen by an individual under arrest. The trial court granted dismissal. The Commonwealth Court affirmed holding that the motor vehicle exception to governmental immunity did not apply as the police officer was not operating the vehicle at the time of the accident. *Gale v. City of Philadelphia,* 86 A.3d 318 (Pa. Cmwlth. 2014).

Plaintiff officer brought an action against Defendant suspect after he was injured attempting to arrest the Defendant for public urination. The trial court dismissed the case. The Superior Court reversed holding that a suspect owed a duty of care to the officer arresting him not to place him at risk of being injured. *Schemberg v. Smicherko,* 85 A.3d 1071 (Pa. Super. 2014).

Police

Decedent's estate brought action against police officer after the decedent was killed in a collision while the officer was involved in a high-speed chase of another motorist. The trial court dismissed the preliminary objections to dismiss the action. The Commonwealth Court affirmed. The Commonwealth Court held that a police officer is immune from negligence claims arising out of police pursuit only when the negligence is based upon the actions of the suspect being pursued. The court held that an officer was not immune from a negligence claim if it involved his negligent operation of his vehicle during the pursuit causing injury to bystander. ***Cornelius v. Roberts*, 71 A.3d 345 (Pa. Cmwlth. 2013).**

Estate of decedent passenger brought action against police department after the decedent was killed in a motor vehicle accident during a high speed police chase. The trial court granted summary judgment to the defendant. The Commonwealth Court affirmed holding that police did not owe a duty to a passenger in a vehicle whose driver was involved in a high speed chase as the passenger was not an innocent bystander. ***Sellers v. Township of Abington*, 67 A.3d 863 (Pa. Cmwlth. 2013).**

Plaintiff brought suit against Defendant police officer after he was struck making a left turn at an intersection by the Defendant. The officer was responding to a disturbance call and exceeding the speed limit, but was not using his lights or siren. The jury found in favor of the Defendant. The Commonwealth Court reversed, holding that the trial court had erred in failing to provide a negligence per se instruction as the officer was responding to a non-emergency call and had been exceeding the posted speed limit without emergency lights or a siren. ***Sodders v. Fry*, 32 A.3d 882 (Pa. Cmwlth. 2011).**

Estate brought cause of action for negligent spoliation of evidence after the Defendant state police failed to preserve evidence for the estate's lawsuit against a tree stand safety-harness manufacturer. The trial court granted summary judgment for the Defendant. The Commonwealth Court affirmed. The Pennsylvania Supreme Court held that under Pennsylvania law there is no cause of action for spoliation of evidence. ***Pyeritz v. Commonwealth of Pennsylvania*, 32 A.3d 687 (Pa. Cmwlth. 2011).**

Driver struck and injured by a police officer driving the wrong way down a one-way road while in pursuit of a suspect brought a claim of negligence against the officer. The trial court entered a directed verdict in favor of the Plaintiff, granting a new trial on the issue of contributory negligence. The Superior Court affirmed, holding that the Defendant had failed to meet its burden at trial that it qualified for special privileges to disregard the speed and directional mandates of the vehicle code and therefore the Defendant was negligent per se for violating these statutes. ***Lahr v. City of York*, 972 A.2d 41 (Pa. Super. 2009).**

The Commonwealth Court determined that a police officer's car, stopped on the road facing against traffic at night, with its lights pointing at oncoming traffic, was not "operating" under motor vehicle exception to governmental immunity and so suit by motorcycle operator for injuries sustained when rider struck police car should have been dismissed. ***North Sewickley Township v. LaValle*, 786 A.2d 325 (Pa. Cmwlth. 2001)**.

Plaintiff police officer was injured when he tripped on old fencing on lot adjacent to house at which a search warrant was being served. Lower court granted summary judgment to defendant property owners holding that police officer was a trespasser and so defendants had a duty only to avoid wanton or willful negligence or misconduct. Superior Court affirmed and Supreme Court granted allocatur and also affirmed holding that Section 345 of Restatement (2d) Torts relating to duty to trespassers entering pursuant to a privilege is not adopted in Pennsylvania and police and firefighters are to be accorded trespasser status. ***Rossino v. Kovacs*, 718 A.2d 755 (Pa. 1998)**.

Police officer who did not see accident in question would not be qualified by experience or training as expert unless foundation were laid for that qualification. Even if officer was qualified as expert, his deposition testimony based on post-accident interviews with parties to accident is inadmissible without his own independent knowledge of actual circumstances of accident. ***Bennett v. Graham*, 714 A.2d 393 (Pa. 1998)**.

Plaintiff pedestrian injured by impact of police car is entitled to reversal of nonsuit where evidence indicates that all elements of negligence claim were established at trial. Trial court's determination that plaintiff failed to prove that his injury was permanent or of a serious nature so as to impair a bodily function is reversible abuse of discretion. Nonsuit removed; remanded for new trial. ***Boyer v. City of Philadelphia*, 692 A.2d 259 (Pa. Cmwlth. 1997)**.

Municipal defendants are neither afforded blanket immunity nor entitled to judgment as a matter of law in each and every tort claim where the victim's injuries were caused in part by the intervening criminal conduct of third parties or where the criminal acts of a third party merely form a link in the chain of causation. It is for the jury to determine whether municipal defendants' conduct was a substantial contributing factor in causing the victim's injuries and, if so, whether intervening criminal conduct of third parties was so extraordinary as not to be reasonably foreseeable by the municipal defendants. Summary judgment reversed. ***Jones v. Chieffo*, ___ Pa. Super. ___, 664 A.2d 1091 (1995)**.

Police officer's failure to provide protection for specific individual shot on bus terminal platform is not a recognized exception to governmental immunity. Despite city ordinance purporting to waive governmental immunity for negligent acts of police officers, City cannot waive its immunity. Ordinance held retroactively invalid under *City of Philadelphia v. Gray*, 534 Pa. 467, 633 A.2d 1090 (1993). Summary judgment affirmed. ***Johnson v. City of Philadelphia*, ___ Pa. Cmwlth. ___, 657 A.2d 87 (1995)**.

Police officer who enters upon another's land in his official capacity and in response to a call for assistance is a licensee. Landowner's duty is to inform licensee of dangerous, hidden conditions. Obviously rowdy crowd of patrons at social hall was not a dangerous, hidden condition. Although violation of Dram Shop Act is negligence *per se*, mere fact that patrons who assaulted police officer were intoxi-

Police

cated neither proves that they had been served when visibly intoxicated nor causation of officer's injuries. Summary judgment for defendant affirmed. *Holpp v. Fez, Inc.*, **440 Pa. Super. 512, 656 A.2d 147 (1995).**

State police failed to rescue passenger in vehicle carried away by flood waters. Police not liable. *Peak v. Petrovitch*, **161 Pa. Cmwlth. 261, 636 A.2d 1248.**

Woman died of hypothermia after being left outside by police. Police not liable. *Philadelphia v. Estate of Dennis*, **161 Pa. Cmwlth. 69, 636 A.2d 240.**

Plaintiffs injured in collision with police vehicles brought actions based on city code section waiving immunity. Code section invalid. *City of Philadelphia Police Department v. Williams*, **534 Pa. 467, 633 A.2d 1090.**

Police and fire personnel took no action to resuscitate subway passenger who died of heart attack. City not liable. *Welsh v. City of Philadelphia*, **156 Pa. Cmwlth. 299, 627 A.2d 248.**

Police officer not liable for injuries to third parties involved in collision with fleeing vehicle. *White v. Mayo Laverda (S.R.L.)*, **152 Pa. Cmwlth. 488, 620 A.2d 52.**

Pedestrian injured in hit-and-run accident. Held: inability of plaintiff to produce police report did not preclude recovery. *Hatcher v. Travelers Insurance Company*, **421 Pa. Super. 225, 617 A.2d 808.**

Shooting victim killed by spouse of police officer with officer's revolver. Summary judgment in favor of city and officer vacated. *Nelson v. City of Philadelphia*, **149 Pa. Cmwlth. 611, 613 A.2d 674.**

Police officer who witnessed man being crushed to death in trash compactor brought action for negligent infliction of emotional distress. Owner of compactor not liable. *Covello v. Weis Markets, Inc.*, **415 Pa. Super. 610, 610 A.2d 50.**

Motorist brought action against police for failure to adequately warn of icy highway and vehicles blocking highway. Police not liable. *Miseo v. Ross Township Police Department*, **147 Pa. Cmwlth. 263, 607 A.2d 806.**

Subway passenger stabbed by other passenger. Police officer helped victim from train then ceased assistance. Held: summary judgment for city inappropriate. Officer owed duty to victim. *Rankin v. SEPTA*, **146 Pa. Cmwlth. 429, 606 A.2d 536.**

Bystander shot and killed by police officer during arrest. Administratrix brought actions for wrongful death, survival and loss of consortium. Separate recovery for loss of consortium denied. *Mease v. Commonwealth*, **145 Pa. Cmwlth. 407, 603 A.2d 679.**

Police officer injured in fall while chasing trespasser. Landowner not liable. No duty to erect fence to protect from hazards on adjacent land. *Hauch v. Samuel Geltman & Company*, **400 Pa. Super. 534, 583 A.2d 1244.**

Police

Motorist injured in collision with police car. City liable. City waived immunity when it enacted Chapter 21–700 of the Philadelphia Code. ***City of Philadelphia v. Gray,*** **133 Pa. Cmwlth. 396, 576 A.2d 411.**

Police officer injured when attempting to arrest former state hospital patient. Hospital immune. Medical-professional exception to sovereign immunity applies only to patient injuries. ***Harrisburg State Hospital v. Sherk,*** **128 Pa. Cmwlth. 150, 562 A.2d 1025.**

Plaintiff playing basketball in city-owned recreation center was injured when intruders entered building and assaulted him. Held: not within any exceptions to governmental immunity act (Political Subdivision Tort Claims Act). ***Johnson v. City of Philadelphia,*** **93 Pa. Cmwlth. 87, 500 A.2d 520.**

Suit against SEPTA and City for injuries sustained by plaintiff in mugging which occurred in subway concourse. Held: complaint did state a cause of action against City as possessor of land and within exception to Political Subdivision Tort Claims Act. ***Johnson v. SEPTA,*** **91 Pa. Cmwlth. 587, 498 A.2d 22.**

Police officer suffered heart attack shortly after arriving at police station with fleeing driver defendant. Defense verdict affirmed. Held: risk that officer would have heart attack could not reasonably be foreseen. Driver owed officer no duty of care for purposes of negligence action. ***Zanine v. Gallegher,*** **345 Pa. Super. 119, 497 A.2d 1332.**

City police officers, allegedly responding to call to pick up "hospital case," instead took decedent to jail where he died three hours later. Held: city *not* immune from suit for alleged negligence of policy which causes injury. Grant of city's preliminary objections reversed. ***Capanna v. City of Philadelphia,*** **89 Pa. Cmwlth. 349, 492 A.2d 761.**

Auto accident. Issue of whether vehicle negligently hit guardrail and thereafter front wheel came off car, or whether wheel came off car, causing it to go out of control. Defense verdict after officer was qualified as expert and opined that wheel came off first. Error to qualify police officer as expert under these circumstances. New trial ordered. ***Reed v. Hutchinson,*** **331 Pa. Super. 404, 480 A.2d 1096.**

Child shot in eye by neighbor. Racial tension in neighborhood. Suit against city for nonfeasance of police and Human Relations Commission. Plaintiff unable to establish that special relationship existed between individual and city. No such relationship shown. ***Melendez v. City of Philadelphia,*** **320 Pa. Super. 59, 466 A.2d 1060.**

Plaintiff assaulted on train platform in city. Demurrer of city sustained. Duty of city to provide police protection is a public one and may not be claimed by an individual unless special relationship exists. Does not exist because plaintiff is in high crime area. ***Chapman v. City of Philadelphia,*** **290 Pa. Super. 281, 434 A.2d 753.**

Off-duty police officer shot neighbor during argument with gun that was not issued by police department. Verdict against individual and City employer. Denial of judgment *n.o.v.* as to City reversed for lack of evidence of connection between tor-

Police

tious act and employer. ***Fitzgerald v. McCutcheon,*** 270 Pa. Super. 102, 410 A.2d 1270.

Death action. Verdict for plaintiff sustained by equally divided court. Plaintiff shot by police officer while lying face down and spread eagle. Cocked gun discharged. Extraordinary care required when dealing with loaded firearm. ***Everette v. City of New Kensington,*** 262 Pa. Super. 28, 396 A.2d 467.

Plaintiff painting a building—shot by police chasing a suspect—sovereign immunity abolished. ***Laughlin v. Pittsburgh,*** 226 Pa. Super. 431, 310 A.2d 289.

Police officer expert testified as to who was driving from after-accident photographs. Judge should have permitted other side to produce expert to say that photographs were inconclusive even though general rule is that expert should not be permitted to state inference or judgment as to ultimate facts for jury determination. ***Ryan v. Furey,*** 225 Pa. Super. 294, 303 A.2d 221.

Plaintiff's decedent, a boy of 18, found wandering semiconscious in cold weather and taken into police custody—boy given no attention and died next day—amended complaint held on appeal to state a cause of action against police officers—good discussion of liability of public officers. ***Ammlung v. Platt,*** 224 Pa. Super. 47, 302 A.2d 491.

Plaintiff operating a police vehicle going to a fire—collision in intersection with vehicle of defendant—cross suits by defendant and borough for property damage—jury denied claims of all contending parties—error assigned was failure to charge that police officer would only be responsible if operating car in a reckless manner—verdicts sustained below on ground that trial judge had properly charged as to the operation of the police car—action sustained on appeal. ***Fullen v. Boory,*** 440 Pa. 644, 270 A.2d 624.

Police officer of City of Harrisburg shot and killed plaintiff's decedent—City sued—preliminary objections properly sustained—City not responsible as matter involved a governmental function. ***Smeltz v. Harrisburg,*** 440 Pa. 224, 269 A.2d 466.

Police officer had automobile mechanical experience prior to entering police service—he tested brakes of car involved in occurrence and found them defective—within discretion of trial court to permit him to testify as an expert. ***Flavin v. Aldrich et al.,*** 213 Pa. Super. 420, 250 A.2d 185.

Police officer arrived on scene of accident some 10 to 15 minutes after occurrence—testifying as to brake failure of one of cars as a result of tests made after arrival—improperly admitted—such testimony hearsay—new trial properly granted. ***Andrews v. Jackson et al.,*** 211 Pa. Super. 166, 235 A.2d 452.

Plaintiff's decedent was a guest passenger in defendant's car—car went out of control on curve and left highway—verdict for defendant—new trial properly granted—car being pursued by police and going 90 miles per hour just before occurrence—jury should have been instructed as to wanton misconduct. ***Fugagli v. Camasi,*** 426 Pa. 1, 229 A.2d 735.

Ponds and pools

Plaintiff brought negligence suit on behalf of his daughter against Defendant property owner after she was injured when she fell into a decorative pond. Trial court granted summary judgment for the Defendant. The Superior Court affirmed holding that for a property owner to be liable for damages caused by an artificial condition on his property, as the result of a child trespassing, he must know or have reason to know that children were likely to trespass on their property. *G.W.E. v. R.E.Z., Jr.*, **77 A.3d 43 (Pa. Super. 2013).**

Administratrix of teenager who drowned in city-owned pond may not recover under Political Subdivision Tort Claims Act based on allegations of city's willful or malicious failure to warn of dangerous condition of pond. Recovery under Political Subdivision Tort Claims Acts is available only for acts of negligence. Public and private lands are covered by Recreation Use of Land and Water Act. Order refusing to grant judgment *n.o.v.* reversed. *Lory v. City of Philadelphia,* **544 Pa. 38, 674 A.2d 673 (1996).**

Willful or malicious failure to guard or warn exception to immunity under the Recreation Use of Land and Water Act applied to action by personal representative of minor's estate where minor drowned in natural pond located in city park. Evidence of prior unrelated swimming accidents inadmissable. Verdict for plaintiff reversed and remanded. *Barr v. City and County of Philadelphia,* ___ **Pa. Cmwlth.** ___**, 653 A.2d 1374 (1995).**

Twelve year-old boy drowned in indoor pool owned by Seminary, during swimming party for altar boys. Boy drowned while Father Flynn was in next room ordering pizza. New trial ordered after plaintiff's verdict and a directed verdict in favor of Father Flynn. Recreation Use of Land and Water Act held not to apply to public bathing places and pools. Reversible error under facts here to charge on §323 of Restatement (2d) Torts, relating to Seminary undertaking duty. *Rivera v. Philadelphia Theological Seminary,* **326 Pa. Super. 509, 474 A.2d 605.**

Plaintiff rendered quadriplegic from dive off dock into canal during private party. New Jersey law governs. Verdict $1.8 million reversed. Error to instruct jury that plaintiff was invitee. Landowner has no duty to inspect as to licensee. Issue of licensee or invitee for jury. *Hager v. Etting,* **268 Pa. Super. 416, 408 A.2d 856.**

Plaintiff injured when he struck portion of defendant's pool when diving from diving board. Expert in water safety and pool design not permitted to testify since from description of pool, water content and design by lay witnesses, the jury should have been able to apply their own experience and not be swayed by conclusions of expert. Defense verdict affirmed. *Maholland v. Bird,* **230 Pa. Super. 431, 326 A.2d 528.**

Defendant borough maintained a swimming pool—minor plaintiff dived from one meter board and struck bottom of pool and was seriously injured—evidence that depth of water at point was below standard of safe maintenance of a swimming pool—error for court below to grant judgment *n.o.v.* for the defendant. *Cummings v. Nazareth Borough,* **427 Pa. 14, 233 A.2d 874.**

Possessor

Possessor

Painting contractor sued by property owner in contract and negligence for failure to abate lead paint during job. Dismissal of contract claim affirmed. Dismissal of negligence claim reversed on grounds that a party to a contract has two duties: a contractual duty and a legal duty to act without negligence toward both the other party to the contract and third parties. One who creates a condition on behalf of a possessor of land has the same liability as the possessor of the land for physical harm to others caused by the dangerous condition. ***Reformed Church v. Hooven*, 764 A.2d 1106 (Pa. Super. 2000).**

Plaintiff was injured when she slipped on ice on public street and fell while going towards church. Summary judgment for church granted and affirmed on appeal because church was not "possessor" of street on which plaintiff fell. Summary judgment for municipality affirmed on basis that snow and ice on street was not a condition "of" the street and therefore action fell outside of streets exception to governmental immunity. ***Walinsky v. St. Nicholas Ukranian Catholic Church*, 740 A.2d 318 (Pa. Cmwlth. 1999).**

Summary judgment reversed where owners of property adjoining parking lot on which plaintiff slipped and fell had easement across parking lot and, therefore, question existed as to whether property owners were liable as possessor of parking lot. ***Blackman v. Federal Realty Inv. Trust*, 444 Pa. Super. 411, 664 A.2d 139 (1995).**

Possibility of injury

Individual contractor working on roof of smaller building within larger building, knocked off roof by crane. He knew of danger after years of working there. Held: crane operator not negligent, but employer-owner of crane/property owner (one entity) negligent for violation of §341A of Restatement (2d) Torts. Possessor should anticipate danger despite knowledge of danger to invitee. ***Skalos v. Higgins*, 449 Pa. Super. 601, 449 A.2d 601.**

Possible cause of occurrence

Expert had not examined bowling area where occurrence took place and only offered to show a possible cause of accident—testimony offer properly rejected as expert's assumptions not based on the testimony produced and not positive that the use of steel wool under foot caused occurrence—court acted within its discretion in rejecting this testimony—nonsuit properly entered. ***Houston et vir v. Canon Bowl, Inc.*, 443 Pa. 383, 278 A.2d 908.**

Post-operative care

Patient treated by defendant orthopedic surgeon filed suit for negligently performed corrective surgery and continuing pain and suffering after the surgery. Verdict for plaintiff apportioning negligence 60/40 between defendant and plaintiff. New trial granted by trial court based on reasoning of *Gentile v. Devergilis*, 290 Pa. 50, 138 A. 540 in which it was held that where a patient refuses to follow directions for post-operative care, there can be no verdict against the treating physician who recommended the care for any negligent act because there can be no determination of which failure to treat- the original physician's or the patient's who refused to follow treatment directions - caused the harm. Superior Court affirmed and Supreme Court reversed stating that a patient's mere failure to attend post-operative appointments does not make it impossible as a matter of law for a jury to determine whether, and to what degree, the physician's negligence caused the injury. *Ferguson v. Panzarella,* **700 A.2d 917 (Pa. 1997).**

Plaintiff who fails to participate significantly in post-operative care risks loss of any claim for alleged negligence of physician in performing surgery. The Comparative Negligence Act is not applicable in such cases because of the inability to apportion liability between both parties. ***Ferguson v. Panzarella,* 445 Pa. Super. 23, 664 A.2d 989 (1995).**

Pothole

Motorcyclists brought negligence claim against the Department of Transportation after he was injured when his motorcycle struck a pothole on the highway. The trial court granted summary judgment to the Defendant. The Commonwealth Court reversed holding that a letter from a state senator expressing concern over the condition of the roadway was sufficient to establish notice of a dangerous condition to preclude the defense of sovereign immunity. ***Walthour v. Commonwealth of Pennsylvania Department of Transportation,* 31 A.3d 762 (Pa. Cmwlth. 2011).**

Pedestrian who tripped over pothole in state road brought action against city based on home rule charter. City not liable. ***Phillips v. City of Philadelphia,* 148 Pa. Cmwlth. 175, 610 A.2d 509.**

Motorcyclist injured in accident caused by potholes in highway. Commonwealth not liable. Statutory requirement that PennDOT be notified in writing of dangerous condition was held to be not unconstitutional. ***Ketterer v. Com., Dept. of Transp.,* 133 Pa. Cmwlth. 92, 574 A.2d 735.**

Pedestrian who fell in pothole brought action against Commonwealth. Trial judge entered judgment *n.o.v.* in favor of Commonwealth. Commonwealth Court overturned judgment *n.o.v.* Jury had sufficient evidence to find Commonwealth had required notice of defect in highway. ***Pallante v. City of Philadelphia,* 133 Pa. Cmwlth. 441, 575 A.2d 980.**

Accident allegedly occurred owing to pothole in state highway. Evidence of repair five days after accident and that pothole was located 1-1/2 miles from Department's local maintenance shed, insufficient to charge department with actual notice as required by statute. Nonsuit as to Commonwealth affirmed. ***Stevens v. Commonwealth,* 89 Pa. Cmwlth. 309, 492 A.2d 490.**

Power lines

Architect has no duty to warn contractor employees of visible overhead power lines that came into contact with metal scaffolding killing or injuring workers. Summary judgment in favor of architect affirmed. ***Frampton v. Dauphin Distribution Services Co.,* 436 Pa. Super. 486, 648 A.2d 326 (1994).**

Prank

Prank

School student prank—one of group dared other to knock trash can off balcony railing. Was tapped inadvertently during horseplay, falling on plaintiff below. Nonsuit affirmed. Settled before trial with two obvious participants. Suit tried against others preset who allegedly encouraged and dared actors. Held: evidence did not present fault of individuals or group as a whole. ***Kline v. Ball*, 306 Pa. Super. 284, 452 A.2d 727.**

Pre-employment physical

Physician failed to diagnose patient's cancer after reading x-ray taken during pre-employment physical. Physician not liable. ***Tomko v. Marks*, 412 Pa. Super. 54, 602 A.2d 890.**

Preemption

Stock trader brought negligent supervision claim against a stock exchange after he was assaulted by another trader on the floor of the stock exchange. Pennsylvania Supreme Court reversed the Superior Court's grant of judgment as a matter of law holding that the Federal Securities Exchange Act did not preempt a state tort claim arising out of personal injuries suffered on a stock exchange floor by a securities industry employee. ***Dooner v. DiDonato*, 971 A.2d 1187 (Pa. 2009).**

When a Health Maintenance Organization makes a treatment decision that affects the type of care or the time in which a patient receives care, the HMO may be liable for negligence under state law for injuries sustained as a result of that decision. Federal preemption under the Employee Retirement Income Security Act of 1974 relates to eligibility determinations only. ***Pappas v. Asbel*, 768 A.2d 1089 (Pa. 2001).**

Federal Employee Retirement Income Security Act provisions regarding federal preemption of state laws which "relate to" ERISA benefits and plans do not preempt negligence claims against HMO for failure to approve in timely manner emergency treatment to patient-plaintiff who suffered permanent injury by reason of delay. ***Pappas v. Asbel*, 724 A.2d 889 (Pa. 1998).**

Plaintiffs are parents of a son who developed mental and physical limitations as a result of encephalitis following administration of a measles, mumps and rubella vaccination. Suit against hospital and physician who administered vaccination. After suit first brought, plaintiffs accepted judgment under federal National Vaccine Injury Compensation Program and then recommenced suit in state court. Held: acceptance of judgment in federal program bars recovery in state action absent some claim that an action other than administration or effect of vaccination was cause of injury. ***Harman v. Borah*, 720 A.2d 1058 (Pa. Super. 1998).**

Husband and wife sued pest-control company and Dow chemical company for injuries suffered by husband and wife as a result of husband's exposure o Dursban 2E pesticide. Only causes of action specifically or by necessary implication preempted by federal legislation are unavailable to a state court plaintiff. If plaintiff can establish a violation of Federal Insecticide, Fungicide and Rodenticide Act not predicated on failure to warn or inadequate labeling (e.g., gross negligence in reporting to EPA or negligence in testing regimen), that claim is actionable in state court. Plaintiffs' failure to cite additional newly-discovered facts in support of a new cause of action or lack of proof that additional facts were unavailable to plaintiff until disclosed by defendant precludes amendment of complaint after statute of limitations had passed. If plaintiff could establish that defendant prevented plaintiff from acquiring knowledge that would support new cause of action, and there was no other reasonable source for such information, statute of limitation would be tolled. ***Romah v. Hygienic Sanitation, Inc.*, 705 A.2d 841 (Pa. Super. 1997).**

A state claim that FDA requirements have not been met arising out of the use of a collagen implant is cognizable, despite preemption provisions of the medical device amendments to the Federal Food, Drug and Cosmetic Act. State negligence claims that mirror FDA standards for medical devices are not preempted. Order granting summary judgment reversed. ***Green v. Dolsky,* 546 Pa. 400, 685 A.2d 110 (1996).**

State law claims for manufacture and sale of defective surgical repair screws and plates were not preempted by medical device amendments to Federal Food, Drug and Cosmetic Act. Actions for failure to warn, strict liability, negligence, and implied warranty are preempted by medical device amendment to federal food and drug act. Summary judgment affirmed in part and reversed in part. ***Burgstahler v. Acromed Corporation,* 448 Pa. Super. 26, 670 A.2d 658 (1996).**

Medical device amendments to the Federal Food, Drug and Cosmetic Act of 1938 preempt state court action for breach of implied warranties of merchantability and fitness for a particular purpose regarding surgical bone plates and screws. Express warranties as to condition or properties of bone plates and screws are not preempted by the amendments. Learned intermediary doctrine does not preclude patient's suit against manufacturer on an express warranty made in connection with the sale of a prescription device. Order granting summary judgment affirmed in part and reversed in part. ***Rosci v. Acromed, Inc.,* ___ Pa. Super. ___, 669 A.2d 959 (1995).**

Following in-depth analysis of federal preemption law, Superior Court held that state common law causes of action are expressly not preempted by the National Traffic and Motor Vehicle Safety Act. Therefore, motorist may raise claim at trial that airbag that contributed to his injuries in head-on collision with another vehicle was defective, because Congress intended such issues to go to the jury. Order denying manufacturer's preliminary objections affirmed. ***Heiple v. C.R. Motors, Inc.,* 446 Pa. Super. 310, 666 A.2d 1066 (1995).**

Premature birth

Wrongful death and survival actions brought based on death of premature triplet. Held: trial court erroneously granted motion to dismiss. ***Hudak v. Georgy,* 535 Pa. 151, 634 A.2d 600.**

Prenatal injuries

Medical malpractice action by parents for injuries suffered by newborn before delivery resulting from nurses failure to monitor and recognize signs of fetal

Presumptions

distress. Very clear elemental analysis of negligence law. ***Cruz v. Northeastern Hospital*, 801 A.2d 602 (Pa. Super. 2002)**.

Pregnant woman injured in automobile accident brought wrongful death action after consenting to abortion. No liability. Non-viable fetus not person. ***Conelski v. Bubnis*, 535 Pa. 166, 634 A.2d 608.**

Accident involving school bus resulted in death of ten-week-old fetus. Death of non-viable fetus not applicable. ***Askew v. Cruciani*, 149 Pa. Cmwlth. 397, 613 A.2d 147.**

Pregnant woman injured in automobile accident brought action to recover for injuries to herself and to fetus. Fetus was aborted to avoid risk of damage. Held: wrongful death and survival action may not be brought on behalf of non-viable fetus. ***Coveleski v. Bubnis*, 391 Pa. Super. 409, 571 A.2d 433.**

Injuries received by child while *en ventre sa mere* formerly could form basis for survival or wrongful death actions as maintained only on behalf of child born alive. Live birth now held no longer to be a limiting prerequisite to maintenance of such action. Case remanded for further proceedings. ***Amadio v. Levin*, 509 Pa. 199, 501 A.2d 1085.**

Estate of stillborn child has no action for damages which occurred owing to allegedly negligent prenatal care. Parents have no cause of action for emotional stress without showing physical injury. ***Justice v. Booth Maternity Center*, 345 Pa. Super. 529, 498 A.2d 950.**

Woman slipped and fell on sidewalk. Gave birth prematurely. Child died after birth. Remanded for trial on issues of control and agency. ***Juarbe v. City of Philadelphia*, 288 Pa. Super. 330, 431 A.2d 1073.**

Suit on behalf of stillborn child who died a a result of injuries received *en ventre sa mere* in auto accident. Dismissed. Infant must be born alive in order to sustain claim. ***Scott v. Kopp*, 494 Pa. 487, 431 A.2d 959.**

Presumptions

Defense of decedent's contributory negligence is not eliminated from consideration merely because of negligence *per se* of tavern that served decedent while he was visibly intoxicated. Remand for new trial to determine plaintiffs' decedent's comparative negligence in driving while intoxicated after having been served while visibly intoxicated. Decedent could not have legally assumed risk of driving while intoxicated following determination of tavern's negligence in serving visibly intoxicated decedent. To pierce corporate veil, against which there is a strong legal presumption, plaintiff must prove undercapitalization, intermingling of individual and corporate affairs, failure to adhere to corporate formalities, and use of the corporate form to perpetrate a fraud. ***Miller v. Brass Rail Tavern, Inc.*, 702 A.2d 1072 (Pa. Super. 1997).**

In action by personal representative of deceased plaintiff, trial court charged that the law presumes that at the time of the accident causing his death the decedent was using due care for his safety. On reconsideration of dissenting opinions in case of *Waddle v. Nelkin*, 511 Pa. 641, 515 A.2d 808 (1986), the Supreme Court held that there is no presumption of due care in favor of a deceased or incapacitated plaintiff. Therefore, the charge was error but not so prejudicial in context of entire charge as to require reversal. **Marks v. Swayne, 701 A.2d 224 (Pa. 1997).**

Driver who collided with garbage truck situated diagonally on road was entitled to jury instruction on sudden emergency doctrine. Where evidence is such that reasonable minds could differ as to whether sudden emergency existed, both assured clear distance and sudden emergency instructions should be given. Assured clear distance charge to jury which failed to detail effect of presumption that rule applies where driver was proceeding in safe and prudent manner was legally insufficient. **Lockhart v. List, 542 Pa. 141, 665 A.2d 1176 (1995).**

Cross over head-on accident. Verdict for defendant affirmed. Defendant testified that he pulled to berm to avoid accident in his lane, then tried to swerve around telephone pole when he lost control of his car, crossing four lanes of roadway and striking plaintiff. Although driver who crosses center line of highway is negligent *per se,* this can be rebutted by competent evidence that vehicle was there through no negligence on defendant's part. **Farelli v. Marko, 349 Pa. Super. 102, 502 A.2d 1293.**

Pedestrian struck by auto. Evidence admitted at trial that pedestrian intoxicated. Charge given based on presumption of intoxication contained in Vehicle Code. Held: error to charge on presumption of intoxication. Other evidence of intoxication, however, was relevant. Verdict for defendant reversed. **Ackerman v. Delcomico, 336 Pa. Super. 569, 486 A.2d 410.**

Defense verdict affirmed. Patron consumed three double shots of whiskey plus beer, then went out and had one-vehicle accident. Charge affirmed—no presumption that plaintiff visibly intoxicated as a result of blood alcohol taken at hospital. Also proper to instruct jury to disregard whether plaintiff was negligent in ordering and consuming the alcohol. Only issue was visible intoxication when served. **Suskey v. Moose Lodge, 325 Pa. Super. 94, 472 A.2d 663.**

Compulsory nonsuit entered; reversed on appeal. Dredger had created sharp drop-off in Ohio River, at boat launch area. Decedent had parked there with girlfriend—car rolled forward over drop-off. Presumption of due care precludes trial court from ruling decedent was contributorily negligent as a matter of law. **Hawthorne v. Dravo Corp., 313 Pa. Super. 436, 460 A.2d 266.**

Auto-bicycle accident causing death to bicycle operator. Defense verdict affirmed. Enough evidence of potential negligence on decedent-plaintiff to overcome presumption of due care. **Yandrich v. Radic, 291 Pa. Super. 75, 435 A.2d 226.**

There is a rebuttable presumption that children between ages 7 and 14 are incapable of negligence. In pedestrian knock down case, it was for jury to decide whether plaintiff, 11 year old, acted reasonably for his age. **Ross v. Vereb, 481 Pa. 446, 392 A.2d 1376.**

Priest

Where plaintiff was killed in accident, it was error to fail to charge on presumption of due care unless court below found contributory negligence as a matter of law. ***Condo v. Caris,* 255 Pa. Super. 16, 386 A.2d 112.**

Late notice to insurer of accident in violation of policy provision and in absence of extenuating circumstances creates rebuttable presumption of prejudice to the insurer. ***Brakeman v. Potomac Insurance Co.,* 236 Pa. Super. 320, 344 A.2d 555.**

When driver crosses center of highway, presumption of negligence—driver then has burden of showing freedom from negligence. ***Fair v. Snowball Express,* 226 Pa. Super. 295, 310 A.2d 386.**

Rental agreement insured only the signor of contract—presumption that he was driving. ***Ryan v. Furey,* 225 Pa. Super. 294, 303 A.2d 221.**

Collision case—plaintiff alive but defendant's decedent dead as the result of causes unrelated to the accident in question—trial judge charged deceased defendant had the benefit of the presumption of due care—Held: charge was correct even though plaintiff died as the result of causes unrelated to the occurrence and that presumption applies to both plaintiff and defendant. ***Dilliplaine v. Lehigh Valley Trust Co.,* 223 Pa. Super. 245, 297 A.2d 826.**

Crossing over center line—head on collision—when a driver is on the wrong side of the road at the time of collision, there is a presumption of negligence—there is no presumption merely by a finding that the auto was on the wrong side of the road after the accident. ***O'Donnell v. Hail,* 343 Pa. 559, 277 A.2d 360.**

When pedestrian's mind a blank, there exists a presumption that he did all the law required him to do and was not guilty of contributory negligence per se. ***Kmetz v. Lochiatto,* 421 Pa. 363, 219 A.2d 588.**

Priest

Estate brought negligence action against Defendant after the decedent committed suicide when the Defendant stopped paying for the decedent's mental health treatment. The trial court dismissed the case. The Superior Court affirmed holding that that Plaintiff had failed to state a claim upon which relief can be granted as there was no allegation that the decedent was at a greater risk of harming himself due to the treatment provided by the Defendant. ***Unglo v. Zubik,* 29 A.3d 810 (Pa. Super. 2011).**

While Section 317 of Restatement (2d) Torts imposes liability upon a master for acts of a servant committed outside the scope of the servant's employment, liability will not lie unless the acts are performed by the servant "upon the premises in possession of the master." Church and religious officials not liable for conduct of priest who molested minor on non-diocesan property. Judgment against Church, bishop and diocese vacated. ***Hutchison v. Luddy,* 453 Pa. Super. 420, 683 A.2d 1254 (1996).**

Prison and prisoners

Prior accident

Falling accident—victim had history of a prior fall—extensive cross-examination concerning prior accident held not error—strong dissent. ***Levant v. L. Wasserman, Inc.*, 218 Pa. Super. 116, 275 A.2d 678.**

Prior injuries

Evidence admissible to establish that plaintiff had a prior rear-end automobile accident involving injury to her back—claiming in instant case similar injuries—cross-examination involving same permitted. ***McCay v. Phila. Electric Co.*, 447 Pa. 490, 291 A.2d 759.**

Prison and prisoners

Prisoner brought negligence action against prison officials for the destruction or loss of his personal property while he was incarcerated. The trial court dismissed the case. The Superior Court affirmed holding that the Pennsylvania Litigation Reform Act did not require exhaustion of administrative remedies prior to filing suit and the prisoner failed to exhaust his administrative remedies to toll the statute of limitations. ***Paluch v. Palakovich*, 84 A.3d 1109 (Pa. Cmwlth. 2014).**

Prisoner brought negligence action against county prison after he was injured when another prisoner backed into him with a tractor while mowing the lawn. Trial court dismissed the complaint. The Commonwealth Court reversed holding that a prisoner operating a tractor was a county employee that permitted an exception to governmental immunity. The Court also held that the county's failure to maintain the back-up warning signal could constitute an exception to governmental immunity. ***Allen v. County of Wayne*, 88 A.3d 1035 (Pa. Cmwlth. 2013).**

Inmate brought claim for negligence against prison after he was injured in a fall from his bunk while trying to open a malfunctioning cell door. The trial court granted summary judgment in favor of the prison. The Commonwealth Court upheld the trial court's ruling holding that a prison only owed a duty to inmates for reasonably foreseeable harm and that it was not reasonably foreseeable that an inmate would try to open a cell door from the top bunk and also that the inmate assumed the risk of falling by attempting to open the cell door from the top bunk knowing of the danger that he could fall. ***Cochrane v. Kopko*, 975 A.2d 1203 (Pa. Cmwlth. 2009).**

Plaintiff inmates sued the Department of Corrections for negligently failing to release them from the Capital Case Unit after their death sentences were vacated. The Commonwealth Court held that it lacked original jurisdiction in an action for a writ of mandamus that sought money damages for a negligent tort claim. The court also held that death row inmates whose death sentences are vacated do not have a protected liberty interest in not being confined on death row for which damages can be obtained. ***Clark v. Beard*, 918 A.2d 155 (Pa. Cmwlth. 2007).**

Prisoner filed claim in negligence against correction officers for the destruction of his television, which was broken while being held in their custody. The trial court dismissed the claim on governmental immunity grounds, but was reversed.

Prison and prisoners

The appellate court held that personal property damaged while in possession of a Commonwealth party is an enumerated exception to sovereign immunity in Pennsylvania. *Williams v. Stickman*, **917 A.2d 915 (Pa. Cmwlth. 2007).**

Inmate sued employees of the Inmate Parole Board on the basis of variety of constitutional law claims and negligence claim. The court dismissed his claim ruling that a claim of negligent deprivation of liberty in violation of due process rights was merely an appeal of the Parole Board's decision to revoke his parole, a claim which was no longer considered timely. *Wilson v. Marrow*, **917 A.2d 357 (Pa. Cmwlth. 2007).**

Prisoner appealed dismissal of his complaint for gross negligence against defendant district attorney. The court found that the prisoner failed to establish probable cause for a misconduct action against the defendant district attorney. *Wilkins v. Marsico, Jr.*, **903 A.2d 1281 (Pa. Super. 2006).**

Inmate injured when he fell on wet, slippery waxed floor was not entitled to trial as condition of floor was not "dangerous condition of real estate" under the real estate exception in the Sovereign Immunity Act. *Raker v. Pa. Dept. of Corrections*, **844 A.2d 659 (Pa. Cmwlth. 2004).**

Inmate in state police holding cell hanged himself with shoelaces that had not been removed far enough from his cell by state troopers. In survival action by parents against state police, held that shoelaces were not "personal property within the care, custody and control" of the commonwealth for personal property exception and holding cell that was not visible to troopers at all times so as to prevent suicide was not subject to real estate exception to sovereign immunity. Compelling dissent. ***Pennsylvania State Police v. Klimek*, 839 A.2d 1173 (Pa. Cmwlth. 2003).**

State prison inmate properly stated a cognizable cause of action for negligence against prison doctor and health system administrator under medical-professional exception to sovereign immunity. Inmate had been prescribed incorrect medication which resulted in low blood pressure and fall with injury to back and administrator transferred inmate to a facility that lacked capacity to care for inmate"s resulting injuries. *Williams v. Syed*, **782 A.2d 1090 (Pa. Super. 2001)**.

Inmate filed suit against county correctional facility for injury to his head received when the "grab bar" in the prison shower broke free causing him to fall. Despite county's argument that the shower stall was only personal property, lack of evidence by county that shower stall was not a fixture and resulting presumption that it was in the nature of real property maintained by the county, precludes summary judgment under Political Subdivision Tort Claims Act. *Davis v. Brennan*, **698 A.2d 1382 (Pa. Cmwlth. 1997).**

A state agency has no duty to remove or treat natural accumulations of ice and snow. A natural accumulation of ice, snow or frost on prison sidewalk is not a defect of property within the real property exception to governmental immunity; therefore, prisoner not entitled to recovery. Order granting summary judgment affirmed. *Hill v. Dragovich*, ___ **Pa. Cmwlth.** ___, **679 A.2d 1382 (1996).**

Proceeding on highway

Suspect killed during police chase following unsuccessful arrest. City liable. Police did not follow proper procedures. *Agresta v. Gillespie,* **158 Pa. Cmwlth. 230, 631 A.2d 772.**

Inmate brought action against prison nurse for dispensing improper medication. Nurse not liable. *Navarro v. George,* **150 Pa. Cmwlth. 229, 615 A.2d 890.**

Suspect committed suicide with police officer's firearm while being detained by township and county police. Officers and departments immune. *Simmons v. Township of Moon,* **144 Pa. Cmwlth. 198, 601 A.2d 425.**

Inmate being held for intoxication hanged herself in police cell. City not liable. Chapter 21–701 of City Code not applicable. *City of Philadelphia v. Kluska,* **134 Pa. Cmwlth. 511, 579 A.2d 1006.**

Prisoner committed suicide shortly after being counseled by parole officer. City and officer not liable. Parole officers not health care personnel under exceptions to government immunity. *Freedman v. City of Allentown,* **128 Pa. Cmwlth. 126, 562 A.2d 1012.**

Private nuisance

Property owners brought an action against the Department of Transportation, townships and school district alleging private nuisance, because the waterway easement that flowed through their property was being eroded, causing them to have to build larger and larger bridges to cross over it. The appellate court held that the Department of Transportation was immune from damages to return the waterway to its 1979 condition and that evidence was insufficient that the actions of any of the defendants had caused the increase in water flow in the waterway. *Swift v. Department of Transportation of the Commonwealth of Pennsylvania,* **937 A.2d 1162 (Pa. Cmwlth. 2007).**

Probate of will

Son of deceased mother filed suit alleging legal malpractice against attorney for his father because attorney did not immediately probate mother's will which established substantial trust for son. Son alleged two theories: He was third party beneficiary of contract between father and attorney and incurred damages in being required to force probate of mother's will and attorney was negligent *per se* because he had, prior to son's forcing of probate of will, concealed the existence of mother's will. Held that criminal statute imposing criminal penalty for concealment of a will is designed to protect society at large, not beneficiaries and so there can be no negligence *per se* for violation; and son was not owed any duty by attorney, despite his beneficiary status, as father's interests in managing his deceased wife's estate was primarily obligation of attorney's representation. *Minnich v. Yost,* **817 A.2d 538 (Pa. Super. 2003).**

Proceeding on highway

Plaintiff to right stopped for red light at intersection—when light changed looked in both directions and saw nothing approaching—then proceeding and did

Professional insurance

not see defendant's car until about point of contact—defendant's car proceeding against a red light—Held: plaintiff was entering an unoccupied intersection and was not apprised that defendant would disregard light—verdict for plaintiff—motions refused below and action affirmed on appeal. ***Fouser v. Cantola*, 438 Pa. 549, 264 A.2d 169.**

Plaintiff proceeding at an intersection with traffic light in his favor—defendant's truck 80 feet to his left when plaintiff 15 feet from intersection—proceeding—collision—plaintiff's possible contributory negligence was for the jury. ***Andrews v. Long*, 425 Pa. 152, 228 A.2d 760.**

Plaintiff on stop street—stopping at curb and observing no vehicles in intersecting street—while in center saw defendant's car 200 feet distant—struck when rear of car within 5 feet of opposite curb line—for jury—plaintiff not guilty of contributory negligence as a matter of law in proceeding. ***Wynkoop v. McLendon*, 208 Pa. Super. 81, 220 A.2d 904.**

Professional insurance

Hospital does not have duty to ensure that its staff maintains professional liability insurance coverage. Order granting summary judgment affirmed. ***Domineck v. Mercy Hospital*, 449 Pa. Super. 313, 673 A.2d 959 (1996).**

Bringing out the fact that one of plaintiff's doctors had professional insurance not sufficient grounds for a new trial. ***Price v. Yellow Cab Co.*, 443 Pa. 56, 278 A.2d 161.**

Professional negligence: Accounting

Contributory negligence of husband and wife physicians who sued their accountant for negligence in preparation of their corporate and personal tax returns precluded recovery, particularly in light of their criminal convictions for tax fraud. ***Columbia Medical Group v. Herring & Roll, P.C.*, 829 A.2d 1184 (Pa. Super. 2003).**

Accountants can be sued for negligence in performance of services to insurance company which leads to misstatements and loss to creditors, policy holders and general public. ***Koken v. Steinberg*, 825 A.2d 723 (Pa. Cmwlth. 2003).**

Professional negligence: Engineering

Property owner brought negligence claim against engineering firm due to the engineering firm's storm water management design. The trial court granted the Defendant's motion for judgment of non pros. The Superior Court affirmed, holding that an engineering firm qualified as a licensed professional requiring the filing of a certificate of merit despite the fact that the Plaintiff failed to identify the defendant as a licensed professional in its complaint. ***Dental Care Associates, Inc. v. Keller Engineers, Inc.*, 954 A.2d 597 (Pa. Super. 2008).**

Property owner brought a claim for negligence against an engineering firm claiming its storm water management system was improperly designed. The property owner failed to file a certificate of merit regarding its allegations arguing that

Protruding objects or body parts

the claim was within the realm of common knowledge. The appellate court affirmed the trial court's decision to deny the property owner's petition to open the judgment of non pros, because the engineering firm qualified as a licensed professional despite the fact that the corporation itself was not a licensed professional. *Dental Care Associates, Inc. v. Keller Engineers, Inc.*, **954 A.2d 597 (Pa. Super. 2008).**

Property owner brought suit against engineering firm, water authority, and contractor for negligently installing a water line on his property without obtaining authorization or consent. The defendant engineering firm was granted a judgment non pros after the plaintiff failed to file a certificate of merit. The appellate court reversed, holding that the property owner's negligence complaint did not require a filing of a certificate of merit, because it was not a professional liability claim since the claim was related to judgment within the realm of common knowledge. ***Merlini v. Gallitzin Water Authority*, 934 A.2d 100 (Pa. Super. 2007).**

Professional negligence: Investment advisor

Bank investment advisor who served as manager of trust account surcharged for negligence in management of trust funds. Decisions to diversify, extend investment horizon and change nature of investments were not made in light of particular circumstances of the actual needs of the life beneficiaries. ***In re: Scheidmantel, Appeal of Sky Trust*, 868 A.2d 464 (Pa. Super. 2005).**

Professional negligence: Vocational rehabilitation

Injured employee permitted to proceed with suit alleging negligence of vocational rehabilitation firm resulting in emotional distress despite plaintiff's referral to vocational rehabilitation firm after work related injury. Exclusivity provisions of Workers' Compensation Act do not bar action against third party provider of services. ***Taylor v. Woods Rehabilitation Service*, 846 A.2d 742 (Pa. Super. 2004).**

Protruding objects or body parts

Minor passenger whose elbow was protruding from open window was injured when bus struck utility pole. Issue of child's contributory negligence was properly submitted to jury. Damages not excessive. ***White v. SEPTA*, 359 Pa. Super. 123, 518 A.2d 810.**

Pedestrian while standing on sidewalk allegedly struck by protruding mirror of defendant's truck—trial court in error in excluding from jury's consideration the fact that mirror may have extended over sidewalk even though the truck was still on the travelled portion of the cartway—new trial awarded to plaintiff. ***Russell v. Helm's Express, Inc.*, 221 Pa. Super. 292, 293 A.2d 78.**

Steel truss being transported by defendant's vehicle struck rear of plaintiff's milk wagon—contact slight—property damage not in excess of $20 to $25—plaintiff alleged excessive personal injuries—verdict for defendant not disturbed. ***Brodhead v. Brentwood Ornamental Iron Co.*, 435 Pa. 7, 255 A.2d 120.**

Property damage

Property damage

There is no requirement that motorist's claim for property damages under the No-Fault Act be joined with motorist's claim for personal injuries under the Act, since the claims are based on causes of action which accrued at different times: 2 years from the date of the accident in the case of property damage claims, and 2 years from date plaintiff knows that the Section 301 threshold has been reached in the case of personal injury claims. ***Branoff v. Fitzpatrick*, 313 Pa. Super. 562, 460 A.2d 330.**

Property owner liability

Plaintiff brought negligence action against former steel mill owner for injuries suffered in an explosion even though the steel mill was no longer owned by the Defendant at the time of the injuries. Plaintiff claimed the removal of an emergency drawbridge by the Defendant led to his injuries while he was employed by current mill owner. The trial court entered summary judgment for the Defendant. The Superior Court affirmed. The Pennsylvania Supreme Court affirmed holding that a former property owner could not be liable for negligent construction based upon alterations it made to a property it no longer owned. ***Gresik v. PA Partners, LP,* 33 A.3d 594 (Pa. 2011).**

Plaintiff, a plumber/pipe-fitter employee of an independent contractor for a power plant, died from asbestos exposure. Plaintiff's personal representative sued possessor of real estate where he worked. Held that possessor of land had no greater knowledge of risks of asbestos than plaintiff and his employer and so was insulated from liability. ***Rudy v. A-Best Products Company*, 870 A.2d 330 (Pa. Super. 2005).**

Proof of assumption of the risk requires the following: the defendant establish that the plaintiff consciously appreciated the risk attendant to a certain endeavor; assumed the risk of injury by engaging in the endeavor despite the appreciation of the risk involved; and injury sustained was, in fact, the same risked injury that was appreciated and assumed. Case includes a thorough analysis of the doctrine and its history. The court addresses liability of an owner who alleges that he is "out of possession" of residence under construction when he actually has retained control of the project. ***Bullman v. Giuntoli*, 761 A.2d 566 (Pa. Super. 2000).**

Slip and fall accident at tavern by patron. Plaintiff sued titled owners of the property despite the fact that the business was operated and managed by a purchaser under a land sale contract, who had full use and possession of the tavern premises and business. The court held that bare legal title alone is not adequate to establish possession and control over premises and subject a party to liability for tortious conduct of the party who is actually in possession. ***Hubert v. Greenwald*, 743 A.2d 977 (Pa. Super. 1999).**

Building owner was liable to elevator mechanic who was injured when she fell from a ladder which was so close to the wall of an elevator shaft as to make it dangerous. Building owner was aware of danger by reason of prior complaints by other elevator mechanics but did not remedy problem. In granting new trial to defendant after verdict for plaintiff, trial court abused its discretion when it substituted its opinion of how the fall occurred for that of the jury. ***Mammoccio v. 1818 Market Partnership*, 734 A.2d 23 (Pa. Super. 1999).**

Plaintiff appeals from grant of summary judgment to defendants based on common-enemy doctrine relating to natural surface water runoff in urban area. Plaintiff was injured when she slipped and fell on ice that had accumulated in alley next to defendant's business location. Held: so long as defendant had not artificially changed natural course of water or substantially changed quality or quantity of surface water, no injury will fall to lower landowner or to another. The record is devoid of evidence that defendants modified natural course of water in any way. ***Fazio v. Fegley Oil Co, Inc.*, 714 A.2d 510 (Pa. Cmwlth. 1998).**

Co-owner of entireties property with actual knowledge of sexual abuse by their co-owner on their minor grandchildren within residence does not have duty to protect or warn grandchildren of grandfather's proclivities. Multimillion dollar compensatory and punitive damages award against grandmother reversed. While landowner may be liable for dangerous condition on the land, landowner is not liable for criminal or tortious acts of third parties. ***T.A. v. Allen*, 447 Pa. Super. 302, 669 A.2d 360 (1995).**

Defendant injured when car struck dumpster he was rummaging through did not state cause of action against owners of property who lawfully placed dumpster in front of house and who had no awareness of plaintiff's presence. Plaintiff failed to show any proximate causation between owner's placement of dumpster and his injuries. Proximate causation exists where wrongful conduct is a substantial factor in bringing about the harm incurred. Order granting summary judgment affirmed. ***Amarhanov v. Fassel*, 442 Pa. Super. 111, 658 A.2d 808 (1995).**

In negligence action against corporate defendant and officers, officers are not liable for failing to maintain clean bathroom absent proof of their participation in creating or allowing continued existence of dangerous condition. Party's failure to answer request for admission that states a conclusion of law does not establish plaintiff's case. Judgment in favor of plaintiff vacated and remanded for consideration of scope of involvement and liability of owners. ***Brindley v. Woodland Village Restaurant, Inc.*, 438 Pa. Super. 385, 652 A.2d 865 (1995).**

Motorist injured in collision with vehicle exiting driveway on commercial property. Property owner not liable for failure to warn of dangerous condition. ***Cruet v. Certain-Teed Corporation*, 432 Pa. Super. 554, 639 A.2d 478.**

Passenger injured when vehicle collided with stone pillar at entrance to private driveway. Property owner not liable. ***Braxton v. Com., Dept. of Transp.*, 160 Pa. Cmwlth. 32, 634 A.2d 1150.**

Abutting landowners to common driveway were all properly joined in case alleging injury from defect in driveway where all had deeds with equal covenant to repair. ***Mscisz v. Russell*, 338 Pa. Super. 38, 487 A.2d 839.**

In action by motorist against landowner for failure to remove plant growth causing visual obstruction at intersection where collision occurred—test of liability of landowner is not the passive "natural v. artificial" analysis of condition, but

Property to be insured

one of factual causation for jury. *Harvey v. Hansen,* **299 Pa. Super. 474, 445 A.2d 1228.**

69 year old woman injured while entering terminal of defendant when door was let go by another patron. Issue of whether plaintiff was a passenger or licensee for jury. Error to charge that plaintiff was a passenger. *Kiely v. SEPTA,* **485 Pa. Super. 205, 401 A.2d 366.**

Patron struck at car wash by car exiting while he was in vacuum area. Error to grant summary judgment on theory of negligent design. For jury even though 200,000 vehicles had used car wash without incident. *Amabile v. Auto Kleen,* **249 Pa. Super. 240, 376 A.2d 247.**

Mannequin fell on plaintiff while shopping in defendant's store. No evidence as to how and why it fell. Nonsuit reversed. Jury could reasonably infer that store was negligent in allowing mannequin to be in such a position and improperly secured. Proof need be slight. *Paul v. Hess Bros., Inc.,* **226 Pa. Super. 92, 312 A.2d 65.**

Jar of olives fell from a high shelf above the ordinary reach of a customer and struck plaintiff—Held: stocking of merchandise in such a manner may subject customers to unwarranted risk and entry of nonsuit below was in error—matter for jury. *Dougherty v. Great A. & P. Tea Co.,* **221 Pa. Super. 221, 289 A.2d 747.**

Property to be insured

Insurance company brought action against contractor in tort and contract for negligently investigating property to be insured. Company permitted to proceed under both theories. *Grode v. Mutual Fire, Marine, and Inland Insurance Company,* **154 Pa. Cmwlth. 366, 623 A.2d 933.**

Prostatectomy

Where patient who underwent perineal urethrotomy and cauterization, rather than planned transurethral prostatectomy, failed to establish a causal connection between resulting injuries and physician's conduct through expert testimony, compulsory nonsuit was proper. Patient should have been allowed to introduce evidence of alleged lack of consent to surgery that was admittedly not discussed by physician and patient prior to its performance. Order granting compulsory nonsuit on question of negligence affirmed. Case remanded on claim for lack of informed consent. *Hoffman v. Mogil,* **445 Pa. Super. 252, 665 A.2d 478 (1995).**

Protective equipment

Non-jury verdict, $83,190 to minor; $1,810 to parents. Minor plaintiff, 5th grade 11 year old student injured in school floor hockey game—organized extracurricular activity. Struck in mouth by hockey stick severing five teeth. Held: negligent not to supply mouth guards. Requests made were denied by school board. Minor plaintiff unaware of injuries in previous games. Presumption that minor incapable of contributory negligence not rebutted. Affirmed. *Berman v. Philadelphia Board of Education,* **310 Pa. Super. 153, 456 A.2d 545.**

Proximate cause

Protestors

University owes no duty to students to control protestors. Student who sees open and obvious impediment to her path of travel should choose an alternate path, rather than attempting to jump from four-foot wall. Order granting summary judgment affirmed. ***Banks v. Trustees of University of Pennsylvania*, 446 Pa. Super. 99, 666 A.2d 329 (1995).**

Prothonotary

Savings and loan brought action against prothonotary and office of prothonotary for failure to index writ of revival of judgment. Prothonotary not personally liable for negligence of employees. Office of prothonotary not liable owing to plaintiff's contributory negligence. ***Commonwealth Federal Savings and Loan Association v. Pettit*, 137 Pa. Cmwlth. 523, 586 A.2d 1021.**

Proximate cause

Plaintiff, a psychiatric patient, brought suit against an ambulance service for negligently transporting him after he escaped from their care and later robbed a bank resulting in a criminal conviction. The appellate court reversed the trial court's ruling holding that under the no felony conviction recovery rule Plaintiff could not profit from his own criminal acts and also that his criminal acts were too remote to establish proximate causation. ***Holt v. Navarro*, 932 A.2d 915 (Pa. Super. 2007).**

Plaintiff rescue worker was struck and injured by a second driver who fell asleep at the wheel and struck plaintiff as he attended to an earlier hit and run accident. Plaintiff filed suit against the hit and run driver claiming his actions were the proximate cause of plaintiff's injuries because his flight forced the only officer securing the accident scene to leave, increasing the danger to plaintiff. The court held that the hit and run driver's flight was too remote to have brought about plaintiff's injury, since the actual cause was the second motorist falling asleep at the wheel. Additionally, the court found that plaintiff's claim of negligence per se based upon the defendant's violation of a hit and run statute still required proximate causation and ultimately failed as well. ***Lux v. Gerald Ort Trucking, Inc.*, 887 A.2d 1281 (Pa. Super. 2005).**

Pennsylvania has not yet adopted the market share liability theory as an exception to the general rule of negligence law that a plaintiff must establish that a particular defendant proximately caused his or her injury. Summary judgment affirmed in favor of lead manufacturers and trade organization sued by minor injured by lead poisoning. ***Skipworth v. Lead Industries Association, Inc.*, 547 Pa. 224, 690 A.2d 169 (1997).**

In legal malpractice action by criminal defendant against his attorney, plaintiff's failure to allege facts in support of his claim that he was innocent of the criminal charges prohibits recovery. Plaintiff must demonstrate attorney's culpable negligent representation as the proximate cause of conviction. ***Slaugher v. Rushing*, 453 Pa. Super. 379, 683 A.2d 1234 (1996).**

Proximate cause

Defendant utility pole inspection company did not have duty to protect bystander from injuries sustained when bystander came into contact with downed electrical wires while assisting victims of automobile accident that damaged utility pole. Defendant inspection company's alleged negligent inspection of pole was too remote to constitute proximate cause of bystander's injuries. Bystander was not third party beneficiary of contract between inspection company and utility company which required inspection company only to inspect and report condition of poles. Order sustaining preliminary objections of defendant inspection company affirmed. *Hicks v. Metropolitan Edison Company,* ___ Pa. Cmwlth. ___, 665 A.2d 529 (1995).

Absent proof that a patron was visibly intoxicated when served additional alcoholic beverages, no action for wrongful death or survival is established. Statutory violation of serving alcohol after hours does not establish liability for acts of third parties absent proof that such service was proximate cause of the injury. *Hiles v. Brandywine Club,* 443 Pa. Super. 462, 662 A.2d 16 (1995).

In action arising out of explosion of boiler caused by defective emergency shut-off valve, manufacturer of valve held strictly liable for defective product. Manufacturer's liability for its defective product is outlined in Section 402A of Restatement (2d) Torts, which provides that a plaintiff must prove that the product was sold in a defective condition dangerous to the user and that the defect was the proximate cause of the injury. An actor is relieved from liability due to an intervening or superseding cause only if the intervening or superseding negligent acts were so extraordinary as not to have been reasonably foreseeable. Summary judgment affirmed in part and reversed in part. *Dougherty v. Edward J. Meloney, Inc.,* 443 Pa. Super. 201, 661 A.2d 375 (1995).

Defendant injured when car struck dumpster he was rummaging through did not state cause of action against owners of property who lawfully placed dumpster in front of house and who had no awareness of plaintiff's presence. Plaintiff failed to show any proximate causation between owner's placement of dumpster and his injuries. Proximate causation exists where wrongful conduct is a substantial factor in bringing about the harm incurred. Order granting summary judgment affirmed. *Amarhanov v. Fassel,* 442 Pa. Super. 111, 658 A.2d 808 (1995).

Emergency medical technician injured by automobile accident victim while providing treatment. Held: neither pedestrian victim nor driver tortfeasor liable due to lack of proximate cause. *Bell v. Irace,* 422 Pa. Super. 298, 619 A.2d 365.

Rear-end collision. Plaintiff's tail lights not working. Issue of whether defective tail lights were proximate cause of accident for jury. Error to direct verdict against plaintiff. *Correll v. Werner,* 293 Pa. Super. 88, 437 A.2d 1004.

Visitor to hospital slipped on freshly mopped floor. Floor wet from wall to wall. Had observed floor being mopped earlier. Plaintiff's evidence weak as to whether wetness caused fall. For jury. Verdict for plaintiff affirmed. Strong dissent. *Calhoun v. Jersey Shore Hospital,* 250 Pa. Super. 567, 378 A.2d 1294.

Proximate cause

Plaintiff involved in chain reaction collision. Plaintiff died of heart attack several months later. Verdict for defendant. Judge charged that foreseeability of injuries a test for determining proximate cause. Since jury never properly instructed on causation, charge on foreseeability reversible error. New trial ordered. ***McCloy v. Penn Fruit*, 245 Pa. Super. 251, 369 A.2d 389.**

Plaintiff dismounting from gondola car, following stoppage of train, to investigate as his duties prescribed. Slipped and fell. Defect in locomotive caused train to stop. Negligence of railroad in having defective engine which stopped causing plaintiff to climb out not a proximate cause of injury. ***Ledford v. Pittsburgh and Lake Erie R.R.*, 236 Pa. Super. 65, 345 A.2d 218.**

Suit by plaintiff against auto driver and phone company for injuries sustained when auto struck phone booth in which plaintiff was making a call. Verdict against phone company and driver affirmed. For jury, whether location of phone booth was dangerous, and whether location was a proximate cause of accident. ***Noon v. Knavel, et al.*, 234 Pa. Super. 198, 339 A.2d 545.**

Illegally parked truck blocking vision of driver edging out at intersection. Car then involved in collision with third vehicle on main street. Illegally parked truck a proximate cause of accident. Verdict against both defendants affirmed. ***Bell v. Cohen, et al.*, 228 Pa. Super. 872, 322 A.2d 704.**

Pile of dirt left near highway by contractor which allegedly obstructed view of driver leaving parking lot—operator collided with motorcyclist on highway—judgment *n.o.v.* reversed and verdict for plaintiff against contractor reinstated. ***Flickinger, et al. v. Marona Const. Co.*, 452 Pa. 66, 305 A.2d 19.**

Plaintiff's truck went off a bridge owned and maintained allegedly defectively by defendant—court not in error in charging jury that any contributory negligence of plaintiff must be a proximate cause of the occurrence—doctrine of *Crane v. Neal* (389 Pa. 329) inferentially repudiated. ***Cebulskie v. Lehigh Valley R. R. Co.*, 441 Pa. 230, 272 A.2d 171.**

Action by motorcyclist for injuries sustained in collision at intersection—defendant motorist filed complaint to join as additional defendant individual who had parked car so near intersection as to obstruct motorist's view—Court held motorist's complaint stated cause of action on theory that conduct of person parking vehicle constituted superseding cause and not proximate cause—remanded; for jury. ***Clevenstein v. Rizzuto*, 438 Pa. 397, 266 A.2d 623.**

The "but for" rule in the concept of proximate cause not overruled but the concept of proximate cause set forth in Section 432 (1) of Restatement (2d) Torts favored—also the phrase "legal cause" held preferable to the phrase "proximate cause." ***Whitner v. Lojeski*, 437 Pa. 448, 263 A.2d 889.**

Plaintiff operating a leased truck which was not equipped with flares, flashers and flags—truck stalled—plaintiff directing traffic—struck by car of one of defendants who saw disabled truck 100 yards away—lessor defendant not legally responsible as its negligence was not proximate cause. ***Klena v. Rutkowski*, 432 Pa. 509, 248 A.2d 9.**

Psychiatric patient

Plaintiff fell from scaffold because a brace slipped suddenly—plaintiff fell into a hole 16 feet deep which defendant had dug and failed to cover—existence of hole not the proximate cause—preliminary objections properly sustained. ***Barber v. Kohler Co.*, 428 Pa. 219, 237 A.2d 224.**

Plaintiff while properly operating his car forced to swerve by the action of an unknown car and to collide with an unlighted trailer illegally parked—Supreme Court by a divided court held that the illegal parking of unlighted trailer the proximate cause. ***Slawson v. C.A.B.Y. Trans.*, 425 Pa. 489, 229 A.2d 888.**

Psychiatric patient

Patient committed to hospital under Mental Health Procedures Act died by drowning while taking an unsupervised bath. Despite clear medical testimony by affidavit that the staff of the hospital breached their duty of care to the patient, it was held that such negligence was not established to be the "gross negligence" required to be proved to avoid the immunity set forth in the Mental Health Procedures Act. ***Downey v. Crozer-Chester Medical Center*, 817 A.2d 517 (Pa. Super. 2003).**

Plaintiff's decedent killed by her mentally ill husband after the husband informed his therapist that he was going to kill his wife. Suit commenced alleging professional negligence by therapist in failing to warn wife or inform police. After judgment on pleadings in favor of defendants, Superior Court affirmed, as did Supreme Court. Supreme Court formally adopts duty to warn doctrine in Pennsylvania if there is a specific and immediate threat of serious bodily injury to a specifically identified victim that has been communicated to the professional. While the Supreme Court found that both criteria to establish a duty to warn were met, it also determined that the telephonic warning that had been given by the therapist to the wife-victim was adequate. Two dissents suggest adequacy of warning should have gone to jury and legal standard for adequacy of warning was too broad and ineffective. ***Emerich v. Philadelphia Center for Human Development*, 720 A.2d 1032 (Pa. 1999).**

Psychiatric patient who died from injuries suffered as a result of crashing through second floor window of hospital and falling two stories was not being treated by hospital so as to clothe hospital with immunity under Mental Health Procedures Act. Judgment affirmed. ***Fogg v. Paoli Memorial Hospital*, 455 Pa. Super. 81, 686 A.2d 1355 (1996).**

Children of mother killed by former mental patient brought action against hospital and psychiatrist for failure to warn of patient's violent tendencies. Defendants not liable. ***Leonard v. Latrobe Hospital*, 425 Pa. Super. 540, 625 A.2d 1228.**

Employee of state hospital raped by patient. Hospital not liable. Medical-professional exception to sovereign immunity did not apply. Workmen's Compensation only remedy. ***Holland v. Norristown State Hospital*, 136 Pa. Cmwlth. 655, 584 A.2d 1056.**

Waiver of immunity as applied to physicians employed by Commonwealth, allows suits by third parties against said physician for releasing mental patient improperly, which patient thereafter assaulted plaintiff. Denial of preliminary objec-

Public Employee Relations Act

tions affirmed. *Allentown State Hospital v. Gill,* **88 Pa. Cmwlth. 331, 488 A.2d 1211.**

Suit alleging damage due to negligent supervision of psychiatric patient, who needed additional care following fatal fire which he set, sufficiently sets forth cause of action. Demurrer denied. *Vattimo v. Lower Bucks Hospital,* **502 Pa. 240, 465 A.2d 1231.**

Wrongful death and survival action by estate of patient at mental hospital killed by another patient. Alleged failure to adequately supervise patient with known homicidal tendencies. Preliminary objections dismissed on allegation of gross negligence against officials and employees of state. *Rhines v. Herzel,* **481 Pa. 165, 392 A.2d 298.**

Patient at mental hospital walked out without being seen, went to her apartment and got gun, then went to boyfriend's apartment and shot and killed girl there. Verdict against patient only. No liability found on part of hospital. *Evanuik v. U. of Pittsburgh Western Psychiatric Institute,* **234 Pa. Super. 287, 338 A.2d 636.**

Psychic injury

Summary judgment reversed where trial court failed to consider medical evidence of psychic injuries that may have qualified as serious impairment of a body function under limited tort coverage provided for in Motor Vehicle Financial Responsibility Law before granting summary judgment. Minor children injured in accident while riding in their mother's uninsured vehicle are held to have the same deemed limited tort coverage as their uninsured mother. *Hames v. Philadelphia Housing Authority,* **696 A.2d 880 (Pa. Cmwlth. 1997).**

Psychotic episode

Mental health care providers had no duty to police officer for injuries caused by patient who, one day after visiting health care facility in agitated state, drove his car into police van while experiencing a psychotic episode, injuring officer. Summary judgment affirmed. *Heil v. Brown,* **443 Pa. Super. 502, 662 A.2d 669 (1995).**

Public defender

Prisoner brought malpractice action against public defender for failure to file petition for allowance of appeal. Defendant not liable even though not immune. *Veneri v. Pappano,* **424 Pa. Super. 394, 622 A.2d 977.**

Prisoner brought negligent representation action against public defender who represented him. Public defender not immune. *Williams v. Office of the Public Defender of the County of Lehigh,* **402 Pa. Super. 188, 586 A.2d 924.**

Public Employee Relations Act

Prison guard injured on job brought action against union and Commonwealth claiming injuries would not have occurred had he received transfer he was entitled to. Action barred by Public Employee Relations Act. *Runski v. American Federation of State, County, and Municipal Employees, Local 2500,* **142 Pa. Cmwlth. 662, 598 A.2d 347.**

Public nuisance

Public nuisance

Suit by electric company for purely economic losses suffered when water company negligently released chlorine gas into the atmosphere requiring evacuation and shut-down of electric generating plant. Summary judgment for water company affirmed on basis that there is no recovery for purely economic loss resulting from negligent acts. Additionally, Pennsylvania does not recognize private right of action for public nuisance. ***Duquesne Light Company v. Pennsylvania American Water Company*, 850 A.2d 701 (Pa. Super. 2004).**

Public Utility Code

Barn owner's suit against electric utility for oversupply of electricity that allegedly caused fire properly initiated in Common Pleas Court. Court of Common Pleas has original jurisdiction to entertain a suit for damages against a public utility, based on its asserted failure to provide adequate services, even though subject matter of complaint against public utility is encompassed by the public utility code. P.U.C. order dismissing complaint vacated and remanded. ***Poorbaugh v. Pennsylvania P.U.C.*, ___ Pa. Cmwlth. ___, 666 A.2d 744 (1995).**

Public Utility Commission

Barn owner's suit against electric utility for oversupply of electricity that allegedly caused fire properly initiated in Common Pleas Court. Court of Common Pleas has original jurisdiction to entertain a suit for damages against a public utility, based on its asserted failure to provide adequate services, even though subject matter of complaint against public utility is encompassed by the public utility code. P.U.C. order dismissing complaint vacated and remanded. ***Poorbaugh v. Pennsylvania P.U.C.*, ___ Pa. Cmwlth. ___, 666 A.2d 744 (1995).**

—Q—

Quadriplegic

Plaintiff's deceased quadriplegic husband suffered head injuries when he fell from an exam table after he was left alone in his doctor's examination room. Where evidence was presented that he could not move independently and he fell from the table, trial court's failure to charge on res ipsa loquitur was reversible. ***Quinby v. Burmeister*, 850 A.2d 667 (Pa. Super. 2004).**

Quasi-judicial immunity

Plaintiff sued an investigative consultant for the Bureau of Program Integrity for negligently conducting his investigation into the Plaintiff's dental practice on behalf of the Department of Public Welfare. The trial court denied the investigator's preliminary objections asserting quasi-judicial immunity. The Superior Court affirmed holding that the Bureau of Program Integrity's investigation did not involve discretionary decision making authority as required for quasi-judicial immunity to apply. ***Pollina v. Dishong*, 2014 Pa. Super. 153 (2014).**

Quick-release mechanism

Plaintiff sued bicycle manufacturer, assembler and seller for injuries sustained when front wheel allegedly fell off bicycle due to defective "quick-release" mechanism. Defendant's expert testified on cross-examination it was his opinion that the front wheel which he had examined was not on plaintiff's bicycle at the time of the accident. This testimony on cross was beyond the scope of his report, contradicted the opinion expressed in his report and contradicted his direct testimony. Trial court denied plaintiff's motion to strike testimony and post trial motions. Trial court affirmed by Superior Court; Supreme Court reversed because of defendants' expert's intentional misrepresentation to the court and jury during his direct examination. New trial granted. ***Factor v. Bicycle Technology, Inc.*, 707 A.2d 504 (Pa. 1998).**

—R—

Racing

Driver of vehicle killed while drag racing. Held: wanton nature of drag racing while intoxicated precludes recovery by one party from another. ***Lewis v. Miller*, 374 Pa. Super. 515, 543 A.2d 590.**

Radiation treatment

Patient brought malpractice action against surgeon and radiologist for treatment of cancer. Informed consent doctrine found not applicable to radiation treatment. ***Dible v. Vagley*, 417 Pa. Super. 302, 612 A.2d 493.**

Radio

Truck driver who knew of propensity of radio to fall from overhead rack found to be seventy percent negligent for injuries sustained when radio fell from

Railing

rack. Judgment for installer of radio affirmed. ***Dath v. Marano Truck Sales and Service, Inc.,* 437 Pa. Super. 571, 650 A.2d 901 (1994).**

Railing

Five-year old playing on outside stairway fell through narrow opening in railing. Jury verdict for defendant. Charge of court approved stating that possessor of land not responsible for acts of bravado or immature recklessness, even in five-year old. Strong dissent. ***Slavish v. Ratajczak,* 277 Pa. Super. 272, 419 A.2d 767.**

Plaintiff was a guest at the residence of the defendant for a limited time to await the arrival of an automobile mechanic—railing on porch gave way and plaintiff injured—verdict for defendant—improper charge—various trial errors—new trial granted on appeal. ***Hamilton v. Fean,* 422 Pa. 373, 221 A.2d 309.**

Railroads

Plaintiff landowner brought negligence action against the Southeastern Pennsylvania Transportation Authority (SEPTA) for failing to maintain a railroad bridge, which caused a stream to flood plaintiff's hotel. The trial court granted summary judgment to the defendant. The Commonwealth Court affirmed, holding that under the Federal Railroad Safety Act the U.S. Department of Transportation had promulgated regulations requiring railroads to keep bridges free of obstruction to accommodate expected water flow, which preempted any state law claim. The court also held that the savings clause of the Federal Railroad Safety Act did not apply as the danger of flooding was not a local hazard; there was no room in the federal regulations to allow additional state regulation of railroad bridges; and, allowing each state to promulgate its own regulations for railroad bridges would burden interstate commerce. ***Miller v. Southeastern Pennsylvania Transportation Authority,* 65 A.3d 1006 (Pa. Cmwlth. 2013).**

Homeowners brought a state court negligence claim against the Southeastern Pennsylvania Transportation Authority (SEPTA) after temporary tracks constructed by their home caused vibrations that damaged their home's foundation and walls. The appellate court reversed and granted SEPTA's motion for judgment n.o.v. because the Federal Railroad Safety Act preempted state law. ***Mastrocola v. Southeastern Pennsylvania Transportation Authority,* 941 A.2d 81 (Pa. Cmwlth. 2008).**

Plaintiff sued railroad after he drove into a stationary freight train and then was dragged several feet when the train began moving again. The court held that the adoption of comparative negligence by the Pennsylvania General Assembly did not negate the continued viability of the occupied crossing rule, which ordinarily absolves a railroad of its duty to warn of its train obstructing a highway. The court also held that the Federal Railroad Safety Act preempted Pennsylvania's blocked-crossing statute. ***Krentz v. Consolidated Rail Corporation,* 589 Pa. 576, 910 A.2d 20 (2006).**

Negligence claim by plaintiff who drove his vehicle under a train stopped at a crossing and was injured when the train moved and dragged his vehicle barred by Occupied Crossing Rule which provides that the existence of a train in a crossing is warning enough of its presence. Negligence *per se* claim of plaintiff was also

Railroads

barred by federal preemption of Federal Rail Safety Act, 49 U.S.C. § 20101 *et seq.* ***Krentz v. Consolidated Rail Corporation*, 865 A.2d 889 (Pa. Super. 2005).**

Plaintiffs' decedent was killed when her vehicle was struck by a train at an un-gated, at-grade railroad crossing. In suit against borough where the crossing was located, PennDOT as owner of the crossing road and the railroad company, summary judgment motion by PennDOT was denied on the grounds that PennDOT had assumed liability for dangerous condition of the crossing when it entered into an agreement with the borough to seek upgrades to crossing from PA Public Utility Commission. Commonwealth Court reversed denial of summary judgment to PennDOT on grounds that the plaintiffs had not proved the applicability of the real estate exception to sovereign immunity as the crossing was not a dangerous condition of the highway under PennDOT's control. ***Sickles v. Consolidate Rail Corporation*, 777 A.2d 1240 (Pa. Cmwlth. 2001).**

This is a thorough review of the Recreation Use of Land and Water Act ("RULWA"). Plaintiff was injured when he fell from at former rail trestle that had been converted to a wooden walkway over a depression located on property owned by Conrail. Suit was brought, alleging negligence in design of trestle. Conrail filed summary judgment motion, alleging it was immune from suit because the trestle and the property on which it was located were subject to the RULWA. In order to determine whether or not the RULWA provides immunity to a landowner, five factors must be considered: 1) use of the land; 2) size of the parcel; 3) location of the parcel; 4) openness of the parcel; and 5) extent of any improvement on the property. ***Yanno v. Consolidated Rail Corp.*, 744 A.2d 279 (Pa. Super. 1999).**

In action by motorist for injuries sustained when she collided with side of a hopper car being pulled by defendant's train, railroad company whose train was actually on and moving over a crossing did not owe motorist a duty to warn of train's presence. Occupied crossing rule survived enactment of the Comparative Negligence Act. Order sustaining preliminary objections affirmed. ***Sprenkle v. Conrail*, 446 Pa. Super. 377, 666 A.2d 1099 (1995).**

Where no evidence that trunk was too large or unwieldy to be placed in overhead rack of railroad car, employee could not maintain action for negligence of employer in providing safe place to work when trunk fell on employee's foot causing injury. Summary judgment affirmed. ***Lehman v. National R.R. Passenger Corp.*, 443 Pa. Super. 185, 661 A.2d 17 (1995).**

Pedestrian killed while crossing railroad tracks in non-designated area. Held: contractor out of possession may be liable for harm to third persons caused by defects in property. Whether deceased was more than 50% negligent was question for jury. ***Gilbert v. Consolidated Rail Corporation*, 154 Pa. Cmwlth. 249, 623 A.2d 873.**

Child run over by train while lying on tracks. Permissive crossing theory held not applicable since child was lying on tracks and not crossing them. ***Gaul v. Consolidated Rail Corp.*, 383 Pa. Super. 250, 556 A.2d 892.**

Rainwater

Railroad which owned land adjacent to electrical tower from which minor received shock and fell could not be held liable because child crossed its land to reach tower. Summary judgment for railroad affirmed. ***Thomas v. Duquesne Light*, 347 Pa. Super. 492, 500 A.2d 1163.**

Plaintiff-decedent riding on top of roof of truck in course of summer employment. Facing to rear. Head struck on overpass as truck passed underneath on highway. Original clearance of 14 feet reduced to 10 feet 2 inches due to numerous road repairs. Railroad held negligent for failure to maintain proper clearance. ***Marinelli v. Montour R.R. Co.*, 278 Pa. Super. 403, 420 A.2d 603.**

Plaintiff unloading box car on defendant's siding—some of contents fell on him—evidence insufficient to establish that defendant's crew pushed another car into standing box car—court below properly granted judgment *n.o.v.* for defendant. ***Flaherty v. Penna. R.R. Co.*, 426 Pa. 83, 231 A.2d 179.**

Plaintiff, while using a railroad bridge, fell through same as the result of a missing plank—railroad company held responsible and Pennsylvania rule as to not having permissive rights to use right of way longitudinally seriously questioned or abrogated. ***Franc v. Penna. R.R. Co.*, 424 Pa. 99, 225 A.2d 528.**

Rainwater

For real property exception to apply against school district, dangerous condition must be of or attached to the pavement or property and not on the subject pavement or property. Rainwater on floor of school building did not constitute dangerous condition of or attached to property. Directed verdict for defendant affirmed. Dissent would apply exception based on school district's use of terrazzo floor tile, which school district knew became dangerously slippery when wet. ***Shedrick v. William Penn School District*, ___ Pa. Cmwlth. ___, 654 A.2d 163 (1995).**

Rape

An employee who is sexually assaulted and raped by a co-employee may still pursue a negligence claim against the employer under the "personal animus" or "third party attack" exception to the exclusivity provisions of the workers compensation act. Because the attack in the instant case was based on purely personal motives, unrelated to the employment, plaintiff was entitled to proceed with her common law action. ***Krasevic v. Goodwill Industries, Inc.*, 764 A.2d 561 (Pa. Super. 2000).**

Victim who was raped in building being renovated brought action against contractor. Contractor not liable. Duty to secure building was to owner and not contractor. ***Glick v. Martin and Mohler, Inc.*, 369 Pa. Super. 428, 535 A.2d 626.**

Customer of defendant raped by a former employee of defendant at plaintiff's home. Complaint dismissed, but reinstated on appeal. Although employee terminated, if employer negligently hired said person, he may owe duty to customers to whose homes employee had been previously sent, to warn of firing. ***Coath v. Jones*, 277 Pa. Super. 479, 419 A.2d 1249.**

Rave

"Rave" party promoter that was not alleged to have provided any drugs or alcohol to adult party-guest driver could not be liable as social host for injuries sustained by party-guest passenger injured in automobile accident on way home. *Looby v. Local 13 Productions*, 751 A.2d 220 (Pa. Super. 2000).

Reactive Airways Dysfunction Syndrome (RADS)

Plaintiff appealed from jury award of $12,000.00 which she considered inadequate for injuries suffered when she inhaled smoke from Port Authority bus which caught fire in front of her car in tunnel. Plaintiff's expert testified to her affliction a Reactive Airways Dysfunction Syndrome ("RADS"). Hotly contested case relating to extent of her injury and when her condition improved to point of plaintiff being completely recovered. Held: there was adequate evidence for jury to accept Port Authority's version of facts rather than plaintiff's. Verdict was not so low as to shock the sense of justice. *Labbett v. Port Authority of Allegheny County*, 714 A.2d 522 (Pa. Cmwlth. 1998).

Real estate agent or broker

Buyers sued sellers and real estate agent for negligent misrepresentation for failing to disclose that the prior owners had been killed in the house in a murder suicide. The trial court dismissed the case on summary judgment. The Pennsylvania Superior Court affirmed. The Pennsylvania Supreme Court held that as a matter of first impression sellers and real estate agents had no duty to disclose psychological stigmas associated with property. *Milliken v. Jacono*, 48 MAP 2013 (Pa. 2014).

Plaintiff brought negligent misrepresentation action against realtors and real estate agency for failing to disclose that a murder/suicide had been committed in the property. The trial court granted summary judgment to the defendants. The Superior Court affirmed, holding that a murder/suicide was not a material defect that had to be disclosed on a mandatory disclosure form and there is no duty to disclose purely psychological defects in a home. *Milliken v. Jacono*, 60 A.3d 133 (Pa. Super. 2012).

Plaintiffs brought tort action against real estate agency, lender and personal property removal service for removing their personal property and locking them out of a home after a foreclosure. The trial court granted the defendants' motion to dismiss. The Superior Court affirmed, holding that tort claims related to the removal of personal property and trespass had been resolved in the prior foreclosure action requiring dismissal of any civil actions related to the process of removal of property from a foreclosed home. *Gray v. Buonopane*, 53 A.3d 829 (Pa. Super. 2012).

Rear-end collision

Plaintiff brought negligence action against tow truck driver and his employers after he rear ended the tow truck as it attempted to make a u-turn at a median opening in a highway. A jury found in favor of the defendants. The Superior Court affirmed, holding that a tow truck operator was authorized to use a median opening

Rear-end collision

to make a u-turn on a highway. ***Keffer v. Bob Nolan's Auto Service, Inc.*, 59 A.3d 621 (Pa. Super. 2013).**

Plaintiff passenger brought negligence action against the unlicensed intoxicated driver of the vehicle she was in and a dram shop action against the bar where they had been drinking. The trial court granted summary judgment on behalf of the Defendant. The Superior Court affirmed holding that the Plaintiff passenger was vicariously liable for the intoxicated driver's actions as she permitted him to drive her vehicle knowing he did not have a license. ***Price v. Leibfried*, 34 A.3d 1279 (Pa. Super. 2011).**

Plaintiff brought claim for personal injuries as a result of a rear end collision by the Defendant. Defendant appealed the trial court's ruling that she was collaterally estopped at trial from disputing the amount of damages suffered by the Plaintiff based upon a prior UIM arbitration proceeding as both the Plaintiff and Defendant had the same insurance carrier. The Superior Court reversed the trial court's decision holding that there was no privity at the UIM arbitration proceeding between the Defendant and her insurance carrier as she did not participate in the proceeding. ***Catroppa v. Carlton*, 998 A.2d 643 (Pa. Super. 2010).**

Apportionment of liability for harm to plaintiff is question of law. Where tortious conduct of two or more persons causes a single harm that cannot be apportioned, the actors are joint tortfeasors even though they acted independently. Jury verdict in favor of driver injured as a result of two separate collisions affirmed. ***Smith v. Pulcinella*, 440 Pa. Super. 525, 656 A.2d 494 (1995).**

Motorist injured when vehicle struck from behind by trash truck. City found negligent but not liable. ***Kaufman v. City of Philadelphia*, 144 Pa. Cmwlth. 444, 601 A.2d 910.**

Passenger in vehicle struck from behind brought action against driver of other vehicle. Driver not liable. Injuries result of previous incident. ***Gigliotti v. Machuca*, 409 Pa. Super. 50, 597 A.2d 655.**

Motorists involved in rear-end collision after lead vehicle braked to avoid snow plow. New trial granted. Verdict against weight of evidence. ***Housknecht v. Walters*, 404 Pa. Super. 85, 590 A.2d 20.**

Motorist injured in rear-end collision at traffic light. Trial judge found damages to be inadequate owing to erroneous interpretation of facts. Held: trial court's granting of delay damages and *additur* not in error. ***Fiarenza v. Kohn*, 395 Pa. Super. 578, 577 A.2d 1384.**

Rear-end accident severely injuring passenger in lead auto. Jury verdict $2,360,000 affirmed. Verdict not excessive under circumstances. Proper to charge on sudden emergency where striking truck driver testified that he saw auto 100 feet away and that truck was capable of stopping within 50-60 feet. ***Mineo v. Tancini*, 349 Pa. Super. 115, 502 A.2d 1300.**

Rear-end collision

Plaintiff, an attorney, injured when his vehicle was struck in rear by SEPTA vehicle. Plaintiff's verdict reversed as to damages only. ***Ferngold v. SEPTA,* 339 Pa. Super. 15, 488 A.2d 284.**

Rear-end collision when Borough stopped traffic on state highway for Memorial Day parade. Alleged negligent traffic control (accident prior to Tort Claims Act), negligence of striking vehicle and negligence of plaintiff for defective tail lights. Verdict for plaintiff affirmed. ***Elder v. Orluck,* 334 Pa. Super. 329, 483 A.2d 474.**

Rear-end collision. Defense was that collision did not cause an injury. Alleged soft tissue neck and back injuries. Previous accident one year earlier. No allegation of or proof of aggravation of preexisting injury. Jury finding of negligence but no injury, affirmed. ***Holland v. Zelnick,* 329 Pa. Super. 469, 478 A.2d 885.**

Rear-end collision. Proper and permissible to charge that jury may infer negligence on the part of driver who has stricken standing vehicle from rear on highway. New trial granted. ***Wisniewski v. Ehemann,* 310 Pa. Super. 99, 456 A.2d 201.**

Defendant entering road from driveway when collision occurred near center of road. Each side claimed to be on proper side of roadway. Jury found defendant negligent—but not cause of plaintiff's injuries. Reversed trial judge's grant of judgment *n.o.v.* Verdict not one to shock senses of court. ***Hilbert v. Katz,* 309 Pa. Super. 466, 455 A.2d 704.**

Jury verdict for defendant. Truck stopped on interstate exit ramp, rear-ended by plaintiff. Defendant stopped truck due to electrical system failure. Accident occurred before driver could put out flares. Plaintiff found 75% negligent. Affirmed. ***Stubbs v. Frazer,* 308 Pa. Super. 257, 454 A.2d 119.**

Rear-end collision. Testimony indicated that plaintiff's tail lights were not working. Issue of whether defective tail lights were a proximate cause of accident should have been for jury. Error to direct verdict against defendant. ***Correll v. Werner,* 293 Pa. Super. 88, 437 A.2d 1004.**

Rear-end collision. Plaintiff in plain view for some period. No excuse given by defendant. No evidence of contributory negligence. Defense verdict overturned and new trial ordered. ***Antolik v. Kerstetter,* 278 Pa. Super. 55, 419 A.2d 1353.**

Rear-end collision with parked dump truck which was parked on highway to protect workers in front of it. Driver in stopped truck and driver of auto sued contractor for failure to properly post warnings. Auto veered into dump truck when cut-off by garbage truck which fled scene. Verdict in favor of both plaintiffs changed by jury after confusing charge. New trial ordered. ***Osterritter v. Holl,* 259 Pa. Super. 112, 393 A.2d 742.**

Rear-end collision. Non-jury verdict for defendant. Defendant testified that as he was slowing to stop his brakes failed. Expert testimony that ruptured brake hose could not have been anticipated. ***Floravit v. Kronenwetter,* 255 Pa. Super. 581, 389 A.2d 130.**

Reasonable care

Plaintiff just turning onto street and struck defendant's car pulling out of parking space. Verdict for defendant. Evidence that plaintiff going 35–40 m.p.h. in 25 m.p.h. zone. Affirmed. **Radogna v. Hester, 255 Pa. Super. 517, 388 A.2d 1087.**

Driving on snow covered interstate, plaintiff pulled into left lane to go around stalled vehicle. Struck in rear by defendant who was already in left lane. Dispute on turn signal. Verdict for plaintiff affirmed. **Havens v. Toner, 243 Pa. Super. 371, 365 A.2d 1271.**

Plaintiff backed car into street onto steep grade. Stopped car in center of street to talk. Defendant came over top of hill with clear view of 300 to 400 feet. Night. Defendant had on high beams but struck side of plaintiff's car. Vehicle Code requires high beams to show 350 feet. Failure to stop within assured clear distance. Verdict for plaintiff affirmed. **Farbacher v. Frank, 228 Pa. Super. 35, 323 A.2d 233.**

Plaintiff had turn signal on for 450 to 500 feet prior to stopping—passed several intersections with turn signal on—rear end collision—verdict for defendant affirmed. **McCay v. Philadelphia Electric Co., 447 Pa. 490, 291 A.2d 759.**

Female plaintiff aged 25 was guest in the car of the defendant Stawski—occurrence took place on a rainy and foggy night—the Stawski car collided with the stopped automobile of the additional defendant—this car stopped on fast lane as the result of a blown-off hood—verdict solely against Stawski—motions denied—action affirmed on appeal. **Arras v. Stawski et al., 439 Pa. 611, 266 A.2d 268.**

Wife plaintiff testified that her car was struck in rear by defendant's bus—bus operator denied collision—issue of fact for jury and judgment for plaintiff affirmed. **Brown v. Phila. T. Co., 437 Pa. 348, 263 A.2d 423.**

Car passed by a bus which threw up a snow swirl—driver of passed car continued on and collided with rear of another car and injuring plaintiff, a passenger therein—jury held both operator of car colliding and bus company responsible—judgment *n.o.v.* properly entered for bus company as its bus was some 1500 to 2000 feet ahead when collision took place. **Metts v. Griglak, 438 Pa. 392, 264 A.2d 684.**

Plaintiff's machine standing motionless at intersection—struck in rear by defendant's machine—verdict for defendant—new trial properly granted—error in charge—under facts burden on defendant to come forward with evidence to exculpate. **Kralik v. Cromwell, 435 Pa. 613, 258 A.2d 654.**

Plaintiff, a passenger in additional defendant's car, had alighted and while crossing in front of car was struck by reason of car of original defendant colliding with rear of car of added defendant—compulsory nonsuit properly granted as to added defendant—point of stopping not proximate cause of occurrence. **Barg v. Shedaker, 420 Pa. 122, 216 A.2d 325.**

Reasonable care

There is but one standard of care in a negligence action, which is reasonable care. Reasonable care will vary based on the circumstances and instrumentalities in each situation. Action by customer against garage and mechanic for injuries

Recreation Use of Land and Water Act

sustained when gasoline exploded after being poured into carburetor did not warrant a jury instruction on a standard of care higher than reasonable care. Judgment for defendants affirmed. *Stewart v. Motts*, **539 Pa. 596, 654 A.2d 535 (1995).**

Reckless conduct

Seventeen-year old plaintiff riding on pickup truck running board—fell from truck. Cause of action prior to Comparative Negligence Act. Held: plaintiff contributorily negligent as matter of law. Proper holding, but new trial awarded. Jury to determine wanton and reckless conduct of plaintiff driver, or whether he had last clear chance to avoid injury. *Hill v. Crawford*, **308 Pa. Super. 502, 454 A.2d 647.**

Recorder of Deeds

Failure of recorder of deed's docketing clerk to correctly index a mortgage led to financial damages to plaintiff. In granting j.n.o.v. to recorder as defedant, held that Political Subdivision Tort Claims Act applies to actions of recorder of deeds alleged to be negligent and alleged negligence was not within exceptions to immunity conferred by act. Affirmed holding that mortgagee's attorney's failure to check that mortgage was properly recorded was negligent. *Antonis v. Liberati*, **821 A.2d 666 (Pa. Cmwlth. 2003).**

In action against Recorder of Deeds by title insurance company, Recorder of Deeds has no duty to index mortgage by location. Summary judgment affirmed. *Penn Title Ins. Co. v. Deshler*, **___ Pa. Cmwlth. ___, 661 A.2d 481 (1995).**

Recreation Use of Land and Water Act

Plaintiff brought negligence action against owner of a public lake after plaintiff was injured when his boat was struck by another boat operator on the defendant's lake. The trial court entered summary judgment on behalf of the defendant. The Superior Court affirmed, holding that a lake was "land" within the meaning of the Recreational Use of Land and Water Act and a landowner must have actual knowledge of a danger to be precluded from statutory immunity under the act. *Ruspi v. Glatz*, **69 A.3d 680 (Pa. Super. 2013).**

Plaintiff brought suit against defendant township and athletic association for injuries suffered after she fractured her ankle after stepping in a hole at a municipal park. The trial court granted summary judgment in favor of the defendant on the basis of immunity under the Recreational Use of Land Water Act (RULWA). The Commonwealth Court reversed holding that immunity under RULWA did not apply, because the field where the plaintiff fell had been altered from its original state and was not unimproved property. *Hatfield v. Penn Township*, **12 A.3d 482 (Pa. Cmwlth. 2010).**

Plaintiff brought suit against the city and sports club after he broke his leg in a flag football league game when he tripped and fell in a depression on a field owned by the city of Philadelphia. The trial court entered summary judgment in favor of the Defendants. The Commonwealth Court affirmed that the mere fact that the field was regularly mowed did not remove the field from exemption of liability

Recreation Use of Land and Water Act

for the city under the Recreational Use of Land and Water Act. *Davis v. City of Philadelphia*, 987 A.2d 1274 (Pa. Cmwlth. 2010).

Parents brought suit on behalf of their minor child against a power company whose easement their child injured himself on while riding a motor bike when he struck a gate the power company had erected on the easement. The appellate court upheld the trial court's decision that a gate on an easement was insufficient to remove the immunity provided by the Recreational Use of Land and Water Act, because the land remained in a vastly unaltered original state. *Stanton v. Lackawanna Energy, Ltd.*, 951A.2d 1181 (Pa. Super. 2008).

Plaintiff minor's guardians filed suit against easement holder for negligence, after the minor plaintiff was injured while riding a motorbike on defendant electric utility's easement. The court held that under the Recreational Use of Land and Water Act (RULWA) private owners of undeveloped land that open it up to recreational public use free of charge are entitled to immunity. The court found that easement holders that exercised control over the easement were for statutory purposes within the definition of owners used by the statute and entitled to immunity under RULWA. *Stanton v. Lackawanna Energy, LTD.*, 585 Pa. 550 (2005)

Owner of property which was improved with recreation equipment and partially fenced was not afforded immunity protections of Recreation Use of Land and Water Act against claim by child injured while snow-tubing. Thorough analysis of various applications of RULWA. *Murtha v. Joyce*, 875 A.2d 1154 (Pa. Super. 2005).

Minor injured when his motorcycle struck a fence while riding on 123 acres of vacant land. Electric power utility which had 70' easement over the area for transmission line purposes held to be an "owner or possessor" under the Recreation Use of Land and Water Act and so immune from suit on basis of compliance with other terms of the act. Allegation of mere negligence rather than willful or malicious conduct, preclude relief from bar of RULWA. *Stanton v. Lackawanna Energy, Ltd.*, 820 A.2d 1256 (Pa. Super. 2003).

Municipal park which contains lake and low-head dam are within purview of Recreation Use of Land and Water Act. Municipality given immunity for death and injury to two minors. Decided one month after *Stone v. York Haven Power Co.*, 749 A.2d 452 (Pa. 2000) but does not cite that decision. *Pagnotti v. Lancaster Township*, 751 A.2d 1226 (Pa. Cmwlth. 2000).

Recreation Use of Land and Water Act provides immunity to owner of manmade lake created when river is dammed to create a water supply for commercial venture, where lake is open to public free of charge. Dam that creates the lake is improvement to the real estate and so dam owner is not entitled to RULWA immunity afforded to lake owner. *Stone v. York Haven Power Co.*, 749 A.2d 452 (Pa. 2000).

Plaintiff injured when she stopped suddenly and was thrown forward at the bottom of a "Giant Slide" located on county-owned property. County claimed immunity under Recreation Use of Land and Water Act. Held: giant slide was improvement to real estate outside RULWA immunity in that county recognized its ob-

Recreation Use of Land and Water Act

ligation to perform daily maintenance on the slide to insure safety of visitors. ***Bashioum v. County of Westmoreland*, 747 A.2d 441 (Pa. Cmwlth. 2000).**

This is a thorough review of the Recreation Use of Land and Water Act ("RULWA"). Plaintiff was injured when he fell from at former rail trestle that had been converted to a wooden walkway over a depression located on property owned by Conrail. Suit was brought, alleging negligence in design of trestle. Conrail filed summary judgment motion, alleging it was immune from suit because the trestle and the property on which it was located were subject to the RULWA. In order to determine whether or not the RULWA provides immunity to a landowner, five factors must be considered: 1) use of the land; 2) size of the parcel; 3) location of the parcel; 4) openness of the parcel; and 5) extent of any improvement on the property. ***Yanno v. Consolidated Rail Corp.*, 744 A.2d 279 (Pa. Super. 1999).**

Plaintiff's decedents were killed when their boat was trapped in the main channel of a dam on the Susquehanna River which created "Lake Frederick." Plaintiffs allege that the owner of the dam was negligent in failing to warn of the location of the dam. Defendants allege that they are immune from suit under the provisions of the Recreation Use of Land and Water Act (68 P.S. §477-1 *et seq.*). Trial court determined that the dam was a substantial improvement to the real property and therefore the immunity granted by the act was not available. Affirmed on basis that the act is designed to protect owners of large unimproved tracts of land that have not been altered. ***York Haven Power Co. v. Stone*, 715 A.2d 1164 (1998).**

Park visitor who slipped on embankment between picnic pavilion and parking lot in County park was precluded from any recovery for injuries sustained against the County under Recreation Use of Land and Water Act. Land was unimproved and no fee was charged to plaintiff for use of the park. Order denying summary judgment reversed and complaint dismissed. ***Brezinski v. County of Allegheny*, 694 A.2d 388 (Pa. Cmwlth. 1997).**

Pedestrian injured after stepping into hole created where tree trunk removed from township-owned park grounds may not recover against township which has immunity under both Political Subdivision Tort Claims Act and Recreation Use of Land and Water Act. Summary judgment for township affirmed. ***Wilkinson v. Conoy Township*, 677 A.2d 876 (Pa. Cmwlth. 1996).**

Administratrix of teenager who drowned in city-owned pond may not recover under Political Subdivision Tort Claims Act based on allegations of city's willful or malicious failure to warn of dangerous condition of pond. Recovery under Political Subdivision Tort Claims Acts is available only for acts of negligence. Public and private lands are covered by Recreation Use of Land and Water Act. Order refusing to grant judgment *n.o.v.* reversed. ***Lory v. City of Philadelphia*, 544 Pa. 38, 674 A.2d 673 (1996).**

Because bleachers constituted a defective improvement to the land, Recreation Use of Land and Water Act did not bar spectator's claim against Township for injuries sustained in fall from bleachers at Township ball field. Order granting summary judgment reversed. ***Brown v. Tunkhannock Township*, ___ Pa. Cmwlth. ___, 665 A.2d 1318 (1995).**

Recreation Use of Land and Water Act

Willful or malicious failure to guard or warn exception to immunity under the Recreation Use of Land and Water Act applied to action by personal representative of minor's estate where minor drowned in natural pond located in city park. Evidence of prior unrelated swimming accidents inadmissable. Verdict for plaintiff reversed and remanded. ***Barr v. City and County of Philadelphia***, ___ **Pa. Cmwlth. ___, 653 A.2d 1374 (1995).**

Pedestrians injured in falls at Penn's Landing Recreation Area. No immunity under Recreation Use of Land and Water Act because land was improved. ***Mills v. Commonwealth*, 534 Pa. 519, 633 A.2d 1115.**

Child drowned in swimming pool leased to township. Real estate exception to Tort Claims Act not applicable. ***Sims v. Silver Springs-Martin Luther School*, 155 Pa. Cmwlth. 619, 625 A.2d 1297.**

Softball player injured on field owned by borough. Held: facts insufficient to determine whether Recreation Use of Land and Water Act applied. ***Thomas v. Borough of Blossburg*, 146 Pa. Super. 220, 604 A.2d 1230.**

Basketball player injured at city-owned playground. City not immune. Recreation Use of Land and Water Act not applicable. Real property exception to governmental immunity applied. ***Walsh v. City of Philadelphia*, 526 Pa. 226, 585 A.2d 445.**

Child injured at city-owned playground. City not immune under Recreation Use of Land and Water Act. Real property exception to governmental immunity may also apply. ***Wurth by Wurth v. City of Philadelphia*, 136 Pa. Cmwlth. 629, 584 A.2d 403.**

Child injured in fall from exercise bars at city-owned playground. City found not liable. Recreation Use of Land and Water Act applies to small inner-city playgrounds. City also immune if injury resulted from willful or malicious conduct of employee. ***Marko v. City of Philadelphia*, 133 Pa. Cmwlth. 574, 576 A.2d 1193.**

Child injured at playground adjacent to underground cave. Owner immune under Recreation Use of Land and Water Act even though admission charged for entrance to cave but not playground. ***Zackhery v. Crystal Cave Company, Inc.*, 391 Pa. Super. 471, 571 A.2d 464.**

Hunter injured while hunting on posted sanitary land fill. Owner found immune under Recreation Use of Land and Water Act even though land was not open for public use and hunter was trespasser. ***Friedman v. Grand Central Sanitation, Inc.*, 524 Pa. 270, 571 A.2d 373.**

Child injured in playground operated by borough and school district. Held: defendants immune under the Recreation Use of Land and Water Act. ***DiMino v. Borough of Pottstown*, 129 Pa. Cmwlth. 154, 564 A.2d 1329.**

Hiker injured when he stepped into mud hole in hiking trail. Commonwealth immune under Recreation Use of Land and Water Act. Hiking trail is not considered improved land. ***Pomeren v. Com., Dept. of Environmental Resources*, 121 Pa. Cmwlth. 287, 550 A.2d 852.**

Register of Wills

Child drowned while swimming in creek at township-owned park. Township immune from suit under Recreation Use of Land and Water Act. ***Jones v. Cheltenham Township,*** **117 Pa. Cmwlth. 440, 543 A.2d 1258.**

Plaintiff injured while attending volunteer fire department picnic in borough-owned park. Held: borough immune under the Recreation Use of Land and Water Act even though fee charged for bingo game. ***Kniaz v. Benton Borough,*** **112 Pa. Cmwlth. 416, 535 A.2d 308.**

Child struck by baseball at high school baseball game. Owner of land immune under Recreation Use of Land and Water Act. School District may be liable under real property exception to the Political Subdivision Tort Claims Act. ***Lowman v. Indiana School District,*** **96 Pa. Cmwlth. 389, 507 A.2d 1270.**

Altar boy drowned while attending swim party at seminary pool. Seminary not immune under Recreation Use of Land and Water Act. Failure to provide lifeguard violated standard of due care. ***Rivera v. Philadelphia Theological Seminary,*** **510 Pa. 1, 507 A.2d 1.**

Owner of land definition in Recreation Use of Land and Water Act does not apply to Commonwealth. Therefore, person injured on snowmobile when he struck concealed tree stump can maintain action against Commonwealth. Grant of Commonwealth's preliminary objections reversed. ***Auresto v. Commonwealth,*** **88 Pa. Cmwlth. 476, 490 A.2d 492.**

Referring physician

A referring physician cannot be held liable under theory of failure to obtain informed consent where he had no physical contact with plaintiff who suffered injury as a result of recommended surgery. Suit for failure to obtain informed consent grounded in battery, not negligence. Verdict for plaintiff vacated and remanded. ***Shaw v. Kirschbaum,*** **439 Pa. Super. 24, 653 A.2d 12 (1994).**

Reflectors

In automobile accident involving drunk driver who struck a stone-wall culvert that did not bear reflectors, issue of dangerous nature of stone wall precludes summary judgment in favor of PennDOT. ***Com., Dept. of Transp. v. Koons,*** **___ Pa. Cmwlth. ___, 661 A.2d 490 (1995).**

Register of Wills

Administratrix brought lawsuit against County Register of Wills for issuing a grant of letters of administration without securing a bond resulting in the estate losing funds. The trial court granted summary judgment on the basis that the register was immune under the Political Subdivision Tort Claims Act. The Commonwealth Court reversed and remanded. The Pennsylvania Supreme Court affirmed the Commonwealth Court holding that the Political Subdivision Tort Claims Act does not immunize Registers for violations of the Probate Estates and Fiduciary Code §3712. ***Dorsey v. Redman,*** **96 A.3d 332 (Pa. 2014).**

Relined brakes

Relined brakes

Plaintiff injured while using a car which left highway on application of brakes—brakes recently relined by defendant—testimony of plaintiff's expert refuted in part by plaintiff's exhibit of brake mechanism at trial—verdict for plaintiff—new trial granted on ground that credibility of witness was "devastated"—Held: order properly entered—strong dissent. *Stover v. Fiveway S. Center,* **220 Pa. Super. 335, 286 A.2d 380.**

Relying on light

Plaintiff on road making a "T" intersection with another highway—proceeding with green light to make a right turn—struck by defendant proceeding on highway to which plaintiff was entering—court below in error in entering judgment *n.o.v.* for defendant—plaintiff did make an observation and could rely on light, although not blindly. *Fowler v. Smith,* **217 Pa. Super. 244, 269 A.2d 340.**

Remote cause

Fire-damaged elevator shaft collapsed during demolition and damaged adjoining property. Owner not liable. Causation too remote. *American Truck Leasing, Inc.,* **400 Pa. Super. 530, 583 A.2d 1242.**

Car left with defendant for repairs—left outside place of business double parked—stolen by stranger who injured plaintiff pedestrian while operating same—no liability—leaving double parked outside place of business a remote cause. *Liney v. Chestnut Motors, Inc.,* **421 Pa. 26, 218 A.2d 336.**

Rental agency

Defendant made a lease to rent an 8 ton truck to one K.—K. struck an overhead railroad bridge with top of truck—plaintiff passenger injured—no recovery from defendant lessor. *Littles et al. v. Avis Rent-A-Car System,* **433 Pa. 72, 248 A.2d 837.**

Rental vehicle

Coverage question—rental vehicle—who was driving. Charge that if jury unable to determine driver then verdict for defendant improper. Must also charge that there is a presumption and jury must decide if overcome. *Ryan v. Furey,* **225 Pa. Super. 294, 303 A.2d 221.**

Rescue van

Negligent maintenance of city's fire department rescue van falls within operation of motor vehicle exception to governmental immunity. "Operation" requires only that the vehicle be in motion. Order granting summary judgment in favor of plaintiff affirmed. *Mickle v. City of Philadelphia,* ___ **Pa. Cmwlth.** ___**, 669 A.2d 520 (1995).**

Rescuer

Plaintiff firefighter brought a claim against his insurer for underinsured motorist benefits after he was injured traveling to the scene of an accident when a bridge on his own property collapsed. The trial court affirmed an arbitration panel denial of benefits on the basis that the bridge collapse was a supervening cause extinguishing liability on behalf of the driver that caused the accident to which the plaintiff was responding. The Pennsylvania Supreme Court affirmed, holding that an original tortfeasor could not be held liable for injuries attributable to a superseding cause. ***Bole v. Erie Ins. Exchange*, 50 A.3d 1256 (Pa. 2012).**

Rescuer injured during attempted rescue of driver of stopped automobile. Comparative Negligence Statute found to apply in cases involving rescue doctrine. Rescuer entitled to full recovery when rescue attempted in a reasonable manner. ***Pachesky v. Getz*, 353 Pa. Super. 505, 510 A.2d 776.**

Res Ipsa Loquitur

Plaintiff brought medical malpractice lawsuit against the Defendants alleging a surgical sponge was left inside him after surgery. The trial court dismissed on the basis that no expert testimony was produced by the Plaintiff. The Superior Court reversed holding that the doctrine of res ipsa loquitur could be applied in medical malpractice cases of obvious negligence. ***Fessenden v. Robert Packer Hospital*, 2014 Pa. Super. 154 (2014).**

Parents brought medical malpractice suit on behalf of their infant against a physician after their infant's arm was paralyzed due to nerves in its neck being torn during delivery. The jury rendered a verdict in favor of the Defendant. The Superior Court reversed holding that the trial court erred by providing a res ipsa loquitur instruction in favor of the Plaintiff, but then providing a second instruction contradicting the res ipsa loquitor instruction. ***Pringle v. Rapaport*, 980 A.2d 159 (Pa. Super. 2009).**

Plaintiff brought suit under a res ipsa loquitor theory against a hospital after she was admitted for a complaint related to Crohn's disease and later while in the hospital developed a shoulder injury requiring surgery. The appellate court reversed the trial court's judgment on the basis that Plaintiff could not proceed on a res ipsa loquitor theory, because she had failed to rule out other responsible causes for her shoulder injury including herself. ***Griffin v. University of Pittsburgh Medical Center-Braddock Hospital*, 950 A.2d 996 (Pa. Super. 2008).**

Plaintiff brought suit against a physician and hospital after he suffered a chemical burn to his shoulder while he was unconscious during surgery. The appellate court held that the doctrine of res ipsa loquitor could not be used by the Plaintiff to create an inference of negligence, because the defense expert testified that the injury was an outbreak of shingles and therefore could have occurred without negligence. ***MacNutt v. Temple University Hospital, Inc.*, 932 A.2d 980 (Pa. Super. 2008).**

Wife of quadriplegic decedent sued physician after her husband fell off an examination table and died of injuries suffered in the fall. The court held that the trial court erred in failing to give an instruction of res ipsa loquitur where the decedent could not have contributed to his injury, no one else could have cause the ac-

Res Ipsa Loquitur

cident, and in the absence of negligence the injury could not have occurred. ***Quinby v. Plumsteadville Family Practice, Inc.*, 589 Pa. 183, 907 A.2d 1061 (2006).**

Plaintiff's deceased quadriplegic husband suffered head injuries when he fell from an exam table after he was left alone in his doctor's examination room. Where evidence was presented that he could not move independently and he fell from the table, trial court's failure to charge on res ipsa loquitur was reversible. ***Quinby v. Burmeister*, 850 A.2d 667 (Pa. Super. 2004).**

Plaintiff who suffered pneumothorax resulting in a collapsed lung sued physician who administered injection that allegedly caused the problem. Due to plaintiff's failure to produce expert medical testimony as to standard of care in the procedure, plaintiff went to trial on theory of *res ipsa loquitur*. After verdict in favor of plaintiff was affirmed by Superior Court, Supreme Court reversed on grounds that failure to provide expert medical testimony on standard of care precludes *res ipsa loquitur* case based purely on jury's lay knowledge or expectations. ***Toogood v. Rogal*, 824 A.2d 1140 (Pa. 2003).**

Plaintiff automobile operator sued PennDOT for damages sustained when his car struck a metal expansion joint that had risen approximately two feet above the roadway. On res ipsa loquitur claim held that plaintiff did not prove the elements set forth in Restatement (Second) of Torts, § 328(d) (1965). ***Biddle v. PennDOT*, 817 A.2d 1213 (Pa. Cmwlth. 2003).**

Plaintiff who was injured when she tripped on a raised metal drain grate in a grocery store was not permitted by the trial court to raise the *res ipsa loquitur* defense in opposition to a motion for nonsuit. Following analysis of transitory defects versus a defect in the building itself, the court held that the existence of a defect that compromises the safety of the building itself permits the plaintiff, at the compulsory nonsuit stage, to raise *res ipsa loquitur* as a defense. ***Neve v. Insalaco's*, 771 A.2d 786 (Pa. Super. 2001).**

Plaintiff's decedent died near the conclusion of spinal fusion surgery when her blood pressure and heart rate dropped dramatically without apparent cause. After a verdict for defendants, a new trial was denied. In *dicta*, the court (which reversed on other grounds) described *res ipsa loquitur* as an event of a kind that does not ordinarily occur in the absence of negligence; where other responsible causes, including the conduct of the plaintiff and third persons, were sufficiently eliminated by the evidence; and the indicated negligence was within the scope of the defendant's duty to plaintiff under Restatement (2d) Torts § 328D. ***Magette v. Goodman*, 771 A.2d 775 (Pa. Super. 2001).**

Res ipsa loquitur allows a jury to infer the existence of negligence and causation where the injury at issue is one that does not ordinarily occur in the absence of negligence, other responsible causes have been sufficiently eliminated by the evidence, and the indicated negligence is within the scope of the defendant's duty to the plaintiff. ***Toogood v. Rogal*, 764 A.2d 552 (Pa. Super 2000).**

Plaintiff was injured when a SEPTA utility pole fell on his car. No error by trial court in refusing to reverse jury verdict for defendant when plaintiffs failed to

Res Ipsa Loquitur

present evidence that there were no other responsible causes, including the conduct of the plaintiff or third parties in support of his *res ipsa loquitur* claim. **Joyner v. SEPTA, 736 A2d 35 (Pa. Cmwlth. 1999).**

Plaintiff minor was injured when his shoe was caught in escalator. Plaintiffs raised negligence and *res ipsa loquitur* claims in complaint (even though *res ipsa* is rule of evidence and not cause of action). Trial court refused to give *res ipsa* charge because plaintiffs had introduced evidence tending to show specific acts of negligence. Held: *res ipsa* charge is permissible as long as plaintiff has not presented evidence which tends to support a single cause of incident causing injury. When plaintiff presents as specific a case of negligence as possible, yet is unable to demonstrate exact cause of accident, plaintiff is entitled to *res ipsa loquitur* charge. **D'Arnenne v. Strawbridge & Clothier, 712 A.2d 318 (Pa. Super. 1998).**

Expert medical testimony in a medical malpractice case involving damage to a laryngeal nerve and resulting hoarseness which establishes (1) that the type of injury complained of does not usually occur without negligence, (2) that other responsible causes, including the conduct of plaintiff or other persons are sufficiently eliminated by evidence, and (3) that the indicated negligent act was performed within the scope of the defendant's duty to the plaintiff prohibits a compulsory nonsuit and calls for an instruction on *res ipsa loquitur*. **Hightower-Warren v. Silk, 698 A.2d 52 (Pa. 1997).**

Plaintiff elevator inspector who tripped on misaligned elevator floor failed to produce evidence that product was defective and that defendant was seller. Products liability claim dismissed and verdict for defendant affirmed. Plaintiff not entitled to *res ipsa loquitur* instruction. **Micciche v. Eastern Elevator Co., 435 Pa. Super. 219, 645 A.2d 278 (1994).**

Patient suffered nerve damage after arthroscopic knee surgery. Held: doctrine of *res ipsa loquitur* applicable in medical malpractice cases. **Leone v. Thomas, 428 Pa. Super. 217, 630 A.2d 900.**

Patient who had sciatic nerve severed during surgery brought action against surgeon based on lack of informed consent and *res ipsa loquitur*. Held: standard of care for informed consent is that of reasonable man and *res ipsa loquitur* is applicable in medical malpractice cases. **Clemons v. Tranovich, 403 Pa. Super. 427, 589 A.2d 260.**

Department store customer injured hand when spring loaded spigot in washroom recoiled violently. Store not liable. Doctrine of res ipsa loquitur not applicable. **Lonsdale v. Joseph Horn Company, 403 Pa. Super. 12, 587 A.2d 810.**

Patient brought malpractice action against surgeon for damage to vocal cords. Trial court refused to give instruction on *res ipsa loquitur*. Reversed and remanded. **Sedlitsky v. Pareso, 400 Pa. Super. 1, 582 A.2d 1314.**

Worker of paving contractor injured when he fell through sewer grate. Trial court erred by not instructing jury on doctrine of *res ipsa loquitur*. **Smith v. City of Chester, 357 Pa. Super. 24, 515 A.2d 303.**

Residential treatment facility

Malpractice case with alleged negligence in damaging facial nerve during ear operation. Nonsuit entered. Expert witness deposition excluded due to failure to comply with pretrial order. *Res ipsa loquitur* theory rejected due to lack of evidence and finding of no common fund of knowledge from which jury could reach conclusion of negligence. Nonsuit affirmed. **Gallegor v. Felder, 329 Pa. Super. 204, 478 A.2d 34.**

Fatal airplane crash. Suit against estate of pilot. Lower court failed to charge on *res ipsa loquitur*—error. Under facts here, with no adequate explanation for crash other than pilot inexperience and negligence, charge should have been given. New trial ordered. **Halsband v. Union National Bank, 318 Pa. Super. 597, 465 A.2d 1014.**

Plaintiff walked between parked truck and his car intending to enter car through left door. Truck turned to left, allegedly causing plaintiff to be struck by rear of truck. Plaintiff's verdict affirmed. Defense argument that accident could not have happened as described rejected with no supporting evidence. Court said *res ipsa* may apply to case—dissent on this issue. **Siravo v. AAA Trucking, 306 Pa. Super. 217, 452 A.2d 521.**

Affirms Superior Court at *Jones v. Harrisburg Polyclinic*, 487 Pa. Super. 506, 410 A.2d 303. **Jones v. Harrisburg Polyclinic, 496 Pa. 465, 437 A.2d 1134.**

During surgery, plaintiff allegedly mispositioned causing severe neck pain, and pain in left shoulder and arm due to nerve palsy. Verdict $56,000.00 reversed. *Res ipsa loquitur* applied to malpractice case but reversed due to failure of plaintiff to eliminate other responsible causes or actions of third persons. **Jones v. Harrisburg Polyclinic, 269 Pa. Super. 373, 410 A.2d 303.**

Plaintiff injured when she pushed against stuck screen door which then gave way. Plaintiff and others had used screen door many times earlier with no problem. *Res ipsa* not applicable as to owner of chalet. **Winkler v. Seven Springs Farm, 240 Pa. Super. 641, 359 A.2d 440.**

§328D of Restatement (2d) Torts accepted as law of Commonwealth. *Res ipsa loquitur* can be used under the terms and conditions set forth in Restatement. Exclusive control not required. Boy of four caught foot in escalator in store. Although Korvette's had day-to-day responsibility, Otis by contract assumed responsibility of regular maintenance, therefore proper to prove negligence circumstantially under §328D. *Res ipsa* doctrine is circumstantial evidence which creates a permissible inference of fault. Error to call it a rebuttable presumption. **Gilbert v. Korvette's and Otis Elevator, 457 Pa. 602, 327 A.2d 94.**

Residential treatment facility

Suit by parents of minor child who was raped by a mental health patient who had been released from a residential treatment facility to the community without adequate supervision. Plaintiffs claimed that base service unit and residential treatment facility were negligent in allow individual defendant into community without adequate supervision and with knowledge of his propensity to deviant sexual behavior. Held that mental health facilities and staff have no duty to unknown and unforeseen victims absent some special relationship. Held further that only a showing of gross negligence will allow recovery from mental health professionals. **F.D.P. and J.A.P. v. Ferrara, 804 A.2d 1221 (Pa. Super. 2002).**

Respiratory therapist

Respiratory therapist who contracted tuberculosis from exposure to patient brought negligence action against employer hospital for failure to diagnosis and treat her condition promptly and not to obtain remedy for contracting disease. Jury verdict for plaintiff reversed on grounds that her sole remedy was workers' compensation. **Snyder v. Pocono Medical Center, 440 Pa. Super. 606, 656 A.2d 534 (1995).**

Respondeat Superior

Bank employees, manager and assistant manager held liable for undue influence in convincing depositor to name employees as sole beneficiaries of substantial accounts and bank held liable for negligent supervision of the employees. **Owens v. Mazzei, 847 A.2d 700 (Pa. Super. 2004).**

Trial court properly granted summary judgment in favor of employer of schizophrenic truck driver who shot and killed one man and wounded another after driving employer's truck into front yard of first victim. Driver's criminal activity was wholly outside scope of his employment. Employer's failure to investigate driver's past criminal behavior, other than driving record, was permitted. Employer's duty is simply to hire competent drivers. Employer is not required to insure safety of those who come into contact with employee by reason other than his employment. **Brezenski v. World Truck Transfer, Inc., 755 A.2d 36 (Pa. Super. 2000).**

Plaintiffs were potential buyers of one of defendant's custom homes who were "fleeced" by defendant's agent in scam he ran without defendant's knowledge. Evidence established that defendant's agent had enticed plaintiffs to invest nearly $49,000 of their money with agent in "get rich quick" scheme designed to allow plaintiffs to upgrade home they were going to pay defendant to build. Trial court found that evidence also established defendant completely failed to supervise their agent when there was substantial evidence that agent was fleecing many clients. Superior Court affirmed on basis of defendant's failure to supervise agent. **Heller v. Patwil Homes, Inc., 713 A.2d 105 (Pa. Super. 1998).**

Plaintiff was head of security at defendant hospital and was attacked by an employee who had been brought to supervisor's office for submission to urinalysis. Plaintiff alleged that tortfeasor was acting in his capacity as employee of the hospital and therefore hospital was liable under doctrine of *respondeat superior*. Defendant's motion for summary judgment sustained and affirmed on appeal. Tortfeasor's intentional act of injuring plaintiff was in no way related to his job description as laundry worker and there was no evidence from plaintiff of any expectation on the part of the defendant employer that the tortfeasor would act violently. **Costa v. Roxborough Memorial Hospital, 708 A.2d 490 (Pa. Super. 1998).**

Restatement (2d) Torts § 315

Restatement (2d) Torts § 315

Co-owner of entireties property with actual knowledge of sexual abuse by other co-owner on their minor grandchildren within residence does not have duty to protect or warn grandchildren of grandfather's proclivities. Multimillion dollar compensatory and punitive damages award against grandmother reversed. While landowner may be liable for dangerous condition on the land, landowner is not liable for criminal or tortious acts of third parties. *T.A. v. Allen,* **447 Pa. Super. 302, 669 A.2d 360 (1995).**

Restatement (2d) Torts § 317

While Section 317 of Restatement (2d) Torts imposes liability upon a master for acts of a servant committed outside the scope of the servant's employment, liability will not lie unless the acts are performed by the servant "upon the premises in possession of the master." Church and religious officials not liable for conduct of priest who molested minor on non-diocesan property. Judgment against Church, bishop and diocese vacated. ***Hutchison v. Luddy,*** **453 Pa. Super. 420, 683 A.2d 1254 (1996).**

Restatement (2d) Torts § 323

Personal representative of estate of deceased personal care home resident brought suit alleging negligence of PCH, staff and administration under § 323 of Restatement 2nd Torts, negligent performance of an undertaking to render services, after the resident was not prevented from leaving the PCH without medications, becoming lost and drowning in a local river. Summary judgment in favor of PCH reversed. ***Feeney v. Disston Manor Personal Care Home,*** **849 A.2d 590 (Pa. Super. 2004).**

Restatement (2d) Torts § 343

Mall patron's suit for injuries sustained in fall caused by alleged "slippery substance" dismissed on summary judgment for lack of any proof that mall manager had constructive or actual notice of existence of any foreign matter on floors. ***Porro v. Century III Associates,*** **846 A.2d 1282 (Pa. Super. 2004).**

Restatement (2d) Torts § 388

Summary judgment for defendant truck driver affirmed where there was no evidence that he knew that driving on an under-inflated tire would create or increase the risk of injury to a mechanic who was severely injured while reinflating the tire during the repair process. Without more, driver's knowledge that he drove on tire that was low or "super low" is inadequate to establish negligence. §388 of Restatement (2d) Torts requires both knowledge of dangerous condition and failure to inform the person to whom control of the chattel in the dangerous condition is transferred. ***Overbeck v. Cates,*** **700 A.2d 970 (Pa. Super. 1997).**

Plaintiff's decedent welder was killed when fumes inside gasoline tank truck in which he was working caught fire and exploded. Motion for compulsory nonsuit granted because plaintiff's decedent was fully aware of the risks attending the work he was performing. Recovery prohibited under Section 388 of Restatement (2d)

Retroactive effect

Torts which imposes duty to warn owner of chattel who has reason to believe that those for whose use the chattel is supplied will not realize its dangerous condition. *Erdos v. Bedford Valley Petroleum Co.,* **452 Pa. Super. 555, 682 A.2d 806 (1996).**

Restaurant

In negligence action against corporate defendant and officers, officers are not liable for failing to maintain clean bathroom absent proof of their participation in creating or allowing continued existence of dangerous condition. Party's failure to answer request for admission that states a conclusion of law does not establish plaintiff's case. Judgment in favor of plaintiff vacated and remanded for consideration of scope of involvement and liability of owners. *Brindley v. Woodland Village Restaurant, Inc.,* **438 Pa. Super. 385, 652 A.2d 865 (1995).**

Restraining vest

In action by guardian of incapacitated, mental health patient for brain damages sustained as result of choking by restraining vest, immunity of physicians under Mental Health Procedures Act is not afforded to physician providing standard medical treatment at non-mental health facility. Judgment on jury verdict for defendant reversed and remanded. *Allen v. Montgomery Hospital,* **447 Pa. Super. 158, 668 A.2d 565 (1995).**

Retarded child

Suit against Schuylkill County and Boy Scouts for damages arising out of injuries sustained by retarded child on camping trip. County dismissed as defendant. Allegation of negligent supervision not within exception to Sovereign Immunity Act. *Silkowski v. Hacker,* **95 Pa. Cmwlth. 226, 504 A.2d 995.**

Retina

Plaintiff received as one of her injuries a splitting of the retina—causal connection with trauma of occurrence established—error to refuse to permit expert to express an opinion as to the possible effect of such an injury on a future operation or the removal of a cataract—also error to refuse to permit expert to express an opinion to the possibility of effect on the good eye—new trial granted. *Walsh v. Brody,* **220 Pa. Super. 293, 286 A.2d 666.**

Retrieving ball

Boy of 4 with young companion on sidewalk—cartway 34 feet wide—boy going into street to retrieve ball—child proceeded at least 17 feet in view of motorist—struck—facts sufficient to take case from purely darting out status—for jury. *Schwegel v. Goldberg,* **209 Pa. Super. 280, 228 A.2d 405.**

Retroactive effect

Plaintiff injured on December 17, 1965, in connection with a sewage disposal plant—defendant sought to amend answer by asserting the defense of the limitation of 12 years provided by the Act of December 22, 1965, P.L. 1183—petition to amend properly reused—Act of 1965 not retroactive—accident happened 5 days

Retrograde amnesia

before the passage of the Act. *Misitis v. Steel City Piping Co.,* **441 Pa. 339, 272 A.2d 883.**

Retrograde amnesia

Minor plaintiff crossing rural highway when struck by defendant's car—minor had traversed within 2 inches of opposite side of highway—minor suffering from retrograde amnesia and unable to recall circumstances—defendant gave a questionable explanation why she did not see minor plaintiff—error to enter summary judgment—matter for jury on merits. *Moore v. Zimmerman,* **221 Pa. Super. 359, 292 A.2d 458.**

Rigger

Plaintiff, a member of an expert independent contractor rigging operator, injured allegedly as the result of the presence of a rack in moving area—owner possessor held not responsible—no duty on owner to warn or remove rack—plaintiff an expert rigger, condition evident, and injury resulted from an act of a fellow employee. *Crane v. I.T.E. Circuit Breaker Co.,* **443 Pa. 442, 278 A.2d 362.**

Right of way

Department of Transportation sued the Borough of West View for damages caused to a state highway by the Borough's water main breaking. The court held that the Tort Claims Act did not provide a defense to liability for the Borough, since it was contractually obligated to repair the damages to the highway as a condition of its occupancy of the right-of-way. *Commonwealth v. Municipal Authority of the Borough of West View,* **919 A.2d 343 (Pa. Cmwlth. 2007).**

Plaintiff widower stated cause of action under real estate exception to sovereign immunity for death of motorist/wife caused by limb falling from tree that had been "topped" twenty years earlier and was growing above PennDOT's right of way at 45° angle. Judgment on verdict for plaintiff affirmed. *Patton v. Com., Dept. of Transp.,* **___ Pa. Cmwlth. ___, 669 A.2d 1090 (1995).**

Where plaintiff sustained injuries after striking utility pole, utility company liable for improper placement of electric pole in highway right-of-way. Compulsory nonsuit reversed. *Talarico v. Bonham,* **168 Pa. Cmwlth. 467, 650 A.2d 1192 (1994).**

Risk of harm

Summary judgment for defendant truck driver affirmed where there was no evidence that he knew that driving on an under-inflated tire would create or increase the risk of injury to a mechanic who was severely injured while reinflating the tire during the repair process. Without more, driver's knowledge that he drove on tire that was low or "super low" is inadequate to establish negligence. §388 of Restatement (2d) Torts requires both knowledge of dangerous condition and failure to inform the person to whom control of the chattel in the dangerous condition is transferred. *Overbeck v. Cates,* **700 A.2d 970 (Pa. Super. 1997).**

In medical malpractice action for delayed diagnosis of liver disease, the "two disease rule" from asbestos-related cases will be applied to preclude plaintiff's claim for increased risk and fear of liver cancer until such disease actually occurs. Second judge's grant of summary judgment on plaintiff's claim for increased risk of harm after first judge denied summary judgment on the same issue is reversible error. Order granting summary judgment as to increased risk of harm reversed. ***Klein v. Weisberg,*** **___ Pa. Super. ___, 694 A.2d 644 (1997).**

Robber

Plaintiff brought negligence action against Defendant drug store after he was robbed by 3 men as he tried to exit the store. The trial court granted dismissal based upon a failure to join the indispensable robbers. The Superior Court reversed holding that the robbers were not indispensable parties in determining the Plaintiff's negligence claim against the Defendant store. ***Martin v. Rite Aid of Pennsylvania, Inc.*, 80 A.3d 813 (Pa. Super. 2013).**

Summary judgment entered against plaintiff who was shot by a robber while a passenger on defendant's stopped train. Plaintiff alleged that defendant's trainman's failure to open the door of the train to allow plaintiff to escape before he was shot was a concurrent cause of his injury and that failure to act involved the operation of the motor vehicle. The Commonwealth Court distinguishes concurrent negligent acts from a negligent act by defendant and a criminal assault by a third party and also holds by implication that the failure to open the door was not "operation" of the motor vehicle. ***Greenleaf v. SEPTA*, 698 A.2d 170 (Pa. Cmwlth. 1997).**

Roller skating

Patron injured while skating at roller skating rink. Defendant found 60% negligent, skater found 40% negligent. ***Berman v. Radnor Rolls, Inc.*, 374 Pa. Super. 118, 542 A.2d 525.**

Roof

Peculiar risk doctrine did not apply to make contractor liable for injuries sustained by subcontractor's employee who fell from roof of building on which he was working where both contractor and subcontractor were aware of dangerous condition of roof. ***Edwards v. Franklin and Marshall College*, 444 Pa. Super. 1, 663 A.2d 187 (1995).**

Political Subdivision Tort Claims Act exception for dangerous condition of property does not extend to plaintiff who became trespasser when he climbed to roof of school building to retrieve tennis ball. School district took sufficient steps to prevent entry onto roof. Summary judgment in favor of school district affirmed. ***Longbottom v. Sim-Kar Lighting Fixture Co.*, ___ Pa. Cmwlth. ___, 651 A.2d 621 (1994).**

Farmer brought action against manufacturer of roof trusses after barn collapsed. Held: 12 year statute of repose did not apply. ***McConnaughey Building Components, Inc.*, 536 Pa. 95, 637 A.2d 1331.**

Rounding sharp curve

Plaintiff employed by heating contractor. Injured on roof of customer when he stepped off roof in dark and fell to ground at night. No evidence of negligence on part of property owner. No duty to warn under these circumstances. **Kalin v. Delaware Valley Telephone Co., 228 Pa. Super. 849, 316 A.2d 912.**

Rounding sharp curve

Wife plaintiff was operating a car around a sharp curve during a highway construction operation and collided with defendant's truck partly double parked—nonsuit granted—assured clear distance rule applied—evidence of excessive speed under circumstances. **Haines v. Dulaney, 424 Pa. 608, 227 A.2d 625.**

Rowdyism

Spitball battle on school bus. Minor passenger lost sight of right eye. Verdict versus owner of bus company and driver. New trial ordered to consider only the liability of the participants. **Sommers v. Hessler, 227 Pa. Super. 41, 323 A.2d 17.**

Minor plaintiff of two attended a picnic with parents—apparently struck in eye by a piece of glass and lost sight of eye—some evidence of rowdyism in park—operator of park held responsible—strong dissent. **Barakos v. Kollas, 433 Pa. 258, 249 A.2d 568.**

Municipality maintained a public swimming pool—minor plaintiff pushed into pool allegedly as result of rowdyism of other boys—minor seriously injured—verdict for defendant—case properly submitted to the jury—refusal of new trial not error. **Zeman v. Canonsburg Borough, 423 Pa. 450, 223 A.2d 728.**

Rugs

Expert testimony of a witness with 25 years experience with fiber rugs permitted where testimony established a curled condition of rug on floor of defendant's premises—not a matter capable of valuation by a jury alone. **Reardon v. Meehan, 424 Pa. 460, 227 A.2d 667.**

Rules of the road

Plaintiff motorist injured in collision with township garbage truck entitled to new trial after trial court incorrectly instructed jury that garbage truck driver was entitled to drive against traffic flow in the same manner as Motor Vehicle Code defined Type I and Type II vehicles such as emergency vehicles. New trial granted. **Sawchzuk-Serge v. Township of Cheltenham, ___ Pa. Super. ___, 670 A.2d 210 (1996).**

Snowy highway—parked car—pulling out and colliding with plaintiff's car—court below properly refused to charge that operator did not violate Section 1004 of Code requiring vehicles to drive on right half of highway. **Houlihan v. Hazlett, 435 Pa. 284, 254 A.2d 615.**

Defendant pulled around standing cars to his left side and collided with car in which plaintiff riding—defendant "bucking traffic" at such time and held responsible for the injuries occasioned. **Rogers v. Moody, 430 Pa. 121, 242 A.2d 276.**

Running board

Seventeen-year old plaintiff riding on pickup truck running board—fell from truck. Cause of action prior to Comparative Negligence Act. Held: plaintiff contributorily negligent as matter of law. Proper holding, but new trial awarded. Jury to determine wanton and reckless conduct of plaintiff driver, or whether he had last clear chance to avoid injury. *Hill v. Crawford,* **308 Pa. Super. 502, 454 A.2d 647.**

Section 1024 B of Code as to riding on running board constructed—minor of 8 injured—charge of court thereon held proper. *Mount v. Bulifant,* **438 Pa. 265, 265 A.2d 627.**

Safer position

—S—

Safer position

Decedent assumed an awkward position in removing a spouting—contacting electrical line—evidence as to whether safer method and position should have been taken not sufficient evidence of contributory negligence to take the case from the jury. ***Groh v. Phila. Electric Co.*, 441 Pa. 345, 271 A.2d 265.**

Safety features or standards

Plaintiff brought suit against forklift manufacturer and forklift lessor for negligence for failing to install a backup warning system after he was injured when a fellow employee hit him while operating the forklift in reverse. The court held that evidence of industry standards and regulations are admissible in strict liability actions where negligence is also alleged. ***Arnoldy v. Forklife L.P.*, 927 A.2d 257 (Pa. Super. 2007).**

Bridge ironworker was injured when he fell from a construction site without a safety net or a connected safety line. In suit against the general contractor, summary judgment was entered because the contractors had no presence at the site and no contractual obligation to oversee safety standards and so no duty to plaintiff. Only subcontractor, plaintiff's employer, had a duty to insure his safety and in the event of a breach, workman's compensation provided recovery. ***Leonard v. Com., Dept. of Transp.*, 771 A.2d 1238 (Pa. 2001).**

In an action by passenger against PennDOT and vehicle manufacturer, compliance with federal motor vehicle safety standards and regulations does not preclude state cause of action sounding in negligence for failure to incorporate additional safety features. Order granting summary judgment against manufacturer reversed. ***Muntz v. Com., Dept. of Transp.*, ___ Pa. Cmwlth. ___, 674 A.2d 328 (1996).**

Safety of goods

An innkeeper's liability at common law for the safety of the goods of his guests is absolute—negligence need not be established—failure of the innkeeper to comply with the provisions of the Act of June 12, 1913, P.L. 481, as to location of a safe place to deposit possessions—summary judgment entered for plaintiff as to liability but innkeeper entitled to jury trial as to extent of damages. ***Buck v. Hankin*, 217 Pa. Super. 262, 269 A.2d 344.**

Salesman

Plaintiff roofing supply salesman was injured when he stepped into unguarded hole in floor of defendant's house that was under construction. At conclusion of plaintiff's case against homeowner, trial court granted compulsory nonsuit on grounds that plaintiff had not presented adequate evidence to establish he was entitled to status greater than trespasser. Record contained references to defendant homeowner's approval of plaintiff's offer to deliver roof vents to plaintiff's house and to implication from workmen at house that plaintiff was permitted to enter house to leave roof vents inside, safe from theft and exposure. Reversal of nonsuit because there were adequate facts to take issue of plaintiff's status as business invitee to jury. *Emge v. Hagosky*, 712 A.2d 315 (Pa. Super. 1998).

Scaffolding

Plaintiff independent contractor, a sandblaster/painter, was injured when he fell from scaffolding below elevated rail tracks after the light on his sandblaster failed and he tripped on a hose he could not see. Plaintiff alleged that SEPTA was liable at common law for failure to provide a safe work area and that lack of lights on SEPTA property he was working on was a defect in SEPTA property. Held: there is no liability of an employer to an independent contractor absent special danger or peculiar risk conditions - working on a scaffold is neither - and that lack of lights on SEPTA is not a dangerous condition "of" the real estate. ***Donnelly v. SEPTA*, 708 A.2d 145 (Pa. Cmwlth. 1998).**

Plaintiff's decedent electrocuted while applying stucco to building in proximity to uninsulated electrical wires. Political Subdivision Tort Claims Act precludes imposition of liability upon governmental unit based on a theory of vicarious liability for work performed by contractor. Order granting summary judgment affirmed. ***Thomas v. City of Philadelphia*, ___ Pa. Cmwlth. ___, 668 A.2d 292 (1995).**

Architect has no duty to warn contractor employees of visible overhead power lines that came into contact with metal scaffolding killing or injuring workers. Summary judgment in favor of architect affirmed. ***Frampton v. Dauphin Distribution Services Co.*, 436 Pa. Super. 486, 648 A.2d 326 (1994).**

Employee of subcontractor injured in fall from scaffold brought action against general contractor and Commonwealth. Held: Commonwealth immune, contractor may be liable and subcontractor not obligated to indemnify general contractor. ***Donaldson v. Com., Dept. of Transp.*, 141 Pa. Cmwlth. 474, 596 A.2d 269.**

Employee of subcontractor injured when scaffold collapsed. General contractor and owner found not liable under special danger or peculiar risk doctrine. Risk of harm was not different from usual risk associated with the work. ***Ortiz v. Ra-El Development Corporation*, 365 Pa. Super. 48, 528 A.2d 1355.**

Homeowners climbed onto scaffold to inspect work done by masonry contractor, fell off scaffold and died. Charge of court held to be in error for not instructing jury on significance of O.S.H.A. standards as to scaffolds. New trial awarded. ***Wood v. Smith*, 343 Pa. Super. 547, 495 A.2d 601.**

Scam by agent

Plaintiffs were potential buyers of one of defendant's custom homes who were "fleeced" by defendant's agent in scam he ran without defendant's knowledge. Evidence established that defendant's agent had enticed plaintiffs to invest nearly $49,000 of their money with agent in "get rich quick" scheme designed to allow plaintiffs to upgrade home they were going to pay defendant to build. Trial court found that evidence also established defendant completely failed to supervise their agent when there was substantial evidence that agent was fleecing many clients. Su-

Scar

perior Court affirmed on basis of defendant's failure to supervise agent. ***Heller v. Patwil Homes, Inc.*, 713 A.2d 105 (Pa. Super. 1998).**

Scar

Violation of a statute, although negligence *per se*, does not constitute a ground for imposing liability unless it can be shown to be a substantial factor in causing plaintiff's injuries which resulted from a trip and fall. Failure to produce evidence of separate and distinct damages attributable to a scar precludes a specific jury instruction regarding the scar. Judgment affirmed. ***Gravlin v. Fredavid Builders and Developers*, 450 Pa. Super. 655, 677 A.2d 1235 (1996).**

School bus

Minor injured when struck by a school bus sustained a permanent 4 millimeter scar on his right wrist. In suit against school bus owned and operated by school district, jury's determination that the scar, although permanent, was not disfiguring was proper and so kept case out of governmental immunity exception for injuries which cause permanent loss of a bodily function or permanent disfigurement. ***Alexander v. Benson*, 812 A.2d 785 (Pa. Cmwlth. 2002).**

Plaintiff's minor son was injured when crossing the street in front of a school bus from which he had just disembarked after having been "waved across" by the bus driver. Lower court granted summary judgment to school district of Philadelphia on basis that bus driver waving to student was not "operation" of the motor vehicle and so not an exception to governmental immunity. Commonwealth Court reversed and Supreme Court reversed Commonwealth Court holding that the driver's wave was not part of the "operation" of the motor vehicle. ***White v. School District of Philadelphia*, 718 A.2d 778 (Pa. 1998).**

Child injured crossing highway at school bus stop. School district not liable for selecting stop location. ***Combs v. Borough of Ellsworth*, 151 Pa. Cmwlth. 21, 615 A.2d 462.**

Fatal injury to student struck by car after alighting from school bus. Held: school district immune from suit. Stopped school bus with flashing lights is not a traffic control as defined by governmental immunity statute. ***Aberant v. Wilkes-Barre Area School District*, 91 Pa. Cmwlth. 27, 492 A.2d 1186.**

Six and one-half year old boy struck by car in area where children were waiting for school bus. Child "ran into street." Issue as to how quickly child entered street. Jury verdict for motorist, affirmed. ***Heffner v. Schad*, 330 Pa. Super. 101, 478 A.2d 1372.**

Spitball battle on school bus. Minor passenger lost sight of right eye. Verdict versus owner of bus company and driver. New trial ordered to consider only the liability of the participants. ***Sommers v. Hessler*, 227 Pa. Super. 41, 323 A.2d 17.**

Scope of employment

Trial court properly granted summary judgment in favor of employer of schizophrenic truck driver who shot and killed one man and wounded another after driving employer's truck into front yard of first victim. Driver's criminal activity was wholly outside scope of his employment. Employer's failure to investigate driver's past criminal behavior, other than driving record, was permitted. Employer's duty is simply to hire competent drivers. Employer is not required to insure safety of those who come into contact with employee by reason other than his employment. ***Brezenski v. World Truck Transfer, Inc.*, 755 A.2d 36 (Pa. Super. 2000).**

While Section 317 of Restatement (2d) Torts imposes liability upon a master for acts of a servant committed outside the scope of the servant's employment, liability will not lie unless the acts are performed by the servant "upon the premises in possession of the master." Church and religious officials not liable for conduct of priest who molested minor on non-diocesan property. Judgment against Church, bishop and diocese vacated. ***Hutchison v. Luddy*, 453 Pa. Super. 420, 683 A.2d 1254 (1996).**

Motor Vehicle Financial Responsibility Law precludes employee injured during the scope of his employment as a result of automobile accident in which co-employee was driving from recovering common law damages against coemployee in addition to workers' compensation benefits. ***Ducjai v. Dennis*, 540 Pa. 103, 656 A.2d 102 (1995).**

Seatbelts

Evidence of non-use of an available seatbelt is not admissible in any civil action. Judgment for defendant vacated and remanded. ***Nicola v. Nicola*, 449 Pa. Super. 293, 673 A.2d 950 (1996).**

Before 1987 amendment of Motor Vehicle Code, there was no common law duty to wear a seat belt and no "seatbelt defense." After 1987 amendment, there is a statutory duty to wear a seatbelt but still no "seatbelt defense." *Stouffer v. PennDOT*, 127 Pa. Cmwlth. 610, 562 A.2d 922 (1989) holding that there was a common-law duty to wear a seatbelt before 1987 amendment of Motor Vehicle Code expressly reversed. ***Solonoski v. Yuhas*, ___ Pa. Cmwlth. ___, 657 A.2d 137 (1995).**

Mother and daughter injured in multi-vehicle collision. Prohibition against testimony concerning the lack of use of safety belts held constitutional. Jury instructions on comparative negligence and sudden emergency doctrine not in error. ***Drango v. Winterhalter*, 359 Pa. Super. 578, 577 A.2d 1349.**

Automobile driver injured in collision with truck. Held: failure of plaintiff to use seat belt is not an affirmative defense in Pennsylvania. ***Grim v. Betz*, 372 Pa. Super. 614, 539 A.2d 1365.**

Proper for judge to refuse charge on effects of failure to use seat belts and possibility of contributory negligence due to said failure where defense presented no evidence that said failure aggravated injuries. ***Paress v. Fehnel*, 267 Pa. Super. 79, 406 A.2d 345.**

Second accident

Second accident

Plaintiff further injured by a fall down steps some three months after occurrence—expert testimony that fall resulted from injuries sustained in occurrence sued on—matter properly left to jury. ***Kinee v. Penn Radio Cab Co.*, 435 Pa. 387, 257 A.2d 554.**

Plaintiff's home damaged by collision of car of original defendant with it—defendant brought in added defendant—motion for summary judgment by added defendant—court below granted it—if plaintiff's home damaged by car of added defendant, it was the result of a separate and different accident from that initially involved—action proper. ***Mallesky v. Stevens*, 427 Pa. 352, 235 A.2d 154.**

Secondary liability

Fall on sidewalk. Suit against property owners. Property owners sought to join city. Joinder disallowed as liability of city only secondary to property owners abutting public sidewalk ***Graham v. Roberts*, 254 Pa. Super. 589, 386 A.2d 610.**

Security guard

Verdict for bank teller plaintiff in suit against security company for negligent and negligent *per se* hiring of security guard who robbed bank during off-duty hours reversed because bank robber's unforeseeable violent criminal act was a superseding cause of the harm. ***Maban v. Am-Guard, Inc.*, 841 A.2d 1052 (Pa. Super. 2004).**

Seizures

Physician was sued for a failure to follow his statutory duty to report a patient's lack of fitness to operate a motor vehicle to the Pennsylvania Department of Transportation. The court held that a physician's failure to comply with the Motor Vehicle Code's reporting requirements by not reporting seizures does not create a private cause of action against the physician for an accident caused by his patient. ***Hospodar v. Schick*, 885 A.2d 986 (Pa. Super. 2005).**

Husband suffering from seizures was treated by a partial lobectomy that resulted in more serious seizures and severe memory and speech problems. Informed consent to medical treatment requires that the patient have a "true understanding of the nature of the operation ... and the possible results." Judgment *n.o.v.* permitted only in "clear case." Judgment *n.o.v.* reversed and jury verdict reinstated. ***Rowinsky v. Sperling*, 452 Pa. Super. 215, 681 A.2d 785 (1996).**

Proper to permit physician to testify from statistical knowledge the probability of a child with a skull fracture and brain damage having epileptic seizures in the future. ***Schwegel v. Goldberg*, 209 Pa. Super. 280, 228 A.2d 405.**

Serious bodily injury or impairment of bodily function

Plaintiff was struck from behind in a motor vehicle accident injuring his wrist. A showing by plaintiff that he could no longer control a jackhammer at his job as a construction worker was sufficient to show a serious impairment to a body function. A determination for the severity of an injury should contemplate the nega-

Service station

tive effect the injury had on the victim's ability to perform their chosen profession. ***Long v. Mejia,* 896 A.2d 596 (Pa. Super. 2006).**

The question of whether a plaintiff has sustained a permanent loss of a bodily function as required by section 8553 of the Judicial Code, 42 Pa.C.S. §8553, in a claim against a local agency under the Political Subdivision Tort Claims Act is a question for the jury. ***Laich v. Bracey,* 776 A.2d 1022 (Pa. Cmwlth. 2001).**

Summary judgment for defendant reversed when limited tort plaintiff established that statute of limitations began not on date of accident but on date that she became aware or reasonably could have become aware that her injuries were "serious" under limited tort policy and so compensable under that statute. ***Walls v. Scheckler,* 700 A.2d 533 (Pa. Super. 1997).**

Plaintiff injured in motor vehicle accident offered four medical reports that showed she had suffered serious soft tissue injury in the accident. Trial court granted defendant's motion for summary judgment based on findings in law that plaintiff's injuries were not compensable under the statutorily imposed limited tort restrictions. Superior Court reversed on its own review of reports by physicians and testimony adduced in summary judgment proceeding. ***Leonelli v. McMullen,* 700 A.2d 525 (Pa. Super. 1997).**

Summary judgment reversed where trial court failed to consider medical evidence of psychic injuries that may have qualified as serious impairment of a body function under limited tort coverage provided for in Motor Vehicle Financial Responsibility Law before granting summary judgment. Minor children injured in accident while riding in their mother's uninsured vehicle are held to have the same deemed limited tort coverage as their uninsured mother. ***Hames v. Philadelphia Housing Authority,* 696 A.2d 880 (Pa. Cmwlth. 1997).**

Plaintiff pedestrian injured by impact of police car is entitled to reversal of nonsuit where evidence indicates that all elements of negligence claim were established at trial. Trial court's determination that plaintiff failed to prove that his injury was permanent or of a serious nature so as to impair a bodily function is reversible abuse of discretion. Nonsuit removed; remanded for new trial. ***Boyer v. City of Philadelphia,* 692 A.2d 259 (Pa. Cmwlth. 1997).**

Pedestrian struck by automobile failed to establish serious injury or serious impairment of bodily function. Factors to be considered in determining severity of bodily impairment for purposes of recovery under limited tort option include extent of the impairment, particular body function impaired, duration of the impairment, treatment required to correct the impairment and any other relevant factors. Judgment in favor of plaintiff for only out-of-pocket medical expenses affirmed. ***Murray v. McCann,* 442 Pa. Super. 30, 658 A.2d 404 (1995).**

Service station

Oil company who supplied gasoline to independent contractor service station had no duty to service station attendant who was assaulted and raped during course of employment. Demurrer to complaint granted. ***Smith v. Exxon Corporation,* 436 Pa. Super. 221, 647 A.2d 577 (1994).**

Sewage enforcement officer

Sewage enforcement officer

Plaintiffs sued local sewage enforcement officer for negligent performance of his duty. Individual and borough defendants' motion for judgment on the pleadings granted because of governmental immunity. Trial court's denial of plaintiff's motion to amend complaint to allege intentional acts by sewage enforcement officer also affirmed because six month statute of limitation had expired before amendment. *Stoppie v. Johns*, **720 A.2d 808 (Pa. Cmwlth. 1998).**

Sewers

Plaintiff brought claim for damages against the city for negligent maintenance of its sewers after the sewer system backed up and flooded her home. The trial court entered summary judgment for the city based upon Commonwealth immunity. The Superior Court reversed, holding that there was a genuine issue of material fact as to whether the city's negligent maintenance and repairs of the sewers were sufficient to fall under the utility service facilities exception under the Political Subdivision Tort Claims Act. *McCarthy v. City of Bethlehem*, **962 A.2d 1276 (Pa. Cmwlth. 2008).**

In action by bus passenger who stepped off of bus and onto broken storm sewer, possessor of land may be liable for physical harm to a licensee caused by conditions on land of which possessor has actual or constructive knowledge. Order granting motion for nonsuit affirmed. *Colston v. SEPTA*, **679 A.2d 299 (Pa. Cmwlth. 1996).**

Condominium owner brought action against condominium association for damage caused by sewer backup. Compulsory nonsuit in favor of association upheld. *Smith v. King's Grant Condominium*, **418 Pa. Super. 260, 614 A.2d 261.**

Work done by employees of city-owned utility caused sewer to back up into basement of home. Homeowner fell because of backwash. Held: utility covered by governmental immunity statute and question of whether immunity attached for fact finder. *Brennan v. Philadelphia Gas Works*, **146 Pa. Cmwlth. 312, 605 A.2d 475.**

Fraudulent misrepresentation of condition of sewer in home by sellers to buyers when known to be defective and to have backed up several times in past makes them liable for cost of repair and damage. §353 of Restatement (2d) Torts. *Shane v. Hoffman*, **227 Pa. Super. 176, 324 A.2d 532.**

Plaintiff fell while on pavement by reason allegedly of a raised concrete sewer cover—in broad daylight—no excuse for not seeing condition—guilty of contributory negligence—nonsuit proper. *Beil v. Allentown*, **434 Pa. 10, 252 A.2d 692.**

Employees of a contractor of a sewage disposal plant injured by reason of the presence allegedly of explosive gas in vault—Sewer Authority not responsible—it could not be held responsible to protect employees of an independent contractor from hazards created by contractor—nonsuit proper. *Celender et al. v. Allegheny County Sanitary Authority*, **208 Pa. Super. 390, 222 A.2d 461.**

Sexual abuse or assault

Sexual abuse or assault

Patient brought medical malpractice and intentional infliction of emotional distress claims against general practitioner treating her for anxiety and depression after he had consensual sex with her, while treating her. The trial court dismissed Plaintiff's complaint on preliminary objections. Superior Court reversed holding that there is a potential cause of action where a patient being treated for emotional symptoms experiences a worsening of their symptoms due to a sexual relationship with a physician providing treatment for those specific emotional symptoms. ***Thierfelder v. Wolfert*, 2009 Pa. Super. 92 (Pa. Super. 2009).**

Twenty-six year old plaintiff brought suit against priest and church administration for injuries sustained as a result of alleged sexual abuse while plaintiff attended high school. Motions for judgment on the pleadings by all defendants sustained due to plaintiff's failure to timely file complaint following actual injury. ***Baselice, III v. Franciscan Friars Assumption BVM Province, Inc.*, 879 A.2d 270 (Pa. Super. 2005).**

Plaintiffs who did not file suit against clergy and church officials who participated in or covered up alleged clergy sexual abuse for at least twenty one years were barred by statute of limitations. ***Meehan v. Archdiocese of Philadelphia*, 870 A.2d 912 (Pa. Super. 2005).**

A residential care center operated by the Commonwealth's Department of Public Welfare is immune from suit alleging "institutional negligence" for failure to properly screen employee who sexually abused minor residents. Institutional negligence does not fall within the medical-professional liability exception to sovereign immunity. ***Dashner v. Hamburg Center of the Department of Public Welfare*, 845 A.2d 935 (Pa. Cmwlth. 2004).**

Plaintiffs sued minister and church alleging minister had sexually molested their daughter, and church had been negligent in investigation prior to hiring minister and in monitoring his behavior after his employment. On appeal from grant of summary judgment in favor of church, the court held that evidence presented by plaintiffs was insufficient to present a question of fact for the jury to decide as to either negligent hiring or supervision. ***R.A. v. First Church of Christ*, 748 A.2d 692 (Pa. Super. 2000).**

Pedophilic sexual molestation is an intentional act and, as such, the doctrine of comparative negligence does not apply. Additionally, a victim of sexual abuse has no duty to avoid placing himself in the position to be harmed. ***Hutchinson ex rel. Hutchinson v. Luddy*, 763 A.2d 826 (Pa. Super. 2000).**

Local and national Big Brother/Big Sister organization does not owe minor who was sexually abused by organization member with prior history of abuse a duty to warn where minor does not have any ties to the organization. Summary judgment affirmed. ***J.E.J. v. Tri-County Big Brothers/Big Sisters, Inc.*, ___ Pa. Super. ___, 692 A.2d 582 (1997).**

Sexual contact

Co-owner of entireties property with actual knowledge of sexual abuse by other co-owner on their minor grandchildren within residence does not have duty to protect or warn grandchildren of grandfather's proclivities. Multimillion dollar compensatory and punitive damages award against grandmother reversed. While landowner may be liable for dangerous condition on the land, landowner is not liable for criminal or tortious acts of third parties. *T.A. v. Allen,* **447 Pa. Super. 302, 669 A.2d 360 (1995).**

Victim of sexual harassment brought action against employer claiming attack by third party and intentional infliction of emotional distress. Employer not liable. *Kryeski v. Schott Glass Technologies, Inc.,* **426 Pa. Super. 105, 626 A.2d 595.**

Parents of altar boy sexually assaulted by priest brought action against diocese, parish, and priest for intentional infliction of emotional distress. Defendants not liable. *Johnson v. Caparelli,* **425 Pa. Super. 404, 625 A.2d 668.**

Patient brought action against psychiatrist alleging sexual misconduct. Held: statute of limitations began to run when patient ceased treatment. *A. McD v. Rosen,* **423 Pa. Super. 304, 621 A.2d 128.**

Sexual contact

Plaintiff, patient of psychiatrist, filed suit for damages resulting from psychiatrist's alleged sexual contact with patient. Motion for summary judgment granted, and affirmed by Superior Court, because plaintiff failed to file suit within two years of date when she could reasonably be expected to know of her injury with the exercise of reasonable diligence. Reasonable diligence is an objective and external standard that is the same for all persons. Plaintiff's allegation that she did not recognize inappropriateness of sexual contact by treating psychiatrist until informed by a later therapist is inadequate to toll statute of limitations. Discovery rule is not appropriate for plaintiff because she knew of existence of sexual contact at all times and a reasonable person would have recognized that such behavior was inappropriate. *Haggart v. Cho,* **703 A.2d 522 (Pa. Super. 1997).**

Shadow

Plaintiff fell in defendant's parking lot. Daylight. Tripped over exposed wires which may or may not have been in shadow. Judgment on the record, after hung jury, reversed. Retrial ordered. *Gregoris v. Stockwell Rubber,* **235 Pa. Super. 71, 340 A.2d 570.**

Sharp curve

Wife plaintiff was operating a car around a sharp curve during a highway construction operation and collided with defendant's truck partly double parked—nonsuit granted—assured clear distance rule applied—evidence of excessive speed under circumstances. *Haines v. Dulaney,* **424 Pa. 608, 227 A.2d 625.**

Sheriff's sale

Plaintiff in legal malpractice action failed to establish he had suffered any discernible injury or damage. Fact that plaintiff lost security interest in property as junior lienholder does not establish that he was unable to enforce his security purely by reason of attorney's failure to provide him with notice of sheriff's sale by senior lienholder. ***Boyer v. Walker*, 714 A.2d 458 (Pa. Super. 1998).**

Shock treatment

Plaintiff, an aged woman, was suffering from a mental condition known as agitated depression—the defendant, her physician, recommended shock treatment and referred her to a hospital equipped to give such treatment—while receiving treatment plaintiff sustained bilateral fractures of the acetabulae—Held on appeal: defendant was not personally negligent and not responsible under doctrine of *respondeat superior* as not having control of those administering treatment. ***Collins v. Hand,* 431 Pa. 378, 246 A.2d 398.**

Shop class - See Municipal liability: Schools and school districts

Shopping cart

Customer fell down a step in store as the result of a shifting shopping cart—fractured hip—Held: cross-examination concerning a prior accident not error—verdict of $2,500.00 with expenses of $2,013.49 not inadequate—new trial refused plaintiff—strong dissent. ***Levant v. L. Wasserman, Inc.*, 218 Pa. Super. 116, 275 A.2d 678.**

Shopping center

Proprietor of a shopping center must exercise reasonable care—previous entrance to center blocked off by high curbing—plaintiffs injured—previous occurrences—case for jury. ***Colangelo v. Penn Hills Center, Inc.*, 221 Pa. Super. 381, 292 A.2d 490.**

Shoring

An employee of a carpenter subcontractor injured by reason of improper shoring—general contractor had employed a subcontractor to do excavation work—this subcontractor employed a highlift truck and operator—Held: verdict solely against excavating subcontractor proper as the operator was not a borrowed or loaned employee—whether general contractor was a statutory employer not passed upon on appeal. ***Hamler v. Waldron et al.*, 445 Pa. 262, 284 A.2d 725.**

Shower

Inmate filed suit against county correctional facility for injury to his head received when the "grab bar" in the prison shower broke free causing him to fall. Despite county's argument that the shower stall was only personal property, lack of evidence by county that shower stall was not a fixture and resulting presumption that it was in the nature of real property maintained by the county, precludes summary judgment under Political Subdivision Tort Claims Act. ***Davis v. Brennan,* 698 A.2d 1382 (Pa. Cmwlth. 1997).**

County's failure to install nonslip tile in drying off area of county prison shower constituted improper design or inherent defect of the governmental real estate. Therefore, inmate may recover under real property exception to Political Sub-

Sideswipe collision

division Tort Claims Act for injuries sustained in fall. Order granting summary judgment in favor of defendant reversed. ***Bradley v. Franklin County Prison,*** **674 A.2d 363 (Pa. Cmwlth. 1996).**

Sideswipe collision

Auto accident caused death of driver and passenger. Sideswipe forced car onto guardrail and thereafter into head-on collision. Evidence of instantaneous death. Verdict exceeded proven money damages, therefore new trial on damages only ordered. ***Nye v. Com., Dept. of Transp.,*** **331 Pa. Super. 209, 480 A.2d 318.**

Eakin driving north on highway, when passed on right by Polimeni, sideswiping Eakin vehicle, then crossing highway striking Caldwell vehicle. Three suits with cross claims. Only Polimeni held to be negligent. Verdict sustained. ***Churchill v. Eakin, et al,*** **233 Pa. Super. 466, 335 A.2d 378.**

Plaintiff injured by reason of contact with a tractor-trailer—one of named defendants skidded into opposite lane and stopped—tractor-trailer endeavored to pass stalled vehicle and caused contact with plaintiff's car—jury exonerated defendant who had skidded and held owner of tractor-trailer and its operator responsible—such finding upheld on appeal. ***Boyd v. Hertz Corp. et al.,*** **219 Pa. Super. 488, 281 A.2d 679.**

Sidewalks

Plaintiff brought a personal injury action against property owner after tripping on an uneven portion of sidewalk. The trial court granted summary judgment as the defect in the sidewalk was only one and 1½ inches deep and thus trivial. The Superior Court reversed holding that there is no definite or mathematical rule for depth or size of a depression to determine if a defect is trivial as a matter of law and that the facts did not establish that the defect was trivial. In addition, it held that the trial court could not consider prior knowledge in determining if a defect is trivial. ***Mull v. Ickes,*** **994 A.2d 1137 (Pa. Super. 2010).**

Plaintiffs injured in a slip and fall crossing a sidewalk brought a negligence claim against the city for failing to remove snow and ice from the sidewalk abutting the city's police station. The trial court found in favor of the Plaintiffs and the Commonwealth Court affirmed. The Supreme Court reversed holding that the real property exception to governmental immunity does not apply to injuries arising from sidewalks even if the sidewalk abuts local agency property. ***Reid v. City of Philadelphia,*** **598 Pa. 389, 957 A.2d 232 (2008).**

Plaintiff sued husband property owner as "resident" of property house on whose sidewalk plaintiff tripped and fell, suffering injuries. Defendant moved for summary judgment for failure to join husband's wife as an indispensable party and trial court granted motion. Trial court's opinion acknowledged error in granting summary judgment rather than dismissal under R.C.P. 1032(b) (failure to join an indispensable party). Superior Court reversed, holding that naming husband as "resident" of house and not "owner" avoids need to name wife (co-owner by entireties) as additional party. ***Gaynor v. Gyuris,*** **707 A.2d 5354 (Pa. Super. 1998).**

Single cause of injury

Pedestrian tripped over raised grate in sidewalk in front of restaurant. Pedestrian licensee and not invitee. ***Palange v. City of Philadelphia Law Department*, 433 Pa. Super. 373, 640 A.2d 1305.**

Minor injured in fall caused by hole in sidewalk. Summary judgment improperly granted. Question existed whether hole extended into sidewalk in front of defendant's home. ***Harris by Harris v. Hanberry*, 149 Pa. Cmwlth. 300, 613 A.2d 101.**

Legally blind patient fell on sidewalk outside of ophthalmologist's office. Patient found lying near hole in sidewalk. Held: summary judgment for defendants improper. ***Morlas v. Tasman*, 527 Pa. 132, 589 A.2d 205.**

Jury verdict $41,770—fractured right ankle. Slip and fall over metal band on otherwise crumbling sidewalk. Medical bills—$1,165. Affirmed. Charge of court approved on loss of earning capacity. ***Donlin v. Newberry*, 319 Pa. Super. 310, 466 A.2d 174.**

Evidence of "V" shaped defect in sidewalk of at least one month's duration sufficient to go to jury on notice and negligence on part of landowner. ***Kardibin v. Associated Hardware*, 284 Pa. Super. 586, 426 A.2d 649.**

Pedestrian-tenant fell on defect in sidewalk which had been present for some time although covered by leaves at time of injury. Held: issue of contributory negligence for jury. Entry of compulsory nonsuit reversed. ***Landy v. Romeo*, 274 Pa. Super. 75, 417 A.2d 1260.**

Plaintiff forced to walk in street due to failure of property owner to clear sidewalk and further required to walk out in roadway due to three foot high bank of snow caused by city snowplows. While walking in street, either slipped, fell, or struck by car—testimony confusing. Compromise verdict against property owner and city. ***Bacsick v. Barnes, et al.*, 234 Pa. Super. 616, 341 A.2d 157.**

Pedestrian falling allegedly due to drop in level of sidewalk—four inch overhang of building held sufficient excuse for not seeing drop—verdict for plaintiff sustained. ***Kobi v. Bau*, 218 Pa. Super. 139, 279 A.2d 297.**

Single cause of injury

Plaintiff minor was injured when his shoe was caught in escalator. Plaintiffs raised negligence and *res ipsa loquitur* claims in complaint (even though *res ipsa* is rule of evidence and not cause of action). Trial court refused to give *res ipsa* charge because plaintiffs had introduced evidence tending to show specific acts of negligence. Held: *res ipsa* charge is permissible as long as plaintiff has not presented evidence which tends to support a single cause of incident causing injury. When plaintiff presents as specific a case of negligence as possible, yet is unable to demonstrate exact cause of accident, plaintiff is entitled to *res ipsa loquitur* charge. ***D'Arnenne v. Strawbridge & Clothier*, 712 A.2d 318 (Pa. Super. 1998).**

Six-month notice

Six-month notice

Plaintiff was injured in an automobile accident allegedly caused by defective road design and condition. On the day of trial, the trial court granted PennDOT's motion for nonsuit based on plaintiff's failure to notify PennDOT of action within six months of accident under 42 Pa. C.S. §5522(a)(1) based on presumption of prejudice and hardship for failure to notify PennDOT. Held: presentation of motion on day of trial was untimely given substantial amount of time during which PennDOT could earlier have made the same motion, there is no presumption of prejudice or hardship attendant to lack of required notice. Negligence of plaintiff's counsel in providing notice coupled with lack of undue hardship to Commonwealth constituted adequate reason for delay in providing notice. Remanded to trial court for hearing on actual prejudice on PennDOT with burden of proof on PennDOT. ***Leedom v. Com., Dept. of Transp.*, 699 A.2d 815 (Pa. Cmwlth. 1997).**

Skating rink

Plaintiff, a business invitee in a skating rink owned and operated by defendant, fell allegedly as the result of a "soft spot" in ice—evidence that ice manufacturing machine was defective—operator held responsible. ***Dean v. Allegheny County*, 209 Pa. Super. 310, 228 A.2d 40.**

Skidmarks and skidding

Charge of court held adequate on issue of shifting of burden of proof when auto crosses center line. Verdict for defendant contrary to weight of evidence; new trial ordered. Defendant crossed center of highway—claims skidded on wet road when car ahead slowed suddenly. This was an inadequate explanation and therefore verdict contrary to weight of evidence. ***Bohner v. Stine*, 316 Pa. Super. 426, 463 A.2d 438.**

Pedestrian struck by auto. Defense verdict reversed. Proper, within discretion of trial judge, to allow police officer to estimate speed from skid marks. Error to refuse charge that if driver saw pedestrian standing ahead, and perceived possibility of crossing, there was a duty to sound horn. ***Morris v. Moss*, 290 Pa. Super. 587, 435 A.2d 184.**

Plaintiff a passenger in auto which skidded on gravel when deer was spotted on highway. Plaintiff warned driver of bad curve ahead. Error to charge on sudden emergency or on contributory negligence. ***Hanlon v. Sorenson*, 289 Pa. Super. 268, 433 A.2d 60.**

Proper to refuse plaintiff's request for charge that mere fact that defendant's vehicle skidded established negligence. ***Kuhn v. Michael*, 283 Pa. Super. 101, 423 A.2d 735.**

Plaintiff, passenger in defendant's car, injured when car went out of control on loose gravel. Error to charge on sudden emergency. Where gravel was stationary, proper charge should have been on assured clear distance doctrine. ***Brown v. Schriver*, 254 Pa. Super. 468, 386 A.2d 45.**

Skiing

Plaintiff injured when vehicle in which he was passenger skidded on icy overpass. Commonwealth has exclusive jurisdiction over control and maintenance of state highways. Township through which highway passes has no duty even to warn of known dangers. Dismissal of Newtown Twp. affirmed. *Haas v. Commonwealth,* **84 Pa. Cmwlth. 522, 79 A.2d 100.**

Skier's Responsibility Act

Skier brought a negligence action against snowboarder, who collided with him at a ski resort. The Plaintiff appealed the trial court's grant of summary judgment. The Superior Court upheld the trial court's decision holding that the State Skier's Responsibility Act preserved the defense of assumption of the risk with respect to downhill skiing. *Bell v. Dean,* _____ A.2d _____, **2010 WL 3211956 (Pa. Super. 2010).**

Skier brought a personal injury action against ski resort after falling from a ski lift. Trial court granted summary judgment to resort because plaintiff had signed a release of any negligence claim. The Superior Court reversed, holding that there was an issue of fact as to whether a promise by the lift operator to stop the lift superseded the terms of the release. The Supreme Court reversed the Superior Court and reinstated the original grant of summary judgment because the plaintiff had assumed inherent risks, including boarding a moving lift. *Chepkevich v. Hidden Valley Resort, L.P.,* _____ A.2d _____, **2010 WL 2482363 (Pa. 2010).**

Plaintiff's acceptance of the inherent risks of skiing does not include acceptance of the risk that he would be hit from behind by a fellow sportsman using the resort's facilities while under the influence of alcohol. *Crews v. Seven Springs Mountain Resort,* **874 A.2d 100 (Pa. Super. 2005).**

A skier who was struck by an uphill skier while traversing the base of the hill towards a ski lift sued facility for injuries. Facility raised assumption of risk as an affirmative defense and also the Skier's Responsibility Act, 42 Pa.C.S. § 7102. Supreme Court analyzed sport of skiing under assumption of risk doctrine and legislation and held that participation in any aspect of sport of downhill skiing, even while not skiing "down" the hill, is covered by assumption of risk and statute. *Hughes v. Seven Springs Farm, Inc.,* **762 A.2d 339 (Pa. 2000).**

High school skier was injured when struck by an unidentified skier while she was stopped at the base of a hill. Summary judgment entered in favor of ski resort based on assumption of risk created by Pennsylvania Skier's Responsibility Act, 42 Pa.C.S. §7102(c). Reversed by Superior Court because question of whether or not non-moving plaintiff at the bottom of a hill was actually "skiing" was for jury. *Hughes v. Seven Springs,* **727 A.2d 135 (Pa. Super. 1999).**

Skiing

Plaintiffs were injured after they fell off a ski lift, when the lift operator failed to stop the lift as agreed. The court held that there was a genuine issue of fact, whether an agreement by a lift operator to stop a ski lift could supersede a signed release of liability form. *Chepkevich v. Hidden Valley Resort,* **L.P., 911 A.2d 946 (Pa. Super. 2006).**

Skylight

Plaintiff's acceptance of the inherent risks of skiing does not include acceptance of the risk that he would be hit from behind by a fellow sportsman using the resort's facilities while under the influence of alcohol. ***Crews v. Seven Springs Mountain Resort*, 874 A.2d 100 (Pa. Super. 2005).**

A skier who was struck by an uphill skier while traversing the base of the hill towards a ski lift sued facility for injuries. Facility raised assumption of risk as an affirmative defense and also the Skier's Responsibility Act, 42 Pa.C.S. § 7102. Supreme Court analyzed sport of skiing under assumption of risk doctrine and legislation and held that participation in any aspect of sport of downhill skiing, even while not skiing "down" the hill, is covered by assumption of risk and statute. ***Hughes v. Seven Springs Farm, Inc.*, 762 A.2d 339 (Pa. 2000).**

High school skier was injured when struck by an unidentified skier while she was stopped at the base of a hill. Summary judgment entered in favor of ski resort based on assumption of risk created by Pennsylvania Skier's Responsibility Act, 42 Pa.C.S. §7102(c). Reversed by Superior Court because question of whether or not non-moving plaintiff at the bottom of a hill was actually "skiing" was for jury. ***Hughes v. Seven Springs*, 727 A.2d 135 (Pa. Super. 1999).**

Skier injured during race. Owner of slope not liable. Releases and exculpatory clauses valid. ***Kotovsky v. Ski Liberty Operating Corporation*, 412 Pa. Super. 442, 603 A.2d 663.**

Plaintiff rented ski equipment and was injured when bindings did not release in fall. Signed lease for equipment contained exculpatory clause. Summary judgment in favor of lessor affirmed. Counts against other defendants unaffected. Strong dissent. ***Zimmer v. Mitchell and Ness*, 490 Pa. 428, 416 A.2d 1010.**

Skylight

School laborer injured when he fell through skydome on roof. Summary judgment for defendants affirmed. Skydome properly an improvement to real property subject to strict 12 year statute of repose. ***Catanzaro v. Wasco Products*, 339 Pa. Super. 481, 489 A.2d 262.**

Slight contact

Contact in collision slight—serious injuries alleged—undoubtedly most had existed prior to occurrence—jury disbelieved plaintiff—verdict for defendant—motion for new trial dismissed below and action sustained on appeal. ***Brodhead v. Brentwood Ornamental Iron Co.*, 435 Pa. 7, 255 A.2d 120.**

Slip and fall

Plaintiff brought negligence action for slip and fall against property owner. Trial court dismissed for Plaintiff's failure to name the estate of the property owner as a party prior to the expiration of the 2-year statute of limitations. The Superior Court held that an estate's failure to transfer ownership from a decedent to the estate was not sufficient to show an act of concealment permitting a tolling of the statute of limitations. ***McClean v. Djerassi*, 84 A.3d 1067 (Pa. Super. 2013).**

Slip and fall

Plaintiff, a trainee with a non-profit, brought negligence action against Defendant city after he slipped and fell while helping to clean up flood damage. The trial court granted summary judgment in favor of the city on the basis that the city had immunity under the Workers' Compensation Act. The Commonwealth Court affirmed holding that under the Borrowed Servant Doctrine the city was the Plaintiff's employer because the non-profit had loaned its workers to the city and the city had controlled the performance of the work and the Plaintiff's hours of work. *Canot v. City of Easton,* **37 A.3d 53 (Pa. Cmwlth. 2012).**

Plaintiff brought negligence claim against Defendant transportation agency after she slipped on an icy wooden step on the train platform, while attempting to board a train. The trial court entered summary judgment for the Defendant. The Commonwealth Court affirmed holding that allegations of improper maintenance resulting in ice were insufficient as the ice did not result from a defect in the real property itself. *Nardella v. Southeastern Pennsylvania Transportation Authority,* **34 A.3d 300 (Pa. Cmwlth. 2011).**

Plaintiff filed negligence action against the food service company that operated the plant's cafeteria after he slipped and fell on cooking oil that had leaked from a dumpster. The trial court entered summary judgment for the Defendant. The Superior Court held that as the Defendant had undertaken a duty to dispose of cooking oil in sealed containers and since cooking oil had been found in the dumpster not in a sealed container it was a question of fact for the jury to determine if the Defendant was negligent. *Casselbury v. American Food Service,* **30 A.3d 510 (Pa. Super. 2011).**

Tenant brought a claim of negligence against landlord after she fell on ice outside her apartment. The trial court granted summary judgment for the landlord. The Superior Court reversed and remanded, holding that Plaintiff's medical records that indicated she stated she fell on ice were sufficient to withstand a motion for summary judgment as statements to medical personnel regarding how a person sustained injury were relevant to treatment and diagnosis under the medical treatment exception to the hearsay rule. *Turner v. Valley Housing Development Corp.,* **972 A.2d 531 (Pa. Super. 2009).**

Plaintiffs injured in a slip and fall crossing a sidewalk brought a negligence claim against the city for failing to remove snow and ice from the sidewalk abutting the city's police station. The trial court found in favor of the Plaintiffs and the Commonwealth Court affirmed. The Supreme Court reversed, holding that the real property exception to governmental immunity does not apply to injuries arising from sidewalks even if the sidewalk abuts local agency property. *Reid v. City of Philadelphia,* **598 Pa. 389, 957 A.2d 232 (2008).**

Plaintiff slipped and fell on black ice, while walking on a recently plowed road owned by a subdivision developer. The court held that based upon the "hills and ridges" doctrine the developer was protected from liability, since the developer had not permitted the ice to unreasonably accumulate to create the dangerous condition. *Harvey v. Rouse Chamberlain, LTD.,* **901 A.2d 523 (Pa. Super. 2006).**

Slip and fall

[Mall patron's suit for injuries sustained in fall caused by alleged "slippery substance" dismissed on summary judgment for lack of any proof that mall manager had constructive or actual notice of existence of any foreign matter on floors. ***Porro v. Century III Associates*, 846 A.2d 1282 (Pa. Super. 2004).**

Inmate injured when he fell on wet, slippery waxed floor was not entitled to trial as condition of floor was not "dangerous condition of real estate" under the real estate exception in the Sovereign Immunity Act. ***Raker v. Pa. Dept. of Corrections*, 844 A.2d 659 (Pa. Cmwlth. 2004).**

Debris and dead cat which had accumulated on steps leading into basement of building owned by Philadelphia Housing Authority were not conditions that "derived, originated or had as their source" the municipal realty itself so as to fall within the real estate exception to governmental immunity. ***Lingo v. Philadelphia Housing Authority*, 820 A.2d 859 (Pa. Cmwlth. 2003).**

Evaluation of the real estate exception to sovereign immunity statute and the historically applied "on/of" distinction. The proper method for determining whether the real estate exception to sovereign immunity applies is to focus on whether or not a dangerous condition created by rock salt on a train platform derived from, originated from, or had its source in the real estate itself and if not, the real estate exception did not apply. "On/of" analysis formally rejected. Important distinction between language of Sovereign Immunity Act and the Political Subdivision Tort Claims Act. ***Jones v. SEPTA*, 772 A.2d 435 (Pa. 2001).**

Tenant of county housing authority who was injured when she slipped and fell on snow and ice-covered parking area could not recover against local agency, because snow and ice were condition *on* the real estate, not condition *of* the real estate. Supreme Court's seemingly different determination on similar facts under the Sovereign Immunity Act does not control under different language of the Political Subdivision Tort Claims Act. ***Irish v. Lehigh County Housing Authority*, 751 A.2d 1201 (Pa. Cmwlth. 2000).**

Plaintiff was injured when she slipped and fell on rock salt located *on* defendant's train platform. Held: "of / on" distinction continues to apply to cases where the real property exception to governmental immunity applies. ***Jones v. SEPTA*, 748 A.2d 1271 (Pa. Cmwlth. 2000).**

Plaintiff slipped and fell on sidewalk in front of city building that fronted on Commonwealth highway. City argued it was immune from liability under the sidewalk exception to the governmental immunity statute, because the sidewalk did not abut a city-owned street. After a very thorough review of the history of the sovereign and governmental immunity acts and cases, the court held that the city could be liable under the real estate exception to governmental immunity. ***Sherman v. City of Philadelphia*, 745 A.2d 95 (Pa. Cmwlth. 2000).**

Slip and fall accident at tavern by patron. Plaintiff sued titled owners of the property despite the fact that the business was operated and managed by a purchaser under a land sale contract, who had full use and possession of the tavern premises and business. The court held that bare legal title alone is not adequate to establish

Slip and fall

possession and control over premises and subject a party to liability for tortious conduct of the party who is actually in possession. ***Hubert v. Greenwald*, 743 A.2d 977 (Pa. Super. 1999).**

Wife plaintiff filed suit against school district alleging that water left from "damp mopping" of school hallway caused her to slip and fall and suffer injuries. After grant of motion for summary judgment by defendant based on plaintiffs' failure to prove facts which would take case under real estate exception to governmental immunity, Commonwealth Court affirmed. On appeal, Supreme Court reversed and remanded to Commonwealth Court which reversed and remanded its prior affirmance of trial court grant of summary judgment. Held: "...for government immunity purposes, it is no longer of any consequence that the injury does not result from a defect in, or condition of, the real property itself, and that the real property exception should no longer be considered *in pari materia* with the sidewalk exception to governmental immunity or the real estate exception to sovereign immunity." ***Hanna v. West Shore School District*, 717 A.2d 626 (Pa. Cmwlth. 1998).**

Plaintiff was injured when she slipped and fell on floor of SEPTA train. Plaintiff argued that train was improperly cared for personal property of Commonwealth and so exempt from protection of Sovereign Immunity Act. Held: SEPTA train is vehicle for purposes of Sovereign Immunity Act and not personal property. Grant of compulsory nonsuit was affirmed. ***Ross v. SEPTA*, 714 A.2d 1131 (Pa. Cmwlth. 1998).**

Plaintiff appeals from grant of summary judgment to defendants based on common-enemy doctrine relating to natural surface water runoff in urban area. Plaintiff was injured when she slipped and fell on ice that had accumulated in alley next to defendant's business location. Held: as long as defendant had not artificially changed natural course of water or substantially changed quality or quantity of surface water, no injury will fall to lower landowner or to another. The record is devoid of evidence that defendants modified natural course of water in any way. ***Fazio v. Fegley Oil Co, Inc.*, 714 A.2d 510 (Pa. Cmwlth. 1998).**

Plaintiff who fell on thin layer of "black ice" in motel parking lot suffered injuries and sued motel owner. Plaintiff argued that "hills and ridges" doctrine, which requires showing of accumulation of ice and snow, should not apply to business premises; they are not so burdened by substantial size of area to be cleared of ice and snow as municipalities and local agencies, which organizations the doctrine is designed to protect. Plaintiff also argued that custodian who had placed salt and sand on portions of premises was negligent for not salting and sanding entire parking lot. Held: "hills and ridges" applies to business invitees and local agencies equally and because plaintiff could not show accumulation had been allowed to form without any effort to cure problem, summary judgment was proper. ***Morin v. Travelers Rest Motel, Inc.*, 704 A.2d 1085 (Pa. Super. 1997).**

Plaintiff who was injured when he fell on defective or missing city-owned and maintained steps presented proof that city employees cleaned or shoveled damaged steps four or five times per year and that those employees were obligated to

Slip and fall

report defects or problems with steps. Plaintiff also offered credible evidence that there was a continuous deterioration of the steps from the date of the last repair more than one and one-half years before plaintiff's injury; therefore, city had actual or constructive notice of defective condition. City's defense of Political Subdivision Tort Claims Act was inadequate in light of plaintiff's evidence of defective condition of steps and notice to city. ***Ellis v. City of Pittsburgh*, 703 A.2d 593 (Pa. Cmwlth. 1997).**

Accumulation of ice and snow into ridges and hills on which plaintiff slipped, fell and was injured is not a dangerous condition of the sidewalk under sovereign immunity act and summary judgment in favor of Commonwealth sustained. The Court closely reviewed *Grieff v. Reisinger*, 548 Pa. 13, 693 A.2d 195 (1997) but remains bound by facts of this case and those in *Finn v. Philadelphia,* 541 Pa. 596, 664 A.2d 1342 (1995) as distinguished from those in *Grieff.* ***Abella v. City of Philadelphia*, 703 A.2d 547 (Pa. Cmwlth. 1997).**

Decedent's failure to establish hospital's knowledge of water on floor in bathroom, which may represent a dangerous or defective condition of the property, prohibits recovery. A business invitee must prove either that the landowner created the harmful condition or had actual or constructive notice of the condition. Summary judgment affirmed. ***Swift v. Northeastern Hospital of Philadelphia,* 456 Pa. Super. 330, 690 A.2d 719 (1997).**

Defense verdict reversed and remanded for trial court to hold evidentiary hearing on whether circumstances surrounding another fall by plaintiff at another of defendant's supermarkets were sufficiently similar to instant slip and fall to warrant admission of evidence of prior fall. ***Valentine v. Acme Markets, Inc.,* 455 Pa. Super. 256, 687 A.2d 1157 (1997).**

Plaintiff injured after slip and fall on wet porch sued homeowner and paint company. Inconsistencies between two releases executed by plaintiff on the same day, one of which released paint company and "all others who may be liable" preserved genuine issue of material fact as to which of the two releases took precedence. Summary judgment reversed. ***Mackay v. Sauerland,* 454 Pa. Super. 666, 686 A.2d 840 (1996).**

In action by guest at wedding reception, testimony that there were two dangerous areas on portable dance floor is sufficient to preclude summary judgment where jury would not be required to speculate impermissibly as to cause of plaintiff's slip and fall on dance floor. Summary judgment reversed. ***First v. Zem Zem Temple,* 454 Pa. Super. 548, 686 A.2d 18 (1996).**

Summary judgment reversed where plaintiff insulation installer on stilts held not to have assumed the risk of slipping on construction debris left at job site by defendants. Assumption of risk should only preclude recovery where it is beyond question that the plaintiff voluntarily and knowingly proceeded in the face of an obvious and dangerous condition. ***Barrett v. Fredavid Builders, Inc.,* 454 Pa. Super. 162, 685 A.2d 129 (1996).**

Slip and fall

Accumulation of water on school district property, which condition contributed to fall of high school student on crutches does not fall within real property exception to Political Subdivision Tort Claims Act. Order granting summary judgment for school district affirmed. ***Leonard v. Fox Chapel Area School District,*** **674 A.2d 767 (Pa. Cmwlth. 1996).**

County's failure to install nonslip tile in drying off area of county prison shower constituted improper design or inherent defect of the governmental real estate. Therefore, inmate may recover under real property exception to Political Subdivision Tort Claims Act for injuries sustained in fall. Order granting summary judgment in favor of defendant reversed. ***Bradley v. Franklin County Prison,*** **674 A.2d 363 (Pa. Cmwlth. 1996).**

Order granting summary judgment in favor of school district affirmed where plaintiff who slipped on ice in school district parking lot failed to establish that injuries were caused by improper design, construction, deterioration, or inherent defect of real estate. Real property exception to Political Subdivision Tort Claims Act not applicable. ***Metkus v. Pennsbury School District,*** **674 A.2d 355 (Pa. Cmwlth. 1996).**

Buildup of grease and oil on city-owned sidewalk is not a dangerous condition "of" the sidewalk; therefore, city is immune from liability under the Political Subdivision Tort Claims Act for injuries sustained by pedestrian who slipped and fell on sidewalk. ***Finn v. City of Philadelphia,*** **541 Pa. 596, 664 A.2d 1342 (1995).**

Summary judgment reversed where owners of property adjoining parking lot on which plaintiff slipped and fell had easement across parking lot and, therefore, question existed as to whether property owners were liable as possessor of parking lot. ***Blackman v. Federal Realty Inv. Trust,*** **444 Pa. Super. 411, 664 A.2d 139 (1995).**

Hills and ridges of ice on school district property are not dangerous condition of the property itself and, therefore, do not fall within real property exception to Political Subdivision Tort Claims Act. Order granting judgment on pleadings affirmed. ***McRae v. School District of Philadelphia,*** **___ Pa. Cmwlth. ___, 660 A.2d 209 (1995).**

For real property exception to apply against school district, dangerous condition must be of or attached to the pavement or property and not on the subject pavement or property. Rainwater on floor of school building did not constitute dangerous condition of or attached to property. Directed verdict for defendant affirmed. Dissent would apply exception based on school district's use of terrazzo floor tile which school district knew became dangerously slippery when wet. ***Shedrick v. William Penn School District,*** **___ Pa. Cmwlth. ___, 654 A.2d 163 (1995).**

Sidewalk exception to governmental immunity and real property exception to governmental immunity are to be read consistently. For real property exception to apply against school district, dangerous condition must be of or attached to the pavement or property and not on the subject pavement or property. Milk on sidewalk did not constitute dangerous condition of or attached to property. Jury ver-

Slip and fall

dict for defendant affirmed. ***DeLuca v. School District of Philadelphia***, ___ Pa. Cmwlth. ___, **654 A.2d 29 (1994).**

Release entered into with hotel defendant for injuries sustained in federal slip and fall case did not release defendants in subsequent state court action for medical malpractice in surgery to repair wrist injured during slip and fall at hotel, where release specifically designated federal court action and caption as subject of release. Summary judgment for physicians and surgeons reversed. ***Harrity v. Medical College of Pennsylvania Hospital,* 439 Pa. Super. 10, 653 A.2d 5 (1995).**

In a negligence action against corporate defendant and officers, officers are not liable for failing to maintain a clean bathroom absent proof of their participation in creating or allowing continued existence of a dangerous condition. Party's failure to answer request for admission that states a conclusion of law does not establish plaintiff's case. Judgment in favor of plaintiff vacated and remanded for consideration of scope of involvement and liability of owners. ***Brindley v. Woodland Village Restaurant, Inc.,* 438 Pa. Super. 385, 652 A.2d 865 (1995).**

Evidence of dangerous condition in store sufficient to preclude granting of compulsory nonsuit. Monetary sanction against plaintiff for delay of trial to acquire expert testimony affirmed. ***Zito v. Merit Outlet Stores,* 434 Pa. Super. 213, 647 A.2d 573 (1994).**

"Dangerous condition of real estate" exception to governmental immunity was fact question for jury. Summary judgment in favor of defendant reversed. ***Berhane v. SEPTA,* 166 Pa. Cmwlth. 196, 646 A.2d 1268 (1994).**

Patron did not assume risk of injury when she observed wet floor immediately before stepping onto it and falling. Nonsuit reversed. ***Hardy v. Southland Corporation,* 435 Pa. Super. 237, 645 A.2d 839 (1994).**

Municipality immune from liability to plaintiff who slipped and fell on grease on sidewalk. Verdict in favor of plaintiff reversed. ***Finn v. City of Philadelphia,* 165 Pa. Cmwlth. 255, 645 A.2d 320 (1994).**

Passenger fell on slippery spot on subway platform. Held: whether dangerous condition was "on" or "off" platform a question of fact. ***Shubert v. SEPTA,* 155 Pa. Cmwlth. 129, 625 A.2d 102.**

Commuter injured in fall caused by grease and debris that accumulated on Authority property. Authority held not liable. ***Fitchett v. SEPTA,* 152 Pa. Cmwlth. 18, 619 A.2d 805.**

Customer who fell in supermarket brought action claiming injuries caused by excess wax or presence of grapes on floor. Market not liable. ***Myers v. Penn Traffic Company,* 414 Pa. Super. 181, 606 A.2d 926.**

Parishioner who fell in church parking lot brought action against parish and diocese. Held: failure to exclude jurors who were members of diocese proper and doctrine of hills and ridges applicable. ***Harmotta v. Bender,* 411 Pa. Super. 371, 601 A.2d 837.**

Pedestrian who slipped on debris on train platform brought action against city. City not liable. Injuries not caused by artificial condition or defect in land. ***Wellons v. SEPTA,*** **141 Pa. Cmwlth. 622, 596 A.2d 1169.**

Customer who slipped on water in front of ice machine brought action against store owner and contractor who stocked machine. New trial ordered. Evidence of post-accident remedial measures improperly admitted. ***Miller v. Peter J. Schmitt & Company, Inc.,*** **405 Pa. Super. 502, 592 A.2d 1324.**

Customer slipped and fell in supermarket. Supermarket not liable. Failure of trial court to grant judgment *n.o.v.* and new trial not error. ***Goldman v. Acme Markets, Inc.,*** **393 Pa. Super. 245, 574 A.2d 100.**

Health club member slipped and fell in shower. Exculpatory clause in membership agreement held not to have released club from liability. ***Brown v. Racquetball Centers, Inc.,*** **369 Pa. Super. 13, 534 A.2d 842.**

Plaintiff fell on patch of ice in parking lot of chiropractic clinic. Jury verdict $70,000 reflecting 35% comparative negligence. Ice was next to car, although rest of lot was clear. Plaintiff became aware of ice while still seated in car. Wore prosthesis at time—fractured left hip. Verdict reversed. Where plaintiff sees risk, possessor of land relieved of responsibility and duty of care to invitee who, under circumstances here was held to have assumed risk as matter of law. Comparative negligence statute not applicable. ***Carrender v. Fitterer,*** **503 Pa. 178, 469 A.2d 120.**

Plaintiff slipped and fell on cherry on floor of supermarket. Absent proof of negligence of employee or actual or constructive notice, plaintiff cannot recover. ***Moultrey v. A & P,*** **281 Pa. Super. 525, 422 A.2d 593.**

Milk hauler slipped on manure on steps in milking pit. Plaintiff, a farmer, familiar that manure was often in milking area. Contributorily negligent as a matter of law. ***Jewell v. Beckstine,*** **255 Pa. Super. 238, 386 A.2d 597.**

Visitor to hospital slipped on freshly mopped floor. Had observed floor being mopped upon entering. Floor wet from wall to wall. For jury even though plaintiff's evidence weak as to whether wetness caused fall. Strong dissent. ***Calhoun v. Jersey Shore Hospital,*** **250 Pa. Super. 567, 378 A.2d 1294.**

Sliver of metal

Sliver of metal entered eye of workman taking old sign off building. Verdict against property owner for not supplying goggles, oil, or giving adequate warning. Plaintiff found 49% negligent. Final verdict including delay damages $27,277.86 affirmed. Issues of assumption of risk and causation were for jury. ***Seewagen v. Vanderklvet,*** **338 Pa. Super. 534, 488 A.2d 21.**

Smoke inhalation

Plaintiff appealed from jury award of $12,000.00 which she considered inadequate for injuries suffered when she inhaled smoke from Port Authority bus which caught fire in front of her car in tunnel. Plaintiff's expert testified to her affliction as Reactive Airways Dysfunction Syndrome ("RADS"). In hotly contested case relat-

Smokestack

ing to extent of her injury and when her condition improved to point of plaintiff being completely recovered, the court held there was adequate evidence for jury to accept Port Authority's version of facts rather than plaintiffs. Verdict was not so low as to shock the sense of justice. **Labbett v. Port Authority of Allegheny County, 714 A.2d 522 (Pa. Cmwlth. 1998).**

Smokestack

Employee of independent contractor injured while working in smokestack. Owner joined contractor on basis of indemnification agreement. Reversed and remanded. Contractor improperly joined. **Fulmer v. Duquesne Light Company, 374 Pa. Super. 537, 543 A.2d 1100.**

Snow tube riding

Plaintiff brought suit against the Defendant snow tube facility and its employee after she was struck on a snow tube slope as a result of the employee sending snow tubers down the slope prior to her being able to clear the slope. The trial court granted summary judgment to the Defendant on the basis of a release signed by the Plaintiff releasing it of all liability for injuries caused by snow tubing. The Supreme Court reversed in part and remanded holding that a pre-injury exculpatory release could not release a party from reckless behavior as it was against public policy. **Tayar v. Camelback Ski Corp. Inc., 47 A.3d 1190 (Pa. 2012).**

Snowtubing patron brought claim of negligence against snowtube facility after they were injured when an employee sent another patron down the slope before the patron was off the slope. The trial court granted summary judgment for the Defendant. The Superior Court reversed and remanded, holding the release language on the lift ticket did not explicitly disclaim claims for reckless or intentional conduct and that the Plaintiff had specifically alleged reckless conduct preventing an award of summary judgment. **Tayar v. Camelback Ski Corporation, 957 A.2d 281 (Pa. Super. 2008).**

Plaintiff brought claim against resort alleging she suffered personal injury after being struck by a fellow snow tuber, because she was improperly instructed on how to exit the snow tube run by a resort employee. The appellate court upheld the trial court's decision that the release signed by the Plaintiff was enforceable because it stated it was a release for those risks associated towith snow tubing at the resort. **Wang v. Whitetail Mountain Resort, 933 A.2d 110 (Pa. Super. 2007).**

Despite a disclaimer printed on their entrance tickets plaintiffs sued for injuries suffered while they were snow tubing at defendant's facility. The court held that for language in a document to disclaim an implied warranty of fitness the language must be so conspicuous that a reasonable person would be put on notice that they were waiving their legal rights. **Beck-Hummel v. Ski Shawnee, Inc., 902 A.2d 1266 (Pa. Super. 2006).**

Owner of property which was improved with recreation equipment and partially fenced was not afforded immunity protections of Recreation Use of Land and Water Act against claim by child injured while snow-tubing. Thorough analysis

Social host

of various applications of RULWA. *Murtha v. Joyce*, 875 A.2d 1154 (Pa. Super. 2005).

Snowmobile

Recreational vehicle riders injured when vehicle struck cable blocking road at coal mine. Actions of mine owner were not willful or wanton. Plaintiffs not entitled to jury instruction on §335 of Restatement (2d) Torts. ***Graham v. Sky Haven Coal, Inc.*, 386 Pa. Super. 598, 563 A.2d 891.**

Plaintiff made a test of a snowmobile furnished by defendant—injured as a result of the condition of the track—court below treated plaintiff as testing a known danger and entered a nonsuit—case really involved an issue of contributory negligence and was for jury. ***Watson v. Zanotti Motor Co.*, 219 Pa. Super. 96, 280 A.2d 670.**

Social host

"Rave" party promoter that was not alleged to have provided any drugs or alcohol to adult party-guest driver could not be liable as social host for injuries sustained by party-guest passenger injured in automobile accident on way home. ***Looby v. Local 13 Productions*, 751 A.2d 220 (Pa. Super. 2000).**

Summary judgment in favor of social host affirmed where no evidence that host had actual notice that minors were consuming alcohol. Summary judgment in favor of telephone company affirmed because causal connection between location of pole and accident too remote in law to impose liability. ***Novak v. Kilby*, 167 Pa. Cmwlth. 217, 647 A.2d 687(1994).**

Social host who serves alcohol to minor may be found liable for damages caused by fire started by intoxicated minor. ***Alumni Association v. Sullivan*, 369 Pa. Super. 585, 535 A.2d 1095.**

Noncommercial organization which sponsored private social gathering and which acted strictly as social host supplying liquor, with no sales and no license under liquor code involved, could not be held liable to third party injured by intoxicated guest. ***Sites v. Cloonan*, 328 Pa. Super. 481, 477 A.2d 547.**

Social hosts can be held liable to minors injured as a result of being served alcoholic beverages, and to third parties injured by the action of the intoxicated minor. Liability, cannot, however, be based upon negligent entrustment of a non-owned auto or on duty as a landowner. ***Congini v. Portersville Valve Co.*, 504 Pa. 157, 470 A.2d 515.**

Social hosts who serve alcoholic beverages held not responsible in third-party actions by later-injured plaintiffs. ***Klein v. Raysinger*, 504 Pa. 141, 470 A.2d 507.**

Dram shop-type complaint against private party dismissed as stating no cause of action. Pennsylvania does not recognize cause of action by persons injured by intoxicated driver against social host who had served intoxicants to driver. But see concurring opinion and footnotes on possibility of pure negligence action. ***Klein v. Raysinger*, 298 Pa. Super. 246, 444 A.2d 753.**

Softball - See Sports injuries

Softball - See Sports injuries

Soft tissue

Plaintiff injured in motor vehicle accident offered four medical reports that showed that she had suffered serious soft tissue injury in the accident. Trial court granted defendant's motion for summary judgment based on findings in law that plaintiff's injuries were not compensable under the statutorily imposed limited tort restrictions. Superior Court reversed on its own review of reports by physicians and testimony adduced in summary judgment proceeding. ***Leonelli v. McMullen*, 700 A.2d 525 (Pa. Super. 1997).**

Jury cannot disregard evidence of soft-tissue damage, cervical sprain, and herniated disk, which are injuries of the kind that normally cause pain and suffering for which plaintiff should be compensated. Order granting new trial on issue of damages reinstated. ***Neison v. Hines*, 539 Pa. 516, 653 A.2d 634 (1995).**

Specific acts of negligence

Plaintiff minor was injured when his shoe was caught in escalator. Plaintiffs raised negligence and *res ipsa loquitur* claims in complaint (even though *res ipsa* is rule of evidence and not cause of action). Trial court refused to give *res ipsa* charge because plaintiffs had introduced evidence tending to show specific acts of negligence. Held: *res ipsa* charge is permissible as long as plaintiff has not presented evidence which tends to support a single cause of incident causing injury. When plaintiff presents as specific a case of negligence as possible, yet is unable to demonstrate exact cause of accident, plaintiff is entitled to *res ipsa loquitur* charge. ***D'Arnenne v. Strawbridge & Clothier*, 712 A.2d 318 (Pa. Super. 1998).**

Spectator

Plaintiff attending Philadelphia Phillies game was struck in the eye and injured by a ball thrown into the stands at the end of the inning by a player. The court held that according to the No Duty Rule, spectators may not recover from operators of places of amusement for injuries suffered due to common or expected risks inherent during the activity. ***Loughran v. The Phillies*, 888 A.2d 872 (Pa. Super. 2005).**

Plaintiff was a professional football game spectator who was tackled and trampled after he caught a football that had cleared the goal posts after a field goal. Summary judgment in favor of security company responsible for fan control and stadium authority reversed on basis that no-duty rule relied on by trial court only applies to hazardous circumstances that are common, frequent and expected. Disorderly fans of which stadium authority and security company were previously aware are not a regular part of a football game. ***Telega v. Security Bureau, Inc.*, 719 A.2d 372 (Pa. Super. 1998).**

Because bleachers constituted a defective improvement to the land, Recreational Use of Land and Water Act did not bar spectator's claim against Township for injuries sustained in fall from bleachers at Township ball field. Order granting summary judgment reversed. ***Brown v. Tunkhannock Township*, ___ Pa. Cmwlth. ___, 665 A.2d 1318 (1995).**

Speed

Fan assaulted at football game in view of security guard. City not liable. ***Poulos v. City of Philadelphia,* 156 Pa. Cmwlth. 648, 628 A.2d 1198.**

Spectator struck by tree limb at little league baseball game. Property owner immune under Recreation Use of Land and Water Act even though property partly developed. ***Redinger v. Clapper's Tree Service, Inc.,* 419 Pa. Super. 487, 615 A.2d 743.**

Spectator at high school sporting event injured in fall on ice. Summary judgment for school district not appropriate. Doctrine of hills and ridges probably not applicable. ***Mahoney Area School District v. Budwash,* 146 Pa. Cmwlth. 72, 604 A.2d 1156.**

Spectator at roller hockey game played in city-owned facility injured while attempting to break up fight. City not liable. ***City of Philadelphia v. Buck,* 138 Pa. Cmwlth. 250, 587 A.2d 875.**

Spectator brought action against city for injuries resulting from fall from temporary bleachers. City immune. Alleged negligence of police improperly pleaded. ***DeRitis v. City of Philadelphia,* 136 Pa. Cmwlth. 244, 582 A.2d 738.**

Spectator injured when struck by football during pre-game activities. School district immune. ***Johnson v. Woodland Hills School District,* 135 Pa. Cmwlth. 43, 582 A.2d 395.**

Speed

Parents of child struck and killed by automobile while riding bicycle brought action against PennDOT, municipality, and adjoining landowner. Defendants not liable. Failure to set speed limit below fifty-five and permitting vegetation to grow along highway not cause of accident. ***Salerno v. LaBarr,* 159 Pa. Cmwlth. 99, 632 A.2d 1002.**

Witness on cross-examination permitted to read statement given shortly after accident. In statement, witness said defendant was not travelling at excessive speed. During reading, but before speed part, plaintiff's counsel objected—overruled. Held: new trial should be awarded to plaintiff. ***Catina v. Maree,* 498 Pa. 443, 447 A.2d 228.**

Collision between auto turning onto street and car pulling out of parking place. Evidence that plaintiff was going 35-40 m.p.h. in 25 m.p.h. zone admissible within the discretion of lower court, even in absence of distance over which observation made. ***Radogna v. Hester,* 255 Pa. Super. 517, 388 A.2d 1087.**

Failure of plaintiff-passenger to protest speed of auto, standing alone, is not evidence of contributory negligence. No evidence that he knew how fast the vehicle was going, that he was a licensed driver, or knew how to operate car. ***Palmer v. Brest,* 254 Pa. Super. 532, 386 A.2d 77.**

Decedent pedestrian struck at night by defendant's car between intersections—evident that decedent was thrown 63 feet through the air—jury could infer

Sperm donor

excessive speed from such testimony—nonsuit improperly entered—case for jury. ***McNett v. Briggs*, 217 Pa. Super. 322, 272 A.2d 202.**

Opinion evidence of speed properly excluded at trial even though admitted by an adverse party at time of taking depositions—adverse witness admitted speed to be "excessive"—deposition stipulation reserved objections to time of trial. ***Starner v. Wirth*, 440 Pa. 177, 269 A.2d 674.**

Facts held sufficient to permit a witness to testify as to speed of vehicle—strong dissent on ground that witness did not have an opportunity to adequately describe speed of vehicle. ***Blinn v. DeBolt Transfer, Inc.*, 213 Pa. Super. 477, 249 A.2d 373.**

Speed of automobile three-tenths of mile from scene of occurrence relevant and admissible—care being pursued by police and leaving highway—plaintiff's decedent, a passenger, killed. ***Fugagli v. Camasi*, 426 Pa. 1, 229 A.2d 735.**

Sperm donor

Plaintiff, surrogate mother, sued infertility clinic under wrongful death and survival statutes, for negligent infliction of emotional distress, for fraud and for breach of fiduciary duty for the death of child murdered by sperm-donor father one month after the child's birth. After determining that clinic had waived any claim that mother lacked standing, Held: mother had stated cause of action under wrongful death and survival statutes but lacked sufficient factual basis for negligent infliction of emotional distress, fraud and breach of fiduciary duty. For-profit infertility clinic was in a "special relationship" with all parties to the transaction—surrogate mother, sperm-donor and resulting child—so as to create a duty imposed by law to effectively provide safeguards that might reasonably prevent foreseeable injuries to the parties, such as abuse of the child. ***Huddleston v. Infertility Center of America*, 700 A.2d 453 (Pa. Super. 1997).**

Spigot

Department store customer injured hand when spring loaded spigot in washroom recoiled violently. Store not liable. Doctrine of *res ipsa loquitur* not applicable. ***Lonsdale v. Joseph Horne Company*, 403 Pa. Super. 12, 587 A.2d 810.**

Spitball battle

Spitball battle on school bus. Minor passenger lost sight of right eye. Verdict versus owner of bus company and driver. New trial ordered to consider only the liability of participants. ***Sommers v. Hessler*, 227 Pa. Super. 41, 323 A.2d 17.**

Spoliation

Estate brought cause of action for negligent spoliation of evidence after the Defendant state police failed to preserve evidence for the estate's lawsuit against a tree stand safety-harness manufacturer. The trial court granted summary judgment for the Defendant. The Commonwealth Court affirmed. The Pennsylvania Supreme Court held that under Pennsylvania law there is no cause of action for spoliation of

Sports injuries

evidence. *Pyeritz v. Commonwealth of Pennsylvania,* 32 A.3d 687 (Pa. Cmwlth. 2011).

Sponge left in body

Not every wrong constitutes a legally cognizable cause of action. A physician who fails to remove sponges following an episiotomy resulting in no more than a foul odor is not subject to liability where no causal link between an act of negligence and legally cognizable injury is established. Order granting motion for nonsuit affirmed. *Gregorio v. Zeluck,* 451 Pa. Super. 154, 678 A.2d 810 (1996).

Spontaneous abortion

Tenant suffered spontaneous abortion of seventeen-week fetus due to collapse of apartment. Actions for wrongful death, survivorship, and loss of consortium not maintainable. *McCaskill v. Philadelphia Housing Authority,* 419 Pa. Super. 313, 615 A.2d 382.

Sports injuries

Plaintiff brought suit against the city and sports club after he broke his leg in a flag football league game when he tripped and fell in a depression on a field owned by the city of Philadelphia. The trial court entered summary judgment in favor of the Defendants. The Commonwealth Court affirmed that the flag football club, by using the field once a week and painting lines on it, did not provide evidence of possession or control to hold it liable for the Plaintiff's injuries. *Davis v. City of Philadelphia,* 987 A.2d 1274 (Pa. Cmwlth. 2010).

Plaintiff golfer filed suit against another golfer for injuries suffered when he was struck in the face by a golf ball. The trial Court granted summary judgment in favor of Defendant. The Superior Court reversed and remanded holding there was a genuine issue of material fact as to whether the Defendant owed a duty of care to the Plaintiff as the Defendant teed off prior to the Plaintiff returning to their tee box after trying to determine if the group in front of them was out of range of the Defendant's tee shot. *Zeidman v. Fisher,* 980 A.2d 637 (Pa. Super. 2009).

A hockey player, in an adult no-check league, brought a claim against another player after he was checked into the boards and suffered injuries. The Superior Court reversed the trial court's grant of summary judgment for the defendant. The Court held that the applicable standard of care to recover for personal injuries suffered in an adult sports league due to a violation of a sports league's rules is reckless or intentional conduct. *Archibald v. Kemble,* 971 A.2d 513 (Pa. Super. 2009).

Amateur softball player brought suit against an amateur softball association for breach of duty for failing to recommend that a helmet be worn during games. The appellate court affirmed the trial court's ruling that under the no duty rule the softball association had no duty to warn of a risk inherent in softball. *Craig v. Amateur Softball Association of America,* 951 A.2d 372 (Pa. Super. 2008).

Inherent danger of attending a baseball game is that you may be hit by a foul ball and injured as happened to plaintiff. Sports team had no duty to protect plaintiff

Sports injuries

from inherent danger of foul ball. ***Pakett v. The Phillies, L.P.,* 871 A.2d 304 (Pa. Cmwlth. 2005).**

Plaintiff filed suit against softball pitching coach alleging negligence for teaching an illegal and dangerous pitching style. Summary judgment in favor of pitching coach reversed based on expert reports provided by plaintiff in support of her contentions of negligence. 42 Pa.C.S. § 8332.1 which establishes negligence standard for volunteer managers, coaches, umpires, referees or non-profit organizations only applies to volunteers, not paid personnel. ***Reeves v. Middletown Athletic Association,* 866 A.2d 1115 (Pa. Super. 2005).**

Summary judgment in favor of volunteer fire department affirmed against child who was injured by a softball hit beyond the boundaries of a softball into a display area near the field. The condition of the fire department's real estate was not itself the cause of the injury, it merely facilitated the injury by a third party. ***Gaylord v. Morris Township Fire Department,* 853 A.2d 1112 (Pa. Cmwlth. 2004).**

Plaintiff who was injured by a hockey puck brought suit against the hockey facility owner alleging negligence in design. Defendant's summary judgment motion granted on basis that it owed no duty to plaintiff to prevent injuries sustained by a common, frequent and expected occurrence at a hockey game and plaintiff had failed to show that some aspect of the design or operation of the facility departed from normal standards or customs. ***Petrongola v. Comcast-Spectacor, L.P.* 789 A.2d 204 (Pa. Super. 2001).**

Plaintiff was injured when struck in the face by a foul ball at a baseball game. The Superior Court affirmed the trial court's decision to sustain the defendant's preliminary objections for failure to state a cause of action under the "no-duty" theory applied to baseball and other sports venues where a patron is injured in circumstances commonly understood to entail some risk of harm. ***Romeo v. The Pittsburgh Associates,* 787 A.2d 1027 (Pa. Super. 2001).**

Plaintiff college baseball player sustained severe injury to knee when he tripped in a depression in center field while fielding a ball. In suit against college which maintained field, summary judgment in favor of college sustained on appeal where plaintiff admitted that he was aware of risks of rutted field, voluntarily consented to playing despite knowledge, and was injured by the same risks of which he was previously aware. ***Zachardy v. Geneva College,* 733 A.2d 648 (Pa. Super. 1999).**

Minor child injured by what may have been a part of a goal post lying "on" city-owned park property. Summary judgment in favor of city reversed because city may have been negligent in care, custody and control of real property for failure to remove the dangerous condition "on" the property. Local agency liability for negligent care, custody or control of real property does not require the instrumentality causing the harm to be "of" the real estate in the sense of being affixed to it. ***Martin v. City of Philadelphia,* 696 A.2d 909 (Pa. Cmwlth. 1997).**

Sports injuries

Spectator injured when struck by bat weight brought to game by player. Held: owner of weight not liable. Weight used by other player without permission. ***Ptak v. Masontown Men's Softball League*, 414 Pa. Super. 425, 607 A.2d 297.**

Basketball player injured when he stepped into hole at city-owned recreation center. City immune under Recreation Use of Land and Water Act. ***Walsh v. City of Philadelphia*, 126 Pa. Cmwlth. 27, 558 A.2d 192.**

Injury to child in stickball game was not the result of negligence when game was played in a normal, reasonable manner. ***Johnson by Johnson v. Walker*, 376 Pa. Super. 291, 545 A.2d 947.**

Student injured sliding into second base during high school baseball game. Judgment on pleadings in favor of school district reversed. Issue remained as to whether base was realty or personalty. Plaintiff permitted to amend to more specifically allege details of how base was attached to ground. ***Beardell v. Western Wayne School District*, 91 Pa. Cmwlth. 348, 496 A.2d 1373.**

Non-jury verdict, $83,190 to minor; $1,810 to parents. Minor plaintiff, 5th grade 11 year old student injured in school floor hockey game—organized extracurricular activity. Struck in mouth by hockey stick severing five teeth. Held: negligent not to supply mouth guards. Requests made were denied by school board. Minor plaintiff unaware of injuries in previous games. Presumption that minor incapable of contributory negligence not rebutted. Affirmed. ***Berman v. Philadelphia Board of Education*, 310 Pa. Super. 153, 456 A.2d 545.**

Nine-year old, playing softball in school yard, struck in head with bat. Not organized school activity. Alleged improperly painted markings on ground required catcher to be too close to plate. Held: plaintiff, a public invitee. School district said painting done for ballgame with no bat. Summary judgment for school district, reversed. Jury issue. ***Bersani v. School District of Philadelphia*, 310 Pa. Super. 1, 456 A.2d 151.**

High school football player sustained severe eye injury in extracurricular football game which was encouraged by coaches. Plaintiff found to have assumed risk of injury. ***Rutter v. Northeastern Beaver Co. School*, 283 Pa. Super. 155, 423 A.2d 1035.**

Patron at ball game injured in concourse area while walking to food stand. Not an assumed risk. Verdict of $125,000 based upon negligent design which allowed batted balls into this area where patrons might not expect them. Superior Court reversal overruled. ***Jones v. Three Rivers Management*, 483 Pa. 75, 394 A.2d 546.**

Minor plaintiff, a golf caddie, struck by golf ball while on defendant's course—no recovery—no negligence shown—assumed risk and probably covered by Workmen's Compensation. ***Taylor v. Churchill Valley Country Club*, 425 Pa. 266, 228 A.2d 768.**

Sprinkler system

Plaintiff struck by an object which jury could infer came from a concession at a fair using balls for public to throw at objects for prizes—nonsuit improper. ***Devenney v. North Franklin Twp. V.F. Dept.,* 209 Pa. Super. 378, 228 A.2d 61.**

Sprinkler system

Plaintiff insurance carrier covered its assured for damages by water—claim paid and company subrogated—damage resulted from defects in sprinkler system which allegedly existed prior to the date of leasing—exculpatory clause in lease held not to necessarily relieve landlord from responsibility—nonsuit improper. ***Employers L.A.C. Ltd. v. Greenville Business Mens Association,* 423 Pa. 288, 423 A.2d 620.**

Plaintiffs were tenants of first four floors of building owned by one of defendants—rental agents also defendants—a sprinkler pipe broke as a result of freezing on fifth floor and damaged plaintiff's property—exculpatory clause in lease agreements held not to exculpate agents as release clause did not expressly include negligence prior to leasing. ***Kotwasinski et al. v. Rasner et al.,* 436 Pa. 32, 258 A.2d 865.**

Stabbing

Plaintiff stabbed in supermarket parking lot. Evidence of previous crimes within store and store policy to limit cash in registers. Verdict for plaintiff affirmed. ***Murphy v. Penn Fruit,* 274 Pa. Super. 427, 418 A.2d 480.**

Stage

Plaintiff injured when she fell from temporary stage. Defendant's negligence not substantial factor in injury. Order for new trial reversed and jury verdict reinstated. ***Arcidiacono v. Timeless Towns of America, Inc.,* 363 Pa. Super. 521, 526 A.2d 804.**

Stairs

Plaintiffs brought negligence action against Defendant after they were injured in a fall when an exterior stairway gave out at the Defendant's facility due to rusted bolts. A jury found in favor of the Plaintiffs. On appeal the Superior Court affirmed holding that the Defendant owed a duty to the Plaintiffs to inspect its exterior stairway for signs of failure. ***Gillingham v. Consol Energy, Inc.,* 2012 Pa. Super. 133 (Pa. Super. 2012).**

Debris and dead cat which had accumulated on steps leading into basement of building owned by Philadelphia Housing Authority were not conditions that "derived, originated or had as their source" the municipal realty itself so as to fall within the real estate exception to governmental immunity. ***Lingo v. Philadelphia Housing Authority,* 820 A.2d 859 (Pa. Cmwlth. 2003).**

Plaintiff wife, school book salesperson, was injured when she attempted to gain entrance to school building which had been constructed in 1902. Plaintiff complained that entrance was not in compliance with current building codes and that noncompliance created an unsafe condition that caused her to fall and become injured. Trial court prohibited any testimony from plaintiff's building code compliance expert reasoning that school, because of its age, was not required to be in compliance with current building codes and to allow that issue to be raised to jury would confuse negligence issue. Additionally, photographs and plans of area in question were adequate to allow jury to make its own determination of whether landing and entrance were unsafe. Trial court's instructions as to defendant's duties to plaintiff were also adequate where they correctly described the plaintiff's status as business invitee and school's responsibilities to her as invitee. ***Kiehner v. School District of Philadelphia*, 712 A.2d 830 (Pa. Cmwlth. 1998).**

Plaintiff who was injured when he fell on defective or missing city-owned and maintained steps presented proof that city employees cleaned or shoveled damaged steps four or five times per year and that those employees were obligated to report defects or problems with steps. Plaintiff also offered credible evidence that there was a continuous deterioration of the steps from the date of the last repair more than one and one-half years before plaintiff's injury; therefore, city had actual or constructive notice of defective condition. City's defense of Political Subdivision Tort Claims Act was inadequate in light of plaintiff's evidence of defective condition of steps and notice to city. ***Ellis v. City of Pittsburgh*, 703 A.2d 593 (Pa. Cmwlth. 1997).**

"Dangerous condition of real estate" exception to governmental immunity was fact question for jury. Summary judgment in favor of defendant reversed. ***Berhane v. SEPTA*, 166 Pa. Cmwlth. 196, 646 A.2d 1268 (1994).**

Resident in building owned by housing authority fell in unlighted stairway. Debris left in stairway by third person. Held: cause of fall question of fact. ***Floyd v. Philadelphia Housing Authority*, 154 Pa. Cmwlth. 303, 623 A.2d 901.**

Employee who fell down stairs leading to employer's office brought action against owner and builder of office building. Defendants not liable. ***Dilauro v. One Bala Avenue Associates*, 419 Pa. Super. 191, 615 A.2d 90.**

Pedestrian injured when he fell on stairs owned and maintained by municipal transportation authority. Former provision of Municipal Transportation Authority Act requiring notice to Authority within six months of incident, held to be constitutional and a bar to recovery if not met. ***James v. SEPTA*, 505 Pa. 137, 477 A.2d 1302.**

Fall down steps in friend's home, while looking for restroom. Entered wrong door; fell as door opened onto cellar steps. Error to grant compulsory nonsuit. New trial ordered. ***Fisher v. Findlay*, 319 Pa. Super. 214, 465 A.2d 1306.**

Tenant stepped onto wooden stairway and fell through onto pavement. For jury on issues of §17.6 of Restatement (2d) Property, and issue of implied warranty of habitability. ***Rivera v. Selfton Home Repairs*, 294 Pa. Super. 41, 439 A.2d 739.**

Wife plaintiff fell on an outside flight of steps while descending same—evidence of defective condition of steps—only means of access to place of employment—verdict for plaintiff sustained—motion for new trial and judgment *n.o.v.* refused. ***Naponic v. Carlton Motel, Inc.*, 221 Pa. Super. 287, 289 A.2d 473.**

Stalled cars

Plaintiff entered defendant's store to purchase meat and on leaving fell on steps—evidence that sawdust, wood chips and fine gravel were on steps—no handrail—jury disagreed—judgment entered on whole record—reversed on appeal—matter for jury. ***Kuminkoski v. Daum,* 429 Pa. 494, 240 A.2d 524.**

Stalled cars

Plaintiff a passenger in car that became disabled at night, in middle of and perpendicular to road. Plaintiff struck while standing near center of road, at front of car attempting to wave on traffic. Plaintiff found 70% at fault. Proper to refuse charge on "discovered peril" doctrine under facts here. No evidence to indicate that defendant knew or should have known of plaintiff's perilous position. Defense verdict affirmed. ***Emerick v. Carson,* 325 Pa. Super. 308, 472 A.2d 1133.**

Vehicles in which plaintiffs were passengers stalled while turning and was struck by oncoming car. Snowing heavily. Driver of oncoming car busy wiping inside of windshield due to inadequate defroster. Verdict against both drivers. ***Poltorak v. Sandy,* 236 Pa. Super. 355, 345 A.2d 201.**

Plaintiff's car stalled in intersection—her situation was apparent or should have been to defendant's bus driver when he was 160 feet away—driver continued on and collided with plaintiff's machine—verdict for defendant—new trial granted on ground that trial judge should have charged on the theory of wanton misconduct. ***Williams v. Phila. Trans. Co.,* 219 Pa. Super. 134, 280 A.2d 612.**

Plaintiff's decedent had been a passenger in a car which stalled in highway—decedent got out to help push car to a nearby gas station—at night—decedent struck by defendant's car coming from rear while he was pushing car—for jury—decedent could not be said to be contributorily negligent as a matter of law. ***Schofield v. Scott,* 442 Pa. 642, 277 A.2d 143.**

Defendant D was pushing stalled car of defendant H—at top of grade D detached his car and H proceeded approximately 175 feet by gravity and then collided with plaintiffs—verdict for defendants—error to grant a new trial as to D—judgment on verdict for him ordered by Supreme Court. ***Miller v. Duncan,* 420 Pa. 249, 215 A.2d 906.**

Standard of care

Paraplegic sued medical center for pressure wounds incurred during his rehabilitation stay allegedly caused by substandard nursing care. Trial court granted compulsory nonsuit against Plaintiff due to lack of causation after the Plaintiff presented a registered nurse to testify regarding the relevant standard of care without presenting a doctor. The Superior Court reversed. The Pennsylvania Supreme Court affirmed the Superior Court holding that a properly qualified nurse could testify as to medical causation under the Professional Nursing Law. The proper test for a nurse to testify regarding causation and the relevant nursing standard of care was whether the witness had specialized knowledge on the subject of testimony as set forth in *Miller v. Brass Rail Tavern, Inc.*, 541 Pa. 474, 480, 664 A.2d 525, 528 (1995). ***Freed v. Geisinger Medical Center,* 971 A.2d 1202 (Pa. 2009).**

Standard of care

Paraplegic sued medical center for pressure wounds incurred during his rehabilitation stay by allegedly substandard nursing care. The court reversed the trial court's decision to bar a nurse from testifying as an expert witness as to a breach of standard of care in treating the plaintiff. The court held that a qualified non-medical expert could give a medical opinion as long as the witness had sufficient specialized knowledge to aid the jury in determining the facts of the case. *Freed v. Geisinger Medical Center,* **910 A.2d 68 (Pa. Super. 2006).**

Plaintiff filed a negligence suit based upon a doctor's failure to follow up with the plaintiff after learning the result of an abnormal CT scan. The court held that the plaintiff was required to present an expert report on the standard of care to be used and to show that the standard was breached proximately causing the injury to plaintiff. The standard of care of a family practitioner who verbally advised of an abnormal CT scan was not within the comprehension or experience of ordinary persons. *Papach v. Mercy Suburban Hospital,* **887 A.2d 233 (Pa. Super. 2005).**

In automobile accident, testimony by State Trooper with familiarity of truck inspection procedures properly disallowed as to standard of care required by truck driver. Comparative Negligence Act requires that jury apportion liability between plaintiff and all defendants against whom recovery is sought. Trial court's bifurcation to allow apportionment of liability between fewer than all defendants reversed. *Christiansen v. Silfies,* **446 Pa. Super. 464, 667 A.2d 396 (1995).**

Plaintiff who contracted AIDS following transfusion of tainted blood filed suit against treating physicians and family physician for medical malpractice. Claim against one defendant dismissed for plaintiff's failure to establish through medical testimony that defendant's actions deviated from good and acceptable medical standards. Proof of compliance with medical standard of care need not be expressed in precisely the language used to annunciate the legal standard. Physician not required to obtain patient's informed consent before blood transfusion which was administered separately from a surgical procedure. *Hoffman v. Brandywine Hospital,* **443 Pa. Super. 245, 661 A.2d 397 (1995).**

There is but one standard of care in a negligence action which is reasonable care. Reasonable care will vary based on the circumstances and instrumentalities in each situation. Action by customer against garage and mechanic for injuries sustained when gasoline exploded after being poured into carburetor did not warrant a jury instruction on a standard of care higher than reasonable care. Judgment for defendants affirmed. *Stewart v. Motts,* **539 Pa. 596, 654 A.2d 535 (1995).**

Standard of care for a child is the exercise of ordinary care appropriate for a child. Driver and Borough not liable where child who darts out into street found seventy percent negligent. *Smith v. Stribling,* **168 Pa. Cmwlth. 188, 649 A.2d 1003 (1994).**

Minor plaintiff injured alighting from trampoline in neighbor's backyard. Defense verdict reversed. Held: error to exclude evidence of industry standard on safe use of both recreational and instructional trampolines. New trial ordered. *Walheim v. Kirkpatrick,* **305 Pa. Super. 590, 451 A.2d 1033.**

Staph infection

Jury verdict $1,000,000—malpractice action; $10,000—auto negligence action. Rear-end collision—injuries to neck and back. Low back surgery. Infection followed—neomycin antibiotic used allegedly caused kidney failure, partial paralysis of lower limbs and total hearing loss. Could walk on crutches at time of trial. Verdict affirmed. Evidence of negligent administration of neomycin. Hospital held in case because the resident-employee actively participated in neomycin therapy and made some dosage decisions. Charge on agency of residents upheld. Residents held to standard of specialist, not general practitioner. *Pratt v. Stein,* **298 Pa. Super. 92, 444 A.2d 674.**

Auto-truck accident. Court declined to adopt higher standard of care for truck drivers. Ordinary charge on negligence upheld. *Fredericks v. Castora,* **241 Pa. Super. 211, 360 A.2d 696.**

Staph infection

Failure to follow Department of Health standards that suggest 48 hour limit for catheterization is not negligence *per se*. Medical malpractice causation requires proof of increased risk of harm. Causation is question for trier of fact where artificial hip replacement patient developed staph infection from catheterization. *Edwards v. Brandywine Hospital,* **438 Pa. Super. 673, 652 A.2d 1382 (1995).**

State-of-the-art

Plaintiff injured back while lifting 450 lb. barrel with drum truck made by defendant more than 20 years earlier. Claimed defective design put strain on user's back. Charge on "state of art" defense held in error. Reasonableness of what defendant should have known about the then "state of art" in the industry not the test. New trial ordered. *Carrecter v. Colson Equipment Co.,* **346 Pa. Super. 95, 499 A.2d 326.**

Station platform

Summary judgment in favor of defendant affirmed because plaintiff's allegations that she was injured by an unknown assailant on SEPTA platform do not constitute defect of the land itself so as to constitute waiver of sovereign immunity. *Warnecki v. SEPTA,* **689 A.2d 1023 (Pa. Cmwlth. 1997).**

Suit against SEPTA and City for injuries sustained by plaintiff as a result of mugging which occurred in subway concourse. Held: complaint did state cause of action against City as possessor of land and within exception to Political Subdivision Tort Claims Act. *Johnson v. SEPTA,* **91 Pa. Cmwlth. 587, 498 A.2d 22.**

Statute of Repose

Plaintiff's decedent was killed when he was struck by the door to a coke oven battery. Issue before the court was whether the door, which was of massive size and rolled on wheels, was a fixture and therefore subject to the 12 year statute of repose or personalty subject to suit for defective design or construction. Held: door was not a fixture and 12 year statute of repose did not apply. *Vargo v. Koppers,* **715 A.2d 423 (1998).**

Statutory employment

Immense coke oven door installed 35 years prior to accident which caused plaintiff's decedent's death and which is movable by means of wheels on tracks is still an "improvement" under statute of repose and so action by coke oven employee is extinguished. Trial court order denying motion for judgment *n.o.v.* reversed. ***Vargo v. Koppers Co., Inc.*, 452 Pa. Super. 275, 681 A.2d 815 (1996).**

In homeowner's action against gas utility for damages to home following gas explosion, gas utility's effort to join as additional defendant original contractor who performed allegedly negligent work was time-barred. Twelve-year statute of repose is not unconstitutional. Order granting judgment on pleadings in favor of additional defendants affirmed. ***Columbia Gas of PA, Inc. v. Carl E. Baker, Inc.*, 446 Pa. Super. 481, 667 A.2d 404 (1995).**

Statutory employment

Plaintiff subcontractor's employee brought negligence action against general contractor for injuries suffered in a fall at the work site. Trial court entered judgment on the verdict in favor of the Plaintiff. The Superior Court, on appeal, held that the general contractor was entitled to statutory immunity under the Workers' Compensation Act based upon the statutory employer doctrine. ***Sheard v. J.J. DeLuca Co., Inc.*, 92 A.3d 68 (Pa. Super. 2014).**

Plaintiff subcontractor brought negligence claim for injuries suffered in a fall against general contractor after he was injured when he drove a scissor lift into a hole in the floor at the construction site. A jury found in favor of the Plaintiff. The Superior Court affirmed holding that as the jury found the Plaintiff was an independent contractor and the Defendant was not immune based upon the statutory employer defense. ***Patton v. Worthington Associates, Inc.*, 43 A.3d 479 (Pa. Super. 2012).**

Summary judgment against employee of subcontractor sustained after he filed negligence action against property owner and general contractor who was afforded immunity as statutory employer. ***Emery v. Leavesly McCollum*, 725 A.2d 807 (Pa. Super. 1999).**

General contractor is "statutory employer" of employee of subcontractor and so is immune from suit for negligence under Workers' Compensation Act. ***McCarthy v. Lepore*, 724 A.2d 938 (Pa. Super. 1998).**

Summary judgment in favor of general contractor who was sued for negligence by worker injured on jobsite was affirmed by Superior and Supreme Courts on basis that general contractor was a statutory employer under Workers' Compensation Act even though the subcontractor who hired worker carried his own workers' compensation insurance. ***Fonner v. Shandon, Inc.*, 724 A.2d 903 (Pa. 1999).**

School laborer injured when he fell through skydome on roof. Summary judgment for defendants affirmed. Skydome properly an improvement to real property subject to strict 12 year statute of repose. ***Catanzaro v. Wasco Products*, 339 Pa. Super. 481, 489 A.2d 262.**

Steel cable

Employee of company which had contract with Bell Telephone to work on phone lines injured in fall. Held: Bell, under facts here, was statutory employer. ***Wiltrout v. Circle Mobile Home,* 293 Pa. Super. 131, 437 A.2d 1240.**

An employee of a carpenter subcontractor injured by reason of improper shoring—general contractor had employed a subcontractor to do excavation work—this subcontractor employed a highlift truck and operator—Held: verdict solely against excavating subcontractor proper as the operator was not a borrowed or loaned employee—whether general contractor was a statutory employer not passed upon appeal. ***Hamler v. Waldron et al.,* 445 Pa. 262, 284 A.2d 725.**

Steel cable

Motorcyclist riding on private property ran into a 1-1/2 inch steel cable strung across roadway to deter trespassers. Admitted, plaintiff was trespasser. Duty to trespasser is not to act in reckless disregard for safety. Landowner knew dirt bikes traversed property. New trial ordered. Submission of case to jury on negligence theory—misleading. Court questions viability of doctrine of landowner immunity. ***Antonace v. Ferri Contracting Co.,* 320 Pa. Super. 519, 467 A.2d 833.**

Steel truss

Steel truss being transported by defendant's vehicle struck rear of plaintiff's milk wagon—contact slight—property damage not in excess of $20 to $25—plaintiff alleged excessive personal injuries—verdict for defendant not disturbed. ***Brodhead v. Brentwood Ornamental Iron Co.,* 435 Pa. 7, 255 A.2d 120.**

Sterilization

Although entire complaint arising out of birth of Down's Syndrome child and sterilization was inartfully drafted, two distinct claims were asserted: one for wrongful birth and one for performance of sterilization procedure without informed consent. Plaintiff's proposed amendments to complaint did not create new cause of action but clarified and strengthened claim based on lack of informed consent and, therefore, should have been allowed. Order granting judgment on the pleadings and denying leave to amend reversed. ***Sejpal v. Corson, McKinley,* 445 Pa. Super. 427, 665 A.2d 1198 (1995).**

Patient brought malpractice action against physician and hospital for unsuccessful sterilization. Patient entitled to collect damages for costs related to childbirth but not for expenses in raising child. ***Butler v. Rolling Hills Hospital,* 400 Pa. Super. 141, 582 A.2d 1384.**

Negligent performance of sterilization operation would allow recovery for costs of pregnancy and delivery. However, Court holds as matter of law that benefits of joy, companionship and affection of normal healthy child outweigh costs of raising child. ***Mason v. Western Pennsylvania Hospital*, 499 Pa. 484, 453 A.2d 974.**

Stick

Six-year old injured by five-year old who swung a stick at him. Summary judgment for defendant affirmed. Conclusive presumption that five-year old incapable of negligence. ***Dunn v. Teti*, 280 Pa. Super. 399, 421 A.2d 782.**

Stillborn child

Injuries received by child while *en ventre sa mere* formerly could form basis for survival or wrongful death actions as maintained only on behalf of child born alive. Live birth now held no longer to be a limiting prerequisite to maintenance of such action. Case remanded for further proceedings. ***Amadio v. Levin*, 509 Pa. 199, 501 A.2d 1085.**

Suit on behalf of stillborn child who died as a result of injuries received *en ventre sa mere* in auto accident, dismissed. Infant must be born alive in order to sustain a claim. ***Scott v. Kapp*, 494 Pa. 487, 431 A.2d 959.**

Dismissal of death action brought by parents of stillborn child who died *in utero* as a result of auto accident. No cause of action. ***Scott v. Kopp*, 261 Pa. Super. 89, 395 A.2d 956.**

Stilts

Summary judgment reversed where plaintiff insulation installer on stilts held not to have assumed the risk of slipping on construction debris left at job site by defendants. Assumption of risk should only preclude recovery where it is beyond question that the plaintiff voluntarily and knowingly proceeded in the face of an obvious and dangerous condition. ***Barrett v. Fredavid Builders, Inc.*, 454 Pa. Super. 162, 685 A.2d 129 (1996).**

Stipulated facts

Plaintiff pedestrian injured by impact of police car is entitled to reversal of nonsuit where evidence indicates that all elements of negligence claim were established at trial. Trial court's determination that plaintiff failed to prove that his injury was permanent or of a serious nature so as to impair a bodily function is reversible abuse of discretion. Nonsuit removed; remanded for new trial. ***Boyer v. City of Philadelphia*, 692 A.2d 259 (Pa. Cmwlth. 1997).**

Stolen vehicles

Police officer severely injured by delinquent minor driving stolen car filed suit against auto dealer/owner who had left locked car on auto auction lot. Summary judgment in favor of auto dealer and auto auction affirmed based on lack of duty to police officer. ***Roche v. Ugly Duckling Car Sales, Inc.*, 879 A.2d 785 (Pa. Super. 2005).**

Defendant insurance company had acquired title to a previously stolen vehicle which it had insured. After sale of the recovered car to an auction house, plaintiff, who purchased the car from a subsequent dealer, was arrested for driving a stolen vehicle because "stolen" status of title had not be revoked by police department. In suit by plaintiff against insurance company; held, no duty of insurance company

Stomach-stapling

to plaintiff to clear title to vehicle. *Salvatore v. State Farm Mutual Automobile Insurance Company*, 869 A.2d 511 (Pa. Super. 2005).

Jury verdict as to liability only in favor of defendant used car dealership affirmed. Plaintiff injured by driver of stolen car failed to state a cause of action, where sole allegation of negligence was that dealership employees left keys in newly delivered vehicles in violation of unattended motor vehicle section of the Pennsylvania Vehicle Code. *Santarlas v. Leaseway Motorcar Transport Company*, 456 Pa. Super. 34, 689 A.2d 311 (1997).

Transportation authority not liable under operation of motor vehicle exception to governmental immunity where bus involved in accident with plaintiff was driven by unauthorized user and not employee of transportation authority. Summary judgment affirmed. *Pana v. SEPTA*, ___ Pa. Cmwlth. ___, 657 A.2d 1320 (1995).

Action by passenger of stolen pizza delivery vehicle after vehicle crashed into pole dismissed against delivery driver and his employer for plaintiff's failure to establish causation. *Matos v. Rivera*, 436 Pa. Super. 509, 648 A.2d 337 (1994).

Defendant's car stolen from its parked position—while being operated by thieves and being chased by police struck the rear of car in which plaintiffs were located—plaintiffs contended that car was not locked and ignition on—nonsuit properly entered. *Ferkler v. Rosenstein*, 437 Pa. 574, 260 A.2d 738.

Uninsured pedestrian injured when struck by stolen automobile. Held: insurer of owner of stolen automobile liable for uninsured motorist benefits. *Ector v. Motorist Insurance Companies*, 391 Pa. Super. 458, 571 A.2d 457.

Plaintiff struck and injured by an automobile driven by a 14 year old boy—car had been stolen from an airport limousine parking lot—majority of Superior Court felt that there existed no liability and that case was ruled by *Line v. Chestnut Motors, Inc.* (421 Pa. 26). *Canavin v. Wilmington Trans. Co.*, 208 Pa. Super. 506, 223 A.2d 902.

Car left with defendant for repairs—left outside place of business double parked—stolen by a stranger who injured plaintiff while operating same—no liability on defendant. *Liney v. Chestnut Motors, Inc.*, 421 Pa. 26, 218 A.2d 336.

Stomach-stapling

Patient who suffered complications after stomach stapling surgery brought action against physician and nurse based on lack of informed consent. Nurse not liable. Negligence theory of informed consent not recognized. *Foflygen v. R. Zemel, M.D. (PC)*, 420 Pa. Super. 18, 615 A.2d 1345.

Stone mason

General contractor defendant engaged other defendant to do certain specialized stone work in a home improvement operation—subcontractor specialized in this type of work, was paid a lump sum, furnished his own tools and equipment and own employees—general contractor interested only in result—Held: relationship was that of independent contractorship and general contractor not responsible for operation of a car by subcontractor—Superior Court reversed. ***Cox v. Caeti,* 444 Pa. 143, 279 A.2d 756.**

Stones

Plaintiffs injured by rocks thrown at their cars by unknown persons from bridge over State highway. History of similar incidents alleged. Held: "condition" within terms of 42 Pa. C.S.A. §5110(a)(4). Transferred to Common Pleas for trial. ***Mistecka v. Commonwealth,* 46 Pa. Cmwlth. 267, 408 A.2d 159.**

Plaintiff injured while passenger on elevated-subway by rock throwing teenager. Evidence by cashier from another station that she had heard that station where incident occurred was dangerous held to be inadmissible hearsay. Verdict for plaintiff reversed. ***Carswell v. SEPTA,* 259 Pa. Super. 167, 393 A.2d 770.**

Minor plaintiff struck in eye by stone thrown by minor defendant during horseplay. Issue of assumption of risk properly submitted to jury. Verdict for defendant. ***McIntyre v. Cusick,* 247 Pa. Super. 354, 372 A.2d 864.**

Minor plaintiff injured by a stone probably thrown by one of additional defendants—contractor and land owner sued—defendants bringing in 12 boys who were throwing stones—court below in error in sustaining preliminary objections on ground not averred which boy had thrown stone—matter controlled by Section 433B (3) of Restatement (2d) Torts—all defendants could be sued—leave to amend should have been given. ***Snoparsky v. Baer,* 439 Pa. 140, 266 A.2d 707.**

Stop, Look, and Listen Doctrine

Decedent operator with two passengers approached a grade crossing and collided with a locomotive on crossing—clear evidence of failure to stop, look and listen—guests familiar with crossing—verdict for defendant railroad and estate of operator proper—error to grant a new trial as to estate of operator. ***Tomasek v. Monongahela Rwy. Co.,* 427 Pa. 371, 235 A.2d 359.**

Stopped traffic

Plaintiff's decedent killed when he struck stopped traffic on I-95 three miles in advance of a construction site. Plaintiff alleged that PennDOT was negligent in failing to place warning signs in advance of location where cars backed up and stopped. Plaintiff also alleged PennDOT's failure to erect signs was negligence *per se*. Held: expert testimony as to need for advance signs three miles from construction site was required. PennDOT regulations that were silent on exact placement of warning signs could not be basis for claim of negligence *per se*, if PennDOT did not place the signs where plaintiff thought they should have been. ***Young v. PennDOT*, 744 A.2d 1276 (Pa. 2000).**

Plaintiffs appeal from grant of summary judgment to defendant PennDOT which was based on plaintiff's failure to procure expert report to support their claim that PennDOT was negligent in not placing warning signs in advance of construction zone. PennDOT argued successfully that it was immune from suit under Sovereign Immunity Act in that placement of warning signs was not necessary to insure

Stopping

safe condition of real estate for its intended use. Reversed by Commonwealth Court. Necessity of warning signs advising of stopped traffic on interstate highway in advance of traffic construction is within everyday knowledge of jury and so does not require expert testimony. Whether lack of warning signs, as described, constitutes dangerous condition of state maintained roadway for its intended purpose is proper question for jury. ***Young v. Com., Dept. of Transp.*, 714 A.2d 475 (Pa. Cmwlth. 1998).**

Stopping

Plaintiff was injured when he fell on a bus that stopped suddenly. Trial court properly granted compulsory nonsuit when evidence of severity of stop failed to show that the stop had the "extraordinarily disturbing effect on other passengers" required to allow the case to go to the jury. ***Meussner v. Port Authority of Allegheny County*, 745 A.2d 719 (Pa. Cmwlth. 2000).**

Plaintiff, a passenger in defendant's bus, was injured by its sudden stopping—evidence that bus was traveling at an excessive speed in a congested area—sudden stop as the result of a truck cutting in front of bus—driver of bus did not testify—matter for the jury. ***Connolly v. Phila. Trans. Co.*, 420 Pa. 280, 216 A.2d 60.**

Storm Water Management Act

250 employees of a tire manufacturing plant sued landowners whose property abutted the plant property for loss of wages and benefits during repair and reconstruction of the plant necessitated by storm water runoff redirected by construction performed by one or more of the adjoining landowners. Held that the Economic Loss Doctrine provides that no cause of action exists in negligence absent physical injury or property damage. Recovery of purely economic losses alleged by plaintiffs are not recoverable. ***Adams v. Copper Beach Townhome Communities, L.P.*, 816 A.2d 301 (Pa. Super. 2003).**

Land owner brought action against city for damage caused by backfilling and regrading adjacent parcel of land. City not liable under Storm Water Management Act. ***Bahor v. City of Pittsburgh*, 158 Pa. Cmwlth. 150, 631 A.2d 731.**

Street railways

Driver an passenger injured in accident caused by streetcar tracks. City iable. Evidence of prior accident and subsequent repairs admissible. ***Fernandez v. City of Pittsburgh*, 164 Pa. Cmwlth. 622, 643 A.2d 1176.**

Passenger on trolley injured in collision with automobiles brought action against insurance company under Financial Responsibility Law. Insurance company found not liable. Trolley on tracks not motor vehicle within statute. ***Ellis v. SEPTA*, 524 Pa. 398, 573 A.2d 216.**

Plaintiff injured alighting from trolley when struck by passing auto. Verdict in favor of plaintiff but city absolved. Reversed issue of city's duty to erect traffic island at dangerous stops should have been for jury. ***Litwinko v. SEPTA*, 267 Pa. Super. 541, 407 A.2d 42.**

Plaintiff waiting on subway platform when struck by subway. Did not remember accident at all. Train was a work train and did not stop at station, and contrary to rules did not slow or signal. Verdict for plaintiff affirmed. ***Canery v. SEPTA*, 267 Pa. Super. 382, 406 A.2d 1093.**

69 year old woman injured while entering terminal of defendant when door let go by another patron struck her knee. Whether plaintiff was a passenger should have been left to jury. ***Kiely v. SEPTA*, 485 Pa. Super. 205, 401 A.2d 366.**

Plaintiff injured while passenger on elevated-subway by rock throwing teenager. Duty of care proscribed by §344 of Restatement (2d) Torts. Reliance on local people not in itself enough as a matter of law. Plaintiff's verdict reversed on evidentiary issues. ***Carswell v. SEPTA*, 259 Pa. Super. 167, 393 A.2d 770.**

Trackless trolley struck open door of parked vehicle while turning. Point of contact with rear of trolley. Operator must be aware that rear of vehicle can be dangerous while making turn. §290 of Restatement (2d) Torts. ***Lebesco v. SEPTA*, 251 Pa. Super. 415, 380 A.2d 848.**

Action brought on last day of two year period against SEPTA, et al for damages allegedly arising from defective trackage—failure to comply with Metropolitan Trans. Authority Act (66 P.S. §2036) by giving prescribed notice within 6 months—summary judgment granted on appeal. ***Micalizzi v. Darby Borough et al.*, 222 Pa. Super. 251, 294 A.2d 779.**

Motorman of defendant company left street car unattended—a thief started car and damaged plaintiff—traction company held responsible by court below and action affirmed by majority without opinion. ***Dolan v. Phila. Trans. Co.*, 217 Pa. Super. 368, 271 A.2d 881.**

Plaintiff was a passenger in defendant's street car—she testified that she was struck by door which opened prematurely before car stopped—case for jury—error to enter nonsuit. ***Whitley v. Phila. Trans. Co.*, 211 Pa. Super. 288, 234 A.2d 922.**

Streptococcus infection

Plaintiff parents of minor who acquired streptococcus infection soon after birth commenced action against medical care providers and hospitals by praecipe for writ of summons and began discovery. After 16 months of discovery and motions, and before a complaint had been filed, parents requested permission to discontinue action without prejudice so they could have time to engage in additional discovery, have their experts review the additional information, and acquire funds on their own for that purpose or engage counsel who would advance the discovery costs. Court granted an additional four months to engage in discovery and file a complaint, which plaintiffs were unable to do; common pleas court entered *non pros*. The Superior Court held that lower court's decision to discontinue without prejudice a case that was 16 months old did not outweigh the burden already imposed on defendants and the additional burden of the potentially long wait for plaintiffs to recommence suit. The Minority Tolling Statute does not preclude compelling a case to proceed rather than allowing a reversion to the protection of tolled status,

Stress

once a case filed on behalf of a minor has been commenced. *Fancsali v. University Health Center of Pittsburgh*, **700 A.2d 962 (Pa. Super. 1997).**

Stress

Held: error to exclude testimony that stress caused by accident caused substantial aggravation of heart condition, leading to open heart surgery, even though surgery at some point in plaintiff's life probably inevitable. ***Walsh v. Snyder*, 295 Pa. Super. 94, 441 A.2d 365.**

Strip mine

Plaintiffs injured when they fell into strip mine adjacent to state road brought action against Commonwealth. Commonwealth immune because injuries occurred on private property. ***Snyder v. Harmon*, 522 Pa. 424, 562 A.2d 307.**

Student

Parents of children expelled from Catholic grade school sued diocese, diocesan oard of Education and principal after diocese and bishop had confirmed expulsion following hearing before diocesan Board of Education. Trial court sustained preliminary objections of defendants on grounds that state court did not have jurisdiction to determine controversies under ecclesiastic rule, custom or law, as upheld and affirmed by bishop of Roman Catholic Church. Affirmed by Commonwealth Court pursuant to same reasoning as elucidated by Pennsylvania Supreme Court in *Presbytery of Beaver-Butler v. Middlesex Presbyterian Church*, 507 Pa. 255, 489 A.2d 1317, *cert.* denied 474 U.S. 887, 106 S.Ct. 198, 88 L.Ed.2d 167. (1985). ***Gaston v. Diocese of Allentown*, 712 A.2d 757 (Pa. Super. 1998).**

Student injured while crossing street on way to school bus stop. School district not liable for negligently selecting location of bus stop. ***Brelish v. Clarks Green Borough*, 146 Pa. Cmwlth. 232, 604 A.2d 1235.**

Student injured when he stepped into hole in field during lacrosse practice. Held: school district not immune under Recreation Use of Land and Water Act. ***Seifirth v. Downingtown Area School District*, 145 Pa. Cmwlth. 562, 604 A.2d 757.**

Student struck by automobile while crossing state highway on way to school brought action against Commonwealth, school district and township for failure to provide crosswalks and traffic control devices. All defendants immune. ***Majestic v. Com., Dept. of Transp.*, 144 Pa. Cmwlth. 109, 601 A.2d 386.**

Highschool student struck by vehicle while crossing state highway brought action against school district, township, and Commonwealth. All defendants immune. ***Stein v. Com., Dept. of Transp.*, 144 Pa. Cmwlth. 105, 601 A.2d 384.**

Student injured when struck by automobile while crossing street after alighting from Transportation Authority bus. Authority immune. ***Lehman v. County of Lebanon Transportation Authority*, 143 Pa. Cmwlth. 416, 599 A.2d 259.**

Student injured in fall on snow-covered lawn while walking to gymnasium. University not liable. Doctrine of hills and ridges not applicable. ***Gilligan v. Villanova University*, 401 Pa. Super. 113, 584 A.2d 1005.**

Student

College student died of alcohol poisoning as a result of being served alcohol by friends on day before 21st birthday. Held: serving alcohol on day before 21st birthday negligence *per se*. *Herr v. Booten,* **398 Pa. Super. 166, 580 A.2d 1115.**

College student convicted of murder brought action against estate of victim and against fraternity for negligently enticing him to party and for serving him drugs and alcohol. Dismissal of complaint upheld. *Van Mastright v. Delta Tau Delta,* **393 Pa. Super. 142, 573 A.2d 1128.**

Student injured in fall during school-sponsored race. Held: real property exception to governmental immunity did not apply. Injury not caused by artificial condition or defect in land. *Faber v. Pennsbury School District,* **131 Pa. Cmwlth. 642, 571 A.2d 546.**

Motorist killed in accident involving students driving between schools. School district not liable. Vehicle exception to governmental immunity did not apply. *Capuzzi v. Heller,* **125 Pa. Cmwlth. 678, 558 A.2d 596.**

Minor student who was served alcohol in university dormitory and at fraternity house started fire that destroyed building. University and fraternity not liable to owner of building. Did not furnish alcohol. *Alumni Association v. Sullivan,* **524 Pa. 356, 572 A.2d 1209.**

Student sexually assaulted by another student. School district immune from suit for actions of third party and for negligent supervision. *Cotter v. School District of Philadelphia,* **125 Pa. Cmwlth. 596, 562 A.2d 1029.**

Highschool wrestler was injured by door during running drill inside school. Held: plaintiff brought claim that fell within the real property exception to the Political Subdivision Tort Claims Act. *Gump v. Chartiers-Houston School District,* **125 Pa. Cmwlth. 596, 558 A.2d 589.**

Student injured while performing stunt in school gymnasium. Held: because complaint alleged negligence concerning care, custody and control of landing surface around vaulting horse, the real property exception to governmental immunity applies. *Singer v. School District of Philadelphia,* **99 Pa. Cmwlth. 553, 513 A.2d 1108.**

Plaintiff injured during cheerleading practice at school. Suit against school district dismissed by granting of order of summary judgment. School district immune where allegation was lack of supervision. *Messina v. Blairsville-Saltsburg School District,* **94 Pa. Cmwlth. 100, 503 A.2d 89.**

School district held not liable for injuries to person assaulted by unknown assailant, on adjacent sidewalk, and subsequent assault on school grounds. Under circumstances, criminal acts not foreseeable use of school property. *Joner v. Board of Education of Philadelphia,* **91 Pa. Cmwlth. 145, 496 A.2d 1288.**

Fatal injury to student struck by car after alighting from school bus. Held: school district immune from suit. Stopped school bus with flashing lights is not a traffic control as defined by governmental immunity statute. *Aberant v. Wilkes-Barre Area School District,* **91 Pa. Cmwlth. 27, 492 A.2d 1186.**

Subjective belief

Minor plaintiff injured in school gymnasium when another pupil tripped her and she fell into a rack of gymnasium equipment—plaintiff contended that school was maintaining a nuisance as gymnasium was being repaired and that "pieces of wood," "nails" and other debris on floor—preliminary objections properly sustained—case not within "nuisance exception." *Young v. Philadelphia School District,* **442 Pa. 638, 276 A.2d 301.**

Subjective belief

A party's subjective belief that they are represented by an attorney and their failure to plead the basic elements of negligence preclude recovery against the attorney. Order sustaining preliminary objections affirmed. *Cost v. Cost,* **450 Pa. Super. 685, 677 A.2d 1250 (1996).**

Subrogation

Workers' compensation carrier brought a subrogation claim against Defendant seeking to recover workers' compensation payments made for indemnity and medical payments to an injured worker. Trial court dismissed the complaint. The Superior Court affirmed holding that a workers' compensation carrier under the Workers' Compensation Act did not have a right to independently sue a third party tortfeasor. *Liberty Mutual Insurance Company v. Domtar Paper Co.,* **77 A.3d 1282 (Pa. Super. 2013).**

Substantial factor

Finding of negligence and injury alone by a jury do not require finding of liability if negligence was not a substantial factor in causing injury and resulting damages. *Daniel v. William R. Drach Co., Inc.,* **849 A.2d 1265 (Pa. Super. 2004).**

Where both plaintiffs' and defendant's experts agree that there were injuries as a result of negligent activities, a jury's determination that the tortious activity was not a substantial factor is against the weight of the evidence. *Campagna v. Rogan,* **829 A.2d 322 (Pa. Super. 2003)**

Where both plaintiff's and defendant's medical expert opine that the plaintiff suffered some physical injury as a result of an automobile accident, and the jury determines that the defendant's negligence caused the accident, a defense verdict based on the jury's belief that the accident was not a substantial factor in causing the injuries is against the weight of the evidence and must be vacated. *Campagna v. Rogan,* **829 A.2d 322 (Pa. Super. 2003).**

Reversal of j.n.o.v. in favor of plaintiff following verdict for defendant where plaintiff alleged injury resulting from automobile accident. Following testimony of plaintiff's expert and no expert testimony from defendant, the trial court held that defense verdict in face of plaintiff's claim of injury was against the weight of the evidence. Held that where plaintiff's and defendant's experts agree that injury followed accident, failure to award damages is not permitted, but where there is no agreement between competing experts as to existence of injury caused by accident, defense verdict may stand, even in the face of injury. *Peterson v. Shreiner,* **822 A.2d 833 (Pa. Super. 2003).**

Substantial factor

Where all medical experts testify that the plaintiff passenger suffered injury in an automobile accident caused by defendant, a jury's determination that the defendant's negligence was not a substantial factor in causing plaintiff's injuries is against the weight of the evidence. ***Lemmon v. Ernst*, 822 A.2d 768 (Pa. Super. 2003)**.

Decedent died as a result of a burst abdominal aortic aneurysm that had not been properly diagnosed well before it burst. Suit was against hospital that took x-ray that clearly showed aneurysm and physician that did not review the x-ray. Summary judgment in favor of hospital and verdict in favor of physician were reversed on determination that question of whether hospital properly notified physician of results of x-ray was for jury and jury's finding that doctor was negligent but that negligence was not a substantial factor was obvious error. ***Cangemi v. Cone*, 774 A.2d 1262 (Pa. Super. 2001)**.

Grant of new trial to plaintiff affirmed after jury returned special iterrogatories that established that defendant was negligent in the operation of his car but defendant's negligence was not a substantial factor when undisputed facts at trial indicate that there were no substantial factors other than defendant's negligent actions which caused the accident in which plaintiff was injured. ***Craft v. Hetherly*, 700 A.2d 520 (Pa. Super. 1997)**.

Plaintiff was injured and his wife was killed when their car was struck by a vehicle fleeing a police vehicle that was operating its emergency lights but no siren. The trial court granted summary judgment to the pursuing officer, his superiors and city under the Political Subdivision Tort Claims Act pursuant to *Dickens v. Horner*, 531 Pa. 127. 611 A.2d 693 (1992). Supreme Court affirmed Commonwealth Court reversal of trial court and overruling of *Dickens, supra.*, holding that it is a question for the jury to decide whether the police officer's/supervisor's/city's negligence was a substantial factor causing plaintiffs' harm and whether the fleeing driver's actions were a superseding cause precluding governmental liability. ***Jones v. Chieffo*, 700 A.2d 417 (Pa. 1997)**.

Violation of a statute, although negligence *per se*, does not constitute a ground for imposing liability unless it can be shown to be a substantial factor in causing plaintiff's injuries which resulted from a trip and fall. Failure to produce evidence of separate and distinct damages attributable to a scar precludes a specific jury instruction regarding the scar. Judgment affirmed. ***Gravlin v. Fredavid Builders and Developers*, 450 Pa. Super. 655, 677 A.2d 1235 (1996)**.

Defendant injured when car struck dumpster he was rummaging through did not state cause of action against owners of property who lawfully placed dumpster in front of house and who had no awareness of plaintiff's presence. Plaintiff failed to show any proximate causation between owner's placement of dumpster and his injuries. Proximate causation exists where wrongful conduct is a substantial factor in bringing about the harm incurred. Order granting summary judgment affirmed. ***Amarhanov v. Fassel*, 442 Pa. Super. 111, 658 A.2d 808 (1995)**.

Substitution

Charge on contributory negligence upheld. Plaintiff's actions must have been a substantial factor in bringing about harm to himself. *Love v. Harrisburg Coca-Cola*, 273 Pa. Super. 210, 417 A.2d 242.

Substitution

Plaintiff who named original defendant as "John Doe I" may not substitute corporate defendant for "John Doe I" after applicable statute of limitations has expired. Order allowing plaintiff to amend complaint reversed. Corporation dismissed from action. *Anderson Equipment Company v. Huchber*, 456 Pa. Super. 535, 690 A.2d 1239 (1997).

Named defendant dead at time of issuance of writ—decedent not a party and personal representative cannot be substituted in action—one year period provided by the Fiduciaries Act of 1949 controlling—preliminary objections properly sustained to rule for substitution of parties. *Ehrhardt v. Costello*, 437 Pa. 556, 264 A.2d 620.

Subway

"Dangerous condition of real estate" exception to governmental immunity was fact question for jury. Summary judgment in favor of defendant reversed. *Berhane v. SEPTA*, 166 Pa. Cmwlth. 196, 646 A.2d 1268 (1994).

Passenger fell on slippery spot on subway platform. Held: whether dangerous condition was "on" or "off" platform a question of fact. *Shubert v. SEPTA*, 155 Pa. Cmwlth. 129, 625 A.2d 102.

Subway passenger stabbed by other passenger. Police officer helped victim from train then ceased assistance. Held: summary judgment for city inappropriate. Officer owed duty to victim. *Rankin v. SEPTA*, 146 Pa. Cmwlth. 429, 606 A.2d 536.

Commuter attacked by unknown assailant in subway station. Authority not liable. *Glenn v. SEPTA*, 137 Pa. Cmwlth. 19, 587 A.2d 24.

Plaintiff assaulted in subway concourse. Held: real estate exception to the Political Subdivision Tort Claims Act not applicable in cases of criminal assault by third party. *Johnson v. SEPTA*, 516 Pa. Cmwlth. 312, 532 A.2d 409.

Suit against SEPTA and City for injuries sustained by plaintiff in mugging which occurred in subway concourse. Held: complaint did state a cause of action against City as possessor of land and within exception to Political Subdivision Tort Claims Act. *Johnson v. SEPTA*, 91 Pa. Cmwlth. 587, 498 A.2d 22.

Plaintiff waiting on subway platform when struck by subway. Did not remember accident at all. Train was a work train and did not stop at station, and contrary to rules did not slow or signal. Verdict for plaintiff affirmed. *Canery v. SEPTA*, 267 Pa. Super. 382, 406 A.2d 1093.

Sudden Emergency Doctrine

Successive collisions

Chain reaction collision caused by brake problems. Jury verdict for defendant. Sudden emergency doctrine does not include sudden mechanical failures. Whether defects are attributable to negligence is determined by regular duty of care standards. New trial ordered. ***Chiodo v. Gargloff & Downham Trucking*, 308 Pa. Super. 498, 454 A.2d 645.**

Plaintiff's vehicle stopped—car to immediate rear collided with plaintiff's car—evidence sufficient for jury to infer that third car collided with second car which in turn collided with plaintiff's car—verdict solely against operator of third car and operator of second car exonerated—motions by operator of third car on ground that there was no evidence that it was moving—motion properly dismissed—plaintiff only testified—affirmed on appeal. ***Stoll v. Miller and Cherry*, 217 Pa. Super. 861, 270 A.2d 244.**

Collision on turnpike—first car out of gas pulled onto berm—a second car partially blocked highway to siphon gas into stalled car—third car (plaintiffs') caused to collide with guard rail—fourth car negotiated space without contact with standing cars—fifth car contacted fourth car and then plaintiffs' car—summary judgment granted as to operator of first and fourth cars proper. ***Stanik v. Steuber*, 439 Pa. 327, 266 A.2d 703.**

Three car successive or chain collision—plaintiff's car in middle—car ahead stopped—plaintiff's car allegedly stopped suddenly—defendant's car, the third in line, collided with plaintiff's car—error for trial judge to remove question of plaintiff's possible contributory negligence from the jury—new trial granted. ***Toff v. Rohde*, 208 Pa. Super. 411, 222 A.2d 434.**

Sudden Emergency Doctrine

Plaintiff driver filed suit after the Defendant driver swerved into the Plaintiff's lane as the Plaintiff was passing the Defendant on the left. The trial court denied instructions on the sudden emergency doctrine and negligence per se. The Superior Court, on appeal, held that a jury instruction on the sudden emergency doctrine is warranted when: 1) the driver suddenly and unexpectedly found himself confronted with a perilous situation; 2) the situation permitted no opportunity to assess the danger; 3) the driver responded appropriately; and 4) the driver established he did not create the emergency. ***Drew v. Work*, 2014 Pa. Super. 137 (Pa. Super. 2014)**.

Plaintiff brought negligence action against driver's estate for injuries suffered in a motor vehicle accident caused when the decedent driver struck plaintiff's vehicle after suffering a cardiac dysrhythmia prior to the collision. The trial court granted summary judgment to the defendant based upon the sudden emergency doctrine. The Superior Court reversed and remanded holding that there was a genuine issue of material fact as to whether the decedent's loss of consciousness was unforeseen based upon the plaintiff's expert's opinion that the decedent had suffered previous cardiac events. ***Shiner v. Ralston*, 64 A.3d 1 (Pa. Super. 2013).**

Sudden Emergency Doctrine

Grant of new trial to plaintiff, bus passenger, reversed when trial judge determined that he did not believe the testimony of the bus driver who alleged that sudden emergency necessitated sudden change of direction and contact of bus with Jersey barrier. Analysis of sudden emergency doctrine. ***Divilly v. Port Authority of Allegheny County*, 810 A.2d 755 (Pa. Cmwlth. 2002).**

The court ruled in verse, short but not terse, and addressed all the issues presented. Two dogs and their walker, came in for a shocker, when defendant's car made one dog dented. The vet's fee at issue, for damaged dog tissue, composed the poor plaintiff's pup's claim. Driver argued contrib, cut short for this squib, as the reason the poor dog was maimed. He loudly protested, the dog was molested, because it came into the road. Unfortunately, for the driver you see, the transcript defies that contention. Sudden emergency, last clear chance, both theories were raised and were argued. The superior court, to excuse the tort, found naught in the facts or the pleadings. Payment is due, from you know who, and the dogs and their owner keep strolling. Though written in verse, which some find perverse, this case is correct and controlling. ***Zangrando v. Sipula*, 756 A.2d 73 (Pa. Super. 2000).**

The Sudden Emergency Doctrine is not an affirmative defense thatmust be specifically pleaded. Thorough analysis of history and purpose of doctrine. ***Leahy v. McClain*, 732 A.2d 619 (Pa. Super. 1999).**

In three-car accident, plaintiff was driver of car in front of which another car turned. Defendant driving behind plaintiff struck plaintiff's and other defendant's cars. Plaintiff was allowed by trial court to offer sudden emergency defense to turning defendant's claim of plaintiff's negligence but following defendant was not. Affirmed by Superior Court but reversed by Supreme Court in opinion which clearly explains difference and interrelationship between assured clear distance rule and sudden emergency doctrine. Both plaintiff and following driver are entitled to argue sudden emergency doctrine under facts of case. ***Levey v. DeNardo*, 725 A.2d 733 (Pa. 1999).**

Plaintiff was rear seat passenger in car driven by defendant which encountered fog bank, left road and struck tree, injuring plaintiff. Trial court charged on sudden emergency doctrine to which plaintiff objected. Plaintiff argued that defendant's summary citation for breaking statutory assured clear distance rule precluded her from claiming sudden emergency; a tree is not a sudden emergency and amount of time it took for defendant to react argues against any suddenness. Held: summary charges, particularly when defendant did not even attend hearing on charge, cannot be admitted in civil cases as a general rule. Tree was not sudden emergency, the fog was. There was adequate evidence that defendant acted quickly and thoroughly to minimize sudden appearance of fog. Plaintiff's second argument that jury's distaste with trial court's habit of chewing tobacco during trial and spitting into a cup as prejudicial to plaintiff is totally unfounded. ***Dickens v. Barnhart*, 711 A.2d 513 (Pa. Super. 1998).**

Driver who collided with garbage truck situated diagonally on road was entitled to jury instruction on sudden emergency doctrine. Where evidence is such that reasonable minds could differ as to whether sudden emergency existed, both assured

Sudden Emergency Doctrine

clear distance and sudden emergency instructions should be given. Assured clear distance charge to jury that failed to detail effect of presumption that rule applies where driver was proceeding in safe and prudent manner was legally insufficient. **Lockhart v. List, 542 Pa. 141, 665 A.2d 1176 (1995).**

Mother and daughter injured in multi-vehicle collision. Prohibition against testimony concerning the lack of use of safety belts held constitutional. Jury instructions on comparative negligence and sudden emergency doctrine not in error. **Drango v. Winterhalter, 359 Pa. Super. 578, 577 A.2d 1349.**

Passenger in automobile injured in collision with vehicle being chased by another automobile. Held: sudden emergency rule not applicable where driver being chased had other options available other than fleeing. **McKee by McKee v. Evans, 380 Pa. Super. 120, 551 A.2d 260.**

Motorist injured while stopped at traffic signal when struck from behind. Sudden emergency doctrine held not to apply. It was defendant's duty to show that brakes failed through no fault of his own. **Papandrea v. Hartman, 352 Pa. Super. 163, 507 A.2d 822.**

Rear-end collision. Borough of Harrisville stopped traffic on state highway for Memorial Day parade. Alleged negligent traffic control (accident occurred before Tort Claims Act), negligence of striking vehicle, and negligence of plaintiff for defective tail lights. Although error here to charge on sudden emergency (this is not sudden confrontation of perilous situation), found to be harmless error. Sudden emergency doctrine and assured clear distance are mutually exclusive. **Elder v. Orluck, 334 Pa. Super. 329, 483 A.2d 474.**

Truck driver faced with vehicle coming across his lane of travel at right angle and only having one or two seconds at most to react is entitled to judgment *n.o.v.* following jury verdict. Sudden emergency doctrine applies. **Polumbo v. DeStefano, 329 Pa. Super. 360, 478 A.2d 828.**

Chain reaction collision caused by brake problems. Jury verdict for defendant. Held: error to charge on sudden emergency. Doctrine not to include sudden mechanical failures. New trial ordered. **Chiodo v. Gargloff & Downham Trucking, 308 Pa. Super. 498, 454 A.2d 645.**

Car skidded on gravel, going around a curve when deer spotted on highway. Error to charge on sudden emergency. Deer 55 feet ahead not an emergency. Gravel was stationary and only subject to assured clear distance ahead doctrine. **Hanlon v. Sorenson, 289 Pa. Super. 268, 433 A.2d 60.**

Charge on sudden emergency in error. All that is required is that actor exercise honest judgment when confronted with sudden emergency, even if not the best judgment under the circumstances. Further, with two defendants, each should be judged independently in their response and not tied to each other's negligence. **Potenburg v. Vainer and Petka, 284 Pa. Super. 19, 424 A.2d 1370.**

Suicide

Improper to charge on sudden emergency doctrine where accident occurred due to wet highway due to heavy rain. Condition was preexisting and static. *McErlean v. McCartan,* 280 Pa. Super. 531, 421 A.2d 849.

Plaintiff robbed at train station and then stripped of his clothes. Killed while climbing atop train to retrieve clothing. Error to charge on sudden emergency. Emergency ended when assailant fled. *Carpenter v. Penn Central,* 269 Pa. Super. 9, 409 A.2d 37.

Skidding accident on icy road. Error to charge on sudden emergency since hazard should have been clearly visible. *Sullivan v. Wolson,* 262 Pa. Super. 397, 396 A.2d 1230.

Head-on collision. Proper to charge on sudden emergency where party's mind is a blank as to what she did in face of emergency and where evidence is that she had only 1 to 2 seconds to react. *Lewis v. Mellor,* 259 Pa. Super. 509, 393 A.2d 941.

Car went out of control on loose gravel injuring passenger. Error to charge on sudden emergency where alleged gravel was stationary object. *Brown v. Schriver,* 254 Pa. Super. 468, 386 A.2d 45.

Defendant's cement truck swerved into oncoming lane of traffic to avoid suddenly stopped vehicle, turning over and striking plaintiff's vehicle which had stopped seeing actions ahead. For jury whether emergency existed. Assured clear distance doctrine does not apply when sudden and clear emergency presents itself. *Stacy v. Thrower Trucking,* 253 Pa. Super. 150, 384 A.2d 1274.

Mrs. Stout driving on turnpike at night when she entered dense fog. Jammed on brakes and skidded into opposite lanes where car stalled. Struck by oncoming car in fog. Sudden emergency doctrine and reasonableness of actions for jury. Verdict against Mrs. Stout and company which owned cooling tower from which fog was emanating—affirmed. *Westerman v. Stout, et al.,* 232 Pa. Super. 195, 335 A.2d 741.

Suicide

Estate brought negligence action against Defendant after the decedent committed suicide when the Defendant stopped paying for the decedent's mental health treatment. The trial court dismissed the case. The Superior Court affirmed holding that Plaintiff had failed to state a claim upon which relief can be granted as there was no allegation that the decedent was at a greater risk of harming himself due to the treatment provided by the Defendant. *Unglo v. Zubik,* 29 A.3d 810 (Pa. Super. 2011).

Widow, individually and as administratrix of her husband's estate, brought a claim for negligence against a hospital and its director after her husband, an anesthesiologist, committed suicide after the hospital confronted him with allegations of his drug abuse relapse. The trial court dismissed Plaintiff's complaint. The Superior Court affirmed, holding that the hospital owed no duty to the decedent as it did not render services or aid to the decedent. ***Cooper v. Frankford Healthcare System, Inc.*, 960 A.2d 134 (Pa. Super. 2008).**

Plaintiffs brought wrongful death and survival action against medical providers who plaintiffs allege caused their son's suicide. Sole substantive issue before Superior Court was whether witness in wrongful death and survival action suit is barred from testimony by Dead Man's Act. Although technically there should not be any testimony allowed by person with interest adverse to decedent's interests in survival action because decedent's interest has passed to his or her personal representative, there is no such restriction as to wrongful death action. Practically, court will not impose Dead Man's Act restrictions in either wrongful death or survival actions because of attendant impracticalities. ***Gibbs v. Herman*, 714 A.2d 432 (Pa. Super. 1998).**

Worker attempted suicide after negotiations on his workman's compensation claim collapsed. Insurance carrier not liable for negligent and intentional infliction of emotional distress. ***Santiago v. Pennsylvania National Mutual Casualty Insurance Company*, 418 Pa. Super. 178, 613 A.2d 1235.**

Client's suicide was not a reasonably foreseeable consequence of attorney's alleged negligent representation. ***McPeake v. Cannon Esquire P.C.*, 381 Pa. Super. 227, 553 A.2d 439.**

Plaintiff-decedent hanged himself with hospital robe ties while patient in psychiatric unit of defendant hospital, having been admitted after suicide attempt. Lower court erred in ruling as matter of law that treating physician was not agent of hospital. New trial as to doctor's agency and negligence only, and damages if appropriate. ***Simmons v. St. Clair Memorial Hospital*, 332 Pa. Super. 444, 481 A.2d 870.**

Nineteen-year old son of plaintiff killed by auto. Father did not witness accident. Father committed suicide three months later. Suit by father's estate against driver of auto dismissed. ***Yandrich v. Radic*, 495 Pa. 243, 433 A.2d 459.**

Plaintiff's decedent jumped to her death from roof of defendant's high rise apartment—complaint averred a failure to restrict access to roof as ground of negligence—preliminary objections in the nature of a demurrer properly sustained—defendant apartment house operator had breached no duty owed to decedent. ***Engel v. Parkway Co.*, 439 Pa. 559, 266 A.2d 685.**

Summary citation

Plaintiff was rear seat passenger in car driven by defendant which encountered fog bank, left road and struck tree, injuring plaintiff. Trial court charged on sudden emergency doctrine to which plaintiff objected. Plaintiff argued that defendant's summary citation for breaking statutory assured clear distance rule precluded her from claiming sudden emergency; a tree is not a sudden emergency and amount of time it took for defendant to react argues against any suddenness. Held: summary charges, particularly when defendant did not even attend hearing on charge, cannot be admitted in civil cases as a general rule. Tree was not sudden emergency, the fog was. There was adequate evidence that defendant acted quickly and thoroughly to minimize sudden appearance of fog. Plaintiff's second argument that jury's distaste

Summer recreation program

with trial court's habit of chewing tobacco during trial and spitting into a cup as prejudicial to plaintiff is totally unfounded. ***Dickens v. Barnhart*, 711 A.2d 513 (Pa. Super. 1998).**

Summer recreation program

School district provided premises for summer recreation programmade no charge—minor plaintiffs injured on premises—preliminary objections sustained—Held: governmental function—affirmed on appeal with strong dissent. ***Kitchen v. Wilkinsburg School District*, 222 Pa. Super. 479, 293 A.2d 84.**

Supermarket

Defense verdict reversed and remanded for trial court to hold evidentiary hearing on whether circumstances surrounding another fall by plaintiff at another of defendant's supermarkets were sufficiently similar to instant slip and fall to warrant admission of evidence of prior fall. ***Valentine v. Acme Markets, Inc.*, 455 Pa. Super. 256, 687 A.2d 1157 (1997).**

Customer who fell in supermarket brought action claiming injuries caused by excess wax or presence of grapes on floor. Market not liable. ***Myers v. Penn Traffic Company*, 414 Pa. Super. 181, 606 A.2d 926.**

Plaintiff injured when struck in buttocks by automatic door at supermarket, as she bent over rail to reach for trading stamp book. Jury verdict for defendant affirmed. Held: not latent or unusual defect. ***Brancato v. Kroger Co., Inc.*, 312 Pa. Super. 448, 458 A.2d 1377.**

Superseding cause

Verdict for bank teller plaintiff in suit against security company for negligent and negligent *per se* hiring of security guard who robbed bank during off-duty hours reversed because bank robber's unforeseeable violent criminal act was a superseding cause of the harm. ***Maban v. Am-Guard, Inc.*, 841 A.2d 1052 (Pa. Super. 2004).**

Plaintiff's decedent allegedly fell asleep at the wheel and his car, wit his wife and family on board, crossed into opposing traffic, struck and slid along a guardrail and struck a bridge abutment causing his death. After verdict for plaintiff molded to reflect jury's finding of 40% comparative negligence of deceased driver, trial court granted new trial at request of PennDOT because it had failed to charge on superseding cause as PennDOT had requested. Commonwealth Court reversed trial court and Supreme Court held that superseding cause requires the act of a third party, not act of plaintiff or defendant. Acts of a plaintiff that contribute to the injury sustained are addressed by the law of comparative negligence, not superseding cause. ***Von Der Heide v. Com., Dept. of Transp.*, 718 A.2d 286 (Pa. 1998).**

Plaintiff was injured and his wife was killed when their car was struck by a vehicle fleeing a police vehicle that was operating its emergency lights but no siren. The trial court granted summary judgment to the pursuing officer, his superiors and city under the Political Subdivision Tort Claims Act pursuant to *Dickens v. Horner,* 531 Pa. 127, 611 A.2d 693 (1992). Supreme Court affirmed Commonwealth Court

Superseding cause

reversal of trial court and overruling of *Dickens, supra*, holding that it is a question for the jury to decide whether the police officer's/supervisor's/city's negligence was a substantial factor causing plaintiffs' harm and whether the fleeing driver's actions were a superseding cause precluding governmental liability. ***Jones v. Chieffo,*** **700 A.2d 417 (Pa. 1997).**

A minor/owner who provides an air powered pellet gun to another minor may be liable to minor plaintiff injured by a pellet for providing the gun without instruction. The reasonably anticipated negligent firing of the pellet gun by other minor is not a superseding, intervening cause that insulates minor/owner from liability. Order sustaining preliminary objections reversed. ***Frey v. Smith,*** **454 Pa. Super. 242, 685 A.2d 169 (1996).**

In suit by decedent's estate against minor passenger in other vehicle, an individual who is simply a passenger in a vehicle operated by an intoxicated driver may not be held responsible for the driver's negligence. Rather, liability may only be imposed where sufficient facts indicate that the passenger substantially assisted or encouraged the driver's negligent conduct. Order granting summary judgment in favor of minor passenger affirmed. ***Welc v. Porter,*** **450 Pa. Super. 112, 675 A.2d 334 (1996).**

Municipal defendants are neither afforded blanket immunity nor entitled to judgment as a matter of law in each and every tort claim where the victim's injuries were caused in part by the intervening criminal conduct of third parties or where the criminal acts of a third party merely form a link in the chain of causation. It is for the jury to determine whether municipal defendants' conduct was a substantial contributing factor in causing the victim's injuries and, if so, whether intervening criminal conduct of third parties was so extraordinary as not to be reasonably foreseeable by the municipal defendants. Summary judgment reversed. ***Jones v. Chieffo,*** **___ Pa. Super. ___, 664 A.2d 1091 (1995).**

In action arising from explosion of boiler caused by defective emergency shut off valve, manufacturer of valve held strictly liable for defective product. Manufacturer's liability for its defective product is outlined in Section 402A of Restatement (2d) Torts, which provides that a plaintiff must prove that the product was sold in a defective condition dangerous to the user and that the defect was the proximate cause of the injury. An actor is relieved from liability owing to an intervening or superseding cause only if the intervening or superseding negligent acts were so extraordinary as not to have been reasonably foreseeable. Summary judgment affirmed in part and reversed in part. ***Dougherty v. Edward J. Meloney, Inc.,*** **443 Pa. Super. 201, 661 A.2d 375 (1995).**

The determination of whether an individual is a trespasser, licensee or invitee is for the jury. A licensee may become an invitee, thereby increasing duty of care owed by landowner. Plaintiff may recover damages where two or more substantial causes combine to cause an injury, even if no one cause standing alone would have brought about the injury. Although action of third party in pushing plaintiff off a guide wall was an intervening cause, its occurrence was not so extraordinary or unforeseeable as to make it a superseding cause, which would excuse property own-

Supplier of chattels

er for negligent maintenance of wall, which condition substantially contributed to plaintiff's injuries. ***Trude v. Martin,* 442 Pa. Super. 614, 660 A.2d 626 (1995).**

In automobile accident case by decedent's administrator against intoxicated driver and PennDOT, whether PennDOT's alleged negligence for improper road design and maintenance was substantial factor in accident was question for jury. Existence of two tortfeasors does not automatically excuse one or the other from liability. Question of concurrent or joint causation and determination of whether an act is so extraordinary as to constitute a superseding cause are for the jury. Order sustaining preliminary objections of PennDOT reversed. ***Powell v. Drumheller,* 539 Pa. 484, 653 A.2d 619 (1995).**

Passengers in vehicle driven by diabetic injured when driver lost consciousness. Held: Commonwealth and city not liable for failure to install warning and speed limit signs. Driver's loss of consciousness superseding cause. ***Chacho v. Com., Dept. of Transp.,* 148 Pa. Cmwlth. 494, 611 A.2d 1346.**

The Supreme Court approved Section 447 of Restatement (2d) Torts definition of superceding cause—a subsequent negligent act will not relieve the original actor if it is a normal consequence of a situation created by the actor's conduct and the manner in which it is done is not extraordinarily negligent. ***Whitner v. Lojeski,* 437 Pa. 448, 263 A.2d 889.**

Supplier of chattels

Plaintiff injured while operating punch press supplied by defendant— §388 of Restatement (2d) Torts: one who supplies chattel who knows or who has reason to know of danger is liable unless he takes reasonable steps to warn—for jury. ***McKenna v. Art Pearl Works,* 225 Pa. Super. 362, 310 A.2d 677.**

Auto agency sold car to one of defendants—within one-half hour after delivery of car, it collided with rear of another car—evidence of defective brakes—for jury as to supplier and operator. ***Flavin v. Aldrich et al.,* 213 Pa. Super. 420, 250 A.2d 185.**

Plaintiff injured while operating a glass cutting machine—Held: strict liability under Section 402A of Restatement (2d) Torts did not apply—plaintiff obviously guilty of contributory negligence in putting hand in moving machinery—supplier of machine not responsible. ***Bartkewich v. Billinger et al.,* 432 Pa. 351, 247 A.2d 603.**

Plaintiffs were breeders of cattle and purchased feed from defendant P. a retailer of cattle feed—feed blended with a compound of corporate defendant Central Soya—blend contained an ingredient which caused cattle to abort and bull to become sterile—action in assumpsit based on breach of implied warranty—Supreme Court overruled doctrine of privity and upheld plaintiff's claim. ***Kassab v. Central Soya,* 432 Pa. 217, 246 A.2d 848.**

Defendant was the supplier of a tractor trailer to plaintiff's employer—while plaintiff operating machine the same left road, struck something and then traveled over highway and down an embankment—plaintiff contended that occurrence was due to locking of wheels and that machine had left highway on prior occasions and

Surgery

had been repaired—case for jury. ***Griffith v. Clearfield Truck Rentals, Inc.,* 427 Pa. 30, 233 A.2d 896.**

Defendant supplied a paint product to plaintiff's employer—plaintiff allegedly sustained serious injury to his eyes in using product—ample warning given plaintiff's employer—suit against supplier and manufacturer and employer joined—verdict against employer only—affirmed on appeal. ***Thomas v. Arvon Products Co.,* 424 Pa. 365, 227 A.2d 897.**

Plaintiff, a handyman, directed by defendant to prune certain trees on defendant's premises—saw and ladder provided—plaintiff fell from ladder—employer not responsible at common law. ***Gilkes v. Levinson,* 421 Pa. 128, 218 A.2d 722.**

Surgery

While informed consent is required from a patient in any surgical or operative rocedure, it is not required when only nonsurgical procedures are performed. Administration of anesthetics, steroids or other medications by injection does not require informed consent. ***Morgan v. MacPhail,* 704 A.2d 617 (Pa. 1997).**

Plaintiff who contracted AIDS following transfusion of tainted blood filed suit against treating physicians and family physician for medical malpractice. Claim against one defendant dismissed for plaintiff's failure to establish through medical testimony that defendant's actions deviated from good and acceptable medical standards. Proof of compliance with medical standard of care need not be expressed in precisely the language used to annunciate the legal standard. Physician not required to obtain patient's informed consent before blood transfusion that was administered separately from a surgical procedure. ***Hoffman v. Brandywine Hospital,* 443 Pa. Super. 245, 661 A.2d 397 (1995).**

A cause of action for failure to obtain informed consent has been steadfastly limited to "surgical or operative medical procedures." Lack of informed consent for a touching states cause of action for battery. Because chiropractors are statutorily proscribed from performing any surgical procedures, a cause of action against a chiropractor for failure to obtain informed consent before performing nonsurgical procedure will not lie as a matter of law. Order dismissing complaint affirmed. ***Matukonis v. Trainer,* 441 Pa. Super. 570, 657 A.2d 1314 (1995).**

A referring physician cannot be held liable under theory of failure to obtain informed consent where he had no physical contact with plaintiff who suffered injury as a result of recommended surgery. Suit for failure to obtain informed consent grounded in battery, not negligence. Verdict for plaintiff vacated and remanded. ***Shaw v. Kirschbaum,* 439 Pa. Super. 24, 653 A.2d 12 (1994).**

Patient died of complications following elective surgery. Husband and daughter asserted claims for negligent infliction of emotional distress. Held: action will not lie unless the bystander personally observes an identifiable traumatic event. ***Halliday v. Beltz,* 356 Pa. Super. 375, 514 A.2d 906.**

Surrogacy

Surrogacy

Plaintiff, surrogate mother, sued infertility clinic under wrongful death and survival statutes, for negligent infliction of emotional distress, for fraud and for breach of fiduciary duty for the death of child murdered by sperm-donor father one month after the child's birth. After determining that clinic had waived any claim that mother lacked standing, Held: mother had stated cause of action under wrongful death and survival statutes but lacked sufficient factual basis for negligent infliction of emotional distress, fraud and breach of fiduciary duty. For-profit infertility clinic was in a "special relationship" with all parties to the transaction—surrogate mother, sperm-donor and resulting child—so as to create a duty imposed by law to effectively provide safeguards that might reasonably prevent foreseeable injuries to the parties, such as abuse of the child. ***Huddleston v. Infertility Center of America,* 700 A.2d 453 (Pa. Super. 1997).**

Swerving

Defendant's truck swerved into oncoming traffic to avoid suddenly stopped vehicle. Verdict for defendant truck driver affirmed. For jury as to whether clear emergency existed, thereby superseding assured clear distance doctrine. ***Stacy v. Thrower Trucking,* 253 Pa. Super. 150, 384 A.2d 1274.**

Swimming and swimming pools

Willful or malicious failure to guard or warn exception to immunity under the Recreation Use of Land and Water Act applied to action by personal representative of minor's estate where minor drowned in natural pond located in city park. Evidence of prior unrelated swimming accidents inadmissable. Verdict for plaintiff reversed and remanded. ***Barr v. City and County of Philadelphia,* ___ Pa. Cmwlth. ___, 653 A.2d 1374 (1995).**

Swimmer injured diving into pool brought action against manufacturer of starting blocks. Trial court denied motion to amend answer to plead statute of repose. Remanded. ***Noll v. Paddock Pool Builders, Inc.,* 416 Pa. Super. 284, 611 A.2d 219.**

Child injured when she dived into swimming pool owned by city. City not immune under Recreation Use of Land and Water Act. Real estate exception to government immunity applicable. ***City of Philadelphia v. Duda,* 141 Pa. Cmwlth. 88, 595 A.2d 206.**

Swimmer injured in pool owned by city. City not immune under Recreation Use of Land and Water Act. Act applies only to unimproved land. ***Ithier v. City of Philadelphia,* 137 Pa. Cmwlth. 103, 585 A.2d 564.**

Altar boy drowned while swimming in seminary pool. Life guard not present. Seminary liable. Delay damages of 10% reduced to 6%. ***Rivera v. Philadelphia Theological Seminary,* 398 Pa. Super. 264, 580 A.2d 1342.**

Handicapped swimmer drowned in university pool. University not liable. Failure to provide lifeguard did not fall into real property exception to sovereign immunity. ***Musheno v. Lock Haven University,* 132 Pa. Cmwlth. 643, 574 A.2d 129.**

Swinging door

City employee stole quantity of swimming pool sanitizer and gave it to another employee in brown paper bag. While in car, plaintiff, a passenger was burned when chemical spontaneously ignited. Improper to direct verdict against manufacturer. Theft irrelevant since adequacy of warnings still at issue as was defect in design which allowed flash fires. ***Pegg v. General Motors,* 258 Pa. Super. 59, 391 A.2d 1074.**

Defendant borough maintained a swimming pool—minor plaintiff dived from one meter board and struck bottom of pool and was seriously injured—evidence that depth of water at point was below standard of safe maintenance of a swimming pool—error for court below to enter judgment *n.o.v.* for defendant. ***Cummings v. Nazareth Borough,* 427 Pa. 14, 233 A.2d 874.**

Municipality maintained a public swimming pool—minor plaintiff pushed into pool allegedly as result of rowdyism of other boys—minor seriously injured—verdict for defendant—case properly submitted to the jury—refusal of new trial not error. ***Zeman v. Canonsburg Borough,* 423 Pa. 450, 223 A.2d 728.**

Swinging door

Plaintiff injured while entering store of defendant by reason of acts of children shoving and pushing a swinging door—preliminary objections improperly sustained—matter for jury. ***Regelski v. F. W. Woolworth Co.,* 423 Pa. 524, 225 A.2d 561.**

"T" Intersections

—T—

"T" Intersections

Plaintiff travelling on street ending at "T" intersection. Defendant travelling on cross street. All three approaches have stop signs. Plaintiff stopped at stop sign with intention of turning left—looked both ways and, seeing nothing, proceeded. When turn almost completed, struck in rear by defendant who went through stop sign. Lower court entered compulsory nonsuit holding plaintiff contributorily negligent as matter of law for failing to look again to his right before entering intersection. Reversed, new trial ordered. ***Zumbo v. Ellis*, 232 Pa. Super. 566, 334 A.2d 770.**

Table saw

Plaintiff's hand was severely injured while attempting a "groove cut" in woodshop class on a table saw. The court affirmed judgment for the plaintiff under the real property exception to immunity under the Political Subdivision Tort Claims Act because the saw was real property under the definition used within the act. ***Wells v. Harrisburg Area School District*, 884 A.2d 946 (Pa. Cmwlth. 2005).**

Tail gates

Jury verdict $838,400. Plaintiff killed while operating dump truck dumping hot asphalt when tailgate on truck broke, burying him. Verdict against seller and manufacturer of truck and then molded to provide indemnity to seller from manufacturer as matter of law. Affirmed. ***Walasavage v. Marinelli*, 334 Pa. Super. 396, 483 A.2d 509.**

Tail lights

Rear-end collision. Testimony indicated that plaintiff's tail lights were not working. Issue of whether defective tail lights were a proximate cause of accident should have been for jury. Error to direct verdict against defendant. ***Correll v. Werner*, 293 Pa. Super. 88, 437 A.2d 1004.**

Tarmac

Airport tarmac is not a sidewalk under sidewalk exception to Political Subdivision Tort Claims Act. Plaintiff's allegation that airport authority's failure to design safety standards for tarmac is not sufficient allegation of defective design or construction of real estate so as to fall within real estate exception to Political Subdivision Tort Claims Act. Order granting summary judgment affirmed. ***Bullard v. Lehigh-Northampton Airport Authority*, ___ Pa. Cmwlth. ___, 668 A.2d 223 (1995).**

Telephone booth

Verdict for plaintiff against driver and telephone company affirmed. Plaintiff making call in phone booth when car struck booth. Evidence that location of booth was such that cars coming downgrade might miss second "S" curve and strike booth. ***Noon v. Knavel, et al.*, 234 Pa. Super. 198, 339 A.2d 545.**

Telephone company

Plaintiff may proceed under theory of negligence against telephone company for placing old ad under expired contract in new yellow pages despite existence of prior contractual relationship. *McDole v. Bell Telephone of Pennsylvania,* **441 Pa. Super. 88, 656 A.2d 933 (1995).**

Telephone directory

Plaintiff may proceed under theory of negligence against telephone company for placing old ad under expired contract in new yellow pages despite existence of prior contractual relationship. *McDole v. Bell Telephone of Pennsylvania,* **441 Pa. Super. 88, 656 A.2d 933 (1995).**

Telephone pole

Summary judgment in favor of social host affirmed where no evidence that host had actual notice that minors were consuming alcohol. Summary judgment in favor of telephone company affirmed because causal connection between location of pole and accident too remote in law to impose liability. *Novak v. Kilby,* **167 Pa. Cmwlth. 217, 647 A.2d 687 (1994).**

Telephone wire

Telephone company wire pulled down by passing truck, blocking street. Defendant taxi company driver drove down street even though asked to stop by plaintiff, thereby hitting wire which tangled in plaintiff's feet causing injury. Negligence of phone company based on previous instances of trucks hitting wire. Verdict against both defendants affirmed. *Miller v. Checker Cab, et al.,* **465 Pa. 82, 348 A.2d 128.**

Termites

Buyer of home infested with termites brought action against seller and termite inspection company. Failure to instruct jury on contributory negligence was reversible error. Buyer had opportunity to inspect infested area. *Rizzo v. Michener,* **401 Pa. Super. 47, 584 A.2d 973.**

Test drive

Plaintiff sued driver of car that veered into her lane and hit her car, used car salesman who had authorized defendant driver to test drive the car, and dealership for which used car salesman worked. Jury returned verdict against all three parties and apportioned liability among them, which was molded to joint and several liability by trial court. On appeal, Superior Court reversed denial of post trial motions of salesman and dealership who argued that they had no knowledge that defendant driver was other than a licensed driver (which he was) and so no duty to plaintiff which would support a claim of negligent entrustment by plaintiff. *Ferry v. Fisher,* **709 A.2d 399 (Pa. Super. 1998).**

Therapeutic purpose

Therapeutic purpose

Plaintiff who was not hired because of positive drug test sued testing company alleging negligence in testing. Summary judgment in favor of testing company affirmed due to lack of required therapeutic purpose for medical service provided by testing company and consequent lack of duty. *Ney v. Axelrod*, **723 A.2d 719 (Pa. Super. 1999).**

Therapist

Plaintiff's decedent killed by her mentally ill husband after the husband informed his therapist that he was going to kill his wife. Suit commenced alleging professional negligence by therapist in failing to warn wife or inform police. After judgment on pleadings in favor of defendants, Superior Court affirmed, as did Supreme Court. Supreme Court formally adopts duty to warn doctrine in Pennsylvania if there is a specific and immediate threat of serious bodily injury to a specifically identified victim that has been communicated to the professional. While the Supreme Court found that both criteria to establish a duty to warn were met, it also determined that the telephonic warning that had been given by the therapist to the wife-victim was adequate. Two dissents suggest adequacy of warning should have gone to jury and legal standard for adequacy of warning was too broad and ineffective. *Emerich v. Philadelphia Center for Human Development*, **720 A.2d 1032 (Pa. 1999).**

Thermostat

Business invitee, a serviceman, not required to make independent investigation to determine location of thermostat controlling air conditioning—could rely on assumption defendant's general manager knew proper location of control—error to enter judgment on pleadings. *Eckborg v. Hyde-Murphy Co.*, **442 Pa. 283, 276 A.2d 513.**

Thimerosal

Exclusive original jurisdiction for vaccine latent and patent vaccine related negligence cases is in "Vaccine Court" established by National Childhood Vaccine Injury Act, 42 U.S. 300aa. *Ashton v. Aventis Pasteur*, **851 A.2d 908 (Pa. Super. 2004).**

Negligence action by parents on behalf of minor child injured by exposure to thimerosal in vaccines dismissed for failure to exhaust administrative remedies under federal legislation National Childhood Vaccine Act, 42 U.S. § 300aa-1, *et seq. Chieskiewicz v. Aventis Pasteur, Inc.*, **843 A.2d 1258 (Pa. Super. 2004).**

Third-party beneficiary

Defendant utility-pole inspection company did not have duty to protect bystander from injuries sustained when bystander came into contact with downed electrical wires while assisting victims of automobile accident that damaged utility pole. Defendant inspection company's alleged negligent inspection of pole was too remote to constitute proximate cause of bystander's injuries. Bystander was not third-party beneficiary of contract between inspection company and utility company, which required inspection company only to inspect and report condition of poles. Order sustaining preliminary objections of defendant inspection company affirmed. ***Hicks v. Metropolitan Edison Company,* 665 A.2d 529 (Pa. Cmwlth. 1995).**

Thrown from seat

Plaintiff injured while passenger on subway-elevated by rock-throwing teenager. Duty of care proscribed by §344 of Restatement (2d) Torts. Reliance on local people not in itself enough as a matter of law. Plaintiff's verdict reversed on evidentiary issues. ***Carswell v. SEPTA,* 259 Pa. Super. 167, 393 A.2d 770.**

Defendant attempted to turn truck in highway with view blocked—evidence that decedent was thrown 63 feet through the air—jury could infer excessive speed from such testimony—nonsuit improperly entered—case for jury. ***McNett v. Briggs,* 217 Pa. Super. 322, 272 A.2d 202.**

Plaintiff a passenger in a bus—bus had been standing for red light—started up and stopped suddenly because car of other defendant had turned sharply in front—no contact—plaintiff thrown from seat—injury to neck—verdict against both defendants—motion of plaintiff based solely on inadequacy—motion dismissed—action affirmed on appeal. ***DiPietro v. Zeiders et al.,* 216 Pa. Super. 860, 266 A.2d 568.**

Tires and tire marks

Summary judgment for defendant truck driver affirmed where there was no evidence that he knew that driving on an under-inflated tire would create or increase the risk of injury to a mechanic who was severely injured while reinflating the tire during the repair process. Without more, driver's knowledge that he drove on tire that was low or "super low" is inadequate to establish negligence. §388 of Restatement (2d) Torts requires both knowledge of dangerous condition and failure to inform the person to whom control of the chattel in the dangerous condition is transferred. ***Overbeck v. Cates,* 700 A.2d 970 (Pa. Super. 1997).**

Contributory negligence does not preclude recovery in a products liability case. In action arising out of a tire explosion which injured garage mechanic, defendant failed to prove plaintiff assumed specific risk attendant to procedure of changing tire. Voluntary assumption of a risk is a defense in products liability case and requires proof that the plaintiff fully understands the specific risk and yet chooses voluntarily to encounter the risk. ***Robinson v. B.F. Goodrich Tire Company,* 444 Pa. Super. 640, 664 A.2d 616 (1995).**

Truck driver injured in accident by tire left on turnpike after prior accident brought action against State Police and Turnpike Commission. Defendants immune. ***Nubert v. Commonwealth State Police,* 148 Pa. Cmwlth. 505, 611 A.2d 1353.**

Mere fact that tire blew out with 37,000 miles of otherwise trouble-free driving is not evidence of defect. Compulsory nonsuit granted and affirmed. ***Woelfel v. Murphy Ford Co.,* 337 Pa. Super. 433, 487 A.2d 23.**

Jury verdict $800,000 in favor of 16 year old female passenger in car, involved in auto accident and rendered quadriplegic due to fracture-dislocation of cer-

Title Search

vical spine. Alleged cause of accident was combining radial and non-radial tire on front axle. New trial ordered. ***Dambacher v. Malles*, 336 Pa. Super. 22, 485 A.2d 408.**

Tire manufactured by one defendant, sold under name of another and installed by third defendant—tire exploded and plaintiff injured—nonsuit below—plaintiff claimed explosion resulted from combination of defective manufacture and improper mounting—unable to establish improper mounting—affirmed by an equally divided appellate court. ***Forry v. Gulf Oil Corporation*, 428 Pa. 334, 237 A.2d 593.**

Title Search

Title insurer brought action against title search company which performed "last owner" search for a refinance. The search failed to disclose a substantial judgment against the refinancing owner and insurer paid. Held that insurer was not contributorily negligent in failing to ask for a full title search because it would not have found anymore relative to the judgment than the last owner search. ***Fidelity National Title Insurance Company of New York v. Suburban West Abstractors*, 852 A.2d 318 (Pa. Super. 2004).**

Tortious interference with marital relationship

Plaintiff wife sued doctor who had disclosed to wife's husband that test results were consistent with sexually transmitted disease. Plaintiff's claim that physician breached physician-patient relationship was recognized as valid but its dismissal affirmed on grounds that wife had impliedly consented to disclosure of medical information to husband. Doctrine of tortious interference with the marital relationship abolished. ***Haddad v. Gopal*, 787 A.2d 975 (Pa. Super. 2002)**

Tow Truck

Plaintiff brought negligence action against defendant tow truck driver and his employers after he rear-ended the tow truck as it attempted to make a u-turn at a median opening in a highway. A jury found in favor of the defendants. The Superior Court affirmed, holding that a tow truck operator was authorized to use a median opening to make a u-turn on a highway. ***Keffer v. Bob Nolan's Auto Service, Inc.*, 59 A.3d 621 (Pa. Super. 2013).**

Toxic chemicals

In suit that alleged decedent contracted malignant nodular lymphoma from occupational exposure to toxic chemicals, plaintiff may proceed with wrongful death cause of action until there is a final determination whether the disease was covered under the Worker's Compensation Act or Occupational Disease Act. Superior Court's reversal of trial court's order sustaining preliminary objections affirmed by evenly divided court. ***Lord Corporation v. Pollard*, 695 A.2d 767 (Pa. 1997).**

Tractor

Jury verdict $80,000—reduced to $64,000 due to finding of 20% contributory negligence. Defendant's auto struck plaintiff's garden tractor head-on, as he

Traffic control devices

was plowing snow from driveway near berm of highway. Exact locations of vehicles at impact disputed. Held: assured clear distance rule does apply at night on snowy road. Driver must take attending circumstances into account. *Fish v. Gosnell,* **316 Pa. Super. 565, 463 A.2d 1042.**

Operator of car in which passenger plaintiff situate contended that the reason that he did not observe tractor of defendant sooner was that it was so dirty as to be virtually camouflaged until he was within 20 feet of it—collision—verdict for passenger sustained but new trial granted as to suit by operator to determine whether contribution should be had. *Stano v. Rearick,* **441 Pa. 72, 271 A.2d 251.**

Plaintiff was a volunteer worker helping blacktop a parking lot—struck by a tractor used to roll blacktop—defendant operator left engine running when leaving machine—his seven year old son started machine and plaintiff injured—owner of premises and operator of tractor held jointly responsible. *Glass v. Freeman,* **430 Pa. 21, 240 A.2d 825.**

Traffic control devices

Passenger injured when automobile struck by truck that went through red light. Truck driver liable. Evidence that truck driver relied on C.B. transmission as to status of traffic signal held admissible. *Smith v. Brooks,* **394 Pa. Super. 327, 575 A.2d 926.**

Motorist injured in collision at intersection. Defendant went through red light at high rate of speed. Plaintiff did not look to left. Defendant found 75% negligent, plaintiff 25% negligent. *Cooper v. Burns,* **376 Pa. Super. 276, 545 A.2d 935.**

Accident at intersection where admittedly overhead traffic signal turned green in two directions at once. Error to admit evidence of 36 motor vehicle accidents between 1965 and 1978. Other accidents from different causes are irrelevant. Correspondence between City of Scranton and PennDOT was admissible concerning maintenance of signals at this intersection. Evidence (letter) focused on deficiencies in maintenance of many items including traffic lights. Response to letters was an admission of party, therefore all letters admitted as exception to hearsay rule. *Whitman v. Riddell,* **324 Pa. Super. 177, 471 A.2d 521.**

Truck coming down steep hill unable to stop at stop sign, skidded on ice through intersection causing accident. Jury verdict for defendant. Held: unavoidable accident. Negligence *per se* (going through sign) not same as strict liability. Jury could find valid excuse, despite due care, for going past sign. Error for judge to grant new trial. Verdict reinstated. *Bumbarger v. Kaminsky,* **311 Pa. Super. 177, 457 A.2d 552.**

Jury verdict against driver with red light and in passenger's favor. Right angle collision. Jury found car with green light not negligent, even though did not look for traffic just before entering intersection. Affirmed. *Spraggins v. Shields,* **310 Pa. Super. 408, 456 A.2d 1000.**

Plaintiff passenger in defendant's car involved in accident with second car whose driver was not a party. Defendant had flashing yellow light. Other car went

Trains and platforms

through flashing red light. Sole issue was negligence of defendant who testified that he did not see other car until it was 15 feet from him. Trial judge charged that defendant did not exercise proper care in proceeding on yellow flasher. Grant of new trial after defense verdict affirmed. **Hayter v. Sileo, 230 Pa. Super. 329, 326 A.2d 462.**

Plaintiff had turn signal on for 450 to 500 feet prior to stopping—passed several intersections with turn signal on—rear end collision—verdict for defendant affirmed. **McCay v. Philadelphia Electric Co., 447 Pa. 490, 291 A.2d 759.**

Rear-end collision—plaintiff in forward car injured—error for trial judge to charge that plaintiff might be found guilty of contributory negligence if she did not give a hand signal of intention to stop—Code also provides for mechanical signals. **Buckalew v. DeAngelis, 424 Pa. 292, 227 A.2d 672.**

Trains and platforms

Evaluation of real estate exception to sovereign immunity statute and historically applied "on/of" distinction. Proper method for determining whether real estate exception to sovereign immunity applies is to focus on whether a dangerous condition created by rock salt on a train platform derived from, originated from, or had its source in the real estate itself and if not, the real estate exception did not apply. "On/of" analysis formally rejected. Important distinction between language of Sovereign Immunity Act and the Political Subdivision Tort Claims Act. **Jones v. SEPTA, 772 A.2d 435 (Pa. 2001).**

Plaintiff was injured when she slipped and fell on rock salt located *on* defendant's train platform. Held: "of / on" distinction continues to apply to cases where the real property exception to governmental immunity applies. **Jones v. SEPTA, 748 A.2d 1271 (Pa. Cmwlth. 2000).**

Plaintiff was injured when the train he was boarding began moving unexpectedly. Independent witnesses testified that train was stopped when plaintiff began to board. After verdict for plaintiff, defendant appealed alleging trial court erred in failing to charge on assumption of risk. Held: if there is no testimony to support any risk to be assumed by plaintiff, charge is improper. Also, assumption of risk is for court to consider in legal analysis of duty aspect of claim, not for jury to determine. **Wallis v. SEPTA, 723 A.2d 267 (Pa. Cmwlth. 1999).**

Summary judgment entered against plaintiff who was shot by robber while a passenger on defendant's stopped train. Plaintiff alleged that defendant's trainman's failure to open the door of the train to allow plaintiff to escape before he was shot was a concurrent cause of his injury and that failure to act involved the operation of the motor vehicle. The Commonwealth Court distinguishes concurrent negligent acts from a negligent act by defendant and a criminal assault by a third party and also holds by implication that the failure to open the door was not "operation" of the motor vehicle. **Greenleaf v. SEPTA, 698 A.2d 170 (Pa. Cmwlth. 1997).**

In action by motorist for injuries sustained when she collided with side of a hopper car being pulled by defendant's train, railroad company whose train was actually on and moving over a crossing did not owe motorist a duty to warn of train's presence. Occupied crossing rule survived enactment of the Comparative Negligence Act. Order sustaining preliminary objections affirmed. *Sprenkle v. Conrail,* **446 Pa. Super. 377, 666 A.2d 1099 (1995).**

Pedestrian who slipped on debris on train platform brought action against city. City not liable. Injuries not caused by artificial condition or defect in land. *Wellons v. SEPTA,* **141 Pa. Cmwlth. 622, 596 A.2d 1169.**

Plaintiff assaulted on train platform in City. Demurrer of City granted. Duty to provide police protection is public and cannot be claimed by individual. *Chapman v. City of Philadelphia,* **290 Pa. Super. 281, 434 A.2d 753.**

Plaintiff's railroad train struck tractor-trailer stalled on a grade crossing—rig remained on tracks some 15 or 20 minutes—operator failing to set out flares or otherwise warn train crew—damage to leading diesel engine—some evidence of defects in crossing—verdict for plaintiff sustained on appeal. *Baltimore & Ohio R.R. Co. v. Campbell and Taylor Lumber Co.,* **218 Pa. Super. 904, 279 A.2d 215.**

Trampoline

Minor plaintiff injured alighting from trampoline in neighbor's backyard. Defense verdict reversed. Held: error to exclude evidence of industry standards on safe use of both recreational and instructional trampolines. New trial ordered. *Walheim v. Kirkpatrick,* **305 Pa. Super. 590, 451 A.2d 1033.**

Transfusion

Plaintiff who contracted AIDS following transfusion of tainted blood filed suit against treating physicians and family physician for medical malpractice. Claim against one defendant dismissed for plaintiff's failure to establish through medical testimony that defendant's actions deviated from good and acceptable medical standards. Proof of compliance with medical standard of care need not be expressed in precisely the language used to annunciate the legal standard. Physician not required to obtain patient's informed consent before blood transfusion which was administered separately from a surgical procedure. *Hoffman v. Brandywine Hospital,* **443 Pa. Super. 245, 661 A.2d 397 (1995).**

Trapdoor

Plaintiff on premises to inspect plywood—falling into open trapdoor and injured—case for jury against parties in control of building—error to direct verdict for defendant. *Pastuszek v. Murphy Plywood Corp. et al.,* **219 Pa. Super. 59, 280 A.2d 644.**

Traumatic amnesia

Plaintiff's vehicle struck by defendant's train at a grade crossing—plaintiff's testimony disclosed that plaintiff had a clear view from 1365 to 1849 feet before entering crossing—incontrovertible physical facts rule applied and action of court below entering nonsuit affirmed—the fact that plaintiff was suffering from traumatic amnesia not controlling. *Reynolds v. Cen. R.R. of N.J. et al.,* **448 Pa. 415, 292 A.2d 924.**

Traumatic cervical syndrome

Traumatic cervical syndrome

Jury verdict $110,000 for economic loss and $140,000 for noneconomic loss affirmed. Permanent traumatic cervical syndrome to woman in her 50s. Work life expectancy of 16.5 years. At time of accident, working as bundle work binder at dress manufacturing plant. Also a licensed beautician working part-time at home. Had been full-time beautician in past. Injuries also included lacerations of lip requiring surgery and leaving scar. Left with headaches and neck pain leaving her incapable of returning to beautician work. Under facts, proper to allow evidence of earning capacity as beautician. Defendant found 100% liable in head-on collision where he drove vehicle which he knew to be leaking carbon monoxide in passenger compartment. Verdict affirmed with setoff for No Fault wage loss benefit actually received. ***Lewis v. Pruitt,* 337 Pa. Super. 419, 487 A.2d 16.**

Traumatic onset of disease

$15,455 verdict for questionable traumatic onset of amyotrophic lateral sclerosis—4 year life expectancy of plaintiff at time of trial. Error to allow testimony of receipt of workmen's compensation benefits, but here not prejudicial—verdict adequate—affirmed. ***Downey v. Weston,* 451 Pa. 259, 301 A.2d 635.**

Trees

Driver brought a claim of negligence for injuries he suffered while driving on a state highway, after a decayed tree fell on his car. Trial Court granted a motion for nonsuit to Defendants based upon immunity. The Commonwealth Court affirmed, holding that PennDOT was entitled to sovereign immunity as the Plaintiff failed to establish that the decayed tree originated on Commonwealth property or that a part of the tree overhanging the highway constituted a dangerous condition that caused the accident. ***Clark v. Pennsylvania Department of Transportation,* 962 A.2d 692 (Pa. Cmwlth. 2008).**

Plaintiff's decedent was killed when his truck struck a tree that had fallen across the road. After verdict for plaintiff, municipality appealed claiming that it was entitled to governmental immunity because the tree "on" the road was not a condition "of" the road. Commonwealth Court reversed on that basis following *Finn v. City of Philadelphia*, 541 Pa. 596, 664 A.2d 1342 (1995). ***Osborne v. Cambridge Township,* 736 A.2d 715 (Pa. Cmwlth. 1999).**

Plaintiff was rear seat passenger in car driven by defendant which encountered fog bank, left road and struck tree, injuring plaintiff. Trial court charged on sudden emergency doctrine to which plaintiff objected. Plaintiff argued that defendant's summary citation for breaking statutory assured clear distance rule precluded her from claiming sudden emergency; a tree is not a sudden emergency and amount of time it took for defendant to react argues against any suddenness. Held: summary charges, particularly when defendant did not even attend hearing on charge, cannot be admitted in civil cases as a general rule. Tree was not sudden emergency, the fog was. There was adequate evidence that defendant acted quickly and thoroughly to minimize sudden appearance of fog. Plaintiff's second argument that jury's distaste with trial court's habit of chewing tobacco during trial and spitting into a cup as

Trees

prejudicial to plaintiff is totally unfounded. ***Dickens v. Barnhart*, 711 A.2d 513 (Pa. Super. 1998).**

To recover against Commonwealth under real property exception to sovereign immunity, plaintiff, whose decedent was killed when tree limb on Commonwealth property fell on her car, must establish that PennDOT had actual or constructive notice of the dangerous condition. Trial court's refusal to charge on notice was reversible error. New trial granted. ***Com. Dept. of Transp. v. Patton*, 546 Pa. 561, 686 A.2d 1302 (1997).**

Pedestrian injured after stepping into hole created where tree trunk removed from township-owned park grounds may not recover against township which has immunity under both Political Subdivision Tort Claims Act and Recreation Use of Land and Water Act. Summary judgment for township affirmed. ***Wilkinson v. Conoy Township*, 677 A.2d 876 (Pa. Cmwlth. 1996).**

Failure of personal representative of decedent driver's estate to prove that tree which fell on decedent's car and killed her was located on Commonwealth property precluded recovery against Commonwealth under real property exception to sovereign immunity. Judgment reversed and judgment *n.o.v.* entered in favor of PennDOT. ***Marker v. Com., Dept. of Transp.*, 677 A.2d 345 (Pa. Cmwlth. 1996).**

Plaintiff widower stated cause of action under real estate exception to sovereign immunity for death of motorist/wife caused by limb falling from tree that had been "topped" twenty years earlier and was growing above PennDOT's right of way at 45° angle. Judgment on verdict for plaintiff affirmed. ***Patton v. Com., Dept. of Transp.*, ___ Pa. Cmwlth. ___, 669 A.2d 1090 (1995).**

Passenger killed when automobile struck tree that had fallen across state road. Township police placed flares and cones around tree. Township immune. ***Mylett v. Adamsky*, 139 Pa. Cmwlth. 637, 591 A.2d 341.**

Pedestrian tripped over sidewalk that was raised because of roots from tree planted by city. Property owner and not city held primarily liable. ***Pischos v. Sauvion*, 103 Pa. Cmwlth. 517, 520 A.2d 945.**

Two vehicles collided at intersection. Plaintiff sued abutting property owner among others for maintaining shrub and trees which obstructed view. Lower court granted summary judgment in favor of property owner. Reversed. Issues of superceding cause, comparative negligence and violations of statutes, for jury. ***Harvey v. Hansen*, 299 Pa. Super. 474, 445 A.2d 1228.**

Limb of tree fell onto plaintiff's car, which he was driving on adjacent road, killing him. Property owner, and electric company which had been trimming and inspecting trees along this highway for 24 years, held responsible. Additional evidence that tree had been decaying for four years. ***Beury v. Hicks*, 227 Pa. Super. 476, 323 A.2d 788.**

Branch of tree extended into cartway and injured an occupant of a passing van—suit against municipality and property owners—verdict against both sustained

Trench

on appeal—property owner not primarily responsible—joint obligation of both defendants. ***Green v. Freeport Borough*, 218 Pa. Super. 334, 280 A.2d 412.**

Trench

Absent proof that a particular trenching effort presented a peculiar risk or danger, an employer, in this case a municipal sewer authority, will not be held vicariously liable for the negligent conduct of its contractors. ***Dunkle v. Middleburg Municipal Authority*, 842 A.2d 477 (Pa. Cmwlth. 2004).**

Plaintiff's decedent was killed in a trench collapse while a representative of the project design engineer was at the site. In affirming dismissal of the action against the engineer, the court held that a design professional does not have a duty to protect workers from hazards on a construction site unless there was an undertaking, either by contract or course of conduct, to supervise or control the construction and/or to maintain safe conditions at the site. ***Herczeg v. Hampton Township*, 766 A.2d 866 (Pa. Super. 2001).**

Action brought against general contractor for death of plumbing contractor killed when walls of trench caved in. Held: Plumber did not assume risk by voluntarily working in dangerous trench. ***Handschuh v. Albert Development*, 393 Pa. Super. 444, 574 A.2d 693.**

Trespassers

Plaintiff's decedent was killed while driving intoxicated without license in uninspected, unregistered car at too high a rate of speed. He entered highway ramp at twice the posted speed limit despite having been on the ramp on daily basis. Jury returned verdict in amount of $250,000.00 and apportioned liability to plaintiff and PennDOT at fifty percent each. Plaintiff appealed, alleging inadequacy of verdict. PennDOT appealed, alleging error by trial court in refusing to allow evidence of lack of license, registration, and inspection, error in refusing to find plaintiff's decedent to be a trespasser, and error in finding any duty on PennDOT because plaintiff's decedent was not licensed driver. Affirmed on basis that verdict was compromise by jury, PennDOT owes duty to all persons operating vehicles on its roads regardless of state of their license and lack of license, registration, and inspection were, while relevant, more prejudicial than probative. ***Quinn v. Com., Dept. of Transp.*, 719 A.2d 1105 (Pa. Cmwlth. 1998).**

Plaintiff police officer was injured when he tripped on old fencing on lot adjacent to house at which a search warrant was being served. Lower court granted summary judgment to defendant property owners holding police officer was trespasser and defendants had duty only to avoid wanton or willful negligence or misconduct. Superior Court affirmed. Supreme Court granted allocatur and affirmed holding Section 345 of Restatement (2d) Torts relating to duty to trespassers entering pursuant to a privilege is not adopted in Pennsylvania and police and fire fighters are to be accorded trespasser status. ***Rossino v. Kovacs*, 718 A.2d 755 (Pa. 1998).**

Plaintiff roofing supply salesman was injured when he stepped into unguarded hole in floor of defendant's house that was under construction. At conclusion of plaintiff's case against homeowner, trial court granted compulsory nonsuit on grounds that plaintiff had not presented adequate evidence to establish he was entitled to status greater than trespasser. Record contained references to defendant homeowner's approval of plaintiff's offer to deliver roof vents to plaintiff's house and to implication from workmen at house that plaintiff was permitted to enter house to leave roof vents inside, safe from theft and exposure. Reversal of nonsuit because there were adequate facts to take issue of plaintiff's status as business invitee to jury. ***Emge v. Hagosky*** **, 712 A.2d 315 (Pa. Super. 1998).**

Plaintiff teenager brought suit against above ground pool owner for injuries suffered when she dove into four feet of water and suffered serious injuries to her neck. Order granting motion for compulsory nonsuit affirmed where evidence by plaintiff established that she was aware of danger of diving into shallow water; she was aware of depth of the water in the pool; and she proceeded to dive into the pool "on a dare." Plaintiff's status as licensee or trespasser not a factor in light of her knowledge of danger. Property owner's duty does not extend to those conditions the existence of which is obvious even to children, and the risk of which is fully realized by them, particularly when the child chooses to encounter the risk through recklessness or bravado. ***Long v. Manzo,*** **452 Pa. Super. 451, 682 A.2d 370 (1996).**

Political Subdivision Tort Claims Act exception for dangerous condition of property does not extend to plaintiff who became trespasser when he climbed to roof of school building to retrieve tennis ball. School district took sufficient steps to prevent entry onto roof. Summary judgment in favor of school district affirmed. ***Longbottom v. Sim-Kar Lighting Fixture Co.,*** **651 A.2d 621 (Pa. Cmwlth. 1994).**

Trespasser electrocuted while attempting to steal copper cable. Property owner not liable. ***Dudley v. USX Corporation,*** **414 Pa. Super. 160, 606 A.2d 916.**

Trespasser at city-owned swimming pool died as a result of injuries. City not immune under Recreation Use of Land and Water Act but is immune under Political Subdivision Tort Claims Act. ***Mitchell v. City of Philadelphia,*** **141 Pa. Cmwlth. 695, 596 A.2d 1205.**

Trespasser injured when he tripped over debris left on city property after employees trimmed tree. City not liable. ***Hedglin v. City of Scranton,*** **139 Pa. Cmwlth. 201, 590 A.2d 62.**

Scoutmaster injured when attempting to stop trespasser from driving ATV through camp grounds. Land owner not liable. Scoutmaster assumed risk. ***Chiricos v. Forest Lakes Council Boy Scouts of America,*** **391 Pa. Super. 491, 571 A.2d 474.**

Hunter injured while hunting on posted sanitary land fill. Owner found immune under Recreation Use of Land and Water Act even though land was not open for public use and hunter was trespasser. ***Friedman v. Grand Central Sanitation, Inc.,*** **524 Pa. 270, 571 A.2d 373.**

Motorcyclist riding on private property ran into 1-1/2 inch steel cable strung across a road to deter trespassers. Admitted that plaintiff was a trespasser. Duty to trespasser is not to act in reckless disregard for safety. Landowner knew dirt bikes traversed property. New trial ordered. Submission of case to jury on negligence the-

Trip and fall

ory—misleading. Court questions viability of doctrine of landowner immunity. *Antonace v. Ferri Contracting Co.,* **320 Pa. Super. 519, 467 A.2d 833.**

Minor plaintiff injured by bullets found in car in defendant's garage. Defendant towed and stored abandoned cars for City of Easton. Nonsuit affirmed. Possessor of land only liable to trespasser for conditions of which he knows or should have known, despite fact that children played in lot. *Norton v. City of Easton,* **249 Pa. Super. 520, 378 A.2d 417.**

Minor plaintiff trespassed on defendant's land at a point not used for play—injured by being impaled by a surveyor's stake—summary judgment properly entered—Section 339 of Restatement (2d) Torts not complied with by plaintiff. *Whigham v. Pyle,* **224 Pa. Super. 6, 302 A.2d 498.**

Trip and fall

Plaintiff brought negligence action against Defendant airport after she tripped and fell on a stage in the airport. The trial court granted summary judgment to the Defendant. The Commonwealth Court affirmed holding that for the real property exception to immunity to apply the dangerous condition must be attached to the floor. *Sanchez-Guardiola v. City of Philadelphia,* **87 A.3d 934 (Pa. Cmwlth 2014).**

Plaintiff brought negligence claim against the Defendant university and city after she tripped and fell on their sidewalk due to a 2-2 ½ inch elevation change. The trial court granted summary judgment to the city. The Superior Court reversed holding that a sidewalk defect may be so trivial that a court as a matter of law may grant summary judgment, but unless it was obviously trivial the question should be determined by the jury. *Shaw v. Thomas Jefferson University,* **80 A.3d 540 (Pa. Cmwlth 2013).**

Plaintiff filed negligence action against the Defendant city after she tripped and fell on an allegedly uneven sidewalk. The trial entered a compulsory nonsuit in favor of the city. The Superior Court affirmed holding that the trial judge's decision to grant nonsuit did not violate the coordinate jurisdiction rule due to a prior judge's decision to deny the city's motion for summary judgment. *Hunter v. City of Philadelphia,* **80 A.3d 533 (Pa. Cmwlth 2013).**

Plaintiff brought negligence action against Defendant after she tripped and fell on stairs at a property she was renting. Trial court granted a new trial on damages only after the jury awarded no damages, but found both parties 50% liable for the Plaintiff's injuries. The Superior Court reversed holding that a new trial on damages only may only be granted if: 1) liability was not intertwined with the question of damages; and 2) the issue of liability is not contested or has been fairly determined. *Banohashim v. R.S. Enterprises, Inc.,* **77 A.3d 14 (Pa. Super. 2013).**

Tenant brought negligence action against a property owner and a paving company after he tripped on the edge of an asphalt driveway. The trial court entered summary judgment in favor of the defendants. The Superior Court reversed in part and affirmed in part. The Superior Court held that the defendant paving company could not be held liable as it had not made the driveway dangerous in a way the landowner was unlikely to discover. The Superior Court reversed as to the landowner on the basis that there was a genuine issue of material fact as to whether the tenant voluntarily and knowingly proceeded in the face of an obvious and dangerous condition in the form of the drop off of the driveway. ***Longwell v. Giordano*, 57 A.3d 163 (Pa. Super. 2012).**

Plaintiff brought negligence action against a casino after he tripped and fell over an electrical cord. The trial court transferred the case based upon preliminary objections to venue. The Superior Court affirmed, holding that the operations of sister corporations could not be used to establish venue unless the Defendant itself actually conducted business in that venue as well. ***Wimble v. Parx Casino v. Greenwood Gaming & Entertainment, Inc.*, 40 A.3d 174 (Pa. Super. 2012).**

Plaintiff brought a personal injury action against property owner after tripping on an uneven portion of sidewalk. The trial court granted summary judgment as the defect in the sidewalk was only 1½ inches deep and thus trivial. The Superior Court reversed holding that there is no definite or mathematical rule for depth or size of a depression to determine if a defect is trivial as a matter of law and that the facts did not establish that the defect was trivial. In addition, it held that the trial court could not consider prior knowledge in determining if a defect is trivial. ***Mull v. Ickes*, 994 A.2d 1137 (Pa. Super. 2010).**

Pedestrian injured in a trip and fall due to street resurfacing brought negligence action against the city. The trial court found for the Plaintiff. The Superior Court reversed, holding that the city was not the owner of the street as it was designated a state highway and also that the Plaintiff had failed to prove a contractual relationship between the city and Commonwealth to maintain the road, which was required for the street exception to the Political Subdivision Tort Claims Act to be applied to the city. ***Leiphart v. City of Philadelphia*, 972 A.2d 1239 (Pa. Cmwlth. 2009).**

Delivery driver brought a claim for negligence against a University after he tripped and fell due to a raised bumper on the loading dock. On appeal the Superior Court affirmed the jury verdict in favor of the delivery driver on the basis that the University failed to warn its business invitee of a known unreasonably dangerous condition and failed to exercise reasonable care to protect the delivery driver as it had reason to expect that he might be distracted and fail to protect himself. ***Walker v. Drexel University*, 971 A.2d 521 (Pa. Super. 2009).**

Plaintiff brought a claim against a property owner after he slipped and fell on ice in their parking lot. The appellate court reversed the trial court's grant of summary judgment holding that when a property owner retains control of a part of the leased premises he is liable for physical harm caused by dangerous conditions that exist on that part of the property over which that he retained control. ***Jones v. Levin*, 940 A.2d 451 (Pa. Super. 2007).**

Plaintiff brought a claim against a property owner after he tripped and fell on sidewalk outside of the property owner's home. The appellate court reversed the trial court's denial for a new trial solely on damages, because the jury's award of zero dollars to the plaintiff, despite a holding of 50% negligence on the part of both

Trip and fall

parties, was against the weight of the evidence. *Casselli v. Powlen*, **937 A.2d 1137 (Pa. Super. 2007).**

City, which owns sidewalk abutted by private owner and Commonwealth highway, is liable for maintenance of sidewalk, regardless of dedication of the highway. Under the Political Subdivision Tort Claims Act, it is control of the sidewalk, not ownership that determines liability for maintenance and injuries. This case abrogates a substantial number of prior cases. ***Walker v. Eleby*, 842 A.2d 389 (Pa. 2004).**

Suit by pedestrian against city and PennDOT for injuries sustained when she tripped on the raised "header" portion of a crosswalk on a city street that had been adopted by PennDOT as a state highway. Held that city-maintained crosswalk was a traffic control device and so city was liable for negligent maintenance. ***Ryals v. City of Philadelphia*, 848 A.2d 1101 (Pa. Cmwlth. 2004).**

Plaintiff who was injured when she tripped on a raised metal drain grate in a grocery store was not permitted by the trial court to raise the *res ipsa loquitur* defense in opposition to a motion for nonsuit. Following analysis of transitory defects versus a defect in the building itself, the court held that the existence of a defect that compromises the safety of the building itself permits the plaintiff, at the compulsory nonsuit stage, to raise *res ipsa loquitur* as a defense. ***Neve v. Insalaco's*, 771 A.2d 786 (Pa. Super. 2001).**

Plaintiff sued city for injuries sustained when she was caused to fall by defective condition of sidewalk that abutted state highway and city-owned property. Trial court granted city's summary judgment motion on grounds that city is immune from liability to suit for injuries sustained by plaintiff where defect is in sidewalk adjacent to state highway and not city street. Held: exception to governmental immunity for dangerous condition of sidewalk owned and maintained by city is unaffected by fact that sidewalk is adjacent to state highway and not city street. ***White v. City of Philadelphia*, 712 A.2d 345 (Pa. Cmwlth. 1998).**

Plaintiff tripped and fell on a crack in sidewalk immediately adjacent to street level "head house" of subway entrance. Plaintiff sued SEPTA and City of Philadelphia, alleging that under lease between City and SEPTA, one or both of those entities was responsible for maintenance of sidewalk. Trial court determined that lease was ambiguous as to responsibility for area of sidewalk at issue and so allowed parol evidence. Jury found that SEPTA was responsible for maintenance. Jury verdict was entered against both City and SEPTA. Post trial motions by City and SEPTA were denied. Held on appeal: if SEPTA were found to be responsible, City should have been granted judgment *n.o.v.* Remand to enter judgment *n.o.v.* in favor of City of Philadelphia. ***Smith v. SEPTA*, 707 A.2d 604 (Pa. Cmwlth. 1998).**

A median on which alighting bus passenger tripped and sustained injuries is part of the highway and not a traffic control device; therefore, PennDOT, as owner of highway, may be subject to liability under exception to sovereign immunity. Verdict against City reversed; verdict against Commonwealth affirmed. ***Slough v. Com., Dept. of Transp.*, 686 A.2d 62 (Pa. Cmwlth. 1996).**

Violation of a statute, although negligence *per se*, does not constitute a ground for imposing liability unless it can be shown to be a substantial factor in causing plaintiff's injuries which resulted from a trip and fall. Failure to produce evidence of separate and distinct damages attributable to a scar precludes a specific jury instruction regarding the scar. Judgment affirmed. ***Gravlin v. Fredavid Builders and Developers,*** **450 Pa. Super. 655, 677 A.2d 1235 (1996).**

For real property exception to governmental immunity to apply to municipality, sidewalk must be within right of way of a street owned by the municipality. Pedestrian who tripped on pipe projecting from sidewalk owned by municipality could not recover from municipality because underlying street right of way was owned by PennDOT. Because sidewalk was not realty for purposes of exception, pipe was not realty by reason of its connection to sidewalk. Summary judgment in favor of borough affirmed. ***Gray v. Logue,*** **___ Pa. Cmwlth. ___, 654 A.2d 109 (1995).**

Plaintiff elevator inspector who tripped on misaligned elevator floor failed to produce evidence that product was defective and that defendant was seller. Products liability claim dismissed and verdict for defendant affirmed. ***Micciche v. Eastern Elevator Co.,*** **435 Pa. Super. 219, 645 A.2d 278 (1994).**

Plaintiff while making a delivery allegedly tripped over a rug on floor of defendant's premises and was seriously injured—recovery allowed—court found actionable negligence. ***Reardon v. Meehan,*** **424 Pa. 460, 227 A.2d 667.**

Truck

Plaintiff brought negligence action against Defendant airport after she tripped and fell on a stage in the airport. The trial court granted summary judgment to the Defendant. The Commonwealth Court affirmed holding that for the real property exception to immunity to apply the dangerous condition must be attached to the floor. ***Sanchez-Guardiola v. City of Philadelphia,*** **87 A.3d 934 (Pa. Cmwlth. 2014).**

Plaintiff brought negligence claim against the Defendant university and city after she tripped and fell on their sidewalk due to a 2-2 ½ inch elevation change. The trial court granted summary judgment to the city. The Superior Court reversed holding that a sidewalk defect may be so trivial that a court as a matter of law may grant summary judgment, but unless it was obviously trivial the question should be determined by the jury. ***Shaw v. Thomas Jefferson University,*** **80 A.3d 540 (Pa. Cmwlth. 2013).**

Plaintiff filed negligence action against the Defendant city after she tripped and fell on an allegedly uneven sidewalk. The trial court entered a compulsory nonsuit in favor of the city. The Superior Court affirmed holding that the trial judge's decision to grant nonsuit did not violate the coordinate jurisdiction rule due to a prior judge's decision to deny the city's motion for summary judgment. ***Hunter v. City of Philadelphia,*** **80 A.3d 533 (Pa. Cmwlth. 2013).**

Plaintiff brought negligence action against Defendant after she tripped and fell on stairs at a property she was renting. Trial court granted a new trial on damag-

Truck

es only after the jury awarded no damages, but found both parties 50% liable for the Plaintiff's injuries. The Superior Court reversed holding that a new trial on damages only may be granted only if: 1) liability was not intertwined with the question of damages; and 2) the issue of liability is not contested or has been fairly determined. ***Banohashim v. R.S. Enterprises, Inc.*, 77 A.3d 14 (Pa. Super. 2013).**

Plaintiff injured when he collided with stopped and abandoned city-owned truck could not recover because the truck's position and abandoned status removed it from "operation of a motor vehicle" exception to political subdivision tort claims act immunity. ***Merz v. City of Philadelphia*, 719 A.2d 1131 (Pa. Cmwlth. 1998).**

Plaintiff was injured when struck by truck being backed up by defendant. Conflicting facts before jury included truck position, who was driving other vehicle, location of plaintiff, preparations to back up made by driver. On conflicting factual record, jury returned verdict in favor of defendant and against plaintiff. On post trial motion, trial court granted new trial on basis that verdict shocked court's sense of justice. The Superior Court affirmed and Supreme Court reversed, holding that determination of credibility is solely within province of jury. A trial court may not disregard a jury's credibility determination and substitute its own. ***Martin v. Evans*, 711 A.2d 458 (Pa. 1998).**

Jury returned verdict in favor of plaintiff and against first driver's company only and allocated 41% liability to plaintiff. On appeal, Commonwealth Court held there was adequate evidence to support jury verdict in favor of plaintiff and against only one defendant. Affirmed with modification, allowing plaintiff's employer to file a subrogation according to Indiana law. ***Burlington Motor Carriers v. Com., Dept. of Transp.*, 710 A.2d 148 (Pa. Cmwlth. 1998).**

Homeowners may recover for damage to property caused by city-owned truck that rolled backward into plaintiffs' home. Truck was improperly parked and left unattended with engine running and therefore was in "operation" under motor vehicle exception to Political Subdivision Tort Claims Act. Judgment on the pleadings against City affirmed and remanded for trial. ***Cacchione v. Wieczorek*, ___ Pa. Cmwlth. ___, 674 A.2d 773 (1996).**

In negligence action by truck driver for damages resulting from cow wandering onto roadway, turnpike commission had no duty of care, custody, or control of cow. Summary judgment affirmed. ***Mason & Dixon Lines, Inc. v. Mognet*, 166 Pa. Cmwlth. 1, 645 A.2d 1370 (1994).**

Truck driver injured when vehicle skidded on ice and snow on highway. PennDOT not liable for failure to clear ice and snow or for failure to warn. ***Hunt v. Com., Dept. of Transp.*, 137 Pa. Cmwlth. 588, 587 A.2d 37.**

Plaintiff to right had his view blocked by a truck turning right—had green light in his favor—struck by car from left when he had traversed more than half of the intersection—evidence such that it could not be ruled as a matter of law that he did not look and relied solely on the light—nonsuit improperly granted—case for jury. ***Robinson v. Raab*, 216 Pa. Super. 397, 268 A.2d 225.**

Trustee

Bank investment advisor who served as manager of trust account surcharged for negligence in management of trust funds. Decisions to diversify, extend investment horizon and change nature of investments were not made in light of particular circumstances of the actual needs of the life beneficiaries. *In re: Scheidmantel, Appeal of Sky Trust*, **868 A.2d 464 (Pa. Super. 2005).**

Tuberculosis

Nurse who sought treatment at employer/hospital for tuberculosis contracted at hospital must seek recovery for injuries sustained as a result of misdiagnosis and mistreatment through workers compensation proceedings. Superior Court order reversing verdict for plaintiff affirmed by equally divided court. *Snyder v. Pocono Medical Center,* **547 Pa. 415, 690 A.2d 1152 (1997).**

Respiratory therapist who contracted tuberculosis from exposure to patient brought negligence action against employer hospital for failure to diagnosis and treat her condition promptly and not to obtain remedy for contracting disease. Jury verdict for plaintiff reversed on grounds that her sole remedy was workers' compensation. *Snyder v. Pocono Medical Center,* **440 Pa. Super. 606, 656 A.2d 534 (1995).**

Tumor

Wife plaintiff diagnosed with lung cancer filed suit against radiology association and radiologist who had taken and interpreted chest x-ray at request of insurance company for failure to diagnose cancerous tumor. No physician-patient relationship is created where a physician examines a patient at the request of an insuranance company. Summary judgment affirmed. *Promubol v. Hackett,* **454 Pa. Super. 622, 686 A.2d 417 (1996).**

Turning vehicles

Left turn accident. Jury found neither driver negligent. Lower court refused to grant new trial. Held: proper as to driver's cross-claims but improper as to passenger. New trial for passenger only. *Myers v. Gold,* **277 Pa. Super. 66, 419 A.2d 663.**

Intersection collision. Both cars had green light. Defendant making left turn. Left turn driver guilty of negligence as a matter of law for not continuing to look for oncoming traffic as he was making left turn, especially where view of oncoming traffic was partially obstructed. *Lind v. Thomas,* **265 Pa. Super. 121, 401 A.2d 830.**

Defendant initiated left turn in front of plaintiff's oncoming vehicle. Impact occurred a split second after initiation of turn. No evidence of plaintiff's speeding. Verdict for defendant against the weight of evidence. *Ditz v. Marshall,* **259 Pa. Super. 31, 393 A.2d 701.**

Vehicle in which plaintiffs were passengers stalled while turning and struck by oncoming car. Snowing heavily. Driver of oncoming car busy wiping inside of windshield. Poor visibility. Verdict against both drivers. Some evidence that driver

Two different accidents

of stalled car negligent in making very sharp turn under the circumstances. ***Poltorak v. Sandy,* 236 Pa. Super. 355, 345 A.2d 201.**

    Plaintiff passing defendant's truck on highway when truck turned left into her. Truck driver stated turn signals were on that he was turning into plant driveway and that there were two blind spots which he could not see using the mirrors. Verdict for defendant affirmed. ***Delp v. Heath,* 234 Pa. Super. 607, 340 A.2d 530.**

    Section 1012, as amended, of Vehicle Code construed with respect to intention to make a left turn—failure to charge on duty of one making left turn held error—new trial granted. ***McMahon v. Young,* 442 Pa. 484, 276 A.2d 534.**

    Sections 1011 (b), 1012 (a) of Vehicle Code construed as not to apply to motorist who was not by nature of highway at point required to make left turn—only required to follow a curve in highway. ***Vescio v. Rubolino,* 433 Pa. 253, 249 A.2d 914.**

Two different accidents

    Plaintiff died in hospital after being injured by roll of fencing that fell from vehicle. After settlement with individual who secured fencing, court ordered dismissal of settled defendants from case. Physicians accused of malpractice appealed. Affirmed. Held: parties not joint tortfeasors under facts here. ***Harlea v. Nabati,* 337 Pa. Super. 617, 487 A.2d 432.**

    Pedestrian struck and killed by one or more autos as he stepped off medial strip at night. Settled with first striking vehicle. Nonsuit as to all others. Evidence insufficient as to whether others actually struck plaintiff, or whether he died from first impact. ***Pio v. Letarec,* 294 Pa. Super. 196, 439 A.2d 818.**

    Auto accident and subsequent malpractice. Plaintiff settled with auto driver. Doctor in malpractice case joined driver. Joinder improper. Release valid. Plaintiff's proof limited to aggravation caused by doctor and/or hospital. ***Lasprogata v. Qualls,* 263 Pa. Super. 174, 397 A.2d 803.**

    Auto accident and subsequent medical malpractice. Death of plaintiff not attributable to accident but to subsequent malpractice. Proper to mold verdict since injuries and damages clearly delineated and so found by special interrogatories. ***Embrey v. Borough of West Mifflin,* 257 Pa. Super. 168, 390 A.2d 765.**

Two falls in same place

    Plaintiff fell on deteriorated sidewalk and was injured. Had fallen in essentially the same place 5 days earlier. Plaintiff held 15% at fault. Condition had existed for years. Proper for jury to apportion responsibility. ***Peair v. Home Assoc. of Enola,* 287 Pa. Super. 400, 430 A.2d 665.**

Two or more equally probable causes

    One-vehicle motorcycle accident. Jury verdict at $1,750,000. Driver of cycle suffered loss of most of right arm and multiple fractures of left arm. Plaintiff alleged defective assembly of front end assembly. Trial court excluded evidence that driver was going 100 m.p.h. when accident occurred. Error to exclude and new trial ordered. Was admissible to show alternate cause of accident. Error also to exclude evidence that plaintiff knew that screws assembling front end were inadequate or not used with proper securing compound. This went to assumption of risk. New trial ordered. **Bascelli v. Randy, Inc., 339 Pa. Super. 254, 488 A.2d 1110.**

Pedestrian struck and killed by one or more autos as he stepped off medial strip at night. Settled with first striking vehicle. Nonsuit as to all others. Evidence insufficient as to whether others actually struck plaintiff, or whether he died from first impact. **Pio v. Letarec, 294 Pa. Super. 196, 439 A.2d 818**

Plaintiff lying prone in roadway after spending the day in several bars. Struck first by McCleary's car and then several minutes later by Senft's car. No evidence to conclude that one defendant did more damage than the other. Verdict should have been molded to find defendants jointly and severably liable. **Lehman v. McCleary, 229 Pa. Super. 508, 329 A.2d 862.**

Plaintiff allegedly struck on head by stone from defendant's construction work—court below in error in charging that ulcerous condition must have resulted without concurrence of contributing cause—defendant only relieved if contributing cause would have produced the injury complained of independently of defendant's negligence. **Boushell et ux. v. J. H. Beers, Inc., 215 Pa. Super. 439, 258 A.2d 682.**

Two-disease Rule

In medical malpractice action for delayed diagnosis of liver disease, the "two disease rule" from asbestos-related cases will be applied to preclude plaintiff's claim for increased risk and fear of liver cancer until such disease actually occurs. Second judge's grant of summary judgment on plaintiff's claim for increased risk of harm after first judge denied summary judgment on the same issue is reversible error. Order granting summary judgment as to increased risk of harm reversed. **Klein v. Weisberg, ___ Pa. Super. ___, 694 A.2d 644 (1997).**

Worker who brought action based on non-malignant asbestos later contracted cancer. Two-disease Rule adopted. Action for cancer may be brought after statute of limitations had run on original cause of action. **Mariani v. Asbestos Corp., LTD, 417 Pa. Super. 440, 612 A.2d 1021.**

"U" Turns

—U—

"U" Turns

Plaintiff brought negligence action against defendant tow truck driver and his employers after he rear-ended the tow truck as it attempted to make a u-turn at a median opening in a highway. A jury found in favor of the defendants. The Superior Court affirmed, holding that a tow truck operator was authorized to use a median opening to make a u-turn on a highway. ***Keffer v. Bob Nolan's Auto Service, Inc.*, 59 A.3d 621 (Pa. Super. 2013).**

Plaintiff passenger in vehicle making "U" turn. Then involved in collision. Auto owned by Turnpike Commission. Verdict against auto driver. ***Fredericks v. Castora*, 241 Pa. Super. 211, 360 A.2d 696.**

Ulcer

Plaintiff alleged that excessively greasy doughnut caused severe gastritis and ulcer flare-up, leading to surgery. Defense verdict by jury affirmed. Court found that there was no evidence of causation, therefore all complaints of error were harmless. Expert opinion here did not have certainty required to allow jury to find causation. ***McCann v. Amy Joy Donut Shops*, 325 Pa. Super. 349, 472 A.2d 1149.**

Plaintiff injured by blasting operation in road construction—had an ulcer and contended occurrence aggravated condition—defendant urged other causes—court erred in charge—to escape liability defendant must show that contributing causes would have brought about injury without wrongful act—new trial granted. ***Boushell v. J. H. Beers, Inc.*, 215 Pa. Super. 439, 258 A.2d 682.**

Ultrahazardous activities

Blast furnace collapsed injuring workmen. Work not being done in normal course and posed unusual dangers. Verdict for plaintiffs reversed. Charge held inadequate on basis of §413 of Restatement (2d) Torts —Duty to provide for taking of precautions against dangers involved in work intrusted to contractors. ***Gonzalez v. U.S. Steel*, 248 Pa. Super. 95, 374 A.2d 1334.**

Plaintiff decedent employed by independent contractor to work at U.S. Steel piling iron ore atop huge pile using large truck. Had to drive on top of 50 foot pile at night with no other lights than headlights. Ran off edge where it had broken away and truck rolled over killing driver. Abnormally dangerous, ultrahazardous activity. Evidence of similar past accidents. Employer of independent contractor liable under §416 of Restatement (2d) Torts. ***McDonough v. U.S. Steel*, 228 Pa. Super. 268, 324 A.2d 542.**

Defendant engaged in road building as an independent contractor—plaintiff's property allegedly damaged by blasting—recovery allowed—Supreme Court held that the fact that the matter was a public construction operation would not bring it into exception granted governmental bodies—doctrine of ultrahazardous occupations applied. ***Lobozzo v. Adam Eidemiller*, 437 Pa. 360, 263 A.2d 432.**

Ultrasound test

Parents of child born with severe diabetes brought action for failure to perform ultrasound test. Physicians not liable. ***Bianchini v. N.K.D.S. Associates LTD.,* 420 Pa. Super. 294, 616 A.2d 700.**

Unauthorized practice of the law

An attorney exclusively employed by a railroad company sought to represent the railroad company in an action of trespass—certain attorneys sought to intervene, urging that the attorney was engaging in the unauthorized practice of law—petition to intervene properly refused—not within Pa. R.C.P. 2327(4). ***Penna. Railroad Co. v. Hughart,* 422 Pa. 615, 222 A.2d 736.**

Unauthorized use

Transportation authority not liable under operation of motor vehicle exception to governmental immunity where bus involved in accident with plaintiff was driven by unauthorized user and not employee of transportation authority. Summary judgment affirmed. ***Pana v. SEPTA,* ___ Pa. Cmwlth. ___, 657 A.2d 1320 (1995).**

Unavoidable accident

Truck coming down steep hill unable to stop at stop sign—skidded on ice through intersection causing accident. Jury verdict for defendant. Held: unavoidable accident. Negligence *per se*—going through sign not same as strict liability. Error to grant new trial. Verdict reinstated. ***Bumbarger v. Kaminsky,* 311 Pa. Super. 177, 457 A.2d 552.**

Charge on unavoidable accident proper where evidence showed ice on highway. However, new trial awarded due to error in charge on skidding. Violation of statute puts burden upon defendant to show lack of proximate cause or reasonable excuse—applies to skidding where vehicle came to rest on wrong side of highway. ***Kenworthy v. Burghart,* 241 Pa. Super. 267, 361 A.2d 335.**

Uncertain medical testimony

Plaintiff's expert stated that plaintiff's physical condition was consistent with the trauma of the occurrence and probably a cause and effect relationship—held insufficient—must state that the result in question came from the cause alleged—testimony inadmissible—new trial granted. ***McMahon v. Young,* 442 Pa. 484, 276 A.2d 534.**

Underground tank

In buyers' action against seller of gasoline station equipment and property, action for strict liability based on leaking underground storage tanks will not lie. The operation of underground storage tanks at a gasoline station is not an abnormally dangerous activity. Order granting preliminary objection to strict liability claim affirmed. ***Smith v. Weaver,* ___ Pa. Super. ___, 665 A.2d 1215 (1995).**

Undue hardship

Property damage—seepage from underground cistern—liability based on failure to reasonably maintain upheld. ***Moss Rose Mfg. Co. v. Foster,* 226 Pa. Super. 448, 314 A.2d 25.**

Undue hardship

Plaintiff was injured in an automobile accident allegedly caused by defective road design and condition. On the day of trial, the trial court granted PennDOT's motion for nonsuit based on plaintiff's failure to notify PennDOT of action within six months of accident under 42 Pa. C.S. §5522(a)(1) based on presumption of prejudice and hardship for failure to notify PennDOT. Held: presentation of motion on day of trial was untimely given substantial amount of time during which PennDOT could earlier have made the same motion, there is no presumption of prejudice or hardship attendant to lack of required notice. Negligence of plaintiff's counsel in providing notice coupled with lack of undue hardship to Commonwealth constituted adequate reason for delay in providing notice. Remanded to trial court for hearing on actual prejudice on PennDOT with burden of proof on PennDOT. ***Leedom v. Com., Dept. of Transp.,* 699 A.2d 815 (Pa. Cmwlth. 1997).**

Unevenness of pavement

Plaintiff was 72 years of age and a retired miner—fell on defendant's abutting sidewalk—evidence that it was snowing at time or shortly before—plaintiff attempted to prove notice by offering two photographs taken some 6 months later—photographs disclosed unevenness of pavement and were rejected—action proper—mere unevenness not sufficient to take case to the jury—nonsuit entered—motions dismissed and action affirmed on appeal. ***Silich v. Wissinger,* 438 Pa. 548, 264 A.2d 169.**

Unfitness to cross street

Plaintiff pedestrian appeals verdict for defendant in negligence action where trial court admitted evidence of plaintiff's history of drug and alcohol abuse and his legal intoxication at time of accident which caused his injuries. Plaintiff argues that such evidence is prejudicial and irrelevant to his claim for damages and should have been excluded. Held: allowing plaintiff to pursue a claim for permanent injury, while simultaneously barring defendant from access to plaintiff's long history of drug and alcohol abuse, "would be manifestly unfair and grossly prejudicial." Further holding that evidence of plaintiff's intoxication "as a pedestrian" was relevant and admissible if evidence would prove unfitness to cross street. ***Kraus v. Taylor,* 710 A.2d 1142 (Pa. Super. 1998).**

Uniform Contribution Among Tortfeasors Act

In action where jury found plaintiff to be 30% negligent, one defendant to be 45% negligent and second defendant 25% negligent, plaintiff may still recover against defendant found to be less negligent than plaintiff because collectively defendants were more negligent than plaintiff. Where strictly liable defendant and negligent defendant acted as joint tortfeasors, contribution among them properly can be awarded. Judgment on molded jury verdict affirmed. ***Smith v. Weissenfels, Inc.,* 441 Pa. Super. 328, 657 A.2d 949 (1995).**

Uniform Fiduciaries Act

Negligence protections afforded to banks under the Uniform Fiduciaries Act are not available when the bank acts in bad faith. ***Melley v. Pioneer Bank, N.A.,* 834 A.2d 1191 (Pa. Super. 2003).**

Unimproved land

Park visitor who slipped on embankment between picnic pavilion and parking lot in County park was precluded from any recovery for injuries sustained against the County under Recreation Use of Land and Water Act. Land was unimproved and no fee was charged to plaintiff for use of the park. Order denying summary judgment reversed and complaint dismissed. ***Brezinski v. County of Allegheny,* 694 A.2d 388 (Pa. Cmwlth. 1997).**

Unlighted corridor

Workman for subcontractor fell in unlighted corridor. Jury found negligence on behalf of general contractor in failing to light job site. Plaintiff held to be statutory employer and therefore unable to recover. ***Rosenbaum v. Kennedy House,* 254 Pa. Super. 628, 387 A.2d 123.**

Unlighted excavation

Plaintiff on a motorcycle was following a car ahead—that car suddenly swerved to avoid an excavation made by defendant and plaintiff unaware of excavation injured in jumping from his vehicle—court erred in instructing jury that existence of car ahead obstructing view would excuse plaintiff's otherwise violation of assured clear distance rule—new trial awarded. ***Koelle v. Phila. Electric Co.,* 443 Pa. 35, 277 A.2d 350.**

Unlighted stairway

Resident in building owned by housing authority fell in unlighted stairway. Debris left in stairway by third person. Held: cause of fall question of fact. ***Floyd v. Philadelphia Housing Authority,* 154 Pa. Cmwlth. 303, 623 A.2d 901.**

Unsafe speed

Driving at unsafe speed in violation of statute constituted negligence *per se* in personal injury action brought by occupants of vehicle with which defendant collided. ***Folino v. Young,* 368 Pa. Super. 220, 553 A.2d 1034.**

Used car

Plaintiff sued driver of car that veered into her lane and hit her car, used car salesman who had authorized defendant driver to test drive the car, and dealership for which used car salesman worked. Jury returned verdict against all three parties and apportioned liability among them, which was molded to joint and several liability by trial court. On appeal, Superior Court reversed denial of post trial motions of salesman and dealership who argued that they had no knowledge that defendant driver was other than a licensed driver (which he was) and so no duty to plaintiff

Utility pole

which would support a claim of negligent entrustment by plaintiff. ***Ferry v. Fisher*, 709 A.2d 399 (Pa. Super. 1998).**

Jury verdict as to liability only in favor of defendant used car dealership affirmed. Plaintiff injured by driver of stolen car failed to state a cause of action, where sole allegation of negligence was that dealership employees left keys in newly delivered vehicles in violation of unattended motor vehicle section of the Pennsylvania Vehicle Code. ***Santarlas v. Leaseway Motorcar Transport Company*, 456 Pa. Super. 34, 689 A.2d 311 (1997).**

Utility pole

Pedestrian brought negligence action against electric utility on the basis that the utility's streetlight failed to adequately illuminate the entire roadway causing her to be struck by a motorist. The trial court granted summary judgment in favor of the defendant. The Superior Court reversed, holding that whether the defendant exercised reasonable care in undertaking its duty to maintain the streetlight precluded summary judgment due to testimony that it had updated other street lights in the area. ***Wilson v. PECO Energy Co.*, 61 A.3d 229 (Pa. Super. 2012).**

Plaintiff brought a negligence action against Defendant electric utility after Defendant repaired a utility pole damaged in an accident and a fire broke out in the Plaintiff's basement electrical panel after the Defendant restored power to the Plaintiff's building. The trial court entered summary judgment in favor of the electric utility. The Superior Court reversed holding that there was a genuine issue of material fact as to whether an electric utility owes a duty to warn its customers that it would be reconnecting electrical lines to its property or owes a duty to inspect its customers electrical system prior to restoring power. ***Alderwoods, Inc. v. Duquesne Light Co.*, 2012 Pa. Super. 153 (Pa Super. 2012).**

Plaintiff was injured when a SEPTA utility pole fell on his car. No error by trial court in refusing to reverse jury verdict for defendant when plaintiffs failed to present evidence that there were no other responsible causes, including the conduct of the plaintiff or third parties in support of his *res ipsa loquitur* claim. ***Joyner v. SEPTA*, 736 A.2d 35 (Pa. Cmwlth. 1999).**

In suit by decedent's estate against minor passenger in other vehicle, an individual who is simply a passenger in a vehicle operated by an intoxicated driver may not be held responsible for the driver's negligence. Rather, liability may only be imposed where sufficient facts indicate that the passenger substantially assisted or encouraged the driver's negligent conduct. Order granting summary judgment in favor of minor passenger affirmed. ***Welc v. Porter*, 450 Pa. Super. 112, 675 A.2d 334 (1996).**

Plaintiff's decedent died after crashing into utility pole following high-speed chase. The decedent's criminal and negligent acts preclude imposition of liability on municipalities whose police officers were engaged in pursuit. Therefore, decedent's widow could not recover from municipalities under wrongful death theory as such action is derivative to any action the decedent may have had. Order granting summary judgment affirmed. ***Tyree v. City of Pittsburgh***, ___ Pa. Cmwlth. ___, 669 A.2d 487 (1995).

Defendant utility-pole inspection company did not have duty to protect bystander from injuries sustained when bystander came into contact with downed electrical wires while assisting victims of automobile accident which damaged utility pole. Defendant inspection company's alleged negligent inspection of pole was too remote to constitute proximate cause of bystander's injuries. Bystander was not third-party beneficiary of contract between inspection company and utility company, which required inspection company only to inspect and report condition of poles. Order sustaining preliminary objections of defendant inspection company affirmed. ***Hicks v. Metropolitan Edison Company***, ___ Pa. Cmwlth. ___, 665 A.2d 529 (1995).

Where plaintiff sustained injuries after striking utility pole, utility company liable for improper placement of electric pole in highway right-of-way. Compulsory nonsuit reversed. ***Talarico v. Bonham***, 168 Pa. Cmwlth. 467, 650 A.2d 1192 (1994).

No duty of care by police to driver fleeing police. Utility company not liable for placement of utility pole struck by fleeing driver. ***Beck v. Zabrowski***, 168 Pa. Cmwlth. 385, 650 A.2d 1152 (1994).

Police officer injured when motorcycle struck utility pole brought action against electric company and PennDOT. Company and department not liable. Injuries would have occurred even if pole not present. Evidence of subsequent relocation of pole not admissible to show negligence. ***Henry v. McCrudden***, 133 Pa. Cmwlth. 231, 575 A.2d 666.

Plaintiff's vehicle allegedly struck utility pole owned by defendant. Utility pole in grassy medial strip. Evidence of rain at time and that vehicle had flipped over several times before striking pole. Nonsuit affirmed. ***Frangis v. Duquesne Light Co.***, 232 Pa. Super. 420, 335 A.2d 796.

Plaintiff's-passengers in a vehicle which veered right at dangerous curve to allow vehicle coming in opposite direction to pass—struck utility pole—unlit pole with no reflectors. Summary judgment in favor of utility company reversed. For jury. ***Scheel v Tremblay and Phila. Elec. Co.***, 226 Pa. Super. 45, 312 A.2d 45.

Utility provisions

Boy of 9-1/2 years fell from a concrete block wall of a building being constructed—children have knowledge of danger of falling—Supreme Court adopted Section 339 of Restatement (2d) Torts and denied recovery. ***Jesko v. Turk***, 421 Pa. 434, 219 A.2d 591.

Vacant building

—V—

Vacant building

Victim who was raped in vacant building brought action against owner. Building owner not liable. Owner's promise to authorities to secure building did not create duty to plaintiff. **Glick v. Olde Town Lancaster, Inc., 369 Pa. Super. 419, 535 A.2d 621.**

Vacant lot

Child injured while walking across vacant lot owned by Lewis. City was granted judgment on pleadings—no duty of care owned to plaintiff due to disrepair of private property. This incident occurred prior to enactment of Political Subdivision Tort Claims Act. **Williams v. Lewis and City of Philadelphia, 319 Pa. Super. 552, 466 A.2d 682.**

Vaccination

Exclusive original jurisdiction for vaccine latent and patent vaccine related negligence cases is in "Vaccine Court" established by National Childhood Vaccine Injury Act, 42 U.S. 300aa. **Ashton v. Aventis Pasteur, 851 A.2d 908 (Pa. Super. 2004).**

Negligence action by parents on behalf of minor child injured by exposure to thimerosal in vaccines dismissed for failure to exhaust administrative remedies under federal legislation National Childhood Vaccine Act, 42 U.S. § 300aa-1, *et seq.* *Chieskiewicz v. Aventis Pasteur, Inc.*, **843 A.2d 1258 (Pa. Super. 2004).**

Plaintiffs are parents of a son who developed mental and physical limitations as a result of encephalitis following administration of a measles, mumps and rubella vaccination. Suit against hospital and physician who administered vaccination. After suit first brought, plaintiffs accepted judgment under federal National Vaccine Injury Compensation Program and then recommenced suit in state court. Held: acceptance of judgment in federal program bars recovery in state action absent some claim that an action other than administration or effect of vaccination was cause of injury. **Harman v. Borah, 720 A.2d 1058 (Pa. Super. 1998).**

Vaccine Act

Exclusive original jurisdiction for vaccine latent and patent vaccine related negligence cases is in "Vaccine Court" established by the National Childhood Vaccine Injury Act, 42 U.S. 300aa. **Ashton v. Aventis Pasteur, 851 A.2d 908 (Pa. Super. 2004).**

Negligence action by parents on behalf of minor child injured by exposure to thimerosal in vaccines dismissed for failure to exhaust administrative remedies under federal legislation National Childhood Vaccine Act, 42 U.S. § 300aa-1, *et seq.* *Chieskiewicz v. Aventis Pasteur, Inc.*, **843 A.2d 1258 (Pa. Super. 2004).**

Vicarious liability

Valet

Plaintiff's estate brought lawsuit against the Defendant casino after casino's valet failed to prevent the intoxicated decedent from driving and he was later killed in a car accident. The trial court granted summary judgment to the casino. The Superior Court affirmed holding that a casino valet has no affirmative duty to refuse to return car keys to a drunk driver. ***Moranko v. Downs Racing L.P.*, 2014 Pa. Super. 128 (Pa. Super. 2014).**

Vegetation along highway

Parents of child struck and killed by automobile while riding bicycle brought action against PennDOT, municipality, and adjoining landowner. Defendants not liable. Failure to set speed limit below fifty-five and permitting vegetation to grow along highway not cause of accident. ***Salerno v. LaBarr*, 159 Pa. Cmwlth. 99, 632 A.2d 1002.**

Ventilation system

Ventilation system malfunction resulted in death of farmer's pigs. System installer's attempt to join suppliers of cable not permitted. Could not identify which supplier sold cable that failed. ***Pennfield Corporation v. Meadow Valley Electric, Inc.*, 413 Pa. Super. 187, 604 A.2d 1082.**

Vicarious liability

A hospital may not be held vicariously liable for the negligence of its agents and employees if they have been previously been absolved of liability in a prior proceeding. ***Bordlemay v. Keystone Health Plans, Inc.*, 789 A.2d 748 (Pa. Super. 2001).**

Plaintiffs' decedent died as a result of injuries sustained in a motor vehicle accident when the driver, who was unlicensed and intoxicated, lost control of the vehicle. In suit against the bar, the driver and the owner of the car, held that owner was vicariously liable for negligence of driver even though owner"s failure to insure that driver was licensed when there was reasonable cause to suspect lack of license was not a substantial factor in harm. Trial court also found driver liable and determined that plaintiffs" decedent was 20% negligent. Good discussion of vicarious liability as distinguished from contributory negligence. ***Terwilliger v. Kitchen*, 781 A.2d 1201 (Pa. Super 2001).**

Plaintiff's decedent electrocuted while applying stucco to building in proximity to uninsulated electrical wires. Political Subdivision Tort Claims Act precludes imposition of liability upon governmental unit based on a theory of vicarious liability for work performed by contractor. Order granting summary judgment affirmed. ***Thomas v. City of Philadelphia*, ___ Pa. Cmwlth. ___, 668 A.2d 292 (1995).**

General release of claims against emergency medical technician and ambulance service for overdose precluded claim of vicarious liability against hospital. Compulsory nonsuit in favor of hospital affirmed. ***Riffe v. Vereb Ambulance Service, Inc.*, 437 Pa. Super. 613, 650 A.2d 1076 (1994).**

View obstructed

View obstructed

Plaintiff motorcyclist injured by reason of an unlighted excavation created by defendant in highway—case for jury but error in charge that existence of car ahead obscuring view could excuse plaintiff from otherwise complying with assured clear distance rule. **Koelle v. Phila. Electric Co., 443 Pa. 35, 277 A.2d 350.**

View of intersection

Plaintiff to right stopped at intersection for light and did not have a good view from such point—starting up with change of light and gliding into a point where she had view and observed nothing—struck by defendant's car coming from left and disregarding light—plaintiff not guilty of contributory negligence *per se* and case for jury. **Fouser v. Cantola, 438 Pa. 549, 264 A.2d 169.**

Plaintiff on through highway—embankment prevented a view of vehicles on stop street—observant—first observing defendant in middle of intersection when plaintiff 10 to 15 feet from intersection—collision—matter still for the jury. **Rhode v. Kearney, 208 Pa. Super. 8, 220 A.2d 378.**

Vision

Opthalmologist's failure to report patient's poor vision to PennDOT, despite statutory obligation to do so, does not give rise to a private cause of action to plaintiff's decedent, who was killed when struck by patient's car. **Estate of Witthoeft v. Kiskaddon, 733 A.2d 623 (Pa. 1999).**

In action by estate of decedent hit by automobile while bicycling, ophthalmologist has no duty to patient to inform PennDOT of patient's poor vision. Order sustaining preliminary objections affirmed. **Estate of Witthoeft v. Kiskaddon, 450 Pa. Super. 364, 676 A.2d 1223 (1996).**

Minor plaintiff, aged 12, was operating his bicycle at night on berm of road—struck by car operated by defendant who had defective vision—case for jury. **Masters v. Alexander, 424 Pa. 65, 225 A.2d 905.**

Visitor

Visitor to home bitten by dog owned by another visitor. Where young victim was warned only to be careful, *not* an assumption of risk to pet dog. Evidence of subsequent dog bites admitted only to show dangerous propensities. Verdict for plaintiff affirmed. **Crance v. Sohanic, 344 Pa. Super. 526, 496 A.2d 1230.**

Vocal cords

Patient brought malpractice action against surgeon for damage to vocal cords. Trial court refused to give instruction on *res ipsa loquitur*. Reversed and remanded. **Sedlitsky v. Pareso, 400 Pa. Super. 1, 582 A.2d 1314.**

Vocational expert

Plaintiff injured in automobile accident filed suit against defendant who admitted liability. Jury returned verdict for plaintiff, but awarded only $600.00 despite substantial evidence of injury and medical treatment. While trial court admitted it was shocked by low verdict, it held plaintiff had waived right to demand new trial because there was no objection to verdict before jury was dismissed. Plaintiff had also been prohibited from introducing testimony of vocational expert relating to lost wages, benefits and earning potential. On appeal, Superior Court reversed on issue of damages because jury's verdict, although low, was not based on inadequate charge or insufficient evidence and so there was no basis for an objection before the jury was discharged. Proper method of attacking low verdict was by post trial motion directed to the conscience of the court which plaintiff had done. As to vocational expert, lack of medical testimony supporting plaintiff's absolute inability to perform work as to which vocational expert would testify should not have prevented jury from having the question based on reasonable certainty of loss of plaintiff's ability to perform work. ***King v. Pulaski*, 710 A.2d 1200 (Pa. Super. 1998).**

Vocational rehabilitation

Injured employee permitted to proceed with suit alleging negligence of vocational rehabilitation firm resulting in emotional distress despite plaintiff's referral to vocational rehabilitation firm after work-related injury. Exclusivity provisions of Workers' Compensation Act do not bar action against third party provider of services. ***Taylor v. Woods Rehabilitation Service*, 846 A.2d 742 (Pa. Super. 2004).**

Voice

Verdict in favor of woman whose voice was irreparably damaged following intubation procedure vacated, and judgment entered for appellant hospital where plaintiff's complaint stated cause of action in negligence against hospital, but proof at trial focused only on family physician's negligence in follow-up care of plaintiff; no amendment to plaintiff's original complaint was filed. ***Reynolds v. Thomas Jefferson University Hospital*, 450 Pa. Super. 327, 676 A.2d 1205 (1996).**

Voluntary Assumption of the Risk Doctrine

Plaintiff motorcyclist was injured when he struck a car that pulled out in front of him. Driver of car alleged that he did not see motorcycle because its headlight was not operating. Plaintiff admitted that he frequently drove without operating headlight. Judgment in favor of plaintiff against motorcycle reseller and car driver vacated on basis that plaintiff assumed the risks that attend riding a motorcycle without a functioning headlight. ***Frey v. Harley Davidson*, 734 A.2d 1 (Pa. Super. 1999).**

Plaintiff college baseball player sustained severe injury to knee when he tripped in a depression in center field while fielding a ball. In suit against college which maintained field, summary judgment in favor of college sustained on appeal where plaintiff admitted that he was aware of risks of rutted field, voluntarily consented to playing despite knowledge, and was injured by the same risks of which he was previously aware. ***Zachardy v. Geneva College*, 733 A.2d 648 (Pa. Super. 1999).**

High school skier was injured when struck by an unidentified skier while she was stopped at the base of a hill. Summary judgment entered in favor of ski resort based on assumption of risk created by Pennsylvania Skier's Responsibility Act,

Voluntary Assumption of the Risk Doctrine

42 Pa.C.S. §7102(c). Reversed by Superior Court because question of whether or not non-moving plaintiff at the bottom of a hill was actually "skiing" was for jury. ***Hughes v. Seven Springs*, 727 A.2d 135 (Pa. Super. 1999).**

Plaintiff was injured when the train he was boarding began moving unexpectedly. Independent witnesses testified that train was stopped when plaintiff began to board. After verdict for plaintiff, defendant appealed alleging trial court erred in failing to charge on assumption of risk. Held: if there is no testimony to support any risk to be assumed by plaintiff, charge is improper. Also, assumption of risk is for court to consider in legal analysis of duty aspect of claim, not for jury to determine. ***Wallis v. SEPTA*, 723 A.2d 267 (Pa. Cmwlth. 1999).**

Defense of decedent's contributory negligence is not eliminated from consideration merely because of negligence *per se* of tavern that served decedent while he was visibly intoxicated. Remand for new trial to determine plaintiffs' decedent's comparative negligence in driving while intoxicated after having been served while visibly intoxicated. Decedent could not have legally assumed risk of driving while intoxicated following determination of tavern's negligence in serving visibly intoxicated decedent. To pierce corporate veil, against which there is a strong legal presumption, plaintiff must prove undercapitalizing, intermingling of individual and corporate affairs, failure to adhere to corporate formalities and use of the corporate form to perpetrate a fraud. ***Miller v. Brass Rail Tavern, Inc.*, 702 A.2d 1072 (Pa. Super. 1997).**

Summary judgment reversed where plaintiff insulation installer on stilts held not to have assumed the risk of slipping on construction debris left at job site by defendants. Assumption of risk should only preclude recovery where it is beyond question that the plaintiff voluntarily and knowingly proceeded in the face of an obvious and dangerous condition. ***Barrett v. Fredavid Builders, Inc.*, 454 Pa. Super. 162, 685 A.2d 129 (1996).**

Where evidence indicates that foundry worker knew that silicosis was a risk associated with being exposed to silica sand and voluntary exposed himself to the risk, employer could not be held strictly liable for failure to warn of dangers associated with silica sand as a matter of law. Order entering judgment notwithstanding the verdict in favor of employer affirmed. ***Phillips v. A-Best Products Company*, 542 Pa. 124, 665 A.2d 1167 (1995).**

Student of military academy injured when toy cannon prematurely discharged did not assume the risk of injury where student had fired cannon more than 200 times without incident. Only necessary jury instruction was on comparative negligence. Judgment on jury verdict affirmed. ***Struble v. Valley Forge Military Academy*, 445 Pa. Super. 224, 665 A.2d 4 (1995).**

Contributory negligence does not preclude recovery in a products liability case. In action arising out of tire explosion which injured garage mechanic, defendant failed to prove that plaintiff assumed the specific risk attendant to the procedure of changing a tire. Voluntary assumption of a risk is a defense in a products liability case and requires proof that the plaintiff fully understands the specific risk and yet

Voluntary Assumption of the Risk Doctrine

chooses voluntarily to encounter the risk. ***Robinson v. B.F. Goodrich Tire Company,*** **444 Pa. Super. 640, 664 A.2d 616 (1995).**

Plaintiff injured after he slipped while dodging lowering hydraulic lift that he knew lowered sporadically was entitled to jury determination on question of assumption of the risk. Order granting summary judgment reversed. ***Long v. Norriton Hydraulics, Inc.,*** **443 Pa. Super. 532, 662 A.2d 1089 (1995).**

Patron did not assume risk of injury when she observed wet floor immediately before stepping on to it and falling. Nonsuit reversed. ***Hardy v. Southland Corporation,*** **435 Pa. Super. 237, 645 A.2d 839 (1994).**

Injured water skier brought action against operator of boat. Operator not liable. Doctrine of assumption of risk applicable in comparative negligence cases. ***Pagesh v. Ucman,*** **403 Pa. Super. 549, 589 A.2d 747.**

Spectator injured when homemade cannon exploded. Held: a nonsuit may be granted based on assumption of the risk only when evidence fails to demonstrate a breach of duty of care. ***Howell v. Clyde,*** **383 Pa. Super. 611, 557 A.2d 419.**

Visitor to home bitten by dog owned by another visitor. Where young victim was warned only to be careful, *not* an assumption of risk to pet dog. Evidence of subsequent dog bites admitted only to show dangerous propensities. Verdict for plaintiff affirmed. ***Crance v. Sohanic,*** **344 Pa. Super. 526, 496 A.2d 1230.**

One-vehicle motorcycle accident. Jury verdict $1,750,000. Driver of cycle suffered loss of most of right arm and multiple fractures of left arm. Plaintiff alleged defective assembly of front-end assembly. Error to exclude evidence that plaintiff knew that screws assembling front end were inadequate or not used with proper compound. This went to assumption of risk. New trial ordered. ***Bascelli v. Randy, Inc.,*** **339 Pa. Super. 254, 488 A.2d 1110.**

Sliver of metal entered eye of workman taking old sign off building. Verdict against property owner for not supplying goggles, oil, or giving adequate warning. Plaintiff found 49% negligent. Final verdict including delay damage $27,277.86 affirmed. Issues of assumption of risk and causation were for jury. ***Seewagen v. Vanderklvet,*** **338 Pa. Super. 534, 488 A.2d 21.**

Plaintiff fell on patch of ice in parking lot of chiropractic clinic. Jury verdict $70,000 reflecting 35% comparative negligence. Ice was next to car, although rest of lot was clear. Plaintiff became aware of ice while still seated in car. Wore prosthesis at time—fractured left hip. Verdict reversed. Where plaintiff sees risk, possessor of land relieved of responsibility and duty of care to invitee who, under circumstances here was held to have assumed risk as matter of law. Comparative negligence statute not applicable. ***Carrender v. Fitterer,*** **503 Pa. 178, 469 A.2d 120.**

Plaintiff injured while unclogging electric lawnmower that started spontaneously. Designed defect claimed: lack of "deadman's switch." Jury verdict $20,000. Amputation, index and middle fingers; ring finger immobilized; thumb and little finger shortened. Lower Court ordered General Electric to wholly indemnify Sears. Held: determination of whether plaintiff, by inserting hand into stalled mower, had

Voluntary undertaking

assumed risk of injury—for jury. Court affirmed verdict and holding, requiring complete indemnification. ***Burch v. Sears, Roebuck & Co.*, 320 Pa. Super. 444, 467 A.2d 615.**

In enacting the comparative negligence statute, the legislature did not intend to extend the application of the assumption of risk defense in cases that had been traditionally evaluated primarily according to contributory negligence principles. ***Fish v. Gosnell*, 316 Pa. Super. 565, 463 A.2d 1042.**

Plaintiff, then 16, injured during supervised summer football practice. No protective gear worn. Trial court held that plaintiff assumed risk as a matter of law. On appeal, assumption of risk doctrine abolished except where specifically preserved by statute. Issue should be limited to negligence and contributory negligence. Reverses *Rutter v. Northeastern Beaver Co. School,* 283 Pa. Super. 155, 423 A.2d 1035. ***Rutter v. Northeastern Beaver School*, 496 Pa. 590, 437 A.2d 1198.**

High School football player sustained severe eye injury in sanctioned intramural football game. Plaintiff a football player for the school. Plaintiff found as a matter of law to have assumed the risk of injury. ***Rutter v. Northeastern Beaver Co. School*, 283 Pa. Super. 155, 423 A.2d 1035.**

Head-on collision. Both drivers and passenger killed. Passenger's estate sued. Driver of passenger's car intoxicated as both driver and passenger had spent afternoon drinking. Verdict for defendant on basis that plaintiff had assumed risk. ***Weaver v. Clabaugh*, 255 Pa. Super. 532, 388 A.2d 1094.**

Minor plaintiff struck in eye by stone thrown by minor defendant during horseplay. Issue of assumption of risk properly submitted to jury. Verdict for defendant. ***McIntyre v. Cusick*, 247 Pa. Super. 354, 372 A.2d 864.**

Where a pedestrian in broad daylight and with full knowledge of a defective pavement sidesteps to avoid another pedestrian and falls into a known defect which she observed, she will be held to have assumed the risk as a matter of law. ***Kresovich v. Fitzsimmons*, 439 Pa. 10, 264 A.2d 585.**

Voluntary undertaking

Motorist injured when vehicle hydroplaned on highway leading to bridge owned by commission. Commission incorporated in New Jersey. Commission liable since it voluntarily attempted to correct dangerous condition of highway. ***Laconis v. Burlington County Bridge Commission*, 400 Pa. Super. 483, 583 A.2d 1218.**

Jury verdict $200,000 for crush injury with permanent disability—male warehouse employee, in dark parking lot. Employee guiding tractor-trailer rigs, by voice, with hand on rig. Fell in parking lot hole. Issue of plaintiff's circumstances with lease silent. Lessor has, over years, undertaken to keep parking area in repair. Held: therefore, a continuing duty to keep it reasonably safe for tenants use. ***McDevitt v. Terminal Warehouse Co.*, 304 Pa. Super. 438, 450 A.2d 991.**

—W—

Waiver of immunity

Pedestrian struck and killed by bus. Held: Since transportation authority could not waive immunity, limitation of damages provisions of Act 152 of 1978 applicable. Wrongful death and survival actions separate causes of action. ***Tulewicz v. SEPTA*, 529 Pa. 588, 606 A.2d 427.**

Waiver of immunity as applied to physicians employed by Commonwealth, allows suits by third parties against said physician for releasing mental patient improperly, which patient thereafter assaulted plaintiff. Denial of preliminary objections affirmed. ***Allentown State Hospital v. Gill*, 88 Pa. Cmwlth. 331, 488 A.2d 1211.**

Walking

Plaintiff and five other Boy Scouts hiking along two lane road. Walking on roadway when they came to ditch. Defendant truck saw scouts and ditch and moved to left. Boys moved to street after seeing truck move to left. Driver moved back to right too soon striking plaintiff. Driver's actions held to be a superseding cause to any negligence on part of plaintiff. ***Grainy v. Campbell*, 269 Pa. Super. 225, 409 A.2d 860.**

Walls

University owes no duty to students to control protestors. Student who sees open and obvious impediment to her path of travel should choose an alternate path, rather than attempting to jump from four-foot wall. Order granting summary judgment was affirmed. ***Banks v. Trustees of University of Pennsylvania*, 446 Pa. Super. 99, 666 A.2d 329 (1995).**

In automobile accident involving drunk driver who struck a stone-wall culvert that did not bear reflectors, issue of dangerous nature of stone wall precludes summary judgment in favor of PennDOT. ***Com., Dept. of Transp. v. Koons*, ___ Pa. Cmwlth. ___, 661 A.2d 490 (1995).**

The determination of whether an individual is a trespasser, licensee, or invitee is for the jury. A licensee may become an invitee, thereby increasing duty of care owed by landowner. Plaintiff may recover damages where two or more substantial causes combine to cause an injury, even if no one cause standing alone would have brought about the injury. Although action of third party in pushing plaintiff off a guide wall was an intervening cause, its occurrence was not so extraordinary or unforeseeable as to make it a superseding cause which would excuse property owner for negligent maintenance of wall, which condition substantially contributed to plaintiff's injuries. ***Trude v. Martin*, 442 Pa. Super. 614, 660 A.2d 626 (1995).**

Party wall of building under demolition collapsed, killing occupant of adjacent building. Jury verdict against contractor, landowner, and City. City hired allegedly unapproved contractor and provided inadequate inspection for this emergency demolition. Under facts, none of the concurrently negligent tortfeasors entitled to indemnity. ***Sirianni v. Nugent Brothers*, 331 Pa. Super. 145, 480 A.2d 285.**

Wanton misconduct

Plaintiffs pouring concrete in warehouse when recently constructed wall fell on top of them. Verdict for plaintiffs against owner, masonry contractor and employer. Evidence indicating that owner planned and designed wall in question plus general control over project. Further, wall failed to meet industry and City standards. ***Hargrove v. Frommeyer,* 229 Pa. Super. 298, 323 A.2d 300.**

Collapse of wall in a shopping center construction operation—workman injured—evidence that wall was weakened by cutting of a pipe chase—sufficient testimony to hold a piping contractor responsible. ***Abbott v. Steel City Piping Co.,* 437 Pa. 412, 263 A.2d 881.**

Boy of 9-1/2 years fell from a concrete block wall of a building being constructed—Section 339 of Restatement (2d) Torts adopted by Supreme Court and action of the Superior Court in entering judgment *n.o.v.* affirmed—plaintiff did not bring case within the "utility" provision of Section 339. ***Jesko v. Turk,* 421 Pa. 434, 219 A.2d 591.**

Wanton misconduct

Motorcycle riders were killed on private road owned by railroad. Railroad's conduct held willful and wanton. Comparative negligence did not apply. ***Krivijanski v. Union Railroad Company,* 357 Pa. Super. 196, 515 A.2d 933.**

Seventeen-year old plaintiff riding on running board of pickup truck, fell from truck. Cause of action prior to Comparative Negligence Act. Plaintiff held to be contributorily negligent as matter of law. Proper holding, but new trial awarded. Jury to determine wanton and reckless conduct of defendant driver, or whether he had last clear chance to avoid injury. ***Hill v. Crawford,* 308 Pa. Super. 502, 454 A.2d 647.**

Head-on collision. Defendant in wrong lane approaching blind intersection without due regard for the situation. Sufficient to submit issue of reckless misconduct to jury. ***Turner v. Smith,* 237 Pa. Super. 161, 346 A.2d 806.**

Plaintiff's car stalled in intersection—her situation was apparent or should have been to defendant's bus driver when he was 160 feet away—driver continued on and collided with plaintiff's machine—verdict for defendant—new trial granted on ground that trial judge should have charged on the theory of wanton misconduct. ***Williams v. Phila. Trans. Co.,* 219 Pa. Super. 134, 280 A.2d 612.**

Minor plaintiff of 8 fell from the running board of a tractor and injured—trial court properly instructed jury that actual knowledge of presence of minor is not required to constitute wanton misconduct—charge as a whole correct and verdict for defendant upheld on appeal. ***Mount v. Bulifant,* 438 Pa. 265, 265 A.2d 627.**

Plaintiff's decedent was a guest passenger in defendant's car—car went out of control on curve and left highway—verdict for defendant—new trial properly granted—car being pursued by police and going 90 miles per hour just before occurrence—jury should have been instructed as to wanton misconduct. ***Fugagli v. Camasi,* 426 Pa. 1, 229 A.2d 735.**

Water

Supreme Court adopts Section 500 of Restatement (2d) Torts which defines wanton misconduct to be where actor realizes existing peril for such time as to take measures to avoid accident and fails to do so. ***Parker v. Jones*, 423 Pa. 15, 223 A.2d 229.**

Water

Plaintiff downstream property owner brought an action against an upstream school district due to the construction of a stormwater drainage system that increased erosion on the Plaintiff's property. The trial court entered judgment in favor of the Plaintiff. The Commonwealth Court reversed holding that an upstream property owner may be held liable for damages caused by artificially directing stormwater onto a downstream owner's land. In addition, it held that obtaining township approval of a project did not preclude Plaintiff from obtaining equitable relief. ***Bretz v. Central Bucks School District*, 86 A.3d 306 (Pa. Cmwlth. 2014).**

Plaintiff filed negligence action against Defendants upstream property owner and former owners based upon ongoing damage to their property from a stormwater management system. The trial court granted summary judgment in favor of the Defendants. The Commonwealth Court reversed holding that flooding damage was an ongoing trespass, which was not subject to a 2-year statute of limitations and that equitable relief is not subject to strict statute of limitations requirements. ***Lake v. Hankin Group*, 79 A.3d 748 (Pa. Cmwlth 2013).**

Property owners brought an action against the Department of Transportation, townships and school district alleging private nuisance, because the waterway easement that followed through their property was being eroded, causing them to build larger and larger bridges to cross over it. The appellate court held that the Department of Transportation was immune from damages to return the waterway to its 1979 condition and that evidence was insufficient that the actions of any of the defendants had caused the increase in water flow in the waterway. ***Swift v. Department of Transportation of the Commonwealth of Pennsylvania*, 937 A.2d 1162 (Pa. Cmwlth. 2007).**

Plaintiff appeals from grant of summary judgment to defendants based on common-enemy doctrine relating to natural surface water runoff in urban area. Plaintiff was injured when she slipped and fell on ice that had accumulated in alley next to defendant's business location. Held: so long as defendant had not artificially changed natural course of water or substantially changed quality or quantity of surface water, no injury will fall to lower landowner or to another. The record is devoid of evidence that defendants modified natural course of water in any way. ***Fazio v. Fegley Oil Co, Inc.*, 714 A.2d 510 (Pa. Cmwlth. 1998).**

Decedent's failure to establish hospital's knowledge of water on floor in bathroom, which may represent a dangerous or defective condition of the property, prohibits recovery. A business invitee must prove either that the landowner created the harmful condition or had actual or constructive notice of the condition. Summary judgment affirmed. ***Swift v. Northeastern Hospital of Philadelphia*, 456 Pa. Super. 330, 690 A.2d 719 (1997).**

Water

Accumulation of water on school district property, which condition contributed to fall of high school student on crutches does not fall within real property exception to Political Subdivision Tort Claims Act. Order granting summary judgment for school district affirmed. ***Leonard v. Fox Chapel Area School District*, 674 A.2d 767 (Pa. Cmwlth. 1996).**

For real property exception to apply against school district, dangerous condition must be of or attached to the pavement or property and not on the subject pavement or property. Rainwater on floor of school building did not constitute dangerous condition of or attached to property. Directed verdict for defendant affirmed. Dissent would apply exception based on school district's use of terrazzo floor tile that school district knew became dangerously slippery when wet. ***Shedrick v. William Penn School District*, ___ Pa. Cmwlth. ___, 654 A.2d 163 (1995).**

"Dangerous condition of real estate" exception to governmental immunity was fact question for jury. Summary judgment in favor of defendant reversed. ***Berhane v. SEPTA*, 166 Pa. Cmwlth. 196, 646 A.2d 1268 (1994).**

Class action suit brought against power company for damage caused by flood waters released from company's dam. Company not liable. Evidence of property damage upstream of dam properly admitted. ***Engle v. West Penn Power Company*, 409 Pa. Super. 486, 598 A.2d 291.**

Commercial tenant brought negligence action against landlord for damage caused by leaking water in apartment above. Landlord liable. Exculpatory clause in lease not enforceable. ***Topp Copy Products, Inc. v. Singletory*, 404 Pa. Super. 459, 591 A.2d 298.**

Non-jury verdict $319,419.92 against PennDOT, $39,927.49 each against Logan Fire Co. and PennDOT assistant county superintendent. Decedent, a husband and father of four minor children. Accident caused by ice patch, causing plaintiff's vehicle to spin out of control. Ice patch created by fire company pumping out flooded basement of adjacent landowner. PennDOT found 80% liable and other two defendants each found 10% liable. ***Commonwealth v. Phillips*, 87 Pa. Cmwlth. 504, 488 A.2d 77.**

Head-on collision with multiple deaths allegedly due to flooded road. Alleged defective road design. Verdict against township and owner of land which drained onto road. On appeal, property owner let out of case as they did not have control over drainage system. ***Piekarski v. Club Overlook*, 281 Pa. Super. 162, 421 A.2d 1198.**

Seepage from underground cistern—liability based on failure to reasonably maintain upheld. ***Moss Rose Mfg. Co. v. Foster*, 226 Pa. Super. 448, 314 A.2d 25.**

Broken water main—trial judge made plaintiff prove specific negligence—refused charge on exclusive control—defense verdict upheld by evenly divided court. ***Banet v. City of Philadelphia*, 226 Pa. Super. 452, 313 A.2d 253.**

Wife plaintiff, a pedestrian, fell in daylight over a water box cover—evidence conflicting as to how much cover was depressed from the level of the crossing—jury found for defendant—court below in error in granting a new trial on ground that jury was confused. ***Imbrescia et vir. v. Charleroi Borough,*** **211 Pa. Super. 371, 236 A.2d 535.**

Water box cover

Wife plaintiff, a pedestrian, fell in daylight over a water box cover—evidence conflicting as to how much cover was depressed from the level of the crossing—jury found for defendant—court below in error in granting a new trial on ground that jury was confused. ***Imbrescia et vir. v. Charleroi Borough,*** **211 Pa. Super. 371, 236 A.2d 535.**

Water Company

Plaintiff brought class action lawsuit against Defendant water company for overcharging its customers under various tort and contract theories. The trial court dismissed Plaintiff's complaint. The Commonwealth Court affirmed holding that the public utility commission had exclusive jurisdiction over claims for over billing. ***Pettko v. Pennsylvania American Water Co.,*** **39 A.3d 473 (Pa. Cmwlth. 2012).**

Water line

Plaintiff was injured when he tripped on a pile of dirt left on Commonwealth owned street by a water line repair contractor. In suit against city and others, court held that nonsuit in favor of city was proper. Plaintiff failed to prove that utility exception to municipal immunity was applicable as water line break was on private property, not city property, and real estate exception to immunity did not apply as plaintiff failed to prove that city had contractual obligation to Commonwealth to maintain Commonwealth owned street. ***Leone v. Commonwealth Department of Transportation,*** **780 A.2d 754 (Pa. Cmwlth. 2001).**

Plaintiffs injured when they fell into strip mine adjacent to state road brought action against Commonwealth. Commonwealth immune because injuries occurred on private property. ***Snyder v. Harmon,*** **522 Pa. 424, 562 A.2d 307.**

Water meter

Plaintiff recovered from city water authority after establishing that city's water meter located in plaintiff's residence was defective when it broke and flooded plaintiff's basement. Held: the broken water meter was a dangerous condition of a utility service facility under the Political Subdivision Tort Claims Act and that it was located on a "right of way" owned by the city, even though it was in plaintiff's residence. ***Primiano v. City of Philadelphia,*** **739 A.2d 1172 (Pa. Cmwlth. 1999).**

Waving through intersection

Bus driver waved plaintiff through intersection. Plaintiff had stopped for stop sign on cross street. Bus then moved prematurely and struck car. Plaintiff not under duty to continue looking at bus once waved on. ***Farley v. SEPTA,*** **279 Pa. Super. 570, 421 A.2d 346.**

Welding

Welding

Plaintiff's decedent welder was killed when fumes inside gasoline tank truck in which he was working caught fire and exploded. Motion for compulsory nonsuit granted because plaintiff's decedent was fully aware of the risks attending the work he was performing. Recovery prohibited under Section 388 of Restatement (2d) Torts which imposes duty to warn owner of chattel who has reason to believe that those for whose use the chattel is supplied will not realize its dangerous condition. ***Erdos v. Bedford Valley Petroleum Co.*, 452 Pa. Super. 555, 682 A.2d 806 (1996).**

Summary judgment in favor of defendant, affirmed. Welding at maritime facility not a distinctively maritime role, therefore, traditional two-year tort statute of limitations applied. Statute began running when welder knew of injury and its cause. ***Volpe v. Johns-Manville*, 323 Pa. Super. 130, 470 A.2d 164.**

Well

Petroleum products from service station contaminated neighbors' wells. Neighbors brought action for negligent infliction of emotional distress. Held: there can be no recovery in the absence of attendant physical injury. ***Houston v. Texaco, Inc.*, 371 Pa. Super. 399, 538 A.2d 502.**

Wheelchair

Plaintiff injured when she fell over in her wheel chair while being transported in a local transportation agency van. Summary judgment in favor of local agency by reason of governmental immunity defense sustained because plaintiff did not provide proof of permanent loss of a bodily function. ***Smith v. Endless Mountain Transportation Authority*, 878 A.2d 177 (Pa. Cmwlth. 2005).**

Whiteout

Real estate exception to sovereign immunity held not to apply in suit against PennDOT for negligent design of road on which family was killed in "whiteout" snow conditions. ***Kosmack v. Jones*, 807 A.2d 927 (Pa. Cmwlth. 2002).**

Wild animal

Zoo volunteer whose fingertip was bitten off by Chuckles, a South American river dolphin, may not recover against City. City is immune from suit because care, custody, and control of animals exception to governmental immunity does not include wild animals. Order denying judgment *n.o.v.* reversed. ***Sakach v. City of Pittsburgh*, ___ Pa. Cmwlth. ___, 687 A.2d 34 (1996).**

Willful misconduct

Plaintiffs were injured when a grader's blade struck their car while plowing snow from the road during a state of emergency declared by the governor. Plaintiff's alleged negligence only, not willful misconduct. Under Section 7704(a) of the Pennsylvania Emergency Code, only willful misconduct is an exception to the general immunity afforded to Commonwealth employees. ***Zuppo v. Com., Dept. of Transp.*, 739 A.2d 1148 (Pa. Cmwlth. 1999).**

Windshield wiper

Plaintiff's decedent killed in an automobile accident with his wife operating car—bad weather—windshield wiper defective—driving into guard rail—suit against wife—verdict for defendant—refusal to grant a new trial affirmed on appeal. *Campana v. Bower,* **424 Pa. 383, 227 A.2d 887.**

Windstorm

The Pennsylvania modification of the rule invoked where a pedestrian injured by glass falling from a plate glass window as the result of a wind storm—plaintiff's expert testified that the defective construction of the building was the proximate cause of the window blowing out—Superior Court reversed. *Jones v. Treegobb,* **433 Pa. 225, 249 A.2d 352.**

Wires

Architect has no duty to warn contractor employees of visible overhead power lines that came into contact with metal scaffolding killing or injuring workers. Summary judgment in favor of architect affirmed. *Frampton v. Dauphin Distribution Services Co.,* **436 Pa. Super. 486, 648 A.2d 326 (1994).**

Jury verdict $490,000 to injured plaintiff and $47,000 to wife for loss of consortium. Plaintiff guiding rail for crane operator when crane hit high tension wires, causing severe electrical burns. Held: crane operator not co-employee of plaintiff under circumstances. Proper to submit negligence of operator to jury. Reversed 402A verdict as improperly submitted under facts here. Plaintiff's proof of negligence was a reasonable secondary cause. Negligence verdict affirmed. *Thompson v. Anthony Crane Rental,* **325 Pa. Super. 386, 473 A.2d 120.**

Wire of telephone company pulled down by passing truck, blocking street. Defendant taxi company driver proceeded down street even though asked to stop by plaintiff, thereby hitting wire which tangled in plaintiff's feet causing injury. Negligence of phone company based on previous instances of trucks hitting wire. Verdict against both defendants affirmed. *Miller v. Checker Cab, et al.,* **465 Pa. 82, 348 A.2d 128.**

Violation by utility company of National Electrical Code in installation of 2400 volt line too close to peak of a roof is evidence of negligence in injury case. Verdict for plaintiff affirmed. *Yocum v. Honold,* **234 Pa. Super. 766, 345 A.2d 741.**

Witness Immunity Doctrine

Plaintiff's claims of professional negligence of its witness in prior litigation was not barred by witness immunity doctrine where alleged errors by witness were professionally negligent and not merely unsuccessful efforts to advance an opinion. *LLMD of Michigan v. Jackson-Cross Company,* **740 A.2d 186 (Pa. 1999).**

Workmen injured while working

Plaintiff, an employee of a subcontractor, brought a claim for negligence against the Defendant school district after he fell from a ladder when the decorative column he had leaned the ladder up against gave way. The trial court entered sum-

Workmen injured while working

mary judgment for the defendant. The Commonwealth Court affirmed holding that a duty cannot be imposed upon a landowner if the defective condition was created by the work of the independent contractor. In addition, a landowner has no further liability where it turns work over to an independent contractor, who selects his own equipment and employees. ***Wombacher v. Greater Johnstown School District*, 20 A.3d 1240 (Pa. Cmwlth. 2011).**

Plaintiff filed negligence action against the defendant college, general contractor and subcontractor after he fell while climbing scaffolding erected by the subcontractor. A jury rendered a verdict against all three defendants. The Superior Court reversed and remanded for entry of judgment notwithstanding the verdict in favor of the college. On appeal the Superior Court affirmed its prior ruling holding that a property owner retaining a certain degree of authority over safety issues such as supervising and enforcing safety requirements or even imposing its own safety requirements does not constitute control sufficient to impose liability. In addition, regulating the use and access to a building is not sufficient to establish control regarding the manner or methods of the work being performed to impose liability. ***Beil v. Telesis Construction, Inc.*, 11 A.3d 456 (Pa. Super. 2011).**

Employee of subcontractor brought suit against the borough, fire company, contractor, and inspection company after he was injured in a fall from scaffolding while building the borough's firehouse. The trial court granted summary judgment in favor of the Defendants. The Commonwealth Court held that the contractor was precluded from being sued by an employee of one of its subcontractors based upon the Workers' Compensation Act and that there was no evidence that the inspection company was required to conduct or address safety issues at the worksite. ***Hain v. Borough of West Reading*, 986 A.2d 961 (Pa. Cmwlth. 2009).**

Guardian of ironworker injured on a construction project filed negligence claim after falling from a beam. The trial court granted nonsuit in favor of the general contractor. The Superior Court affirmed holding that the general contractor was a statutory employer entitled to immunity under the Worker's Compensation Act. ***Braun v. Target Corporation*, 983 A.2d 752 (Pa. Super. 2009).**

Plaintiff's decedent was killed in automobile accident following employer-sponsored Christmas party. Where no factual determination as to whether injury was work-related, action against employer not barred by workers' compensation exclusivity provision. Order granting summary judgment in favor of employer reversed. ***Vetter v. Fun Footwear Co.*, 447 Pa. Super. 84, 668 A.2d 529 (1995).**

Summary judgment reversed where plaintiff insulation installer on stilts held not to have assumed the risk of slipping on construction debris left at job site by defendants. Assumption of risk should only preclude recovery where it is beyond question that the plaintiff voluntarily and knowingly proceeded in the face of an obvious and dangerous condition. ***Barrett v. Fredavid Builders, Inc.*, 454 Pa. Super. 162, 685 A.2d 129 (1996).**

Architect has no duty to warn contractor employees of visible overhead power lines that came into contact with metal scaffolding killing or injuring work-

Workmen injured while working

ers. Summary judgment in favor of architect affirmed. ***Frampton v. Dauphin Distribution Services Co.,* 436 Pa. Super. 486, 648 A.2d 326 (1994).**

Employee brought action against employer who did not purchase worker's compensation insurance. Held: employee not required to obtain formal declaration that employer was not insured. ***Liberty v. Adventure Shops, Inc.,* 433 Pa. Super. 586, 641 A.2d 615.**

Employer of worker injured on job did not carry worker's compensation coverage. Held: employee's claim against general liability carrier not enforceable. ***Inman v. Nationwide Mutual Insurance Company,* 433 Pa. Super. 534, 641 A.2d 329.**

Employee of subcontractor brought action against contractor and owner of construction site. Held: employer not liable for indemnification absent express agreement. ***Snare v. Ebensburg Power Company,* 535 Pa. Super. 595, 637 A.2d 296.**

Employee injured in fall down steps brought action against building owners. Owners officers in corporation employing plaintiff. Held: issues of material fact existed that precluded summary judgment. ***Fern v. Usser,* 428 Pa. Super. 210, 630 A.2d 896.**

Employee of independent contractor injured in fall from ladder. Telephone company not liable. Peculiar Risk Doctrine not applicable. ***Steiner v. Bell Telephone of Pennsylvania,* 426 Pa. Super. 84, 626 A.2d 584.**

Employee of independent contractor injured in fall from ladder. Owner of land not liable. Peculiar Risk Doctrine not applicable. ***Lorah v. Luppold Roofing Company, Inc.,* 424 Pa. Super. 439, 622 A.2d 1383.**

Blood bank employee contracted AIDS after being splashed with HIV-infected blood. Blood not tested. Blood bank director negligent but not liable. ***James v. Nolan,* 418 Pa. Super. 425, 614 A.2d 709.**

Employee of contractor injured in fall brought action against owner of construction site based on §§411, 416, and 427 Restatement (2d) Torts. Owner not liable. ***Mentzer v. Ognibene,* 408 Pa. Super. 578, 597 A.2d 604.**

Employee of subcontractor injured in fall from scaffold brought action against general contractor and Commonwealth. Held: Commonwealth immune, contractor may be liable and subcontractor not obligated to indemnify general contractor. ***Donaldson v. Com., Dept. of Transp.,* 141 Pa. Cmwlth. 474, 596 A.2d 269.**

Employee of subcontractor injured in fall from ladder brought action against owner of construction site. Owner not liable. ***Peffer v. Penn 21 Associates,* 406 Pa. Super. 460, 594 A.2d 711.**

Employee of subcontractor injured at construction site. Both general contractor and subcontractor found negligent. Indemnification clause in contract held to be valid. ***Woodburn v. Consolidation Coal Company,* 404 Pa. Super. 359, 590 A.2d 1273.**

Workmen injured while working

Employee of subcontractor brought negligence action against general contractor for on-the-job injury. General contractor was statutory employer and therefore not liable. Contract language to the contrary not controlling. ***Pastore v. Anjo Construction Company,* 396 Pa. Super. 58, 578 A.2d 21.**

Employee of subcontractor injured on job brought action against engineering firm that signed contract on behalf of power company. Engineering firm not immune. Was not party to contract and not statutory employer. ***Travaglia v. C. H. Schwertner & Son, Inc.,* 391 Pa. Super. 61, 570 A.2d 513.**

Employee of independent contractor injured while working in smokestack. Owner joined contractor on basis of indemnification agreement. Reversed and remanded. Contractor improperly joined. ***Fulmer v. Duquesne Light Company,* 374 Pa. Super. 537, 543 A.2d 1100.**

Employee of subcontractor injured while riding in hoist brought action against general contractor. Judgment for plaintiff. Hoist operated contrary to safety regulations. General contractor not statutory employer. ***Cox v. Turner Construction Company,* 373 Pa. Super. 214, 540 A.2d 944.**

Employee of subcontractor injured when scaffold collapsed. General contractor and owner found not liable under special danger or peculiar risk doctrine. Risk of harm was not different from usual risk associated with the work. ***Ortiz v. Ra-El Development Corporation,* 365 Pa. Super. 48, 528 A.2d 1355.**

Worker's Compensation Act does not bar wrongful death action in case where employee of subcontractor is killed as a result of negligence of different subcontractor. ***Grant v. Riverside Corp.,* 364 Pa. Super. 593, 528 A.2d 962.**

Passenger in truck leased to carrier was injured when brakes failed. Lessee held vicariously liable under Interstate Common Carrier Act for injury to member of the traveling public. ***Wilkerson v. Allied Van Lines,* 360 Pa. Super. 523, 521 A.2d 25.**

Worker of paving contractor injured when he fell through sewer grate. Trial court erred by not instructing jury on doctrine of *res ipsa loquitur.* ***Smith v. City of Chester,* 357 Pa. Super. 24, 515 A.2d 303.**

Employee of subcontractor who was injured in fall down uncovered elevator shaft brought action against other subcontractor. Defendant had no duty of care and therefore was not liable. ***Weiser v. Bethlehem Steel Corporation,* 353 Pa. Super. 10, 508 A.2d 1241.**

Claimant fell while descending tank truck which he had mounted for purpose of priming a pump thereon. Directed verdict reversed. For jury, as to whether this act of alighting from vehicle covered by No-Fault Act. ***Cooke v. Travelers Insurance Co.,* 350 Pa. Super. 467, 504 A.2d 935.**

Welder injured while repairing air tank which exploded when pressurized for testing. Nonsuit granted as to owner of tank. Section 388 of Restatement (2d) Torts applies. No reason to believe owner knew of dangerous condition or that experi-

Workmen injured while working

enced welder wouldn't himself realize the danger under facts here. Affirmed. ***Herleman v. Trumbauer Auto Sales,* 346 Pa. Super. 494, 499 A.2d 1109.**

School laborer injured when he fell through skydome on roof. Summary judgment for defendants affirmed. Skydome properly an improvement to real property subject to strict 12 year statute of repose. ***Catanzaro v. Wasco Products,* 339 Pa. Super. 481, 489 A.2d 262.**

Sliver of metal entered eye of workman taking old sign off building. Verdict against property owner for not supplying goggles, oil, or giving adequate warning. Plaintiff found 49% negligent. Final verdict including delay damages $27,277.86 affirmed. Issues of assumption of risk and causation were for jury. ***Seewagen v. Vanderklvet,* 338 Pa. Super. 534, 488 A.2d 21.**

Painter injured by spray painter without guard. Leased by Sherwin-Williams to plaintiff's employer with knowledge by him that guard was missing and with contractual indemnification signed by plaintiff's employer. Error to grant summary judgment in favor of employer on contract claim. ***Rankia v. Sherwin-Williams,* 337 Pa. Super. 78, 486 A.2d 489.**

Independent contractor repairing water leak at PECO substation received severe electrical shock while breaking up concrete. Not warned of location of underground power lines. Improper to grant directed verdict in favor of PECO. For jury whether liability could be based on theories contained in §416 or §427 of Restatement (2d) Torts. New trial ordered. ***Colloi v. Philadelphia Electric Co.,* 332 Pa. Super. 284, 481 A.2d 616.**

Plaintiff-decedent killed when crushed by backhoe. Plaintiff's counsel's failure to specifically object to curative charge on products liability after original charge, waived right to object on appeal. Under Worker's Compensation Law, widow and children of deceased employee are limited to the recovery provided for by Act and have, therefore, no right of action against employer. ***DiSerafino v. Bucyrus-Erie Corp.,* 323 Pa. Super. 247, 470 A.2d 574.**

Jury verdict $25,000 against employer only. Manufacturer exonerated. Verdict molded to defense verdict. Affirmed. Steam hammer sold to employer 43 years earlier. Die flew off ram striking plaintiff. ***Brogley v. Chambersburg Engineering,* 306 Pa. Super. 316, 452 A.2d 743.**

Plaintiff working at construction site injured when he pulled block from under wheel of truck and it moved in opposite direction expected. Verdict against truck driver affirmed. ***Fahringer v. Rinehimer,* 283 Pa. Super. 93, 423 A.2d 731.**

Industrial accident. Plaintiff's glove caught in machine causing injury. Judge's charge on assumption of risk held in error. Use of gloves must have been a "substantial factor" in bringing about the harm. ***Takach v. Root Co.,* 279 Pa. Super. 167, 420 A.2d 1084.**

Plaintiff killed while in construction trench which collapsed. Defendant required to supervise work and inspect pursuant to contract. Verdict for plaintiff affirmed. ***Heath v. Huth Engineers,* 279 Pa. Super. 90, 420 A.2d 758.**

Workmen injured while working

Independent contractor working at defendant's plant injured when ladder slipped on floor on which water accumulated while he was on ladder. Verdict for plaintiff affirmed. ***Love v. Harrisburg Coca-Cola,* 273 Pa. Super. 210, 417 A.2d 242.**

Workman injured on construction job stepping on loose concrete block. Installer of block had not finished and would have done so on next work day. Plaintiff's nonsuit reversed. Accident on a Saturday. Failure to post warnings should have been for jury. ***McKenzie v. Cost Brothers,* 487 Pa. 303, 409 A.2d 362.**

Workman injured in fall from temporary platform used for passage to house under construction. Had traversed platform several times without problem. No evidence of cause of platform failure. Jury verdict for plaintiff reversed and judgment entered for defendant. ***Szumski v. Lohman Homes,* 267 Pa. Super. 478, 406 A.2d 1142.**

Blast furnace collapsed injuring workmen. Work not being done in normal course and posed unusual dangers. Verdict for plaintiffs reversed. Charge held inadequate on basis of §413 of Restatement (2d) Torts —Duty to provide for taking of precautions against dangers involved in work intrusted to contractors. ***Gonzales v. U.S. Steel,* 484 Pa. 277, 398 A.2d 1378.**

Plaintiff injured while working at construction site—walking on incomplete wall which gave way. Nonsuit affirmed by evenly divided court. Plaintiff failed to show breach of industry standards, negligence in scheduling work, or knowledge by defendants that he would be working on Saturday when accident occurred. ***McKenzie v. Cost Brothers,* 260 Pa. Super. 295, 394 A.2d 559.**

Verdict for defendant affirmed. Plaintiff, a truck driver, injured while defendant's employees were loading his truck. Defense contended employees only following plaintiff's instructions. ***Pepin v. Bethlehem Steel,* 257 Pa. Super. 643, 390 A.2d 312.**

Workman for subcontractor fell in unlighted corridor. Jury found negligence on behalf of general contractor in failing to light job site. Plaintiff held to be statutory employer and therefore unable to recover. ***Rosenbaum v. Kennedy House,* 254 Pa. Super. 628, 387 A.2d 123.**

Plaintiff fell while erecting a coal hopper when V-clip which had been welded by PBI gave way. Whether use of V-clip under the circumstances was foreseeable by PBI as a secondary use, was for jury. Contributory negligence of plaintiff in failing to use safety belt also for jury. Verdict for plaintiff. ***Lambert v. PBI Industries,* 244 Pa. Super. 118, 366 A.2d 944.**

Plaintiff injured when steel plate running from loading platform to compactor gave way. Suit versus installer of plate who joined employer and trash hauler. Verdict against installer and employer only. ***Hinton v. Waste Techniques,* 243 Pa. Super. 189, 364 A.2d 724.**

Verdict of $900,000.00 affirmed. Plaintiff painting electrical towers of defendant. Told by his employer that power was off. Erroneous information. Severe burns

Workmen injured while working

over 35 percent of body. *Piso v. Weirton Steel Co., et al.,* **235 Pa. Super. 517, 345 A.2d 728.**

Employee of independent contractor injured when employee of owner of plant started a machine which plaintiff was adjusting. Court below refused to charge on duty owed by possessor of land to business visitor and charged only on negligence. Error on these facts. New trial ordered. ***Crotty v. Reading Industries,* 237 Pa. Super. 1, 345 A.2d 259.**

Plaintiff injured when industrial split wheel separated and struck him in head. Plaintiff worked for company which replaced tires on forklift trucks with this type of wheel. Court held that plaintiff could not be barred from recovery even though jury found that plaintiff's employer failed to exercise duty of reasonable inspection. ***Lambert v. Pittsburgh Iron Works,* 463 Pa. 237, 344 A.2d 810.**

Foley—electrical subcontractor. Armstrong—plastering contractor. Plaintiff employed by Armstrong—on job pushing wheelbarrow which struck a conduit sticking up through cement floor causing handle to strike groin. Judgment against Foley upheld but new trial ordered as to damages only. Armstrong judgment reversed due to late joinder. ***Moore v. Foley,* 235 Pa. Super. 310, 340 A.2d 519.**

Plaintiff working, remodeling office building when ceiling, installed 26 years earlier, fell on him. Suit against company which designed and installed ceiling, plus owners at time and all subsequent owners. Motion for summary judgment by current owner under 12 P.S. §65.1 et seq. [now 42 Pa. C.S.A. §5536] which limits time for bringing suits to 12 years for injuries arising out of deficiencies in design, construction, etc. of improvements to real property against person performing construction or furnishing design. Owner held not to be protected by statute. ***Leach v. P.S.F.S.,* 234 Pa. Super. 486, 340 A.2d 491.**

Plaintiff injured when aluminum siding he was installing came into contact with uninsulated electric wire of defendant. Fell off scaffold supplied by employer. Judge did not charge on possibility of verdict against employer (additional defendant) only. New trial ordered. ***Burke v. Duquesne Light Co.,* 231 Pa. Super. 412, 332 A.2d 544.**

Plaintiff, decedent, employed by independent contractor to work at U. S. Steel piling iron ore atop huge pile using large truck. Night—had to drive on top of 50 foot pile with no other light but headlights. Ran off edge where it had broken off. Ultrahazardous activity. Evidence of previous similar accidents. §416 of Restatement (2d) Torts involving peculiar risk of physical harm. Verdict for plaintiff affirmed. ***McDonough v. U.S. Steel,* 228 Pa. Super. 268, 324 A.2d 542.**

Plaintiffs pouring concrete in warehouse when recently constructed wall fell on top of them. Verdict for plaintiffs against owner, masonry contractor and employer. Evidence that design and construction failed to meet industry and City standards. ***Hargrove v. Frommeyer,* 229 Pa. Super. 298, 323 A.2d 300.**

Plaintiff working at building being renovated. Injured when 16 year old child of owner dropped a prefabricated staircase section on his leg. Plaintiff had com-

Work place

plained to owner that his children were playing on site. Verdict for plaintiff against owner and general contractor. ***Byrd v. Merwin, et al.,* 456 Pa. 516, 317 A.2d 280.**

Plaintiff employed by heating contractor. Injured on roof of customer when he stepped off roof in dark and fell to ground at night. No evidence of negligence on part of property owner. No duty to warn under these circumstances. ***Kalin v. Delaware Valley Telephone Co.,* 228 Pa. Super. 849, 316 A.2d 912.**

Decedent, a workman, was removing a piece of spouting and contacted defendant's 13.2 KV transmission line—sustaining injuries which resulted in his death—line 6 feet, 3 inches from side of building and not 8 feet—conflicting expert testimony—held: case for jury as to death action only. ***Groh v. Phila. Electric Co.,* 441 Pa. 345, 271 A.2d 265.**

Plaintiff in ditch struck by rear wheel of defendant's bus which partially ran over ditch—case for jury. ***Jackson v. Phila. Trans. Co.,* 433 Pa. 606, 248 A.2d 766.**

Plaintiff was a volunteer worker helping blacktop a parking lot—struck by a tractor used to roll blacktop—defendant operator left engine running when leaving machine—his seven year old son started machine and plaintiff injured—owner of premises and operator of tractor held jointly responsible. ***Glass v. Freeman,* 430 Pa. 21, 240 A.2d 825.**

Work place

Plaintiff, a plumber/pipe-fitter employee of an independent contractor for a power plant, died from asbestos exposure. Plaintiff's personal representative sued possessor of real estate where he worked. Held that possessor of land had no greater knowledge of risks of asbestos than plaintiff and his employer and so was insulated from liability. ***Rudy v. A-Best Products Company,* 870 A.2d 330 (Pa. Super. 2005).**

Where no evidence that trunk was too large or unwieldy to be placed in overhead rack of railroad car, employee could not maintain action for negligence of employer in providing safe place to work when trunk fell on employee's foot, causing injury. Summary judgment affirmed. ***Lehman v. National R.R. Passenger Corp.,* 443 Pa. Super. 185, 661 A.2d 17 (1995).**

Work release

City's failure to supervise and control criminal detainee in work-release facility who left facility and murdered plaintiffs' decedent is not a recognized exception to governmental immunity. City's indemnification of lessor of work release facility was not a waiver of governmental immunity in favor of plaintiffs. Summary judgment affirmed. ***Rodriguez v. City of Philadelphia, Dept. of Human Services,* ___ Pa. Cmwlth. ___, 657 A.2d 105 (1995).**

Wrong side of highway

Crossover head-on accident. Verdict for defendant. Defendant testified that he pulled to berm to avoid accident in his lane, then tried to swerve around telephone pole when he lost control of his car, crossing four lanes of roadway and striking plaintiff. Verdict affirmed. Although driver who crosses center line of highway is

Wrong side of highway

negligent *per se,* this can be rebutted by competent evidence that vehicle was there through no negligence on part of defendant. Failure to charge on sudden emergency doctrine is of no significance considering verdict and holding. ***Farrelli v. Marko,* 349 Pa. Super. 102, 502 A.2d 1293.**

Charge of court held adequate on issue of shifting of burden of proof when auto crosses center line. Verdict for defendant contrary to weight of evidence, new trial ordered. Defendant crossed center of highway—claims skidded on wet road when car ahead slowed suddenly. This was an inadequate explanation and therefore verdict contrary to weight of evidence. ***Bohner v. Stine,* 316 Pa. Super. 426, 463 A.2d 438.**

Jury verdict $800,000 for teenage boy. Severe blow to forehead causing complete loss of forehead bone and damage to frontal lobes of brain. Proper to direct verdict against defendant where accident occurred on wrong side of road without explanation by defendant. Evidence clear as to point of impact. Oral evidence rule applies only where there are no clear physical facts. ***Krupz v. Williams,* 316 Pa. Super. 408, 463 A.2d 429.**

Passenger in auto injured when car in which he was riding was driven off road to avoid oncoming car. Verdict in favor of both drivers. Extent of injuries in sharp dispute. Driver who came across highway offered reasonable explanation for cause. Affirmed. ***Troutman v. Tabb,* 285 Pa. Super. 353, 427 A.2d 673.**

Head-on collision on snowy street. Each side claimed he was in his own lane. Defense verdict. Cars parked on both sides of street and plaintiff's car stopped to permit defendant to pass. Charge in error on stopping vehicle on highway. All circumstances must be considered. New trial ordered. ***Kuhn v. Michael,* 283 Pa. Super. 101, 423 A.2d 735.**

Head-on collision when southbound vehicle crossed medial barrier. Passenger in northbound vehicle sued both drivers. Verdict against northbound vehicle only. Southbound vehicle in northbound lanes for several seconds. Witness stated that "with luck and skill" on part of northbound vehicle, she possibly could have avoided the accident. Affirmed. ***Lewis v. Mellor,* 259 Pa. Super. 509, 393 A.2d 941.**

Auto accident between auto and truck. Truck driver claimed auto swerved into his lane. Auto driver claimed truck in her lane so she swerved back into his lane. Impact in lane of truck. Verdict against truck driver. ***Lininger v. Kromer,* 238 Pa. Super. 259, 358 A.2d 89.**

Plaintiff a pedestrian struck by defendant's truck which was pulling between two stopped buses discharging passengers on opposite sides of the street. Plaintiff lost memory of accident. Only witness stated that she didn't know if plaintiff looked for traffic. Defendant's truck operated partially on wrong side of road. For jury. ***Gregorich v. Pepsi-Cola,* 230 Pa. Super. 144, 327 A.2d 171.**

Each driver claimed other crossed medial barrier—passenger in one of the vehicles killed—verdict for both defendants reversed—when a driver crosses the center of highway it then becomes his burden to explain why—here each driver had burden to prove freedom from negligence—in absence of exculpatory evidence, the

Wrongful accusation

collision must have resulted from negligence of one of the drivers. *Fair v. Snowball Express,* **226 Pa. Super. 295, 310 A.2d 386.**

Minor pedestrian injured by auto. Testimony that boy asked for ice cream money—picked up in front of defendant's car three feet from ice cream truck. From this it could be inferred that defendant was on wrong side of highway. For jury. *DeLio v. Hamilton,* **227 Pa. Super. 581, 308 A.2d 607.**

Crossing over center line—head-on collision—when a driver is on the wrong side of the road at the time of collision, there is a presumption of negligence—there is no presumption merely by a finding that the auto was on the wrong side of the road after the accident. *O'Donnell v. Hail,* **343 Pa. 559, 277 A.2d 360.**

Plaintiff's and defendant's cars going in opposite directions—cars rounding a curve—defendant testified that he panicked, slammed on the brakes and skidded into plaintiff's car on plaintiff's side of the road—verdict for defendant—new trial awarded on appeal—court below abused its discretion in not granting same. *Anzelone v. Jesperson,* **436 Pa. 28, 258 A.2d 510.**

Plaintiff was a passenger in one of colliding cars—snowy and highway icy—car of defendant skidded and went over into lane for vehicles proceeding in the opposite direction—defendant contended that his car was at rest when colliding vehicle was several hundred feet away—verdict for defendant upheld—fact question for jury as to whether defendant proceeding properly. *Keba v. Pickett,* **434 Pa. 148, 252 A.2d 675.**

Wrongful accusation

Employee who was wrongfully reassigned for allegedly making suggestive remarks to a customer brought action for intentional infliction of emotional distress against employer. Held: there is no liability for the mere negligent infliction of emotional distress. *Jackson v. Sun Oil Company,* **361 Pa. Super. 54, 521 A.2d 469.**

Wrongful death and survival actions

Administrator appealed a trial court's molded verdict of zero dollars to the estate based upon health insurance benefits already received. The Pennsylvania Supreme Court held that the failure to present affirmative evidence does not make the other party's opinion evidence uncontroverted and the amount of damages is a question for the jury. *Carroll v. Avallone,* **565 Pa. 676, 939 A.2d 872 (2007).**

Administrator brought a claim of wrongful death and survival against physicians, social workers and a hospital after they allegedly refused to commit the individual and he later committed suicide. The appellate court reversed the trial court holding that the mother of the deceased had reported she believed her son had previously attempted suicide, which was sufficient to provide a genuine issue of material fact as to his intent to commit suicide to survive a motion for summary judgment. *Zator v. Coachi,* **939 A.2d 349 (Pa. Super. 2007).**

Plaintiffs filed suit asserting wrongful death and survival actions for failure to investigate and failure to transmit x-rays. The court upheld dismissal on the basis of defendants' lis pendens defense. Defendants had shown that the parties, the

Wrongful death and survival actions

causes of action, and the relief sought were the same in both of the plaintiff's actions. ***Rostock v. Anzalone*, 904 A.2d 943 (Pa. Super. 2006).**

Plaintiffs filed suit on their own behalf and on behalf of decedent's estate for wrongful death due to prolonged exposure to sewage sludge. The court upheld dismissal on the basis that the Discovery Rule could not be applied to toll the statute of limitations in a wrongful death action. Death puts survivors on notice to determine the cause of death and any claims that might flow from it. ***Pennock v. Lenzi*, 882 A.2d 1057 (Pa. Cmwlth. 2005).**

Plaintiffs brought wrongful death and survival action against medical providers who plaintiffs allege caused their son's suicide. Sole substantive issue before Superior Court was whether witness in wrongful death and survival action suit is barred from testimony by Dead Man's Act. Although technically there should not be any testimony allowed by person with interest adverse to decedent's interests in survival action because decedent's interest has passed to his or her personal representative, there is no such restriction as to wrongful death action. Practically, court will not impose Dead Man's Act restrictions in either wrongful death or survival actions because of attendant impracticalities. ***Gibbs v. Herman*, 714 A.2d 432 (Pa. Super. 1998).**

Plaintiff, surrogate mother, sued infertility clinic under wrongful death and survival statutes, for negligent infliction of emotional distress, for fraud and for breach of fiduciary duty for the death of child murdered by sperm-donor father one month after the child's birth. After determining that clinic had waived any claim that mother lacked standing, Held: mother had stated cause of action under wrongful death and survival statutes but lacked sufficient factual basis for negligent infliction of emotional distress, fraud and breach of fiduciary duty. For-profit infertility clinic was in a "special relationship" with all parties to the transaction—surrogate mother, sperm-donor and resulting child—so as to create a duty imposed by law to effectively provide safeguards that might reasonably prevent foreseeable injuries to the parties, such as abuse of the child. ***Huddleston v. Infertility Center of America*, 700 A.2d 453 (Pa. Super. 1997).**

In suit which alleged that decedent contracted malignant nodular lymphoma from occupational exposure to toxic chemicals, plaintiff may proceed with wrongful death cause of action until there is a final determination whether the disease was covered under the Worker's Compensation Act or Occupational Disease Act. Superior Court's reversal of trial court's order sustaining preliminary objections affirmed by evenly divided court. ***Lord Corporation v. Pollard*, ___ Pa. ___, 695 A.2d 767 (1997).**

Plaintiff's decedent died after crashing into utility pole following high-speed chase. The decedent's criminal and negligent acts preclude imposition of liability on municipalities whose police officers were engaged in pursuit. Therefore, decedent's widow could not recover from municipalities under wrongful death theory because such action is derivative to any action the decedent may have had. Order granting summary judgment affirmed. ***Tyree v. City of Pittsburgh*, ___ Pa. Cmwlth. ___, 669 A.2d 487 (1995).**

Wrongful death and survival actions

In wrongful death and survival action by widow of motorist whose automobile crossed opposing lane and left highway, PennDOT entitled to jury charge on contributory negligence where no evidence presented regarding external cause of accident. Following plaintiff's inquiry into other causes of accident, State Trooper permitted to testify as to possibility of driver having fallen asleep. *Burkholz v. Com., Dept. of Transp.,* ___ **Pa. Cmwlth.** ___, **667 A.2d 513 (1995).**

In automobile accident, testimony by State Trooper with familiarity of truck inspection procedures properly disallowed as to standard of care required by truck driver. Comparative Negligence Act requires that jury apportion liability between plaintiff and all defendants against whom recovery is sought. Trial court's bifurcation to allow apportionment of liability between less than all defendants reversed. *Christiansen v. Silfies,* **446 Pa. Super. 464, 667 A.2d 396 (1995).**

Plaintiff's decedent who was informed that mesothelioma was a rare, asbestos-induced form of lung cancer is not entitled to benefit of discovery rule where products liability action commenced more than two years after diagnosis of lung cancer. *Baumgart v. Keene Bldg. Products Corp.,* **542 Pa. 194, 666 A.2d 238 (1995).**

Absent proof that a patron was visibly intoxicated when served additional alcoholic beverages, no action for wrongful death or survival is established. Statutory violation of serving alcohol after hours does not establish liability for acts of third parties absent proof that such service was proximate cause of the injury. *Hiles v. Brandywine Club,* **443 Pa. Super. 462, 662 A.2d 16 (1995).**

City's failure to supervise and control criminal detainee in work release facility who left facility and murdered plaintiffs' decedent is not a recognized exception to governmental immunity. City's indemnification of lessor of work release facility was not a waiver of governmental immunity in favor of plaintiffs. Summary judgment affirmed. *Rodriguez v. City of Philadelphia, Dept. of Human Services,* ___ **Pa. Cmwlth.** ___, **657 A.2d 105 (1995).**

Wrongful death and survival actions based on medical malpractice for failure to diagnose breast cancer are to be treated separately as to applicable statute of limitations. Failure to commence survival action within two years following death of decedent did not preclude wrongful death action filed within two years of death, as underlying cause of action for medical malpractice was not yet time barred as of decedent's death. *Moyer v. Rubright,* **438 Pa. Super. 154, 651 A.2d 1139 (1994).**

Wrongful death and survival actions brought against physician and hospital. Amended complaint removed hospital from action. Held: if action against hospital is discontinued estate must be allowed to join hospital as additional defendant. *Hileman v. Morelli,* **413 Pa. Super. 316, 605 A.2d 377.**

Parents of child killed by automobile agreed to settlement without court approval. Father later brought wrongful death and survival actions. Held: wrongful death action barred but survival action allowed. *Schuster v. Reeves,* **403 Pa. Super. 518, 589 A.2d 731.**

Wrongful death and survival actions

Wrongful death action brought against cigarette manufacturer based on defective design and failure to warn. Held: 1) Federal Cigarette Labeling Act preempted state action for failure to warn; 2) while action for defective design not preempted, plaintiff failed to state cause of action. *Hite v. R. J. Reynolds Tobacco Company,* **396 Pa. Super. 82, 578 A.2d 417.**

Injuries received by child while *en ventre sa mere* formerly could form basis for survival or wrongful death actions as maintained only on behalf of child born alive. Live birth now held no longer to be a limiting prerequisite to maintenance of such action. Case remanded for further proceedings. *Amadio v. Levin,* **509 Pa. 199, 501 A.2d 1085.**

Administrator of an estate of a deceased pedestrian could not recover punitive damages in a survival action based on the gross negligence of the defendant motorist. *Harvey v. Hassinger,* **315 Pa. Super. 97, 461 A.2d 814 (1983).**

Non-jury verdict—$11,234.51, wrongful death; $128,173.77—survival. Motorcycle accident. Clear evidence of conscious pain and suffering. 55 year old decedent—excellent health, earning $19,688.68/year plus fringe benefits. Actuary testified loss of future earnings, straight line basis—$133,542 to 65; $187,939 to age 70. Under Wrongful Death Act, widow and family entitled to compensation for loss of contributions decedent would have made for food, shelter, clothing, etc. Widow also entitled to loss of society, comfort and assistance. Wrongful death verdict shockingly low. Verdicts vacated. *Slaseman v. Myers,* **309 Pa. Super. 537, 455 A.2d 1213.**

Jury verdict $3,283.70—wrongful death; nothing in survival. Wrongful death verdict reducd 50% contribution. Survival verdict held unreasonable. Eighteen-year old passenger drinking with driver prior to getting into car—both intoxicated. Decedent earning $3.00/hr. as mechanic. Life expectancy—50.6 years. Minimum net loss of earnings, after maintenance—$77,659.00. With 50% contribution found, verdict unexplainable. New trial—damages only. *Bortner v. Gladfelter,* **302 Pa. Super. 492, 448 A.2d 1386.**

Suit on behalf of stillborn child who died as a result of injuries received *en ventre sa mere* in auto accident, dismissed. Infant must be born alive in order to sustain a claim. *Scott v. Kapp,* **494 Pa. 487, 431 A.2d 959.**

Filing of death action before appointment of administrator formalized, in that bond not yet filed, after appointment validated filing would be related back so that initiation of action was held timely filed within statute of limitations. *McGuire v. Erie Lackawanna Rwy.,* **253 Pa. Super. 531, 385 A.2d 466.**

Death of 5 year old boy following tonsillectomy. Verdict of $455,199.75 reversed and new trial ordered as to damages only. Error to charge that item of damage was loss of amenities of life. *Willinger v. Mercy Catholic Medical Center,* **241 Pa. Super. 456, 362 A.2d 280.**

By provisions of the Wrongful Death Act of 1855, as amended, distribution is to be made in accordance with the provisions of the Intestate Act—decedent left a widow and a daughter by a previous marriage—held: each take a one-half interest in net proceeds—strong dissent. *Seymour v. Rossman,* **449 Pa. 515, 297 A.2d 804.**

Wrongful life

Court below properly ordered distribution of the proceeds of a recovery under the Wrongful Death Act by awarding fiftypercent to widow and fifty percent to a surviving child—the same was in accordance with the provisions of the Interstate Act. ***Seymour v. Rossman,* 220 Pa. Super. 92, 283 A.2d 495.**

Error to permit an amendment to aver a cause of action under the Survival Act when made more than 2 years after cause of action arose. ***Groh v. Phila. Electric Co.,* 441 Pa. 345, 271 A.2d 265.**

Mother, while six months pregnant, was allegedly injured by an electric shock while passenger in defendant's car—child stillborn—no right of action exists under Pennsylvania Wrongful Death and Survival Afacts. ***Marko v. Phila. T. Co.,* 420 Pa. 124, 216 A.2d 502.**

Wrongful life

Plaintiffs brought wrongful birth and wrongful life action against defendant physicians and hospital after the physicians failed to advise them that Plaintiff-mother was a carrier of a genetic mutation that the mother maintained would have led her to terminate her pregnancy. The trial court dismissed the action on preliminary objections. The Superior Court on appeal reversed and remanded holding that 42 Pa.C.S. § 8305, which precludes wrongful birth and wrongful life actions, was unconstitutional on the basis that it was passed in violation of the single-subject constitutional rule. ***Sernovitz v. Dershaw,* 57 A.3d 1254 (Pa. Super. 2012).**

Although entire complaint arising out of birth of Down's Syndrome child and sterilization was unartfully drafted, two distinct claims were asserted: one for wrongful birth and one for performance of sterilization procedure without informed consent. Plaintiff's proposed amendments to complaint did not create new cause of action but clarified and strengthened claim based on lack of informed consent and, therefore, should have been allowed. Order granting judgment on the pleadings and denying leave to amend reversed. ***Sejpal v. Corson, McKinley,* 445 Pa. Super. 427, 665 A.2d 1198 (1995).**

Mother brought wrongful birth and malpractice actions against hospital and physicians. Judgment on pleadings granted for wrongful birth. Held: judgment appealable. Wrongful birth statute not retroactive. ***Jenkins v. Hospital of Medical College of Pennsylvania,* 535 Pa. 252, 634 A.2d 1099.**

Patient brought malpractice action against physician and hospital for unsuccessful sterilization. Patient entitled to collect damages for costs related to childbirth but not for expenses in raising child. ***Butler v. Rolling Hills Hospital,* 400 Pa. Super. 141, 582 A.2d 1384.**

Damages for infant plaintiff, with birth defect not detected by early tests *in utero*, had no cause of action. Case dismissed. ***Ellis v. Sherman,* 330 Pa. Super. 42, 478 A.2d 1339.**

Child born with birth defect has no cause of action against lab or physician who allegedly failed to determine, prenatally, and in sufficient time to prevent birth,

Wrongful use of civil proceedings

that child was afflicted with defect. ***Rubin v. Hamot Medical Center,* 329 Pa. Super. 439, 478 A.2d 869.**

Negligent performance of sterilization operation would allow recovery for costs associated with pregnancy and delivery. However, Court holds as matter of law that benefits of joy, companionship and affection of normal, healthy child outweigh costs of raising the child. ***Mason v. Western Pennsylvania Hospital,* 499 Pa. 484, 453 A.2d 974.**

Parents' right to cause of action in tort against physicians to recover expenses attributable to birth and raising of child affirmed. Parents also entitled to recover for mental distress and physical inconvenience attributable to the birth; by evenly divided Court, affirmed denial of child's cause of action. ***Speck v. Finegold,* 497 Pa. 77, 439 A.2d 110.**

Child born after tubal ligation with birth defect. Measure of damages defined as cost of raising child, mother's pain and suffering and loss of income, and father's expenses for birth and wife's medical bills. ***Stribling v. deQuevedo,* 288 Pa. Super. 436, 432 A.2d 239.**

Healthy baby born to plaintiff despite tubal ligation by defendant doctor. Demurrer granted to defendants reversed under previous cases. Not relevant that baby born healthy. Damages will be cost of rearing child reduced by benefit of value of child's aid, comfort and society during parents' life expectancy. ***Mason v. Western Pa. Hospital,* 286 Pa. Super. 359, 428 A.2d 1366.**

Child born to plaintiffs despite vasectomy to father and abortion attempt by mother. Child born with crippling hereditary disease. Claim on behalf of child dismissed. Parents' claim allowed to go forward for breach of duty on part of doctors to properly treat and advise parents. Damages, if proven, may include pecuniary losses they will have to bear for care and treatment of their child. Claim for emotional distress denied. ***Speck v. Finegold,* 268 Pa. Super. 342, 408 A.2d 496.**

Wrongful use of civil proceedings

Plaintiff trucking company brought wrongful use of civil proceeding action against Defendant estate for bringing wrongful death action against it on the basis that it was clear the decedent had died of natural causes prior the accident. The trial court entered summary judgment in favor of the Defendant estate. The Superior Court affirmed holding that Defendant's reliance on an expert medical report that the decedent had died of blunt force trauma and an accident reconstruction report that Plaintiff's employee was careless in his driving was sufficient probable cause to file the action. ***Keystone Freight Corporation v. Stricker,* 31 A.3d 967 (Pa. Super. 2011).**

Yellow Pages

—XYZ—

Yellow Pages

Plaintiff may proceed under theory of negligence against telephone company for placing old ad under expired contract in new yellow pages despite existence of prior contractual relationship. *McDole v. Bell Telephone of Pennsylvania,* **441 Pa. Super. 88, 656 A.2d 933 (1995).**

Dentist brought action for failure to publish advertisement in Yellow Pages. Held: action was properly in contract and not in tort. *Bash v. Bell Telephone of Pennsylvania,* **411 Pa. Super. 347, 601 A.2d 825.**

Index

A

Abandoned vehicle 1
Abdominal aneurysm 1
Abduction from parking lot 1
Abortion 1
Absolute liability 1
Absolute negligence 2
Accelerated speed 2
Accounting 2
Acidosis 2
Actual loss 3
Adjacent property 3
Administrative remedy 3
Adoption 3
Adoption of road 4
Advertising 4
AED Good Samaritan Act 4
Affirmative defense 4
Affirmative duty 5
Agency 5
Aggravating injury 6
Aiding injured person on highway 6
AIDS (HIV) 6
Airbags 7
Air conditioning unit 7
Aircraft accidents 8
Airport tarmac 8
Air quality testing 9
Air tank 9
Alcoholism 9
Alighting from vehicle 9
Allergic reaction 10
All-terrain vehicle (ATV) 10
Alternate path 10
Ambiguous language 10
Ambulance 11
Amnesia 12
Amputation 12
Anesthesia 12
Angioplasty 13

Antenna 13
Anticipating negligence 13
Apartments 13
Apportionment of liability 14
Architect 14, 15
Arm 15
Armed robbery 15
Arrest 15
Arthroscopic surgery 15
Asbestos 16
Assault and battery 16
Assumption of the Risk Doctrine 19
Assured Clear Distance Rule 20
Attorney 24
Attractive nuisances 24
Authority of client 24
Automated External Defibrillator 24
Automatic door 25
Automatic door locks 25
Automobile dealer 25
Autopsy 25
Autopsy report changed 26

B

Baby sitter 27
Backing 27
Back injuries 27
Back up warning 27
Bailing wire 28
Bailments 28
Bakery products 28
Bank 28
Barricades 29
Barrier 29
Bathroom 29
Battery 29
BB gun 27
Bendectin 30
Beryllium plant 30
Bicycles 30
Bifurcation 32
Big Brother and Big Sister Organization 32
Bingo game 32
Birth defect 32

Blast furnace 33
Blasting 33
Bleachers 33
Blinded by lights 34
Blindness 34
Blood alcohol content 34
Blood bank employee 35
Blood Shield Statute 35
Blood transfusion 35
Boating accidents 35
Body 36
Boiler 36
Bone plate and screws 37
Bone tumor 37
Bottles 37
Bowling 38
Box making machine 38
Brain damage 38
Brain surgery 38
Brakes 39
Brawl 40
Breach of guarantee 40
Breast cancer 41
Bridges 42
Broken wrist 42
Bucking traffic 42
Building code 42
Burden of proof 43
Burial 44
Bus 44
Business invitee 49
Bus station 49
Buyout agreement 50
Bystander 50

C

Cadmium 52
Cannon 52
Canon law 52
Captain of the Ship Doctrine 52
Card game 53
Car leaving highway 53
Car wash 53
Cast 54

Caterer 54
Catheterization 54
Catholic grade school 54
Catwalk 55
Causation 55
Cauterization 61
Cave in 61
C.B. radio 61
Ceiling 61
Cellar doors 62
Center of road 62
Cervical sprain 62
Cesarean section 62
Chain 63
Chain collision 63
Chain sling 63
Chair 64
Change of direction 64
Charities 64
Charter school 64
Chase 65
Chemistry class 65
Chest tube 65
Child abuse 65
Child Protective Services Act 65
Children 65
  and alcohol 67
  causing injury 68
  contributorily negligence 69
  injured by conditions on property 72
  in street 70
Children and Youth Services 68
Chiropractic 74
Choice of Ways Doctrine 74
Choking 75
Christmas party 75
Church 75
Cigarette 76
Cigarette lighter 76
Clamp 76
Class action 76
Clearance 77
Clear view 77
Clergy Sexual Abuse 77
Club 78
Club foot 78
Coaching negligence 78

Coin-operated machine 79
Coke oven 79
Collagen 79
Collapse 79
Coma 80
Combination of circumstances 80
Combustible liquid 80
Common carrier 81
Commonwealth liability 81
  Care, custody and control of animals 81
  Education 81
  Emergency medical technicians 82
  Government function 82
  Medical care 83
  Miscellaneous 85
  Motor vehicles 86
  Personal property 88
  Police 88
  Real estate 89
  Sidewalks 93
  Streets and highways 93
  Traffic control 104
  Utility service facilities 105
Company physician 107
Comparative negligence 107
Concert patron 111
Concurrent causation 111
Concurrent negligence 111, 112
Condominium owner 112
Confidentiality 112
Consciously listening and observing 112
Consent 112
Construction 113
Contagious disease 115
Continuing negligence 115
Continuing to look 115
Continuing to operate truck 115
Contract for specific result or cure 116
Contractors 116
Contributory cause 118
Contributory negligence 120
  Falling 118
  Legal malpractice 119
  Miscellaneous 120
  Motor vehicles 121
  Real estate 124
Control 124

Controlled Substance, Drug, Device, and Cosmetics 125
Control of vehicle 124
Convenience store 125
Conveyor belt 125
Coroner 125
Corporate liability 126
Corporate officer liability 127
County health facility 127
Cousin 127
Cows 127
Credit union 128
Creeping disease 129
Crest of hill 129
Criminal acts 129
Criminal assault 130
Criminal defense 131
Criminal suspect 131
Crossing center line 131
Crossing guard 131
Crossing zone 131
Crosswalk 132
Crowds 132
Curb 132
Curve 133
Custom and method 133

D

Dam 134
Dance floor 134
Dangerous activity 134
Dangerous condition
Darkness 136
Darting out 137
Daycare 138
Dead body 138
Deck 139
Deer 139
Defamation 139
Defective assembly 140
Defective condition
Defective design
Defective equipment 141
Delivery driver 143
Delivery vehicle 143

Demolition 143
D.E.S. case 144
Diabetes 144
Diesel fumes 144
Dilapidated buildings 145
Director 145
Disability of party 145
Disaster Emergency 145
Discharge of passenger 145
Disclosure of statements 145
Discovered Peril Doctrine 146
Discovery Rule 146
Disfigurement 148
Display rack 148
Disregard of safety of others 149
Dissolution of corporation 149
Ditch 149
Diversion of water 149
Diving 149
Divorce 150
Dogs 150
Dolphin 153
Doors 153
Down's Syndrome 153
Drag racing 154
Drain grate 154
Dram Shop Act 154
Drifting vehicle 156
Drill 156
Drive-in theater 156
Driver 156
Driver's license 157
Driveway 157
Drowning 158
Drugs and drug companies 159
Drug testing 159
Drunk driver 161
Dumpster 162
Dursban 162
Duty of care
  Drug testing 162
  Miscellaneous 162
  Of business proprietor 166
  Of carrier 166
  Of professional 167
  Of property owner 168
  To children 170

To fraternity initiate 171
  To licensee 171
  To motor vehicle operator 172
  To trespasser 172
  To worker 172
Duty to warn 173

E

Easement 178
E-coli bacteria 178
Economic Loss Doctrine 178
Electricity 179
Electric Utility 179
Elements of negligence 183
Elevators 183
Embankment 185
Embolism 185
Emergency Management Service Code 185
Emergency medical care 186
Emergency Medical Services Act 186
Emergency medical technician 187
Emergency responder 187
Emergency room 187
Emergency Vehicle Doctrine 188
Emergency vehicles 188
Emotional distress 188
Emphysema 193
Employee 193
Employee of contractor or subcontractor 194
Employee pension plan 195
Employer's duty 195
Employer's liability 195
Encephalitis 197
Engine running 197
Entering highway 197
En ventre sa mere 198
Epilepsy 198
Episiotomy 198
ERISA 198
Errand 198
Escalators 198
Escaped patient 199
Escaped prisoner 199
Estate planning 199

Excavation 200
Exclusive Control Doctrine 200
Expansion joint 201
Expectation of violence 201
Experimental procedure 201
Expert testimony required or allowed 201
Explosions 207
Extramarital affair 209
Eye injuries 209
Eyewitness 210

F

Failing to observe 211
Failing to stop 211
Failure to discover defect 211
Failure to inspect 211
Failure to supervise 211
Failure to warn 212
Fall
  By business invitee 213
  Caused by objects or foreign matter 214
  In industrial setting 215
  On personal property 216
  On public property 217
Falling asleep 220
Falling objects 220
False representations 221
Family use doctrine 221
Farm 623
Farm tractor 221
Faulty construction or condition 221
Fear or fright 222
Federal agency 223
Federal Employee's Health Benefits Act 223
Federal Insecticide, Fungicide and Rodenticide Act 223
Federal statutes 223
Federal Tort Claims Act 225
Fellow Servant Rule 225
Fence 226
Fetus 226
Fiduciary negligence 226
Fighting 227
Fill 227
Fire 227

Fire and Panic Act 230
Firearms 232
Fire department 230
Fireworks 233
Fixture 234
Flares 234
Flooding 235
Floors 235
Flow of traffic 237
Foam padding 237
Fog 237
Food 237
Food and Drug Administration 237
Food, Drug and Cosmetics Act of 1938 238
Food poisoning 238
Foot 238
Foreclosure 239
Foreign defendan 239
Foreign defendant 239
Foreign Sovereign Immunities Act 239
Foreign substance 239
Foreseeability 240
Foul ball 242
Four in front seat 242
Fraternity 242
Freezing 242
Fumes 243
Fundraising 244
Funeral parlor 244

G

Garbage truck 245
Gas main 245
Gas range 245
Gas station 245
Gas tank 246
Gastric-bypass surgery 247
Gastroscopic examination 247
Gas utility 246
Gas valve 246
General contractor 247
Gist of the Action Doctrine 248
Glass 248
Gloves 248

Good Samaritan Rule 248
Government contractor defense 249
Grab bar 249
Grade crossings 249
Grading of property 251
Grease 251
Gross negligence 251
Guard rails 251
Guests 253
Guilty plea 254
Gum disease 254
Gunshot 255

H

Habitability 256
Hallway 256
Hamil/Mitzelfelt Test 256
Handicapped child 256
Handicapped curb cuts 256
Handrails 256
Hands off steering wheel 256
Harrassment 257
Hazards created by contractor 257
Headlights 257
Head-on collision 257
Health care centers 259
Health Care Services Malpractice Act 259
Health regulations 259
Health spas 260
Heart attack 260
Heart valve 260
Heparin lock 260
Hepatitis 260
Herniated disk 260
Hidden approach 260
High beams 261
Highway construction 261
Hitchhiker 262
HMO liability 262
Hoarseness 262
Holes and depressions 262
Homeowner's association 263
Horseplay 263
Horses 263

Host liability 263
Hotel 264
Hunter 264
Husband and wife 264
Hydraulic lift 265
Hydroplaning 265
Hypoxia 266

I

Ice and snow 267
Ice skating 274
Identity 274
Imputed negligence 274
Incontrovertible Physical Facts Rule 275
Independent contractor 275
Industrial accidents 277
Industrial development corporation 279
Industrial standards 279
Inherent risks 279
Injection 279
Injury without damage 279
Innkeeper 280
Inspection 280
Institutional negligence 281
Insurance 281
Insurance agent/Broker malpractice 282
Intentional acts 282
Intentional infliction of emotional distress 283
Intersection accidents
  Between intersections 284
  Location of parties 285
  Miscellaneous 286
  Traffic control device present 287
Intervening negligence or cause 289
Intoxication 291
Intra-family Immunity 302
Intubation 301, 302
Invitees 301, 302
Ischemia 305, 306

J

Janitor 307

Jar 307
Jerk or Jolt Doctrine 307
Joint enterprise 307
Joint tortfeasor 307
Joists 311
Jones Ac 311
Judicial immunity 623

K

Knee 312
Knee immobilizer 312
Knife 312
Knockdown at crosswalk 312
Knowledge of danger 312

L

Labor dispute 315
Laches 315
Ladder 315
Landlord and tenant 315
Landslide 319
Lanes of travel 319
Laryngeal nerve 319
Last Clear Chance Doctrine 320
Latent defects 320
Lawn 320
Lawn mower 320
Lead poisoning 321
Learned Intermediary Doctrine 322
Leased equipment or vehicle 322
Leases 322
Leaves 323
Left turn 323
Legal malpractice 324
Lessor of vehicle 331
Licensee 331
Lights and lighting 333
Limited tort option 333
Liver disease 334
Livestock 334
Loading and unloading 334
Lobectomy 335

Lock 335
Log 335
Log homes 335
Looking—Observation 335
Loss of consortium 336
Loss of control 337
Lung disease 337
Lying in roadway 338

M

Machinery 339
Maintenance of vehicle 339
Malfunction theory 339
Malingering 340
Mammogram 340
Manhole cover 340
Man-made lake 340
Manure 340
Market share liability 340
Mastectomy 341
Master and servant 341
Mat 343
Mechanic 343
Mechanical failure 343
Mechanical signal 343
Medial barrier 343
Median strip 344
Medical Device Amendments of 1976 344
Medical malpractice 345
  Abatement of action 345
  Anesthesia 345
  Dental 345
  Failure to diagnose 347
  HMO 352
  Hospital 353
  Informed Consent Doctrine 361
  Miscellaneous 367
  Nurse 368
  Nursing home 370
  Physician 370
  Physician's assistant 384
Medical monitoring 385
Medical records 385
Medical reports 385

Memory 386
Mental distress damages 386
Mental Health Procedures Act 386
Mental illness 387
Mental shock and anguish 388
Mere happening of accident 388
Mesothelioma 389
Metastasis 389
Meter reader 389
Microvascular decompression surgery 390
Minority Tolling Statute 390
Mirror of car 390
Miscarriage 390
Missing plank 390
Mistaken identity 391
Molestation 391
Moral duty 391
Mortality tables 391
Mortgages and mortgagees 391
Motorcycles and motorscooters 393
Motor Vehicle Financial Responsibility Act 392
Moving machinery 396
Muffler 396
Multiple impacts 396
Multi-vehicle accident 396
Municipal liability
  Care, custody, and control of animals 396
  Fire departments and fire fighters 397
  Government function 398
  Miscellaneous 400
  Motor vehicles 402
  Nursing home 405
  Police 405
  Police pursuit 410
  Prisons 623
  Real estate 413
  Schools and school districts 419
  Sidewalks 426
  Streets amd highways 429
  Structures 434
  Traffic control 434, 435
  Utility service facilities 437
  Volunterer ambulance company 438
Murder 438

N

Nail 439
National Traffic and Motor Vehicle Safety Act 439
Neck surgery 439
Negligence per se 439
Negligent design 442
Negligent destruction of evidence 442
Negligent entrustment 442
Negligent hiring or supervision 443
Negligent identification 444
Negligent infliction of emotional distress 444
Negligent misrepresentation 448
Negligent referral 448
Negligent supervision 449
Neither driver negligent 449
Neomycin 449
New injuries 449
Newspaper delivery driver 449
Notice of condition 450
Not looking 449
Nullum tempus 452
Numerous accidents 452
Nursing home 452

O

Obstructed view 454
Obstruction 454
Occupied Crossing Rule 455
Odor 455
Odorizing gas 455
Only Reasonable Inference Rule 455
Open and obvious danger 456
Opportunity and occasion 456
Opposite lane 456
Opthalmologist 456
Other accidents or occurrences 457
Other causes 457
Out of possession 457
Oven door 457
Overdose 457
Overhanging limb 457
Overpass 458

Overturned rig on highway 458

P

Paint 459
Painter 459
Paint thinner 459
Panicked driver 460
Paralysis 460
Paramedics 460
Paranoid psychosis 460
Parents 460
Parked cars 461
Parking garage or lot 462
Partially constructed building 465
Participation theory 465
Partners 465
Passengers 465
Passing 468
Passing lane 469
Patella 470
Peculiar Risk Doctrine 470
Pedestrians 470
Pellet gun 476
Pennsylvania National Guardsmen 476
Perineal urethrotomy 477
Permanent disfigurement 477
Permissive path and ways 477
Personal care home 477
Personal property 478
Physical education class 478
Physical therapy 478
Physician-patient confidentiality 478
Piercing corporate veil 479
Pile of dirt 479
Pipe and pipeline 479
Plaintiff's own testimony 480
Plain view 480
Plate glass window 480
Platelets 480
Playgrounds, parks, and recreation areas 481
Plumber 484
Poles 484
Police 485
Ponds and pools 491

Possessor 492
Possibility of injury 492
Possible cause of occurrence 492
Post-operative care 492
Pothole 493
Power lines 493, 494
Prank 494
Pre-employment physical 494
Preemption 494
Premature birth 495
Prenatal injuries 495
Presumptions 496
Priest 498
Prior accident 499
Prior injuries 499
Prison and prisoners 499
Private nuisance 501
Probate of will 501
Proceeding on highway 501
Professional insurance 502
Professional negligence
  Accounting 502
  Engineering 502
  Investment advisor 503
  Vocational rehabilitation 503
Projecting objects or parts 503
Property damage 504
Property owner liability 504
Property to be insured 506
Prostatectomy 506
Protective equipment 506
Protestors 507
Prothonotary 507
Proximate cause 507
Psychiatric patient 510
Psychic injury 511
Psychotic episode 511
Public defender 511
Public Employee Relations Act 511
Public nuisance 512
Public Utility Code 512
Public Utility Commission 512

Q

Quadriplegic 513
Quasi-judicial immunity 623
Quick release mechanism 513

R

Racing 513
Radiation treatment 513
Radio 513
Railing 514
Railroads 514
Rainwater 516
Rape 516
Rave 517
Reactive Airways Dysfunction Syndrome (RADS) 517
Real estate agent or broker 517
Rear-end collision 517
Reasonable care 520
Reckless conduct 521
Recorder of Deeds 521
Recreation Use of Land and Water Act 521
Referring physician 525
Reflectors 525
Register of Wills 623
Relined brakes 526
Relying on light 526
Remote cause 526
Rental agency 526
Rental vehicle 526
Rescuer 526
Rescue van 526
Res Ipsa Loquitur 527
Respiratory therapist 531
Respondeat Superior 531
Restatement (2d) Torts § 315 532
Restatement (2d) Torts § 317 532
Restatement (2d) Torts § 323 532
Restatement (2d) Torts § 343 532
Restatement (2d) Torts § 388 532
Restaurant 533
Restraining vest 533
Retarded child 533
Retina 533
Retrieving ball 533
Retroactive effect 533

Retrograde amnesia 534
Rigger 534
Right of way 534
Risk of harm 534
Robber 535
Roof 535
Rounding sharp curve 536
Rowdyism 536
Rugs 536
Rules of the road 536
Running board 537

S

Safer position 538
Safety features or standards 538
Safety of goods 538
Salesman 538
Scaffolding 539
Scam by agent 539
Scar 540
School bus 540
Scope of employment 540
Seatbelts 541
Second accident 542
Secondary liability 542
Security guard 542
Seizures 542
Serious bodily injury or impairment of bodily func 542
Service station 543
Sewage enforcement officer 544
Sewers 544
Sexual abuse or assault 545
Sexual contact 546
Shadow 546
Sharp curve 546
Sheriff's sale 546
Shock treatment 547
Shopping cart 547
Shopping center 547
Shoring 547
Shower 547
Sideswipe collision 548
Sidewalks 548
Single cause of injury 549

Six month notice 550
Skating rink 550
Skidmarks and skidding 550
Skier's Responsibility Act 551
Skiing 551
Skylight 552
Slight contact 552
Slip and fall 552
Sliver of metal 559
Smoke inhalation 559
Smokestack 560
Snowmobile 561
Snow tube riding 560
Social host 561
Softball - See Sports injuries 562
Soft tissue 562
Specific acts of negligence 562
Spectator 562
Speed 563
Sperm donor 564
Spigot 564
Spitball battle 564
Sponge left in body 565
Spontaneous abortion 565
Sports injuries 565
Sprinkler system 568
Stabbing 568
Stage 568
Stairs 568
Standard of care 570
Staph infection 572
State-of-the-art 572
Station platform 572
Statute of Repose 572
Statutory employment 573
Steel cable 574
Steel truss 574
Sterilization 574
Stick 575
Stillborn child 575
Stilts 575
Stipulated facts 575
Stolen vehicles 575
Stomach stapling 576
Stone mason 576
Stones 577
Stop, Look, and Listen Doctrine 577

Stopped traffic 577
Storm Water Management Act 578
Street railways 578
Stress 580
Strip mine 580
Student 580
Subjective belief 582
Substantial factor 582
Substitution 584
Subway 584
Successive collisions 585
Sudden Emergency Doctrine 585
Suicide 588
Summary citation 589
Summer recreation program 590
Superseding cause 590
Surgery 593
Surrogacy 593
Swerving 594
Swimming and swimming pools 594
Swinging door 595

T

Table saw 596
Tail gates 596
Tail lights 596
Tarmac 596
Telephone
  booth 596
  company 597
  directory 597
  pole 597
  wire 597
Termites 597
Test drive 597
Therapeutic purpose 598
Therapist 598
Thermostat 598
Thimerosal 598
Third-party beneficiary 598
Thrown from seat 599
"T" Intersections 596
Tire and tire marks 599
Title Search 600

To invitee 171
Tortious interference with marital relationship 600
Tow Truck 600
Toxic chemicals 600
Tractor 600
Traffic control devices 601
Trains and platforms 602
Trampoline 603
Transfusion 603
Trapdoor 603
Traumatic amnesia 603
Traumatic cervical syndrome 604
Traumatic onset of disease 604
Trees 604
Trench 606
Trespassers 606
Trip and fall 608
Truck 611
Trustee 613
Tuberculosis 613
Tumor 613
Turning vehicles 613
Two different accidents 614
Two-disease Rule 615
Two falls in same place 614
Two or more equally probable causes 614

U

Ulcer 616
Ultrahazardous activities 616
Ultrasound test 617
Unauthorized practice of the law 617
Unauthorized use 617
Unavoidable accident 617
Uncertain medical testimony 617
Underground tank 617
Undue hardship 618
Unevenness of pavement 618
Unfitness to cross street 618
Uniform Contribution Among Tortfeasors Act 618
Uniform Fiduciaries Act 619
Unimproved land 619
Unlighted corridor 619
Unlighted excavation 619

Unlighted stairway 619
Unsafe speed 619
Used car 619
Utility pole 620
Utility provisions 621
"U" Turns 616

V

Vacant building 622
Vacant lot 622
Vaccination 622
Vaccine Act 622
Valet 623
Vegetation along highway 623
Ventilation system 623
Vicarious liability 623
View obstructed 624
View of intersection 624
Vision 624
Visitor 624
Vocal cords 624
Vocational expert 624
Vocational rehabilitation 625
Voice 625
Voluntary Assumption of the Risk Doctrine 625
Voluntary undertaking 628

W

Waiver of immunity 629
Walking 629
Walls 629
Wanton misconduct 630
Water 631
  box cover 633
  line trench 633
  meter 633
Waving through intersection 633
Welding 634
Well 634
Wheelchair 634
Whiteout 634
Wild animal 634

Willful misconduct 634
Windshield wiper 635
Windstorm 635
Wires 635
Witness Immunity Doctrine 635
Workmen injured while working 635
Work place 642
Work release 642
Wrongful accusation 644
Wrongful death and survival actions 644
Wrongful life 648
Wrong side of highway 642

Y

Yellow Pages 650